The Tax Law of Charities and Other Exempt Organizations

The Tax Law of Charities and Other Exempt Organizations

FOURTH EDITION

David A. Brennen
Frost, Brown & Todd Professor of Law
University of Kentucky J. David Rosenberg College of Law

Darryll K. Jones
Associate Dean for Research and Faculty Development
& Professor of Law
Florida A&M University School of Law

Beverly I. Moran
Professor Emerita of Law
Vanderbilt Law School

Steven J. Willis
Professor of Law
University of Florida Levin College of Law

CAROLINA ACADEMIC PRESS
Durham, North Carolina

ISBN 978-1-5310-2286-0
e-ISBN 978-1-5310-2287-7
LCCN 2021935677

Carolina Academic Press
700 Kent Street
Durham, NC 27701
(919) 489-7486
www.cap-press.com

Printed in the United States of America

Contents

PART THREE • CHARITABLE EXEMPT ORGANIZATIONS — PRIVATE FOUNDATIONS

PART FOUR • NON-CHARITABLE EXEMPT ORGANIZATIONS

Preface

The first edition of this, our scholastic labor of love published nearly two decades ago, owed its genesis to the work of our senior co-author, Steven Willis, who taught two of us the law of exempt organizations as University of Florida LLM students. As students we were exposed—in some cases "subjected"—to different typeface and mimeograph quality because, there being no published text on the subject, Professor Willis constantly gathered, collated, and distributed material as events warranted. Of course, this was all well before the IT revolution. The successive editions have been immeasurably improved, not only by the wonders of IT, but by our second senior colleague, Beverly Moran, who recently retired from Vanderbilt University but graciously continues with our quest to bring tax exempt organizations law more into the mainstream of both JD and LLM curricula.

The changes to the Independent Sector have been many and significant since our first edition. In those days, economic issues such as exempt hospital joint ventures and intermediate sanctions on private inurement (now more often referred to as "excess benefit transactions") comprised the fuel driving the evolution of exempt organization tax law. These days, socio-political issues, e.g., exempt organizations' increasing involvement in politics and social wars, issues relating to so called "dark money," the emergence of social justice groups such as Black Lives Matter (exempt under 501(c)(3)) and reactionary groups such as the Alt-Right (also exempt under 501(c)(3)), seem to command more attention. The Supreme Court's decision in *Citizens United* no doubt had something to do with the trend. Regardless, the world of exempt organizations continues to evolve and grow as demonstrated by a 2019 Report by the National Center for Charitable Statistics reporting that:

- Approximately 1.54 million nonprofits were registered with the Internal Revenue Service (IRS) in 2016, an increase of 4.5 percent from 2006.
- The nonprofit sector contributed an estimated $1,047.2 trillion to the US economy in 2016, composing 5.6 percent of the country's gross domestic product (GDP).
- Of the nonprofit organizations registered with the IRS, 501(c)(3) public charities accounted for just over three-quarters of revenue and expenses for the nonprofit sector as a whole ($2.04 trillion and $1.94 trillion, respectively) and just under two-thirds of the nonprofit sector's total assets ($3.79 trillion).

- In 2018, total private giving from individuals, foundations, and businesses totaled $427.71 billion (Giving USA Foundation 2019), a decrease of 1.7 percent from 2017 (after adjusting for inflation). According to Giving USA (2018) total charitable giving rose for consecutive years from 2014 to 2017, making 2017 the largest single year for private charitable giving, even after adjusting for inflation.
- An estimated 25.1 percent of US adults volunteered in 2017, contributing an estimated 8.8 billion hours. This is a 1.6 percent increase from 2016. The value of these hours is approximately $195.0 billion.

Attorneys of all stripes are usually active members of at least one charitable, civic or religious organization and are almost invariably asked to "lend" their expertise to an issue regarding their organization's legal status. And yet, because of its specialized nature, most of those attorneys have little exposure to the field. There is much more to exempt organization tax law than just completing the Form 1023. It seems to us also that legal scholarly attention paid to the Independent Sector ebbs and flows. Tax Analyst's Exempt Organization Tax Review, for example, was once required weekly, if not monthly, reading. Now it is no longer published. On the other hand, there are still online blogs, such as the Nonprofit Tax Professor Blog, exclusively devoted to the law of tax exemption. There are still centers and think tanks devoted to the study of exempt organizations, such as NYU's National Center on Philanthropy and the Law and Iowa's Larned A. Waterman Iowa Nonprofit Resource Center to name only two.

This fourth edition continues with our initial goal of providing sufficient coverage to allow for broad, deep, or broad *and* deep coverage. The goal, as always, is to provide a resource for the acquisition of fundamental knowledge regarding our topic. Knowledgeable observers know that the tax law of exempt organizations has become increasingly regulated. For example, provisions in the Affordable Care Act (which seems to have survived fierce efforts at repeal) demand greater accountability (particularly regarding "community benefit") from exempt health care. The extent to which exempt organizations may engage in political activities, although always controversial, has become even more of an issue since the last edition. In this regard, we have sought to consolidate political activities into one chapter, rather than examine the issue as it relates to the different types of exempt organizations covered in different chapters. The book continues to provide coverage of as many of the exempt organizations as there are statutory authorizations. Professors may therefore select which areas are most important according to their own pedagogical beliefs and even geographical regions. Labor organizations, for example, may not be as important to law students in southern states where organized labor has less influence than in midwestern and northeastern regions. While we have consolidated some of the materials regarding private foundations, there is still enough (and probably more) for coverage of the important subject in a survey course, or for use of the book in a seminar (for example) solely on private foundations. We hope, too, that the fourth edition remains in students' personal libraries well after graduation, as it is useful to those attorneys unversed in the area but who, we believe, will inevitably be called upon to lend efforts to their own charitable, civic, or religious organizations.

David A. Brennen
Darryll K. Jones
Beverly I. Moran
Steven J. Willis

PART ONE

Charitable Exempt Organizations — Exempt Purpose Requirement

Chapter 1

A Brief Overview of Tax-Exempt Organizations

A. Introduction

Those who are new to the world of tax-exempt organizations might be surprised to learn that "non-profit organization," "tax-exempt organization," and "charitable organization" are not synonymous phrases. The phrase "non-profit organization" tends to refer to state law issues—incorporation under a state not-for-profit corporation act or organized as a trust. Though there are many differences between corporations and trusts, the primary differences between nonprofit corporations and nonprofit trusts emanate from their structure. A nonprofit corporation operates pursuant to its bylaws as determined by a board of directors, whereas a nonprofit trust operates for the benefit of its trust beneficiaries as determined by its trustees. Such a "non-profit corporation" or non-profit trust that is organized under state law may or may not be taxable under federal law. The status of being "non-profit" tells one little about the federal tax consequences the entity faces. An organization, even one that does nothing but give away all of its wealth, must still comply with intricate and detailed requirements to gain recognition and treatment as a federally "tax-exempt organization."

Similarly, not all "non-profit" or "tax-exempt organizations" are "charitable," as that term is commonly understood. Internal Revenue Code § 501(c) specifies 29 different classifications of tax-exempt organizations only one of which—that specified in § 501(c)(3)—comprises what we refer to as "charities" or charitable organizations. In addition, there are seven other types of tax-exempt organizations described in § 501(d), (e), (f), (k), (l), (n) and (q). But of the approximately two million tax-exempt organizations as of 2010, nearly 1.3 million of those are charities granted tax exemption under § 501(c)(3). Social welfare organizations (§ 501(c)(4)), representing 139,125 tax exempt entities, make up the next largest group, followed by business leagues (§ 501(c)(6)) at 92,331, social clubs (§ 501(c)(7)) at 79,718, fraternal benefit societies (§ 501(c)(8)) at 63,391 and labor/agricultural organizations (§ 501(c)(5)) at 63,012. See Chart 1.

One other important but often overlooked type of entity is exempt from federal taxation. Any guesses? The answer is state governments and their related entities, including Native American governing bodies and their related entities. Governing bodies—such as a state or county—derive significant income through taxation or

Chart 1: 501 Organizations

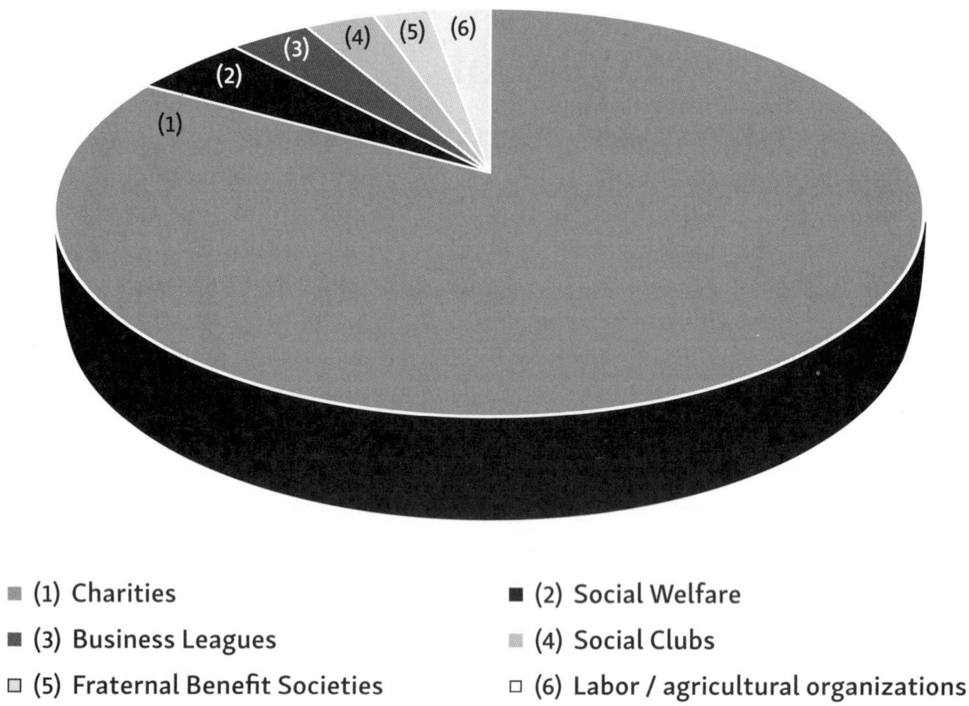

from the sale of goods and services, yet the genesis and operation of their federal tax exemption is often ignored. We therefore include a study of such governing bodies, which are exempt primarily under § 115.

B. Charities

Throughout this book we use the term "charity" in its general sense, referring to those organizations described both in §§ 501(c)(3) and 170(c)(2); mostly those that are not only exempt from federal income tax, but to which contributions are tax deductible in calculating the federal income tax liability of the individual or corporate contributor. To satisfy §§ 501(c)(3) and 170(c)(2), a tax-exempt organization must meet five statutory criteria:

1. It must be *organized* exclusively for an exempt purpose.
2. It must be *operated* exclusively for an exempt purpose.
3. It must avoid any *private inurement.*
4. It must avoid substantial *lobbying.*
5. It must avoid any *political activity.*

The "organizational" and "operational" tests each have three sub-parts:

1. The *exclusivity* requirement.
2. The *exempt purpose* requirement.
3. The *procedural rules* requirement.

Courts have added three additional tests:

1. The entity must provide *public benefit.*
2. The entity must not violate established *public policy.*
3. The activities must *not* be *illegal.*

We begin our focus—in Chapters 2 through 6—with the three judicial tests for charitable tax exemption (the public benefit, public policy, and legality requirements) and the "exempt purpose" requirement, a sub-part of both the organizational and operational tests.

Chapter 2 focuses on general notions of the term "charitable," with a particular emphasis on the three judicial tests for charitable exemption. We include a mostly unedited version of a United States Supreme Court case, *Bob Jones University v. United States*, which outlines each of these tests. Of the three judicial tests, "illegality" is by far the least difficult conceptually. In contrast, "public benefit" and "public policy" can sometimes be very unclear. Indeed, with the exception of racial discrimination against black people at religious schools, the federal courts have yet to delineate examples of established public policies that charities cannot violate.

Chapters 3 through 6 highlight various aspects of particular types of charitable activities, namely religious, educational, scientific, health care, and public interest law. Though we recognize that there are many other types of charitable activities—for instance, environmental, community development, and artistic—we chose these particular activities to demonstrate many of the common approaches to analyzing exempt purpose.

Chapters 7, 8 and 9 focus on the "exclusivity" requirement, another sub-part of both the organizational and operational tests. This requirement overlaps with the "exempt purpose" requirement, essentially looking at it from a different angle. Not only must a charity have an appropriate exempt purpose, but it must also be organized and operated *exclusively* for that purpose. While "exclusively" does not mean 100%—or even anything very close to that—it is a profoundly important, albeit sometimes slippery, requirement. These three chapters also cover the related "commerciality" doctrine, which focuses on whether the charity's purpose—both in organization and especially operation—is too commercial. If it is, the entity is not "exclusively" charitable and thus not entitled to exempt status, at least not as a § 501(c)(3) charity. Even if the level of the entity's commercial activity is not so much at to cause it to lose its status as a § 501(c)(3) charity, the entity may nonetheless be subject to federal tax on the income generated by the commercial activity. This is the subject of chapters 25 through 30, which are outlined below in this introductory chapter.

Chapters 7, 8 and 9 require particular attention, lest they be confusing. The exclusivity and commerciality doctrines not only overlap with the "exempt purpose" requirement (Chapters 2 through 6), but they also have some overlap with the private inurement prohibition and private benefit restrictions discussed in Chapter 11 and Chapter 12. Theoretically, each of these doctrines (exempt purpose, exclusivity, private inurement and private benefit) is distinct . . . but not entirely so. Thus, the reader must be careful not only in keeping them separate, but also in understanding the relationships and overlaps. And, as if that were not enough, the discussion in Chapters 7, 8 and 9 of the commerciality doctrine is best understood with knowledge of Chapters 25 through 30 of this text that cover unrelated business income taxation. Many cases dealing with commerciality also deal with unrelated business income taxation. Similarly, the lines between an activity being too commercial to be charitable versus acceptably commercial but taxable (to the extent commercial) versus acceptably commercial because the commercial activity is itself inherently charitable, are not easy lines to draw. Presenting these various doctrines (exclusivity, private inurement, private benefit, and unrelated business income taxation) as separate concepts is best, because the student will likely learn them best that way; however, as separate concepts — and presented in separate Parts of the book — the doctrines may appear artificially distinct. Thus, we will continually try to relate back and forth.

Chapter 10 then looks at the procedural rules, another sub-part of both the *organizational* and *operational* tests. In particular, we look at the mechanical aspects of an application for exemption.

Four aspects of the *procedural rules* are noteworthy:

1. The *Initial Filing* and *Notice Requirement*. This ensures that the organization is actually organized for the proper exempt purpose.

2. *Judicial Review of the Ruling Process.*

3. *Annual Filing Requirements* and *Disclosure Rules*. These ensure that the organization actually operates for the proper purposes for which it received exemption.

4. *State and Local Issues*. These can be particularly important because some organizations seek federal exemption not for the federal advantages, but rather for the concomitant state advantages. For example, an organization might have no taxable income and thus might not care about federal income tax exemption; it might receive insignificant donations and thus might not care about charitable tax deductions. But, it may desire state or local property tax exemption. Often, that is realistically available only if the entity first achieves federal exempt status under § 501(c)(3). Thus, federal status is not the object, but merely a tool to obtain the desired result.

Part II (Chapters 11 through 14) then looks more specifically at prohibitions or restrictions on charities. Chapter 11 focuses on the private inurement prohibition, including forms of inurement and excess benefit transactions. Chapter 12 focuses on the private benefit restrictions. Chapter 13 outlines the lobbying restrictions, including the safe harbor provisions that allow prescribed levels of lobbying as measured by expenditures spent on lobbying. Finally, Chapter 14 deals with the general prohibition against charities engaging in political campaign activities, including outlining ways in which a charity might get involved politically yet keep its § 501(c)(3) charity status intact. Generally, a charity's violation of any of these prohibitions or restrictions could lead to loss of the federal tax exemption and associated benefits, imposition of some intermediate type of penalty short of loss of exemption or some combination of the two.

C. Private Foundation Status

Part III of this text (Chapters 15 through 19) covers private foundations in depth. Section 509 defines the term "private foundation" as including all § 501(c)(3) organizations — those we refer to as "charities" (which are also described in § 170(c)(2)). In addition, according to § 4947(a)(1) and (a)(2), certain trusts are treated as if they were § 501(c)(3) organizations solely for purposes of the private foundation rules. Traditional parlance refers to charities that are not private foundations as "public charities." The term "public charity," however, is never defined or even used in the Code. The policy behind the two categories — private foundation and public charity — relates to the general notion that exempt organizations are not heavily regulated through the United States tax system. Public charities, in particular, operate largely without federal government supervision or regulation despite the important fact of their receiving substantial government benefits: tax exemption plus the ability to receive tax deductible contributions. Many courts and commentators liken these benefits to government subsidies. Whether they are indeed equivalent to subsidies — and thus deserving of special constitutional scrutiny — is discussed later. For now, we can at least stipulate that they are very important government-sanctioned benefits. As such, special scrutiny is justified. How to provide it is the issue.

Very generally, public charities are those that receive "substantial" public support. As such, they rely on pleasing the "public" for their continued existence. In theory at least, if they were to violate that public trust — such as through excessive economic entanglement with donors or by providing benefits only to very narrow groups — they would jeopardize their very existence because the public would withdraw support. Theoretically, they would lose their "substantial" public support if they failed to provide real public benefits. Whether the theory works in practice — and particularly whether the definition of "substantial" is realistic to accomplish the theory — is beside the point for now. In a real sense, charities that satisfy one of several mechanical "public support" tests are subject to very little government oversight. Charities that fail to satisfy one of the mechanical public support tests, however, face some very strict rules: the private foundation excise taxes found in §§ 4940 to 4945. Part III of this text covers these private foundation excise taxes.

Given the enormous impact that private foundation status has on a charitable organization, a brief overview of private foundations is essential to an understanding of the charitable exemption. Thus, here are a few very general observations regarding private foundations:

1. **Private Foundation status is not desirable.** Granted, being a private foundation is probably better than not being exempt at all; however, "public charity" status is preferable for several reasons, including:

- Charitable contribution reductions are generally lower under § 170(e) for contributions to public charities as compared to contributions to private foundations.
- Charitable contribution limitations are generally higher under § 170(b) for contributions to public charities as compared to contributions to private foundations.
- The harsh excise taxes of §§ 4940 through 4945 do not apply to public charities, but they apply to most private foundations.

2. **Private Foundation status applies *only* to § 501(c)(3) organizations—those we call "charities."** Other exempt organizations, such as § 501(c)(4) social welfare groups, (c)(5) labor unions, (c)(6) business leagues, and (c)(7) social clubs need not be concerned about private foundation status. An exception applies to (c)(4) organizations that once were (c)(3) private foundations.

3. **Private Foundation status is difficult to get rid of.** Section 507(b)(1) provides two methods of voluntary termination: either transfer all assets to a five-year-old (or older) public charity or operate as a public charity for 60 months. Section 508 provides for involuntary termination (imposed for willful or repeated violations of the Chapter 42 excise taxes) by imposing a harsh termination tax potentially equal to the net assets of the entity.

Next, for some good news: three types of charities are never private foundations. They are:

1. **Churches.** Per §§ 170(b)(1)(A)(i) and 509(a)(1), "churches" and some related organizations are never private foundations. Be cautious, however; while the reference to "church" includes organizations of any religious faith, it is narrower than the category "religious" organization. In essence, while all churches are religious organizations, not all religious organizations are churches.

2. **Schools.** Per §§ 170(b)(1)(A)(ii) and 509(a)(1), "schools" are never private foundations. Be cautious, however. The definition of "schools"—a term defined, but not specifically used in the Code—is narrower than the category "educational" organization. Thus, while all schools are educational organizations, all educational organizations are not schools.

3. Hospitals. Per §§ 170(b)(1)(A)(iii) and 509(a)(1), "hospitals" and some related organizations are never private foundations. Be cautious, however; the reference to "hospitals" is narrower than the category "medical" organization. Thus, while all hospitals are medical organizations, not all medical organizations are hospitals.

Finally, the tax system provides for different levels of private foundation status—"operating" and "non-operating." While private foundation status is never great, operating status is usually better than non-operating status. "Private operating foundations," for example, receive many of the "public charity" benefits as provided in §§ 4942(j) and 170(b)(1)(F), while non-operating private foundations do not. Chapters 16 through 18 cover this in much greater depth. We should add that while public charity status is preferred over private foundation status, most well-known private foundations—the MacArthur Foundation, for example—are wealthy enough to hire counsel fully competent to easily deal with the arguably overwrought private foundation statutes and regulations. We need not weep too long for their private foundation status.

D. Other Types of Exempt Organizations

Although the main focus of this book is on "charities"—§ 501(c)(3) and § 170(c)(2) organizations—we also cover several other important types of exempt entities in Part IV (Chapters 20–24).

Chapter 20 covers § 501(c)(4) "social welfare" organizations. Not only are they exempt from tax, but they are often indistinguishable from "charities" under § 501(c)(3) because their purposes are generally the same. Contributions to them, however, are not deductible because they are not described in § 170(c). Why would anyone want that classification? For one, they are not (typically) subject to the onerous private foundation rules. Second, lobbying and political restrictions are significantly more lenient than they are for "charities." Third, many "charities" create related "social welfare" entities under § 501(c)(4) precisely to use the more lenient lobbying and political activity rules. As noted in Chapter 19, a charity must be careful in creating and operating such a related entity; however, with proper advice and careful accounting, it is a very useful tool. A similar but opposite structural tool involves a (c)(4) creating and controlling a separate (c)(3) organization. This would be motivated by a desire of the parent social welfare organization to take advantage of the charitable contribution deduction available to the (c)(3)'s contributors. With careful advice, the resulting (c)(3) can avoid private foundation status as a function of the parent social welfare organization's public support rather than its own.

Chapter 21 covers § 501(c)(5) "labor unions." Again, they are exempt from tax, but contributions to them are not deductible. They, too, need not worry about private foundation status. In addition, their lobbying and political activity restrictions are also more lenient than those imposed on "charities." Frequently, a § 501(c)(5) entity will create a related charity to gain advantage of the charitable contribution benefits. As explained above, such a plan requires careful advice and accounting, but can be a very useful tool. A special private foundation rule can also protect the related § 501(c)(3) by classifying it as a public charity based on the labor union's public support rather than its own.

Chapter 22 covers § 501(c)(6) "business leagues." These include entities organized to support a "line of business." Common examples involve local or state bar associations and medical societies. While they are exempt from tax, contributions to them are not deductible. They, too, need not worry about private foundation status. And, as with social welfare organizations ((c)(4)s) and labor unions ((c)(5)s), their lobbying and political activity restrictions are more lenient than those imposed on "charities." Just as do labor unions, business leagues will frequently establish related (and often controlled) charities to take advantage of the charitable contribution rules. Again, a special private foundation rule can also protect the related § 501(c)(3) by classifying it as a public charity based on the labor union's public support rather than its own.

Chapter 23 covers § 501(c)(7) social clubs. These include myriad organizations, such as country clubs, dinner clubs, and college fraternities and sororities. They are exempt from tax but contributions to them are not deductible. They also need not worry about private foundation status. They, too, often create separate § 501(c)(3) organizations — to which contributions are deductible — to carry on charitable activities such as scholarship or library funds. Such entities need to pay special attention to the "exclusivity" requirement of the organizational and operational tests. For example, a scholarship fund would be a typical § 501(c)(3) charity; however, if limited to a particular sorority, it may run afoul of the "exclusivity" requirement if it insufficiently benefits the general public and overly benefits the parent sorority. Social clubs are also unique as non-charitable tax-exempt organizations because they are subject to a special statutory provision — § 501(i). Section 501(i) prohibits social clubs from discriminating on the basis of "race, color or religion" in certain contexts. In some ways, this non-discrimination requirement is similar to the public policy requirement for charitable exempt organizations. But there are some differences. We discuss these differences and the many other aspects of the social club exemption in Chapter 23.

Finally, in Chapter 24 we discuss states and state-related organizations. This is a very technical area that is significantly influenced by non-statutory sources (such as case law and constitutional law — state and federal). Thus, in this chapter, we outline the federal tax exemption of such entities and associated issues of intergovernmental tax immunity. We also address tax-exempt issues associated with state-related entities and Native American governing bodies.

Thus, while we focus in this text primarily on § 501(c)(3) charities, we also cover other organizations that exist alongside charities. As explained above — and later in greater detail — such other entities often operate very closely with charities, thus we cannot study the different types in a vacuum. Sometimes the operations are too interrelated, causing problems—perhaps serious ones. Other times, the operations are insufficiently related, causing other problems. So, once again, in studying charities, one must keep an eye open to how they relate to other tax-exempt organizations.

E. Commercial Activity

Because of the "nonprofit" misnomer referenced earlier in this introductory chapter, many assume that charities and similar entities are noncommercial. However, such an assumption couldn't be further from the truth. Of the total $21.7 trillion comprising the nation's gross domestic product in 2019, $1.2 trillion, or 5.5%, was produced by the nonprofit sector alone. To put that figure better into perspective, consider that the GDP contribution of American farms for that year was $140 billion, or a tenth of the product added by nonprofits. In addition, much of this commercial productivity came as a result of activity that is in direct competition with other for-profit entities. For instance, nonprofit YMCA facilities often compete directly with for-profit gyms and other types of work-out facilities.

Part V (Chapters 25 through 30) of this text takes a close look at the federal laws that attempt to level the playing field between nonprofit and for-profit organizations by imposing an income tax on certain prescribed commercial activity. Chapters 25 through 27 lay the groundwork by outlining the basics of the so-called *unrelated business income tax*, including the "trade or business," "regularly carried on" and "substantially related" requirements. Finally, Chapters 28 through 30 outline the exceptions to the unrelated business income tax, including exceptions for royalty income, special rules for income tax imposed on membership organizations that are otherwise exempt, deductions for directly connected expenses, income generated by controlled entities and unrelated debt financed income. Overall, these six chapters outline the elaborate system of federal income taxes imposed on otherwise tax-exempt organizations.

F. The Charitable Contributions Deduction

Part VI of this text (Chapters 31 and 32) covers the deductibility of charitable contributions in depth. For now, however, an overview is important for perspective. Just as not all "non-profit organizations" are "tax-exempt" and not all "tax-exempt entities" are "non-profit," not all "tax-exempt entities" enjoy the benefit of tax-deductible contributions.

Sections 501 and 115 cover the status of being tax-exempt—a misnomer itself, as no entity, including state and local governments, is ever fully exempt. Section 170, however, covers the deductibility of contributions for *income* tax purposes, while §§ 2055 and 2522 cover most aspects of deductibility for *estate* (§ 2055) and *gift* (§ 2522) taxes.

Of the 29 different exempt entities described in § 501, only four are listed in § 170(c) as capable of receiving contributions deductible for *income tax* purposes. In addition, contributions to state and local governments are also income tax deductible. The five listed entities are:

1. **States, possessions, political subdivisions, the United States, and the District of Columbia.** This category mostly — but not completely — overlaps with § 115 status.

2. **"Charitable organizations" (as we use that term).** This category mostly — but not completely — overlaps with § 501(c)(3) entities.

3. **War Veterans' posts.** This category mostly — but not completely — overlaps with § 501(c)(19).

4. **Domestic Fraternal Societies.** This category mostly — but not completely — overlaps with § 501(c)(10). It does not include college fraternities and sororities, which are themselves exempt under § 501(c)(7) as social clubs. Contributions to social clubs are not deductible under § 170(c).

5. **Cemetery Organizations.** This category mostly — but not completely — overlaps with § 501(c)(13).

Clearly, obtaining exempt status under § 501 is only part of the charitable deduction process: a charity must also concern itself with its § 170 status. For example, contributors to a school will (or at least *should*) inquire into whether the proposed recipient has determinations under both §§ 501(c)(3) (for exempt status) and 170(c)(2) (for charitable contributions). These two statuses, however, say nothing about the deductibility of contributions for either estate or gift tax purposes. Subtitle A of the Internal Revenue Code, which includes § 170, covers the *income tax* deduction only. Subtitle B, which includes §§ 2055 and 2522, covers the *estate and gift tax* deductions.

Chapter 2

The Exempt Purpose Requirement: Public Policy and Illegality Doctrines

A. The Public Policy Doctrine

CODE: § 501(c)(3), (p)

TREAS. REG.: § 1.501(c)(3)-1(c), (d)(2)

Eventually—perhaps by the end of Chapter 9—readers should have an epiphany: charity, for tax purposes, is a vague and elusive concept, but not completely unrecognizable. We "sort of" know what charity is and when tax exemption is appropriate; but we cannot quite pin it down. Rather than ask, "what is charity?" perhaps we should ask both "what is not charity?" and "when is tax exemption *in*appropriate?"

By and large, the second question is relatively easy. According to many economists, for example, one theory is that tax exemption is inappropriate when the marketplace adequately supplies a good or service. Chapters 7, 8 and 9 explore that point in relation to the commerciality doctrine and the doctrine of commercial feasibility. *Bob Jones University v. United States*, 461 U.S. 574 (1983), the case that follows, attempts to answer the harder question "What is charity?", but is probably successful only in answering the question "What is not charity?" Because the *Bob Jones* opinion is so valuable in a global sense, we include it largely unedited.

Bob Jones is valuable in many respects because it raises some still unresolved issues. The majority discussed the common law origins of the term "charity" as it relates to tax exemption and focused on the "public good" theory of tax exemption: the idea that the loss of revenue resulting from tax exemption is compensated for by the provision of public goods and services. Such discussion begs the question whether tax exemption is a government subsidy or "tax expenditure," a topic Chapter 3 explores. Writing for the majority, Chief Justice Burger discussed diversity and pluralism as a theory of tax exemption. In his view, tax-exempt status exists to allow for a diversity of viewpoints and governance with respect to public policy. Justice Rehnquist's dissent, too, is valuable particularly in putting the whole concept of tax exemption in historical context. He focused, at least in part, on whether the Court, or Congress, should create law. Essentially, he asked whether we should read the tax statutes literally or, instead, in light of general trust law principles. The question is somewhat profound and continues to be debated in many fact situations other than those involving tax exemption.

In addition, the decision is important for a general legal doctrine with both tax and non-tax implications: the doctrine of legislative acquiescence. See *United States v. Rapanos*, 547 U.S. 715, 750 (2006). Very generally, the doctrine of legislative acquiescence suggests Congress sometimes passively acquiesces in administrative or judicial interpretations of statutes. Such acquiescence is not immediate. Rather, it can occur — under the doctrine (which can be controversial) — after many years and particularly if Congress amends the relevant statute with regard to other matters but fails to address the particular interpretation. In *Bob Jones*, the Court found Congress to have acquiesced in a long-standing revenue ruling, albeit one that had been withdrawn by the time of the litigation.

Authors' Notes: **Bob Jones University and Goldsboro Christian Schools** *in Historical and Contemporary Context*

Consolidated for their similarities, these two cases created political havoc, if not nightmares. The Reagan Administration faced a Hobson's choice: argue for a strict interpretation of law (and thus support a racially discriminatory educational policy) or oppose the discrimination (and thus risk charges of hypocrisy in its fundamental approach to the judiciary). Alas, the Administration chose the first option, a choice that haunted it throughout its tenure.[1]

Bob Jones, historically a school that discriminated against African Americans in its admissions policies, was associated with a "religious" philosophy (though no particular religion), as were many southern (and probably northern) private schools. Until 1970, such discriminatory bodies routinely received exempt status — assuming they met other exemption requirements (such as lack of private inurement,

1. Indeed, the *Bob Jones* case was filled with controversy. So much so that, instead of the Solicitor General arguing the case at the U.S. Supreme Court, the government hired a private African American attorney — Mr. William Coleman — to do so. Interestingly, Coleman was also the first African American to clerk at the High Court. On April 21, 1982, the New York Times had this to say about Coleman's involvement:

> The Court often assigns lawyers to represent the indigent but it rarely has to retain a lawyer to defend an entire court. In this instance the lawyer will defend the judgment of the United States Court of Appeals for the Fourth Circuit, which followed a decade of sound precedent in a case involving [two universities] and their financial supporters. The court held that they were not entitled to the tax breaks the Federal Government permits for charitable donations that benefit the public.
>
> Initially, the Reagan Justice Department endorsed that view of the law[.] But suddenly, in January [of 1982], it reversed policy. Astonishingly, the department with responsibility for protecting civil rights came out for tax exemptions for segregated schools[.] As a result, government lawyers were no longer available to argue for their former stand when the case went to the Supreme Court. A friend of the Court [] was required.

Opinion, *A True Friend of the Court*, N.Y. Times, Apr. 21, 1982, at A22.

insubstantial lobbying, and no political activities). Then, in response to a federal injunction, the Internal Revenue Service (during the Nixon Administration) announced that it could no longer continue such a policy. *Green v. Kennedy*, 309 F. Supp. 1127 (D.D.C.), *appeal dismissed sub nom. Cannon v. Green*, 398 U.S. 956 (1970). Revenue Ruling 71-447 provided:

> Both the courts and the Internal Revenue Service have long recognized that the statutory requirement of being "organized and operated exclusively for religious, charitable, . . . or educational purposes" was intended to express the basic common law concept [of "charity"] . . . . All charitable trusts, educational or otherwise, are subject to the requirement that the purpose of the trust may not be illegal or contrary to public policy.

1971-2 C.B. 230, 1 (1971).

Citing the "national policy to discourage racial discrimination in education," the Service ruled that a private school must have a racially nondiscriminatory policy as to students; otherwise, it could not be considered "charitable" within the common law concepts reflected in §§ 170 and 501(c)(3).

By 1975, Bob Jones' policy evolved at least to the extent it would admit students of all races; however, it forbade interracial marriage or dating, ostensibly on religious grounds.[2] This policy change followed—and appears to have been prompted by—the Fourth Circuit decision in *McCrary v. Runyon*, 515 F.2d 1082 (4th Cir. 1975), *aff'd*, 427 U.S. 160 (1976), which prohibited racial exclusion from private schools. Congress, however, moved more slowly. While (in 1976) it added subsection 501(i) to preclude exemption for discriminatory private social clubs, it said nothing explicit about racial discrimination by other exempt entities, be they religious, educational, scientific, or other.

In 1976 (during the Ford Administration), the Service revoked Bob Jones University's exempt status, retroactive to 1970. This followed an unsuccessful attempt by the University to enjoin such government action. *Bob Jones University v. Simon*, 416 U.S. 725 (1974), (holding the Anti-Injunction Act, 26 U.S.C. § 7421(a), prohibited judicial review prior to the assessment or collection of any tax). After the University paid nominal unemployment taxes and failed to obtain a refund, it filed suit in the

2. The Supreme Court summarized the University's policy as follows:

> Since May 29, 1975, the University has permitted unmarried Negroes to enroll; but a disciplinary rule prohibits interracial dating and marriage. That rule reads:
>
> *"There is to be no interracial dating.*
>
> "1. Students who are partners in an interracial marriage will be expelled.
>
> "2. Students who are members of or affiliated with any group or organization which holds as one of its goals or advocates interracial marriage will be expelled.
>
> "3. Students who date outside of their own race will be expelled.
>
> "4. Students who espouse, promote, or encourage others to violate the University's dating rules and regulations will be expelled."

The University continues to deny admission to applicants engaged in an interracial marriage or known to advocate interracial marriage or dating.

district court for a refund of $21. The Service counterclaimed for federal unemployment taxes of $89,675.59 for the years 1971 through 1975, plus interest.

Citing the First Amendment protections for religious freedom, the district court granted the refund and denied the counterclaim. 468 F. Supp. 890, 907 (D.S.C. 1978). A divided Court of Appeals for the Fourth Circuit reversed the opinion, reading § 501(c)(3) against the background of charitable trust law. To be eligible for an exemption under that section, according to that Court, an institution must be "charitable" in the common-law sense, and therefore must not be contrary to public policy. 461 U.S. at 582.

Goldsboro Christian Schools had a similar history, though it never obtained exempt status. Based in North Carolina, it almost exclusively limited enrollment to white students. Following an audit for years 1969 through 1972, the school paid federal withholding, Social Security, and unemployment taxes of $3,459.93. After an unsuccessful refund claim, the school filed suit in district court and the government counterclaimed for an additional $160,073.96. The district court, although finding the discriminatory policies were based on "sincerely held religious beliefs," denied the refund, granted the counterclaim, and held Goldsboro not entitled to exempt status. *Goldsboro Christian Schools, Inc. v. United States*, 436 F. Supp. 1314 (E.D.N.C. 1977). The Fourth Circuit affirmed, *per curiam*, based on its then recent holding in *Bob Jones*, 644 F.2d 879 (4th Cir. 1981) (per curiam).

After the Supreme Court granted *certiorari* in both cases, 454 U.S. 892 (1981), the Service announced that it would withdraw Revenue Ruling 71-447 and thereafter grant exempt status to both institutions, pending action by Congress. According to a report prepared by the Joint Committee Staff:

> On January 12, 1982, the White House issued a statement concerning the tax-exempt status of nonprofit, private, educational institutions. In that statement, President Reagan said that "I am unalterably opposed to racial discrimination in any form" and that "I am also opposed to administrative agencies exercising powers that the Constitution assigns to the Congress." The President further stated that "I believe the right thing to do on this issue is to enact legislation which will prohibit tax exemptions for organizations that discriminate on the basis of race. Therefore, I will submit legislation and will work with the Congress to accomplish this purpose."
>
> On January 18, 1982, President Reagan transmitted to Congress proposed legislation to deny tax-exempt status to schools that are racially discriminatory. The proposal, which would be retroactive to July 10, 1970, would prohibit the granting of tax-exempt status to private schools with racially discriminatory policies.

Background Relating to the Effect of Racially Discriminatory Policies on the Tax-Exempt Status of Private Schools, Joint Committee Staff, 24 (Jan. 29, 1982).

The Court of Appeals for the D.C. Circuit, however, quickly enjoined the government from granting exempt status to any school that discriminated on the basis of race. *Wright v. Regan*, 1982 U.S. App. LEXIS 21708 (Feb. 18, 1982) (*per curiam* order). Thereafter, the proposed legislation never passed Congress.[3]

In 1983, the Supreme Court affirmed both circuit opinions. The majority addressed two main issues:

1. Does § 501 implicitly bar exempt status for racially discriminatory schools?

2. Do Constitutional protections involving religion force a separate standard for religious schools as compared to non-religious schools?

The Court answered "yes" to the first question and "no" to the second: rooted in historic charitable trust law, § 501 implicitly and constitutionally bars exempt status for racially discriminatory schools, whether they are religious or non-religious in nature.

The decision has been controversial. Much of the controversy stems not from the Court's answers to the above two questions; instead, criticism of *Bob Jones* centers on the Court's answer to a third question: must tax-exempt organizations promote some public benefit or public good? The majority opinion not only suggested "yes," but also that they must do so "demonstrably." Concurring, however, Justice Powell doubted the wisdom of such a requirement, finding it unnecessary to reach the correct result:

> With all respect, I am unconvinced that the critical question in determining tax-exempt status is whether an individual organization provides a clear "public benefit" as defined by the Court. Over 106,000 organizations filed § 501(c)(3) returns in 1981.... I find it impossible to believe that all or even most of those organizations could prove that they "demonstrably serve and [are] in harmony with the public interest" or that they are "beneficial and stabilizing influences in community life."

461 U.S. at 608–09 (Powell, J., concurring in part).

---

3. [U]nder the Administration proposal, an organization that normally maintains a regular faculty and curriculum (other than an exclusively religious curriculum) and that normally has a regularly enrolled body of students in attendance at the place where its educational activities are regularly carried on will not be exempt from tax if the organization has a racially discriminatory policy.

Under the proposal, such an organization would have a racially discriminatory policy (and therefore be denied exemption) if (1) it refuses to admit students of all races to the rights, privileges, programs, and activities generally accorded or made available to students by that organization, or if (2) it refuses to administer its educational policies, admissions policies, scholarship and loan programs, athletic programs, or other programs administered by the organization in a manner that does not discriminate on the basis of race.

BACKGROUND RELATING TO THE EFFECT OF RACIALLY DISCRIMINATORY POLICIES ON THE TAX-EXEMPT STATUS OF PRIVATE SCHOOLS, Joint Committee Staff, 29 (Jan. 29, 1982).

In hindsight, little evidence exists that organizations have faced any significant additional burden stemming from the language that so concerned Justice Powell: the need to prove they "demonstrably serve . . . the public interest." The future is naturally uncertain and some future Administration (or bureaucrat) may assert, or even abuse, the power to define public interest. Chapter 3 explores the possibility in greater depth; however, nearly 40 years of experience surely provide substantial reassurance that Justice Powell's fears have not become common.

A second controversial aspect of the case has nothing in particular to do with tax-exempt organizations. Some commentators—supported in large part by Justice Rehnquist's dissent and the Reagan Administration's statement on transmittal of its proposed legislation—criticize the majority for "legislating." They also criticize Congress for failing to do its job. Indeed, the *Bob Jones* majority stressed Congress' clear acquiescence in Revenue Ruling 71-447, which initially barred exempt status for racially discriminatory schools. One cannot help but speculate: if Congress felt so strongly on the subject, why did it not simply say so? This matter spanned 13 years—surely the majority in Congress could have found the opportunity to put into statutory law such a clear fundamental public policy; after all, it found the time (in 1976) to amend the rules on private social clubs prohibiting such discrimination. Did Congress fail to act in relation to charities because it (collectively) viewed the matter as clear and settled—and thus such legislation was superfluous? Did it fail to act, at least in part, to force the Hobson's Choice faced by the Executive Branch: support discrimination or support judicial activism? Or, perhaps, are such profoundly important public policies best set by courts rather than through legislation?

No matter how one might answer these questions, the following case is both critical and interesting reading—not just for its dealing with the subject at hand, but also for its description of the role charities play in our society.

Bob Jones University v. United States

461 U.S. 574 (1983)

CHIEF JUSTICE BURGER delivered the opinion of the Court.

. . . In Revenue Ruling 71-447, the IRS formalized the policy, first announced in 1970, that § 170 and § 501(c)(3) embrace the common-law "charity" concept. Under that view, to qualify for a tax exemption pursuant to § 501(c)(3), an institution must show, first, that it falls within one of the eight categories expressly set forth in that section, and second, that its activity is not contrary to settled public policy.

Section 501(c)(3) provides that "[corporations] . . . organized and operated exclusively for religious, charitable . . . or educational purposes" are entitled to tax exemption. Petitioners argue that the plain language of the statute guarantees them tax-exempt status. They emphasize the absence of any language in the statute expressly requiring all exempt organizations to be "charitable" in the common-law sense, and they contend that the disjunctive "or" separating the categories in § 501(c)(3) precludes such a reading. Instead, they argue that if an institution falls within one or more of the specified categories it is automatically entitled to exemption, without regard to whether it also qualifies as "charitable." The Court of Appeals rejected that contention and concluded that petitioners' interpretation of the statute "tears section 501(c)(3) from its roots." 639 F.2d, at 151.

It is a well-established canon of statutory construction that a court should go beyond the literal language of a statute if reliance on that language would defeat the plain purpose of the statute:

The general words used in the clause . . . , taken by themselves, and literally construed, without regard to the object in view, would seem to sanction the claim of the plaintiff. But this mode of expounding a statute has never been adopted by any enlightened tribunal—because it is evident that in many cases it would defeat the object which the Legislature intended to accomplish. And it is well settled that, in interpreting a statute, the court will not look merely to a particular clause in which general words may be used, *but will take in connection with it the whole statute . . . and the objects and policy of the law . . .* *Brown v. Duchesne*, 19 How. 183, 194 (1857) (emphasis added).

Section 501(c)(3) therefore must be analyzed and construed within the framework of the Internal Revenue Code and against the background of the congressional purposes. Such an examination reveals unmistakable evidence that, underlying all relevant parts of the Code, is the intent that entitlement to tax exemption depends on meeting certain common-law standards of charity—namely, that an institution seeking tax-exempt status must serve a public purpose and not be contrary to established public policy.

This "charitable" concept appears explicitly in § 170 of the Code. That section contains a list of organizations virtually identical to that contained in § 501(c)(3). It is apparent that Congress intended that list to have the same meaning in both sections.[4] In § 170, Congress used the list of organizations in defining the term "charitable contributions." On its face, therefore, § 170 reveals that Congress' intention was to provide tax benefits to organizations serving charitable purposes.[5] The form of

4. [10] The predecessor of § 170 originally was enacted in 1917, as part of the War Revenue Act of 1917, ch. 63, § 1201(2), 40 Stat. 330, whereas the predecessor of § 501(c)(3) dates back to the income tax law of 1894, Act of Aug. 27, 1894, ch. 349, 28 Stat. 509, see n. 14, *infra*. There are minor differences between the lists of organizations in the two sections, *see generally* Liles & Blum, *Development of the Federal Tax Treatment of Charities*, 39 Law & Contemp. Prob. 6, 24–25 (No. 4, 1975) (hereinafter Liles & Blum). Nevertheless, the two sections are closely related; both seek to achieve the same basic goal of encouraging the development of certain organizations through the grant of tax benefits. The language of the two sections is in most respects identical, and the Commissioner and the courts consistently have applied many of the same standards in interpreting those sections. *See* 5 J. Mertens, Law of Federal Income Taxation § 1.12 (1980); 6 *id.*, §§ 34.01–34.13 (1975); B. Bittker & L. Stone, Federal Income Taxation 220–222 (5th ed. 1980). To the extent that § 170 "aids in ascertaining the meaning" of § 501(c)(3), therefore, it is "entitled to great weight," *United States v. Stewart*, 311 U.S. 60, 64–65 (1940). *See Harris v. Commissioner*, 340 U.S. 106, 107 (1950).

5. [11] The dissent suggests that the Court "quite adeptly avoids the statute it is construing," *post*, at 612, and "seeks refuge . . . by turning to § 170," *post*, at 613. This assertion dissolves when

§ 170 simply makes plain what common sense and history tell us: in enacting both § 170 and § 501(c)(3), Congress sought to provide tax benefits to charitable organizations, to encourage the development of private institutions that serve a useful public purpose or supplement or take the place of public institutions of the same kind.

Tax exemptions for certain institutions thought beneficial to the social order of the country as a whole, or to a particular community, are deeply rooted in our history, as in that of England. The origins of such exemptions lie in the special privileges that have long been extended to charitable trusts.[6] More than a century ago, this Court announced the caveat that is critical in this case:

> "[It] has now become an established principle of American law, that courts of chancery will sustain and protect . . . a gift . . . to public charitable uses, *provided the same is consistent with local laws and public policy. . . ." Perin v. Carey*, 24 How. 465, 501 (1861) (emphasis added).

Soon after that, in 1877, the Court commented:

> "A charitable use, *where neither law nor public policy forbids*, may be applied to almost any thing *that tends to promote the well-doing and well-being of social man." Ould v. Washington Hospital for Foundlings*, 95 U.S. 303, 311 (emphasis added). . . .

In 1891, in a restatement of the English law of charity[7] which has long been recognized as a leading authority in this country, Lord MacNaghten stated:

---

one sees that § 501(c)(3) and § 170 are construed together, as they must be. The dissent acknowledges that the two sections are "mirror" provisions; surely there can be no doubt that the Court properly looks to § 170 to determine the meaning of § 501(c)(3). It is also suggested that § 170 is "at best of little usefulness in finding the meaning of § 501(c)(3)," since "§ 170(c) simply tracks the requirements set forth in § 501(c)(3)," *post*, at 614. That reading loses sight of the fact that § 170(c) defines the term "charitable contribution." The plain language of § 170 reveals that Congress' objective was to employ tax exemptions and deductions to promote certain *charitable* purposes. While the eight categories of institutions specified in the statute are indeed presumptively charitable in nature, the IRS properly considered principles of charitable trust law in determining whether the institutions in question may truly be considered "charitable" for purposes of entitlement to the tax benefits conferred by § 170 and § 501(c)(3).

6. [12] The form and history of the charitable exemption and deduction sections of the various income tax Acts reveal that Congress was guided by the common law of charitable trusts. *See* Simon, *The Tax-Exempt Status of Racially Discriminatory Religious Schools*, 36 Tax L. Rev. 477, 485–489 (1981) (hereinafter Simon). Congress acknowledged as much in 1969. The House Report on the Tax Reform Act of 1969, Pub. L. 91-172, 83 Stat. 487, stated that the § 501(c)(3) exemption was available only to institutions that served "the specified charitable purposes," H. R. Rep. No. 91-413, pt. 1, p. 35 (1969), and described "charitable" as "a term that has been used in the law of trusts for hundreds of years." *Id.*, at 43. We need not consider whether Congress intended to incorporate into the Internal Revenue Code any aspects of charitable trust law other than the requirements of public benefit and a valid public purpose.

7. [13] . . . .

> "'Charity' in its legal sense comprises four principal divisions: trusts for the relief of poverty; *trusts for the advancement of education*; trusts for the advancement of religion; and trusts for *other purposes beneficial to the community*, not falling under any of the preceding heads." *Commissioners v. Pemsel*, [1891] A. C. 531, 583 (emphasis added).

See, *e.g.*, 4 A. Scott, Law of Trusts § 368, pp. 2853–2854 (3d ed. 1967) (hereinafter Scott). These statements clearly reveal the legal background against which Congress enacted the first charitable exemption statute in 1894:[8] charities were to be given preferential treatment because they provide a benefit to society. What little floor debate occurred on the charitable exemption provision of the 1894 Act and similar sections of later statutes leaves no doubt that Congress deemed the specified organizations entitled to tax benefits because they served desirable public purposes. See, *e.g.*, 26 Cong. Rec. 585-586 (1894); *id.*, at 1727. In floor debate on a similar provision in 1917, for example, Senator Hollis articulated the rationale: "For every dollar that a man contributes for these public charities, educational, scientific, or otherwise, the public gets 100 per cent." 55 Cong. Rec. 6728. See also *e.g.*, 44 Cong. Rec. 4150 (1909); 50 Cong. Rec. 1305–1306 (1913). In 1924, this Court restated the common understanding of the charitable exemption provision: "Evidently the exemption is made in recognition of the benefit which the public derives from corporate activities of the class named, and is intended to aid them when not conducted for private gain." *Trinidad v. Sagrada Orden*, 263 U.S. 578, 581.[9]

In enacting the Revenue Act of 1938, ch. 289, 52 Stat. 447, Congress expressly reconfirmed this view with respect to the charitable deduction provision: "The exemption from taxation of money or property devoted to charitable and other purposes is based upon the theory that the Government is compensated for the loss of revenue by its relief from financial burdens which would otherwise have to be met by appropriations from other public funds, and by the benefits resulting from the promotion of the general welfare." H.R. Rep. No. 1860, 75th Cong., 3d Sess., 19 (1938).[10]

---

8. [14] Act of Aug. 27, 1894, ch. 349, § 32, 28 Stat. 556–557. The income tax system contained in the 1894 Act was declared unconstitutional, *Pollock v. Farmers' Loan & Trust Co.*, 158 U.S. 601 (1895), for reasons unrelated to the charitable exemption provision. The terms of that exemption were in substance included in the corporate income tax contained in the Payne-Aldrich Tariff Act of 1909, ch. 6, § 38, 36 Stat. 112. A similar exemption has been included in every income tax Act since the adoption of the Sixteenth Amendment, beginning with the Revenue Act of 1913, ch. 16, § II(G), 38 Stat. 172. *See generally* Reiling, *Federal Taxation: What Is a Charitable Organization?*, 44 A.B.A.J. 525 (1958); Liles & Blum.

9. [15] That same year, the Bureau of Internal Revenue expressed a similar view of the charitable deduction section of the estate tax contained in the Revenue Act of 1918, ch. 18, § 403(a)(3), 40 Stat. 1098. The Solicitor of Internal Revenue looked to the common law of charitable trusts in construing that provision, and noted that "generally bequests for the benefit and advantage of the general public are valid as charities." Sol. Op. 159, III-1 Cum. Bull. 480, 482 (1924).

10. [16] The common-law requirement of public benefit is universally recognized by commentators on the law of trusts. For example, the Bogerts state: "In return for the favorable treatment

A corollary to the public benefit principle is the requirement, long recognized in the law of trusts, that the purpose of a charitable trust may not be illegal or violate established public policy. In 1861, this Court stated that a public charitable use must be "consistent with local laws and public policy," *Perin v. Carey*, 24 How., at 501. Modern commentators and courts have echoed that view. *See, e.g.*, Restatement (Second) of Trusts § 377, Comment *c* (1959); 4 Scott § 377, and cases cited therein; Bogert § 378, at 191–192.

When the Government grants exemptions or allows deductions, all taxpayers are affected; the very fact of the exemption or deduction for the donor means that other taxpayers can be said to be indirect and vicarious "donors." Charitable exemptions are justified on the basis that the exempt entity confers a public benefit—a benefit that the society or the community may not itself choose or be able to provide, or that supplements and advances the work of public institutions already supported by tax revenues.[11] History buttresses logic to make clear that, to warrant exemption under § 501(c)(3), an institution must fall within a category specified in that section and must demonstrably serve and be in harmony with the public interest.[12] The institution's purpose must not be so at odds with the common community conscience as to undermine any public benefit that might otherwise be conferred.

---

accorded charitable gifts which imply some disadvantage to the community, the courts must find in the trust which is to be deemed 'charitable' some real advantages to the public which more than offset the disadvantages arising out of special privileges accorded charitable trusts." G. Bogert & G. Bogert, Law of Trusts and Trustees § 361, p. 3 (rev. 2d ed. 1977) (hereinafter Bogert). For other statements of this principle, see, *e.g.*, 4 Scott § 348, at 2770; Restatement (Second) of Trusts § 368, Comment *b* (1959); E. Fisch, D. Freed, & E. Schachter, Charities and Charitable Foundations § 256 (1974).

11. [18] The dissent acknowledges that "Congress intended . . . to offer a tax benefit to organizations . . . providing a public benefit," *post*, at 614–615, but suggests that Congress itself fully defined what organizations provide a public benefit, through the list of eight categories of exempt organizations contained in § 170 and § 501(c)(3). Under that view, any nonprofit organization that falls within one of the specified categories is automatically entitled to the tax benefits, provided it does not engage in expressly prohibited lobbying or political activities. *Post*, at 617. The dissent thus would have us conclude, for example, that any nonprofit organization that does not engage in prohibited lobbying activities is entitled to tax exemption as an "educational" institution if it is organized for the "'instruction or training of the individual for the purpose of improving or developing his capabilities,' " 26 CFR § 1.501(c)(3)-1(d)(3) (1982). See *post*, at 623. As Judge Leventhal noted in *Green v. Connally*, 330 F. Supp. 1150, 1160 (DC), summarily *aff'd sub nom. Coit v. Green*, 404 U.S. 997 (1971), Fagin's school for educating English boys in the art of picking pockets would be an "educational" institution under that definition. Similarly, a band of former military personnel might well set up a school for intensive training of subversives for guerrilla warfare and terrorism in other countries; in the abstract, that "school" would qualify as an "educational" institution. Surely Congress had no thought of affording such an unthinking, wooden meaning to § 170 and § 501(c)(3) as to provide tax benefits to "educational" organizations that do not serve a public, charitable purpose.

12. [19] The Court's reading of § 501(c)(3) does not render meaningless Congress' action in specifying the eight categories of presumptively exempt organizations, as petitioners suggest. To be entitled to tax-exempt status under § 501(c)(3), an organization must first fall within one of the categories specified by Congress, and in addition must serve a valid charitable purpose.

B

We are bound to approach these questions with full awareness that determinations of public benefit and public policy are sensitive matters with serious implications for the institutions affected; a declaration that a given institution is not "charitable" should be made only where there can be no doubt that the activity involved is contrary to a fundamental public policy. But there can no longer be any doubt that racial discrimination in education violates deeply and widely accepted views of elementary justice. Prior to 1954, public education in many places still was conducted under the pall of *Plessy v. Ferguson*, 163 U.S. 537 (1896); racial segregation in primary and secondary education prevailed in many parts of the country. *See, e.g.*, SEGREGATION AND THE FOURTEENTH AMENDMENT IN THE STATES (B. Reams & P. Wilson eds. 1975).[13] This Court's decision in *Brown v. Board of Education*, 347 U.S. 483 (1954), signaled an end to that era. Over the past quarter of a century, every pronouncement of this Court and myriad Acts of Congress and Executive Orders attest a firm national policy to prohibit racial segregation and discrimination in public education.

An unbroken line of cases following *Brown v. Board of Education* establishes beyond doubt this Court's view that racial discrimination in education violates a most fundamental national public policy, as well as rights of individuals. "The right of a student not to be segregated on racial grounds in schools . . . is indeed so fundamental and pervasive that it is embraced in the concept of due process of law." *Cooper v. Aaron*, 358 U.S. 1, 19 (1958). In *Norwood v. Harrison*, 413 U.S. 455, 468–469 (1973), we dealt with a nonpublic institution:

> "[A] private school—even one that discriminates—fulfills an important educational function; *however, . . . [that] legitimate educational function cannot be isolated from discriminatory practices. . . . [Discriminatory] treatment exerts a pervasive influence on the entire educational process.*" (Emphasis added.) See also *Runyon v. McCrary*, 427 U.S. 160 (1976)[].

Congress, in Titles IV and VI of the Civil Rights Act of 1964, Pub. L. 88-352, 78 Stat. 241, 42 U.S.C. §§ 2000c, 2000c-6, 2000d, clearly expressed its agreement that racial discrimination in education violates a fundamental public policy. Other sections of that Act, and numerous enactments since then, testify to the public policy against racial discrimination. . . .

---

13. [20] In 1894, when the first charitable exemption provision was enacted, racially segregated educational institutions would not have been regarded as against public policy. Yet contemporary standards must be considered in determining whether given activities provide a public benefit and are entitled to the charitable tax exemption. In *Walz v. Tax Comm'n*, 397 U.S. 664, 673 (1970), we observed: "Qualification for tax exemption is not perpetual or immutable; some tax-exempt groups lose that status when their activities take them outside the classification and new entities can come into being and qualify for exemption." Charitable trust law also makes clear that the definition of "charity" depends upon contemporary standards. *See, e.g.*, RESTATEMENT (SECOND) OF TRUSTS § 374, Comment *a* (1959); BOGERT § 369, at 65–67; 4 SCOTT § 368, at 2855–2856.

The Executive Branch has consistently placed its support behind eradication of racial discrimination. Several years before this Court's decision in *Brown v. Board of Education, supra,* President Truman issued Executive Orders prohibiting racial discrimination in federal employment decisions, Exec. Order No. 9980, 3 CFR 720 (1943–1948 Comp.), and in classifications for the Selective Service, Exec. Order No. 9988, 3 CFR 726, 729 (1943–1948 Comp.). In 1957, President Eisenhower employed military forces to ensure compliance with federal standards in school desegregation programs. Exec. Order No. 10730, 3 CFR 389 (1954–1958 Comp.). And in 1962, President Kennedy announced:

"[The] granting of Federal assistance for . . . housing and related facilities from which Americans are excluded because of their race, color, creed, or national origin is unfair, unjust, and inconsistent with the public policy of the United States as manifested in its Constitution and laws." Exec. Order No. 11063, 3 CFR 652 (1959–1963 Comp.).

These are but a few of numerous Executive Orders over the past three decades demonstrating the commitment of the Executive Branch to the fundamental policy of eliminating racial discrimination. . . .

Few social or political issues in our history have been more vigorously debated and more extensively ventilated than the issue of racial discrimination, particularly in education. Given the stress and anguish of the history of efforts to escape from the shackles of the "separate but equal" doctrine of *Plessy v. Ferguson*, 163 U.S. 537 (1896), it cannot be said that educational institutions that, for whatever reasons, practice racial discrimination, are institutions exercising "beneficial and stabilizing influences in community life," *Walz v. Tax Comm'n*, 397 U.S. 664, 673 (1970), or should be encouraged by having all taxpayers share in their support by way of special tax status.

There can thus be no question that the interpretation of § 170 and § 501(c)(3) announced by the IRS in 1970 was correct. That it may be seen as belated does not undermine its soundness. It would be wholly incompatible with the concepts underlying tax exemption to grant the benefit of tax-exempt status to racially discriminatory educational entities, which "[exert] a pervasive influence on the entire educational process." *Norwood v. Harrison, supra*, at 469. Whatever may be the rationale for such private schools' policies, and however sincere the rationale may be, racial discrimination in education is contrary to public policy. Racially discriminatory educational institutions cannot be viewed as conferring a public benefit within the "charitable" concept discussed earlier, or within the congressional intent underlying § 170 and § 501(c)(3).[14]

---

14. [21] In view of our conclusion that racially discriminatory private schools violate fundamental public policy and cannot be deemed to confer a benefit on the public, we need not decide whether an organization providing a public benefit and otherwise meeting the requirements of § 501(c)(3) could nevertheless be denied tax-exempt status if certain of its activities violated a law or public policy.

C

Petitioners contend that, regardless of whether the IRS properly concluded that racially discriminatory private schools violate public policy, only Congress can alter the scope of § 170 and § 501(c)(3). Petitioners accordingly argue that the IRS overstepped its lawful bounds in issuing its 1970 and 1971 rulings.

Yet ever since the inception of the Tax Code, Congress has seen fit to vest in those administering the tax laws very broad authority to interpret those laws. In an area as complex as the tax system, the agency Congress vests with administrative responsibility must be able to exercise its authority to meet changing conditions and new problems. Indeed as early as 1918, Congress expressly authorized the Commissioner "to make all needful rules and regulations for the enforcement" of the tax laws. Revenue Act of 1918, ch. 18, § 1309, 40 Stat. 1143. The same provision, so essential to efficient and fair administration of the tax laws, has appeared in Tax Codes ever since, see 26 U.S.C. § 7805(a); and this Court has long recognized the primary authority of the IRS and its predecessors in construing the Internal Revenue Code. . . .

Congress, the source of IRS authority, can modify IRS rulings it considers improper; and courts exercise review over IRS actions. In the first instance, however, the responsibility for construing the Code falls to the IRS. Since Congress cannot be expected to anticipate every conceivable problem that can arise or to carry out day-to-day oversight, it relies on the administrators and on the courts to implement the legislative will. Administrators, like judges, are under oath to do so.

* * *

Guided, of course, by the Code, the IRS has the responsibility, in the first instance, to determine whether a particular entity is "charitable" for purposes of § 170 and § 501(c)(3). This in turn may necessitate later determinations of whether given activities so violate public policy that the entities involved cannot be deemed to provide a public benefit worthy of "charitable" status. We emphasize, however, that these sensitive determinations should be made only where there is no doubt that the organization's activities violate fundamental public policy.

On the record before us, there can be no doubt as to the national policy. In 1970, when the IRS first issued the ruling challenged here, the position of all three branches of the Federal Government was unmistakably clear. The correctness of the Commissioner's conclusion that a racially discriminatory private school "is not 'charitable' within the common law concepts reflected in . . . the Code," Rev. Rul. 71-447, 1971-2 Cum. Bull., at 231, is wholly consistent with what Congress, the Executive, and the courts had repeatedly declared before 1970. Indeed, it would be anomalous for the Executive, Legislative, and Judicial Branches to reach conclusions that add up to a firm public policy on racial discrimination, and at the same time have the IRS blissfully ignore what all three branches of the Federal Government had declared.[15] Clearly an educational institution engaging in practices affirmatively at odds with this declared position of the whole Government cannot be seen as exercising a "beneficial and stabilizing [influence] in community life," *Walz v. Tax Comm'n*, 397 U.S., at 673, and is not "charitable," within the meaning of § 170 and § 501(c)(3). We therefore hold that the IRS did not exceed its authority when it announced its interpretation of § 170 and § 501(c)(3) in 1970 and 1971.

D

The actions of Congress since 1970 leave no doubt that the IRS reached the correct conclusion in exercising its authority. It is, of course, not unknown for independent agencies or the Executive Branch to misconstrue the intent of a statute; Congress can and often does correct such misconceptions, if the courts have not done so. Yet for a dozen years Congress has been made aware — acutely aware — of the IRS rulings of 1970 and 1971. As we noted earlier, few issues have been the subject of more vigorous and widespread debate and discussion in and out of Congress than those related to racial segregation in education. Sincere adherents advocating contrary views have ventilated the subject for well over three decades. Failure of Congress to modify the IRS rulings of 1970 and 1971, of which Congress was, by its own studies and by public discourse, constantly reminded, and Congress' awareness of the denial of tax-exempt status for racially discriminatory schools when enacting other and related legislation make out an unusually strong case of legislative acquiescence in and ratification by implication of the 1970 and 1971 rulings.

Ordinarily, and quite appropriately, courts are slow to attribute significance to the failure of Congress to act on particular legislation. [] We have observed that "unsuccessful attempts at legislation are not the best of guides to legislative intent," *Red Lion Broadcasting Co. v. FCC*, 395 U.S. 367, 382, n. 11 (1969). Here, however, we do not have an ordinary claim of legislative acquiescence. Only one month after the IRS announced its position in 1970, Congress held its first hearings on this precise issue. Equal Educational Opportunity: Hearings before the Senate Select Committee on Equal Educational Opportunity, 91st Cong., 2d Sess., 1991 (1970). Exhaustive hearings have been held on the issue at various times since then. These include hearings in February 1982, after we granted review in this case. Administration's Change in Federal Policy Regarding the Tax Status of Racially Discriminatory Private Schools: Hearing before the House Committee on Ways and Means, 97th Cong., 2d Sess. (1982).

---

15. [23] Justice Powell misreads the Court's opinion when he suggests that the Court implies that "the Internal Revenue Service is invested with authority to decide which public policies are sufficiently 'fundamental' to require denial of tax exemptions," *post*, at 611. The Court's opinion does not warrant that interpretation. Justice Powell concedes that "if any national policy is sufficiently fundamental to constitute such an overriding limitation on the availability of tax-exempt status under § 501(c)(3), it is the policy against racial discrimination in education." Since that policy is sufficiently clear to warrant Justice Powell's concession and for him to support our finding of longstanding congressional acquiescence, it should be apparent that his concerns about the Court's opinion are unfounded.

Nonaction by Congress is not often a useful guide, but the nonaction here is significant. During the past 12 years there have been no fewer than 13 bills introduced to overturn the IRS interpretation of § 501(c)(3).[16] Not one of these bills has emerged from any committee, although Congress has enacted numerous other amendments to § 501 during this same period, including an amendment to § 501(c)(3) itself. . . . It is hardly conceivable that Congress — and in this setting, any member of Congress — was not abundantly aware of what was going on. In view of its prolonged and acute awareness of so important an issue, Congress' failure to act on the bills proposed on this subject provides added support for concluding that Congress acquiesced in the IRS rulings of 1970 and 1971. . . .

The evidence of congressional approval of the policy embodied in Revenue Ruling 71-447 goes well beyond the failure of Congress to act on legislative proposals. Congress affirmatively manifested its acquiescence in the IRS policy when it enacted the present § 501(i) of the Code, Act of Oct. 20, 1976, Pub. L. 94-568, 90 Stat. 2697. That provision denies tax-exempt status to social clubs whose charters or policy statements provide for "discrimination against any person on the basis of race, color, or religion."[17] Both the House and Senate Committee Reports on that bill articulated the national policy against granting tax exemptions to racially discriminatory private clubs. . . . .

Even more significant is the fact that both Reports focus on this Court's affirmance of *Green v. Connally*, 330 F. Supp. 1150 (DC 1971), as having established that "discrimination on account of race is inconsistent with an *educational institution's* tax-exempt status." S. Rep. No. 94-1318, *supra*, at 7–8, and n.5; H. R. Rep. No. 94-1353, *supra*, at 8, and n. 5 (emphasis added). These references in congressional Committee Reports on an enactment denying tax exemptions to racially discriminatory private social clubs cannot be read other than as indicating approval of the standards applied to racially discriminatory private schools by the IRS subsequent to 1970, and specifically of Revenue Ruling 71-447.

III

Petitioners contend that, even if the Commissioner's policy is valid as to nonreligious private schools, that policy cannot constitutionally be applied to schools that engage in racial discrimination on the basis of sincerely held religious beliefs.[18] As to such schools, it is argued that the IRS construction of § 170 and § 501(c)(3) violates

16. [25] . . .

17. [26] Prior to the introduction of this legislation, a three-judge District Court had held that segregated social clubs were entitled to tax exemptions. *McGlotten v. Connally*, 338 F. Supp. 448 (DC 1972). Section 501(i) was enacted primarily in response to that decision. See S. Rep. No. 94-1318, pp. 7–8 (1976); H. R. Rep. No. 94-1353, p. 8 (1976).

18. [28] The District Court found, on the basis of a full evidentiary record, that the challenged practices of petitioner Bob Jones University were based on a genuine belief that the Bible forbids interracial dating and marriage. 468 F. Supp., at 894. We assume, as did the District Court, that the same is true with respect to petitioner Goldsboro Christian Schools. *See* 436 F. Supp., at 1317.

their free exercise rights under the Religion Clauses of the First Amendment. This contention presents claims not heretofore considered by this Court in precisely this context.

This Court has long held the Free Exercise Clause of the First Amendment to be an absolute prohibition against governmental regulation of religious beliefs, *Wisconsin v. Yoder*, 406 U.S. 205, 219 (1972)[]. As interpreted by this Court, moreover, the Free Exercise Clause provides substantial protection for lawful conduct grounded in religious belief, see *Wisconsin v. Yoder, supra*, at 220; *Thomas v. Review Board of Indiana Employment Security Div.*, 450 U.S. 707 (1981)[]. However, "[not] all burdens on religion are unconstitutional.... The state may justify a limitation on religious liberty by showing that it is essential to accomplish an overriding governmental interest." *United States v. Lee*, 455 U.S. 252, 257–258 (1982). []

On occasion this Court has found certain governmental interests so compelling as to allow even regulations prohibiting religiously based conduct. In *Prince v. Massachusetts*, 321 U.S. 158 (1944), for example, the Court held that neutrally cast child labor laws prohibiting sale of printed materials on public streets could be applied to prohibit children from dispensing religious literature. The Court found no constitutional infirmity in "excluding [Jehovah's Witness children] from doing there what no other children may do." *Id.*, at 171. See also [] *United States v. Lee, supra; Gillette v. United States, supra.* [] Denial of tax benefits will inevitably have a substantial impact on the operation of private religious schools, but will not prevent those schools from observing their religious tenets.

The governmental interest at stake here is compelling. As discussed in Part II-B, *supra*, the Government has a fundamental, overriding interest in eradicating racial discrimination in education[19]—discrimination that prevailed, with official approval, for the first 165 years of this Nation's constitutional history. That governmental interest substantially outweighs whatever burden denial of tax benefits places on petitioners' exercise of their religious beliefs. The interests asserted by petitioners cannot be accommodated with that compelling governmental interest, see *United States v. Lee, supra*, at 259–260; and no "less restrictive means," see *Thomas v. Review Board of Indiana Employment Security Div., supra*, at 718, are available to achieve the governmental interest.[20]

---

19. [29] We deal here only with religious *schools*—not with churches or other purely religious institutions; here, the governmental interest is in denying public support to racial discrimination in education. As noted earlier, racially discriminatory schools "[exert] a pervasive influence on the entire educational process," outweighing any public benefit that they might otherwise provide, *Norwood v. Harrison*, 413 U.S. 455, 469 (1973). *See generally* Simon 495–496.

20. [30] Bob Jones University also argues that the IRS policy should not apply to it because it is entitled to exemption under § 501(c)(3) as a "religious" organization, rather than as an "educational" institution. The record in this case leaves no doubt, however, that Bob Jones University is both an educational institution and a religious institution. As discussed previously, the IRS policy properly extends to all private schools, including religious schools. See n. 29, *supra*. The IRS policy thus was properly applied to Bob Jones University.

... The IRS properly denied tax-exempt status to Goldsboro Christian Schools.

Petitioner Bob Jones University, however, contends that it is not racially discriminatory. It emphasizes that it now allows all races to enroll, subject only to its restrictions on the conduct of all students, including its prohibitions of association between men and women of different races, and of interracial marriage. Although a ban on intermarriage or interracial dating applies to all races, decisions of this Court firmly establish that discrimination on the basis of racial affiliation and association is a form of racial discrimination.... We therefore find that the IRS properly applied Revenue Ruling 71-447 to Bob Jones University.[21]

The judgments of the Court of Appeals are, accordingly,

Affirmed.

JUSTICE POWELL, concurring in part and concurring in the judgment.

* * *

Federal taxes are not imposed on organizations "operated exclusively for religious, charitable, scientific, testing for public safety, literary, or educational purposes...." 26 U.S.C. § 501(c)(3). The Code also permits a tax deduction for contributions made to these organizations. § 170(c). It is clear that petitioners, organizations incorporated for educational purposes, fall within the language of the statute. It also is clear that the language itself does not mandate refusal of tax-exempt status to any private school that maintains a racially discriminatory admissions policy. Accordingly, there is force in JUSTICE REHNQUIST's argument that §§ 170(c) and 501(c)(3) should be construed as setting forth the only criteria Congress has established for qualification as a tax-exempt organization. See *post*, at 612–615 (REHNQUIST, J., dissenting). Indeed, were we writing prior to the history detailed in the Court's opinion, this could well be the construction I would adopt. But there has been a decade of acceptance that is persuasive in the circumstances of these cases, and I conclude that there are now sufficient reasons for accepting the IRS's construction of the Code as proscribing tax exemptions for schools that discriminate on the basis of race as a matter of policy.

I cannot say that this construction of the Code, adopted by the IRS in 1970 and upheld by the Court of Appeals below, is without logical support. The statutory terms are not self-defining, and it is plausible that in some instances an organization seeking a tax exemption might act in a manner so clearly contrary to the purposes

21. [32] Bob Jones University also argues that the IRS policy should not apply to it because it is entitled to exemption under § 501(c)(3) as a "religious" organization, rather than as an "educational" institution. The record in this case leaves no doubt, however, that Bob Jones University is both an educational institution and a religious institution. As discussed previously, the IRS policy properly extends to all private schools, including religious schools. *See* n. 29, *supra*. The IRS policy thus was properly applied to Bob Jones University.

of our laws that it could not be deemed to serve the enumerated statutory purposes.[22] And, as the Court notes, if any national policy is sufficiently fundamental to constitute such an overriding limitation on the availability of tax-exempt status under § 501(c)(3), it is the policy against racial discrimination in education. Finally, and of critical importance for me, the subsequent actions of Congress present "an unusually strong case of legislative acquiescence in and ratification by implication of the [IRS's] 1970 and 1971 rulings" with respect to racially discriminatory schools. In particular, Congress' enactment of § 501(i) in 1976 is strong evidence of agreement with these particular IRS rulings.[23]

II

I therefore concur in the Court's judgment that tax-exempt status under §§ 170(c) and 501(c)(3) is not available to private schools that concededly are racially discriminatory. I do not agree, however, with the Court's more general explanation of the justifications for the tax exemptions provided to charitable organizations. The Court states:

> "Charitable exemptions are justified on the basis that the exempt entity confers a public benefit—a benefit which the society or the community may not itself choose or be able to provide, or which supplements and advances the work of public institutions already supported by tax revenues. History buttresses logic to make clear that, to warrant exemption under § 501(c)(3), an institution must fall within a category specified in that section and must demonstrably serve and be in harmony with the public interest. The institution's purpose must not be so at odds with the common community conscience as to undermine any public benefit that might otherwise be conferred."

Applying this test to petitioners, the Court concludes that "[clearly] an educational institution engaging in practices affirmatively at odds with [the] declared position of the whole Government cannot be seen as exercising a 'beneficial and stabilizing [influence] in community life,' . . . and is not 'charitable,' within the

22. [1] I note that the Court has construed other provisions of the Code as containing narrowly defined public-policy exceptions. See *Commissioner v. Tellier*, 383 U.S. 687, 693–694 (1966); *Tank Truck Rentals, Inc. v. Commissioner*, 356 U.S. 30, 35 (1958).

23. [2] The District Court for the District of Columbia in *Green v. Connally*, 330 F. Supp. 1150 (three-judge court), summarily *aff'd sub nom. Coit v. Green*, 404 U.S. 997 (1971), held that racially discriminatory private schools were not entitled to tax-exempt status. The same District Court, however, later ruled that racially segregated social clubs could receive tax exemptions under § 501(c)(7) of the Code. *See McGlotten v. Connally*, 338 F. Supp. 448 (1972) (three-judge court). Faced with these two important three-judge court rulings, Congress expressly overturned the relevant portion of *McGlotten* by enacting § 501(i), thus conforming the policy with respect to social clubs to the prevailing policy with respect to private schools. This affirmative step is a persuasive indication that Congress has not just silently acquiesced in the result of *Green*. *Cf. Merrill Lynch, Pierce, Fenner & Smith, Inc. v. Curran*, 456 U.S. 353, 402 (1982) (Powell, J., dissenting) (rejecting theory "that congressional intent can be inferred from silence, and that legislative inaction should achieve the force of law").

meaning of § 170 and § 501(c)(3)." (quoting *Walz v. Tax Comm'n*, 397 U.S. 664, 673 (1970)).

With all respect, I am unconvinced that the critical question in determining tax-exempt status is whether an individual organization provides a clear "public benefit" as defined by the Court. Over 106,000 organizations filed § 501(c)(3) returns in 1981. . . . I find it impossible to believe that all or even most of those organizations could prove that they "demonstrably serve and [are] in harmony with the public interest" or that they are "beneficial and stabilizing influences in community life." Nor am I prepared to say that petitioners, because of their racially discriminatory policies, necessarily contribute nothing of benefit to the community. It is clear from the substantially secular character of the curricula and degrees offered that petitioners provide educational benefits.

Even more troubling to me is the element of conformity that appears to inform the Court's analysis. The Court asserts that an exempt organization must "demonstrably serve and be in harmony with the public interest," must have a purpose that comports with "the common community conscience," and must not act in a manner "affirmatively at odds with [the] declared position of the whole Government." Taken together, these passages suggest that the primary function of a tax-exempt organization is to act on behalf of the Government in carrying out governmentally approved policies. In my opinion, such a view of § 501(c)(3) ignores the important role played by tax exemptions in encouraging diverse, indeed often sharply conflicting, activities and viewpoints. As Justice Brennan has observed, private, nonprofit groups receive tax exemptions because "each group contributes to the diversity of association, viewpoint, and enterprise essential to a vigorous, pluralistic society." *Walz, supra*, at 689 (concurring opinion). Far from representing an effort to reinforce any perceived "common community conscience," the provision of tax exemptions to nonprofit groups is one indispensable means of limiting the influence of governmental orthodoxy on important areas of community life.[24]

24. [3] Certainly § 501(c)(3) has not been applied in the manner suggested by the Court's analysis. The 1,100-page list of exempt organizations includes—among countless examples—such organizations as American Friends Service Committee, Inc., Committee on the Present Danger, Jehovahs Witnesses in the United States, Moral Majority Foundation, Inc., Friends of the Earth Foundation, Inc., Mountain States Legal Foundation, National Right to Life Educational Foundation, Planned Parenthood Federation of America, Scientists and Engineers for Secure Energy, Inc., and Union of Concerned Scientists Fund, Inc. See Internal Revenue Service, Cumulative List of Organizations Described in Section 170(c) of the Internal Revenue Code of 1954, pp. 31, 221, 376, 518, 670, 677, 694, 795, 880, 1001, 1073 (Revised Oct. 1981). It would be difficult indeed to argue that each of these organizations reflects the views of the "common community conscience" or "demonstrably . . . [is] in harmony with the public interest." In identifying these organizations, largely taken at random from the tens of thousands on the list, I of course do not imply disapproval of their being exempt from taxation. Rather, they illustrate the commendable tolerance by our Government of even the most strongly held divergent views, including views that at least from time to time *are* "at odds" with the position of our Government. We have consistently recognized that such disparate groups are entitled to share the privilege of tax exemption.

Given the importance of our tradition of pluralism,[25] "[the] interest in preserving an area of untrammeled choice for private philanthropy is very great." *Jackson v. Statler Foundation*, 496 F.2d 623, 639 (C.A.2 1974) (Friendly, J., dissenting from denial of reconsideration en banc).

I do not suggest that these considerations always are or should be dispositive. Congress, of course, may find that some organizations do not warrant tax-exempt status. In these cases I agree with the Court that Congress has determined that the policy against racial discrimination in education should override the countervailing interest in permitting unorthodox private behavior.

I would emphasize, however, that the balancing of these substantial interests is for *Congress* to perform. I am unwilling to join any suggestion that the Internal Revenue Service is invested with authority to decide which public policies are sufficiently "fundamental" to require denial of tax exemptions. Its business is to administer laws designed to produce revenue for the Government, not to promote "public policy." As former IRS Commissioner Kurtz has noted, questions concerning religion and civil rights "are far afield from the more typical tasks of tax administrators—determining taxable income." Kurtz, *Difficult Definitional Problems in Tax Administration: Religion and Race*, 23 CATHOLIC LAWYER 301 (1978). This Court often has expressed concern that the scope of an agency's authorization be limited to those areas in which the agency fairly may be said to have expertise,[26] and this concern applies with special force when the asserted administrative power is one to determine the scope of public policy. As JUSTICE BLACKMUN has noted:

> "[Where] the philanthropic organization is concerned, there appears to be little to circumscribe the almost unfettered power of the Commissioner. This may be very well so long as one subscribes to the particular brand of social policy the Commissioner happens to be advocating at the time . . . ,

25. [4] "A distinctive feature of America's tradition has been respect for diversity. This has been characteristic of the peoples from numerous lands who have built our country. It is the essence of our democratic system." *Mississippi University for Women v. Hogan*, 458 U.S. 718, 745 (1982) (POWELL, J., dissenting). Sectarian schools make an important contribution to this tradition, for they "have provided an educational alternative for millions of young Americans" and "often afford wholesome competition with our public schools." *Wolman v. Walter*, 433 U.S. 229, 262 (1977) (POWELL, J., concurring in part, concurring in judgment in part, and dissenting in part).

26. [5] *See, e.g.*, Community Television of Southern California v. Gottfried, 459 U.S. 498, 510–511, n. 17 (1983) ("[An] agency's general duty to enforce the public interest does not require it to assume responsibility for enforcing legislation that is not directed at the agency"); Hampton v. Mow Sun Wong, 426 U.S. 88, 114 (1976) ("It is the business of the Civil Service Commission to adopt and enforce regulations which will best promote the efficiency of the federal civil service. That agency has no responsibility for foreign affairs, for treaty negotiations, for establishing immigration quotas or conditions of entry, or for naturalization policies"); NAACP v. FPC, 425 U.S. 662, 670 (1976) ("The use of the words 'public interest' in the Gas and Power Acts is not a directive to the [Federal Power] Commission to seek to eradicate discrimination, but, rather, is a charge to promote the orderly production of supplies of electric energy and natural gas at just and reasonable rates").

> but application of our tax laws should not operate in so fickle a fashion. Surely, social policy in the first instance is a matter for legislative concern."

Commissioner v. "Americans United" Inc., 416 U.S. 752, 774–775 (1974) (dissenting opinion).

III

The Court's decision upholds IRS Revenue Ruling 71-447, and thus resolves the question whether tax-exempt status is available to private schools that openly maintain racially discriminatory admissions policies. There no longer is any justification for Congress to hesitate—as it apparently has—in articulating and codifying its desired policy as to tax exemptions for discriminatory organizations. Many questions remain, such as whether organizations that violate other policies should receive tax-exempt status under § 501(c)(3). These should be legislative policy choices. It is not appropriate to leave the IRS "on the cutting edge of developing national policy." Kurtz, *supra*, at 308. The contours of public policy should be determined by Congress, not by judges or the IRS.

JUSTICE REHNQUIST, dissenting.

The Court points out that there is a strong national policy in this country against racial discrimination. To the extent that the Court states that Congress in furtherance of this policy could deny tax-exempt status to educational institutions that promote racial discrimination, I readily agree. But, unlike the Court, I am convinced that Congress simply has failed to take this action and, as this Court has said over and over again, regardless of our view on the propriety of Congress' failure to legislate we are not constitutionally empowered to act for it.

In approaching this statutory construction question the Court quite adeptly avoids the statute it is construing. This I am sure is no accident, for there is nothing in the language of § 501(c)(3) that supports the result obtained by the Court. . . . .

With undeniable clarity, Congress has explicitly defined the requirements for § 501(c)(3) status. An entity must be (1) a corporation, or community chest, fund, or foundation, (2) organized for one of the eight enumerated purposes, (3) operated on a nonprofit basis, and (4) free from involvement in lobbying activities and political campaigns. Nowhere is there to be found some additional, undefined public policy requirement.

The Court first seeks refuge from the obvious reading of § 501(c)(3) by turning to *§ 170* of the Internal Revenue Code, which provides a tax deduction for contributions made to § 501(c)(3) organizations. In setting forth the general rule, § 170 states:

> "There shall be allowed as a deduction any charitable contribution (as defined in subsection (c)) payment of which is made within the taxable year. A charitable contribution shall be allowable as a deduction only if verified under regulations prescribed by the Secretary." 26 U.S.C. § 170(a)(1).

The Court seizes the words "charitable contribution" and with little discussion concludes that "[on] its face, therefore, § 170 reveals that Congress' intention was to provide tax benefits to organizations serving charitable purposes," intimating that this implies some unspecified common-law charitable trust requirement.

The Court would have been well advised to look to subsection (c) where, as § 170(a)(1) indicates, Congress has defined a "charitable contribution":

* * *

Plainly, § 170(c) simply tracks the requirements set forth in § 501(c)(3). Since § 170 is no more than a mirror of § 501(c)(3) and, as the Court points out, § 170 followed § 501(c)(3) by more than two decades, it is at best of little usefulness in finding the meaning of § 501(c)(3).

Making a more fruitful inquiry, the Court next turns to the legislative history of § 501(c)(3) and finds that Congress intended in that statute to offer a tax benefit to organizations that Congress believed were providing a public benefit. I certainly agree. But then the Court leaps to the conclusion that this history is proof Congress intended that an organization seeking § 501(c)(3) status "must fall within a category specified in that section *and must demonstrably serve and be in harmony with the public interest.*" (emphasis added). To the contrary, I think that the legislative history of § 501(c)(3) unmistakably makes clear that *Congress has decided* what organizations are serving a public purpose and providing a public benefit within the meaning of § 501(c)(3) and has clearly set forth in § 501(c)(3) the characteristics of such organizations. In fact, there are few examples which better illustrate Congress' effort to define and redefine the requirements of a legislative Act.

The first general income tax law was passed by Congress in the form of the Tariff Act of 1894. A provision of that Act provided an exemption for "corporations, companies, or associations organized and conducted solely for charitable, religious, or educational purposes." Ch. 349, § 32, 28 Stat. 556 (1894). The income tax portion of the 1894 Act was held unconstitutional by this Court, see *Pollock v. Farmers' Loan & Trust Co.*, 158 U.S. 601 (1895), but a similar exemption appeared in the Tariff Act of 1909 which imposed a tax on corporate income. The 1909 Act provided an exemption for "any corporation or association organized and operated exclusively for religious, charitable, or educational purposes, no part of the net income of which inures to the benefit of any private stockholder or individual." Ch. 6, § 38, 36 Stat. 113 (1909).

With the ratification of the Sixteenth Amendment, Congress again turned its attention to an individual income tax with the Tariff Act of 1913. And again, in the direct predecessor of § 501(c)(3), a tax exemption was provided for "any corporation or association organized and operated exclusively for religious, charitable, scientific, or educational purposes, no part of the net income of which inures to the benefit of any private stockholder or individual." Ch. 16, § II(G)(a), 38 Stat. 172 (1913). In subsequent Acts Congress continued to broaden the list of exempt purposes. The Revenue Act of 1918 added an exemption for corporations or associations organized "for the prevention of cruelty to children or animals." Ch. 18, § 231(6), 40 Stat. 1057, 1076 (1918). The Revenue Act of 1921 expanded the groups to which the exemption applied to include "any community chest, fund, or foundation" and added "literary" endeavors to the list of exempt purposes. Ch. 136, § 231(6), 42 Stat. 253 (1921). The exemption remained unchanged in the Revenue Acts of 1924, 1926, 1928, and 1932. In the Revenue Act of 1934 Congress added the requirement that no substantial part of the activities of any exempt organization can involve the carrying on of "propaganda" or "attempting to influence legislation." Ch. 277, § 101(6), 48 Stat. 700 (1934). Again, the exemption was left unchanged by the Revenue Acts of 1936 and 1938.

The tax laws were overhauled by the Internal Revenue Code of 1939, but this exemption was left unchanged. Ch. 1, § 101(6), 53 Stat. 33 (1939). When the 1939 Code was replaced with the Internal Revenue Code of 1954, the exemption was adopted in full in the present § 501(c)(3) with the addition of "testing for public safety" as an exempt purpose and an additional restriction that tax-exempt organizations could not "participate in, or intervene in (including the publishing or distributing of statements), any political campaign on behalf of any candidate for public office." Ch. 1, § 501(c)(3), 68A Stat. 163 (1954). Then in 1976 the statute was again amended adding to the purposes for which an exemption would be authorized, "to foster national or international amateur sports competition," provided the activities did not involve the provision of athletic facilities or equipment. Tax Reform Act of 1976, Pub. L. 94-455, § 1313(a), 90 Stat. 1730 (1976).

One way to read the opinion handed down by the Court today leads to the conclusion that this long and arduous refining process of § 501(c)(3) was certainly a waste of time, for when enacting the original 1894 statute Congress intended to adopt a common-law term of art, and intended that this term of art carry with it all of the common-law baggage which defines it. Such a view, however, leads also to the unsupportable idea that Congress has spent almost a century adding illustrations simply to clarify an already defined common-law term.

Another way to read the Court's opinion leads to the conclusion that even though Congress has set forth *some* of the requirements of a § 501(c)(3) organization, it intended that the IRS additionally require that organizations meet a higher standard of public interest, not stated by Congress, but to be determined and defined by the IRS and the courts. This view I find equally unsupportable. Almost a century of statutory history proves that Congress itself intended to decide what § 501(c)(3) requires. Congress has expressed its decision in the plainest of terms in § 501(c)(3) by providing that tax-exempt status is to be given to any corporation, or community chest, fund, or foundation that is organized for one of the eight enumerated purposes, operated on a nonprofit basis, and uninvolved in lobbying activities or political campaigns. The IRS certainly is empowered to adopt regulations for the enforcement of these specified requirements, and the courts have authority to resolve challenges to the IRS's exercise of this power, but Congress has left it to neither the IRS nor the courts to select or add to the requirements of § 501(c)(3).

The Court suggests that unless its new requirement be added to § 501(c)(3), nonprofit organizations formed to teach pickpockets and terrorists would necessarily acquire tax-exempt status. Since the Court does not challenge the characterization of *petitioners* as "educational" institutions within the meaning of § 501(c)(3), and in fact states several times in the course of its opinion that petitioners *are* educational institutions, it is difficult to see how this argument advances the Court's reasoning for disposing of petitioners' cases.

But simply because I reject the Court's heavyhanded creation of the requirement that an organization seeking § 501(c)(3) status must "serve and be in harmony with the public interest," does not mean that I would deny to the IRS the usual authority to adopt regulations further explaining what Congress meant by the term "educational." The IRS has fully exercised that authority in Treas. Reg. § 1.501(c)(3)-1(d)(3).... I have little doubt that neither the "Fagin School for Pickpockets" nor a school training students for guerrilla warfare and terrorism in other countries would meet the definitions contained in the regulations.

Prior to 1970, when the charted course was abruptly changed, the IRS had continuously interpreted § 501(c)(3) and its predecessors in accordance with the view I have expressed above. This, of course, is of considerable significance in determining the intended meaning of the statute....

In 1970 the IRS was sued by parents of black public school children seeking to enjoin the IRS from according tax-exempt status under § 501(c)(3) to private schools in Mississippi that discriminated against blacks. The IRS answered, consistent with its longstanding position, by maintaining a lack of authority to deny the tax exemption if the schools met the specified requirements of § 501(c)(3). Then "[in] the midst of this litigation," *Green v. Connally*, 330 F. Supp. 1150, 1156 (DC), summarily aff'd *sub nom. Coit v. Green*, 404 U.S. 997 (1971), and in the face of a preliminary injunction, the IRS changed its position and adopted the view of the plaintiffs.

Following the close of the litigation, the IRS published its new position in Revenue Ruling 71-447, stating that "a school asserting a right to the benefits provided for in section 501(c)(3) of the Code as being organized and operated exclusively for educational purposes must be a common law charity in order to be exempt under that section." Rev. Rul. 71-447, 1971-2 Cum. Bull. 230. The IRS then concluded that a school that promotes racial discrimination violates public policy and therefore cannot qualify as a common-law charity. The circumstances under which this change in interpretation was made suggest that it is entitled to very little deference. But even if the circumstances were different, the latter-day wisdom of the IRS has no basis in § 501(c)(3).

Perhaps recognizing the lack of support in the statute itself, or in its history, for the 1970 IRS change in interpretation, the Court finds that "[the] actions of Congress since 1970 leave no doubt that the IRS reached the correct conclusion in exercising its authority," concluding that there is "an unusually strong case of legislative acquiescence in and ratification by implication of the 1970 and 1971 rulings." *Ante*, at 599. The Court relies first on several bills introduced to overturn the IRS interpretation of § 501(c)(3). But we have said before, and it is equally applicable here, that this type of congressional inaction is of virtually no weight in determining legislative intent.

See *United States v. Wise*, 370 U.S. 405, 411 (1962) []. These bills and related hearings indicate little more than that a vigorous debate has existed in Congress concerning the new IRS position.

The Court next asserts that "Congress affirmatively manifested its acquiescence in the IRS policy when it enacted the present § 501(i) of the Code," a provision that "denies tax-exempt status to social clubs whose charters or policy statements provide for" racial discrimination. *Ante*, at 601. Quite to the contrary, it seems to me that in § 501(i) Congress showed that when it wants to add a requirement prohibiting racial discrimination to one of the tax-benefit provisions, it is fully aware of how to do it. *Cf. Commissioner v. Tellier*, 383 U.S. 687, 693, n. 10 (1966).

The Court intimates that the Ashbrook and Dornan Amendments also reflect an intent by Congress to acquiesce in the new IRS position. The amendments were passed to limit certain enforcement procedures proposed by the IRS in 1978 and 1979 for determining whether a school operated in a racially nondiscriminatory fashion. The Court points out that in proposing his amendment, Congressman Ashbrook stated: "'My amendment very clearly indicates on its face that all the regulations in existence as of August 22, 1978, would not be touched.'" The Court fails to note that Congressman Ashbrook also said:

> The IRS has no authority to create public policy. . . . So long as the Congress has not acted to set forth a national policy respecting denial of tax exemptions to private schools, it is improper for the IRS or any other branch of the Federal Government to seek denial of tax-exempt status. . . . There exists but a single responsibility which is proper for the Internal Revenue Service: To serve as tax collector.

125 Cong. Rec. 18444 (1979).

In the same debate, Congressman Grassley asserted: "Nobody argues that racial discrimination should receive preferred tax status in the United States. However, the IRS should not be making these decisions on the agency's own discretion. Congress should make these decisions." *Id.*, at 18448. The same debates are filled with other similar statements. While on the whole these debates do not show conclusively that Congress believed the IRS had exceeded its authority with the 1970 change in position, they likewise are far less than a showing of acquiescence in and ratification of the new position.

This Court continuously has been hesitant to find ratification through inaction. See *United States v. Wise*, *supra*. This is especially true where such a finding "would result in a construction of the statute which not only is at odds with the language of the section in question and the pattern of the statute taken as a whole, but also is extremely far reaching in terms of the virtually untrammeled and unreviewable power it would vest in a regulatory agency." *SEC v. Sloan*, 436 U.S. 103, 121 (1978). Few cases would call for more caution in finding ratification by acquiescence than the present ones. The new IRS interpretation is not only far less than a longstanding administrative policy, it is at odds with a position maintained by the IRS, and unquestioned by Congress, for several decades prior to 1970. The interpretation is unsupported by the statutory language, it is unsupported by legislative history, the interpretation has led to considerable controversy in and out of Congress, and the interpretation gives to the IRS a broad power which until now Congress had kept for itself. Where in addition to these circumstances Congress has shown time and time again that it is ready to enact positive legislation to change the Tax Code when it desires, this Court has no business finding that Congress has adopted the new IRS position by failing to enact legislation to reverse it.

I have no disagreement with the Court's finding that there is a strong national policy in this country opposed to racial discrimination. I agree with the Court that Congress has the power to further this policy by denying § 501(c)(3) status to organizations that practice racial discrimination. But as of yet Congress has failed to do so. Whatever the reasons for the failure, this Court should not legislate for Congress.

Petitioners are each organized for the "instruction or training of the individual for the purpose of improving or developing his capabilities," 26 CFR § 1.501(c)(3)-1(d)(3) (1982), and thus are organized for "educational purposes" within the meaning of § 501(c)(3). Petitioners' nonprofit status is uncontested. There is no indication that either petitioner has been involved in lobbying activities or political campaigns. Therefore, it is my view that unless and until Congress affirmatively amends § 501(c)(3) to require more, the IRS is without authority to deny petitioners § 501(c)(3) status. For this reason, I would reverse the Court of Appeals.

Questions

One commentator wrote the following about *Bob Jones*:

> The influence of societal views on race discrimination was an important factor in *Bob Jones University* because, according to the Court, to be tax-exempt, a charitable institution "must demonstrably serve and be in harmony with the public interest . . . [and] must not be so at odds with the common community conscience as to undermine any public benefit that might otherwise be conferred." The Court in *Bob Jones* further reasoned that denial of tax benefits would not "prevent [the organization] from observing . . . [its] . . . tenets."
>
> In light of the Court's rationale in *Bob Jones University*, some scholars have queried whether the Boy Scouts' sexual orientation-based discrimination is so at odds with the "community conscience" on homosexuality that it would serve as a legitimate reason for revoking an organization's tax-exempt status.

J. Christine Harris, *Should Boy Scouts' Policy on Gays Preclude Tax Exempt Status?*, 31 Exempt Org. Tax Rev. 32, 33 (2001).

In recent years, the public's perception of public policy has changed alongside that of the Court's. For nearly the entire twentieth century, the Boy Scouts of America followed a strict policy of banning homosexual scouts and leaders: the Supreme Court, in *Boy Scouts of America v. Dale*, 530 U.S. 640 (2000), endorsed this practice as not inconsistent with the Constitution. However, in 2013, the Boy Scouts' governing body voted to allow openly gay youth participants. A few years later, in 2015, they also voted to allow openly gay adults to serve as leaders within the organization. *See Boy Scouts of America Amends Adult Leadership Policy*, Boy Scouts of America Newsroom Blog, https://web.archive.org/web/20160902071556/http://scoutingnewsroom.org/blog/boy-scouts-of-america-amends-adult-leadership-policy (last visited Sept. 14, 2020); Kurtis Lee, *Here Is How the Boy Scouts Has Evolved on Social Issues over the Years*, Los Angeles Times (Feb. 5, 2017, 3 A.M.), https://www.latimes.com/nation/la-na-boy-scouts-evolution-2017-story.html.

In addition, the Supreme Court ruled in 2020 that a landmark federal civil rights law from the 1960s protects gay and transgender workers. *See Bostock v. Clayton County, Georgia*, 140 S. Ct. 1731 (2020). In *Bostock*, Justice Neil M. Gorsuch and Chief Justice John G. Roberts Jr. joined the Court's liberal wing in the 6-to-3 ruling. They said Title VII of the Civil Rights Act of 1964, which prohibits discrimination "because of sex," includes gay and transgender employees.

1. Even though the *Bostock* decision does not explicitly apply to 501(c)(3) tax exemptions, what bearing does (or should) this case have on delineating "clearly defined public policy" for tax exemption purposes?

2. Does the public policy rationale preclude tax exemption for a Boy Scout Council if a particular Council does not allow openly gay men to serve as scout leaders? *See* "Boy Scouts of America Statement" (May 23, 2013) (changing the organization's policy to admit gay youth, but retaining the existing policy regarding adult leaders). What about for an employer that discriminates against gay or transgender employees in apparent violation of Title VII of the Civil Rights Act of 1964?

3. If there is not now a "clearly defined public policy" against discrimination based on sexual orientation or transgender persons, when, if ever, will we know that such public policies have come about and who should decide that such policies do or do not exist?

4. What are the pros and cons of injecting a public policy requirement into § 501(c)(3)?

One of us has thought long and hard about the whole notion of injecting a public policy requirement into § 501(c)(3) to achieve an otherwise laudable goal (such as eradicating racial discrimination). With regard to question 1, see David A. Brennen, *Charities and the Constitution: Evaluating the Role of Constitutional Principles in Determining the Scope of Tax Law's Public Policy Limitation for Charities*, 5 Fla. Tax Rev. 779, 831–44 (2002) (discussing the public policy doctrine in the context of homosexuality). With regard to questions 2 and 3, see *Charities and the Constitution*, *supra* (discussing whether the constitution should be used as a guide for determining the existence of particular public policies); David A. Brennen, *Tax Expenditures, Social Justice, and Civil Rights: Expanding the Scope of Civil Rights Laws to Apply to Tax-Exempt Charities*, 2001 BYU L. Rev. 167 (discussing whether statutory civil rights laws could be used as a substitute for the public policy doctrine); David A. Brennen, *The Power of the Treasury: Racial Discrimination, Public Policy and "Charity" in Contemporary Society*, 33 U.C. DAVIS L. REV. 389, 389–447 (2000) (discussing overall concerns with the public policy doctrine, including enforcement concerns). *See also* Samuel D. Brunson & David J. Herzig, *A Diachronic Approach to Bob Jones: Religious Tax Exemptions After* Obergefell, 92 IND. L.J. 1175 (2017) (advocating for "three tiers of examination as proxies for the standard of fundamental public policy," including "strict scrutiny analysis," using "the Civil Rights Act as the proxy for fundamental public policy," and "utilizing the equal protection test under the Fourteenth Amendment."); Nicholas A. Mirkay, *Globalism, Public Policy, and Tax-Exempt Status: Are U.S. Charities Adrift at Sea?*, 91 N.C. L. REV. 851 (2013) (examining the public policy doctrine's applicability to charities that potentially violate U.S. foreign policy).

B. The Illegality Doctrine

The federal tax consequences of illegal activities are generally straightforward: courts apply various statutes and doctrines so as not to encourage crime. As a result, receipts from illegal activities are taxed, consistent with § 61 (requiring the inclusion of gross income from whatever source derived) and *Glenshaw Glass* (defining gross income as "an undeniable accession to wealth, clearly realized, and over which the taxpayers have complete dominion."). *Commissioner v. Glenshaw Glass*, 348 U.S. 426 (1955). Without question, proceeds from illegal drug sales, prostitution, gambling, theft, and similar criminal enterprises constitute an accession to wealth. This is true even though the taxpayer is obligated to return stolen property or forfeit illegal gains. *James v. United States*, 366 U.S. 213 (1961); *United States v. Sullivan*, 274 U.S. 259 (1927); Treas. Reg. § 1.61-14(a).

Costs associated with such illegal activities, however, present a more difficult question. Permitting them as deductions would encourage crime. In 1955, the Supreme Court decided two cases dealing with the issue. In *Tank Truck Rentals*, the Court decided against deductibility of fines assessed for violation of state trucking weight laws. Allowing such a deduction would frustrate public policy. *Tank Truck Rentals, Inc. v. Commissioner*, 356 U.S. 30 (1958). In a case decided the same day, however, the Supreme Court permitted deduction of rent and salary expenses associated with illegal gambling activities. *Commissioner v. Sullivan*, 356 U.S. 27 (1958). The two cases can be difficult to reconcile, although both were arguably consistent with § 162 as then written, which allowed deductions for ordinary and necessary business expenses. Fines for overweight trucks are not "ordinary and necessary" expenses; however, rent and salaries are indeed "ordinary and necessary," even for illegal businesses. Such reconciliation relegates the decisions to those based on statutory analysis rather than broad public policy. *See also* Treas. Reg. § 1.162-1(a) (disallowing deductions that contravene sharply defined public policy).

Congress partially resolved the issue of "illegal deductions" in 1970 with the enactment of § 162(c). The section generally disallows deductions for "illegal payments" if the law prohibiting them is "generally enforced." While explicitly applying to illegal bribes and kickbacks, the provision also can be used to deny deductions for costs and expenses associated with illegal activities, such as drug sales.

In light of the above statutes and cases, no one should be surprised to learn of similar principles in relation to tax laws affecting tax-exempt entities. The *Bob Jones* decision prohibits exemption for organizations that violate clearly defined public policy. More specifically, the following Revenue Ruling prohibits exemption for organizations that encourage or foment illegal activities. Pay attention to the standard used in the ruling, i.e., what portion of the purpose (under the organizational test) or of the activities (under the operational test) must be illegal so as to trigger the doctrine prohibiting exemption for illegal activities?

Revenue Ruling 75-384

1975-2 C.B. 204

* * *

Advice has been requested whether a nonprofit organization formed to promote world peace and disarmament by nonviolent direct action including acts of civil disobedience qualifies for exemption from Federal income tax under section 501(c)(3) or 501(c)(4) of the Internal Revenue Code of 1954.

The purposes of the organization are to educate and inform the public on the principles of pacifism and nonviolent action including civil disobedience. Its primary activity is the sponsoring of protest demonstrations and nonviolent action projects in opposition to war and preparations for war.

Protest demonstrations are conducted at military establishments, federal agencies, and industrial companies involved with military and defense operations. Other activities consist of peace matches and protests against the use of tax monies for war purposes. The protest demonstrations constitute the primary activity of the organization. They are designed to draw public attention to the views of the organization and to exert pressure on governmental authorities. To derive the maximum publicity of an event, demonstrators are urged to commit acts of civil disobedience. Participants deliberately block vehicular or pedestrian traffic, disrupt the work of government, and prevent the movement of supplies. These activities are violations of local ordinances and breaches of public order. Incidental to demonstrations, leaflets are dispersed presenting the views of the organization.

* * *

As a matter of trust law, one of the main sources of the general law of charity, no trust can be created for a purpose which is illegal. The purpose is illegal if the trust property is to be used for an object which is in violation of the criminal law, or if the trust tends to induce the commission of crime, or if the accomplishment of the purpose is otherwise against public, policy. IV *Scott on Trusts* Sec. 377 (3d. ed. 1967). Thus, all charitable trusts (and by implication all charitable organizations, regardless of their form) are subject to the requirement that their purposes may not be illegal or contrary to public policy. . . .

In this case the organization induces or encourages the commission of criminal acts by planning and sponsoring such events. The intentional nature of this encouragement precludes the possibility that the organization might unfairly fail to qualify for exemption due to an isolated or inadvertent violation of a regulatory statute. Its activities demonstrate an illegal purpose which is inconsistent with charitable ends. Moreover, the generation of criminal acts increases the burdens of government, thus frustrating a well recognized charitable goal, i.e., relief of the burdens of government. Accordingly, the organization is not operated exclusively for charitable purposes and does not qualify for exemption from Federal income tax under section 501(c)(3) of the Code.

* * *

Illegal activities, which violate the minimum standards of acceptable conduct necessary to the preservation of an orderly society, are contrary to the common good and the general welfare of the people in a community and thus are not permissible means of promoting the social welfare for purposes of section 501(c)(4) of the Code. Accordingly, the organization in this case is not operated exclusively for the promotion of social welfare and does not qualify for exemption from Federal income tax under section 501(c)(4).

Authors' Analysis

Notice two things about that ruling: it applies both the organizational and operational tests (under § 501(c)(3) an entity must be *both* organized *and* operated exclusively for charitable purposes). A substantial purpose of the entity was to promote civil disobedience. Operationally, such activities were also substantial; indeed, the ruling speaks of the demonstrations as being the "primary" activity. That could create some confusion: the organization failed for having a substantial illegal *purpose*. In addition, it also failed for having *primary* illegal *activities*. Surely, mere *substantial* illegal activities would also have been fatal.

Compare Rev. Rul. 75-384 to Rev. Rul. 97-21, which dealt with exempt hospitals. The 1997 ruling posits six exempt hospitals with varying physician recruitment methods. It approves five, but disapproves of the sixth, which involved illegal kickbacks:

> Hospital F is located in City Z, a medium to large size metropolitan area. Because of its physician recruitment practices, Hospital F has been found guilty in a court of law of knowingly and willfully violating the Medicare and Medicaid anti-kickback statute, 42 U.S.C. § 1320a-7b(b), for providing recruitment incentives that constituted payments for referrals. The activities resulting in the violations were substantial.

* * *

> Hospital F has engaged in physician recruiting practices resulting in a criminal conviction. As in Rev. Rul. 75-384, the recruiting activities were intentional and criminal, not isolated or inadvertent violations of a regulatory statute. An organization that engages in substantial unlawful activities, including activities involving the use of the organization's property for an objective that is in violation of criminal law, does not qualify as an organization described in § 501(c)(3). Because Hospital F has knowingly and willfully conducted substantial activities that are inconsistent with charitable purposes, it does not comply with the requirements of § 501(c)(3) and § 1.501(c)(3)-1.

This ruling effectively expands the application of the illegality doctrine: the kickbacks were neither a primary nor even a substantial purpose, although they were "substantial" activities. Many organizations commit crimes — perhaps a violation of a gambling statute or fundraising law. At least under these rulings, such behavior endangers the charity's exempt status if it is substantial, intentional, knowing, and willful. *See* Steven J. Willis, *People in Glass Houses*, 113 Tax Notes 477 (2006).

C. Writing and Planning Exercise

People for the Ethical Treatment of Animals (PETA) is a § 501(c)(3) organization dedicated to animal rights. On Monday, its president hands you a file with the following three documents (among others not included here) and asks you to prepare a letter in response to Congressman McInnis (whose letter is included in the file below). She has also scheduled a meeting with you at 2:00 p.m. that afternoon to discuss PETA's exempt status and any other legal and strategic concerns relating to the file. Prepare a draft letter to the congressman and an outline of issues to discuss with PETA's president.

1. ABC News Broadcast on Ecoterror

Dean Schabner, New Front on Ecoterror? Some Want to Target High-Profile Activists in Battle on Ecoterror

ABC News, Feb. 26, 2002

Summary:

- Members of Congress and lobbyists have asked the Administration to examine well-known animal rights and environmental groups, suggesting they be shut down — or at least be denied tax exemptions — because they are supporters of terrorism.
- According to sources, PETA gave $1,500 to ELF, which has been involved in vandalism to the tune of $43,000,000. The Animal Liberation Front, which is allegedly related to ELF and PETA, firebombed a Colorado ski

resort, causing approximately $12,000,000 in damages. According to the FBI, each group amounts to a "terrorist operation."

- PETA's response:

  We have an annual budget of $17 million and [they] . . . go back two years to find something for $1,500. [W]e don't fund anything that's illegal."

2. *Wall Street Journal* Editorial

Animal House (Editorial)

Wall Street Journal

Feb. 22, 2002

Summary:

- "PETA used tax-free dollars to support other advocates of violence, such as the $45,200 contribution it gave to the 'support committee' of Rodney Coronado, an arsonist who pleaded guilty to setting fire to a University lab."
- PETA denied doing anything "illegal" and suggested this contribution and several similar ones were "tiny items in multimillion-dollar annual budgets." A PETA spokesman described Mr. Coronado as "very nice" and "idealistic." She even distinguished violence to property and violence to people.
- The editorial finished with the curt statement: "You might try telling that to a fireman."

3. Letter to PETA from Chairman McInnis

March 4, 2002

Ms. Ingrid Newkirk
President, PETA
501 Front Street
Norfolk, Virginia 23510

Dear Ms. Newkirk:

When the House Resources Subcommittee on Forests and Forest Health held an oversight hearing probing the increasing threat of ecoterrorism on National Forest lands last month, evidence was submitted by one of the Subcommittee's witnesses showing that the People for the Ethical Treatment of Animals (PETA) contributed to the Earth Liberation Front, the public face of an organization described by the FBI as America's single largest domestic terrorism threat. The purpose of the contribution to ELF is listed on PETA's Form 990 tax return as to "support their program activities." Subsequent reporting in the media appears to substantiate these allegations.

As a non-profit organization with tax-exempt privileges and the incumbent public policy obligations that status entails, PETA has a responsibility to explain the full extent of its involvement with and contributions to environmental terror groups like ELF and ALF. With that in mind, I respectfully request that you respond to the following questions, the answers to which will be made part of the hearing's public record.

- Since 1993, how much and on how many occasions has PETA made financial contributions to either the Earth Liberation Front and/or its press office, the Animal Liberation Front and/or its press office, and suspected or convicted persons associated with ELF and ALF?

  Does PETA have any internal policies or guidelines either encouraging or discouraging financial support of unlawful groups like ELF and ALF? If so, what are they?
- Under what rationale did PETA make a contribution(s) to ELF?
- What steps did PETA take to ensure that these funds would not be used for unlawful purposes?
- Whose signature appeared on the returned check that PETA gave ELF?
- Does PETA condone the violent activities of organizations like ELF? Should PETA's contribution to ELF be seen as an endorsement?
- Does PETA have any intention of contributing to ELF, ALF, or other similarly motivated groups in the future?

As local, state, and federal law enforcement officials grapple with this formidable threat, careful scrutiny must be applied to any and all persons or organizations that lend financial aid and comfort to this radical band of extremists. In the future, I hope that PETA will cut-off its financial ties with ELF and ALF, and join America's largest mainstream environmental groups in publicly condemning these and other eco-terrorist groups.

I look forward to your response.

Sincerely,

Scott McInnis
Chairman, House Resources Subcommittee on Forests and Forest Health
cc: Internal Revenue Service
Federal Bureau of Investigation

Questions

1. Assume all the groups mentioned in the article and editorial are § 501(c)(3) organizations (indeed, most of them are). Do you see a sufficient public policy/illegality basis for revoking the tax-exempt status of any or all of the groups? What are some of the dangers inherent in relying upon a public policy doctrine? Do you detect any constitutional issues with regard to the call to revoke the organizations' tax exemption?

2. In 2003, Congress enacted § 501(p), which directs the Service to suspend the tax-exempt status of an organization designated or identified as a terrorist organization or as supporting terrorism. During the period of suspension, contributions to the organization are not tax deductible. The provision also states that no person may challenge the suspension or denial of tax deductibility of contributions via a tax case. Apparently, an aggrieved party or organization would need to proceed against the designation or identification in a separate action. Does this provision raise any concerns in your mind? In light of the already existing public policy and illegality doctrines, is § 501(p) necessary?

Chapter 3

The Exempt Purpose Requirement: *Religious*

CODE: §§ 501(c)(3); 170(b)(1)(A)(i); 170(c)(2)

TREAS. REGS.: §§ 1.501(c)(3)-1(c)-(d); 1.170A-9(a)

A. Overview of Religious Exemption

This Chapter continues our exploration of the meaning of "charity" with a consideration of what exactly constitutes "exempt purposes." The primary exempt purposes under §§ 501(c)(3) and 170(c)(2) are: religious, educational, scientific, and charitable. As previously noted, the term "charitable" encompasses most, if not all, other purposes. An applicant for exemption need not list a specific purpose—such as "religious" or "charitable"—on Form 1023 (the application for exempt status).[1] It must, however, provide a detailed narrative of proposed activities, which will necessarily identify the entity as being "organized and operated" for an exempt purpose, such as "religious." Thus, viewing "religious" as a distinct category is helpful.

Even someone with only a passing interest in constitutional law will recognize that the grant of tax exemption to religious organizations implicates the establishment and free exercise clauses of the First Amendment. We are tempted simply to inform our readers that the Supreme Court has concluded, as a matter of broad principle, that granting tax exemption to religious organizations does not violate the First Amendment. But doing so would only reinforce the too-often held assumption that tax law is made, studied, and applied in a vacuum, without regard to other legal and non-legal disciplines. Indeed, we all need to be reminded that tax law is perhaps the epitome of interdisciplinary arts—it relates to birth, marriage, divorce, death, spirituality, and many, if not all, events in between. In particular instances, tax laws can be understood only in conjunction with an understanding of other legal disciplines, such as environmental law, securities law, family law, and even constitutional law, to name just a few.

1. The instructions for IRS Form 1023 state the following: "Limiting your purposes by reference to section 501(c)(3) generally will be sufficient." *See* IRS Form 1023 Instructions (Part III, Line 1—Purpose Clause). Internal Revenue Service, Instructions for Form 1023 (01/2020) (2020), https://www.irs.gov/instructions/i1023#idm139883039998304.

We begin, then, with a study of the historical and constitutional implications of granting tax exemption to religious organizations. Both historical and constitutional concerns are always lurking about with regard to any issue regarding tax exemption of religious organizations. As a result, the grant, administration, and policing of exemption to religious organizations is accomplished via special rules and considerations.

B. Constitutional Implications of Religious Tax Exemption

Are state and local property tax exemptions granted to religious organizations constitutional? Yes, answered a nearly unanimous Supreme Court in 1970. Logically, the same analysis applies to federal tax exemption. As a result, the § 501(c)(3) income tax exemption granted to "religious" organizations appears constitutional:

> For so long as federal income taxes have had any potential impact on churches—more than 75 years—religious organizations have been expressly exempt from the tax. Such treatment is an "aid" to churches no more and no less in principle than the real estate tax exemption granted by States.

Walz v. Tax Commission, 397 U.S. 664, 676 (1970).

At issue in *Walz* was whether the granting of tax exemption constituted the "establishment" of a religion. Similarly, denial (or revocation) of tax exemption might be considered to infringe the "free exercise" of religion. The *Walz* majority argued forcefully that taxing religiously owned property involves as much or more entanglement with religion as does granting an exemption.

The dissent, and one concurring Justice, however, found no real difference between a tax exemption and a direct subsidy. The two Justices, however, focused on different aspects of the similarity between exemption and subsidy. Justice Harlan, concurring, found no economic difference. In contrast, Justice Douglas found the two constitutionally indistinguishable. Quoting from a Brookings Institution report, he explained:

> Tax exemption ... is essentially a government grant or subsidy. Such grants would seem to be justified only if the purpose for which they are made is one for which the legislative body *would be equally willing to make* a direct appropriation from public funds equal to the amount of the exemption.

Finally, Justice Douglas, dissenting alone, concluded that "[d]irect financial aid to churches or tax exemptions to the church *qua* church is not, in my view, even arguably permitted." *Walz v. Tax Commission*, 397 U.S. at 710 (1970) (Douglas, J., dissenting).

Although the dissent raised an important question—whether exemption and subsidies are constitutionally distinguishable—the proposed Brookings Institution test goes to the heart of the Chapter 2 discussion regarding ideology. Perhaps income tax exemption—and similarly the ability to receive deductible contributions—should occur only in cases "for which the legislative body would be *equally willing [and within its constitutional authority] to make a direct appropriation.*" But what does that do to the legitimate fears of inappropriate government ideological tests? Arguably, broad categories of tax exemption exist to promote pluralism and ideas that could not realistically receive political favor, at least not consistently. Does anyone believe that most animal rights or environmental groups would receive majority congressional—and thus political—support, consistently, year after year? If not, then at least *political* differences exist between exemption and subsidy.

Fundamentally, do provisions for exempt status and tax-deductible contributions exist with an eye toward support for the Red Cross or Girl Scouts or similar organizations with overwhelming public esteem? Probably not. Surely Congress—or the states—could just as easily (and *arguably* more efficiently) directly subsidize such entities. They could not, however, directly subsidize a great many controversial organizations. Perhaps, then, the wisdom of exemptions and deductions really is rooted in a desire to support the unsupportable (at least politically) if not constitutionally unsupportable.

This is not to suggest that Justice Douglas was wrong—or even correct when he concluded that tax exemption and direct government subsidy were constitutionally indistinguishable. One scholar suggests that "groups seeking public largesse prefer tax relief, as a matter of political strategy, because, for a critical segment of the public, public subsidy framed as tax relief is different from, and less objectionable than, equivalent cash payments." *See generally* Edward A. Zelinsky, *Do Tax Expenditures Create Framing Effects? Volunteer Firefighters, Property Tax Exemptions, and the Paradox of Tax Expenditure Analysis*, 24 VA. TAX REV. 797, 823 (Spring 2005). Instead, the point here is that arguments supporting or opposing the very existence of exempt status transcend any one category, be it religious or education or support for the arts. For a discussion of the constitutional equivalence of tax exemptions and direct government outlays, see Linda Sugin, *Tax Expenditure Analysis and Constitutional Decisions*, 50 HASTINGS L.J. 407 (1999); Edward A. Zelinsky, *Are Tax "Benefits" Constitutionally Equivalent to Direct Expenditures?*, 112 HARV. L. REV. 379, 380–81 (1998). For a discussion of this equivalence issue in the context of statutory civil rights law, see David A. Brennen, *Tax Expenditures, Social Justice, and Civil Rights: Expanding the Scope of Civil Rights Laws to Apply to Tax-Exempt Charities*, 2001 BYU L. REV. 167 (concluding that, for purposes of civil rights statutes that apply to recipients of "federal financial assistance," tax exemption and direct government outlays are economically equivalent, even if not constitutionally so).

Walz v. Tax Commission of City of New York

397 U.S. 664 (1970)

Appellant, owner of real estate in Richmond County, New York, sought an injunction in the New York courts to prevent the New York City Tax Commission from granting property tax exemptions to religious organizations for religious properties used solely for religious worship. The exemption from state taxes is authorized by Art. 16, § 1, of the New York Constitution, which provides in relevant part:

> "Exemptions from taxation may be granted only by general laws. Exemptions may be altered or repealed except those exempting real or personal property used exclusively for religious, educational or charitable purposes as defined by law and owned by any corporation or association organized or conducted exclusively for one or more of such purposes and not operating for profit."

The essence of appellant's contention was that the New York City Tax Commission's grant of an exemption to church property indirectly requires the appellant to make a contribution to religious bodies and thereby violates provisions prohibiting establishment of religion under the First Amendment which under the Fourteenth Amendment is binding on the States.

* * *

[F]or the men who wrote the Religion Clauses of the First Amendment the "establishment" of a religion connoted sponsorship, financial support, and active involvement of the sovereign in religious activity. . . . The exclusivity of established churches in the 17th and 18th centuries, of course, was often carried to prohibition of other forms of worship. . . .

The Establishment and Free Exercise Clauses of the First Amendment are not the most precisely drawn portions of the Constitution. . . . The Court has struggled to find a neutral course between the two Religion Clauses, both of which are cast in absolute terms, and either of which, if expanded to a logical extreme, would tend to clash with the other. For example, in *Zorach v. Clauson, 343 U.S. 306 (1952)*, . . . the Court, noted:

> "The First Amendment, however, does not say that in every and all respects there shall be a separation of Church and State." *Id., at 312.*

. . . The course of constitutional neutrality in this area cannot be an absolutely straight line; rigidity could well defeat the basic purpose of these provisions, which is to insure that no religion be sponsored or favored, none commanded, and none inhibited. The general principle . . . is this: that we will not tolerate either governmentally established religion or governmental interference with religion. . . .

Each value judgment under the Religion Clauses must therefore turn on whether particular acts in question are intended to establish or interfere with religious beliefs and practices or have the effect of doing so. . . .

Adherents of particular faiths and individual churches frequently take strong positions on public issues including, as this case reveals in the several briefs *amici*, vigorous advocacy of legal or constitutional positions. Of course, churches as much as secular bodies and private citizens have that right. No perfect or absolute separation is really possible; the very existence of the Religion Clauses is an involvement of sorts—one that seeks to mark boundaries to avoid excessive entanglement.

The hazards of placing too much weight on a few words or phrases of the Court is abundantly illustrated within the pages of the Court's opinion in *Everson* [*v. Board of Education*, 330 U.S. 1 (1947)]. MR. JUSTICE BLACK, writing for the Court's majority, said the First Amendment "means at least this: Neither a state nor the Federal Government can ... pass laws which aid one religion, aid all religions, or prefer one religion over another." 330 U.S., at 15. Yet he had no difficulty in holding that:

> "Measured by these standards, we cannot say that the First Amendment prohibits New Jersey from spending tax-raised funds to pay the bus fares of parochial school pupils as a part of a general program under which it pays the fares of pupils attending public and other schools. *It is undoubtedly true that children are helped to get to church schools. There is even a possibility that some of the children might not be sent to the church schools if the parents were compelled to pay their children's bus fares out of their own pockets....*" *Id.*, at 17. (Emphasis added.)

The Court did not regard such "aid" to schools teaching a particular religious faith as any more a violation of the Establishment Clause than providing "state-paid policemen, detailed to protect children ... [at the schools] from the very real hazards of traffic ..." *Ibid.*

... In *Everson* the Court declined to construe the Religion Clauses with a literalness that would undermine the ultimate constitutional objective as illuminated by history. Surely, bus transportation and police protection to pupils who receive religious instruction "aid" that particular religion to maintain schools that plainly tend to assure future adherents to a particular faith by having control of their total education at an early age. No religious body that maintains schools would deny this as an affirmative if not dominant policy of church schools. But if as in *Everson* buses can be provided to carry and policemen to protect church school pupils, we fail to see how a broader range of police and fire protection given equally to all churches, along with nonprofit hospitals, art galleries, and libraries receiving the same tax exemption, is different for purposes of the Religion Clauses.

Similarly, making textbooks available to pupils in parochial schools in common with public schools was surely an "aid" to the sponsoring churches because it relieved those churches of an enormous aggregate cost for those books. Supplying of costly teaching materials was not seen either as manifesting a legislative purpose to aid or as having a primary effect of aid contravening the First Amendment. *Board of Education v. Allen*, 392 U.S. 236 (1968). In so holding the Court was heeding both its own prior decisions and our religious tradition. MR. JUSTICE DOUGLAS, in *Zorach v. Clauson, supra*, after recalling that we "are a religious people whose institutions presuppose a Supreme Being," went on to say:

> "We make room for as wide a variety of beliefs and creeds as the spiritual needs of man deem necessary. . . . *When the state encourages religious instruction . . . it follows the best of our traditions.* For it then respects the religious nature of our people and accommodates the public service to their spiritual needs." 343 U.S., at 313–314. (Emphasis added.) With all the risks inherent in programs that bring about administrative relationships between public education bodies and church-sponsored schools, we have been able to chart a course that preserved the autonomy and freedom of religious bodies while avoiding any semblance of established religion. This is a "tight rope" and one we have successfully traversed. . . .

The legislative purpose of the property tax exemption is neither the advancement nor the inhibition of religion; it is neither sponsorship nor hostility. New York, in common with the other States, has determined that certain entities that exist in a harmonious relationship to the community at large, and that foster its "moral or mental improvement," should not be inhibited in their activities by property taxation or the hazard of loss of those properties for nonpayment of taxes. It has not singled out one particular church or religious group or even churches as such. . . .

Governments have not always been tolerant of religious activity, and hostility toward religion has taken many shapes and forms — economic, political, and sometimes harshly oppressive. Grants of exemption historically reflect the concern of authors of constitutions and statutes as to the latent dangers inherent in the imposition of property taxes; exemption constitutes a reasonable and balanced attempt to guard against those dangers. The limits of permissible state accommodation to religion are by no means co-extensive with the noninterference mandated by the Free Exercise Clause. To equate the two would be to deny a national heritage with roots in the Revolution itself. . . . We cannot read New York's statute as attempting to establish religion; it is simply sparing the exercise of religion from the burden of property taxation levied on private profit institutions.

We find it unnecessary to justify the tax exemption on the social welfare services or "good works" that some churches perform for parishioners and others — family counseling, aid to the elderly and the infirm, and to children. Churches vary substantially in the scope of such services; programs expand or contract according to resources and need. As public-sponsored programs enlarge, private aid from the church sector may diminish. The extent of social services may vary, depending on whether the church serves an urban or rural, a rich or poor constituency. To give emphasis to so variable an aspect of the work of religious bodies would introduce an element of governmental evaluation and standards as to the worth of particular social welfare programs, thus producing a kind of continuing day-to-day relationship which the policy of neutrality seeks to minimize. Hence, the use of a social welfare yardstick as a significant element to qualify for tax exemption could conceivably give rise to confrontations that could escalate to constitutional dimensions.

Determining that the legislative purpose of tax exemption is not aimed at establishing, sponsoring, or supporting religion does not end the inquiry, however. We must also be sure that the end result—the effect—is not an excessive government entanglement with religion. The test is inescapably one of degree. Either course, taxation of churches or exemption, occasions some degree of involvement with religion. Elimination of exemption would tend to expand the involvement of government by giving rise to tax valuation of church property, tax liens, tax foreclosures, and the direct confrontations and conflicts that follow in the train of those legal processes.

Granting tax exemptions to churches necessarily operates to afford an indirect economic benefit and also gives rise to some, but yet a lesser, involvement than taxing them.... Obviously a direct money subsidy would be a relationship pregnant with involvement and, as with most governmental grant programs, could encompass sustained and detailed administrative relationships for enforcement of statutory or administrative standards, but that is not this case. The hazards of churches supporting government are hardly less in their potential than the hazards of government supporting churches; each relationship carries some involvement rather than the desired insulation and separation. We cannot ignore the instances in history when church support of government led to the kind of involvement we seek to avoid.

The grant of a tax exemption is not sponsorship since the government does not transfer part of its revenue to churches but simply abstains from demanding that the church support the state.... The exemption creates only a minimal and remote involvement between church and state and far less than taxation of churches. It restricts the fiscal relationship between church and state, and tends to complement and reinforce the desired separation insulating each from the other....

All of the 50 States provide for tax exemption of places of worship, most of them doing so by constitutional guarantees. For so long as federal income taxes have had any potential impact on churches—over 75 years—religious organizations have been expressly exempt from the tax.[2] Such treatment is an "aid" to churches no more and no less in principle than the real estate tax exemption granted by States. Few concepts are more deeply embedded in the fabric of our national life, beginning with pre-Revolutionary colonial times, than for the government to exercise at the very least this kind of benevolent neutrality toward churches and religious exercise generally so long as none was favored over others and none suffered interference.

* * *

2. [4] Act of August 27, 1894, § 32, 28 Stat. 556. Following passage of the Sixteenth Amendment, federal income tax acts have consistently exempted corporations and associations, organized and operated exclusively for religious purposes along with eleemosynary groups, from payment of the tax. Act of Oct. 3, 1913, § IIG (a), 38 Stat. 172. *See* Int. Rev. Code of 1954, § 501 et seq., 26 U.S.C. § 501 et seq.

[N]o one acquires a vested or protected right in violation of the Constitution by long use, even when that span of time covers our entire national existence and indeed predates it. Yet an unbroken practice of according the exemption to churches, openly and by affirmative state action, not covertly or by state inaction, is not something to be lightly cast aside. Nearly 50 years ago Mr. Justice Holmes stated:

> "If a thing has been practised for two hundred years by common consent, it will need a strong case for the Fourteenth Amendment to affect it . . ." *Jackman v. Rosenbaum Co.*, 260 U.S. 22, 31 (1922).

Nothing in this national attitude toward religious tolerance and two centuries of uninterrupted freedom from taxation has given the remotest sign of leading to an established church or religion and on the contrary it has operated affirmatively to help guarantee the free exercise of all forms of religious belief. Thus, it is hardly useful to suggest that tax exemption is but the "foot in the door" or the "nose of the camel in the tent" leading to an established church. If tax exemption can be seen as this first step toward "establishment" of religion, as Mr. Justice Douglas fears, the second step has been long in coming. . . .

Affirmed.

Mr. Justice Brennan, concurring. . . .

Thomas Jefferson was President when tax exemption was first given Washington churches, and James Madison sat in sessions of the Virginia General Assembly that voted exemptions for churches in that Commonwealth. I have found no record of their personal views on the respective Acts. The absence of such a record is itself significant. It is unlikely that two men so concerned with the separation of church and state would have remained silent had they thought the exemptions established religion. And if they had not either approved the exemptions, or been mild in their opposition, it is probable that their views would be known to us today. Both Jefferson and Madison wrote prolifically about issues they felt important, and their opinions were well known to contemporary chroniclers. . . . Much the same can be said of the other Framers and Ratifiers of the Bill of Rights who remained active in public affairs during the late 18th and early 19th centuries. The adoption of the early exemptions without controversy, in other words, strongly suggests that they were not thought incompatible with constitutional prohibitions against involvements of church and state. . . .

Government has two basic secular purposes for granting real property tax exemptions to religious organizations. First, these organizations are exempted because they, among a range of other private, nonprofit organizations contribute to the well-being of the community in a variety of nonreligious ways, and thereby bear burdens that would otherwise either have to be met by general taxation, or be left undone, to the detriment of the community. . . .

Second, government grants exemptions to religious organizations because they uniquely contribute to the pluralism of American society by their religious activities. . . .

General subsidies of religious activities would, of course, constitute impermissible state involvement with religion.... Tax exemptions and general subsidies, however, are qualitatively different. Though both provide economic assistance, they do so in fundamentally different ways. A subsidy involves the direct transfer of public monies to the subsidized enterprise and uses resources exacted from taxpayers as a whole. An exemption, on the other hand, involves no such transfer.[3] ... Whether Government grants or withholds the exemptions, it is going to be involved with religion.[4] ...

Opinion of MR. JUSTICE HARLAN [concurring].

... I agree with my Brother DOUGLAS that exemptions do not differ from subsidies as an economic matter....

MR. JUSTICE DOUGLAS, dissenting.

... The question in the case therefore is whether believers—organized in church groups—can be made exempt from real estate taxes, merely because they are believers, while nonbelievers, whether organized or not, must pay the real estate taxes....

There is a line between what a State may do in encouraging "religious" activities, *Zorach v. Clauson*, 343 U.S. 306, and what a State may not do by using its resources to promote "religious" activities, *McCollum v. Board of Education*, 333 U.S. 203, or bestowing benefits because of them. Yet that line may not always be clear. Closing public schools on Sunday is in the former category; subsidizing churches, in my view, is in the latter. Indeed I would suppose that in common understanding one of the best ways to "establish" one or more religions is to subsidize them, which a tax exemption does. The State may not do that any more than it may prefer "those who believe in no religion over those who do believe." ...

In affirming this judgment the Court largely overlooks the revolution initiated by the adoption of the Fourteenth Amendment....

The Establishment Clause was not incorporated in the Fourteenth Amendment until *Everson v. Board of Education*, 330 U.S. 1, was decided in 1947.

Those developments in the last 30 years have had unsettling effects. It was, for example, not until 1962 that state-sponsored, sectarian prayers were held to violate the Establishment Clause. *Engel v. Vitale*, 370 U.S. 421. That decision brought many protests, for the habit of putting one sect's prayer in public schools had long been practiced. Yet if the Catholics, controlling one school board, could put their prayer into one group of public schools, the Mormons, Baptists, Moslems, Presbyterians, and others could do the same, once they got control. And so the seeds of

---

3. [10] A real property tax exemption cannot be viewed as the free provision by the State of certain basic services—fire, police, water, and the like.... *See generally* Bittker, *Churches, Taxes and the Constitution*, 78 YALE L. J. 1285, 1304–1310 (1969).

4. [12] The state involvement with religion that would be occasioned by any cessation of exemptions might conflict with the demands of the Free Exercise Clause....

Establishment would grow and a secular institution would be used to serve a sectarian end....

Hence the question in the present case makes irrelevant the "two centuries of uninterrupted freedom from taxation," referred to by the Court. *Ante*, at 678. If history be our guide, then tax exemption of church property in this country is indeed highly suspect, as it arose in the early days when the church was an agency of the state....

With all due respect the governing principle is not controlled by *Everson v. Board of Education, supra. Everson* involved the use of public funds to bus children to parochial as well as to public schools. Parochial schools teach religion; yet they are also educational institutions offering courses competitive with public schools. They prepare students for the professions and for activities in all walks of life. Education in the secular sense was combined with religious indoctrination at the parochial schools involved in *Everson*. Even so, the *Everson* decision was five to four and, though one of the five, I have since had grave doubts about it, because I have become convinced that grants to institutions teaching a sectarian creed violate the Establishment Clause....

This case, however, is quite different. Education is not involved. The financial support rendered here is to the church, the place of worship. A tax exemption is a subsidy. Is my Brother BRENNAN correct in saying that we would hold that state or federal grants to churches, say, to construct the edifice itself would be unconstitutional? What is the difference between that kind of subsidy and the present subsidy? ...

The Court seeks to avoid this historic argument as to the meaning of "establishment" and "free exercise" by relying on the long practice of the States in granting the subsidies challenged here. Certainly government may not lay a tax on either worshiping or preaching. In *Murdock v. Pennsylvania*, 319 U.S. 105, we ruled on a state license tax levied on religious colporteurs as a condition to pursuit of their activities. In holding the tax unconstitutional we said:

> "The power to tax the exercise of a privilege is the power to control or suppress its enjoyment. *Magnano Co.* v. *Hamilton*, 292 U.S. 40, 44–45, and cases cited. Those who can tax the exercise of this religious practice can make its exercise so costly as to deprive it of the resources necessary for its maintenance. Those who can tax the privilege of engaging in this form of missionary evangelism can close its doors to all those who do not have a full purse. Spreading religious beliefs in this ancient and honorable manner would thus be denied the needy. Those who can deprive religious groups of their colporteurs can take from them a part of the vital power of the press which has survived from the Reformation." *Id.*, at 112....

The church *qua* church would not be entitled to that support from believers and from nonbelievers alike. Yet the church *qua* nonprofit, charitable institution is one of many that receive a form of subsidy through tax exemption. To be sure, the New

York statute does not single out the church for grant or favor. . . . While the beneficiaries cover a wide range, "atheistic," "agnostic," or "antitheological" groups do not seem to be included.

* * *

The Brookings Institution, writing in 1933, before the application of the Establishment Clause of the First Amendment to the States, said about tax exemptions of religious groups:

> "Tax exemption, no matter what its form, is essentially a government grant or subsidy. Such grants would seem to be justified only if the purpose for which they are made is one for which the legislative body *would be equally willing to make* a direct appropriation from public funds equal to the amount of the exemption. . . ." (Emphasis added.)

Since 1947, when the Establishment Clause was made applicable to the States, that report would have to state that the exemption would be justified only where "the legislative body *could make*" an appropriation for the cause. . . .

Direct financial aid to churches or tax exemptions to the church *qua* church is not, in my view, even arguably permitted. Sectarian causes are certainly not anti-public and many would rate their own church or perhaps all churches as the highest form of welfare. The difficulty is that sectarian causes must remain in the private domain not subject to public control or subsidy. That seems to me to be the requirement of the Establishment Clause. . . .

The exemptions provided here insofar as welfare projects are concerned may have the ring of neutrality. But subsidies either through direct grant or tax exemption for sectarian causes, whether carried on by church *qua* church or by church *qua* welfare agency, must be treated differently, lest we in time allow the church *qua* church to be on the public payroll, which, I fear, is imminent. . . .

What Madison would have thought of the present state subsidy to churches—a tax exemption as distinguished from an outright grant—no one can say with certainty. The fact that Virginia early granted church tax exemptions cannot be credited to Madison. Certainly he seems to have been opposed. In his paper Monopolies, Perpetuities, Corporations, Ecclesiastical Endowments he wrote: "Strongly guarded as is the separation between Religion & Govt in the Constitution of the United States the danger of encroachment by Ecclesiastical Bodies, may be illustrated by precedents already furnished in their short history." And he referred, *inter alia*, to the "attempt in Kentucky for example, where it was proposed to exempt Houses of Worship from taxes." From these three statements, Madison, it seems, opposed all state subsidies to churches. *Cf.* D. Robertson, Should Churches Be Taxed? 60–61 (1968).

We should adhere to what we said in *Torcaso v. Watkins*, 367 U.S., at 495, that neither a State nor the Federal Government "can constitutionally pass laws or impose requirements *which aid all religions as against nonbelievers*, and neither can aid those religions based on a belief in the existence of God as against those religions founded on different beliefs." (Emphasis added.)

Unless we adhere to that principle, we do not give full support either to the Free Exercise Clause or to the Establishment Clause. If a church can be exempted from paying real estate taxes, why may not it be made exempt from paying special assessments? The benefits in the two cases differ only in degree; and the burden on nonbelievers is likewise no different in kind.

The religiously used real estate of the churches today constitutes a vast domain. See M. Larson & C. Lowell, The Churches: Their Riches, Revenues, and Immunities (1969). Their assets total over $141 billion and their annual income at least $22 billion. *Id.*, at 232. And the extent to which they are feeding from the public trough in a variety of forms is alarming. *Id.*, c. 10. . . .

I conclude that this tax exemption is unconstitutional.

Questions

1. In 2001, President George W. Bush sought the introduction of legislation allowing direct government grants to "faith-based" organizations. Such grants were to be used solely for "non-proselytizing," social welfare activities. One such bipartisan proposal was summarized as follows:

> The Community Solutions Act puts faith-based organizations on a level playing field with other charitable groups. The bill:
>
> a. Allows faith-based organizations to compete for federal grants in the areas of housing, juvenile justice programs, community development block grants, job training, children welfare and child care services, crime prevention programs, senior citizen services, domestic violence programming and hunger relief activities.
>
> b. Prohibits discrimination against an organization on the basis of religion in the distribution of government funds to provide government assistance.

Would the bill, if enacted, be constitutional? Separately analyze the proposal in light of the majority, concurring, and dissenting opinions in *Walz*. How, if at all, does the distinction between tax exemption and direct government outlay affect your analysis? *See* David A. Brennen, *Tax Expenditures, Social Justice, and Civil Rights: Expanding the Scope of Civil Rights Laws to Apply to Tax-Exempt Charities*, 2001 BYU L. Rev. 167 (arguing that no significance should be attached to the form of government expenditure — tax exemption or direct government outlay — for civil rights statutory analysis purposes). Should the results of your analysis change if the government grant money goes to a separate 501(c)(3) that is set up by the religious organization to accept government grants and do good, nonreligious, deeds?

Although the Act never became law, Congress has considered later versions in several years. *E.g.*, H.R. 5533 (111th): Nonprofit Sector and Community Solutions Act of 2010.

2. In light of *Walz* and *Everson* (dealing with transportation provided to parochial students), what if, instead of a direct federal grant of money to religious organizations, the aid is in the form of a voucher given to an individual who in turn decides to give the voucher to a religious organization? For example, would the provision of education vouchers to children attending parochial schools be constitutional? Could government provide such vouchers to children attending private non-sectarian schools, but prohibit their use at religious schools? *See Ariz. Christian Sch. Tuition Org. v. Winn*, 131 S. Ct. 1436 (U.S. 2011), (in which the Court denied standing to taxpayers who objected to a state tax credit for parents of children attending religious schools). *Cf.*, *Christian Legal Society v. Martinez*, 561 U.S. 661 (2010) (holding that Hastings Law School could prohibit religious discrimination by *all* student organizations, but resting its decision on a policy prohibiting all viewpoint discrimination by all organizations, suggesting the state could not target religious viewpoints while favoring other viewpoints).

C. Administration of the Religious Tax Exemption

Code: §§ 501(c)(3), 508(a), 508(c)(1)(A)

Once the *Walz* Court settled the constitutionality of religious tax exemption, the burden of administration and enforcement fell to the Service, particularly since the Internal Revenue Code never defines "religious," although it refers to subcategories, such as "church." § 170(b)(1)(A)(i). The foremost difficulty, of course, is identifying "religious" organizations entitled to tax exemption. A second difficulty is identifying which "religious" organizations constitute a "church," justifying particularly favorable status.

1. What Is a Religion?

While the Treasury Regulations attempt to define *education*, *charity*, and *scientific*, they avoid any attempt whatsoever at defining *religion*. Doing so would necessarily entail value judgments and distinctions with regard to belief systems. Indulging such judgments and distinctions would violate the axiomatic purpose of religious freedom—the very act of government judging beliefs and identifying some as worthy of tax exemption, and others as unworthy, goes against the purpose of the First Amendment. As a result, the Supreme Court has attempted to define "religion" in a manner that can be described as "content neutral." According to a 1965 decision, religion involves a sincere and meaningful belief that "occupies a place in the life of its possessor parallel to that filled by the orthodox belief in God" of one who adheres to a clearly recognized religion. *United States v. Seeger*, 380 U.S. 163 (1965). Per Court instruction, no inquiry may be made into the validity of a person's belief. The task is limited to deciding "whether the beliefs . . . are sincerely held" and whether they are, according to the possessor's own way of thinking, "religious." Significantly, however, the *Seeger* Court explained: "while the 'truth' of a belief is not open to question, there remains the significant question whether [the belief] is 'truly held.'"[5]

A former Commissioner explained the Service's application of this dictate in a 1977 article. As he explained, the Service must concern itself with *actions* based on beliefs. If a group uses beliefs as a basis for exemption, the Service has two inquiries:

> Are the practices and rituals . . . illegal or contrary to clearly defined public policy? If . . . [so] tax preferences are inappropriate. . . . Under this test the Service revoked an exemption granted for ostensibly conventional charitable and religious purposes when we learned the group was actually organized to carry out a vicious, anti-Semitic campaign.

Second, the Service must—to a very limited extent—inquire into whether the applicants' beliefs are sincerely held. The Court, however, ruled "more than a generation ago that citizens may not be put to proof of their religious doctrines or beliefs":

The Fathers of the Constitution were not unaware of the varied and extreme views of religious sects, of the violence of disagreement among them, and of the lack of any one religious creed which all men would agree. They fashioned a charter of government which envisaged the widest possible toleration of conflicting views . . . The religious views espoused by respondents might seem incredible, if not preposterous, to most people. But if the doctrines are subject to trial before a jury charged with finding their truth or falsity, then the same can be done with the religious beliefs of any sect.

Jerome Kurtz, *Difficult Definitional Problems in Tax Administration: Religion and Race*, 23 CATH. LAW. 301, 302–03 (1977) (*quoting* United States v. Ballard, 322 U.S. 78, 87 (1944).

The court in *Church of the Chosen People v. United States* applied the difficult Supreme Court test regarding what is a "religion." The case involved an entity created to espouse a doctrine called the "Gay Imperative." Recognizing that it "must avoid any judgments concerning the truth or validity of the plaintiff's religious beliefs," the court followed a Third Circuit three-part test:

1. whether the beliefs address fundamental and ultimate questions concerning the human condition,
2. whether the beliefs are comprehensive in nature and constitute an entire system of belief instead of merely an isolated teaching, and
3. whether the beliefs are manifested in external forms.

5. For a detailed explanation, from the point of view of the Service, of what is religion and what is a church, *see* INTERNAL REVENUE SERVICE PUBLICATION 1828 (Rev. 8-2015).

Africa v. Commonwealth of Pennsylvania, 662 F.2d 1025, 1032 (3d Cir. 1981), *cert. denied*, 456 U.S. 908 (1982).

Applying the test, the court found the entity not organized "exclusively or substantially" for religious purposes. Readers should pause on that phrase: although the code requires a charity to be "exclusively" organized for a specified purpose, the regulations define that in relation to a "primary" exempt purpose and the lack of any "substantial" non-exempt purpose. Thus, the court should probably have stopped with the word "exclusively."

The court considered, but did not clearly apply, an alternate "analogy approach" that inquires into whether the beliefs espoused hold "the same important position for members of one of the new religions as the traditional faith holds for more orthodox believers. . . ."

Church of the Chosen People v. United States

548 F. Supp. 1247 (D. Minn. 1982)

. . . . Plaintiff Demigod Socko Pantheon (DSP) was incorporated in Minnesota on August 31, 1976. DSP filed federal income tax returns for tax years 1976, 1977, and 1978, and paid taxes in the amounts of $45.60, $1.40, and $425.00 for the respective years. . . .

[T]he plaintiff's primary purpose and activity is the preaching of a doctrine called The Gay Imperative. The plaintiff defines The Gay Imperative as "the philosophic fundamental whereby the Gods direct that ever increasing numbers of persons expand their affectional preferences to encompass loving Gay relationships to hasten their full development for the control of overbreeding, and to ensure the survival of the human species and the multitude of terrestrial ecologies."

. . . Adherents to The Gay Imperative believe that only 10 percent of the population has to reproduce in order to be self-fulfilled; another 10 percent of the population needs a female-female bond for self-fulfillment; and another 10 percent of the population needs a male-male bond for self-fulfillment. According to this doctrine, the remaining 70 percent of the population can be persuaded to join religions advocating any of the three pair-bonds. . . .

In addition to officers and functionaries, the plaintiff has members. The plaintiff presented conflicting evidence concerning the number of its members. In a letter to the IRS dated October 27, 1975, the plaintiff claimed to have 10 members. However, Baker testified that the plaintiff had no list of the members of the congregation. Baker also stated that the secretary of the DSP had not enrolled any members during the period at issue.

In addition to members, the plaintiff has, according to Baker, adherents who "identify" with the DSP and The Gay Imperative. The plaintiff maintains no record of the names or numbers of these adherents. Adherents are not required to attend any ceremonies, to participate in any instruction, or to read any publications. According to Baker, adherents are automatically trained by associating with members of the DSP.

The plaintiff possesses no outward characteristics that are analogous to those of other religions. The plaintiff has no published literature explaining its traditions. The plaintiff's doctrines are not formalized in any written equivalent of the Bible, Talmud, Koran, or Bhagavad-Gita. Nor does the plaintiff claim to have any oral literature reflecting its beliefs or history. During the years in question, the plaintiff conducted only two ceremonies. One of the ceremonies was a memorial to a gay victim; the other was the dedication of an archacy or subunit of the geographic area known as a Panarchate. The plaintiff held no regular religious services although it declared certain parts of an annual Gay Pride Week a "Festival of the Chosen." The plaintiff claims to have performed one marriage between two members of the same sex. The Minnesota Supreme Court has declared that such same sex "marriages" are not authorized and are in fact prohibited under Minnesota statutes. *Baker v. Nelson*, 291 Minn. 310, 191 N.W.2d 185, 186 (1971).

The plaintiff itself emphasizes the secular nature of its ideology. The plaintiff's sacerdotal functions are "all bodily functions normal to the adult human . . ." . . .

Baker testified that the main activity of the plaintiff's adherents is preaching The Gay Imperative which can be done anywhere on the planet and encompasses all of daily life. This "preaching," according to Baker, involves attaining a state of consciousness that can be exhibited anywhere including walking down the street or at poker games. No words are required to "preach" the doctrine.

No clear distinction existed between the plaintiff's business affairs and those of Baker and McConnell. The plaintiff's income from donations and the sale of religious artifacts was used to pay the rent at 2929 South 40th Street, Minneapolis, Minnesota, in 1977. Baker and McConnell used the residence as their personal residence and only one room was occasionally used for church administrative matters. On a few occasions the residence was used for social gatherings by the plaintiff's adherents. The rent was not prorated to reflect a division between personal and church use. The plaintiff's revenues also were used to pay the utilities and telephone bills for the residence. In addition, the plaintiff paid for subscriptions to *Time* magazine, local newspapers, and other periodicals in Baker's and McConnell's names. The plaintiff's bank account was in Baker's name, not its own name. . . .

In determining whether the plaintiff is entitled to an exemption, the Court must avoid any judgments concerning the truth or validity of the plaintiff's religious beliefs. In *Teterud v. Burns*, 522 F.2d 357 (8th Cir. 1975), the United States Court of Appeals for the Eighth Circuit emphasized the first amendment's ban on such inquiries: "It is not the province of government officials or court to determine religious orthodoxy." 522 F.2d at 360 (citations omitted). See also *U.S. v. Seeger*, 380

U.S. 163, 185, . . . (1965) ("while the 'truth' of a belief is not open to question, there remains the significant question whether [the belief] is 'truly held.' ").

Even if the Court determines that the plaintiff organization and its adherents are sincere in their beliefs, they must still establish that their beliefs are religious in nature. The definitions of the words "religion" and "religious" are by no means free of ambiguity. . . . The United States Supreme Court has not established a clear standard for determining which beliefs are religious. The Supreme Court has, however, distinguished between personal secular philosophy and religious beliefs. *See, e.g., Wisconsin v. Yoder*, 406 U.S. 205, 216 (1972) (distinguishing between the religious belief of the Amish and personal philosophy of Thoreau).

In *Africa v. Commonwealth of Pennsylvania*, 662 F.2d 1025 (3d Cir.), cert. denied, 456 U.S. 908 (1982), the court set forth a three-part test for determining whether a plaintiff's goals are religious. The test addresses the questions of: (1) whether the beliefs address fundamental and ultimate questions concerning the human condition, (2) whether the beliefs are comprehensive in nature and constitute an entire system of belief instead of merely an isolated teaching, and (3) whether the beliefs are manifested in external forms. 662 F.2d at 1032. Many courts use a definition by analogy approach, inquiring whether the beliefs espoused hold "the same important position for members of one of the new religions as the traditional faith holds for more orthodox believers . . ." . . .

The Court concludes based on its findings of fact and the standard set forth in *Africa* that the plaintiff was not exclusively or substantially organized for religious purposes. During the period in question, The Gay Imperative, the plaintiff's only major doctrine, was a single-faceted doctrine of sexual preference and secular lifestyle. The plaintiff's ideology did not address the fundamental and ultimate questions concerning the human condition, such as the nature of good and evil, right and wrong, life and death.

The plaintiff's doctrine was not comprehensive in nature nor did it constitute an entire system of belief. Instead, the plaintiff narrowly focused on only one aspect of human existence — sexual preference. . . .

In addition, the plaintiff lacked external manifestations analogous to other religions during the period in question. It possessed no established history or literature, required no formal or informal education of its leaders, conducted no regular ceremonies, and possessed no identifiable membership beyond its small core of leaders. The plaintiff is prohibited by Minnesota law from conducting same-sex "marriages," one of the few activities the plaintiff performed that is analogous to those of mainstream religions. . . .

[The Court affirmed the Service's denial of tax exemption.]

2. What Is a Church?

A sub-category of "religious organization" is that of "church." Church status offers several important advantages to a religious organization:

1. **A church is automatically not a private foundation per §§ 170(b)(1)(A)(i) and 509(a)(1).** As such, it need not be concerned with the many detrimental consequences of private foundation status.

2. **A church is automatically a preferred "50% charity."** Thus, donors may deduct up to 50% of their contribution base annually under § 170(b)(1)(A).

3. **A church is subject to lesser reporting requirements than are other charities.** For example, they need not apply for exempt status and annual reporting requirements are sharply curtailed.

Do not confuse the sub-category with the main category. A religious organization may be exempt under § 501(c)(3) and thus entitled to receive deductible contributions under § 170(c)(2). If the religious organization also satisfies the definition of a "church," it receives the above three advantages. If, however, it fails to satisfy the definition of a "church," all is not lost—it may still be exempt as a religious organization. As such, it is potentially a private foundation and is subject to greater reporting requirements—but it is still exempt.

a. The Service's 14-Part Test

Neither statute nor treasury regulation adequately defines "church," leaving that task to a series of court decisions. Several courts have adopted a 14-part test promulgated by the Service. *See, e.g., United States v. Jeffries*, 854 F.2d 254 (7th Cir. 1988); *Lutheran Social Service of Minn. v. United States*, 758 F.2d 1283, 1286–87 (8th Cir. 1985); *Found. of Human Understanding v. United States*, 88 Fed. Cl. 203 (2009) (using both the 14-part test and the associational test); *Williams Home, Inc. v. United States*, 540 F. Supp. 310, 317 (W.D. Va. 1982); *American Guidance Foundation v. United States*, 490 F. Supp. 304, 306 (D.D.C. 1980), *aff'd* without opinion (D.C. Cir. July 10, 1981); *Church of the Visible Intelligence that Governs the Universe v. United States*, 4 Cl. Ct. 55 (1983). That test focuses on whether the religious organization has:

1. a distinct legal existence;
2. a recognized creed and form of worship;
3. a definite and distinct ecclesiastical government;
4. a formal code of doctrine and discipline;
5. a distinct religious history;
6. a membership not associated with any other church or denomination;
7. an organization of ordained ministers;
8. ordained ministers selected after completing prescribed studies;
9. a literature of its own;

10. established places of worship;
11. regular congregations;
12. regular religious services;
13. Sunday schools for religious instruction of the young; and
14. schools for the preparation of its ministers.

5 Administration, Internal Revenue Manual 7(10)69, EXEMPT ORGANIZATIONS EXAMINATION GUIDELINES HANDBOOK 321.3(3), at 22,455-4 (CCH) (Apr. 5, 1982).

b. Tax Court Rejects the 14-Part Test

As noted above, many courts have adopted the Service's 14-part test. The Tax Court, however, has not. While it considers the test useful, it has refused to adopt it as controlling. *See Good v. C.I.R.*, T.C. Memo. 2012-323 (2012). The Tax Court has explained that few entities could satisfy the entire test. Instead, the Tax Court has focused more on the "association test" and "spiritual togetherness" definition of a church. These two tests, which are essentially the same, define a church as:

> a coherent group of individuals and families that join together to accomplish the religious purposes of mutually held beliefs. In other words, a church's principal means of accomplishing its religious purposes must be to assemble regularly a group of individuals related by common worship and faith.

Church of Eternal Life v. Commissioner, 86 T.C. 916, 924 (1986).

One instance in which the Tax Court applied the associational and spiritual togetherness tests is in *Foundation of Human Understanding v. Commissioner*. Established in 1961, the Foundation focused on meditation, salvation, emotional self-control, and man's relation to God. In 1972, the organization amended its articles of incorporation to become a "church." Counsel thereupon notified the Service that "The Foundation is now a church." It opened a school in 1977 and later began substantial broadcasting activities through which it reached most of its followers. The Commissioner issued an adverse determination letter on February 23, 1983.

Over a strong dissent, the Tax Court found the 20-year-old religious entity to be a church for periods prior to 1983. Later, in a revised determination letter on January 29, 1988, the service confirmed the entity's church status effective August 1, 1979. *Found. of Human Understanding v. United States*, 88 Fed. Cl. 203, 207 (2009). But that was not the end of the matter:

> In a letter dated October 16, 2001, the IRS notified plaintiff that it was commencing a church tax inquiry to resolve questions concerning plaintiff's continued qualification as a church under § 170(b)(1)(A)(i). Def.'s Facts P 17; Pl.'s Resp. to Def.'s Facts 14; Admin. Rec. 1. Plaintiff responded on November 21, 2001. Def.'s Facts P 17; Pl.'s Resp. to Def.'s Facts 14; Admin. Rec. 228. On December 21, 2001, the IRS sent plaintiff a Notice of Church Tax

> Examination. Def.'s Facts P 17; Pl.'s Resp. to Def.'s Facts 14; Admin. Rec. 314. The church tax examination concluded with defendant's issuance of a Technical Advice Memorandum dated June 8, 2004. Def.'s Facts P 4[2]; Pl.'s Resp. to Def.'s Facts 34; Admin. Rec. 8798-824 (IRS National Office Technical Advice Memorandum) (Technical Advice Memorandum). The Technical Advice Memorandum included defendant's conclusion that plaintiff's status as a tax-exempt organization under § 501(c)(3) should not be revoked, but that plaintiff no longer qualified as a church under § 170(b)(1)(A)(i). Def.'s Facts P 4[2]; Pl.'s Resp. to Def.'s Facts 34; Technical Advice Memorandum 27. Defendant's revocation of plaintiff's church status was retroactive in its effect to January 1, 1998. Technical Advice Memorandum 27.

Id. at 207–08. Several things are important in that quotation: (1) notice the procedures for the church audit; (2) the use of a TAM for the audit conclusion retaining exempt status but denying church status; and (3) the six-year retroactivity of the TAM. In 2004, the entity filed a section 7428 action for a declaratory judgment invalidating the TAM in the Court of Federal Claims. The court, however, ruled for the service in 2009. It did not disagree with the Tax Court on the merits; instead, it found sufficiently changed facts to justify denial of church status under both the associational and the 14-part tests. According to the court:

> In explaining its rejection of plaintiff's declaratory judgment action in *VIA*, the Tax Court summarized the key characteristics exhibited by plaintiff in *Foundation I* which were sufficient to support recognition of church status: plaintiff conducted services "three to four times a week by ordained ministers for congregations of no less than 50 to 300 members[;] [Foundation] ministers were ordained only after having completed a three-year apprenticeship under the tutelage of [Foundation's] founder and leader[;] [and] Foundation operated a regular school for children in which the teaching of [Foundation] principles formed part of the curriculum." *VIA*, 68 T.C.M. (CCH) at 216 (describing plaintiff's characteristics essential to meeting the associational standard in *Foundation I*). There is no evidence in the record presently before the court in this case to show that the distinguishing characteristics of plaintiff in *Foundation I*, as delineated by the Tax Court in *VIA*, continue to exist.

Id. at 232–33.

As a result, the following decision is pedagogically important for its discussion of how the Tax Court views the various tests. From the beginning, the dissent essentially considered the broadcast activities too large and the associational activities too small for the entity to constitute a church. The dissent is particularly useful in its description of the associational and spiritual togetherness tests.

Foundation of Human Understanding v. Commissioner

88 T.C. 1341 (1987)

* * *

Petitioner conducts "services" at its Los Angeles building 3 or 4 times a week. These services, which are open to the public, are conducted by one of the ministers of petitioner. The conducting minister is permitted to structure the service as he chooses, ranging from highly Scriptural exhortations to practical suggestions on overcoming sin, weakness, and depression. Afterwards, followers in the congregation are allowed to and regularly do share their recent experiences concerning the Scriptures, meditation, and God. Although ministers may discuss the meditation technique prescribed by Roy Masters, meditation is performed by petitioner's followers in solitude. Ministers have performed weddings; however, the beliefs of petitioner eschew other rites such as baptism and holy communion. Although petitioner does not require its followers to disavow membership in other churches or religious organizations, many of its followers look upon petitioner as their only church....

In 1981, petitioner had nine ordained ministers who were employed full time. The ministers included Roy Masters, his wife, Ann Masters, and his children, David Masters, Dianne Masters, and Michael Masters. In addition, there were five ministers in training. The ministerial training process is a 3-year apprenticeship under the personal tutelage of Roy Masters....

During the years 1971 through 1980, contributions constituted 65.8 percent of petitioner's total receipts with the remainder derived from the sales of religious publications, school tuition, thrift store sales, interest, capital gains, and royalties.... The percentage that petitioner's broadcasting expenditures bore to total expenditures for exempt purposes for the years 1975 through 1980 [ranged from 45 to 49 percent].

* * *

The term "church" is not defined in the Internal Revenue Code. Nor are the regulations promulgated under section 170 helpful in deciding what is a church. They simply restate the statutory language of section 170(b)(1)(A)(i).[6] Sec. 1.170A-9(a),

6. [5] At one time the regulations under sec. 170 contained a cross-reference to the regulations under sec. 511, which define a church as follows:

> (ii) The term "church" includes a religious order or a religious organization if such order or organization (a) is an integral part of a church, and (b) is engaged in carrying out the functions of a church, whether as a civil law corporation or otherwise. In determining whether a religious order or organization is an integral part of a church, consideration will be given to the degree to which it is connected with, and controlled by, such church. A religious order or organization shall be considered to be engaged in carrying out the functions of a church if its duties include the ministration of sacerdotal functions and the conduct of religious worship.... [Sec. 1.511-2(a)(3)(ii), Income Tax Regs.] The Tax Reform Act of 1969 made several changes in the tax treatment of exempt organizations including

Income Tax Regs. It seems clear, however, that Congress intended that the word "church" have a more restrictive definition than the term "religious organization." *American Guidance Foundation v. United States*, 490 F. Supp. 304, 306 (D.D.C. 1980), *aff'd* without opinion (D.C. Cir., July 10, 1981); *Church of the Visible Intelligence that Governs the Universe v. United States*, 4 Cl. Ct. 55 (1983).

In the absence of guidance by Congress and a meaningful regulatory definition, it has been suggested that the term "church" is to be interpreted in light of the generally accepted meaning and usage of the word. *De La Salle Institute v. United States*, 195 F. Supp. 891, 903 (N.D.Cal.1961). However, given the plurality of religious beliefs in this country, the validity of this approach is not without doubt. See *American Guidance Foundation, Inc. v. United States, supra* at 306. We can only approach this question with care for all of us are burdened with the baggage of our own unique beliefs and perspectives. We must recognize that one person's prophet is another's pariah. Consequently, we must also assiduously avoid expanding our inquiry into the merits of petitioner's beliefs or risk running afoul of First Amendment religious protections. *Parker v. Commissioner*, 365 F.2d 792, 795 (8th Cir. 1966), affg. in part, revg. in part, and remanding a Memorandum Opinion of this Court, cert. denied 385 U.S. 1026 (1967); *Unitary Mission Church of Long Island v. Commissioner*, 74 T.C. 507, 514 (1980), affd. without published opinion 647 F.2d 163 (2d Cir. 1981).

Although every church may be a religious organization, not every religious organization is a church. *Chapman v. Commissioner*, 48 T.C. 358, 363 (1967). To classify a religious organization as a church under the Internal Revenue Code, we should look to its religious purposes and, particularly, the means by which its religious purposes are accomplished. See *Chapman v. Commissioner, supra at 367* (Tannenwald, J., concurring). "The means by which an avowedly religious purpose is accomplished separates a 'church' from other forms of religious enterprise. . . . At a minimum, a church includes a body of believers or communicants that assembles regularly in order to worship." *American Guidance Foundation, Inc. v. United States*, supra at 306 (citation omitted); see *Church of Eternal Life and Liberty, Inc. v. Commissioner*, 86 T.C. 916, 924 (1986); *Chapman v. Commissioner, supra* at 367 (Tannenwald, J., concurring). When bringing people together for worship is only an incidental part of the activities of a religious organization, those limited activities are insufficient to

---

repeal of the exemption given to churches from the tax on unrelated business income under sec. 511. Pub. L. 91-172, 83 Stat. 536. Following enactment of the Tax Reform Act of 1969, the Treasury proposed regulations defining "church" for purposes of sec. 170 that closely resembled the definition found in sec. 1.511-2(a)(3)(ii), Income Tax Regs. Sec. 1.170A-9(a), Proposed Income Tax Regs., 36 Fed. Reg. 9298 (May 22, 1971). Because of objections from the public, the proposed regulation defining "church" under sec. 170 was never promulgated as final. Instead the current regulation merely provides that "An organization is described in sec. 170(b)(1)(A)(i) if it is a church or a convention or association of churches." Sec. 1.170A-9(a), Income Tax Regs. *See Whelan, "Church" in the Internal Revenue Code: The Definitional Problems*, 45 FORDHAM L. REV. 885, 916–917 (1977).

label the entire organization a church. *De La Salle Institute v. United States*, supra at 901; see *Chapman v. Commissioner*, supra at 364.

In its efforts to identify organizations that qualify for church status the IRS has developed 14 criteria. [*see* editor's note, above]

Although this Court has not adopted these 14 criteria in deciding whether an organization is a church, other courts have expressly adopted them or at least given them the appearance of judicial imprimatur. See *Lutheran Social Service of Minn. v. United States*, 758 F.2d 1283, 1286–1287 (8th Cir. 1985), revg. and remanding 583 F. Supp. 1298 (D. Minn. 1984); *Williams Home, Inc. v. United States*, 540 F. Supp. 310, 317 (W.D. Va. 1982); *American Guidance Foundation v. United States, supra; Church of the Visible Intelligence that Governs the Universe v. United States, supra.* It is recognized that few traditional churches could meet all of the criteria. . . .

Although the criteria developed by the IRS are helpful in deciding what is essentially a fact question, whether petitioner is a church, we do not adopt them as a test.

Petitioner, a nonprofit corporation incorporated under the laws of California, certainly has a distinct legal existence. Although based on Judeo-Christian principles, the emphasis on emotional self-control through a specific type of meditation as the key to salvation sets petitioner apart from other recognized religions. Petitioner provides regular religious services for established congregations that are served by an organized ministry. Worship takes the form of regular meetings of regular congregations at established places of worship, petitioner's Los Angeles headquarters and the Grant Pass, Oregon, church building. These services are open to the public. Cf. *American Guidance Foundation, Inc. v. United States, supra at 307* (husband, wife, and minor child do not constitute a church). These services were regularly conducted by the ministry for congregations consisting of 50 to 350 persons. Such activity is far from incidental. Cf. *De La Salle Institute v. United States, supra.* Although petitioner does not require its followers to reject membership in other churches, many followers consider petitioner to be their only church. Although the regular services have no set structure or liturgy, they are conducted by petitioner's ordained ministers. Ministers ordained by petitioner must serve a 3-year apprenticeship under the personal tutelage of Roy Masters. Petitioner does not maintain separate physical facilities for the preparation of its ministers. Although petitioner does not separately provide for the religious instruction of the young, such as through Sunday School classes, its school includes religious instruction as part of the general education curriculum.

. . . The record is unclear as to when and how Roy Masters formulated his beliefs or had them revealed to him. Nonetheless, petitioner had existed, at the time the Commissioner made his final adverse determination, for more than 20 years as an association and a corporation.

Petitioner lacks a definite ecclesiastical government. The record does not reveal how religious or doctrinal decisions are made. However as founder, Roy Masters is clearly the leader of petitioner. He is also president of petitioner under civil corporate law. Furthermore, his ample writings illustrate fully the beliefs and doctrine of petitioner. Nonetheless, petitioner lacks a formal code of doctrine and discipline.

Petitioner does not possess all of the criteria. It does, however, possess most of the criteria to some degree. Moreover, most of the factors considered to be of central importance are satisfied. It possesses associational aspects that are much more than incidental. Despite the involvement of several members of Roy Master's family, petitioner is more than a one family church. Cf. *American Guidance Foundation, Inc. v. United States, supra at 307.* Furthermore, petitioner is not a sham organization created solely for tax purposes. See, e.g., *Davis v. Commissioner*, 81 T.C. 806 (1983), affd. without published opinion 767 F.2d 931 (9th Cir. 1985) (Universal Life Church case). Based upon all the facts and circumstances, we conclude that petitioner is a church within the meaning of section 170(b)(1)(A)(i).

We acknowledge that petitioner reaches far more people with its message of emotional self control through its radio broadcasts, books, pamphlets, and magazine. Petitioner's radio broadcasts have the potential to reach 2 million people with a regular listening audience of 30,000. Petitioner's magazine, the Iconoclast, has a subscription circulation of 5,200. In contrast, approximately 2,000 followers relocated to Oregon at petitioner's behest, leaving approximately that many in Los Angeles. Attendance at services at the Los Angeles and Grants Pass, Oregon, locations, ranged from 50 to 350. In financial terms, petitioner's radio broadcast and publishing efforts constitute a large percentage of petitioner's total receipts and expenditures. Nevertheless, petitioner's substantial broadcasting and publishing activities do not overshadow the other indications that petitioner is a church. The call to evangelize or otherwise spread one's religious beliefs is, undeniably, an integral part of many faiths. The fact that in this case, the religious outreach was substantial both before and after petitioner began to possess many church-like characteristics does not change our conclusion. More importantly, despite the breadth of petitioner's broadcasting and publishing efforts, its associational aspects are much more than incidental. Cf. *De La Salle Institute v. United States, supra.* We hold that petitioner has sufficient associational aspects to be considered a church. *American Guidance Foundation, Inc. v. United States, supra;* see *Church of Eternal Life and Liberty v. Commissioner, supra; Chapman v. Commissioner, supra.*

We readily acknowledge that this case presents a close question. Our conclusion is based upon the particular facts of this case.... Despite the lack of guidance from Congress, and in the absence of a more explicit regulatory definition of the term "church," we will continue our efforts to give a distinct meaning to this statutory classification....

Simpson, *J.*, dissenting in part: ... This Court recently embraced the "spiritual togetherness" definition of a church suggested by Judge Tannenwald in *Chapman v. Commissioner*, 48 T.C. 358, 367 (1967); in *Church of Eternal Life v. Commissioner*, 86 T.C. 916, 924 (1986), we defined a church as:

> a coherent group of individuals and families that join together to accomplish the religious purposes of mutually held beliefs. In other words, a

> church's principal means of accomplishing its religious purposes must be to assemble regularly a group of individuals related by common worship and faith. . . .

In my opinion, that definition should be applied in this case, and this petitioner does not satisfy that definition. . . .

The true explanation for the congressional deference to churches is more likely to be due, at least in part, to a belief that traditional churches do not require supervision by the Commissioner. A traditional church involves regular and frequent meetings of members of the community, and although a minister or other employees may be engaged to carry on the day-to-day administrative activities of the church, members of the community are generally active participants in the management and carrying on of the activities. The community is fully aware of all the activities of the church and can assure that those activities are carried on for public purposes. Consequently, in the case of a traditional church, there is no need for the Commissioner to require reports and to oversee the activities of the church.

It has been recognized that a church involves an associational activity. In *American Guidance Foundation v. United States*, 490 F. Supp. 304, 306 (D.D.C. 1980), *aff'd*, without opinion (D.C. Cir., July 10, 1982), the court said:

> At a minimum, a church includes a body of believers or communicants that assembles regularly in order to worship. Unless the organization is reasonably available to the public in its conduct of worship, its educational instruction, and its promulgation of doctrine, it cannot fulfill this associational role.

The same test was adopted by the Claims Court in *Church of the Visible Intelligence v. United States, 4 Cl. Ct. at 65.* This petitioner clearly carries on some associational activity, but is that activity sufficient to justify calling it a church?

In his concurrence in *Chapman*, Judge Tannenwald suggested that for an organization to be treated as a church, the associational activity had to be "the principal means" of carrying out its purposes, and in *Church of Eternal Life*, we declared that the associational activity had to be "the principal means" of accomplishing its religious purposes. . . .

The facts of this case show that this petitioner was not a traditional church. Although it conducted regular meetings for significant numbers of participants, it also sought to spread its beliefs through extensive radio and television activities. Those broadcasts were the principal means of spreading its beliefs; they were not merely broadcasts of services conducted for its members. Under these circumstances, I would hold that this petitioner is not a church for tax purposes.

c. "Church" Status Versus "Religious"

Because being classified as a church, rather than merely as a religious organization, offers significant advantages, many entities have attempted to push the definition of "church." The following case is a good illustration of such an attempt. This entity was at least successful in convincing the government of its "religious" nature and, thus, was entitled to exempt status. Many other organizations have incurred criminal penalties.

VIA, a California entity, promotes the "wellness" of its members through the utilization of the latest discoveries in exercise, nutrition, and stress management. "VIA" is an acronym for vitality, integrity, and ability. Membership in VIA requires payment of an annual five-dollar membership fee. The five-dollar fee entitles members to bimonthly monitoring of: (1) resting and post-exercise heart rates, (2) exercise performance, and (3) percentage of body fat. Additionally, VIA "mentors" tailor-make individualized fitness programs for each member. The entity does not solicit contributions; however, it raises funds by selling a nutritional food supplement.

It has no traditional worship services or ministers. Instead, it has "mentors" who receive brief training. With regard to worship, the application for exemption asserted "our form of worship takes place at all meetings: the enlightenment via the intake of new info and the attendant discussions is vital and it's all imbued via group harmonizing." Harmonizing is a method of meditation advocated by VIA as beneficial prior to physical exercise. These meetings, described as places of worship, are held at members' homes. According to the application, "Services are conducted weekly on days that vary with the schedule of the conducting member." Lastly, VIA added "Our congregation differs from that of most churches primarily in the emphasis placed on exercise and nutrition."

Not surprisingly, the government denied classification as a church. The Service, however, granted exempt status as a religious organization and issued an advanced ruling of non-private foundation status under section 509(a)(2).

In contrast to *Foundation of Human Understanding* (the prior case), the Tax Court (in a memorandum opinion) rejected VIA's claims that it constituted a Church. Again, the court declined to adopt the 14-part IRS test; however, the Court examined the 14 factors and concluded:

> using respondent's criteria only as a reasonable yardstick, we cannot conclude that an organization that lacks most, if not all, of these criteria qualifies as a church within the meaning of section 170(b)(1)(A)(i).

The Court then distinguished *FHU*, emphasizing the "associational aspects" of that entity as opposed to the lack of such association in VIA.

VIA v. Commissioner

T.C. Memo. 1994-349

. . . Although we have declined to adopt these [14 point] guidelines as a formal test, we have concluded that they are helpful in deciding what is essentially a question of fact. *Foundation of Understanding v. Commissioner, supra at 1358.*

In lieu of a rigid test, we opted instead to classify a religious organization as a church by examining its religious purposes and, particularly, the means by which its religious purposes are accomplished. *Id.* at 1357 (citing *Chapman v. Commissioner, supra* at 367 (Tannenwald, J., concurring)). Additionally, as a minimum threshold "a church includes a body of believers or communicants that assembles regularly in order to worship." *Foundation of Understanding v. Commissioner, supra* at 1357 (emphasis added) (citing *American Guidance Foundation v. United States*, 490 F. Supp. at 306; *Church of Eternal Life v. Commissioner*, 86 T.C. at 924; *Chapman v. Commissioner, supra* at 367 (Tannenwald, J., concurring)). It is against this backdrop that we determine petitioner's church status.

Apparently, petitioner's religious purpose is the promotion of "wellness". Petitioner claims that this religious purpose is accomplished through meetings in individual members' homes. By petitioner's own admission "members meet fairly regularly but very optionally." Additionally, petitioner added that meetings are conducted weekly on days that vary with the schedule of the conducting member. In all other respects, the record is devoid of any information evidencing that these meetings take place with regularity or consistency. Petitioner also describes the meetings as its form of worship. Repeatedly, the record evidences that these meetings consist of the exchange of information on exercise, nutrition, and stress management coupled with group harmonizing (meditation).

As regards an ordained ministry for the carrying out of petitioner's religious purpose, we are told by petitioner that Ling's apartment provides an informal school in which "mentors" receive three classes. The record indicates that the primary, if not only, services provided by these mentors is the tailoring and monitoring of member's individual fitness programs. Petitioner provides no school or instruction for the education of its young. By petitioner's own admission, it lacks a definite and distinct ecclesiastical government and its discipline is "completely informal and unstructured". In sum, of all of respondent's 14 criteria, we can conclude at most that petitioner satisfies only two—a distinct legal existence and a literature of its own.

We recognize that few churches could meet all of respondent's criteria. *Foundation of Understanding v. Commissioner, supra* at 1358. However, using respondent's criteria only as a reasonable yardstick, we cannot conclude that an organization that lacks most, if not all, of these criteria qualifies as a church within the meaning of section 170(b)(1)(A)(i). In our opinion, petitioner, even when viewed as a religious organization, falls into this class.

Additionally, petitioner's reliance on *Foundation of Understanding v. Commissioner, supra*, is misplaced. Although, we did find that the Foundation of Human

Understanding (FHU) qualified as a church, that case is distinguishable. Unlike petitioner, FHU provided regular services for established congregations. The services were conducted three to four times a week by ordained ministers for congregations of no less than 50 to 300 members. FHU ministers were ordained only after having completed a three-year apprenticeship under the tutelage of FHU's founder and leader. FHU also operated a regular school for children in which teachings of FHU principles formed part of the curriculum....

Question

The Salem organization is an unincorporated association of priests, priestesses, and other followers of the ancient rites of the mystique, a set of beliefs historically associated with "witchcraft." Members of Salem consider themselves to be pagans engaged in the practice of a religion and claim membership in excess of 5,000 people. The organization publishes a pagan manifesto, complete with periodically issued interpretive writings from the high priest or priestess. Members of Salem implore followers of the ancient rites to adhere to certain standards of behavior and to render obedience to the "horned god." Priests and Priestesses claim to possess certain supernatural powers that are made known to them only after completing years of study and apprenticeship. Certain of its doctrines are completely secret and known only to the High Priest/Priestess and his or her council of sorcerers. The organization holds weekly meetings according to a standard ritual. Attendance is not mandatory, though the organization claims average attendance is around 1,800 people per week. When the local council of religious leaders learned that the Salem organization had voluntarily filed a Form 1023 seeking recognition as a religious organization and church, it sent a detailed scholarly letter to the district counsel explaining that witchcraft has never been accepted as a valid religion and therefore the organization's application should be denied. How should the Service rule?

Writing Exercise

The taxpayer in *Church of the Chosen People* did not take an appeal from the district court's ruling. Assume, though, that taxpayer appealed the decision, and you are the judge to whom the case has been assigned. Prepare a draft opinion affirming or rejecting the district court's reasoning and holding. In particular, address whether the court in *Church of the Chosen People* complied with the admonition to strictly avoid value judgments with respect to whether a set of beliefs constitute a religion. Is it really possible to do so?

D. Policing Religious Tax Exemption: The Church Audit Procedures

CODE: § 7611, Skim § 7609

TREAS. REGS.: § 301.7611-1

At the beginning of this chapter, we noted that the grant of tax exemption to religious organizations obviously implicates First Amendment concerns. That observation, as we have seen, holds true at every step of the procedural and substantive religious tax-exemption process. This section concerns itself with the special, constitutionally inspired process by which the Service may bring enforcement action against a church.[7] The regulations pertaining to the Church Audit Procedure Act (CAPA) are written in question-and-answer format and very nicely summarize the detailed workings of § 7611. Test your understanding of the procedures by answering the questions at the end of this section.

The following case explains certain aspects of the intentionally high barriers that Congress requires the Service to overcome before gaining access to church records or otherwise examining church activities. Note, however, that the procedures do not apply to non-church religious organizations.

United States v. C.E. Hobbs Foundation for Religious Training and Education, Inc.

7 F.3d 169 (9th Cir. 1993)

. . . Criminal investigations of the Foundation and subsequent newspaper reports prompted the IRS to believe that the Foundation was not tax-exempt because it was not being operated for religious purposes and because Foundation profits were inuring to private individuals. A search warrant obtained by local law enforcement officials alleged that one of the Foundation's central teachings was to encourage members to participate in "sharing," which consisted of sexual activity between adult church members and minors. A second search warrant alleged that the Foundation was selling beer and wine without a license. Subsequent newspaper reports described the Foundation's opulent grounds, nightclub-like furnishings, and weekend-long parties for members. One news report stated that the Foundation had transferred its assets to a trust, with Reverend Hobbs' son and his female companion as the sole trustees.

The IRS initiated a church tax inquiry on May 7, 1990, by sending the Foundation a notice of church tax inquiry, as required by 26 U.S.C. § 7611(a)(3), stating that the IRS had reason to believe that the Foundation might not be tax-exempt or might be liable for tax. The letter further stated that the IRS had reason to believe that

7. Note that any organization claiming to be a church, even one that does not meet the vague substantive definition of "church," is entitled to the protections of § 7611. § 7611(h)(1)(A). Treas. Reg. § 301.7611-1, Q & A 3.

the Foundation's character, purpose, or method of operation was different from that stated in its application for tax-exempt status, and that the Foundation was not organized or operated for an exempt purpose. The IRS indicated in the letter that its reasonable belief was based on the police investigations and newspaper articles discussed above.

. . . Subsequently, two conferences were held at which the IRS requested the production of certain documents. The Foundation provided some, but not all of the materials requested by the IRS.

Not satisfied by the documents produced by the Foundation, the IRS issued two summonses, one to the Foundation and one to the Bank. The Foundation summons requests production of all of the church's accounting ledgers and journals, all records of church assets, all organizational and religious records, and all tax-related records. The Bank summons requests all financial records pertaining to the Foundation.

On January 22, 1991, the Foundation moved to quash both summonses, . . .

II. The Foundation Summons

Section 7611 of the tax code affords churches special protections in the audit context. First, the IRS may initiate a church tax inquiry only if certain procedural requirements are met. 26 U.S.C. § 7611(a). These procedural requirements are the heart of the statute, in that they afford religious institutions extensive safeguards from having to defend an audit at all. After an inquiry has been validly initiated, the IRS may examine church records "to the extent necessary to determine liability. . . ." 26 U.S.C. § 7611(b)(1)(A). Likewise, the IRS may examine religious activities "to the extent necessary to determine whether the organization claiming to be a church is a church for any period." 26 U.S.C. § 7611(b)(1)(B).

The district court found that the IRS failed even to show that it was conducting a valid investigation. Thus as a threshold matter we must determine if the IRS properly initiated a church tax inquiry.

In its initial notice of church tax inquiry, the IRS stated in writing that it had reason to believe that the church was operating for purposes other than those that were tax-exempt, citing the criminal investigations, the newspaper articles, and the alleged transfer of church property to non-exempt entities as the reasons for its belief. The IRS then complied with all other procedural requirements of section 7611. No more is required of the IRS in order to initiate an inquiry. See 26 U.S.C. § 7611(a)(1)-(2). The district court stated that the IRS lacked sufficient "evidence" to prove that it was conducting a valid investigation, presumably because the district court felt the evidence was not sufficiently probative. It is clear from the statute that information relied on by the IRS in initiating a valid inquiry need provide the IRS with nothing more than a reasonable belief that an investigation is warranted. . . .

The IRS argues that "to the extent necessary" in section 7611 means nothing more than that the IRS must show that the requested documents are relevant in determining liability. The district court disagreed and, following the reasoning of a First Circuit case, found that section 7611(b)(1) requires the IRS to "'explain why the particular documents it seeks will significantly help to further the purpose of the investigation.' "(quoting *United States v. Church of Scientology of Boston, Inc.*, 933 F.2d 1074, 1079 (1st Cir. 1991)).

Since the district court's decision, we have also held that section 7611(b)(1) requires something more than a showing of relevance. In *United States v. Church of Scientology Western United States*, 973 F.2d 715, 719 (9th Cir. 1992), we upheld a district court's partial enforcement of an IRS summons where the district court required there to be "'some showing that [the requested documents] contain the type of information which has a relation to the purposes of the examination set forth."' *Id.* at 719 (citing to the district court order). We concluded that "the district court did not err when it declined to enforce the summons with respect to categories which did not fall *directly and logically within [the] proper scope [of the examination]*." *Id.* at 721 (emphasis supplied). Thus the district court in the case at bar did not employ an incorrect standard when it held that section 7611(b)(1) requires more than a showing of mere relevance.

The IRS further contends that even if a showing greater than relevance is required by section 7611, it has made that showing with respect to all of the requested Foundation documents. We review for clear error the district court's finding that the requested documents were not necessary within the meaning of 26 U.S.C. § 7611(b)(1). *Church of Scientology Western United States*, 973 F.2d at 721.

To show that the summoned Foundation documents are necessary, the IRS must (1) show that the purposes of its investigation are proper, and (2) explain how the particular documents, or categories of documents, (a) fall directly and logically within the scope of those purposes and (b) will help significantly to further an investigation within the scope of those purposes. *See Church of Scientology of Boston, Inc.*, 933 F.2d at 1079; *Church of Scientology Western United* States, 973 F.2d at 721.

The stated purposes of the IRS investigation are to determine (1) whether the Foundation was operating exclusively for religious purposes and (2) whether the Foundation's property was inuring to the benefit of private individuals. It is clear that the IRS' stated purposes are valid under the statute. *See* 26 U.S.C. §§ 7611(a)(2)(A)–(B); *see also Church of Scientology Western United States*, 973 F.2d at 719.

IRS agent John Lien testified in detail as to how each category of documents would significantly help to further the valid purposes behind the IRS investigation. Agent Lien testified that records of the church's income are necessary to determine whether that income is related to the church's exempt function, or is generated by unrelated businesses. Similarly, records of the Foundation's expenditures are necessary to determine whether the Foundation is spending money for religious purposes, or for the purpose of socially entertaining a closed group of members. Examination of the Foundation's expense records is also necessary to determine whether Foundation earnings are inuring to private individuals. The Foundation's organizational records are necessary for the IRS to determine whether the activities and events conducted by the Foundation are religious, or wholly social or commercial. Similarly, records of the Foundation's assets are necessary to investigate whether the Foundation is indeed a religious organization or instead a private social club.

We recognize that the IRS is asking for production of a vast number of the Foundation's documents. However the principal, and proper, purpose of the IRS investigation is to determine whether the Foundation is in fact a church, rather than a private social club organized to foster illicit sexual conduct. This legitimate purpose is so broad in scope that we are unable to find that any category of documents requested by the IRS will not help significantly to further the investigation nor that any category of requested documents is not directly and logically within the proper scope of the examination. The IRS' proper purpose should not be frustrated simply because the scope of its investigation is broad.

As the First Circuit emphasized, section 7611 "focuses the court's attention on the needs of a competent investigator, not the needs of a prosecutor." *Church of Scientology of Boston, Inc.*, 933 F.2d at 1078–79. Thus we do not require the IRS to have probable cause to examine church documents. Rather, the IRS must initiate a valid church tax inquiry and then explain why examination of the requested documents is necessary to a competent investigation. . . .

III. The Bank Summons

. . . Whether third party records are excluded from the requirements of section 7611 is an issue of statutory interpretation subject to de novo review. *See United States v. Saunders*, 951 F.2d 1065, 1066 (9th Cir. 1991).

In the definitions section of section 7611, church records are defined to *exclude* records acquired "pursuant to a summons to which section 7609 applies. . . ." 26 U.S.C. § 7611(h)(4)(B)(i). Thus the IRS is clearly correct. The Bank summons is not governed by section 7611. Therefore, the IRS only has to show that the summoned documents are relevant to its investigation. *See United States v. Powell*, 379 U.S. 48, 57–58, 85 S.Ct. 248, 13 L.Ed.2d 112 (1964). Based on Agent Lien's testimony and the affidavits of Lien and another IRS agent, the IRS has made a showing of relevance.

IV. Remaining Issues

The Foundation argues that enforcing the Bank summons would violate the Foundation's rights under the First Amendment. In order to prevail, the Foundation must make a showing that the Bank summons burdens the exercise of religious beliefs by Foundation members. *See Kerr v. United States*, 801 F.2d 1162, 1164 (9th Cir. 1986). If the Foundation succeeds in making this prima facie showing, the IRS action will be upheld "only upon demonstration that a compelling governmental interest warrants the burden, and that less restrictive means to achieve the government's ends are not available." *St. German of Alaska Eastern Orthodox Catholic Church v. United States*, 840 F.2d 1087, 1093 (2d Cir. 1988). We note that the IRS' interest in enforcing summonses has been found compelling. *See id.* Whether the

Foundation has made its prima facie showing and whether the IRS could have utilized less restrictive means, however, are matters better left to be decided by the district court on remand. . . .

Questions

1. If the Service issues a summons to Church for any and all of its records pertaining to the parsonage allowance provided to the youth minister (solely to determine the youth minister's tax liability), can Church avoid compliance on the basis of the Service's failure to comply with the first notice requirement of § 7611?

2. If the Service suspects that the youth minister's salary is unreasonable and may support imposition of personal liability (under § 4958) against the minister and certain members of the church's Board of Deacons, must it comply with the § 7611 procedures before requesting information from the church relevant to that suspicion? Assume that Church provides the requested information and the Service determines that, in addition to imposing an excise tax against the youth minister and certain members of the church's Board of Deacons, the church's § 501(c)(3) status should be revoked. May the Service do so without initiating a church tax inquiry?

3. Suppose Church publishes a full-page ad in a major newspaper imploring the public to vote only for libertarian candidates in an upcoming election. If the Service obtains, via subpoena to the newspaper, verification that the advertisement was commissioned and paid for by Church, may it seek revocation of Church's exempt status without issuing one or both of the § 7611 notices?

4. What if Church's leaders are indicted and convicted of fraud in their personal capacities and in their capacities as church leaders. If the Service obtains the transcript of trial (a public record) from the clerk of the court, may it initiate revocation proceedings without first complying with any or all of the § 7611 procedures?

5. If the Service properly conducts an inquiry and examination regarding the inurement of church funds to the senior minister and determines that no violation occurred, how soon thereafter may it conduct another inquiry and examination regarding the inurement of church funds to the senior minister's wholly owned corporation (assuming inurement to the corporation was not the subject of the first audit)?

Chapter 4

The Exempt Purpose Requirement: *Educational*

Code: §§ 501(c)(3); 170(c)(2)

Treas. Regs.: §§ 1.501(c)(3)-1(d)(2)-(3); 1.170A-9(c)

A. Overview of Educational Exemption

This Chapter continues with a consideration of what exactly constitutes "exempt purposes" by focusing on *educational* as an exempt purpose. As with all exempt purposes, an applicant for exemption need not list a specific purpose—such as "educational" or "charitable"—on Form 1023 (the application for exempt status). It must, however, provide a detailed narrative of proposed activities, which will necessarily identify its purpose as within a sub-category of "charitable," such as "educational." Thus, viewing "educational" as a distinct category is helpful.

Educational organizations include typical learning institutions, such as primary and secondary schools, trade schools, colleges and universities. The term "educational" also includes any organization involved in the (a) instruction or training of the individual for the purpose of improving or developing his capabilities, or (b) instruction of the public on subjects useful to the individual and beneficial to the community. Organizations coming within either of these descriptions include those that conduct or operate public forums or lectures, correspondence or "distance" learning, and museums, zoos, planetariums, orchestras, art institutions, theatrical productions, and the like.

Although constitutional issues do not permeate the grant, administration, or policing of educational tax exemption to the same extent as they do with regard to religious tax exemption, the educational purpose is not without controversy. The Service, apparently holding to the admirable, but perhaps idealist belief that "education" is concerned solely with the objective search for truth, includes the following caveat in its regulations pertaining to the definition of educational organizations:

> An organization may be educational even though it advocates a particular position or viewpoint so long as it presents a sufficiently full and fair exposition of the pertinent facts as to permit an individual or the public to form an independent opinion or conclusion. On the other hand, an organization

> is not educational if its principal function is the mere presentation of unsupported opinion.

Treas. Reg. §1.501(c)(3)-1(d)(3)(i) (flush). The quoted language created an occasion to address the educational tax exemption from a constitutional viewpoint, as the following cases and revenue procedure demonstrate. It also prompts ideological issues, such as whether the Service (if anyone) should have the power to determine what is "full and fair" versus what is "unsupported opinion."

In 1980, the D.C. Circuit found the above language unconstitutionally vague. *Big Mama Rag, Inc. v. United States*, 631 F.2d 1030 (D.C. Cir. 1980). The government had applied the language to deny educational exempt status to a feminist newspaper because its articles were "controversial" and failed to present a "full and fair exposition of the facts." The District Court, reversed by the Circuit, had found the publication too "doctrinaire." Rather than change the regulations, the government formulated what it called a "methodology test" to clarify the vague terms.

Three years later, the D.C. Circuit affirmed the denial of educational status to a Nazi organization, finding that application of the Service's "methodology test" sufficiently reduced the vagueness problems with the Treasury Regulation. *National Alliance v. United States*, 710 F.2d 868 (D.C. Cir. 1983).

Another three years later, in the 1986 Revenue Procedure quoted below, the Service formally adopted the "methodology test" for organizations that advocate a particular position. Under the test:

> The presence of any of the following factors in the presentations made by an organization is indicative that the method used by the organization to advocate its viewpoints or positions is not educational.
>
> 1. The presentation of viewpoints or positions unsupported by facts is a significant portion of the organization's communications.
>
> 2. The facts that purport to support the viewpoints or positions are distorted.
>
> 3. The organization's presentations make substantial use of inflammatory and disparaging terms and express conclusions more on the basis of strong emotional feelings than of objective evaluations.
>
> 4. The approach used in the organization's presentations is not aimed at developing an understanding on the part of the intended audience or readership because it does not consider their background or training in the subject matter.

Rev. Proc. 86-43, 1986-2 C.B. 729.

Interestingly, "charitable organizations" that advocate a particular position are subject neither to the vague "full and fair exposition test" nor the clearer "methodology test." Instead, they are subject to the "action organization test" found in Treas. Reg. §1.501(c)(3)-1(d)(2). To further complicate the matter, the treasury regulations define "charitable organizations" as including, *inter alia*, educational organizations. Whether an organization could avoid the "full and fair" versus "methodology test" issue simply by "applying" for tax exemption as a "charitable" rather than "educational" organization is unclear. Presumably, the government would attempt to apply the methodology test to any advocacy organization; however, it has not clearly said so. Also, as noted above, an entity does not check an "exempt purpose" box on its Form 1023 application for exemption; thus, applying as "charitable" rather than "educational" may not be particularly realistic.

1. D.C. Circuit Declares Treasury's "Educational" Regulation Unconstitutional

The D.C. Circuit declared in 1980 in *Big Mama Rag, Inc.* that the Treasury's definition of the term "educational," in Treasury Regulation § 1.501(c)(3)-1(d)(3)(i) (flush), was unconstitutionally vague. In *Big Mama Rag, Inc.*, a feminist organization, BMR, Inc., applied for exempt status in 1974. Its purpose was "to create a channel of communication for women that would educate and inform them on general issues of concern to them." Its primary activity was the publication of a monthly newspaper, Big Mama Rag, which printed articles, editorials, calendars of events, and other information of interest to women. It also devoted significant time to promoting women's rights through workshops, seminars, lectures, a weekly radio program, and a free library.

The organization had a predominantly volunteer staff and distributed a large majority of its newspapers free. It sold very little advertising and relied on contributions for a majority of its revenue. The District Director denied exemption largely because the activities were not "educational." The IRS National Office affirmed the denial on three separate grounds:

1. the commercial nature of the newspaper;
2. the political and legislative commentary found throughout; and
3. the articles, lectures, editorials, etc., promoting lesbianism.

Big Mama Rag, Inc. v. United States

631 F.2d 1030 (D.C. Cir. 1980)

... Because we find that the definition of "educational" contained in Treas. Reg. § 1.501(c)(3)-1(d)(3) is unconstitutionally vague in violation of the First Amendment, we reverse the order of the court below....

The district court found that BMR, Inc. was not entitled to tax-exempt status because it had "adopted a stance so doctrinaire" that it could not meet the "full and fair exposition" standard articulated in the definition quoted above....

Even though tax exemptions are a matter of legislative grace, the denial of which is not usually considered to implicate constitutional values, tax law and constitutional law are not completely distinct entities. In fact, the First Amendment was partly aimed at the so-called "taxes on knowledge," which were intended to limit the circulation of newspapers and therefore the public's opportunity to acquire information about governmental affairs.... In light of their experience with such taxes, the framers realized, in the words of Mr. Justice Douglas, that "(t)he power to tax the exercise of a privilege is the power to control or suppress its enjoyment." *Murdock v. Pennsylvania*, 319 U.S. 105 (1943). Thus, although First Amendment activities need not be subsidized by the state, the discriminatory denial of tax exemptions can impermissibly infringe free speech. *Speiser v. Randall*, 357 U.S. 513, 518 (1958). Similarly, regulations authorizing tax exemptions may not be so unclear as to afford latitude for subjective application by IRS officials. We find that the definition of "educational," and in particular its "full and fair exposition" requirement, is so vague as to violate the First Amendment and to defy our attempts to review its application in this case.

III. Vagueness Analysis

* * *

These standards are especially stringent, and an even greater degree of specificity is required, where, as here, the exercise of First Amendment rights may be chilled by a law of uncertain meaning. *Hynes [v. Mayor of Oradell]*, 425 U.S. at 620; *Goguen*, 415 U.S. at 573; *NAACP v. Button*, 371 U.S. at 432–33. Vague laws touching on First Amendment rights, noted the Supreme Court in Baggett, require (those subject to them) to "steer far wider of the unlawful zone," than if the boundaries of the forbidden areas were clearly marked, ... by restricting their conduct to that which is unquestionably safe. Free speech may not be so inhibited. 377 U.S. at 372 (quoting *Speiser v. Randall*, 357 U.S. 513, 526 (1958)) (citation omitted). Measured by any standard, and especially by the strict standard that must be applied when First Amendment rights are involved, the definition of "educational" contained in Treas. Reg. §1.501(c)(3)-1(d)(3) must fall because of its excessive vagueness.

We do not minimize the difficulty and delicacy of the task delegated to the Treasury by Congress under section 501(c)(3) of the Code. Words such as "religious," "charitable," "literary," and "educational" easily lend themselves to subjective definitions at odds with the constitutional limitations we describe above. Treasury bravely made a pass at defining "educational," but the more parameters it tried to set, the more problems it encountered.

The first portion of the regulation relied upon to deny BMR, Inc.'s request for tax-exempt status measures an applicant organization by whether it provides "instruction of the public on subjects useful to the individual and beneficial to the community." Treas. Reg. §1.501(c)(3)-1(d)(3)(i)(b) (1959). The district court rejected that test with barely a murmur of disagreement from appellees. That standard, held the court below, "would be far too subjective in its application to pass constitutional muster." 494 F. Supp. at 479 n.6.

We find similar problems inherent in the "full and fair exposition" test, on which the district court based affirmance of the IRS's denial of tax-exempt status to BMR, Inc. That test lacks the requisite clarity, both in explaining which applicant organizations are subject to the standard and in articulating its substantive requirements.

A. Who is Covered by the "Full and Fair Exposition" Test?

According to the terms of the Treasury regulation, only an organization that "advocates a particular position or viewpoint" must clear the "full and fair exposition" hurdle. Appellant maintains that the definition of an advocacy organization is to be found in the preceding subsection of the regulation, which defines the term "charitable":

The fact that an organization, in carrying out its primary purpose, advocates social or civic changes or presents opinion on controversial issues with the intention of molding public opinion or creating public sentiment to an acceptance of its views does not preclude such organization from qualifying under section 501(c)(3) so long as it is not an "action" organization of any one of the types described in paragraph (c)(3) of this section. Treas. Reg. § 1.501(c)(3)-1(d)(2) (1959). The district court held that this part of the regulation was designed to cover charitable institutions and that BMR, Inc., an educational rather than a charitable organization, must meet the "full and fair exposition" standard rather than the more lenient "action organization" standard of section 1.501(c)(3)-1(d)(2). Obviously, if BMR, Inc. is an advocacy group and is not a charitable organization, it may not take cover under the "action organization" standard but must instead meet the "full and fair exposition" test.

The initial question, however, is whether or not BMR, Inc. is an advocacy group at all. What appellant turns to Treas. Reg. § 1.501(c)(3)-1(d)(2) for is the definition of "advocacy," not for the appropriate standard to be applied to advocacy organizations seeking tax-exempt status. The district court did not deal with that question, and, indeed, it is difficult to ascertain from the language of the regulation defining "educational" exactly what organizations are intended to be covered by the "full and fair exposition" standard and whether or not the definitions of advocacy groups are the same for both educational and charitable organizations.

The uncertainty of the coverage of the "full and fair exposition" standard is evidenced by its application over the years by the IRS. The Treasury Department's Exempt Organizations Handbook has defined "advocates a particular position" as synonymous with "controversial."[1] Such a gloss clearly cannot withstand First Amendment scrutiny. It gives IRS officials no objective standard by which to judge which applicant organizations are advocacy groups-the evaluation is made solely on the basis of one's subjective notion of what is "controversial." And, in fact, only a

---

1. [11] "Organizations doing research or educating the public on controversial public issues must stick to the reasoned approach and avoid unsupported opinion." 3 INT.REV.MANUAL-ADMIN. (CCH) pt. 7751, § 345.(12), at 20,572 (Apr. 28, 1977).

very few organizations, whose views are not in the mainstream of political thought, have been deemed advocates and held to the "full and fair exposition" standard. The one tax-exempt homosexual organization cited by the Government as evidence that the IRS does not discriminate on the basis of sexual preference was required to meet the "full and fair exposition" standard even though it admittedly did not "advocate or seek to convince individuals that they should or should not be homosexuals." Rev. Rul. 78-305, 1978-2 C.B. 172, 173.

The Treasury regulation defining "educational" is, therefore, unconstitutionally vague in that it does not clearly indicate which organizations are advocacy groups and thereby subject to the "full and fair exposition" standard. And the latitude for subjectivity afforded by the regulation has seemingly resulted in selective application of the "full and fair exposition" standard-one of the very evils that the vagueness doctrine is designed to prevent.

B. What Does the "Full and Fair Exposition" Test Require?

. . . What makes an exposition "full and fair"? Can it be "fair" without being "full"? Which facts are "pertinent"? How does one tell whether an exposition of the pertinent facts is "sufficient . . . to permit an individual or the public to form an independent opinion or conclusion"? And who is to make all of these determinations?

The regulation's vagueness is especially apparent in the last clause [an organization is not educational if its principal function is the mere presentation of unsupported opinion.] . . . That portion of the test is expressly based on an individualistic-and therefore necessarily varying and unascertainable-standard: the reactions of members of the public. The Supreme Court has recognized that statutes phrased in terms of individual sensitivities are suspect and susceptible to attack on vagueness grounds. See *Coates v. City of Cincinnati*, 402 U.S. 611, 614 (1971) ("Conduct that annoys some people does not annoy others. Thus, the ordinance is vague . . . in the sense that no standard of conduct is specified at all."). . . .

An additional source of unclarity lies in the relationship between the two sentences comprising the "full and fair exposition" test. Appellant argues that the two should be read as counter-examples-an organization fails to satisfy the test only if "its principal function is the mere presentation of unsupported opinion." The Government, on the other hand, contends that tax-exempt status must be denied BMR, Inc. if a substantial portion of its newspaper consists of unsupported opinion. Again, the language of the regulation does not resolve this issue.[2]

---

2. [13] The IRS has adopted a list of specific guidelines to implement the Treasury definition of "educational." But those guidelines use the same conclusory terms as the regulation and are not helpful in clarifying its meaning: An organization . . . may qualify . . . if (1) the content of the publication is educational, (2) the preparation of material follows methods generally accepted as "educational" in character, (3) the distribution of the materials is necessary or valuable in achieving the organization's educational and scientific purposes, and (4) the manner in which the distribution is accomplished is distinguishable from ordinary commercial publishing practices. Rev. Rul. 67-4, 1967-1 C.B. 121, 122; *see* Rev. Rul. 77-4, 1977-1 C.B. 141.

* * *

One of the five examples cited by the Government as evidence of BMR's failure to meet the "full and fair exposition" test may be used to illustrate our point. Most of the article, discussing Susan Saxe's 1975 plea of guilty to charges stemming from a bank robbery in Philadelphia, is simple journalistic reporting. It discusses the terms of the plea bargain, the reaction of local feminists, the differential treatment accorded Saxe supporters and white men who went to observe the pretrial hearing, and police questioning of women in Philadelphia. In return for Saxe's plea, the Government apparently agreed, among other things, to "call off its investigation of the women's and lesbian communities" in the area and not to ask Saxe to testify against "anyone she has known or know (sic) about in the last five years." By forcing Saxe to choose between her own interests and those of other women, the article continues, "the Government has clarified for us, once again, that we, as women, are inextricably bound up with each other in the struggle." *Big Mama Rag*, July, 1975, at 1, cols. 1–3, reprinted in App. 447.

Certainly, the author's viewpoint is not disguised in the last sentence. But is the statement one of fact or opinion? If the latter, is the author's description of the terms of the guilty plea sufficient to inform readers of the basis underlying her opinion? Or is further proof of the existence of "the struggle" necessary? If so, would the article satisfy the "full and fair exposition" test without that final statement? Neither the Treasury regulation nor the proposed fact/opinion distinction is responsive to these questions. And one's answers will likely be colored by one's attitude towards the author's point of view.[3]

. . . Appellees suggest that the Treasury regulation at issue here embodies a related distinction-between appeals to the emotions and appeals to the mind.[4] Material is educational, they argue, if it appeals to the mind, that is, if it reasons to a conclusion from stated facts. Again, the required line drawing is difficult, a problem which is compounded if the difference between the two relies on the aforementioned fact/opinion distinction. Moreover, the Treasury regulation does not support such a narrow concept of "educational" and we cannot approve it. Nowhere does the regulation hint that the definition of "educational" is to turn on the fervor of the organization or the strength of its language. . . .

3. [15] Ironically, an article appearing in the same issue of BMR as the Saxe piece criticizes another feminist group, which had accused Gloria Steinem of collaborating with the CIA, for "slant(ing) the information it presents in such a way as to make certain conclusions inevitable, rather than presenting the facts and leaving the reader to reach her own conclusions." *Big Mama Rag*, July, 1975, at 5, cols. 1, 4, reprinted in App. 451.

4. [16] The court below also seemed to endorse this distinction: it read the Treasury regulation as requiring that a publication be "sufficiently dispassionate as to provide its readers with the factual basis from which they may draw independent conclusions." 494 F. Supp. at 479 (emphasis supplied). One can only speculate how a poetry publication would be classified under such a dichotomy.

An example raised by appellees in their brief and discussed at oral argument is illustrative. The American Cancer Society's cause may be better served by a bumper sticker picturing a skull and crossbones and saying "Smoking rots your lungs" than by one that merely states "Smoking is hazardous to your health." Both are intended to impart the same message, and they are identical in degree of specificity of the underlying facts. Although the first may be said to appeal more to the emotions, and the second to the mind, that distinction should not obscure the similarities between the two. They should be considered equal in educational content.

Even if one could in fact differentiate fact from unsupported opinion, or emotional appeals from appeals to the mind, these proposed distinctions would be inadequate definitions of "educational" because material often combines elements of each. In such cases, appellees suggested at oral argument, a quantitative test would be appropriate. But the Treasury regulation makes no mention of such a test. Even if a quantitative approach were authorized, it is unclear how much of a publication's content would have to be factual, or appeal to the mind, in order to satisfy the "full and fair exposition" standard. Also unanswered is who would apply the test and determine the requisite amount of factual material. Certainly, the Treasury regulation itself gives no clue.[5]

* * *

The district court's decision was based on the value-laden conclusion that BMR was too doctrinaire. Similarly, IRS officials earlier advised appellant's counsel that an exemption could be approved only if the organization "agree(d) to abstain from advocating that homosexuality is a mere preference, orientation, or propensity on par with heterosexuality and which should otherwise be regarded as normal." Whether or not this view represented official IRS policy is irrelevant. It simply highlights the inherent susceptibility to discriminatory enforcement of vague statutory language.

We are sympathetic with the IRS's attempt to safeguard the public fisc by closing revenue loopholes. And we by no means intend to suggest that tax-exempt status must be accorded to every organization claiming an educational mantle. Applications for tax exemption must be evaluated, however, on the basis of criteria capable of neutral application. The standards may not be so imprecise that they afford latitude to individual IRS officials to pass judgment on the content and quality of an applicant's views and goals and therefore to discriminate against those engaged in protected First Amendment activities.

5. [18] In addition to advancing the two distinctions discussed above to elucidate the Treasury's definition of "educational," appellees also rely on the notion of one sidedness. They point to BMR's editorial policy of "not print(ing) any material which, by our judgment, does not affirm our struggle." *Big Mama Rag*, Sept., 1976, at 4, col. 2, reprinted in App. 667. We agree with the court below that the Treasury regulation may not be read to compel an educational organization to "present views inimical to its philosophy." 494 F. Supp. at 479.

We are not unmindful of the burden involved in reformulating the definition of "educational" to conform to First Amendment requirements. But the difficulty of the task neither lessens its importance nor warrants its avoidance. Objective standards are especially essential in cases such as this involving those espousing non-majoritarian philosophies. In this area the First Amendment cannot countenance a subjective "I know it when I see it" standard. And neither can we. . . .

2. The Methodology Test Cures Constitutional Concerns

In *National Alliance v. United States* (included below), the federal circuit that declared the Treasury's "educational" regulation unconstitutional concluded that the Service's "methodology test" essentially eliminates any vagueness concerns. National Alliance, a Virginia Corporation, was primarily a racist, anti-Semitic organization. It published a monthly newsletter and membership bulletin, organized lectures and meetings, issued occasional leaflets, and distributed books, all for the stated purpose of arousing in white Americans of European ancestry "an understanding of and a pride in their racial and cultural heritage and an awareness of the present dangers to that heritage." The news articles even promoted violence to disadvantage or to injure persons who are members of named racial, religious, or ethnic groups.

The organization applied for exempt status, claiming to be educational. The Service denied exemption, finding the entity failed to satisfy the "full and fair exposition" standard. This, of course, was the standard declared unconstitutionally vague by the D.C. Circuit in *Big Mama Rag*. To remedy the questionable nature of the "full and fair exposition" test, the government presented four criteria that it designated the "Methodology Test," contending that the new test was an explanatory gloss to the test held vague in *Big Mama Rag*. The government then argued that National Alliance material was not "educational" under the Methodology Test.

The district court concluded that the Methodology Test was itself vague and would not cure the faults of the regulation found in *Big Mama*. The D.C. Circuit, however, disagreed, finding the test useful. It also chose to focus more broadly on the statutory meaning of "educational," finding that National Alliance could not satisfy any meaning of that term. In response to a constitutional argument, the Court also concluded:

> We have no doubt that publication of the National Alliance material is protected by the First Amendment from abridgement by law. But it does not follow that the First Amendment requires a construction of the term "educational" which embraces every continuing dissemination of views. See *Taxation With Representation*, 461 U.S. 540, 546, (quoting *Cammarano*, 358 U.S. at 515, (Douglas, J., concurring)) ("We again reject the 'notion that First Amendment rights are somehow not fully realized unless they are subsidized by the State.'"); *Big Mama*, 631 F.2d at 1040 ("And we by no means

intend to suggest that tax-exempt status must be accorded to every organization claiming an educational mantle.").

National Alliance v. United States

710 F.2d 868 (D.C. Cir. 1983)

* * *

In response to an IRS request, National Alliance supplemented its application for exemption with back copies of its monthly newsletter, *Attack*!, and its membership bulletin, *Action*. It is these materials the IRS found noneducational.

The nature of these publications may be summarized as follows. *Attack*! is the organization's principal publication; it contains stories, pictures, feature articles and editorials in a form resembling a newspaper. The general theme of the newsletter is that "non-whites"—principally blacks—are inferior to white Americans of European ancestry ("WAEA"), and are aggressively brutal and dangerous; Jews control the media and through that means—as well as through political and financial positions and other means—cause the policy of the United States to be harmful to the interests of WAEA. A subsidiary proposition is that communists have persuaded "neo-liberals" of equality among human beings, the desirability of racial integration, and the evil of discrimination on racial grounds. In support of these themes, each newsletter contains one or two news stories reporting incidents of murder or other violence by black persons, and identifying as Jews persons holding important media or other positions. Reports of black violence are presented as brief factual accounts—though usually without reference to source—accompanied by assertions of a media coverup and the inborn savagery of blacks.... Identifications of Jews as individuals holding significant positions are accompanied by assertions of resulting Jewish manipulation of American society.... Other articles and editorials attribute political and social events deemed detrimental to WAEA to the integration of non-whites into society or to Jewish manipulation of society....

The organization's newsletter describes its themes of black savagery or Jewish manipulation as warnings to WAEA of the "dangers which arise from the presence of so many alien groups in our midst." A National Alliance membership bulletin states that these perceived dangers can only be averted by the removal of non-whites and Jews from society.... Issues of *Attack*! advocate that the removal be violent.... The terms "non-whites," "blacks," and "Jews" are not defined.

In sum, National Alliance repetitively appeals for action, including violence, to put to disadvantage or to injure persons who are members of named racial, religious, or ethnic groups. It both asserts and implies that members of these groups have common characteristics which make them sufficiently dangerous to others to justify violent expulsion and separation.

Even under the most minimal requirement of a rational development of a point of view, National Alliance's materials fall short. The publications before us purport to state demonstrable facts—such as the occurrence of violent acts, perpetrated by black persons, the presence of Jews in important positions, and other events consistent with National Alliance themes. The real gap is in reasoning from the purported facts to the views advocated; there is no more than suggestion that the few "facts" presented in each issue of *Attack*! justify its sweeping pronouncements about the common traits of non-whites and Jews or the need for their violent removal from society. It is the fact that there is no reasoned development of the conclusions which removes it from any definition of "educational" conceivably intended by Congress. The material may express the emotions felt by a number of people, but it cannot reasonably be considered intellectual exposition.

Significantly, National Alliance has not suggested before the IRS or the district court or here *any* definition of "educational" which would arguably be met by its material. The exposition of propositions the correctness of which is readily demonstrable is doubtless educational. As the truth of the view asserted becomes less and less demonstrable, however, "instruction" or "education" must, we think, require more than mere assertion and repetition.

> We recognize the inherently general nature of the term "educational" and the wide range of meanings Congress may have intended to convey. In attempting a definition suitable for all comers, the IRS, or any legislature, court, or other administrator is beset with difficulties which are obvious. We do not attempt a definition, but we are convinced that the National Alliance material is far outside the range Congress could have intended to subsidize in the public interest by granting tax exemption.

II.

Aside from vagueness, it is clear that in formulating its regulation, IRS was attempting to include as educational some types of advocacy of views not generally accepted. But in order to be deemed "educational" and enjoy tax exemption some degree of intellectually appealing development of or foundation for the views advocated would be required. Hence, the portion of the regulation which requires that the organization "present a sufficiently full and fair exposition of the pertinent facts as to permit an individual or the public to form an independent opinion or conclusion. On the other hand, an organization is not educational if its principal function is the mere presentation of unsupported opinion." It is clear that the National Alliance material is not educational under that test.

One of the concerns in this area, because of First Amendment considerations, is that the government must shun being the arbiter of "truth." Material supporting a particular point of view may well be "educational" although a particular public officer may strongly disagree with the proposition advocated. Accordingly IRS has attempted to test the method by which the advocate proceeds from the premises he furnishes to the conclusion he advocates rather than the truth or accuracy or general acceptance of the conclusion.

Thus the Methodology Test presented in this proceeding contains the following four criteria: . . . [Editor's Note: the four criteria appear below in Rev. Proc. 86-43.]

Nothing in these criteria would suggest that the National Alliance material could be deemed educational. . . .

We assume that the court in *Big Mama* viewed the activity of BMR, Inc. as falling within the range of reasonable interpretation of "educational" as used in the statute, or at least not clearly outside such range. Thus the vague test posed a real risk that BMR, Inc. might have been denied exemption under the test while others not distinguishable on any principled objective basis might be granted exemption.

In the present case we see no possibility that the National Alliance publication can be found educational within any reasonable interpretation of the term. . . .

We observe that . . . application by IRS of the Methodology Test would move in the direction of more specifically requiring, in advocacy material, an intellectually appealing development of the views advocated. The four criteria tend toward ensuring that the educational exemption be restricted to material which substantially helps a reader or listener in a learning process. The test reduces the vagueness found by the *Big Mama* decision. . . .

3. Service Formally Adopts the Methodology Test

Three years after the D.C. Circuit spoke favorably of the Service's "Methodology Test" in *National Alliance*, the government formally adopted it in the following Revenue Procedure. Despite the 1980 *Big Mama Rag* finding of Treasury Regulation § 1.501(c)(3)-1(d)(3) as unconstitutionally vague, the Treasury has failed to withdraw or amend the regulation. Instead, it has chosen merely to modify application of it through the Revenue Procedure.

Revenue Procedure 86-43

1986-2 C.B. 729

. . . The Service has attempted to eliminate or minimize the potential for any public official to impose his or her preconceptions or beliefs in determining whether the particular viewpoint or position is educational. It has been, and it remains, the policy of the Service to maintain a position of disinterested neutrality with respect to the beliefs advocated by an organization. The focus of section 1.501(c)(3)-1(d)(3), and of the Service's application of this regulation, is not upon the viewpoint or position, but instead upon the method used by the organization to communicate its viewpoint or positions to others.

. . . The Service recognizes that the advocacy of particular viewpoints or positions may serve an educational purpose even if the viewpoints or positions being advocated are unpopular or are not generally accepted.

. . . The method used by the organization will not be considered educational if it fails to provide a factual foundation for the viewpoint or position being advocated, or if it fails to provide a development from the relevant facts that would materially aid a listener or reader in a learning process.

.03 The presence of any of the following factors in the presentations made by an organization is indicative that the method used by the organization to advocate its viewpoints or positions is not educational.

> 1. The presentation of viewpoints or positions unsupported by facts is a significant portion of the organization's communications.
>
> 2. The facts that purport to support the viewpoints or positions are distorted.
>
> 3. The organization's presentations make substantial use of inflammatory and disparaging terms and express conclusions more on the basis of strong emotional feelings than of objective evaluations.
>
> 4. The approach used in the organization's presentations is not aimed at developing an understanding on the part of the intended audience or readership because it does not consider their background or training in the subject matter.

.04 There may be exceptional circumstances, however, where an organization's advocacy may be educational even if one or more of the factors listed in section 3.03 are present. The Service will look to all the facts and circumstances to determine whether an organization may be considered educational despite the presence of one or more of such factors. . . .

4. Application of the Methodology Test

A 1994 Tax Court opinion approved Rev. Proc. 86-43, finding it is not overbroad and does not violate the First and Fourteenth Amendments to the Constitution. *Nationalist Movement v. Commissioner*, 102 T.C. 558, *aff'd*, 37 F.3d 216 (5th Cir. 1994). The taxpayer in *Nationalist Movement* was an organization whose activities were focused on supporting racist beliefs.

A 2000 Tax Court Memorandum opinion also used the Methodology Test. That case, however, stands more for the consequences of an incomplete record than it does for its application of the Test. The critical placement of the burden of proof appeared in the following language:

> In order to gain section 501(c)(3) status, a taxpayer must openly and candidly disclose all facts bearing upon the organization, its operations, and its finances so that the Court may be assured that it is not sanctioning an abuse of the revenue laws by granting a claimed exemption. Where such a disclosure is not made, the logical inference is that the facts, if disclosed, would show that the taxpayer fails to meet the requirements of section 501(c)(3).

Nationalist Foundation v. Commissioner, T.C. Memo. 2000-318.

Concluding that the *taxpayer* failed to prove its qualification as an exempt organization, the Court denied exempt status. The Court somewhat harshly criticized the entity for the incomplete record. In addition, based on the record before it, the Court found some pronouncements of the taxpayer to be distorting or inflammatory and thus inconsistent with the second and third standards of the Methodology Test.

The Court rejected the entity's First and Fourteenth Amendment claims based on free speech and equal protection. Essentially, the taxpayer argued that even if it indeed used inflammatory language, so do many exempt organizations that arguably sit far to the left of the taxpayer on the political spectrum. The Court was unpersuaded.

Questions

1. Suppose that for hundreds of years, society believed that the earth was the center of the universe. Suppose also that our system of tax exemption applied throughout those years. Would Nicolaus Copernicus had been able to obtain tax exemption for an organization that advocated that the sun and not the earth was the center of our Universe? Would Frederick Douglass have been granted tax exemption for an organization that taught that slavery was wrong during a time when slavery was viewed as acceptable? In what manner does the "methodology test" support or undermine your conclusion?

2. The Tax Court, in denying exempt status to the Nationalist Foundation, cited the organization's depiction of the NAACP Legal Defense Fund and the ACLU as "the leftist threat to our liberties." The Court later characterized the taxpayer as follows: "Petitioner's actions serve the purpose of increasing social activism of pro-majority and rightist beliefs and are antithetical to these examples [of activities decreasing tensions]." Rev. Proc. 86-43 begins with the following ideal: "It has been, and it remains, the policy of the Service to maintain a position of disinterested neutrality with respect to the beliefs advocated by an organization." Is that standard realistic? Should the Court aspire to it, as well? Can you reconcile this statement with the following Revenue Procedure statement: "The Service recognizes that the advocacy of particular viewpoints or positions may serve an educational purpose even if the viewpoints or positions being advocated are unpopular or are not generally accepted"?

B. Schools

CODE: §§ 170(b)(1)(A)(ii); 509(a)(1)

TREAS. REG.: § 1.170A-9(c)(1)

A safe bet is that all schools are educational organizations, but not all educational organizations are schools. Educational organizations, subject to the restrictions discussed in Part II of this book, qualify as § 501(c)(3) organizations and are thus tax-exempt. They also qualify as § 170(c)(2) organizations. Thus, contributions to them are income tax deductible. They must, however, concern themselves with the onerous private foundation rules. Generally, as long as they satisfy either the § 170(b)(1)(A)(vi) or § 509(a)(2) public support test, they will be public charities and need not worry about private foundation status.

Schools, however, are automatically public charities and need not meet a public support test. As demonstrated in Part III of this text, that is very significant. Public charity status carries not only benefits to the organization, but it also benefits to donors. What, then, is a school? The Code itself provides a helpful answer:

> an educational organization which normally maintains a regular faculty and curriculum and normally has a regularly enrolled body of pupils or students in attendance at the place where its educational activities are regularly carried on

§ 170(b)(1)(A)(ii). Section 509(a)(1) exempts from private foundation status any entity satisfying the above language. Treasury Regulations supply additional gloss to the school definition:

> An educational organization is described in section 170(b)(1)(A)(ii) if its primary function is the presentation of formal instruction and it normally maintains a regular faculty and curriculum and normally has a regularly enrolled body of pupils or students in attendance at the place where its educational activities are regularly carried on. The term includes institutions such as primary, secondary, preparatory, or high schools, and colleges and universities. It includes Federal, State, and other public-supported schools which otherwise come within the definition. It does not include organizations engaged in both educational and noneducational activities unless the latter are merely incidental to the educational activities. A recognized university which incidentally operates a museum or sponsors concerts is an educational organization within the meaning of section 170(b)(1)(A)(ii). However, the operation of a school by a museum does not necessarily qualify the museum as an educational organization within the meaning of this subparagraph.

Treas. Reg. § 1.170A(a)-9(c)(1). But see *Mayo Clinic v. United States*, 412 F. Supp. 3d 1038 (D. Minn. 2019) (invalidating Treas. Reg. § 1.170A(a)-9(c)(1) to the extent that it adds to § 170(b)(1)(A)(ii) a requirement that an educational organization have education as its "primary function" and does not engage in "noneducational activities" unless they are "merely incidental to the educational activities").

Question

Note the similarity in favorable "public charity" status treatment of a "church" (a place where religion may be practiced) and a "school" (a place where education may be delivered). These "places" are usually physical in nature. Why do you suppose Congress provides more favorable tax treatment to entities organized to deliver "charitable" services at a physical "place" than for those that do not?

Chapter 5

The Exempt Purpose Requirement: *Scientific*

CODE: § 501(c)(3); Skim § 512(b)(7)-(9)

TREAS. REG.: § 1.501(c)(3)-1(d)(5)

A. Overview of Scientific Exemption

This Chapter continues with a consideration of what exactly constitutes "exempt purposes" by focusing on "scientific" as an exempt purpose. Given the preeminence of scientific activities in commercial ventures (e.g., research and development), our study of the scientific exemption offers us an opportunity to introduce the topic of the commerciality doctrine as it relates to the exclusivity requirement. This discussion also naturally lends itself to a discussion of the unrelated business income tax. Each of these topics (i.e., exclusivity and unrelated business income) are discussed in great detail in later chapters. *See* Chapters 7 through 9 and Chapters 25 through 30.

B. General Issues of Exemption

By now, readers should be painfully aware that everyday words—religion and education, for example—are by no means subject to precise legal definition. That observation holds true, too, with regard to scientific and charitable organizations, though the imprecision is not so much the result of constitutional concerns. A brief observation regarding tax exemption under § 501(c)(3) is thus appropriate, just in case the reader is beginning to be frustrated by the lack of precision.

Whether purposefully or not, Congress and the Service exhibit unmistakable wisdom in leaving operative terms largely undefined. How useful would tax exemption be in encouraging "good" works if activities thought to be "good" were defined by reference to a certain time and place in history? Thus, even if a precise and exclusive definition were constitutionally permissible, Congress and the Service would be better advised to leave the meaning of certain terms open-ended. The risk of imprecision, however, involves the potential for bureaucratic abuse.

The familiar and necessary pattern of imprecision holds with regard to the exemption of scientific organizations. Neither Congress nor the Service attempts to define "science" or "scientific." Case law suggests that the issue is rather easily dispatched by reference to an ordinary dictionary. In one 1985 case, the Claims Court stated:

> The terms "science" and "scientific" are not defined in the Internal Revenue Code, Congress apparently having chosen to rely on the commonly understood meaning of the term. The *McGraw-Hill Dictionary of Scientific and Technical Terms* (Lapedes ed., 2d ed. 1978), p. 1414, defines "science" as a "branch of study in which facts are observed, classified, and, usually, quantitative laws are formulated and verified; [or] involves the application of mathematical reasoning and data analysis to natural phenomenon." The *Random House Dictionary of the English Language*, p. 1279 (Stein ed. 1967), defines "science" as "[k]nowledge, as of facts and principles, gained by systemic study." Thus, in the context of this litigation, "science" will be defined as the process by which knowledge is systematized or classified through the use of observation, experimentation, or reasoning.

IIT Research Institute v. United States, 9 Cl. Ct. 13, 20 (1985). In an earlier case, a district court opinion stated:

> Webster's Third New International Dictionary refers to science as "a branch of study that is concerned with observation and classification of facts and especially with the establishment . . . of verifiable general laws chiefly by induction and hypotheses." In the Court's view, while projects may vary in terms of degree of sophistication, if professional skill is involved in the design and supervision of a project intended to solve a problem through a search for a demonstrable truth, the project would appear to be scientific research.

Midwest Research Inst. v. United States, 554 F. Supp. 1379, 1386 (W.D. Mo. 1983).

The Treasury's definition of the term "research" is contained in Treasury Regulation § 1.501(c)(3)-1(d)(5), which provides in relevant part:

> [T]he term scientific, as used in section 501(c)(3), includes the carrying on of scientific research in the public interest. Research when taken alone is a word with various meanings; it is not synonymous with scientific; and the nature of particular research depends upon the purpose which it serves. For research to be scientific, within the meaning of section 501(c)(3), it must be carried on in furtherance of a scientific purpose. The determination as to whether research is scientific does not depend on whether such research is classified as fundamental or basic as contrasted with applied or practical. On the other hand, for purposes of the exclusion from unrelated business taxable income provided by section 512(b)(9), it is necessary to determine whether the organization is operated primarily for purposes of carrying on fundamental, as contrasted with applied, research.

Treas. Reg. § 1.501(c)(3)-1(d)(5)(i). The regulation continues in this vein by outlining various instances in which scientific research either is, or is not, *scientific* for purposes of the § 501(c)(3).

A first reading of the "scientific" regulation might lead one to the following conclusion: all scientific organizations are research organizations, but not all research organizations are scientific organizations. The latter clause is correct, the former incorrect. An organization need not engage in original research to be scientific for tax exemption purposes, although the conduct of research certainly helps. The regulation concerning scientific organizations is exclusively devoted to organizations that conduct scientific research, but an organization may obtain scientific tax exemption via a variety of different activities.

As briefly noted in *Washington Research Foundation v. Commissioner*, T.C. Memo. 1985-570, an organization may qualify for *scientific* tax exemption if it engages in publishing or manufacturing activities for the purpose of advancing science.[1] Nevertheless, failure of an entity actually to conduct research does not predict well for exempt status. Washington Research Foundation initially lost its bid for exempt status not only because it conducted no actual research, but also because it was heavily commercial. Granted, almost any trade or business activity will support tax exemption "if the operation of such trade or business is in furtherance of the organization's exempt purpose." Treas. Reg. §1.501(c)(3)-1(e) (discussed in detail below). But, as covered in Chapters 7 through 9 (dealing with the commerciality doctrine), overly commercial activities can negate any otherwise charitable or exempt purpose.

Earlier cases might leave the impression that imprecise terms always receive broad meaning—certainly what constitutes religious, a church, or educational might lead to that conclusion. The conclusion, however, does not always hold, at least not in the construction of the term "scientific."

An initial reading of the *American Kennel Club* case (reprinted below) facts might cause the reader to predict an easy grant of exempt status—if not as scientific, then as educational, or even perhaps "charitable," which sometimes seems to mean anything or everything. That initial guess, however, would be incorrect—at least in the view of the Second Circuit Court of Appeals.

The well-known entity existed to "adopt and enforce uniform rules regulating and governing dog shows and field trials, to regulate the conduct of persons interested in exhibiting, running, breeding, registering, purchasing, and selling dogs, to detect, prevent and punish frauds in connection therewith, to protect the interests of its members, to maintain and publish an official stud book and an official kennel gazette, and generally to do everything to advance the study, breeding, exhibiting, running and maintenance of the purity of thoroughbred dogs." Funding came from

1. In Revenue Ruling 66-147, 1966-1 C.B. 137, the Service held that an organization that employed technical personnel to survey the world's medical and scientific publications soon after publication was organized for educational and scientific purposes. The reviewers were all "highly trained in the particular fields of medicine, chemistry [or] biology, and most spoke a foreign language." The staff persons selected and summarized articles appearing in world literature and then complied the summaries in monthly publications distributed free of charge.

dog show license and registration fees for dog shows, fees for certification of pedigrees, kennel names, and superintendents' and handlers' licenses, and the sale of its publications. Expenses included those for publications, awards, library maintenance, and overhead. No funds benefited members. Other publicly beneficial activities included:

> [G]enealogical records resulting from an accumulation, condensation, classification and systematization of facts relating to the genealogy of registered dogs since 1908 . . . are available for inspection and use by the public. Records are published in a monthly stud book and a monthly magazine, "The American Kennel Gazette," which also contains articles dealing with the history and breeding of dogs and the like, and includes articles by veterinarians on the health and care of dogs. The "Gazette" is sold publicly, but has always been published at a loss. The plaintiff maintains a library of some 4,000 volumes dealing with the origin and history and breeding of dogs; it includes five volumes on psychology and philosophy as applied to dogs. This library is open to the public.

Despite the many laudable organization activities, the Court denied exempt status. Although the non-research activity resulted in useful information and the entity assisted in the dissemination of useful information, it did not apparently undertake the activities for the purpose of *generating* such information. Thus, it was not scientific.

That may seem a bit conclusionary—probably because it is. The decision is important, if not for its holding, then at least as an illustration of just how *ad hoc* some tax-exempt decisions can be. Essentially, the Court found the club not to be scientific *because it was not scientific.* Perhaps, the case is defensible for its construction of the term "exclusively": although the organization had scientific research elements, they certainly were not the exclusive activity. Read the excerpt below and decide for yourself the Court's rationale.

American Kennel Club v. Hoey

148 F.2d 920 (2d Cir. 1945)

. . . The fact that an organization derives income from services not "scientific" does not preclude exemption. *Cf. Bohemian Gymnastic Ass'n v. Higgins*, 2 Cir., 147 F.2d 774; *Oklahoma State Fair and Exposition v. Jones*, D.C., 44 F. Supp. 630. But the exemption granted by the statute is only for those organizations whose "purposes" are "exclusively . . . scientific." The word "scientific" has a large variety of meanings. Thus, among savants, there has been much disputation as to whether, with accuracy, history or politics or economics or sociology or law is or can be a science. . . . Fortunately, we are not here required to decide whether in this statute Congress intended to use "scientific" in a restricted or a latitudinarian manner. For, patently, the taxpayer's prime function is the maintenance, at a high sportsmanlike level, of the sport of dog shows and field trials. Its chief aim is to see that the dog shows are staffed by proper judges and that a fair trial is given to all entrants. However worthy this aim may be, it is not scientific. Doubtless, as plaintiff doggedly asserts, much of the data resulting from taxpayer's activities can be used scientifically by geneticists, and probably is. But this is not enough. Gambling furnished the data to Pascal and Fermat for working out the mathematical theory of probability, a theory mathematicians and physicists, for their purposes, still studied what went on in gambling houses, [but] such institutions were [not] organized and operated for purposes "exclusively . . . scientific." The instant case cannot be distinguished — as was the *Bohemian* case, *supra* — from our decision in *Jockey Club v. Helvering*, 2 Cir., 76 F.2d 597.

Notes

Washington Research Foundation v. Comm'r, T.C. Memo. 1985-570, is instructive about the scientific exemption for several reasons. First, it details two important issues: how do science researchers transfer their ideas and technology to the market? And can the process of technology transfer be exempt? Second, the case includes a good discussion of the commerciality doctrine — a topic covered in Chapters 7 through 9. Last, the case illustrates a creative solution: if you cannot win before the Service or the Courts, try Congress. Following the Tax Court's denial of exempt status, Congress passed special legislation providing for the exempt status of organizations exactly like — indeed only for — the Washington Research Foundation.

The organization proposed to assist universities by obtaining patent, copyright, trade secrets, and other rights for the purpose of licensing them to third parties. Petitioner explained that it intended to do this because academic institutions and individual researchers usually do not have the resources or ability to develop a patentable product. It also planned seminars and publications available to the public at no charge.

Although the entity planned activities beyond the State of Washington, its initial agreement was with the University of Washington. Under the agreement:

> The University agreed to make its technology available to petitioner. Once the technological information was received petitioner would use its best efforts to introduce the technology into public use and to secure royalties or other compensation. After notification by petitioner, the University would assign all rights to petitioner in such technology and agree to execute any other instruments to place the ownership, right, title, and interest in petitioner. Petitioner would thereafter undertake the commercialization of the technology. The basic concept of the agreement is that the major portion of the revenues received from the licensing activities would flow directly to the University after petitioner had covered its out-of-pocket expenses. The monies flowing to the University would be used for further research and to meet its obligation to the inventors. Any monies that petitioner received in excess of that required to cover expenses would be returned to the University in the form of grants for further research.

The Court denied exempt status largely because the entity's activities were overly commercial and, more specifically, were competitive with for-profit businesses. Further, the Court believed the public benefits — including those to the University — were indirect and largely financial. As explained in Chapters 7 through 9, dealing with the commerciality doctrine, a proposed exempt activity is not exempt merely because it results in financial benefits to other exempt entities.

The case also relied significantly and favorably on an earlier questionable Tax Court decision, *Edward Orton, Jr., Ceramic Foundation v. Commissioner*, 56 T.C. 147 (1971).[2] *Edward Orton* involved an exempt organization whose primary activity is the manufacture and sale of ceramic cones — items used in the making of pottery. Orton conducts some scientific research and provides scholarships and training; however, it also competes with for-profit manufacturers and is primarily commercial. Unfortunately, the *Washington Research* court failed to convincingly explain why Orton was an exempt scientific organization, but Washington Research was not.

Following denial of its exempt status, the Washington Research Foundation appealed to a higher authority — Congress — and in 1986 Congress responded by enacting a bill granting tax exemption. Note: the statute is *not* part of the Internal Revenue Code.

Public Law 99-514

Sec. 1605. Tax-Exempt Status for an Organization Introducing Into Public Use Technology Developed by Qualified Organizations

(a) IN GENERAL. — For purposes of the Internal Revenue Code of 1986, an organization shall be treated as an organization organized and operated exclusively for charitable purposes if such organization —

(1) is organized and operated exclusively —

(A) to provide for (directly or by arranging for and supervising the performance by independent contractors) —

(i) reviewing technology disclosures from qualified organizations,

(ii) obtaining protection for such technology through patents, copyrights, or other means, and

(iii) licensing, sale, or other exploitation of such technology,

(B) to distribute the income therefrom, to such qualified organizations after paying expenses and other amounts as agreed with the originating qualified organizations, and

2. Chapter 8, dealing with the commerciality doctrine, covers the *Edward Orton* decision in greater depth.

(C) to make research grants to such qualified organizations,

(2) regularly provides the services and research grants described in paragraph (1) exclusively to 1 or more qualified organizations, except that research grants may be made to such qualified organizations through an organization which is controlled by 1 or more organizations each of which—

(A) is an organization described in section 501(c)(3) of the Internal Revenue Code of 1986 or the income of which is excluded from taxation under section 115 of such Code, and

(B) may be a recipient of the services or research grants described in paragraph (1),

(3) derives at least 80 percent of its gross revenues from providing services to qualified organizations located in the same State as the State in which such organization has its principal office, and

(4) was incorporated on July 20, 1981.

Question

Read the law carefully. Is it possible for a newly created technology transfer company or entity to achieve tax exemption under the enactment? Particularly, note section (a)(4). What does Congress' action in enacting the laws tell us about the theory, if any, Congress follows in granting tax exemption?

C. Sponsored Research

The bulk of the scientific exemption regulation is devoted to distinguishing between research deserving of scientific tax exemption and research that will not qualify for such exemption. The Service explains the distinction by a particularized application of concepts relevant to all organizations seeking exemption under § 501(c)(3).

- An organization will not be entitled to scientific tax exemption if its research is incidental to ordinary commercial or industrial activities. Treas. Reg. § 1.501(c)(3)-1(d)(5)(ii). This requirement is essentially a particularized application of the "exclusively operated" requirement.
- An organization will not be entitled to tax exemption if its research is not "carried on in the public interest." This requirement is a particularized application of the private benefit prohibition.[3]

3. Both requirements—that "scientific" activities do not include those that are merely incidental to normal commercial activities and must be for public rather than private benefit—have been most extensively discussed in the context of the cases regarding unrelated business income tax. To avoid confusion, while also ensuring sufficient coverage of the subject, we will revisit those two

Both issues frequently arise when an organization engages in research at the behest of a for-profit sponsor. For example, a pharmaceutical company might endow a fund for research and, in return, the organization will agree that the sponsor shall retain any patent rights arising from the research. In such circumstances an appropriate question involves whether the organization is merely engaged in ordinary product testing prior to marketing, and also whether it is operating for public rather than the sponsor's private benefit.

While this Chapter covers exempt status itself, an important related issue involves the taxation of unrelated business activities, covered in Part V of this text. In particular, §§ 512(b)(7), (8), and (9) relate to research activities. Paragraph (7) excludes from taxation any income of any tax-exempt entity resulting from research conducted for the U.S. government, a State, or a political subdivision. Paragraph (8) excludes income of colleges, universities, and hospitals resulting from research for any person. Paragraph (9) more generally excludes income for "fundamental research" if the results are "freely available" to the "general public."

For now, our inquiry focuses on whether sponsored or other research supports exempt status. In the later chapter on the unrelated business income tax, we will consider the extent to which such research results in taxable income to the exempt entity. For now, students should realize that the UBIT (unrelated business income tax) reaches only unrelated activities. Thus, if the sponsored "research" is found to accomplish or to further an exempt purpose, it is, by definition, not subject to taxation. In contrast, if the sponsored research is unrelated, it may—or may not—be taxed under § 512.

1. Product Testing: Rev. Rul. 68-373

Drug and pharmaceutical testing is a common venture of exempt organizations, particularly those associated with hospitals. Such testing has clear societal benefits and at least seems to be "scientific." It also might appear to fit within the commonsense definition of "testing for public safety"—another permitted exempt purpose under § 501(c)(3). But such testing also has significant commercial overtones: drug companies clearly benefit, even if they pay fair value for the testing.

In a 1968 Ruling, the Service published its view that drug testing for for-profit companies does not constitute an exempt activity. The Ruling explained:

> Clinical testing is an activity ordinarily carried on as an incident to a pharmaceutical company's commercial operations. The fact that the testing must be done by highly qualified professionals does not change its basic nature. Therefore, such testing does not constitute scientific research within the meaning of section 1.501(c)(3)-1(d)(5)(i) of the regulations.

---

requirements as part of the materials related to the unrelated business income tax in Chapters 25 through 30.

> Until a drug is approved for marketing by the Food and Drug Administration, it is not a "consumer product," available for general use by the public. The clinical testing of a drug for safety and efficacy in order to enable the manufacturer to meet FDA requirements for marketing is not "testing for public safety" but is merely a service performed for the manufacturer. Such testing principally serves the private interest of the manufacturer rather than the public interest.

Rev. Rul. 68-373, 1968-2 C.B. 206. The Service found support for its position in various Treasury Regulations:

> Section 1.501(c)(3)-1(d)(4) of the regulations defines the term "testing for public safety" as used in section 501(c)(3) to include the testing of consumer products, such as electrical products, to determine whether they are safe for use by the general public.
>
> Section 1.501(c)(3)-1(d)(5)(i) of the regulations, in defining the term "scientific," provides that because an organization may meet the requirements of section 501(c)(3) only if it serves a public rather than a private interest, a "scientific" organization must be organized and operated in the public interest.
>
> Section 1.501(c)(3)-1(d)(5)(ii) of the regulations further provides that scientific research does not include activities of a type ordinarily carried on as an incident to commercial or industrial operations, as, for example, the ordinary testing or inspection of materials or products.

Informally, the Service has limited Revenue Ruling 68-373 to *situations immediately preceding* an intention to engage in product manufacturing. The issue is more difficult, however, when an organization is commissioned by a for-profit entity to engage in research in the search of a prototype or pilot product that may eventually prove commercially viable after clinical trials. Thus, the Service has stated:

> [Revenue Ruling 68-373 has] limited utility when applied to commercially sponsored research projects funded by private high technology enterprises such as, for example, firms engaged in producing advanced biomedical equipment. The "ordinary commercial activity" of such a firm may include scientific research projects and the design and testing of experimental prototypes of new equipment. Instead of conducting the research or experimental testing itself, the biomedical firm may contract for these tasks to be performed by an exempt scientific research organization. When the nonprofit research organization performs the research, is it engaged in activities of a type ordinarily carried on as an incident to the commercial operations of the sponsor?

1986 IRS Exempt Organizations CPE Technical Instruction Program Textbook: Chapter 0: Scientific Research Under IRC 501(c)(3).

In answering its own question, the Service looked to the distinction between "research and experimental expenditures" and "ordinary testing" for purposes of the Research and Experimental Credit under section 174. In general, section 174 research and experimental expenditures relate to the *development* or *improvement* of a new product, invention, or process. *See generally* Treas. Reg. § 1.174-2. Because Congress grants a deduction (a tax exemption of sorts) for commercial R & D, the Service reasoned that the Section 174 definition of "exempt" activities should apply to the question of commercially sponsored research as well. Thus, the Service does not consider an exempt organization's participation in the development or improvement of prototypes as an incident to commercial or industrial operations.

> Scientific research can be performed by a commercial enterprise or by an exempt organization. It is scientific research in either case. Therefore, the question posed earlier can be answered this way: A commercial enterprise engaged in scientific research can either do its own research or contract it out to an exempt scientific research organization. If the commercial firm contracts out scientific research to an exempt organization, such research will not become, by virtue of that fact alone, ordinary testing incident to commercial operations for the exempt organization performing the research.

1986 CPE text. Thus, the development or improvement of a prototype or other new invention or process will always be scientific, whether it is undertaken at the organization's own behest or at the behest of a taxable entity that could have done the research in-house.

The regulations do a fair job of answering the second concern identified at the beginning of this section: whether the research is conducted in the public interest. Research, though commissioned by a for-profit organization, is *presumptively* in the public interest if:

- the results thereof are made available to the public on a nondiscriminatory basis,
- the research is performed for a state or federal governmental agency, or
- the research is directed toward benefiting the public. Research engaged in aid of higher education, scholarly publication, curing disease, or attracting new industry to a community or geographic agency is directed toward benefiting the public. Treas. Reg. 1.501(c)(3)-1(d)(5)(iii)(c). If privately funded "sponsored" research is "directed towards benefiting the public," the sponsoring party may retain the right of exclusive ownership of any patent or copyright resulting therefrom.

Note the similarity between the categories of "public interest"—relating to exempt status of the research—and the three categories of exclusion from unrelated business taxable income found in §§ 512(b)(7), (8), and (9). Interestingly, paragraph (9) adds the additional requirement that income from only "fundamental" research freely available to the general public escapes taxation if the research is unrelated.

2. Satisfying the Public Interest through Publication

The following important ruling applies a "publication test" from the treasury regulations. Under the test, commercially sponsored research can satisfy the "public interest" requirement if the results are adequately published. This requires more information disclosure than normally appears in a patent application. Critically, publication need not occur immediately: it can await a patent application by the sponsor. Sponsored research that fails the publication test is, according to the ruling, subject to tax under § 513 and is not excluded per § 512(b)(9) because it fails the "freely available" standard therein.

Revenue Ruling 76-296

1976-2 C.B. 141

Advice has been requested whether the commercially sponsored scientific research in the situations described below is scientific research carried on in the public interest within the meaning of section 501(c)(3) . . . .

The organization that performs the research is one that otherwise qualifies as a scientific organization exempt from Federal income tax under section 501(c)(3) of the Code. As part of its activities, the organization regularly undertakes what is termed "commercially sponsored scientific research," which is scientific research undertaken pursuant to contracts with private industries. Under the contracts for such research, the sponsor pays for the research and receives the right to the results of the research and all the ownership rights in patents resulting from work on the project.

Situation 1

The results of the commercially sponsored projects, including all relevant information, are generally published in such form as to be available to the interested public either currently, as developments in the project warrant, or within a reasonably short time after completion of the project. If patent rights are involved, publication is delayed pending reasonable opportunity to establish such rights, such as through the filing of application for patents.

Situation 2

On occasion, however, the organization will agree, at the request of the sponsor to forego publication of the results of a particular project in order to protect against disclosure of processes or technical data which the sponsor desires to keep secret for various business reasons. In other instances, the organization may agree to extend delay in the publication of results in cases in which the sponsor, for business reasons, desires to protect its patent rights under the project, but desires to defer initiation of patent procedures so as to delay or control the timing of public disclosure of the results of the project.

. . . Because a "scientific" organization must be organized and operated in the public interest, the regulations further provide that the term "scientific," as used in section 501(c)(3), includes the carrying on of scientific research in the public interest.

Section 1.501(c)(3)-1(d)(5)(iii) of the regulations provides that scientific research will be regarded as carried on in the public interest if (a) the results of such research (including any patents, copyrights, processes, or formulae resulting therefrom) are made available to the public on a non-discriminatory basis; (b) such research is performed for the United States, or any of its agencies or instrumentalities, or for a State or political subdivision thereof; or (c) such research is directed toward benefiting the public.

This section of the regulations further provides that scientific research will be considered as directed toward benefiting the public, and, therefore, regarded as carried on in the public interest if it is carried on for the purpose of obtaining scientific information, which is published in a treatise, thesis, trade publication, or in any other form that is available to the interested public. In addition, the regulations explicitly provide that such research will be regarded as carried on in the public interest even though such research is performed pursuant to a contract or agreement under which the sponsor or sponsors of the research have the right to obtain ownership or control of any patents, copyrights, processes, or formulae resulting from such research.

Thus, commercially sponsored scientific research that otherwise qualifies as scientific research under section 501(c)(3) of the Code and that meets the publication test of the regulations constitutes scientific research carried on in the public interest. To meet the test, the publication must be adequate and timely. Some public disclosure beyond that which flows naturally from the issuance of a patent is required. In addition, the publication must disclose substantially all of the information concerning the results of the research which would be useful or beneficial to the interested public.

Although the timing of the publication may vary depending upon the circumstance, the publication must be reasonably prompt because the public disclosure as an addition to the body of useful scientific knowledge is the reason for considering the activity as directed toward benefiting the public. It should be noted that section 102 of Title 35 of the United States Code provides, in effect, that the right to a patent may be lost by publication of a description of the invention in a printed publication more than twelve months prior to the date of the application for the patent. Since the regulations recognize the right of the sponsor to obtain patents or copyrights resulting from the research, publication is not required in advance of the time at which it can be made public without jeopardy to the sponsor's right by reasonably diligent action to secure any patents or copyrights resulting from the research. However, adequate publication of the results of the research should be made as promptly after the completion of the research as is reasonably possible without jeopardizing the sponsor's right to secure patents or copyrights necessary to protect its ownership or control of the results of the research.

The "publication test" is satisfied in Situation 1 because the results of the commercially sponsored research, including all relevant information, are not withheld beyond the time reasonably necessary to obtain patents or copyrights. Therefore, the scientific research is carried on for the purpose of obtaining scientific information which is published in some form available to the interested public. Since such research is regarded as carried on in the public interest even though it is performed pursuant to a contract under which the sponsor has the right to obtain ownership of the patent, it constitutes scientific research in the public interest within the meaning of section 501(c)(3) of the Code.

With respect to Situation 2, however, in which publication of the results of commercially sponsored scientific research is withheld entirely or delayed significantly beyond the time reasonably necessary to establish patent or other ownership rights in the results of the research in order to accommodate the sponsor's business interest in maintaining the secrecy of certain processes or to control the timing of public disclosure of the results, the requirements of the publication test are not met. The research connected with such projects, therefore, is not scientific research carried on in the public interest within the meaning of section 501(c)(3) of the Code.

The term "unrelated trade or business" is defined in section 513 of the Code to mean, in the case of any organization subject to the tax imposed by section 511, any trade or business the conduct of which is not substantially related (aside from the need of such organization for income or funds or the use it makes of the profits derived) to the exercise or performance by such organization of its exempt purposes or functions.

* * *

The organization, by agreeing to undertake commercially sponsored scientific research in the manner described above in Situation 2, is engaging in activity which is not exclusively scientific within the meaning of section 501(c)(3) of the Code and the regulations. Such activity, other than through the production of income, does not contribute importantly to the purposes for which exemption is granted to the organization.

Accordingly, the carrying on of the sponsored research in the manner described in Situation 2 is the conduct of unrelated trade or business within the meaning of section 513.

Question

Is sponsored research an exempt purpose if the results are transferred under an exclusive contract to the sponsor and there is never any publication of the results? Read the last sentence of Treas. Reg. § 1.501(c)(3)-1(d)(5)(iii) carefully before answering.

D. Technology Transfer

Many exempt entities, particularly large research universities, seek not only to conduct research but also to market it to the highest bidder. While the conduct of the research itself may be scientific, of what relevance is the process or purpose behind the resulting marketing efforts? Are these merely efforts to generate "royalties" excluded from unrelated business taxable income per § 512(b)(2)? Or, might the process of marketing — the technology transfer — affect the exempt status of the research entity? The answers are not always clear and have been controversial.

As stated in Revenue Ruling 76-296, if an organization performs research *only* for its non-exempt creators, it is not operating for *public benefit* and will not be entitled to tax exemption as a scientific organization. Treas. Reg. § 1.501(c)(3)-1(d)(5)(iv). The word "only" in the regulation presents some confusion: the regulation does not disclose precisely what will qualify. Some guidance, however, is available.

Research funded by a state or federal agency is axiomatically for public benefit. However, if the results of government-funded research are made available only to a select few, the organization may not be entitled to tax exemption. Under the Bayh-Dole Act, a scientific organization may retain ownership in any patent or other intellectual property right arising from government-funded research.[4] The issue, however, arises whether the scientific organization is "sitting" on technology such that the research is not beneficial to the public or is granting access to the technology on a discriminatory basis.[5] In either of those events, the research creating the intellectual asset will not meet the public benefit test. Treas. Reg. § 1.501(c)(3)-1(d)(5)(iv)(b).

In essence, the tax regulations imply that the organization may retain ownership of any intellectual property, but must normally make that property available to the public via license or similar legal arrangement on a non-discriminatory basis (i.e., nonexclusive license). The regulations explicitly acknowledge, though, that the ultimate goal is to increase the amount of knowledge available to the public, and that in some instances, it may be necessary to grant an exclusive license to a user of intellectual property in order to achieve that goal. For example, certain scientific knowledge may require significant amounts of concentrated venture capital to achieve its full public potential. If tax law required that knowledge to be made available to all takers, it is possible that no single user could attract the capital, or retain the profit motivation, necessary to convert the knowledge into usable public goods.

In reality, this apparent "exception" — that in certain circumstances *exclusive* (rather than nonexclusive) licensing of research results is permissible — is really

4. *See generally* 35 U.S.C. § 200–04 (2001). The Bayh-Dole Act contains provisions that essentially force the scientific organization to grant license(s) under reasonable terms to end-users of technology developed with federal funds. *See* 35 U.S.C. § 203 (2001).

5. *See id.*

the rule. Large research universities, for example, are particularly interested in "technology transfer" whereby know-how is marketed to the highest bidder on an exclusive basis. Exclusive licenses bring in higher (tax exempt) royalties than do nonexclusive licenses. Thus, a scientific organization may agree beforehand that a commercial sponsor will have exclusive ownership of resulting intellectual property rights, provided the research is "directed towards benefiting the 'public'"(as that phrase has been previously defined), or the research was government sponsored. Despite the public benefit requirement, the grant of ownership or exclusive license to intellectual property developed using government funds or under grant of tax exemption has sometimes sparked congressional inquiry and public debate. See John Copeland, *Scientific Research—A Look Back, A Look Forward*, 8 Exempt Org. Tax Rev. 874 (1993), and William E. Nelson, *Letter to the Editor of the Exempt Org. Tax Review* (February 9, 1994) (responding to Copeland).

Questions

1. Private University has the opportunity to aid NASA in developing a new fuel that will be useful for the Space Shuttle. Does conducting this exclusive research affect the exempt status of the University? Would your answer differ if it were a public university? Suppose Private University created a wholly owned subsidiary to conduct the research. Would that subsidiary be exempt?

2. Private University Teaching Hospital has the opportunity to aid ABC Pharmaceuticals, Inc., in testing a new drug that will prove useful in treating childhood leukemia. Does conducting this exclusive research affect the exempt status of University? May ABC retain the patent rights to the drug without the activity adversely affecting the exempt status of University?

3. Gatorade was invented in 1965 by two University of Florida scientists, Drs. Dana Shires and Robert Cade. At the time, the University of Florida had no policy with regard to faculty inventions and had to sue the inventors to obtain rights in the invention. David Villano, *Big Money on Campus*, Florida Trend, Dec. 1, 1995 at 66. The University eventually won a judgment granting it a 20% royalty on Gatorade sales. *Id.* It is estimated that as of 1995, the University was receiving $4.5 million per year in royalties and that Gatorade sales continued to increase. *Id.* Gatorade commands approximately 85% (by total annual sales) of the sports drink market. In 1999, revenues from the sale of Gatorade reached $1.8 billion worldwide (i.e., from sales in 47 countries). Betsy McKay, *PepsiCo Asks More of Gatorade Despite Its 85% Market Share*, Wall. St. J., June 11, 2002, at B4. Assume the University of Florida was exempt under § 501(c)(3) when Gatorade was invented (actually, the University has never applied for tax exemption but is instead exempt as an agency of the state). How would the granting of the exclusive rights in Gatorade be viewed under the scientific rulings and regulations (do not concern yourself with the exclusively operating requirement). Does the granting of the exclusive license in tax exemption-financed technology (Gatorade) achieve a public or private interest?

Chapter 6

The Exempt Purpose Requirement: *Charitable*

A. An Overview of Charitable Exemption

Code: § 501(c)(3)

Treas. Reg.: § 1.501(c)(3)-1(d)(2)

Undoubtedly, the pursuit of religion, education, and science are not the only "good" activities deserving of special tax treatment. Historically, "charity" most often connoted activities designed to relieve the burdens of poverty. According to prevailing thought, the inclusion of "charitable" amongst the permitted exempt purposes referred only to assistance to the poor. Under such reasoning, the term "charitable" could not have been meant to refer to the broadest idea of good works because Congress took the time to specifically enumerate certain categories of good works. Today, however, according to Treasury Regulations, the term "charitable" not only includes the specifically enumerated purposes in § 501(c)(3), but also a much broader and indefinite range of activities beneficial to society. The regulations provide that the term *charitable* is used "in its generally accepted legal sense" and is "not to be construed as limited by the separate enumeration . . . of other tax-exempt purposes which may fall within the broad outlines of charity as developed by judicial decisions." *See* Treas. Reg. § 1.501(c)(3)-1(d)(2).

The different activities for which charitable tax exemption has been granted are far too numerous to list. Those activities include employment counseling (Revenue Ruling 68-71), home delivery of meals (Revenue Ruling 76-244), volunteer fire departments (Revenue Ruling 74-361), jazz appreciation (Revenue Ruling 65-271), film festivals (Revenue Ruling 75-471), environmental preservation (Revenue Ruling 76-204), and neighborhood beautification (Revenue Ruling 68-14), to name just a very few. Certainly, it would be impossible to include a judicial or administrative ruling for all of the different activities and still maintain this text at a manageable length. The relevant regulation defines charitable as including:

> Relief of the poor and distressed or of the underprivileged; advancement of *religion*; advancement of *education* or *science*; erection or maintenance of public buildings, monuments, or works; *lessening of the burdens of Government*; and promotion of social welfare by organizations designed to accomplish any of the above purposes, or (i) to lessen neighborhood tensions; (ii) to eliminate prejudice and discrimination; (iii) to defend human and civil

> rights secured by law; or (iv) to combat community deterioration and juvenile delinquency.

Treas. Reg. §1.501(c)(3)-1(d)(2) (emphasis added).

In this chapter, we focus on only *two* of the more common types of activities giving rise to charitable tax exemption—healthcare entities (hospitals and health maintenance organizations) and public interest law firms.

> 1. The first, involving *healthcare entities*, is included because of its overall importance to tax exempt jurisprudence. Some of the most important tax issues affecting non-profit organizations in general have been, or are being, hashed out within the context of health care.
>
> 2. The second, involving *public interest law firms*, seems appropriate in light of our assumption that our readers are primarily law students or scholars, and many are interested in public interest law.

Although healthcare entities and law firms are ubiquitous in society, some pay taxes while others do not. Why? What factors make some, but not all, healthcare entities and law firms tax exempt? The answers teach us not only about charitable health care and public interest law firms, but also more generally, they help clarify the factors from which tax distinctions among seemingly identical activities are drawn.

What factor distinguishes a tax-exempt soup kitchen or a homeless shelter from taxable restaurants and hotels? The answer is rather obvious. Likewise, the same factor distinguishes a thrift store from a normal clothing boutique. We know that assistance to the poor characterizes the most limited meaning of charity. But if the category "charity" is broader than assistance to the poor, what factors characterize its most expansive meaning? The factors that distinguish charitable health care entities and tax-exempt law firms from the non-charitable taxable health care entities and law firms are useful in answering the latter question, and thus drawing broad general tax distinctions among identical activities. We might conclude that in the broadest sense "charitable" refers not only to the substance of an activity, but also to *the manner by which an activity is conducted.* Thus, almost any activity can support charitable tax exemption if it is conducted in a certain manner, which manner we hope can be derived from the following cases and rulings.

B. Charitable Hospitals

In the not-too-distant past, hospital care substantially involved treating the poor. The wealthy received care at home. By the end of World War II, however, hospitals in the United States had become the common place for paying customers to receive medical care. The following revenue ruling reflects that climate. To be exempt . . . at least in 1956 . . . a hospital initially had to provide substantial care for the indigent for free or at a reduced price. But even in 1956, if only "nominal" demands for indigent care arose in the community, the hospital could retain its exempt status.

1. Indigent Care Required

The following ruling can be difficult to reconcile with the general § 501(c)(3) requirement that an exempt entity be "exclusively" charitable. Indeed, the ruling required a hospital merely to treat the poor "to the extent of its financial ability . . . and not [operate] exclusively for those who are able and expected to pay." Clearly, requiring an entity to be less than "exclusively" for-profit is a far cry from requiring it to be "exclusively" charitable. In that light, the ruling seems to assume that the provision of health care . . . if conducted in a particular manner . . . is itself "per se" charitable, with one caveat: at least some indigent care must be available.

Caution: do not stop reading with this ruling, as it is only an early part of a progression of rulings affecting charitable health care.

Revenue Ruling 56-185

1956-1 C.B. 202

. . . The only ground upon which a hospital may be held to be exempt under section 501(c)(3) of the Code is that it is organized and operated primarily for educational, scientific or public charitable purposes. Usually, the ground for exemption is that it is organized and operated for public charitable purposes. The Supreme Court of the United States in *Helvering v. Susan D. Bliss et al.*, 293 U.S. 144, Ct. D. 884, C. B. XIII-2, 191 (1934), held that the provisions of law granting exemption of income devoted to charity are liberalizations of the law in the taxpayer's favor, were begotten from motives of public policy, and are not to be narrowly construed. Thus, in regard to hospitals and similar organizations, the Internal Revenue Service takes the position that the term "charitable" in its legal sense and as it is used in section 501(c)(3) of the Code contemplates an implied public trust constituted for some public benefit, the income or beneficial interest of which may not inure to the benefit of any private shareholder or individual.

In order for a hospital to establish that it is exempt as a public charitable organization within the contemplation of section 501(c)(3), it must, among other things, show that it meets the following general requirements:

1. It must be organized as a nonprofit charitable organization for the purpose of operating a hospital for the care of the sick. A nonprofit hospital chartered only in general terms as a charitable corporation can meet the test as being organized exclusively for charitable purposes. See *Commissioner v. Battle Creek*. 126 Fed.2d 405.

2. It must be operated to the extent of its financial ability for those not able to pay for the services rendered and not exclusively for those who are able and expected to pay. It is normal for hospitals to charge those able to pay for services rendered in order to meet the operating expenses of the institution, without denying medical care or treatment to others unable to pay. The fact that its charity record is relatively low is not conclusive that a hospital is not operated for charitable purposes to the full extent of its financial ability. It may furnish services at reduced rates which are

below cost, and thereby render charity in that manner. It may also set aside earnings which it uses for improvements and additions to hospital facilities. It must not, however, refuse to accept patients in need of hospital care who cannot pay for such services. Furthermore, if it operates with the expectation of full payment from all those to whom it renders services, it does not dispense charity merely because some of its patients fail to pay for the services rendered.

3. It must not restrict the use of its facilities to a particular group of physicians and surgeons, such as a medical partnership or association, to the exclusion of all other qualified doctors. Such limitation on the use of hospital facilities is inconsistent with the public service concept inherent in section 501(c)(3) and the prohibition against the inurement of benefits to private shareholders or individuals. It is recognized, however, that in the operation of a hospital there must of necessity be some discretionary authority in the management to approve the qualifications of those applying for the use of the medical facilities. The size and nature of facilities may also make it necessary to impose limitations on the extent to which they may be made available to all reputable and competent physicians in the area....

A community hospital of the type supported partly by contributions from the general public and/or public grants from a city, county or state, normally meets the requirements of section 501(c)(3) as a public charitable organization. It is formed for the purpose of furnishing hospital facilities to all persons in the community at the lowest possible cost and necessarily accepts patients who are unable to pay for hospital facilities in order to retain the support of the community. A nominal charity record for a given period of time, in the absence of charitable demands of the community, will not affect its right to continued exemption. On the other hand, a hospital formed by one or more physicians in a community who may own the capital stock thereof or rent the hospital facilities to a corporation which they control requires careful study to determine whether it is being operated in part to serve their interest, directly or indirectly.

A hospital formed to operate on a membership basis to provide, at fixed rates, prepaid hospitalization to its members is not a charitable organization within the meaning of section 501(c)(3) of the Code. Compare G. C. M. 22554, C. B. 1941-1, 243. But exemption will not be denied merely because the hospital maintains a prepayment plan, so long as such plan is available to all persons living in the area and so long as the hospital makes available its facilities to the indigent as well as to pay patients to the same extent as any other hospital not operated for profit....

2. Only Emergency Room Indigent Care Required for Exempt Status

The provision of medical care in the United States, however, did not remain static. The 1960s saw enactment of Medicare and Medicaid legislation, which resulted in satisfying many demands for indigent care. In that light, the government issued the following ruling, which further reduced the amount of indigent care required of exempt hospitals. It also expanded the notion that the provision of health care in a hospital format can be charitable in and of itself, even absent significant indigent care.

The following ruling is important for many purposes:

It modifies Revenue Ruling 56-185 by removing most of the indigent care requirement. In its place, the ruling imposed an "emergency room" indigent care requirement.

It illustrates the "public benefit" or "public purpose" requirement for hospital exemption, foreshadowing the *Bob Jones* public benefit test.

It illustrates the "selfish motive" test: a hospital—otherwise identical to an exempt hospital—organized for the selfish motive of servicing its founders' patients is not exempt. This "selfish motive" aspect is important in an understanding of the private inurement test.

It illustrates the frequent misuse of the term "non-profit" as a charitable requirement. At one point the ruling speaks of Hospital A as having a "nonprofit" purpose; however, in the next paragraph, it finds regular profits to be consistent with such a purpose. Indeed, the "non-profit" requirement is a fiction: nothing in § 501(c)(3) requires an entity to be organized or operated for nonprofit purposes. *But see* § 501(c)(4) which, at least facially, has a non-profit requirement.

It illustrates a significant inconsistency in what the statute requires and what practice requires: ostensibly, charities must be exclusively charitable. Treasury regulations require a "primary" charitable purpose and forbid more than insubstantial unrelated activities. The ruling, however, rests at least in part on the existence of free medical care in an emergency room—surely an activity that is less than "primary" to Hospital A. Without the free care in the emergency room, the hospital would not likely have been exempt in 1969; yet that suggests a relatively small purpose and activity effectively overwhelmed the rest.

Revenue Ruling 69-545

1969-2 C.B. 117

... *Situation 1.* Hospital *A* is a 250-bed community hospital. Its board of trustees is composed of prominent citizens in the community. Medical staff privileges in the hospital are available to all qualified physicians in the area, consistent with the size and nature of its facilities. The hospital has 150 doctors on its active staff and 200 doctors on its courtesy staff. It also owns a medical office building on its premises with space for 60 doctors. Any member of its active medical staff has the privilege of leasing available office space. Rents are set at rates comparable to those of other commercial buildings in the area.

The hospital operates a full time emergency room and no one requiring emergency care is denied treatment. The hospital otherwise ordinarily limits admissions to those who can pay the cost of their hospitalization, either themselves, or through private health insurance, or with the aid of public programs such as Medicare. Patients who cannot meet the financial requirements for admission are ordinarily referred to another hospital in the community that does serve indigent patients.

The hospital usually ends each year with an excess of operating receipts over operating disbursements from its hospital operations. Excess funds are generally applied to expansion and replacement of existing facilities and equipment, amortization of indebtedness, improvement in patient care, and medical training, education, and research.

Situation 2. Hospital *B* is a 60-bed general hospital which was originally owned by five doctors. The owners formed a nonprofit organization and sold their interests in the hospital to the organization at fair market value. The board of trustees of the organization consists of the five doctors, their accountant, and their lawyer. The five doctors also comprise the hospital's medical committee and thereby control the selection and the admission of other doctors to the medical staff. During its first five years of operations, only four other doctors have been granted staff privileges at the hospital. The applications of a number of qualified doctors in the community have been rejected.

Hospital admission is restricted to patients of doctors holding staff privileges. Patients of the five original physicians have accounted for a large majority of all hospital admissions over the years. The hospital maintains an emergency room, but on a relatively inactive basis, and primarily for the convenience of the patients of the staff doctors. The local ambulance services have been instructed by the hospital to take emergency cases to other hospitals in the area. The hospital follows the policy of ordinarily limiting admissions to those who can pay the cost of the services rendered. The five doctors comprising the original medical staff have continued to maintain their offices in the hospital since its sale to the nonprofit organization. The rental paid is less than that of comparable office space in the vicinity. No office space is available for any of the other staff members. . . .

In the general law of charity, the promotion of health is considered to be a charitable purpose. . . . A nonprofit organization whose purpose and activity are providing hospital care is promoting health and may, therefore, qualify as organized and operated in furtherance of a charitable purpose. If it meets the other requirements of section 501(c)(3) of the Code, it will qualify for exemption from Federal income tax under section 501(a).

Since the purpose and activity of Hospital *A*, apart from its related educational and research activities and purposes, are providing hospital care on a nonprofit basis for members of its community, it is organized and operated in furtherance of a purpose considered "charitable" in the generally accepted legal sense of that term. The promotion of health, like the relief of poverty and the advancement of education and religion, is one of the purposes in the general law of charity that is deemed beneficial to the community as a whole even though the class of beneficiaries eligible to receive a direct benefit from its activities does not include all members of the community, such as indigent members of the community, provided that the class is not so small that its relief is not of benefit to the community.... By operating an emergency room open to all persons and by providing hospital care for all those persons in the community able to pay the cost thereof either directly or through third party reimbursement, Hospital *A* is promoting the health of a class of persons that is broad enough to benefit the community.

The fact that Hospital *A* operates at an annual surplus of receipts over disbursements does not preclude its exemption. By using its surplus funds to improve the quality of patient care, expand its facilities, and advance its medical training, education, and research programs, the hospital is operating in furtherance of its exempt purposes.

Furthermore, Hospital *A* is operated to serve a public rather than a private interest. Control of the hospital rests with its board of trustees, which is composed of independent civic leaders. The hospital maintains an open medical staff, with privileges available to all qualified physicians. Members of its active medical staff have the privilege of leasing available space in its medical building. It operates an active and generally accessible emergency room. These factors indicate that the use and control of Hospital *A* are for the benefit of the public and that no part of the income of the organization is inuring to the benefit of any private individual nor is any private interest being served.

Accordingly, ... Hospital *A* is exempt from Federal income tax....

Hospital *B* is also providing hospital care. However, in order to qualify under section 501(c)(3) of the Code, an organization must be organized and operated *exclusively* for one or more of the purposes set forth in that section. Hospital *B* was initially established as a proprietary institution operated for the benefit of its owners. Although its ownership has been transferred to a nonprofit organization, the hospital has continued to operate for the private benefit of its original owners who exercise control over the hospital through the board of trustees and the medical committee. They have used their control to restrict the number of doctors admitted to the medical staff, to enter into favorable rental agreements with the hospital, and to limit emergency room care and hospital admission substantially to their own patients. These facts indicate that the hospital is operated for the private benefit of its original owners, rather than for the exclusive benefit of the public....

Accordingly, ... Hospital *B* does not qualify for exemption.... In considering whether a nonprofit hospital claiming such exemption is operated to serve a private benefit, the Service will weigh all of the relevant facts and circumstances in each case. The absence of particular factors set forth above or the presence of other factors will not necessarily be determinative.

... Revenue Ruling 56-185 is hereby modified to remove therefrom the requirements relating to caring for patients without charge or at rates below cost....

3. Indigent Care Not Required

In 1974, a public interest group—The Eastern Kentucky Welfare Rights Organization—challenged the validity of Revenue Ruling 69-545. According to the organization, the government abused its discretion to interpret the Internal Revenue Code to the extent it modified the Revenue Ruling 56-185 requirement of indigent care. The federal district court agreed. The Circuit Court for the D.C. Circuit, however, approved Revenue Ruling 69-545. The Court recounted the history of hospital care, finding that "to continue to base the 'charitable' status of a hospital strictly on the relief it provides for the poor fails to account for these major changes in the area of health care."

The decision is noteworthy for its well-documented discussion of the history of medical care in the United States. Readers might also ponder its treatment of the legislative acquiescence doctrine—so important in the *Bob Jones* decision (Chapter 2): in *Bob Jones*, the Supreme Court found inaction by Congress to constitute legislative acquiescence in a revenue ruling. The Eastern Kentucky district court, in contrast, found inaction by Congress to be grounds for *discarding* a ruling. The Circuit Court properly reversed, at least when viewed in isolation. Arguably, however, Congress acquiesced in the prior ruling—56-185; if so, one might ask "Under what authority could the Executive alter congressional acquiescence?" The Court answered the question with a lengthy discussion of changing views regarding the meaning of "charitable," but never explained the authority of the Service, rather than the Congress, to implement such changes.

Further, the Court emphasized the provision of emergency room indigent care as critical for tax exemption under Rev. Rul. 69-545—without noting the relative insignificance of such care in relation to the total care provided. The Court also noted how important emergency room care was (and is today) for the poor. One might wonder whether a society efficiently provides indigent care through emergency rooms. If one thinks not, one might also ponder the extent to which the practice of providing so much indigent care in emergency rooms resulted from those two revenue rulings, rather than from deliberate and considered congressional debate. Could one then conclude that perhaps the Service should administer the law rather than foment broad social policies, which arguably is the province of Congress?

Eastern Kentucky Welfare Rights Organization v. Simon

506 F.2d 1278 (D.C. Cir. 1974)

... Hospitals and other health organizations have never been expressly categorized as tax exempt organizations and have achieved that status only by qualifying as "charitable" organizations under the Code. Long established Internal Revenue Service (I.R.S.) policy held that hospitals qualified as charitable organizations under 501(c)(3) only if they provided free or below cost service to those unable to pay. This policy was articulated in Revenue Ruling 56-185 ....

The I.R.S. modified this position in 1969 with the issuance of Revenue Ruling 69-545. The new ruling broadly defines "charitable" in terms of community benefit....

Based on this community benefit concept, a nonprofit hospital can qualify as a charitable organization under § 501(c)(3) "By operating an emergency room open to all persons and by providing hospital care for all those persons in the community able to pay the cost thereof either directly or through third party reimbursement ..." [e.g. private health insurance, Medicare, or Medicaid]. Thus, for a hospital to qualify as a tax exempt organization, the provision of free or below cost service to those unable to pay is no longer essential.

Alleging harm from this new ruling, the plaintiffs-appellees, a group of health and welfare organizations and indigent persons, brought this action seeking to declare Revenue Ruling 69-545 invalid and to enjoin its implementation. They submitted affidavits recounting incidents in various parts of the country involving the denial of hospital services to indigents by institutions enjoying tax exempt status as "charitable" organizations.

* * *

In holding that "Revenue Ruling 69-545 was improperly promulgated ...", the district court concluded that "based on relevant judicial, legislative, and administrative decisions" the new Ruling constituted an unauthorized reversal of a long-established policy of requiring exempt hospitals "to offer special financial consideration to persons unable to pay". The court recognized that "as a matter of jurisdiction and efficient tax administration ... courts have regularly paid deference to the expertise attributed to the I.R.S. in tax related matters and therefore judicial interference has been reluctantly employed". The court continued: "However, this exhibition of restraint is predicated upon the assumption that administrative rulings will do no more than effectuate, implement and clarify the provisions of the Code which have been Congressionally enacted.... When this assumption is proven wrong, the courts must act to rectify any administrative determination which is not in accord with the Code."

We do not disagree with these principles of judicial interpretation of administrative rulings, but our own analysis of the judicial, legislative, and administrative decisions leads to a contrary result. We conclude that Revenue Ruling 69-545 is not inconsistent with 26 U.S.C. § 501(c)(3) and that the modification of the prior ruling was authorized.

The definition of the term "charitable" has never been static and has been broadened in recent years. Prior to 1959, Treasury Regulations generally defined charitable organizations as those operated for the relief of the poor.[1] In 1959, however, a comprehensive set of regulations interpreting § 501(c)(3) was issued. These regulations adopted a broad concept of "charitable". . . .

This Treasury Regulation was cited in *Green v. Connally* . . . :

> ". . . clearly, the term 'charitable' is used 'in its generally accepted legal sense,' Treas. Reg. § 1.501(c)(3)-1(d)(2), and not in a street or popular sense (such as, e.g., benevolence to the poor and suffering). . . . Thus, 'strong analogy' can be derived from the general common law of charitable trusts, at least for close interpretative questions." . . . [2]

In promulgating Revenue Ruling 69-545, the Commissioner did rely on an analogy to the law of charitable trusts. As indicated earlier, the Commissioner cited both the Restatement (Second) of Trusts, sec. 368 and sec. 372,[3] and IV Scott on Trusts (3rd ed. 1967) sec. 368 and sec. 372[4] in holding that the promotion of health is a charitable purpose within the meaning of § 501(c)(3).

The term "charitable" is thus capable of a definition far broader than merely the relief of the poor. The law of charitable trusts supports the broader concept. The question involved here then is whether the term "charitable" as used in § 501(c)(3) may be broadly interpreted as was done in Revenue Ruling 69-545 or is to be restricted to its narrow sense of relief of the poor.

We cannot conclude, as did the district court, that Congress intended the latter construction. While it is true that in the past Congress and the federal courts have conditioned a hospital's charitable status on the level of free or below cost care that it provided for indigents,[5] there is no authority for the conclusion that the determination of "charitable" status was always to be so limited. Such an inflexible construction

---

1. [13] See e.g., Treas. Reg. § 39.101(b)-1(b) (1939 Code) which stated:

> "Corporations organized and operated exclusively for charitable purposes comprise, in general, organizations for the relief of the poor."

See also, I.T. 1800, II-2 Cum. Bull. 152 (1923), a ruling of the Commissioner of the I.R.S., which held that the term "charitable" in the predecessor of § 501(c)(3) was used in its more restrictive sense of relief of the poor, rather than its broader legal sense in the law of charities.

2. [15] The court said in part: "Changes in the courts' conceptions of what is charitable are wrought by changes in moral and ethical precepts generally held, or by changes in relative values assigned to different and sometimes competing and even conflicting interests of society." *Id.* at 1159.

3. [16] . . .

4. [17] . . .

5. [18] *Commissioner of Internal Revenue v. Battle Creek, Inc.*, 126 F.2d 405 (5 Cir. 1942); *Davis Hospital, Inc.*, 4 CCH Tax. Ct. Memo. 312 (1945); *Inter-City Hospital Association v. Squire*, 56 F. Supp. 472 (W.D. Wash. 1944); *Goldsby King Memorial*, 3 CCH Tax. Ct. Memo. 693 (1944); *Lorain Avenue Clinic*, 31 T.C. 141 (1958); *Robert C. Olney*, 1958 T.C. Memo. 200, 17 CCH Tax Ct. Mem. 982 (1958); *Sonora Community Hospital*, 46 T.C. 519 (1966), *aff'd per curiam*, 397 F.2d 814 (9th Cir. 1968).

fails to recognize the changing economic, social and technological precepts and values of contemporary society.

In the field of health care, the changes have been dramatic. Hospitals in the early part of this nation's history were almshouses supported by philanthropy and serving almost exclusively the sick poor.[6] Today, hospitals are the primary community health facility for both rich and poor. Philanthropy accounts for only a minute percentage of the hospital's total operating costs.[7] Those costs have soared in recent years as constant modernization of equipment and facilities is necessitated by the advances in medical science and technology. The institution of Medicare and Medicaid in the last decade combined with the rapid growth of medical and hospital insurance has greatly reduced the number of poor people requiring free or below cost hospital services. Much of that decrease has been realized since the promulgation of Revenue Ruling 56-185. Moreover, increasingly counties and other political subdivisions are providing nonemergency hospitalization and medical care for those unable to pay. Thus, it appears that the rationale upon which the limited definition of "charitable" was predicated has largely disappeared.[8] To continue to base the "charitable" status of a hospital strictly on the relief it provides for the poor fails to account for these major changes in the area of health care.

In holding Revenue Ruling 69-545 void, the district court placed undue emphasis on the fact that Congress in 1969 failed to amend the Internal Revenue Code by including language which would have conformed the Code to the new ruling. The

---

6. [19] As noted by one commentator:

> "General hospitals were established in the United States as early as the 18th century to serve the sick, poor and offer a roof and bed for the homeless or for those whose homes were inadequate. These institutions were primarily the last resort of the sick. Their standards of care did not approach those for the simplest custodial care today." John H. Hayes, ed., Financing Hospital Care in the United States, Vol. I, "Factors Affecting the Cost of Hospital Care (1954), p. 9.

7. [20] Professor William Thomas speaking before a special Senate subcommittee in 1965 stated:

> "The image of a voluntary institution as a charitable organization, financing its care of patients to a substantial degree through philanthropy . . . is largely anachronistic. Philanthropy, though increasing, has not been able to match the redoubled demands for health care." Hearings on Conditions and Problems of the Nation's Nursing Homes, Subcommittee on Long Term Care, Spec. Committee on Aging, U.S. Senate, 89th Cong., 1st Sess., Pt. 2 (Feb. 15, 1965), p. 559.

8. [23] The state courts have recognized these changes in the health care field. As stated by the Supreme Court of Nebraska in *Evangelical Lutheran Good Samaritan Society v. County of Gage*, 181 Neb. 831, 151 N.W.2d 446, 449 (1967):

> "Formerly all institutions furnishing services of this nature, including hospitals and nursing homes, were providing care for many patients without compensation and extended charity in the sense of alms-giving or free services to the poor. With the advent of present day social security and welfare programs, this type of charity is not often found because assistance is available to the poor under these programs. Yet, . . . the courts have defined 'charity' to be something more than mere alms-giving or the relief of poverty and distress, and have given it a significance broad enough to include practical enterprises for the good of humanity operated at a moderate cost to those who receive the benefits."

Senate Finance Committee in deleting a House provision which would have allowed exempt status to institutions "organized and operated exclusively for the providing of hospital care" stated:

> The committee deleted from the bill those provisions which would have conformed the code to the result reached by the 1969 ruling. The committee decided to reexamine this matter in connection with pending legislation on Medicare and Medicaid.[9]

This action or inaction by Congress cannot be interpreted as disapproving the new ruling. Congress could have rejected the ruling had it determined that it was not in conformity with the Code. Instead, it committed the matter for further study in the light of Medicare and Medicaid. No further action has been taken by Congress since the ruling became effective in 1969.

It is important to note also that Revenue Ruling 69-545 rather than overruling Revenue Ruling 56-185 simply provides an alternative method whereby a nonprofit hospital can qualify as a tax exempt charitable organization. That method entails the operation of an emergency room open to all regardless of their ability to pay and providing hospital services to those able to pay the cost either directly or through third party reimbursement. Thus, to qualify as a tax exempt charitable organization, a hospital must still provide services to indigents.

The required provision of emergency room services is of great import to the indigent. Emergency room service is often the only means of access that the poor have to medical care.[10] Furthermore, the fact that hospitals seeking to qualify as charities pursuant to Revenue Ruling 69-545 must accept Medicare and Medicaid patients is also significant. A large percentage of the indigent populace of the nation is now covered by either Medicare or Medicaid. In the final analysis, Revenue Ruling 69-545 may be of greater benefit to the poor than its predecessor Ruling 56-185.[11] Certainly Ruling 69-545 is more in conformity with the concept of "charitable" as

---

9. [24] Actually the provision of the House bill which was deleted provided a broader exemption than Revenue Ruling 69-545. It would have afforded exempt status to all nonprofit hospitals. Ruling 69-545 requires the operation of an emergency room open to all regardless of ability to pay as well as acceptance of Medicare and Medicaid patients and patients whose hospital costs will be paid by third parties.

10. [25] "Finding a physician and getting health care is particularly difficult for families who change communities. A significant portion of these are poor. When health needs become critical, families that do not have adequate financial resources may find the emergency rooms and outpatient clinics of general hospitals the only available resource. These families, along with poor families, who often have no other alternative, have contributed to the 150 million emergency room and outpatient visits in 1967, an increase of 250% during the past two decades." National Advisory Commission on Health Facilities: A Report of the President (1969), p. 20.

11. [26] Moreover, Revenue Ruling 69-545 sets forth a more definite and specific standard. Under Revenue Ruling 56-185 hospitals were required to provide free care only to the extent of their financial ability. Hospitals operating at a deficit would have no obligation under Ruling 56-185. In addition the Ruling qualified the "financial ability" standard by providing:

defined in the Treasury Regulation adopted, after extensive study, in 1959 and interpreting § 501(c)(3).

In summary, we conclude that Revenue Ruling 69-545 is founded on a permissible definition of the term "charitable" and is not contrary to any express Congressional intent.

4. Emergency Indigent Care Not Required If Provided Elsewhere in the Community

In 1983, the government further reduced the amount of indigent care required of exempt hospitals, eliminating the need for free emergency care whenever such care was available elsewhere in the community. Of considerable significance, the ruling illustrates a "community standard" (as opposed to the traditional "community benefit standard") evident in some other rulings (and cases). *See Plumstead Theatre Society, Inc. v. Commissioner*, 675 F.2d 244 (9th Cir. 1982). Under such a standard, what qualifies for exemption in one part of the country might not qualify elsewhere.

Revenue Ruling 83-157

1983-2 C.B. 94

. . . A nonprofit hospital is identical to Hospital A, described in Situation 1 of Rev. Rul. 69-545, 1969-2 C.B. 117, except that it does not operate an emergency room. A state health planning agency has determined that the operation of an emergency room by the hospital is unnecessary because it would duplicate emergency services and facilities that are adequately provided by another medical institution in the community. . . .

In Rev. Rul. 69-545, after examining all the facts, it was determined that Hospital *A* promoted the health of a class of persons that was broad enough to benefit the community. A major factor in this determination was the operation by Hospital *A* of an emergency room open to all persons regardless of ability to pay.

Generally, operation of a full time emergency room providing emergency medical services to all members of the public regardless of their ability to pay for such services is strong evidence that a hospital is operating to benefit the community. Nevertheless, there are other significant factors that may be considered in determining whether a hospital promotes the health of a class of persons broad enough so that the community benefits.

"The fact that its charity record is relatively low is not conclusive that a hospital is not operated for charitable purposes to the full extent of its financial ability. . . . It may also set aside earnings which it uses for improvements and additions to hospital facilities. . . . A nominal charity record for a given period of time, in the absence of charitable demands of the community, will not affect its right to continued exemption."

The hospital in this case does not operate an emergency room because the state health planning agency has made an independent determination that this operation would be unnecessary and duplicative. Consequently, the hospital is unable to rely on the operation of an emergency room open to all regardless of ability to pay as strong evidence that the hospital promotes the health of a sufficiently broad class of persons to benefit the community. Other significant factors, however, including a broad of directors drawn from the community, an open medical staff policy, treatment of persons paying their bills with the aid of public programs like Medicare and Medicaid, and the application of any surplus to improving facilities, equipment, patient care, and medical training, education, and research, indicate that the hospital is operating exclusively to benefit the community.

Certain specialized hospitals, such as eye hospitals and cancer hospitals, offer medical care limited to special conditions unlikely to necessitate emergency care and do not, as a practical matter, maintain emergency rooms. These organizations may also qualify under section 501(c)(3) if there are present similar, significant factors that demonstrate that the hospitals operate exclusively to benefit the community. . . .

5. Requirements for 501(c)(3) Hospitals Under the Affordable Care Act — § 501(r)

26 U.S.C. § 501(r), enacted March 23, 2010, as part of the Patient Protection and Affordable Care Act (ACA), codifies new requirements for hospitals that otherwise satisfy the requirements of § 501(c)(3) and Revenue Ruling 69-545. The ACA also added new reporting requirements for hospitals and a new excise tax. The new requirements are imposed on a facility-by-facility basis and include the following:

1. Community Health Needs Assessment (CHNA)
2. Financial Assistance Policy and Emergency Medical Care Policy
3. Limitations on Charges
4. Billings and Collections

Community Health Needs Assessment—Section 501(r)(3)(A) requires a hospital organization to conduct a community health needs assessment every three years and to adopt an implementation strategy to meet the community health needs identified through the CHNA.

Section 501(r)(3)(B) provides that the CHNA must:

- Take into account input from persons who represent the broad interests of the community served by the hospital facility, including those with special knowledge of or expertise in public health, and
- Be made widely available to the public.

Financial Assistance Policy and Emergency Medical Care Policy—Section 501(r)(4) requires a hospital organization to establish a written financial assistance policy (FAP) and a written emergency medical care policy for a hospital facility it operates.

Limitation on Charges

> A hospital organization meets the requirements of Section 501(r)(5) with respect to a hospital facility it operates only if the hospital facility (and any substantially-related entity) limits the amount charged for any emergency or other medically necessary care it provides to a FAP-eligible individual to not more tha[n] the amount generally billed (AGB) to individuals who have insurance covering such care.
>
> The amounts charged to FAP-eligible individuals for all other medical care covered under the FAP is limited to less than the gross charges for that care

Billing and Collections

> Section 501(r)(6) requires a hospital organization to make reasonable efforts to determine whether an individual is eligible for assistance under the hospital organization's financial assistance policy (FAP) before engaging in extraordinary collection actions (ECAs) against that individual.

On December 29, 2014, the Treasury issued final regulations interpreting § 501(r). Essentially, a hospital or hospital organization that fails to meet the requirements of 501(r) with respect to one or more of its facilities it operates may be subject to loss of 501(c)(3) tax-exemption.

Questions

1. What is "charity"? Are you able to derive a definition of the term "charitable" or "charity" from *Eastern Kentucky Welfare Rights Organization*? Try to articulate and write a definition that you think would be appropriate as a statute or regulation.

2. In the penultimate paragraph of the *Eastern Kentucky Welfare Rights Organization* opinion, the D.C. Circuit found significance in the requirement of Revenue Ruling 69-545 that an exempt hospital "must accept Medicare and Medicaid patients." Is that a correct statement of the ruling?

3. Would Hospital B (in Rev. Rul. 69-545) be exempt if organized by five non-doctor community-minded individuals? If so, what — other than ethics — would prevent the founders from finding five "straw men" to found and operate the hospital?

4. If a tax-exempt hospital can operate without an emergency room open to all comers, maintain a policy of referring indigent patients to other hospitals within the community and still be tax-exempt, then what distinguishes such a hospital from taxable hospitals?

5. Should Congress simply specify in § 501(c)(3) that the provision of health care is an exempt purpose, the way education and religion are so designated? Does enactment of 501(r) in 2010 indicate Congress' acceptance of Revenue 56-185 and its progeny?

6. What makes education and religion so special that they should be singled out for specific attention? Is health care different somehow, or should it be automatically exempt?

C. Health Maintenance Organizations

Sound Health Association v. Commissioner, 71 T.C. 158 (1978), is an early case (1978) in which the Tax Court approved exempt status for an HMO. The court traced the many changes that occurred in the provision of health care during the twentieth century. Relying on those changes, the Court essentially concluded that the provision of health care itself is an appropriate exempt purpose, regardless of the provision of indigent care other than emergency care. While the Court discussed at some length the Association's provision of indigent emergency care, the relevance of this factor should be viewed in light of the date of the opinion—1978—which predates Revenue Ruling 83-157.

The Tax Court also downplayed the "insurance" component of the HMO, finding that such "risk sharing" did not in and of itself preclude exempt status. The Court found such "risk sharing" to constitute a benefit to members, but also found such benefits to be irrelevant. The "private benefit" proscription precludes exempt status to organizations that inappropriately benefit their founders or insiders, rather than the broader group of persons to whom their efforts are directed. Indeed, as the Court explained, if no private benefit of human beings was permissible, few organizations would ever qualify as exempt.

In a 1993 opinion, however, the Third Circuit disagreed with the Tax Court, denying exempt status to an HMO. *Geisinger Health Plan v. Commissioner,* 985 F.2d 1210 (3d Cir. 1993). The Geisinger Plan differed from the Sound Health plan significantly, however. While Sound Health actually provided health care to members, Geisinger merely arranged for health care provided by others. The Tax Court approved the Geisinger plan, relying on its reasoning from *Sound Health*. The Third Circuit, however, disagreed.

Although the two cases are distinguishable on the issue of health care provision, significant differences in the two court approaches are evident. The Tax Court was not particularly concerned about the "community benefit" standard, finding sufficient benefit from the health care provision and the various benefits to the many members. The Third Circuit, however, explained its position differently:

> The test remains one of community benefit, and GHP cannot demonstrate that it benefits anyone but its subscribers....
>
> [T]he *Sound Health* court ventured too far when it reasoned that the presence of a subsidized dues program meant that the HMO in question served a large enough class that it benefited the community. The court ruled that because there was no economic barrier to subscribership, "the class of persons potentially benefitted [sic] by the Association is not so small that its relief is of no benefit to the community." *Sound Health,* 71 T.C. at 185. In doing so, however, the court misconstrued the relevant inquiry by focusing on whether the HMO benefited the community at all rather than whether it primarily benefited the community, as an entity must in order to qualify for tax-exempt status.

Geisinger Health Plan, 985 F.2d at 1219 (1993).

In summary, both *Sound Health* and *GHP* recognize that the direct provision of health care services is a charitable activity worthy of tax exemption. Both also recognize that the concept of "charity" implies broadly dispersed benefit, rather than benefit to a small or identifiable group of persons. Where the two courts differ, however, is in the need for the very characteristic that defines health maintenance organizations—prepaid membership. The organization in *GHP* asserted that a membership requirement—particularly one that contains a subsidized dues component—may result in broadly dispersed benefit. But, according to the Third Circuit, the primary goal or effect of a membership requirement is the promotion of the organization itself; the benefit to the public was considered secondary. Both *Sound Health* and *GHP*'s focus on the beneficial effect of an activity to determine whether that activity is "charitable" introduces the concept of "private benefit"—a separate doctrine that is relevant regardless of the claimed purpose. In fact, an activity serves no exempt purpose—educational, scientific, religious, or charitable—to the extent it serves private benefit. We study the doctrine of private benefit in greater detail later, but it is particularly relevant to the study of the "charitable" purpose, because identifying that purpose relies upon the method by which an activity is carried out and the effect of that activity rather than by reference to definable activities.

But the idea that "promotion of the organization itself," even in the absence of some identifiable benefit to individuals, seems a strange and puzzling basis upon which to find private benefit. Why should the law conclude that individuals are unduly benefited when the organization is beholden to no identifiable group? We might have left both cases and an attempted resolution of this question to our consideration of the private benefit doctrine. But the answer we settle upon is relevant to the study of what activities prove a charitable purpose. The explanatory implication we find is that a broker, even one who deals in charitable goods and services—i.e., a person who brings together producer and consumer—does not serve a charitable purpose and therefore is not entitled to tax exemption. Thus, the organization in *Washington Research Foundation* was not entitled to tax exemption merely because its activities consisted of licensing scientific information produced by others to potential customers. Likewise, *GHP* could not claim tax exemption, according to the Third Circuit, on the sole basis that it brought together producers and consumers of health care services. Ultimately, this is the finding that separates *Sound Health* and *GHP*. Note, too, that the Third Circuit would have granted tax exemption to *Sound Health*, but only on the grounds that the organization in that case was a producer—that is, it directly provided a charitable product or service—not just a broker of charitable services.

On remand in *Geisinger*, the Tax Court considered whether the plan could be exempt as an *integral part* of a larger group of organizations that indeed provided substantial health care. The Court decided that it could not so qualify, largely because the Geisinger plan contracted as much as 20% of its hospital services to non-member hospitals. Nevertheless, the case essentially formulated a two-pronged test for HMOs:

1. Does the HMO benefit the "community"?

2. If not, is the HMO an "integral part" of a group of entities that benefit the community?

In a 2001 memorandum opinion—*IHC*—the Tax Court again considered the exempt status of an HMO that was associated with health care providers. Although the case was not appealable to the Third Circuit, the Tax Court appeared to apply the reasoning of the Third Circuit *Geisinger* decision. It found the HMO failed both the *community benefit test* as well as the *integral part test*. The entity failed the community benefit test because it:

1. lacked sufficient programs to help the indigent,

2. had a board composed of persons who were not representative of the community at large, and

3. had a premium rating program that differentiated based on experience, suggesting a benefit for larger employers rather than for the entire community.

The following excerpt from *IHC* illustrates the Tax Court's evolving view of HMOs.

IHC Health Plans, Inc. v. Commissioner

T.C. Memo. 2001-246

In *Sound Health Association v. Commissioner, supra*, we first considered whether an HMO may qualify as an organization described in section 501(c)(3). The Commissioner determined that Sound Health Association did not qualify for tax-exempt status pursuant to section 501(c)(3) on the ground that the organization served the private interests of its members as opposed to the interests of the community.

In *Sound Health Association v. Commissioner, supra* at 182–183, we utilized the same factors deemed significant by the Commissioner in granting tax-exempt status to one of two hospitals under review in Rev. Rul. 69-545, 1969-2 C.B. 117, and referred to the factors cited favorably in that ruling as the community benefit test. In Sound Health Association, we concluded that the subject organization shared several characteristics with the hospital deemed exempt in Rev. Rul. 69-545, supra. In particular, like the hospital in the revenue ruling, Sound Health Association operated a medical clinic and employed physicians and nurses to provide medical services, and opened its emergency room to all persons requiring emergency care whether they were members or not and regardless of whether they were financially able to pay. Sound Health Association also established a research program to study health care delivery systems, conducted a health education program open to the general public, and was governed by a board of directors the majority of whom were elected by Sound Health Association members from the community at large. *Sound Health Association v. Commissioner, supra* at 184.

We found that Sound Health Association provided community benefits beyond those offered by the hospital deemed exempt in Rev. Rul. 69-545, supra. Specifically, Sound Health Association adopted a plan to accept contributions for the purpose of subsidizing membership for those who could not otherwise afford to pay the full amount of monthly dues. Further, Sound Health Association's practice of offering membership to the public at large demonstrated that the class of persons eligible to benefit from the organization's activities was practically unlimited. *Sound Health Association v. Commissioner, supra* 71 T.C. at 184–185.

We rejected the Commissioner's argument that Sound Health Association provided an unwarranted private benefit to its members. We reasoned that, like the hospital deemed exempt in *Rev. Rul. 69-545*, supra, which (except in emergency cases) limited its treatment to paying patients, Sound Health Association was permitted to restrict its services to paying members. *Sound Health Association v. Commissioner, supra* 71 T.C. at 186–187.

The tax-exempt status of an HMO arose again in *Geisinger Health Plan v. Commissioner*, T.C. Memo. 1991-649 (*Geisinger I*), revd. and remanded (*Geisinger II*), opinion on remand 100 T.C. 394 (1993) (*Geisinger III*), aff'd, 30 F.3d 494 (3d Cir. 1994) (Geisinger IV). Geisinger HMO, like petitioner in the instant case, was part of a group of related organizations forming a large health care network (the Geisinger system).

Geisinger HMO arranged for its enrollees to receive hospital services by contracting for such services with other Geisinger entities (Geisinger hospitals and outpatient clinics that were recognized as exempt organizations) and independent hospitals. Geisinger HMO arranged for its enrollees to receive physician services by contracting for such services with Clinic—a tax-exempt Geisinger affiliate. Clinic provided physician services through a combination of 400 staff physicians and by contracting with independent physicians for their services. Geisinger HMO was organized as a separate entity to avoid regulatory difficulties and to simplify operations from an organizational and managerial standpoint.

Geisinger HMO offered enrollment to groups (with a minimum of 100 eligible enrollees) and individuals (and certain dependents) residing in 17 of the 27 counties in which the Geisinger system operated. Individual enrollees were required to be at least 18 years of age. Individual enrollees were required to complete a medical questionnaire, whereas group enrollees were not subject to this requirement. All enrollees generally paid the same premium based on a community rating system. During the period in question, Geisinger HMO had approximately 71,000 individual and group enrollees.

Geisinger HMO also enrolled slightly more than 1,000 Medicare recipients at a reduced rate under a "wraparound" plan that covered medical expenses not reimbursed by Medicare. Geisinger HMO also enrolled a small number of Medicaid recipients. Geisinger HMO planned to initiate a subsidized dues program to assist enrollees who might be unable to continue to pay their membership fees as the result of some financial misfortune.

At the conclusion of the administrative proceedings, the Commissioner determined that Geisinger HMO did not qualify for exemption as an organization described in section 501(c)(3) on the grounds that: (1) Geisinger HMO did not satisfy the criteria for exemption outlined in *Sound Health Association v. Commissioner, supra;* and (2) Geisinger HMO was not an integral part of its tax-exempt parent.

In *Geisinger I*, we held that the Commissioner erred in determining that Geisinger HMO did not qualify for exemption pursuant to section 501(c)(3). We based our holding largely on a comparison of the Geisinger HMO with the organization in *Sound Health Association v. Commissioner, supra.* In particular, we found that, like Sound Health Association, Geisinger HMO was operated for the charitable purpose of promoting health insofar as its class of possible enrollees was practically unlimited, it had adopted a subsidized dues program for its enrollees, it offered health care services to Medicare recipients at a reduced rate, and it was not operated for the private benefit of its enrollees. *Geisinger Health Plan v. Commissioner,* T.C. Memo. 1991-649.

In *Geisinger II*, the United States Court of Appeals for the Third Circuit reversed and remanded our decision in *Geisinger I. Geisinger Health Plan v. Commissioner,* 985 F.2d 1210, 1218–1219 (3d Cir. 1993). Although the Court of Appeals agreed with the Court that an HMO seeking tax-exempt status must provide a community benefit, see *id.* at 1218–1219, the Court of Appeals concluded that Geisinger HMO did not provide a primary benefit to the community but, rather, provided benefits solely to its members. The Court of Appeals, looking at the totality of the circumstances, stated:

> GHP standing alone does not merit tax-exempt status under section 501(c)(3). GHP cannot say that it provides any health care services itself. Nor does it ensure that people who are not GHP subscribers have access to health care or information about health care. According to the record, it neither conducts research nor offers educational programs, much less educational programs open to the public. It benefits no one but its subscribers. [*Id.* at 1219.]

Further, the Court of Appeals attached little significance to Geisinger HMO's subsidized dues program, stating in pertinent part:

> The mere fact that a person need not pay to belong does not necessarily mean that GHP, which provides services only to those who do belong, serves a public purpose which primarily benefits the community. The community benefited is, in fact, limited to those who belong to GHP since the requirement of subscribership remains a condition precedent to any service. Absent any additional indicia of a charitable purpose, this self-imposed precondition suggests that GHP is primarily benefiting itself (and, perhaps, secondarily benefiting the community) by promoting subscribership throughout the areas it serves. [*Id.* at 1219.]

... The community benefit test requires consideration of a variety of factors that indicate whether an organization is involved in the charitable activity of promoting health on a communitywide basis. Considering all the facts and circumstances surrounding petitioner's operations, we conclude that petitioner did not provide a meaningful community benefit, and, therefore, petitioner does not qualify for exemption pursuant to section 501(a) as an organization described in section 501(c)(3).

Much like the HMOs under consideration in *Sound Health Association v. Commissioner, supra*, and *Geisinger Health Plan, supra*, petitioner offered its health plans to a broad cross-section of the community including individuals, the employees of both large and small employers, and individuals eligible for Medicaid benefits. Petitioner offered several different health plans encompassing a range of health services at varying prices. There is no indication in the record that petitioner rejected any potential enrollees, although it was petitioner's practice to deny an enrollee coverage with respect to certain preexisting conditions for the first 12 months of enrollment.

During 1999, petitioner's enrollees represented approximately one-fifth of Utah's total population and petitioner's IHC Access plan enrollees constituted nearly 50 percent of Utah residents that were eligible for managed Medicaid benefits.

Despite petitioner's open enrollment policy and the wide acceptance of its plans by individuals and groups alike, petitioner's operations differed materially from the operations of Sound Health Association HMO and Geisinger HMO. Significantly, petitioner did not own or operate its own medical facilities, did not employ (to any significant extent) its own physicians, and did not offer free medical care to the needy. Additionally, petitioner did not institute any program whereby individuals were permitted to become members while paying reduced premiums, and, aside from the few free health screenings that petitioner conducted in 1999, petitioner did not provide or arrange to provide any free or low cost health care services. The record does not reflect whether petitioner applied surplus funds to improve facilities, equipment, patient care, or to enhance medical training, education, and research. *See* Rev. Rul. 83-157, 1983-2 C.B. 94.

Importantly, the record does not reveal why petitioner applied an adjusted community rating methodology to determine premiums for individual and small employer group enrollees while setting premiums for large employer group enrollees based upon past claims experience. If the difference in treatment of the enrollees caused a disparity in premium costs between the classes of enrollees, there could be an inference that petitioner was benefiting larger employers. However, the record contains no explanation of the difference in treatment of enrollees.

In conjunction with the premium disparity issue, we note that, unlike the arrangement adopted by Sound Health Association, petitioner's bylaws stated that its board of trustees would be composed of a plurality of representatives from the buyer-employer community, with an approximately equal number of physicians and hospital representatives. The composition of petitioner's board of trustees, lacking in representation of the community at large, furthers the inference that petitioner predominantly served the private interests of the larger employers participating in its plans. In the absence of an explanation in the record, the Court is left with doubt as to petitioner's provision of a community benefit. Petitioner has the burden of proof. *See* Rule 217(c)(2)(A); *Geisinger Health Plan v. Commissioner*, 100 T.C. at 406.

In sum, we hold that petitioner has not established that it provided a community benefit that qualifies it for tax-exempt status pursuant to section 501(c)(3). Put another way, it has failed to show that it provides any community benefit that accomplishes a charitable purpose....

2. Whether Petitioner Satisfies the Integral Part Test

In *Geisinger III*, we concluded that an organization may qualify for exemption as an integral part of a tax-exempt affiliate if: (1) The organization's activities are carried out under the supervision or control of a tax-exempt affiliate, and (2) such activities would not constitute an unrelated trade or business if conducted by a related tax-exempt entity. *Geisinger Health Plans v. Commissioner*, 100 T.C. at 402–405. There is no dispute that petitioner's activities were carried out under the supervision and control of IHC—a tax-exempt affiliate. Thus, we need only consider whether petitioner's activities would constitute an unrelated trade or business if conducted by a related tax-exempt entity.

In *Geisinger III*, we held that, because Geisinger HMO enrollees received some hospital services from independent hospitals, Geisinger HMO had to show that its overall operations were substantially related to the functions of its tax-exempt affiliates. *Id.* at 405. We stated:

> If petitioner's activities are "conducted on a scale larger than is 'reasonably necessary'" to accomplish the purposes of the exempt entities, there is no substantial relationship within the meaning of the regulations. *Hi-Plains Hospital v. United States*, 670 F.2d 528, 530–531; sec. 1.513-1(d)(3), Income Tax Regs. [*Id.* at 406.]

Although Geisinger HMO enrollees received all of their physician services through Clinic, an exempt affiliate, Geisinger HMO enrollees received approximately 20 percent of their hospital services from independent hospitals. Because the record did not disclose why Geisinger HMO enrollees received hospital services from hospitals outside of the Geisinger system, we were unable to conclude that Geisinger HMO's operations were substantially related to the functions of its tax-exempt affiliates. *Id.* at 404–406.

Like Geisinger HMO, petitioner neither owned nor operated any medical facilities and did not employ a significant number of physicians or health care professionals. Petitioner fulfilled its obligation to provide medical services to its enrollees by contracting with physicians (both physicians employed by Health Services and independent physicians) and hospitals (both Health Services hospitals and independent hospitals) to provide such services. In contrast to *Geisinger III*, however, the administrative record in this case indicates that the medical services that petitioner's enrollees received from independent hospitals were largely attributable to admissions to either UMC or Davis Hospital and Medical Center. Further, these admissions were undertaken to: (1) Take advantage of specialized services (such as burn treatment and pain management) provided at UMC; (2) address occasional shortages of psychiatric beds in Health Services hospitals; and (3) accommodate petitioner's enrollees living in Davis County, Utah, where Health Services lacked a hospital. Because the circumstances under which petitioner's enrollees received hospital services from independent hospitals were limited to situations where Health Services was unable to provide specialized hospital services or were due to geographical expediency, or both, we are satisfied that petitioner's method for arranging for its enrollees to receive hospital services was substantially related to Health Services' tax-exempt function.

However, we do not end our analysis here. In particular, the administrative record reveals that petitioner's enrollees received a substantial portion of their physician services from independent physicians.

In *Geisinger III*, we did not discuss the provision of physician services to Geisinger enrollees inasmuch as Geisinger HMO arranged for its enrollees to receive all their physician services from Clinic—a tax-exempt affiliate of Geisinger HMO. Clinic in turn arranged to provide physician services to Geisinger enrollees through its approximately 400 physician/employees (approximately 84 percent of services) and through contracts with independent physicians (approximately 16 percent of services). In contrast, in the instant case, petitioner's enrollees received approximately 20 percent of their physician services from physicians employed by or contracting with Health Services, while petitioner contracted for the remaining 80 percent of such physician services directly with independent physicians. In other words, petitioner's enrollees received nearly 80 percent of their physician services from physicians with no direct link to one of petitioner's tax-exempt affiliates.

Petitioner contends that its contracts with independent physicians are not relevant to the question of whether it qualifies for tax-exempt status as an integral part of its tax-exempt IHC affiliates because all such independent physicians were required to maintain privileges at Health Services' hospitals. We disagree with the basic premise underlying petitioner's argument.

Health Services comprised the hospital division, which operated a large number of hospitals and clinics, and the physician division, which employed approximately 400 primary care and specialist physicians who generally practiced in Health Services' clinics and other community-based settings. Considering that petitioner does not provide free or low cost health services, we fail to see how petitioner's operations, including its heavy reliance on independent physicians, would be essential to or substantially related to Health Services' exempt functions. To the contrary, petitioner's method of arranging for its enrollees to receive physician services suggests that petitioner conducted its operations on a scale "larger than is reasonably necessary to accomplish the purposes of the exempt entities". *Geisinger Health Plans v. Commissioner*, 100 T.C. at 406. Based on the record presented, we hold that petitioner does not satisfy the integral part test....

Questions

1. Under early interpretations, in order to be charitable, an organization had to provide assistance to the poor. In the HMO context, the Third Circuit rejects the corollary—assistance to the poor does not necessarily mean an organization is charitable. Why isn't it enough in the HMO cases that the HMO provide a subsidized dues program to assist people who are unable to afford the dues? If the reason for denying tax exemption to Geisinger HMO is that it looks just like a for-profit HMO, can you think of a for-profit HMO that allows for free or below-market premiums?

2. Write a brief memorandum explaining the factors relevant to whether an HMO might receive § 501(c)(3) exempt status.

D. Public Interest Law Firms

Public interest law firms present three issues, two relatively simple and one complex. The simple issues involve exempt status and the receipt of fees. The complex issue involves the fundamental purpose of many such firms—to challenge government or large corporate interests, often at odds with what might be viewed as majority (or at least controlling) public opinion. Such ideological issues are particularly difficult because they prompt accusations that such firms may exist to foment controversial political or social change.

First, let's deal with the simple issues.

1. Exemption

Public interest law firms are entitled to exempt status as charitable organizations. According to Revenue Ruling 75-75 (which paraphrases Rev. Rul. 75-74):

> the recognition of a public interest law firm as charitable is based on its providing legal representation for the resolution of issues of broad public importance where such representation is not ordinarily provided by traditional private law firms.

2. Receipt of Fees by Public Interest Law Firms

Exempt public interest law firms may receive fees, but with significant restrictions. First, a policy of charging or accepting attorneys' fees from clients was historically fatal. As explained by Revenue Ruling 75-75 (revoked in 1992), such a policy was viewed as indistinguishable from that of a private law firm. Under that view, such a firm did not operate exclusively for charitable purposes: it also operated significantly for the purpose of generating fees. As such, it had a significant commercial purpose and was not entitled to § 501(c)(3) exempt status.

Arguably, even if all such generated fees support clearly exempt activities, the result does not change. That scenario would simply result in the entity being a forbidden "feeder organization" under § 501(c)(2). See also § 513(c), which provides, in part, that the process of earning money for charitable purposes is not itself a charitable purpose.

Second, however, is the good news for exempt public interest firms: they may indeed accept fees from opposing parties when such fees are awarded or approved by a court or administrative agency. Revenue Ruling 75-76 approved exempt status for a firm with such a policy. The firm also assured the government that it would not select cases or clients on the basis of any potential fee recovery. The firm anticipated that most support would come from grants and contributions, rather than awarded fees. The favorable ruling explained:

> As a general rule, United States courts do not award attorneys' fees to the prevailing party. Fees are awarded only under a specific statutory authorization or in special circumstances in which the court concludes that equity compels the award of fees. *Mills v. Electric Auto-Lite Co.*, 396 U.S. 375 (1970). In either case, the award of attorneys' fees serves to effectuate some legislative or judicial policy in deterring or encouraging certain actions, for which the Court determines that the opposing party should pay all or part of the cost. *See Newman v. Piggie Park Enterprises, Inc.*, 309 U.S. 400 (1968). Thus, the award or acceptance of attorneys' fees by public interest law firms in these situations is consistent with and tends to support the statutory and public policy objectives in awarding such fees.
>
> Unlike fees paid by clients described in Rev. Rul. 75-75, the after-the-fact award of attorneys' fees does not necessarily indicate that the case involved a sufficient economic interest to warrant the utilization of private counsel. Ordinarily, there is little correlation between the award of a fee and the economic feasibility of the litigation to the client. Accordingly, the receipt of fees awarded against an opposing party is not necessarily inconsistent with the basis of charitable exemption of public interest law firms.
>
> However, the likelihood or certainty of an award of fees is a factor affecting the appropriateness of the particular litigation for a public interest law firm. Certainty of an award of fees, or even a strong probability, would suggest that the issue may be economically feasible for the client and thus may not be proper for the public interest law firm to undertake. In order for its exempt status to be unaffected by the receipt of awarded fees, it must be clear that neither the expectation nor the possibility, however remote, of an award of fees is a substantial motivating factor in the selection of cases. As legal precedent in developed indicating the strong possibility of the recovery of fees, certain issues may become economically feasible for private litigants and thus inappropriate for public interest law firm participation.

In 1992, the government further revised its policies concerning the exempt status of public interest law firms. Revenue Procedure 92-59 revoked the absolute prohibition of firms accepting client fees. It also amplified and explained the process by which a firm could accept awarded fees.

Revenue Procedure 92-59

1992-2 C.B. 411

Sec. 3. General Guidelines

.01 The engagement of the organization in litigation can reasonably be said to be in representation of a broad public interest rather than a private interest. Litigation will be considered to be in representation of a broad public interest if it is designed to present a position on behalf of the public at large on matters of public interest. Typical of such litigation may be class actions in which the resolution of the dispute is in the public interest; suits for injunction against action by government or private interests broadly affecting the public; similar representation before administrative boards and agencies; test suits where the private interest is small; and the like.

.02 The litigation activity does not normally extend to direct representation of litigants in actions between private persons where the financial interests at stake would warrant representation from private legal sources. In such cases, however, where the issue in litigation affects a broad public interest or will have an impact on the broad public interest, the organization may serve as a friend of the court.

.03 The organization does not attempt to achieve its objectives through a program of disruption of the judicial system, illegal activity, or violation of applicable canons of ethics.

.04 The organization files with its annual information return a description of cases litigated and the rationale for the determination that they would benefit the public generally.

.05 The policies and programs of the organization (including compensation arrangements) are the responsibility of a board or committee representative of the public interest, which is not controlled by employees or persons who litigate on behalf of the organization nor by any organization that is not itself an organization described in section 501(c)(3) of the Code.

.06 The organization is not operated, through sharing of office space or otherwise, in a manner so as to create identification or confusion with a particular private law firm.

.07 There is no arrangement to provide, directly or indirectly, a deduction for the cost of litigation that is for the private benefit of the donor.

.08 The organization does not accept fees for its service except in accordance with the procedures set forth in Sections 4 and 5 below.

* * *

.10 A public interest law firm may accept reimbursement from clients or from opposing parties for direct out-of-pocket expenses incurred in the litigation. Courts have traditionally distinguished out-of-pocket costs such as filing fees, travel expenses, and expert witness fees from attorneys' fees. These expenses are usually nominal in comparison to the amount of attorneys' fees.

Sec. 4. Acceptance of Attorneys' Fees

.01 The organization may accept attorneys' fees in public interest cases if such fees are paid by opposing parties and are awarded by a court or administrative agency or approved by such a body in a settlement agreement.

.02 The organization may accept attorneys' fees in public interest cases if such fees are paid directly by its clients provided it adopts additional procedures as set forth in Section 5 of this revenue procedure.

.03 The likelihood or probability of a fee, whether court awarded or client-paid, may not be a consideration in the organization's selection of cases. The selection of cases should be made in accordance with the procedures set forth in Section 3 of this revenue procedure.

.04 Cases in which a court awarded or client-paid fee is possible may not be accepted if the organization believes the litigants have a sufficient commercial or financial interest in the outcome of the litigation to justify retention of a private law firm. The organization may, in cases of sufficient broad public interest, represent the public interest as *amicus curiae* or intervenor in such cases.

.05 The total amount of all attorneys' fees (court awarded and received from clients) must not exceed 50 percent of the total cost of operation of the organization's legal functions. This percentage will be calculated over a five-year period, including the taxable year in which any fees are received and the four preceding taxable years (or any lesser period of existence). Costs of legal functions include: attorneys' salaries, nonprofessional salaries, overhead, and other costs directly attributable to the performance of the organization's legal functions. An organization may submit a ruling request where an exception to the above 50 percent limitation appears warranted.

.06 The organization will not seek or accept attorneys' fees in any circumstances that would result in a conflict with state statutes or professional canons of ethics.

.07 All attorneys' fees will be paid to the organization, rather than to individual staff attorneys. All staff attorneys and other employees will be compensated on a straight salary basis, not exceeding reasonable salary levels and not established by reference to any fees received in connection with the cases they have handled.

.08 In addition to the information required by Section 3.04 of this revenue procedure, the organization will file with its annual information return a report of all attorneys' fees sought and recovered in each case.

Sec. 5. Additional Rules Applicable to Client-paid Fees

.01 Client-paid fees may not exceed the actual cost incurred in each case, *viz.*, the salaries, overhead, and other costs fairly allocable to the litigation in question. Costs may be charged against a retainer, with any balance remaining after the conclusion of the litigation refunded to the litigant.

.02 Once having undertaken a representation, a public interest law firm may not withdraw from the case because the litigant is unable to pay the contemplated fee. . . .

Questions

1. In determining the broad contours of charitable law firms, why does the Service impose explicit limitations on the amount of fees that may be collected? Why is there no such explicit concern with respect to health care organizations, educational organizations, or other organizations seeking exemption under § 501(c)(3)?

2. Does it appear, now that you have completed your study of charitable health and law, that "charity" means one thing with regard to certain endeavors and another with respect to others? If so, should Congress eliminate the "charitable" exempt purpose and instead provide a specific list of activities that justify tax exemption?

3. Ideological Issues Involving Public Interest Law Firms

The following decision—*Center on Corporate Responsibility v. Schultz*—illustrates one court's reasoning regarding exempt status for a public interest law firm. CCR focused on improving corporate "social responsibility." To further its goal, the organization supported litigation, among other activities. In response to government pressure during the application process, it agreed not to be involved in proxy fights—activities that, it agreed, would be conducted by a related, non-exempt organization. The entity's activities raised considerable concerns at the White House during the Nixon Administration. During most of the application process, the organization realistically expected a favorable ruling; ultimately, however, the service denied exemption. The court viewed the resulting White House "interference" in the exemption process as inappropriate.

Center on Corporate Responsibility is thus valuable as more than just an example of judicial interpretation of the concept of "charity" *vis-à-vis* public interest law firms. It asks whether the definition of "charity" varies according to one's ideology. Clearly, the organization in *Center on Corporate Responsibility* was involved, maybe intentionally, perhaps unwillingly so, in a larger and seemingly timeless battle between political ideologies. Public interest law firms are almost by definition involved in such battles and we therefore think it appropriate to pause here and consider the bigger picture regarding the impact of ideology on the grant and maintenance of tax exemption.

Initially, the case provides an opportunity to consider and preview the role of charities and other non-profit organizations in shaping or influencing public policy. Section 501(c)(3) organizations are prohibited from taking an active role in the political process. But the formal political arena is not the sole arbiter of public policy. Many institutions—both public and private—shape, formulate, and implement public policy. Charities, particularly public interest law firms, can legitimately and significantly influence public policy despite the general prohibitions against political activity.

But as *Center on Corporate Responsibility* demonstrates in the extreme, because of their potential influence, charities may be required to fend off some of the more "rough and tumble" tactics that often predominate in the battle for hearts and minds. Often, for example, an organization that seeks to operate a homeless shelter or a soup kitchen must confront and deal with the vocal opposition of well-meaning business or homeowners who would rather not be located next to a facility that will attract the not-so-beautiful people who need or depend on homeless shelters or soup kitchens. Fortunately, both sides most often fight these battles with legitimate weapons. Open and logical debate, and even seeking the appropriate involvement of elected representatives on one side of the issue or another, is legitimate. It is not uncommon, for example, that third parties, having learned that an organization has filed an application for tax exemption, will send unsolicited letters to the Service urging it to grant or deny exemption on various ideological or economic grounds. Most would agree, though, that stonewalling, politically motivated expedient reinterpretations of legal precedent, and unequal application of the law are illegitimate.

Although the Watergate-era manipulation of the Service with regard to tax exemption may seem incredible and unlikely to recur, one should remember that laws are interpreted and applied by fallible human beings who are sometimes tempted to make decisions based upon their own view of what's best for the world. It therefore happens, even after Watergate, that the qualifications of an ostensibly exempt organization are attacked as part of a broader battle to thwart a certain political ideology. During the mid-1990s for example, House Speaker Newt Gingrich (R-Ga.) was successfully dethroned in part because of his relationship to a tax-exempt educational organization. Allegedly, the educational organization existed solely to achieve and implement a Republican political agenda; therefore, Speaker Gingrich was allegedly violating tax laws (i.e., the organization should not have been tax-exempt) and he was therefore unfit to be Speaker. Ultimately, Speaker Gingrich resigned. The Service later ruled in a technical advice memorandum that the organization had not actually violated any requirements for tax exemption under § 501(c)(3). For the full text of the technical advice memorandum (which was not officially numbered or released), see 23 EXEMPT ORG. TAX REV. 512 (1999). Still later, as this edition goes to press, the media in 2014 is filled with allegations of political involvement in the review of exempt organization applications, particularly relating to § 501(c)(4) organizations.

Center on Corporate Responsibility, Inc. v. Shultz

368 F. Supp. 863 (D.D.C. 1973)

... Plaintiff was incorporated ... as a non-profit corporation on February 19, 1970, under the name "Project on Corporate Responsibility, Inc." ...

Defendants' representatives ... informally expressed the view that the Plaintiff would qualify as a tax exempt organization if the Plaintiff would cease to participate in its proxy contest activities.

The Plaintiff's amended application stated its activities would continue to focus both on corporate involvement in various social problems and conditions, and on the social impact of various corporate policies, but that after August 18, 1972, these purposes would be realized entirely by sponsoring and performing research, conducting educational programs, issuing publications, conducting public interest litigation and other such related activities which the IRS employees indicated were clearly consistent with exempt status. All future proxy contest activities would be undertaken by the Plaintiff's sister organization....

On May 16, 1973, the Service issued a ruling that the Plaintiff was not exempt from federal income taxes under section 501(c)(3) and not qualified to receive deductible charitable contributions under section 170(c)(2).

On June 29, 1973, Plaintiff's counsel sent the Court a letter listing several indicia that White House influence may have been used to induce the IRS to enter the unfavorable ruling even though the Service had given all indication that it would enter a favorable ruling. Plaintiff's counsel pointed to: (1) The testimony of John W. Dean III before the Senate Select Committee on Presidential Campaign Activities, in which Mr. Dean submitted several memoranda dated in August and September, 1970 and in the fall of 1971 which indicated that attempts were made to use IRS administrative actions against tax exempt organizations, described as "left wing" or "activist," whose views the White House found offensive; ... (2) the extreme delay, two years and eight months, in processing the application, and the fact that the ruling was finally rendered only after this suit was instituted, and the fact that the final ruling was totally contrary to the views expressed by the IRS representatives at the June 9, 1972 meeting; and (3) the fact that Mr. Roger V. Barth, Deputy Counsel of the Internal Revenue Service, a political appointee and addressee of one of the memorandum described in (1) *supra*, was in charge of processing the ruling request in its concluding stages, despite the fact that he had no ordinary responsibility for the ruling processes, no special background in tax exempt organizations law, and had performed a number of functions for the White House at the Internal Revenue Service.

In response to this letter the Court held a hearing and entered an order on July 6, 1973 allowing the Plaintiff to conduct discovery on the question of political intrusion or influence in the processing of the Plaintiff's application....

Pursuant to this Order, the Plaintiff was allowed to inspect the IRS files relative to the Plaintiff's application for exemption and copy those documents which showed some form of impropriety, if the Defendants agreed the documents showed some impropriety.... While inspecting the file, the Plaintiff discovered seven pages of hand-written notes by Mr. Richard Cox ... with the notation "*perhaps White House pressure*."

The files also disclosed certain unusual procedures in the final processing of the application.... Following submission of additional information which indicated compliance with the IRS representatives' requested modifications, a favorable ruling letter was drafted in the fall of 1972 by the Rulings Section of the Exempt Organizations Branch and referred to the conference and Review Staff of the Exempt Organizations Branch. At this point in time, all disqualifying aspects of the Plaintiff's former operations had been eliminated and the "novel" question the case presented was moot, and the Plaintiff was in compliance with IRS standards for exempt status.

Having learned that a favorable ruling was contemplated for the Plaintiff, on January 16, 1973, Mr. Lee H. Henkel, Chief Counsel of the Internal Revenue Service, requested to see the file before such a ruling was issued. . . .

It appears that during the period of inactivity (February 20–May 2, 1973), the file was referred to Mr. Roger V. Barth, then Deputy Chief Counsel and a political appointee. About April 25, 1973, Mr. Barth referred the file to a Mrs. June Norris, then employed in the Office of the Director of the Miscellaneous and Special Provisions Tax Division, under the Assistant Commissioner (Technical). Although she had neither direct or indirect responsibility to the Chief Counsel, nor any prior involvement regarding the application, it was Mrs. Norris, who working on her own time, at home, prepared by May 1, 1973, the draft of an adverse ruling approximately 80 pages in length. The draft appears to have been the basis in part for the adverse ruling ultimately issued by the IRS. . . .

The question of political influence or political considerations intruding into the Internal Revenue Services' consideration of the Plaintiff's exemption application has loomed large in this case. . . .

At a hearing on July 18, 1973, on the Motion to Compel Answers to the Plaintiff's Interrogatories, . . . the Court specifically indicated the breadth of the search it wanted the Defendants to undertake regarding this issue. . . .

Subsequent to the Court's Order the Defendants conducted two separate searches of the "White House Files." The first by Bruce A. Kehrli, who stated in an affidavit that his search had failed to reveal any materials in the files and records of the White House relating to or mentioning the Plaintiff. The Plaintiff's deposition of Mr. Kehrli, taken July 17, 1973, indicated that his search was limited not only regarding the particular files he investigated but also in the scope of the subject matter of his search. . . .

The second search was conducted under the direction of J. Fred Buzhardt, Special Counsel to the President. . . . His search revealed only four documents which fell within the scope of the Court's Order. These he submitted to the Court for its *in camera* inspection. . . . Mr. Buzhardt stated that he searched the central and special files of the White House for (1) writings relating to or mentioning the Plaintiff, the Project on Corporate Responsibility, or Campaign GM, and (2) writings "relating to White House interest in the tax exempt status of left-wing activist organizations."[12]

---

12. [14] In describing his search of the impounded White House files of Charles W. Colson, John D. Ehrlichman, H. R. Haldeman, John N. Mitchell, Maurice H. Stans, John W. Dean, III, and John J. Caulfield, Mr. Buzhardt stated he searched these files "for documents" relative to the Plaintiff, to the Project on Corporate Responsibility, or to Campaign GM, or which mention the Plaintiff, the Project on Corporate Responsibility, Campaign GM, or "documents" relating to White House

On October 2, 1973, the Court entered a Show Cause Order to determine why the Sanctions of Rule 37 of the Federal Rules of Civil Procedure should not be applied against the Defendants for their failure to comply with the Court's Order of July 6. In the October 2 Order the Court specifically stated that included within the scope of the July 6 Order were "materials referring to White House interest in, concern with, or intervention in the decisions or actions of the Internal Revenue Service or the Treasury Department on tax-exempt organizations, including the granting or withholding of tax exemption rulings or the conducting of audits from January 20, 1969 to the present date." The Defendants responded that they had complied with the Court's July 6 Order in that they had provided the access to the IRS Files which in any way pertained to the Plaintiff.... The Defendants' affidavit stated further that a search of all Treasury and IRS files regarding tax-exempt organizations since January 20, 1969 would be burdensome. The Defendants referred to Mr. Buzhardt's affidavit as its response to the Order regarding the search of the White House files for materials pertaining to the issue of political intervention.

The two remaining aspects of the October 2 Order required the production of the tape recording of the meeting between the President, John Dean and H. R. Haldeman ... regarding the use of taxing mechanisms against White House "enemies" and whether the White House would claim executive privilege regarding any of the requested documents, memoranda or writings....

A looming issue in this case has been whether political interference or intrusion has played a role in the Internal Revenue Service's consideration of the Plaintiff's exemption application.... Should this specter prove to have substance, the complexion of this case changes. A showing of political influence renders the Service's ruling null and void. It is outside the law.

The Court is concerned not only with direct political intervention, but also with the creation of a political atmosphere generated by the White House in the Internal Revenue Service which may have affected the objectivity of those participating in the ruling in the Plaintiff's case. The inference of political intervention has been unmistakenly raised: (1) by the handwritten memo in the Plaintiff's file indicating "*perhaps White House pressure*"; (2) by John Dean's testimony before the Ervin Committee; (3) by the memoranda Mr. Dean submitted to the Ervin Committee; (4) by the testimony of Patrick J. Buchanan, White House Staff Member, before the same committee (September 27, 1973);[13] (5) by the Deposition of Roy Kinsey, Assistant to Mr. Dean, (July 30, 1973, at 10–18); and (6) by the four documents submitted

---

interest in the tax-exempt status of left-wing activist organizations, or tax-exempt organizations, and found no documents so relating. Mr. Buzhardt limited his search of these files to "documents," while his search of the other files included "any documents, memoranda or other writings" as the Court's Order specifically required of all searches.

13. [18] Mr. Buchanan's testimony referred to a memorandum from himself to the President, dated March 31, 1971, which discussed the Administration's intent to use the IRS to combat those "anti-Administration institutions like the Stern Foundation." *See* New York Times, September 27, 1973, p. 31.

for *in camera* inspection. These indicia of political intervention, combined with the unusual and protracted processing of the Plaintiff's application, have triggered a warning signal requiring the Court to fully investigate the issue. Through its Discovery Orders, the Court has endeavored to obtain all the information necessary to make an informed evaluation of the issue. However, the time has come for the Court to make that evaluation, and the Court is without the requested materials to do so.

The Defendants have failed to comply with the Court's Order of July 6. . . .

Neither of the two searches of the White House files met the scope of the Order. The first was limited solely to materials in the White House files which mentioned the Plaintiff. In addition, Mr. Kehrli's affidavit regarding the first search of "all White House files" was misleading. As his deposition indicates, he did not in fact search all of the White House files. He did not search the impounded files of Messrs. Colson, Ehrlichman, Haldeman, Dean or Caulfield.

. . . Mr. Buzhardt's affidavit indicated that he conducted a complete search of the files which produced four documents which he submitted for *in camera* inspection.[14] Mr. Buzhardt's complete search, however, failed to produce the documents, memoranda, and writings.

As to the Defendants' duty to search the Treasury and IRS files, they have simply replied that the Order is "excessively burdensome." They made no request for a protective order. They provided no objective facts to support their claim, which would have allowed the Court to treat the reply as a form of protective request and determine if there was "good cause" under Rule 26(c), F.R.C.P., to limit the scope of the search.

In addition to failing to comply with the Court's general discovery orders, the Defendants have failed to comply fully with the Court's Order Compelling Answers to Interrogatories in either substance or in deadlines. The Court can only consider this is another example of the Defendants' efforts to evade the Court's orders. Considering both the necessity for the information sought in the discovery orders and the fact that the Defendants have sole possession of that information, failure to comply with the orders is grounds for imposition of Rule 37(b), F.R.C.P. Sanctions. . . .

There is one other facet of the Defendants' Response to the Court's Show Cause Order which concerns the Court. The tape[15] of the conversation between the Presi-

14. [19] The four documents demonstrate that the White House staff did in fact consider using the IRS against their "enemies." This conduct is at best reprehensible. The Court finds that the documents contain information relevant to this action, and are discoverable. The Court has summarized the reasons for this finding in a statement which it has submitted to the U.S. Court of Appeals for the District of Columbia Circuit for their *in camera* review pursuant to their direction at page 39 in *Nixon v. Sirica*, 487 F.2d 700, D.C. Cir., 1973. See Appendix for statement of reasons. Should the Court of Appeals' requirement for a sealed review apply solely to that suit and not to the circumstances of this case, the Court shall make the documents part of the record *sua sponte*.

15. [19a] The October 2 Order ordered the production of the tape of the conversation on September 15, 1972 between the President, John Dean and John Erhlichman. Mr. Buzhardt's affidavit

dent, Mr. Dean and Mr. Haldeman regarding the use of the IRS against White House "enemies", will not be produced because of "executive privilege". Mr. Buzhardt's affidavit states that he is "authorized" to say that the White House was claiming "executive privilege" as to any and all tapes as well as the four documents submitted for the Court's *in camera* inspection. Evidently this single statement is intended to be a claim of executive privilege. *United States v. Reynolds*, 345 U.S. 1, 97 L.Ed. 727, 73 S. Ct. 528 (1954) at 7–8, requires that a valid claim of executive privilege can be made only by the head of the agency which has custody of the documents in issue.... The President, as head of the "agency," the White House, must make the formal claim. A mere statement by Mr. Buzhardt that he is authorized to advise the Court that the White House is claiming executive privilege is wholly insufficient to activate a formal claim of executive privilege. *See*, *Nixon v. Sirica and Cox*, 487 F.2d 700, (D.C. Cir. 1973), in which the President himself asserted the privilege. Thus the Defendants have again failed to comply with the Court's Order without a proper claim of executive privilege. This is also grounds for imposing Rule 37(b) sanctions....

Plaintiff... meets the requirements of Section 501(c)(3) ....

In its ruling letter of May 16, the Service's *sole* basis for denial of the exemption was the Plaintiff's alleged involvement in proxy contests. The Service set out at length its belief that proxy contests are not charitable activities.... The Service's emphasis is puzzling, since the Plaintiff had so modified its articles and operation that it could not (and does not) engage in proxy contests. Yet, the Service pointed to the Plaintiff's relationship with its sister organization (and citing indefiniteness of the roles of the two organizations' apparent common control, overlapping personnel, serving as its counsel, confusion concerning the relationship of proposed litigation and research programs) ... as indication that the Plaintiff's purposes and intended operation contemplate a "substantial role in the carrying on and support of proxy contests." Ruling Letter at 28.

In its Motion for Summary Judgment, the Defendants articulated three grounds for the Plaintiff's exemption denial: First, from August 14, 1973 until its termination, the Plaintiff's funds were used to support[16] Project operations, thus making it ineligible (a) because it was not operated exclusively for charitable purposes, and (b) its earnings inured to the benefit of a noncharitable organization, the Project....

Litigation in the public interest is a recognized charitable activity. Rev. Proc. 71-39, 1971-2 Cum. Bull. 575.... The Plaintiff met every guideline and is, and was, entitled to an advance ruling letter.

The three requirements which the Defendants now say the Plaintiff's public interest litigation program failed to meet, ... appear to have been created for this case.

---

informed the Court that the taped conversation of that date was between the President, Mr. Dean and H. R. Haldeman.

16. [23] The defendants conducted a six-week audit of the Plaintiff and the Project to provide support for this point.

Nowhere does Revenue Procedure 71-39 require: "objectivity" in suit selection, a separate "independent" board to govern policies and programs, or that the subject matter of the suit involve charitable activities. What the Revenue Procedure 71-39 does say is that the area of representation may be in some specific area of public concern or "more broadly upon any subject of public interest as determined by the applicant." Sec. 2.01 (emphasis added). This language does not say that only those suits whose subject matter involves charitable activities will be recognized as public interest litigation, nor can it be read to require "objectivity" of an undefined nature. There has been no allegation that the suits, undertaken since the Plaintiff's reorganization, have not been in the public interest or have not met the spirit and letter of Revenue Procedure 71-39. Furthermore, under Sec. 3.05 of the Revenue Procedure, the only requirements of the board which is responsible for the policies and programs of the organization is that it be representative of the public interest, and that it not be controlled by employees or persons who litigate on behalf of the organization or by any organization that is not itself a § 501(c)(3) organization. The Plaintiff's sixteen member Board of Directors meets these criteria. See, Memorandum: Here We Stand, *supra*, at 16–17. There has been no allegation that it is not representative of the public interest. And without affirmative proof to the contrary, it is impossible to infer that four Board members who are also employees "control" the Board. . . .

The Plaintiff's litigation program so obviously meets the guidelines of Revenue Procedure 71-39, it appears that the Defendants were grasping at straws when they raised points two and three. As it has been said before, the Plaintiff's relationship with its sister organization, who can carry on proxy contests: their interlocking directorate, sharing of personnel and office space, is what the Defendants relied upon to make their initial denial. Evidently the Service envisions the Plaintiff and the Project as one entity since they have the same purposes and goals, and participate in several of the same type of activities (education and research) . . . to achieve those goals.

The Defendants admit, however, the fact that a charitable organization is affiliated with a non-charitable organization is not necessarily fatal to charitable qualification. The Service permits interlocking directorates and overlapping personnel, between a charitable organization and its non-charitable affiliate. . . . [17] The Plaintiff and the Project are two separate organizations: separately registered, separate bank accounts and holding themselves out as separate entities. If interlocking directorates and overlapping personnel do not destroy the separateness of a charitable

17. [27] A noteworthy example of permitted interlocking directorates and personnel between a tax-exempt and non-tax-exempt organization is the set up between the American Civil Liberties Union and its tax-exempt affiliate, the ACLU Foundation. Both have the same directors and corporate officials. The Board of the ACLU governs the expenditure of the Foundation's tax-exempt funds, determines the Foundation's programs and policies which are carried out by ACLU personnel. Affidavit of Alan Reitman and exhibit, attached to Plaintiff's Brief to Support Motion for Summary Judgment. The ACLU's case presents far greater interlocking of directors and overlap of personnel than exists in the Plaintiff's/Project's situation.

organization and its non-charitable affiliate, then the fact that the Plaintiff may represent the Project in the litigation aspect of its activities does not make the two entities one. It has long been recognized that a solid demarcation line is drawn between an attorney and his client in the attorney-client relationship.

* * *

The Defendants maintain that the Plaintiff has financially supported the Project and its activities. They have two alternative arguments as to why this justifies disqualification for exemption: Such support allows the Plaintiff's tax-free revenues to enrich a non-charitable organization, or in the alternative, such support contributes to proxy contests, which are non-charitable activities, and thus the Plaintiff is not operated exclusively for charitable purposes.

As evidence of their allegation, the Defendants have attached exhibits collected in a six-week audit of the Plaintiff and the Project covering the period from August 14, 1972 to July 31, 1973. Assuming the Defendants' factual allegations are true, $89.16 is the amount that the Plaintiff has contributed to the Project's benefit in the first quarter of 1973.[18]

The Defendants' Revenue Rulings as well as case law clearly permit charitable organizations to contribute their proceeds both to individuals ... and to non-charitable activities in the furtherance of its charitable purposes.... Not only is the amount that the Plaintiff contributed to the Project so miniscule, particularly in comparison to overall expenditures of $80,000 plus, but any contribution to the Project's activities would be in furtherance of the Plaintiff's purposes as both seek the same goal—increased corporate social responsibility. There has been no allegation that the Project has done anything other than pursue its purposes in good faith. The complaint is with the means the Project uses to achieve those goals. The means that the Project has used to attain these goals differ from those of the Plaintiff in one principal respect—the use of proxy contests.[19] Even if the Defendants remain steadfast in their determination that proxy contests are not charitable activities

18. [29] The Plaintiff admits this amount is in contention based on an analysis of the Affidavits filed with the Defendants' Motion for Summary Judgment and the Plaintiff's October 26 Response. The Defendants have not denied this. The Plaintiff's total expenditures from January 1 to July 31, 1973 amounted to $84,764.87. The Plaintiff alleges that the great preponderance of these expenditures occurred during the first quarter of the year since due to the Plaintiff's acute financial crisis staff salaries were terminated on March 15, 1973 and the expenditures thereafter dropped radically. See Plaintiff's Reply to Defendants' Supplemental Memorandum, November 15, 1973.

19. [31] During the period covered by the audit, the Project undertook three principal activities (1) research concerning the feasibility of a mutual fund investor awareness program, which never materialized, (2) the Shareholder Joint Action Program, which the Defendant even characterizes as a program for educating the individual shareholders as to the levels of corporate responsibility of those corporations in which they hold stock and the means to achieve a greater degree of corporate responsibility. (Defendant's brief at 13) and (3) their proxy contest activities. The Project is also empowered to engage in lobbying activities to attain its goal. This aspect of the Project's activities has been dormant.

(see footnote 21, *supra*), in light of the holdings and clear language of Revenue Rulings 73-313, 72-559, and 71-29, *supra*, and [*Edward Orton, Jr., Ceramic Foundation v. Commissioner*, 56 T.C. 147 (1971)], *supra*, this is irrelevant to the exemption question. The means employed by the charitable organization to achieve its purposes do not make the end results uncharitable. So it is in this case. Proxy contests are the instruments, both legal and not against public policy, which can be used to achieve the Plaintiff's purposes.

Assuming, however, for the sake of argument, that proxy contests cannot be considered charitable activities. The Plaintiff's contribution to an organization conducting activities not in the furtherance of the Plaintiff's exempted purposes has been so insubstantial[20] that this is a totally insufficient argument to legitimize an exemption denial. . . .

Taking all of the Defendants' allegations at their face value and examining them in light of Treasury Regulations and Rulings as well as the case law, it is self-evident that the Defendants' exemption denial is without basis in the law. The Plaintiff has met the requirements necessary for exemption status and is entitled to a refund of the employment taxes it paid in the first quarter of 1973. Furthermore, since the Plaintiff's purposes and activities were the same throughout the period of the audit, as it was the first quarter of 1973, the ruling letter's denial of exemption had no more legal basis than the denial of the refund.

* * *

The Court finds that under the standards of *Enochs v. Williams Packing & Navigation Co.*, 370 U.S. 1, 82 S. Ct. 1125, 8 L. Ed. 2d 292 (1962), the Court has jurisdiction to enter an injunction to prevent the Defendants from denying the Plaintiff its tax exempt status for as long as its operations do not conflict with its amended exemption application. The Court's finding does not preclude the Defendants from examining the Plaintiff's future operations and revoking this exemption on the proper grounds.

20. [32] The Defendants' examples of support (from August, 1972 through July, 1973) fall in the following categories: seven incidents of paying a bill part of which allegedly should have been allocated to the Project; partial allocation of salaries in the final months of 1972; refund of a phone bill payment; payment of employees' insurance; allocation of rent; and two appearances before legislative committees.

Chapter 7

Exclusivity and the Commerciality Doctrine

A. The Exclusively Operated Requirement

CODE: § 501(c)(3)

REGS.: §§ 1.501(c)(3)-1(b)(3), 1.501(c)(3)-1(c)(1), 1.501(c)(3)-1(e)

Charitable tax exemption has always been conditioned upon an organization operating "exclusively" for exempt purposes. But that requirement has never applied literally, though during the early years of tax exemption jurisprudence (i.e., prior to 1940), the Service sought to require exclusivity. Arguably, the courts defined "exclusively" to mean "primarily" because, in enacting the unrelated business income tax (whereby an organization is allowed to engage in a small amount of non-exempt activities without jeopardizing tax exemption), Congress implicitly condoned small deviations from the charitable purpose justifying tax exemption. In accord with this explanation, requiring absolute exclusivity would be contrary to the assumptions underlying the unrelated business income tax. Although this explanation appears to make sense, it has one major problem: the word "exclusively" was redefined to mean "primarily" several years before Congress enacted the unrelated business income tax. Thus, the courts could not have been seeking to solve an inconsistency, because the inconsistency had not yet arisen. More likely, the judiciary simply cleaned up the statute by defining "exclusively" as "primarily" and, in the process, created a *de minimis* exception to the exclusivity requirement.

A close reading of the regulations elucidates several categories of permitted activities:

1. Activities that accomplish an exempt purpose.
2. Activities that further an exempt purpose.
3. Unrelated activities.

Treasury Regulation § 1.501-1(c)(3)-1(b)(1) prohibits more than an "insubstantial" amount of activities that fail to "further" an exempt purpose. Treasury Regulation § 1.501(c)(3)-1(c)(1) adds further gloss: it requires an organization to have "primary" activities that "accomplish" an exempt purpose. It then, consistent with the earlier regulation, restricts activities that fail to "further" an exempt purpose to being "insubstantial." To complete the picture, Treasury Regulation § 1.501(c)(3)-1(e) expressly permits "substantial" trades or businesses so long as the activity "furthers" an exempt purpose. Confusingly, the regulation then allows exemption only if the entity is not organized and operated "for the primary purpose of carrying on an unrelated trade or business." One would have thought the regulation would prohibit "substantial" unrelated businesses, rather than "primary" ones.

The Code also describes permitted activities in a variety of ways. In addition to operations that are "exclusively" or "primarily" charitable, the code and regulations speak of activities which "further" an exempt purpose, that are "functionally related to" an exempt purpose, "related" to an exempt purpose or "substantially related" to an exempt purpose. In addition, regulations address activities that are "directly related" to the active conduct of a "related" activity, as well as activities that "accomplish" an exempt purpose.

Once we recognize the categories of permitted activities, we must then endeavor to quantify them. Most courts refuse to adopt a percentage test, relying instead on "all the facts and circumstances" as required by the regulations. Some guidance, however, is available. Presumably, the word "primary" indicates a majority and "substantial" indicates an amount more than *de minimis*, but less than "primary." As we will see in later chapters, these terms exist in a sea of similar terms. For example

- § 170 (charitable contribution deduction) uses the term "exclusively";
- Treas. Reg. § 1.170A-9(f)(3)(iii)(B)); refers to "almost all";
- § 501(c)(3) restriction on lobbying (covered in Chapter 13) depends on whether the activities are "substantial";
- § 501(c)(7) (tax exempt social clubs), § 528 (certain homeowners' associations), § 4942 (taxes on failure to distribute income) and § 4945 (taxes on taxable expenditures) use the term "substantially";
- § 507(d)(2)(C)(i)(III) (termination of private foundation status) refers to "insignificant";
- § 512 (unrelated business taxable income) and § 4944 (taxes on investments which jeopardize charitable purpose) use the term "primarily";
- § 513 (unrelated trade or business) and § 514 (unrelated debt-finance income) use both "substantially" and "primarily";
- § 4911 (tax on excess expenditure to influence legislation) — if elected — defines "substantial" for purposes of lobbying as up to 20% of an entity's expenditures (or even up to 30% with adverse tax consequences);
- § 4942(j)(3)(B)(i) refers to "substantially more than half," which is defined as 65% in Treas. Reg. § 53.4942(b)-2(a)(5); and
- § 4946 (definition and special rules) uses the term "substantially all," which is defined as 85% in:
  - Treas. Reg. § 1.514(b)-1(b)(1)(ii),
  - Treas. Reg. § 53.4942(b)-1(c), and
  - Treas. Reg. § 53.4946-1(b)(2).

While nothing clearly defines "substantial" in relation to lobbying, one court defined it as something more than 5% of the organization's activities. *Seasongood v. Commissioner*, 227 F.2d 907 (6th Cir. 1955). Further, as explained in Chapter 13, most charitable entities may elect an "expenditure test," which mechanically defines "substantial lobbying" in relation to expenditures (as opposed to volunteer efforts, which do not involve expenditures).

As a general rule, if a charity's unrelated activities—those that neither further nor accomplish an exempt purpose—exceed 10%, the entity should be concerned. Fifteen or 20 percent might be acceptable; but that level is likely very close to too much. Of note, quantification of unrelated activities is cumulative—all non-furthering, non-accomplishing activities lumped together cannot exceed the forbidden amount (however it may be quantified or measured).

A legitimate question would be: a percentage of what? Unfortunately, we cannot provide much clarity. The regulations refer to all facts and circumstances, but which facts and which circumstances remain unclear. Thus, one might consider the percentage of expenditures, time (probably including that of *volunteers*), reputation, or perhaps even the physical square footage of a building devoted to charitable purposes.

If an organization conducts only one activity, the answer to the commerciality question oftentimes determines the substantiality issue. If there is only one activity, the purpose is presumptively "substantial" whether it is commercial or exempt. But when an organization engages in more than one activity, one of which is unquestionably non-exempt, or when a single activity is said to further both exempt and non-exempt purposes, how much is "substantial"? In a few cases, the Tax Court has taken a quantitative approach to defining substantiality while at the same time cautioning that no single quantitative formula is appropriate.

1. More than 20% Non-Exempt Activity Is Probably Too Much

In *Church in Boston v. Commissioner*, 71 T.C. 102 (1978), the Tax Court ruled that making expenditures amounting to 20% of an organization's revenues in furtherance of a non-exempt purpose was "substantial."

2. Less than 10% Non-Exempt Activity Is Probably Acceptable

In *World Family Corporation v. Commissioner*, 81 T.C. 958 (1983) (reprinted in Chapter 11), the court found that a religious organization that engaged in a non-exempt activity was nevertheless entitled to tax exemption because no more than 10% of its expenditures were devoted to the non-exempt activity. The Tax Court noted that it had previously ruled in *Church in Boston* that 20% of an organization's revenues in furtherance of a non-exempt purpose was "substantial," but explained that that there was no set percentage for determining the substantiality issue.

3. Between 10% and 20% Non-Exempt Activity Is Highly Suspect

In *Manning Association v. Commissioner*, 93 T.C. 596 (1989), an organization claiming exempt status argued that *World Family Corporation* established a 10% safe harbor, and that because 90% of its efforts were devoted to the exempt purpose of preserving a historical site for educational purposes, it was entitled to tax exemption. The Tax Court questioned those figures, noting that, in addition to the educational purpose, the organization also engaged in the substantial non-exempt activities of renting property for commercial purposes (i.e., the rental of the historical site for use as a restaurant) and the conduct of family reunions. In any event, the Court specifically rejected the argument that *World Family Corporation* created a 10% "safe harbor," reiterating instead that each case must be judged according to its unique facts and circumstances.

These fluctuating percentages prove that nothing is certain. Nevertheless, when an organization's expenditures or efforts on non-exempt purposes exceed 10%, it may be time to seriously assess creating a taxable subsidiary.

Better Business Bureau of Washington, D.C. v. United States, 326 U.S. 279 (1945), is most often cited with respect to the meaning of "exclusively." But it also represents a subtle introduction of another important doctrine related to tax exemption. In discussing the "commercial hue" of the organization, the Court previews what has come to be known as the "commerciality doctrine." The commerciality doctrine recognizes that, historically, "good" works may be conducted for profit as much as for the public good. And though the courts are not quite as explicit, legal economists might suggest that, if an activity is the subject of sufficient demand such that it involves a profit potential, then the activity should not be tax-exempt. In other words, an activity should not be supported by tax exemption when there is a ready market sufficient to encourage its natural occurrence. To grant tax exemption to an otherwise commercial activity—i.e., one for which there is a sufficient paying market—would create a distortion in the marketplace by suppressing the natural conduct of the activity by those who would otherwise be motivated by the activity's profit potential. Thus, the relevance of "competition"—particularly "unfair competition"—has arisen as an important aspect of commerciality. We will see later that the commerciality doctrine affects other areas of tax exemption jurisprudence.

Of note, this case arose under the Social Security Act, which exempted employees of various charities, defined almost exactly as the predecessor to § 501(c)(3) defined them.[1] As the Court held, the BBB qualified as a business league but not as a charity.

1. Employment Covered Under the Social Security Program 1935-84, https://www.ssa.gov/policy/does/ssb/v48m4/v48m4p33.pdf.

In 1951, Congress continued Social Security tax exemptions for employees of charities, although it permitted charities to elect into Social Security coverage.[2] Beginning in 1984, Congress expanded the social security system to cover employees of charities other than those with specified religious objections. *See*, § 3127.

Better Business Bureau of Washington, D.C., Inc. v. United States

326 U.S. 279 (1945) (emphasis added)

Mr. Justice Murphy delivered the opinion of the Court.

Here our consideration is directed to the question of whether the petitioner, the Better Business Bureau of Washington, D. C., Inc., is exempt from social security taxes as a corporation organized and operated exclusively for scientific or educational purposes within the meaning of Section 811 (b)(8) of the Social Security Act.

From the stipulated statement of facts it appears that petitioner was organized in 1920 as a non-profit corporation under the laws of the District of Columbia. It has no shares of stock and no part of its earnings inures to the benefit of any private shareholder or individual. Its officers are elected annually from its membership; they have merely nominal duties and are paid no salary. Only the managing director and a small number of employees are paid. Membership is open to "any person, firm, corporation or association interested in better business ethics" as may be elected by the board of trustees and pay "voluntary subscriptions" or dues.

The charter of petitioner states that "the object for which it is formed is for the mutual welfare, protection and improvement of business methods among merchants and other persons engaged in any and all business or professions and occupations of every description whatsoever that deal directly or indirectly with the public at large, and for the educational and scientific advancements of business methods among persons, corporations or associations engaged in business in the District of Columbia so that the public can obtain a proper, clean, honest and fair treatment in its dealings or transactions with such merchants, tradesmen, corporations, associations or persons following a profession and at the same time protecting the interest of the latter classes of businesses to enable such as are engaged in the same to successfully and profitably conduct their business and for the further purposes of endeavoring to obtain the proper, just, fair and effective enforcement of the Act of Congress approved May 29th, 1916, otherwise known as 'An Act to prevent fraudulent advertising in the District of Columbia.'"

In carrying out its charter provisions, petitioner divides its work roughly into five subdivisions:

(1) Prevention of fraud by informing and warning members and the general public of the plans and schemes of various types of swindlers.

2. *Id.*

> (2) Fighting fraud by bringing general and abstract fraudulent practices to the attention of the public.
>
> (3) Elevation of business standards by showing and convincing merchants that the application of "the doctrine of caveat emptor is not good business" and by showing and convincing them that misleading advertising, extravagant claims and price comparisons are not good business.
>
> (4) Education of consumers to be intelligent buyers.
>
> (5) Cooperation with various governmental agencies interested in law enforcement.

Information which the petitioner compiles is available to anyone without charge and is communicated to the members and the public by means of the radio, newspapers, bulletins, meetings and interviews. This information is also exchanged with the approximately eighty-five other Better Business Bureaus in the United States.

After paying the social security taxes for the calendar years 1937 to 1941, inclusive, petitioner filed claims for refunds, which were disallowed. This suit to recover the taxes paid was then filed by petitioner in the District Court, which granted a motion for summary judgment for the United States. The court below affirmed the judgment, . . . and we granted certiorari. . . .

Petitioner claims that it qualifies as a corporation "organized and operated exclusively for . . . scientific . . . or educational purposes . . . no part of the net earnings of which inures to the benefit of any private shareholder or individual" within the meaning of § 811(b)(8) of the Social Security Act and hence is exempt from payment of social security taxes. No serious assertion is made, however, that petitioner is devoted exclusively to scientific purposes. The basic contention is that all of its purposes and activities are directed toward the education of business men and the general public. Merchants are taught to conduct their businesses honestly, while consumers are taught to avoid being victimized and to purchase goods intelligently. We join with the courts below in rejecting this contention.

* * *

[T]o fall within the claimed exemption, an organization must be devoted to educational purposes exclusively. **This plainly means that the presence of a single noneducational purpose, if substantial in nature, will destroy the exemption regardless of the number or importance of truly educational purposes.** It thus becomes unnecessary to determine the correctness of the educational characterization of petitioner's operations, it being apparent beyond dispute that an important, if not the primary, pursuit of petitioner's organization is to promote not only an ethical but also a profitable business community. The exemption is therefore unavailable to petitioner.

The commercial hue permeating petitioner's organization is reflected in its corporate title and in the charter provisions dedicating petitioner to the promotion of the "mutual welfare, protection and improvement of business methods among merchants" and others and to the securing of the "educational and scientific advancements of business methods" so that merchants might "successfully and profitably conduct their business." Petitioner's activities are largely animated by this commercial purpose. Unethical business practices and fraudulent merchandising schemes are investigated, exposed and destroyed. Such efforts to cleanse the business system of dishonest practices are highly commendable and may even serve incidentally to educate certain persons. But they are directed fundamentally to ends other than that of education. Any claim that education is the sole aim of petitioner's organization is thereby destroyed. . . .

The legislative history of § 811(b)(8) of the Social Security Act confirms the conclusion that petitioner is not exempt under that section. This provision was drawn almost verbatim from § 101(6) of the Internal Revenue Code, [now I.R.C. § 501(c)(3)] dealing with exemptions from income taxation. And Congress has made it clear, from its committee reports, that it meant to include within § 811(b)(8) only those organizations exempt from the income tax under § 101(6). Significantly, however, Congress did not write into the Social Security Act certain other exemptions embodied in the income tax provisions, especially the exemption in § 101(7) of "business leagues, chambers of commerce, real-estate boards, or boards of trade." Petitioner closely resembles such organizations and has, indeed, secured an exemption from the income tax under § 101(7) as a "business league." Thus Congress has made, for income tax exemption purposes, an unmistakable demarcation between corporations organized and operated exclusively for educational purposes and those organizations in the nature of business leagues and the like. Its manifest desire to include only the former within the meaning of § 811(b)(8) of the Social Security Act prevents us from construing the language of that section to include an organization like petitioner.

. . . *Affirmed.*

B. Substantial Non-Exempt Purpose Aspect of the Commerciality Doctrine

CODE: § 501(c)(3)

REGS.: §§ 1.501(c)(3)-1(b)(3), 1.501(c)(3)-1(c)(1), 1.501(c)(3)-1(e)

The enduring black letter lesson of *Better Business Bureau* is that the presence of a single non-exempt purpose — "if substantial in nature" — will preclude tax exemption no matter how many exempt purposes are present. We will see that in the commerciality cases the courts typically face an organization that has only one activity and the court's task is to determine whether that sole activity is conducted for an exempt or non-exempt purpose. Indeed, Treasury Regulation § 1.501(c)(3)-1(e) recognizes that an activity may appear entirely commercial, yet nevertheless support tax exemption, if the motivations of those undertaking the activity is consistent with an exempt purpose. That is, "purpose" is not necessarily determined merely by the generic nature of the activities.

Determining whether an organization is exclusively operated for an exempt purpose might, at first thought, be viewed as a question automatically answered by the converse: if the activity is not within any of the broadly defined exempt purposes, it must be motivated by a non-exempt purpose and the task is therefore to determine the substantiality of that purpose. But because of the changing nature of economic activity—changes that oftentimes make it profitable to do good works—the first question is not so easily answered. An activity may be "good" in the historical sense underlying tax exemption, but it may be said to be motivated by commercial purposes. That is, the activity may seem to fit whatever technical meaning we ascribe to the several exempt purposes, and yet still be non-exempt!

The presence of the prohibition against private inurement indicates that "commercial purpose" does not mean "engaged in for private profit." If the commerciality doctrine was about private profit, then it would be unnecessary, because § 501(c)(3) explicitly prohibits profit taking. If the commerciality doctrine is not about improper profit-taking, what is it about? What policy do the courts protect with a doctrine that prohibits tax exemption for an organization whose stewards forego profit but utilize successful business techniques in pursuit of activities that are otherwise tax exempt? Think about these questions as you read the following cases.

1. General Aspects of the Commerciality Doctrine

a. Presence (or Absence) of Free or Below Market Goods or Services

Federation Pharmacy Services, Inc. v. Commissioner

625 F.2d 804 (8th Cir. 1980), affirming 72 TC 687

Roy, Judge.

This is an appeal by the Federation Pharmacy Services, Inc., (Federation) from the decision of the United States Tax Court that it is not a tax-exempt organization as described in § 501(c)(3) of the Internal Revenue Code of 1954....

... The record reflects that Metropolitan Senior Federation (Metropolitan), a nonprofit Minnesota corporation whose purpose is to enhance the well-being of Minneapolis-St. Paul senior citizens, organized the Federation. Prior to Federation's formation, Script Shoppes, Inc., (Script), a commercial pharmacy, had agreed with Metropolitan to provide senior citizens with prescription drugs at 10 percent off the lowest retail price in the Minneapolis-St. Paul area and to make free or low-cost delivery of those drugs to certain senior citizens. But Script incurred substantial losses and consequently was forced to discontinue its operation in December 1976. In order to preserve the services that Script had rendered to the elderly, Metropolitan acquired its remaining assets and transferred them to Federation.

According to its articles of incorporation, Federation was organized for the purposes of operating a nonprofit pharmaceutical service for the general public, with special discount rates for senior citizens and handicapped citizens in the Minneapolis-St. Paul metropolitan area.

In its application for recognition of exemption under § 501(c)(3) of the Internal Revenue Code of 1954, the Federation proposed to sell prescription drugs to its members at a price of 5 percent below the lowest price charged for such items at local for-profit pharmacies, as established by a price survey. Nonmembers would be obliged to pay the established survey price for their drug purchases. . . .

In its application for tax-exempt status Federation stated that all customers, whether members or not, would be required to pay for their drug purchases. Federation gave no commitment that it would reduce prices in any instance below cost, and the organization was not obligated to provide free drugs to any indigent persons.

In order to meet its operating costs Federation expected to rely on the assistance of volunteers to perform certain duties and financial contributions. However, it was admitted that the primary source of income would be derived from its prescription drug sales and that Federation had not formulated a program for soliciting contributions. . . . After adverse rulings from the Tax Commission, Federation then petitioned the Tax Court for a declaratory judgment relating to its classification as a § 501(c)(3) organization. The majority of the Court held that Federation must be denied tax-exempt status because "it is operated for a substantial commercial purpose." The Court emphasized that the selling of prescription drugs at a discount to the elderly and the handicapped does not in itself manifest a charitable purpose. The only issue before this Court is whether the Tax Court correctly decided that Federation does not qualify as a tax-exempt organization.

Federation contends that its activities accomplish two exempt purposes—the promotion of health and the relief of financial distress of the aged and the handicapped. The burden of proving entitlement to an exemption lies with the party claiming it. In the instant case, the Tax Court held that Federation failed to carry that burden and that it operated for a substantial commercial purpose rather than for an exclusively charitable purpose. This factual finding of the Tax Court may not be disturbed on appeal unless it is shown to be clearly erroneous.

* * *

The income of all persons, natural or corporate, is subject to tax unless it comes within a specific statutory exception. . . . One of the exceptions to the general rule is § 501(a) of the Internal Revenue Code of 1954, . . . exempting the income of organizations described in Code § 501(c) (26 U.S.C.) from taxation. Organizations exempt under Code § 501(c)(3) include "Corporations . . . organized and operated exclusively for . . . charitable . . . purposes, . . . no part of the net earnings of which inures to the benefit of any private shareholder or individual. . . ." If an organization fails to meet either the operational or organizational test, it will not come within the provisions of § 501(c)(3) of the Code. Nor will an organization be considered organized or operated exclusively for a charitable purpose established in § 501(c)(3) unless it serves a public, as opposed to a private, interest.

In order to operate "exclusively" for a charitable purpose, an organization must engage "primarily in activities which accomplish" such a purpose and its exempt status will be lost "if more than an insubstantial part of its activities is not in furtherance of an exempt purpose." In *Northern Cal. Cent. Services, Inc. v. United States*, 591 F.2d 620 (Ct. Cl. 1979), the Court stated:

> ... The test of "exclusivity" has been defined by Treasury Regulations and case law to mean that a substantial nonexempt purpose or activity will disqualify the organization's exempt status, but insubstantial nonexempt activities do not destroy the exemption. *Better Business Bureau of Washington, D.C., Inc. v. United States*, 326 U.S. 279, 283 ....

The term "charitable", as used in § 501(c)(3), is to be construed in "its generally accepted legal sense" and includes within its scope "Relief of the poor." § 1.501(c)(3)-1(d)(2). More recently the concept of "charitable" has been broadened to encompass, inter alia, the promotion of health. ...

In the case at bar the selling of prescription drugs by Federation may serve to promote health, but it does not, without more, further a charitable purpose within the scope of § 501(c)(3). See *Sonora Community Hospital v. Commissioner*, 46 T.C. 519, 526 (1966) in which it was stated that the cure of disease merely lays the "foundation" for characterizing an activity as charitable.

An organization which does not extend some of its benefits to individuals financially unable to make the required payments reflects a commercial activity rather than a charitable one. In *Sonora Community Hospital v. Commissioner, supra*, the Tax Court denied tax-exempt status to a hospital which provided only a de minimis amount of free care. The Court said ... "a 'charitable' hospital may impose charges or fees for services rendered, and indeed its charity record may be comparatively low depending upon all the facts ... but a serious question is raised where its charitable operation is virtually inconsequential." (citation omitted)

A similar conclusion was reached by the Court in *Hassett v. Associated Hospital Service Corp.*, 125 F.2d 611 (1st Cir. 1942) .... There an organization instituted a "nonprofit hospital service plan" to provide health care to its subscribers at a set fee. Any surplus proceeds were used to reduce future subscription rates or increase services and the corporate officers performed their duties without compensation. But the corporation solicited no charitable contributions and its subscribers were required to pay the fee charged in order to receive its benefits. The Court held that such an arrangement was commercial in nature, and although the rates were "as low as possible," the corporation was not organized and operated exclusively for a charitable purpose. ...

Again, in *B.S.W. Group, Inc. v. Commissioner*, 70 T.C. 352 (1978), a corporation whose purpose was to furnish consulting services to exempt and other not-for-profit organizations sought to be classified as a § 501(c)(3) organization. As in *Hassett*, its officers received no compensation. But the corporation here, too, solicited no contributions and, therefore, while giving some consideration to the client's ability to pay, planned to charge a sufficient fee which would enable it to recover its costs plus a small profit. The Tax Court pointed out that the corporation was engaged in a business normally pursued by commercial enterprises and appeared to be in competition with them, which is "strong evidence of the predominance of nonexempt commercial purposes." ... The Court, moreover, was not impressed by the corporation's statement that it would charge a lesser fee than that imposed by other firms.

In the recent case of *Christian Manner International, Inc. v. Commissioner*, 71 T.C. 661, 670 (1979), the Court held that a corporation which sold books of a religious nature at a profit was pursuing principally a commercial purpose and was thus ineligible for tax-exempt status. As one factor indicating such a purpose, the court cited that the corporation there was in direct competition with other businesses that sold religious literature.

Federation has admitted that it has no program for raising charitable contributions and intends to rely financially on the "patrons of the pharmacy." As pointed out in *B.S.W. Group, Inc.*, and *Harding Hospital, Inc.* [*Inc. v. United States*, 505 F.2d 1068 (6th Cir. 1974)], *supra*, *Lorain Avenue Clinic v. Commissioner*, 31 T.C. 141 (1958), and *Hassett, supra*, the absence of contributions or of a plan to solicit contributions, which are characteristic of a charitable institution, militated against the finding of tax-exempt status for those respective organizations.

Federation is not an adjunct to a tax-exempt entity or even servicing one. (Compare *United Hospital Services, Inc. v. United States*, 384 F. Supp. 776, 778 (S.D. Ind. 1974), in which an organization that provided laundry services exclusively for tax-exempt hospitals was found to qualify as a § 501(c)(3) organization). Rather, Federation engages in the sale of prescription drugs to the general public and holders of VIP cards. Such an activity is as presumptively commercial as the sale of religious books (*Christian Manner International*) ... or the sale of consulting services (*B.S.W. Group*) ... or the sale of any other product. The granting of a tax exemption to Federation would necessarily disadvantage other for-profit drug stores with which Federation competes. ...

Federation also requires that all its customers pay for their prescription drug purchases. Although its members are allowed a 5 percent discount,[3] there is no evidence that Federation has ever offered or is committed to offer its products to any customer below cost. Further, it should be noted that the use of volunteers by Federation to defray its costs does not negate the existence of a commercial purpose. ...

3. [5] As even Federation concedes, the establishment of a discount is not enough to warrant tax exemption.... The Court also takes judicial notice of the fact that many banks, restaurants, transportation carriers, and other competitive for-profit establishments give special discounts or other preferred treatment to senior citizens.

It is immaterial that Federation's objectives may be laudable. In the case of *Est of Hawaii v. Commissioner*, 71 T.C. 1067, p. 1082) (1979), the Tax Court stated:

> We do not question the sincerity or dedication of petitioner's members. But it is petitioner's activities and not its members' devotion to their work that determines whether it is entitled to exemption from taxation....

Moreover, in order for an organization to qualify for exemption under § 501(c)(3) the organization must "establish" that it is neither organized nor operated for the "benefit of private interests." Only Federation's card-holding members are eligible to purchase drugs at a discount. There is no showing one needs financial assistance or is indigent to receive a card. Thus, it has not been "established" that the recipients of any benefits derived from Federation do not represent "private interests."

To summarize, we find Federation relies financially on the sale of prescription drugs to the public with no accommodation made for those unable to pay. As a consequence, it is engaged in competition with for-profit pharmacies in the area. Nor does the administrative record indicate any other activity on Federation's part which establishes the requisite charitable purpose.

Accordingly, we find that the Tax Court's decision that Federation operates for a substantial commercial purpose and does not qualify as a charitable organization exempt from tax under § 501(c)(3) of the Code is not clearly erroneous, but is supported by substantial evidence.

The decision of the Tax Court is affirmed.

Questions

1. Wait a minute! Don't cases and rulings like *Eastern Kentucky Welfare Rights Organizations*, Rev. Rulings 69-545 and 83-157 stand for the proposition that the free or below-cost delivery of goods or services is not an absolute requirement of tax exemption? If that is correct, then why shouldn't *Federation Pharmacy* be tax-exempt?

2. The Court criticized Federation Pharmacy for failing to provide "some" of its benefits to those unable to pay. Why merely "some"? Would not the requirement that an entity be "exclusively" charitable require much more than "some"?

3. What harm would there be in granting tax exemption to Federation Pharmacy and other similarly situated organizations? What good might be achieved from doing so, and is there a more efficient way of achieving that good? Notice the emphasis on competition: if Federation were exempt, would that not undercut the ability of for-profit competitors to compete?

4. What is the relevance to the commerciality doctrine of an organization's failure to solicit contributions from the general public? Could Federation Pharmacy have obtained tax exemption if it operated as described, but also simply maintained a public fund-raising campaign? Consider also the relevance of volunteers.

5. One of the key statements in the decision is: "Federation is not an adjunct to a tax-exempt entity or even servicing one." If Federation Pharmacy were owned and operated by an exempt hospital, would its activities "further" an exempt purpose? Does this case stand for the proposition that some commercial activities cannot stand alone as exempt—because they do not "accomplish" an exempt purpose; however, such activities may "further" an exempt purpose and thus effectively be exempt if part of a larger endeavor?

6. Note that the Court of Appeals in *Federation Pharmacy* states that only when the Tax Court's decision with regard to the commerciality doctrine is clearly erroneous should the Court of Appeals reverse that decision. If the Tax Court had ruled that Federation Pharmacy was not operated for commercial purposes, could the Service have successfully argued that the Tax Court's decision was "clearly erroneous"?

b. Success (or Failure) of a Commercial Activity

As noted earlier, charities may have commercial activities that constitute their primary purpose or that further their activities. The following two cases illustrate some significant issues regarding what those terms mean.

The activities in *Presbyterian and Reformed Publishing Co.* involved publishing and distributing books on reformed theology. Initially, that was an acceptable primary purpose. Essentially, the entity was performing a service not otherwise provided: publishing books on reformed theology. But, starting in 1969, the entity started to become quite successful when one of its authors became popular. The entity began to earn profits. Making profits and conducting the commercial activity was not in and of itself bad: conducting the commercial activity was one of its original purposes. In 1980, the government sought to withdraw its exempt status retroactive to 1969. The Tax Court, however, permitted the retroactive withdrawal only to 1975: the year the entity developed a "commercial hue." The Court criticized the entity for not lowering prices. One might question, however, whether the lowering of prices might discourage competition rather than enhance it. If "commerciality" was the problem, would it not be associated with "unfair competition"? If so, then the Tax Court solution would seem to make the matter worse.

The Third Circuit reversed the Tax Court and permitted the activity to continue with an exemption. In so doing, the court appeared to adopt a standard under which an entity loses its exempt status when it becomes "overly commercial." However, is that standard the same as the standard that would prevent the entity from obtaining exempt status in the first place? Would the Third Circuit have granted the entity exempt status under an original application rather than a government withdrawal of an application?

Presbyterian and Reformed Publishing Co. v. Commissioner

743 F.2d 148 (3d Cir. 1984) (emphasis added)

ADAMS, Circuit Judge.

This is an appeal from a decision of the United States Tax Court affirming the . . . revocation of tax-exempt status for a religiously-oriented publishing house. The Tax Court's decision affirming the termination of the publisher's 52-year-old tax-exemption under 26 U.S.C. § 501(c)(3) (1982), was based on its conclusion that the publisher had become a profitable venture with only an attenuated relationship to the church with which it claims an affiliation. For the reasons set forth below, the decision of the Tax Court will be reversed.

I.

In 1931, the Presbyterian and Reformed Publishing Company (P & R) was incorporated to

> . . . state, defend and disseminate (through every proper means connected with or incidental to the printing and publishing business) the system of belief and practice taught in the Bible, as that system is now set forth in the Confession of Faith and Catechisms of the Presbyterian Church in the United States of America. . . .

P & R's charter requires that any income otherwise available as a dividend be used to improve its publications, extend their influence, or assist institutions "engaged in the teaching or inculcating" of the "system of belief and practice" of the Orthodox Presbyterian Church (OPC). *Id.*

The IRS granted P & R tax-exempt status in 1939, stating,

> Your actual activities consist of publishing a religious paper known as "Christianity Today," a Presbyterian journal devoted to stating, defending, and furthering the gospel. Your income is derived from subscriptions, contributions and gifts and is used to defray maintenance and general operating expenses.

From the beginning, P & R has been closely linked—although not formally affiliated—with the OPC, a Presbyterian group dedicated to its view of reformed Presbyterian theology and, in particular, to the doctrine of Biblical Christianity set forth in the Westminster Confession of Faith. P & R's central editorial criterion is whether a book chosen for publication would make a "worthy contribution . . . to the reformed [Presbyterian] community." One independent publisher characterized P & R's books as lacking in "common ground" with the "nonreformed mind" and "offensive" to all but the "truly reformed."

One of P & R's three incorporators and original directors founded the OPC in 1932, one year after P & R's incorporation. Seven of P & R's nine directors are either officials at Westminster Theological Seminary of Philadelphia or pastors of OPC or OPC-affiliated denominations. On January 1, 1976, P & R changed its charter to specify OPC's seminary, the Westminster Theological Seminary of Philadelphia, as the recipient of all P & R assets in case of dissolution, citing Westminster's common dedication to Biblical Christianity and the Westminster Confession.

The organizational structure of P & R further underscores its close ties to the OPC. Since 1931, the publishing house has been run by three successive generations of the Craig family. Samuel, Charles, and Bryce Craig each worked without compensation at what amounted to a family concern whose business was conducted at the Craigs' kitchen table; all three Craigs were ministers. The record is devoid of evidence indicating any lessening or attenuation of ties between P & R and the OPC.

From its inception until 1969, the company could claim no income over and above expenses. Indeed, the Craigs themselves often contributed personal funds in order to keep the corporation afloat (Samuel donated \$500 in 1939 and \$3,000 in 1954; Charles donated a total of \$19,600 from 1955 to 1963). Until 1973, P & R relied exclusively on volunteers to help the Craigs with editing, packing, shipping, and clerical work.

Beginning in 1969, however, P & R experienced a considerable increase in economic activity as a result of the sudden and unexpected popularity of books written by Jay Adams, a Westminster Theological faculty member. P & R reported gross profits of over \$20,000 for 1969, almost twice as much in 1970, and subsequent escalations culminating in over \$300,000 in gross profits in 1979. By 1979, P & R had seven paid employees assisting Bryce Craig, one with a salary of \$12,500, and five with salaries under \$6,250 (all five full-time employees were OPC officials or members). Bryce Craig himself began receiving a salary of \$12,000 in 1976, which after yearly increases, reached \$15,350 in 1979.

After an audit, the IRS issued a final revocation of P & R's tax-exempt status in 1980 on the grounds that P & R was not "operating exclusively for purposes set forth in 501(c)(3)" and was "engaged in a business activity which is carried on similar to a commercial enterprise." **The IRS made this revocation retroactive, to apply from January 1, 1969 onward.**

The Tax Court affirmed the revocation, . . . , but held that the IRS abused its discretion in making the revocation retroactive to 1969. Instead, it set the effective revocation date at 1975, based upon its declaration that as of that year P & R "had acquired a truly commercial hue" and the company "was aware . . . that IRS agents had been raising serious questions [about its exemption]." . . . . To support its determination that P & R came to be "'animated' by a substantial commercial [and thus nonexempt] purpose" in 1975, . . . **the Tax Court relied primarily on three lines of evidence: first, P & R's "soar[ing] net and gross profits" between 1969 and 1979; second, the fact that P & R set prices which generated "consistent and comfortable net profit margins," rather than lowering prices to encourage a broader readership**; and, third, P & R's purchase and sale of books to and from Baker Book Stores (a commercial publishing house), which "must have . . . overlapp[ed] in subject matter" with commercial publishers. . . . . The Tax Court deemed this sufficient to support the proposition that P & R was in "competition with commercial publishers."[4]

* * *

The principal issue this Court must address is at what point the successful operation of a tax-exempt organization should be deemed to have transformed that organization into a commercial enterprise and thereby to have forfeited its tax exemption. The Tax Court answered this question by looking at the composite effects of the broad-scale increase in commercial activity, the accumulation of capital, the company's "profitability," and the development of a professional staff. Although these indicia of non-exempt business activity are all relevant, we are troubled by the inflexibility of the Tax Court's approach. It is doubtful that any small-scale exempt operation could ever increase its economic activity without forfeiting its tax-exempt status under such a definition of non-exempt commercial character. Thus, we believe that the statutory inclusion or exclusion of P & R should be considered under a two-prong test: first, what is the purpose of an organization claiming tax-exempt status; and, second, to whose benefit does its activity inure?

This two-prong inquiry is drawn directly from the wording of § 501(c)(3) and the legislative history of its enactment. The statute explicitly cites as qualifying for exemption from taxation those entities "organized exclusively for religious, charitable . . . or educational purposes." Indeed, the statute's original sponsor cited the religious publishing house as the archetypal example of the contemplated tax-exempt organization. In the words of the sponsor, Senator Bacon:

> The corporation which I had particularly in mind as an illustration at the time I drew this amendment is the Methodist Book Concern, which has its headquarters in Nashville, which is a very large printing establishment, and in which there must necessarily be profit made, and there is a profit made

---

4. [2] The Tax Court appended a list of additional "profit motivated" decisions:

> Other activities as well indicate that petitioner was animated by a substantial commercial purpose. It consciously attempted to transform itself into a more mainline commercial enterprise: It searched out more readers; it employed paid workers; it dropped money-losing plans; it paid substantial royalties; it made formal contracts with some authors; and, of course, it expanded into a new facility from which it could continue to reap profits. Further, petitioner was not affiliated or controlled by any particular church organization and this nondenominational character "contributes to the resemblance between its publishing activities and those of commercial, non-exempt publishers of Christian literature with whom . . . [it] competes."
>
> Petitioner argues that it accumulated profits to expand so that it could publish more books and thus reach more readers. We recognize that petitioner used a large amount of its accumulated profits for the new Harmony facility; this new facility probably aided petitioner in increasing its productivity and distribution. Such increase, however, may also be indicative of a commercial enterprise. We are not convinced that one of the significant reasons for expansion was not the commercial one of wishing to expand production for profit.

> exclusively for religious, benevolent, charitable, and educational purposes, in which no man receives a scintilla of individual profit....

44 Cong. Rec., pt. 4, at 4151 (1909).

This passage directly supports the two-part test set forth today. The legislative history refers to a "very large printing establishment ... in which there must necessarily be profit made" as within the scope of the exemption. Significantly, Senator Bacon's remarks point to the purpose of the publishing house and the absence of personal profit, rather than the volume of business, as the hallmarks of non-taxable activity. Assuming that large religious or educational publishers may qualify for an exemption, and assuming that not all such publishers are created as large entities, the question becomes one of defining the standards by which the growth in volume of a publisher will not in itself jeopardize the tax exemption.

In the case at hand, the "purpose" prong of the two-part test is the more difficult to administer. Therefore, we will turn first to the question of inurement, and then return to the question of purpose.

A.

* * *

There is no basis in the record for concluding that P & R's increased commercial activity inured to the personal benefit of any individual....

Therefore, if P & R is to be denied tax-exempt status, it must be as a result of the first prong of the test set forward today: the purpose of P & R would have to be incompatible with § 501(c)(3).

B.

In order to come within the terms of § 501(c)(3), an organization seeking tax-exempt status must establish that it is organized "exclusively" for an exempt purpose. In the leading case elucidating the purposes considered exempt under § 501(c)(3), the Supreme Court in *Better Business Bureau v. U.S.*, 326 U.S. 279, 283 ... (1945), stated, "the presence of a single [non-exempt] purpose, ... substantial in nature, will destroy the exemption." The Court found that the Better Business Bureau of the District of Columbia was not exempt because a substantial purpose was "the mutual welfare, protection and improvement of business methods among merchants." *Id.* at 281. Nevertheless, *Better Business Bureau* is a relatively straightforward case because of the presence of an explicit non-exempt commercial purpose by the organization claiming the exemption. P & R, to the contrary, claims that it is animated by no commercial motive and therefore falls squarely within the statutory exemption. Thus, the Tax Court's decision in the present case rests on the evaluation of what it deemed to be the true but unspoken motive of P & R.

Any exploration of unarticulated or illicit purpose necessarily involves courts in difficult and murky problems. When the legality of an action depends not upon its surface manifestation but upon the undisclosed motivation of the actor, similar acts can lead to diametrically opposite legal consequences. In the field of equal protection law, for instance, similar state actions having disproportionate impacts upon minorities may be upheld or struck down depending upon the weighing of the various indicia of "discriminatory intent." *Compare Rogers v. Lodge*, 458 U.S. 613 (1982) (striking down at-large election systems in Burke County, Georgia as invidiously motivated) with *City of Mobile v. Bolden*, 446 U.S. 55 (1980) (upholding identical election scheme in Mobile, Alabama).

The difficulties inherent in any legal standard predicated upon the subjective intent of an actor are further compounded when that actor is a corporate entity. In such circumstances, courts forced to pass upon a potentially illicit purpose have looked for objective indicia from which the intent of the actor may be discerned. . . . In reviewing the decision of the Tax Court in the present case, therefore, the question is whether the proper indicia were relied upon in concluding that P & R was animated by a purpose alien to the statutory exemption of § 501(c)(3).

There are two aspects of the Tax Court's opinion regarding P & R's purpose that require careful examination. First is the Tax Court's conclusion that "petitioner was not affiliated or controlled by any particular church and [that] this nondenominational character 'contributes to the resemblance between its publishing activities and those of commercial, non-exempt publishers of Christian literature with whom . . . [it] competes.'" . . . , quoting *Inc. Trustees of Gospel Wkr. Soc. v. United States*, 510 F. Supp. 374, 379 n.16 (D.D.C. 1981). Given the close connection between P & R and the OPC, the absence of formal control of P & R by any particular church is not dispositive of the question of the fundamental ties between its goals as a publishing house and the dogma espoused by the OPC. In *Inc. Trustees*, the court's decision that a gospel-oriented press failed to qualify for § 501(c)(3) status did not turn on the extent of the press' formal affiliation with a church. Rather, the court focused on the virtually complete cessation of religious activity by the church, the church's unexplained accumulation of millions of dollars, and the fact that some officers of the affiliated publishing concern were drawing salaries ranging from $42,000 to over $100,000. The Tax Court itself seems to have recognized the non-dispositive nature of formal affiliation in its decision on the motion for reconsideration, where it stated, "the denominational or nondenominational character of an organization has never been a controlling criterion." . . . .

The second point, P & R's accumulation of "profits," causes greater difficulty. Although the profits of P & R constituted only one of the factors enumerated and discussed by the Tax Court in its opinion, the memorandum filed upon P & R's motion for reconsideration makes clear that the Tax Court's principal concern was the "presence of substantial profits." . . .

We do not read § 501(c)(3) or its legislative history to define the purpose of an organization claiming tax-exempt status as a direct derivative of the volume of business of that organization. Rather, the inquiry must remain that of determining the purpose to which the increased business activity is directed. As the Tax Court itself observed, "the presence of profit making activities is not per se a bar to qualification of an organization as exempt if the activities further or accomplish an exempt purpose." *Aid to Artisans, Inc. v. Commissioner*, 71 T.C. 202, 211 (1978). Despite the long history of § 501(c)(3) and the numerous organizations that have claimed its coverage, no regulation or body of case law has defined the concept of "purpose" under this provision of the Tax Code with sufficient clarity to protect against arbitrary, ad hoc decision-making.

* * *

There is no doubt that unexplained accumulations of cash may properly be considered as evidence of commercial purpose. Although no regulations govern cash accumulations in the 501(c)(3) context, we are guided by the accumulated earnings tax, 26 U.S.C. § 531 et seq. (1982). The accumulated earnings provision of the Tax Code was designed to weed out illegitimate non-payment of dividends by corporations seeking to avoid the higher tax exposure of shareholders. 26 U.S.C. § 532. A violation of this section is established by a corporation's accumulation of earnings beyond the reasonable needs of the business, 26 U.S.C. § 533, which may include reasonably anticipated future needs of the enterprise. 26 U.S.C. § 537. The legislative history of this provision reveals congressional concern that an inflexible application of the tax laws not stifle legitimate business expansion.... The legislative concern was directly incorporated by the IRS in its regulations, particularly 26 C.F.R. § 1.537-2(b)(1) (1984) which cites as a reasonable basis for the accumulation of earnings and profits the need to "provide for bona fide expansion of business or replacement of plant...."

Given the absence of regulations governing the accumulation of cash by § 501(c)(3) organizations, it is reasonable to take notice of the regulations developed by the IRS in 26 C.F.R. § 1.537 in reviewing the case at bar. In light of the clear notice to the IRS of P & R's need to expand its physical capacity, the claim that the accumulated profits would be used for this purpose, and the recognition by the IRS of such expansion as a legitimate reason for cash accumulation, we are unable to affirm the Tax Court's determination that P & R's cash-on-hand situation was a strong indicator of a non-exempt purpose.

Although we recognize that the Tax Court is entitled to deference in determining the existence of a substantial, non-exempt purpose, that court must focus on facts which indicate a purpose falling outside the ambit of section 501(c)(3). In this case, the Tax Court focused primarily on two factors—the lack of affiliation with a particular church and the accumulation of profits. As we have shown, neither factor indicates the presence of a non-exempt purpose here. Therefore, we must consider the balance of the record to determine whether all the evidence taken together supports a finding of non-exemption. Such an examination reveals no additional evidence of improper motives.

III.

Two competing policy considerations are present in situations where tax-exempt organizations begin to expand the scope of their profit-generating activities. On the one hand, the simple act of accumulating revenues may properly call into question the ultimate purpose of an organization ostensibly dedicated to one of the enumerated pursuits under § 501(c)(3). **On the other hand, success in terms of audience reached and influence exerted, in and of itself, should not jeopardize the tax-exempt status of organizations which remain true to their stated goals.**

Our concern is that organizations seeking § 501(c)(3) status may be forced to choose between expanding their audience and influence on the one hand, and maintaining their tax-exempt status on the other. If this were a stagnant society in which various ideas and creeds preserve a hold on a fixed proportion of the population, this concern would evaporate. A large religious institution with a broad base of support, such as one of the more established churches, could be the springboard for large-scale publishing houses dedicated to advancing its doctrines and be assured of qualifying for § 501(c)(3) coverage. A small denomination, such as the OPC, could then have within its penumbra only a small-scale operation run off a kitchen table. In such circumstances, any attempt by a publisher adhering to the views of the small denomination to expand its scope of activities would properly raise questions relating to its continued eligibility for tax-exempt status.

This view does not reflect either the dynamic quality of our society or the goals that generated the grant of tax-exempt status to religious publishers. The sudden popularity of an erstwhile obscure writer, such as Jay Adams, cannot, by itself, be the basis for stating that P & R has departed from its professed purpose any more than an increase in congregations would call into question the OPC's continued designation as a church. Such a standard would lead to an inequitable disparity in treatment for publishers affiliated with mainstream churches as opposed to small offshoots.

Accordingly, the decision of the Tax Court will be reversed.

Living Faith, Inc. v. Commissioner

950 F.2d 365 (7th Cir. 1991)

Living Faith, Inc. (Living Faith) appeals the Tax Court's affirmance of a determination by the Commissioner of the Internal Revenue Service (Commissioner) that Living Faith was not operated for exempt purposes within the meaning of § 501(c)(3) of the Internal Revenue Code (I.R.C.), 26 U.S.C. § 501(c)(3). This Court has jurisdiction to review the Tax Court's ruling pursuant to I.R.C. § 7482, 26 U.S.C. § 7482.... Upon review of the record, we find that the Tax Court's determination was not clearly erroneous and affirm its decision.

I.

Living Faith was incorporated as a not-for-profit corporation on September 4, 1986, under the laws of Illinois. According to its articles of incorporation, Living Faith was established for the purpose of keeping with the doctrines of the Seventh-day Adventist Church. Living Faith is a member of the Association of Self-Supporting Institutions of the Seventh-day Adventist Church, but, like all members, is independent from the church and receives no direct funding. Seventh-day

Adventists believe that the concept of health is permeated with religious meaning. Good health, according to Seventh-day Adventists, promotes virtuous conduct, and is furthered by a vegetarian diet and abstention from tobacco, alcohol, and caffeine. Ill health, in contrast, promotes sin, with the original sin consisting of eating food condemned by God.

Living Faith operates two vegetarian restaurants and health food stores, in Oak Brook Terrace, Illinois, and Glen Ellyn, Illinois, in a manner consistent with these religious beliefs. These two facilities—the subject of this litigation—are open to the public, and operate under the name "Country Life." Country Life is a worldwide chain of independently operated restaurants and food stores. Living Faith is licensed to use the name, without charge, by Oak Haven, Inc., a wholesale food distributor. Oak Haven's guidelines require Country Life facilities to employ Seventh-day Adventist management and maintain a good working relationship with the local Seventh-day Adventist Church. They also require that management have business ability, undergo six months training in operating a Country Life restaurant, and maintain good business relations with suppliers and the community.

The Oak Brook Terrace facility operates out of a 3,200 square foot leased space in a shopping center, of which 2,400 square feet is used for the restaurant. . . . Operations at the Glen Ellyn facility are substantially similar to those at Oak Brook Terrace. Living Faith sets its meal and food prices at market rates. Buffet prices at its restaurants are set at approximately three times the wholesale cost of food, a formula commonly used in the food business, and retail prices at its health food stores are maintained at levels recommended by its wholesalers. According to Living Faith, its prices are similar to, and in some instances higher than, other vegetarian restaurants and health food stores. Products sold at the health food stores include grocery items, such as packaged and bulk foods, as well as vitamins, spices, and toiletries.

In addition to purveying food and health products, Living Faith disseminates various informational materials which promote both "the healing message of Jesus Christ" and the "world famous" Country Life restaurants. The literature is placed by the counter, the door, at the end of the buffet line, and on each table. Living Faith also offers books on religious subjects at no charge to its patrons. Customers are not required to take or read the literature. Living Faith states that its "literature evangelism" is currently limited to this in-store distribution, and estimates that 10 to 12 people have joined the Seventh-day Adventist Church as a result of its efforts.

Each day before the facilities open, Living Faith conducts a devotional talk by a staff member, hymn singing, and a Bible reading for workers. One Saturday each month, Living Faith provides the public an opportunity to sample vegetarian cooking by offering free meals. Those who attend may also peruse the Seventh-day Adventist literature and obtain information about the Church. Living Faith offers to the public a five-week cooking school which promotes vegetarian cooking. Classes meet on a weekly basis, during hours when the restaurants and food stores are closed, and are priced at $20 per person, or $25 per married couple, plus $15 for a cookbook. The organization also offers weekly Bible study class, free of charge, during hours when the facilities are closed. It occasionally provides meals to the needy in exchange for chores, such as washing dishes, and has collected and donated to charity approximately 100 plastic bags of used clothing.

* * *

Stipends for Living Faith's five-member staff totaled $25,663.67 for the fiscal year ending September 30, 1987, and increased to $63,673.93 the following fiscal year. According to Living Faith, its staff is composed of people who otherwise might have difficulty in finding employment. Several staff members also serve as officers and directors of Living Faith. Three of these—the president, vice president, and secretary—are ordained deacons of the Seventh-day Adventist Church. The chairperson, who is not on the staff, is an ordained Elder of the Church.

According to Living Faith, any profits realized from its operations will be used to expand its health ministry in accordance with Seventh-day Adventist tenets. Its application for § 501(c)(3) tax exemption states that its future plans include the establishment of an "outpost evangelism program" where people "may live in harmony with the principles of the Bible and the writings of Ellen G. White," a founder of the Seventh-day Adventist Church. However, its current operations are limited to the two restaurants and health food stores.

Living Faith filed its application for tax-exempt status on March 29, 1988. The Commissioner denied Living Faith's application, finding that it was not operated exclusively for exempt purposes within the meaning of § 501(c)(3). Living Faith timely protested the ruling, and the Commissioner subsequently sent notice of the final adverse ruling. Living Faith filed a petition for a declaratory judgment with the Tax Court, pursuant to I.R.C. § 7428(a), requesting tax-exempt status pursuant to § 501(a) as an organization described in § 501(c)(3).

The Tax Court upheld the Commissioner's ruling, finding that Living Faith conducts its operations with a substantial commercial purpose and therefore does not qualify as a tax-exempt organization. *Living Faith, Inc. v. Commissioner*, 60 T.C.M. (CCH) 710 (1990). We now examine the Tax Court's decision.

II.

Living Faith contends that it operates its restaurants and health food stores with the exclusive, tax-exempt purpose of furthering the religious work of the Seventh-day Adventist Church as a health ministry. As the taxpayer claiming the exemption, Living Faith bears the burden of proving entitlement to it. . . . . Section 501(c)(3) establishes a tax exemption, pursuant to § 501(a), for organizations "organized and operated exclusively for religious, charitable . . . or educational purposes, . . . no part of the net earnings of which inures to the benefit of any private shareholder or individual . . ." To comport with these provisions, an entity must be both "organized and operated exclusively" for at least one of the listed exempt purposes. Treas. Reg. § 1.501(c)(3)-1(a). The parties do not dispute that Living Faith satisfies the "organizational" test, or that its net earnings do not inure to any individual's benefit. The sole issue, therefore, is whether Living Faith is "operated exclusively" for exempt purposes within the meaning of § 501(c)(3).

In evaluating this issue, we focus on "the purposes toward which an organization's activities are directed, and not the nature of the activities." *B.S.W. Group, Inc. v. Commissioner*, 70 T.C. 352, 356–57 (1978). The purposes need not be solely religious; courts recognize that a non-exempt purpose, even "somewhat beyond a de minimis level," may be permitted without loss of exception. . . . The nonexempt purpose, however, cannot be substantial. "The presence of a single non-exempt purpose, if substantial in nature, will destroy the exemption regardless of the number or importance of truly [exempt] purposes." . . . (quoting *Better Business Bureau v. United States); see also* Treas. Reg. § 501(c)(3)-1(c)(1) (organization not "operated exclusively" for exempt purposes "if more than an insubstantial part of its activities is not in furtherance of an exempt purpose.").

A single activity may be carried on for more than one purpose. The fact that an organization's primary activity may constitute a trade or business does not, of itself, disqualify it from classification under § 501(c)(3), provided the trade or business furthers or accomplishes an exempt purpose. . . . If one of the activity's purposes, however, is substantial and nonexempt (e.g., commercial), the organization will be denied exempt status under § 501(c)(3), even if its activity also furthers an exempt (*e.g.*, religious) purpose. *Schoger Found. v. Commissioner*, 76 T.C. 380, 386 (1981).

Living Faith contends that the Tax Court erred in upholding the Commissioner's determination that its operations have a substantial commercial purpose. It makes essentially three claims. First, Living Faith argues the Tax Court applied an incorrect legal standard, therefore requiring this Court to undertake a plenary review of the decision. Second, Living Faith maintains that, even under a clearly erroneous standard, the Tax Court's determination was incorrect. Finally, Living Faith asserts that the Tax Court unconstitutionally discriminated against it by judging the merits of its beliefs in denying it tax-exempt status. We first determine the proper standard of review.

A.

Whether an activity has a substantial nonexempt purpose is a question of fact to be determined under the facts and circumstances of each case. . . . The Tax Court's factual finding that an organization is not operated exclusively for exempt purposes cannot be disturbed on appeal unless clearly erroneous. . . . Here, however, Living Faith argues that we should apply a de novo standard of review, apparently on the ground that the Tax Court's finding of fact that Living Faith has a substantial commercial purpose is predicated on a misunderstanding of the governing rule of law.

* * *

Because we find that the Tax Court based its factual findings on a proper legal standard, we accept them unless clearly erroneous. The critical inquiry, therefore, is whether sufficient evidence exists in the record to support the Tax Court's finding that Living Faith operates for a substantial commercial purpose.

B.

When undertaking this inquiry, we look to various objective indicia. The particular manner in which an organization's activities are conducted, the commercial hue of those activities, competition with commercial firms, and the existence and amount of annual or accumulated profits, are all relevant evidence in determining whether an organization has a substantial nonexempt purpose. *See B.S.W. Group*, 70 T.C. at 357; *United Missionary Aviation, Inc.*, 60 T.C.M. (CCH) at 1156–57. Living Faith argues that the Tax Court unduly relied on such factors, however, and inordinately emphasized the nature of its activities. Living Faith maintains that "great weight [should] be given to the assertions of religious purpose made in good faith on behalf of the organization." In this regard, it asserts that good health is an especially important component of the Seventh-day Adventist Church, and that its Country Life operations further this religious purpose.

While we agree with Living Faith that an organization's good faith assertion of an exempt purpose is relevant to the analysis of tax-exempt status, we cannot accept the view that such an assertion be dispositive. Put simply, saying one's purpose is exclusively religious doesn't necessarily make it so.

This Court and others have consistently held that an organization's purposes may be inferred from its manner of operations. *See, e.g., Bethel Conservative Mennonite Church v. Commissioner*, 746 F.2d 388, 391 (7th Cir. 1984) (facts "must be explored to ascertain the predominant or primary purpose for which the organization was formed, and also the manner of its operation.") . . . *United Missionary Aviation*, 60 T.C.M. (CCH) at 1156 ("The manner in which an organization conducts its activities is relevant evidence of a forbidden purpose."). An organization's activities, and not solely its members' devotion to their work, determines entitlement to tax exemption. . . . Indeed, this Court previously has stated that "it is necessary and proper . . . to survey all the activities of [an] organization, in order to determine whether what the organization in fact does is to carry out a religious mission or to engage in commercial business." . . . While "the inquiry must remain that of determining the purpose to which the . . . business activity is directed," *Presbyterian & Reformed Publishing Co. v. Commissioner*, 743 F.2d 148, 156 (3d Cir. 1984), the activities provide a useful indicia of the organization's purpose or purposes. Thus, keeping in mind Living Faith's good faith assertion of a religious purpose, we examine Living Faith's activities and manner of operations.

Although an organization is not disqualified from tax-exempt status solely because its primary activity constitutes a business, when it conducts a business with an apparently commercial character as its primary activity, "that fact weighs heavily against exemption." *B.S.W. Group*, 70 T.C. at 359. Living Faith, whose primary activity consists of operating restaurants and food stores, engages in precisely such conduct. Its operations are "as presumptively commercial" as the sale of prescription drugs to the general public and holders of special VIP cards, *see Federation Pharmacy Servs., Inc. v. Commissioner*, 625 F.2d 804, 808 (8th Cir. 1980), the sale of consulting services, *see B.S.W.*, 70 T.C. at 358, "or the sale of any other product." *Federation Pharmacy*, 615 F.2d at 808.

It is significant that Living Faith is in direct competition with other restaurants. "Competition with commercial firms is strong evidence of the predominance of non-exempt commercial purposes." *B.S.W. Group*, 70 T.C. at 358 .... Living Faith has failed to demonstrate that its business, which operates in a shopping center, does not compete with other restaurants and food stores. Living Faith's prices, for example, are set "competitively with area businesses," using pricing formulas common in the retail food business. This lack of below-cost pricing militates against granting an exemption. *See Federation Pharmacy*, 625 F.2d at 807 .... Indeed, the profit-making price structure looms large in our analysis of its purposes....

That Living Faith competes with other commercial enterprises is also indicated by its informational materials, which are apparently promotional as well. The use of promotional materials and "commercial catch phrases" to enhance sales are relevant factors in determining whether an organization "operate[s] in the same manner as that of any profitable commercial enterprise." ... A few examples are illustrative. A tract dated June 1988 contains not only religious references ("The Lord has helped us to provide a haven of rest to nourish body, mind and soul"), but significant commercial overtones as well ("If you bring this story to our restaurant we will give you one meal free when you buy one. Limit one meal per story."). A mailing distributed by Living Faith states its religious purpose ("Country Life is a 'not for profit' health ministry whose goal is to help people achieve a better life through the intelligent application of the laws of health and spiritual renewal in Christ"), but also contains language that is clearly commercial in nature (Country Life offers "world famous restaurants, superb vegetarian cuisine since 1963"). Another tract promotes Living Faith's various activities, including the Bible study classes and vegetarian cooking classes, and states, "We want to serve you better with expanded hours and services." These materials contain a strong "commercial hue," *see B.S.W. Group*, 70 T.C. at 357, and thus provide an indicia of a forbidden commercial purpose.

Living Faith's advertising — totaling $15,500 over a two-year period — is another relevant factor in determining that it is engaging in activities for a nonexempt purpose.... So, too, is its lack of plans to solicit contributions. *See Federation Pharmacy*, 625 F.2d at 808. Although Living Faith states that it has received donations from members of the Seventh-day Adventist Church (its financial statements show that it received approximately $101,000 in "donations" for the 1987 operating year and $46,000 for 1988), the record does not document the sources of these donations. Living Faith relies exclusively on its own financial statements, and on memoranda it submitted to the Commissioner during the application process. However, its own arguments and statements, solely by virtue of being included in the administrative record, are insufficient to establish the source of the donations.... Similarly, although Living Faith states that it occasionally provides free meals to the needy, in exchange for chores, and has provided more than 100 bags of clothing to charity, the record provides no documentation other than Living Faith's own statements....

Living Faith's financial statements show that its operations grossed $280,000 from paying customers during the 1988 fiscal year. Despite these gross profits, Living Faith asserts that its lack of net profits indicates that its purpose is indeed tax exempt. Although Living Faith is correct that a failure to show a profit is relevant in determining the presence or absence of commercial purposes, . . . , it is only one factor among several, and does not per se entitle an organization to exempt status. . . . This is especially so where, as here, the lack of profits occur during an organization's early period of existence. . . . Other factors reveal additional evidence of a commercial purpose. Living Faith's hours of operation, for example, are substantially competitive with other commercial enterprises; although closed on Saturdays, the Sabbath for members of the Seventh-day Adventist Church, its Country Life restaurants are open 40 hours each week, and the health food stores for 55. The various activities sponsored by Living Faith, such as the Bible study classes and the free meals periodically offered to the public, are offered after hours and thus do not interfere with routine business operations.

In urging us to reverse the Tax Court's determination, Living Faith relies heavily upon *Golden Rule Church Association v. Commissioner*, 41 T.C. 719 (1964). The petitioners in *Golden Rule* were a church and two of its subsidiaries, one of which operated several businesses as vehicles for spreading the church's religious doctrines, and the other of which held property for the church. The Commissioner sought to tax income the property-holding subsidiary had derived from the sale of timber on property it had purchased. In denying a tax exemption, the Commissioner relied on various other activities, unrelated to the timber sale, which had given rise to net operating losses over a period of more than ten years. The Tax Court reversed the Commissioner's adverse determination. Living Faith argues that *Golden Rule* is analogous to the instant case, and maintains further that *Golden Rule* appeared to give "controlling significance" to the petitioners good faith assertion of religious purpose. . . .

We find the scenario in *Golden Rule* distinguishable from the present case. First, unlike Living Faith, which conducts the primary activity of operating two restaurants and health food stores, the organization in *Golden Rule* operated a variety of small businesses, the very purpose of which was to illustrate to the public that the "golden rule" can be applied to one's daily business activities. *Id.* at 726. Indeed, the petitioners in *Golden Rule* had closed at least one of these businesses, because it had turned out to be "a poor illustration of the concepts the church tried to demonstrate to the public." *Id.* at 724. Additionally, the petitioners had sustained "consistent and substantial" operating losses for most of the businesses over an eleven-year period. *Id.* at 731. In contrast, Living Faith's financial figures—which include its fledgling period—reflect a substantial increase in gross profits, from $73,000 for the fiscal year ending September 30, 1987, to $280,000 the following year, and a decline in operating losses during the same periods. Moreover, the businesses in *Golden Rule* were operated by "student ministers," who, unlike the Living Faith "volunteers," received no salaries and whose total time was under ecclesiastical direction. Living

Faith's records indicate it paid salaries of more than $25,000 in fiscal year 1987 and $63,000 in 1988. Finally, the student ministers in *Golden Rule* were rotated among various projects "to maximize the variety of their experiences with the public," *id.* at 725, and the organization made no effort to create specialists in order to foster efficiency of operation. *Id.* The Country Life guidelines under which Living Faith operates, however, require that, among other things, its management have business ability and six months training in a Country Life store. Given the numerous distinguishing factors, the result in *Golden Rule* is not compelled here.

We also reject Living Faith's claim that the Tax Court in *Golden Rule* gave "controlling significance" to the petitioners' assertion of religious purpose. Although the court recognized the petitioners' espoused purpose, it specifically stated that it "must always be guided by the character of the organization and its activities," *id.* at 729, and further noted that "it does not necessarily follow that we must accept all claims that activities are religious simply because those claims are sincere." *Id.* at 730 n.10.

Living Faith's situation is closer to that of the organization denied exempt status in *Schoger Foundation v. Commissioner*, 76 T.C. 380 (1981). The petitioner in *Schoger*, a not-for-profit corporation, operated a lodge located in the mountains of Colorado, and promoted the facility as a lodge "for Christian families." The lodge offered various recreational activities. It also offered religious activities — operated without a set program — including daily devotions and Scripture reading after breakfast, Sunday morning worship for guests requesting the service, and discussion seminars, Christian song sessions, and "share sessions" conducted by staff members. *Id.* at 382. Attendance at both the recreational and religious activities was strictly optional. *Id.* at 382–83. Although the lodge conducted only minimal advertising, a brochure — which referenced recreational activities and accommodations as well as religion — was provided to potential guests. *Id.* at 383–84. While the court recognized that "specific mandatory religious activities are not necessarily required" to obtain exempt status, it added:

> There must be something more than the fact that Christ Haven Lodge is promoted as a lodge "for Christian families." . . . It is difficult to see how that experience differs, if it does, from the same experience one can have at any quiet inn or lodge located in the beautiful mountains of Colorado.

Id. at 388.

Similarly, it is difficult to see how the experience of dining or shopping at Living Faith's restaurant and health food stores differs, if it does, from the same experience one might have while dining or shopping at other vegetarian restaurants and health food stores. Granting a tax exemption to Living Faith would necessarily disadvantage its for-profit competitors. . . . We do not doubt the sincerity of Living Faith's beliefs, and we recognize its good faith in asserting a religious purpose of health promotion. Based on the record before us, however, we must uphold the Tax Court's determination that Living Faith operates with a substantial commercial purpose as well, and is therefore not entitled to § 501(c)(3) tax-exempt status.

C.

Living Faith further argues that the Tax Court's method of determining the existence of a substantial nonexempt purpose violates the free exercise clause of the first amendment by unconstitutionally discriminating against less orthodox religions. . . .

We disagree. In our view, the Tax Court cast no aspersions on the sincerely held beliefs of Living Faith. Rather, it applied § 501(c)(3) on a neutral basis, relying on appropriate factors to determine whether Living Faith's operations advance a substantial nonexempt purpose. . . .

* * *

As we have stated previously, "the IRS has the same monitoring function with respect to all [§ 501(c)] groups, namely to determine whether their actual activities conform to the requirements which Congress has established as entitling them to tax exempt status." . . . Examining an organization's activities allows the IRS and the courts to make a determination regarding exempt status "without entering into any subjective inquiry with respect to religious truth which would be forbidden by the First Amendment." . . . The Tax Court in this case appropriately made such a determination, based on the facts as contained in the administrative record and not on the merits of the Seventh-day Adventist faith.

We find that the Tax Court's decision that Living Faith operates for a substantial commercial purpose and does not qualify as a tax-exempt organization under § 501(c)(3) is not clearly erroneous, but is supported by substantial evidence in the administrative record. The decision of the Tax Court is

AFFIRMED.

Note on Very Successful Commercial Activities

As the Court in *Presbyterian and Reformed Publishing, Inc.*, suggests, the commerciality doctrine is a "catch-22" of sorts for any charity that pursues its exempt purpose with fervor and dedication. On the one hand, the organization strives to be successful (and we want it to be, don't we?) and success often requires the adoption of the same strategies that drive for-profit business to new heights (e.g., advertising and more efficient means of production). On the other hand, however, when a charity generates demand for its good work or generates significant profits, it also proves the existence of a market or profit potential sufficient to encourage and support the conduct of the activity for which tax exemption has previously been granted. In proving the existence of a market or profit potential, the charity attacks one of the economic justifications for tax exemption. If, however, that results in a loss of exempt status, practitioners will be tempted to tell clients "Do a good job, but not too good a job, lest you lose your exempt status." Clearly, such advice would be counter-productive, but how else should one read the government and the Tax Court's approaches in *Presbyterian*?

In relation to *Living Faith*, would the entity have been exempt if it were located on church property rather than in a shopping mall? Would its activities constitute "furthering" activities under Treas. Reg. § 1.501(c)(3)-1(c)(1)? If the Living Faith restaurant could be a furthering activity, though not a primary one, how and where must it operate?

Questions

1. CBN is a religious organization exempt under § 501(c)(3). Its main activity is to spread the Christian Gospel via the media, and it operates a television station in pursuit of its purpose. On Monday morning, you learn of a news article describing its soaring success in the television industry. The article describes how Pat Robertson purchased a small radio station in 1959 from which he broadcasts religious programs. With the revenues from the radio station, he later purchased a group of television stations and began broadcasting religious programs, including "The 700 Club." CBN continued to seek contributions from the general public but it also began to sell advertising on its television networks. It began to broadcast "wholesome" family television that contained no explicit religious themes, but also no sex, violence, or themes thought inconsistent with Christian values. CBN changed its name to "CBN Cable Network—The Family Entertainer" and began advertising its shows to attract more viewers. The changes resulted in a huge increase in CBN's television audience and advertising revenues. The advertising revenues from the wholesome shows generated $41 million dollars per year as of 1993, while the explicitly religious programs generated about $750,000 per year for that same year. Still, CBN continued to attract about $50 million in contributions per year. Is CBN still entitled to a tax exemption?

2. Read Treas. Reg. § 1.501(c)(3)-1(e) again. What factors might the Service have pointed to in arguing that CBN was engaged in broadcasting activities primarily for commercial purposes? What factors might CBN have asserted in arguing that its broadcasting activity was motivated by an exempt purpose?

Chapter 8

Special Application of Commerciality Doctrine — Feeder Organizations and the Integral Part Test

A. Feeder Organizations: A Single Entity

CODE: § 502

REGS.: § 1.502-1

Prior to 1951, an organization that operated what appeared to be a normal trade or business might still be deemed "exclusively operated" for an exempt purpose (and, thus, be entitled to tax exemption) if all of its profits were devoted to an exempt purpose. For example, a macaroni manufacturer was entitled to tax exemption because it was wholly owned by New York University and its profits were thus devoted to educational purposes. *C.F. Mueller Co. v. Commissioner*, 190 F.2d 120 (3d Cir. 1951). Likewise, an organization that operated a beach resort was entitled to tax exemption because all of its profits were paid to an organization that provided relief for destitute women and children. *Roche's Beach, Inc. v. Commissioner*, 96 F.2d 776 (2d Cir. 1938). The "destination of income," rather than the source of income, led to the conclusion that these organizations had exempt purposes. *See Trinidad v. Sagrada Orden de Predicadores*, 263 U.S. 578 (1924). With the enactment of § 502, the destination of income became an insufficient basis for tax exemption. So-called "feeder" organizations are no longer conducting an activity for exempt purposes, even though all profits are devoted exclusively to exempt purposes. Instead, feeder organizations are conclusively presumed engaged in commercial purposes not entitled to tax exemption. Thus, § 502 draws a distinction between the active, direct conduct of a "good" activity and the indirect, passive support of a "good" activity.

After Congress enacted § 502, the indirect, passive support of an exempt purpose no longer justified tax exemption. Still, the application of § 502 depends, in the first instance, on determining whether the organization is directly conducting a charitable activity or is instead engaged in a commercial activity, the profits of which are dedicated to charity. As shown in the famous case that follows, there is reason to question whether the threshold determination is always correctly made.

Edward Orton, Jr., Ceramic Foundation v. Commissioner

56 T.C. 147 (1971)

* * *

We are to decide whether petitioner for the years in issue fails to qualify as an organization exempt from taxation under section 501(c)(3), or is a feeder organization under section 502, or, in the alternative, is the recipient of unrelated-business income under sections 511, 512, and 513.

* * *

Petitioner was established under the will of Edward Orton, Jr., deceased, which was admitted to probate February 28, 1932. Edward Orton, Jr. . . . was an outstanding authority on ceramics. His particular interest lay in scientific research and education in the field of ceramics and ceramic engineering. He received a degree as an engineer of mines from Ohio State University and later became a member of the faculty. He procured the establishment, by legislative enactment, and became the head of the Department of Ceramics at Ohio State University. He first began the manufacture of pyrometric cones in the university laboratory.

* * *

Pyrometric cones are used in the manufacture of ceramics for testing the firing process and maturing of various clay products. They are described as small, slender, trihedral pyramids made of a mixture of minerals very similar to the minerals of which the ceramic bodies are composed. The cone bodies and the ceramic bodies are sufficiently alike that they react approximately the same thermochemically. The function of the pyrometric cone is to provide a convenient means of measuring the combined effect, during firing, of temperature, time, and firing atmosphere on ceramic ware. Thus the cones provide a reference standard and serve as a means of measuring and communicating the results of heat treatment of ceramic ware within the ceramic industry. In addition to being a production control, the cones are tools for basic research, and fundamental aids in ceramic education.

* * *

The board of trustees, according to the will, is composed of seven individuals who are: The president of Ohio State University, a representative from the National Bureau of Standards, the head of the Engineering Experiment Station of Ohio State University, the head of the Ceramic Engineering Department of Ohio State University, the secretary of the American Ceramic Society, one other representative from the American Ceramic Society, and an attorney at law. The trustees receive from the petitioner $1 per year plus expenses incurred in relation to trust business. The attorney on the board, however, receives compensation for legal services he renders to the trust.

* * *

If the trust is dissolved, all of its assets are required to be turned over to Ohio State University.

* * *

The manufacturing of cones has been carried on by the trustees under the terms of the will since 1933 and during the years in issue. Most of petitioner's sales are to manufacturers of ceramic products. Some sales are made to scientific and research laboratories and to ceramic art studios throughout the United States. Substantial sales are also made outside the United States.

The American Standard Materials Society specifies Orton Standard Pyrometric Cones be used in the Pyrometric Cone Equivalent Test. This is a test which evaluates the refractoriness of refractory materials. The PCE value resulting from the test is an important specification of refractory material, and is utilized in describing and purchasing such material. The American Ceramics Society cooperates with ASTM in establishing this standard. The Orton Pyrometric Cones have been accurately established as a reference standard by the National Bureau of Standards.

During the years before the Court another manufacturer, Bell Research, Inc., Chester, W. Va., competed with petitioner in the production of standard pyrometric cones in the United States. The Bell series of cones is not as long as petitioner's and does not deal with as wide a temperature range. Pyrometric cones produced by Bell do not perform identically to petitioner's; they appear to have a greater variability within a lot. The prices on petitioner's cones were higher than those on the Bell-produced cones. German-manufactured cones have been tested by petitioner and found to have an even greater variability within a lot than the Bell cones.

There are two other known devices designed to measure the combined effect of temperature and time in the firing of ceramics. They are the "Fire-Chek Keys" manufactured by Bell Research, Inc., and the "Veritas Ring" manufactured by Fortune Ceramics, Trenton, N.J. In addition the ceramic industry also relies upon the use of separate devices measuring time or measuring temperature, such as clocks and pyrometers, which are used for both measurement and control of one or all the other factors in connection with the regulation of the heat treatment of ceramic products. Some of these devices are the "Tempilstiks" manufactured by the Burrell Corp., Pittsburgh, Pa., and "Thermochrom Crayons" and "Detecto-Temp Paints" manufactured by H.V. Hardman Co., Inc., Belleville, N.J., and Curtiss-Wright Corp., East Paterson, N.J. Although these products are available, the pyrometric cone is a control over the firing aspect of production for which industry has no substitute.

* * *

Research activities conducted in the petitioner's physical plant have been confined primarily to problems directly connected with the manufacture and use of the pyrometric cone.

The research which the petitioner sponsored in certain universities was funded by the net income realized from the cone-manufacturing operation and the few investments the petitioner had.

* * *

When we analyze respondent's present contention that petitioner is not an exempt organization under section 501(c)(3), we find part of the answer in our earlier decision and its affirmation by the Sixth Circuit. It was there determined that petitioner was indeed organized for the requisite exempt purpose. Since there has been no change in the law on that score, we fail to see how our decision could change.

For the sake of completeness of this decision we note briefly that the following provisions in the founding testamentary trust justify our reaffirmation:

1. The trust was founded for the "first and principal purpose" of continuing the manufacture of Standard Pyrometric Cones "of the highest quality and most exact accuracy" and for the "second and subsidiary purpose" of providing "a Research Organization for the prosecution of studies and researches . . . , and for thus advancing the ceramic arts and industries in the United States."

2. While profit was essential to the continuance of the enterprise, testator's purpose from the first was:

> to make financial profit incidental to the principal idea of furnishing to ceramic manufacturers, a mode of controlling or regulating the firing process of their wares with the highest attainable degree of dependability at the lowest reasonable cost.

3. The price at which the cones could be sold is limited to produce a 20-percent profit which must be "expended upon Research."

4. Testator said it was his intention:

> To provide an organization, not for profit, whose real or ultimate objects are altruistic, and wholly devoted to producing industrial, scientific and social betterments, without any personal or private gain to anyone, ... To this end, . . . the surplus produced by the manufacturing and vending organization, . . . shall be expended by the Research Organization, whose product is knowledge, given free to all who are interested.

5. The results of the research are to be published and thus be freely available to the public and the ceramic industry "to the end that all surplus . . . made upon the sale of Standard Pyrometric Cones shall be returned to the Ceramic Industries in the form of technical knowledge."

6. The trustees are authorized to cease manufacture and close up the cone-manufacturing business "if scientific progress makes it no longer necessary or advisable to continue" and the assets are to be distributed upon dissolution to the Ohio State University.

Further, we find that petitioner has met the operating requirements for exemption of section 501(c)(3). As our findings of fact state, petitioner's mode of operation has not changed significantly since our prior decision. We there stated, 9 T.C. at 539, that "The predominate purpose for which the petitioner was organized . . . was to promote the science or art of ceramics" and that purpose was an exempt one. Section 1.501(c)(3)-1(c), Income Tax Regs., provides with respect to the "operational test" that "An organization will be regarded as 'operated exclusively' for one or more exempt purposes only if it engages primarily in activities which accomplish one or more of such exempt purposes."

Pursuant to the terms of the will petitioner has continued the manufacture of Orton Standard Pyrometric Cones since the foundation was established. The cones must be sold for no more than a 20-percent profit. Thus, unlike the normal commercial operation the sale of cones can produce only a limited profit. In addition to a return from the manufacture of cones, petitioner also realized income from interest on savings accounts, Government and corporate bonds, dividends on mutual funds, and rent on real property.

Utilizing its net income from manufacturing and nonoperating sources, petitioner sponsored research in other institutions concerning the ceramic firing process. Most of the research expenditures were in the form of fellowships awarded to selected graduate students in ceramic engineering departments of colleges and universities. Although the funds were channeled through a given school, the funding took the form of a specific grant to a selected candidate who was to work on a given project. The candidate and project were selected by petitioner's board of trustees.

Normally the fellowship grantee would write a thesis setting out the results of his research. Many of the theses resulting from the research sponsored by petitioner were published in journals concerning ceramic arts. To induce higher quality research and its publication, petitioner paid honorariums, normally of $200, to the individual who supervised the researching student if the research was published.

Petitioner also made grants for equipment and special projects to universities and other institutions conducting research in the field of ceramics. In one or two instances petitioner made grants to established endowments run by Ohio State University which reserved to itself the selection of student distributees.

A comparison of petitioner's annual net income with its distributions in pursuit of its fellowship and grant program reveals that it always expended a major portion of, and sometimes an amount exceeding, its net income on that program:

* * *

The present matter contrasts sharply with *Scripture Press Foundation v. United States*, 285 F.2d 800 (Ct. Cl. 1961); *Parker v. Commissioner*, 365 F.2d 792 (C.A. 8, 1966), affirming in part a Memorandum Opinion of this Court; and *Fides Publishers Ass'n. v. United States*, 263 F. Supp. 924 (N.D. Ind. 1967). Fundamental to determinations in those cases that the organizations in question were not exempt were findings of large profits, substantial accumulations of income, and relatively small amounts of actual exempt activity. Petitioner on the other hand was not a business of burgeoning profits, and greatly increasing accumulations of income in relation to distributions.

Ninety percent of petitioner's net income for the period in issue was expended on its fellowship and grant program. During the period January 1, 1962, through June 30, 1965, petitioner realized net income in the total amount of $143,434.64. Of that amount, $129,641 was expended on the program. Petitioner had no program for accumulating income for expansion. Compensation for employees was moderate. Members of petitioner's board of directors were given a dollar a year plus the expenses of attending meetings.

The aforenoted 20-percent limitation on profit prescribed by the testator is analogous to our finding of fact in *Forest Press, Inc.*, 22 T.C. 265, 267 (1954), wherein we noted that:

> The price for an edition of the system is determined by the manufacturing expense, plus the estimated cost of carrying the small staff until the date of a subsequent edition. *The price is not fixed with any intent to make a profit over and above the expenses involved in running the corporation and publishing the system*.... [Emphasis added.]

This Court went on to conclude that the organization there at issue was entitled to its tax exemption. We might note, too, that the item produced and sold by Forest Press, a Dewey Decimal Classification System and Related Index, is more analogous to the pyrometric cone, in terms of the relationship between the function of the item sold and the exempt purposes of the organization, than to the items involved in the other cases cited.

The facts in this case are quite close to those of Rev. Rul. 64-182, 1964-1 C.B. (Part 1) 186. There a charitable organization derived its income principally from the rental of space in a commercial office building, and pursued its exempt program by aiding other charitable organizations, selected at the discretion of its governing body, through contributions and grants. Such organization is deemed by the ruling to meet the primary purpose test of section 1.501(c)(3)-1(e)(1), Income Tax Regs., and to be exempt where its program is shown to be commensurate with its financial resources. See also Rev. Rul. 55-406, 1955-1 C.B. 73.

Respondent contends that certain provisions of the Revenue Act of 1950, 64 Stat. 210, have in effect vitiated the force of our decision and its affirmance in *Edward Orton, Jr. Ceramic Foundation, supra.* Section 301 of the Revenue Act of 1950 introduced into the law the feeder organization and the unrelated business income provisions. Feeders were unconditionally declared nonexempt, and unrelated business income was made subject to tax. Congress opted for this solution to rectify the problem of unfair business competition made possible because of exempt income, and exacerbated in no small measure by a liberal application of the destination-of-income test....

A close reading of the legislative history of the Revenue Act of 1950 indicates that Congress was quite specific in choosing a remedy for the problem it saw, and that it did not intend to alter the meaning of what is now section 501(c)(3). The only type of organization whose eligibility for exempt status Congress professed to deal with was the feeder organization. By enacting what is now section 502, Congress said no organization operated primarily to carry on a trade or business for profit will be exempt merely because all its profits are payable to an organization exempt under section 501. When enacting this provision Congress expressed the judgment that "such an organization is not itself carrying out an exempt purpose." H. Rept. No. 2319, 1950-2 C.B. 412. As to other organizations involved in exempt activities, Congress chose to impose a tax on income realized from an unrelated business regularly carried on rather than deny them an exemption. Speaking of the unrelated-business income provisions, Congress said:

> In fact it is not intended that the tax imposed on unrelated business income will have any effect on the tax-exempt status of any organization. An organization which is exempt prior to the enactment of this bill, if continuing the same activities, would still be exempt after this bill becomes law. [Emphasis supplied. S. Rept. 2375, 1950-2 C.B. 504–505.]

Thus it appears that in the Revenue Act of 1950 Congress effected a very deliberate and specific change in the qualifications an organization must have to be exempt under section 501. This change was not so sweeping as to cause courts to define anew, on a more narrow basis, what is charitable, educational, scientific, etc. To hold otherwise is to engage in judicial legislation....

Now we turn to the question of whether petitioner was a feeder organization within the meaning of section 502. Under the statute an organization operated primarily for carrying on a trade or business will not be exempt merely because its profits are payable to another exempt organization. Whether petitioner was operated primarily to carry on a trade or business is a question of fact.... A court should view all phases of an organization's operations in making this determination.... Petitioner was, as found above, actually carrying on a program of exempt activities of a scientific and educational nature....

The primary purpose of the foundation was to carry on its exempt program, which it did in its operations and with its net income from operating and non-operating sources in accordance with the testator's will. The evidence clearly indicates that distributions for fellowships were based on a determination by petitioner's board of trustees that a fellowship candidate was capable of doing significant research and that his proposed topic was of value in the field of ceramic engineering. These determinations were not made by any of the institutions through which the funds were channeled. This clearly indicates that the petitioner, in its fellowship program, was involved in the selection of individuals and not institutions. Additionally, petitioner had no obligation to distribute funds or equipment to or through specific institutions, nor did it in fact always make distributions to or through the same institutions each year. Petitioner was not owned or controlled by any of the institutions to or through which it made grants. Upon a consideration of the evidence as to the nature of petitioner's operations, we conclude that the foundation was not a feeder organization during the years in issue.

Finally we direct ourselves to the question of whether petitioner during 1962, 1963, and 1964 received unrelated-business taxable income. This turns on whether petitioner's cone-manufacturing operation was a trade or business, regularly carried on, and substantially related to its exempt function....

The record also shows that the manufacturing effort was pursued on a regular basis rather than a sporadic basis. Consequently we find that the cone manufacturing was a trade or business regularly carried on by petitioner.

The remaining question under this issue is whether petitioner's trade or business was related to its exempt function....

Petitioner's exempt purpose in general is to promote the science or art of ceramics. The testator in his will stated he entered the manufacture and sale of cones with the purpose of better controlling the firing of ceramic products and facilitating the freer exchange of exact information concerning that process.

* * *

The intention was not that the manufacturer of pyrometric cones would be merely a source of income but rather that it would serve as the necessary predicate to furthering the foundation's scientific and educational purposes.... Since the testator's will was executed in October of 1928, its directory terminology cannot be equated with code words for tax avoidance.

Orton Standard Pyrometric Cones are the most reliable cones available. They have been calibrated by the National Bureau of Standards and are the only cones which can be used in the American Standard Materials Society Pyrometric Cone Equivalent Test of refractoriness. While other devices perform similar functions, pyrometric cones are essential to the ceramic industry. Thus an invaluable and irreplaceable standard of measurement, tool for research, and means of communication concerning the firing of ceramic ware has been continuously available to the ceramic industry and to the ceramic engineering profession. Cf. *Forest Press, Inc., supra.*

There is no evidence showing extensive accumulations of income by petitioner for use in expanding the manufacturing operation. Further there is no evidence that petitioner used its exempt status to gain an unfair competitive advantage; indeed petitioner's cones were higher priced than those of the only other manufacturer of cones made known to this Court.

Having the burden of proof the respondent is bound to see that there is before us evidence sufficient to show that the cone business did not have as a principal purpose the furtherance (other than through the production of income) of the foundation's exempt purpose, or to suffer us finding against him on this issue. Upon a consideration of the whole record we are not satisfied that there is sufficient evidence to decide that the manufacture of pyrometric cones as conducted by petitioner did not have as its primary purpose the furtherance of the foundations' exempt purpose.

For the reasons given, we hold that during the years in issue petitioner's manufacturing of pyrometric cones was not an unrelated trade or business. . . .

* * *

Raum, J., dissenting: The majority holds an organization primarily and directly engaged in the manufacture and sale of a commercial product at a profit to be exempt from taxation. It also holds that the income received by the organization from its commercial activities is not unrelated-business taxable income and must therefore altogether escape taxation. I dissent from both conclusions. They are completely at odds with the purposes of the applicable congressional legislation. . . .

* * *

The conclusion is virtually inescapable that the taxpayer's manufacturing operations, not its charitable distributions, dominated the organization's activities, and that the scale of the taxpayer's manufacturing operations far exceeded that which might be appropriate and helpful to furthering the organization's scientific and educational purposes.

The social or economic utility of the taxpayer's product does not render its manufacture and sale to the public at a profit any less commercial, or more charitable than the manufacture and sale of other products. In any event, the manufacture and sale of the pyrometric cone is certainly no less commercial than the publication and sale of religious literature, . . . , the publication and sale of the results of economic research, . . . , the operation of bingo games for the purpose of financing medical services for children, . . . , or the furnishing of medical services, ... Moreover, the fact that the taxpayer may not have accumulated substantial funds but applied such funds instead to the development of its product does not adequately differentiate this case from those cited and distinguished by the majority. Indeed, to the extent that the taxpayer's exempt status permits it to finance the development of its product at a faster rate than its nonexempt competitors can develop theirs, the effect of the majority's decision may be to promote the very sort of anticompetitive advantage which Congress sought to eliminate in 1950.

1. With regard to the majority's decision that the taxpayer is exempt from taxation, I would add the following: The majority, I fear, has too mechanically relied upon our prior decision in *Edward Orton, Jr. Ceramic Foundation*, 9 T.C. 533, *aff'd*, 173 F.2d 483 (C.A. 6), which in 1947 upheld the exempt status of the taxpayer now before us. There we relied heavily upon the then-current doctrine that the destination of an organization's income (i.e., for charitable purposes) was more important than its source (i.e., a commercial enterprise) in determining the organization's exempt status (9 T.C. at 540):

> The manufacture and sale of the standard cones was not the ultimate purpose of the foundation. That was merely a means of accomplishing its real purpose. The income from this business was to be used for financing the research work. In applying the exemption clause of the statute, the test is not the origin of the income, but its destination. *Trinidad v. Sagrada Orden*

de Predicadores, 263 U.S. 578; *Roche's Beach, Inc. v. Commissioner*, 96 Fed. (2d) 776. . . .

However, in 1950 Congress enacted legislation designed to terminate the so-called "destination-of-income" test and thereby curtail the anticompetitive abuses which were thought to have developed under it: An exempt organization which conducted a business enterprise could charge lower prices, earn a higher rate of return, or invest its profits (unreduced by corporate taxation) in improvements at a faster rate than could its tax-paying competitors. . . . The approach taken in the 1950 legislation was two-pronged: (1) An organization which otherwise qualified for exemption as a charity but which was also engaged directly in the conduct of an active trade or business was to be taxed on its "unrelated business taxable income," that is, on income generated by activities not integrally related to the performance of the organization's exempt functions. (2) And where a charitable organization conducted an active trade or business indirectly through a "feeder" (a separately incorporated subsidiary), the feeder would be taxed in the same manner as competitive corporations. The underlying purpose was to tax commercial enterprises operated by charitable organizations on the same basis as their tax-paying rivals, regardless of whether such enterprises were operated directly as divisions of charitable organizations, or indirectly as separately incorporated feeders. The congressional effort was thus to deal comprehensively with the problems created by previously exempt organizations which had engaged in commercial activities, irrespective of differences in corporate structure. See H. Rept. No. 2319, 81st Cong., 2d Sess., p. 37 (1950); S. Rept. No. 2375, 81st Cong., 2d Sess., p. 29 (1950):

> Some of the witnesses who appeared before your committee took the position that this unrelated business income should be taxed only if received by a subsidiary organization. However, it is difficult to see why a difference in tax treatment should be allowed merely because in one case the income is earned directly by an educational or charitable organization, while in the other it is earned by a subsidiary of such an organization. In both cases the income is derived from the same type of activities and disposed of in the same manner. Moreover, in most cases the business functions now carried on by subsidiaries could be transferred to the parent if the tax were applied only to the income of the subsidiaries.

Thus, it is clear that Congress understood that it was taxing the income generated by a commercial enterprise regardless of the organizational mechanism that was selected as a means for carrying on that enterprise; it intended to leave no loophole. Notwithstanding the 1950 legislation, the majority today asserts that "there has been no change in the law" since the date of the first *Orton* case and concludes that it must rely upon our decision in that case.

To be sure, Congress did not amend section 101(6), I.R.C. 1939 (the statutory predecessor of section 501(c)(3)), in 1950. But by terminating the "destination-of-income" test and by attempting to remedy the anticompetitive advantages described above, Congress radically altered the entire statutory context. Accordingly, the weight to be accorded to the first *Orton* case must be evaluated in the light of that change. The correct principles to be applied in this situation are indicated by *Commissioner v. Sunnen*, 333 U.S. 591, which approved a different result for a later tax year from that reached in prior litigation for an earlier tax year in respect of the same taxpayer, the same controlling instrument and the same statutory language. Although the Supreme Court's opinion was focused upon res judicata and collateral estoppel, which it held to be inapplicable where there had been a significant change in "the legal atmosphere" (333 U.S. at 600) between the dates of the two cases, its decision of necessity represents a conclusion also that the doctrine of *stare decisis* is similarly inapplicable in such circumstances. The Court made clear that the change in "the legal atmosphere" might be wrought by any of a variety of circumstances, such as the rendition of a judicial declaration by a State court or the intervening development of legal principles by the Supreme Court itself (333 U.S. at 600) and that the earlier decision would likewise not have any binding effect if there were "an interposed alteration in the pertinent statutory provisions or Treasury regulations" (333 U.S. at 601).

Surely, the changes introduced by the 1950 Act and the accompanying extensive legislative history which made plain the intention of Congress to tax the profits of a commercial enterprise regardless of the fact that they were committed to be paid out for charitable purposes represent as much a change in "the legal atmosphere" within the meaning of *Sunnen* as any of the other intervening events referred to in that opinion. In my judgment the change in "the legal atmosphere" created by the 1950 legislation was of such character as to call for reconsideration of the decision in the first *Orton* case. The majority avoids this task by asserting that to do so would amount to "judicial legislation." But the cry of "judicial legislation" in the context of this case merely raises a bugaboo. Congress did not decide the *Orton* case; that decision represents judge-made law. Indeed, far from codifying *Orton* in 1950, Congress terminated the "destination-of-income" test upon which that case relied. Accordingly, since the courts were the source of that judge-made law they have a particular responsibility for it. To wait for Congress to take care of a problem that the courts themselves have created is an abdication of that responsibility, and to characterize an exercise of that responsibility disparagingly as "judicial legislation" is hardly warranted in the circumstances of this case.

Equally remarkable is the majority's misuse of an excerpt from the following paragraph from the Senate Finance Committee's report . . . :

> In neither the House bill nor your committee's bill does this provision deny the exemption where the organizations are carrying on unrelated active business enterprise, nor require that they dispose of such businesses. Both provisions merely impose the same tax on income derived from an unrelated trade or business as is borne by their competitors. In fact it is not intended that the tax imposed on unrelated business income will have any effect on the tax-exempt status of any organization. *An organization which is exempt prior to the enactment of this bill*, if continuing the same

> activities, *would still be exempt* after this bill becomes law. In a similar manner any reasons for denying exemption prior to enactment of this bill would continue to justify denial of exemption after the bill's passage. [Emphasis supplied.]

From the italicized fragments of the paragraph, the majority would infer that in enacting the 1950 legislation Congress intended that all organizations previously treated as tax-exempt would continue to be so treated. However, a fair reading of the entire paragraph reveals that the Finance Committee's intention was simply that if an organization were *otherwise entitled to exemption*, it would not *automatically* lose that exemption because it had unrelated business income. In passing upon the 1950 legislation, neither Congress nor the Finance Committee intended to freeze the exempt status of any specific organization which may have resulted from a prior judicial opinion based on criteria that are erroneous when considered in the light of the 1950 Act. We continue to have the responsibility for inquiring into the validity of such individual exemptions, giving appropriate weight to the congressional objective reflected in the 1950 legislation.

Forest Press, Inc., 22 T.C. 265, affords no basis for concluding that this responsibility has been discharged by the majority. That case involved a taxable year antedating the 1950 legislation. Moreover, the focus of that decision was upon the fact that although the terms of its certificate of incorporation did not restrict the scope of its activities, in fact the taxpayer was organized for and performed an exclusively noncommercial educational function. It is not without significance that *Forest Press, Inc.*, omitted any reference to our earlier *Orton* decision.

2. I would also note the following with regard to the majority's conclusion that the taxpayer was not the recipient of unrelated-business taxable income. By imposing a tax on only unrelated-business income of an otherwise bona fide exempt charitable organization, Congress attempted to avoid taxing business income derived from an exempt organization's activities which were necessarily and integrally part of the organization's exempt functions. Thus, the regulations, which follow the intent of Congress as reflected in the reports of the congressional committees, make explicit that the sort of activity intended to escape the tax is (1) a relatively small-scale enterprise (in comparison with the organization's charitable activities), (2) which is integrally related to the performance of the organization's exempt functions, and (3) which has as its primary purpose the advancement of such exempt functions.... Here the taxpayer's activities were dominated by its manufacturing and sales operations. Moreover, the manufacturing and sales operations were conducted on a scale that far exceeded that which might have been appropriate to furthering the organization's scientific and educational purposes. They were hardly incidental or related to the taxpayer's charitable activities within the understanding of Congress or the terms of the regulations.

* * *

Writing Exercise

The government did not appeal the Tax Court's decision in *Edward Orton, Jr.*, but did issue a Commissioner's Nonacquiescence. 1972-2 C.B. 4. Assume the government did appeal and that you have been assigned to write the majority opinion. Write an opinion affirming or reversing the Tax Court's decision. Address the following issues:

1. Whether the Edward Orton, Jr., Ceramic Foundation satisfies the exempt purpose requirement;

2. Whether the Edward Orton, Jr., Ceramic Foundation meets the exclusivity requirement and does not violate the "commerciality doctrine;" and

3. Whether § 502 would dictate denial of charitable exempt status to the Edward Orton, Jr., Ceramic Foundation.

You should not restate the facts except insofar as doing so provides emphasis to your opinion (i.e., eliminate the fact section of your written opinion). Discuss the significance of the following factors: (a) the composition of Orton Cone's Board of Directors; (b) the significance of its relationship to Ohio State University; (c) the relevance of Orton Cone's advertising activities; and (d) the impact of Orton Cone's pricing structure — i.e., its decision to sell cones at profit. Be prepared to deliver and defend your opinion in class.

B. The Integral Part Doctrine: Separate Related Entities

Despite the holding in *Edward Orton Jr., Ceramic Foundation, Inc.*, it is generally settled that an organization that engages in what is normally viewed as an ordinary trade or business is precluded by § 502 from being tax exempt even though its profits are dedicated to charitable purposes. Of course, an organization that is directly engaged in an exempt activity might also be required (or find it beneficial) to conduct, many activities preliminary to the accomplishment of the direct activity and some of those preliminary activities may generate income. For instance, a college or university may be primarily engaged in education, an exempt purpose. But it may find it beneficial to also operate a bookstore. A university's operation of a bookstore, *per se*, is not an exempt purpose, but the university bookstore nevertheless *furthers* the university owner's exempt educational purpose by making available needed books and supplies. The activity, then, will not detract from the University's exempt purpose because it is undertaken in furtherance of an exempt purpose. *See* Treas. Reg. § 1.501(c)(3)-1(e).

We will have further confirmation in part V (concerning the unrelated business income tax) that even though most campus bookstores are operated in a commercial manner, they escape taxation (for the most part) because they directly further the university's primarily engaged-in exempt purpose and are operated for the convenience of the university's students. What if, for liability, legal, or other business reasons, the University decides to operate its bookstore through a wholly owned subsidiary or other entity having the characteristics of a subsidiary? That separate entity would be engaging in a non-exempt activity. As a technical matter, it would not be entitled to tax exemption. But the incidence of taxation in that circumstance would only prevent — unnecessarily — the exempt parent from structuring an otherwise nontaxable activity in the most efficient manner. If the activity could be conducted by the parent without taxation (i.e., the activity is substantially related to the exempt purpose), what reason is there to tax the activity when it is conducted solely for the parent's benefit via a separate entity? Fortunately, form has not been elevated over substance in this regard and the parent is allowed to conduct the activity via a separate entity without sacrificing tax exemption with regard to that activity. *See Squire v. Students Book Corp.*, 191 F.2d 1018 (9th Cir. 1951); *see also* section 1.502-1(b).

Glance at § 501(b)(13), which permits exempt entities to operate for-profit (non-exempt) subsidiaries. That may provide an alternative for commercial activities that are too large to further exempt activities.

1. General Rule Permitting Separate Entities to Be Exempt as Integral Parts of a Charitable Function

University Medical Resident Services, P.C. v. Commissioner

71 TCM 3130 (1996).

Petitioners, University Medical Resident Services, P.C. (UMRS), and University Dental Resident Services, P.C. (UDRS), seek a declaratory judgment under section 7428(a) that they are exempt from Federal income taxation under section 501(a) as organizations meeting the requirements of section 501(c)(3).

* * *

Background

Petitioners are professional service corporations organized under the not-for-profit corporation law of the State of New York. Each petitioner's principal place of business was in Buffalo, New York, at the time their respective petitions were filed.

Prior to 1983, the State University of New York at Buffalo, New York (the University), sponsored graduate clinical training programs in medicine and dentistry. Within the University, these programs were administered by the School of Medicine and Biomedical Sciences and the School of Dental Medicine (collectively, the Schools). The clinical training provided is a prerequisite to the professional licensing of doctors and dentists in New York State.

The University does not maintain its own medical center. To provide the necessary clinical training, the University relies on its affiliation with several teaching hospitals in the Buffalo area. All clinical programs are conducted at one or more teaching hospitals.

Prior to 1983, the Schools and the affiliated teaching hospitals administered their own programs for the clinical education of medical and dental residents and fellows (hereinafter residents and fellows will be referred to collectively as residents)....

In 1981, new accreditation standards, effective beginning in 1982, were announced by the Accreditation Council for Graduate Medical Education (ACGME). These standards required greater centralization of decision-making where two or more institutions join together to provide medical education. In such cases, the standards required the establishment of mechanisms to ensure that the operations of individual institutions are consistent with the overall mission of the group of institutions.

In 1983, the Schools and the affiliated teaching hospitals responded to the new accreditation standards by entering into a contract entitled "The Graduate Medical and Dental Education Consortium of Buffalo" (the Consortium Agreement). The Consortium Agreement created a membership organization (the Consortium) comprising the Schools and several affiliated teaching hospitals.

Through the Consortium Agreement, decision-making related to the conduct of clinical training programs was centralized, and the Consortium became the sole sponsoring institution with ultimate responsibility for all clinical training programs conducted at any of the hospitals....

All decisions relating to program operations, resource allocations, residents' grievances, disciplinary actions, and policy development are made by the Consortium. It makes and implements these decisions through meetings of the Consortium, a coordinating board that makes recommendations to the Consortium, and three standing committees. Each of these organizational units consists of representatives from the Schools and the affiliated teaching hospitals. Prior to 1991, the Schools and the member hospitals employed their own residents.

In June of 1991, UMRS and UDRS were incorporated. The certificates of incorporation, ..., state that the corporations were formed to render those professional services that a doctor ... or a dentist ... is authorized to render. They further state that the corporations may engage in any activity that a professional service corporation is permitted to engage in under New York law, subject to the limitation that the corporations may not engage in any activity that would prevent them from qualifying under section 501(c)(3) as tax-exempt organizations.

* * *

In July of 1991, the Consortium, affiliated teaching hospitals, UMRS, and UDRS entered into the "Graduate Medical and Dental Education Consolidation Contract" (the Consolidation Contract). The Recitals section of the Consolidation Contract provides as follows:

> I. . . . [The Consortium] is the institution of record for governing graduate medical and dental education programs in Western New York to comply with the requirements of the Accreditation Council on Graduate Medical Education, and . . . [the Consortium] provides overall management and program control for that graduate medical and dental education. . . . [UMRS] AND . . . [UDRS] . . . are professional service corporations controlled by . . . [the Consortium].
>
> II. To promote the pooling of resources dedicated to graduate medical and dental education, to improve hospital and ambulatory care and related health care for patients in the Western New York area and to coordinate more closely the academic medical and dental programs in the Teaching Hospitals, the Teaching Hospitals and . . . [the Consortium] desire to provide for the direct employment by . . . [UMRS] of the medical residents and fellows and the direct employment by . . . [UDRS] of the dental residents and fellows who are enrolled in . . . [the University] training programs conducted at the Teaching Hospitals, with coordination of the medical and dental education aspects of this employment by the Administrative Committee of . . . [the Consortium]. . . . [UMRS] and . . . [UDRS] have been established to provide for that respective direct employment of the medical and dental residents and fellows.

The Consolidation Contract allocates responsibility among the Schools, the hospitals, the Consortium, and petitioners. It provides that, commencing July 1, 1991, all residents enrolled in academic medical programs administered by the Consortium "shall become employed by" UMRS, and all residents enrolled in academic dental programs administered by the Consortium "shall become employed by" UDRS. It further provides that the affiliated teaching hospitals would contract with petitioners for the provision of residents. Petitioners serve only the Schools and the affiliated teaching hospitals, each of which is a tax-exempt organization qualified under section 501(c)(3).

Under the Consolidation Contract, the Schools and the hospitals follow specific procedures with respect to the allocation of residents. The program directors at each of the teaching hospitals project their hospital's needs for residents and communicate that estimate to the Consortium. Applicants for residency positions submit an application to the Consortium. The Schools, the Consortium, and the teaching hospitals then select residents to meet each hospital's needs and communicate that selection to UMRS . . . or UDRS. . . . Thereafter, a certificate of residency is issued by the Consortium, and the resident is assigned to the appropriate hospital.

* * *

The Consolidation Contract also states that petitioners have the power to "hire and fire" residents. The affiliated teaching hospitals, however, supervise the residents and have the right to refuse to accept the assignment of a particular resident. . . .

Once a resident is selected and allocated to a member hospital, the relevant petitioner assumes responsibility for the payment of all wages, benefits, and related payroll taxes and deductions in connection with the resident's employment. The Consortium determines the amount of compensation and benefits. At least 5 days prior to the date UMRS or UDRS makes a payment for compensation, the relevant school or hospital remits to UMRS or UDRS funds equal to the amount of the payment. Petitioners do not engage in fund-raising activities and receive all of their funding from the Schools and hospitals.

Under the Consolidation Contract, petitioners must provide the Schools and hospitals with quarterly reports describing all receipts and disbursements, and the Consortium has the right to audit petitioners' books and records. Because petitioners have no administrative employees, petitioners' administrative activities (i.e., processing invoices sent to the Schools and hospitals and salary payments made to residents) are performed by employees of the Schools. . . .

On August 26, 1994, respondent issued final adverse rulings notifying petitioners that they did not qualify for tax exemption. The rulings each stated in pertinent part:

> You have failed to establish that you will be operated exclusively for exempt purposes as required by section 501(c)(3) of the Code. Your primary activity is to provide administrative services to teaching hospitals affiliated through the Consortium with the State University of New York at Buffalo residency training program by paying salaries and fringe benefits of the residents working in these hospitals. This activity does not advance education within the meaning of section 1.501(c)(3)-1(d)(1) of the Income Tax Regulations. You also do not qualify under section 501(e) of the Code because you are not operating on a cooperative basis.

Discussion

I. In General

Section 501(a) provides an exemption from Federal income tax for organizations described in section 501(c). Section 501(c) sets forth a list of exempt organizations. The list includes organizations "organized and operated exclusively for . . . charitable . . . or educational purposes". Sec. 501(c)(3).

Section 501(e), entitled "Cooperative Hospital Service Organizations", provides that an organization will be treated as meeting the requirements of section 501(c)(3) if the organization is: (1) Organized and operated exclusively to provide listed services solely to two or more hospitals meeting certain requirements; (2) organized on a cooperative basis and paying net earnings to members within a specified time period; and (3) wholly owned by the members if the organization has capital stock. Sec. 501(e).

Petitioners contend that they are charitable and educational organizations within the meaning of section 501(c)(3). Respondent counters that petitioners are neither charitable nor educational organizations and that they are operated for a substantial nonexempt purpose. Respondent further argues that petitioners do not fit within section 501(e), and that, pursuant to the Supreme Court's decision in *HCSC-Laundry v. United States*, 450 U.S. 1 (1981), petitioners cannot qualify under section 501(c)(3).

As a preliminary matter, we note that, in this case, section 501(e) does not preclude an analysis under section 501(c)(3). In *HCSC-Laundry v. United States, supra*, the Supreme Court held that section 501(e) is the exclusive provision for hospital cooperatives to qualify under section 501(c)(3) and that a hospital cooperative that does not satisfy section 501(e) cannot qualify independently under section 501(c)(3). To qualify as a hospital cooperative under section 501(e), the organization must provide services "solely for two or more hospitals". Petitioners serve schools in addition to hospitals. Thus, they are not hospital cooperatives, and section 501(e) does not preclude petitioners from qualifying under section 501(c)(3).

To qualify under section 501(c)(3), petitioners must establish that they are both "organized and operated" exclusively for exempt purposes. Sec. 1.501(c)(3)-1(a)(1), Income Tax Regs. Respondent concedes that petitioners are organized exclusively for exempt purposes but argues that petitioners are not operated exclusively for such purposes. An organization will be regarded as operated exclusively for exempt purposes only if it engages primarily in activities that accomplish one or more exempt purposes listed in section 501(c)(3). Sec. 1.501(c)(3)-1(c)(1), Income Tax Regs. Whether an organization is operated exclusively for one or more exempt purposes is a question of fact to be resolved on the basis of all the evidence in the administrative record. *B.S.W. Group, Inc. v. Commissioner*, 70 T.C. 352, 357 (1978) .... Petitioners have the burden of establishing that the grounds for denying exemption stated in the final notices of determination were inadequate.....

II. Qualification as "Charitable" Under Section 501(c)(3)

Petitioners argue that they are operated exclusively for "charitable" purposes. The term charitable is used in section 501(c)(3) in its generally accepted legal sense, which includes the "advancement of education" and "lessening the burdens of Government".... Sec. 1.501(c)(3)-1(d)(2), Income Tax Regs.

A. Advancement of Education

Petitioners contend that they advance education in two ways. We reject both of petitioners' contentions. First, petitioners argue that they advance education by assisting the Schools in meeting several requirements imposed by the ACGME accreditation standards. Petitioners contend that they assist in the provision of uniform pay and benefits for residents of similar experience levels, as required by the accreditation standards. The Consortium Agreement, however, states that the Consortium, not petitioners, determines resident compensation levels. Petitioners contend that they assist in the provision of professional liability insurance for residents, as required by the accreditation standards. The Consolidation Contract, however, states that the member hospitals, not petitioners, provide such insurance. Petitioners contend that they assist in the provision of adequate financial support to residents, as required by the accreditation standards. The Consolidation Contract, however, states that the Schools and hospitals, not petitioners, provide all funding of resident salaries and benefits. Indeed, the Consortium Agreement states that it is the Consortium, not petitioners, that generally has responsibility for ensuring compliance with the accreditation standards. Consequently, we conclude that petitioners provide the Schools and hospitals minimal, if any, assistance in meeting these standards.

Second, petitioners argue that they advance education by working with the Schools and hospitals to manage program-related activities. Petitioners, however, do not manage any educational programs. Petitioners emphasize that they have the right to hire and fire residents. The Schools and hospitals, however, have an effective veto over petitioners' hiring decisions because the Schools and hospitals have the right to refuse to allow a resident to perform his or her duties. In addition, the Consortium handles all resident grievances including matters of termination of employment. Thus, even if the Consolidation Contract grants petitioners the right to hire and fire residents, other provisions of the contract supersede that right by delegating substantial responsibility to the Consortium and its members. Further, even if petitioners did have responsibility for the program, they have no administrative employees, so it is unclear how they would discharge this responsibility. Petitioners have not met their burden of establishing that they advance the education of residents.

* * *

III. Qualification as "Educational" under Section 501(c)(3)

Petitioners' final argument is that they qualify as "educational" organizations. Generally, the term "educational" as used in section 501(c)(3) relates to (1) the instruction or training of an individual for the purpose of improving or developing his capabilities or (2) the instruction of the public on subjects useful to an individual and beneficial to the community. Sec. 1.501(c)(3)-1(d)(3), Income Tax Regs. Petitioners do not claim to qualify independently as educational organizations, but contend, under the integral part doctrine, that they are entitled to share in the Consortium members' exempt status. See *Hospital Bureau of Standards & Supplies, Inc. v. United States*, 158 F. Supp. 560, 141 Ct. Cl. 91 (1958).

The integral part doctrine is not a codified rule, but is a judicial doctrine recognized in cases, regulations, and revenue rulings as a basis for derivative exemption under section 501(c)(3). The cases applying this doctrine have held that where an organization (1) bears a "close and intimate relationship" to the operation of one or more tax-exempt organizations, and (2) provides a "necessary and indispensable" service solely to those tax-exempt organizations, it will take on the exempt status of those organizations. *See, e.g., Hospital Bureau of Standards & Supplies, Inc. v. United States, supra* at 562; *Council for Bibliographic & Info. Technologies v. Commissioner*, T.C. Memo. 1992-364.

The rationale behind the integral part doctrine is that an organization that takes over an essential task which would otherwise have to be performed by the organizations served should be exempt because the members would continue to be exempt if they performed the task themselves.... In cases granting exemption based on the integral part doctrine, the organization seeking exemption invariably contributed to the attainment of its members' exempt purpose. *Nonprofits' Ins. Alliance v. United States, supra;* cf. *Northern Cal. Cent. Servs., Inc. v. United States,* 591 F.2d 620, 219 Ct. Cl. 60 (1979) (involving an independent corporation that provided higher quality laundry services for member hospitals at lower cost in furtherance of their exempt purpose) ....

In the present case, petitioners' function is merely incidental to the exempt purpose of the organizations they serve. Indeed, the Consolidation Contract states that "the employment of the ... [residents] is ancillary to the primary purpose of graduate medical and dental education". (Emphasis added.) A comparison of the facts in *Hospital Bureau* and *Council for Bibliographic & Info. Technologies* with those in the present case further establishes this point. In *Hospital Bureau* and *Council for Bibliographic & Info. Technologies,* the organizations seeking exemption took over functions previously performed by the organizations they served in order to achieve cost reductions and better achieve the organizations' exempt purpose. *Hospital Bureau of Standards & Supplies v. United States, supra* (involving a corporation that took over the purchasing of hospital supplies in order to achieve volume discounts for its members); *Council for Bibliographic & Info. Technologies v. Commissioner, supra* (involving a corporation that took over operation and maintenance of a computerized library research system enabling member libraries to better perform their exempt functions). In the present case, petitioners are superfluous corporate shells that make no cognizable contribution to the education of residents. Despite petitioners' incorporations, all funds continue to be provided by the Schools and hospitals, and all program-related decisions continue to be made through the Consortium. The Schools and the hospitals continue to supervise and train the residents and pay their salaries. In addition, the Consortium continues to make the policy decisions, just as it has since 1983. The only change since the incorporation of petitioners is that the money used to pay residents is funneled through petitioners before it reaches the residents. As the Consolidation Contract states, the Consortium has "overall management and program control" with respect to the education of residents. Petitioners are merely "corporations controlled by ... [the Consortium]." In substance, petitioners appear to be appendages rather than integral parts.

IV. Conclusion

We hold that petitioners have not satisfied their burden of establishing that respondent's final adverse determinations were erroneous. Our holding is consistent with the policy underlying section 501(c)(3). The Supreme Court has stated that Congress, in enacting section 501(c)(3), sought to "encourage the development of private institutions that serve a useful public purpose or supplement or take the place of public institutions of the same kind." *Bob Jones Univ. v. United States,* 461 U.S. 574, 588 (1983). In essence, an organization obtains exemption from tax under section 501(c)(3) in recognition of its contribution to the public. Petitioners make no such contribution.

To reflect the foregoing,

Decisions will be entered for respondent.

Question

If the organization's activities in *University Medical Resident Services, PC v. Commissioner* were indeed incidental to the operations of their exempt owners, what sense does it make to allow the owners to conduct the activities themselves, without taxation, but to tax the activities if they are conducted via a separate, wholly owned subsidiary? Why must the activity be "essential" rather than just "incidental"? In the note below, we cite to a 1938 ruling in which the Service stated that what an organization may do itself without taxation, it may also do via a separate entity. Why might the Service have changed its view?

Note on Origin of the Integral Part Doctrine

University Medical Resident Services incorrectly states that the integral part doctrine is an uncodified judicial doctrine. The first judicial mention of the doctrine occurred in *Squire v. Students Book Corp.*, 191 F.2d 1018 (9th Cir. 1951), one year before the enactment of Treas. Reg. § 1.502-1, so it may be that the doctrine has judicial origins. On the other hand, in G.C.M. 20853, 1938-2 C.B. 166 (declared obsolete in Rev. Rul. 67-46, C.B. 1967-1), the Service stated "[W]hat a corporation, exempt under [§ 501(c)(3)], may do directly without forfeiting its exemption . . . it may do through a corporation organized for that purpose, and . . . a corporation so organized and operated is entitled to exemption." Treas. Reg. § 1.502-1(b) purports to be the Service's codification of the doctrine. Whether the doctrine has a judicial or statutory origin is important because of some significant differences between the articulation of that doctrine in *University Medical Resident Services* and Treas. Reg. § 1.502-1. *University Medical Resident Services* indicates more than once that an organization can serve several exempt organizations and thereby obtain derivative tax exemption. Moreover, the opinion contains no requirement that the benefited exempt organizations be related as a condition for tax exemption of the "consolidation" entity. By contrast, Treas. Reg. § 1.502-1 allows derivative tax exemption only when the consolidation entity is owned by a single exempt "parent" and serves only that parent or other exempt entities owned by that parent, (i.e., sister organizations), or both the parent and sister organizations. Service to an organization outside of the corporate family, according to the regulation, will preclude tax exemption. The noted differences are especially important in light of the Service's refusal to grant tax exemption to charitable cooperatives, unless such cooperatives are explicitly recognized in § 501. We will consider cooperatives soon, but first we return to HMOs because those are the entities with regard to which the contours of the integral part doctrine are being defined.

2. Enhancement of Related Entity's Exempt Character

Geisinger Health Plan v. Commissioner of Internal Revenue Service

30 F.3d 494 (3d Cir. 1994)

In *Geisinger Health Plan v. Commissioner of Internal Revenue*, 985 F.2d 1210 (3d Cir. 1993) ("*Geisinger I*"), we held that the Geisinger Health Plan ("GHP"), a health maintenance organization ("HMO"), was not entitled to exemption from federal income taxation as a charitable organization under 26 U.S.C. § 501(c)(3). We remanded the case for determination of whether GHP was entitled to exemption from taxation by virtue of being an integral part of the Geisinger System (the "System"), a comprehensive health care system serving northeastern and north-central Pennsylvania. We will affirm the Tax Court's decision that it is not exempt as an integral part of the System.

I.

GHP is a prepaid health care plan which contracts with health care providers to provide services to its subscribers. The facts relevant to GHP's function are detailed in our opinion in Geisinger I, and we need not repeat them here. Instead, far more relevant to this appeal is GHP's relationship with the Geisinger System and its other constituent entities, a relationship which we must examine in some detail to decide the issue before us.

The Geisinger System consists of GHP and eight other nonprofit entities, all involved in some way in promoting health care in 27 counties in northeastern and northcentral Pennsylvania. They are: the Geisinger Foundation (the "Foundation"), Geisinger Medical Center ("GMC"), Geisinger Clinic (the "Clinic"), Geisinger Wyoming Valley Medical Center ("GWV"), Marworth, Geisinger System Services ("GSS") and two professional liability trusts. All of these entities are recognized as exempt from federal income taxation under one or more sections of the Internal Revenue Code.

The Foundation controls all these entities, as well as three for-profit corporations. It has the power to appoint the corporate members of GHP, GMC, GWV, GSS, the Clinic and Marworth, and those members elect the boards of directors of those entities. The Foundation also raises funds for the Geisinger System. Its board of directors is composed of civic and business leaders in the area.

GMC operates a 569-bed regional medical center. As of March 31, 1988, it had 3,512 employees, including 195 resident physicians and fellows in approved postgraduate training programs. It accepts patients without regard to ability to pay, including Medicare, Medicaid and charity patients. It operates a full-time emergency room open to all, regardless of ability to pay. It also serves as a teaching hospital.

GWV is a 230-bed hospital located in Wilkes-Barre, Pennsylvania. It accepts patients regardless of ability to pay, and it operates a full-time emergency room open to all, regardless of ability to pay. The Clinic provides medical services to patients at 43 locations throughout the System's service area. It also conducts extensive medical research in conjunction with GMC and physicians who perform medical services for GMC, GWV and other entities in the Geisinger System. As of March 31, 1988, it employed 401 physicians. It accepts patients without regard to their ability to pay.

Marworth operates two alcohol detoxification and rehabilitation centers and offers educational programs to prevent alcohol and substance abuse. GSS employs management and other personnel who provide services to entities in the Geisinger System. As we noted in *Geisinger I*, the Geisinger System apparently decided to create GHP after GMC experimented with a pilot prepaid health plan between 1972 and 1985. The experience was positive, and the Geisinger System formed GHP to provide its own prepaid health plan.

GHP's interaction with other Geisinger System entities is varied. Its most significant contact is with the Clinic, from which it purchases the physician services its subscribers require by paying a fixed amount per member per month, as set forth in a Medical Services Agreement. Eighty-four percent of physician services are provided by doctors who are employees of the Clinic; the remaining 16 percent are provided by doctors who are not affiliated with the Clinic but who have contracted with the Clinic to provide services to GHP subscribers. GHP has similarly entered into contracts with GMC and GWV, as well as 20 non-related hospitals. When its subscribers require hospital care, these hospitals provide it pursuant to the terms of their contracts, for either a negotiated per diem charge or a discounted percentage of billed charges. GHP has also contracted with GSS to purchase office space, supplies and administrative services.

Except in emergency situations, only physicians who either work for the Clinic or have contracted with the Clinic may order that a GHP subscriber be admitted to a hospital. When such admission is ordered, it generally must be to GMC, GWV or one of the 20 other hospitals with which GHP has contracted. The only exceptions to this requirement are in a medical emergency outside of GHP's service area or when approved in advance by GHP's medical director; in those instances, a subscriber may be admitted to a hospital with which GHP has no contractual relationship.

GHP has also entered into contracts with pharmacies, durable medical equipment suppliers, ambulance services and physical therapists. Those entities' services are available to subscribers only (1) in a medical emergency or (2) when prescribed by a doctor who is employed by the Clinic or who is under contract with the Clinic to provide care to GHP subscribers.

The Tax Court considered GHP's role in the Geisinger System when, on remand from *Geisinger I*, it decided that GHP did not qualify for exempt status under the integral part doctrine. *Geisinger Health Plan v. Commissioner of Internal Revenue*, 100 T.C. 394 (1993) ("*Geisinger II*"). The court first distinguished a series of "group practice cases," in which incorporated groups of doctors on hospital or faculty medical staffs were held to be exempt from taxation as integral parts of the tax-exempt hospitals or medical schools with which they were associated. The Tax Court found that those cases did not control its decision because "for [them] to apply here, the population of [GHP's] subscribers would have to overlap substantially with the patients of the related exempt entities [and t]he facts indicated that it does not." *Geisinger II*, 100 T.C. at 404. Moreover, it held, GHP was not entitled to tax-exempt status as an integral part of the System because it would produce unrelated business income for the Clinic, GMC or GWV if one of those entities were to absorb its activities. *Id.* at 404–06. A timely appeal followed; as noted previously, we will affirm, although we will do so on grounds which differ from those on which the Tax Court rested. Specifically, because we deem it unnecessary to decide, we will not reach the issue whether GHP would produce unrelated business income if it were part of some entity created by merging its operations with one of the other Geisinger System entities.

II.

Generally, separately incorporated entities must qualify for tax exemption on their own merits. *Mutual Aid Association of the Church of the Brethren v. United States*, 759 F.2d 792, 795 n.3 (10th Cir. 1985) . . . . In *Geisinger I*, we decided that GHP cannot qualify for tax exemption on its own merits. The question before us now is whether it comes within the "integral part doctrine," which may best be described as an exception to the general rule that entitlement to exemption is derived solely from an entity's own characteristics. . . .

A.

In *Geisinger I*, we described the integral part doctrine as follows:

> The integral part doctrine provides a means by which organizations may qualify for exemption vicariously through related organizations, as long as they are engaged in activities which would be exempt if the related organizations engaged in them, and as long as those activities are furthering the exempt purposes of the related organizations.

Geisinger I, 985 F.2d at 1220. The Tax Court on remand stated:

> The parties agree that an organization is entitled to exemption as an integral part of a tax-exempt affiliate if its activities are carried out under the supervision or control of an exempt organization and could be carried out by the exempt organization without constituting an unrelated trade or business.

Geisinger II, 100 T.C. at 402; see 26 C.F.R. § 1.502-1(b).

GHP argues that these statements require us to examine whether the Clinic or GMC could retain tax-exempt status if it were to absorb GHP. It thus compares the attributes of a hypothetically merged Clinic/GHP or GMC/GHP entity to the attributes of the HMO held to be exempt in *Sound Health Association v. Commissioner*, 71 T.C. 158 (1978), acq. 1981-2 C.B. 2. Concluding that the merged entity would display more indicia of entitlement to exemption than the Sound Health HMO, GHP urges that it is exempt because of the characteristics of the hypothetical merged entity. Despite its superficial appeal, we reject this argument and hold that the integral part doctrine does not mean that GHP would be exempt solely because either GMC or the Clinic could absorb it while retaining its tax-exempt status. While this is a necessary condition to applying the doctrine, it is not the only condition. GHP is separately incorporated for reasons it found administratively and politically advantageous. While it may certainly benefit from that separate incorporation, it must also cope with the consequences flowing from it. . . .

We acknowledge that interpreting the integral part doctrine in the manner GHP urges might enable entities to choose their organizational structures based on efficiency concerns rather than perverting those concerns by making tax considerations relevant. In our view, however, there are countervailing policy concerns which justify determining each entity's tax status based upon its own organizational structure. It is less complex and more certain for courts and administrators to assess an entity's tax status in light of its unique organizational composition and its association with another entity, and only to have to take into account some hypothetical combination of organizations as a second step in those relatively rare instances when an organization meets the other precondition of integral part status we set forth below. See II.C. infra. We recognize that it may appear overly technical to tax GHP differently from a GMC/GHP or a Clinic/GHP combination, for instance, merely because it is incorporated separately. On the other hand, to tax GHP differently merely because it is related to those entities, without searching for indicia that its association with them enhances its own tax-exempt characteristics, would be inconsistent with the narrow construction generally accorded tax exemptions. . . .

Accordingly, we will determine whether GHP is exempt from taxation when examined not only in the context of its relationship with the other entities in the System, but also based upon its own organizational structure. . . .

B.

As the Tax Court recognized, 100 T.C. at 401, the integral part doctrine is not codified. Its genesis may be found in a phrase contained within a regulation which speaks of a subsidiary being exempt "on the ground that its activities are an integral part of the activities of the parent organization." 26 C.F.R. § 1.502-1(b); see generally General Counsel Memorandum 39,830 (August 30, 1990). This reference to the doctrine is only fully understood, however, when one considers it in the context of the regulation and the statute it implements. Section 502 of the Internal Revenue Code (the "feeder organization rule") provides that an organization engaged in a trade or business for profit will be taxed even if it pays all of its profits over to an exempt organization. 26 U.S.C. § 502(a). . . . The regulation interpreting this section of the Code makes clear that in the case of an organization operated for the primary purpose of carrying on a trade or business for profit, exemption is not allowed . . . on the ground that all the profits of such organization are payable to one or more [exempt] organizations. . . . 26 C.F.R. § 502-1(b).

The integral part doctrine arises from an exception to this "feeder organization" rule. Regulation 502-1(b) states that despite the general rule of taxation of "feeder organizations,"

> if a subsidiary organization of a tax-exempt organization would itself be exempt on the ground that its activities are an integral part of the exempt activities of the parent organization, its exemption will not be lost because, as a matter of accounting between the two organizations, the subsidiary derives a profit from its dealings with the parent organization[.]

26 C.F.R. § 502-1(b) (emphasis added). To illustrate how this exemption might apply to an entity, the regulation describes "a subsidiary organization which is operated for the sole purpose of furnishing electric power used by its parent organization, a tax-exempt organization, in carrying out its educational activities." *Id. See also* Rev. Rul. 78-41, 1978-1 C.B. 148 (trust existing solely as a repository of funds set aside by nonprofit hospital for the payment of malpractice claims against the hospital, and as the payor of those claims, was exempt as an integral part of the hospital); Rev. Rul. 63-235, 1963-2 C.B. 210 (incidental publication and sale of law journals did not prevent journal corporation from being exempt as "adjunct to" an exempt law school); Rev. Rul. 58-194, 1958-1 C.B. 240 (bookstore used almost exclusively by university faculty and students was exempt as an integral part of the university with which it was associated).

GHP contends that as long as it would not generate unrelated business income if it were merged into any one of the other Geisinger System entities, it is exempt as an integral part of the System. The Tax Court, in fact, utilized unrelated business income concepts in analyzing GHP's claim for exemption. *See Geisinger II*, 100 T.C. at 404–07.... We agree that an entity seeking exemption as an integral part of another cannot primarily be engaged in activity which would generate more than insubstantial unrelated business income for the other entity. That much is demonstrated by the remainder of 26 C.F.R. § 1.502-1(b), which cautions that:

> the subsidiary organization is not exempt from tax if it is operated for the primary purpose of carrying on a trade or business which would be an unrelated trade or business (that is, unrelated to exempt activities) if regularly carried on by the parent organization. For example, if a subsidiary organization is operated primarily for the purpose of furnishing electric power to consumers other than its parent organization (and the parent's tax-exempt subsidiary organizations), it is not exempt since such business would be an unrelated trade or business if regularly carried on by the parent organization. Similarly, if the organization is owned by several unrelated exempt organizations, and is operated for the purpose of furnishing electric power to each of them, it is not exempt since such business would be an unrelated trade or business if regularly carried on by any one of the tax-exempt organizations.

Id.

Although 26 C.F.R. § 502-1(b) clearly makes the absence of activity constituting an unrelated trade or business a necessary qualification for the operation of the integral part doctrine, because this regulation speaks in terms of disqualification from exemption rather than qualifications for exemption, it does not indicate or explain whether there are any other necessary qualifications — the issue we face in this case.

Both the revenue rulings cited earlier and case law similarly fail to state a comprehensive rule to assist in determining when an entity is exempt as an integral part of another. In *Squire v. Students Book Corp.*, 191 F.2d 1018 (9th Cir. 1951), for example, the court ruled that a corporation operating a bookstore and restaurant which sold college texts, was wholly owned by a college, used college space free of charge, served mostly faculty and students, and devoted its earnings to educational purposes was exempt because it "obviously bears a close and intimate relationship to the functioning of the college itself." *Squire*, 191 F.2d at 1020. It did not, however, provide further explication for its rationale. . . .

C.

Distilling § 1.502-1(b) and these cases into a general rule leads us to conclude that a subsidiary which is not entitled to exempt status on its own may only receive such status as an integral part of its § 501(c)(3) qualified parent if (i) it is not carrying on a trade or business which would be an unrelated trade or business (that is, unrelated to exempt activities) if regularly carried on by the parent, and (ii) its relationship to its parent somehow enhances the subsidiary's own exempt character to the point that, when the boost provided by the parent is added to the contribution made by the subsidiary itself, the subsidiary would be entitled to § 501(c)(3) status.

Whether income received by an HMO operated by an entity which also directly operates a health care facility would be deemed unrelated business income was answered in the negative by *Sound Health*. Nevertheless, this is a complex issue which will probably be further explored by the courts and Congress as the entities which pay for health care, and those which provide it, begin to intertwine. Because we find that GHP does not meet the second prong of the integral part test articulated above, we need not probe the legal soundness of the *Sound Health* opinion.

In considering whether the boost received by GHP from its association with GMC or the Clinic might be sufficient, when added to its own contribution, to merit § 501(c)(3) treatment, we must first look at the nature of the boost which was sufficient in those instances where the integral part doctrine has been applied. The electric company discussed in 26 C.F.R. § 1.502-1(b), for example, would not be entitled to an exemption standing alone, because the provision of electric power to others is not a charitable purpose.

However, the fact that the electric company is a subsidiary of an exempt university eliminates the characteristic which prevented the company from being exempt on its own. As a subsidiary of the university, the electric company acquires the purpose of the university — it produces electricity solely for the purpose of allowing education to occur. The "boost" it receives from its association with the educational institution transforms it from a company without to a company with a charitable purpose and thus enables it to qualify for tax-exempt status as an integral part of that institution. Like the electric company, the bookstores in *Squire* and Rev. Rul. 58-194, and the law journal in Rev. Rul. 63-235 had insufficiently charitable purposes to qualify for exempt status when considered alone. Selling books or a journal to the general public is not educational enough to qualify for exempt status as a charitable institution. But because these particular bookstores and this particular law journal were subsidiaries of universities and aided the universities' exempt missions of educating their students, the purposes of the bookstores and journal became more charitable, and they were entitled to an exemption. Absent receipt of such a "boost," we do not think that an institution is entitled to a tax exemption as an integral part. To hold otherwise might enable an organization that is not entitled to an exemption on its own to become tax-exempt merely because it happens to be controlled by an organization that is itself exempt.

Here, we do not think that GHP receives any "boost" from its association with the Geisinger System. In *Geisinger I*, we determined that while GHP helps to promote health, it does not do so for a significant enough portion of the community to qualify for tax-exempt status on its own. *See Geisinger I*, 985 F.2d at 1219–20. Cf. Rev. Rul. 69-545, 1969-2 C.B. 117 (promotion of health is a charitable purpose "provided that the class [served] is not so small that its relief is not of benefit to the community"). And, unlike the electric company, university bookstores or law journal in the regulations and case law, the contribution that GHP makes to community health is not increased at all by the fact that GHP is a subsidiary of the System rather than being an independent organization which sends its subscribers to a variety of hospitals and clinics.

As our examination of the manner in which GHP interacts with other entities in the System makes clear, its association with those entities does nothing to increase the portion of the community for which GHP promotes health — it serves no more people as a part of the System than it would serve otherwise. It may contribute to the System by providing more patients than the System might otherwise have served, thus arguably allowing the System to promote health among a broader segment of the community than could be served without it, but its provision of patients to the System does not enhance its own promotion of health; the patients it provides — its subscribers — are the same patients it serves without its association with the System. To the extent it promotes health among non-GHP-subscriber patients of the System, it does so only because GHP subscribers' payments to the System help finance the provision of health care to others. An entity's mere financing of the exempt purposes of a related organization does not constitute furtherance of that organization's purpose so as to justify exemption. . . . Thus, it is apparent that GHP merely seeks to "piggyback" off of the other entities in the System, taking on their charitable characteristics in an effort to gain exemption without demonstrating that it is rendered "more charitable" by virtue of its association with them.

D.

It has not escaped our attention, of course, that both our decision today and our decision in Geisinger I may either set the tone for, or be superseded by, legislative activity in the near future. The executive and the legislative branches are currently debating the appropriate parameters of future governmental involvement in the provision and financing of health care in this country. The legislation which may result could significantly transform the structure and financing of health care delivery systems in ways both anticipated and unanticipated. Academic commentary on our decision in Geisinger I reinforces our common-sense impression that questions regarding the tax-exempt status of integrated delivery systems under 26 U.S.C. § 501(c)(3) may be addressed during these debates. *See generally* Loren Callan Rosenzweig, Geisinger, *HMOs and Health Care Reform*, TAXES, January 1994, at 20; Kenneth L. Levine, *Geisinger Health Plan Likely to Adversely Affect HMOs and Other Health Organizations*, J. TAXATION, August 1993, at 90.

Whatever changes are wrought by the legislature in the future, however, today we are constrained to apply the law in its current form and to construe tax exemptions narrowly. Our interpretation of the integral part route to exemption under section 501(c)(3) reflects those constraints. Obviously, we express no opinion as to whether HMOs, whether structured like GHP or like the Sound Health HMO, can or should be exempt from federal income taxation after whatever transformation of the health care industry may be forthcoming.

III.

In sum, GHP does not qualify for exemption as an integral part of the Geisinger System because its charitable character is not enhanced by virtue of its association with the System. We will affirm the decision of the Tax Court.

Question

Why would we ever need an "integral part doctrine" if, as stated in *Geisinger*, the subsidiary already has a charitable purpose of its own?

3. Substantially Related to Related Entity's Exempt Purpose or Function

IHC Health Plans, Inc. v. Commissioner

T.C. Memo. 2001-246 (2001).

[Editor's Note: The facts of *IHC Health Plans, Inc.* are set out in Chapter 6.]

Integral Part Test

In *Geisinger III*, we held that the administrative record did not support Geisinger HMO's claim that it was entitled to tax-exempt status as an integral part of the Geisinger system. *Geisinger Health Plan v. Commissioner*, 100 T.C. at 404–405. As a preliminary matter, we concluded that an HMO may qualify for tax-exempt status as an integral part of a related tax-exempt entity if its activities are carried out under the supervision or control of a related tax-exempt entity and the HMO's activities would not constitute an unrelated trade or business if conducted by the related tax-exempt entity. *Id.* at 402, 404–405. We looked to section 513(a) which defined an unrelated trade or business in pertinent part as:

> "any trade or business the conduct of which is not substantially related (aside from the need of such organization for income or funds or the use it makes of the profits derived) to the exercise or performance by such organization of . . . [the] purpose or function constituting the basis for its exemption."

[*Id.* at 405.]

Because Geisinger HMO enrollees received medical services from hospitals outside of the Geisinger system, and because the administrative record lacked evidence as to whether such services were substantial, we were unable to conclude that Geisinger HMO's activities were substantially related to the activities of its tax-exempt affiliates. *Id.* at 405–406.

In *Geisinger IV*, the Court of Appeals affirmed our holding in *Geisinger III*, albeit on slightly different grounds. *Geisinger Health Plan v. Commissioner*, 30 F.3d at 501. The Court of Appeals held that an organization may qualify for tax-exempt status as an integral part of its tax-exempt parent if: (1) The organization is not carrying on a trade or business which would be an unrelated trade or business if regularly carried on by its tax-exempt parent; and (2) the organization's relationship with its tax-exempt parent somehow enhances or "boosts" its own tax-exempt character to the point that the organization would qualify for tax-exempt status. *Id.* at 501. Focusing solely on the latter issue, the Court of Appeals concluded that Geisinger HMO was not entitled to tax-exempt status because it did not receive the necessary boost from its relationship with exempt Geisinger entities. In particular, the Court of Appeals held:

> As our examination of the manner in which . . . [Geisinger HMO] interacts with other entities in the System makes clear, its association with those entities does nothing to increase the portion of the community for which . . .

> [Geisinger HMO] promotes health—it serves no more people as a part of the System than it would serve otherwise....

[*Id.* at 502.]

Under the circumstances, the Court of Appeals concluded that it was unnecessary to consider whether Geisinger HMO's activities would constitute an unrelated trade or business if regularly carried on by a related tax-exempt entity. *Id.* at 501.

* * *

2. Whether Petitioner Satisfies the Integral Part Test

In *Geisinger III*, we concluded that an organization may qualify for exemption as an integral part of a tax-exempt affiliate if: (1) The organization's activities are carried out under the supervision or control of a tax-exempt affiliate, and (2) such activities would not constitute an unrelated trade or business if conducted by a related tax-exempt entity. *Geisinger Health Plans v. Commissioner*, 100 T.C. at 402–405. There is no dispute that petitioner's activities were carried out under the supervision and control of IHC—a tax-exempt affiliate. Thus, we need only consider whether petitioner's activities would constitute an unrelated trade or business if conducted by a related tax-exempt entity.

In *Geisinger III*, we held that, because Geisinger HMO enrollees received some hospital services from independent hospitals, Geisinger HMO had to show that its overall operations were substantially related to the functions of its tax-exempt affiliates. *Id.* at 405. We stated:

> If petitioner's activities are "conducted on a scale larger than is 'reasonably necessary'" to accomplish the purposes of the exempt entities, there is no substantial relationship within the meaning of the regulations. *Hi-Plains Hospital v. United States*, 670 F.2d 528, 530–531; sec. 1.513-1(d)(3), Income Tax Regs. [*Id.* at 406.]

Although Geisinger HMO enrollees received all of their physician services through Clinic, an exempt affiliate, Geisinger HMO enrollees received approximately 20 percent of their hospital services from independent hospitals. Because the record did not disclose why Geisinger HMO enrollees received hospital services from hospitals outside of the Geisinger system, we were unable to conclude that Geisinger HMO's operations were substantially related to the functions of its tax-exempt affiliates. *Id.* at 404–406.

Like Geisinger HMO, petitioner neither owned nor operated any medical facilities and did not employ a significant number of physicians or health care professionals. Petitioner fulfilled its obligation to provide medical services to its enrollees by contracting with physicians (both physicians employed by Health Services and independent physicians) and hospitals (both Health Services hospitals and independent hospitals) to provide such services. In contrast to Geisinger III, however, the administrative record in this case indicates that the medical services that petitioner's enrollees received from independent hospitals were largely attributable to admissions to either UMC or Davis Hospital and Medical Center. Further, these admissions were undertaken to: (1) Take advantage of specialized services (such as burn treatment and pain management) provided at UMC; (2) address occasional shortages of psychiatric beds in Health Services hospitals; and (3) accommodate petitioner's enrollees living in Davis County, Utah, where Health Services lacked a hospital. Because the circumstances under which petitioner's enrollees received hospital services from independent hospitals were limited to situations where Health Services was unable to provide specialized hospital services or were due to geographical expediency, or both, we are satisfied that petitioner's method for arranging for its enrollees to receive hospital services was substantially related to Health Services' tax-exempt function.

However, we do not end our analysis here. In particular, the administrative record reveals that petitioner's enrollees received a substantial portion of their physician services from independent physicians.

In *Geisinger III*, we did not discuss the provision of physician services to Geisinger enrollees inasmuch as Geisinger HMO arranged for its enrollees to receive all their physician services from Clinic—a tax-exempt affiliate of Geisinger HMO. Clinic in turn arranged to provide physician services to Geisinger enrollees through its approximately 400 physician/employees (approximately 84 percent of services) and through contracts with independent physicians (approximately 16 percent of services). In contrast, in the instant case, petitioner's enrollees received approximately 20 percent of their physician services from physicians employed by or contracting with Health Services, while petitioner contracted for the remaining 80 percent of such physician services directly with independent physicians. In other words, petitioner's enrollees received nearly 80 percent of their physician services from physicians with no direct link to one of petitioner's tax-exempt affiliates.

Petitioner contends that its contracts with independent physicians are not relevant to the question of whether it qualifies for tax-exempt status as an integral part of its tax-exempt IHC affiliates because all such independent physicians were required to maintain privileges at Health Services' hospitals. We disagree with the basic premise underlying petitioner's argument.

Health Services comprised the hospital division, which operated a large number of hospitals and clinics, and the physician division, which employed approximately 400 primary care and specialist physicians who generally practiced in Health Services' clinics and other community-based settings. Considering that petitioner does not provide free or low cost health services, we fail to see how petitioner's operations, including its heavy reliance on independent physicians, would be essential to or substantially related to Health Services' exempt functions. To the contrary, petitioner's method of arranging for its enrollees to receive physician services suggests that petitioner conducted its operations on a scale "larger than is reasonably necessary to accomplish the purposes of the exempt entities". *Geisinger Health Plans v. Commissioner*, 100 T.C. at 406. Based on the record presented, we hold that petitioner does not satisfy the integral part test.

In sum, petitioner did not provide the community benefit required for petitioner to qualify as an organization described in section 501(c)(3). Further, petitioner's operations were not essential to or substantially related to Health Services' exempt functions. Consequently, petitioner is not entitled to the declaratory judgment it seeks.

To reflect the foregoing,

Decision will be entered for respondent.

Note on Confusion with Respect to Integral Part Doctrine

Are you completely confused by the explanation of the integral part doctrine in both *Geisinger* and *IHC*? You should be. The doctrine is easily enough understood outside the context of health care. But in the context of health care, the doctrine seems incomprehensible. Professor John Colombo published a well-written article in 2001 on the *IHC* case that does not make the health care application of the integral part doctrine comprehensible but does help us understand the source of our confusion. In the process, the author also provides some much-needed clarifying context to the whole area of charitable health care. *See* John D. Colombo, *The IHC Cases: A Catch-22 for Integral Part Doctrine, a Requiem for Rev. Rul. 69-545*, 34 EXEMPT ORG. TAX REV. 401 (2001).

Chapter 9

Select Commercial Activities: Cooperatives and Commercial Insurance

A. Note on Relationship of Integral Part Analysis to Cooperatives

Cooperatives are functionally similar to "integral part entities" in that they seek to provide a central point from which several exempt organizations may obtain necessary goods or services. In the absence of a specific statutory recognition of tax exemption, the Service will deny tax exemption to cooperatives unless they limit the provision of goods and services to family members (i.e., a single parent entity or organizations having the same parent as the first entity). As we noted earlier, *University Medical Resident Services* strongly indicates that a cooperative or consolidation entity may serve several unrelated exempt organizations and still be entitled to tax exemption.

Three factors suggest that the Service's contrary view, that cooperatives are not entitled to tax exemption under § 501(c)(3) unless the goods and services are provided to corporate-type family members, will prevail (if it has not already prevailed). First, *University Medical Resident Services* is a Tax Court Memorandum opinion, which means it is less authoritative than a regular opinion. The opinion might also be discounted for its failure to discuss Treas. Reg. § 1.502-1, which has been on the books since 1952. Second, the practicing bar seems to have acquiesced to the Service's insistence that a consolidation entity must serve a single organization, or structurally related organizations, to be tax exempt. Rather than directly challenging the Service's view, practitioners have developed a rather complicated contractual structure, known as joint operating agreements, to get around that requirement. Joint Operating Agreements are discussed in greater detail following a closer study of statutorily recognized cooperative organizations.

B. Cooperative Organizations: Separate Unrelated Entities

Code: § 501(e), Skim § 501(f)

Regs.: §§ 1.501(e)-1; 1.502-1(b) [last sentence]

1. General Rule Treating the Provision of Goods or Services to Unrelated Cooperatives as a Nonexempt Commercial Activity

For reasons largely unexplained, the Service has adhered to the conclusion that an organization, the sole purpose of which is to provide needed goods or services to unrelated charitable organizations, is pursuing a non-exempt, commercial activity and is therefore not entitled to tax exemption. In Revenue Ruling 54-305, an organization acted as a purchasing agent for hospital supplies for the benefit of unrelated hospitals exempt under § 501(c)(3). By purchasing supplies on a cooperative basis, the several unrelated organizations could demand lower prices and thereby devote more of their aggregate wealth to health care. This goal seems to make obvious sense. But the Service, relying on the last sentence of Treas. Reg. § 1.502-1(b), ruled that the cooperative purchasing organization was not entitled to 501(c)(3) recognition. Treas. Reg. § 1.502-1(b) is ostensibly based on § 502 and its rejection of feeder organizations. In an early judicial opinion, a federal district court found the relationship between feeders and cooperatives so unsupported by law or logic that it explicitly refused to apply the regulation. *United Hospital Services v. United States*, 384 F. Supp. 776 (S.D. Ind. 1974). That court rhetorically asked, "What does IRC § 502 have to do with two or more [charitable] organizations setting up a not-for-profit corporation, wholly controlled by them and not serving the public, in order to affect the economies in their own charitable operations?" *Id.* at 782. The Tax Court later complained that Rev. Rul. 54-305 "made no effort to analyze the commercial aspects of the subject corporation's activities." *Associated Hospital Services, Inc. v. Commissioner*, 74 T.C. 213, 218–19 (1980). The Tax Court also complained that the rationale used in Rev. Rul. 54-305 to conclude that the organization was engaged in a nonexempt, commercial activity (i.e., service to several unrelated charitable organizations, rather than a parent or sister organizations, constituted a commercial activity according to Treasury Regulation 1.502-1(b)) was "totally beside the point." *Id. See also Hospital Bureau of Standards and Supplies, Inc. v. United States*, 158 F. Supp. 560, 564 (Ct. Cl. 1958) (reasoning that an organization that sells goods and services only to unrelated charitable member organizations does not demonstrate the indicia of commercial activity).

Despite these explicit misgivings, the Service's view prevailed insofar as hospital cooperatives are concerned when Congress enacted § 501(e). That provision specifically grants § 501(c)(3) status to hospital cooperatives performing certain enumerated functions. The question then became whether an organization that does not qualify under § 501(e) may still obtain tax exemption under § 501(c)(3) as a charitable cooperative or consolidation entity. The Supreme Court resolved that issue in *HCSC-Laundry v. United States*, which follows.

2. Non-501(e) Hospital Cooperative Services

HCSC-Laundry v. United States

450 U.S. 1 (1981)

Petitioner HCSC-Laundry is a Pennsylvania nonprofit corporation. It was organized in 1967 under the law of that Commonwealth "[to] operate and maintain a hospital laundry and linen supply program for those public hospitals and non-profit hospitals or related health facilities organized and operated exclusively for religious, charitable, scientific, or educational purposes that contract with [it]."

Petitioner provides laundry and linen service to 15 non-profit hospitals and to an ambulance service. All these are located in eastern Pennsylvania. Each organization served possesses a certificate of exemption from federal income taxation under § 501(c)(3) of the Internal Revenue Code of 1954, 26 U.S.C. § 501(c)(3). Each participating hospital pays petitioner annual membership dues based upon bed capacity. The ambulance service pays no dues. Petitioner's only other income is derived from (a) a charge for laundry and linen service based upon budgeted costs and (b) a charge of 1 1/2 cents per pound of laundry. Budgeted costs include operating expenses, debt retirement, and linen replacement. The amounts charged in excess of costs have been placed in a fund for equipment acquisition and replacement.

No part of petitioner's net earnings inures to the benefit of any individual.

Petitioner was formed after the Lehigh Valley Health Planning Council determined that a shared, nonprofit, off-premises laundry would best accommodate the requirements of the member hospitals with respect to both quality of service and economies of scale. The Council had investigated various alternatives. It had rejected a joint service concept because no member hospital had sufficient laundry facilities to serve more than itself. A commercial laundry had declined an offer for the laundry business of all the hospitals, and most of the other available commercial laundries were not capable of managing the heavy total volume.

Petitioner's laundry plant was built and equipped at a cost of about $2 million. This was financed through loans from local banks, with 15-year contracts from 10 of the hospitals used as collateral. Petitioner employs approximately 125 persons.

In 1976, petitioner applied for exemption under § 501(c)(3) from federal income taxation. The Internal Revenue Service denied the exemption application on the grounds that § 501(e) of the Code was the exclusive provision under which a cooperative hospital service organization could qualify as "an organization organized and operated exclusively for charitable purposes" and therefore exempt. Because subsection (e)(1)(A) does not mention laundry, the Service reasoned that petitioner was not entitled to tax exemption.

Petitioner duly filed its federal corporate income tax return for its fiscal year ended June 30, 1976. That return showed taxable income of $123,521 and a tax of $10,395. The tax was paid. Shortly thereafter, petitioner filed a claim for refund of that tax and, when the Internal Revenue Service took no action on the claim within six months, *see* 26 U.S.C. § 6532(a)(1), petitioner commenced this refund suit in the United States District Court for the Eastern District of Pennsylvania.

On stipulated facts and cross-motions for summary judgment, the District Court ruled in favor of petitioner, holding that it was entitled to exemption as an organization described in § 501(c)(3). . . . The United States Court of Appeals for the Third Circuit, however, reversed. It held that § 501(e) was the exclusive provision under which a cooperative hospital service organization could obtain an income tax exemption, and that the omission of laundry services from § 501(e)(1)(A)'s specific list of activities demonstrated that Congress intended to deny exempt status to cooperative hospital service laundries. . . . Because the ruling of the Court of Appeals is in conflict with decisions elsewhere, we grant certiorari, and we now affirm.

This Court has said: "The starting point in the determination of the scope of 'gross income' is the cardinal principle that Congress in creating the income tax intended 'to use the full measure of its taxing power.'" *Commissioner v. Kowalski*, 434 U.S. 77, 82 (1977) . . . . Under our system of federal income taxation, therefore, every element of gross income of a person, corporate or individual, is subject to tax unless there is a statute or some rule of law that exempts that person or element.

Sections 501(a) and (c)(3) provide such an exemption, and a complete one, for a corporation fitting the description set forth in subsection (c)(3) and fulfilling the subsection's requirements. But subsection (e) is also a part of § 501. And it expressly concerns the tax status of a cooperative hospital service organization. It provides that such an organization is exempt if, among other things, its activities consist of "data processing, purchasing, warehousing, billing and collection, food, clinical, industrial engineering, laboratory, printing, communications, record center, and personnel (including selection, testing, training, and education of personnel) services." Laundry and linen service, so essential to a hospital's operation, is not included in that list and, indeed, is noticeable for its absence. The issue, thus, is whether that omission prohibits petitioner from qualifying under § 501 as an organization exempt from taxation. The Government's position is that subsection (e) is controlling and exclusive, and because petitioner does not qualify under it, exemption is not available. Petitioner takes the opposing position that § 501(c)(3) clearly entitles it to the claimed exemption.

Without reference to the legislative history, the Government would appear to have the benefit of this skirmish, for it is a basic principle of statutory construction that a specific statute, here subsection (e), controls over a general provision such as subsection (c)(3), particularly when the two are interrelated and closely positioned, both in fact being parts of § 501 relating to exemption of organizations from tax. . . . Additionally, however, the legislative history provides strong and conclusive support for the Government's position. It persuades us that Congress intended subsection (e) to be exclusive and controlling for cooperative hospital service organizations. Prior to the enactment of subsection (e) in 1968, the law as to the tax status of shared hospital service organizations was uncertain. The Internal Revenue Service took the position that if two or more tax-exempt hospitals created an entity to perform commercial services for them, that entity was not entitled to exemption. *See* Rev. Rul. 54-305, 1954-2 Cum. Bull. 127. *See also* § 502, as amended, of the 1954 Code, 26 U.S.C. § 502. This position, however, was rejected by the Court of Claims in *Hospital Bureau of Standards and Supplies, Inc. v. United States*, 158 F. Supp. 560, 141 Ct. Cl. 91 (1958). After expressly noting the uncertainty in the law, Congress enacted subsection (e). *See* Revenue and Expenditure Control Act of 1968, Pub. L. 90-364, § 109 (a), 82 Stat. 269.

In considering the provisions of the tax adjustment bill of 1968 that ultimately became subsection (e), the Senate sought to include laundry in the list of services that a cooperative hospital service organization could provide and still maintain its tax-exempt status. The Treasury Department supported the Senate amendment. *See* 114 Cong. Rec. 7516, 8111–8112 (1968). At the urging of commercial interests, however . . . , the Conference Committee would accept only a limited version of the Senate amendment. In recommending the adoption of subsection (e), the managers on the part of the House emphasized that shared hospital service organizations performing laundry services were not entitled to tax-exempt status under the new provision. See H. R. Conf. Rep. No. 1533, 90th Cong., 2d Sess., 43 (1968); Senate Committee on Finance and House Committee on Ways and Means, Revenue and Expenditure Control Act of 1968, Explanation of the Bill H. R. 15414, 90th Cong., 2d Sess., 1, 20 (Comm. Print 1968).

Later, in 1976, at the urging of the American Hospital Association, the Senate Committee on Finance proposed an amendment that would have added laundry to the list of services specified in subsection (e)(1)(A). Hearings on H. R. 10612 before the Senate Committee on Finance, 94th Cong., 2d Sess., 2765–2772 (1976); S. Rep. No. 94-938, pt. 2, pp. 76–77 (1976). The amendment, however, was defeated on the floor of the Senate. 122 Cong. Rec. 25915 (1976). In view of all this, it seems to us beyond dispute that subsection (e)(1)(A) of § 501, despite the seemingly broad general language of subsection (c)(3), specifies the types of hospital service organizations that are encompassed within the scope of § 501 as charitable organizations. Inasmuch as laundry service was deliberately omitted from the statutory list and, indeed, specifically was refused inclusion in that list, it inevitably follows that petitioner is not entitled to tax-exempt status. The Congress easily can change the statute whenever it is so inclined.

The judgment of the Court of Appeals is affirmed.

Justice Stevens, dissenting.

Today the Court summarily decides that § 501, read in light of the legislative history of § 501(e), requires that nonprofit cooperative hospital laundries be denied an exemption from federal income tax, even though they may satisfy the requirements of §§ 501(a) and 501(c)(3). In my opinion, the Court's summary disposition is ill-advised because a full understanding of the question presented in this case requires an examination of the history underlying the present state of the law with respect to the tax status of cooperative hospital service organizations. When the statute is read against that background — indeed, even when it is read in isolation — its plain language unambiguously entitles this petitioner to an exemption.

I

In 1950, Congress amended § 101 of the Internal Revenue Code of 1939 by adding to that section a paragraph dealing with so-called "feeder organizations." Revenue Act of 1950, § 301 (b), Pub. L. 814, ch. 994, 64 Stat. 953. This paragraph was subsequently reenacted without substantial change as § 502(a) of the Internal Revenue Code of 1954. In 1952, the Treasury Department adopted a regulation designed to implement the feeder provision of § 101. Treas. Regs. 111, § 29.101-3 (b). Although this regulation did not specifically address cooperative hospital service organizations, it did indicate that the Treasury considered cooperative ventures operated by tax-exempt entities for the purpose of providing necessary services to those entities nonexempt feeder organizations.

The Internal Revenue Service first applied this regulation to cooperative hospital service organizations in a 1954 Revenue Ruling, Rev. Rul. 54-305 .... In that Ruling, the Service held that a corporation organized and operated for the primary purpose of operating and maintaining a purchasing agency for the benefit of its members — tax-exempt hospitals and other charitable institutions — fell within the feeder regulation and thus was not entitled to an income tax exemption. The corporation at issue realized substantial profits from its operations and distributed only a portion of those profits to its members. *Ibid.* Accordingly, the Service found that the corporation was operated for the primary purpose of carrying on a trade or business for profit within the meaning of § 101 of the 1939 Code. This Revenue Ruling, and the regulation on which it was based, are the sources of the Treasury's pre-1968 position that cooperative hospital service organizations were not entitled to tax-exempt status.

The first judicial consideration of this position came in 1958 in *Hospital Bureau of Standards & Supplies, Inc. v. United States*, 158 F. Supp. 560, 141 Ct. Cl. 91. In that case, a group of nonprofit, tax-exempt hospitals formed a nonprofit corporation to act as their joint purchasing agent and to perform certain research functions on their behalf. The corporation brought suit against the Government to recover income taxes assessed for 1952 and 1953, alleging that it was entitled to a tax exemption under § 101(6) of the 1939 Code, the predecessor of present § 501(c)(3). The Government opposed the claimed exemption, arguing primarily that the corporation was a feeder organization under Treas. Regs. 118, § 39.101-2(b) (1953). The Court of Claims held that the feeder provision was inapplicable in that case because the corporation was not organized and operated for the primary purpose of carrying on a trade or business for profit as required by the statute, even though it had reported net income for the two tax years in question. ... Accordingly, the court ruled that the corporation was entitled to a tax exemption under § 101(6).

Almost 10 years passed before the next important development in this area. In 1967, in connection with the Social Security Amendments of 1967, the original version of § 501(e) was proposed as an amendment to § 501. The proposed amendment provided that a cooperative hospital service organization would be exempt from income taxation as long as it satisfied certain requirements, among them a requirement that it perform only services which, if performed by the member hospitals themselves, would constitute an integral part of their exempt activities. See S. Rep. No. 744, Social Security Amendments of 1967, Report of the Senate Committee on Finance, 90th Cong., 1st Sess., 201–202, 318–319 (1967). The legislative history indicates that laundry services were considered within the scope of the proposed amendment. *Id.*, at 201. The legislative history also indicates that Congress was aware of the Treasury's belief that such cooperative ventures were not tax exempt because of the Code's feeder provision. *Id.*, at 200–201. However, the Senate Report noted as well that the Court of Claims in *Hospital Bureau*, "the leading case in point," had rejected the Treasury's position. S. Rep. No. 744, at 201, and n.1.

The proposed amendment was not accepted by the House in its original form. See H. R. Conf. Rep. No. 1030, 90th Cong., 1st Sess., 73 (1967). Rather, during 1968, § 501(e) in its present form was enacted into law as part of the Revenue and Expenditure Control Act of 1968. The 1968 legislative history is set forth in adequate detail in the majority opinion, . . . and does not warrant repetition here. As I read that legislative history, it establishes that Congress deliberately omitted laundry services from § 501(e) and clearly intended that joint hospital laundries not be entitled to claim an income tax exemption under § 501(e). These conclusions are reinforced by Congress' rejection in 1976 of a proposed amendment to § 501(e) that would have added laundry services to that subsection's list of eligible services. See *ante*, at 7.

Despite the enactment of § 501(e) in 1968, it was not until 1980 that a federal court decided that nonprofit cooperative hospital laundries were not entitled to an income tax exemption under § 501. Between 1968 and 1980, six federal courts rejected the Treasury's contention that hospital service organizations providing services other than those listed in § 501(e) were not entitled to claim an exemption under § 501(c)(3). These courts also rejected the Treasury's alternative contention that, even if such entities were not automatically excluded from consideration under § 501(c)(3), they nonetheless were nonexempt feeder organizations under § 502(a) and Treas. Reg. § 1.502-1(b). In 1980, however, three Courts of Appeals concluded that § 501(e) provides the exclusive means by which a hospital service organization may acquire an income tax exemption. These courts relied primarily upon the 1968 and 1976 legislative history cited by the majority. The decision of the Third Circuit, the first in this series of Court of Appeals decisions, is presently before us.

II

In the District Court in this case, the Government argued, as it had on five previous occasions, that because Congress deliberately omitted hospital laundries from § 501(e), it necessarily followed that they also were outside the scope of § 501(c)(3). See 473 F. Supp. 250, 252 (E.D. Pa. 1979). The District Court rejected this argument, choosing instead to align itself with the then-unbroken line of precedent. *Id.*, at 253–254. The District Court also rejected the Government's alternative argument based upon § 502(a). On appeal, the Government abandoned this argument, . . . , and relied solely upon § 501(e). Thus, as shaped by the proceedings below, the question presented here is whether Congress, in enacting § 501(e), intended that cooperative hospital service organizations must qualify for tax exemption under that statute or not at all. The Court concludes that the statutory language and legislative history require an affirmative answer to that question. Neither factor, in my judgment, supports the Court's conclusion.

A

Correct analysis of the income tax exemption provisions at issue in this case should focus upon the language of the statutory provision which actually creates the exemption. That provision is § 501(a), which states:

> "An organization described in subsection (c) or (d) or section 401 (a) shall be exempt from taxation under this subtitle unless such exemption is denied under section 502 or 503." 26 U.S.C. § 501(a).

This language is clear and unambiguous. Insofar as relevant in this case, it provides that organizations meeting the requirements of § 501(c)(3) shall be exempt from the federal income tax. Such organizations are to be denied exemption only if they fall within the provisions of §§ 502 or 503. Section 501(a) contains no reference to § 501(e), nor does § 501(c)(3) indicate that it is in any way limited by § 501(e).

Applying this plain statutory language to the facts of this case, it is clear that, but for § 501(e), petitioner is entitled to a tax exemption under §§ 501(a) and 501(c)(3). It is undisputed that petitioner satisfies the requirements of § 501(c)(3). Therefore, under § 501(a) petitioner is exempt from taxation unless one of the two express exceptions identified in that subsection applies. The District Court found § 502 inapplicable because petitioner was not operated on a "for profit" basis. . . . This finding has not been challenged by the Government. Section 503 is simply irrelevant in this case. Therefore, the plain language of the relevant statutes clearly states that petitioner is a tax-exempt organization.

The majority overrides this plain statutory language by construing § 501(e) as an exception to the broad charitable exemption created by §§ 501(a) and 501(c)(3). Construed in this manner, § 501(e) operates to deny a tax exemption to organizations that otherwise satisfy the express statutory requirements for exemption. The § 501(e) exception itself, however, is not express: rather than identifying particular organizations as nonexempt, § 501(e) identifies particular organizations as exempt and, apparently by implication, denies all similar but unlisted organizations the exemption otherwise available under §§ 501(a) and 501(c)(3).

The Court silently dismisses the fact that §§ 501(a) and 501(c)(3) contain no reference indicating that § 501(e) is to have this limiting effect; the necessary connection between the statutes is supplied instead by the Court's finding that § 501(e) is "interrelated" with and "closely positioned" to § 501(c)(3). It cannot be denied that § 501(e) is close in position to § 501(c)(3). But a statute's text is surely more significant than its physical location. And to state, as the majority does, that §§ 501(c)(3) and 501(e) are "interrelated" is to substitute conclusion for analysis. Apart from their proximity to one another, the only express relationship between these statutes is that certain entities described in § 501(e) are to be treated as charitable organizations under § 501(c)(3) for federal income tax purposes. Nothing in any of the relevant statutes suggests that § 501(e) is to have the effect of denying an exemption to organizations that satisfy the requirements of § 501(c)(3). When Congress wanted a statute to have such an effect, it had no difficulty making its intention unmistakably plain, as is evident from § 501(a)'s reference to §§ 502 and 503. The language Congress employed in § 501(e) reflects an intention to enlarge, not to reduce, the category of organizations entitled to exemption under § 501(c)(3).

B

The Court supports its interpretation of § 501 with a discussion of legislative history. However, this discussion makes no reference to the legislative history of the statutory provisions primarily at issue in this case, §§ 501(a) and 501(c)(3). Instead, the Court focuses upon the legislative history of § 501(e). In my opinion, insofar as the Court relies upon this legislative history, its decision rests upon a non sequitur. Because the text and legislative history of § 501(e), which was enacted in 1968, persuade the Court that petitioner is not entitled to an exemption under that section, the Court concludes that petitioner also is not entitled to claim exemption under § 501(c)(3), which was enacted in 1954. Unless the later statute limited the scope of the earlier statute, the conclusion is not supported by the premise.

The legislative history of § 501(e) might support the Court's position if it unambiguously revealed: (1) that Congress in 1968 believed that no cooperative hospital service organization could satisfy the requirements of § 501(c)(3) and it therefore enacted § 501(e) to extend a tax exemption to certain entities previously not entitled to exemption; or (2) that Congress in 1968 believed that cooperative hospital service organizations were at least arguably entitled to tax exemption under § 501(c)(3) and it enacted § 501(e) to withdraw this exemption from some, but not all, of these entities. The legislative history provides persuasive support for neither proposition.

In my opinion, § 501(e) unambiguously granted a tax exemption to certain entities that arguably already were entitled to an exemption under § 501(c)(3). There is absolutely no evidence that the 1968 statute was intended to withdraw any benefits that were already available under the 1954 Act. Proper analysis, therefore, should focus on the question whether petitioner would have been entitled to an exemption under pre-1968 law.

The 1954 Act created a broad category of exempt organizations, including corporations "operated exclusively for . . . charitable . . . purposes." That hospitals could qualify for exemption has always been clear. The question whether a cooperative organization formed by a group of tax-exempt hospitals to provide services for the hospitals could also qualify for exemption was less clear. As discussed in Part I, *supra*, prior to 1968 the Treasury took the position that such a cooperative was a "feeder organization" within the meaning of § 502 of the Code. This position, however, was rejected by the Court of Claims which — quite properly in my opinion — held that such a cooperative was not a "feeder" and was exempt under what is now § 501(c)(3). See *Hospital Bureau of Standards & Supplies, Inc. v. United States*, 158 F. Supp. 560, 141 Ct. Cl. 91 (1958).

As a matter of history — presumably because cooperative service organizations were fairly common in the hospital industry — the § 502 issue arose in disputes between the Treasury Department and hospital affiliates. Conceptually, however, there is no reason why the identical issue could not arise if other tax-exempt entities, such as schools or churches, might find it advantageous to form cooperatives to perform some of their essential functions for them. In any event, when the issue was brought to the attention of Congress in 1967 and 1968, the focus of the dispute still concerned hospital affiliates. Congress then made an unequivocal policy choice rejecting the position of the Treasury and granting an unambiguous exemption to cooperative hospital service organizations performing certain described functions. Nothing in the 1968 legislation explicitly or implicitly qualified the exemption previously available under § 501.[1]

Section 501(e) does not confer an exemption on cooperative educational or religious service organizations. If such organizations would previously have been exempt under § 501(c)(3), should the 1968 Act be construed to have withdrawn the exemption by reason of the fact that Congress saw fit to confine the benefit of its clarifying amendment to "cooperative hospital service organizations"? I think the

1. [22] In fact, since the Treasury's opposition to tax-exempt status for hospital service organizations was based on § 502, rather than § 501(c)(3), it is more reasonable to construe the enactment of § 501(e) as a congressional attempt to limit § 502, rather than § 501(c)(3). Some of the language of § 501(e) supports this view. For example, § 501(e)(2) provides that a cooperative hospital service organization qualifying for exemption under that subsection must allocate or pay to its members all net earnings within 8 1/2 months after the close of its taxable year. Section 502, which was the congressional response to the series of "destination of income" cases culminating in the famous case involving the New York University School of Law's noodle factory, *C. F. Mueller Co.* v. *Commissioner*, 190 F.2d 120 (C.A.3 1951), was directed precisely at organizations which funneled their net income to tax-exempt institutions. Thus, organizations which might otherwise reasonably be considered feeder organizations are entitled to exemption under § 501(e). However, there is no reason why a cooperative organization that operates on a nonprofit basis and does not funnel earnings back to its members, such as the petitioner in this case, cannot qualify for an income tax exemption under § 501(c)(3). Such an organization, deprived of the shield of § 501(e), should nonetheless be tax exempt if it can avoid challenge as a feeder on its own merits.

The conclusion that § 501(e) was designed as a shield for certain organizations that otherwise would be considered nonexempt feeders is also supported by the fact that the exemption available under § 501(e) is more restrictive than that available under § 501(c)(3). As the District Court in *Chart, Inc. v. United States*, 491 F. Supp. 10 (D.C. 1979), appeal pending, Nos. 80-1138, 80-1139 (CADC), observed, organizations which qualify for tax exemption under § 501(c)(3) are able to operate with a great deal more flexibility than those qualifying under § 501(e). *Id.*, at 13–14. Congress may well have designed § 501(e) to provide a limited form of tax exemption for previously nonexempt feeder organizations.

answer is clear and that the same answer should apply to a hospital cooperative that is not expressly covered by the 1968 Act. Its tax status should be evaluated on the basis of the remaining relevant provisions of the Internal Revenue Code.

I recognize that both in 1968 and in 1976 attempts were made to extend the explicit § 501(e) exemption to encompass hospital laundry cooperatives and that these attempts were rejected. This legislative history proves nothing more than what is already plainly stated in the statute itself: the § 501(e) exemption is not available to petitioner. That is equally true of a cooperative educational service organization. But that fact does not evidence any intent by Congress to withdraw whatever exemption would be available to such organizations under other provisions of the Code.

Nor does logic compel the conclusion that Congress intended to withdraw a pre-existing exemption. As a matter of tax policy, nothing that I have read provides any obvious legitimate basis for giving hospital service organizations more favorable treatment than other charitable service organizations, or for giving a data processing or food service organization better treatment than a laundry service organization. Furthermore, I cannot accept the kind of reasoning — which unfortunately may characterize our summary dispositions — that interprets a statute that was plainly intended to do nothing more than extend a certain benefit to some taxpayers as though it were intended to withdraw a benefit otherwise available to other taxpayers.

Question

On what possible basis does the Service conclude in Treas. Reg. § 1.502-1(b) that an organization that provides goods or services solely to several unrelated exempt organizations is engaged in a commercial activity and therefore not entitled to tax exemption? Would we consider a taxable entity that sold only to a small group of customers at cost to be engaged in a commercial endeavor?

3. Advanced Application: Joint Operating Agreements — A Way to Avoid Unrelated Cooperative Treatment

As a result of Treasury Regulation § 1.502-1(b), the primary hurdle for unrelated charitable organizations that want to consolidate their efforts and thereby increase the amount of benefits to common beneficiaries (i.e., by eliminating duplicative costs) is their technically independent existence. Under the regulation, a single charitable organization can create a subsidiary to handle its payroll, purchasing or other administrative functions (e.g., legal, insurance, billing), and that subsidiary will be exempt under the integral part doctrine provided it serves only the exempt parent. The servicing-subsidiary entity is not functionally independent but is entirely controlled by the parent-recipient. The regulation also grants tax exemption when a consolidation entity serves other organizations that have the same parent as the consolidation entity. What this means is that sister organizations can provide services to one another (or the common parent) without jeopardizing their tax exemptions. Thus, a charitable hospital, for example, can create several subsidiaries, one of which may handle all payroll functions for every other corporate member of the group, another billing, another claims processing, etc.

But the ability to have administrative services performed by a separate legal entity that is also tax exempt under § 501(c)(3) only holds, according to the regulation, when all participants are legally related through stock ownership or, as later rulings indicated, something analogous to stock ownership (common governance and control). As we have seen, the result does not apply when several exempt organizations wish to maintain independence but still wish to consolidate those routine administrative functions, the central accomplishment of which would have no effect on their separate identities. For example, religious or other philosophical differences might prevent two social service organizations from actually merging but may not prevent them from pooling their resources with regard to routine administrative matters not inherently related to their philosophical views. An obvious example might involve one charitable hospital that provides abortion counseling and another that is against abortions, but the differences need not be so dramatic. It may simply involve two organizations that focus their similar efforts on different constituents. But since the hospitals are not technically related, any cooperative or "consolidation" entity they create will not be tax-exempt because of Treas. Reg. § 1.502-1(b).

Instead of challenging the regulation's essential premise (that providing needed goods and services exclusively to two or more unrelated charitable organization is non-charitable), practitioners, with the Service's approval, have engaged in rather complex "virtual mergers" whereby unrelated charitable entities enter into a contractual "joint operating agreement" (JOA). The JOA allows the participants to claim that they are subject to a common source of control (similar to a parent-subsidiary type relationship), while also maintaining a certain degree of independence. Having achieved the parent-subsidiary type relationship with respect to some (but not all) matters, the participants then claim the benefit of the integral part doctrine with respect to their consolidation efforts. For a more detailed discussion of joint operating agreements, see Darryll K. Jones, *Creating Complex Monsters: Joint Operating Agreements and the Logical Invalidity of Treasury Regulation 1.502-1(b)*, 3 FLA. TAX REV. 563 (1997).

Questions

Tax attorneys are often asked or required to provide informed speculation as to how the Service might rule or approach a particular transaction or proposal. If the attorney thinks the Service might rule against the client's interest, she or he may be asked to render an opinion regarding the logic and legal vulnerability of the Service's conclusion (among other things, such as whether the cost of challenging the Service's position is worth incurring, given the organization's goals). The following fact situations are taken from two revenue rulings (although the second is modified). How might the Service rule on those facts? If you think the Service would deny tax exemption, state any logical flaws or vulnerabilities in the Service's likely conclusions that might support a challenge.

1. The organization was incorporated without stock by a church to provide a standardized source of educational and religious material for the church's parochial school system. Its affairs are managed by a board of directors composed of clergymen appointed by the church and responsible to the church for the organization's finances and operations. The organization prints material, which is prepared and edited by the school system. The organization sells the material exclusively to the parochial school system. All profits are returned annually to the school system.

2. The organization is a non-profit corporation formed by several unrelated churches of differing denominations to promote and provide financial support for the charitable programs of its member/owners through the performance of certain printing functions and the production of income for jointly conducted charitable activities. It seeks to accomplish these charitable objectives by printing religious materials solely for its owners. The organization derives a better than modest profit from the provision of such material to its member churches. The publication functions performed for the church account for all of the overall publishing activities of the organization. In accordance with an express requirement in the articles of incorporation, all the net income of the organization is to be used for a little league baseball league organized by the member churches (which activity is part of the churches' religious community outreach efforts).

C. Commercial-Type Insurance: Section 501(m) — An Industry-Specific Codification of the Commerciality Doctrine

1. The General Rule Denying Exemption to Commercial-Type Insurers: 501(m)

Code: § 501(m), 501(n)

Although the commerciality doctrine originated in the courts, Congress seems to approve of the underlying assumption that tax exemption should not provide a basis from which certain organizations may succeed in the for-profit marketplace or preempt for-profit vendors. One example is in the 1986 enactment of § 501(m), which denies tax exemption to an organization that provides "commercial type insurance" as a substantial part of its activities. The provision was motivated by a desire to deny tax exemption to Blue Cross/Blue Shield organizations, but its ramifications extend well beyond such organizations. As we will see in the note following the next two cases, § 501(m) may have gone too far, leading Congress to enact § 501(n), which essentially provides an exception for charities that band together to provide self-insurance in a cooperative noncommercial manner. It might have been better had Congress more carefully drafted § 501(m) — thereby avoiding the need to enact

§ 501(n). In any event, both provisions can be viewed as rather clumsy attempts to codify the commerciality doctrine as it relates to a particular industry. The following case involves the application of § 501(m) as well as a summary of the commerciality concerns that lead to denial of tax exemption in other contexts.

Paratransit Insurance Corporation v. Commissioner

102 T.C. 745 (1994)

RAUM, Judge: The Commissioner determined that petitioner is not an organization described in section 501(c)(3) and that it is not exempt from Federal income tax under section 501(a) for the taxable year 1988 and subsequent years. Petitioner has invoked the jurisdiction of this Court pursuant to section 7428 to obtain a declaratory judgment as to whether it meets the requirements of section 501(c)(3) and therefore qualifies for tax-exempt status under section 501(a). The case was submitted on the basis of a stipulated administrative record.

At the time of filing its petition, petitioner's principal place of business was in Oakland, California. It is a California non-profit mutual benefit insurance corporation, organized in 1988. During the 4-year period from 1983 to 1987, a 239-percent increase in automobile insurance caused serious disruptions and reductions in needed social service transportation provided by California transportation agencies. Because of this automobile insurance crisis, the California Department of Transportation (CALTRANS) applied for and received a technical studies grant from the U.S. Department of Transportation, Urban Mass Transportation Administration, to conduct a study of insurance alternatives for California social service transportation providers. The study report was issued in July 1987; it recommended that CALTRANS and the California Association for Coordinated Transportation assist private social service transportation providers to develop a mechanism for managing and limiting their liability risks and losses.

Pursuant to the recommendation of the study report, a steering committee made up of representatives of various private and public social service transportation providers was created to incorporate petitioner. Petitioner was incorporated on March 16, 1988.

To qualify for membership in petitioner, an organization must be a section 501(c)(3) tax-exempt private social service entity that uses automobiles to furnish transportation for the elderly, the handicapped, the needy, etc., and that uses such vehicles to provide other transportation services such as those familiarly known as "meals on wheels". Such organizations have been referred to as paratransit providers. Petitioner's objectives and purposes were stated in its bylaws as follows:

> The primary objectives and purposes of this Corporation shall be to create and administer a group self-insurance pool pursuant to section 5005.1 of the California Corporations Code. Such pool is formed by private paratransit providers which are tax exempt under section 501(c)(3) of the Internal Revenue Code in order to provide the necessary financing for

comprehensive automobile liability, risk management, and related services for pool members.

In addition to providing funding and payment of member vehicular losses, petitioner also provides members with assistance and education on the control and management of losses arising from the operation of their vehicles.

Promptly after its incorporation on March 16, 1988, petitioner engaged in startup activities, enrolling eligible member organizations. It actually began its first year substantive operation as a nonprofit mutual benefit insurance corporation on July 1, 1988. It thus commenced the insurance business of risk spreading in July 1988 with a membership of 74 unrelated private, tax-exempt paratransit providers. Its membership increased to 142 by January 1991.

Upon becoming a member of the pool, a joining organization enters into a "member agreement" with petitioner committing the organization to the pool for 3 years. Under the terms of the membership agreement, each member pays a one-time $25 per vehicle registration fee, and thereafter pays premiums ("contributes funds") to cover insured losses for each year and to assist in covering the costs of risk management programs, driver safety programs, and other technical assistance provided by petitioner. The amount of a member's premiums ("contributions") is determined actuarially to take into account a number of factors, such as the deductibles selected by the member, the number of vehicles the member operates, the number of passengers carried by each vehicle, and the radius of the member's operations. At the time of petitioner's application for exemption, each member paid an average of $800 a year per vehicle.

Petitioner has provided a series of estimates which suggests that, depending upon a member's locale, the premiums range from 20 to 50 percent less than the premiums charged by regular commercial insurance companies for comparable automobile insurance. At other points in the record, however, petitioner has stated that in a random sampling of its member "contributions" (premiums) they were "30% to 80% below the commercial market"; and that "The estimates for 1991/92, . . . demonstrate a cost to members that range from 60% to 80% below the low estimate of commercial premiums." In comparing the cost of the insurance it provides its members with the cost of insurance from commercial vendors, petitioner increased the cost of insurance from commercial vendors by $5,000 for each member (regardless of the number of vehicles insured by such member) to reflect "an estimate of the cost to each member to individually . . . purchase . . . services" comparable to the risk management/safety services provided by petitioner.

The member agreement provides as follows with respect to the treatment of accumulated surplus contribution funds:

Article VII

Return Premiums:

Any surplus funds accumulated during a fiscal year in excess of the amounts necessary to fulfill all obligations for incurred claims, administrative and other program expenses, may be refunded by the Board as return

> Premiums or as reduced Premiums. For the purposes of determining such return or reduced Premiums the Board shall receive advice from a qualified casualty actuary. The actuary shall calculate the amount of incurred losses, which shall include paid and reserved claims, incurred-but-not-reported claims, loss development, loss trending, and a contingency reserve.
>
> * * *
>
> The self-insurance pool established by petitioner insures the first $100,000 of its members' claims. Coverage for claims in excess of that amount is obtained by purchasing reinsurance on the commercial market.

* * *

In June 1990, petitioner applied for exemption from Federal income tax under section 501(c)(3) by submitting a Form 1023 to the IRS district office for Los Angeles, California. The exemption application was referred to the IRS National Office for a ruling. After an initial adverse ruling, a final ruling by the IRS National Office was issued denying tax-exempt status to petitioner for the following stated reasons:

> You are not operated exclusively for exempt purposes. You are operating for a substantial nonexempt, commercial purpose. Furthermore, because a substantial part of your activities consists of providing commercial-type insurance, you are disqualified from exemption by virtue of section 501(m) of the Code. Finally, because you provide services to unrelated exempt organizations, you are a "feeder" within the meaning of section 502 of the Code.

Petitioner thereafter sought review by this Court. We sustain the Commissioner.

Organizations described in section 501(c)(3) are ordinarily exempt from Federal income tax pursuant to section 501(a). However, under section 501(m), such organizations qualify for exempt status under section 501(a) only if "no substantial part" of their activities consists of providing "commercial-type insurance." Sec. 501(m)(1). Section 501(m) reads in pertinent part as follows:

> SEC. 501(m). Certain Organizations Providing Commercial-Type Insurance Not Exempt From Tax.—
>
> (1) Denial of tax exemption where providing commercial-type insurance is substantial part of activities.—An organization described in paragraph (3) or (4) of subsection (c) shall be exempt from tax under subsection (a) only if no substantial part of its activities consists of providing commercial-type insurance.
>
> * * *
>
> (3) Commercial-type insurance.—For purposes of this subsection, the term "commercial-type insurance" shall not include—
>
> (A) insurance provided at substantially below cost to a class of charitable recipients,

Section 501(m), as currently written, was added to the Code by section 1012(a) of the Tax Reform Act of 1986, Pub. L. 99-514, 100 Stat. 2085, 2390–2391. The House Ways and Means Committee report strongly indicates that Congress intended a broad definition of the term "commercial-type insurance" when it added the current version of section 501(m). See H. Rept. 99-426, at 662–665 (1985), 1986-3 C.B. (Vol. 2) 1, 662–665. Pertinent portions of the House report read as follows:

> 2. Taxation of Tax-Exempt Organizations Engaged in Insurance Activities (sec. 1012 of the bill and sec. 501(m) of the Code)
>
> **Present Law**
>
> * * *
>
> The providing of insurance benefits by an organization otherwise described in sec. 501(c)(3) generally is considered a commercial activity that does not meet the requirements for tax-exempt status. For example, *if two or more unrelated tax-exempt organizations pool funds for the purpose of accumulating and holding funds to be used to satisfy malpractice claims against the organizations, the organization holding the pooled funds is not entitled to tax exemption because the activity (i.e., the provision of insurance) is inherently commercial in nature.*
>
> * * *
>
> **Reasons for Change**
>
> The committee is concerned that exempt charitable and social welfare organizations that engage in insurance activities are engaged in an activity whose nature and scope is so inherently commercial that tax exempt status is inappropriate. The committee believes that *the tax-exempt status of organizations engaged in insurance activities provides an unfair competitive advantage to these organizations.* The committee further believes that the provision of insurance to the general public at a price sufficient to cover the costs of insurance generally constitutes an activity that is commercial.
>
> * * *
>
> **Explanation of Provision**
>
> Under the bill, an organization described in sections 501(c)(3) and (4) of the Code is exempt from tax only if no substantial part of its activities consists of providing commercial-type insurance. For this purpose, no substantial part has the meaning given to it under present law applicable to such organizations. *See, e.g., Haswell v.* U.S., 500 F.2d 1133 (Ct. Cl. 1974); *Seasongood v. Comm'r*, 227 F.2d 907 (6th Cir. 1955) . . . .
>
> * * *
>
> **[C]ommercial-type insurance generally is any insurance of a type provided by commercial insurance companies. . . .**

Several aspects of the House report deserve comment. First, in the portion entitled "Present Law", the House report provides an example which describes petitioner's situation almost perfectly: two or more unrelated tax-exempt organizations pooling funds in a separate entity "to be used to satisfy malpractice claims against the organizations". And in that example, the House report unequivocally states that "the organization holding the pooled funds is not entitled to tax exemption because the activity (i.e., the provision of insurance) is inherently commercial in nature." Significantly, the House report refers generically to "insurance", and its reference to malpractice insurance was introduced by the phrase "For example". Certainly, there is no basis whatsoever to conclude that automobile liability insurance would not be regarded the same as malpractice insurance in this context.

In the portion entitled "Reasons for Change", the House report again refers in general terms to "insurance" activity, which it describes as "an activity whose nature and scope is so inherently commercial that tax exempt status is inappropriate." H. Rept. 99-426, *supra* at 664, 1986-3 C.B. (Vol. 2) at 664. Also, the portion of the House report captioned "Explanation of Provision" states that "commercial-type insurance generally is *any* insurance of a type provided by commercial insurance companies." H. Rept. 99-426, *supra* at 665, 1986-3 C.B. (Vol. 2) at 665 (emphasis added). It is clear from the passages in the report of the House Ways and Means Committee that the term "commercial-type insurance", as used in section 501(m), encompasses every type of insurance that can be purchased in the commercial market.

Every relevant aspect of the administrative record indicates that petitioner provides "commercial-type insurance" within the meaning of section 501(m). First, the purpose of the insurance pool established by petitioner is to shift the risk of potential tort liability from each of the individual insured paratransit organizations to petitioner. Through its receipt of premiums from multiple member organizations, petitioner diversifies the risk of liability for each individual member. The fact that petitioner in addition peripherally provides education and other forms of assistance to help member organizations control and manage losses does not alter the fact it fundamentally provides a means for spreading their individual risks of tort liability. Furthermore, the *type* of insurance petitioner offers to its members is basic automobile liability insurance, a type of insurance provided by a number of commercial insurance carriers.

Finally, the *manner* in which petitioner insures its members clearly bespeaks a commercial nature. Petitioner does not offer insurance to members based on need, or even at a uniform charge. Instead it determines member contributions by reference to factors affecting the level of risk insured by petitioner, e.g., total number of vehicles, number of passengers per vehicle, radius of operation, etc. In short, petitioner calculates member premiums actuarially in precisely the same way that commercial insurers determine premiums for their customers. The commercial hue of such insurance fee arrangements has been noted by courts in cases decided under "pre-section 501(m)" law. . . . Moreover, it should also be noted that petitioner directly insures members only up to a $100,000 level of coverage. Coverage above

$100,000 is effected through reinsurance obtained by petitioner in the commercial market.

Petitioner on brief argues that Congress, by using the phrase "commercial-type insurance" in section 501(m), intended to cover only those situations where insurance is offered to the general public. Petitioner relies on the following sentence in the House report:

> The committee further believes that the provision of insurance to the general public at a price sufficient to cover the costs of insurance generally constitutes an activity that is commercial.

[H. Rept. 99-426, *supra* at 664, 1986-3 C.B. (Vol. 2) at 664.]

This reference to the "general public" was deleted from the report of the Staff of the Joint Committee on Taxation in its General Explanation of the Tax Reform Act of 1986, at 504 (J. Comm. Print 1987). Furthermore, it must be remembered that section 501(m) was enacted to restrict rather than enlarge the categories of organizations that qualify for tax-exempt status under section 501(c)(3). And it is obvious from the example cited in the "Present Law" section of the House report that insurance pool arrangements — including those, which like petitioner, involve unrelated, tax-exempt organizations — were viewed as taxable activities even prior to enactment of section 501(m). The fact that the insurance provided by such pools was not available to the general public did not prevent them from having taxable status.

Moreover, if Congress had intended the phrase "commercial-type insurance" in section 501(m)(1) to apply only to insurance available to the general public, then it would not have needed to enact the exceptions in section 501(m)(3)(C) and (D) to the definition of commercial-type insurance. Both section 501(m)(3)(C) ("property or casualty insurance provided . . . by a church or convention . . . for such church or convention") and section 501(m)(3)(D) ("retirement or welfare benefits . . . [provided by] a church or a convention . . . for the employees . . . of such church or convention") describe insurance arrangements to which members of the general public clearly would not have access. Viewed against this backdrop of statutory provisions and legislative history, petitioner's argument is simply unpersuasive. Petitioner clearly provides "commercial-type insurance" as defined in section 501(m).

Even if, as we have concluded above, petitioner does provide "commercial-type insurance" within the meaning of section 501(m)(1), it is not disqualified from tax exemption under section 501(a) by reason of section 501(m) if the proscribed activity, i.e., provision of commercial-type insurance, is not a "substantial part" of petitioner's overall activities. Sec. 501(m)(1). The House report states that the phrase "no substantial part", for purposes of section 501(m), "has the meaning given to it under present law applicable to such organizations." . . . The cases referred to in the House report defined substantiality in regard to an organization's legislative or political activities. However, as the House report makes clear, Congress obviously intended to rely on that existing body of law in defining the term "substantial" for purposes of the proscription in section 501(m)(1) on insurance activities. In *Seasongood v. Commissioner*, 227 F.2d 907, 912 (6th Cir. 1955), revg. 22 T.C. 671 (1954), the Court of Appeals concluded that where "less than 5% of the time and effort of . . . [an organization] was devoted to . . . activities . . . found to be 'political'", such political activities "were not in relation to all of its other activities *substantial*, within the meaning of the section." In *Haswell v. United States*, 500 F.2d 1133, 205 Ct. Cl. 421, 443–444 (1974), the Court of Claims held that where an organization applied approximately 16 to 20 percent of its total expenditures toward political activities during the years 1967 and 1968, its political activities were "more than [an] insubstantial" part of its overall activities, and therefore the organization did not qualify for tax exemption under section 501(c)(3).

We recognize that neither *Seasongood* nor *Haswell* purported to fix an automatic percentage for substantiality. Nevertheless, even the most cursory examination of petitioner's operations reveals that its insurance-related expenditures far exceed the percentages involved in *Seasongood* and *Haswell*. For example, on the basis of the figures provided in petitioner's letter dated July 19, 1991, petitioner's "Total Claims Expenses" during the calendar years 1988, 1989, and 1990 were 40.11 percent, 67.74 percent, and 74.64 percent, respectively, of its total expenditures during each of those years. Petitioner's insurance activities are unquestionably a substantial part of its operations within the meaning of section 501(m).

Petitioner nonetheless contends that it should not be denied tax exemption by reason of section 501(m), because it falls within the exception in section 501(m)(3)(A) applicable to "insurance provided at substantially below cost to a class of charitable recipients". Petitioner's contention is without merit.

Passing the question whether petitioner's tax-exempt members are the "class of charitable recipients" contemplated by the statute, it is clear that petitioner has in any event failed to insure them at "substantially below cost", within the meaning of section 501(m)(3)(A). In an attempt to clarify the meaning of this phrase, the House report states "*See, e.g.*, Rev. Rul. 71-529, 1971-2 C.B. 234 (relating to the meaning of substantially below cost)." H. Rept. 99-426, *supra* at 665, 1986-3 C.B. (Vol. 2) at 665. Rev. Rul. 71-529, 1971-2 C.B. 234, involved an organization formed to aid tax-exempt educational institutions "by assisting them to manage more effectively their endowment or investment funds". In the ruling, it was stated that

> Most of the operating expenses of the organization, including the costs of the services of the investment counselors and the custodian banks, are paid for by grants from independent charitable organizations. The member organizations pay only a nominal fee for the services performed. These fees represent less than fifteen percent of the total costs of operation. [*Id.*] The ruling concluded that, by performing such functions for the tax-exempt

> institutions at "a charge that is substantially below cost," the organization was "performing a charitable activity within the meaning of section 501(c)(3) of the Code." *Id.*

Applying this standard to petitioner's operations, as described in its July 19, 1991, letter to the IRS, it is clear that petitioner comes nowhere near the mark. Revenues from member contributions, i.e., the sum of the amounts designated as "application fees" and "premiums-pooled layer", totaled $28,065, $930,327, and $1,212,757, respectively, for the years 1988, 1989, and 1990. Petitioner's total expenditures, including in-kind expenses (i.e., donated services), totaled $542,918, $1,164,381, and $1,444,429, respectively, during each of those years. Thus, even if we accept petitioner's questionable inclusion of its so-called in-kind expenses in its total expenditures, its revenues from member contributions as a percentage of total expenditures are 60.43 percent, 79.90 percent, and 83.96 percent for the years 1988, 1989, and 1990, respectively. If in-kind expenses are subtracted, then member contributions approach 100 percent of petitioner's total expenditures during each of those years.

Petitioner also contends that "in determining *substantially below costs* the test should be applied against its administrative operating costs only" rather than its total expenditures, "including . . . [costs relating to] members' pool claim payments or reserve accounts." (Pet. Opening Brief at 11.) However, nothing in the legislative history or elsewhere supports such a notion. Indeed, the ruling cited in the House report, Rev. Rul. 71-529, 1971-2 C.B. 234, in describing the percentage of organizational costs attributable to member fees, specifically refers to "the *total* costs of [the organization's] operation." (Emphasis added.) Moreover, petitioner's contention flies in the face of common sense. It would require that, in determining whether insurance was provided at a price substantially below cost, we exclude from the calculation the very costs that relate to the insurance itself.

Petitioner further argues that in determining what is substantially below cost, we should look to the percentages referred to in *Haswell v. United States, supra*, and other cases. But *Haswell* and the other cases have no relevance in this connection. The House report is quite clear on this point. *Haswell* is relevant only in determining the substantiality of an organization's commercial type insurance activities vis-a-vis its other activities. It is not the standard to be used in determining whether such insurance has been provided at substantially below cost. Petitioner does not qualify for the exception in section 501(m)(3)(A) for insurance provided at substantially below cost to a charitable class of recipients.

In view of the conclusion that we have reached in respect of section 501(m), we need not consider the Government's alternative positions that petitioner is disqualified for exemption either because it does not otherwise qualify as a section 501(c)(3) organization or because it is a feeder organization within the meaning of section 502.

Decision will be entered for respondent.

2. Group Self-Insurers

Nonprofits' Insurance Alliance of California v. United States

32 Fed. Cl. 277 (1994)

This case is before the court after argument on plaintiff's action for a declaratory judgment pursuant to 26 U.S.C. 7428(a) (Supp. V 1993). The central question presented is whether plaintiff, an organization formed to administer a group self-insurance risk pool, qualifies for tax-exempt status under section 501(a) of the Internal Revenue Code of 1954, 26 U.S.C. § 501(a) (1988) (the "I.R.C."). Section 501(a) indicates that organizations described in I.R.C. § 501(c)(3) shall be exempt from taxation. First to be decided is whether plaintiff's organization constitutes an "exempt organization" as that term is defined in I.R.C. § 501(c)(3). Assuming that plaintiff's organization satisfies this definition, the issue becomes whether plaintiff is precluded from qualifying as tax-exempt by operation of I.R.C. § 501(m)(1), which disallows exemption for the provision of commercial-type insurance, or whether plaintiff's exempt status is preserved under I.R.C. § 501(m)(3)(A) because it provides insurance "at substantially below cost."

Facts

On September 15, 1988, the Nonprofits' Insurance Alliance of California ("plaintiff"), a group self-insurance risk pool with a membership consisting entirely of nonprofit organizations, was incorporated under the California Corporations Code (the "California Code") as a "mutual benefit corporation." Section 5005.1 of the California Code, enacted in response to concerns of California nonprofit organizations regarding the price and availability of commercial insurance, authorizes the existence of such group self-insurance pools. According to the terms of section 5005.1, plaintiff's insurance pooling arrangement neither qualifies as insurance, nor is subject to regulation under the California Insurance Code. In addition, plaintiff qualifies as a tax exempt charitable organization for purposes of California state income and franchise tax law.

... On August 7, 1991 ... plaintiff submitted an application, dated June 20, 1991, for recognition of exempt status under I.R.C. § 501(c)(3) as an insurer operated exclusively for exempt purposes ... [T]he IRS issued a final decision denying plaintiff's exemption application on February 24, 1993. The grounds cited to support the denial included:

> You are not operated exclusively for exempt purposes. You are operating for a substantial nonexempt, commercial purpose. Furthermore, because a substantial part of your activities consists of providing commercial-type insurance you are disqualified from exemption by virtue of section 501(m) of the Code. Finally, because you provide services to unrelated exempt organizations, you are a "feeder" within the meaning of section 502 of the Code.

On May 24, 1993, plaintiff filed suit in the United States Court of Federal Claims seeking a declaration pursuant to I.R.C. §7428(a) that it qualifies as an exempt corporation under section 501(c)(3). Disposition of this action hinges on the following factual allegations set forth in the administrative record concerning the nature of plaintiffs corporation.

In support of its application for exempt status under I.R.C. §501(c)(3), dated June 20, 1991, plaintiff described itself as an organization formed "to provide reasonably priced liability coverages to its [nonprofit] members at stable prices not available from commercial insurers." Plaintiff's formation took place in response to the results of a study conducted by the Liability Insurance Task Force, a group sponsored by the California Association of Nonprofits. The Task Force reported that California nonprofit organizations had encountered difficulties obtaining affordable insurance and had endured periods of large price increases, coverage reductions, and cancellations. Nonprofit organizations particularly are affected by price increases because their rigid budget structure and funding schedule disables them from swiftly adapting to market changes.

According to the Task Force study, the existence of an insurance risk-pool enables member organizations to pool their risks and resources so as to secure insurance at regular prices on a continual basis. Plaintiff maintains that by providing insurance at stable prices, it "directly advances the charitable purposes of nonprofit organizations because it substantially impacts the services that those organizations ... [can] provide." As plaintiff notes:

> While there was no concern regarding periods of a "soft" market (i.e., a market in which insurance coverage was readily available to nonprofit organizations at a reasonable cost), the advent of a "hard" market (i.e., a market in which insurance coverage was either unavailable to nonprofits entirely, or was available only at highly inflated costs) could and would make it much more difficult, or even impossible, for nonprofit corporations to continue their charitable missions ...

Id. at 3–4.

Plaintiff provides four basic activities to its member organizations, which include "providing liability insurance," developing educational materials and making educational presentations, providing loss control and risk management services free of charge, and serving as a resource for insurance-related questions by operating a toll-free telephone line. As plaintiff admitted in its section 501(c)(3) application, "commercial insurers provide similar coverages, but at wildly fluctuating prices...." Nonetheless, plaintiff maintains that its corporation differs from other commercial insurance companies in that plaintiff provides insurance at substantially below cost to its members and further provides loss control and risk management services free of charge. Plaintiff also argues that it differs from a commercial insurance company because it shares claims and loss data with the community in an attempt to encourage commercial companies to adjust their rates favorably toward nonprofit organizations.

Plaintiff's membership consists entirely of nonprofit organizations that both qualify as tax-exempt organizations under I.R.C. § 501(c)(3) and operate to fund or provide health or human services. The materials submitted by plaintiff in support of its exemption application indicate a membership of approximately 487 unrelated nonprofits. . . .

An organization seeking membership in plaintiff's organization must complete a membership application to be approved by the Board of Directors. Membership remains contingent on whether the nonprofit organization makes timely payment of both its premium payments and one-time "contribution" or membership fee. Failure to make the requisite payments results in termination of all membership benefits. The one-time non-refundable membership fee serves as a contribution to the operating surplus of the corporation and is approximately 10 percent of the member's commercial general liability premium. Once the payments are made, each member becomes an owner of the corporation. The benefits of ownership include the guarantee that any profits received by plaintiff will inure only to the benefit of the owners in the form of reduced future insurance premiums.

In terms of insurance coverage, plaintiff provides commercial general liability, automobile liability, employer's non-owned and hired automobile liability, and miscellaneous professional liability. Plaintiff determines the amount of a member's premium payment based on a variety of criteria set forth in the membership application form. Such factors include, but are not limited to, potential hazards, the type of services provided by the organization, the existence of a safety program, and past claims history. Annual member premiums ranged from $69.00 to $92,328.00 in 1990, and typical liability limits were an annual aggregate of between $1 and $2 million.

To complement the in-house underwriting, plaintiff contracts with other companies to provide reinsurance for any risks in excess of $50,000.00. Several of these companies require plaintiff to maintain a two-to-one ratio of net premiums to surplus. Plaintiff contends that the standard insurance industry financial guidelines also recommend that insurers maintain a similar ratio of premiums to surplus.

Plaintiff achieved the requisite surplus level, after receiving $1.3 million in loans from six foundations, including the Ford Foundation. Each foundation entered into a separate loan agreement with plaintiff concerning the terms and conditions of the loan. The Ford Foundation loan, which is representative of all the loan agreements, 1) was evidenced by a promissory note; 2) characterized the creditor as unsecured; 3) specified a 2 percent rate of interest; 4) included certain financial reporting requirements; 5) specified terms of default; and 6) indicated a repayment schedule. The loan agreement, dated September 18, 1989, further stated that plaintiff must make payments on principal and interest from earned surplus and that such payments shall be made only when an Actuary "certif[ies] that [the] Borrower had Earned Surplus as of the . . . [relevant payment date] in an amount which equaled or exceeded the amount of . . . [the] payment." The agreement also indicated that in cases wherein the interest or principal payments exceed earned surplus, the borrower shall pay to the lender the amount of earned surplus accrued as of the specified payment date. Finally, the loan agreement stipulated in section 3.3 that "the Loan Agreement and the Note (the 'Loan Documents') will constitute the legal, valid and binding obligations of the borrower. . . ."

Plaintiff and defendant dispute the proper characterization of the foundation loans. Plaintiff emphasizes the charitable nature of the loans, claiming that the loans constitute a subsidy or "contribution[]" rather than "true debt." Plaintiff also notes that the IRS characterized these loans as "program-related investments" for purposes of the tax consequences to the respective foundations. Plaintiff argues that "implicit in . . . [this] ruling is . . . [the IRS'] classification of the 'loans' as grants for purposes of IRC § 4945(h) and 4945(d)(4) (sic) . . . ." (citation omitted). In contrast, defendant emphasizes the strict terms of the loan agreements and argues that the financial arrangements between plaintiff and the foundations can be interpreted in no way other than as loan agreements.

Plaintiff also received grants from twelve foundations in the amount of $330,100.00 to cover plaintiff's initial operating costs. Other entities donated $31,055.00 in equipment and $60,536.00 toward risk management programs.

Discussion

* * *

2. Tax-exempt status under I.R.C. § 501(c)(3)

* * *

Accordingly, based on the administrative record, the court finds that plaintiff has not sustained its burden of proof and that the IRS properly determined that plaintiff failed the operational test under I.R.C. § 501(c)(3) because of the existence of a substantial nonexempt, commercial purpose.

3. Organizations providing commercial-type insurance as that term is defined in I.R.C. § 501(m)(3)(A)

Even assuming that plaintiff qualifies as an organization described in I.R.C. § 501(c)(3), plaintiff, serving as a group self-insurance risk pool, must demonstrate that I.R.C. § 501(m)(1) does not preclude its exempt status. Section 501(m)(1) specifically provides that an organization described in section 501(c)(3) is exempt under I.R.C. § 501(a) "only if no substantial part of its activities consists of providing commercial-type insurance." Section 501(m)(3)(A) stipulates that for purposes of section 501(m), the term "commercial-type insurance" shall not include "insurance provided at substantially below cost to a class of charitable recipients." This provision forms the basis of the parties' dispute on point. Specifically, plaintiff and defendant disagree as to what qualifies as "substantially below cost" and what amounts are to be employed in calculating whether plaintiff meets the "substantially below cost" threshold.

Both parties acknowledge the lack of authority concerning the meaning of the phrase "substantially below cost." Although the statute does not define the term, both the House Ways and Means and Joint Committee on Taxation Reports addressing section 501(m) refer to Rev. Rul. 71-529, 1971-2 C.B. 234, as "relating to the meaning of substantially below cost." . . . Rev. Rul. 71-529 stipulates that where a taxpayer provides a subsidy of 85 percent, i.e., members pay 15 percent of an organization's total costs, the taxpayer qualifies as tax-exempt under I.R.C. § 501(c)(3).

Plaintiff argues that the citation to Rev. Rul. 71-529 should not control the court's disposition of the "substantially below cost" analysis, because the Revenue Ruling is cited only as an example of what constitutes the provision of services at "substantially below cost." . . . Plaintiff further notes that the IRS acknowledged that the standard set forth in Rev. Rul. 71-529 should not be adopted as a bright-line rule for determining what qualifies as substantially below cost. See G.C.M. 37,257 (Sept. 15, 1977). Plaintiff relies heavily on the IRS' statement in a footnote to G.C.M. 37,257 that "although we are not prepared to suggest another percentage, we think that something significantly in excess of 15 percent [of costs] would be acceptable."

In contending that plaintiff does not satisfy the "substantially below cost" standard, defendant relies principally on the recent Tax Court decision in *Paratransit* and Rev. Rul. 71-529. Rather than seeking adoption of the 85-percent subsidy, defendant asks the court to examine *Paratransit* and look to the Revenue Ruling for guidance as to what constitutes "substantially below cost."

The Tax Court in *Paratransit* addressed the issue of whether an organization which provided automobile insurance to a group of exempt organizations under section 501(c)(3) qualified under the section 501(m)(3)(A) exception to the definition of "commercial-type insurance." The corporation in *Paratransit*, like plaintiff, was organized under section 5005.1 of the California Corporations Code as a group self-insurance pool. The characteristics of the organization mimic many of the features of plaintiff's organization. For example, the organization offered automobile insurance, determined member contributions according to the level of risk, and provided reinsurance for certain claims.

In analyzing whether the taxpayer in *Paratransit* satisfied the "substantially below cost" threshold, the court relied heavily upon Rev. Rul. 71-529 given that the ruling constituted the only guidance provided by Congress for interpreting section 501(m)(3)(A). The ruling involved an organization formed to aid entities exempt under I.R.C. § 501(c)(3) to manage their investment funds in an effective and efficient manner. Each member contributed capital for investment and such funds were invested according to the advice of an independent investment officer. The IRS found that the organization provided investment services at "substantially below cost" because the member organizations paid "*only a nominal fee*." Rev. Rul. 71-529 (emphasis added). The fees assessed the member organizations constituted "less than fifteen percent of the total costs of operation," *i.e.*, an 85 percent subsidy, and the majority of the operating expenses were paid from grants by charitable organizations. *Id.*

Employing this standard, the Tax Court held that an arrangement whereby an organization's members, for the taxable years 1988–90, contributed 60.43, 79.90, and

83.96 percent, respectively, of the total costs of providing insurance "comes nowhere near the mark" for purposes of qualifying under I.R.C. § 501(m)(3)(A).... The court derived these numbers by comparing the total amount of member revenues with petitioner's total costs or expenditures. Both plaintiff and defendant agree with this general methodology. The parties, however, disagree as to the components of "total costs."

Plaintiff argues that "only those items of operational income and expense not attributable to the risk pool itself" should be considered in the calculation of total cost. Under this theory plaintiff maintains that it provides a 57-percent subsidy, thereby requiring members to pay only 43 percent of operational costs. The taxpayer in *Paratransit* made an identical argument, stating that in determining "substantially below cost," the court should examine only its "administrative operating costs," as opposed to its total expenditures, which included costs related to claim payments and reserve accounts. Slip op. at 21. The Tax Court's conclusion that such a proposition of considering only operational expenses "flies in the face of common sense," *id.*, is persuasive. In discussing costs, Rev. Rul. 71-529 specifically states that the fees charged member organizations represent "less than fifteen percent of the total costs of operation." This court cannot define plaintiff's total costs of operation to exclude the costs related to the provision of insurance, especially when plaintiff's raison d'etre is to provide insurance to nonprofit organizations. The 57-percent subsidy figure advanced by plaintiff is rejected given it does not properly reflect total costs.

Even accounting for the costs associated with the provision of insurance, plaintiff maintains that it still provides insurance substantially below cost. Specifically, plaintiff asserts that from 1988–92, it provided "an aggregate charitable subsidy of approximately 35 percent" to its member organizations, thereby requiring members to pay only 65 percent of the total costs of plaintiff's operations. According to plaintiff, such a subsidy satisfies the intendment of the section 501(m)(3)(A) exception. The Tax Court held that a 35-percent subsidy does not fall within the realm of the exception. Providing insurance to members at approximately a 40-percent subsidy, where members pay 60 percent of costs "comes nowhere near the mark."... Thus, even including the disputed foundation loans in total costs and examining the costs on an aggregate basis as plaintiff suggests, plaintiff's numbers do not suffice.

This result is consistent with Rev. Rul. 71-529, which discussed the "substantially below cost" standard in evaluating whether an organization qualified as exempt under I.R.C. § 501(c)(3). The ruling illustrates that prior to the existence of I.R.C. § 501(m), incorporated into the Tax Code as a result of the 1986 Tax Amendments, the IRS performed an identical cost/below cost analysis in determining whether an organization qualified as exempt under section 501(c)(3). Arguably, the policy and analysis governing exemptions granted under I.R.C. § 501(c)(3) bear on the section 501(m)(3)(A) analysis.

In examining the "cost/below cost" analysis, the IRS in G.C.M. 38,877 (July 16, 1982), noted that the "provision of goods and services to other organizations described in section 501(c)(3) may be considered an activity similar to those carried on *by a grant-making charity*. . . . [Such] activity will be considered to be conducted in a charitable manner only if the price charged is *substantially below cost*." G.C.M. 38,877 (emphasis added; citation omitted). The IRS further defined "substantially below cost" by stating "that the activities of the organization are clearly distinguishable from those of its commercial counterparts *by manifestation of donative intent*." *Id.* (emphasis added); see Rev. Rul. 71-529 (emphasizing that member organizations paid only a "*nominal fee*" and that "*most* of the operating expenses" were paid by grants from charitable entities) (emphasis added). Providing members a 35-percent subsidy in obtaining insurance benefits, thereby requiring them to pay 65 percent of the costs of plaintiff's operation, does not qualify under the rubric of "donative intent."

Finally, the result in *Paratransit* is supported by legislative history. In enacting I.R.C. § 501(m), Congress particularly was concerned that non-profit organizations would take advantage of their tax-exempt status to compete unfairly with commercial, for-profit insurance companies. The Joint Committee on Taxation Report summarizes these concerns, as follows:

> Congress was concerned that exempt charitable and social welfare organizations that engage in insurance activities are engaged in an activity whose nature and scope is inherently commercial rather than charitable; hence, tax-exempt status is inappropriate. Congress believed that the tax-exempt status of organizations engaged in insurance activities provided an unfair competitive advantage to these organizations. . . .

General Explanation of the Tax Reform Act of 1986 at 584. This report indicates that Congress enacted section 501(m) to restrict, not enlarge, the scope of organizations that qualify for tax-exempt status under section 501(c)(3). . . . The record reflects that plaintiff directly competes with commercial firms during the soft period of the insurance cycle, a period which has existed since plaintiff's inception. Providing exempt status to organizations such as plaintiff or the taxpayer in *Paratransit* would contravene congressional intent. The Tax Court in *Florida Hospital* so acknowledged, noting that Congress specifically sought to deny exempt status to group self-insurance pools to ensure that such inherently commercial "organizations would not enjoy an unfair competitive advantage. . . ." Although this court is not prepared to draw a bright line demarcating what constitutes "substantially below cost," plaintiff has not sustained its burden in that the aggregate 35 percent subsidy from 1988–92 does not fall within the boundaries of the section 501(m)(3)(A) exception.

Plaintiff attempts to distinguish *Paratransit* by arguing that the Tax Court's decision hinged on the fact that "in-kind expenses" comprised a significant portion of the taxpayer's charitable subsidy, whereas its charitable subsidy consists "exclusively of 'hard' dollar costs." The fact the Tax Court included the value of in-kind services in determining the taxpayer's overall costs benefits plaintiff, because such a computation resulted in higher subsidy estimates for the taxpayer in *Paratransit*. In the alternative, plaintiff distinguishes the case based on the substantial amount of the foundation loans, which provided plaintiff the ability to significantly subsidize its operations. Plaintiff argues that without the loans, it would have been required to ask for an additional $1.3 million from its members. The court acknowledges that the foundation loans enabled plaintiff to obtain the required reserves set forth by the insurance industry. In using plaintiff's figures, the court has considered these loans. Moreover, the existence of the loans standing alone does not warrant a finding that plaintiff provided its services substantially below cost, because, as the parties agree, the proper analysis under I.R.C. § 501(m)(3)(A) requires an examination of total revenues as compared with total costs. Finally, plaintiff urges the court not to follow this Tax Court precedent.

Even examining plaintiff's annual, as opposed to aggregate, figures for the tax period at issue, plaintiff's numbers miss the mark under the standard adopted by the authorities discussed above. Using plaintiff's figures, defendant derived annual percentage subsidies for 1990 through 1992, whereby plaintiff provided a subsidy of 53, 35, and 22 percent, respectively, from 1990 through 1992, i.e., members contributed 47, 65, and 78 percent of costs, respectively. Although plaintiff commenced operations in November 1989, the subsidy for that year based on only two months of data is not properly reflective of plaintiff's overall costs and therefore is not considered.

Plaintiff's members have contributed as much as 78 percent of the total costs of operation most recently in 1992 and as little as 47 percent in 1990. Contributing 47 percent of costs, however, does not satisfy the policy underlying the "substantially below cost" analysis. Such a figure is neither a "nominal fee," Rev. Rul. 71-529, nor does it manifest donative intent. G.C.M. 38,877; see *Paratransit*, slip op. at 20 (holding that where member organizations bear approximately 60 percent of the costs of operation, such figure "comes nowhere near the mark"). At argument plaintiff asserted that the "nominal fee" language in Rev. Rul. 71-529 should not control the disposition of the case. Although the court does not interpret the provision of services at "substantially below cost" to mean that members contribute only a "nominal" amount, the court does find that the fees paid by members of organizations such as plaintiff's should, at a minimum, be "insubstantial." Plaintiff's fees do not meet this threshold.

Even employing plaintiff's figures, which included the disputed foundation loans, plaintiff does not fall within the intendment of section 501(m)(3)(A) and therefore cannot qualify as exempt under I.R.C.§ 501(a). As defendant properly notes, "wherever the dividing line [exists] between [providing insurance] 'substantially below cost' and not [providing insurance] 'substantially below cost,' . . . the minimal subsidies involved in this case fall squarely and easily on the wrong side of . . . [the] line. . . ." In light of this conclusion, the court need not consider the IRS' determination that plaintiff qualifies as a feeder organization within the meaning of I.R.C. § 502.

Conclusion

Accordingly, based on the foregoing, the service properly determined that plaintiff does not qualify for tax-exempt status under § 501(c)(3). The Clerk of the Court shall enter judgment dismissing the complaint.

Note on Charitable Risk Pools and 501(n)

In 1996, Congress enacted § 501(n) as an exception to § 501(m). In general, § 501(n) provides tax exemption for organizations such as that described in *Paratransit*. Thus, an insurance cooperative composed solely of exempt organizations may achieve tax exemption. The cooperative risk pool must receive at least $1 million in start-up capital from other charitable organizations that are not members of the risk pool. There are other organizational requirements. Significantly, though, the risk pool can provide insurance for all risks except those related to medical malpractice. Thus, charitable hospitals that band together to provide self-insurance against medical malpractice claims will likely still not qualify under § 501(c)(3). *See Florida Hospital Trust Fund v. Comm'r*, 103 T.C. 140 (1994).

Questions

1. What does Congress' enactment of § 501(n) — providing tax exemption for an insurance company wholly owned by its charitable clients — implicitly say about the Service's conclusion in Treas. Reg. § 1.502-1(b) that an organization that provides goods or services solely to unrelated charitable organizations is engaged in a commercial activity?

2. Does the definition of "substantially below cost" as used in § 501(m) mean that an organization seeking to prove its non-commerciality cannot do so unless it provides goods or services free or almost free? How should this rule affect the commerciality question in other contexts?

3. Suppose a group of organizations in other cities through a single state conduct spring festivals every year. The festivals include animal rides, mechanical rides, etc. The organizations cannot afford to buy insurance to cover the tort liabilities inherent in the festivals. If they want to create a self-insurance pool to cover those liabilities, how should they structure it? What should be the terms and conditions for each member? Prepare an outline of the governing document.

3. Health Maintenance Organizations as "Insurers" for § 501(m) Purposes

The two previous cases concern the applicability of § 501(m) to arrangements that all parties agree constitute insurance. The issue was whether the insurance was of a commercial type. In other instances, primarily those involving health maintenance organizations, there is a threshold question of whether an organization is providing insurance, never mind whether the insurance is of a commercial type. The issue, insofar as it relates to HMOs, remains unresolved, with the Service taking a broad view as demonstrated in the following Technical Advice Memorandum. Although the courts have had a few occasions to consider § 501(m) as it relates to HMOs, they have managed to avoid a definitive ruling to date. Thus, the Service's position remains as a possible and viable interpretation.

Technical Advice Memorandum 200033046

Apr. 27, 2000

1. Whether the provision of services under Plan B where the medical providers are compensated on either a discounted fee-for-service basis with no withholds or under a point of service arrangement is commercial-type insurance as described in section 501(m)(3) of the Code.

2. Whether the provision of services under Plan B is an insubstantial part of X's activities and would be subject to unrelated business income tax.

3. Whether the unrelated business income tax would be calculated under subchapter L rather than section 511.

Facts:

[2] X is a licensed IPA model HMO recognized as an organization described in section 501(c)(4). X arranges for comprehensive preventive and therapeutic health care services, on a prepaid basis, to subscribing individuals and groups.

[3] X arranges for the delivery of health care services to its subscribers through agreements with independent health care providers who form a network of contracted providers working in private offices and with hospitals within designated service areas.

[4] X offers its subscribers a choice of two medical plans when choosing their medical benefits. The A plan provides that subscribers utilize only an in-network primary care physician or physicians authorized by an in-network primary care physician. Subscribers are only responsible for a preset co-payment for each physician office visit. No claim forms are submitted. If an emergency situation arises, care may be provided by an out-of-network physician without authorization from the subscriber's in-network primary care physician. The B plan contains a point of service (POS) option and is administered by Y, a taxable affiliate of X. Under Plan B, subscribers can utilize any physician, either in network or out-of-network. The POS option can also be used in emergency situations where the member is out of the service area. However, the subscriber is subject to a co-payment based on the total physician charges if an unauthorized, out-of-network physician is selected.

[5] The number of subscribers enrolled in Plan A makes it the predominant plan offered by X. The number of subscribers in Plan B is insignificant compared to X's total health plan subscribers.

[6] The physicians are compensated by X based upon the type of plan that the subscriber purchased. If the subscriber is enrolled in Plan A, then the physician

is compensated on a capitated basis. If the in-network physician sees individuals enrolled in Plan B, then the physician is paid 70 percent of the in-network charges with no withhold feature. Out-of-network physicians providing services to Plan B enrollees receive 100 percent of their typical charges, a portion of which is paid by the enrollees as a co-payment.

[7] X shares the income/loss on Plan B with Y. The risk sharing with Y is 50 percent of the income or loss and is capped at 5 percent of the premium revenue.

[8] X originally reported as UBI only premiums received from Plan B. X's return was subsequently amended to include as UBI premiums stemming from Plan B relating to out-of-network primary care physicians for non-authorized services. X's return was amended a second time to exclude from UBI the total premiums received from Plan B.

Law:

[9] Section 501(m)(1) of the Code provides that an organization described in section 501(c)(4) shall be exempt only if no substantial part of its activities consists of providing commercial-type insurance. Consequently, where an organization's activities resemble those of commercial insurers, section 501(m) would serve to deny exemption under section 501(c)(4).

[10] Section 501(m)(2) of the Code provides that a section 501(c)(3) or (4) organization that provides commercial-type insurance as an insubstantial part of its activities shall treat the activity as an unrelated trade or business (as defined in section 513), and in lieu of the tax imposed by section 511 with respect to such activity shall treat the organization as an insurance company for purposes of applying subchapter L with respect to that activity.

[11] Section 501(m)(3)(B) of the Code provides that commercial-type insurance does not include "incidental health insurance provided by a health maintenance organization of a kind customarily provided by such organizations."

[12] The legislative history of section 501(m) of the Code provides that commercial-type insurance generally is any insurance of a type provided by commercial insurance companies.

[13] Commercial-type insurance does not include arrangements that are not treated as insurance in the absence of a sufficient risk shifting and risk distribution for the arrangement to constitute insurance. *See Helvering v. Legierse*, 312 U.S. 531 (1941).

[14] In reporting on technical corrections to section 501(m) of the Code that were made in the Technical and Miscellaneous Revenue Act of 1988 (TAMRA), the Conference Committee stated:

> The provision relating to organizations engaging in commercial-type insurance activities did not alter the tax-exempt status of health maintenance organizations. HMOs provide physician services in a variety of practice settings primarily through physicians who are either employees or partners of

> the HMO or through contracts with individual physicians or one or more groups of physicians. The conference committee clarifies that, in addition to the general exemption for HMOs, organizations that provide supplemental HMO type services (such as dental or vision services) are not treated as providing commercial-type insurance if they operate in the same manner as a health maintenance organization.

[15] Rev. Rul. 68-27, 1968-1 C.B. 315, concludes that an organization that issued medical service contracts to groups or individuals and furnished direct medical services to the subscribers by means of a salaried staff of medical personnel was held not to be an insurance company. In this revenue ruling, a medical clinic employed a staff of salaried physicians, nurses and technicians to provide a major portion of the contracted medical services. In the event the clinic had to treat a patient with an illness or injury, the revenue ruling concluded that any risk the clinic incurred was predominately a normal business risk. The clinic's costs for its medical providers was fixed because the clinic paid its providers a salary. As a result, if a patient were to suffer a serious illness or injury, the clinic would not incur any substantial additional costs. Thus, the clinic's economic risk was fixed regardless of the presence or extent of any illness or injury.

[16] In *Jordan, Superintendent of Insurance v. Group Health Association*, 107 F.2d 239 (1939), the U.S. Court of Appeals for the District of Columbia held that an HMO was not an insurance company. In this case, the HMO did not employ salaried physicians to provide medical services but paid contracted physicians a "fixed annual compensation, paid in monthly installments, not specific fees for each treatment or case."

[17] Neither the Internal Revenue Code nor the Income Tax Regulations define the term insurance contract. Rev. Rul. 68-27, *supra*, citing *Jordan*, defined an insurance contract as one that:

> Must involve the element of shifting or assuming the risk of loss of the insured and must, therefore, be a contract under which the insurer is liable for a loss suffered by its insured. Case law has defined an insurance contract as a contract whereby for an adequate consideration one party undertakes to indemnify another against loss from certain specific contingencies or perils. It is contractual security against anticipated loss. *Epmeier v. U.S.*, 199 F.2d 508, 509–510 (7th Cir. 1952).

* * *

[19] Moreover, case law has established that risk shifting and risk distribution are the fundamental characteristics of a contract of insurance. *Helvering v. LeGierse, supra*. In this case, the Supreme Court stated that "historically and commonly insurance involves risk-shifting and risk-distributing." 312 U.S. at 539.

[20] Finally, the risk transferred must be a risk of economic loss. The risk for which insurance coverage is provided is an insurance risk; that is, it must occur fortuitously and must result in an economic loss to the insurer. *Allied Fidelity Corp. v. Commissioner*, 66 T.C. 1068 (1976). In this case, the Court of Appeals stated:

> The common definition for insurance is an agreement to protect the insured against a direct or indirect economic loss arising from a defined contingency whereby the insurer undertakes no present duty of performance but stands ready to assume the financial burden of any covered loss. 1 COUCH ON INSURANCE 2d, 1:2 (1955). As the Tax Court below noted, an insurance contract contemplates a specified insurable hazard or risk with one party willing, in exchange for the payment of premiums, to agree to sustain economic loss resulting from the occurrence of the risk specified and, another party with an insurable interest in the insurable risk. It is important here to note that one of the essential features of insurance is this assumption of another's risk of economic loss. 1 COUCH ON INSURANCE 2D, 1:3 (1959).

[21] Risk shifting occurs when a person facing the possibility of an economic loss transfers some or all of the financial consequences of the loss to the insurer. Rev. Rul. 88-72, 1988-2 C.B. 31, clarified by Rev. Rul. 89-61, 1989-1 C.B. 75.

Rationale:

[22] Under section 501(m)(1) of the Code, an organization that otherwise qualifies for exemption under section 501(c)(3) or section 501(c)(4) is precluded from qualifying for exemption if a substantial part of its activities consists of providing commercial-type insurance. If the provision of commercial-type insurance is an insubstantial part of an organization's activities, then section 501(m)(2) provides that the activity is from an unrelated trade or business and tax shall be calculated under subchapter L of the Code relating to insurance companies.

[23] When individuals enroll in an HMO and directly or indirectly pay the HMO fixed premiums, the HMO agrees that it will furnish health care services to treat their injuries and illnesses. Under this arrangement, enrollees protect themselves against the risk that they would suffer economic loss from having to pay for health care services that are necessary because of injuries and illnesses. By enrolling in an HMO, individuals shift their risk of economic loss to the HMO.

[24] For an HMO that operates on a staff model basis, the HMO assumes the financial risk associated with furnishing medical services. Since a staff model HMO pays physicians on a salaried basis, it does not incur additional fees when its employed physicians treat its enrollees. Therefore, the risk the HMO assumes is predominately a normal business risk of an organization engaged in furnishing medical services on a fixed-price basis, rather than an insurance risk. Rev. Rul. 68-27, *supra.*

[25] On the other hand, a non-staff model HMO that does not pay its health care providers on a fixed-price basis assumes a financial risk that is greater than a normal business risk associated with its obligation to furnish medical services to its enrollees. Therefore, this obligation constitutes a contract of insurance.

[26] An HMO that compensates its non-employee health care providers on a fixed fee basis is treated the same as a staff model HMO that pays its health care

providers on a salaried basis because the HMO has transferred to its health care providers a substantial portion of its financial risk associated with its obligation to furnish medical services to its enrollees. The remaining risk is only the normal business risk associated with operating the HMO.

[27] For example, an HMO that pays its contracted health care providers almost exclusively on fixed monthly fees based on the number of enrollees (capitated fees), transfers to these providers a substantial portion of its financial risk associated with its obligation to furnish medical services to its enrollees. Therefore, the remaining risk is only the normal business risk associated with operating the HMO.

[28] Similarly, an HMO that pays its contracted health care providers almost exclusively fees-for-service under a fee schedule that represents a meaningful discount from the physicians' usual and customary charges (discounted fee-for-service) and withholds from these payments a significant percent of the fees otherwise payable, pending compliance with periodic budget or utilization standards, transfers to these providers, in effect, a substantial portion of its financial risk associated with its obligation to furnish medical services to its enrollees. Therefore, the remaining risk is only the normal business risk associated with operating the HMO.

[29] On the other hand, when an HMO pays its contracted providers on a fee-for-service basis that is not discounted and where no significant portion of the fees has been withheld, the HMO does not transfer to these providers its financial risk associated with its obligation to furnish medical services to its enrollees. Thus, the HMO retains the financial risk associated with its obligation to furnish medical services to its enrollees. The financial risk constitutes a contract of insurance. A discounted fee arrangement, even if the discount is meaningful, without a significant withhold does not transfer financial risk to providers. In return for accepting discounted fees, the providers are assured a flow of patients from the HMO. It is a common commercial practice for vendors of goods or providers of services to accept lower prices or fees in return for greater sales.

[30] The health care providers are compensated based upon the type of plan purchased by an enrollee. If a physician sees an enrollee who is a subscriber of the A plan, then the physician is compensated by capitated fees. If a physician sees an enrollee of Plan B, then the in-network physician is paid on a discounted fee-for-service with no withhold and the out-of-network physician is paid at 100 percent of his or her typical charges.

[31] Under the A plan, a substantial amount of the financial risk associated with X's obligation to arrange for the provision of health care services to its enrollees is being shifted to the primary care providers. The provision of services by the health care providers on a capitated basis shifts a substantial portion of risk to the health care providers because they have to provide the medical care without receiving additional funds. But, X retains substantial financial risk associated with Plan B, because the physicians are on a fee-for-service basis while it retains financial risk to furnish medical services. Therefore, the provision of services under the A policy

would not be commercial-type insurance as described in section 501(m)(1), but the provision of medical services under Plan B would be commercial-type insurance.

[32] X has argued that the proceeds from the sale of the POS policies satisfy the exception to section 501(m)(3)(B) because the POS product is incidental health insurance customarily provided by a health maintenance organization. The section 501(m)(3)(B) exception would not be applicable since the legislative history of section 501(m)(3)(B) does not include the point of service provisions as examples of the type of insurance that would satisfy this exception. Only dental and vision services are mentioned in the Conference Committee Report on TAMRA.

[33] Even though Plan B is commercial-type insurance for purposes of section 501(m)(3), it is not a substantial part of X's activities since it is an insubstantial portion of X's total activities. Therefore, under section 501(m)(2) of the Code all income from Plan B would be from an unrelated trade or business and tax liability will be calculated in accordance with the provisions set forth in subchapter L.

[34] CONCLUSION:

1. The provision of services under Plan B where the medical providers are compensated on either a discounted fee-for-service basis with no withhold or under a point of service arrangement is commercial-type insurance as described in section 501(m)(3) of the Code.

2. The provision of services under Plan B is an insubstantial part of X's activities and would be subject to unrelated business income tax.

3. The unrelated business income tax would be calculated under subchapter L rather than section 511.

Chapter 10

Organizational Requirement: Procedural Rules

A. Introduction

Recall from Chapter 1 that in order to satisfy §§ 501(c)(3) and 170(c)(2), a tax-exempt organization must meet five *statutory* criteria:

1. It must be *organized* exclusively for an exempt purpose.
2. It must be *operated* exclusively for an exempt purpose.
3. It must avoid any *private inurement.*
4. It must avoid substantial *lobbying.*
5. It must avoid any *political activity.*

The "organizational" and "operational" tests each have three sub-parts:

1. The "exclusivity" requirement.
2. The "exempt purpose" requirement.
3. The procedural rules.

Chapters 2 through 6 covered the "exempt purpose" sub-part of both the *organizational* and *operational* tests. Chapters 7 through 9 covered the "exclusivity" requirement of both the *organizational* and *operational* tests. This Chapter covers the procedural aspects of both tests.

B. The Filing and Notice Requirement

Code: §§ 501(c)(3); 508(a)–(c)

Treas. Regs.: §§ 1.501(a)-1, 1.501(c)(3)-1(a)–(b); 1.508-1(a)

1. Application Form

To be exempt, most charities must file an application for exemption. Being non-profit and/or operating consistently with § 501 is insufficient. Treasury Regulations presume an organization to be taxable as a corporation, unless and until it complies with the administrative requirements discussed in this chapter. The regulations under § 501 hold that an organization is not tax-exempt merely because it operates in accordance with the substantive requirements for tax exemption. Treas. Reg. § 1.501(a)-1(a)(2). The regulations under § 7701 treat an organization presuming to be tax-exempt under § 501 as a corporation until such time as the Service affirmatively determines that the organization meets what are known as the "organizational" requirements.[1] Treas. Reg. § 301.7701-3(c)(1)(v).

Charities—those organizations exempt under § 501(c)(3)—apply for exemption using Form 1023.[2] Those comprise the majority of applicants. Other organizations—those applying under most of the rest of § 501(c) use Form 1024 and Form 8718.[3] Social welfare organizations under § 501(c)(4)—use Form 1024-A rather than Form 1023 or 1024. Under § 506(a), a social welfare organization must notify the IRS of its existence within 60 days of its organization. Social welfare organizations use Form 8976 Electronic Notice Registration System for this purpose. A perusal of the forms is instructive at this point. Notice both the length of the forms, as well as the considerable amount of detailed information required, even for brand-new organizations with no operational history.

As a general matter, the forms must be substantially complete before the Service will issue a "determination letter." However, the application process is decidedly non-adversarial and, though an incomplete application will result in delay, the Service will normally inform the organization exactly what is needed if the application is incomplete. Thus, the *organizational* test is not so much a "test," as it is a prerequisite—entities rarely fail the "test" because those that initially fail have ample opportunity to amend the application. They may, of course, fail to receive exempt status because they fail another test—exclusivity, exempt purpose, private inurement, or the statutory requirements restricting lobbying or political activity.

A "simple" exempt organization can file a 1023-EZ instead of the usual Form 1023. You can quickly determine whether an exempt organization is eligible to use the Form 1023-EZ by filling out a worksheet included with the Form 1023-EZ Instructions. The only meaningful limitation on the worksheet is that anticipated annual donations cannot exceed $50,000 in any of the first three years of existence. Foundations, whether simple or complex, can be corporations or trusts under state law (see discussion of Articles of Creation below). If a simple foundation is a trust, then the trust document, requesting a tax number, filing Form 1023-EZ, and paying a $275 filing fee, creates a "simple private foundation." The cost in time and money is much

1. Upon the revocation of a tax exemption, a former tax-exempt organization is treated as a taxable corporation until it elects to be treated as a partnership or sole proprietorship. Treas. Reg. § 301.7701-3(c)(1)(v) (1999).

2. In addition, Form 1023 is used for recognition under § 501(e) (cooperative hospital service organizations), 501(f) (cooperative service organization of operating educational organization), 501(k) (child care organizations), and 501(n) (charitable risk pools).

3. Organizations filing Form 1024 are described in § 501(c)(2), (5)–(10), (12)–(13), (15), (17), (19)–(20). Form 1028 is used for organizations claiming exemption under § 521 (farming associations), and Form 1120-H is used by organizations claiming exemption under § 528 (homeowners associations).

less than the months and significant legal fees generated by forming complex private foundations.

2. Articles of Creation

A primary part of the application-review process, particularly with regard to organizations seeking recognition as a § 501(c)(3) organization, involves a review of the organization's "articles of organization." The term "articles of organization" refers to the trust instrument, corporate charter, articles of association, or any other document by which the organization was created and is governed. The essence of the organizational requirement is that the authorizing documents must contain a detailed statement of the organization's proposed activities and that statement must describe an "exempt purpose." In addition, the authorizing documents must contain statements obligating the organization to comply with the various other substantive requirements pertaining to tax exemption, and may not contain any statements authorizing the organization to violate any substantive requirement. Treas. Reg. § 1.501(c)(3)-1(b).[4] Thus, counsel should include the federal tax organizational provisions in the articles of incorporation or in the trust agreement.

Sample proposed articles appear in IRS Publication 557. As you will note, powers need not be detailed—a general provision limiting activities to those permitted by § 501(c)(3) will suffice. Form 1023, however, requires greater specificity in the description of proposed activities. Often the application process is delayed because the applicant failed to describe what it planned to do in sufficient detail.

3. Filing Deadline

Prior to 1969, an organization was entitled to tax exemption without an application, so long as it operated in accordance with the substantive requirements for tax exemption.[5] But Congress believed that the resulting lack of information-reporting prevented the Service from enforcing the tax laws. As a result, Congress enacted § 508, which precludes tax exemption under § 501(c)(3) unless the organization "notifies" the Service that it is claiming § 501(c)(3) status.

---

4. The substantive requirements are discussed in separate chapters. They are: the requirement to operate "exclusively" for one or more exempt purposes, the private benefit prohibition; the private inurement/excess benefit prohibitions; and the prohibition/limitations pertaining to lobbying and political activity.

5. This was so, despite Treas. Reg. § 1.501(a)-1, which admonished that organizations must actually file before being treated as tax-exempt. *See* S. Rep. No. 91-552, 91st Cong., 1st Sess., 53–54 (1969). Treas. Reg. 1.501(a)-1 still applies to all organizations seeking exemption under a provision other than § 501(c)(3), but the Service will nevertheless grant retroactive recognition of an organization claiming exemption under a subsection other than § 501(c)(3), even if the organization did not file a timely application (assuming the organization met the substantive requirements during the retroactive period). *See* Rev. Rul. 80-108, 1980-1 C.B. 119 (1980) (granting retroactive § 501(c)(4) status to an organization that failed to timely file an application for recognition).

Section 508 applies only to organizations claiming § 501(c)(3) status, probably because the vast majority of tax-exempt organizations seek that status. To comply with § 508(a), an organization must file Form 1023 within 15 months from the end of the month in which it was organized. Treas. Reg. § 1.508-1(a)(2). For many years, one had to check a box on Form 1023 to receive a 12-month extension. More recently, the form grants an automatic extension, effectively altering the statutory 15-month requirement to 27 months.[6]

In addition, the Commissioner has discretion, upon a showing of good cause by a taxpayer, to grant a reasonable extension of time for applying, provided:

1. the time for applying is not expressly prescribed by the statute;
2. the request for the extension is filed with the Commissioner within a period of time the Commissioner considers reasonable under the circumstances; and
3. it is shown to the Commissioner's satisfaction that granting the extension will not jeopardize the government's interests.[7]

In 2015, Congress passed § 506(a). That section requires a social welfare organization under § 501(c)(4) to notify the IRS "that it is operating as a social welfare organization." The notice is given by filing Form 8976 (Notice of Intent to Operate Under section 501(c)(4)). The organization must file the Form "not later than 60 days after the organization is established." The IRS can extend the 60-day period for reasonable cause. IRC § 506(d). Failure to file subjects the organization to a penalty of $20 for each day of delinquency, up to a maximum of $5,000. IRC § 6652(c)(4)(A). If

6. For an organization incorporated under state law, the "organized" month is the month during which existence was recognized for state law purposes (generally, the month during which the articles of incorporation are filed with the appropriate state office). Rev. Rul. 77-469, 1977-2 C.B. 196. However, an unincorporated association is deemed to be in existence on the date it actually came into existence without regard to § 508(a). Treas. Reg. § 1.508-1(a)(2)(iii). Thus, unless an unincorporated association files a timely notice within the fifteen month period beginning on the last day of the month in which it began operations, it will not be in compliance with § 508(a) for the period from the start of its operations. It cannot remedy that noncompliance by incorporating and then seeking recognition. In such case, the incorporated entity will be treated as a new entity separate from the old unincorporated association. The "new" entity, if it files an application within twenty-seven months of incorporation, will be recognized to the date of incorporation but not for any period prior to its incorporation (when it operated as an unincorporated association without complying with the filing requirement). *Id.*

7. Rev. Proc. 79-63, 1979-2 C.B. 578, provides information and sets forth the representations that taxpayers must furnish to obtain such relief. It also discusses some factors that will be taken into consideration in determining whether such extensions will be granted. Although Rev. Proc. 79-63 was superseded by Rev. Proc. 92-85, 1992-2 C.B. 490, T.D. 8378 states that: "Until the issuance of further guidance, the Service will apply Rev. Proc. 79-63 to elections under all the subtitles now included in § 301.9100-1 of the regulations taking into account their special characteristics, if any." The Service will give consideration to applying the Commissioner's discretionary authority under § 301.9100-1 of the regulations to extend the time for satisfying the notice requirement of § 508(a) of the Code.

the organization does not file a notice after an IRS demand, the person within the organization with responsibility for filing the notice may become liable for the penalty. IRC § 6652(c)(4)(B).

Organizations that operated as § 501(c)(4) social welfare organizations before the enactment of § 506(a) are required to notify the Service of their existence. However, meeting the notification requirement does not constitute a determination of exempt status. For that determination, an organization may voluntarily file Form 1024-A, "Application for Recognition of Exemption Under Section 501(a)," but is not required to do so. Alternatively, an organization that intends to operate as a § 501(c)(4) organization may file an annual information return, Form 990, in which case the initial Form 990 serves as a request for recognition of exempt status as an organization described in § 501(c)(4).

An all-too-common scenario involves an entity in existence for many years—sometimes decades—without ever having filed for exempt status, believing itself to be exempt and contributions to it to be deductible. The resulting mountain of unfilled tax returns and unpaid corporate taxes may seem daunting; however, such failure to meet the application deadline is not the disaster it might seem to be. Late applicants receive § 501(c)(3) exempt status—and § 170(c)(2) charitable deduction status—prospectively, from the date of application. As a result, contributions to the organization will not be deductible prior to the date of the application—and all those made earlier were non-deductible, despite the beliefs of the donors and recipients.

4. Exemption from the Filing Requirement

Two categories of 501(c)(3) organization are exempt from the § 508 notice requirement. They need not file for exempt status. Indeed, they will be treated as exempt under § 501(c)(3) so long as they are organized and operated in accordance with the substantive requirements. The two categories are:

1. *Churches* and their affiliated organizations, as well as organizations covered by a group exemption letter.[8]

8. Under Revenue Procedure 80-27, 1980-1 C.B. 677, a central organization may obtain an exemption letter pertaining to it and all subordinate organizations. Very generally, the central organization must establish its tax exemption, and all subordinate organizations must be (1) exempt, (2) not private foundations, and (3) subject to the central organization's general supervision and control. The central organization's application for exemption must contain detailed information on each subordinate organization, and the central organization must file annual reports pertaining to the continued inclusion of all subordinate organizations in the group exemption letter.

2. *Small public charities*: organizations that are not private foundations[9] and the gross receipts of which are "normally" not more than $5,000.[10]

Many churches and affiliated organizations file a Form 1023 despite their exemption from the § 508 notice requirement. Why? They do so because the formal application process results in their being listed in Publication 78—a government listing of all organizations described in § 170(c) of the Internal Revenue Code. Section 170(c) organizations can receive deductible contributions. Although churches (and affiliated organizations) are automatically described in § 170(c) (which is essentially identical with § 501(c)(3)), potential patrons may not know that. Some people (arguably all those who are well-advised) limit their charitable contributions to organizations on the government list. It provides a guarantee of sorts that the contribution is tax deductible: most people may rely on a listing even if facts exist justifying withdrawal of exempt status. Thus, many churches—particularly those that are less well-known—file the non-required (for them) Form 1023 solely for the purpose of getting themselves listed in Publication 78.

C. Two Revenue Rulings and a Revenue Procedure

1. Revenue Ruling 90-100

Revenue Ruling 90-100, 1990-2 C.B. 156, details several examples involving application deadlines. One example involves an organization that timely filed a Form 1023, but later withdrew the application fearing a negative result. After curing whatever problems existed, the entity re-filed. The Service ruled the application late (the withdrawn Form 1023 did not constitute § 508 notice) and thus granted prospective exemption only. A second example illustrates the simultaneous filing of Forms 1023 and 1024 for late filing—the Form 1023 filing resulting in prospective § 501(c)(3) status only. Finally, the ruling illustrates the consequences of a group exemption—which relieves member organizations from having to file separately, subject to separate deadlines.

---

9. The distinction between public charities and private foundations is discussed in Chapters 15 through 19.

10. Whether an organization normally has gross receipts in excess of $5,000 is determined by an objective set of rules set forth in Treasury Regulation § 1.508-1(a)(3)(ii). If the organization's gross receipts do not exceed $7,500 in its first year of existence, it will be exempt from the notice requirement for that year. If its aggregate gross receipts for its first two years of existence do not exceed $12,000, it will be exempt for the second year. Thereafter, the determination is based upon a rolling three-year period. The organization must determine its aggregate gross receipts for its current and the two immediately preceding years. If the aggregate gross receipts during the three-year period do not exceed $15,000, the organization will be exempt from the § 508 notice requirement for the current year. If the organization's aggregate gross receipts exceed the limitation pertaining to any year, it must file Form 1023 within 90 days of the close of that year and, upon the failure to do so, will violate the § 508 requirement as of the beginning of the that year. Treas. Reg. § 1.508-1(a)(3)(i).

2. Revenue Ruling 80-259

Another interesting ruling illustrates the technical application triggers for very small organizations—another common scenario. Revenue Ruling 80-259, 1980-2 C.B. 192, dealt with an organization that began with annual gross receipts of:

Taxable Year Ending	
1973	$3,600
1974	2,900
1975	400
1976	12,600
1977	76,400
1978	96,200
1979	142,400

The § 508 filing requirement applies to entities with annual gross receipts "normally" above $5000. For this purpose, the term "normally" involves an objective moving average. An entity can have up to $7,500 in receipts its first year, $12,000 in its first two years, or $15,000 in its first three years (or three-year period thereafter) without being required to file for exemption. The entity discussed in Revenue Ruling 80-259 did not meet the requirement in 1976 because its cumulative three-year receipts exceeded $15,000. As a result, the entity had 90 days to file a Form 1023. After that 90-day period, absent a discretionary extension, the entity could only seek *prospective* § 501(c)(3) status.

Revenue Procedure 2019-5

Revenue Procedure 2019-5, 2019-1 IRB 230, sets forth the procedures the IRS follows for issuing determination letters to organizations on their exempt status under § 501 or § 521, private foundation status, the exhaustion of administrative remedies for purposes of declaratory judgment under § 7428, and other determinations related to exempt organizations, such as revocation or modification of determination letters. Important information from the revenue procedure includes that:

1. Most applications report proposed activities rather than actual activities because the organization is not yet operating. Applications must include detailed narratives of what the entity plans to do. Insufficient detail will prompt government questions or will delay the process until substantial operations have occurred.

2. Among other information, a Form 1023 requires the inclusion of a multi-year budget—including a proposed two-year budget for new organizations. This requirement frustrates applicants but is essential.

3. The Service charges a user fee for the application.

4. If the application for recognition of exemption involves an issue for which contrary authorities exist, failure to disclose and distinguish such

significant contrary authorities may result in requests for additional information, which will delay action on the application.

5. No determination of exemption is permanent: the government (with cause) may withdraw exempt status — even retroactively.

6. A material change in an organization's purpose or operations necessitates a new application.

7. The IRS has centralized application processing.

The IRS updates this Revenue Procedure every year.

The following decision demonstrates that exempt status can be revoked retroactively for many years. The watchword is: Beware!

Partners in Charity, Inc. v. Commissioner of Internal Revenue

141 T.C. 151 (2013)

P was established as a nonprofit corporation under the laws of Illinois. P applied for recognition of tax-exempt status, explaining that its primary activity was to provide down-payment assistance grants to home buyers. R determined that P was a charitable organization described in I.R.C. sec. 501(c)(3). In actual operation, P required each home seller to pay to P the down-payment amount along with a fee. R retroactively revoked his determination, and P filed for a declaratory judgment under I.R.C. sec. 7428.

Held: P's down-payment assistance program was not operated for a charitable purpose, and P engaged in substantial commercial activities that did not further an exempt purpose. Therefore, P is not an organization described in I.R.C. sec. 501(c)(3).

Held, further, R did not abuse his discretion in making his adverse determination retroactive to the date of P's incorporation.

* * *

Gustafson, Judge: After examining the activities of petitioner, Partners In Charity, Inc. ("PIC"), for the years 2002 and 2003, the Internal Revenue Service ("IRS") issued to PIC a final adverse determination letter dated October 22, 2010, revoking its recognition of PIC's tax-exempt status. The revocation was retroactively effective to the date of PIC's incorporation on July 10, 2000.

* * *

The issues for decision are:

* * *

(2) whether, in retroactively revoking its determination that PIC was an organization described in section 501(c)(3), the IRS abused its discretion (we hold that it did not).

* * *

PIC's application for recognition of tax-exempt status

In July 2000 PIC submitted to the IRS Form 1023, "Application For Recognition of Exemption Under Section 501(c)(3) of the Internal Revenue Code", on which PIC reported:

> Partners In Charity will provide down payment assistance program for low income individuals and families to allow individuals who could not otherwise do so to own their own home. Partners in Charity [sic] will also engage in other affordable housing efforts, using excess contributions to develop low-income apartments for seniors and families, the acquisition and rehabilitation of single-family homes, and contributions to other housing related charitable organizations such as faith based charities, community based charities and national charities such as Habitat for Humanity.

* * *

On October 2, 2000, the IRS asked PIC to provide assurances (1) that PIC would serve a charitable class (mentioning the safe harbor guidelines in Rev. Proc. 96-32, 1996-1 C.B. 717) and (2) that no private interests of individuals with a financial stake in the project would be furthered. On October 9, 2000, PIC submitted to the IRS a "Statement of Policy" signed by Mr. Konkus as "President/Treasurer/Director" of PIC, which stated:

> Partners In Charity, Inc. has adopted a policy to comply with the low income housing safe harbor guidelines in that at least 75% of units for a given project will be made available for families earning 60% or less of the area's median income as adjusted for family size. The remaining 25% of the units for a given project will be made available to persons on the lower end of the economic spectrum who may not necessarily be members of a charitable class.
>
> The Directors and Officers in Partners In Charity, Inc. are not real estate developers, property managers or owners of significant parcels of undeveloped lands. Partners In Charity, Inc. intends to have a community-based Board of Directors once it established a track record and can attract qualified community-based individuals to serve.

The IRS's prior determination

On November 9, 2000, the IRS ruled favorably on PIC's application and issued to PIC a determination letter that stated: "[B]ased on information you supplied, and assuming your operations will be as stated in your application for recognition of exemption, we have determined you are exempt from federal income tax under section 501(a) of the Internal Revenue Code as an organization described in section 501(c)(3)." This determination was effective as of PIC's incorporation date, July 10, 2000.

The DPA program

As its title suggests, PIC's "down payment assistance" ("DPA") program provided home buyers with funds to use for down payments for home purchases. However, it obtained those funds (along with a fee) from home sellers; and in only two-tenths of 1% of its transactions did PIC make a DPA grant where the seller was not reimbursing the down payment and PIC's fee. A seller's payment to PIC equaled the down payment amount that PIC gave to the buyer plus PIC's fee—i.e., either 0.75% of the final sale price or, in the case of a professional home builder, $500.

* * *

The buyers' incomes

Although PIC collected information about grantee buyers' annual incomes and ethnicities, PIC did not use this or any other information to assure that a grantee was a member of the class described in the policy statement ("families earning 60% or less of the area's median income as adjusted for family size") that PIC provided when the IRS was considering its application. PIC did not collect any information concerning the buyer's marital or parental status (and so could not know "family size"). PIC made the DPA program available indiscriminately to a broad range of buyers, not just those with low incomes or in under-served populations.[11] Mr. Konkus testified at trial about an example of an $85,000 home ("certainly a modest house, Your Honor") that was financed by a loan from the Federal Housing Authority ("FHA")[12] that required a down payment of 3%—calling for PIC to make a DPA grant of $2,550. However, throughout 2002 and 2003 almost 600 of PIC's DPA grants exceeded $10,000, and PIC made at least two DPA grants of $100,000 or more to assist buyers purchasing property priced over $1 million.

* * *

Payment by and benefits to sellers

PIC advertised that its DPA program financially benefited sellers by (1) providing sellers with ready buyers, (2) enabling the sellers to sell for higher prices,[13] and (3)

11. [4] One of PIC's fliers advertised: "If you can get the mortgage, we'll give you the down payment. It's extremely easy to receive your FREE gift from PIC. In fact, there is only one requirement you must meet. You must qualify for any eligible loan program with your lender. Don't worry; they have many programs to meet your needs." Another flyer advertised: "No Income, Asset, or First Time Buyer Restrictions".

12. [5] Congress created the FHA through the National Housing Act of 1934, ch. 847, sec. 2, 48 Stat. at 1246 (codified as amended at 12 U.S.C. sec 1709 (2006)). FHA was established primarily for the purpose of insuring mortgage lenders against default by borrowers. *Id.*, sec. 1709 (b)(9). Before FHA can insure a single-family home mortgage, the loan must meet certain eligibility requirements set forth in the National Housing Act. 12 U.S.C. sec. 1709. One of these eligibility requirements involves the 3% down payment of the home's acquisition cost. *Id.* sec. 1709 (b)(9).

13. [7] Several of PIC's promotional materials claimed that PIC's DPA program generally increased sellers' net proceeds. One particular flyer listed step-by-step instructions for seller, and, after stating that sellers were required to pay PIC the down payment amount and a fee, the flyer stated:

allowing them to sell faster because of the larger pool of potential buyers.[14] Consistent with the language in the "Seller Participation Agreement" that PIC's benefits to sellers were "in consideration for" sellers' contributions and fees, we find that in PIC's transactions with sellers, the seller paid PIC a fee for a service. PIC received virtually all of its funding from payments by sellers for the services it provided to them, and when considered in combination with PIC's marketing strategy, commission-like fee structures, and significant revenues, we find that PIC's commercial activity with sellers was a substantial part of PIC's operation This commercial activity was in fact PIC's primary purpose.

PIC's other activities

In conjunction with the DPA program, PIC educated potential buyers about purchasing a home and about various responsibilities associated with home ownership. The educational materials provided by PIC also helped buyers to develop action plans for buying a home. PIC's educational programs were evidently informative and, we assume, beneficial to prospective home buyers. However, we find that providing education to home buyers was neither PIC's exclusive nor its primary purpose.

* * *

PIC's finances

PIC's income and expenditures greatly exceeded the expectations it reported on its Form 1023. According to annual financial reports, PIC received payments from home sellers participating in the DPA program totaling $28, 644,173 in 2002 and $32,439,723 in 2003. Revenues from home sellers were PIC's primary source of income in 2002 and 2003,[15] and PIC did not receive any charitable contributions, gifts, or grants in those years.

In 2002, PIC made 5,743 DPA grants totaling $25,206,041. Similarly, in 2003 PIC made 5,704 DPA grants totaling $29,058,724.

To make the transaction fair for you, the buyer will most likely offer full value on your property. This benefits you dramatically. To illustrate this, you need to know that on average, sellers take a reduction in the price to sales price of 5-7%. This means that a home listed at $100,000 would normally sell for $93,000 to $95,000 if the buyer didn't use the PIC Program. If they use the program, you will most likely sell your home for the list price of $100,000 and contribute $3,000 of the downpayment plus a fee of only .75% of the sales price to PIC. This means you'll net $96, 250 instead of $93,000-$95,000.
<u>That's $1,250 MORE FOR USING PIC! We're Helping You PIC Your Future!</u>

14. [8] Another PIC flyer that was directed to sellers and builders stated:

Participating in the PIC program opens up the seller's market by 30-40% because more buyers qualify. *** There are no restrictions, like many bond or local affordable housing programs. NO First Time Homebuyer Requirements; NO Income Asset Restrictions; NO Recapture Clauses (the borrower never needs to pay it back); NO Reserved Required; NO Geographic Boundaries; Use With Any Program.

15. [9] PIC also reported revenue from interest on cash investments, dividends, and gain from the sales of securities.

Apart from the DPA grant obligations, PIC incurred expenses in 2002 totaling $1,641,125. Of this amount, $564,933 was for marketing expenses paid to Royale Dynamics, Inc. (RDI), a company (discussed below) that was wholly owned by Mr. Kronkus's wife. Similarly, in 2003 PIC incurred expenses totaling $2,266,831, which included $580,234 paid to RDI. Apart from DPA grants, PIC's aggregate payments to RDI accounted for its largest expenditures in both 2002 and 2003.

By the end of 2003, PIC had accumulated unrestricted net assets totaling $3,592,271.

* * *

IRS's revocation

The IRS examined PIC's activities during the years 2002 and 2003, and on October 22, 2010, the IRS issued a final adverse determination, revoking its recognition of PIC's tax-exempt status. The IRS concluded that PIC did not operate exclusively for an exempt purpose, as required under section 501 (c)(3). The IRS's conclusion was based on its findings that: (1) PIC's net earnings inured to the benefit of private individuals or shareholders; (2) more than an insubstantial part of PIC's activities was not in furtherance of an exempt purpose; (3) PIC operated for the benefit of private interests; and (4) PIC operated for the primary purpose of carrying on an unrelated trade or business. . . .

The IRS made its adverse determination retroactive to PIC's incorporation date.

* * *

Opinion

I Procedural Issues

Section 7428 (a) confers jurisdiction on the Tax Court "[i]n a case of actual controversy" to "make a declaration" with respect to an organization's "continuing qualification" as an organization described section 501 (c)(3) that is exempt from tax under section 501 (a). For purposes of section 7428, "a determination with respect to continuing qualification . . . includes any revocation of or other change in a qualification". Sec. 7428(a).

* * *

On the issue of the retroactivity of the IRS's adverse determination, our standard of review is different. Section 7805(b)(8) provides that "[t]he Secretary [of the Treasury] may prescribe the extent, if any, to which any ruling (including any judicial decision or any administrative determination other than by regulation) relating to the internal revenue laws shall be applied without retroactive effect." Pursuant to this authority the Secretary has given the IRS discretion to retroactively revoke exemption rulings or determination letters where "the organization omitted or misstated a material fact, [or] operated in a manner materially different from that originally represented". 26 C.F.R. sec. 601.201(n)(6)(i), Statement of Procedural Rules. A retroactive revocation of a tax-exemption ruling will not be disturbed in the absence of an abuse of discretion, *Auto. Club v. Commissioner*, 353 U.S. 180, 184 (1957), and we therefore review that retroactive determination for abuse of discretion.

* * *

III. Retroactive effect

The last issue we must address is the propriety of the IRS's making its revocation retroactive. As we explained above in part I, section 7805(b)(8) and 26 C.F.R. sec. 601.201(n)(6)(i) give the IRS discretion to retroactively revoke exemption rulings or determination letters where "the organization omitted or misstated a material fact, [or] operated in a manner materially different from that originally represented"; and we review that retroactive revocation for abuse of discretion.

PIC operated in a manner that was different from what it represented to the IRS in its application. PIC represented there that its purpose was to "provide down payment assistance program for low income individuals and families", that its "down payment assistance will be provided only to individuals who have a financial need for such services", and that PIC intended to meet the safe harbor guidelines set forth in Rev. Proc. 96-27, *supra*, which would assure that certain percentages of individuals PIC served had incomes at specified levels below the area's median income. Despite these representations, both the administrative record and the trial record show that PIC did not have any income limitations for its grantees, nor did it screen buyers for down payment assistance based on income. Rather, PIC provided a grant to any home buyer who qualified for a loan.

PIC reported on its Form 1023 that it would "solicit gifts from corporations, foundations, and individuals with whom the members, directors, and officers have personal relationships." However, PIC received virtually all of its funding from sellers; and contrary to PIC's characterization, seller payments were not gifts nor did PIC have personal relationships with sellers. Instead, those receipts were in consideration for the services PIC provided the sellers.

For these reasons, we conclude that the IRS did not abuse its discretion in revoking its initial determination retroactively.

Decision will be entered for respondent.

Questions

1. Charity files its articles of incorporation on June 1, year one. What is the last date by which it must file its Form 1023 to be exempt from June 1, year one?

2. If Charity files its Form 1023 three months late, will donors who made contributions prior to the date of filing be precluded from taking a charitable contribution deduction under § 170?

3. Charity's gross receipts for its first six years are $6,500, $3,000, $5,000, $8,000, $4,000, and $15,000. In which taxable year must Charity file a Form 1023? What are the consequences for failure to file a Form 1023 and for what years will the consequences apply?

D. Judicial Review of the Ruling Process

Code: § 7428

Prior to 1976, organizations denied a favorable ruling could not directly challenge the denial. Similarly, organizations that had prior favorable rulings withdrawn by the Service also could not directly challenge the withdrawal. Their solutions were either to cease operations as an exempt entity or to proceed, risking a negative audit examination. They could, of course, litigate the issue of their exempt status after exhausting their administrative audit procedures. In addition to the risk of operating without a favorable ruling, such organizations suffered two other negative consequences. As a practical matter, they could not successfully solicit charitable contributions because many donors were unwilling to risk disallowance of their contributions: they would not donate to an organization lacking a favorable ruling and a listing in Publication 78. Moreover, the organization would be deprived of many state benefits that are conditioned upon the organization being recognized as tax-exempt at the federal level—e.g., sales tax exemption, property tax exemption, or the ability to participate in various state programs.

Congress enacted § 7428 to solve these problems: to provide the means by which to get an early resolution of conflicts regarding tax-exempt status and status as an entity to which charitable contributions can be made.

1. Tax Reform Act of 1976

Senate Report No. 94-938

94th Cong. 2d Sess. 585–591 (1976)

The Senate Finance Committee report, excerpted below, explains both the problem prior to the enactment of § 7428 and the solution contained in § 7428. Note in particular several factors:

1. Section 7428 applies both to the Service's refusal to recognize an entity and its decision to revoke an entity's previously granted tax-exempt status.

2. Section 7428 applies only to § 501(c)(3) organizations.

3. Jurisdiction lies in the Tax Court, Claims Court, or the District Court for the District of Columbia.

4. Individual contributions—up to $1,000—may remain deductible during the declaratory judgment proceeding in cases involving the withdrawal of exempt status.

5. A case or controversy must exist, i.e., an entity that voluntarily (even under pressure) amends its application and then receives a favorable ruling has no right to a declaratory judgment.

Senate Report No. 94-938

94th Cong. 2d Sess. 585–591 (1976)

... [Review of the law prior to 1976].

[A]s a practical matter, most organizations hoping to qualify for exempt status find it imperative to obtain a favorable ruling letter from the Service and to be listed in the Service's "blue book" (Cumulative List of Organizations Described in 170(c) of the Internal Revenue Code of [1986], Publication 78). An exemption letter and listing in the blue book assure potential donors in advance that contributions to the organization will qualify as charitable deductions under section 170(c)(2). In general, potential donors may rely upon these indicia even though the organization may not in fact be qualified under the statute for this treatment at the time of the gift.

In two cases decided in 1974 (*Bob Jones University v. Simon*, 416 U.S. 725 and *Alexander v. "Americans United" Inc.*, 416 U.S. 752) the Supreme Court held that an organization could not obtain the assistance of the courts to restrain the Internal Revenue Service from withdrawing a favorable ruling letter or withdrawing its listing in the blue book. In effect, this means that a judicial determination as to the organization's status cannot be had by the organization or its contributors, except in the context of a suit to redetermine a tax deficiency or to determine eligibility for a refund of taxes....

In *Bob Jones University v. Simon*, the Supreme Court ... noted ...:

> Congress has imposed an especially harsh regime on 501(c)(3) organizations threatened with loss of tax-exempt status and with withdrawal of advance assurance of deductibility of contribution.... The degree of bureaucratic control that, practically speaking, has been placed in the Service over those in petitioner's position [*i.e.*, the position of Bob Jones University] is susceptible to abuse, regardless of how conscientiously the Service may attempt to carry out its responsibilities. Specific treatment of not-for-profit organizations to allow them to seek pre-enforcement review may well merit consideration.

... Accordingly, the committee has agreed to ... a declaratory judgment procedure under which an organization can obtain a judicial determination of its own status ..., its status as an eligible charitable contribution donee, its status as a private foundation, or its status as a private operating foundation. Also, the committee amendment provides assurances regarding contributions made during the litigation period....

Explanation of provision

... [T]he Federal district court for the District of Columbia, the United States Court of Claims, and the United States Tax Court are to have jurisdiction in the case of an actual controversy involving a determination (or failure to make a determination) by the Internal Revenue Service with respect to the initial or continuing qualification or classification of an organization as an exempt charitable, etc., organization (sec. 501(c)(3)), as a qualified charitable contribution donee (sec. 170(c)(2)), as a private foundation (sec. 509), or as a private operating foundation (sec. 4942(j)(3)). A suit under this provision can be brought only by the organization whose qualification or status is at issue. . . .

The judgment . . . is to be binding upon the parties to the case based upon the facts as presented to the court in the case for the year or years involved. This, of course, does not foreclose Service action for later years (within the limits of the legal doctrines of estoppel and *stare decisis*) if the governing law or the organization's operations have changed since the years to which the declaratory judgment applies, or (especially in the case of a new organization) if the organization does not in operation meet the requirements for qualification.

This provision . . . is not intended to supplant the normal avenues of judicial review. . . . Consequently, it is expected that the courts will not entertain a declaratory judgment suit with regard to a period for which a notice of deficiency has already been issued, except upon a showing by the organization that the declaratory judgment route is likely to substantially reduce the time necessary to attain a final judicial review of the Service's determination. . . .

Contributions made during the litigation period. — . . . [T]o reduce the likelihood of the litigation "drying up" the resources of an organization's support . . . , contributions made during the litigation period may be deductible even though the court ultimately determines that the organization had lost its status as an eligible charitable donee under section 170(c)(2) of the Code.

This protection is to apply only where the organization had previously been declared to be an eligible donee, the Service has published a notice of the revocation of its advance assurance of deductibility of contributions, and the organization has initiated its proceeding before the 91st day after the Service mailed its adverse determination to the organization. . . .

However, the aggregate of deductions by any individual contributor to be given this protection with regard to contributions to or on behalf of any one organization is not to exceed $1,000 for the entire period. (For these purposes, a husband and wife are to be treated as one contributor.) This benefit is not to apply to any individual who was responsible, in whole or in part, for the actions (or failures to act) on the part of the organization which were the basis for the revocation.

From time to time, the Internal Revenue Service, in announcing its revocations of assurance as to exempt status, has applied this revocation retroactively, to the date of the asserted improper actions or failures to act (sec. 7805(b)). The committee understands that in such cases the retroactive revocation is not applied to those contributors who were innocent of the improper actions or failures to act. The committee intends that the Service continue to follow this course, which is consistent with the rule provided in this amendment.

Exhaustion of administrative remedies required.—For an organization to receive a declaratory judgment under this provision, it must demonstrate to the court that it has exhausted all administrative remedies which are available to it within the Internal Revenue Service. Thus, it must demonstrate that it has made a request to the Internal Revenue Service for a determination and that the Internal Revenue Service has either failed to act, or has acted adversely to it, and that it has appealed any adverse determination by a district office to the national office of the Internal Revenue Service or has requested or obtained through the district director technical advice of the national office. To exhaust its administrative remedies, the organization must satisfy all appropriate procedural requirements of the Service. For example, the Service may decline to make a determination if the organization fails to comply with a reasonable request by the Service to supply the necessary information on which to make a determination.

An organization is not to be deemed to have exhausted its administrative remedies in a case where there is a failure by the Internal Revenue Service to make a determination, before the expiration of 270 days after the request for such a determination had been made. Once this 270-day period has elapsed, an organization which has taken all reasonable steps to secure a determination may bring an action even though there has been no notice of determination from the Internal Revenue Service....

2. Case or Controversy: *AHW Corporation v. Commissioner of Internal Revenue*, 79 T.C. 390 (1982)

Although the section 7428 declaratory judgment procedure solved many problems, it did not solve them all. A 1982 Tax Court decision illustrated a difficult practical issue faced by many applicants. During the application process, the Service sometimes questions proposed activities. An applicant unable to convince the Service of its position faces a difficult choice:

1. Proceed with the proposal, receive an adverse ruling, and then seek a declaratory judgment.
2. Amend the Form 1023 application, deleting the controversial activity. It can then either operate without the activity, or operate with it, risking an adverse audit and/or the withdrawal of its exempt status. It can then seek judicial review.

Neither choice is particularly palatable. Effectively, the organization will be strongly tempted to succumb to the Service's views, however much it may disagree with them.

In *AHW Corporation*, the litigating organization was a subsidiary of an existing charity. It proposed providing various services to its parent, including property management and consulting. In addition, it proposed providing the same services, at cost, to unrelated tax exempt entities. The Service balked at the plan in relation to unrelated organizations, suggesting that such services provided significantly below cost would be "charitable"; however, the "at cost" proposal was non-charitable, rendering the organization less than "exclusively" charitable. The Service thus preliminarily proposed an adverse ruling.

Following a conference, the organization amended its application for exemption — the Form 1023–eliminating the controversial provision of services to unrelated organizations. Thereafter, the Service issued a favorable ruling of exemption.

Did this present a case or controversy justifying a declaratory judgment proceeding? No, ruled the Tax Court:

> *New Community* [*Sr. Citizen Housing v. Commissioner*, 72 T.C. 372 (1979)] prevents an organization already recognized as tax exempt from obtaining judicial review of an adverse ruling on a proposed transaction other than by actually performing the proposed transaction.

AHW v. Commissioner, 79 T.C. 390, 395 (1982).

The Court, despite ruling against the organization, was sympathetic with its predicament:

> We sympathize with petitioner's plight here, as well as with that of taxpayers in the situation considered in *New Community Sr. Citizen Housing v. Commissioner*, 72 T.C. 372 (1979). In both situations, taxpayers realistically knew they would not be recognized by respondent as exempt organizations if they engaged in particular proposed activities but could obtain judicial review of respondent's position only after actually losing such recognition. This is a harsh price to pay to obtain judicial review, but we note that prior to the enactment of sec. 7428, it was the only available route to judicial review. Although it can be argued as a matter of policy that taxpayers in these situations should not be deprived of the right to declaratory judgment review where the "case or controversy" requirement is met, this Court has interpreted the statutory language to preclude jurisdiction in this circumstance.

AHW, 79 T.C. at 397, n. 4.

Questions

1. Suppose a high-ranking IRS official publicly announces — at a speech given during a bar association meeting to which she was invited — the Service's intention to seek retroactive revocation of tax exemption with regard to any charity that engages in fundraising arrangements allowing fundraisers to retain 40% of all monies raised on behalf of and using the charity's name. Your client, New Charity, relies heavily on such fundraising and probably will not survive without the ability to enter into such arrangements. Can New Charity file an action under § 7428 in response to the announcement? What if the Service made its intentions known through the issuance of an IRS Notice published in the federal register? *See Anclote Psychiatric Center, Inc. v. Commissioner*, 98 T.C. 374 (1992).

2. Assume that five years ago, the Service issued a revenue ruling stating that charities that engaged in joint ventures whereby a non-exempt partner is granted a right to a share of the profits from the venture will not risk revocation of their tax-exempt status. However, earlier this year, the Service issued a revenue ruling revoking the prior ruling and providing for a period of amnesty during which charities subject to such arrangements may terminate those arrangements. After the amnesty period, according to the new ruling, the Service will treat the arrangements as grounds to revoke tax exemption. Can your client file an action under § 7428 if it is a party to such a joint venture?

3. Supporting Organization is a public charity because it is operated in connection with Private University. If the Service proposes to revoke Private University's tax exemption because of its failure to comply with certain requirements, may Supporting Organization file an action under § 7428?

4. What if Private University in question 3 files an action under § 7428 and, while the suit is pending, Donor contributes $8,000 to Private University and $1,000 to Supporting Organization? Ultimately, the court decides that Private University's tax exemption should be revoked as of the date specified in the Service's notice. How much, if any, of donor's contributions are deductible?

E. Filing and Public Disclosure Requirements

CODE: §§ 6033(a), (b); 6104(a)(1)(A), 6104(d); 6652(c)

TREAS. REGS.: §§ 301.6104(d)-1(a), (b)(3)–(5), (c)–(d), (g), 301.6104(d)-2, 301.6104(d)-3

1. Annual Information Returns: § 6033

Per § 6033(a)(1), exempt organizations must file an annual information return. Four exempt organizations are excused from the annual filing requirement:

1. churches, their integrated auxiliaries, and conventions or associations of churches, § 6033(a)(3)(A)(i)
2. most organizations with annual gross receipts normally not more than $5,000 [actually $50,000, as explained below], § 6033(a)(3)(A)(ii)
3. the exclusively religious activities of any religious order, § 6033(a)(3)(A)(iii), and
4. any organization excused under the discretionary authority of the Secretary, § 6033(a)(3)(B).

The *first* exception extends to organized religious groups of any faith. The *second* exception extends broadly to most public charities, but specifically does not apply to private foundations. An organization meets the test if the average of its gross receipts for the return year and the two previous years is not more than $5,000 under the statute, but actually $50,000 per the *fourth* exception, which gives the Secretary of Treasury discretion, under § 6033(a)(3)(B), to excuse an exempt organization from filing an annual return. Treasury Regulation § 1.6033-2(g)(6) delegates this authority to the Commissioner. Thus, in Revenue Procedure 2011-15, the Service announced that public charities that normally have gross receipts of $50,000 or less need not file an annual return. A charity that is not exempted from the filing requirement is required, under § 6033(b), to include a list of information relevant to whether the charity has violated the substantive requirements for tax exemption, including the exclusively operated requirement, the private inurement prohibition, the excess benefit prohibition, as well as the lobbying and political activity provision. The annual return is made on Form 990. If an organization has gross receipts less than $200,000 and total assets less than $500,000 it can file Form 990EZ instead of Form 990. In addition, exempt organizations report their unrelated trade or business income on Form 990T.

2. Public Disclosure of Returns and Other Information: § 6104

Congress imposed public disclosure requirements on organizations with § 6104(a) which allows the public to request from the Service copies of an organization's application and supporting documents.

Enacted in 1958, § 6104(a) is no longer as relevant or important as it once was. In 1987, Congress added § 6104(d), which mandates that exempt organizations *themselves* make their exemption application and annual information reports available for public inspection and public copying at no charge other than the reasonable costs of the copying. However, an organization need not provide an individual copy of its exemption application or information return if either document is otherwise "widely available." One way of making the application and information return widely available is by posting those documents on the Internet. The regulations recognize that method. Treas. Reg. § 301.6104(d)-2(b). Note, however, that making a document widely available does not mean that an organization may prevent a member of the public from personally inspecting the document at the organization's national or regional offices.

As we will see in later chapters, exempt organizations often seek to be agents of social change. As a result, they are often lightning rods with respect to different perspectives. The public inspection and copying requirements may therefore be viewed as a means to distract an organization from its social changing issue. Section 6104(d)(4) gives the Service authority to exempt an organization from complying with a request for copies if the Service determines that the request is part of a harassment campaign and compliance with the request would not be in the "public interest." Treasury Regulation section 301.6104(d)-3 implements that authority. If an organization believes that it has received a harassing request, it must first apply for a determination from the Service finding a harassment campaign. While the request is pending, the organization may suspend compliance with the request. If there is a determination that a harassment campaign is ongoing, the organization need not comply with requests for copies that it "reasonably believes" are part of the campaign. Other requests made during the time the harassment campaign is ongoing—that is, requests that are not related to the campaign—must be satisfied. The organization will be subject to sanction if it refuses to comply with a request without a reasonable basis for concluding that the request was part of the campaign. If the Service determines that there is no harassment campaign, the organization must comply with requests within 30 days and will be subject to sanction for failure to timely comply with the request only if there was no reasonable basis upon which to request a determination.

In addition to the organized campaign exception, an organization may ignore a request from an individual if it has previously complied with two previous requests from that individual within a 30-day period or with four previous requests from that individual within a one-year period.

a. Tax Analysts v. CBN, *214 F.3d 179 (D.C. Cir. 2000)*

The breadth of § 6104's public disclosure obligation is not entirely clear. A 2000 D.C. Circuit opinion illustrated two issues:

1. No private right of action against the organization exists. If an organization refuses to disclose required information, the requesting party cannot seek a remedy directly against the organization. Instead, it may complain to the government, which has discretion to seek enforcement of disclosure.

2. The statute's apparent reach of "all documents" related to an application cannot be taken literally, as some documents are exempt. Nevertheless, some apparently "exempt" documents may indeed be discoverable from the Service, depending on their individual contents. In short, the label placed on a document—such as "closing agreement"—does not determine whether the document is discoverable; instead, its contents control.

The case involved an interesting fight between Tax Analysts—a well-known publisher—and the Christian Broadcasting Network (CBN). Long exempt, CBN entered into a closing agreement with the Service denying it exempt status for 1985 and 1986 because of political activities. The organization then reapplied for exemption and received a favorable ruling retroactive to 1987. Tax Analysts sought copies of all documents related to the new application, including the closing agreement.

The D.C. Circuit held that Tax Analysts had no right of action against CBN directly, finding that it could seek the same documents from the government. The Court explained that the statute was silent on the private right of action issue, but Congress apparently did not intend for such an action to exist.[16] The Court also

16. An earlier case, also relying on Congress' intent to deny a private right of action, was *Schuloff v. Queens College Foundation*, 994 F. Supp. 425 (E.D.N.Y. 1998).

discussed various exceptions to the disclosure requirements, particularly those involving "return information." It declined to hold that a "closing agreement" is automatically exempt from public disclosure. Instead, the Circuit remanded the case to the District Court for an *in camera* hearing regarding the contents of the requested documents.

b. Sklar v. Commissioner, *282 F.3d 610 (9th Cir. 2002)*

In 1993, the Service entered into a closing agreement with the Church of Scientology, an organization exempt under § 501(c)(3). The agreement settled several issues pertaining to the Church's tax exemption, as well as the deductibility of "auditing" fees, which adherents of Scientology claimed were charitable contributions eligible for deduction under § 170. Although the fees could easily be viewed as being paid in exchange for services, the closing agreement nevertheless allowed a deduction. The closing agreement apparently interpreted the "auditing" services as involving a purely religious benefit. That conclusion has been soundly criticized, though never overturned.

Taxpayers in *Sklar* sought to deduct a portion of the fees paid to an Orthodox Jewish school under the same reasoning. At trial, the Service refused to divulge the Scientology closing agreement to the Taxpayer, the Court or even the Justice Department (though we suspect that Justice may have counseled the Service to take that position), claiming that the closing agreement was exempt from disclosure. The Ninth Circuit, however, required disclosure:

> We agree with the D.C. Circuit. Disclosure of closing agreements is not categorically prohibited by § 6103, which is subject to § 6104; in appropriate circumstances, disclosure may be required under § 6104 or otherwise. Similarly, we reject the notion that § 6103 prohibits the disclosure of the entire closing agreement whenever part of the agreement contains return information. We also conclude that there are several reasons why the closing agreement in the case before us likely is subject to disclosure, at least in substantial part. First, just as in the Tax Analysts case the settling of the Church of Scientology's tax liability through the closing agreement was required in order for the organization to regain the tax-exempt status it had previously lost. Therefore the closing agreement would appear to constitute documentation in support of the exemption application which must be publicly disclosed pursuant to § 6104(a)(1)(A). See Alison H. Eaton, *Can the IRS Overrule the Supreme Court?* 45 Emory L.J. 987, 987–89 (1996) (discussing the fact that, as part of the closing agreement, the main Church of Scientology regained the tax-exempt status it had lost in the 1960s). This is fully consistent with the already extensive disclosure generally required of tax-exempt organizations under § 6104: in this case, the publication of the Church of Scientology's application for tax-exempt status, which contains detailed financial information about the organization, including its revenues and expenses. I.R.C. § 6104(a)(1)(A); 26 U.S.C. 6104(d)-1; IRS Form 1023.

Second, public disclosure of agreements that affect not just one taxpayer or a discrete group of taxpayers, but a broad and indeterminate class of taxpayers with a large and constantly changing membership, is also necessary as a practical matter. In the case of the Church of Scientology agreement, there are potentially tens, if not hundreds, of thousands of taxpayers who were not parties to the agreement and must be informed of the nature of the tax deductions available to them. . . . Indeed, the IRS, likely in recognition of that fact, has itself already disclosed some of the terms of this agreement, further confirming its adoption of the position that policymaking closing agreements can and must be disclosed. See Letter from Derome O. Bratvold, Chief, Adjustments Branch, IRS, to petitioners Michael and Marla Sklar (Feb. 4, 1994) ER 32 ("The settlement agreement between the Internal Revenue Service and the Church of Scientology allows individuals to claim, as charitable contributions, 80 percent of the cast [sic] of qualified religious services.").

Third, where a closing agreement sets out a new policy and contains rules of general applicability to a class of taxpayers, disclosure of at least the relevant part of that agreement is required in the interest of public policy. That this is the IRS's understanding as well is demonstrated by the fact that public disclosure has been a requirement contained in at least two such policymaking closing agreements. The IRS required publication of its closing agreement with Hermann Hospital of Houston, Texas, a tax-exempt entity, concluded following the hospital's disclosure to the IRS of certain physician recruitment practices which might have constituted prohibited transactions for a tax-exempt entity. John W. Leggett, *Physician Recruitment and Retention by Tax-Exempt Hospitals: The Hermann Hospital Physician Recruitment Guidelines*, 8 HEALTH LAW. 1, 6 (Spring 1995). Under the closing agreement, the hospital was required to engage only in permissible physician recruitment activities, as detailed extensively in an attached set of "Guidelines." Leggett at 1–3. Public disclosure of the closing agreement put other non-profit hospitals on notice of the IRS's definition of permissible physician recruitment activities. . . . That such was the purpose of requiring publication is clear from the fact that the agreement included provisions that did not apply to Hermann Hospital, but that might in the future be applicable to other tax-exempt hospitals. Leggett at 6 n. 35. Similarly, publication on the Internet was required of the IRS's closing agreement with the Kamehameha Schools Bishop Estate, a tax-exempt educational trust in Hawaii. The agreement was concluded after the IRS threatened to revoke the trust's tax-exempt status because the trustees had engaged in serious financial misconduct and self-dealing. Evelyn Brody, *A Taxing Time for the Bishop Estate: What is the I.R.S. Role in Charity Governance?*, 21 U. HAW. L. REV. 537, 539–540 (1999). It required that the incumbent trustees be removed, that the estate pay a penalty of nine million dollars, and that

> future governance of the estate conform to the agreement's provisions, including restrictions on who could become trustees and a requirement that the estate make its financial records publicly available. Brody at 21 U. HAW. L. REV. 539–40. Because the IRS had not traditionally intervened to this extent in matters of estate governance, the publication of the closing agreement served to put the members of other trusts on notice that the failure to administer trusts along the lines that the IRS required of the Bishop Estate might lead to loss of tax-exempt status.[17] Here, there is a strong public interest in the disclosure of the contents of the IRS's agreement with the Church of Scientology, especially as the agreement establishes a new policy governing charitable contributions to a particular religious organization which, while the pertinent statute may be unclear, clearly contravenes a prior Supreme Court holding.
>
> Therefore, we reject the argument that the closing agreement made with the Church of Scientology, or at least the portion establishing rules or policies that are applicable to Scientology members generally, is not subject to public disclosure. The IRS is simply not free to enter into closing agreements with religious or other tax-exempt organizations governing the deductions that will be available to their members and to keep such provisions secret from the courts, the Congress, and the public.

Nevertheless, despite the *Sklar* and *Tax Analysts* decisions, the Service announced in 2000:[18]

> [Pre-filing Agreements] (PFAs) are closing agreements entered into pursuant to I.R.C. § 7121. As such, it is the position of the IRS that both PFAs and the information generated or received by the IRS during the PFA process constitute confidential return information as defined by I.R.C. § 6103(b)(2)(A), that PFAs are not written determinations under I.R.C. § 6110, and, accordingly, are exempt from disclosure to the public under the Freedom of Information Act (FOIA). However, the issue of whether certain closing agreements must be disclosed under the FOIA has been the subject of recent litigation; thus far, courts addressing this issue have agreed with the IRS position. *See Tax Analysts v. IRS*, 53 F. Supp. 2d 449 (D.D.C. 1999); *Tax Analysts v. IRS*, 1999 U.S. Dist. LEXIS 16733 (D.D.C. Aug. 6, 1999), appeal docketed, No. 5284 (D.C. Cir. Aug. 13, 1999).

PFAs were judged a success, and the program continues to this day.

---

17. [12] Evelyn Brody, *The Limits of Charity Fiduciary Law*, 57 MD. L. REV. 1400, 1410–1411 & n. 49 (1998) ("Lately, perhaps responding to criticism that closing agreements create a secret body of law, some [IRS] regulators have conditioned settlement on the charity's assenting to public disclosure of the agreement.").

18. Notice 2000-12.

The tide appears to be turning away from the Service's position and in favor of disclosure of closing agreements under section 6104. Nevertheless, the issue remains open in other Circuits.

F. State and Local Filing Requirements

Most states — as well as most counties and municipalities — have their own statutes regulating charitable solicitation. Such statutes and ordinances typically have filing requirements as well as disclosure requirements. Some require entities to use particular words in charitable solicitations. Many also require entities soliciting the public to file, or to provide upon request, detailed information regarding the charity, often including a copy of the annual Form 990 information returns. Counties and localities often have "permit" ordinances, requiring registration prior to charitable solicitation. Many require solicitors (including sellers of merchandise, the proceeds of which benefit a charity) to carry a copy of such permits.

Violation of such statutes and ordinances varies. While many violations simply result in a fine, others amount to crimes, including felonies. For example, the Florida statute requires the following words to appear in relation to any charitable solicitation:

> A COPY OF THE OFFICIAL REGISTRATION AND FINANCIAL INFORMATION MAY BE OBTAINED FROM THE DIVISION OF CONSUMER SERVICES BY CALLING TOLL-FREE, WITHIN THE STATE. REGISTRATION DOES NOT IMPLY ENDORSEMENT, APPROVAL OR RECOMMENDATION BY THE STATE.[19]

The words not only must appear, but they also must be printed in capital letters. Printing them in lowercase letters technically constitutes a third-degree felony, punishable by up to five years in prison. While enforcement of such a technicality is rare, if it occurs at all, the statute nevertheless is clear. Counsel for exempt organizations would be well-advised to be aware of all such state statutes and local ordinances — and to inform their clients.

---

19. F.S. §496.411(3). Disclosure requirements and duties of charitable organizations and sponsors. In addition, each charitable solicitation must include:

- The name of the organization and the state of its principal place of business.
- A description of the purpose of the solicitation.
- Upon request, the name and address or telephone number of a representative.
- Upon request, the amount of the contribution which may be deducted.
- Upon request, the source from which a financial statement may be obtained.
- This statement must contain particular information.
- It must be provided within 14 days of a request.
- This is in addition to the financial disclosure information — generally a Form 990 — required to be filed with the state.

Writing and Research Exercise

1. Assume you are counsel for an exempt college. A member of your client's governing body informs you that she has been told that the person requesting information from the organization is doing so not because of a real need or desire to know about the organization's operations and finances, but only in hopes that an organization will inadvertently violate the law. The Board of Trustees asked you to prepare a memorandum discussing whether the request can be ignored since it is made for an improper purpose (i.e., in hopes of generating a lawsuit) and is merely a form of harassment. Prepare a brief memorandum for the Board. *See Schuloff v. Queens College Foundation*, 994 F. Supp. 425 (E.D.N.Y. 1998).

2. How would your analysis differ if instead of the requests being made by Anita Schluoff, (per Question 1), the requests were made by Tax Analysts and you knew that a reporter from that industry news magazine was simply seeking to find out whether organizations in the New York area were complying with § 6104?

3. What are some reasons why exempt organizations would be reluctant to divulge application and return information to such an extent that Congress felt obliged to enact a statute and the issue is frequently litigated?

4. Suppose your client hopes to build a controversial new cement plant. An environmental group, exempt under § 501(c)(3), opposes your plans. Would you seek information under § 6104, hoping to find the organization in violation of the statute? Would you seek similar information under state statutes or local ordinances? At what point would your actions amount to harassment rather than zealous representation of your client?

5. Go to www.guidestar.org and find a Form 990 and a Form 1023 relating to an organization concerned with animal welfare. It should be relatively easy to find a Form 990, but it may be difficult to find a Form 1023, because the "widely available" standard was made applicable to Form 1023s years after most such applications were filed. Whenever you are filing a Form 1023 for an organization, it is always helpful to have a completed and accepted Form 1023 with which to compare your own work. Note also that Guidestar normally includes a link to the referenced organization and you can use that link to request a copy of the organization's Form 1023 and accompanying materials.

6. Create a hypothetical (or real) organization and complete Form 1023 and all related forms.

PART TWO

Charitable Exempt Organizations — Restricted Activities

Chapter 11

Private Inurement Prohibition

A. Introduction

What began as a single rule — the prohibition of private inurement — has morphed into four distinct doctrines with overlapping factors:

1. The traditional § 501(c)(3) private inurement prohibition.
2. The 1995 § 4958 excess benefit prohibition for public charities.
3. The § 4941 self-dealing excise tax for private foundations.
4. The amorphous private benefit doctrine emanating from the courts and the service.

Chapter 11 covers the first two topics: the traditional prohibition and what significantly amounts to its statutory replacement. By 1995, Congress realized the traditional restriction was often ineffective.

Chapter 17 covers the third topic. Students should carefully note the striking differences between public charity private inurement — controlled by §§ 501(c) and 4958 along with the private benefit doctrine — as compared to private foundation self-dealing (§ 4941), a far more draconian set of rules.

Chapter 12 covers the private benefit doctrine, which arguably overlaps with private inurement. Because courts and the Service often treat it as a set of rules distinct from private inurement, we treat it separately as well. Be prepared, however, for some issue overlap between the chapters.

B. The General Rule Prohibiting Private Inurement

CODE: § 501(c)(3), (4), (6), (7)

REGS.: §§ 1.501(a)-1(c), 1.501(c)(3)-1(c)(2)

Perhaps the one assumption most associated with tax exemption, by laypersons and scholars alike, is that those who conduct charitable activities are not in it for the money. Supposedly, things money cannot buy motivate Samaritans, at least those who seek tax exemption. Indeed, when the Tax Code first formally recognized charitable tax exemption, the only explicitly stated requirement was that any financial surplus derived from conducting the charitable endeavor could not be distributed to those who control the entity by which charity is delivered. *See* Corporation Excise Tax of 1909, Ch. 6, Sec. 38, 36 Stat. 11, 115.

Specified entities received tax exemption provided no person received a "scintilla of individual profit" from the entity. 44 Cong. Rec. 4150–51 (1909) (statement of Sen. Bacon). Never has the law required or even assumed that the charitable entity, as opposed to the individuals controlling the entity, will not derive what might accurately be described as "profit." Indeed, an entity will often have more revenue (contributions, grants, service income) than expenses (expenditures in furtherance of the charitable goal). What is facially prohibited by the private inurement doctrine is the distribution of the excess revenue or inside appreciation—the increase in value of the entity's assets—to persons commonly referred to as "insiders." More practically, application of the rule effectively ignores the "net earnings" factor and prohibits the distribution or use of assets to or by insiders. More broadly—as covered in Chapter 12—the private benefit doctrine prohibits the operation of the entity from benefitting insiders—or even persons who do not qualify as insiders—regardless of whether the benefit results from a distribution or use of assets.

Although the Code articulates the private inurement doctrine simply—"no part of the net earnings [of the charitable organization may] inure to the benefit of any private shareholder or individual"—its application over the years has hardly been characterized by an identifiable principle or theory. For the most part, practitioners, judges, and scholars have been content with a doctrine seemingly devoid of theoretical thread from one case to another, and instead entirely dependent upon particular facts and circumstances. Two developments, one in the marketplace and one in the legal arena, have combined to make the facts and circumstances approach insufficient.

First, the emergence of "managed care" during the late 1980s and early 1990s placed great pressure on tax exempt hospitals to devise ways to compete with for-profit hospitals that were busily consolidating and gobbling up independent physician practices in order to provide a wider range of services in-house and at less cost. Employers and insurance companies—those who ultimately bear the variable costs of health care—naturally preferred entering into medical service provider contracts with hospitals that were best able to control the cost of health care. To maintain its niche and market competitiveness, the tax-exempt health care sector also began adopting similar consolidation strategies. Because all strategies depended on the hospital's monopolization of physician services, particularly family practitioners, exempt health care entities necessarily had to offer the same sorts of compensation packages to health care providers as were available from the for-profit sector. In many instances, this meant offering health care providers an explicit or implicit share of what would otherwise be the health care organization's revenue surplus. The lack of an identifiable principle with regard to the private inurement prohibition made the imperative to consolidate within the tax-exempt health care sector a difficult and dangerous one indeed. To preserve the traditional role of charitable health care, exempt health care providers needed to compete with for-profit health care. Yet, the amorphous private inurement doctrine hampered those efforts.

The second development showing the insufficiency of the facts and circumstances approach was the enactment of § 4958. Prior to 1995, the only consequence of "private inurement" was the loss of tax exemption. With § 4958, for the first time in the nearly one hundred year history of charitable tax exemption, violations of the private inurement doctrine could result in personal liability of the organization's directors as well as the person to whom the benefit inured. As a result, pressures arose to identify, in broader terms than particularized facts and circumstances, the meaning and theory of the private inurement prohibition. Section B of this chapter discusses § 4958, and the implications it has on the theory of private inurement and valuation of "net earnings."

This section begins with a discussion of the two requirements for a finding of private inurement: (1) the participation of an "insider" and (2) the "inurement" of "net earnings." Notice how, as with the overall prohibition against private inurement, the two requirements are simply stated, yet chock full of unresolved theoretical questions. Notice also, the consequence of violation is implicit: a loss of exempt status, which would result in subjecting the entity to general taxation and donors to loss of charitable deductions.

1. "Private Shareholder or Individual"

Who Is an Insider? The statutory language makes the prohibition against private inurement applicable only to "private shareholders and individuals." The regulations provide little assistance, stating that the phrase "private shareholder or individual" means any person having a "personal and private interest" in the activities of the organization. Treas. Reg. § 1.501(a)-1(c). The reference to "private shareholder" is somewhat antiquated, as nearly all states now provide that not for profit entities have members or directors rather than shareholders.

Also, one must not take the term "individual" too literally: of course, charities may benefit individual people. The prohibition applies only to the benefit of "insiders," as the regulation attempts to clarify.

Arguably, every employee of a tax-exempt organization is an insider under the regulation, and the Service has once so argued. *See* GCM 39670 (Oct. 14, 1987). The following case, *United Cancer Council v. Commissioner*, 165 F.3d 1173 (7th Cir. 1999), provides a judicial "insider" definition and also demonstrates one court's view of the Service's expansive definition of the phrase "private shareholder or individual." The case has prompted extensive criticism. As discussed in Chapter 12, the court arguably should have decided it under the private benefit doctrine.

The matter involved a nearly defunct charity that had a clear charitable purpose: encouraging preventive and ameliorative approaches to cancer. By 1984, its annual budget was merely $35,000. As the court explained, "it was on the brink of bankruptcy because several of its larger member societies had defected to its rival, the American Cancer Society." The charity hired an outside fundraiser—Watson & Hughey Company (W & H)—to re-invigorate the entity. Over a five-year period, fundraising activities generated $28.8 million of proceeds accompanied by $26.5 million of expenses. Arguably, some $12.2 million of expenses constituted "education."

The government revoked UCC's tax exemption, claiming violations of both the private inurement and private benefit doctrines. Arguably, the fundraiser so controlled the entity that it became an insider. Also, according to the government, operation of the "charity" essentially served little purpose other than to provide a business opportunity to the fundraiser. The Tax Court upheld the revoked exemption, but decided the case solely on private inurement grounds and did not reach the issue of private benefit. The Seventh Circuit disagreed, finding two things: W & H was not an insider (and thus the private inurement rules did not apply) and also the government failed to prove any excessive benefit to W & H.

United Cancer Council, Inc. v. Commissioner

165 F.3d 1173 (7th Cir. 1999)

POSNER, Chief Judge.

* * *

It is important to understand what the IRS does not contend. It does not contend that any part of UCC's earnings found its way into the pockets of any members of the charity's board; the board members, who were medical professionals, lawyers, judges, and bankers, served without compensation. It does not contend that any members of the board were owners, managers, or employees of W & H, or relatives or even friends of any of W & H's owners, managers, or employees. It does not contend that the fundraiser was involved either directly or indirectly in the creation of UCC, or selected UCC's charitable goals. It concedes that the contract between charity and fundraiser was negotiated at an arm's length [sic] basis. But it contends that the contract was so advantageous to W & H and so disadvantageous to UCC that the charity must be deemed to have surrendered the control of its operations and earnings to the noncharitable enterprise that it had hired to raise money for it.

... Because of UCC's perilous financial condition, the committee wanted W & H to "front" all the expenses of the fundraising campaign, though it would be reimbursed by UCC as soon as the campaign generated sufficient donations to cover those expenses. W & H agreed. But it demanded in return that it be made UCC's exclusive fundraiser during the five-year term of the contract, that it be given co-ownership of the list of prospective donors generated by its fundraising efforts, and that UCC be forbidden, both during the term of the contract and after it expired, to sell or lease the list, although it would be free to use it to solicit repeat donations. There was no restriction on W & H's use of the list. ...

Over the five-year term of the contract, W & H mailed 80 million letters soliciting contributions to UCC. Each letter contained advice about preventing cancer, as well as a pitch for donations; 70 percent of the letters also offered the recipient a chance to win a sweepstake. The text of all the letters was reviewed and approved by UCC. As a result of these mailings, UCC raised an enormous amount of money (by its standards)—$28.8 million. But its expenses—that is, the costs borne by W & H for postage, printing, and mailing the letters soliciting donations, costs reimbursed by UCC according to the terms of the contract—were also enormous—$26.5 million. The balance, $2.3 million, the net proceeds of the direct-mail campaign, was spent by UCC for services to cancer patients and on research for the prevention and treatment of cancer. The charity was permitted by the relevant accounting conventions to classify $12.2 million of its fundraising expenses as educational expenditures because of the cancer information contained in the fundraising letters.

Although UCC considered its experience with W & H successful, it did not renew the contract when it expired by its terms in 1989. Instead, it hired another fundraising organization—with disastrous results. The following year, UCC declared bankruptcy, and within months the IRS revoked its tax exemption retroactively to the date on which UCC had signed the contract with W & H. The effect was to make the IRS a major creditor of UCC in the bankruptcy proceeding....

The term "any private shareholder or individual" in the inurement clause of section 501(c)(3) of the Internal Revenue Code has been interpreted to mean an insider of the charity.... A charity is not to siphon its earnings to its founder, or the members of its board, or their families, or anyone else fairly to be described as an insider, that is, as the equivalent of an owner or manager. The test is functional. It looks to the reality of control rather than to the insider's place in a formal table of organization. The insider could be a "mere" employee—or even a nominal outsider, such as a physician with hospital privileges in a charitable hospital,... a licensor,... or for that matter a fundraiser....

The Tax Court's classification of W & H as an insider of UCC was based on the fundraising contract. Such contracts are common. Fundraising has become a specialized professional activity and many charities hire specialists in it. If the charity's contract with the fundraiser makes the latter an insider, triggering the inurement clause of section 501(c)(3) and so destroying the charity's tax exemption, the charity sector of the economy is in trouble. The IRS does not take the position that every such contract has this effect. What troubles it are the particular terms and circumstances of UCC's contract. It argues that since at the inception of the contract the charity had no money to speak of, and since, therefore, at least at the beginning, all the expenses of the fundraising campaign were borne by W & H, the latter was like a founder,... of the charity. The IRS points out that 90 percent of the contributions received by UCC during the term of the contract were paid to W & H to defray the cost of the fundraising campaign that brought in those contributions, and so argues that W & H was the real recipient of the contributions. It argues that because W & H was UCC's only fundraiser, the charity was totally at W & H's mercy during the five-year term of the contract—giving W & H effective control over the charity. UCC even surrendered the right to rent out the list of names of donors that the fundraising campaign generated. The terms of the contract were more favorable to the fundraiser than the terms of the average fundraising contract are.

Singly and together, these points bear no relation that we can see to the inurement provision. The provision is designed to prevent the siphoning of charitable receipts to insiders of the charity, not to empower the IRS to monitor the terms of arm's length [sic] contracts made by charitable organizations with the firms that supply them with essential inputs, whether premises, paper, computers, legal advice, or fundraising services.

Take the Service's first point, that W & H defrayed such a large fraction of the charity's total expenses in the early stages of the contract that it was the equivalent of a founder. Pushed to its logical extreme, this argument would deny the charitable tax exemption to any new or small charity that wanted to grow by soliciting donations, since it would have to get the cash to pay for the solicitations from an outside source, logically a fundraising organization. We can't see what this has to do with inurement. The argument is connected to another of the Service's points, that W & H was UCC's only fundraiser during the period of the contract. If UCC had hired ten fundraisers, the Service couldn't argue that any of them was so large a recipient of the charity's expenditures that it must be deemed to have controlled the charity. Yet in terms of the purposes of the inurement clause, it makes no difference how many fundraisers a charity employs. W & H obtained an exclusive contract, and thus was the sole fundraiser, not because it sought to control UCC and suck it dry, but because it was taking a risk; the exclusive contract lent assurance that if the venture succeeded, UCC wouldn't hire other fundraisers to reap where W & H had sown.

And it was only at the beginning of the contract period that W & H was funding UCC. As donations poured into the charity's coffers as a result of the success of the fundraising campaign, the charity began paying for the subsequent stages of the campaign out of its own revenues. True, to guarantee recoupment, the contract with W & H required UCC to place these funds in an escrow account, from which they could be withdrawn for UCC's charitable purposes only after W & H recovered the expenses of the fundraising campaign. But this is a detail; the important point is that UCC did not receive repeated infusions of capital from W & H. All the advances that W & H had made to UCC to fund the fundraising campaign were repaid. Indeed, it is an essential part of the government's case that W & H profited from the contract.

The other point that the Service makes about the exclusivity provision in the contract—that it put the charity at the mercy of the fundraiser, since if W & H stopped its fundraising efforts UCC would be barred from hiring another fundraiser until the contract with W & H expired—merely demonstrates the Service's ignorance of contract law. When a firm is granted an exclusive contract, the law reads into it an obligation that the firm use its best efforts to promote the contract's objectives.... If W & H folded its tent and walked away, it would be in breach of this implied term of the contract and UCC would be free to terminate the contract without liability.

* * *

The Service's point that has the most intuitive appeal is the high ratio of fundraising expenses, all of which went to W & H because it was UCC's only fundraiser during the term of the contract, to net charitable proceeds. Of the $28-odd million that came in, $26-plus million went right back out, to W & H....

[T]he ratio of expenses to net charitable receipts is unrelated to the issue of inurement. For one thing, it is a ratio of apples to oranges: the gross expenses of the fundraiser to the net receipts of the charity. For all that appears, while UCC derived a net benefit from the contract equal to the difference between donations and expenses plus the educational value of the mailings, W & H derived only a modest profit; for we know what UCC paid it, but not what its expenses were. The record does contain a table showing that W & H incurred postage and printing expenses of $12.5 million, but there is nothing on its total expenses.

* * *

UCC's low net yield is no doubt related to the terms of the fundraising contract, which were more favorable to the fundraiser than the average such contract. But so far as appears, they were favorable to W & H not because UCC's board was disloyal and mysteriously wanted to shower charity on a fundraiser with which it had no affiliation or overlapping membership or common ownership or control, but because UCC was desperate. The charity drove (so far as the record shows) the best bargain that it could, but it was not a good bargain. Maybe desperate charities should be encouraged to fold rather than to embark on expensive campaigns to raise funds. But that too is a separate issue from inurement. W & H did not, by reason of being able to drive a hard bargain, become an insider of UCC. If W & H was calling the shots, why did UCC refuse to renew the contract when it expired, and instead switch to another fundraiser?

We can find nothing in the facts to support the IRS's theory and the Tax Court's finding that W & H seized control of UCC and by doing so became an insider, triggering the inurement provision and destroying the exemption. There is nothing that corporate or agency law would recognize as control. A creditor of UCC could not seek the satisfaction of his claim from W & H on the ground that the charity was merely a cat's paw or alter ego of W & H.... The Service and the Tax Court are using "control" in a special sense not used elsewhere, so far as we can determine, in the law, including federal tax law.... It is hard enough for new, small, weak, or marginal charities to survive, because they are likely to have a high expense ratio, and many potential donors will be put off by that. The Tax Court's decision if sustained would make the survival of such charities even more dubious, by enveloping them in doubt about their tax exemption.

* * *

There was no diversion of charitable revenues to an insider here, nothing that smacks of self-dealing, disloyalty, breach of fiduciary obligation or other misconduct of the type aimed at by a provision of law that forbids a charity to divert its earnings to members of the board or other insiders.

REVERSED AND REMANDED.

Questions

1. In rejecting the Service's assertion of private inurement, Judge Posner relies in part on the lack of any intentional misconduct by the charity's board members. "There was no diversion of charitable revenues to an insider here, nothing that smacks of self-dealing, disloyalty, breach of fiduciary obligation or other misconduct of the type aimed at by a provision of law that forbids a charity to divert its earnings to members of the board or other insiders." Is there any language in the statute or regulations that makes intentional misconduct a condition precedent to a finding of private inurement?

2. The Service appeared to argue, and the Tax Court agreed, that a charity might become so beholden to an outside creditor or contracting party that the creditor or contracting party is able to control the charity and therefore becomes an "insider." Did Judge Posner disagree with the premise that the charity was too beholden to the fundraiser, or was his ultimate conclusion a function of his view that private inurement requires a finding of misconduct?

3. What standard did Judge Posner apply in determining insider status in response to the "facts and circumstances" which he found to be "no standard at all"?

4. If the potential for individual profit is the best guarantor of prudent and efficient behavior by a charity's governing body, as Judge Posner suggests, why should the law prohibit profit-taking? Is there some other means by which to ensure that tax-exempt organizations devote their full resources to charities without depriving the human managers of the incentive to be as efficient and prudent as possible?

5. The court stated: "For all that appears, while UCC derived a net benefit from the contract equal to the difference between donations and expenses plus the educational value of the mailings, W & H derived only a modest profit; for we know what UCC paid it, but not what its expenses were." Why would the government litigate a case grounded on private inurement by W & H if it had no evidence regarding the net dollar amount of inurement?

Note on United Cancer Council v. Commissioner

After nearly nine years of litigation in which the only issue settled was "who is an insider," UCC and the Service entered into a Closing Agreement (i.e., a settlement), whereby UCC's tax exemption was revoked for the years 1986 through 1989 and tax exemption was granted for the year 1990 and beyond, provided UCC refrained from public fundraising.

2. Forms of Inurement

How do net earnings "inure" to the benefit of an insider? Rarely, if ever, will a tax- exempt organization openly divide its surplus wealth amongst its insiders at the end of each year. Malevolent persons masquerading as Samaritans would not be that obvious. Instead, those seeking to profit from their close relationship with a tax-exempt organization must take their profits in disguise. Disguised profit taking is often accomplished by an insider overcharging the entity for goods or services he sells to the entity, or causing the entity to sell goods or services to the insider at less than market rates. In other cases, profit might inure to an insider because the insider has what amounts to an unlimited expense account.

Generally, private inurement cases fall into one of three categories:

1) direct monetary benefits to insiders;

2) indirect benefits to insiders resulting from the operation of the entity; and

3) "selfish motive" cases in which the underlying purpose of the entity is to benefit an insider.

Direct Monetary Benefits. The Technical Advice Memorandum below provides multiple egregious examples of direct benefits. A subtler example—one that often surprises readers—involves *Wendy L. Parker Rehabilitation Foundation v. Commissioner*, 1986 Tax Ct. Memo LEXIS 272. The case involved a coma victim who needed funding for care. Members of her family created and operated an organization with the following goals:

> [T]o aid the victims of coma, resulting from motor vehicular accidents, stroke, drowning, and other related causes; to provide such coma victims, who are in various stages of rehabilitation and recovery, with funds and therapeutic equipment and devices used in conjunction with accepted coma recovery programs; to run fund-raising affairs and social functions in aid of coma victims; to exchange and disseminate information concerning the care and treatment of coma victims in all stages of recovery.

Id. at *2-3. The entity claimed:

> [I]ts expected source of income if from contributions, and disbursements are for contributions to other coma recovery organizations; purchase of related equipment and devices; and payments to nurses and physicians. Twenty percent of the income will be distributed to organizations and 80 percent to coma patients. Thirty percent of petitioner's income is expected to be expended for the benefit of Wendy L. Parker.

Id. at *4. The government denied exemption and the entity brought an action in the Tax Court, which found for the government:

> The distribution of funds for the benefit of Wendy Parker assists the Parker family in providing for her care. These funds will be used to pay for the medical and rehabilitative care of Wendy Parker. This relieves the Parker family of the economic burden of providing such care. Consequently, there is a prohibitive benefit from petitioner's funds that inures to the benefit of private individuals. See *Founding Church of Scientology v. United States,* 188 Ct.Cl. 490, 412 F.2d 1197 (1969), cert. denied 397 U.S. 1009 (1970) (payments made to family members of organization's founder); *Charleston Chair Company v. United States,* 203 F. Supp. 126 (E.D.S.C. 1962) (scholarship aid given to son of officer and director); *Rueckwald Foundation, Inc. v. Commissioner,* T.C. Memo. 1974-298 (payments made for nursing home and medical expenses of mother and college expenses of son of officer and director).
>
> The Parker family's control over petitioner is not in itself fatal to petitioner's cause. However, petitioner's selection of Wendy Parker as a substantial beneficiary of its disbursements is the determinative factor in this case. Inurement of a benefit to "private individuals," whether monetary or not, as a result of contributions made to a purportedly exempt organization is proscribed. See *Lowry Hospital Association v. Commissioner,* [66 T.C. 850, 857 (1976),] *supra* at 857 n. 8; *People of God Community v. Commissioner,* [75 T.C. 127 (1980),] *supra* at 133; *Horace Heidt Foundation v. United States,* 145 Ct.Cl. 322, 170 F. Supp. 634, 638 (1959). The benefit to the Parker family is no less tangible because payment is directed not to be Parkers but to others for Wendy Parker's care.
>
> We do not doubt that the Parkers are sincere in their efforts to help coma patients, but these good intentions cannot rectify petitioner's failure to meet the standards for tax exemption. We cannot say that respondent has erred in its determination and we so hold.

Id. at *9–11 (citation omitted). Had strangers created and operated the organization and had Wendy Parker merely been a chosen beneficiary, the result likely would have been different. Readers, however, should not draw the lesson that the use of "straw-men" to organize and operate a charity will eliminate some risk of a private inurement attack. Such actions would be both misleading and unethical, although likely successful.

Indirect Benefits from Operations. Ginsburg v. Commissioner, 46 T.C. 47 (1966) involved an entity organized to dredge a channel near Long Island Sound. Ostensibly, the organization would benefit the community — a small village — by providing navigable waters, providing safe harbors for boats, and reducing foul oders during low tides. As a practical matter, it improved the property values of one or more founders. Nothing suggested the "net earnings" or assets were distributed to any "insiders"; however, the operations clearly benefitted insiders and thus justified denial of exempt status.

Selfish Motives. Section 501(c)(3) requires an organization to be both organized and operated "for" a charitable purpose. That word "for" prompts occasional questions regarding the motives behind creation of the organization. In all cases, organizations state selfless intentions — one can hardly imagine an entity with a stated purpose to aid the founders. Nevertheless, sometimes aiding the founders is exactly the underlying purpose of the entity. Understandably, proof of such "selfish motives" can be difficult for the government to come by, as few people provide it openly. Both the *Wendy Parker* and *Ginsberg* cases illustrate this type of inurement, although both courts decided the cases on more traditional grounds. A famous revenue ruling and two important cases provide further examples. The ruling is important for two reasons, only one of which is relevant in the chapter. First, it removed the requirement — dating from 1955 — that exempt hospitals provide indigent care; instead, it replaced the requirement with one of emergency room indigent care. Later, Revenue Ruling 83-157 eliminated even that amount of aid to indigents. Second — and relevant for this chapter — the ruling compared two hypothetical hospitals — one open generally to all local doctors and their patients and the other restricted to the founding doctors. Otherwise, the two hospitals were similar. Not surprisingly, the first would be exempt and the latter would not. The reason for denial of the second was not based on strict private inurement to insiders; instead, it rested on the lack of a charitable purpose and the existence of a "private" or selfish purpose.

Revenue Ruling 69-545

1969-2 C.B. 117

Examples illustrate whether a nonprofit hospital claiming exemption under section 501(c) (3) of the Code is operated to serve a public rather than a private interest * * *

Situation 1. Hospital *A* is a 250-bed community hospital. Its board of trustees is composed of prominent citizens in the community. Medical staff privileges in the hospital are available to all qualified physicians in the area, consistent with the size and nature of its facilities. The hospital has 150 doctors on its active staff and 200 doctors on its courtesy staff. It also owns a medical office building on its premises with space for 60 doctors. Any member of its active medical staff has the privilege of leasing available office space. Rents are set at rates comparable to those of other commercial buildings in the area.

The hospital operates a full time emergency room and no one requiring emergency care is denied treatment. The hospital otherwise ordinarily limits admissions to those who can pay the cost of their hospitalization, either themselves, or through private health insurance, or with the aid of public programs such as Medicare. Patients who cannot meet the financial requirements for admission are ordinarily referred to another hospital in the community that does serve indigent patients.

The hospital usually ends each year with an excess of operating receipts over operating disbursements from its hospital operations. Excess funds are generally applied to expansion and replacement of existing facilities and equipment, amortization of indebtedness, improvement in patient care, and medical training, education, and research.

Situation 2. Hospital *B* is a 60-bed general hospital which was originally owned by five doctors. The owners formed a nonprofit organization and sold their interests in the hospital to the organization at fair market value. The board of trustees of the organization consists of the five doctors, their accountant, and their lawyer. The five doctors also comprise the hospital's medical committee and thereby control the selection and the admission of other doctors to the medical staff. During its first five years of operations, only four other doctors have been granted staff privileges at the hospital. The applications of a number of qualified doctors in the community have been rejected.

Hospital admission is restricted to patients of doctors holding staff privileges. Patients of the five original physicians have accounted for a large majority of all hospital admissions over the years. The hospital maintains an emergency room, but on a relatively inactive basis, and primarily for the convenience of the patients of the staff doctors. The local ambulance services have been instructed by the hospital to take emergency cases to other hospitals in the area. The hospital follows the policy of ordinarily limiting admissions to those who can pay the cost of the services rendered. The five doctors comprising the original medical staff have continued to maintain their offices in the hospital since its sale to the nonprofit organization. The rental paid is less than that of comparable office space in the vicinity. No office space is available for any of the other staff members.

* * *

In the general law of charity, the promotion of health is considered to be a charitable purpose. *Restatement (Second), Trusts*, sec. 368 and sec. 372; IV *Scott on Trusts* (3d ed. 1967), sec. 368 and sec. 372. A nonprofit organization whose purpose and activity are providing hospital care is promoting health and may, therefore, qualify as organized and operated in furtherance of a charitable purpose....

Since the purpose and activity of Hospital *A*, apart from its related educational and research activities and purposes, are providing hospital care on a nonprofit basis for members of its community, it is organized and operated in furtherance of a purpose considered "charitable" in the generally accepted legal sense of that term. The promotion of health, like the relief of poverty and the advancement of education and religion, is one of the purposes in the general law of charity that is deemed beneficial to the community as a whole even though the class of beneficiaries eligible to receive a direct benefit from its activities does not include all members of the community, such as indigent members of the community, provided that the class is not so small that its relief is not of benefit to the community.... By operating an emergency room open to all persons and by providing hospital care for all those persons in the community able to pay the cost thereof either directly or through third party reimbursement, Hospital *A* is promoting the health of a class of persons that is broad enough to benefit the community.

The fact that Hospital *A* operates at an annual surplus of receipts over disbursements does not preclude its exemption. By using its surplus funds to improve the quality of patient care, expand its facilities, and advance its medical training, education, and research programs, the hospital is operating in furtherance of its exempt purposes.

Furthermore, Hospital *A* is operated to serve a public rather than a private interest. Control of the hospital rests with its board of trustees, which is composed of independent civic leaders. The hospital maintains an open medical staff, with privileges available to all qualified physicians. Members of its active medical staff have the privilege of leasing available space in its medical building.... It operates an active and generally accessible emergency room. These factors indicate that the use and control of Hospital *A* are for the benefit of the public and that no part of the income of the organization is inuring to the benefit of any private individual nor is any private interest being served.

Accordingly, it is held that Hospital *A* is exempt from Federal income tax under section 501(c)(3) of the Code.

Hospital *B* is also providing hospital care. However, in order to qualify under section 501(c)(3) of the Code, an organization must be organized and operated *exclusively* for one or more of the purposes set forth in that section. Hospital *B* was initially established as a proprietary institution operated for the benefit of its owners. Although its ownership has been transferred to a nonprofit organization, the hospital has continued to operate for the private benefit of its original owners who exercise control over the hospital through the board of trustees and the medical committee. They have used their control to restrict the number of doctors admitted to the medical staff, to enter into favorable rental agreements with the hospital, and to limit emergency room care and hospital admission substantially to their own patients. These facts indicate that the hospital is operated for the private benefit of its original owners, rather than for the exclusive benefit of the public. See *Sonora Community Hospital v. Commissioner*, 46 T.C. 519 (1966), *aff'd*, 397 F. 2d 814 (1968).

Accordingly, it is held that Hospital *B* does not qualify for exemption from Federal income tax under section 501(c)(3) of the Code. In considering whether a nonprofit hospital claiming such exemption is operated to serve a private benefit, the Service will weigh all of the relevant facts and circumstances in each case. The absence of particular factors set forth above or the presence of other factors will not necessarily be determinative.

* * *

Revenue Ruling 56-185 is hereby modified to remove therefrom the requirements relating to caring for patients without charge or at rates below cost....

Note on Revenue Ruling 69-545

Arguably, this ruling belongs in Chapter 12, which covers the "private benefit" doctrine, rather than in Chapter 11 on "private inurement." That point illustrates the common difficulty in distinguishing the doctrines. One distinction involves "insiders." In *American Campaign Academy*, included in Chapter 12, the court found the benefitting persons or entities were not "insiders." In the Revenue Ruling, the five doctors would constitute "insiders."

A similar analysis appeared in Revenue Ruling 71-395, 1971-2 C.B. 228 (1971) — an organization devoted to operating an art gallery. Fifty artists in one community created and operated the entity, which sold their artwork. Not surprisingly, the IRS ruled the entity not to be exempt: "The cooperative gallery in this case is engaged in showing and selling only the works of its own members and is a vehicle for advancing their careers and promoting the sale of their work. It serves the private purposes of its members, even though the exhibition and sale of paintings may be an educational activity in other respects." *Id.* Compare that to *Goldsboro Art League*, 75 T.C. 337 (1980), which held a similar entity to be exempt:

> Among the factors we consider in determining whether an organization is operated to further a substantial commercial purpose are the particular manner in which an organization's activities are conducted, the commercial hue of these activities, and the existence and amount of profit from these activities.
>
> In the instant case, since there are no other art museums or galleries in the area, petitioner has found difficulty attracting artists to exhibit their work without the incentive of the Art Gallery and Art Market. Petitioner has a jury to select which works will be displayed, and we find it significant that the works are chosen not for their salability but for their representation of modern trends. Exhibiting an artist's more daring works in a part of the country where there are no nearby art museums or galleries illustrates that petitioner's purpose is primarily to educate rather than to sell.
>
> Moreover, petitioner's activities with respect to the Art Market and Art Gallery must be viewed in connection with petitioner's other activities. The clear impression that we get from the record is one of petitioner's dedication to teach the public, through a variety of means, to appreciate art. We find that petitioner's sales activities are incidental to its other activities and serve the same overall objective of art education. This is not a case where the other activities are adjunct to petitioner's sales, but, rather, where petitioner's sales activities are secondary and incidental to furthering its exempt purpose. See *Aid to Artisans, Inc. v. Commissioner*, 71 T.C. 202 (1978); *Pulpit Resource v. Commissioner*, 70 T.C. 594 (1978); *Golden Rule Church Association v. Commissioner*, 41 T.C. 719 (1964); *Saint Germain Foundation v. Commissioner*, 26 T.C. 648 (1956); cf. *Senior Citizens Stores, Inc. v. United States, supra; Christian Manner International v. Commissioner*, 71 T.C. 661 (1979).

> We are convinced, moreover, that petitioner is not operating these galleries for a profit. Petitioner retains only approximately 20 percent of the gross receipts from the sales and uses this amount to defray its expenses. A review of petitioner's books for 3 years shows that petitioner has either made no profit or, at most, a negligible one, for these years.
>
> Finally, we reject respondent's contention that petitioner is operated for the private benefit of individuals. Firstly, we find that petitioner's purpose in operating these two galleries is art education for the benefit of the public. Secondly, the private benefit prohibited under section 501(c)(3) relates to a benefit to "designated individuals, the creator or his family, shareholders of the organization, or persons controlled, directly or indirectly, by such private interests.... The artists exhibited in these two galleries had their works selected by a jury which these artists did not control. Similarly, the proscription against private inurement to the benefit of any shareholder or individual does not apply to unrelated third parties. *People of God Community v. Commissioner*, 75 T.C. 127 (1980); *Broadway Theatre League of Lynchburg, Va. v. United States, supra*. Of the more than 100 artists exhibited in the two galleries, only 2 members of petitioner have exhibited their works in these galleries and neither of these members is on petitioner's board of directors.

Id. at 344-46 (footnotes omitted). *Goldsboro* involved two significant distinctions from Revenue Ruling 71-395. First, the *Goldsboro* entity had many other activities in addition to operating the art gallery. How much additional activity was needed is unclear. Arguably, the extra activities were "window dressing" made to achieve exempt status for an art gallery. The court, however, did not see it that way. Second, the artists themselves did not control the gallery—which was likely the most important distinction.

Another "selfish motive" case is *Easter House v. United States*, 12 Cl. Ct. 476 (1987), *aff'd*, 846 F.2d 78 (Fed. Cir. 1988). The case involved an Illinois not-for-profit entity that cared for unwed mothers, mostly those in need and unemployed. It charged $1,500 to investigate prospective parents and $16,500 to adopt.

Easter House v. United States

12 Cl. Ct. 476 (1987)

* * *

One result of plaintiff's fee structure was to put its adoption service beyond the reach of a sizeable segment of the population. Thus, qualified applicants who cannot afford to pay $16,500 are unable to adopt through plaintiff or, at best, reduced to taking a problem placement at a lower placement fee.

Plaintiff concedes that in most cases the fees paid by the adoptive parents more than cover the costs of the services it provided mother, child and adoptive parents. Although plaintiff has represented otherwise, the record clearly indicates that prospective adoptive parents are informed by plaintiff in the information literature furnished to them, that they are responsible for all legal expenses relative to the adoption process.

The fees charged adoptive parents are plaintiff's sole source of income. Plaintiff states it depends upon these fees to perform its services to mother, child and adoptive parents. It neither solicits nor receives contributions. Plaintiff neither receives nor seeks funding from state or federal government sources. Plaintiff claims that its fee system is not designed to produce a profit (over the costs of providing the services and maintaining a "reasonable reserve"). For the calendar year 1983 plaintiff had a "total service income" of $1,032,575 and net income of $257,338.78, a profit margin of approximately 25 percent.

The dominant influence in plaintiff's affairs is Seymour Kurtz (Kurtz), its president and only "life member." The life member elects every other member of the corporation. Kurtz is also one of plaintiff's directors. He had no active role as an officer until 1974. In 1962 and 1963 Kurtz, as attorney, provided some legal services for plaintiff and received approximately $2,000 in fees for these services. In 1973 Kurtz became one of plaintiff's directors. At this time, i.e., 1973, plaintiff was considering closing down because of the shortage of children available for adoption. Kurtz became president of plaintiff in 1974. During the period 1974–1977, the plaintiff's activities were minimal and they placed only a few children for adoption. As the only life member Kurtz elects and qualifies all of the other directors. On its IRS form 1023, plaintiff lists five other directors in addition to Kurtz.

As the sole life member of plaintiff, Kurtz enjoyed many powers. Only the life member can recommend the expulsion or suspension of another member (for or without cause). Only the life membership is transferable by inter vivos or testamentary instrument. No other membership is transferable. The life member decides what corporate affairs will be managed by the board of directors and what corporate affairs will be managed by the life member. The life member has the power, even without a board of directors' resolution, to enter into contracts and execute drafts, notes and other forms of indebtedness on plaintiff's behalf. For Kurtz's services in 1983, he received a salary of $45,125.05. In 1982, Kurtz received a salary of $32,000.

Kurtz was associated with three other child welfare organizations at times material herein. He was a compensated officer of Friends of Children, Inc. (Friends), a Georgia not-for-profit agency which provided services similar to the ones provided by plaintiff. Plaintiff and Friends shared a common principal director—Margot Hamilton. Kurtz was also an officer of Tzyril Foundation (Tzyril), a not-for-profit organization established to coordinate adoptions of foreign children by parents in the United States. Tzyril began its operations in the mid-1970's and ceased activity in 1982. Finally, Kurtz was the sole owner and "wholly controlled" Suko Corporation (Suko), a for-profit corporation established to provide legal services for adoption of Latin American children. At times pertinent to plaintiff's application for exemption Kurtz had "other sources of income," not otherwise explained in the record, in addition to that received from plaintiff and Friends.

Plaintiff has engaged in financial transactions with all of the entities listed above. For the period ending December 31, 1982 plaintiff held a note from Friends in the amount of $7,500. It also held Tzyril's note for $86,681.20. Finally, Suko was indebted to plaintiff for a $6,250.00 loan. In plaintiff's 1983 financial statement it lists the note due from Tzyril. It also lists a note due from Friends, but this one is for $75,000. Apparently the Suko loan was repaid because it is not on plaintiff's 1983 financial statement. The record contains no terms or payment schedule relative to the Tzyril loan. The Friends loan was explicitly made without any terms of repayment schedule.

* * *

All of the services provided by plaintiff to the unwed mothers and children could ostensibly be provided without the adoption service. Plaintiff argues that the adoption service is integral to the unwed mothers' prenatal care because it provides them with "peace of mind" that their babies will have a good home after delivery. Yet this hardly seems to support a contention that the adoption service is operated *primarily* for accomplishing educational and charitable purposes.

Of course plaintiff contends that the adoption service is operated in furtherance of providing educational and charitable services to the unwed mothers and children because the adoption service provides the funding for the exempt purposes. Funding an exempt activity can in and of itself constitute an exempt activity. See *World Family Corp. v. Commissioner*, 81 T.C. 958, 963 (1983). This contention calls into question whether providing funding for the educational and charitable services is the *primary* purpose for which plaintiff operates the adoption agency or whether there is some other purpose(s) served by the adoption agency which removes the "primary" from the purpose of providing funds.

This consideration dovetails into the second of the guidelines set forth above. The adoption service provided by plaintiff is in the nature of a trade or business. Operation of a trade or business does not automatically negate an organization qualifying for an exemption.... However, the organization must be operated primarily to carry on an exempt purpose. Thus the relevant inquiry again is: does plaintiff's adoption service primarily further exempt purposes or other purposes. Put another way, is the promotion of exempt purposes primary to business purposes or vice versa? This is a question of fact to be decided on the evidence in the record. *B.S.W. Group, Inc. v. Commissioner, supra,* 70 T.C. at 357 (citations omitted).

The court finds that the business purpose, and not the advancement of educational and charitable activities purpose, of plaintiff's adoption service is its primary goal. Plaintiff is in competition with other adoption services. Thus it is competing with other commercial organizations providing similar services. This is far different than an organization which solicits charitable contributions. Plaintiff's competition provides its activities with a commercial hue. *See American Institute for Economic Research v. United States, supra,* 157 Ct. Cl. at 555, 302 F.2d at 938. "Competition with commercial firms is strong evidence of the predominance of non-exempt commercial purposes." *B.S.W. Group, Inc. v. Commissioner, supra,* 70 T.C. at 358.

Plaintiff in past years has accumulated very substantial profits. The court realizes that the presence of profits does not automatically prevent an organization from qualifying under section 501(c)(3). *See Industrial Aid for the Blind v. Commissioner,* 73 T.C. 96, 101 (1979). However, the existence of profits certainly can be indicative of a business purpose. *See Scripture Press Foundation v. United States, supra,* 152 Ct. Cl. at 468, 285 F.2d at 803; *B.S.W. Group, Inc. v. Commissioner, supra,* 70 T.C. at 357. The substantial fees plaintiff charged were not incidental to plaintiff's exempt purposes but rather admittedly were designed to make a profit. *See Scripture Press Foundation v. United States, supra,* 152 Ct. Cl. at 472, 285 F.2d at 804. The profit-making fee structure of the adoption service looms so large as to overshadow any of its other purposes. *See id.* at 475, 225 F.2d at 807. It is also noted that plaintiff's only source of income was the fees charged adoptive parents. This is a factor indicating the commercial character of the operation. *See B.S.W. Group, Inc. v. Commissioner, supra,* 70 T.C. at 359-60. The fact that plaintiff never solicited, nor does it plan to solicit charitable contributions to further its operation is another factor indicating a commercial operation. *Id.* at 359. *See also Federation Pharmacy Services, Inc. v. Commissioner,* 625 F.2d 804, 808 (8th Cir. 1980).

In its moving brief, plaintiff offers three reasons why it must accumulate profits. In its reply brief plaintiff offers a fourth reason. None are persuasive. First, it cites to a state law requiring that an adoption agency maintain financial stability. Yet this law indicates only that an agency must maintain "financial solvency". It says nothing about accumulating profits. Next, it says that the profits are needed as a sort of self insurance for certain contingencies. There is nothing in the record to suggest that insurance for these contingencies is not available through conventional insurers. Additionally, it says that it needs the profits to provide for various services to the unwed mothers and children. However, plaintiff also claims that the fees paid by the adoptive parents cover these services. Finally, plaintiff states it is planning to purchase a residential facility because the cost of rent is so high. The record is devoid of any evidence of this. The pages plaintiff cites merely says that plaintiff had to expend high sums of rental property it would not have had to spend if it owned its own facility.

Plaintiff's response to the deficiencies in the record relative to the above discussion on the reasons for accumulation is as follows. In various submissions to the IRS during the application process plaintiff made some of the same arguments it makes here concerning the reasons for accumulating profits. These arguments were made in memoranda which are now included in the administrative record. Therefore, says plaintiff, these reasons for profit accumulation contained in these memos must be accepted as true. Plaintiff fails to distinguish the difference between its arguments and facts. An argument made by plaintiff during the administrative process is not somehow converted into an unreviewable fact by having been included in the administrative record. The court is not precluded from examining the merits of plaintiff's argument which is presented to it.

The IRS also found that plaintiff failed to qualify as an organization described in section 501(c)(3) because plaintiff failed to establish that no part of its net earnings inured to private individuals or that plaintiff served private individuals. Pursuant to section 501(c)(3) an organization does not qualify for tax exempt status if any of its net earnings inures to the benefit of any private shareholder or individual.[1] The phrase "private shareholder or individual" refers to persons having a personal and private interest in the activities of the organization. . . . Furthermore, an organization is not organized and operated exclusively for section 501(c)(3) purposes if it serves a public rather than private interest. Treas. Reg. 1.501(c)(3)-1(d)(1)(ii).

Plaintiff argues that the IRS never named the individuals to whom its net earnings inured nor named the private individuals plaintiff served. Therefore, plaintiff contends, the IRS determination was wrong. This argument appears to be an attempt on the part of plaintiff to shift the burden of proof it must satisfy in order to establish its exemption. It is the taxpayer who must prove its entitlement to an exemption. *The Founding Church of Scientology v. United States,* 188 Ct. Cl. 490, 496, 412 F.2d 1197, 1200 (1969). It is the taxpayer who must demonstrate that no part of its earnings inured to the benefit of any private individual. *The Basic Unit Ministry of Karl Schurig v. Commissioner,* 670 F.2d 1210, 1211, 1213 (D.C. Cir. 1982). Likewise, it is the responsibility of an organization to establish that it serves a public rather than private interest. Treas. Reg. § 1.501(c)(3)-1(d)(1)(ii). Plaintiff cannot make up for the lack of an affirmative showing on its part that there is not any inurement or service to private interests by claiming that the IRS has not proven that there is. The IRS does not have to "prove" anything. It is plaintiff's burden to prove its net earnings do not inure to the benefit of a private shareholder or individual or that it does not serve a private interest.

The term "net earnings" in section 501(c)(3) allows an organization to incur ordinary and necessary expenditures in its operations without losing its tax exempt status. *The Founding Church of Scientology v. United States, supra,* 188 Ct. Cl. at 496, 412 F.2d at 1200. One of those ordinary and necessary expenditures is the payment of reasonable salaries. Thus payment of a reasonable salary to an employee of the organization does not automatically result in inurement. *Id.; Fraternal Medical Specialist Services, Inc. v. Commissioner, supra,* 49 T.C.M. at 292. However, payment of an excessive salary will result in inurement. *The Founding Church of Scientology v. United States, supra,* 188 Ct. Cl. at 496, 412 F.2d at 1200; *Unitary Mission Church v. Commissioner, supra,* 74 T.C. at 514. Whether a salary is reasonable or excessive is a question of fact. *Unitary Mission Church v. Commissioner, supra,* 74 T.C. at 514.

1. [15] The Tax Court has held on more than one occasion that the requirement prohibiting inurement to private shareholders and individuals is redundant to the operational test since in order to qualify as operating for an exempt purpose an organization must provide a public not a private benefit. *Unitary Mission Church v. Commissioner,* 74 T.C. 507, 512 n. 7 (1980), *aff'd,* 647 F.2d 163 (2d Cir. 1981); *Western Catholic Church, v. Commissioner,* 73 T.C. 196, 209 n. 27, 213 (1979), *aff'd,* 631 F.2d 736 (7th Cir. 1980). Nevertheless, in the case at hand, the IRS separately stated that plaintiff was not operated for an exempt purpose and had not proven its net earnings did not inure to the benefit of a private shareholder or individual. As a result, the court will undertake a separate analysis of the inurement issue in the interest of sequential completeness.

One of the factors used in determining the reasonableness of a salary is whether or not an individual works for an organization full time. Income received from other sources is an indication that the recipient is not employed on a full time basis by the organization. *The Founding Church of Scientology v. United States, supra,* 188 Ct. Cl. at 498, 412 F.2d at 1201.

Net earnings may inure to an individual in ways other than the payment of excessive salaries. For example, the existence of a private source of loan credit from an organization's earnings may amount to inurement. *The Founding Church of Scientology v. United States, supra,* 188 Ct. Cl. at 499, 412 F.2d at 1201; *Unitary Mission Church v. Commissioner, supra,* 74 T.C. at 515.

It is also important to note that section 501(c)(3) specifically provides that "no part" of the organization's net earnings may inure to a private shareholder or individual. This means that any inurement, regardless of amount, will prevent an organization from qualifying under section 501(c)(3). *The Founding Church of Scientology v. United States, supra,* 188 Ct. Cl. at 497, 412 F.2d at 1200; *Unitary Mission Church v. Commissioner, supra,* 74 T.C. at 513.

As mentioned above, the IRS determined that plaintiff failed to prove that none of its net earnings inured to the benefit of a private individual. Defendant argues that inurement is supported by two factors: (1) the size of Kurtz's salary and the amount of any other income from other sources and (2) loan transactions made by plaintiff. Plaintiff asserts these issues were never raised until the present litigation. However, the record shows that the IRS was concerned about, and placed plaintiff on notice relative to these two issues during the administrative process.

The court finds the IRS conclusion supportable on the record before it. It is well settled that plaintiff must satisfy all the requirements for a tax exempt organization. *See Western Catholic Church v. Commissioner,* 73 T.C. 196, 207, *aff'd,* 631 F.2d 736 (7th Cir. 1980). Indeed, on this record, the court is persuaded that plaintiff could not make such a showing because part of its net earnings clearly inured to the benefit of Kurtz, plaintiff's president and sole life member. As president and sole life member, Kurtz qualifies as a private shareholder or individual as defined by the pertinent regulations....

Kurtz was paid a salary of in excess of $45,000 for his work for plaintiff in the year 1983. That same year, he was also compensated by another adoption agency, Friends, and also received income from "other sources." The record does not disclose how many hours per week Kurtz worked for plaintiff. As pointed out above, the presence of at least two other sources of income would indicate Kurtz's salary of over $45,000 was for part time employment with plaintiff. *See The Founding Church of Scientology v. United States, supra,* 188 Ct. Cl. at 498, 412 F.2d at 1201.

Additionally, plaintiff has provided loans to three organizations which Kurtz was either employed by or owned. Coupled with his status as a "life member" of plaintiff, this factor takes on added significance. A loan in excess of $86,000 was made by plaintiff to the Tzyril Foundation. The record contains nothing concerning any terms or repayment schedule relative to this loan. However, plaintiff's 1983 financial statement does indicate that plaintiff planned to write off the Tzyril loan as a bad debt. The 1983 financial statement also showed a loan outstanding to Friends in the amount of $75,000. The record shows that this loan to Friends was expressly made without any terms or repayment schedule. Finally a smaller loan for over $6,000 was made by plaintiff to the Suko Corporation. From all indications in the record, this loan was repaid.

Plaintiff claims that the Friends and Tzyril loans should not disqualify it from exempt status because they were made to organizations similar to itself for charitable purposes. There is absolutely no evidence in the record relative to the purposes of these loans. The loan to Suko was made to a for-profit corporation. Apparently the loan was not outstanding at the time of plaintiff's application. Nevertheless the fact that it was made shows that companies controlled by Kurtz had a *source* of loan credit in plaintiff. The existence of a source of credit is what it important. *The Founding Church of Scientology v. United States, supra,* 188 Ct. Cl. at 499, 412 F.2d at 1201; *Unitary Mission Church v. Commissioner, supra,* 74 T.C. at 515.

The totality of facts contained in the record certainly shows that a portion of plaintiff's net earnings inured to the benefit of Kurtz. His $45,000 salary for part time employment and utilization of plaintiff as a source of credit for other corporations add up to inurement as defined by the pertinent regulations and case law.

Note on Easter House

As the Claims Court noted in footnote 15, this case involves both the private inurement and the private benefit doctrines. Significantly, the court — citing the Tax Court — questioned whether the doctrines are distinct. We include the case here because it illustrates how an organizer might create an entity for the selfish purpose of employing himself. Arguably, the "private benefit" doctrine involves benefits to non-insiders; here, the private benefit — in addition to the private inurement of excessive income and low-interest loans — involved an "insider." Whether that distinction justifies a separate legal doctrine is debatable: arguably the case illustrates how private inurement has morphed into three doctrines. First, the case involves direct inurement as in Easter House's salaries and Wendy Parker's relief of family obligations. Second, it involves the lack of a public purpose (with a private or selfish one existing instead). Third, it involves the private benefit doctrine that, at least in the eyes of some, is distinct from the other two.

Significantly, the court noted extensive instances of direct private inurement — high salaries and low interest loans. However, even without those facts, the government's claim that the "purpose" was private rather than public remained. Would that have been sufficient for the government to win? One cannot be certain, which probably explains why cases involving a "private" motive tend to involve other "violations" as well.

The case also involves the "commerciality doctrine" discussed in Chapters 7 through 9. Suppose both the direct private inurement and the private motive (or private benefit) facts disappeared. Would the commercial nature of the entity be sufficient to deny exempt status?

Lastly, note the bolded language about halfway through. The court broadly stated that providing funds for a charitable purpose could itself be a charitable purpose. Is that correct? How would you reconcile that with the 1954 repeal of the "destination of income test"? *See*, the discussion in Chapter 8.

In Technical Advice Memorandum (TAM) 9451001 the Service revoked a health care facility's tax-exempt status because of private inurement. The health care facility subsequently challenged the revocation. *LAC Facilities, Inc. v. United States*, No. 94-604T, U.S.Ct. Fed. Cl. That action was later dismissed by stipulation of both parties. *See Notice of Disposition of Declaratory Judgment Proceedings under Section 7428*, 1998-52 IRB 88.

We make two prefatory points regarding TAM 9451001. First, the TAM tediously and laboriously details the extreme facts leading to its finding of private inurement. Indeed, it is rare to find such gross violations of the prohibition and we admit that the situation is atypical. The TAM is nonetheless valuable because it exemplifies in one ruling the many ways profit may be improperly distributed to insiders. There are many private inurement cases demonstrating a vast number of profit taking devices. The TAM provides exposure to those devices, while alleviating the need to read all those cases. Second, the TAM's use of letters makes it difficult to follow the transactions. The use of letters in technical advice memoranda, though, is typical. Read the TAM lightly once to get oriented. Then read it again closely to identify the several instances of private inurement. Afterwards, you should have a fair understanding of private inurement in the majority of its manifestations.

Questions

1. Read (TAM) 9451001. How many separate instances of private inurement did the Service identify? How many did it need to find to revoke the organization's tax-exempt status?

2. Scholars and practitioners often express frustration and bewilderment at the apparent inability to articulate broad principles concerning the occurrence of private inurement. They note that a finding of private inurement is so fact specific that there is little comfort in comparing a client's compensation practices with available case law. One scholar, though, has attempted to identify an overriding theory and label what he believes are the three generic types of private inurement. Darryll K. Jones, *The Scintilla of Individual Profit: In Search of Private Inurement and Excess Benefit*, 19 VA. TAX REV. 575 (2000). Jones argues that any arrangement which essentially renders the entity's wealth "synonymous" with that of the insider's wealth constitutes private inurement. He identifies three generic types of private inurement:

(1) strict accounting private inurement, whereby an entity pays too much or charges too little for some good or service provided by or to an insider, (2) incorporated pocketbook private inurement, whereby an insider freely uses the entity's money and property for purposes unrelated to the entity's charitable goals, and (3) joint venture private inurement, whereby an insider causes the entity to conduct its operations through or in conjunction with a taxable business in which the insider has a financial interest (e.g., causing the entity to purchase all of its necessary goods from the insider's separate taxable business). See if you can identify the different types of private inurement in Technical Advice Memorandum 9451001. How does the overall theory of synonymity of wealth between individual and entity apply to the TAM?

3. What is the significance of the organization's failure to show documentation with regard to certain transactions with insiders?

4. What is the significance of the organization's failure to maintain records pertaining to expenditures and to use an independent compensation committee? Had the organization maintained records and utilized an independent committee, might the result have changed?

5. Is the Service's conclusion that the physician's are "insiders" correct under the reasoning of *United Cancer Council v. Commissioner*? Why or why not?

C. The General Rule Prohibiting Private Inurement

CODE: § 4958, 4961, 4963(b and c)

REGS.: §§ 53.4958-1(a)–(d), 53.4958-3, 53.4958-4, 53.4958-6

TREAS.. REGS.: §§ 1.501(c)(3)–1(f)

One problem with the prohibition against private inurement is its drastic effect. Technically, one incident of profit-taking, no matter how small, is sufficient to revoke an entity's tax exemption. Prior to enactment of § 4958 the Service had no other weapon with which to combat such profit-taking. As one might expect, the "nuclear bomb" that revocation represents was rarely used and, in an ironic twist of circumstance, the harshness of the rule encouraged more profit-taking to occur than if the rule were not so harsh. Suppose, for example, that a high ranking employee of a private university engaged in private inurement. The Service's revocation of the university's tax-exempt status might not even have an impact on the actual wrongdoer (i.e., the insider). Instead, it might only harm the students who attend the university. Revocation would increase the university's cost and that cost might be passed on to the students. Moreover, revocation might adversely limit the university's ability to hire employees, thereby affecting both the quality of the education and the local economy. The Service was naturally reluctant to revoke an entire organization's tax exemption solely because of the actions of a single employee.

1. Origins of Intermediate Sanctions Statute

In 1993, Congress began considering proposals to impose "intermediate sanctions" in response to violations of the private inurement prohibition. The term "intermediate sanctions" refers to sanctions less than total revocation of tax exemption. The Stark Bill would have imposed excise taxes only on health care organizations that engaged in certain defined transactions. H.R. 3697, 103rd Cong., 2nd Sess. (1994). These transactions were (1) leasing property between insider and entity, (2) loans from entity to insider, and (3) the entity's payment of unreasonable compensation. In effect, the Stark Bill went further than the prohibition against private inurement by essentially penalizing certain transactions regardless of their reasonableness. Thus, an entity could engage in the transaction, but it would pay a penalty tax. Around the same time, the Treasury Department pushed its own proposal for intermediate sanctions. S. 2351, 103rd Cong., 2nd Sess. (1994). Both proposals were essentially part and parcel of the Clinton administration's health care reform proposals and when those proposals died, the intermediate sanctions proposals died along with them. Finally, in 1996, Congress adopted a broad proposal to provide sanctions against those who actually benefited from or authorized the distribution of profit to insiders.

2. Mechanics of § 4958

Mechanically, § 4958 presents practitioners with three separate problems: 1) record-keeping involving "disqualified persons"; 2) defining an excess benefit and obtaining appraisals so as to avoid excess benefits; and 3) application and computation of the tax.

a. Lists of Disqualified Persons

Maintaining records regarding "disqualified persons" is daunting. In reality, public charities must maintain three separate, over-lapping lists with similar labels. Under § 4958, they must keep track of "disqualified persons." If they did not, how would they possibly evaluate potential or actual excess benefit transactions, which only apply if a disqualified person is involved? In addition, most charities must maintain lists of § 4946 "disqualified persons," a list based on a very different set of definitions. This second list is essential for application of the § 509(a)(1) and (2) public support tests to determine whether the entity is a public charity or a private foundation. Without the second list, many charities will have difficulty in evaluating their § 509 status. To further complicate the matter, charities may want to maintain a list of "disqualified individuals" for purpose of applying the § 507 rules providing for elimination of "substantial contributor" status. Each list is often essential. Each serves a very different purpose. Each functions with its own definitions, which differ substantially; yet, each is denominated with a deceptively similar title.

To make matters worse, maintaining just the § 4958 list is complicated. Under § 4958(f)(1)(A), the list includes persons who are "in a position to exercise substantial influence over the affairs of the organization." Regulations provide details regarding who fits that category. A person on this initial list remains on the list for five years after he or she no longer fits the category. Hence anyone who serves on a charity board must be cognizant of potential excess benefit transactions with the organization for years after leaving the board.

Section (f)(1)(B) then includes family members of category (A) persons. Section 4958(f)(4) defines family members with a modified definition stemming from § 4946. This includes a person's "spouse, ancestors, children, grandchildren, great grandchildren, and the spouses of children, grandchildren, and great grandchildren," as well as siblings and their spouses. Naturally, it includes new family members added during the five-year period following an "influential" person's cessation of influence.

Section (f)(1)(C) then includes entities controlled (defined as 35% of voting power for a corporation) by persons on the list. That means a charity must track the investment portfolio of its board members, former board members, as well as of the family members of such persons. But the rule is still far more complicated. Section 4958(f)(3)(B) adopts constructive ownership rules based on §§ 4946 and 267. Hence, one must count investments owned by an entity owned by a person otherwise on the list. Thus, an entity must also track the investment portfolios of disqualified persons' investments.

As if that were not sufficiently complicated, § 4958(b)(1)(A) defines an "excess benefit transaction" as one affecting a disqualified person either "directly or indirectly." Thus, a transaction might be with a person not on the list, but nevertheless "indirectly" benefit someone on the list, and thus result in a substantial excise tax. Treasury Regulation § 53.4958-4(a)(2) provides some examples of "indirect" benefit.

Sections 4958(f)(1)(E) and (F) provide special rules for defining disqualified persons for donor advised funds. In some cases, these rules include investment advisors as well as their family members and controlled entities. *See*, § 4958(f)(8).

b. Defining and Avoiding Excess Benefit

As explained below, appraisals and valuations can be tricky, especially if they involve the sale of the entire exempt organization. But even lesser matters present complicated issues. For compensation, the entity may rely on independent directors who have "appropriate data" which is "adequately documented." Treasury Regulation § 53.4958-6. For general transactions, regulation § 53.49584(b) provides valuation standards. Because § 4958(b) imposes a tax on the participation of any "organizational manager," such persons must be aware of what constitutes "participation." Silence and inaction can constitute participation. Treasury Regulation § 53.4958-1(d)(3).

c. Computing the Tax

Section 4958 imposes two "tiers" of tax on excess benefit transactions. Effectively, § 6684 applies a third tier.

1) The first tier—under § 4958(a)(1)—imposes a tax of 25% of the amount involved, imposed on the benefitting disqualified person. Subsection (a)(2) also imposes a tax of 10% on the participation of managers with a cap of $20,000 per transaction. Management liability is joint and several. Managers are exempt from the tax if their participation is not "willful" and is due to "reasonable cause."

2) The second tier—under § 4958(b)—imposes an additional 200% tax on the disqualified person. This tax applies if the disqualified person fails to "correct" the transaction within the "taxable period." Section (f)(6) defines "correction" as generally undoing the transaction to the extent possible and placing the entity in a position no worse than it would have been had normal fiduciary duties applied. The "taxable period" begins with the date of the transaction and ends with the earlier of the mailing of a notice of deficiency or assessment of the tax. Practitioners should heed this last rule carefully. Section 6033(b)(11) imposes a reporting requirement on exempt organizations regarding § 4958 taxes imposed on managers or disqualified persons. Section 6011 requires the persons subject to the tax to file a Form 4720. Typically, reporting a tax results in an assessment of the tax, which would end the "taxable period" and thus foreclose the possibility of timely correction. Thus, an entity will want to carefully weigh prompt correction of such transactions prior to the reporting of them.

3) The third tier—under § 6684—imposes a penalty equal to the amount of any chapter 42 tax, essentially doubling the 10% rate to 20%, the 25% rate to 50%, and the 200% rate to 400%. The penalty applies to any person who has previously been liable for *any* Chapter 42 tax (including excises on private foundations as well as the § 4958 excise on public charity excess benefit transactions). It also applies to a first instance of tax if the taxpayer's actions were willful and flagrant.

3. Intermediate Sanctions Regulations

The Service adopted final regulations under § 4958 in January 2002, amended in 2007. Those regulations, quite naturally, follow the expectations expressed in the legislative history. Here, we note a few rules, not discussed in the legislative history, but adopted in the final regulations.

> ***Joint and Several Liability***: If an excess benefit transaction is not fully corrected within the applicable time period, any disqualified person who received an excess benefit from that transaction will be subject to the 200 percent second tier penalty. For example, suppose two disqualified persons sell their jointly owned land to a charity for an inflated price. One of the disqualified persons corrects the overpayment by giving back his

portion thereof but the other does not. The 200 percent second tier tax can be imposed on either disqualified person. Treas. Reg. § 53.4958-1(c)(2).

Reasoned Written Opinion: Note, too, that the regulations provide a specific method by which an organizational manager may avoid liability for the 10% tax imposed on managers who approve or acquiesce in (where the manager has a duty to speak or act) an excess benefit transaction. Managers, defined as individuals having powers or responsibilities similar to those of officers, directors, or trustees, are liable only if they knowingly participate in the transaction willfully and without reasonable cause. Treas. Reg. § 53.4958-1(d). A manager can obtain immunity, in effect, if she fully discloses the facts of the proposed transaction to legal counsel, a CPA, or a valuation expert, and receives back a "reasoned written opinion" that the transaction will not violate IRC § 4958. Treas. Reg. § 53.4958-1(d)(4)(iii). The immunity afforded to the manager applies even if the opinion is later shown to be incorrect.

501(c)(3) Application Requirement: Another notable rule stated in the regulation relates to the definition of an "applicable tax-exempt organization." Section 4958 applies only to such organizations. § 4958(c)(1)(A). Prior to the adoption of the final regulations there was concern as to whether 4958 applied to an entity that was tax-exempt under some other rule or provision of tax law, but which had not actually applied for § 501(c)(3) status. A public university is a prime example. It is generally assumed that public universities are exempt even without § 501(c)(3) under the doctrine of intergovernmental tax immunity (discussed in Chapter 24, States and State Related Organizations). Thus, some public universities never seek exemption under § 501(c)(3). Are those entities nevertheless "applicable tax-exempt organizations"? The regulation answer is "no." Not only are they exempted because they are governmental units or affiliates thereof, but the regulations also exclude all organizations that have not applied for § 501(c)(3) status in accordance with § 508 (discussed in Chapter 1). Treas. Reg. § 53.4958-2(a)(2).

Application to Churches. Treasury Regulations specifically include churches and church-related organizations as "applicable organizations," even though churches are exempt from the § 508 application requirement. Treas. Reg. § 53.4958-2(3)(ii). In 2007, Senator Grassley—ranking member of the Senate Finance Committee—sent letters to six prominent "media-based" ministries. In the letters, he expressed concerns raised by various media reports: "The allegations involve governing boards that aren't independent and allow generous salaries and housing allowances and amenities such as private jets and Rolls-Royces," he said. "I don't want to conclude that there's a problem, but I have an obligation to donors and the taxpayers to find out more. People who donated should have their money spent as intended and in adherence with the tax code." Press Release, Nov. 6, 2007. Because the entities are exempt from filing Form 990's, the senator requested audited financial statements. Church audit restrictions under section 7611 have hampered the government's ability to discover information regarding church finances, which would include information regarding possible section 4958 taxes. *See U. S. v. Living Word Christian Ctr.*, 2009 U.S. Dist. LEXIS 6902 (D. Minn. Jan. 30, 2009). According to news reports, the IRS has suspended all church audits until it can finalize section 7611 regulations specifying the appropriate government official to approve church audits. *See*, http://www.bna.com/church-tax-audits-n17179870390/.

Statutory Categories of Disqualified Persons: In a further effort to eliminate the subjectivity complained about in *United Cancer Council* (recall Judge Posner's lamentation that the determination of insider status based upon facts and circumstances was "no standard at all"), the regulations identify "statutory categories of disqualified persons," Treas. Reg. § 53.4958-3(b), as well as persons who will be presumed to be in a position to exercise substantial influence over the organization. Treas. Reg. § 53.4958-3(c). We do not repeat the list here, but only point out that the Service seems conscious of the need to provide a bit more predictability. The regulations retain the facts and circumstances as the final fallback method of determining who is and is not a disqualified person (i.e., an insider). Treas. Reg. § 53.4958-3(e).

Initial Contract Exception: The last significant new wrinkle concerns what has sometimes been referred to as the "first bite" rule. When the Service first proposed regulations under § 4958, many in the tax-exempt community argued that the intermediate sanctions (and by logical extension, the prohibition against private inurement) should not apply when a person receives unreasonable compensation by virtue of an arrangement or contract entered into before the person is actually in a position to exercise control or influence over the organization. Under this rule, a person who has no previous relationship to an entity, but who negotiates a contract by which he is hired as CEO and paid an unreasonable amount would not be in violation of either profit taking prohibitions because he was not an insider at the time the contract was made. Thus, the latter day insider would be granted an opportunity to take a free "first bite" of the organization's profit without sanction (at least not under the prohibitions against private inurement or excess benefit). The Service initially resisted adoption of the rule, but after its defeat in *United Cancer Council,* it decided to adopt the rule.

Thus, Treas. Reg. § 53.4958-4(a)(3) adopts what is called an "initial contract" exception. Under that rule, § 4958 will not apply to the first contract between the organization and an individual or entity even though the contract may provide for unreasonable payment or other excess benefit. The contract must call for a "fixed payment," defined as a payment that can be objectively determined from the terms of the contract and which is not subject to any person's discretion as to amount. The fixed payment may be determined by a formula stated in the contract. The Service disclaims any ability to challenge the payment as violative of the profit-taking prohibitions, except when the recipient fails to substantially perform under the contract or when the contract is materially amended.

Planning and Writing Exercise

A state law in Mississippi restricts the operation of nursing homes to nonprofit organizations exempt under § 501(c)(3). Your client, Out To Pasture, Inc., is a tax-exempt organization that has operated several such nursing homes for many years. Out To Pasture is owned equally by John and Susan Young, husband and wife who are the only members of the board of directors. John and Susan Young, along with their four children, also own a for-profit medical supply partnership. The four children are also Vice Presidents (for Finance, Human Resources, Quality Care, and Legal Affairs, respectively) of Out to Pasture, Inc. Recently, Mississippi repealed the law limiting the operation of nursing homes to exempt organizations, thus allowing for-profit entities to operate nursing homes. John asks you to prepare a plan whereby Out to Pasture, Inc. may be converted into a taxable LLC ("LLC") owned by John, Susan, and Med-Supply, Inc. Essentially, John wants Out To Pasture to sell all of its fixed assets (building, land, beds, supplies, etc.) to John, Susan and the children. The buyers will then contribute the assets to an LLC, through which they will operate the nursing homes as a profit-making venture. John tells you that he wants to complete the conversion quickly because he is aware that national commercial entities will soon be entering the market. In this regard he gives you a list of assets he wants transferred, along with values he derived from his own informed estimations. He tells you he does not want to hire an outside firm to value the assets because that would seriously delay the conversion. Evaluate John's proposal with regard to potential tax consequences. Identify potential disqualified persons and state the legal standards applicable to the sale of assets from Out to Pasture to the individual buyers. Would your analysis change if Out to Pasture instead sold the assets to Med-Supply or a previously formed LLC owned by the buyers?

Question

Charity is exempt under § 501(c)(3). It provides technical and animal husbandry training for students who do not wish to pursue a college degree. It was founded via a post-secondary "charter school" grant provided by the state to a former high school educator, his brother, and his sister-in-law, also former high school educators. The founders serve as President and Vice-Presidents, respectively and are paid salaries which are at the lower end of the salary range paid to administrators of similar technical, post-secondary institutions. All faculty members are part-time technicians, and none work year-round for Charity. In June, the President and his wife traveled to France using funds ($18,000) provided by Charity. The ostensible purpose was to study European post-secondary technical education methods, but in that regard, the President spoke to only one person who works for a French textbook publisher. He has no documentation showing any other consultations or observations regarding teaching methods. Late that summer, the President and his son traveled to Texas and were reimbursed their travel expenses ($1200) by Charity. That trip was said to be motivated by a desire to recruit students, but as it turned out, no out of state residents received applications or applied for admission to Charity. When the examining agent questioned the President regarding these trips, the President stated that the trips related to Charity's activities, and even if they were not, "I deserved a raise anyway." Analyze the consequences under IRC § 4958.

Note on Standards for 501(c)(3) Exemption If Charity Engaged in Excess Benefit Transaction

On April 29, 2008, the Service issued final regulations on the standards that apply in determining tax-exempt status of a charity that engages in an excess benefit transaction. See 73 Fed. Reg. 23069. Regulation § 1.501(c)(3)-1(f) clarifies 1) that the § 4958 excess benefit transaction rules only apply to organizations that are exempt under § 501(c)(3); 2) that the § 4958 rules are not determinative of whether an entity is entitled to § 501(c)(3) tax exemption; and 3) identifies standards for determining whether revocation of tax exemption is appropriate when § 4958 excise taxes also apply. The regulation also contains various examples.

Note on Applicability of Excess Benefit Transaction Rules to Supporting Organizations and Donor Advised Funds

As discussed above, the § 4958 excise taxes on excess benefit transactions apply to public charities and 501(c)(4) organizations but not private foundations. § 4958(e). One type of public charity is a "supporting organization," so called because its tax-exempt status derives from its support of another public charity. § 509(a)(3). In the Pension Protection Act of 2006, Congress made clear that an excess benefit transaction under § 4958 includes any "grant, loan, compensation or other similar payment" from a supporting organization to a "substantial contributor" or a substantial contributor's family member or a 35% enrolled entity. § 4958(c)(3). An excess benefit transaction also occurs when a supporting organization makes a loan to a disqualified person.

A donor advised fund allows the donor to make a contribution to the fund while retaining at least an "advisory" role in where his donation will go. Under § 4958(c)(2), effective in 2006, an excess benefit transaction occurs whenever a donor advised fund makes a "grant, loan, compensation or similar payment" from the fund to a donor, his family member or 35% controlled entity.

4. Valuation for Purposes of Private Inurement Prohibition and Intermediate Sanctions

Occasionally, exempt organizations decide to re-organize as for-profit entities. To accomplish this goal, an entity may sell its assets to another entity, subject to unrelated income provisions of §§ 512(b)(5), 514, and 1245. Serious problems arise if the purchasers are either "insiders" under the private inurement rules or "disqualified persons" under § 4958. Two cases illustrate the potential consequences.

In one particularly egregious case—litigated under the private inurement rules—an entity's Board members proposed to sell all the entity assets and operations to a for-profit organization owned by them. They sought a private letter ruling in which the government approved such a sale on the condition the price paid equaled the fair market value. Ultimately, the members—represented by the attorney who represented the organization in the PLR application—purchased the assets for approximately $6.6 million. The entity continued to operate as a research organization, largely in conjunction with the new for-profit psychiatric hospital. Two years later, they sold the business for $29 million—a 350% profit. In a memorandum opinion, the Tax Court held the organization was not exempt for all years following the sale. The Court found the sale price to be at least $1.2 million inadequate, which amounted to private inurement. As a result of the loss of exempt status, the entity's taxable income increased by approximately $1.2 million over a six-year period. The case illustrates a significant flaw in the private inurement prohibition: loss of exempt status resulted in increased taxes of several hundred thousand dollars; however, at least under federal law, the Board members retained their profit. Whether the entity ever sought recovery from its Board or attorney is not publicly available information. *Anclote Psychiatric Center v. Comm'r*, T.C. Memo. 1998-273.

In another notable example—litigated under § 4958—the operators of an exempt health care provider sought to convert the entity to for profit status. After several years of losses, they felt the entity could obtain easier financing if it ended its exempt status. An appraisal put the fair market value as negative; hence, the purchasers paid nothing. The operators issued shares in the new entity to themselves and to various family members. The government, however, valued the entity at over $18 million. As a result, it asserted § 4958 excise taxes in excess of $250 million. That number included asserted deficiencies against multiple family members who were jointly and severally liable; hence, the actual proposed tax was closer to $49 million.

The Tax Court painstakingly reviewed the various appraisals and ultimately adopted its own, which was a modification of the government's approach. The Court found an excess benefit of over $5 million, resulting in § 4958 taxes of over $11 million. In an opinion harshly critical of both the Tax Court and the government, the Fifth Circuit reversed and found for the taxpayer/purchasers. *Caracci v. Commissioner*, 456 F.3d 444 (5th Cir. 2006).

The *Caracci* opinions are very complicated. They illustrate competing valuation methods and the enormous consequences that can flow from expert opinions. Although no federal law precludes either "insiders" or "disqualified persons" from purchasing all the assets of an exempt entity, one must wonder whether they ever "should" do so. As both *Anclote* and *Caracci* illustrate, conflicts of interest are inherent, which will likely raise government suspicions.

We re-print part of the Fifth Circuit opinion below; however, we suggest students also read the Tax Court decision. We caution: the detailed appraisal explanations are quite complicated both in the Tax Court and Circuit opinions.

Caracci v. Commissioner of Internal Revenue

456 F.3d 444 (5th Cir. 2006)

* * *

The Tax Court's factual determinations are reviewed for clear error and its conclusions of law are reviewed de novo. The determination of fair market value is a mixed question of fact and law; "the factual premises [are] subject to review on a clearly erroneous standard, and the legal conclusion[s are] subject to de novo review." *Id.* Although the mathematical computation of fair market value is an issue of fact, the determination of the appropriate valuation method is an issue of law.

* * *

The Commissioner began the cascade of errors by issuing deficiency notices based on a brief, intermediate internal analysis. That analysis stated on its face that it was intermediate and that a final economic study had to be performed. Ignoring this disclaimer, the Commissioner issued valuation-based deficiency notices asserting § 4958 excise tax penalties against the Sta-Home entities and the Caracci family totaling $250,729,866 . . . and retroactively revoking the exempt status of the Sta-Home exempt agencies. Internal IRS documents reveal that the IRS issued the notices on the basis of an intermediate rather than final economic study to prevent the Caraccis from correcting what the IRS viewed as prohibited transactions, which would have reduced the § 4958 "intermediate sanction" penalties. The second reason the IRS issued these premature notices was its concern over the statute of limitations. . . . Even more disturbing, . . . the Commissioner defended the correctness of those notices for several years into this litigation and only conceded that the notices overstated the Commissioner's tax claim when the trial began in the Tax Court. . . .

The legal effect of the Commissioner's concession of error in the Tax Court is clear. "In a Tax Court deficiency proceeding, once the taxpayer has established that the assessment is arbitrary and erroneous, the burden shifts to the government to prove the correct amount of any taxes owed." The Tax Court, however, did not place the burden of proof on the Commissioner. . . . Instead, the Tax Court rejected most of the only support the Commissioner provided for the net excess benefit finding, the testimony of the Commissioner's valuation expert. At that point, the Commissioner failed to meet his burden of proof. At that point, the Tax Court should have found in the taxpayers' favor. Its failure to do so was error, as a matter of law.

In rejecting most, but not all, of the Commissioner's valuation expert's opinions, the Tax Court made a number of errors in the valuation method it selected and in the facts it found in selecting and applying that method. The Tax Court's use of Wilhoite's modified MVIC-Revenue method for valuing Sta-Home's assets, particularly its intangible assets, is wrong as a matter of law. Wilhoite had no experience in appraising healthcare companies and knew very little about the Sta-Home entities or their assets and liabilities. Wilhoite did not value Sta-Home's specific assets, but instead used a variation on an invested-capital valuation method to do a general and indirect valuation of Sta-Home's assets. The Tax Court adopted a modified version of Wilhoite's valuation approach, which is designed to value invested capital, . . . to value the assets of a company that had no capital. The Tax Court did so with no legal support. . . . The Tax Court then compounded this error by deriving the invested-capital multiple it applied to the Sta-Home entities using the seven public companies Wilhoite selected as "comparables." . . .

The Tax Court considered the Commissioner's expert testimony against a record of stipulated or undisputed facts. Those facts included that between 95 and 97 percent of Sta-Home's revenues came from Medicare, compared to a national average of 38 percent, and that Medicare only reimbursed up to actual costs and disallowed .7 percent of Sta-Home's annual costs, thereby ensuring that the Sta-Home entities would continue to build liabilities, not assets, and could not profit. . . . The parties did not dispute that the Sta-Home exempt agencies had $13.5 million in debts and liabilities that the newly created nonexempt entities assumed. . . . Despite these undisputed facts, the Tax Court's valuation method used an invested-capital valuation method that compared the Sta-Home entities with solvent, publicly traded companies with significant equity and a present ability to generate profits. This aspect of Wilhoite's analysis, accepted by the Tax Court, excluded distressed companies from the "comparables." . . .

A "comparable" must be substantially similar to the entity or asset that is at issue. As noted, none of the publicly traded entities Wilhoite chose were similar to Sta-Home. They were publicly traded. They had capital. They were profitable. They were not limited to offering basic, and unprofitable, therapies. Most important, they did not depend on Medicare for over 95 percent of their revenues, were not limited to recovery of actual costs, and did not have a portion of their actual costs disallowed every year. . . . The Tax Court recognized some of these differences, but assumed—without explanation—that the publicly traded entities could still be used as "comparables" as long as the amount of the multiple derived was adjusted. The Tax Court did not explain how it arrived at the amount of the adjustment or how that amount transformed fundamentally different financial entities into "comparables."

Using an adjusted version of the Wilhoite MVIC-Revenue invested capital method, the Tax Court concluded that the value of the assets the nonexempt Sta-Home entities received exceeded the value of the $13.5 million in liabilities and debts they assumed by $5.1 million. As the taxpayers point out, the Tax Court concluded that a willing buyer would assume $13.5 million in liabilities and pay $5.1 million to acquire the right to lose money on an ongoing basis. The Tax Court explained why it believed this apparently illogical conclusion made sense: it found that Sta-Home had the potential to make a profit, which demonstrated that its assets had substantial fair market value. This finding was clearly erroneous.

The Tax Court based its finding that the Sta-Home entities had the potential to make a profit on the finding that if Sta-Home had not paid a year-end bonus to its staff in 1995, it would have reported nontaxable income of approximately $1.78 million, "more than enough to eliminate the accumulated deficit in net asset value." ... The statement ignores the fact that under the Medicare system that accounted for between 95 and 97 percent of Sta-Home's revenues, there is no reimbursement unless there is an actual expense incurred. If Sta-Home had not paid the bonuses, the Medicare reimbursements it received would have been reduced by an equal amount, leaving the same level of company losses. The Tax Court did not take into account this effect of the Medicare reimbursement system on the Sta-Home entities.... The Tax Court also overlooked the reason for the bonuses and what they revealed about the Sta-Home entities' finances. These "bonuses" were unpaid, deferred employee pay, rather than discretionary bonuses. The deferred wages for existing employees, along with deferred first-month wages for newly hired employees, were mechanisms the taxpayers used to continue to operate despite their perennial cash-flow problems, their lack of profitability, their increasing operating losses, and their increasing deficits. The Commissioner acknowledged before the Tax Court that the salaries and bonuses were neither excessive nor unreasonable.... In short, these "bonuses" evidenced the unprofitable nature of the Sta-Home entities, not the potential for profitability, as the Tax Court erroneously stated.

* * *

This case began and ends with the Commissioner's refusal to recognize the legal effect of its own errors. The Commissioner issued erroneous and excessive deficiency notices, yet persisted in defending them for nearly two years of litigation before the Tax Court. After the Commissioner admitted his erroneous deficiency notices, he failed to meet his burden of proving that the excise taxes he sought to collect were correct. The Commissioner presented an expert who used an inappropriate valuation method and lacked basic factual information essential to the asset valuation he was called on to provide. The Tax Court erred as a matter of law when it failed to find for the taxpayers after it rejected much of the Commissioner's expert's opinion and instead proceeded to use bits and pieces from that opinion to value the Sta-Home assets transferred to the newly created nonexempt entities. The Tax Court erred as a matter of law in the valuation method it selected. In the process of arriving at and applying that method, and in struggling to make that method make sense, the Tax Court made a number of clearly erroneous factual findings. These errors led the Tax Court to reject the taxpayers' expert, whose adjusted balance sheet valuation method provided the only rational and justifiable valuation available in the record, and to find that a willing buyer would have paid $18.6 million for the

Sta-Home exempt agencies despite their unprofitability. These errors require this court to reverse. . . .

III. Conclusion

The Commissioner failed to perform a legitimate asset valuation analysis throughout the audit, discovery, and litigation of this case. The Tax Court erred as a matter of law in failing to hold the Commissioner to his burden of proof and in selecting an inappropriate and incorrect method to value the assets of the Sta–Home entities and made clearly erroneous factual findings in applying this valuation method. The Tax Court's errors do not require remand because the record makes it clear that the Commissioner cannot meet his burden of proof under 26 U.S.C. § 6213, Portillo, and Dunn. The Tax Court's decision is reversed and judgment is rendered in favor of the taxpayers.

Note on Valuation Misstatements

As *Caracci* makes clear, how one values property is a tricky business and experts can (and often do) disagree. Nevertheless, under IRC § 6662(e) taxpayers are subject to accuracy related penalties when they understate their tax liability by using substantially inaccurate property values. A "substantial valuation misstatement" exists when the taxpayer claims a value that is 150% or more of the "correct" value and a "gross valuation misstatement" occurs when the claimed value is 200% more than (or 50% less than) the "correct" value. A substantial misstatement merits a 20% tax on the underpayment. A gross misstatement earns a 40% tax. Further, a person who knowingly prepares an appraisal that contains a substantial or gross misstatement of value is also subject to a penalty under § 6695A.

Questions

1. According to the Fifth Circuit, what are the various approaches to valuing a charity's goods and services? Describe the approaches and how they differ.

2. Was the Fifth Circuit correct in criticizing the Tax Court for making a $1.75 million mistake? Was the government correct in stipulating to the "mistake"? Regardless of the Medicare consequences involving the bonuses, did not the cash-flow nevertheless exist and thus affect the government expert's valuation based, at least in part on a cash-flow analysis?

3. As a practical matter, what does the Fifth Circuit's decision mean in terms of what a tax advisor or attorney who is hired to assess significant events should ask a client to obtain in terms of documentation for such transactions as: (a) conversion from non-profit to for-profit? (b) hiring a paid executive director? (c) renting excess space in its building to a board member?

4. According to the Fifth Circuit in *Caracci*, what is the standard of review that will be applied in determining whether a trial court properly determined the fair market value? What are the factual issues? What are the legal issues? How did the Fifth Circuit resolve these various issues?

D. Advanced Application: Revenue Sharing as a Form of Private Inurement

CODE: §§ 501(c)(3), 4958(c)(2)

REGS.: § 53.4958-5

When an insider's compensation is determined by reference to a tax-exempt entity's gross or net revenues, the compensation method is referred to as a "revenue sharing arrangement." *See* H. R. Rep. No. 506, 104th Cong., 2nd Sess. 56 (1996). For example, an insider or disqualified person might be paid $100 plus 25% of the entity's net income from certain sales. Such arrangements implicate the literal prohibition against private inurement because, as a purely technical matter, a portion of the entity's "net earnings" are being transferred to the insider. However, for many years, whether such arrangements necessarily resulted in private inurement remained an open question. The courts generally viewed the matter solely as a function of the total compensation paid to the insider. If the total compensation was reasonable, it mattered not that the total was determined by taking a percentage of the entity's revenues. The Service took a more expansive view, asserting that even if the total compensation turned out to be reasonable, a revenue sharing arrangement would nevertheless violate the prohibition against private inurement if the arrangement placed the insider's interest in conflict with the entity's charitable interests. At times, the Service has indicated that a conflict between an insider's own interest and that of the organization was inevitable in such circumstances. This view gave rise to the notion of "private inurement, per se." That is, the arrangement was thought to be so inherently fraught with conflict that it violated the private inurement prohibition regardless of whether the insider was paid $1.00 or $1 million dollars. *See* GCM 39876. At other times, the Service has taken a less prohibitive view (as indicated below), relying instead on proof of actual conflict, or actual profit distribution.

As the case reproduced after the GCM shows, the judiciary has never fully accepted the Service's view. Readers must understand the *judicial* approach to revenue sharing arrangements because Congress authorized the Service to declare such arrangements improper under § 4958(c)(4), but only if such arrangements resulted in private inurement under § 501(c)(3) before the enactment of IRC § 4958. Readers should also note, however, that Treasury Regulation § 53.4958-5 has yet to be drafted—now 18 years after the initial enactment. Hence, the Service has yet to declare such revenue sharing arrangements subject to § 4958.

GCM 39674 (July 29, 1992)

Whether the establishment of "profit-sharing" incentive compensation plans for hospital employees results in the inurement of the net earnings of the hospitals to the employees or in other private benefit inconsistent with exemption under § 501(c)(3).

Conclusion

The mere establishment of the "profit-sharing" incentive compensation plans does not result in prohibited inurement or other private benefit that will cause the hospitals to lose their exempt status under section 501(c)(3). The plans are not inconsistent with exempt status as devices to distribute profits to principals or transform the organizations' activities into joint ventures and are the result of arm's length [sic] bargaining. However, if the compensation paid under the plans, when considered with the other compensation paid to the plan participants, is determined to be unreasonable on examination, the hospitals' exempt status under section 501(c)(3) will be jeopardized.

Facts

. . . (Hospital A) is exempt under section 501(c)(3) and proposes to adopt an incentive compensation plan for its employees (Plan A). Plan A will not be a qualified employee plan under section 401(a) or 403(a). All management and nonmanagement employees of Hospital A would be eligible to participate in Plan A. Employee-directors of Hospital A would be prohibited from voting on any matter affecting Plan A, including any decisions regarding the amount to be set aside to pay bonuses under Plan A.

The total amount payable under Plan A would be determined solely by the board of directors, as a percentage (not to exceed 50 percent) of the excess of the actual margin of revenues from operations over expenses compared to the budgeted margin. Results achieved under a quality assurance plan adopted by the board and implemented through separate committees of the board, the medical staff, and the hospital management, would be considered in determining the gross amount payable under Plan A, as would amounts allocated for patient guarantee expenses and amounts expected to be required for capital expenditures. The amount allocated to Plan A for the 1984–85 fiscal year is expected to be 50 percent of the excess of the actual margin over the budgeted margin, subject to approval by the board.

Payments would be allocated to employees as a uniform percentage of compensation, excluding nonproductive time (leave). The maximum bonus allocated to any employee-participant cannot exceed 10 percent of the employee's regular compensation.

Hospital A's stated purposes in adopting Plan A are to recognize and reward employee performance, encourage cost containment, motivate and reinforce efficiency and quality of service, and provide compensation competitive with that offered by other employers. Hospital A has represented that its charges for patient care are subject to review by an agency of the state it is located in, and that this review process "effectively prevents management of the Hospital from artificially raising Hospital charges in order to directly benefit from such increases through Plan A."

. . . (Hospital B), an exempt hospital under section 501(c)(3), also proposes to adopt a "profit-sharing", incentive compensation plan that is not intended to qualify under section 401(a) or 403(a) (Plan B). Under Plan B, eligible employees would include all full-time, regularly scheduled part-time, and PRN registered nurse employees, other than administrative managers and collective bargaining unit employees. Hospital B represents that 304 of its 454 employees would be eligible; that doctors are excluded because they are not considered employees of the hospital; and that none of the eligible employees is an officer, director, or member of the committee that will administer the plan.

The total amount payable to employees under Plan B will be one-third of the amount remaining after Hospital B's net income from operations is reduced by between 3% and 5% of gross patient revenue.

Payments under Plan B are related to each employee's allocable share of the total amount payable and the performance of the employee's department with respect to standards designed to measure quality of patient care and patient satisfaction. Quality of patient care is measured by detailed objective standards reviewed and approved by Hospital B's chief executive officer and board of directors. Patient satisfaction is measured by a short questionnaire that asks patients to evaluate the timeliness, efficiency, accuracy, and courtesy of service; the quality of room and dietary service; and the education and information provided with respect to diagnostic and treatment procedures and results.

An employee may not receive incentive compensation under Plan B greater than 50 percent of his or her gross salary (without regard to the compensation received under Plan B).

Hospital B states that Plan B is expected to improve the quality of patient care and productivity, thereby reducing (or limiting increases in) patient costs.

Analysis

Section 501(a) exempts organizations described in section 501(c) from federal income taxation. Section 501(c)(3) describes in pertinent part corporations organized and operated exclusively for charitable purposes no part of the net earnings of which inures to the benefit of any private shareholder or individual. Treas. Reg. § 1.501(c)(3)-1(a) provides that, in order to be exempt as an organization described in section 501(c)(3), an organization must be both organized and operated exclusively for one or more exempt purposes.

Section 1.501(c)(3)-1(c)(2) provides that an organization is not operated exclusively for one or more exempt purposes if its net earnings inure in whole or in part to the benefit of private shareholders or individuals as defined in section 1.501(a)-1(c). Section 1.501(a)-1(c) provides that the terms "private shareholder or individual" in section 501 refer to persons having a personal and private interest in the activities of the organization. Section 1.501(c)(3)-1(d)(1)(ii) provides that an exempt organization must serve a public rather than a private interest. The organization must demonstrate that it is not organized to benefit private interests such as "designated individuals, the creator or his family, shareholders of the organization, or persons controlled, directly or indirectly, by such private interests."

On numerous occasions, we have considered whether particular forms of compensation plans for persons providing services to a section 501(c) organization cause the organization to be operated to benefit private interests rather than for public purposes, or to be operated so that there is prohibited inurement of net earnings to the benefit of private shareholders or individuals.

Most recently, in . . . GCM 39670 . . . , we examined nonqualified deferred compensation plans and addressed the issue of whether a particular form of compensation arrangement could per se violate the proscriptions against private benefit and prohibited inurement. We reexamined our earlier views that certain forms of compensation plans per se resulted in prohibited inurement or private benefit.

For example, in . . . GCM 35865, . . . we had originally expressed the view that the establishment of profit-sharing plans intended to qualify under section 401(a) resulted in private inurement per se. That position was subsequently reversed in . . . , GCM 38283, I-44-74 . . . . With respect to the inurement and private benefit issues, we concluded in GCM 38283 that an exempt organization will not violate the requirements of exemption merely by adopting and operating an incentive compensation plan in which profits are a factor in the compensation formula. We reasoned that, with respect to a plan intended to qualify under section 401(a), the principles of subchapter D of chapter 1 and chapter 43 of the Code, as well as Title 1 of the Employee Retirement Income Security Act of 1974 (ERISA), would usually be sufficient to ensure that the operation of the plan would not jeopardize the exempt status of the organization. . . .

Similarly, in . . . GCM 37180, . . . we stated that a nonqualified deferred compensation plan maintained by a hospital for staff physicians that provided that participants shared in investment gains and losses of the plan resulted in per se prohibited inurement to the physicians. This result obtained even though the compensation was reasonable and the result of arm's length [sic] bargaining. In GCM 39670, however, we modified that position and recognized that a deferred compensation plan under which deferred amounts are invested does not automatically jeopardize the exempt status of the organization maintaining the plan. We noted that section 457 . . . and section 1.457-1(b)(1) specifically contemplate that deferred amounts can be invested. We further stated that this office will rely on the principles of Rev. Rul. 69-383, 1969-2 CB 113 . . . to determine whether a particular plan of compensation results in prohibited inurement or private benefit.

Rev. Rul. 69-383 considered a hospital that, after arm's length [sic] negotiations, entered into an agreement with a hospital-based radiologist to compensate him on the basis of a fixed percentage of the radiology department's gross billings. The radiologist did not have any management authority with respect to the hospital itself, but did have the right to approve the amounts charged by the hospital for radiology services. The amount received by the radiologist under the contract was not excessive when compared with amounts received by other radiologists having similar responsibilities and handling a comparable patient volume at other hospitals. . . .

Rev. Rul. 69-383 outlines the factors that we will examine in testing whether a compensation plan results in prohibited inurement. Thus, a compensation plan of an exempt organization does not result in prohibited inurement if: (1) the compensation plan is not inconsistent with exempt status, such as merely a device to distribute profits to principals or transform the organization's principal activity into a joint venture, (2) the compensation plan is the result of arm's length [sic] bargaining and (3) the compensation plan results in reasonable compensation. Whether these criteria are met depends upon the facts and circumstances of each case.

We have previously examined compensation plans of health care organizations and have generally applied the criteria of Rev. Rul. 69-383 to determine whether prohibited inurement or private benefit exists. In GCM 32453, . . . we considered whether the adoption of a contingent compensation plan which paid participants a percentage of revenues was inconsistent with exempt status as a section 501(c)(3) organization. In GCM 32453, an exempt organization, (HP), had contracted with subscribers to establish and operate prepaid medical service and hospitalization plans. HP paid private physicians who actually performed the services a flat fee per member-month plus 50 percent of the "Net Health Plan Revenue" (which was specifically defined in the contracts). The other 50 percent of the Net Health Plan Revenue was payable to hospitals that also provided services to HP's subscribers. The purpose of the percentage fee was to maximize the efficiency of service and shift most of the risk under the plan to the physician groups and hospitals. Through this arrangement, HP could operate without large, insurance-type reserves. In practice, the per capita fees constituted 92–97 percent of the total amount paid under the contract, and the incentive compensation could not exceed 10 percent of the total compensation payable. We concluded that the arrangement was not inconsistent with exempt status because it served a valid business purpose of providing compensatory incentives to contain costs and prevent unnecessary utilization of hospital services in prepaid medical care programs. GCM 32453 at 8–9.

GCM 35638, . . . involved a plan in which participants shared savings generated by productivity improvements with patients and in which management personnel and physicians did not participate. We stated that,

> So long as an arrangement of the subject type has all the earmarks of being worked out on an arm's length [sic] basis as a means of providing reasonable compensation to employees without any potential for reducing the charitable services or benefits otherwise being provided, and does not amount to the establishment of a joint venture or comparable program for individual participation in net profits as such, we think the Service should hold that it does not adversely affect the Hospital's exempt status under section 501(c)(3).

GCM 35638 at 8–9.

In GCM 36918, . . . which involved a "productivity-incentive" program, we stated that a representation that all compensation was reasonable would not shield the plan from scrutiny as to whether the plan was inconsistent with exempt purposes. We also noted the Service's view that a "profit-sharing" arrangement automatically resulted in inurement but found that the plan in question was based on limiting expenditures rather than profit-sharing. Because the plan was not inconsistent with exempt purposes, we advised that a favorable ruling on the plan should be issued, conditioned on the compensation payments under the plan remaining in the reasonable range. GCM 36918 at 3.

In GCM 38394, . . . we explained that, with respect to medical organizations, those compensation arrangements which are most inconsistent with exempt status are generally those which are not the result of arm's length [sic] bargaining and involve the division of profits so that it is apparent that the organization functions basically as a billing and collection agency for private medical practitioners. . . .

In the context of whether arrangements are the result of arm's length [sic] bargaining, we stated in GCM 38294 that compensation for controlling employees of a medical organization should be established by an independent compensation committee. This eliminates the potential for abuse inherent when those in control of an organization are responsible for establishing their own compensation. GCM 38394 at 9.

More recently, in GCM 39498, . . . we examined guaranteed minimum annual salary contracts under which the physicians' salaries were subsidized in order to induce them to commence employment at a hospital. In applying the criteria of Rev. Rul. 69-383, we acknowledged that the compensation plans did not per se constitute devices to distribute profits or transform the arrangement into a joint venture. We also found that the contracts were the result of arm's length [sic] bargaining between the physicians and the hospitals. We examined at length the requirement that compensation must be reasonable and noted that various forms of compensation could be provided in addition to the guaranteed salary contracts, such as, payment of household and office moving expenses, financial assistance in connection with home purchases, financing for office equipment, furniture and remodeling, assistance in leasing an office, and the provision of office and administrative services in connection with a physician's private medical practice. We concluded that the entire compensation package (rather than just the portion of the compensation plan in question) must be examined to determine whether it is reasonable. GCM 39498 concluded that it was impossible to determine, in connection with an advance ruling request, whether the compensation considered as a whole constituted reasonable compensation. . . .

GCM 39498 also discussed whether private interests were served other than incidentally by reason of the guaranteed annual salary contracts and noted, at 6, "If an organization serves a public interest, and also serves a private interest other than incidentally, it is not entitled to exemption under section 501(c)(3)." GCM 39498 stated that, as in testing for private inurement, the entire compensation package must be examined to determine whether it is reasonable and serves to benefit private interests only incidentally. See also GCM 38394 (which explains that whether private interests are served more than incidentally depends on the facts and circumstances of each case).

As we have discussed, we believe that whether a particular compensation plan adversely affects an organization's exempt status is an inherently factual question. So long as the compensation plan is not inconsistent with exempt status as discussed above, is the result of arm's length [sic] bargaining and the compensation under the plan, as well as all other compensation provided, is reasonable, the plan should not jeopardize the exempt status of the organization. However, whether compensation is reasonable is an inquiry which is best left to field examination....

In these cases, the mere establishment of incentive compensation plans to pay a percentage of the "profits" of the hospitals as additional compensation is not inconsistent with exempt status, such as when the compensation transforms the activity into a joint venture or is a mere device to distribute profits to principals. Both Plan A and Plan B have been established to advance the exempt purpose of the hospital by improving the quality and efficiency of patient care and appear reasonably designed to accomplish the exempt purpose. In addition, these plans are not the result of other than arm's length [sic] bargaining. Plan A covers a broad class of noncontrolling employees and is designed to avoid increases in compensation predicated on increases in fees charged to patients. Likewise, Plan B covers only a broad class of nonmanagement employees.

With respect to whether the compensation is reasonable, however, as stated previously, we will not determine in advance whether, under the facts and circumstances of this case, the compensation is reasonable. We therefore suggest that your letters to both Hospitals A and B be caveated to provide that a favorable ruling is conditioned on the requirement that the compensation as a whole constitutes reasonable compensation and that no determination is being made with respect to that issue.

* * *

World Family Corporation v. Commissioner

81 T.C. 958 (1983)

Nims, Judge:

Petitioner brought this action for a declaratory judgment pursuant to section 7428 and Rule 211 on the ground that respondent had failed to determine whether petitioner qualifies as an organization exempt from taxation under sections 501(a) and 501(c)(3). The issues presented are whether petitioner is operated exclusively for religious, charitable, scientific or other exempt purposes and whether part of petitioner's net earnings inures to the benefit of private individuals.

* * *

Petitioner, World Family Corporation ("WFC"), was organized as a nonprofit corporation in Utah on December 13, 1977. On November 27, 1978, it submitted to respondent an application for recognition of exemption under section 501(c)(3) (Form 1023). During the following two years, respondent requested and petitioner supplied supplemental information on two occasions. Finally, on November 30, 1981, petitioner filed the petition in this case, having exhausted its administrative remedies in accordance with the requirements of section 7428(b)(2). At the time its petition was filed, WFC had its principal office at Salt Lake City, Utah.

Petitioner essentially is a fund raising and fund dispensing organization. Its primary purpose is to provide grants and interest-free loans to missionaries sent out by the Church of Jesus Christ of Latter–Day Saints (hereinafter the "LDS Church"). The administrative record shows the missionary program of the LDS Church to be conducted as follows:

> Each congregation (known as a Ward, of which there are thousands in the Church), is headed by a Bishop. It is the policy of the Church to have all worthy young men, who are able, fulfill a two year full time mission for the Church at about age 19, and some worthy young women who are able to fulfill an 18 month full time mission for the Church at about age 21. The Bishop in each Ward keeps track of the young people as they grow up and notifies the Church headquarters of those who fulfill these qualifications. Thereafter the call to fulfill a mission comes directly from the First Presidency of the Church. Any given missionary may be called to any of the hundreds of missions throughout the world, and this is controlled solely by the Church. . . .
>
> The primary work of a missionary is to make contact with people in the assigned area and teach them the doctrines of the Church, i.e., Christianity, to the end that such people will be converted and become members of the Church. This is full time for approximately two years. By full time it is meant not just a 40 hour week but basically all day, seven days a week.

The missionaries are always dispatched to locations away from their homes and they are obliged to meet their own expenses. Most missionaries are supported by their parents but some must look to other sources for financial assistance.

The availability of financial assistance from WFC will be communicated to prospective missionaries through the Bishops of the various Wards. Candidates will apply to the Board of Trustees of petitioner, which will select missionaries for assistance "based on need, recommendations from church leaders, availability of funds and various other factors." The dollar value of a grant or loan will vary with the cost of living in the missionary's assignment area, the missionary's other sources of support and the availability of funds in WFC's treasury. The amounts will be calculated to provide bare subsistence; the average grant or loan is anticipated to be "in the neighborhood of $3,000 to $5,000." The funds will be disbursed monthly either directly to the missionaries in the field or to their immediate supervisors to be dispensed to the missionaries at the supervisors' discretion.

* * *

Petitioner plans a fund raising program based on mail solicitations to church and community leaders, business people and others. To attract fund raisers, petitioner also "has plans to offer commissions of up to 20 percent." In response to a question from respondent, petitioner justified its commissions program as follows:

We believe that paying a commission gets the job done better than just hiring solicitors. We have considered the possibility to hire people on a set salary to do solicitation may be less expensive, and it is possible that at some time in the future the company may switch to such a system, however presently the company believes that the commission system better meets its needs—for one thing it doesn't cost anything if the solicitation fails.

Petitioner does not require fund raisers to keep records of their time and expenses: "Since the payment of the fee is strictly a contingency, World Family is not concerned whether the individual spends a dollar, ten thousand dollars, ten minutes or ten weeks."

Petitioner's president, David Yeaman, was responsible for procuring the contributions of stock currently constituting the assets of the company. Accordingly, petitioner's balance sheet carries an accounts payable item due David Yeaman for a commission of $20,000.

* * *

B. Private Inurement

Section 501(c)(3) requires that no part of the net earnings of an exempt organization inure to the benefit of any private shareholder or individual. The regulations define "private shareholder or individual" as any person "having a personal and private interest in the activities of the organization." Section 1.501(a)-1(c), Income Tax Regs. We agree with respondent that David Yeaman, the president and incorporator of petitioner, comes within this definition.

Respondent further contends, however, that petitioner's net earnings will inure to David Yeaman through the fund raising commissions currently credited to him on petitioner's balance sheet. We part ways with respondent at this point.

It is well established that an exempt organization is entitled to pay reasonable compensation for services without endangering its exemption. Such payments are permissible even though they are made to the organization's trustees, officers or founders; the issue is whether the payments are reasonable.

Whether compensation is reasonable is a question of fact to be determined in light of all the circumstances. Initially, we note that a contingent-fee arrangement made by a tax-exempt entity is not per se unreasonable as respondent appears to content:

> We do not, however, mean to imply that all contingent compensation arrangements made by charitable organizations will preclude tax-exempt status. Such arrangements are a part of business life and must occasionally be paid by a charity to salesmen, publishers, support groups, *and even fund raisers.* [Emphasis added.]

People of God Community v. Commissioner, 75 T.C. 127, 133 (1980) (petitioner's founder and "pastor" received varying percentages of the gross tithes and offerings adjusted according to his personal needs).

Indeed, contingent fee payments to fundraisers by charities are expressly recognized and regulated by statute in many States. These statutes specifically sanction such commissions and in many cases endorse percentage commissions higher than the 20-percent ceiling proposed here by petitioner. See, e.g., Fla. Stat. Ann. sec. 496.11 (1976) (professional solicitor's total fee shall not be in excess of 25 percent of gross contributions which he solicits, fundraising costs included).

We must consider then whether a commission which may be reasonable when paid to an unrelated third party becomes unreasonable when paid to an individual having a personal and private interest in the payor organization. Although in some circumstances such a finding may be warranted, it is clear that payment to an interested individual does not make a commission unreasonable as a matter of law. We have observed that "[o]ne factor to consider [in determining the reasonableness of compensation] is whether comparable services would cost as much if obtained from an outside source in an arm's length [sic] transaction." *B.H.W. Anesthesia Foundation, Inc. v. Commissioner*, 72 T.C. 681, 686 (1979). The law places no duty on individuals operating charitable organizations to donate their services; they are entitled to reasonable compensation for their efforts. See also Section 4941(d)(2)(f) ("the payment of compensation . . . by a private foundation to a disqualified person for personal services which are reasonable and necessary to carrying out the exempt purpose of the private foundation shall not be an act of self-dealing if the compensation . . . is not excessive.").

In this case, we find the commission arrangement to be reasonable, notwithstanding that petitioner's president and incorporator may reap some of its benefits. Commissions are payable to any individual who procures contributions for petitioner; payments are not limited to particular individuals. Moreover, commissions are directly contingent on success in procuring funds and as such are tied to services rendered. These elements distinguish petitioner's commission arrangement from other arrangements found by the courts to constitute private inurement.

* * *

Note on World Family Corporation

The Tax Court rejected the government's argument which would prohibit all percentage fundraising arrangements. In so doing, it cited the following case, which held for the government and rejected a particular percentage arrangement. Indeed,

People of God arguably prohibits all percentage of gross receipts agreements. Consider the two cases carefully to understand why Word Family won and People of God lost. Was it merely the higher percentage in *People of God* that was fatal? Or was it more closely related to the lack of justification for the dollar amounts when compared to the workload? Are the cases distinguishable mostly on evidentiary grounds: the taxpayer in one introduced substantial evidence for his position, while the other did not? Or did the Tax Court change positions?

People of God Community v. Commissioner

75 T.C. 127 (1980)

Fay, Judge:

* * *

Petitioner is operated as a Christian church.

* * *

Petitioner has three ministers, Charles Donhowe (Donhowe), Michael Law (Law), and Timothy McCombs (McCombs), who also comprise its board of directors. . . .

Donhowe is petitioner's founder and the "Pastor of the Community." . . .

Since 1975, Donhowe's compensation from petitioner has been based on a percentage of the gross tithes and offerings received. The precise method by which the percentage is determined is not made explicit by the record. Generally, Donhowe's percentage is based on what he received in the prior year, adjusted upward to reflect his increased personal expenses such as "home improvements and rapidly rising taxes" and downward to the extent that larger gross receipts permit an increase in the compensation of petitioner's other ministers, who also receive a (smaller) percentage of gross tithes. No upper limit is set for the total amount Donhowe could receive under the formula. . . . Donhowe's compensation of $29,468 for the period January 1 to October 11, 1978 (about $36,700 per year) was 53 percent of petitioner's receipts for that period (exclusive of loan repayments). Total ministers' salaries made up 86 percent of petitioner's 1978 budget and 69 percent of petitioner's 1977 budget.

The percentage-of-gross-tithes method for determining ministers' compensation was originated by Donhowe in 1974 or 1975 and has been continued by petitioner. Donhowe wanted to keep his newly formed church out of debt so that his ministry would not be a burden on his followers. In the administrative record, Donhowe stated:

> It was my determination that if the people prospered and were blessed, then I too, would prosper and be blessed. But if the people would suffer or experience deprivation, I too would experience it along with them. I find this consistent with scripture, that "if one member suffer, all suffer. That if one member rejoices, we all are to rejoice." From that time on, I began to function on a percentage basis and found that my basic needs and necessities were taken care of.

Donhowe devotes 50 to 100 hours per week to his ministry.

* * *

Respondent argues that petitioner's . . . ministers' compensation each demonstrate both private inurement of net earnings and prohibited private purposes. While not necessarily identical, the prohibitions against private inurement and private purposes overlap to a great extent . . . , and we will confine our discussion herein to the private inurement issue.

Petitioner first contends, and respondent agrees, that it is entitled to pay its ministers reasonable compensation. This principle is well established. . . . Petitioner goes on to argue that the compensation paid Donhowe and its other ministers is reasonable in amount and that the method by which such compensation is determined is not unreasonable per se. We find for respondent.

The burden falls upon petitioner to establish the reasonableness of the compensation paid to Donhowe and petitioner's other ministers. . . . Petitioner has failed to do so inasmuch as the record on this point contains little more than conclusory assertions and the fact that Donhowe's compensation was partly based on his personal needs. Moreover, the method by which ministers' compensation was determined shows clearly that a part of petitioner's net earnings was paid to private shareholders or individuals.

Gemological Institute of America v. Commissioner . . . , involved a corporation formed by Shipley, a jeweler, and his wife for the purpose of offering courses of instruction in the science of gemology. Shipley was employed by the corporation as its executive director in return for a fixed salary plus 50 percent of the organization's net receipts. Deciding that the corporation was not tax exempt, we stated:

> Petitioner argues, because of Shipley's ability and past services, that he "was entitled to receive much more than the nominal amount set up as flat salary." This is not disputed. However, when petitioner further says that Shipley's compensation was not part of its net earnings but was only measured by the amount of its net earnings, we can not accept this argument as it is unsupported by the facts. . . .
>
> Regardless of what these amounts are called, salary or compensation based on earnings, it is obvious that half of the net earnings of petitioner inured to the benefit of an individual, viz, Shipley. . . . Such a distribution of net earnings is unequivocally prohibited by the statute. The petitioner has failed to meet one of the essential tests of section 101 (6). Therefore, it does not qualify for the exemptions because all requirements of the section must coexist. [17 T.C. at 1609–1610.]

This case falls squarely within the rule and the rationale of Gemological Institute. Whatever Donhowe's services are worth, they are not directly related to petitioner's gross receipts; the value of solace and spiritual leadership cannot be measured by the collection box. By basing Donhowe's compensation upon a percentage of petitioner's gross receipts, apparently subject to no upper limit, a portion of petitioner's earnings is being passed on to Donhowe. . . . The statute specifically denies tax exemption where a portion of net earnings is paid to private shareholders or individuals. We hold here that paying over a portion of gross earnings to those vested with the control of a charitable organization constitutes private inurement as well. All in all, taking a slice off the top should be no less prohibited than a slice out of net.

We do not, however, mean to imply that all contingent compensation arrangements made by charitable organizations will preclude tax-exempt status. Such arrangements are a part of business life and must occasionally be paid by a charity to salesmen, publishers, support groups, and even fund raisers. . . . What is prohibited is inurement "to the benefit of any private shareholder or individual." Sec. 501(c)(3); sec. 1.501(c)(3)-1(c)(2), Income Tax Regs. The term "private shareholder or individual" refers to persons who have a personal and private interest in the payor organization. Sec. 1.501(a)-1(c), Income Tax Regs. . . . . The term does not refer to unrelated third parties. . . . In other words, section 501(c)(3) denies exempt status to an organization whose founders or controlling members have a personal stake in that organization's receipts. . . . Such is the case here, where petitioner's ministers, and Donhowe, in particular, completely control its affairs. Petitioner therefore fails to qualify for exemption under section 501(c)(3).

Because we have decided this case on the above ground, we need not consider whether petitioner's loans program evidenced a substantial private purpose nor whether petitioner is a "church" for purposes of section 509.

Questions

1. Recall that Congress, in § 4958(c)(2), authorized the Service to promulgate regulations specifying when revenue sharing arrangements constitute an excess benefit transaction. The sole condition is that to constitute an excess benefit transaction, a revenue sharing arrangement must be considered private inurement under § 501(c)(3). The first set of proposed regulations stated:

> A revenue-sharing transaction may constitute an excess benefit transaction regardless of whether the economic benefit provided to the disqualified person exceeds the fair market value of the consideration provided in return if, at any point, it permits a disqualified person to receive additional compensation without providing proportional benefits that contribute to the organization's accomplishment of its exempt purpose.

The examples in the regulation (which are set out as questions below) sought to demonstrate the "proportional benefits" requirement. Prop. Treas. Reg. § 53.4958-5(d), Examples 1 and 2. The Treasury promulgated this proposed regulation in 1998 at 63 FR 41486.

In 2002, the Treasury adopted final regulations under § 4945 at 67 FR 3076, excluding the examples. State whether the arrangements described below would result in an excess benefit transaction under the proportional benefit standard described above and under the standards applied in the private inurement cases set out earlier:

A. A is the manager of the investment portfolio of M, an applicable tax-exempt organization for purposes of § 4958. A and several other professional investment managers work exclusively for M in an office in M's building. A's compensation consists of a flat base annual salary, health insurance, eligibility to participate in a retirement plan, and a bonus that is equal to a percentage of any increase in the value of M's portfolio over the year (net of expenses for investment management other than the in-house managers' compensation). The revenue-based portion of A's compensation gives A an incentive to provide the highest quality service in order to maximize benefits and minimize expenses to M. A has a measure of control over the activities generating the revenues on which his bonus is based, but A can increase his own compensation only if M also receives a proportional benefit.

B. L, an applicable tax-exempt organization for purposes of § 4958, enters into a contract with H, a company who manages charitable gaming activities for public charities. As a result of the contractual relationship, H becomes a disqualified person with respect to any transaction involving L that provides economic benefits to H directly or indirectly. Under the contract, H agrees to provide all of the staff and equipment necessary to carry out charitable gaming operations on behalf of L, and to pay L z percent of the net profits, which are calculated as the gross revenue less rental for the equipment, wages for the staff, prizes for the winners, and other specified operating expenses. H retains the balance of the proceeds after expenses and after paying L its z percent of the net profits. As manager, H controls the activities generating the revenue on which its compensation is based. In addition, because H owns the equipment and employs the staff needed to operate the charitable gaming activities, H controls what L is charged, including the profit H makes above the cost of these items.

Example 3. R, a professor and faculty member at S, a university that is an applicable tax-exempt organization for purposes of § 4958, is the principal investigator in charge of certain scientific research at S. The research produces an invention. In accordance with S's agreement with its faculty, S owns the invention. R assists S in preparing a patent application. S receives a patent for R's invention, which S owns. Also in accordance with S's agreement with its faculty, S grants R the right to receive v percent of S's royalties on the patent, payable semi-annually.

2. Assume you are IRS counsel. Prepare a rough first draft of a regulation pertaining to revenue sharing arrangements based solely on the case above (i.e., do not include the "proportional benefit" test of the former proposed regulations).

E. Excess Compensation

CODE: §§ 4960, 115

Beginning in 2018, § 4960 imposes an excise tax at section 11 corporate rates on excess compensation for employees of "applicable organizations." Such organizations include all § 501(a) entities, as well as those accruing income under § 511(1). Excessive compensation is the amount exceeding $1,000,000. The tax is imposed on the employer.

The section includes remuneration paid by persons, organizations or governmental entities related to the employing organization. Section 4960(c)(4)(B)(i)-(ii) defines a related person or organization as one controlled by the employing entity or who controls the employer. Arguably, an employer can facilitate highly paid employees receiving compensation directly from entities which neither control nor which are controlled by the employer. For example, a university athletic association might arrange for a football coach to receive endorsement monies directly from a sponsor rather than via the university or athletic association. Whether general assignment of income or step-transaction principles will overcome such transparent schemes is unclear.

The section applies only to the five highest paid employees. It excludes compensation paid to licensed doctors, including veterinarians, for medical services. It includes, however, excess parachute payments, as defined in § 4960(c)(5)(B). That might impact buy-out contracts for coaches; however, the section excludes many deferred compensation arrangements, which may provide a loophole for separation agreements. § 4960(c)(5)(C).

Whether the section applies to state colleges and universities is arguably uncertain. Section 4960(c)(1)(C) includes entities that have income excluded under § 511(a)(1). That excludes "income derived from . . . the exercise of any essential governmental function and accruing to a State or any political subdivision thereof, or the District of Columbia. . . ." Facially, that applies to income of the state, which typically includes colleges and universities.

Indeed, the legislative history of § 115 supports the notion that state income is not taxed; however, the history regarding whether § 115 says so is arguably ambiguous.[2] Government interpretation over many decades has suggested § 115 does not say what it appears to plainly say. Focus on the § 115 language, which applies to income "accruing to" a state, as opposed to accrued "by" the state. A 1935 General Counsel Memorandum and more recent rulings suggest § 115 applies only to entities separate from states which nevertheless perform essential functions. Revenue Ruling 77-261 stated:

2. Ellen P. Aprill, *Excluding the Income of State and Local Governments: The Need for Congressional Action*, 26 GA. L. REV. 421 (1992), at note 12.

> A comprehensive interpretation of section 115(1) of the Code is set forth in G.C.M. 14407, XIV-1 C.B. 103 (1935), as superseded by Rev. Rul. 71-131, 1971-1 C.B. 28, in discussing the corresponding section of a prior statute (section 116(d) of the Revenue Act of 1934). It is indicated therein that the predecessor section of what is now section 115(1) of the Code was intended to refer, not to the income of a State or municipality resulting from its own direct participation in industry, but rather to that part of the income of a corporation engaged in the operation of a public utility or the performance of some governmental function that accrued to a State or municipality.

Rev. Rul. 77-261, 1977-2 C.B. 45.

On its face, § 4940 appears intended to apply to state colleges and universities, and their athletic coaches in particular, because it refers to entities that have "income excluded from taxation" under § 115(1). Anyone reading §§ 4960 and 115, without any administrative gloss, would surely draw that conclusion: the bizarre distinction between accruing to and accruing by is hardly self-evident. The administrative pronouncements, however, are very clear and undoubtedly contrary to the plain statutory language. How they will ultimately apply is uncertain. Perhaps, the Treasury "made its bed" over many decades and must now lie in it. Perhaps only coaches of private universities need worry.

Chapter 12

Private Benefit Restriction

A. The Private Benefit Prohibition in General

CODE: § 501(c)(3)

REGS.: § 1.501(c)(3)-1(d)(1)(ii)

Judges, scholars, and practitioners often approach the private benefit prohibition as though it is merely an expansive form of the private inurement prohibition. Section 501(c)(3) refers only to private inurement and never actually states that an organization, to be exempt, must be operated for public, as opposed to private, benefit. As we point out below, such an approach is not entirely unreasonable or unexpected given the regulatory articulation of the doctrine. Indeed, other than that the private benefit doctrine applies to more than just insiders, we cannot say with any certainty exactly what the private benefit doctrine adds to tax exemption jurisprudence. We think the differences in doctrines goes beyond the mere presence of insiders and outsiders, though we have yet to agree on exactly what the difference is. Compare *American Campaign Academy* and General Counsel Memorandum 39862 (both set out below) with § 501(c)(3) and *United Cancer Council, supra*, Chapter 11: see if you can articulate the differences between the private benefit and private inurement doctrines. Your task will be complicated, of course, because *American Campaign Academy* and the General Counsel Memorandum, which both deal with private benefit, are themselves inconsistent.

In any event, because courts generally recognize the private benefit doctrine as somehow separate, we approach it separately from the private inurement discussion. The danger of assuming that private benefit is synonymous with private inurement is that, as a practical matter, an alleged violation of the tax exemption requirements may be analyzed with regard to private inurement, when in fact it ought to have been analyzed in light of the private benefit doctrine. We saw this phenomenon in *United Cancer Council v. Commissioner*, a case litigated for nine years, only to be remanded because the Service and the Tax Court, according to the Seventh Circuit, mistakenly applied the private inurement doctrine instead of the private benefit doctrine.

1. The Judicial Private Benefit Test?

Treasury Regulations formally articulate the private benefit prohibition, and do so in terms that seem applicable to the prohibition against private inurement. For example, Regulation § 1.501(c)(3)-1(d)(1)(ii) prohibits an organization from operating "for the benefit of private interests such as designated individuals, the creator or his family, shareholders of the organization, or persons controlled, directly or indirectly, by such private interests." The list of prohibited private interests seems to capture and merely repeat the idea underlying the definition of "insider" for purposes of the prohibition against private inurement. *See* Chapter 11, *supra* (relating to the definition of "insider"). In fact, the Tax Court at one time limited the applicability of the private benefit prohibition to those persons who exercised control over an organization, i.e., to insiders. *See Goldsboro Art League, Inc. v. Commissioner*, 75 T.C. 337, 345 (1980). In doing so, the Tax Court might have rendered the private benefit prohibition superfluous. But in *American Campaign Academy v. Commissioner*, 92 T.C. 1053 (1989), the Court faced the argument that the private benefit prohibition did not apply because the party benefited was neither an insider, nor described in the Treasury Regulation. The Tax Court's opinion, though often criticized, remains the most authoritative judicial discussion of private benefit, not only with regard to its relationship to the private inurement prohibition, but also with regard to the doctrine in general.

Focus on the highlighted passages. After describing the test as part of the general requirement that an organization operate exclusively for charitable purposes, the court stressed substantial non-charitable beneficiaries are not permissible. The court emphasized the beneficiaries need not be "insiders."

American Campaign Academy v. Commissioner

92 T.C. 1053 (1989)

* * *

Petitioner, American Campaign Academy . . . is a Virginia corporation incorporated by Jan W. Baran, General Counsel of the National Republican Congressional Committee, on January 24, 1986, exclusively for charitable and educational purposes. . . .

As its primary activity, petitioner operates a school to train individuals for careers as political campaign professionals. Petitioner's school maintains a regularly scheduled curriculum, a regular faculty, and a full-time enrolled student body at the facilities it occupies. Petitioner claims that it is the only school to exclusively offer a highly concentrated and extensive campaign training curriculum. Similar campaign management courses are offered by American University, Kent State University, Westminster College in Utah, Georgia State University, North Florida State, San Francisco State College, University of California-Davis, University of Southern California and Bernard Baruch College in New York. Seminars offering campaign training are also sponsored by such groups as the Republican National Committee Campaign Management College, United States Campaign Academy, The Leadership Institute, Committee for the Survival of a Free Congress, and the Democratic National Committee. Petitioner has no connection with any of these training programs.

Prior to the organization of the Academy, the National Republican Congressional Committee (NRCC), an unincorporated association comprised of Republican members of the United States House of Representatives, sponsored programs designed to train candidates and to train and subsequently place campaign professionals in Republican campaigns. A campaign professional works for a candidate. Campaign professionals typically occupy such strategic campaign positions as communications director, finance director, or campaign manager.

The Academy stated on its . . . Form 1023 . . . that it was an "outgrowth" of the course of instruction run by the NRCC. NRCC contributed physical assets such as furniture and computer hardware to the Academy. Two of the Academy's six full-time faculty were previously involved in the NRCC's training program. One of the Academy's three initial directors, Joseph Gaylord, is the Executive Director of the NRCC. Another initial director, John C. McDonald, is a member of the Republican National Committee.

NRCC continues to offer training for Republican candidates and staff members of incumbent Republican congressmen. The administrative record does not reveal to what extent, if any, NRCC continues to offer training to campaign professionals.

The Academy program for training campaign professionals differs from its predecessor NRCC program. Significantly, . . . the Academy limits its students to "campaign professionals." The Academy does not train candidates nor participate in, nor intervene in, any political campaign on behalf of any candidate. Neither does the Academy engage in any activities tending to influence legislation. Moreover, while the Academy actively refers resumes and provides recommendations of graduates to requesting campaigns, it assumes no formal placement responsibilities.

No training materials developed by the NRCC are used by the Academy. Rather, the Academy has generally hired its own faculty, developed its own courses and enhanced the training curriculum. The Academy's faculty consists of 5–6 full-time . . . and approximately 141 adjunct members. Training materials used by students include compilations and handouts, published textbooks, trade books and articles, and faculty-prepared lecture materials.

The Academy has more applicants for admission than it . . . can accommodate. Thus, its admissions criteria are competitive. The Academy seeks to admit applicants who have a strong commitment to professional campaign involvement on the Congressional level. Each applicant provides the Academy with the details of his or her qualifications in each applicable category. In addition, applicants are asked to provide at least two political and two professional references. And while applicants are not required to formally declare their political affiliation to attend the Academy, such affiliations may often be deduced from the campaign experiences and political references contained in the application. Applicants may freely volunteer their political party affiliation. The Academy maintains no records indicating the number of applicants who are Republicans, Democrats, associated with other parties, or independent.

Completed applications ... to the Academy are evaluated by an admission panel. The Academy has no requirement that a member of the ... panel be affiliated with any particular political party. However, the Academy believes that a substantial number of the members of its admission panel are affiliated with the Republican party. The Academy does not discriminate on the basis of race, color, national, or ethnic origin in admitting students, in administering its educational policies and school-sponsored programs, or in granting financial assistance.

The Academy's curriculum presents a considerable body of knowledge to be learned and skills to be mastered in preparing the student to perform effectively as a campaign professional. The Academy ... offers a single 10-week general program to all students. Current courses ... explore ... campaign strategy, the American political system ..., research techniques, organization basics, campaign strategy, professional ethics, Federal Election Commission rules and regulations, campaign financing techniques, voter surveying, vote targeting, issue development, media communications, speechwriting, volunteer recruiting and organizing, budgeting, coalition building and basic computer applications. Discussions concerning "How some Republicans have won Black votes," "NRCC/RNC/NRSC/State Party naughtiness," and "Use of GOP allies" are included in the campaign strategy and organizational courses.

Following graduation, Academy students are expected to apply their newly acquired knowledge and skills in a political campaign. If a graduate fails to put forth a good faith effort to secure a position in a campaign, the Academy may withhold its recommendation. Approximately 80 percent of the Academy's graduates served on political campaigns during 1986.

Beginning June 6, 1986, the Academy began publishing a monthly newsletter entitled "A Hundred Battles." ... During the months of June through September 1986, the newsletter tracked the activities of 119 of the Academy's 120 graduates. As reported ..., 85 graduates participated in the campaigns of Congressional or Senatorial candidates, four graduates were employed by the NRCC or Republican National Committee Field Divisions, 10 graduates participated in gubernatorial or other statewide or local campaigns, at least three graduates were employed by various State Republican parties, and several graduates worked as political consultants. Many graduates whose candidates were defeated in the 1986 primary elections joined the campaigns of other candidates. In total, Academy graduates filled important positions in approximately 98 Congressional and Senatorial campaign positions during the 1986 election cycle. In addition, one graduate worked in a presidential campaign in a foreign country.

On September 16, 1986, respondent requested petitioner to provide additional information regarding several matters. One matter concerned the affiliation of the candidates served by petitioner's graduates. ...

On October 3, 1986, petitioner answered respondent's inquiry as follows:

> We do not require students to remain in contact with the Academy following graduation. Of those who chose to do so, some have informed the

> Academy of the identity of the candidate(s) for whom they are working. To the best that can be determined, the predominant party affiliation of the candidates for whom Academy graduates are working in 1986 is Republican, but the Academy has no exact numbers.

Following the 1986 Federal election, approximately 46 percent of the Academy's graduates were either unemployed or employed in nonpolitical positions.

Funding for the Academy's activities has been exclusively provided by the National Republican Congressional Trust (NRCT), an organization that collects political contributions and uses such funds for purposes approved by the [FEC]. No funding has been received from any candidate's campaign committee. NRCT funding through August, 1987, reached $972,000. The Academy has estimated that 90 percent of its funding is expended to run its school. The remaining 10 percent of funding has been dedicated to research and the publishing of reports, pamphlets, books, or other materials to be made available to the general public.

Discussion

* * *

Respondent concedes that (1) petitioner is organized exclusively for exempt purposes, i.e., educational purposes, (2) no part of petitioner's net earnings inure to the benefit of a private shareholder or individual, (3) no substantial part of petitioner's activities consists of political or lobbying activities and (4) petitioner is not involved in any proscribed campaign activities. Likewise, respondent makes no contention that the activities of the Academy are contrary to established public policy. Rather, respondent rests his denial of the Academy's application for exempt status solely on the Academy's alleged failure to operate exclusively for exempt purposes. Specifically, respondent's final ruling letter states:

> You have failed to establish that you are operated exclusively for exempt purposes as required by section 501(c)(3). You are operated for a substantial non-exempt private purpose. You benefit Republican Party entities and candidates more than incidentally. Also, your activities serve the private interests of Republican Party entities rather than public interests exclusively.

We note at the outset that petitioner bears the burden of overcoming the grounds set forth in respondent's final ruling letter. Rule 217(c)(2)(i). To prevail herein, petitioner must show, based upon the materials in the administrative record, that it does not operate to benefit Republican Party entities and candidates more than incidentally or that such benefits do not serve a private rather than a public interest. *See Hancock Academy of Savannah, Inc. v. Commissioner*, 69 T.C. 488, 492 (1977); *B.S.W. Group, Inc. v. Commissioner*, 70 T.C. 352, 356 (1978); section 1.501(c)(3)-1(c), Income Tax Regs.

Operational Test

* * *

The Treasury Regulations specify three conditions which must be satisfied for an organization to meet the operational test.... First, the organization must be primarily engaged in activities which accomplish one or more of the exempt purposes specified in section 501(c)(3). . . . Second, the organization's net earnings must not be distributed in whole or in part to the benefit of private shareholders or individuals. . . . Third, the organization must not be an "action" organization, i.e., one which devotes a substantial part of its activities attempting to influence legislation, or participates or intervenes, directly or indirectly, in any political campaign. . . .

Respondent does not contend that petitioner [fails the second or third tests]. Thus, the sole issue for declaration is whether respondent properly determined that petitioner failed to satisfy the first condition of the operational test by not primarily engaging in activities which accomplish exempt purposes.

Operating Primarily for Exempt Purposes

To establish that it operates primarily in activities which accomplish exempt purposes, petitioner must establish that no more than an insubstantial part of its activities does not further an exempt purpose. Section 1.501(c)(3)-1(c)(1), Income Tax Regs. The presence of a single substantial nonexempt purpose destroys the exemption regardless of the number or importance of the exempt purposes. *Better Business Bureau v. United States*, 326 U.S. 279, 283 (1945); *Copyright Clearance Center v. Commissioner*, 79 T.C. 793, 804 (1982).

When an organization operates for the benefit of private interests such as designated individuals, the creator or his family, shareholders of the organization, or persons controlled, directly or indirectly, by such private interests, the organization by definition does not operate exclusively for exempt purposes. Section 1.501(c)(3)-1(d)(1)(ii), Income Tax Regs. Prohibited private benefits may include an "advantage; profit; fruit; privilege; gain; [or] interest." *Retired Teachers Legal Fund v. Commissioner*, 78 T.C. 280, 286 (1982). Occasional economic benefits flowing to persons as an incidental consequence of an organization pursuing exempt charitable purposes will not generally constitute prohibited private benefits. *Kentucky Bar Foundation v. Commissioner*, 78 T.C. at 926. Thus, should petitioner be shown to benefit private interests, it will be deemed to further a nonexempt purpose under section 1.501(c)(3)-1(d)(1)(ii), Income Tax Regs. This nonexempt purpose will prevent petitioner from operating primarily for exempt purposes absent a showing that no more than an insubstantial part of its activities further the private interests or any other nonexempt purposes. Section 1.501(c)(3)-1(c)(1), Income Tax Regs.

Respondent contends that petitioner's activities substantially benefit the private interests of Republican party entities and candidates, thereby advancing a nonexempt private purpose. Petitioner counters that respondent erred in denying its exemption application by incorrectly applying the private benefit analysis of section 1.501(c)(3)-1(d)(1)(ii), Income Tax Regs., to persons other than a "private shareholder or individual" within the meaning of section 1.501(a)-1(c), Income Tax Regs. Section 1.501(a)-1(c), Income Tax Regs., defines the words "private shareholder or individual" as persons having a personal and private interest in the activities of the organization (hereinafter private shareholders or individuals are sometimes referred to as "insiders"). Alternatively, petitioner argues that the private benefits, if any, conferred on various Republican entities and candidates were incidental to the exempt public educational purposes its activities further.

Unrelated Parties and Private Interests

We begin our analysis by considering whether an organization may transgress the "public rather than a private interest" mandate of section 1.501(c)(3)-1(d)(1)(ii), Income Tax Regs., by conferring benefits on persons not having a personal and private interest in the activities of the organization. See sections 1.501(c)(3)-1(c)(2) and 1.501(a)-1(c), Income Tax Regs. Petitioner maintains that the prohibition against private benefit is limited to situations in which an organization's insiders are benefited. Petitioner further contends that since "Republican Party entities and candidates" cannot be construed as insiders of its organization, no transgression of the operational test exists.

In support of limiting the private benefit analysis to insiders, petitioner compares the language of section 1.501(c)(3)-1(d)(1)(ii), Income Tax Regs. to the statutory and regulatory language prohibiting the inurement of organizational earnings to private shareholders and individuals. Section 501(c)(3) and sections 1.501(c)(3)-1(c)(2) and 1.501(a)-1(c), Tax Income Regs. Petitioner asserts that the class of persons illustrated in section 1.501(c)(3)-1(d)(1)(ii), Income Tax Regs. (i.e., designated individuals, the creator or his family, shareholders of the organization or persons controlled directly or indirectly by such private interests), overlaps with the class of persons identified by section 501(c)(3) and section 1.501(a)-1(c), Income Tax Regs., as insiders in the private inurement context (i.e., persons having a personal and private interest in the activities of the organization). Petitioner believes that this overlap "clearly indicates" that both the prohibition against private inurement and the prohibition against conferral of substantial private benefits exclusively target the same class of persons.

Petitioner reasons that because this Court has explicitly excluded unrelated third parties from the ambit of the term "private shareholder or individual" in the earnings inurement context, *People of God Community v. Commissioner*, 75 T.C. 127, 133 (1980), unrelated third parties must likewise be excluded from the class of private persons whose receipt of a substantial benefit would cause the organization to be operated other than exclusively for exempt purposes.... Accordingly, petitioner concludes that since Republican entities and candidates are not interested insiders, the private benefit analysis of section 1.501(c)(3)-1(d)(1)(ii), Income Tax Regs., is inapplicable in the case at bar. We do not agree.

Petitioner misconstrues the overlapping characteristics of the private benefit and private inurement prohibitions. We have consistently recognized that while the prohibitions against private inurement and private benefits share common and often overlapping elements, *Church of Ethereal Joy v. Commissioner*, 83 T.C. 20, 21 (1984), *Goldsboro Art League, Inc. v. Commissioner*, 75 T.C. 337, 345 n. 10 (1980), the two are distinct requirements which must independently be satisfied. *Canada v. Commissioner*, 82 T.C. 973, 981 (1984); *Aid to Artisans, Inc. v. Commissioner*, 71 T.C. at 215.

Nonetheless, we have often observed that the prohibition against private inurement of net earnings appears redundant, since the inurement of earnings to an interested person or insider would constitute the conferral of a benefit inconsistent with operating exclusively for an exempt purpose. . . .

The absence of private inurement of earnings to the benefit of a private shareholder or individual does not, however, establish that the organization is operated exclusively for exempt purposes. Therefore, while the private inurement prohibition may arguably be subsumed within the private benefit analysis of the operational test, the reverse is not true. Accordingly, when the Court concludes that no prohibited inurement of earnings exists, it cannot stop there but must inquire further and determine whether a prohibited private benefit is conferred. *See Aid to Artisans, Inc. v. Commissioner*, 71 T.C. at 215; *Retired Teachers Legal Fund v. Commissioner*, 78 T.C. 280, 287 (1982).

Moreover, an organization's conferral of benefits on disinterested persons may cause it to serve "a private interest" within the meaning of section 1.501(c)(3)-1(d)(1)(ii), Income Tax Regs. *Christian Stewardship Assistance, Inc. v. Commissioner*, 70 T.C. 1037 (1978). *See Kentucky Bar Foundation v. Commissioner, supra*; *Aid to Artisans, Inc. v. Commissioner, supra*; *see also The Martin S. Ackerman Foundation v. Commissioner*, T.C. Memo. 1986-365. In this connection, we use 'disinterested' to distinguish persons who are not private shareholders or individuals having a personal and private interest in the activities of the organization within the meaning of section 1.501(a)-1(c), Income Tax Regs.

Presence of Private Benefits

Having determined that nonincidental benefits conferred on disinterested persons may serve private interests, we now consider whether respondent erred in determining that petitioner conferred nonincidental private benefits upon Republican entities and candidates. Section 1.501(c)(3)-1(d)(1)(ii), Income Tax Regs. Petitioner contends that Rev. Rul. 76-456, 1976-2 C.B. 151, prescribes the proper characterization of all benefits conferred by organizations engaging in its type of activities. In this revenue ruling, an organization collected, collated and disseminated information concerning general campaign practices on a nonpartisan basis. The organization also furnished "teaching aids" to political science and civics teachers. Emphasizing the organization's nonpartisan nature, respondent determined that the organization exclusively served a public purpose by encouraging citizens to increase their knowledge and understanding of the election process and participate more effectively in their selection of government officials.

* * *

In contrast to the nonpartisan activities conducted by the organization in Rev. Rul. 76-456, supra, respondent determined and we find that petitioner conducted its educational activities with the partisan objective of benefiting Republican candidates and entities. Petitioner was incorporated by Jan W. Baran, General Counsel of the NRCC on January 24, 1986. In April, 1986, petitioner stated in its Application for Recognition of Exemption that its training program was an outgrowth of the program run by the NRCC.

Petitioner's activities have been exclusively funded by the National Republican Congressional Trust. Two of petitioner's three initial directors had significant ties to the Republican party: Joseph Gaylord as Executive Director of NRCC and John C. McDonald as a member of the Republican National Committee. Petitioner's bylaws empowered this Republican majority of the Board to "have general charge of the affairs, property and assets of the Corporation." Under their general charge the Academy instituted a curriculum that included studies of the "Growth of NRCC, etc." and "Why are people Republicans."

Following the reorganization of petitioner's curriculum after the 1986 election, additional partisan topics such as "Other Republican givers lists," "How some Republicans have won Black votes," and "NRCC/RNC/NRSC/State Party naughtiness" were added. The Academy's curriculum failed to counterbalance the Republican party focus of these courses with comparable studies of the Democratic or other political parties.

Petitioner does not require that its admission panel members be affiliated with a particular political party, but believes that a substantial number of the panel members are affiliated with the Republican party. Likewise, while no particular political affiliation is required of students, the two political references solicited by petitioner on its application for admission often permit the admission panel to deduce the applicant's political affiliation. In turn, knowledge of an applicant's political affiliation provides the admission panel with a means of limiting enrollment to applicants who are likely to subsequently work in Republican organizations and campaigns.

Petitioner was asked by respondent to identify the affiliation of the candidates served by its graduates. Petitioner responded that although graduates are not required to remain in contact with Academy following graduation, "some" graduates chose to report their whereabouts. To the "best" that petitioner could determine, these graduates served on campaigns of candidates who were predominantly affiliated with the Republican party.

The administrative record reveals that 119 of 120 graduates reported their whereabouts to petitioner. These addresses were reported by petitioner in its June, 1986, monthly newsletter. The addresses of graduates working in Congressional or Senatorial campaigns contained the name of the political committee or organization of the candidate; e.g., Bruce Long for Congress, Friends of Bill Emerson, Jim Hansen Committee, People for Dio Guardi, etc. The June–September, 1986, newsletters disclosed that 85 Academy graduates worked in approximately 98 Congressional and Senatorial candidate campaigns. The newsletters did not, however, specify the political affiliations of the respective candidates.

* * *

A showing that petitioner's graduates served in Congressional and Senatorial campaigns of candidates from both major political parties in substantial numbers would have significantly aided petitioner's contention that its activities only benefited nonselect members of a charitable class. Nevertheless, petitioner did not see fit to include in the administrative record any specific example of a graduate working for a Democratic Senatorial or Congressional candidate. We cannot assume that information regarding the placement of Academy graduates, not shown to be unavailable, would have been favorable to petitioner; i.e., would have reflected nonpartisan placement. In fact the contrary is true. *See Fear v. Commissioner*, T.C. Memo. 1989-211; *see also Wichita Terminal Elevator Co. v. Commissioner*, 6 T.C. 1158 (1946), *aff'd*, 162 F.2d 513 (10th Cir. 1947). Consequently, it is reasonable to infer from petitioner's omission that the affiliation information, had it been included, would have revealed the Republican affiliation of the candidates.

Based upon our review of the administrative record, we find that petitioner operated to advance Republican interests. We also find that the placement of 85 of petitioner's graduates in the campaigns of 98 Republican Senatorial and Congressional candidates conferred a benefit on those candidates. Petitioner's partisan purpose distinguishes the case at bar from Rev. Rul. 76-456. . . .

Petitioner next contends that because all educational programs inherently benefit both the student by increasing his or her skills and future earnings and the eventual employer who profits from the services of trained individuals, the educational benefits it provides should not be construed as prohibited private benefits. (Hereinafter, we will refer to the benefits conferred on the students as primary private benefits and the benefits conferred on the employers as secondary benefits.) In support of this contention, petitioner cites several revenue rulings granting exempt status to training programs and educational facilities sponsored by various industry and professional organizations.

Respondent does not quarrel with the notion that exempt educational organizations must inherently confer private benefits on participating individuals. Indeed, he recognizes that an educational organization exists to confer primary private benefits by instructing or training individuals for the purpose of improving or developing his or her capabilities. . . . Moreover, respondent does not assert that the pool of potential students is so narrowly drawn that the Academy would confer a proscribed primary private benefit. . . .

Instead, respondent objects to the secondary benefit accruing exclusively to the Republican entities and candidates who employ petitioner's skilled alumni. Respondent contends that where the training of individuals is focused on furthering a particular targeted private interest, the conferred secondary benefit ceases to be incidental to the providing organization's exempt purposes. By contrast, respondent contends that when secondary benefits are broadly distributed, they become incidental to the organization's exempt purposes.

Respondent asserts that the case at bar differs from the circumstances described in revenue rulings cited by petitioner. Significantly, respondent contends that the secondary benefit provided in each ruling was broadly spread among members of an industry (i.e., employers of union members within an industry, banks within an urban area, members and designees of a local bar association), as opposed to being earmarked for a particular organization or person. The secondary benefit in each of the cited rulings was therefore incidental to the providing organization's exempt purpose.

Based upon his determination that petitioner targeted Republican entities and candidates to receive the secondary benefit through employing its alumni, respondent concludes that the secondary benefit provided by petitioner was not incidental and that more than an insubstantial part of petitioner's activities were performed to further a nonexempt purpose. We agree with respondent.

The question of whether a benefit is private in nature, within the meaning of 1.501(c)(3)-1(d)(1)(ii), Income Tax Regs., was explored by this Court in *Aid to Artisans, Inc. v. Commissioner*, 71 T.C. 202, 215–216 (1978). In that case, the Commissioner asserted that the organization's purchase of handicrafts from disadvantaged artisans served the private interests of the artisans selling their works. In evaluating the merit of the Commissioner's contention, we stated that:

> The questions whether an organization serves private interests within the meaning of [section 1.501(c)(3)-1(d)(1)(ii), Income Tax Regs.] and whether an organization's activities are conducted for private gain . . . may be resolved . . . by examining the definiteness and charitable nature of the class to be benefited and the overall purpose for which the organization is operated. [71 T.C. at 215.]

Upon finding that (1) the disadvantaged artisans receiving the benefits of the organization's purchases comprised a charitable class, (2) the organization's method of selecting handicrafts for purchase indicated no selectivity with regard to individual artisans to be benefited, and (3) the organization's overall purpose was to benefit disadvantaged communities, we declared the Aid to Artisans organization exempt. 71 T.C. at 215–216. *See also Goldsboro Art League, Inc. v. Commissioner, supra*; *Cleveland Creative Arts Guild v. Commissioner*, T.C. Memo. 1985-316. *Compare St. Louis Science Fiction Limited v. Commissioner*, T.C. Memo. 1985-162. **Similarly, we have found that organizations which further exempt purposes through sponsoring legal or medical referral services did not confer private benefits so long as the referral service was open to a broad representation of professionals and no select group of professionals were the primary beneficiaries of the service.** *Kentucky Bar Foundation v. Commissioner, supra. See also Fraternal Medical Specialist Services, Inc. v. Commissioner*, T.C. Memo. 1984-644.

To prevail herein, petitioner must establish that the Republican entities and candidates benefiting from the employment of its graduates are members of a charitable class, and within that charitable class do not comprise a select group of members earmarked to receive benefits. With regard to the charitable nature of Republican entities and candidates, petitioner contends that because the Republican party is comprised of millions of individuals with like "political sympathies," benefits conferred by the Academy on Republican entities and candidates should be deemed to benefit the community at large. We are not persuaded by petitioner's argument.

* * *

Moreover, even were we to find political entities and candidates to generally comprise a charitable class, petitioner would bear the burden of proving that its activities benefited the members of the class in a nonselect manner. Rule 217(c)(2)(i); Aid to Artisans, Inc. v. Commissioner, supra. The administrative record and the partisan affiliation of the candidates served fail to establish that petitioner broadly distributed its secondary benefits among political entities and candidates in a nonselect manner.

Petitioner contends that should we determine that a private benefit is conferred on Republican entities and candidates, such benefit is incidental and collateral to its primary purpose of benefiting the general public. In support of this contention, petitioner argues that a benefit which it cannot control must be incidental in nature. Petitioner observes that "while it is undoubtedly [petitioner's hope] that its alumni eventually will work for Republican organizations and candidates, Petitioner has in fact no control over whether they will do so or not." Petitioner reasons that absent an ability to control the employment of its students, it lacks the ability to control the conferral of secondary benefits attributable to such employment. Therefore, the secondary benefits conferred on Republicans are the result of happenstance and should in the opinion of petitioner be treated as merely incidental to its exempt purpose of educating campaign professionals.

Petitioner cites no compelling authority in support of its contention that nonincidental benefits must be controllable by the organization. Moreover, as discussed previously, we find the administrative record supports respondent's contention that petitioner was formed with a substantial purpose to train campaign professionals for service in Republican entities and campaigns, an activity previously conducted by NRCC. Petitioner has failed to persuade us that this is not the case. Secondary benefits which advance a substantial purpose cannot be construed as incidental to the organization's exempt educational purpose. . . .

Accordingly, we conclude that petitioner is operated for the benefit of private interests, a nonexempt purpose. Because more than an insubstantial part of petitioner's activities further this nonexempt purpose, petitioner has failed to establish that it operates exclusively for exempt purposes within the meaning of section 501(c)(3). Consequently, petitioner is not entitled to an exemption from taxation under section 501(a).

2. The Service's Private Benefit Test: GCM 39862

Although the Service prevailed in *American Campaign Academy*, it has never completely embraced the underlying reasoning of that case. In General Counsel Memorandum 39862 (Nov. 21, 1991), the Service's Chief Counsel articulated the test for private benefit as follows:

> Any private benefit arising from a particular activity must be "incidental" in both a qualitative and quantitative sense to the overall public benefit achieved by the activity if the organization is to remain exempt. To be qualitatively incidental, a private benefit must occur as a necessary concomitant of the activity that benefits the public at large; in other words, the benefit to the public cannot be achieved without necessarily benefiting private individuals. Such benefits might also be characterized as indirect or unintentional. To be quantitatively incidental, a benefit must be insubstantial when viewed in relation to the public benefit conferred by the activity. It bears emphasis that, even though exemption of the entire organization may be at stake, the private benefit conferred by an activity or arrangement is balanced only against the public benefit conferred by that activity or arrangement, not the overall good accomplished by the organization.

An earlier General Counsel, issued before *American Campaign Academy*, actually first articulated this formulation. *See* GCM 37789 (Dec. 18, 1978). Because the Service issued GCM 39862 after *American Campaign Academy*, the author had the benefit of the Tax Court's instruction on the private benefit issue. Nevertheless, the Chief Counsel's private benefit test is markedly different from that of the Tax Court and indeed the Treasury's own regulation. Do you see the differences? Use the hypothetical that follows to isolate the differences in the Tax Court and Chief Counsel tests.

Questions

1. Hogtown Community Center, exempt under § 501(c)(3), offers outreach and social activities for senior citizens in Hogtown. It conducts field trips to nature preserves, beaches, and performing arts presentations free of charge. It also offers educational classes and seminars on a wide range of subjects for senior citizens. As an insubstantial part of its operations, the Center operates a free lunch program whereby it delivers mid-day meals to homebound seniors. Although more than a dozen restaurants are nearby, the Center purchases the meals at market price exclusively from the Hogtown Bar and Grill, the owner of which otherwise has no connection to the Community Center. Approximately 40% of the Bar and Grill's revenue is comprised of receipts from the Center's purchases.

   a. If the Service sought to revoke the Center's tax exemption on the basis of private benefit, what result under American Campaign Academy?

   b. What result under GCM 39862?

c. Which approach is best from a policy perspective?

d. Does it matter in either case that the Bar and Grill is charging no more than the market price for the food it sells to the Community Center?

KJ's Fund Raisers, Inc. v. Commissioner

T.C. Memo. 1997-424

* * *

Kristine Hurd and James Gould are the sole owners of KJ's Place, a lounge where alcoholic beverages are served. The term KJ is obviously derived from the first initials of the first names of the owners, Kristine and James. In 1992, Kristine and James created petitioner, KJ's Fund Raisers, Inc. They had petitioner incorporated as a Vermont Non-Profit Corporation on October 12, 1992. They also had petitioner file a Form 1023 . . . on November 11, 1992.

Petitioner's business is selling Lucky 7 or other break-open (or lottery or rip) tickets. The lottery tickets are sold exclusively at KJ's Place; no other locations were considered. The tickets are sold during regular business hours by the owners and employees of KJ's Place.

Petitioner was organized purportedly to "raise funds for distribution to charitable causes". Petitioner expects the majority of its funds to come from the sale of lottery tickets and does not plan to solicit public donations, but will accept any donations offered. There is no evidence in the record that any such donations were ever offered or received.

When petitioner was organized, Hurd and Gould were both officers and directors. She was president; he was vice president, secretary, and treasurer. The third member of the board of directors was Karen Gould, a relative of James Gould.

In April 1993, petitioner replaced its board of directors. Of the three new members, two were related to Hurd or Gould. The board has been altered since then. The current board has two members unrelated to Hurd or Gould; the third is Kristine Hurd's sister. In a letter to the IRS, petitioner indicated that it would further revise its board so that none of the members were related to the officers of KJ's Place. However, that change has never been implemented.

In 1993, petitioner paid Hurd and Gould compensation of $6,000 each for bookkeeping, accounting and managerial services. Petitioner also paid $6,000 in rent to KJ's Place. The measure of compensation was determined by Hurd and Gould. On July 1, 1994, changes in Vermont's gambling laws took effect. In accordance with these changes, petitioner stopped paying rent to KJ's Place and stopped paying wages to Hurd and Gould. Currently, there are no business dealings between petitioner's directors and the owners of KJ's Place, and petitioner's books are kept separate from the accounts of KJ's Place.

From the proceeds of the sales of the lottery tickets, petitioner has made grants to a variety of organizations. Some of these grants have been memorialized in local newspapers. Of six clippings sent to the IRS by petitioner, two have a photo of Hurd or Gould in front of KJ's Place handing out a check on behalf of petitioner. One clipping notes that KJ's Fund Raisers is a new corporation located at KJ's Place. Another shows a director of petitioner presenting a check and identifies the proceeds as arising from rip-ticket sales at KJ's Place.

* * *

Petitioner's case is factually similar to *P.L.L. Scholarship Fund v. Commissioner*, 82 T.C. 196 (1984). In that case, the taxpayer was a nonprofit corporation formed to raise money for college scholarships. It planned to raise money through the operation of bingo games held at the Pastime Lounge, a lounge owned by two members of the board of directors. The other board members consisted of an accountant and director of the lounge and two "bingo players." The board was self-perpetuating, with the existing directors selecting future directors. *Id.* at 197.

The owners of the Pastime Lounge ran the bingo games during regular business hours. Employees of the Pastime Lounge solicited orders for food and drink from the bingo players. However, the accounts of the Pastime Lounge were kept separate and distinct from those of the taxpayer. *Id.* at 197–198.

This Court held that the taxpayer had a nonexempt purpose which was "substantial in nature"; i.e., to promote business at the Pastime Lounge through the medium of the bingo games. *Id.* at 199–200. The Court based this conclusion in part on the identity of the taxpayer's board of directors with the owners and associates of the Pastime Lounge. Since the owners controlled the board and appointed its future directors, the Court reasoned, the taxpayer's activities could be used to the advantage of the Lounge. *Id.* at 200.

The taxpayer argued that the separate accounts and the fact that the Lounge received nothing from the taxpayer for wages or rent demonstrated that it was operated exclusively for an exempt purpose. The Court held otherwise: "A realistic look at the operations of these two entities, however, shows that the activities of . . . [the taxpayer] and the Pastime Lounge were so interrelated as to be functionally inseparable. Separate accountings of receipts and disbursements does not change that fact." *Id.*

The manner in which petitioner is operated benefits private interests, KJ's Place and its owners. Like *P.L.L. Scholarship Fund v. Commissioner, supra*, petitioner's lottery tickets are sold at a single location, KJ's Place. As in *P.L.L. Scholarship Fund v. Commissioner, supra*, the lottery tickets are sold during KJ's Place's regular business hours, their sale overseen by the owners of KJ's Place, Hurd and Gould. While in KJ's Place, lottery ticket purchasers are solicited for beverages. As in *P.L.L. Scholarship Fund v. Commissioner, supra*, the accounts of petitioner and KJ's Place are kept separate and apart.

Despite these similarities, petitioner contends that two factors distinguish it from *P.L.L. Scholarship Fund v. Commissioner, supra*. First, the board of directors is responsible for running petitioner, and the majority of the board members are not related to the owners of KJ's Place. Second, KJ's Place has allegedly lost money as patrons prefer to purchase lottery tickets rather than beverages.

Petitioner stresses that the board of directors, independent of Hurd and Gould, controls the distribution of proceeds raised by the sale of the lottery tickets. While the board does decide which charities will receive funds, it is clear from the record that Kristine Hurd and James Gould control sales of the lottery tickets.... It is also clear that their control is realistically independent of the board. In a protest letter to the IRS..., petitioner concedes that the officers of KJ's Place appear able to control petitioner but defend it as necessary.

> It is our opinion, however, that KJ's Fundraisers. Inc. would fold without the original founders of the organization as officers and local charities would go unfunded....

Before July 1, 1994, Hurd and Gould received wages and KJ's Place received rent from petitioner. Although those practices ceased and are not in issue here, the current board of directors is composed of at least the majority of the same members who allowed those amounts to be paid. This strongly suggests that Hurd and Gould are free to set policy for their own benefit without objection from the board. Nothing in the record since July 1, 1994, indicates otherwise.

Petitioner also contends that KJ's Place actually lost money, since patrons preferred to buy lottery tickets rather than use their money to purchase beverages. Thus, petitioner argues, there was no actual benefit. While all facts must be accepted as true for purposes of a declaratory judgment, Rule 217, conjectural statements such as the one above are entitled to no such consideration. Petitioner has presented no evidence that KJ's Place lost money. More important, KJ's Place has benefitted from the publicity surrounding donations given by petitioner. In four of six newspaper articles or picture captions in evidence, KJ's Place is pictured or mentioned, along with Hurd or Gould, who are identified as the owners of KJ's Place rather than officers of petitioner.

Petitioner argues that the clippings are not paid advertising and do not indicate the receipt of an actual benefit by KJ's Place. We find, however, that the publicity, which KJ's Place would not have received but for petitioner's exclusive association with the lounge, is a significant benefit. Moreover, the record discloses that there were other "clubs" or lounges in the area where comparable gambling took place. It is thus a fair inference that one of the real purposes of establishing petitioner in the first place was to induce customers with a proclivity for this type of gambling not to desert KJ's Place in favor of other clubs or lounges. As a result of petitioner's formation, KJ's Place, far from losing revenue, may indeed have prevented at least a portion of its business from being taken elsewhere.

Petitioner engaged in the exempt activity of raising money for charitable purposes. Petitioner also operated for the substantial private benefit of KJ's Place and its owners....

Note on KJ's Fund Raisers

This decision arguably belongs in Chapter 11, along with other "selfish motive" cases. A significant purpose of the organization was to benefit the founders' tavern. Yet the court styled the case as one of "private benefit" rather than "private inurement." Unlike *Easter House*, in Chapter 11, *KJ's* did not involve allegations of excessive compensation or low-interest loans. Also, unlike *American Campaign Academy*, "insiders" benefitted in *KJ's*, rather than outsiders. Ultimately, readers should be less concerned with distinguishing the three doctrines—direct private inurement, a private rather than public purpose, and "private benefit"—and should focus more on insuring they cover their bases in avoiding all three arguments. Recall how in *United Cancer Council* the Circuit Court—unlike the Tax Court—decided the matter solely on "private benefit" grounds and not on private inurement. Significantly, the government in *UCC* failed to prove the dollar amount of the alleged private benefit.

3. Private Benefit and the Meaning of Charity

The question whether an activity is "charitable" and whether it contravenes the private benefit prohibition is often hopelessly intertwined. For example, the Tax Court in *Columbia Park and Recreation Association, Inc. v. Commissioner*, 88 T.C. 1 (1987), denied exemption to a homeowners' association that provided municipal-type services to a private community with a population of 110,000. Its massive size notwithstanding, the community nevertheless lacked a "sufficient public element" and therefore service to the community was not "charitable" within the meaning of § 501(c)(3). As a corollary, the Court concluded that the organization operated for the private benefit of the community residents and property owners. Even though residents and property owners paid for the provided services through property assessments or admission fees for use of recreational facilities, the Court found private benefit. Thus, private benefit is not a function of the entity's provision of goods or services at less than market value, as is the private inurement doctrine. *Columbia Park* is similar to *American Campaign Academy*: Columbia substantially benefited a private neighborhood, and American substantially benefited the Republican Party. Neither were charitable classes.

In some cases, an activity might not be charitable even though no private benefit is present. For example, in *Federation Pharmacy Services, Inc. v. Commissioner*, 72 T.C. 687 (1979), the Tax Court denied tax exemption to a corporation that provided prescription drugs at discount prices to senior citizens. Although the corporation charged the lowest retail price available, less five percent, it did not sell drugs at prices below its own costs. The Court concluded that the corporation was really no different from ordinary commercial drug stores—which also provide discounts to senior citizens—and therefore was not entitled to tax exemption. The Court did not hold that the organization operated for private benefit, however. The pharmacy lacked a charitable purpose and instead had a commercial purpose without sufficiently benefiting a charitable class. In contrast to *American Campaign Academy* and *Columbia Park*, it did not substantially benefit a non-charitable class; instead, it merely benefited itself.

Sometimes the result is simply inexplicable. In *Monterey Public Parking v. United States*, 321 F. Supp. 972 (N.D. Cal. 1970), *aff'd*, 481 F.2d 175 (9th Cir. 1973), the court considered a commercial parking lot in downtown Monterey, California. "Monterey's municipal government, in the opinion of many, could not expeditiously finance and construct needed parking facilities, and as a result several private business and professional persons organized plaintiff corporation." *Id.* at 974. According to the government, "the primary, or at least a substantial, goal of plaintiff corporation is to encourage the general public to patronize those businesses which participate in plaintiff's validation stamp system. This, it is said, constitutes a direct private benefit to certain individuals, with only an incidental benefit to the public." *Id.* at 975. The court sided with the parking lot: "This Court cannot say that plaintiff corporation, organizationally or operationally, subserves, in any substantial way, private interests. . . . [A]ll but one of plaintiff's organizers were businessmen whose establishments would tend to suffer if the traffic problems of downtown Monterey were not soon resolved. Customers, finding themselves unable to find convenient parking, would avoid the center city in favor of suburban shopping centers. But this was a threat not only to plaintiffs, but to all the City of Monterey, and the deliberations of the City Council so state. . . . The City of Monterey, therefore, was the primary beneficiary when plaintiff succeeded in constructing public parking facilities without any significant outlay of public funds." *Id.* at 976.

Aside on Monterey Public Parking

Monterey would appear to be a classic case of "private benefit," except that it is not: the court decided otherwise and the Ninth Circuit almost summarily agreed. The beneficiary was the city rather than the commercial businesses substantially patronized by people parking. While less than self-evident, the conclusion was clear. That alone is an important lesson: some cases are just different and irreconcilable with the majority. But the case also stands for another important proposition — and in this case, the court was consistent with the consensus view. The parking lot sought exempt status under subsection 501(c)(4) as a social welfare organization, rather than under subsection 501(c)(3) as a charity. The primary difference, of course, is that a (c)(3) can receive deductible contributions while a (c)(4) cannot. But another important distinction exists: subsection (c)(4) requires the entity be "not organized for-profit," while subsection (c)(3) has no such limitation. In considering the commercial, profit-making nature of the parking lot, the court chose to ignore the literal words of subsection (c)(4) — as well as the same words in the regulations — holding that the commerciality doctrine applies to each the same. Thus, subsection (c)(4) organizations may make profits. The court chose to follow the "philosophy" behind the law rather than the words chosen by Congress. *Id.*

Questions

1. State whether the following entities should be denied charitable tax exemption based upon private benefit or simply because it is not charitable:

a. A educational organization that provides classes on life skills (family relationships, speaking skills, financial planning, etc.) for its paying members, all of whom must be union employees of the largest coal-mining company in the country.

b. A health maintenance organization that coordinates health services solely for its paying members, but membership is open to any and all willing to pay the membership fee.

c. A thrift shop that sells clothing and household appliances at below cost solely to residents of the large, privately owned condominium complex in which it is situated.

d. A soup kitchen, located in a privately owned condominium complex, that sells clothing and household appliances to any and all customers at discount prices.

Discussion Activity. Prepare a written definition of private benefit. Be prepared to further explain and defend your memo in class with your own hypothetical.

B. Class Size

An important issue related to the "public benefit" requirement involves just how public must the benefit be? The answer is unclear. Traditionally, the service has argued in favor of an indefinite number of potential beneficiaries and has typically rejected charities dedicated to aiding particular individuals.

On August 25, 1995, following the Oklahoma City bombing, the Service issued a Guidance Letter in which it cautioned organizations from accepting donations dedicated to particular individuals. The letter posited and answered several questions, including:

Question 1

What can a charity do to meet long-term concerns such as education for orphans or children injured in a disaster?

Answer

Beneficiaries must constitute a traditionally charitable class (which would include orphans or injured children) and must also be indefinite either by virtue of their large numbers or by defining a class of beneficiaries in an open-ended manner. The class of beneficiaries is open-ended when the charity aids victims of a particular disaster and also others in similar circumstances in the future rather than a finite or fixed group that is identifiable.

The 19-page letter effectively instructed Oklahoma charities that they would not be approved as serving an exempt purpose if they accepted funds dedicated to the victims of the single disaster. The Service preceded its letter with a notice issued on May 17, 1995:

Notice 95-33

1995-1 C.B. 309

As a result of the devastation, personal injury and loss of life caused by the bomb attack on the Alfred P. Murrah Federal Building in Oklahoma City, Oklahoma on April 19, 1995, the President has declared the affected area to be eligible for Federal disaster assistance. The Internal Revenue Service has received questions regarding the tax consequences of private efforts to provide relief to disaster victims in this area. This notice serves as an "administrative pronouncement" within the meaning of section 1.6661-3(b)(2) of the Income Tax Regulations to provide guidance that may be relied on to the same extent as a revenue ruling or revenue procedure.

Contributions earmarked for Oklahoma City federal building bomb attack relief that are made to organizations currently recognized by the Service as tax exempt under section 501(c)(3) of the Internal Revenue Code are fully deductible as charitable contributions. However, the tax law does not allow taxpayers to deduct contributions earmarked for relief of any particular individual or family.

Donors should exercise care before contributing to any organization. With increased public interest in making donations to charitable organizations to assist disaster victims, there is the increased possibility that some organizations (or their fundraisers) may make false or inaccurate claims regarding how contributions will be used or whether these contributions are tax deductible. Donors have advance assurance of deductibility only for contributions to organizations recognized as exempt by the Service under section 501(c)(3) of the Code.

Charitable organizations formed to aid victims of the Oklahoma City bomb attack but not yet recognized as exempt can receive expedited consideration of their application for recognition of exemption by writing "OKLAHOMA CITY FEDERAL BUILDING BOMB ATTACK RELIEF" at the top of Form 1023, which is the form they use to apply for exempt status....

The expedited application processing does not modify or relax the requirement that tax exempt organizations operate exclusively for charitable purposes. However, to the extent that an organization is providing appropriate relief, in good faith, in the designated disaster area, the Service will not raise certain issues that might otherwise affect the organization's qualification for exempt status or, in the case of a private foundation, liability for certain taxes under Chapter 42. Examples of these issues include an organization providing emergency assistance to its own employees or employees of related organizations who have been victimized by the bombing (which raise the issue of prohibited inurement), and a private foundation providing emergency assistance to disqualified persons (as defined in section 4946 of the Code) victimized by the attack.

This relief is also granted to organizations exempt under other paragraphs of section 501(c). For example, the Service will not raise the issue of particular services with respect to a business league exempt under section 501(c)(6) if the organization's good faith relief efforts include aid provided to members victimized by the attack.

This relief is available to both new organizations and existing tax exempt organizations until December 31, 1995, or later if an extension by the Service is determined to be necessary or appropriate.

Note on Notice 95-33

According to news reports, Oklahoma charities complied with the articulated rules; however, charities in other locales—responding to similar disasters—have not. *See* Randy Ellis, *IRS Disaster Fund Advice Followed in OKC, Ignored Elsewhere*, NewsOK, Nov. 19, 2012, http://newsok.com/irs-disaster-fund-advice-followed-in-okc-ignored-elsewhere/article/3729581.

How much the government has modified its position post-9/11 is unclear; however, Publication 3833 provides some current guidance. Pay close attention to the distinction between a "charitable class" and a "smaller group." An entity can exclusively benefit a "class," but it must be indefinite if it initially only benefits a smaller group.

> CHARITABLE CLASS—The group of individuals that may properly receive assistance from a tax-exempt charitable organization is called a "charitable class."
>
> A charitable class must be large enough or sufficiently indefinite that the community as a whole, rather than a pre-selected group of people, benefits when a charity provides assistance. For example, a charitable class could consist of all the individuals in a city, county or state. This charitable class is large enough that the potential beneficiaries cannot be individually identified and providing benefits to this group would benefit the entire community.
>
> If the group of eligible beneficiaries is limited to a **smaller group**, such as the employees of a particular employer, the group of persons eligible for assistance must be indefinite. To be considered to benefit an indefinite class, the proposed relief program must be open-ended and include employees affected by the current disaster and those who may be affected by a future disaster. Accordingly, if a charity follows a policy of assisting employees who are victims of all disasters, present or future, it would be providing assistance to an indefinite charitable class. If the facts and circumstances indicate that a newly established disaster relief program is intended to benefit only victims of a current disaster without any intention to provide for victims of future disasters, the organization would not be considered to be benefiting a charitable class.

Because of the requirement that exempt organizations must serve a charitable class, a tax-exempt disaster relief or emergency hardship organization cannot target and limit its assistance to specific individuals, such as a few persons injured in a particular fire. Similarly, donors cannot earmark contributions to a charitable organization for a particular individual or family.

EXAMPLE 1: Linda's baby, Todd, suffers severe burns in a fire requiring costly treatment that Linda cannot afford. Linda's friends and co-workers form the Todd Foundation to raise funds from fellow workers, family members, and the general public to meet Todd's expenses. Since the organization is formed to assist a **particular individual**, it **would not qualify** as a charitable organization.

Consider this alternative case: Linda's friends and co-workers form an organization to raise funds to meet the expenses of an open-ended group consisting of all children in the community injured by disasters where financial help is needed. Neither Linda nor members of Linda's family control the charitable organization. The organization controls the selection of aid recipients and determines whether any assistance should be provided to Todd. Potential donors are advised that, while funds may be used to assist Todd, their contributions might well be used for other children who have similar needs. The organization does not accept contributions specifically earmarked for Todd or any other individual. The organization, formed and operated to assist an **indefinite** number of current and future disaster victims, **qualifies** as a charitable organization.

* * *

EXAMPLE 2: A hurricane causes widespread damage to property and loss of life in several counties of a coastal state. Over 100,000 homes are damaged or destroyed by high winds and flooding. The **group of people affected by the disaster is large enough** so that providing aid to this group benefits the public as a whole. Therefore, a charitable organization can be formed to assist persons in this group since the eligible recipients comprise a charitable class.

EXAMPLE 3: A hurricane causes widespread damage to property and loss of life in several counties of a coastal state. In one of the affected counties, an existing charitable organization has an ongoing program that provides emergency assistance to residents of the county. A small number of residents of this county suffered significant injury or property damage as a result of the storm. The organization provided assistance to some of these individuals. The organization's assistance was provided to a charitable class because **the group of potential recipients is indefinite** in that it is open-ended to include other victims of future disasters in the county.

Questions

Consider whether a fund dedicated solely to victims of the following disasters might be exempt. If you believe it would not be exempt, how might you modify the fund to satisfy the requirements of § 501, as articulated by the Oklahoma City Guidance Letter and Publication 3833? Consider the relevance, if any, of § 139.

1. The September 11, 2001, attacks on the World Trade Center and the Pentagon.
2. The April 15, 2013, bombings at the Boston Marathon.
3. The Newtown, Connecticut, shootings in December 2012.
4. Hurricane Katrina in August 2005.

See Rochelle Korman, Charitable Class and Need: Whom Should Charities Benefit? (2002), http://www1.law.nyu.edu/ncpl/pdfs/2002/Korman2002.pdf; Robert A. Katz, *A Pig in a Python: How the Charitable Response to September 11 Overwhelmed the Law of Disaster Relief*, 36 Ind. L. Rev. 251 (2003).

C. Advanced Application: Joint Ventures Between Charities and Commercial Entities

1. Ancillary Joint Ventures

In lean economic times, exempt organizations often receive smaller and fewer donations, and have access to even fewer sources of governmental support. Governmental and private funding for the Arts, for example, can usually be counted as one of the first casualties of a recession. At other times, the changing economy simply chokes off familiar sources of revenue, such as fees for services in the health care industry, which support medical research or health care for the indigent. In such circumstances, exempt organizations have been known to seek novel forms of financing, such as joint ventures, which normally involve the participation of a for-profit entity in the exempt organization's activities. As might be expected, the for-profit entity is rarely motivated by the same charitable impulses as the exempt entity: the for-profit typically participates for the benefit it (and its owners) can obtain. The question arises whether, by participating in such schemes, the exempt entity violates the prohibition against private benefit and is therefore organized or operated for a non-exempt purpose.

The Service initially took the position that participation in a joint venture with a for-profit entity was inherently inconsistent with tax exemption because such participation caused the organization to convey a private benefit on the for-profit partner. But in *Plumstead Theatre Society, Inc. v. Commissioner*, 74 T.C. 1324 (1980), an organization formed to promote the performing arts needed money to produce a play. To obtain financing, the organization formed a limited partnership in which it served as the general partner and for-profit investors were granted interests as limited partners. The organization engaged, or planned to engage, in other activities outside of the partnership. The Tax Court responded to the Service's contention that participation in the partnership prevented the organization from being tax exempt thusly:

> Respondent's last argument is that because of the partnership petitioner entered into with two private individuals and a corporation whereby the limited partners provided capital in exchange for an interest in the profits and losses of First Monday [the play] petitioner is operated for private, rather than public interests. We do not agree. After entering into an agreement with the Kennedy Center, petitioner discovered it was in need of funds for its share of the capitalization costs of First Monday.... [I]n an arm's-length transaction, it obtained those funds by selling a portion of its interest in the play itself, for a reasonable price. Petitioner is not obligated for the return of any capital contribution made by the limited partners from its own funds, and the partnership has no interest in petitioner or in any other plays it is planning to produce. The limited partners have no control over the way petitioner operates or manages its affairs, and none of the limited petitioner or in any other plays it is planning to produce. The limited partners have no control over the way petitioner operates or manages its affairs, and none of the limited partners nor any officer or director of Pantheon Pictures, Inc. is an officer or director of petitioner.

74 T.C. 1324, 1333–34 (1980).

Aside on Plumstead Theater

As is true of many decisions, we could place this one in several chapters. It belongs in Chapter 12 because it famously involved a joint venture with a for-profit entity. But it also belongs in Chapters 7 through 9 dealing with the commerciality doctrine. The theater's joint venture involved a commercially-feasible production; however, as the court found, the primary purpose of the entity was to foster very different types of plays in Pasadena, California, a place in which what the entity proposed to do was not commercially feasible. Importantly, the decision illustrates what amounts to a regional standard for commerciality: what might be too commercial in one part of the country can be non-commercial in another. Facts and circumstances trump consistent doctrine.

2. Whole-Entity Joint Ventures

Plumstead dealt only with a situation in which the exempt organization conducted a small portion of its activities via a joint venture with a for-profit entity. The question remained whether an organization could be exempt even if the entirety of its activities were conducted via a joint venture with a for-profit partner. The following ruling and case demonstrate the Service's very cautious approach to joint ventures. Pay close attention to highlighted text which emphasizes important distinctions between partnership C (which can have an exempt partner) and partnership F (which cannot have an exempt partner).

C has two important factors: its governing document limit it to "furthering" a charitable purpose, and a majority of its board represents A, the charitable member of the C partnership. In contrast, F lacks organizational restrictions limiting it to at least "furthering" a charitable purpose. In addition, F's board is split equally between representing D (its charitable partner) and E (a for profit partner). The absence of those two factors for F resulted in D (the charitable partner) not being exempt. Whether adding one, but not both, of the factors would have changed the result is unclear.

Revenue Ruling 98-15

1998-1 C.B. 718 (emphasis added)

Issue

Whether, under the facts described below, an organization that operates an acute care hospital continues to qualify for exemption from federal income tax as an organization described in 501(c)(3) of the Internal Revenue Code when it forms a limited liability company (LLC) with a for-profit corporation and then contributes its hospital and all of its other operating assets to the LLC, which then operates the hospital.

Situation 1

A is a nonprofit corporation that owns and operates an acute care . . . exempt . . . under . . . 501(c)(3) and as other than a private foundation. . . . B is a for-profit corporation that owns and operates a number of hospitals.

A concludes that it could better serve its community if it obtained additional funding. B is interested in providing financing for A's hospital, provided it earns a reasonable rate of return. A and B form a limited liability company, C. A contributes all of its operating assets, including its hospital to C. B also contributes assets to C. In return, A and B receive ownership interests in C proportional and equal in value to their respective contributions.

C's Articles of Organization and Operating Agreement ("governing documents") provide that **C is to be managed by a governing board consisting of three individuals chosen by A and two individuals chosen by B.** A intends to appoint community leaders who have experience with hospital matters, but who are not on the hospital staff and do not otherwise engage in business transactions with the hospital.

The governing documents further provide that they may only be amended with the approval of both owners and that a majority of three board members must approve certain major decisions relating to C's operation . . .

The governing documents require that C operate any hospital it owns in a manner that furthers charitable purposes by promoting health for a broad cross section of its community. The governing documents explicitly provide that the duty of the members of the governing board to operate C in a manner that furthers [such]charitable purposes . . . overrides any duty they may have to operate C for the financial benefit of its owners. Accordingly, in the event of a conflict between operation in accordance with the community benefit standard and any duty to maximize profits, the members of the governing board are to satisfy the community benefit standard without regard to the consequences for maximizing profitability.

The governing documents further provide that all returns of capital and distributions of earnings made to owners of C shall be proportional to their ownership interests in C. The terms of the governing documents are legal, binding, and enforceable under applicable state law.

C enters into a management agreement with a management company that is unrelated to A or B to provide day-to-day management services to C. . . . The management company will be paid a management fee for its services based on C's gross revenues. The terms and conditions of the management agreement, including the fee structure and the contract term, are reasonable and comparable to what other management firms receive for similar services at similarly situated hospitals. C may terminate the agreement for cause.

None of the officers, directors, or key employees of A who were involved in making the decision to form C were promised employment or any other inducement by C or B and their related entities if the transaction were approved. None of A's officers, directors, or key employees have any interest, including any interest through attribution determined in accordance with the principles of 318, in B or any of its related entities.

. . . C will be treated as a partnership for federal income tax purposes.

A intends to use any distributions it receives from C to fund grants to support activities that promote the health of A's community and to help the indigent obtain health care. Substantially all of A's grantmaking will be funded by distributions from C. A's projected grantmaking program and its participation as an owner of C will constitute A's only activities.

Situation 2

D is a nonprofit corporation that owns and operates an acute care hospital . . . exempt under . . . 501(c)(3) and as other than a private foundation. . . . E is a for-profit hospital corporation that owns and operates a number of hospitals and provides management services to several hospitals that it does not own.

D concludes that it could better serve its community if it obtained additional funding. E is interested in providing financing for D's hospital, provided it earns a reasonable rate of return. D and E form a limited liability company, F. D contributes all of its operating assets, including its hospital to F. E also contributes assets to F. In return, D and E receive ownership interests proportional and equal in value to their respective contributions.

F's Articles of Organization . . . provide that F is to be managed by a governing board consisting of three individuals chosen by D and three individuals chosen by E. D intends to appoint community leaders who have experience with hospital matters, but who are not on the hospital staff and do not otherwise engage in business transactions with the hospital.

The governing documents further provide that they may only be amended with the approval of both owners and that a majority of board members must approve certain major decisions relating to F's operation . . .

F's governing documents provide that F's purpose is to construct, develop, own, manage, operate, and take other action in connection with operating the health care facilities it owns and engage in other health care-related activities. . . . [A]ll returns of capital and distributions of earnings made to owners of F shall be proportional to their ownership interests in F.

F enters into a management agreement with a wholly-owned subsidiary of E to provide day-to-day management services to F. . . . F may terminate the agreement only for cause. E's subsidiary will be paid a management fee for its services based on gross revenues. The terms and conditions of the management agreement, including the fee structure and the contract term other than the renewal terms, are reasonable and comparable to what other management firms receive for similar services at similarly situated hospitals.

As part of the agreement to form F, D agrees to approve the selection of two individuals to serve as F's chief executive officer and chief financial officer. These individuals have previously worked for E in hospital management and have business expertise. They will work with the management company to oversee F's day-to-day management. Their compensation is comparable to what comparable executives are paid at similarly situated hospitals.

. . . F will be treated as a partnership for federal tax income purposes.

D intends to use any distributions it receives from F to fund grants to support activities that promote the health of D's community and to help the indigent obtain health care. Substantially all of D's grantmaking will be funded by distributions from F. D's projected grantmaking program and its participation as an owner of F will constitute D's only activities.

Law

* * *

The promotion of health has long been recognized as a charitable purpose. . . . However, not every activity that promotes health supports tax exemption under 501(c)(3). For example, selling prescription pharmaceuticals certainly promotes health, but pharmacies cannot qualify for recognition of exemption under 501(c)(3) on that basis alone. *Federation Pharmacy Services, Inc. v. Commissioner*, 72 T.C. 687 (1979), *aff'd*, 625 F.2d 804 (8th Cir. 1980) . . . . Furthermore, "an institution for the promotion of health is not a charitable institution if it is privately owned and is run for the profit of the owners." 4A AUSTIN W. SCOTT AND WILLIAM F. FRATCHER, THE LAW OF TRUSTS 372.1 (4th ed. 1989). *See also* RESTATEMENT (SECOND) OF TRUSTS, 376 (1959). This principle applies to hospitals and other health care organizations. As the Tax Court stated, "[w]hile the diagnosis and cure of disease are indeed purposes that may furnish the foundation for characterizing the activity as 'charitable,' something more is required." . . .

In evaluating whether a nonprofit hospital qualifies as an organization described in 501(c)(3), Rev. Rul. 69-545, 1969-2 C.B. 117, compares two hospitals. The first hospital discussed is controlled by a board of trustees composed of independent civic leaders. In addition, the hospital maintains an open medical staff, with privileges available to all qualified physicians; it operates a full-time emergency room open to all regardless of ability to pay; and it otherwise admits all patients able to pay (either themselves, or through third party payers such as private health insurance or government programs such as Medicare). In contrast, the second hospital is controlled by physicians who have a substantial economic interest in the hospital. This hospital restricts the number of physicians admitted to the medical staff, enters into favorable rental agreements with the individuals who control the hospital, and limits emergency room and hospital admission substantially to the patients of the physicians who control the hospital. Rev. Rul. 69-545 notes that in considering whether a nonprofit hospital is operated to serve a private benefit, the Service will weigh all the relevant facts and circumstances in each case, including the use and control of the hospital. The revenue ruling concludes that the first hospital continues to qualify as an organization described in s 501(c)(3) and the second hospital does not because it is operated for the private benefit of the physicians who control the hospital.

* * *

Section 512(c) provides that an exempt organization that is a member of a partnership conducting an unrelated trade or business . . . must include its share of the partnership income and deductions attributable to that business (subject to the exceptions, additions, and limitations in 512(b)) in computing its unrelated business income. . . .

In *Butler v. Commissioner*, 36 T.C. 1097 (1961), acq. 1962-2 C.B. 4 . . . the court examined the relationship between a partner and a partnership for purposes of determining whether the partner was entitled to a business bad debt deduction for a loan he had made to the partnership that it could not repay. In holding that the partner was entitled to the bad debt deduction, the court noted that "[b]y reason of being a partner in a business, petitioner was individually engaged in business." . . .

In Plumstead Theatre Society, Inc. v. Commissioner, 74 T.C. 1324 (1980), *aff'd*, 675 F.2d 244 (9th Cir. 1982) . . . the Tax Court held that a charitable organization's participation as a general partner in a limited partnership did not jeopardize its exempt status. . . . **One of the significant factors supporting the Tax Court's holding was its finding that the limited partners had no control over the organization's operations.**

In *Broadway Theatre League of Lynchburg, Virginia, Inc. v. U.S.*, 293 F. Supp. 346 (W.D. Va. 1968) . . . the court held that an organization that promoted an interest in theatrical arts did not jeopardize its exempt status when it hired a booking organization to arrange for a series of theatrical performances, promote the series and sell season tickets to the series because the contract was for a reasonable term and provided for reasonable compensation and the organization retained ultimate authority over the activities being managed.

In *Housing Pioneers v. Commissioner*, 65 T.C.M. (CCH) 2191 (1993), *aff'd*, 49 F.3d 1395 (9th Cir. 1995), . . . the Tax Court concluded that an organization did not qualify as a 501(c)(3) organization because its activities performed as co-general partner in for-profit limited partnerships substantially furthered a non-exempt purpose, and serving that purpose caused the organization to serve private interests. The organization entered into partnerships as a one percent co-general partner of existing limited partnerships for the purpose of splitting the tax benefits with the for-profit partners. Under the management agreement, the organization's authority as co-general partner was narrowly circumscribed. It had no management responsibilities and could describe only a vague charitable function of surveying tenant needs.

In *Est of Hawaii v. Commissioner*, 71 T.C. 1067 (1979), *aff'd in unpublished opinion* 647 F.2d 170 (9th Cir. 1981) . . . several for-profit est organizations exerted significant indirect control over est of Hawaii, a non-profit entity, through contractual arrangements. The Tax Court concluded that the for-profits were able to use the non-profit as an "instrument" to further their for-profit purposes. Neither the fact that the for-profits lacked structural control over the organization nor the fact that amounts paid to the for-profit organizations under the contracts were reasonable affected the court's conclusion. Consequently, est of Hawaii did not qualify as an organization described in § 501(c)(3).

In *Harding Hospital, Inc. v. United States*, 505 F.2d 1068 (6th Cir. 1974) . . . , a non-profit hospital with an independent board . . . executed a contract with a . . . partnership composed of seven physicians. The contract gave the physicians control over care of the hospital's patients and the stream of income generated by the patients while also guaranteeing the physicians thousands of dollars . . . for various supervisory activities. The court held that the benefits derived from the contract constituted sufficient private benefit to preclude exemption.

Analysis

For . . . tax purposes, the activities of a partnership are often . . . the activities of the partners. . . . Aggregate treatment is also consistent with the treatment of partnerships for purpose of the unrelated business income tax under 512(c). . . . [T]he aggregate approach also applies for purposes of the operational test set forth in 1.501(c)(3)-1(c). Thus, the activities of an LLC treated as a partnership for federal income tax purposes are considered to be the activities of a nonprofit organization that is an owner of the LLC when evaluating whether the nonprofit organization is operated exclusively for exempt purposes within the meaning of 501(c)(3).

A 501(c)(3) organization may form and participate in a partnership, including an LLC treated as a partnership for federal income tax purposes, and meet the operational test if participation in the partnership furthers a charitable purpose, and the partnership arrangement permits the exempt organization to act exclusively in furtherance of its exempt purpose and only incidentally for the benefit of the for-profit partners. . . . Similarly, a 501(c)(3) organization may enter into a management contract with a private party giving that party authority to conduct activities on behalf of the organization and direct the use of the organization's assets provided that the organization retains ultimate authority over the assets and activities being managed and the terms and conditions of the contract are reasonable, including reasonable compensation and a reasonable term. . . . However, if a private party is allowed to control or use the non-profit organization's activities or assets for the benefit of the private party, and the benefit is not incidental to the accomplishment of exempt purposes, the organization will fail to be organized and operated exclusively for exempt purposes. . . .

Situation 1

After A and B form C, and A contributes all of its operating assets to C, A's activities will consist of the health care services it provides through C and any grantmaking activities it can conduct using income distributed to C. A will receive an interest in C equal in value to the assets it contributes to C, and A's and B's returns from C will be proportional to their respective investments in C. The governing documents of C commit C to providing health care services for the benefit of the community as a whole and to give charitable purposes priority over maximizing profits for C's owners. Furthermore, through A's appointment of members of the community familiar with the hospital to C's board, the board's structure, which gives A's appointees voting control, and the specifically enumerated powers of the board over changes in activities, disposition of assets, and renewal of the management agreement. A can ensure that the assets it owns through C and the activities it conducts through C are used primarily to further exempt purposes. Thus, A can ensure that the benefit to B and other private parties, like the management company, will be incidental to the accomplishment of charitable purposes. Additionally, the terms and conditions of the management contract, including the terms for renewal and termination are reasonable. Finally, A's grants are intended to support education and research and give resources to help provide health care to the indigent. **All of these facts and circumstances establish that, when A participates in forming C and contributes all of its operating assets to C, and C operates in accordance with its governing documents, A will be furthering charitable purposes and continue to be operated exclusively for exempt purposes.**

Because A's grantmaking activity will be contingent upon receiving distributions from C, A's principal activity will continue to be the provision of hospital care. As long as A's principal activity remains the provision of hospital care, A will not be classified as a private foundation in accordance with s 509(a)(1) as an organization described in s 170(b)(1)(A)(iii).

Situation 2

When D and E from F, and D contributes its assets to F, D will be engaged in activities that consist of the health care services it provides through F and any grant-making activities it can conduct using income distributed by F. However, unlike A, **D will not be engaging primarily in activities that further an exempt purpose.** "While the diagnosis and cure of disease are indeed purposes that may furnish the foundation for characterizing the activity as 'charitable,' something more is required." *Sonora*, 46 T.C. at 525–526. *See also Federation Pharmacy*; *Sound Health*; and *Geisinger*. **In the absence of a binding obligation in F's governing documents for F to serve charitable purposes or otherwise provide its services to the community as a whole, F will be able to deny care to segments of the community, such as the indigent. Because D will share control of F with E, D will not be able to initiate programs within F to serve new health needs within the community without the agreement of at least one governing board member appointed by E.** As a business enterprise, E will not necessarily give priority to the health needs of the community over the consequences for F's profits. The primary source of information for board members appointed by D will be the chief executives, who have a prior relationship with E and the management company, which is a subsidiary of E. The management company itself will have broad discretion over F's activities and assets that may not always be under the board's supervision. For example, the management company is permitted to enter into all but "unusually large" contracts without board approval. The management company may also unilaterally renew the management agreement. Based on all these facts and circumstances, D cannot establish that the activities it conducts through F further exempt purposes. "[I]n order for an organization to qualify for exemption under § 501(c)(3) the organization must 'establish' that it is neither organized nor operated for the 'benefit of private interests.'" *Federation Pharmacy*, 625 F.2d at 809. Consequently, the benefit to E resulting from the activities D conducts through F will not be incidental to the furtherance of an exempt purpose. Thus, D will fail the operational test when it forms F, contributes its operating assets to F, and then serves as an owner to F.

Holding

A will continue to qualify as an organization described in § 501(c)(3) when it forms C and contributes all of its operating assets to C because A has established that A will be operating exclusively for a charitable purpose and only incidentally for the purpose of benefiting the private interests of B. Furthermore, A's principal activity will continue to be the provision of hospital care when C begins operations. Thus, A will be an organization described in 170(b)(1)(A)(iii) and thus, will not be classified as a private foundation in accordance with 509(a)(1), as long as hospital care remains its principal activity.

D will violate the requirements to be an organization described in § 501(c)(3) when it forms F and contributes all of its operating assets to F because D has failed to establish that it will be operated exclusively for exempt purposes.

Questions

1. Does Hospital B in Revenue Ruling 98-15 violate the organizational test? Or does it violate the operational test?

2. Would the Situation 2 result differ if the acute hospital could show that it would have to discontinue all services to the poor without an affiliation with a for-profit entity and that no for-profit entity would enter into such an affiliation except under the terms presented in the ruling? What effect would denial of tax exemption even under those circumstances have on indigent patients? How would American Campaign Academy and GCM 39862 answer these questions?

3. Note that the Ruling never describes the actual operations of either organization and yet it concludes that one operates primarily for a charitable purpose and the other does not. How and why is it that the Ruling focuses on and makes conclusions about the operational requirement without any description of the organization's activities?

Note

The following decision is both complicated and long; yet it is important on many levels. Arguably, it belongs in Chapter 6, dealing with exempt purposes, which raises the question of whether hospitals should be exempt simply because they are hospitals. The decision also belongs here because it deals with an exempt entity that appears to benefit others' commercial endeavors. And it could easily appear in Chapters 7 through 9 dealing with commerciality.

The complex matter involved Redlands Health Systems, a tax-exempt public charity that owned three subsidiaries—two exempt and one for-profit. That structure is itself interesting. From prior Chapters we learned, for example, that a charity may own a for-profit subsidiary. Indeed, in a later Chapter, we will study § 512(b)(13), which specifically addresses the relationship of transactions between such a parent and subsidiary. We will also later raise questions regarding transactions among the various tax-exempt and for-profit subs. For now, we acknowledge the structure was acceptable.

The parent—RHS—became a 46% partner with another for-profit corporation, SCA Surgical, a 54% partner in profits and losses. This partnership then acquired a 61% interest in an existing surgical center. This general partnership became the sole general partner in a limited partnership that owned the surgical center. At this point, things are at least questionable—the tax-exempt parent is involved in a new for-profit venture with other commercial interests, including a for-profit corporation and 31 physicians. This is questionable because the partnership arrangement clearly benefited private interests. The limited partnership then entered a management agreement for a new company—SCA Management—to operate the surgical center in exchange for a percentage of the gross receipts.

Then the trouble started. RHS formed Redlands Surgical Services [RSS] to own its interest in the top partnership. As the sole member of RSS, RHS could select officers and directors. RSS applied for charity status under § 501(c)(3). As the Tax Court explained:

> [RSS] has no activity other than its involvement with the partnerships. The question is whether petitioner is operated exclusively for exempt purposes within the meaning of section 501(c)(3). We hold that it is not.

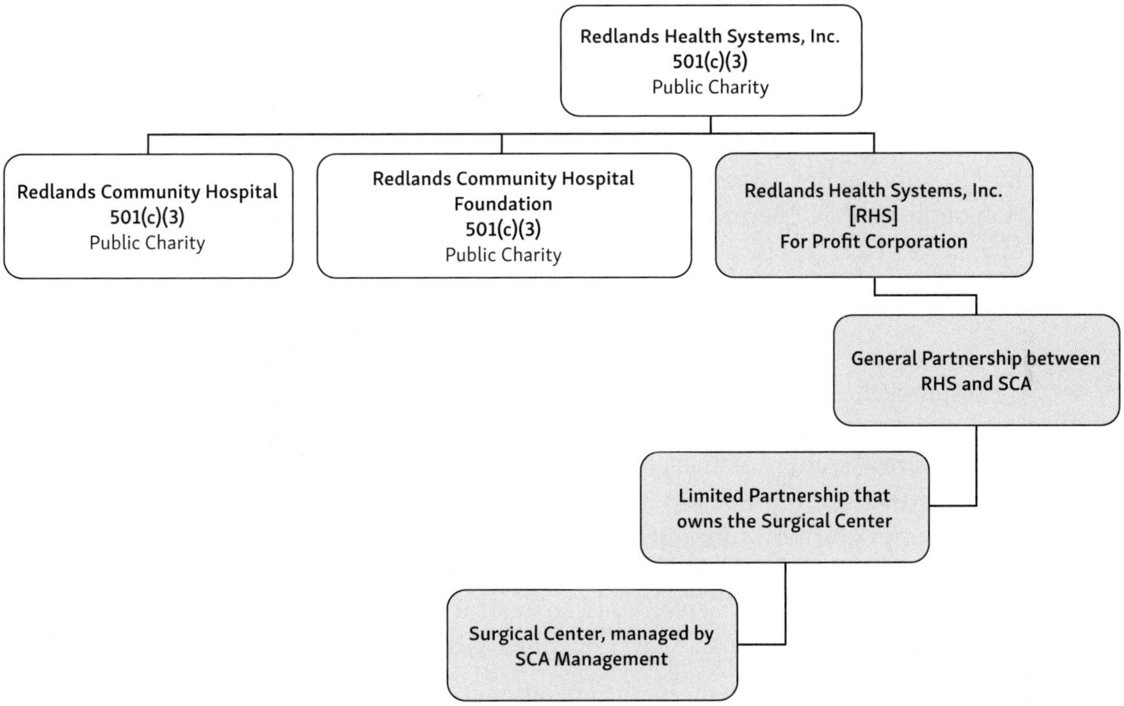

The transfer of the interest into a subsidiary with no other purpose exacerbated whatever questions existed regarding RHS's ability to enter into a partnership with commercial interests. As long as the commercial venture was part of the parent, it at least gained some cover in terms of whether the parent was "exclusively" charitable (which, from Chapter 6 we know means having no more than an insubstantial non-charitable purpose). It likely, as part of the parent, had at least a marginally better chance of asserting the "integral part" doctrine successfully. Also, the parent, as owner, had greater resources with which it could exercise informal, if not formal, control over the partnership. The transfer to a stand-alone subsidiary emphasized—if nothing else—the primary commercial nature of the activity. Thus the transfer raised two questions: one of substance, i.e., whether a charity can be heavily involved in a commercial partnership (and, if so, with what restrictions), and also one of form or strategy, i.e., whether it was wise to make the structure so obvious. That, of course, leads to an ethical and policy dilemma: if we punish taxpayers for transparency, do we not then at least arguably encourage deception?

Redlands Surgical Services v. Commissioner

113 T.C. 47 (1999), aff'd per curium, 242 F.3d 904 (9th Cir. 2001)

Before 1990, Redlands Hospital desired to increase its outpatient surgery capacity but lacked the capital resources and experience to develop and operate its own freestanding outpatient facility. In addition, such a facility would have been in competition with the existing Surgery Center, and there was concern that the Redlands community could not sustain both.

* * *

The Surgery Center operates on a nondiscriminatory basis both as to doctors and patients. There are no restrictions as to whether a surgical patient can be operated on at the Surgery Center, other than a review as to the appropriateness of conducting the surgical procedure in an outpatient setting and the overall medical condition of the patient. There is practically a 100-percent overlap between surgeons who operate at Redlands Hospital and at the Surgery Center.

* * *

I. The Parties' Positions

Respondent contends that petitioner is not operated exclusively for charitable purposes because it operates for the benefit of private parties and fails to benefit a broad cross-section of the community. In support of its position, respondent contends that the partnership agreements and related management contract are structured to give for-profit interests control over the Surgery Center. Respondent contends that both before and after the General Partnership acquired an ownership interest in it, the Surgery Center was a successful profit-making business that never held itself out as a charity and never operated as a charitable health-care provider.

Petitioner argues that it meets the operational test under section 501(c)(3) because its activities with regard to the Surgery Center further its purpose of promoting health for the benefit of the Redlands community, by providing access to an ambulatory surgery center for all members of the community based upon medical need rather than ability to pay, and by integrating the outpatient services of Redlands Hospital and the Surgery Center. Petitioner argues that its dealings with the for-profit partners have been at arm's length [sic], and that its influence over the activities of the Surgery Center has been sufficient to further its charitable goals. Petitioner further contends that it qualifies for exemption because it is organized and operated to perform services that are integral to the exempt purposes of RHS, its tax-exempt parent, and Redlands Hospital, its tax-exempt affiliate.

* * *

C. Proscription Against Benefiting Private Interests

* * *

The proscription against private benefit shares common elements with, but is distinct from, the proscription against the inurement of organizational earnings to private shareholders and individuals.... The proscription against private benefit encompasses not only benefits conferred on insiders having a personal and private interest in the organization, but also benefits conferred on unrelated or disinterested persons....

The mere fact that an organization seeking exemption enters into a partnership agreement with private parties that receive returns on their capital investments does not establish that the organization has impermissibly conferred private benefit. The question remains whether the organization has a substantial nonexempt purpose whereby it serves private interests. Compare *Plumstead Theatre Socy., Inc. v. Commissioner*, 675 F.2d 244 (9th Cir. 1982), affg. per curiam 74 T.C. 1324 (1980) (a nonprofit arts organization furthered its charitable purposes by participating as sole general partner in a partnership with private parties to produce a play), with *Housing Pioneers, Inc. v. Commissioner*, 49 F.3d 1395 (9th Cir. 1995), affg. T.C. Memo. 1993-120 (a nonprofit corporation's participation as co-general partner in low-income housing partnerships, structured to trade off its tax exemption to secure tax benefits for its for-profit partners, had a substantial nonexempt purpose and impermissibly served private interests).

The proscription against private benefit corresponds to a similar proscription in the law of charitable trusts. "A trust is not a charitable trust if the property or the income therefrom is to be devoted to a private use." 2 RESTATEMENT, TRUSTS 2D, sec. 376 (1959). An organization's property may be impermissibly devoted to a private use where private interests have control, directly or indirectly, over its assets, and thereby secure nonincidental private benefits....

III. Petitioner's Claim to Exemption on a "Stand-Alone" Basis

* * *

A. The Relevance of Control — The Parties' Positions

Respondent asserts that petitioner has ceded effective control over its sole activity — participating as a co-general partner with for-profit parties in the partnerships that own and operate the Surgery Center — to the for-profit partners and the for-profit management company.... Respondent asserts that this arrangement is indicative of a substantial nonexempt purpose, whereby petitioner impermissibly benefits private interests.

Without conceding that private parties control its activities, petitioner challenges the premise that the ability to control its activities determines its purposes. Petitioner argues that under the operational test, "the critical issue in determining whether an organization's purposes are noncharitable is not whether a for profit or not for profit entity has control. Rather, the critical issue is the sort of conduct in which the organization is actually engaged." On brief, the parties agree that under an aggregate theory of partnership taxation, the partnerships' activities are considered petitioner's own activities. Petitioner's brief states: "The evidence in the administrative file demonstrates that ... [the Operating Partnership] has been operated in an exclusively charitable manner since

1990". Therefore, petitioner concludes, it should be deemed to operate exclusively for charitable purposes.

We disagree with petitioner's thesis. It is patently clear that the Operating Partnership, whatever charitable benefits it may produce, is not operated "in an exclusively charitable manner". As stated by Justice Cardozo (then Justice of the New York Court of Appeals), in describing one of the "ancient principles" of charitable trusts, "It is only when income may be applied to the profit of the founders that business has a beginning and charity an end." *Butterworth v. Keeler*, 219 N.Y. 446, 449–450, 114 N.E. 803, 804 (1916). The Operating Partnership's income is, of course, applied to the profit of petitioner's co-general partner and the numerous limited partners.[1] It is no answer to say that none of petitioner's income from this activity was applied to private interests, for the activity is indivisible, and no discrete part of the Operating Partnership's income-producing activities is severable from those activities that produce income to be applied to the other partners' profit.

Taken to its logical conclusion, petitioner's thesis would suggest that an organization whose main activity is passive participation in a for-profit health-service enterprise could thereby be deemed to be operating exclusively for charitable purposes. Such a conclusion, however, would be contrary to well-established principles of charitable trust law.

* * *

To the extent that petitioner cedes control over its sole activity to for-profit parties having an independent economic interest in the same activity and having no obligation to put charitable purposes ahead of profit-making objectives, petitioner cannot be assured that the partnerships will in fact be operated in furtherance of charitable purposes. In such a circumstance, we are led to the conclusion that petitioner is not operated exclusively for charitable purposes.

Based on the totality of factors described below, we conclude that petitioner has in fact ceded effective control of the partnerships' and the Surgery Center's activities to for-profit parties, conferring on them significant private benefits, and therefore is not operated exclusively for charitable purposes within the meaning of section 501(c)(3).

B. Indicia of For-Profit Control Over the Partnerships' Activities

1. No Charitable Obligation

Nothing in the General Partnership agreement, or in any of the other binding commitments relating to the operation of the Surgery Center, establishes any obligation that charitable purposes be put ahead of economic objectives in the Surgery

1. [10] In making these observations, we are mindful that it is the status of petitioner, not of the General Partnership or the Operating Partnership, that is in issue. Indeed, it is not meaningful to speak of a partnership's exempt status, given that partnerships are nontaxable entities. *See* sec. 701.

Center's operations. The General Partnership agreement does not expressly state any mutually agreed-upon charitable purpose or objective of the partnership.

After the General Partnership acquired its 61-percent interest, the Operating Partnership—which had long operated as a successful for-profit enterprise and never held itself out as a charity—never changed its organizing documents to acknowledge a charitable purpose. Indeed, in at least one instance the Operating Partnership agreement explicitly acknowledges the partnership's noncharitable objectives. Section 16.5.2 of the Operating Partnership agreement in authorizing the General Partnership to amend the Operating Partnership as necessary to comply with legal requirements, specifies that this authority may be exercised only if "such amendments do not alter the economic objectives of the partnership or materially reduce the economic return to the limited partners."

2. Petitioner's Lack of Formal Control

a. Managing Directors

Under the General Partnership agreement, control over all matters other than medical standards and policies is nominally divided equally between petitioner and SCA Centers, each appointing two representatives to serve as managing directors.... Consequently, petitioner may exert influence by blocking actions proposed to be taken by the managing directors, but it cannot initiate action without the consent of at least one of SCA Center's appointees to the managing directors. For instance, petitioner lacks sufficient control unilaterally to cause the Surgery Center to respond to community needs for new health services, modify the delivery or cost structure of its present health services to serve the community better, or, as discussed in more detail infra, terminate SCA Management, if SCA Management were determined to be managing the Surgery Center in a manner inconsistent with charitable objectives.

The administrative record shows that petitioner has successfully blocked various proposals to expand the scope of activities performed at the Surgery Center. Petitioner's ability to veto expansion of the scope of the Surgery Center's activities, however, does not establish that petitioner has effective control over the manner in which the Surgery Center conducts activities within its predesignated sphere of operations. Nor does it tend to indicate that the Surgery Center is not operated to maximize profits with regard to those activities. Indeed, given that all the partners except petitioner are for-profit interests not shown to be motivated or constrained by charitable objectives, and given that all the limited partners except Beaver Medical Clinic were issued SCA common stock when the General Partnership acquired its interest in the Operating Partnership, and given that SCA Management derives a management fee computed as a percentage of gross revenues, we find, in the absence of evidence to the contrary, that a significant profit-making objective is present in the Surgery Center's operations. The high rates of return earned on the partners' investments (including petitioner's) in the Operating Partnership bolster this finding.

In sum, the composition of the managing directorship evidences a lack of majority control by petitioner whereby it might assure that the Surgery Center is operated for charitable purposes. Consequently, we look to the binding commitments made between petitioner and the other parties to ascertain whether other specific powers or rights conferred upon petitioner might mitigate or compensate for its lack of majority control.

b. Arbitration Process

The General Partnership agreement provides for an arbitration process in the event that the managing directors of the General Partnership deadlock over a matter other than medical standards and medical policies, such as approval of new surgical procedures.... Under the General Partnership agreement, the arbitrators are not required to take into account any charitable or community benefit objective, but are simply required to "apply the substantive law of California"....

c. The Management Contract

* * *

Under the management contract, SCA Management is entitled to receive fees equaling 6 percent of the Operating Partnership's gross revenues each month, in addition to reimbursement of its direct expenses. This revenue-based compensation structure provides SCA Management an incentive to manage the Surgery Center so as to maximize profits.

As a practical matter, the Operating Partnership is locked into the management agreement with SCA Management for at least 15 years. At its sole discretion, SCA Management may renew the agreement for two additional 5-year periods on the same terms and conditions.... Thus, even if petitioner determined that SCA Management were managing the Surgery Center in a manner inconsistent with charitable purposes, petitioner could not be assured of any remedy.

Moreover, neither the General Partnership agreement, the Operating Partnership agreement, nor the management contract itself requires that SCA Management be guided by any charitable or community benefit, goal, policy, or objective....

Respondent asserts, and we agree, that this long-term management contract with an affiliate of SCA Centers is a salient indicator of petitioner's surrender of effective control over the Surgery Center's operations to SCA affiliates, whereby the affiliates were given the ability and incentive to operate the Surgery Center so as to maximize profits. This surrender of effective control reflects adversely on petitioner's own charitable purposes in contracting to have its sole activity managed in this fashion....

d. Medical Advisory Group

The ... Partnership agreement delegates authority for making decisions about care and treatment of patients and other medical matters to the ... Medical Advisory Group....

Only three of the six members of the Medical Advisory Group are selected by the General Partnership. The other three are selected by one of the limited partners, Beaver Medical Clinic. It is telling that the Medical Advisory Group is composed entirely of limited partners of the Operating Partnership, all of whom (except Beaver Medical Clinic) received common stock in SCA when the General Partnership acquired its Operating Partnership interest. Taking all these considerations into account, it is clear that petitioner lacks sufficient influence to determine the resolution of any matter brought before the Medical Advisory Group. Moreover, there is no evidence in the record that the decisions of the Medical Advisory Committee are subject to independent review by petitioner or Redlands Hospital.

e. Termination of Quality Assurance Activities

As required by the General Partnership agreement . . . , SCA Management entered into a quality assurance agreement with RHS. The term of the quality assurance agreement was conditioned on maintenance of a specified level of surgery activity in the Surgery Center. Petitioner concedes that the quality assurance agreement terminated after the first year. Although the agreement required the parties to negotiate a new quality assurance agreement in the event of such a termination, there is no evidence in the record that such negotiations ever occurred.

The termination of the quality assurance agreement vividly evidences petitioner's lack of effective control over vital aspects of the . . . Center. . . . Quality assurance agreements . . . serve the important dual functions of attempting to avoid inappropriate services (e.g., the wrong services for the patient's needs, or services that are improperly rendered), and seeking to assure that enough services are provided to meet the patient's needs. . . . The record does not reflect that petitioner performed any quality assurance work. Likewise, the record is silent as to how petitioner, in the absence of any operable quality assurance agreement, purports to assure itself that these vital functions will be discharged consistently with charitable objectives.

3. Lack of Informal Control

The administrative record provides no basis for concluding that, in the absence of formal control, petitioner possesses significant informal control by which it exercises its influence with regard to the Surgery Center's activities. Nothing in the administrative record suggests that petitioner commands allegiance or loyalty of the SCA affiliates or of the limited partners to cause them to put charitable objectives ahead of their own economic objectives. Indeed, until April 1992, petitioner was in a debtor relationship to SCA. . . .

The administrative record does not establish that petitioner has the resources or ability effectively to oversee or monitor the Surgery Center's operations. Petitioner has almost no resources apart from its assets invested in the General Partnership. The president of Redlands Hospital also serves as petitioner's president and as one of the four managing directors of the General Partnership. . . .

a. Change in Criteria for Procedures Performed at the Surgery Center

Petitioner asserts that after the General Partnership acquired its interest in the Operating Partnership, "the decision to perform a surgery at the Surgery Center was changed from an economic to exclusively a medical decision. Accordingly, RHS achieved its goal of providing complete access to freestanding ambulatory surgery center care for all members of the Redlands community irrespective of their ability to pay."

This proposed finding of fact is not supported by the record. Neither before nor after petitioner's involvement . . . has the . . . Center provided charity care. Moreover, the . . . record indicates that one aspect of ambulatory surgery centers that makes them attractive investment opportunities . . . is that they boast favorable "procedure and payer mixes".

* * *

b. Provision for Indigent Patients

Petitioner concedes that as of December 31, 1993, Medi-Cal patients accounted for only 0.8 percent of total procedures performed at the Surgery Center. Petitioner argues that the type of services which the Service Center offers is not the type of services typically sought by low-income individuals. Petitioner notes that Redlands Hospital has negotiated certain provider agreements that designate the Surgery Center as a subcontractor to provide outpatient services for Medi-Cal patients, and that Redlands Hospital has caused the Surgery Center to increase its number of managed care contracts. Petitioner suggests that these efforts demonstrate petitioner's influence over the operations of the Surgery Center and evidence petitioner's charitable purposes.

We do not find petitioner's arguments convincing. The facts remain that the Surgery Center provides no free care to indigents and only negligible coverage for Medi-Cal patients. That low-income individuals may not typically seek the types of services the Surgery Center offers may partially explain the virtual absence of relief it provides for such individuals. But it provides no independent basis for establishing petitioner's charitable purposes in its involvement with the Surgery Center. Moreover, the activities of Redlands Hospital in effecting some negligible degree of Medi-Cal coverage at the Surgery Center and in increasing the number of managed care contracts do not provide a basis for establishing petitioner's exemption. . . .

Petitioner asserts that the Surgery Center has no requirement that patients demonstrate an ability to pay before receiving treatment. The record does not reflect whether any such policy has been communicated to its patients. . . .

c. Coordination of Activities of Redlands Hospital and the Surgery Center

In arguing that it plays an active role in the conduct of the Surgery Center's activities, petitioner cites a number of ways in which Redlands Hospital has integrated its activities with those of the Surgery Center. . . . These include Redlands Hospital's use of the Surgery Center as a site for training and surgeon proctoring, as well as various other cooperative . . . educational activities. . . . [N]othing in the record suggests that these various cooperative activities are more than incidental to the for-profit orientation of the Surgery Center's activities. *Cf. Harding Hosp., Inc. v. United States, supra* at 1075–1076 (educational, training and community-oriented programs conducted at a hospital and funded by a third party were not sufficient to merit the hospital's tax exemption where other disqualifying factors were present).

C. Competitive Restrictions and Market Advantages

By entering into the General Partnership agreement, RHS . . . not only acquired an interest in the Surgery Center, but also restricted its future ability to provide outpatient services at Redlands Hospital or elsewhere without the approval of its for-profit partner. . . .

The General Partnership agreement also restricts the parties and their affiliates from providing outpatient surgery services and procedures that the agreement does not specifically authorize . . . nonlisted services. . . . Redlands Hospital, but not the co-general partners or any of their other affiliates, is allowed to perform nonlisted outpatient services that were currently available to patients in California at the time the General Partnership agreement was executed. By contrast, neither Redlands Hospital nor the co-general partners or their affiliates are allowed to perform nonlisted outpatient services that first become available in California during the term of the . . . agreement (i.e., until March 31, 2020), unless the managing directors . . . approve. Consequently, RHS effectively restricted its own ability to assess and service community needs for outpatient services until the year 2020. It is difficult to conceive of a significant charitable purpose that would be furthered by such a restriction.

The administrative record contains a market research report on the ambulatory surgery center industry, prepared by Ernst & Young. . . . This report describes the strong movement toward providing health care services in ambulatory settings, driven both by economic considerations and technological advances. The report notes that hospitals face "strong competition" in this market. It cites economic advantages that freestanding ambulatory surgery centers enjoy over hospitals. These advantages include . . . higher turn-over of operating rooms that increases the number of "fee-generating procedures" surgeons can do; lower nurse compensation that in turn leads to "higher margins"; and the "general tendency for private payers to account for a high percentage of a surgery center's mix, since most procedures performed in outpatient settings are elective . . . and are done on younger, non-Medicare patients." The report cites physician relations and capital as two major barriers to entering this market.

The Shearson Lehman Brothers investment summary . . . contains similar facts and conclusions. The report indicates that SCA and Medical Care International are the two main surgical center chains, that they are highly profitable, and that their margins are likely to continue moving higher. . . . [O]ne reason for the high profitability of these chains is that "they typically shadow-price hospitals, which tend to charge very high rates for outpatient surgery so they can shift costs to the private sector and spread out their overhead." The report states that "one might expect hospitals to fight hard for this business by starting up their own FASCs [freestanding ambulatory surgery centers]", but that this had not happened to date because it is very hard for hospitals to do so, due partly to problems hospitals face in throwing off their own "culture" and creating an autonomous unit that is small, friendly, and efficient. The report states: "[SCA's] strategy of developing three-way joint ventures— consisting of a local hospital, surgeons, and the company—represents an attractive opportunity to address these cultural problems." The report notes:

> the FASC niche of the health care services industry has the further attraction of considerable consolidation opportunity. We believe that multispecialty, nonhospital FASCs currently number 600–700, with perhaps another 100 opening each year. Yet there are currently only two chains, Medical Care International and [SCA] affiliates, which have a total of 109 units.... Once a surgical group decides to sell its center, there is generally only one bidder... with the price typically five to seven times pretax income.... The key issue for MDs is not the modest amount of cash that comes from a sale but the operating environment for them once the center changes hands.

* * *

By virtue of this arrangement, petitioner and SCA Centers realized further mutual benefits by eliminating sources of potential competition for patients, as is evidenced by the restrictions on either party's providing future outpatient services outside the Surgery Center, and by Redlands Hospital's agreeing not to expand or promote its existing outpatient surgery facility at the hospital. In light of the statement in the record that it is typical for national chains such as SCA to "shadow-price" hospitals in charging for services at outpatient surgery centers, it seems most likely that one purpose and effect of the containment and contraction of Redlands Hospital's outpatient surgery activities is to eliminate a competitive constraint for setting Surgery Center fees (a matter delegated to SCA Management under the management contract, excluding charges for physicians' services). Moreover, market consolidation provided petitioner and SCA Centers mutual advantages by eliminating pressures to compete in spending for expensive equipment. There is no per se proscription against a nonprofit organization's entering into contracts with private parties to further its charitable purposes on mutually beneficial terms, so long as the nonprofit organization does not thereby impermissibly serve private interests. *Cf. Plumstead Theatre Socy. v. Commissioner*, 75 F.2d 244 (9th Cir. 1982); *Broadway Theatre League v. United States*, 293 F. Supp. 346 (W.D. Va. 1968). In the instant case, however, RHS relied on the established relationship between Redlands Hospital and Redlands physicians to enable RHS and SCA affiliates jointly to gain foothold, on favorable terms, in the Redlands ambulatory surgery market. Then, by virtue of their effective control over the Surgery Center, the SCA affiliates have been enabled to operate it as a profit-making business, with significantly reduced competitive pressures from Redlands Hospital, and largely unfettered by charitable objectives that might conflict with purely commercial objectives. *Cf. est of Hawaii v. Commissioner*, 71 T.C. 1067, 1080 (1979); *Housing Pioneers, Inc. v. Commissioner*, T.C. Memo.1993-120, *aff'd*, 49 F.3d 1395 (9th Cir. 1995). The net result to the SCA affiliates is a nonincidental "advantage; profit; fruit; privilege; gain; [or] interest" that constitutes a prohibited private benefit. *See American Campaign Academy v. Commissioner*, 92 T.C. 1053, 1065 (1989).

D. Conclusion

Based on all the facts and circumstances, we hold that petitioner has not established that it operates exclusively for exempt purposes. . . . [W]e do not view any one factor as crucial, but we have considered these factors in their totality: The lack of any express or implied obligation of the for-profit interests involved in petitioner's sole activity to put charitable objectives ahead of noncharitable objectives; petitioner's lack of voting control over the General Partnership; petitioner's lack of other formal or informal control sufficient to ensure furtherance of charitable purposes; the long-term contract giving SCA Management control over day-to-day operations as well as a profit-maximizing incentive; and the market advantages and competitive benefits secured by the SCA affiliates as the result of this arrangement with petitioner. Taken in their totality, these factors compel the conclusion that by ceding effective control over its operations to for-profit parties, petitioner impermissibly serves private interests.

IV. Petitioner's Claim to Exemption Under the Integral Part Doctrine

Petitioner argues that even if it does not qualify for tax exemption on a "stand alone" basis, it qualifies for exemption under the integral part doctrine.

The integral part doctrine is not codified, but rather is the outgrowth of judicial opinions, rulings, and regulations. The precise contours of this doctrine are not clearly defined. The seminal case of *Squire v. Students Book Corp.*, 191 F.2d 1018 (9th Cir. 1951), held that an organization that operated a bookstore on the premises of a college for the accommodation of students and faculty was exempt because it bore a "close and intimate relationship" to the functioning of the college itself. . . .

Shortly after . . . *Squire*, Treasury regulations acknowledged the existence of the integral part doctrine in providing an exception to the feeder organization rules. . . .[2]

* * *

Since *Squire*, only a relatively small number of cases have applied the integral part doctrine. These cases are fact-specific. *See Geisinger Health Plan v. Commissioner*, 30 F.3d 494, 501 (3d Cir. 1994) . . . . [T]he . . . doctrine requires the organization . . .

2. [23] Although these regulations relate expressly to determining whether an organization is a feeder organization within the meaning of sec. 502 (an issue that respondent does not raise in the instant case), this Court previously has referred to these regulations in applying the integral part doctrine in the context of sec. 501(c)(3) exemptions. . . .

to provide "necessary and indispensable" services solely to an exempt organization to which it bears some legal or significant operational relationship. . . . [T]he integral part doctrine operates to recognize a derivative exemption of an organization which serves only another exempt organization and performs essential services that the client organization otherwise would have performed for itself to accomplish its own exempt purposes. . . . .

Consistent with this rationale, professional group practices serving exempt entities have been granted tax exemption under the integral part doctrine. *See University of Mass. Med. Sch. Group Practice v. Commissioner*, 74 T.C. 1299 (1980); *B.H.W. Anesthesia Found., Inc. v. Commissioner*, 72 T.C. 681 (1979); *University of Md. Physicians, P.A. v. Commissioner*, T.C. Memo.1981-23. These cases involved anesthesiology services or faculty medical activities that were provided solely to the served hospital or medical school and that were essential to the operation of the hospital or medical school. . . .

In *Geisinger Health Plan v. Commissioner, supra*, this Court denied a claim for tax exemption asserted by an HMO under the integral part theory. We reasoned that the group-practice line of cases was not controlling because, unlike the exempt organizations in those cases, the HMO had a population of subscribers that did not overlap substantially with the patients of the related exempt entities. . . .

. . . [P]etitioner has failed to establish that the Surgery Center's patient population overlaps substantially with that of Redlands Hospital. The record does not reveal what percentage of persons served at the Surgery Center are patients of Redlands Hospital. Clearly, however, the Surgery Center was performing ambulatory surgery on a for-profit basis for its own patients before petitioner was ever involved and presumably continued to do so afterward.

Even if we were to assume, arguendo, that the patient populations of the Surgery Center and Redlands Hospital overlap substantially, this circumstance would not suffice to confer exemption . . . under the integral part doctrine. In all the precedents . . . the organization has been under the supervision or control of the exempt affiliate (or a group of exempt affiliates with common exempt purposes) or otherwise expressly limited in its purposes to advancing the interests of the affiliated exempt . . . entities, and serving no private interests. For instance, in Squire . . . all actions of the bookstore's board of trustees were submitted to the president of the college for approval, and the college comptroller acted as ex officio treasurer of the bookstore. The bookstore paid no rebates and no part of its earnings inured to private benefit. It seems clear that such considerations are central to the court's holding in Squire that the bookstore's business enterprise "bears a close and intimate relationship to the functioning of the College itself." By contrast, . . . petitioner's sole activity (the Surgery Center) is effectively controlled by for-profit parties. The operations . . . are not dedicated to advancing the interests of petitioner's exempt affiliates other than as those interests might happen to coincide with the commercial interests of petitioner's for-profit partners. Moreover, . . . petitioner impermissibly serves private interests. Petitioner's activity is not so substantially and closely related to the exempt purposes of its affiliates that these private interests may be disregarded.... Accordingly, petitioner is not entitled to exemption under the integral part doctrine....

Note and Commentary

A three-judge panel of the Ninth Circuit Court of Appeals heard oral arguments on March 5, 2001, and issued a one-paragraph, per curiam opinion affirming the Tax Court on March 15, 2001. *Redlands Surgical Servs. v. Commissioner*, 242 F.3d 904 (9th Cir. 2001). Many observers were surprised by the Ninth Circuit's swift decision. Counsel for Redlands, apparently unaware that the opinion had already been issued, was quoted on the very day the decision issued as saying he expected to wait the normal three to four months after oral arguments before receiving an opinion. That the Court took only 10 days led many to conclude that it wanted to send a strong message to the exempt community regarding the necessity to provide free or below-cost services, at least insofar as tax-exempt health care is concerned. Compare the Court's opinion with regard to free or below-cost services with the requirements for health care tax exemption in Revenue Ruling 69-545. See David M. Flynn, *Tax Court's Decision in Redlands Provides Limited Endorsement for IRS Position on Joint Ventures*, 91 J. Tax'n 241 (1999) (hereafter "Flynn") (describing Redlands as a "major [though incomplete] victory for the IRS").

Lessons from *Redlands* are many. According to the Service, an exempt entity may enter a joint venture with a for-profit entity; however, the exempt partner must ensure the venture:

1. operates to further the exempt entity's charitable purposes;
2. does not operate in an ordinary commercial manner; and
3. does not more than incidentally further the private purposes of the for-profit entity.

As the court explained, provisions in the partnership agreement requiring the venture to further the exempt entity's charitable purposes are significant (as are the absence of such provisions). Voting control in the hands of the exempt entity is not essential, but is an important factor.

As Flynn explained, *Redlands* only dealt with an exempt entity acting as a general partner in a partnership with for-profit entities. Of note, "It does not deal with an EO's participation as a limited partner or as a member of an LLC that is treated as a partnership for federal income tax purposes (although it may prove relevant to an analysis of such situations). Moreover, the activity under scrutiny in *Redlands* was the only activity conducted by the subject organization." Flynn at 242. As Flynn later explained, if an exempt entity is merely a limited partner, the only likely issue raised involves § 512 and unrelated business taxable income. *Id.* at 250. The consequence of an exempt entity's participation in a limited liability company with for-profit investors is unclear: probably the more passive the participation of the exempt entity, the better. Serving as an LLC manager would likely trigger a *Redlands* analysis.

Questions

1. What are the potential private benefits from joint ventures? Just what are the Service and Courts concerned about with regard to an exempt organization's participation in joint ventures with taxable entities? Do the relevant regulations ever really articulate the real concern?

2. How are an organization's charitable goals achieved or furthered by a joint venture?

3. Should the availability of a different method of achieving the charitable goal that results in less private gain be relevant?

St. David's Health Care System, Inc. v. United States

2002 U.S. Dist. LEXIS 10453 (W.D. Tex. June 7, 2002)

[EDITOR'S NOTE: We caution you: the following opinion did not hold up, at least not factually. It is nevertheless entertaining to read the trial court's thoughts regarding the regulations and the consistency of the government arguments. Pay close attention to the court's criticisms, as well as to its attempts to translate regulatory double and triple negatives into positive statements. Ask yourself whether the court's translation is accurate. Be sure to read the note following the case to place this opinion in its proper context.]

... The operational test, as laid out in the Code of Federal Regulations, places three basic requirements on an organization seeking tax exemption under § 501(c)(3). Two of these requirements are not in dispute. The undisputed requirements are that its net earnings may not "inure in whole or in part to the benefit of private shareholders or individuals," ... and that it may not be an "action organization" engaged in lobbying or political activities, ... The only dispute between these parties centers around the remaining requirement of the operational test, the "primary activities" prong.

> An organization will be regarded as operated exclusively for one or more exempt purposes only if it engages primarily in activities which accomplish one or more of such exempt purposes specified in section 501(c)(3). An organization will not be so regarded if more than an insubstantial part of its activities is not in furtherance of an exempt purpose.

26 C.F.R. § 1.501(c)(3)-1(c)(1) .... Sadly, the last sentence of that section is a horrible amalgamation of negatives arranged like an inside joke prompting laughter only from seasoned and sadistic bureaucrats. In plain English, it means that an organization cannot be exempt while devoting a substantial portion of its activities to non-exempt purposes.

A list of exempt purposes is provided, which includes charity as an exempt purpose.... On the issue of whether or not St. David's has a charitable purpose, the government chooses to avert its eyes when Revenue Ruling 69-545 is raised. Specifically, the government turns its eyes to Revenue Ruling 56-185. The government says that "the promotion of health is not per se charitable" and relies on 56-185 for the proposition that an exempt hospital must be "operated to the extent of its financial ability for those not able to pay for the services rendered and not exclusively for those who are able and expected to pay and must not . . . refuse to accept patients in need of hospital care who cannot pay for such services." . . . However, Revenue Ruling 69-545 states, "In the general law of charity, the promotion of health is considered to be a charitable purpose." . . . The ruling does go on to say that more is required to be tax-exempt under 501(c)(3), but the promotion of health is clearly a charitable purpose.

The government also overlooks the final paragraph of 69-545, which expressly removes the requirement of giving care to patients without charge or at rates below cost. The government relies . . . Revenue Ruling 56-185, but this paragraph in 69-545 even cites that prior ruling when removing that requirement. There is therefore absolutely no issue as to whether St. David's has a charitable purpose, and any argument to the contrary appears at least mildly disingenuous.

Admittedly, the government has cited another court's opinion that 69-545 did not overrule 56-185, but merely provided an alternative test for determining tax-exempt status. *See Eastern Kentucky Welfare Rights Org. v. Simon*, 506 F.2d 1278, 1290 (D.C. Cir. 1974). However, there are at least two problems with this statement as related to this case. First, 69-545, if it is merely an alternative test, it is far more relevant to this case than the 56-185 test because it is undisputed that St. David's has a generally accessible emergency room as required by the 69-545 test. The requirement of providing free or below-cost care is removed in specifically such a case, if not in others also. Second, it is difficult to view 69-545 as anything but an overruling of 56-185 when the later ruling says that "56-185 is hereby modified . . ."

A later section of these regulations effectively adds a consideration to the primary activities prong of the operational test. It states,

> An organization is not organized or operated exclusively for [an exempt purpose, e.g., charity] unless it serves a public rather than a private interest. Thus, to meet the requirement of this subdivision, it is necessary for an organization to establish that it is not organized or operated for the benefit of private interests such as designated individuals, the creator or his family, shareholders of the organization, or persons controlled, directly or indirectly, by such private interests.

26 C.F.R. § 1.501(c)(3)-1(d)(1)(ii) . . . . By placing the above-quoted section apart from the operational test, the regulations seem to make this a separate consideration from that test in spite of the apparent overlap. The Court's interpretation is that the operational test requires the organization to operate exclusively for an exempt purpose . . . and Regulation 1(d)(1)(ii) requires that the organization benefit the community and not a private interest. However, it is difficult to conceive of an organization that operates exclusively as a charity, but substantially furthers a private interest. Perhaps a case in which the exempt purpose at issue was science or another exempt purpose

listed in 1(d)(1), this separation would be less confusing. In any event, the overlap is so significant for this case that the Court will consider them simultaneously.

Thus, the parties' dispute can be resolved by answering these two overlapping questions: First, is St. David's operated exclusively for charity, meaning that only insubstantial portions of its activities benefit private, non-exempt purposes? Second, is it operated for the community interest and not for a private interest, specifically, HCA? This is consistent with what was conveyed to St. David's by the government when it revoked the tax-exempt status. As is often the case with statutes and regulations, these are but a starting point. They only begin to take a more definite shape after they have been applied to facts. Fortunately, these regulations have been applied to countless factual situations, and these situations guide the Court's decision. Revenue Ruling 69-545, 1969-2 C.B. 117 is a seminal application of these regulations and is especially relevant to the facts in this case since it involves a similar hospital. It lists several important characteristics of a hospital, imaginatively referred to as "Hospital A," that now comprise what is referred to as the "community benefit" standard. The Court will list these characteristics in the order they appear in the Revenue Ruling, which is not indicative of relative importance.

First, Hospital A has a board of trustees comprised of "prominent citizens in the community." Second, all qualified physicians in the area have medical staff privileges, as the size and nature of its facility allows. Third, Hospital A operates an emergency room that does not deny treatment to anyone requiring emergency care. However, non-emergency care is given only to those who can pay for it, either themselves or via a third party. Those who cannot pay are referred to another hospital in the community that will serve them. Hospital A typically takes in more money than it spends, and that money is applied to expansion and replacement of existing facilities, etc. Finally, and most importantly, this Revenue Ruling holds that Hospital A is exempt from paying federal income taxes. Having gotten past all of the detached rules and standards governing this case, there appear to the Court two things causing the government to revoke St. David's tax-exempt status. First, the government claims that St. David's is not controlled by a community board. Second, the government claims that HCA receives an impermissible private benefit.

A. Community Board

In Revenue Ruling 69-545, Hospital A had a community board, and this became a part of the community benefit standard. However, there is some dispute as to whether a community board is an absolute requirement, or just one point in favor of tax-exemption. Furthermore, there is some dispute as to what constitutes a community board. In this case, half of St. David's Board of Governors (the Board) is appointed by St. David's, and half by HCA.

1. Does the Community Benefit Standard Absolutely Require a Community Board? The Court finds that, as a matter of law, the presence of a community board is a point in favor of exemption, but is not an absolute requirement for exemption. Going back to the original source of the community benefit standard, Revenue

Ruling 69-545 never states that any one factor is an absolute requirement for exemption. Indeed, it lists several of the factors repeated here, then states, "These factors indicate that the use and control of Hospital A are for the benefit of the public ..." Rev. Rul. 69-545, 1969-2 C.B. at 118 (emphasis added). This language suggests that the prongs of the community benefit standard are major factors but also that the absence of one is not absolutely dispositive of the question.

This finding is supported by other applications of the community benefit standard. In *Sound Health Assoc. v. Commissioner of Internal Revenue*, 71 T.C. 158 (1978), the Tax Court found that the HMO's board was made up of prominent members of the community, but they were selected only from the members of the HMO. Furthermore, this particular HMO was owned by its members, so the board was comprised of owners and was not selected from the community at large. Nonetheless, the Tax Court found that the HMO satisfied the community benefit standard and qualified for tax exemption.

The government paints itself into a corner with its arguments in its response to the Magistrate's Report. ... It cites Revenue Ruling 83-157, which held that a hospital that was identical to 69-545's Hospital A in every respect except for the fact that it had no emergency room. 83-157 held that this hospital was tax-exempt in spite of its lack of a generally accessible emergency room because a state agency determined that such an emergency room would unnecessarily duplicate other services provided in the community. The government actually writes that the ... Service will "weigh all of the facts and circumstances" and the "absence of particular factors ... or the presence of other factors will not necessarily be determinative." ...

The government later refers to the community benefit standard as "somewhat flexible," stating that "a core ingredient like control vested in a community board may not be omitted unless the presence of other factors render that ingredient unnecessary." ... Thus, by the government's own implicit admission, the individual factors of the community benefit standard laid out in 69-545 are not absolute requirements.

The government attempts to rely on *Redlands*. ... However, the facts of that case are only vaguely similar to this case. In *Redlands*, the surgery center deemed non-exempt operated no emergency room and provided no free care to indigents. As quoted by the government, the Tax Court stated that the surgery center was "largely unfettered by charitable objectives." *Id.*, 113 T.C. at 92. As described fully below, the structure of this partnership precludes any genuine argument that St. David's is "unfettered by charitable objectives."

2. Is St. David's Run by a Community Board? Even if a community board is an absolute requirement for 501(c)(3) tax exemption, St. David's Board satisfies the requirement. Although exactly half of the members are appointed by a for-profit entity, the purpose of a community board is more complex than giving wealthy self-styled philanthropists something to do on the rare occasion that they are not playing golf. The purpose of the community board is to ensure that the community's

interests are given precedence over any private interests. Thus, if a board is structured to ensure such protection, it is clearly a community board.

The error of the government's position in arguing that St. David's board is not a community board is that it counts possible votes and discovers that members appointed by a non-profit entity can only tie the members appointed by a for-profit entity, and then end the inquiry. Looking further reveals exceptional protections against running this hospital in pursuit of private interests. The partnership contract requires that all hospitals owned by the partnership operate in accord with the community benefit standard. Should the hospitals fail to meet that standard, St. David's has the unilateral right to dissolve the partnership. The chairmen's seat is reserved for a member appointed by St. David's and therefore great control over the board's agenda is exercised.... Even the day-to-day operations ... are disproportionately impacted by the non-profit entity, because St. David's has the power to unilaterally remove the Chief Executive Officer.

Voting strength is more than just a numbers game, and these provisions clearly protect the non-profit, charitable pursuits as well as any community board could. The government seems focused on majority control, but the law is more concerned with control, regardless of whether its control springs from a majority or from a corporate structure. Even if it were slightly ambiguous as to whether the board was structured to protect the charitable purpose of the organization, the other factors from the community benefit standard are met with such overwhelming force as to carry the day for St. David's. Every hospital owned by the partnership provides emergency care without regard to the patient's ability to pay.

The government attempts to quibble about how St. David's differentiates between free care that is charity and free care that is bad debt. The Court thinks that is a silly and meaningless distinction for purposes of this case. When all who need emergency care are treated regardless of willingness or ability to pay, the function is charitable regardless of what the accountants discover later. The government uses ... St. David's attempts to collect payment from all patients before determining whether the care rendered was charity care or bad debt to show that St. David's actually provides no charity care. This implicitly attempts to require St. David's to determine before rendering care whether to expect payment ..., a luxury allowed only to those privileged to live in a bubble constructed by theories without the rude pin prick of practicality that so frequently bursts such bubbles. Not surprisingly, the IRS offers no method by which that determination could be made, perhaps it could be based on skin color, the brand name of clothes worn by the patient upon entering the emergency room, or shaking a magic eight ball.

The IRS states that "a hospital does not dispense charity care merely because some of its patients fail to pay for the services rendered." ... While the Court will not argue with that as a general proposition, this does not preclude attempts at collecting payment before determining the care to be charitable. Knowing that the hospital will not be compensated for much of the care rendered can be sufficient even if it cannot predetermine which patients can pay and which cannot pay. When a hospital operates a generally accessible emergency room, it knows that it will not be paid for much of the care rendered. The statement cited by the IRS is more applicable to non-emergency care.

B. Private Benefit to HCA

The IRS crystallizes the issue and governing standards for a private benefit in Objections to the Report and Recommendation (Doc. No. 59). The Court agrees that not all joint ventures between non-profit and for-profit organizations are either per se exempt or per se non-exempt. Other factors must be considered. The standard under the operational test was set out in *Redlands*, and it focuses on control of the organization. The *Redlands* court stated,

> To the extent that petitioner cedes control over its sole activity to for-profit parties having an independent economic interest in the same activity and having no obligation to put charitable purposes ahead of profit-making objectives, petitioner cannot be assured that the partnerships will in fact be operated in furtherance of charitable purposes. In such a circumstance, we are led to the conclusion that petitioner is not operated exclusively for charitable purposes."

Redlands . . . , 113 T.C. at 78 (1999) . . . . Since the IRS accepts this as the governing law, the Court will use it for purposes of this case without deciding whether it is in fact the governing standard. As discussed in detail above, it is difficult to imagine a corporate structure more protective of an organization's charitable purpose than the one at issue in this case. The purpose stated in Section 3.2 of the Partnership Agreement make the purpose clear, and the voting rules and rights of the non-profit partner prevent any usurpation of that purpose by HCA. The government essentially argues that these protections are all basically irrelevant, but the truth of the matter is that St. David's has the power to ensure that the manager and CEO are to its liking. That, among other protections discussed above gives the non-profit partner substantially more control than the for-profit partner, despite the facial 50-50 split in voting rights on the Board of Governors. Upon application of all of these legal tests and standards to the undisputed facts of this case, it is clear that St. David's was exempt from federal income taxes under 501(c)(3) for the tax year 1996 as a matter of law, and therefore summary judgment must be granted.

Note on Appeal of Summary Judgment Order in St. David's Health Care System, Inc. v. United States

The Fifth Circuit vacated the *St. David's* summary judgment order and remanded it for a trial to determine the facts. *St. David's Health Care System, Inc. v. United States*, 349 F.3d 232 (5th Cir. 2003). Essentially, the tax-exempt hospital joined with a for-profit hospital. The exempt group asserted that it maintained control; however, the government believed otherwise. The Fifth Circuit found the disputed facts legitimate. The following statement from the Circuit opinion summarizes the government's argument:

> The Government argues that St. David's cannot demonstrate the first element of the operational test.... [B]ecause of its partnership with HCA, St. David's cannot show that it engages "primarily" in activities that accomplish its charitable purpose. The Government does not contend that a non-profit organization should automatically lose its tax-exempt status when it forms a partnership with a for-profit entity. Instead, the Government argues that a non-profit organization must sacrifice its tax exemption if it cedes control over the partnership to the for-profit entity. The Government asserts that, when a non-profit cedes control, it can no longer ensure that its activities via the partnership primarily further its charitable purpose. In this case, the Government contends that St. David's forfeited its exemption because it ceded control....

St. David's argued that it must merely show it has a proper charitable purpose which, per prior rulings, includes being a hospital. The Circuit Court, however, also insisted:

> However, we cannot agree with St. David's suggestion that the central issue in this case is whether the partnership provides some (or even an extensive amount of) charitable services.... § 501(c)(3) confers tax-exempt status only on those organizations that operate *exclusively* in furtherance of exempt purposes.... As a result, in determining whether an organization satisfies the operational test, we do not simply consider whether the organization's activities further its charitable purposes. We must also ensure that those activities do *not* substantially further other (non-charitable) purposes. If more than an "insubstantial" amount of the partnership's activities further non-charitable interests, then St. David's can no longer be deemed to operate *exclusively* for charitable purposes.

That position raises serious questions about whether substantial partnerships and joint ventures with for-profit entities can be conducted by charities. If the for-profit partner cannot receive a substantial benefit from the activity, then such arrangements would seem not to be feasible. If, instead, this is merely about "control" and whether the exempt organization asserts ultimate control over the partnership or joint venture, then the issue becomes one of drafting and the reasonableness of the benefit to the for-profit entity (as opposed to whether it is substantial).

Revenue Ruling 98-15, 1998-1 C.B. 718 (1998) provides some guidance:

> [A] non-profit can demonstrate control by showing some or all of the following: (1) that the founding documents of the partnership expressly state that it has a charitable purpose and that the charitable purpose will take priority over all other concerns; (2) that the partnership agreement gives the non-profit organization a majority vote in the partnership's board of directors; and (3) that the partnership is managed by an independent company (an organization that is not affiliated with the for-profit entity).

Additional gloss on this subject appears in Rev. Rul. 2004-51, 2004-1 C.B. 974 (2004).

The fog surrounding the meaning of the private benefit doctrine, and when and how it applies, continues to hover over tax-exempt jurisprudence. Certainly, the district court opinion in St. David's and the Tax Court's opinion in *Redlands* did little to clarify the matter, and neither did the Fifth Circuit's opinion vacating *St. David's*. In the meantime, the Treasury Department might heed the District Court's editorial comments regarding its regulatory articulations and offer some clarification through the administrative process rather than through continuing litigation.

Aside on District Court Criticism

Although the court appropriately criticized the many double and triple negatives found in the Treasury Regulations, it arguably translated them incorrectly to "plain English." The language concerns Treas. Reg. § 1.501(c)(3)-1(c)(1). As discussed in Chapters 7 through 9 that particular language introduces the concept of exempt organizations having three categories of activities: primary, furthering, and unrelated. Primary activities must accomplish an exempt purpose. Furthering activities are related to primary activities, but are collateral to them and do not accomplish an exempt purpose (e.g., a gift shop or food court in a hospital). The court objected to a triple negative: an organization is *not* exempt if more than an *in*substantial portion of its activities is *not* in furtherance of exempt activities. The court's translation, however — that a substantial portion must be related — ignores the existence of the middle category of furthering activities: those that are less than "accomplishing" activities, but that are also more than unrelated. This illustrates the dangers of translating regulations into plain English: one must be careful not to alter the meaning.

Chapter 13

Lobbying Restriction

A. The Prohibition Against "Substantial" Lobbying—Generally

CODE: §§ 501(c)(3); 4912; 4945(d)(1) and (e)

REGS.: §§ 1.501(c)(3)-1(c)(3)(i)–(ii); 53.4945-2(d).

In addition to the private inurement prohibition and private benefit restrictions outlined in the two previous chapters, another tax law limitation imposed on charities is a legislative lobbying restriction. Section 501(c)(3) provides that "no substantial part" of a charity's activities may involve "carrying on propaganda, or otherwise attempting, to influence legislation (except as provided in [Section 501(h)]." Thus, if a charity engages in lobbying that is deemed "substantial," the charity will be considered an "action" organization and will either be denied 501(c)(3) exempt status or its exempt status will be revoked. *See* Treas. Reg. § 1.501(c)(3)-1(c)(3)(i) and (ii). Even without this "no substantial lobbying" requirement, "substantial lobbying" might still be prohibited as either a type of private inurement, or as an indication that the organization is not operated "exclusively" for exempt purposes. Do you see how?

As is the case with many code provisions and clauses, the "no substantial lobbying" requirement was first introduced to the law of tax-exempt organizations by the Service. A 1919 Treasury Regulation provided, in part, that "associations formed to disseminate controversial or partisan propaganda are not educational." *See* T.D. 2831, 21 Treas. Dec. Int. Rev. 1,285 (1919). Later, in *Slee v. Commissioner*, 42 F.2d 184 (2d Cir. 1930), a federal court upheld this Service position. In *Slee*, the Second Circuit held that the American Birth Control League failed to qualify for exemption because of its dissemination of propaganda to legislators and the public supporting repeal of anti-birth control laws. The Court determined that, due to its lobbying, the ABC League's purposes were not exclusively charitable, educational, or scientific.

As a result of the holding in *Slee*, Congress, in 1934, amended § 103(6) of the 1934 Act—the predecessor of § 501(c)(3)—to prohibit substantial lobbying. In 1954, Congress extended the prohibition to *any* political campaign activities—which is addressed in the next chapter. In 1976, Congress added § 501(h)—a safe harbor provision that allows certain lobbying expenditures by certain charities. If a § 501(h) election is made, the exempt entity is no longer subject to the "substantial part" test of § 501(c)(3) for lobbying activities. Instead, the § 501(h) electing entity loses its tax exemption only if it "normally" exceeds spending statutory caps on lobbying expenditures. Additionally, the § 501(h) electing entity becomes potentially liable for certain excise taxes outlined in § 4911 for each year that it exceeds the spending caps, regardless of whether it "normally" does so. In 1987 Congress enacted other excise tax provisions that apply even if a § 501(h) election is not made. *See* § 4912.

What is lobbying? Congress has given little guidance on what it means to "influence legislation" for purposes of the "no substantial lobbying" prohibition. However, the Treasury gives some insights in the regulations. Regulation § 1.501(c)(3)-1(c)(3) provides that an "action organization" is not eligible for § 501(c)(3) tax exemption and defines "action organization" as including a charity where a "substantial part of its activities is attempting to influence legislation." The phrase "influence legislation" is further defined to include either: (1) direct or indirect contacts with legislative officials in order to support or oppose legislation or (2) advocating the adoption or rejection of legislation. Finally, the term "legislation" is defined as meaning legislation at all levels of government—federal, state, local, and public referenda. See Treas. Reg. § 1.501(c)(3)-1(c)(3)(ii). As indicated in the *Anthony Haswell* case below, however, some acts that might ordinarily seem to fit the definition of lobbying are not considered lobbying for purposes of 501(c)(3). Thus, nonpartisan analysis, study, or research; technical advice or assistance; self-defense communications; and examinations and discussions of broad social or economic problems do not generally constitute attempts to "influence legislation." *See* IRC § 4945(e) and (f) and Treas. Reg. § 53.4945-2(d).

What does "no substantial part" mean? The meaning of the term "substantial" in reference to the "no substantial lobbying" restriction for charities that do not elect IRC § 501(h) is unclear. The vagueness surrounding this term is not unlike the vagueness that surrounds the term "exclusively," discussed earlier in this text in reference to the "exclusivity" requirement. One case held that spending less than 5% of an organization's "time & effort" on lobbying is not "substantial."[1] However, one potential problem with using a flat percentage to determine substantiality is that smaller organizations are put at a disadvantage—5% may be significantly less in volume of "time and effort" for them than for larger organizations. Another issue concerns what factors should be examined to determine substantiality. Thus, even if 5% is an acceptable amount of lobbying, what does one apply the 5% to? Is it 5% of the budget? Five percent of total time? Should it matter whether the lobbying is continuous or intermittent? What about the controversial nature of an organization's position on particular issues—should this matter? Thus, the vagueness that is naturally inherent in the term "substantial" is a major concern for organizations trying to comply with the "no substantial lobbying" restriction.

What happens if a charity that has not made a 501(h) election engages in substantial lobbying? The 1987 Act added IRC § 4912, subsection "(a)" of which applies to charities that are not exempt from tax under IRC § 501(c)(3) by reason of the

1. *Seasongood v. Commissioner*, 227 F.2d 907 (CA6 1955).

"no substantial lobbying" requirement. If IRC § 4912(a) applies, the organization, in addition to being denied exemption and denied the right to reorganize as a § 501(c)(4) social welfare organization, is subject to an excise tax equal to 5% of the amount of the lobbying expenditures.[2] Section 4912(b) imposes a similar 5% tax on any manager of the organization who agreed to making the expenditure knowing that the expenditure was improper lobbying. However, the tax on the manager does not apply if the agreement to make the expenditure was not willful and is due to reasonable cause. The excise tax applies to all public charities except those making a § 501(h) election, churches, and other organizations described in § 501(h)(5), and private foundations.

The following case, *Anthony Haswell v. United States*, contains a nice overview of the substantial lobbying restriction as it existed prior to 1974. After that, *Regan v. Taxation with Representation of Washington* examines the issue of whether the lobbying restriction unconstitutionally infringes on a charity's First Amendment free speech rights.

Anthony Haswell v. United States

500 F.2d 1133 (Ct. Cl. 1974), cert. denied (1975)

Plaintiff seeks a refund of income taxes paid in 1967 and 1968 on the theory that his payments to the National Association of Railroad Passengers (NARP) were charitable contributions as then defined in Section 170(c)(2) of the Internal Revenue Code of 1954. In 1967 and 1968, plaintiff timely paid income taxes of $7,783.67 and $23,059.96, respectively, but did not claim a deduction for payments to NARP, which had totaled $41,864.23 in 1967 and $90,000 in 1968. On April 13, 1971, a refund of $2,765.95 was claimed for 1967 and $9,840.06 for 1968. These refund claims were disallowed.

* * *

To be deductible, a charitable contribution must satisfy section 170(c)(2), which, among other requirements, specifies that the payment be made to an organization "organized and operated exclusively" for certain purposes, and "no substantial part of the activities of which is carrying on propaganda, or otherwise attempting, to influence legislation."

* * *

As will be shown, in 1967 and 1968, NARP was not operated exclusively for the purposes required by section 170(c)(2)(B) and a substantial part of its activities involved attempts to influence legislation within the limitation of section 170(c)(2)(D).

* * *

2. IRC § 504 prevents reorganization as a § 501(c)(4).

I

Summary of Facts

In 1967, plaintiff's concern over discontinuances of passenger trains in the United States caused him to undertake a program to preserve, improve, and expand railroad passenger service. As part of this program, plaintiff caused NARP to be incorporated on May 18, 1967, under the "General Not For Profit Corporation Act" of Illinois. The purposes for which NARP was organized were to act as a focal point for, and to undertake, programs designed to encourage and promote maintenance and improvement of passenger services, operations, and facilities of American railroads.

* * *

From the start of his program, plaintiff recognized that attainment of the goal to preserve, improve, and expand railroad passenger service would require political action at the national level. Prior to the incorporation of NARP, plaintiff explored his proposed program with a senior partner of National Counsel Associates (NCA), a Washington consulting firm that specialized in lobbying. In his correspondence with NCA, plaintiff indicated that he expected NCA to represent NARP in legislative matters before Congress and to promote its interests within the executive departments. Plaintiff emphasized that NARP's objectives "will require substantial legislative action by the Congress." NARP's contract with NCA was signed 18 days after NARP was incorporated.

In 1967 and 1968, NARP's legislative activities involved participation in proceedings in both Houses of the United States Congress in connection with legislation to amend Section 13(a) of the Interstate Commerce Act. As executive director of NARP, plaintiff testified four times before subcommittees of the Senate Committee on Commerce or of the Senate Committee on Banking and Currency. In addition to these appearances as executive director of NARP, plaintiff submitted four written statements or letters to the House of Representatives' Interstate and Foreign Commerce Committee or its subcommittees.

Each appearance as a witness or written submission by plaintiff on behalf of NARP was an activity that involved an attempt to influence pending legislation or to secure legislation sought by NARP. Each appearance as a witness or submission of written materials by plaintiff on behalf of NARP was in response to an invitation from the committee that had been arranged by NCA, NARP's Washington representative. In each instance that plaintiff testified, or submitted written materials, the testimony or materials stated NARP's position on behalf of the consumer rail passenger.

* * *

In its attempts to influence legislation, NARP advocated the interest of the consumer railroad passengers of the United States. Testimony by plaintiff and the written materials submitted did not represent nonpartisan analysis, study, or research in that the testimony or the materials were not the type of full and fair objective expositions that would enable the public to reach an independent conclusion on the subject. Plaintiff's testimony on behalf of NARP and the written materials submitted advocated a particular position and were partisan on the issue of the necessity to continue rail passenger service. In view of the complexities of rail industry operations and of its regulation, much of NARP's testimony and written materials necessarily included technical advice and assistance.

NARP's legislative activities were not limited to direct testimony or written submissions to congressional committees. Through NCA or through plaintiff as executive director, NARP made presentations of its views on pending legislation by personal contacts with Members of Congress, their legislative or administrative assistants, or with staff members of congressional committees. These personal presentations were made in informal meetings in legislative offices, at lunch, or over cocktails.

During 1967 and 1968, NCA was host for NARP at two or three cocktail parties to give plaintiff an opportunity to meet with Members of Congress and selected members of the staffs of Members of Congress or of congressional committees. At these cocktail parties, plaintiff and NCA talked about rail passenger problems and NARP's legislative goals for adequate passenger train service. In addition, in 1967 and 1968, NCA entertained at cocktails or lunch, for the purpose of presenting NARP's views on pending legislation, five Members of Congress, 16 legislative or administrative assistants to Members of Congress, and six professional or technical staff members of congressional committees. Plaintiff had personal interviews with approximately five to 10 Members of Congress, most of whom were members of committees or subcommittees which had legislation pending that could affect the rail passenger. In 1967, plaintiff conferred with approximately 12 to 15 congressional staff personnel on pending legislation that could affect the rail passenger and, in 1968, with approximately 30 such staff personnel.

In addition to direct attempts to influence legislation by presentations to congressional committees, Members of Congress, or congressional staff personnel, NCA undertook indirect legislative activities on behalf of NARP that included meetings with personnel of the Department of Transportation and the Interstate Commerce Commission who were concerned with railroad legislation. In these meetings, NCA sought to establish NARP as a legitimate spokesman for railroad passengers.

Background Analysis

Federal revenue laws historically have exempted from taxation organizations created and operated exclusively for religious, charitable, scientific, literary, or educational purposes. In the Internal Revenue Code of 1954, such organizations are included in section 501(c)(3) in the enumeration of entities exempted from federal income taxation. If an organization can qualify for exemption under section 501(c)(3), it acquires not only a tax exempt status, but also the status [(under section 170(c)(2))] of an organization to which deductible contributions can be made.

* * *

Prior to the Revenue Act of 1934, the revenue laws did not impose specific limitations on the political activities of tax exempt organizations. Treasury Department regulations, however, since 1919 had denied an exemption to organizations that disseminated controversial or partisan propaganda on the ground that such action was not within the exempt purposes. The Revenue Act of 1934, in sections 101(6) (exempt organizations) and 23(o)(2) (charitable deductions), added a substantiality test to the exemption for organizations "organized and operated exclusively for religious, charitable, scientific, literary, or educational purposes." These sections granted the exemption or permitted the deduction of contributions to qualified organizations provided that "no substantial part of the activities of which is carrying on propaganda, or otherwise attempting, to influence legislation."

The case which led to the 1934 legislation was *Slee v. Commissioner.*[3] In that case, the court held that the American Birth Control League was not entitled to a charitable exemption because it disseminated propaganda to legislators and to the public aimed at the repeal of laws preventing birth control. A tax exempt status was denied because the League's purpose was not exclusively charitable, educational, or scientific. In 1954, exempt status was further limited in section 501(c)(3) by a condition against participation or intervention in political campaigns on behalf of candidates for public office.

Tax exemptions are matters of legislative grace and taxpayers have the burden of establishing their entitlement to exemptions. The limitations in sections 501(c)(3) and 170(c)(2) of the 1954 Code stem from the policy that the United States Treasury should be neutral in political affairs and that substantial activities directed to attempts to influence legislation should not be subsidized. The Supreme Court in 1958 traced the development of the congressional policy against an exemption for organizations that attempt to promote or defeat legislation and stated:

> . . . These limitations, carried over into the 1939 and 1954 Codes [footnote omitted], made explicit the conclusion derived by Judge Learned Hand in 1930 that "political agitation as such is outside the statute, however innocent the aim. . . . Controversies of that sort must be conducted without public subvention; the Treasury stands aside from them." . . . 358 U.S. 498, 512 (1959)

* * *

Neither the legislative histories of sections 170(c)(2) and 501(c)(3), nor the cases that have arisen thereunder, provide specific guidance as to the content of the phrases "organized and operated exclusively," "no substantial part," and "to influence legislation," as used in those sections.

Treasury regulations under section 170(c)(2) follow the statutory language and provide that, for purposes of determining whether an organization is attempting to

3. [9] 42 F.2d 184 (2d Cir. 1930).

influence legislation or is engaging in political activities, reference should be made to the regulations promulgated under section 501(c)(3). The cases provide guidelines as to the extent and types of activities that disqualify the exemption and the deduction.

An organization that engages in substantial activity aimed at influencing legislation is disqualified from a tax exemption, whatever the motivation. The applicability of the influencing legislation clause is not affected by the selfish and unselfish motives and interests of the organization, and it applies to all organizations whether they represent private interests or the interests of the public. The term "exclusively" is given a connotation that differs from the ordinary meaning of the term, and activities which are minor, and not substantial, do not disqualify charitable and educational organizations from the benefit of the exemption nor do they disqualify individual contributors to such organizations from a deduction. The limitation is remedial and should be liberally construed.

The political efforts of an organization must be balanced in the context of the objectives and circumstances of the organization to determine whether a substantial part of its activities is to influence, or is an attempt to influence, legislation. A percentage test to determine whether the activities are substantial is not appropriate. Such a test obscures the complexity of balancing the organization's activities in relation to its objectives and circumstances in the context of the totality of the organization.

* * *

Whether NARP was operated exclusively for charitable and educational purposes and whether a substantial part of its operations involved attempts to influence legislation are questions of fact to be determined through a comparison of its purely charitable activities to its activities to influence legislation.

Disposition of Claim

NARP's operations may be divided into four categories: administrative; educational; litigation; and legislative. The question then becomes whether the activities concerned with legislation are the type that are proscribed by sections 170(c)(2) and 501(c)(3) or whether those activities are the type of nonpartisan analysis, study, or research or of technical advice or assistance, that remove them from the limitation. For convenient reference, the terms "legislative activities" and "political activities" will be used hereinafter to identify action that is "carrying on propaganda, or otherwise attempting, to influence legislation," within the meaning of section 170(c)(2)(D).

Treasury regulations in effect in 1967 and 1968 under section 501(c)(3) excluded "nonpartisan analysis, study, or research and making the results thereof available to the public" from the definition of advocacy that was one of the two characteristics of an "action" organization. An "action" organization, by definition, was not operated exclusively for an exempt purpose and, accordingly, was not eligible as an exempt organization. The section 501(c)(3) regulations, however, did not define what constitutes "nonpartisan analysis, study, or research" nor did these regulations state that the results of nonpartisan analysis, study, or research may be made available to legislative bodies when legislation is pending.

The Tax Reform Act of 1969 provides more precision. Section 4945(d) includes in the definition of a taxable expenditure of a private foundation amounts paid to carry on propaganda, or otherwise to attempt, to influence legislation "within the meaning of subsection (e)." In subsection (e), the "making available the results of nonpartisan analysis, study, or research" in communications with any member or employee of a legislative body or any other Government official or employee who may participate in the formulation of legislation is permissible and is not considered to be a proscribed attempt to influence legislation. No penalty attaches to a private foundation for making available the results of nonpartisan analysis, study, or research. By analogy, similar language in the section 501(c)(3) regulation in effect in 1967 and 1968 should permit charitable and educational organizations to undertake similar activity and not lose their exemption.

The Treasury regulations add further definition to what constitutes "nonpartisan analysis, study, or research." For the purposes of subsection 4945(e), "nonpartisan analysis, study, or research" means an *independent* and *objective* exposition of a particular subject matter. The term includes any activity which would be "educational," as defined in the regulations under section 501(c)(3).[4] Advocacy of a particular position or viewpoint qualifies as nonpartisan analysis, study, or research as long as there is a sufficiently full and fair exposition of the pertinent facts to enable the public or an individual to form an independent opinion or conclusion. Presentation of unsupported opinion does not qualify. The examples in the regulation make it clear that projects designed to present information merely of one side of a legislative controversy do not qualify as nonpartisan, nor do projects that fail to report available information that would tend to dispute conclusions that are advocated.

"Nonpartisan," as used in the statute and regulations, need not refer to organized political parties. Nonpartisan analysis, study, or research is oriented to issues and requires a fair exposition of both sides of the issue involved. An organization's position on a particular issue may be partisan even though the position advocated has not become identified with any particular organized political party, and, conversely, it can be nonpartisan even though the issue is the subject of hotly contested legislation. The organization's position may be nonpartisan in relation to party politics, and still be partisan on a particular issue, and the issue may or may not be politically significant.

Section 4945(e) of the 1954 Code also permits private foundations to provide "technical advice or assistance" to a legislative body in response to a written request

4. [22] 26 C.F.R. §1.501(c)(3)-1(d)(3)(i)(b) provides that an educational organization may advocate a particular position or viewpoint so long as it presents a sufficiently full and fair exposition of facts as to permit an independent opinion or conclusion to be reached.

without incurring the penalty of having the expense deemed a taxable expenditure. The regulations under section 501(c)(3) do not refer to technical advice or assistance as such. Regulations under section 4945(e) provide that technical advice or assistance need not qualify as nonpartisan analysis, study, or research. Technical advice or assistance must be specifically requested, as must the offering of opinions or recommendations, and must be available to every member of the requesting committee.[5]

In addition to nonpartisan analysis, study, or research and technical advice or assistance, the Treasury regulations under section 4945(e) also exclude from taxable expenditures communications with members of legislative bodies that are an examination or discussion of broad social, economic, or similar problems. Such communications, however, must not be directly addressed to the merits of a specific legislative proposal being considered.[6]

The part of NARP's operations involved in the advocacy of the interests of railroad passenger consumers on legislative matters does not consist of activities which qualify as nonpartisan analysis, study, or research; nor can NARP's efforts on legislative matters properly be categorized as technical advice or assistance. NARP presented its information in a manner which would advance most forcefully its position that rail passenger service must be preserved. NARP was partisan on this issue, and the materials submitted in support of its position were not the full and fair objective expositions that would enable the public or an individual to reach an independent conclusion. NARP was nonpartisan from the standpoint of political party organization. It was partisan, however, on issues of passenger train discontinuances.

Recapitulation of the facts shows that NARP's legislative program was not "analysis, study, or research." Plaintiff, on behalf of NARP, appeared four times to testify and, in addition, made four written submissions to committees of Congress on pending legislation of concern to NARP. In addition, plaintiff made personal presentations to approximately five to 10 Members of Congress and personally conferred with from 15 to 30 congressional staff personnel on pending legislation that could affect the rail passenger. To further its goals and to focus its legislative programs, NARP retained a permanent Washington representative that warranted it possessed expertise in the fields of public relations, education, and congressional lobbying. NARP's Washington representative, on its behalf, performed the myriad activities incident to NARP's appearances before, or submissions to, congressional committees and conducted a continuing research program to keep abreast of railroad-related matters that were legislatively significant. NARP's Washington representative also made personal presentations to Members of Congress and to congressional staff personnel on legislation of concern to NARP. In 1967 and 1968, NCA entertained at cocktails or luncheon for this purpose five Members of Congress,

5. [23] 26 C.F.R. §§ 53.4945-2(d)(2)(i) and (ii) (1973).

6. [24] 26 C.F.R. § 53.4945-2(d)(4) (1973).

16 legislative or administrative assistants to Members of Congress, and six professional or technical staff members of congressional committees. These activities, which were all part of the same partisan program, are more in accord with concepts of attempts to influence legislation rather than concepts that apply to the making available to governmental bodies nonpartisan analysis, study, or research.

NARP's efforts in legislative matters concerned pending legislation, and, for this reason, do not qualify as an examination or discussion of broad social, economic, or similar problems. Materials presented by NARP contained much information that was technical advice. The information, however, does not qualify as the technical advice or assistance contemplated by the statute and regulations. A simple invitation to testify or to submit a statement to a congressional committee is not in itself a request for technical advice or assistance. NARP's invitations had been arranged by NARP's Washington representative as part of its efforts to influence legislation and were not independent requests from the committee for specific technical advice or assistance. In these circumstances, the committees' invitations merely afforded an opportunity for a representative of the railroad passenger segment of the community to advocate its position.

Determination that NARP's operations relative to legislation were political activities and not excusable as nonpartisan analysis, study, or research, as technical advice or assistance, or as examination and discussion of broad social, economic, or similar problems does not dispose of the case. NARP's political activities must be compared with its exempted charitable and educational activities to determine whether the attempts to influence legislation were a substantial part of NARP's operations.

Although a percentage test is not determinative of substantiality, one measure of the relative significance of NARP's various activities in relation to its objectives is the amount of money devoted to each category of operations. In such analysis, the principle employed to allocate expenditures among the various classes of functions is crucial to the ultimate determination.

* * *

Distribution of expenditures is only one measure of the substantiality of NARP's political activities. Plaintiff's arrangements with NCA prior to NARP's incorporation also indicate the importance of legislative efforts in plaintiff's program as a whole. The primary reason for securing NCA's services was to facilitate NARP's effort to make its position known on the ICC's legislative proposals to amend the Interstate Commerce Act. Before NARP was incorporated, plaintiff had acknowledged to NCA that his objective would require "substantial legislative action by the Congress." Further, NARP's brochure—"*Yes—What's the real story about railroad passenger service?*"—asserted a need to maintain permanent Washington representation "to work for the preparation of constructive legislation."

Attempts to influence legislation were not secondary or incidental to NARP's charitable purposes. The legislative program was a primary objective in NARP's total operations for preservation of railroad passenger service and is on an equal footing with its educational and litigative efforts.

* * *

[The court's discussion of the constitutional issues is omitted. See *Regan v. Taxation with Representation*, below].

Regan v. Taxation With Representation of Washington

461 U.S. 540 (1983)

Justice Rehnquist delivered the opinion of the Court.

Appellee Taxation With Representation of Washington (TWR) is a nonprofit corporation organized to promote what it conceives to be the "public interest" in the area of federal taxation. It proposes to advocate its point of view before Congress, the Executive Branch, and the Judiciary. This case began when TWR applied for tax-exempt status under § 501(c)(3) of the Internal Revenue Code, 26 U.S.C. § 501(c)(3). The Internal Revenue Service denied the application because it appeared that a substantial part of TWR's activities would consist of attempting to influence legislation, which is not permitted by § 501(c)(3).

TWR then brought this suit. It claimed the prohibition against substantial lobbying is unconstitutional under the First Amendment and the equal protection component of the Fifth Amendment's Due Process Clause.

* * *

TWR was formed to take over the operations of two other nonprofit corporations. One, Taxation With Representation Fund, was organized to promote TWR's goals by publishing a journal and engaging in litigation; it had tax-exempt status under § 501(c)(3). The other, Taxation With Representation, attempted to promote the same goals by influencing legislation; it had tax-exempt status under § 501(c)(4). Neither predecessor organization was required to pay federal income taxes. For purposes of our analysis, there are two principal differences between § 501(c)(3) organizations and § 501(c)(4) organizations. Taxpayers who contribute to § 501(c)(3) organizations, are permitted by § 170(c)(2) to deduct the amount of their contributions on their federal income tax returns, while contributions to § 501(c)(4) organizations are not deductible. Section 501(c)(4) organizations, but not § 501(c)(3) organizations, are permitted to engage in substantial lobbying to advance their exempt purposes.

In these cases, TWR is attacking the prohibition against substantial lobbying in § 501(c)(3) because it wants to use tax-deductible contributions to support substantial lobbying activities. To evaluate TWR's claims, it is necessary to understand the effect of the tax-exemption system enacted by Congress.

Both tax exemptions and tax deductibility are a form of subsidy that is administered through the tax system. A tax exemption has much the same effect as a cash grant to the organization of the amount of tax it would have to pay on its income. Deductible contributions are similar to cash grants of the amount of a portion of the individual's contributions. The system Congress has enacted provides this kind of subsidy to nonprofit civic welfare organizations generally, and an additional subsidy to those charitable organizations that do not engage in substantial lobbying. In short, Congress chose not to subsidize lobbying as extensively as it chose to subsidize other activities that nonprofit organizations undertake to promote the public welfare.

It appears that TWR could still qualify for a tax exemption under § 501(c)(4). It also appears that TWR can obtain tax-deductible contributions for its nonlobbying activity by returning to the dual structure it used in the past, with a § 501(c)(3) organization for nonlobbying activities and a § 501(c)(4) organization for lobbying. TWR would, of course, have to ensure that the § 501(c)(3) organization did not subsidize the § 501(c)(4) organization; otherwise, public funds might be spent on an activity Congress chose not to subsidize.

TWR contends that Congress' decision not to subsidize its lobbying violates the First Amendment. It claims, relying on *Speiser v. Randall*, 357 U.S. 513 (1958), that the prohibition against substantial lobbying by § 501(c)(3) organizations imposes an "unconstitutional condition" on the receipt of tax-deductible contributions. In *Speiser*, California established a rule requiring anyone who sought to take advantage of a property tax exemption to sign a declaration stating that he did not advocate the forcible overthrow of the Government of the United States. This Court stated that "[to] deny an exemption to claimants who engage in certain forms of speech is in effect to penalize them for such speech." *Id.*, at 518.

TWR is certainly correct when it states that we have held that the government may not deny a benefit to a person because he exercises a constitutional right. *See Perry v. Sindermann*, 408 U.S. 593, 597 (1972). But TWR is just as certainly incorrect when it claims that this case fits the *Speiser-Perry* model. The Code does not deny TWR the right to receive deductible contributions to support its nonlobbying activity, nor does it deny TWR any independent benefit on account of its intention to lobby. Congress has merely refused to pay for the lobbying out of public moneys. This Court has never held that Congress must grant a benefit such as TWR claims here to a person who wishes to exercise a constitutional right.

This aspect of these cases is controlled by *Cammarano v. United States*, 358 U.S. 498 (1959), in which we upheld a Treasury Regulation that denied business expense deductions for lobbying activities. We held that Congress is not required by the First Amendment to subsidize lobbying. *Id.*, at 513. In these cases, as in *Cammarano*, Congress has not infringed any First Amendment rights or regulated any First Amendment activity. Congress has simply chosen not to pay for TWR's lobbying. We again reject the "notion that First Amendment rights are somehow not fully realized unless they are subsidized by the State." *Id.*, at 515 (Douglas, J., concurring).

TWR also contends that the equal protection component of the Fifth Amendment renders the prohibition against substantial lobbying invalid. TWR points out that § 170(c)(3) permits taxpayers to deduct contributions to veterans' organizations that qualify for tax exemption under § 501(c)(19). Qualifying veterans' organizations are permitted to lobby as much as they want in furtherance of their exempt purposes. TWR argues that because Congress has chosen to subsidize the substantial lobbying activities of veterans' organizations, it must also subsidize the lobbying of § 501(c)(3) organizations.

Generally, statutory classifications are valid if they bear a rational relation to a legitimate governmental purpose. Statutes are subjected to a higher level of scrutiny if they interfere with the exercise of a fundamental right, such as freedom of speech, or employ a suspect classification, such as race. *E.g., Harris v. McRae*, 448 U.S. 297, 322 (1980). Legislatures have especially broad latitude in creating classifications and distinctions in tax statutes. More than 40 years ago we addressed these comments to an equal protection challenge to tax legislation:

> "The broad discretion as to classification possessed by a legislature in the field of taxation has long been recognized.... [The] passage of time has only served to underscore the wisdom of that recognition of the large area of discretion which is needed by a legislature in formulating sound tax policies. Traditionally classification has been a device for fitting tax programs to local needs and usages in order to achieve an equitable distribution of the tax burden. It has, because of this, been pointed out that in taxation, even more than in other fields, legislatures possess the greatest freedom in classification. Since the members of a legislature necessarily enjoy a familiarity with local conditions which this Court cannot have, the presumption of constitutionality can be overcome only by the most explicit demonstration that a classification is a hostile and oppressive discrimination against particular persons and classes. The burden is on the one attacking the legislative arrangement to negative every conceivable basis which might support it." *Madden v. Kentucky*, 309 U.S. 83, 87–88 (1940) (footnotes omitted).

See also *San Antonio Independent School District v. Rodriguez*, 411 U.S. 1, 40–41 (1973); *Lehnhausen v. Lake Shore Auto Parts Co.*, 410 U.S. 356, 359–360 (1973).

We have already explained why we conclude that Congress has not violated TWR's First Amendment rights by declining to subsidize its First Amendment activities. The case would be different if Congress were to discriminate invidiously in its subsidies in such a way as to "'[aim] at the suppression of dangerous ideas.'" *Cammarano, supra*, at 513, quoting *Speiser*, 357 U.S., at 519. But the veterans' organizations that qualify under § 501(c)(19) are entitled to receive tax-deductible contributions regardless of the content of any speech they may use, including lobbying. We find no indication that the statute was intended to suppress any ideas or any demonstration that it has had that effect. The sections of the Internal Revenue Code here at issue do not employ any suspect classification. The distinction between veterans' organizations and other charitable organizations is not at all like distinctions based on race or national origin.

The Court of Appeals nonetheless held that "strict scrutiny" is required because the statute *"[affects]* First Amendment rights on a discriminatory basis." 219 U.S. App. D.C., at 130, 676 F.2d, at 728 (emphasis supplied). Its opinion suggests that strict scrutiny applies whenever Congress subsidizes some speech, but not all speech. This is not the law. Congress could, for example, grant funds to an organization dedicated to combating teenage drug abuse, but condition the grant by providing that none of the money received from Congress should be used to lobby state legislatures. Under *Cammarano*, such a statute would be valid. Congress might also enact a statute providing public money for an organization dedicated to combating teenage alcohol abuse, and impose no condition against using funds obtained from Congress for lobbying. The existence of the second statute would not make the first statute subject to strict scrutiny.

Congressional selection of particular entities or persons for entitlement to this sort of largesse "is obviously a matter of policy and discretion not open to judicial review unless in circumstances which here we are not able to find". For the purposes of these cases appropriations are comparable to tax exemptions and deductions, which are also "a matter of grace [that] Congress can, of course, disallow . . . as it chooses." *Commissioner v. Sullivan*, 356 U.S. 27, 28 (1958).

These are scarcely novel principles. We have held in several contexts that a legislature's decision not to subsidize the exercise of a fundamental right does not infringe the right, and thus is not subject to strict scrutiny. *Buckley v. Valeo*, 424 U.S. 1 (1976), upheld a statute that provides federal funds for candidates for public office who enter primary campaigns, but does not provide funds for candidates who do not run in party primaries. We rejected First Amendment and equal protection challenges to this provision without applying strict scrutiny. *Harris v. McRae, supra*, and *Maher v. Roe*, 432 U.S. 464 (1977), considered legislative decisions not to subsidize abortions, even though other medical procedures were subsidized. We declined to apply strict scrutiny and rejected equal protection challenges to the statutes.

The reasoning of these decisions is simple: "although government may not place obstacles in the path of a [person's] exercise of . . . freedom of [speech], it need not remove those not of its own creation." *Harris*, 448 U.S., at 316. Although TWR does not have as much money as it wants, and thus cannot exercise its freedom of speech as much as it would like, the Constitution "does not confer an entitlement to such funds as may be necessary to realize all the advantages of that freedom." *Id.*, at 318. As we said in *Maher*, "[constitutional] concerns are greatest when the State attempts to impose its will by force of law. . . ." 432 U.S., at 476. Where governmental provision of subsidies is not "'aimed at the suppression of dangerous ideas,'" *Cammarano*, 358 U.S., at 513, its "power to encourage actions deemed to be in the public interest is necessarily far broader." *Maher, supra*, at 476.

We have no doubt but that this statute is within Congress' broad power in this area. TWR contends that § 501(c)(3) organizations could better advance their charitable purposes if they were permitted to engage in substantial lobbying. This may well be true. But Congress — not TWR or this Court — has the authority to determine whether the advantage the public would receive from additional lobbying by charities is worth the money the public would pay to subsidize that lobbying, and other disadvantages that might accompany that lobbying. It appears that Congress was concerned that exempt organizations might use tax-deductible contributions to lobby to promote the private interests of their members. *See* 78 Cong. Rec. 5861 (1934) (remarks of Sen. Reed); *id.*, at 5959 (remarks of Sen. La Follette). It is not irrational for Congress to decide that tax-exempt charities such as TWR should not further benefit at the expense of taxpayers at large by obtaining a further subsidy for lobbying.

It is also not irrational for Congress to decide that, even though it will not subsidize substantial lobbying by charities generally, it will subsidize lobbying by veterans' organizations. Veterans have "been obliged to drop their own affairs to take up the burdens of the nation," *Boone v. Lightner*, 319 U.S. 561, 575 (1943), "'subjecting themselves to the mental and physical hazards as well as the economic and family detriments which are peculiar to military service and which do not exist in normal civil life.'" *Johnson v. Robison*, 415 U.S. 361, 380 (1974) (emphasis deleted). Our country has a longstanding policy of compensating veterans for their past contributions by providing them with numerous advantages. This policy has "always been deemed to be legitimate." *Personnel Administrator of Mass.* v. *Feeney*, 442 U.S. 256, 279, n. 25 (1979).

The issue in these cases is not whether TWR must be permitted to lobby, but whether Congress is required to provide it with public money with which to lobby. For the reasons stated above, we hold that it is not. Accordingly, the judgment of the Court of Appeals is

Reversed.

Justice Blackmun, with whom Justice Brennan and Justice Marshall join, concurring.

I join the Court's opinion. Because 26 U.S.C. § 501's discrimination between veterans' organizations and charitable organizations is not based on the content of their speech, *ante*, at 548, I agree with the Court that § 501 does not deny charitable organizations equal protection of the law. The benefit provided to veterans' organizations is rationally based on the Nation's time-honored policy of "compensating veterans for their past contributions." *Ante*, this page. As the Court says, *ante*, at 548 and 550, a statute designed to discourage the expression of particular views would present a very different question.

I also agree that the First Amendment does not require the Government to subsidize protected activity, *ante*, at 546, and that this principle controls disposition of TWR's First Amendment claim. I write separately to make clear that in my view the result under the First Amendment depends entirely upon the Court's necessary assumption—which I share—about the manner in which the Internal Revenue Service administers § 501.

If viewed in isolation, the lobbying restriction contained in § 501(c)(3) violates the principle, reaffirmed today, *ante*, at 545, "that the government may not deny a benefit to a person because he exercises a constitutional right." Section 501(c)(3) does not merely deny a subsidy for lobbying activities, see *Cammarano v. United States*, 358 U.S. 498 (1959); it deprives an otherwise eligible organization of its tax-exempt status and its eligibility to receive tax-deductible contributions for all its activities, whenever one of those activities is "substantial lobbying." Because lobbying is protected by the First Amendment, § 501(c)(3) therefore denies a significant benefit to organizations choosing to exercise their constitutional rights.

The constitutional defect that would inhere in § 501(c)(3) alone is avoided by § 501(c)(4). As the Court notes, *ante*, at 544, TWR may use its present § 501(c)(3) organization for its nonlobbying activities and may create a § 501(c)(4) affiliate to pursue its charitable goals through lobbying. The § 501(c)(4) affiliate would not be eligible to receive tax-deductible contributions.

Given this relationship between § 501(c)(3) and § 501(c)(4), the Court finds that Congress' purpose in imposing the lobbying restriction was merely to ensure that "no tax-deductible contributions are used to pay for substantial lobbying." *Ante*, at 544, n. 6; see *ante*, at 545. Consistent with that purpose, "[the] IRS apparently requires only that the two groups be separately incorporated and keep records adequate to show that tax-deductible contributions are not used to pay for lobbying." *Ante*, at 545, n. 6. As long as the IRS goes no further than this, we perhaps can safely say that "[the] Code does not deny TWR the right to receive deductible contributions to support its nonlobbying activity, nor does it deny TWR any independent benefit on account of its intention to lobby." *Ante*, at 545. A § 501(c)(3) organization's right to speak is not infringed, because it is free to make known its views on legislation through its § 501(c)(4) affiliate without losing tax benefits for its nonlobbying activities.

Any significant restriction on this channel of communication, however, would negate the saving effect of § 501(c)(4). It must be remembered that § 501(c)(3) organizations retain their constitutional right to speak and to petition the Government. Should the IRS attempt to limit the control these organizations exercise over the lobbying of their § 501(c)(4) affiliates, the First Amendment problems would be insurmountable. It hardly answers one person's objection to a restriction on his speech that another person, outside his control, may speak for him. Similarly, an attempt to prevent § 501(c)(4) organizations from lobbying explicitly on behalf of their § 501(c)(3) affiliates would perpetuate § 501(c)(3) organizations' inability to make known their views on legislation without incurring the unconstitutional penalty. Such restrictions would extend far beyond Congress' mere refusal to subsidize lobbying. See *ante*, at 544–545, n. 6. In my view, any such restriction would render the statutory scheme unconstitutional.

I must assume that the IRS will continue to administer §§ 501(c)(3) and 501(c)(4) in keeping with Congress' limited purpose and with the IRS's duty to respect and uphold the Constitution. I therefore agree with the Court that the First Amendment questions in these cases are controlled by *Cammarano v. United States*, 358 U.S. 498, 513 (1959), rather than by *Speiser v. Randall*, 357 U.S. 513, 518–519 (1958), and *Perry v. Sindermann*, 408 U.S. 593, 597 (1972).

B. Section 501(h) Safe Harbor for Lobbying

CODE: §§ 501(h); 4911(a)–(e)

REGS.: §§ 1.501(h)-3(a)–(b)(1), (c); 56.4911-2(a)(1); 56.4911-2(b)(1)–(2)(i); 56.4911-2(b)(2)(v)(H), Examples 1 and 2

In attempting to define "lobbying" for the purpose of the prohibition against substantial lobbying, the *Haswell* court relied on IRC § 4945(d)(1) and the 4945 regulations in effect prior to 1990. That approach was entirely sensible because the 4945(d)(1) tax on lobbying activities used language that was essentially identical to the prohibition against substantial lobbying found in IRC § 501(c)(3). In 1976, two years after the court's decision, Congress implicitly approved the *Haswell* approach by enacting IRC § 501(h) and IRC § 4911. However, it was not until 1990 that the Service finally issued regulations under these two statutory provisions. The new regulations not only interpreted and applied IRC §§ 501(h) and 4911, they also replaced the old regulations under IRC § 4945 (though in substance, they did not differ very much from the old regulations). That is, the substantive analysis under IRC § 4911 is meant to be consistent with the analysis under IRC § 4945. Of course, certain portions of the IRC § 4911 regulations that apply only to public charities are not applicable under IRC § 4945. These differences will be highlighted later when we study the private foundation excise taxes.

Although *Haswell* predates IRC §§ 501(h) and 4911, it nevertheless contains a still-accurate discussion of some of the exceptions to the definition of lobbying under IRC § 4911. The ultimate consequence of IRC §§ 501(h) and 4911 is that an electing organization will not be subject to the prohibition against substantial lobbying under IRC § 501(c)(3). IRC § 501(h)(1). Instead, an electing organization will be subject to a 25% excise on its "excess lobbying expenditures." IRC § 4911(a)(1). More important, an organization's tax exemption may be revoked if its lobbying expenditures normally exceed its lobbying ceiling amount, or if its grass-roots expenditures normally exceed its grass-roots ceiling amount. IRC § 501(h)(1). In essence, IRC § 501(h) provides a safe-harbor for charities that want to lobby, but do not want to violate the vague "substantiality" limit on lobbying imposed by § 501(c)(3). By electing under IRC § 501(h), these lobbying charities eliminate the vagueness and can lobby up to a predetermined dollar amount without fear of losing their § 501(c)(3) tax exemption.

Understanding §§ 501(h) and 4911 is essentially a matter of learning a new vocabulary. The first necessary phrase is "lobbying expenditures," which is defined as the sum of *direct lobbying* and *grass-roots lobbying* expenditures. *See* IRC §§ 501(h)(2)(A); 4911(c). *See also* Treas. Reg. § 56.4911-2(a)(1).

Direct lobbying is any communication with a member or employee of a legislative body or with a government official, or employee who may participate in the formulation of legislation, for the principal purpose of influencing legislation. Treas. Reg. § 56.4911-2(b)(1). A legislative body does not include judicial or executive bodies (i.e., administrative agencies). Treas. Reg. § 56.4911-2(d)(3). Thus, direct lobbying involves an appeal to a government representative with some input into the legislative process (as opposed to the enforcement or interpretive process) but only if the communication is for the purpose of influencing legislation. In the case of referenda or other laws that require approval by the public, the public itself is the government representative to whom the appeal must be made. Treas. Reg. § 56.4911-2(b)(1)(vi). The communication will not be for the purpose of influencing legislation unless it refers to and reflects a view on "specific legislation." Treas. Reg. § 56.4911-2(b)(1)(ii). "Legislation" includes action by federal, state, or local legislative body, or any action that is enacted via public referendum, ballot initiative, or similar procedure. IRC § 4911(e)(2). "Specific legislation" includes legislation that has already been introduced, as well as an action that has not yet been introduced but that is supported or opposed by the organization. Treas. Reg. § 56.4911-2(d)(1)(ii). An action that requires petition signatures to be placed on a public ballot becomes legislation when the first petition is circulated. *Id.*

Grass-roots lobbying is any communication with the general public or any segment thereof in an attempt to influence legislation. IRC § 4911(d)(1)(A). Communications are not attempts to influence legislation unless they meet the same requirements as a direct lobbying expenditure (i.e., refers to and reflects a view on specific legislation) and also encourages the audience to take action with respect to specific legislation. Treas. Reg. § 56.4911-2(b)(2)(ii). An organization directly encourages the public to take action if: (1) it states that recipients of the communication should contact a government official with input into the legislative process as a means of influencing the legislation, (2) provides directory information of a legislator or employee of a legislative body, or (3) provides a petition, postcard, or similar item by which the audience may contact the government official. Treas. Reg. § 56.4911-2(b)(2)(iii)(A)–(C). Indirect encouragement results when a communication identifies legislators who will vote on the legislation as: (1) opposed to the organization's position on the legislation, (2) being undecided on the legislation, (3) being the recipient's legislative representative, or (4) being a member of the committee or subcommittee considering the legislation. Treas. Reg. § 56.4911-2(b)(2)(iii)(D). The distinction between direct and indirect encouragement is important to the application of the exceptions discussed below.

Certain communications are specifically excluded from the definition of lobbying and therefore expenditures related to those communications are not lobbying expenditures (though they are included in total exempt purpose expenditures, see below). First, "nonpartisan analysis, study, or research" constitutes neither direct, nor grass-roots lobbying. IRC § 4911 (d)(2)(A); Treas. Reg. § 56.4911-2(c)(1)(ii). This is so even if the analysis, study, or research advocates a particular position "so long as there is a sufficiently full and fair exposition of the pertinent facts to enable the public or an individual to form an independent opinion or conclusion."[7] However, if the communication otherwise qualifies as nonpartisan analysis, study, or research, but also *directly* (as opposed to indirectly) encourages a recipient to take action, it will not come within the exception. Treas. Reg. § 56.4911-2(c)(1)(v). Second, discussions or communications on broad social, economic, or "similar" problems are excluded even if the subject matter is one that is also the subject of a legislative proposal, if the discussion does not address the merits of the proposal nor encourage direct action. Treas. Reg. § 56.4911-2(c)(2). Third, providing technical advice or assistance to a governmental body or committee is excluded if doing so is in response to a written request by the body or committee. Treas. Reg. § 56.4911-2(c)(3). Certain communications between the organization and its bona fide members regarding legislation of direct interest to the organization and its members, unless the communications directly encourage the members to influence legislation or directly encourage the members to urge nonmembers to influence legislation. IRC § 4911(d)(2)(D). Finally, under the "self-defense" exception, a charity may appear before a legislative body regarding action that affects the charity's existence, powers, and duties, or the deductibility of contributions to the organization. IRC § 4911(d)(2)(C).

The presence of excess lobbying expenditures will trigger the 25% excise tax. An organization has excess lobbying expenditures if its lobbying expenditures (i.e., amounts spent for direct and grass-roots lobbying) exceed its lobbying nontaxable amount, or its grass-roots expenditures exceed its grass-roots nontaxable amount. IRC § 4911(b); Treas. Reg. § 56.4911-1(b). The amount upon which the 25% tax is imposed is the greater of the two excesses. *Id.* The lobbying nontaxable amount is determined by applying a declining percentage to an organization's exempt purpose expenditures; but, in any event, it can never exceed $1,000,000. IRC § 4911(c)(2). For an organization with $500,000 or less in exempt purpose expenditures, the lobbying nontaxable amount is 20% of the exempt purpose expenditures. The lobbying nontaxable amount is increased by 15% of the exempt purpose expenditures over $500,000 but under $1 million, by 10% of the exempt purpose expenditures over $1 million up to $1.5 million, and 5% of the exempt purpose expenditures over $1.5 million. *Id.* An organization's grass-roots nontaxable amount is a flat 25% of its lobbying nontaxable amount. IRC § 4911(c)(4). Thus, in every case (1) it is necessary to determine the lobbying nontaxable amount before determining the grass-roots nontaxable amount, and (2) it will be easier to exceed the grass-roots ceiling amount than it will be to exceed the lobbying ceiling amount.

Because the lobbying nontaxable and grass-roots nontaxable amounts increase as exempt purpose expenditures increase, an organization may engage in more lobbying as it increases its exempt purpose expenditures. For some organizations, this effect may provide an incentive to overstate exempt purpose expenditures. Contrariwise, an organization may seek to understate its lobbying expenditures. The

7. *See Big Mama Rag, Inc. v. United States*, 631 F.2d 1030 (D.C. Cir. 1980).

regulations attempt to address both types of avoidance. In general, exempt purpose expenditures are amounts spent in pursuit of the organization's charitable purpose—including amounts for activities specifically excepted from the definition of grass-roots and lobbying expenditures, and membership communications that are not lobbying expenditures. Exempt purpose expenditures also include direct and grass roots lobbying expenditures, overhead expenses related to these amounts, amounts determined under the straight-line depreciation method on property used in furtherance of the charitable purpose, controlled grants, and fundraising expenditures. Treas. Reg. § 56.4911-4(b). If an organization transfers an amount to another § 501(c)(3) organization in pursuit of the transferor's charitable purpose, the amount of the transfer is an exempt purpose expenditure, provided the amount transferred is not earmarked for a non-charitable purpose. Treas. Reg. § 56.4911-4(d)(2). In Treasury Regulation § 56.4911-(4)(e)(3), however, the Service reserves the right to disregard any transfer if "a substantial purpose of a transfer is to inflate" the organization's exempt purpose transfers. This provision has not yet been tested in court.

One way for a charity to understate its lobbying expenditures is to provide indirect support to non-charities that engage in lobbying. For example, if a charity provides free or below-cost goods or services to a lobbying firm, the substance of the transaction is no different than if the charity itself spent money for lobbying activities. To the extent that the lobbying firm can avoid certain costs of operation, it can increase amounts directly spent for lobbying. The regulations include these discounted transactions as lobbying expenditures. Treas. Reg. § 56.4911-3(c)(3)(ii). The discount or other uncompensated value provided to the organization that engages in lobbying is first treated as the provider-charity's own grass-roots expenditures to the extent of the recipient's actual grass-roots expenditures (determined as if the recipient was a charity). Treas. Reg. § 56.4911-3(c)(3)(iii). The excess, if any, is then treated as the provider charity's direct lobbying expenditures to the extent of the recipient's actual direct lobbying expenditures. *Id.* Any amount remaining after deducting the recipient organization's grass roots and direct lobbying expenditures are not lobbying expenditures to the provider charity.

"Controlled grants"—i.e., grants made for and limited to a specific project that furthers the provider charity's exempt purpose, and for which the provider charity maintains records sufficient to show that the grant was not used for lobbying—are excluded from the indirect lobbying provisions. Treas. Reg. §§ 56.4911-3(c)(3)(i)(B); 56.4911-4(f)(3). In addition, when the discounted provision of goods and services is made widely available to the public as part of an activity that is substantially related to an exempt purpose, and a "substantial" number of unrelated persons actually purchase the goods or services, the provision of a discount to an organization that engages in lobbying will not be viewed as indirect lobbying. Treas. Reg. § 56.4911-3(c)(3)(i)(D).

Direct and grass-roots expenditures include all costs of preparing communications qualifying as either, including salaries and overhead attributable to the preparation of such communications. Treas. Reg. § 56.4911-3. A special rule applies when a communication is for both lobbying and exempt purposes. All costs incurred for communication on the same subject as the lobbying portion of the communication are considered lobbying expenditures. Treas. Reg. § 56.4911-3(a)(2). A communication is on the same subject if it discusses an activity or specific legislation that would be directly affected by the specific legislation that is the subject of the lobbying portion of the communication. *Id.*

Finally, after obtaining even a precarious grasp on the preceding detail, an electing charity should also be aware of a special "lenient" rule applicable to communications made by an electing charity exclusively to its members. Such communications may refer to and reflect a view on specific legislation and may indirectly encourage members to engage in direct or grass roots lobbying, provided the specific legislation is of "direct interest" to the organization and its members. Treas. Reg. § 56.4911-5(b). Expenditures for these communications are not lobbying expenditures. Under other circumstances — i.e., if the communication were made to the general public — such communications would constitute grass-roots lobbying. Under the members-only rule, they are lobbying communications, albeit indirectly, only if the communication *directly* encourages action. Only then will the related costs be counted as lobbying expenditures. If a members-only communication directly encourages members to engage in direct lobbying but not grass-roots communications with nonmembers, it is a direct lobbying communication and the costs of the communications are counted as direct lobbying expenditures. Treas. Reg. § 56.4911-5(c). If the members-only communication directly encourages members to engage in grass roots communications with nonmembers, regardless of whether it also directly encourages members to engage in direct lobbying, it is a grass-roots communications and the costs thereof are counted as grass roots expenditures. Treas. Reg. § 56.4911-5(d).

The § 501(h) election may be made only by "eligible organizations," which include all public charities except religious organizations and public safety testing organizations. IRC § 501(h)(4). An organization will violate the expenditure test and thus forfeit its tax exemption in any taxable year if its lobbying/grass roots expenditures for the taxable year and the three immediately past years (the four years are collectively referred to as the "base period") exceed 150% of the total lobbying/grass roots nontaxable amounts for the same time period. Thus, the organization must sum up its nontaxable amounts for each year in the base period. It must then sum up its lobbying and grass roots expenditures for each year of the base period. If the sum of the lobbying or grass roots expenditures exceed 1.5 times the sum of the lobbying or grass roots nontaxable amounts, respectively, the organization will be in violation of the expenditure test. IRC § 501(h)(2); Treas. Reg. § 1.501(h)-3(b).

Notes About Lobbying

Influencing Judicial Nominations: In IRS Notice 88-76, the Service concludes that attempts to influence the Senate confirmation of a federal judicial nominee are attempts to influence legislation. The Service reasoned that the Senate's action of advice and consent on a nonelective judicial nomination is similar to action with respect to a resolution. Pursuant to this view, a charity that attempts to influence the Senate confirmation vote for a judicial nominee would potentially violate the "no substantial lobbying" prohibition, if its lobbying is deemed "substantial." The Service is probably wrong in Notice 88-76 in concluding that "legislation" includes any matter on which a legislature votes. Congress' legislative power is contained in Article I of the Constitution, whereas its confirmation power is contained in Article II. Thus, the exercise of Article II confirmation power is not necessarily the exercise of Article I legislative power. However, the IRS still maintains its position that influencing the judicial nomination process is lobbying. *See* Christopher Quay, *Charities Allowed to Influence Supreme Court Nominations, Says IRS*, 108 Tax Notes 519 (2005).

Section 501(h) Electors Beware: Charities that make a § 501(h) election should be aware that the election does not make them immune from IRS scrutiny. Some have speculated that one of the possible side effects of making a § 501(h) election is that the IRS will pay *more* attention to your group's lobbying activities than it would otherwise. However, the IRS denies that this is the case. *See, e.g.*, Fred Stokeld, *EO Reps Upset over IRS Audits of Lobbying Charities*, 98 Tax Notes 1967 (2003); Fred Stokeld, *IRS Officials Meet with Nonprofit Reps on Audits of Charities That Lobby*, 99 Tax Notes 625 (2003).

In addition, recall that § 501(c)(3) charities retain their exemption only if their purposes remain "exclusively" charitable, educational, etc. In enacting IRC § 501(h), Congress noted that:

> The Act deals only with whether an organization is to be treated as violating the lobbying limits of the law. The Act does not affect the question of whether an expenditure might cause the organization to lose its charitable status because the expenditure violates the requirement that the organization be organized and operated "exclusively" for charitable, etc., purposes.[8]

This footnote apparently means that meeting the requirements of IRC § 501(h) is a safe harbor for "insubstantial lobbying." However, the exempt organization still has to satisfy the "exclusively for exempt purpose" requirement. As indicated in Part I of this text, the courts have interpreted this "exclusively" requirement to mean that a charity cannot have more than "insubstantial" non-exempt purposes. Thus, if an electing charity (1) expends proceeds on lobbying which satisfy the § 501(h) test, but also (2) has an unrelated trade or business activity, the charity may still lose its exemption for not engaging "exclusively" in exempt purposes.

8. General Explanation of the Tax Reform Act of 1976 (H.R. 10612, 94th Congress, P.L. 94-455), December 29, 1976, at page 411, footnote 7.

Questions

1. Organization T, a non-membership organization exempt under IRC § 501(c)(3) that has made an election under IRC § 501(h), prepares a three-page document that is mailed to 3,000 people on T's mailing list. The first two pages of the three-page document, titled "The Need for Child Care," discuss the need for additional child care programs, and include statistics on the number of children living in homes where both parents work or in homes with a single parent. The two pages also make note of the inadequacy of the number of daycare providers to meet the needs of these parents. The third page of the document, titled "H.R.1" indicates T's support of H.R. 1, a bill pending in the U.S. House of Representatives. The document states that H.R. 1 will provide for $10,000,000 in additional subsidies to child care providers, primarily for providers caring for lower-income children. The third page of the document also notes that H.R. 1 includes new federal standards regulating the quality of child care providers. The document ends with T's request that recipients contact their congressional representatives in support of H.R. 1.

One night, at around 9:00 p.m., T's president calls you and in a frantic, agitated state explains that the bond issuance that T is relying upon to expand its facilities is in jeopardy. In the course of its "due diligence" review, bond counsel came upon copies of the document and is concerned that the document may be in violation of the lobbying restrictions. Bond counsel informed the president that he was having an associate look into the matter. The President wants you to look into the matter as well. Limit your analysis at this point to whether the cost of preparing and distributing the document are lobbying expenditures and, if so, whether they are direct, grass roots, or both.

2. Client has had an annual budget of $1,500,000 for the last six years. Most of the money comes from an annual fundraising drive, although some of it comes from a small endowment. Most of the donors—if not all—are substantially motivated by its § 170(c)(2) status. Client has never been involved in any lobbying and has never made a § 501(h) election. It does not want to increase the size of its budget and does not want to seek new sources of funds; however, it wants to divert part of its expenditures to lobbying starting in year 8. It is willing to set up a separate lobbying organization if you so recommend.

a. Approximately what is the maximum amount client could spend in year 8 for lobbying without endangering its exempt status and without subjecting itself to any excise taxes? Assume a total budget of $250,000 for lobbying, which will reduce money left for exempt purposes to $1,250,000.

b. Assuming Client is willing to be subject to some excise taxes, approximately what is the maximum amount it could spend in Year 8 without endangering its exempt status?

c. If client spends the maximum amount you determined in part a., may it also spend that amount for lobbying in Year 9 without endangering its exempt status?

d. If your answer in "(c)" is "no," what is the maximum amount Client could spend in Year 9 for lobbying, assuming that it wanted to continue indefinitely spending that amount for lobbying and that its total budget will not change? Again, assume Client does not want to endanger its exempt status or be subject to any excise taxes.

e. Do you recommend a § 501(h) election?

Chapter 14

Political Activity Prohibition

A. Prohibition Against Campaign Intervention

CODE: §§ 501(c)(3); 4955; 6852; 7409

REG.: § 1.501(c)(3)-1(c)(3)

In addition to the lobbying restrictions of § 501(c)(3), charities must also abide by a political activities prohibition. Thus, charities cannot "directly or indirectly" participate in or intervene in any political campaign on behalf of, or in opposition to, any candidate for public office. If a charity engages in any prohibited political campaign activities, the organization is an "action" organization and its exemption will be revoked or denied, as appropriate.

Congress instituted the "no political activities on behalf of any candidate" requirement in 1954 as an extension of the prohibition on an exempt organization's involvement in lobbying. Legend has it that then-Senator Lyndon B. Johnson sought to weaken or eliminate a political opponent's funding source when he offered a floor amendment prohibiting charities from intervening in political campaigns. The legislative history confirms only that the prohibition was adopted without hearings or debate. Although Senator Johnson's brief statement indicates that campaign activities were to be treated in the same manner as lobbying activities, the campaign intervention prohibition is absolute, while the lobbying activities restriction is not.

In 1987, Congress amended the law to prohibit political campaigning "in opposition to" any candidate, thus prohibiting "negative campaigning." In 1987 Congress also enacted §§ 4955, 6852, and 7409, which provide penalties and enforcement procedures for certain political campaign expenditures of public charities. Most recently, in December 1995, the Service issued final regulations for the 1987 congressional enactments.

The "no political activities" prohibition is absolute. Contrary to the assertion of the New York City Bar in *Association of Bar of City of New York v. Commissioner* (included below), this "no political" requirement contains no "substantiality" test as there is for lobbying. Nonetheless, both the Service and the courts tend to permit some political activities by public benefit organizations, provided the activity is incidental in comparison to the organization's exempt activities. For example, in *St. Louis Union Trust Co. v. United States*, 374 F.2d 427, 431–32 (8th Cir. 1967), the court remarked that a "slight and comparatively unimportant deviation from the narrow furrow of tax approved activity is not fatal." Presumably, the reason a court would take such a relaxed attitude toward a congressional *requirement* for exemption is that (at the time) the only real remedy for violation of this provision is the death penalty for the exempt organization (i.e., loss of tax-exemption). This view, that a "slight" deviation is permissible, is clearly not the majority viewpoint and not what Congress intended.

The Internal Revenue Code does not explain what political activities are prohibited by § 501(c)(3). However, the regulations provide some guidance within the context of its description of so-called "action" organizations:

> Activities which constitute participation or intervention in a political campaign include but are not limited to *the publication or distribution of written or oral statements on behalf of, or in opposition to, any candidate for public office.*

Treas. Reg. § 1.501(c)(3)-1(c)(3)(iii) (emphasis added). Revenue Ruling 74-574, Revenue Ruling 78-248, Revenue Ruling 80-282, and Revenue Ruling 86-95 (all included below) provide some additional guidance as to what types of activities constitute political activities for purposes of the political activities prohibition. As these various revenue rulings demonstrate, the Service's view is that political-type activities are not banned totally. Only when the political-looking activities are determined to show a bias (either for or against a particular candidate), is the "no political" requirement violated.

Who is a candidate for public office? Whether a person is a candidate, particularly in the era characterized by informal campaigns beginning the day after a prior election, is an open question. The regulations define "candidate for public office" as "an individual who offers himself, or is proposed by others, as a contestant for an elective public office, whether such office be national, State, or local." Treas. Reg. § 1.501(c)(3)-1(c)(3)(iii). The Service has interpreted this definition to exclude candidates for appointed office, such as federal judges and cabinet officials. 1988-2 C.B. 392, Notice 88-76. However, as explained in the prior chapter on lobbying, the Notice goes on to say that commenting on judicial nominations is lobbying for purposes of the "no substantial lobbying" restrictions. But an oft-quoted statement from the Joint Committee on Taxation demonstrates the overriding uncertainty regarding the identification of a "candidate":

> Clear standards do not exist for determining precisely at what point an individual becomes a candidate for purposes of the rule. On the one hand, once an individual declares his candidacy for a particular office, his status as a candidate is clear. On the other hand, the fact that an individual is a prominent political figure does not automatically make him a candidate, even if there is speculation regarding his possible future candidacy for particular offices.

Joint Committee on Taxation, Lobbying and Political Activities of Tax Exempt Organizations, at 54. (1987). In addition to risking revocation of its tax exempt status, an organization and its managers are subject to excise taxes when the organization engages in campaign activity. Internal Revenue Code § 4955 imposes a two-tier tax similar to that imposed under § 4958 — the intermediate sanctions provision, which imposes an excise tax on so-called excess benefit transactions. In addition, the Service may seek to enjoin a charity from "flagrantly" participating or intervening in a political campaign under § 7409, and may accelerate any § 4955 taxes due from an organization that flagrantly participates or intervenes in a political campaign under § 6852.

Political intervention versus voter education. The most troublesome issue with regard to the prohibition against participation and intervention in political campaigns involves the distinction between participation and intervention, on the one hand, and voter education and civic activities (e.g., voter registration drives) on the other. The Service has issued a series of rulings that analyze common activities in light of the prohibition against campaign interventions.

But before considering those rulings, we look at whether nonpartisan activities are immune from the campaign intervention prohibition.

Association of the Bar of the City of New York v. Commissioner

858 F.2d 876 (2d Cir. 1988)

Van Graafeiland, Circuit Judge:

Section 501(c)(3) of the Internal Revenue Code provides for the exemption from federal income tax of organizations operated exclusively for charitable or educational purposes. To qualify under that section, however, an organization must not "participate in, or intervene in (including the publishing or distributing of statements), any political campaign on behalf of (or in opposition to) any candidate for public office." I.R.C. § 501(c)(3).

The Commissioner of Internal Revenue appeals from a decision of the United States Tax Court in which the Association of the Bar of the City of New York was held to qualify as a tax-exempt charitable and educational organization within the meaning of section 501(c)(3). The Tax Court reached this decision by holding that the Association does not engage in forbidden political activity. For the reasons that follow, we reverse.

> The Association was incorporated in 1871 by Special Act of the New York Legislature for the purposes of cultivating the science of jurisprudence, promoting reforms in the law, facilitating the administration of justice, elevating the standard of integrity, honor and courtesy in the legal profession and cherishing the spirit of brotherhood among the members thereof.

In order to carry out these purposes, the Association engages in a variety of activities, many of which are conducted through the Association's more than fifty standing committees.

One of the Association's significant activities is the rating of candidates for both appointive and elective judgeships at the municipal, state and federal level. This task is assigned to the Association's Committee on the Judiciary. The Committee considers a candidate's professional ability, experience, character, temperament and the possession of such special qualifications as the Committee deems desirable for judicial office. It then rates the candidate as either "approved", "not approved", or "approved as highly qualified." The ratings are communicated to the public in the form of press releases and are published in The Record of the Association of the Bar of the City of New York, a regular publication of the Association which is sent out to the Association's members and approximately 120 other subscribers, including libraries and law schools. A "not approved" rating may be accompanied on occasion by a short statement explaining the reasons for the rating.

In 1982, the Association applied to the Commissioner for recognition as a charitable and educational organization exempt from tax under section 501(c)(3). Although the Association already is exempt from federal income taxes under section 501(c)(6), qualifying under section 501(c)(3) would give additional tax advantages to the Association and persons who contribute to it. For example, a section 501(c)(3) organization is eligible to receive charitable contributions which are tax-deductible to the donor for federal income, estate, and gift tax purposes.

The Commissioner denied the Association's application on the ground that the procedure followed by the Association in the rating of candidates for elective judicial office constituted intervention or participation in political campaigns on behalf of candidates for public office. Following this adverse determination, the Association brought an action in Tax Court for a declaratory judgment that it qualifies as a section 501(c)(3) organization. That Court, by a vote of ten to six, held that the Association's conduct in question does not constitute prohibited political activity and that the Association therefore qualifies as a section 501(c)(3) organization. We disagree.

Canon 8 of New York's Code of Professional Responsibility provides "A Lawyer Should Assist in Improving the Legal System." N.Y. Code of Professional Responsibility Canon 8, *reprinted in* N.Y. Jud. Law App. (McKinney 1975). Ethical Consideration 8-6 elaborates on this provision as follows:

> Judges and administrative officials having adjudicatory powers ought to be persons of integrity, competence, and suitable temperament. Generally, lawyers are qualified, by personal observation or investigation, to evaluate the qualifications of persons seeking or being considered for such public offices, and for this reason they have a special responsibility to aid in the selection of only those who are qualified. It is the duty of lawyers to endeavor to prevent political considerations from outweighing judicial fitness in the selection of judges. Lawyers should protest earnestly against the appointment or election of those who are unsuited for the bench and should strive to have elected or appointed thereto only those who are willing to forego pursuits, whether of a business, political, or other nature, that

> may interfere with the free and fair consideration of questions presented for adjudication. (footnotes omitted)

N.Y. Code of Professional Responsibility EC 8–6 (1975).

There can be little question that lawyers take seriously the obligation imposed upon them by this Canon and Ethical Consideration. Bar Associations across the State follow the practice of rating candidates for judicial office, and it is clearly in the public interest for them to do so. The issue in the instant case, however, is not whether Bar Associations serve the public by rating candidates and publicizing their rating. It is whether they may do so and still claim tax exemptions which are not available under section 501(c)(3) to organizations which "participate in, or intervene in (including the publishing or distributing of statements), any political campaign on behalf of (or in opposition to) any candidate for public office."

* * *

The findings of the Tax Court on this issue are ambivalent. The Court says that "the ratings do not support or oppose the candidacy of any particular individual or recommend that the public vote for or against a specific candidate." In almost the same breath, however, the Court states that it is "obvious that the ratings are published with the hope that they will have an impact on the voter." Studies of Bar Associations' judicial ratings indicate that they do influence the voting public. Certainly, a candidate for judicial office who receives a "not approved" Bar Association rating will believe that this is so.

As is evident from legislative history, government subsidization of political activity has been a matter of concern to Congress from the time Judge Learned Hand wrote that "political agitation . . . however innocent the aim. . . . must be conducted without public subvention. . . ." *Slee v. Commissioner*, 42 F.2d 184, 185 (2d Cir. 1930); *see Cammarano v. United States*, 358 U.S. 498 (1959). "A tax exemption has much the same effect as a cash grant to the organization of the amount of tax it would have to pay on its income." *Regan v. Taxation with Representation of Washington*, 461 U.S. 540, 544 (1983). When Congress included tax exemptions to charitable and educational organizations in the Revenue Act of 1934, it excepted from exemption those organizations that devote a substantial part of their activities to "carrying on propaganda, or otherwise attempting, to influence legislation." Ch. 277, § 101(6), 48 Stat. 680, 700. That provision remains intact in present section 501(c)(3).

Section 501(c)(3) of the Internal Revenue Code of 1954 added to the group of excepted organizations those which participate or intervene in the political campaign of a candidate for public office. "This provision merely expressly stated what had always been understood to be the law. Political campaigns did not fit within any of the specified purposes listed in the section." 9 MERTENS, LAW OF FEDERAL INCOME TAXATION § 34.05 at 22; *see Haswell v. United States*, 500 F.2d 1133, 1140 (1974). To remove any doubt as to the scope of this exception, Congress again amended section 501(c)(3) in 1987 to ban participation both "on behalf of" and "in opposition to" candidates for public office. The House Report that accompanied this Bill states that "the prohibition on political campaign activities . . . reflect[s] Congressional policies that the U.S. Treasury should be neutral in political affairs. . . ."

The Association suggests several reasons why the proscription against participation or intervention in the campaigns of judicial candidates does not apply to its rating procedures. It argues, and we assume this to be so, that it evaluates judicial candidates on a nonpartisan basis. However, the statute and pertinent regulations thereunder are not limited in their application to the partisan campaigns of candidates representing recognized political parties. "'Nonpartisan,' as used in the statute and regulations, need not refer to organized political parties." *Haswell, supra*, 500 F.2d at 1144. One need not be a party nominee to be a candidate for public office. "The term 'candidate for public office' means an individual who offers himself, or is proposed by others, as a contestant for an elective public office. . . ." Treas. Reg. 1.501(c)(3)-(1)(c)(3)(iii). Moreover, one may be a candidate without running an organized political campaign. "[A] campaign for a public office in a public election merely and simply means running for office, or candidacy for office, as the word is used in common parlance and as it is understood by the man in the street." *Norris v. United States*, 86 F.2d 379, 382 (8th Cir. 1936). Indeed, a candidate for judicial office is limited in his political campaign activities by Canon 7 of his own Code of Judicial Conduct. N.Y. Code of Judicial Conduct Canon 7 (1975). A candidate who receives a "not qualified" rating will derive little comfort from the fact that the rating may have been made in a nonpartisan manner.

The Association also asserts that its "rating activity involves merely the collection and limited dissemination of objective data." We disagree. Objective data are data that are independent of what is personal or private in our apprehension and feelings, that use facts without distortion by personal feelings or prejudices and that are publicly or intersubjectively observable or verifiable, especially by scientific methods. Objective representations have been described judicially as "representations of previous and present conditions and past events, which are susceptible of exact knowledge and correct statement." A belief that something is so does not make it so. A representation that a candidate is a lawyer or a judge is a readily provable statement of objective fact. A representation that a candidate is able and has proper character and temperament is simply a subjective expression of opinion. The Tax Court recognized quite correctly that "ratings, by their very nature, necessarily will reflect the philosophy of the organization conducting such activities," and they are simply expressions of "professional opinion" concerning the candidates' qualifications. *Association of the Bar v. Commissioner, supra*, 89 T.C. at 610–11.

Published expressions of such opinion, made with an eye toward imminent elections, are a far cry from the revenue rulings upon which the Association relies. *See, e.g.*, 80-282, where, in holding that the publication of a newsletter by an organization otherwise qualifying for section 501(c)(3) exemption did not constitute proscribed political activity, the IRS emphasized the following factors:

1. "The voting records of all incumbents will be presented;"

2. "Candidates for reelection will not be identified;"

3. "No comment will be made on an individual's overall qualifications for public office;"

4. "No statements expressly or impliedly endorsing or rejecting any incumbent as a candidate for public office will be offered;"

5. "The organization will not widely distribute its compilation of incumbents' voting records;"

6. "No attempt will be made to target the publication toward particular areas in which elections are occurring nor to time the date of publication to coincide with an election campaign."

The inapplicability of these criteria to the activities of the Association is readily apparent. Indeed, the Association concedes that it is attempting to "ensure" that candidates whom it considers to be "legally and professionally unqualified" are not elected to office. In pursuing this activity, the Association falls clearly within the definition of an "action" organization, i.e., one that "participates or intervenes, directly or *indirectly*, in any political campaign on behalf of or in opposition to any candidate for public office." Treas. Reg. 1.501(c)(3)-1(c)(3)(iii) (emphasis supplied). *See* Rev. Rul. 67-71.

We note in passing that, except for an occasional attempt to justify a "not qualified" rating, no reasons are given for the ratings assigned by the Association. Although we see no need to reach this issue, we note the possibility of a conflict between this procedure and Treas. Reg. 1.501(c)(3)-1(d)(3)(b), which holds that advocated viewpoints unaccompanied by sufficient pertinent facts to permit members of the public to form their own independent opinions, cannot be considered educational in nature.

Finally, the Association contends that the phrase "substantial part of its activities" as used in the proscription against the influencing of legislation should be carried over into the proscription against participating in any political campaign. "The short answer [to this argument] is that Congress did not write the statute that way." *United States v. Naftalin*, 441 U.S. 768, 773 (1979). As above noted, the exception from section 501(c)(3) exemption of an organization that participates in political campaigns was added to the section some twenty years after the exception based on the influencing of legislation. Had Congress intended the added exception to apply only to those organizations that devote a substantial part of their activity to participation in political campaigns, it easily could have said so. It did not. Indeed, since it is most unlikely as a practical matter that any charitable organization would devote a substantial part of either its activity or its budget to the sporadic and relatively inexpensive rating of candidates for public office, the interpretation of section 501(c)(3) urged by the Association would make this portion of section 501(c)(3) substantially meaningless. Congress did not intend it to be so. "Although the present provisions of Section 501(c)(3) permit some degree of influencing legislation by a Section 501(c)(3) organization, it provides that no degree of support for an individual's candidacy for public office is permitted." H.R. Rep. No. 413, 91st Cong., 1st Sess. 32 (1969); S. Rep. No. 552, 91st Cong., 1st Sess. 47 (1969). "It should be noted that exemption is lost . . . by participation in *any* political campaign on behalf of *any* candidate for public office. It need not form a *substantial* part of the organization's activities." *United States v. Dykema*, 666 F.2d 1096, 1101 (7th Cir. 1981); *see Hutchinson Baseball Enterprises, Inc. v. Commissioner*, 696 F.2d 757, 760 (10th Cir. 1982).

Needless to say, the members of this panel, whose combined years of Bar Association membership total well over a century, empathize with the efforts of such Associations to improve the administration of justice. We recognize, however, that it is not within our province to grant Bar Associations a tax exemption that Congress has not seen fit to grant. "Courts should not 'rewrite a statute because they might deem its effects susceptible of improvement.'".

The decision of the Tax Court is reversed.

Revenue Ruling 74-574

1974-2 C.B. 16

Advice has been requested whether, in the circumstances described below, an organization has participated in political campaigns on behalf of candidates for public office within the meaning of section 501(c)(3) of the Internal Revenue Code of 1954.

The organization, a nonprofit corporation formed exclusively for religious and educational purposes, is recognized as exempt from Federal income tax as an organization described in section 501(c)(3) of the Code. In furtherance of its stated purposes, the corporation operates a noncommercial broadcasting station that presents religious, educational, and public interest programs.

In accordance with the requirements of the Federal Communications Act of 1934, *as amended*, 47 U.S.C. 312(a)(7) (Supp. II, 1972) [the Act], the organization makes reasonable amounts of air time available, without charge, to bona fide legally qualified candidates for elective public office in order that they may present their viewpoints and urge their election to public office. Equal opportunities are afforded all such candidates for the same public office to present their views. Before and after each broadcast, a statement is made by the station that the views expressed are those of the candidate and not those of the station; that the station endorses no candidate or viewpoint; that the presentation is made as a public service in the interest of informing the electorate; and that equal opportunities will be presented to all bona fide legally qualified candidates for the same public office to present their views. In providing free air time to the candidates, the station complies in all respects with the equal opportunities requirements of the Act.

Section 501(c)(3) of the Code provides for the exemption from Federal income tax of organizations that are organized and operated exclusively for educational purposes and that do not participate in any political campaign on behalf of any candidate for public office.

Section 1.501(c)(3)-1(d)(3) of the Income Tax Regulations defines the term "educational" as the instruction of the public on subjects useful to the individual and beneficial to the community.

Section 1.501(c)(3)-1(c)(3)(i) of the regulations provides that an organization is not operated exclusively for one or more exempt purposes if it is an "action" organization.

Section 1.501(c)(3)-1(c)(3)(iii) of the regulations provides, in part, that an organization is an action organization if it participates or intervenes, directly or indirectly, in any political campaign on behalf of or in opposition to any candidate for public office. Activities which constitute participation or intervention in a political campaign on behalf of or in opposition to a candidate include, but are not limited to, the making of oral statements on behalf of or in opposition to such a candidate.

The provision of broadcasting facilities to bona fide legally qualified candidates for elective public office, under the circumstances described above, furthers the education of the electorate by providing a public forum for the exchange of ideas and the debate of public issues which instructs them on subjects useful to the individual and beneficial to the community. Providing of a forum for the presentation of opposing candidates and points of view to the public assists in providing the electorate with information concerning the candidates for public office and better enables them to exercise their voting rights.

The fact that the organization makes its facilities equally available to the candidates for public office does not make the expression of political views by the candidates the acts of the broadcasting station within the intendment of section 501(c)(3) of the Code. Cf. Rev. Rul. 72-512, 1972-2 C.B. 246, which states a university is not participating in political campaigns within the meaning of section 501(c)(3) by providing a political science course that requires the students' participation in political campaigns of their choice and Rev. Rul. 72-513, 1972-2 C.B. 246, which states that the provision of facilities and faculty advisors for a campus newspaper that publishes the students' editorial opinions on political and legislative matters does not constitute an attempt by the university to influence legislation or participate in political campaigns. The broadcasting station, by reason of its disclaimers and the presentation of equal opportunities for all bona fide legally qualified candidates for the same elective public office to express their views, is not participating or intervening on behalf of or in opposition to any candidate for public office and is therefore not an action organization.

Accordingly, the organization's compliance with the requirements of section 312(a)(7) of the Act does not constitute participation in political campaigns on behalf of candidates for public office within the meaning of section 501(c)(3) of the Code.

Revenue Ruling 78-248

1978-1 C.B. 154

Advice has been requested whether certain organizations, which otherwise qualify for exemption from Federal income tax under section 501(c)(3) of the Internal Revenue Code of 1954, will be considered "action" organizations and not exempt under section 501(c)(3) if they undertake "voter education" activities in the situations described below.

Section 501(c)(3) of the Code provides for the exemption from Federal income tax of organizations that are organized and operated exclusively for charitable purposes and that do "not participate in, or intervene in (including the publishing or distributing of statements), any political campaign on behalf of any candidate for public office."

* * *

Whether an organization is participating or intervening, directly or indirectly, in any political campaign on behalf of or in opposition to any candidate for public office depends upon all of the facts and circumstances of each case. Certain "voter education" activities conducted in a non-partisan manner may not constitute prohibited political activity under section 501(c)(3) of the Code. Other so-called "voter education" activities, however, may be proscribed by the statute. The following situations are illustrative:

Situation 1

Organization A has been recognized as exempt under section 501(c)(3) of the Code by the Internal Revenue Service. As one of its activities, the organization annually prepares and makes generally available to the public a compilation of voting records of all Members of Congress on major legislative issues involving a wide range of subjects. The publication contains no editorial opinion, and its contents and structure do not imply approval or disapproval of any Members or their voting records.

The "voter education" activity of Organization A is not prohibited political activity within the meaning of section 501(c)(3) of the Code.

Situation 2

Organization B has been recognized as exempt under section 501(c)(3) of the Code by the Internal Revenue Service. As one of its activities in election years, it sends a questionnaire to all candidates for governor in State *M*. The Questionnaire solicits a brief statement of each candidate's position on a wide variety of issues. All responses are published in a voters guide that it makes generally available to the public. The issues covered are selected by the organization solely on the basis of their importance and interest to the electorate as a whole. Neither the questionnaire nor the voters guide, in content or structure, evidences a bias or preference with respect to the views of any candidate or group of candidates.

The "voter education" activity of Organization B is not prohibited political activity within the meaning of section 501(c)(3) of the Code.

Situation 3

Organization C has been recognized as exempt under section 501(c)(3) of the Code by the Internal Revenue Service. Organization C undertakes a "voter education" activity patterned after that of Organization B in *Situation 2.* It sends a Questionnaire to candidates for major public offices and uses the responses to prepare a voters guide which is distributed during an election campaign. Some questions evidence a bias on certain issues. By using a Questionnaire structured in this way, Organization C is participating in a political campaign in contravention of the provisions of section 501(c)(3) and is disqualified as exempt under that section.

Situation 4

Organization D has been recognized as exempt under section 501(c)(3) of the Code. It is primarily concerned with land conservation matters.

The organization publishes a voters guide for its members and others concerned with land conservation issues. The guide is intended as a compilation of incumbents' voting records on selected land conservation issues of importance to the organization and is factual in nature. It contains no express statements in support of or in opposition to any candidate. The guide is widely distributed among the electorate during an election campaign.

While the guide may provide the voting public with useful information, its emphasis on one area of concern indicates that its purpose is not nonpartisan voter education.

By concentrating on a narrow range of issues in the voters guide and widely distributing it among the electorate during an election campaign, Organization D is participating in a political campaign in contravention of the provisions of section 501(c)(3) and is disqualified as exempt under that section.

Revenue Ruling 80-282

1980-2 C.B. 178

Issue

Would the publication of a newsletter, by an organization otherwise described in section 501(c)(3) of the Internal Revenue Code, containing the voting records of congressional incumbents on selected issues, in the manner described below, constitute participation or intervention in any political campaign within the meaning of section 501(c)(3)?

Facts

The organization is exempt from federal income tax under section 501(c)(3) of the Code. The organization engages in a number of different educational and charitable activities. As one of its activities, the organization maintains an office that monitors and reports on legislative, judicial, administrative, and other governmental activities and developments considered to be of important social interest. As part of the office's activities, it distributes a monthly newsletter to interested members and others, who together number only a few thousand nationwide.

The monthly newsletter contains expressions of the organization's views on a broad range of legislative, judicial, and administrative issues it considers significant. In discussing a particular issue, the reader is sometimes encouraged to contact various governmental officials to express his or her views on the issue.

As soon as practical after the close of each congressional session, the organization intends to publish in an issue of its newsletter a summary of the voting records of all incumbent Members of Congress on selected legislative issues important to it, together with an expression of the organization's position on those issues. Each member's votes will be reported in a way which illustrates whether he or she voted in accordance with the organization's position on the issue. The newsletter is politically non-partisan, and will not contain any reference to or mention of any political campaigns, elections, candidates, or any statements expressly or impliedly endorsing or rejecting any incumbent as a candidate for public office. No mention will be made of an individual's overall qualification for public office, nor will there be any comparison of candidates that might be competing with the incumbents in any political campaign. The voting records of all incumbents will be presented and candidates for reelection will not be identified. The newsletter will point out the limitations of judging the qualifications of an incumbent on the basis of a few selected votes and will note the need to consider such unrecorded matters as performance on subcommittees and constituent service.

Publication usually will occur after congressional adjournment and will not be geared to the timing of any federal election. The newsletter will be distributed to the usual subscribers, and will not be targeted toward particular areas in which elections are occurring.

Law

Section 501(c)(3) of the Code provides for the exemption from federal income tax of organizations organized and operated exclusively for charitable purposes, no substantial part of the activities of which is carrying on propaganda, or otherwise attempting to influence legislation, and which do not participate in, or intervene in (including the publishing or distributing of statements), any political campaign on behalf of any candidate for public office.

Section 1.501(c)(3)-1(c)(i) of the Income Tax Regulations states that an organization is not operated exclusively for one or more exempt purposes if it is an "action" organization. Section 1.501(c)(3)-1(c)(3)(iii) defines an "action" organization as an organization that participates or intervenes, directly or indirectly, in any political campaign on behalf of or in opposition to any candidate for public office. The regulations further provide that activities that constitute participation or intervention in a political campaign on behalf of or in opposition to a candidate include, but are not limited to, the publication or distribution of written statements or the making of oral statements on behalf of or in opposition to such a candidate.

Analysis

Whether an organization is participating or intervening, directly or indirectly, in any political campaign on behalf of or in opposition to any candidate for public office depends upon all of the facts and circumstances of each case. Certain "voter education" activities conducted in a non-partisan manner may not constitute prohibited political activities under section 501(c)(3) of the Code. Other so-called "voter education" activities, however, may be proscribed by the statute. Rev. Rul. 78-248, 1978-1 C.B. 154, sets forth several situations illustrating when an organization has or has not engaged in prohibited political activities within the meaning of section 501(c)(3).

In *Situation 3* of Rev. Rul. 78-248, the organization prepared a questionnaire to all candidates for major public offices that contained questions evidencing a bias on certain issues and made the responses generally available to the public during an election campaign. It was considered to be participating in prohibited political campaign activity. In *Situation 4* of Rev. Rul. 78-248, an organization primarily concerned with land conservation matters published a compilation of incumbents' voting records on selected land conservation issues and widely distributed it to the electorate during an election campaign. It was held that by concentrating on a narrow range of issues and widely distributing the publication among the electorate during an election campaign, the organization was participating in a prohibited political activity.

In this case the format and content of the publication are not neutral, since the organization reports each incumbent's votes and its own views on selected legislative issues and indicates whether the incumbent supported or opposed the organization's view. On the other hand, the voting records of all incumbents will be presented, candidates for reelection will not be identified, no comment will be made on an individual's overall qualifications for public office, no statements expressly or impliedly endorsing or rejecting any incumbent as a candidate for public office will be offered, no comparison of incumbents with other candidates will be made, and the organization will point out the inherent limitations of judging the qualifications of an incumbent on the basis of certain selected votes by stating the need to consider such unrecorded matters as performance on subcommittees and constituent service.

In view of the foregoing, other factors must be examined to determine whether in the final analysis the organization is participating or intervening in a political campaign.

In the instant case, the organization will not widely distribute its compilation of incumbents' voting records. The publication will be distributed to the organization's normal readership who number only a few thousand nationwide. This will result in a very small distribution in any particular state or congressional district. No attempt will be made to target the publication toward particular areas in which elections are occurring nor to time the date of publication to coincide with an election campaign.

In view of these facts, *Situations 3 and 4* of Rev. Rul. 78-248 are distinguishable from the present case, and the organization will not be considered to be engaged in prohibited political campaign activity.

Holding

The publication of a newsletter, by an organization otherwise described in section 501(c)(3) of the Code, containing the voting records of Congressional incumbents on selected issues, in the manner described above, will not constitute participation or intervention in any political campaign within the meaning of section 501(c)(3).

EFFECT ON OTHER REVENUE RULINGS

Rev. Rul. 78-248 is amplified.

Revenue Ruling 86-95

1986-2 C.B. 73

Issue

Would the conduct of public forums involving qualified congressional candidates by an organization otherwise described in section 501(c)(3) of the Internal Revenue Code, in the manner described below, constitute participation or intervention in any political campaign within the meaning of section 501(c)(3)?

Facts

The organization is an educational membership organization exempt from federal income tax under section 501(c)(3) of the Code. As one of its programs, the organization monitors and reports on legislative, judicial, administrative, and other governmental activities and developments considered to be of important interest to its members.

The organization proposes to conduct a series of public forums. These forums will be conducted in congressional districts during congressional election campaigns. All legally qualified candidates for the House of Representatives from the congressional districts in question will be invited to participate in a forum.

The agenda at each of the forums will cover a broad range of issues, including, but not limited to, those issues considered to be of important educational interest to the organization's members. Questions to forum participants will be prepared and presented by a nonpartisan, independent panel of knowledgeable persons composed of representatives of the media, educational organizations, community leaders, and other interested persons. Each candidate will be allowed an equal opportunity to present his or her views on each of the issues discussed. The organization will select a moderator for each forum whose sole function will be limited to assuring that the general ground rules are followed. At both the beginning and end of each forum, the moderator will state that the views expressed are those of the candidates and not those of the organization and that the sponsorship of the forum is not intended as an endorsement of any candidate.

Law and Analysis

Section 501(c)(3) of the Code provides for the exemption from federal income tax of organizations organized and operated exclusively for charitable or educational purposes, no substantial part of the activities of which is carrying on propaganda, or otherwise attempting to influence legislation, (except as otherwise provided in section 501(h)), and which do not participate in, or intervene in (including the publishing or distributing of statements), any political campaign on behalf of any candidate for public office.

Section 1.501(c)(3)-1(c)(3)(i) of the Income Tax Regulations states that an organization is not operated exclusively for one or more exempt purposes if it is an "action" organization. Section 1.501(c)(3)-1(c)(3)(iii) defines an "action" organization as an organization that participates or intervenes, directly or indirectly, in any political campaign on behalf of or in opposition to any candidate for public office. The regulations further provide that activities that constitute participation or intervention in a political campaign on behalf of or in opposition to a candidate include, but are not limited to, the publication or distribution of written statements or the making of oral statements on behalf of or in opposition to such a candidate.

Rev. Rul. 66-256, 1966-2 C.B. 210, holds that a nonprofit organization formed to conduct public forums at which lectures and debates on social, political, and international matters are presented qualifies for exemption from federal income tax under section 501(c)(3) of the Code.

Rev. Rul. 74-574, 1974-2 C.B. 160, holds that a section 501(c)(3) organization operating a broadcast station is not participating in political campaigns on behalf of public candidates by providing reasonable amounts of air time equally available to all legally qualified candidates for election to public office in compliance with the reasonable access provisions of the Communications Act of 1934, 47 U.S.C. § 312(a)(7), (1982).

Whether an organization is participating or intervening, directly or indirectly, in any political campaign on behalf of or in opposition to any candidate for public office depends upon all of the facts and circumstances of each case. For example, certain "voter education" activities conducted in a non-partisan manner may not constitute prohibited political activities under section 501(c)(3) of the Code. Other so-called "voter education" activities may be proscribed by the statute. Rev. Rul. 78-248, 1978-1 C.B. 154, contrasts several situations illustrating when an organization that publishes a compilation of a candidate's position or voting record has or has not engaged in prohibited political activities based on whether the questionnaire or voting guide in content or structure shows a bias or preference with respect to the views of a particular candidate. See also Rev. Rul. 80-282, 1980-2 C.B. 178, that amplified Rev. Rul. 78-248 regarding the timing and distribution of voter education materials.

The presentation of public forums or debates is a recognized method of educating the public. See Rev. Rul. 66-256. Providing a forum for candidates is not, in and of itself, prohibited political activity. See Rev. Rul. 74-574. However, a forum for candidates could be operated in a manner that would show a bias or preference for or against a particular candidate. This could be done, for example, through biased questioning procedures. On the other hand, a forum held for the purpose of educating and informing the voters, which provides fair and impartial treatment of candidates, and which does not promote or advance one candidate over another, would not constitute participation or intervention in any political campaign on behalf of or in opposition to any candidate for public office.

The facts and circumstances of this case establish that both the format and content of the proposed forums will be presented in a neutral manner. All legally qualified congressional candidates will be invited to participate in the forum. The questions will be prepared and presented by a non-partisan, independent panel. The topics discussed will cover a broad range of issues of interest to the public, notwithstanding that the issues discussed may include issues of particular importance to the organization's members. Each candidate will receive an equal opportunity to present his or her views on each of the issues discussed. Finally, the moderator selected by the organization will not comment on the questions or otherwise make comments that imply approval or disapproval of any of the candidates. In view of these facts, the organization will not be considered to be engaged in prohibited political activity.

This conclusion is based on the totality of the circumstances described. The presence or absence of a particular fact here in other similar situations is not determinative of other cases but would have to be considered in light of all the surrounding factors in that case.

Holding

The conduct of public forums involving qualified congressional candidates in the manner described above, by an organization otherwise described in section 501(c)(3) of the Code, will not constitute participation or intervention in any political campaign within the meaning of section 501(c)(3).

EFFECT ON OTHER REVENUE RULINGS

Rev. Rul. 66-256 is amplified.

Branch Ministries v. Rossotti

211 F.3d 137 (D.C. Cir. 2000)

BUCKLEY, Senior Judge:

Four days before the 1992 presidential election, Branch Ministries, a tax-exempt church, placed full-page advertisements in two newspapers in which it urged Christians not to vote for then-presidential candidate Bill Clinton because of his positions on certain moral issues.[1] The Internal Revenue Service concluded that the placement of the advertisements violated the statutory restrictions on organizations exempt from taxation and, for the first time in its history, it revoked a bona fide church's tax-exempt status because of its involvement in politics. Branch Ministries and its pastor, Dan Little, challenge the revocation on the grounds that (1) the Service acted beyond its statutory authority, (2) the revocation violated its right to the free exercise of religion guaranteed by the First Amendment and the Religious Freedom Restoration Act, and (3) it was the victim of selective prosecution in violation of the Fifth Amendment. Because these objections are without merit, we affirm the district court's grant of summary judgment to the Service.

I. Background

A. Taxation of Churches

The Internal Revenue Code ("Code") exempts certain organizations from taxation, including those organized and operated for religious purposes, provided that they do not engage in certain activities, including involvement in "any political campaign on behalf of (or in opposition to) any candidate for public office." 26 U.S.C. § 501(a), (c)(3) (1994). Contributions to such organizations are also deductible from the donating taxpayer's taxable income. *Id.* § 170(a). Although most organizations seeking tax-exempt status are required to apply to the Internal Revenue Service ("IRS" or "Service") for an advance determination that they meet the requirements of section 501(c)(3), *id.* § 508(a), a church may simply hold itself out as tax exempt and receive the benefits of that status without applying for advance recognition from the IRS. *Id.* § 508(c)(1)(A).

B. Factual and Procedural History

Branch Ministries, Inc. operates the Church at Pierce Creek ("Church"), a Christian church located in Binghamton, New York. In 1983, the Church requested and received a letter from the IRS recognizing its tax-exempt status. On October 30, 1992,

1. [The lower court described the ad thusly: "Christian Beware. Do not put the economy ahead of the Ten Commandments." It asserted that Governor Clinton supported abortion on demand, homosexuality and the distribution of condoms to teenagers in public schools. The advertisement cited various Biblical passages and stated that "Bill Clinton is promoting policies that are in rebellion to God's laws." It concluded with the QUESTION: "How then can we vote for Bill Clinton?" 40 F. Supp. at 17. — Eds.]

four days before the presidential election, the Church placed full-page advertisements in *USA Today* and the *Washington Times*. Each bore the headline "Christians Beware" and asserted that then-Governor Clinton's positions concerning abortion, homosexuality, and the distribution of condoms to teenagers in schools violated Biblical precepts. The following appeared at the bottom of each advertisement:

> This advertisement was co-sponsored by the Church at Pierce Creek, Daniel J. Little, Senior Pastor, and by churches and concerned Christians nationwide. Tax-deductible donations for this advertisement gladly accepted. Make donations to: The Church at Pierce Creek. [mailing address].

The advertisements did not go unnoticed. They produced hundreds of contributions to the Church from across the country and were mentioned in a *New York Times* article and an Anthony Lewis column which stated that the sponsors of the advertisement had almost certainly violated the Internal Revenue Code. Peter Applebome, *Religious Right Intensifies Campaign for Bush*, N.Y. Times, Oct. 31, 1992, at A1; Anthony Lewis, *Tax Exempt Politics?*, N.Y. Times, Dec. 1, 1992, at A15.

The advertisements also came to the attention of the Regional Commissioner of the IRS, who notified the Church on November 20, 1992 that he had authorized a church tax inquiry based on "a reasonable belief . . . that you may not be tax-exempt or that you may be liable for tax" due to political activities and expenditures. Letter from Cornelius J. Coleman, IRS Regional Commissioner, to The Church at Pierce Creek (Nov. 20, 1992). The Church denied that it had engaged in any prohibited political activity and declined to provide the IRS with certain information the Service had requested. On February 11, 1993, the IRS informed the Church that it was beginning a church tax examination. Following two unproductive meetings between the parties, the IRS revoked the Church's section 501(c)(3) tax-exempt status on January 19, 1995, citing the newspaper advertisements as prohibited intervention in a political campaign.

The Church and Pastor Little (collectively, "Church") commenced this lawsuit soon thereafter. This had the effect of suspending the revocation of the Church's tax exemption until the district court entered its judgment in this case. *See* 26 U.S.C. § 7428(c). The Church challenged the revocation of its tax-exempt status, alleging that the IRS had no authority to revoke its tax exemption, that the revocation violated its right to free speech and to freely exercise its religion under the First Amendment and the Religious Freedom Restoration Act of 1993, 42 U.S.C. § 2000bb (1994) ("RFRA"), and that the IRS engaged in selective prosecution in violation of the Equal Protection Clause of the Fifth Amendment. After allowing discovery on the Church's selective prosecution claim, the district court granted summary judgment in favor of the IRS. *Branch Ministries, Inc. v. Rossotti*, 40 F. Supp. 2d 15 (D.D.C. 1999).

* * *

II. Analysis

The Church advances a number of arguments in support of its challenges to the revocation. We examine only those that warrant analysis.

* * *

B. First Amendment Claims and the RFRA

The Church claims that the revocation of its exemption violated its right to freely exercise its religion under both the First Amendment and the RFRA. To sustain its claim under either the Constitution or the statute, the Church must first establish that its free exercise right has been substantially burdened. *See Jimmy Swaggart Ministries v. Board of Equalization*, 493 U.S. 378, 384–85 (1990) ("Our cases have established that the free exercise inquiry asks whether government has placed a substantial burden on the observation of a central religious belief or practice and, if so, whether a compelling governmental interest justifies the burden.") (internal quotation marks and brackets omitted); 42 U.S.C. § 2000bb-1(a), (b) ("Government shall not substantially burden a person's exercise of religion" in the absence of a compelling government interest that is furthered by the least restrictive means.). We conclude that the Church has failed to meet this test.

The Church asserts, first, that a revocation would threaten its existence. *See* Affidavit of Dan Little dated July 31, 1995 at P 22, *reprinted in* App. at Tab 8 ("The Church at Pierce Creek will have to close due to the revocation of its tax exempt status, and the inability of congregants to deduct their contributions from their taxes."). The Church maintains that a loss of its tax-exempt status will not only make its members reluctant to contribute the funds essential to its survival, but may obligate the Church itself to pay taxes.

The Church appears to assume that the withdrawal of a conditional privilege for failure to meet the condition is in itself an unconstitutional burden on its free exercise right. This is true, however, only if the receipt of the privilege (in this case the tax exemption) is conditioned

> upon conduct proscribed by a religious faith, or ... denied ... because of conduct mandated by religious belief, thereby putting substantial pressure on an adherent to modify his behavior and to violate his beliefs.

Jimmy Swaggart Ministries, 493 U.S. at 391–92 (internal quotation marks and citation omitted). Although its advertisements reflected its religious convictions on certain questions of morality, the Church does not maintain that a withdrawal from electoral politics would violate its beliefs. The sole effect of the loss of the tax exemption will be to decrease the amount of money available to the Church for its religious practices. The Supreme Court has declared, however, that such a burden "is not constitutionally significant." *Id.* at 391; *see also Hernandez v. Commissioner*, 490 U.S. 680, 700 (1989) (the "contention that an incrementally larger tax burden interferes with religious activities ... knows no limitation").

In actual fact, even this burden is overstated. Because of the unique treatment churches receive under the Internal Revenue Code, the impact of the revocation is likely to be more symbolic than substantial. As the IRS confirmed at oral argument, if the Church does not intervene in future political campaigns, it may hold itself out as a 501(c)(3) organization and receive all the benefits of that status. All that will have been lost, in that event, is the advance assurance of deductibility in the event a donor should be audited. *See* 26 U.S.C. § 508(c)(1)(A); Rev. Proc. 82-39 § 2.03. Contributions will remain tax deductible as long as donors are able to establish that the Church meets the requirements of section 501(c)(3).

Nor does the revocation necessarily make the Church liable for the payment of taxes. As the IRS explicitly represented in its brief and reiterated at oral argument, the revocation of the exemption does not convert bona fide donations into income taxable to the Church. *See* 26 U.S.C. § 102 ("Gross income does not include the value of property acquired by gift. . . ."). Furthermore, we know of no authority, and counsel provided none, to prevent the Church from reapplying for a prospective determination of its tax-exempt status and regaining the advance assurance of deductibility—provided, of course, that it renounces future involvement in political campaigns.

We also reject the Church's argument that it is substantially burdened because it has no alternate means by which to communicate its sentiments about candidates for public office. In *Regan v. Taxation With Representation*, 461 U.S. 540, 552–53 (1983) (Blackmun, J., concurring), three members of the Supreme Court stated that the availability of such an alternate means of communication is essential to the constitutionality of section 501(c)(3)'s restrictions on lobbying. The Court subsequently confirmed that this was an accurate description of its holding. *See FCC v. League of Women Voters*, 468 U.S. 364, 400 (1984). In *Regan*, the concurring justices noted that "TWR may use its present § 501(c)(3) organization for its nonlobbying activities and may create a § 501(c)(4) affiliate to pursue its charitable goals through lobbying." 461 U.S. at 552.

The Church has such an avenue available to it. As was the case with TWR, the Church may form a related organization under section 501(c)(4) of the Code. . . . (tax exemption for "civic leagues or organizations not organized for profit but operated exclusively for the promotion of social welfare"). Such organizations are exempt from taxation; but unlike their section 501(c)(3) counterparts, contributions to them are not deductible. . . . Although a section 501(c)(4) organization is also subject to the ban on intervening in political campaigns . . . , it may form a political action committee ("PAC") that would be free to participate in political campaigns. *Id.* § 1.527-6(f), (g) ("An organization described in section 501(c) that is exempt from taxation under section 501(a) may, [if it is not a section 501(c)(3) organization], establish and maintain such a separate segregated fund to receive contributions and make expenditures in a political campaign.").

At oral argument, counsel for the Church doggedly maintained that there can be no "Church at Pierce Creek PAC." True, it may not itself create a PAC; but as we have pointed out, the Church can initiate a series of steps that will provide an alternate means of political communication that will satisfy the standards set by the concurring justices in *Regan*. Should the Church proceed to do so, however, it must understand that the related 501(c)(4) organization must be separately incorporated; and it must maintain records that will demonstrate that tax-deductible contributions to the Church have not been used to support the political activities conducted by the 501(c)(4) organization's political action arm. *See* 26 U.S.C. § 527(f)(3); 26 C.F.R. § 1.527-6(e), (f).

That the Church cannot use its tax-free dollars to fund such a PAC unquestionably passes constitutional muster. The Supreme Court has consistently held that, absent invidious discrimination, "Congress has not violated [an organization's] First Amendment rights by declining to subsidize its First Amendment activities." *Regan*, 461 U.S. at 548; *see also Cammarano v. United States*, 358 U.S. 498, 513 (1959) ("Petitioners are not being denied a tax deduction because they engage in constitutionally protected activities, but are simply being required to pay for those activities entirely out of their own pockets, as everyone else engaging in similar activities is required to do under the provisions of the Internal Revenue Code.").

Because the Church has failed to demonstrate that its free exercise rights have been substantially burdened, we do not reach its arguments that section 501(c)(3) does not serve a compelling government interest or, if it is indeed compelling, that revocation of its tax exemption was not the least restrictive means of furthering that interest.

Nor does the Church succeed in its claim that the IRS has violated its First Amendment free speech rights by engaging in viewpoint discrimination. The restrictions imposed by section 501(c)(3) are viewpoint neutral; they prohibit intervention in favor of all candidates for public office by all tax-exempt organizations, regardless of candidate, party, or viewpoint. *Cf. Regan*, 461 U.S. at 550–51 (upholding denial of tax deduction for lobbying activities, in spite of allowance of such deduction for veteran's groups).

* * *

III. Conclusion

For the foregoing reasons, we find that the revocation of the Church's tax-exempt status neither violated the Constitution nor exceeded the IRS's statutory authority. The judgment of the district court is therefore

Affirmed.

Note

If our study of improper campaign intervention ended with *Branch Ministries*, we would be doing our readers a disservice. Rarely will there ever be a case of such open and blatant violation of the prohibition against campaign activities. It is more often the case that organizations that seek to influence an election will do so in a way that allows for some deniability. Moreover, controversies are rather predictable—they occur every two or four years (when members of Congress or the President are elected). Usually, the case comes to the attention of the Service because one side or the other is seeking votes and is trying to weaken an opponent or a group it views as supporting an opponent, not because disinterested persons inform the Service of a violation. Thus, the Service is normally in a difficult position when it comes to enforcing the campaign prohibition. If it does nothing, it is subject to an allegation of favoritism toward the ideology most closely associated with the alleged violator. If it takes enforcement action, it is subject to an allegation of favoritism towards the ideology most closely associated with the whistle-blower.

Although some scholars and proponents have, for years, thought the prohibition against political intervention unconstitutional, the issue had never been squarely addressed. One reason for this is that the Service had always been reluctant to enforce the prohibition except in very blatant cases such as was the case in *Branch Ministries*. In 2010, though, the issue became relevant in a case regarding a provision of the Bipartisan Campaign Reform Act of 2002 (aka, the McCain-Feingold Act) generally prohibiting corporations (for profit and not for profit) from purchasing advertisements containing "electioneering communications" naming a federal candidate within 30 days of an election. The Supreme Court's opinion (only the majority opinion is excerpted below) cast even more doubt on the constitutionality of the prohibition against campaign intervention. The organization in *Citizens United* was exempt under IRC 501(c)(4) but the majority opinion is written broadly enough to apply to all organizations exempt under IRC 501. None of the statutes or regulations prohibiting campaign intervention have been changed but one should suspect that the Service is even more loathed to enforce the prohibition.

Citizens United v. FEC

558 U.S. 310 (2010)

Justice Kennedy delivered the opinion of the Court.

Federal law prohibits corporations and unions from using their general treasury funds to make independent expenditures for speech defined as an "electioneering communication" or for speech expressly advocating the election or defeat of a candidate. 2 U.S.C. § 441b. Limits on electioneering communications were upheld in *McConnell v. Federal Election Comm'n*, 540 U.S. 93, 203-209 (2003). The holding of *McConnell* rested to a large extent on an earlier case, *Austin v. Michigan Chamber of Commerce*, 494 U.S. 652 (1990). *Austin* had held that political speech may be banned based on the speaker's corporate identity.

In this case we are asked to reconsider *Austin* and, in effect, *McConnell*. It has been noted that "*Austin* was a significant departure from ancient *First Amendment* principles," *Federal Election Comm'n v. Wisconsin Right to Life, Inc.*, 551 U.S. 449, 490 (2007) (*WRTL*) (Scalia, J., concurring in part and concurring in judgment). We agree with that conclusion and hold that *stare decisis* does not compel the continued acceptance of *Austin*. The Government may regulate corporate political speech through disclaimer and disclosure requirements, but it may not suppress that speech altogether. We turn to the case now before us.

I

A

Citizens United is a nonprofit corporation [exempt from taxation under IRC § 501(c)(4)]. It brought this action in the United States District Court for the District of Columbia. A three-judge court later convened to hear the cause. The resulting judgment gives rise to this appeal.

Citizens United has an annual budget of about $12 million. Most of its funds are from donations by individuals; but, in addition, it accepts a small portion of its funds from for-profit corporations. In January 2008, Citizens United released a film entitled *Hillary: The Movie*. We refer to the film as *Hillary*. It is a 90-minute documentary about then-Senator Hillary Clinton, who was a candidate in the Democratic Party's 2008 Presidential primary elections. *Hillary* mentions Senator Clinton by name and depicts interviews with political commentators and other persons, most of them quite critical of Senator Clinton. *Hillary* was released in theaters and on DVD, but Citizens United wanted to increase distribution by making it available through video-on-demand.

Video-on-demand allows digital cable subscribers to select programming from various menus, including movies, television shows, sports, news, and music. The viewer can watch the program at any time and can elect to rewind or pause the program. In December 2007, a cable company offered, for a payment of $1.2 million, to make *Hillary* available on a video-on-demand channel called "Elections '08." Some video-on-demand services require viewers to pay a small fee to view a selected program, but here the proposal was to make *Hillary* available to viewers free of charge.

To implement the proposal, Citizens United was prepared to pay for the video-on-demand; and to promote the film, it produced two 10-second ads and one 30-second ad for *Hillary*. Each ad includes a short (and, in our view, pejorative) statement about Senator Clinton, followed by the name of the movie and the movie's Web site address. Citizens United desired to promote the video-on-demand offering by running advertisements on broadcast and cable television.

B

Before the Bipartisan Campaign Reform Act of 2002 (BCRA), federal law prohibited—and still does prohibit—corporations and unions from using general treasury funds to make direct contributions to candidates or independent expenditures that expressly advocate the election or defeat of a candidate, through any form of media, in connection with certain qualified federal elections. *2 U.S.C. § 441b (2000 ed.);* see *McConnell, supra*, at 204 and n. 87; *Federal Election Comm'n v. Massachusetts Citizens for Life, Inc.*, 479 U.S. 238, 249 (1986) (*MCFL*). BCRA § 203 amended § 441b to prohibit any "electioneering communication" as well. 2 U.S.C. § 441b(b)(2) (2006 ed.). An electioneering communication is defined as "any broadcast, cable, or satellite communication" that "refers to a clearly identified candidate for Federal office" and is made within 30 days of a primary or 60 days of a general election. § 434(f)(3)(A). The Federal Election Commission's (FEC) regulations further define an electioneering communication as a communication that is "publicly distributed." 11 CFR § 100.29(a)(2) (2009). "In the case of a candidate for nomination for President ... *publicly distributed* means" that the communication "[c]an be received by 50,000 or more persons in a State where a primary election ... is being held within 30 days." § 100.29(b)(3)(ii)(A). Corporations and unions are barred from using their general treasury funds for express advocacy or electioneering communications. They may establish, however, a "separate segregated fund" (known as a political action committee, or PAC) for these purposes. 2 U.S.C. § 441b(b)(2). The moneys received by the segregated fund are limited to donations from stockholders and employees of the corporation or, in the case of unions, members of the union. *Ibid.*

C

Citizens United wanted to make *Hillary* available through video-on-demand within 30 days of the 2008 primary elections. It feared, however, that both the film and the ads would be covered by § 441b's ban on corporate-funded independent expenditures, thus subjecting the corporation to civil and criminal penalties under § 437g. In December 2007, Citizens United sought declaratory and injunctive relief against the FEC. It argued that (1) § 441b is unconstitutional as applied to *Hillary;* and (2) BCRA's disclaimer and disclosure requirements, BCRA §§ 201 and 311, 116 Stat. 88, 105, are unconstitutional as applied to *Hillary* and to the three ads for the movie.

The District Court denied Citizens United's motion for a preliminary injunction, 530 F. Supp. 2d 274 (DC 2008) (*per curiam*), and then granted the FEC's motion for summary judgment. The court held that § 441b was facially constitutional under *McConnell*, and that § 441b was constitutional as applied to *Hillary* because it was "susceptible of no other interpretation than to inform the electorate that Senator Clinton is unfit for office, that the United States would be a dangerous place in a President Hillary Clinton world, and that viewers should vote against her." 530 F. Supp. 2d, at 279. The court also rejected Citizens United's challenge to BCRA's disclaimer and disclosure requirements. It noted that "the Supreme Court has written approvingly of disclosure provisions triggered by political speech even though the speech itself was constitutionally protected under the First Amendment." Id., at 281.

* * *

III

The First Amendment provides that "Congress shall make no law ... abridging the freedom of speech." Laws enacted to control or suppress speech may operate at different points in the speech process. The following are just a few examples of restrictions that have been attempted at different stages of the speech process—all laws found to be invalid: restrictions requiring a permit at the outset, *Watchtower Bible & Tract Soc. of N.Y., Inc. v. Village of Stratton*, 536 U.S. 150, 153 (2002); imposing a burden by impounding proceeds on receipts or royalties, *Simon & Schuster, Inc. v. Members of N.Y. State Crime Victims Bd.*, 502 U.S. 105, 108 (1991); seeking to exact a cost after the speech occurs, *New York Times Co. v. Sullivan*, 376 U.S., at 267; and subjecting the speaker to criminal penalties, *Brandenburg v. Ohio*, 395 U.S. 444, 445 (1969) (*per curiam*).

The law before us is an outright ban, backed by criminal sanctions. Section 441b makes it a felony for all corporations—including nonprofit advocacy corporations—either to expressly advocate the election or defeat of candidates or to broadcast electioneering communications within 30 days of a primary election and 60 days of a general election. Thus, the following acts would all be felonies under § 441b: The Sierra Club runs an ad, within the crucial phase of 60 days before the general election, that exhorts the public to disapprove of a Congressman who favors logging in national forests; the National Rifle Association publishes a book urging the public to vote for the challenger because the incumbent U. S. Senator supports a handgun ban; and the American Civil Liberties Union creates a Web site telling the public to vote for a Presidential candidate in light of that candidate's defense of free speech. These prohibitions are classic examples of censorship.

Section 441b is a ban on corporate speech notwithstanding the fact that a PAC created by a corporation can still speak. See *McConnell*, 540 U.S., at 330-333 (opinion of Kennedy, J.). A PAC is a separate association from the corporation. So the PAC exemption from § 441b's expenditure ban, § 441b(b)(2), does not allow corporations to speak. Even if a PAC could somehow allow a corporation to speak—and it does not—the option to form PACs does not alleviate the First Amendment problems with § 441b. PACs are burdensome alternatives; they are expensive to administer and subject to extensive regulations. For example, every PAC must appoint a treasurer, forward donations to the treasurer promptly, keep detailed records of the identities of the persons making donations, preserve receipts for three years, and file an organization statement and report changes to this information within 10 days. See *id.*, at 330-332 (quoting *MCFL*, 479 U.S., at 253-254 (opinion of Brennan, J.).

And that is just the beginning. PACs must file detailed monthly reports with the FEC, which are due at different times depending on the type of election that is about to occur:

> "'These reports must contain information regarding the amount of cash on hand; the total amount of receipts, detailed by 10 different categories; the identification of each political committee and candidate's authorized or affiliated committee making contributions, and any persons making loans, providing rebates, refunds, dividends, or interest or any other offset to operating expenditures in an aggregate amount over $200; the total amount of all disbursements, detailed by 12 different categories; the names of all authorized or affiliated committees to whom expenditures aggregating over $200 have been made; persons to whom loan repayments or refunds have been made; the total sum of all contributions, operating expenses,

> outstanding debts and obligations, and the settlement terms of the retirement of any debt or obligation.'" 540 U.S., at 331-332 (quoting *MCFL, supra*, at 253-254).

PACs have to comply with these regulations just to speak. This might explain why fewer than 2,000 of the millions of corporations in this country have PACs. . . . PACs, furthermore, must exist before they can speak. Given the onerous restrictions, a corporation may not be able to establish a PAC in time to make its views known regarding candidates and issues in a current campaign.

Section 441b's prohibition on corporate independent expenditures is thus a ban on speech. As a "restriction on the amount of money a person or group can spend on political communication during a campaign," that statute "necessarily reduces the quantity of expression by restricting the number of issues discussed, the depth of their exploration, and the size of the audience reached." *Buckley v. Valeo*, 424 U.S. 1, 19 (1976) (*per curiam*). Were the Court to uphold these restrictions, the Government could repress speech by silencing certain voices at any of the various points in the speech process. See *McConnell*, supra, at 251 (opinion of Scalia, J.) (Government could repress speech by "attacking all levels of the production and dissemination of ideas," for "effective public communication requires the speaker to make use of the services of others"). If § 441b applied to individuals, no one would believe that it is merely a time, place, or manner restriction on speech. Its purpose and effect are to silence entities whose voices the Government deems to be suspect.

Speech is an essential mechanism of democracy, for it is the means to hold officials accountable to the people. See *Buckley, supra*, at 14-15 ("In a republic where the people are sovereign, the ability of the citizenry to make informed choices among candidates for office is essential"). The right of citizens to inquire, to hear, to speak, and to use information to reach consensus is a precondition to enlightened self-government and a necessary means to protect it. The First Amendment "'has its fullest and most urgent application' to speech uttered during a campaign for political office." *Eu v. San Francisco County Democratic Central Comm.*, 489 U.S. 214, 223 (1989) (quoting *Monitor Patriot Co. v. Roy*, 401 U.S. 265, 272 (1971)); . . .

For these reasons, political speech must prevail against laws that would suppress it, whether by design or inadvertence. Laws that burden political speech are "subject to strict scrutiny," which requires the Government to prove that the restriction "furthers a compelling interest and is narrowly tailored to achieve that interest." *WRTL*, 551 U.S., at 464 (opinion of Roberts, C.J.). While it might be maintained that political speech simply cannot be banned or restricted as a categorical matter, see *Simon & Schuster*, 502 U.S., at 124 (Kennedy, J., concurring in judgment), the quoted language from *WRTL* provides a sufficient framework for protecting the relevant *First Amendment* interests in this case. We shall employ it here.

Premised on mistrust of governmental power, the First Amendment stands against attempts to disfavor certain subjects or viewpoints. See, *e.g.*, *United States v. Playboy Entertainment Group, Inc.*, 529 U.S. 803, 813 (2000) (striking down content-based restriction). Prohibited, too, are restrictions distinguishing among different speakers, allowing speech by some but not others. See *First Nat. Bank of Boston v. Bellotti*, 435 U.S. 765, 784 (1978). As instruments to censor, these categories are interrelated: Speech restrictions based on the identity of the speaker are all too often simply a means to control content.

Quite apart from the purpose or effect of regulating content, moreover, the Government may commit a constitutional wrong when by law it identifies certain preferred speakers. By taking the right to speak from some and giving it to others, the Government deprives the disadvantaged person or class of the right to use speech to strive to establish worth, standing, and respect for the speaker's voice. The Government may not by these means deprive the public of the right and privilege to determine for itself what speech and speakers are worthy of consideration. The First Amendment protects speech and speaker, and the ideas that flow from each.

The Court has upheld a narrow class of speech restrictions that operate to the disadvantage of certain persons, but these rulings were based on an interest in allowing governmental entities to perform their functions. See, *e.g.*, *Bethel School Dist. No. 403 v. Fraser*, 478 U.S. 675, 683 (1986) (protecting the "function of public school education"); *Jones v. North Carolina Prisoners' Labor Union, Inc.*, 433 U.S. 119, 129 (1977) (furthering "the legitimate penological objectives of the corrections system" (internal quotation marks omitted)); *Parker v. Levy*, 417 U.S. 733, 759 (1974) (ensuring "the capacity of the Government to discharge its [military] responsibilities" (internal quotation marks omitted)); *Civil Service Comm'n v. Letter Carriers*, 413 U.S. 548, 557 (1973) ("[F]ederal service should depend upon meritorious performance rather than political service"). The corporate independent expenditures at issue in this case, however, would not interfere with governmental functions, so these cases are inapposite. These precedents stand only for the proposition that there are certain governmental functions that cannot operate without some restrictions on particular kinds of speech. By contrast, it is inherent in the nature of the political process that voters must be free to obtain information from diverse sources in order to determine how to cast their votes. At least before *Austin*, the Court had not allowed the exclusion of a class of speakers from the general public dialogue.

We find no basis for the proposition that, in the context of political speech, the Government may impose restrictions on certain disfavored speakers. Both history and logic lead us to this conclusion.

A

1

The Court has recognized that First Amendment protection extends to corporations. [citations omitted] .... This protection has been extended by explicit holdings to the context of political speech. See, *e.g.*, *Button*, 371 U.S., at 428-429; *Grosjean v. American Press Co.*, 297 U.S. 233, 244 (1936). Under the rationale of these precedents, political speech does not lose *First Amendment* protection "simply because its source is a corporation." *Bellotti, supra*, at 784; see *Pacific Gas & Elec. Co. v. Public*

Util. Comm'n of Cal., 475 U.S. 1, 8 (1986) (plurality opinion) ("The identity of the speaker is not decisive in determining whether speech is protected. Corporations and other associations, like individuals, contribute to the 'discussion, debate, and the dissemination of information and ideas' that the First Amendment seeks to foster" (quoting *Bellotti*, 435 U.S., at 783).

The Court has thus rejected the argument that political speech of corporations or other associations should be treated differently under the First Amendment simply because such associations are not "natural persons." *Id.*, at 776; see *id.*, at 780, n. 16. Cf. id., at 828 (Rehnquist, J:, dissenting).

At least since the latter part of the 19th century, the laws of some States and of the United States imposed a ban on corporate direct contributions to candidates. See B. Smith, Unfree Speech: The Folly of Campaign Finance Reform 23 (2001). Yet not until 1947 did Congress first prohibit independent expenditures by corporations and labor unions in § 304 of the Labor Management Relations Act, 1947, 61 Stat. 159 (codified at 2 U.S.C. § 251 (1946 ed., Supp. I)). In passing this Act Congress overrode the veto of President Truman, who warned that the expenditure ban was a "dangerous intrusion on free speech." Message from the President of the United States, H. R. Doc. No. 334, 80th Cong., 1st Sess., 9 (1947).

For almost three decades thereafter, the Court did not reach the question whether restrictions on corporate and union expenditures are constitutional. See *WRTL*, 551 U.S., at 502 (opinion of Scalia, J.). The question was in the background of *United States v. CIO*, 335 U.S. 106 (1948). There, a labor union endorsed a congressional candidate in its weekly periodical. The Court stated that "the gravest doubt would arise in our minds as to [the federal expenditure prohibition's] constitutionality" if it were construed to suppress that writing. *Id.*, at 121. The Court engaged in statutory interpretation and found the statute did not cover the publication. *Id.*, at 121-122, and n. 20. Four Justices, however, said they would reach the constitutional question and invalidate the Labor Management Relations Act's expenditure ban. *Id.*, at 155 (Rutledge, J., joined by Black, Douglas, and Murphy, JJ., concurring in result). The concurrence explained that any "'undue influence'" generated by a speaker's "large expenditures" was outweighed "by the loss for democratic processes resulting from the restrictions upon free and full public discussion." *Id.*, at 143.

In *United States v. Automobile Workers*, 352 U.S. 567 (1957), the Court again encountered the independent expenditure ban, which had been recodified at 18 U.S.C. § 610 (1952 ed.). See 62 Stat. 723-724. After holding only that a union television broadcast that endorsed candidates was covered by the statute, the Court "[r]efus[ed] to anticipate constitutional questions" and remanded for the trial to proceed. 352 U.S., at 591. Three Justices dissented, arguing that the Court should have reached the constitutional question and that the ban on independent expenditures was unconstitutional:

> "Under our Constitution it is We The People who are sovereign. The people have the final say. The legislators are their spokesmen. The people determine

> through their votes the destiny of the nation. It is therefore important—vitally important—that all channels of communication be open to them during every election, that no point of view be restrained or barred, and that the people have access to the views of every group in the community." *Id.*, at 593 (opinion of Douglas, J., joined by Warren, C. J., and Black, J.).

The dissent concluded that deeming a particular group "too powerful" was not a "justificatio[n] for withholding First Amendment rights from any group—labor or corporate." *Id.*, at 597. The Court did not get another opportunity to consider the constitutional question in that case; for after a remand, a jury found the defendants not guilty. See Hayward, Revisiting the Fable of Reform, 45 Harv. J. Legis. 421, 463 (2008).

Later, in *Pipefitters v. United States*, 407 U.S. 385, 400-401 (1972), the Court reversed a conviction for expenditure of union funds for political speech—again without reaching the constitutional question. The Court would not resolve that question for another four years.

2

In *Buckley*, 424 U.S. 1, the Court addressed various challenges to the Federal Election Campaign Act of 1971 (FECA) as amended in 1974. These amendments created 18 U.S.C. § 608(e) (1970 ed., Supp. V), see 88 Stat. 1265, an independent expenditure ban separate from § 610 that applied to individuals as well as corporations and labor unions, *Buckley*, 424 U.S., at 23, 39, and n. 45.

Before addressing the constitutionality of § 608(e)'s independent expenditure ban, *Buckley* first upheld § 608(b), FECA's limits on direct contributions to candidates. The *Buckley* Court recognized a "sufficiently important" governmental interest in "the prevention of corruption and the appearance of corruption." *Id.*, at 25; see *id.*, at 26. This followed from the Court's concern that large contributions could be given "to secure a political *quid pro quo*." *Ibid.*

The *Buckley* Court explained that the potential for *quid pro quo* corruption distinguished direct contributions to candidates from independent expenditures. The Court emphasized that "the independent expenditure ceiling . . . fails to serve any substantial governmental interest in stemming the reality or appearance of corruption in the electoral process," *id.*, at 47-48, because "[t]he absence of prearrangement and coordination . . . alleviates the danger that expenditures will be given as a *quid pro quo* for improper commitments from the candidate," *id.*, at 47. *Buckley* invalidated § 608(e)'s restrictions on independent expenditures, with only one Justice dissenting. See *Federal Election Comm'n v. National Conservative Political Action Comm.*, 470 U.S. 480, 491, n. 3 (1985) (*NCPAC*).

Buckley did not consider § 610's separate ban on corporate and union independent expenditures, the prohibition that had also been in the background in *CIO*, *Automobile Workers*, and *Pipefitters*. Had § 610 been challenged in the wake of *Buckley*, however, it could not have been squared with the reasoning and analysis of that precedent. See *WRTL*, 551 U.S., at 487 (opinion of Scalia, J.) ("*Buckley* might well have been the last word on limitations on independent expenditures"); *Austin*, 494 U.S., at 683 (Scalia, J., dissenting). The expenditure ban invalidated in *Buckley*, § 608(e), applied to corporations and unions, 424 U.S., at 23, 39, n. 45; and some of the prevailing plaintiffs in *Buckley* were corporations, *id.*, at 8. The *Buckley* Court did not invoke the First Amendment's overbreadth doctrine, [citations omitted].

Notwithstanding this precedent, Congress recodified § 610's corporate and union expenditure ban at 2 U.S.C. § 441b four months after *Buckley* was decided. See 90 Stat. 490. Section 441b is the independent expenditure restriction challenged here.

Less than two years after *Buckley, Bellotti*, 435 U.S. 765, reaffirmed the First Amendment principle that the Government cannot restrict political speech based on the speaker's corporate identity. *Bellotti* could not have been clearer when it struck down a state-law prohibition on corporate independent expenditures related to referenda issues:

> "We thus find no support in the First Amendment, or in the decisions of this Court, for the proposition that speech that otherwise would be within the protection of the First Amendment loses that protection simply because its source is a corporation that cannot prove, to the satisfaction of a court, a material effect on its business or property. . . . [That proposition] amounts to an impermissible legislative prohibition of speech based on the identity of the interests that spokesmen may represent in public debate over controversial issues and a requirement that the speaker have a sufficiently great interest in the subject to justify communication.
>
> * * *
>
> "In the realm of protected speech, the legislature is constitutionally disqualified from dictating the subjects about which persons may speak and the speakers who may address a public issue." *Id.*, at 784-785.

It is important to note that the reasoning and holding of *Bellotti* did not rest on the existence of a viewpoint-discriminatory statute. It rested on the principle that the Government lacks the power to ban corporations from speaking.

Bellotti did not address the constitutionality of the State's ban on corporate independent expenditures to support candidates. In our view, however, that restriction would have been unconstitutional under *Bellotti*'s central principle: that the First Amendment does not allow political speech restrictions based on a speaker's corporate identity. See *ibid.*

3

Thus the law stood until *Austin. Austin* "uph[eld] a direct restriction on the independent expenditure of funds for political speech for the first time in [this Court's] history." 494 U.S., at 695 (Kennedy, J., dissenting). There, the Michigan Chamber of Commerce sought to use general treasury funds to run a newspaper ad supporting a specific candidate. Michigan law, however, prohibited corporate independent expenditures that supported or opposed any candidate for state office. A violation of the law was punishable as a felony. The Court sustained the speech prohibition.

To bypass *Buckley* and *Bellotti*, the *Austin* Court identified a new governmental interest in limiting political speech: an antidistortion interest. *Austin* found a compelling governmental interest in preventing "the corrosive and distorting effects of immense aggregations of wealth that are accumulated with the help of the corporate form and that have little or no correlation to the public's support for the corporation's political ideas." 494 U.S., at 660; see *id.*, at 659 (citing *MCFL*, 479 U.S., at 257; *NCPAC*, 470 U.S., at 500-501).

B

The Court is thus confronted with conflicting lines of precedent: a pre-*Austin* line that forbids restrictions on political speech based on the speaker's corporate identity and a post-*Austin* line that permits them. No case before *Austin* had held that Congress could prohibit independent expenditures for political speech based on the speaker's corporate identity. Before *Austin*, Congress had enacted legislation for this purpose, and the Government urged the same proposition before this Court. See *MCFL*, *supra*, at 257 (FEC posited that Congress intended to "curb the political influence of 'those who exercise control over large aggregations of capital'" (quoting *Automobile Workers*, 352 U.S., at 585)); *California Medical Assn. v. Federal Election Comm'n*, 453 U.S. 182, 201 (Congress believed that "differing structures and purposes" of corporations and unions "may require different forms of regulation in order to protect the integrity of the electoral process"). In neither of these cases did the Court adopt the proposition.

In its defense of the corporate-speech restrictions in § 441b, the Government notes the antidistortion rationale on which *Austin* and its progeny rest in part, yet it all but abandons reliance upon it. It argues instead that two other compelling interests support *Austin*'s holding that corporate expenditure restrictions are constitutional: an anticorruption interest, see 494 U.S., at 678 (Stevens, J., concurring), and a shareholder-protection interest, see *id.*, at 674-675 (Brennan, J., concurring). We consider the three points in turn.

1

As for *Austin*'s antidistortion rationale, the Government does little to defend it. See Tr. of Oral Arg. 45-48 (Sept. 9, 2009). And with good reason, for the rationale cannot support § 441b.

If the First Amendment has any force, it prohibits Congress from fining or jailing citizens, or associations of citizens, for simply engaging in political speech. If the antidistortion rationale were to be accepted, however, it would permit Government to ban political speech simply because the speaker is an association that has taken on the corporate form. The Government contends that *Austin* permits it to ban corporate expenditures for almost all forms of communication stemming from a corporation. See Part II-E, *supra;* Tr. of Oral Arg. 66 (Sept. 9, 2009); see also *id.*, at 26-31 (Mar. 24, 2009). If *Austin* were correct, the Government could prohibit a corporation from expressing political views in media beyond those presented here, such as by printing books. The Government responds "that the FEC has never applied this statute to a book," and if it did, "there would be quite [a] good as-applied challenge." Tr. of Oral Arg. 65 (Sept. 9, 2009). This troubling assertion of brooding governmental power cannot be reconciled with the confidence and stability in civic discourse that the First Amendment must secure.

Political speech is "indispensable to decisionmaking in a democracy, and this is no less true because the speech comes from a corporation rather than an individual." *Bellotti,* 435 U.S., at 777 (footnote omitted); see *ibid.* (the worth of speech "does not depend upon the identity of its source, whether corporation, association, union, or individual"); *Buckley,* 424 U.S., at 48-49 ("[T]he concept that government may restrict the speech of some elements of our society in order to enhance the relative voice of others is wholly foreign to the First Amendment"); *Automobile Workers, supra,* at 597 (Douglas, J., dissenting); *CIO,* 335 U.S., at 154-155 (Rutledge, J., concurring in result). This protection for speech is inconsistent with *Austin*'s antidistortion rationale. *Austin* sought to defend the antidistortion rationale as a means to prevent corporations from obtaining "'an unfair advantage in the political marketplace'" by using "'resources amassed in the economic marketplace.'" 494 U.S., at 659 (quoting *MCFL, supra,* at 257). But *Buckley* rejected the premise that the Government has an interest "in equalizing the relative ability of individuals and groups to influence the outcome of elections." 424 U.S., at 48; see *Bellotti, supra,* at 791, n. 30. *Buckley* was specific in stating that "the skyrocketing cost of political campaigns" could not sustain the governmental prohibition. 424 U.S., at 26. The First Amendment's protections do not depend on the speaker's "financial ability to engage in public discussion." *Id.,* at 49.

The Court reaffirmed these conclusions when it invalidated the BCRA provision that increased the cap on contributions to one candidate if the opponent made certain expenditures from personal funds. See *Davis v. FEC,* 554 U.S. 724, 742 (2008) ("Leveling electoral opportunities means making and implementing judgments about which strengths should be permitted to contribute to the outcome of an election. The Constitution, however, confers upon voters, not Congress, the power to choose the Members of the House of Representatives, Art. I, § 2, and it is a dangerous business for Congress to use the election laws to influence the voters' choices"). The rule that political speech cannot be limited based on a speaker's wealth is a necessary consequence of the premise that the First Amendment generally prohibits the suppression of political speech based on the speaker's identity.

Either as support for its antidistortion rationale or as a further argument, the *Austin* majority undertook to distinguish wealthy individuals from corporations on the ground that "[s]tate law grants corporations special advantages — such as limited liability, perpetual life, and favorable treatment of the accumulation and distribution of assets." 494 U.S., at 658-659. This does not suffice, however, to allow laws prohibiting speech. "It is rudimentary that the State cannot exact as the price of those special advantages the forfeiture of First Amendment rights." *Id.*, at 680 (Scalia, J., dissenting).

It is irrelevant for purposes of the First Amendment that corporate funds may "have little or no correlation to the public's support for the corporation's political ideas." *Id.*, at 660 (majority opinion). All speakers, including individuals and the media, use money amassed from the economic marketplace to fund their speech. The First Amendment protects the resulting speech, even if it was enabled by economic transactions with persons or entities who disagree with the speaker's ideas. See *id.*, at 707 (Kennedy, J., dissenting) ("Many persons can trace their funds to corporations, if not in the form of donations, then in the form of dividends, interest, or salary").

* * *

The censorship we now confront is vast in its reach. The Government has "muffle[d] the voices that best represent the most significant segments of the economy." *McConnell, supra*, at 257-258 (opinion of Scalia, J.). And "the electorate [has been] deprived of information, knowledge and opinion vital to its function." *CIO*, 335 U.S., at 144 (Rutledge, J., concurring in result). By suppressing the speech of manifold corporations, both for-profit and nonprofit, the Government prevents their voices and viewpoints from reaching the public and advising voters on which persons or entities are hostile to their interests. Factions will necessarily form in our Republic, but the remedy of "destroying the liberty" of some factions is "worse than the disease." The Federalist No. 10, p. 130 (B. Wright ed. 1961) (J. Madison). Factions should be checked by permitting them all to speak, see *ibid.*, and by entrusting the people to judge what is true and what is false.

The purpose and effect of this law is to prevent corporations, including small and nonprofit corporations, from presenting both facts and opinions to the public. This makes *Austin*'s antidistortion rationale all the more an aberration. "[T]he First Amendment protects the right of corporations to petition legislative and administrative bodies." *Bellotti*, 435 U.S., at 792, n (citing *California Motor Transport Co. v. Trucking Unlimited*, 404 U.S. 508, 510-511; *Eastern Railroad Presidents Conference v. Noerr Motor Freight, Inc.*, 365 U.S. 127, 137-138 (1961)). Corporate executives and employees counsel Members of Congress and Presidential administrations on many issues, as a matter of routine and often in private. An *amici* brief filed on behalf of Montana and 25 other States notes that lobbying and corporate communications with elected officials occur on a regular basis. Brief for State of Montana et al. 19. When that phenomenon is coupled with § 441b, the result is that smaller or nonprofit corporations cannot raise a voice to object when other corporations, including those with vast wealth, are cooperating with the Government. That cooperation may sometimes be voluntary, or it may be at the demand of a Government official who uses his or her authority, influence, and power to threaten corporations to support the Government's policies. Those kinds of interactions are often unknown and unseen. The speech that § 441b forbids, though, is public, and all can judge its content and purpose. References to massive corporate treasuries should not mask the real operation of this law. Rhetoric ought not obscure reality.

Even if §441b's expenditure ban were constitutional, wealthy corporations could still lobby elected officials, although smaller corporations may not have the resources to do so. And wealthy individuals and unincorporated associations can spend unlimited amounts on independent expenditures. See, *e.g.*, *WRTL*, 551 U.S., at 503-504 (opinion of Scalia, J.) ("In the 2004 election cycle, a mere 24 individuals contributed an astounding total of $142 million to [26 U.S.C. §527 organizations]"). Yet certain disfavored associations of citizens—those that have taken on the corporate form—are penalized for engaging in the same political speech.

When Government seeks to use its full power, including the criminal law, to command where a person may get his or her information or what distrusted source he or she may not hear, it uses censorship to control thought. This is unlawful. The First Amendment confirms the freedom to think for ourselves The Government contends further that corporate independent expenditures can be limited because of its interest in protecting dissenting shareholders from being compelled to fund corporate political speech. This asserted interest, like *Austin*'s antidistortion rationale, would allow the Government to ban the political speech even of media corporations. See *supra,* at 352-354. Assume, for example, that a shareholder of a corporation that owns a newspaper disagrees with the political views the newspaper expresses. See *Austin*, 494 U.S., at 687 (Scalia, J., dissenting). Under the Government's view, that potential disagreement could give the Government the authority to restrict the media corporation's political speech. The First Amendment does not allow that power. There is, furthermore, little evidence of abuse that cannot be corrected by shareholders "through the procedures of corporate democracy." *Bellotti*, 435 U.S., at 794; see *ibid*., n. 34.

Those reasons are sufficient to reject this shareholder-protection interest; and, moreover, the statute is both underinclusive and overinclusive. As to the first, if Congress had been seeking to protect dissenting shareholders, it would not have banned corporate speech in only certain media within 30 or 60 days before an election. A dissenting shareholder's interests would be implicated by speech in any media at any time. As to the second, the statute is overinclusive because it covers all corporations, including nonprofit corporations and for-profit corporations with only single shareholders. As to other corporations, the remedy is not to restrict speech but to consider and explore other regulatory mechanisms. The regulatory mechanism here, based on speech, contravenes the First Amendment.

[Citizens United is generally chalked up as a 5-4 decision. Only the majority opinion is included above. Kennedy, J., delivered the opinion of the Court, in which Roberts, C.J., and Scalia and Alito, JJ., joined, in which Thomas, J., joined as to all but Part IV, and in which Stevens, Ginsburg, Breyer, and Sotomayor, JJ., joined as to Part IV. Roberts, C.J., filed a concurring opinion, in which Alito, J., joined. Scalia, J., filed a concurring opinion, in which Alito, J., joined, and in which Thomas, J., joined in part. Stevens, J., filed an opinion concurring in part and dissenting in part, in which Ginsburg, Breyer, and Sotomayor, JJ., joined. Thomas, J., filed an opinion concurring in part and dissenting in part.]

Question

Preacher-Man is a minister to a large congregation that is organized as a tax-exempt religious corporation. Each week, Preacher-Man's congregation airs a nationally televised religious service watched by millions of people. Preacher-Man's sermons are the primary activity of the religious service. Preacher-Man is very influential in the Conservaliberal Party, and during each election cycle, nominees seek his support, although nominees of the opposition Liberalconserve Party do so only half-heartedly. During the most recent election cycle, Preacher-Man gave his personal endorsement to the Conservaliberal candidate for President. On a few occasions, Preacher-Man delivered sermons during the televised services warning true believers to avoid a certain activity most often associated with the opposition, Liberalconserve Party. Normally, Preacher-Man's admonitions are supported by references to the congregation's written book of beliefs.

With funding from his congregation, Preacher-Man has participated in several "get out the vote" campaigns and voter drives, most often in areas that have historically voted for Conservaliberal candidates. Preacher-Man never appeared with a Conservaliberal candidate when he appeared at the voter drives, but whenever he did appear in public with a candidate, the candidate was always from the Conservaliberal Party.

As the election draws near, Preacher-Man normally goes on tour, visiting several other congregations of the same faith and delivering a sermon on issues related to the election and supported by the written book of beliefs.

For one week during the campaign, Preacher-Man traveled around the country in the Conservaliberal's official campaign bus and appeared at rallies with the Conservaliberal candidate. Although he never gave speeches, Preacher-Man was always prominently featured in television and newspaper reports of the rallies.

Assume you are an IRS official and the Commissioner routes to you a letter from a Liberalconserve Congressperson complaining that the congregation is intervening in the political campaign and demanding that the Service revoke the congregation's exempt status. Prepare a short memorandum to the Commissioner outlining the issues that should be resolved before responding to the Congressperson.

B. Political Organizations

CODE: § 527

REGS.: §§ 1.527-2; 1.527-5; 1.527-6.

Branch Ministries is provocative for a number of reasons, not the least of which is its discussion of so called "527 organizations." First, the opinion asserts that a social welfare organization that is exempt under § 504 is subject to the complete ban on campaign intervention. This is almost certainly incorrect, as we will see when we more fully consider social welfare organizations in Chapter 20. The cited regulation, § 1.501(c)(4)-1(a)(2)(ii), merely excludes such activity from the range of activities that promote social welfare. Because a 501(c)(4) organization need only *primarily* engage in activities that promote social welfare, and because there is no explicit ban on campaign intervention, such an organization can engage in insubstantial campaign intervention activities. *See* Treas. Reg. § 1.501(c)(4)-1(a)(2)(ii); S. Rept. No. 93-1357, 2d Sess. at 29, *reprinted in* 1975-1 C.B. 517, 533–34.

Second, the Court resolves the constitutional issue by explaining that a charity is not entirely foreclosed from campaign interventions because it may establish a 501(c)(4) organization. In turn, the 501(c)(4) can create a 527 organization — in effect a second tier subsidiary of the 501(c)(3) — and the 527 organization can engage in campaign activity.[2] The Service, however, maintains that a 501(c)(3) organization cannot establish a 527 organization as a first-tier subsidiary to engage in campaign intervention without the 527 organization's activities being imputed to the 501(c)(3) resulting in the revocation of tax exemption. Its reasoning would seem equally applicable to a second-tier subsidiary even with an intervening 501(c)(4) organization:

> If prohibited political campaign activities conducted by the [527 first tier subsidiary] are not imputed to the [501(c)(3)], section 527 would, in contravention of Congress' express desire, affect the prohibition against section 501(c)(3) organizations conducting such activities. In the absence of such imputation, a section 501(c)(3) organization could indirectly conduct a wide-ranging program of intervention in political campaigns merely by following the formality of establishing a separate [527 organization]. Such a result is clearly not in accordance with the intent of Congress.

GCM 39694 (Jan. 21, 1988).

However sensible the Service's reasoning — that Congress would never welcome through the back door that which it bars through the front — it must still give way to constitutional grounds. And at least one commentator has forcefully argued that completely foreclosing a 501(c)(3) organization from directly engaging in protected political speech — enforcing that prohibition with the loss of tax exemption — is

2. The 501(c)(4) can even have the same board members as the 501(c)(3), and those board members can then dictate the activities of the 501(c)(4), so long as the decision-making process (i.e., meetings and records) are kept separate from the decision making process of the 501(c)(3).

unconstitutional in the absence of a viable alternate method of engaging in the protected activity. Laura Brown Chisolm, *Politics and Charity: A Proposal for Peaceful Coexistence*, 58 GEO. WASH. L. REV. 308 (1990). The Court in *Branch Ministries* implicitly agrees with the argument and then fashions a solution. But if a 501(c)(3) can establish a second-tier subsidiary to engage in campaign intervention, why can't it simply establish a first-tier subsidiary to do the same thing? What substantive or constitutional reason is there to require a second layer of bureaucracy when one layer will do just fine? The answers to such questions we leave for in-class discussion and debate. We turn now to a consideration of the details of IRC § 527.

Prior to 1975, there was uncertainty regarding the proper tax treatment of political parties, campaign committees, and other organizations that primarily worked for the election of persons to public office. The Service did not require such organizations to file tax returns nor pay tax on their income, because it believed that the income was composed entirely of nontaxable gifts. In 1968, however, the Service became concerned that these political organizations were earning income through ordinary trades and business, and also making expenditures for individual personal benefit rather than in an effort to influence elections. In Revenue Procedure 68-19, 1968-1 C.B. 810, the Service announced that amounts expended by political organizations for the personal benefit of a political candidate will constitute taxable income to the candidate. It subsequently stated, in Announcement 73-84, 1973-2 C.B. 461, that it would begin requiring political organizations to file tax returns and pay tax on investment income, income from any ancillary commercial activities and gains from sales of appreciated property. However, it also stated that it would not enforce the requirements of Announcement 73-84 until Congress had an opportunity to consider the matter. Congress subsequently enacted IRC § 527.

Generally consistent with the Service's proposed approach, section 527 taxes political organizations on all of their "political organization taxable income." IRC § 527(b). A political organization is an entity, organization, or fund that is organized and operated primarily to accept contributions or make expenditures for exempt functions. IRC § 527(e)(1). An exempt function is any activity designed to influence the selection, nomination, election, or appointment of a person to federal, state, or local public office, or office in a political organization. The phrase also includes activities seeking to influence the appointment of presidential or vice presidential electors. IRC § 527(e)(2). Political organization taxable income is essentially all income (less deductions directly connected therewith) except "exempt function income." IRC § 527(c). Except for "principal campaign committees," the rate of tax is the highest rate applicable to corporations under IRC § 11(b) for ordinary income, and the applicable capital gains rate for any capital gains. IRC § 527(b). Principle Campaign Committees are taxed under the normal graduated rates of IRC § 11(b). IRC § 527(h).

Exempt function income includes amounts received as a contribution of money or property, dues or assessments from members of the organization, proceeds of political fundraising events, or the sale of campaign materials and proceeds from certain bingo games to the extent these amounts are segregated for use in an exempt function. IRC § 527(c)(3). The regulations state that the sale of campaign materials must be in conjunction with a political activity conducted for purposes other than to raise money (e.g., events designed to rally support for a candidate, not just raise money). Treas. Reg. 1.527-3(e). Exempt function income must be kept separate from all the other funds of the organization or individual establishing the organization and must be used primarily for exempt functions. Treas. Reg. 1.527-2(b). The regulations elaborate by stating that the fund must be clearly identified and if more than an insubstantial amount of the funds are used for purposes other than an exempt function, the fund will not be treated as a section 527 organization.

The statute and regulations confirm that amounts expended for a candidate's personal use will be included in the candidate's gross income. 527(d), Treas. Reg. 1.527-5(a)(1). Moreover, if amounts are spent for other than an exempt function and the organization benefits, the organization must include the amount spent in its taxable income. Certain expenditures, however, will not result in taxable income to the candidate or the organization. If the organization contributes to another political organization, a public charity, or federal, state, or local government, the contributed amount will not be taxable. IRC § 527(d); Treas. Reg. 1.527-5(b). After a campaign has ended, a political organization can transfer any leftover funds to any of the organizations just mentioned (within a reasonable time), or it may retain the funds "in reasonable anticipation" of future exempt functions. Treas. Reg. 1.527-5(c). In such cases, the excess funds will not be taxable to the organization.

IRC § 527(f) and Treasury Regulation 1.527-6 seek to equalize treatment of political organizations and 501(c) organizations that engage in campaign activity. If a 501(c) organization (that is not otherwise prohibited from doing so) makes an exempt function expenditure, it will be taxable on the lesser of its net investment income or the amount of the expenditure. In the absence of this rule, 501(c) organizations would have an advantage over 527 organizations because they could use untaxed earnings — net investment income includes interest, dividends, rents, royalties, and net gains on the sale of assets, all of which would otherwise be exempt from tax under 512(b) — to engage in campaign activities. 527 organizations could not use such untaxed income (since the investment income of 527 organizations is taxable). A 501(c) organization can avoid the tax on its investment income by establishing a "separate segregated fund" into which it deposits political contributions or dues to be used for exempt functions. The separate segregated fund will then be treated as a separate 527 organization and only the investment income earned by the fund will be taxed. IRC § 527(f)(3); Treas. Reg. 1.527-6(f). Political contributions and dues collected by the 501(c) organization and transferred to the separate segregated fund will not constitute an exempt function expenditure by the 501(c) organization. However, as the case below demonstrates, the 501(c) organization has the burden of maintaining adequate records to prove that the funds transferred to the separate segregated fund consisted solely of political contributions and not investment income. If the 501(c) organization fails to meet that burden it will be subject to tax on its net investment income.

Alaska Public Service Employees Local 71 v. Commissioner

T.C. Memo. 1991-650

Memorandum Findings of Fact and Opinion

Respondent determined a deficiency of $11,454 for taxable year 1984. The issues for decision are:

(1) Whether petitioner, a labor organization, is liable for tax under section 527(b) and (f) as the result of its 1984 transfer of $25,000 to its separate segregated political organization account. We hold that it is.

(2) Whether petitioner can, in effect, reverse the transaction and avoid the tax by transferring $25,000 from its political account back to its general account in 1987, after respondent notified petitioner that it intended to assess tax for the transfer. We hold that it cannot.

Findings of Fact

Some of the facts have been stipulated and are so found.

1. Petitioner and Petitioner's Political League

Petitioner Alaska Public Service Employees Local 71 is a labor organization as defined in section 501(c)(5) and is exempt from tax under section 501(a). It is included under Group Exemption Number 121 issued to its parent, the Laborers' International Union of America, AFL-CIO.

Petitioner, an unincorporated association, had its principal offices in Anchorage, Alaska, when it filed its petition in this case.

During 1984, petitioner maintained a general fund in which it deposited dues and other revenue items and from which it paid all expenses. During 1984, the general fund had account No. 3-770818 at the National Bank of Alaska.

Petitioner also maintained a separate segregated fund within the meaning of section 527(f)(3) and section 1.527-2(b), Income Tax Regs., for making political contributions during 1984. It was called the Political League (Political League). During 1984, the Political League had account No. 3-006366 at the National Bank of Alaska.

Most of the funds available to the Political League in 1984 were contributed by union members, including an apportionment of 5 percent of general fund dues to the political fund that could have been discontinued at the election of the member. Some additional contributions were withheld from the salaries of petitioner's office staff pursuant to voluntary payroll deduction agreements. Member contributions to the political fund were normally deposited in the general account as part of member dues. Office staff contributions were simply left in the general account when petitioner issued its payroll checks. The amounts destined for the political fund from these two sources were promptly transferred (up to four times each month) from the general account to the separate account for the political fund. The parties agree that the general fund served only as a conduit for these moneys as provided in section 527.

2. Petitioner's $25,000 Additional Transfer to the Political League

During 1984, petitioner's executive board authorized the transfer of an additional $25,000 from the general fund to the Political League. The transfer was made on October 8, 1984. The $25,000 transfer was in addition to the five percent allocation of member dues and the voluntary contributions to the Political League through payroll deductions described above.

The $25,000 transfer was made from undesignated funds in petitioner's general fund, containing dues and other revenue items. The record contains only the total amount of interest earned by petitioner in 1984, and a list of deposits by date and amount for the months May through September 1984.

On May 29, 1987, respondent notified petitioner that it proposed to assess tax against petitioner under section 527 as a result of the $25,000 transfer in 1984.

At a meeting on July 6, 1987, petitioner's executive board attempted to reverse the $25,000 payment by adopting a motion providing for the transfer of $25,000 from the political fund to the general fund. On July 15, 1987, a $25,000 check was issued from the Political League account to the general fund.

During 1984, petitioner earned and received $59,127 in interest income. Petitioner's net investment income during 1984 was more than $25,000, the amount of the transfer from petitioner's general account to the account of the Political League.

Opinion

The issue for decision is whether petitioner is liable for the tax imposed by section 527 as a result of its transfer in 1984 of $25,000 to its Political League.

The parties agree that petitioner transferred $25,000 from its general account to a separate account maintained to fund political contributions, that petitioner is a section 501(c)(5) labor organization, that the account to which this money was transferred was a separate segregated fund within the meaning of section 527(f)(3), that the Political League is a political organization engaged in influencing the selection of political candidates, and that petitioner's net investment income was in excess of $25,000.

1. Petitioner's Transfer of $25,000 in 1984

Petitioner argues that section 1.527-6(e), Income Tax Regs., allows the transfer of petitioner's dues to its separate segregated fund. Section 1.527-6(e), Income Tax Regs., provides:

(e) Transfer not treated as exempt function expenditures. Provided the provisions of this paragraph (e) are met, a transfer of political contributions or dues collected by a section 501(c) organization to a separate segregated fund as defined in paragraph

(f) of this section is not treated as an expenditure for an exempt function (within the meaning of § 1.527-2(c)). Such transfers must be made promptly after the receipt of such amounts by the section 501(c) organization, and must be made directly to the separate segregated fund. A transfer is considered promptly and directly made if:

(1) The procedures followed by the section 501(c) organization satisfy the requirements of applicable Federal or State campaign law and regulations;

(2) The section 501(c) organization maintains adequate records to demonstrate that amounts transferred in fact consist of political contributions or dues, rather than investment income; and

(3) The political contributions or dues transferred were not used to earn investment income for the section 501(c) organization.

Petitioner contends that: (1) It followed Federal and State campaign laws, (2) it maintained adequate records which demonstrate that the amounts transferred consisted of dues and not investment income, and (3) the dues transferred were not used to earn investment income. Petitioner asserts that because section 1.527-6(e), Income Tax Regs., specifically allows the transfer of dues funds to a separate segregated fund and because petitioner fulfilled the regulatory requirements, petitioner's tax-exempt status should be recognized, and the deficiency should not be sustained.

Respondent argues that all of the requirements of section 527(b) and (f) are met and that petitioner is liable for the tax imposed by section 527.

Respondent notes that because it is undisputed that this separate segregated account was used to fund political contributions, the account is treated as a political organization for purposes of section 527(f)(3) during 1984 and the disbursements from the fund during 1984 clearly would have been toward an exempt function pursuant to section 527(e)(2). See sec. 1.527-6(f), Income Tax Regs. Respondent contends that the transfer from petitioner's general account to its Political League was therefore an expenditure of petitioner's funds for a section 527(e)(2) exempt function. Sec. 1.527-6(b)(1)(ii), Income Tax Regs. Accordingly, pursuant to section 527(f), petitioner is liable for the tax imposed by section 527(b) on the lesser of the amount transferred or its net investment income.

Moreover, respondent contends that the parties have agreed on all of the facts necessary to fix the amount of the deficiency: that is, that the amount transferred was $25,000 and that petitioner's investment income during 1984 was greater than this amount.

We hold that petitioner's transfer of $25,000 from its general fund to its Political League is subject to the tax imposed by section 527(f). The transfer was made from undesignated funds in petitioner's general account, containing dues and other revenue items. The record contains only the total amount of interest earned by petitioner in 1984, and a list of deposits by date and amount for the months May through September 1984. Petitioner did not persuade the Court that the transfer consisted of dues and not investment income, and that the dues were not used to earn investment income (i.e., interest) before transfer. Accordingly, petitioner failed to meet the requirements of section 1.527-6(e), Income Tax Regs.

2. Petitioner's Return of the $25,000 in 1987

Petitioner argues that courts recognize equitable principles which negate the imposition of taxation upon the return and rescission of funds. *United States v. Merrill*, 211 F.2d 297 (9th Cir. 1954); *Gargaro v. United States*, 73 F. Supp. 973, 109 Ct. Cl. 528 (1947); *Lilly v. Commissioner*, 14 B.T.A. 703 (1928) (advances drawn by taxpayer in tax year and repaid in following year do not constitute income). Petitioner further contends that its tax-exempt status should be respected since it returned the funds immediately upon realizing a tax assessment would be imposed. Petitioner maintains that its good faith rescission and return of the funds is sufficient to undo the transaction.

Petitioner further argues that the return of $25,000 in 1987 effectively negates the transaction and that any tax which would otherwise apply under section 527(f)(3) should also be negated.

Under section 527(b), an exempt organization is taxed on an amount equal to the lesser of its political campaign expenditures or its "net investment income." Thus, such an organization effectively loses the tax exemption on its investment earnings to the extent it uses funds to influence or attempt to influence the selection of candidates for government or political party office.

Respondent contends that petitioner's attempt to avoid this tax by its 1987 transfer of $25,000 from its political account to its general account after notice of an IRS examination, should not prevail. Respondent argues that to allow a taxpayer to change the tax consequences of a transaction that occurred in an earlier year simply by reversing the net result of that transaction in a later one is inconsistent with the annual accounting concept that is now well fixed as a part of Federal tax law. *See Healy v. United States*, 345 U.S. 278 (1953); *United States v. Lewis*, 340 U.S. 590 (1951); *North American Oil Consolidated v. Burnet*, 286 U.S. 417 (1932); *Burnet v. Sanford & Brooks Co.*, 282 U.S. 359 (1931). Thus, respondent argues that transactions that are closed and completed in one taxable year are taxed in that year absent some statutory provision that allows the year to be reopened.

Respondent maintains that Federal income taxes are imposed on transactions as they occur. Thus, respondent argues petitioner cannot escape the tax by contending that it would not have made the transfer had it known that the transfer would form the basis for a tax or that another nontaxable transaction could have achieved the same result.

Moreover, respondent claims, to recognize such a reversal when made after the IRS has determined to assess additional tax as a result of the original transaction would substantially interfere with the orderly collection of revenue by making it impossible for the IRS to enforce the provisions of the Internal Revenue Code. *See Healy v. Commissioner, supra* at 284–285.

We agree with respondent. We know of no statutory provision that would afford petitioner the relief it seeks. Section 1341 is clearly inapplicable because there was no prior inclusion of an amount in income under a claim of right and because petitioner's repayment to reverse the taxable transaction was voluntary.

We do not read petitioner's cited cases to stand for the proposition that equitable principles require the imposition of tax be nullified upon the return and rescission of funds. In *United States v. Merrill, supra* at 303, the Ninth Circuit, the circuit to which this case is appealable, followed the Supreme Court's opinion in *North American Oil Consolidated Co. v. Burnet, supra*, and held that, under the claim of right doctrine, a taxpayer who receives earnings under a claim of right and without restriction as to its disposition is ordinarily deemed to have received taxable income, even though he may not be entitled to retain the money and even though he may still be required to restore its equivalent. The Ninth Circuit further explained:

> That rule is founded upon the proposition that, when funds are received by a taxpayer under claim of right, he must be held taxable thereon, for the Treasury cannot be compelled to determine whether the claim is without legal warrant, and repayment of funds in a later year cannot, consistently with the annual accounting concept, justify a refund of the taxes paid.

211 F.2d at 304.

Similarly, petitioner's reliance on *Lilly v. Commissioner, supra*, is misplaced. In *Lilly*, the taxpayer drew $24,113.43 as advances against his salary and commissions but earned only $19,856.76. The taxpayer repaid the advances in a later year. The Court ruled that the taxpayer was taxable only on the amount actually earned by him. We believe that the Court's finding that the advances were repaid is relevant in establishing that the advances involved were loans, and that repayment of the advances in a later year thus had no impact on their taxability in the earlier year.

Petitioner also cites *Gargaro v. United States, supra*, in support of its theory that its transfer of $25,000 from its separate segregated political fund to its general fund negates the tax determined by respondent by, in effect, undoing the taxable transaction. In *Gargaro*, the taxpayer was paid a bonus based on a contemporaneous calculation of the net earnings of his corporate employer. After the corporation refunded a portion of its earnings in a later year and its net income for the earlier year was correspondingly reduced, the taxpayer repaid the portion of his bonus attributable to the returned earnings in a taxable year after the year in which the full bonus was reported. The taxpayer then filed a claim for refund for the year the bonus was originally reported, citing his repayment of a portion of the bonus in the later year. The court in *Gargaro* awarded the taxpayer the refund he requested.

While *Gargaro* arguably supports petitioner's position, we question its continuing validity in view of its reliance on the Supreme Court's decision in *Commissioner v. Wilcox*, 327 U.S. 404 (1946), which was subsequently overruled by *James v. United States*, 366 U.S. 213 (1961).

Moreover, we note that in *Gargaro*, the taxpayer repaid the bonus payment as a result of a bona fide legal obligation. Here, petitioner attempted to undo its transaction simply to avoid the adverse tax consequences attendant thereto.

We view the facts of the instant case as analogous to those in *Healy v. Commissioner*, supra, wherein the Court held that the taxpayer's income tax liability for the year in which he received excess salary is not recomputed so as to exclude from income for that year that part of his salary subsequently determined to be excessive. In *Healy*, the taxpayer was a corporate officer who received a salary in excess of what could be deducted as reasonable compensation by his corporate employer for a given year. The Court held that under annual accounting principles the taxpayer could not avoid tax on the full amount received by returning the nondeductible "unreasonable" portion in a later year, and the adjustment should properly be made in the year of repayment of the amount earlier included in the taxpayer's income.

We note that the tax exemptions granted to petitioner's general fund and Political League pursuant to sections 501(a) and 527, respectively, are not unlimited. While petitioner could (absent the transfer that is in issue) have earned the investment income that it did during 1984 without incurring an income tax liability, petitioner's Political League could not. Political organizations pay tax on their political organization taxable income as defined in section 527(c). Pursuant to section 527(f), petitioner's transfer of $25,000 from its general fund to its Political League voids the tax exemption on its investment earnings to the extent of the amount contributed. We conclude that the $25,000 is taxable as if it had been earned directly by the separate segregated political fund.

Accordingly,

Decision will be entered for the respondent.

Alaska Public Service Employers Local 71 demonstrates a trap for unwary exempt organizations that venture into political campaigns. Another trap involves an exempt organization that engages in issue advocacy under circumstances that might be viewed as campaign intervention. In that instance, too, a 501(c)(4), (c)(5), or (c)(6) organization might find itself faced with an unexpected tax liability. Revenue Ruling 2004-6 attempts to set forth guidance useful to avoid that trap. The ruling holds that (c)(4), (c)(5) and (c)(6) organizations that publicly advocate positions on public policy issues, including lobbying for legislation consistent with these positions, may be subject to tax under § 527(f). Indeed, if the public policy advocacy involves discussion of the positions of public officials who are also candidates for public office, the public policy advocacy communication may constitute an exempt function within the meaning of § 527(e)(2). *See* Revenue Ruling 2004-6, 2004-4 I.R.B. 328.

Note on Filing and Disclosure Requirements for Political Organizations

As discussed in Chapter 8, most charitable organizations are subject to filing and disclosure requirements. Readers may therefore wonder why § 527(i) and (j) impose additional filing and disclosure requirements pertaining to political organizations. These special requirements grow out of a rather long and complicated legal and political background related to political action committees, the Federal Elections Campaign Act (FECA), and the First Amendment to the Constitution. Space limitations simply do not allow us to provide a complete review of that background. We do note, however, that the legal and political issues described below have not yet been fully resolved. For now, we must be content to provide a broad description of this very important issue.

Under the Radar: The Attack of the "Stealth PACs" on Our Nation's Election

COMMON CAUSE, Apr. 7, 2000

* * *

At the time Section 527 was enacted, federal political committees that fell under Section 527 of the federal tax code also were regulated under the Federal Election Campaign Act (FECA). The FECA limits the size and sources of contributions to candidates, political parties, and PACs, and requires public disclosure of all donations of more than $200. Political committees regulated by the FECA are required to register with the Federal Election Commission (FEC) and file public disclosure reports regarding their contributions and expenditures.

But a court ruling in 1996 [*Federal Election Commission v. GOPAC, Inc.*, 917 F. Supp. 851 (D.D.C. 1996),] and recent IRS interpretations [see below] have combined to open the door to a dangerous, new concept: that a political organization formed to influence elections and taxed under Section 527 could actually evade the jurisdiction and limits of election law.

PART THREE

Charitable Exempt Organizations — Private Foundations

Chapter 15

Private Foundation Status

A. Public Charity Status Versus Private Foundation Status

Code: Skim §§ 170(b)(1)(A) and (G), 170(c)(1)–(2); 509(a), (d)–(e)

Regs.: Skim Treas. Reg. § 1.170A-9(f)(1)–(4), (6)–(8)

The first, lasting, and most important determination in the life of a charitable organization is whether that organization is a public charity or a private foundation. From a tax and regulatory standpoint, public charity status is clearly preferable. Donations to public charities generate more favorable tax benefit for the donor, and public charities are subject to none of the expensive and burdensome oversight and operating requirements imposed on private foundations — requirements enforced by a series of complicated excise taxes necessitating expensive and time-consuming compliance measures.[1] Private foundations are defined, essentially, as all charities that are not public charities. That is, all 501(c)(3) organizations are private foundations except those that fall within four categories. As you will soon learn, the four categories attempt to define the universe of charities that are responsive to the public and not controlled by relatively few people who provide most or all of the organization's funding. Thus, although this Chapter is about private foundations, it focuses on the organizations that meet the various tests for public charity status. Any organization that does not meet one of the public charity tests is a private foundation. Before we proceed into the depths, consider one court's reaction to the whole regulatory scheme surrounding private foundations:

> On the basis of the congressional enactment, 26 U.S.C. § 501, et seq., the Internal Revenue Service has drafted fantastically intricate and detailed regulations in an attempt to thwart the fantastically intricate and detailed efforts of taxpayers to obtain private benefits from [private] foundations while avoiding the imposition of taxes.

Windsor Foundation v. United States of America, 77-2 U.S. Tax Cas. (CCH) ¶ 9709 (1977). We would like to assert that the quote overstates the case but, frankly, we cannot. The regulations are intricate and detailed, and we have another reason for drawing your attention to the quote. The discussion of the private foundation regulations below are, by necessity, mere summaries designed to convey the "big

1. We study the private foundation excise taxes in the next chapter.

picture." A more detailed discussion would only prove the fantastic intricacies and details of those regulations without imparting much more necessary knowledge. But if you are faced with an issue with regard to private foundations in your practice, you must bite the bullet and master the regulations in all their glorious detail. It is certainly not an impossible task, but it will require a substantial investment in time. With that, we proceed.

The last, smallest, and easiest to define category of public charities are 501(c)(3) organizations organized and operated exclusively for testing for public safety. IRC § 509(a)(4). Defining the other three categories is not nearly as simple. The first and largest category of 501(c)(3) organizations that are not private foundations are organizations described in § 170(b)(1)(A)(i)-(vi). Thus, 509(a)(1) excludes from private foundation status: (1) a church or a convention or association of churches; (2) a formal educational organization;[2] (3) a hospital whose principle purpose is to provide medical or hospital care, or medical education or research; (4) an organization whose principal purpose is to engage in medical research, if the organization is directly engaged in the continuous active conduct of research;[3] (5) an organization that normally receives a substantial part of its support from the United States or any state, or possession of the United States, and any political subdivision of either or from the general public and whose purpose is to serve as an endowment fund for a public college or university, if the fund meets the § 170 public support test; (6) a government unit; and (7) a domestic charitable organization that can show substantial public support under the § 170 public support test. Internal Revenue Code § 509(a)(2) excludes from private foundation status charitable organizations that meet a different public support test. Organizations that meet either the § 170 or the § 509 support test are generally referred to as "broadly publicly supported organizations." The determination of whether an organization receives broad public support is the source of most of the regulatory detail. Finally, § 509(a)(3) pertains to certain "supporting organizations"—organizations that, essentially, exist for the benefit of one or more broadly publicly supported organizations.

2. That is, an organization which normally maintains a regular faculty and curriculum and normally has a regularly enrolled body of pupils or students in attendance at the place where its educational activities are regularly carried on. IRC § 170(b)(1)(A)(ii).

3. For purposes of § 170(b)(1)(A), the organization must commit to spend all contributions for medical research before January 1 of the fifth year that begins after the contribution is made. IRC § 170(b)(1)(A)(iii). That requirement is not applicable in determining whether an organization is other than a private foundation. Treas. Reg. § 1.509(a)–2(b).

B. Types of Public Charities

1. 509(a)(1) Organizations

CODE: § 509(a); IRC § 170(b)(1)(A)(i)–(vi)

REGS.: § 1.170A-9(f)(1)–(4), (6)–(9)

To be a § 509(a)(1) organization, a charity must be specifically described in § 170(b)(1)(A)(i)–(v) (each category of which is generally described above) or meet the § 170 public support[4] test stated in § 170(b)(1)(A)(vi).

a. The Public Support Test Safe Harbor

An organization meets the § 170 public support test if it "normally receives a substantial part of its support (exclusive of income received in the exercise or performance of such organization of its charitable, educational or other purpose or function constituting the bases for its exemption under § 501(a)) from the United States or any State, or a political subdivision of either,[5] or from direct or indirect contributions from the general public"[6] or from both governmental and general public sources combined.

The regulations provide two tests to determine whether an organization meets the § 170 public support test, one of which is essentially a safe harbor, and the other a less objective, facts and circumstances test. Under the one-third (safe harbor) test, an organization meets the public support test in any year and the immediately succeeding year if at least one-third of its total aggregate support during the immediate past four years came from governmental and public sources. Treas. Regs. § 1.170A-9(f)(2) and (4)(i).

The term "normally" is determined by looking at the percentage of government and public support during the first four years previous to the year of determination. So, for example, an organization that receives $120,000 in total support during the years 1 through 4, inclusive, will meet the § 170 public support test for year 5 and year 6 if at least $40,000 of its support during the years 1 through 4 was from governmental and general public sources.

Note that if there is a shortfall in governmental and general public support in year 5, such that the aggregate amount of such support for the years 2 through 5 is less than one-third of the total support, the organization will nevertheless be treated as meeting the public support test for year 6 because for each year that the

---

4. Although § 170, and its support requirement, is incorporated by reference into § 509, 509(a)(2) contains another support requirement. Thus, we refer to the support requirement under § 509(a)(1) as the § 170 support test. Later, we will discuss the § 509(a)(2) support test.

5. Henceforth, and for ease of comprehension, we refer to this type of support as "governmental support."

6. Henceforth, and for ease of comprehension, we refer to this type of support as "general public support."

organization meets the requirements (in our hypothetical, the organization meets the requirements during year 1), it is treated as satisfying the public support test until the end of the following taxable year (in our hypothetical, the organization is so treated until the end of year 6).

In effect, an organization that once meets the public support test is given one year to cure any shortfall that causes it to fail the test in the year after it meets the test. In our hypothetical, for example, the organization may fail the test in the year 6 (determined by reference to the years 2 through 5), but it will still be treated as meeting the public support test for year 5 because of the years 1–4. If, for the years 3–6, the governmental and public support is at least one-third of the total support for the same period, the organization will be treated as having met the test for years 7 and 8, thus not suffering a break in its public charity status.[7]

b. The Public Support Test: 10% Plus Facts and Circumstances

An organization whose governmental and public contribution support is less than one-third of its total support can still meet the § 170 public support test if at least one-tenth of its total support is from such sources, and it is organized and operated so as to attract new and additional general public or governmental support. Treas. Reg. § 1.170A-9(f)(3)(i)–(ii). To be organized and operated so as to attract new and additional support, an organization must, in all instances, maintain a continuous and bona fide government or public fundraising program that is reasonable in light of its charitable activities. Even if those two requirements are met, however, the organization may still fail the 10 percent facts and circumstances test if other facts indicate that it is not really organized and operated to attract public support.

Some, but not all the facts and circumstances specifically mentioned in the regulation include: (1) the percentage by which the organization does not meet the one-third safe harbor — the higher the shortfall, the less likely the organization is organized and operated to attract the governmental and general public support, (2) the diversity of sources of support — if the organization is dependent primarily on a single family, it will less likely be considered as organized and operated to attract governmental and general public support, (3) whether the organization's governing body is representative of a limited number of donors, rather than a cross section of the community, and (4) the extent to which the organization makes its services and facilities directly available to the general public on a continuing basis. Treas. Reg. § 1.170A-9(f)(3)(iii)(A)-(D).

Whether an organization "normally" meets the one-tenth rule is decided in the same manner as whether the organization "normally" meets the one-third rule (i.e., by looking to the five years immediately preceding the year of determination, and if

7. Although the regulations are not entirely clear on this point, it seems logical to conclude that an organization can meet the § 170 public support requirement by meeting the one-third test during less than the four years in the four-year period, if it meets the one-tenth requirement in the other years during the four-year period. *See* Treas. Reg. § 1.170A-9(f)(4)(iv) Example.

the test is met, treating the organization as such for the year of determination and the next year thereafter). Treas. Reg. § 1.170A-9(f)(4)(v).

The § 170 public support test is determined by dividing aggregate governmental and general public support during the four-year period by total aggregate support during the four-year period. If the result is at least one-third, the organization will automatically qualify. If the result is less than one third but at least one-tenth, the organization may qualify with the assistance of additional facts and circumstances, one of which must be the presence of a continuous fundraising program.

c. Support

Treasury Regulation 1.170A-9(f)(7) incorporates by reference the definition of "support" provided in § 509(d). However, § 509(d)(2) is specifically excluded. Thus, support is the total amount received from gifts, grants, contributions, membership fees, net income from unrelated businesses even if the business is not regularly carried on, taxes collected for the benefit of and paid to, or expended on behalf of the organization, and the value of services and facilities specially provided by a governmental unit without charge to the organization. Receipts from the conduct of related activities are not included in the definition of support, nor are the value of nondeductible contributions of services. Treas. Reg. § 1.170A-9(f)(7)(i). In addition, membership fees are included only if the basic purpose for the payment of such fees is to support the organization, rather than to purchase admission, merchandise, services, or the use of the organization's facilities. Treas. Reg. § 1.170A-9(f)(7)(iv).

Because receipts from the performance of related activities are excluded, an organization that primarily engaged in related trade or business could meet the one-third or one-tenth test by the receipt of a relatively few small donations. For example, an organization that earns $150,000 per year from the conduct of related activities, but attracts $1,500 in contributions, would technically receive broad public support, because 100% of its total support (excluding the receipts from related activities) is public support. Yet, it is inaccurate to say that the organization is directly responsive to public "owners." Instead, the organization may be responsive to the public as "customers"—that is, the organization may operate in accordance with market forces rather than purely public needs. To avoid this outcome, the regulations state that an organization that receives almost all its income from gross receipts from related activities and an insignificant amount from governmental and public sources cannot meet either the one-third or one-tenth public support test. Treas. Reg. § 1.170A-9(f)(7)(ii). The regulations do not define "almost all" and "insignificant" but they do provide an example where an organization received more than 99% of its income from receipts (excluded from the definition of support), and less than one percent from small donations. *Id.*

After determining our denominator—total support—it is necessary to determine the numerator—total governmental and public support. Governmental support includes donations, contributions, and amounts received under a contract with a governmental unit for the performance of services or in connection with a government research grant. Amounts received under a government contract are excluded from governmental support if the amount is paid for the organization's performance of a related activity. Organizations avoid this rule if the purpose of the contract payment (even though for the performance of a related activity) is primarily to enable the organization to provide a service or facility directly to the public (as opposed to providing a facility or service to the government payor). Treas. Reg. § 1.170A-9(f)(8)(ii). General public support may be direct or indirect. It includes contributions from individuals, trusts, or corporations, or another organization that meets the § 170 public support test (the latter contribution being an example of an indirect contribution). Treas. Reg. § 1.170A-9(f)(6)(i).

Contributions from individuals, trusts, or corporations are included in the total public support only to the extent that the contribution does not exceed 2% of the total support during the four-year test period. Treas. Reg. § 1.170A-9(f)(6)(i). Thus, if an organization has total support of $200,000 over the four years immediately preceding the current year, $100,000 of which is from a single donor,[8] it may include only $4,000 of the $100,000 contribution as public support. As a result of the 2% limitation (and assuming other governmental or public support of less than $16,000), the organization will fail both the one-third test and the one-tenth test (its total support will be $200,000, but its governmental and general public support will be less than ten percent of the total support—because its total governmental and general public support is less than $20,000).

d. Exception for Unusual Grants

The failure to achieve public charity status is unjustified if the $100,000 individual, corporate, or trust donor has no previous or future relationship to the organization but is simply acting out of disinterested generosity. The regulations recognize that, in some instances, a single large gift does not necessarily signal the need for the greater regulatory scrutiny imposed on private foundations. Thus, "unusual grants" may be completely excluded from both total support and public support in determining whether the organization meets the one-third or one-tenth test. Treas. Reg. § 1.170A-9(f)(6)(ii)(A). Picking up on our hypothetical again, assume the following sources of total support.

Governmental grant	$15,999
Receipts from unrelated activities	$84,001
Contribution (one person)	$100,000
Total Support	$200,000

8. A "single donor" is any individual, trust, or corporation, and all donors related to the individual, trust, or corporation under § 4946(a)(1)(C) through (G).

Under such circumstances, the organization will fail both tests because its governmental and public support equals $19,999 ($15,999 from the governmental grant, plus $4,000—the $100,000 contribution taken into account only to the extent of 2% of total support). Thus, total governmental and public support is only 9.9%. However, if the contribution from the single benefactor is an "unusual grant," the regulations take that grant out of consideration. Thus, total support will be $100,000 and total governmental and public support will be $15,999. The organization meets the one-tenth test and can achieve public charity status if it maintains the required fundraising activity and there are no other countervailing facts and circumstances.[9] What might be the purpose of the 2% limitation?[10]

The goal, then, of our hypothetical organization is to characterize the large contribution as an "unusual grant." The regulations apply the term to contributions:

(1) from disinterested persons, who are

(2) attracted by reason of the publicly supported nature of the organization, where the grants are

(3) unusual and unexpected with respect to the amount, and that

(4) adversely affect the organization's ability to meet the § 170 public support test for the relevant period.

Id. The regulations further state that other facts and circumstances may be relevant to the determination (but that no single factor will necessarily be determinative), and then refer the reader to Treasury Regulation § 1.509(a)-3(c) for a list of potentially relevant factors.

Rev. Proc. 2018-32, 2018-23 I.R.B. 739

* * *

Section 2. Background

. . .

.05. <u>Prior Reliance Revenue Procedures</u>.

The IRS has issued several revenue procedures to further describe the extent to which grantors and contributors may rely on the IRS's identification of an organization's tax-exempt and foundation status and to provide safe harbors with regard to the effect of grants and contributions on an organization's foundation status.

* * *

9. The exclusion of an "unusual grant" might also result in an organization meeting the one-third test.

10. The effect of the 2% limitation is to ensure that a public charity is one that receives support from more than a limited number of individuals (a classic signal that a charity is a private foundation).

(2) Rev. Proc. 81-7.

Rev. Proc. 81-7 provides a safe harbor to grantors and contributors as to the grants and contributions that will be considered unusual grants. Under §§ 1.170A-9(f)(6)(ii) and 1.509(a)-3(c)(3), the receipt of an "unusual grant" will not result in a grantee organization losing its classification as a public charity and becoming a private foundation because an unusual grant is excluded from both the numerator and the denominator of the applicable support fraction for purposes of determining whether the organization is publicly supported under § 170(b)(1)(A)(vi) and § 509(a)(1) or under § 509(a)(2). Thus, a grantor or contributor who makes a grant or contribution that is an "unusual grant" to a publicly supported organization will not be responsible for an act that results in the organization's loss of classification as a publicly supported organization and is entitled to rely on the organization's classification as a publicly supported organization.

* * *

Section 7. Safe Harbors for Grantors and Contributors When an Organization Loses Its Public Charity Status

* * *

.03. <u>Safe Harbor for "Unusual Grants."</u>

(1) For purposes of §§ 1.170A-9(f)(6)(ii) and 1.509(a)-3(c)(3), a grant or contribution with all of the characteristics described in this section 7.03(1) (see § 1.509(a)-3(c)(4)) will be considered an unusual grant.

(a) By reason of its size, the grant or contribution would adversely affect the status of a recipient organization under §§ 170(b)(1)(A)(vi) and 509(a)(1) or under § 509(a)(2), absent its treatment as an "unusual grant" under §§ 1.170A-9(f)(6)(ii) and 1.509(a)-3(c)(3).

(b) The grant or contribution is not made by a person who created the organization or by a person who was a substantial contributor (within the meaning of § 507(d)(2)) to the organization prior to the grant or contribution (or by a person standing in a relationship described in § 4946(a)(1)(C) through (G) to either person).

(c) The grant or contribution is not made by a person who is in a position of authority with respect to the organization such as a foundation manager within the meaning of § 4946(b)), by a person who otherwise has the ability to exercise control over the recipient organization, or by a person standing in a relationship described in § 4946(a)(1)(C) through (G) to any person who is in a position of authority or control. Similarly, the grant or contribution is not made by a person who, as a consequence of the grant or contribution, becomes a person of authority with respect to the organization, a person who otherwise gains the ability to exercise control over the organization, or a person who will be standing in a relationship described in § 4946(a)(1)(C) through (G) to any person who is in a position of authority or control.

(d) The grant or contribution is in the form of cash, readily marketable securities, or assets that directly further the exempt purpose of the organization, such as a contribution of a painting to a museum.

(e) The recipient organization has received a final determination letter or ruling classifying it as an organization described in §§ 170(b)(1)(A)(vi) and 509(a)(1) or in § 509(a)(2) and the organization is actively engaged in a program of activities in furtherance of its exempt purpose.

(f) The grantor or contributor has not imposed material restrictions or conditions (within the meaning of § 1.507-2(a)(7)) upon the organization in connection with the grant or contribution.

(g) The terms and amount of the grant or contribution are expressly limited to underwriting no more than one year's operating expenses, if the grant or contribution is intended to underwrite operating expenses, and the grant or contribution is not used to finance capital items.

(3) A potential recipient organization may request a determination letter under Rev. Proc. 2018-5, and any successor revenue procedure, concerning whether a proposed grant or contribution that does or does not satisfy the requirements of the safe harbor in section 7.03(1) of this revenue procedure will constitute an unusual grant, as provided for in §§ 1.509(a)-3(c)(5) and 1.170A-9(f)(6)(iv).

* * *

Note

Ensuring donations do not result in Private Foundation Status. The preceding Revenue Procedure states that a donee organization may seek a ruling from the Service regarding the effect of a proposed contribution. In addition, an attorney representing a donor who wishes to make a large contribution should insist upon written assurance from the donee organization that the donor's contribution will not result in the loss of the organization's public charity status. Treasury Regulation § 1.170A-9(f)(5)(iii) provides that if the donor obtains such written assurance and is not viewed as responsible for, or aware of, a substantial and material change in an organization's sources of support, the donor remains entitled to the highest charitable contribution deduction under § 170 even if the organization loses its public charity status as a result of the contribution. The written assurance must be signed by a responsible officer of the donee organization and must set forth sufficient financial and other information to assure a reasonably prudent person that the organization will not lose its public charity status as a result of the contribution.

St. John's Orphanage, Inc. v. United States

16 Cl. Ct. 299 (1989)

Futey, Judge.

St. John's Orphanage, Inc., d/b/a Knoxville Children's Foundation, Inc., a Tennessee corporation, brings this petition for declaratory judgment pursuant to 26 U.S.C. §7428, challenging the Internal Revenue Service classification of the organization as a tax-exempt private foundation. Plaintiff contends that the organization qualifies as a tax-exempt non-private foundation pursuant to §509(a)(1) of the Internal Revenue Code of 1954. For the reasons stated in this opinion plaintiff's petition is denied.

Factual Background

The Church Orphanage of Knoxville was chartered in Tennessee on December 1, 1905, for the purpose of operating a non-profit orphanage. By amendment to its charter the organization later became St. John's Orphanage Incorporated (St. John's). The organization continued running as an orphanage until 1951, when it was dissolved and its assets sold. Using these funds, in addition to memorials and bequests of money and property, the organization entered into a trust agreement with Fidelity Bankers Trust Company (the predecessor of Valley Fidelity Bank and Trust Company). Pursuant to this agreement the bank managed and invested the funds of the organization. In May of 1965, St. John's established the Knox Children's Foundation to distribute the funds held in trust to child welfare projects in the area of Knox County, Tennessee. In 1967 the remaining real property held by the organization was sold and the proceeds were placed into the foundation's "Improvement and Land Sale Fund" (Land Fund).

In May of 1984, plaintiff filed a Form 1023 Application for Recognition of Exemption with the Internal Revenue Service (I.R.S.) requesting tax exempt status pursuant to §501(c)(3) (1982) of the Internal Revenue Code of 1954 (I.R.C.) and non-private foundation classification under I.R.C. §509(a)(1) (1982). By letter dated April 24, 1986, plaintiff was informed that the foundation was determined to be a tax-exempt organization under §501(c)(3). However, the I.R.S. found that St. John's did not qualify as a non-private foundation under §509(a)(1).

Plaintiff protested this preliminary adverse determination in a May 13, 1986 letter, asserting that the organization should be considered a non-private foundation pursuant to §509(a)(1). Specifically, St. John's claimed that it met the "facts and circumstances" test set forth in 26 C.F.R. §1.170A-9(e)(3) (1988), thus qualifying as a non-private organization under I.R.C. §170(b)(1)(A)(vi) (1982), based on the foundation's level of public support and the nature of its activities.

The I.R.S. issued a final adverse decision on January 9, 1987, which stated that only 5.6% of plaintiff's income was considered "public support," thus, St. John's failed to meet the 10% support requirement set forth in the regulations. Accordingly, the organization was found to be a private foundation. Plaintiff subsequently filed this action for declaratory judgment pursuant to I.R.C. § 7428 (1982), asserting that the organization satisfies the requirements of § 509(a)(1), and therefore should not be classified as a private foundation.

Discussion

Every organization exempt from taxation under § 501(c)(3) is presumed to be a private foundation unless it comes within one of the four excepted categories of organizations enumerated in § 509(a). *See Change-All Souls Housing Corp. v. United States*, 671 F.2d 463, 465 (1982). St. John's asserts that it satisfies the criteria of § 509(a)(1) as a publicly supported organization described in § 170(b)(1)(A). Pursuant to the Treasury Regulations, 26 C.F.R. § 1.170A-9, an organization can achieve this status by meeting either of two tests. Plaintiff claims that it meets the facts and circumstances test set forth in 26 C.F.R. § 1.170A-9(e)(3).[11] To satisfy this test, an organization must (1) normally receive a minimum of 10% of its total support from governmental agencies and/or from direct or indirect public contributions, and (2) be organized so as to attract new and additional public support. 26 C.F.R. § 1.170A-9(e)(3)(i-ii). Both parts of this test must be satisfied. *Trustees for the Home for Aged Women v. United States*, 57 AFTR 2d 86-1261, 86-1263 (1986). Thus, if the first part of this test cannot be met, further inquiry is unnecessary.

An organization must satisfy the facts and circumstances test for the four taxable years preceding the taxable year in which classification is sought to qualify as a non-private foundation. 26 C.F.R. § 1.170A-9(e)(4)(ii). In the case at bar, since petitioner filed with the I.R.S. for recognition of this exemption in tax year 1984, the determination is made on the basis of tax years 1980 through 1983. If the organization fulfills the requirements of the test for the taxable year in which the exemption is sought, it will automatically be deemed to satisfy the test in the immediately succeeding taxable year. 26 C.F.R § 1.170A-9(e)(4)(ii).

Pursuant to 26 C.F.R. § 1.170A-9(e)(6)(i), "contributions by an individual, trust, or corporation shall be taken into account as 'support' .... only to the extent that the total amount of the contributions by any such individual, trust, or corporation.... does not exceed 2 percent of the organization's total support for such period...."[12] Thus, contributions to the foundation from an entity may only be used in the calculation of support for up to, but not exceeding, 2% of the organization's total support for the year at issue. 26 C.F.R. § 1.170A-9(e)(6)(i).

The majority of the foundation's support comes from dividends and interest on proceeds from the 1951 sale of the orphanage. In addition, the organization receives investment income from estates and trusts created under various wills. Plaintiff

---

11. [6] The foundation concedes that it cannot meet the requirements of 26 C.F.R. § 1.170A-9(e)(2), which provides that an organization normally receiving at least one-third of its total support from direct or indirect contributions from the general public, will be classified as a non-private foundation.

12. [7] 6 C.F.R. § 1.170A-9(e)(6) sets forth several limited exceptions to this rule; however, none is pertinent to the case at bar.

contends that these funds constitute sufficient public support for classification as a non-private foundation under § 509(a)(1). The following chart from plaintiff's brief represents the total amount of public support the foundation claims for tax years 1980 through 1983, subject to the 2% limitation.

[Editor's Note: The chart asserts public support ranging from 12.1% to 15.56% for the years 1980 through 1983.]

* * *

Defendant argues that this chart is incorrect, thus, contrary to plaintiff's assertions, St. John's does not meet the 10% support requirement of the facts and circumstances test.

The income that the foundation claims for tax years 1980 through 1983 is derived from the investment of the above funds and trusts. The government argues that the investment income from Corpus A and the Land Fund should not be considered as public support. . . .

Under the regulations public support is defined as "direct or indirect contributions from the general public. . . ." 26 C.F.R. § 1.170A-9(e)(6)(i). "'Indirect contributions from the general public' includes contributions received by the organization from organizations (such as section 170(b)(1)(A)(vi) [publicly supported] organizations) which normally receive a substantial part of their support from direct contributions from the general public. . . ." 26 C.F.R. § 1.170A-9(e)(6)(i). Thus, direct contributions are those which are given directly to the organization by the general public. Indirect contributions are those which an organization receives from other publicly supported organizations.

The examples in the Treasury Regulations aid in the determination of whether the investment income from Corpus A and the Land Fund constitutes public support. In examples one and two of 26 C.F.R. § 1.170A-9(e)(9), both support from investment income of an organization's original endowment, and other investment income are not considered public support. Only contributions which come *directly* from the general public or from other publicly supported organizations qualify as public support within the meaning of the regulations. *See* examples, 26 C.F.R. § 1.170A-9(e)(9).

Underlying this determination is the Congressional intent behind the creation of public charities and private foundations. These two classes of charitable organizations, established under the Tax Reform Act of 1969, Pub. L. No. 91-172, 83 stat. 487 (codified in scattered sections of 26 U.S.C.), are primarily distinguished by the degree of public involvement in the organization. Public charities receive a greater portion of support from public sources (i.e., sources unconnected to the organization), whereas private foundations receive the bulk of their support from investment income rather than contributions. *See* § 509. To assure that private foundations employ their funds for charitable purposes and not misuse them, certain restrictions and requirements are imposed on private foundations to compensate for their lack of public accountability. *See* §§ 4940–4945; *Change-All Souls*, 671 F.2d at 465.

Public charities, in contrast, which rely on the public or government for a substantial portion of their support, need to be accountable and responsive to the public or government in order to maintain their support base. *See Wm. F. Quarrie, Mable E. Quarrie, etc. v. C.I.R.*, 70 T.C. 182, 190 (1978), *aff'd*, 603 F.2d 1274, 1277 (7th Cir. 1979). Thus, Congress imposed no restrictions on public charities since the organizations' donors are presumed to provide the necessary oversight. 603 F.2d at 1277.

Defendant states that the funds which the foundation receives from the investment of Corpus A and the Land Fund are not public support since they do not provide the requisite public involvement in the organization as contemplated by the legislation. This conclusion is premised on the fact that the original donors have no input concerning the use or expenditure of the income from these funds. Therefore, there is no independent judgment as to whether the organization is properly fulfilling its charitable purpose.

This court agrees. An organization's investment income is not public support for purposes of the facts and circumstances test as evidenced by the examples in the Treasury Regulations and the legislative intent.

Plaintiff additionally asserts that because these funds are subject to "restrictions" they should qualify as public support. However, the record contains no evidence regarding either the nature of the restrictions or to which funds they apply. Furthermore, investment income derived from restricted funds does not qualify as public support under 26 C.F.R. § 1.170A-9.

In *Trustees*, 57 AFTR 2d 86-1261, the plaintiff taxpayer argued that investment income generated by the organization's endowment fund should be considered public support since the funds were restricted (i.e., the taxpayer could access the investment income but not the principal). The court in that case, however, determined that the taxpayer's investment income did not constitute indirect public support under 26 C.F.R. § 1.170A-9(e)(6)(i), even if the original funds were themselves restricted. *Trustees*, 57 AFTR 2d at 86-1263. This court similarly finds that the income derived from Corpus A and the Land Fund does not qualify as public support even if restrictions have been placed upon these funds, since no restrictions can provide the necessary oversight and judgment. Thus, plaintiff's argument must fail.

In addition to the income that the foundation receives from the investment of Corpus A and the Land Fund, the organization also receives support from the investment of numerous trusts. As identified in plaintiff's April 2, 1985 letter to the I.R.S., these trusts are contained in three accounts. . . .

Plaintiff suggests that each trust in account number 11900-099 should be considered as a separate source of support. However, since St. John's carries the burden of proof, all insufficient or contradictory evidence must be resolved against plaintiff. *See Church of Visible Intelligence that Governs the Universe v. United States*, 4 Cl. Ct. 55, 60 (1983), *aff'd*, 672 F.2d 894 (D.C. Cir. 1981). The record contains no breakdown of these commingled funds, thus, the court must treat this account as one source of income.

Defendant appears to argue that the support which St. John's derives from the investment of these trusts does not qualify as public support. This court need not reach that question. Since these accounts are subject to the 2% support limitation, 26 C.F.R. § 1.170A-9(e)(6), the largest amount of support the foundation could claim in any one year from the income produced by the three accounts is 6%. This does not satisfy the 10% requirement set forth in the first part of the facts and circumstances test. Therefore, it is unnecessary to determine whether St. John's meets the second part of the facts and circumstances test.

Conclusion

Upon review of the Administrative Record, this court finds that plaintiff has failed to meet its burden of proof in order to show that St. John's is a non-private foundation pursuant to § 509(a)(1).

Note on Public Endowments

The Court's treatment of St. John's endowment fund seems incomplete, at best, in light of Treasury Regulation § 1.170A-9(f)(3)(iii)(A). That provision, relating to the 10% facts and circumstances test, states that if endowment funds were originally contributed by a governmental unit or the general public, reliance on the endowment fund will tend to show that the § 501(c)(3) is organized and operated so as to attract new and additional public and governmental support on a continuous basis. It would appear that St. John's sought to use this rule to meet the 10% threshold. The Court, with implicit support from the regulations, appears to require that the 10% threshold be met independently of an endowment, even if the endowment is from public or governmental sources. By this reasoning, only after the 10% threshold is met (without regard to endowment income) can the organization point to the governmental or public source of its endowment (from which it derives investment income) as an indication that it meets the facts and circumstances test.

Questions

Question 1-3 Facts

Charity owns a homeless shelter from which it conducts a drug rehabilitation program. The location of the shelter (near a residential neighborhood) and the methods used as part of the drug rehab program (involving alternative measures not supported by the mainstream health and rehabilitation professionals) are controversial. Thus, Charity tries to maintain a low profile. It conducts a fundraising program only once every two years and solicits only a relatively few people for donations so as not to draw unwanted attention or publicity. Its board of directors consists only of its five founders, as no medical or psychological professional in the locale would agree to join the board. Charity has the following sources of revenue (in thousands) in the indicated years:

	YEARS (AMOUNTS IN THOUSANDS)						
SOURCE	Year 1	Year 2	Year 3	Year 4	Year 5	Year 6	Year 7
Sale of related goods/services	10	8	4	17	12	16	11
Donations	27	52	16	10	0	1	7
Government Grant	0	10	0	0	80	0	0
Sale of unrelated goods/services	2	3	7	6	1	5	4
Rents/Royalties	6	11	3	15	11	12	10
Dividends	4	1	3	7	0	0	17
Value of donated services	12	25	33	19	60	17	19

1. Will Charity be classified as a private foundation or a public charity in Year 5?

2. What if the donation in Year 1 was made by a single corporation and the donation in Year 2 was made by a single individual who sits on Charity's board of directors?

3. What if, in addition to the assumptions made in Question 2, the $80,000 government grant made in Year 4 was for services related to the organization's charitable goals provided directly to a government agency (e.g., training agency personnel with regard to experimental drug intervention techniques), would charity be a private foundation or a public charity in Year 5?

2. 509(a)(2) Organizations

CODE: § 509(a)(2)

REGS.: §§ 1.509(a)-3(a)(1)–(2), (4); 1.509(a)–3(b), (c).

The second major category of § 501(c)(3) organizations excluded from the definition of private foundations is defined in § 509(a)(2). That provision relies upon a two-part public support test (known together as the "§ 509 public support test").

First, the organization must normally receive more than one-third of its support from any combination of gifts, grants, contributions, membership fees, and gross receipts from related activities. Gifts, contributions, membership fees, and gross receipts from related activities are included in the numerator only to the extent they are received from "permitted sources." Treas. Reg. § 1.509(a)-3(a)(2). Permitted sources are persons who are not disqualified under § 4946,[13] governmental units, and § 509(a)(1) organizations. Treas. Reg. § 1.509(a)-3(a)(2)(ii). In addition, gross receipts from a person or a governmental unit are included in the numerator only to the extent they do not exceed the greater of $5,000 or 1% of the organization's

13. We study disqualified persons in detail in Chapter 17.

total support.[14] Treas. Reg. § 1.509(a)-3(b)(1). Second, the organization cannot normally receive more than one-third of its total support from passive investments (of the type excluded from UBIT under IRC 512(b)) and unrelated trades or business income less taxes paid on that UBTI (net unrelated income). Treas. Reg. § 1.509(a)-3(a)(3)(i).

As with the § 509(a)(1) calculation, an organization must first determine its total support — its denominator for each part of the § 509 support test — and then both its active income from permitted sources — the numerator in the more-than-one-third test — and its passive and net unrelated income — the numerator in the not-more-than-one third test.[15]

Whether an organization "normally" meets the more than one-third and not more than one-third tests is determined using the same methodology as used in § 509(a)(1). That is, the aggregate total support, active support, and passive/unrelated support must be determined for each of the four years immediately preceding the year of determination. If, on the aggregate, the more than one-third and the not more than one-third tests are met, the organization is treated as a § 509(a)(2) organization for the determination year and the immediately succeeding year.

"Support" for purposes of § 509(a)(2) is defined as it is for § 509(a)(1) purposes, except that receipts from the conduct of related activities are included. § 509(d). However, as with 509(a)(1) organizations, an organization seeking to qualify under § 509(a)(2) may disregard "unusual grants" — as defined under § 1.170A-9(f)(6).[16]

Questions

Charity owns a homeless shelter from which it conducts a drug rehabilitation program. Every day, Charity publishes and sells "Streetwise," a newspaper devoted to issues of homelessness. In addition, every three months it organizes a community carwash to raise funds from the public. Though Charity is not affiliated with a church, several members of the clergy of different denominations sit on its board and it sends representatives to churches on a regular basis to solicit donations. The shelter provides beds and meals to homeless persons on a space available basis each day. Once per week, health professionals visit the shelter and provide free medical

14. Because the limitation applies only to "gross receipts," it is necessary to distinguish a gift, contribution, grant, or membership fee from a gross receipt. The regulations address the factors for doing so at Treas. Reg. §§ 1.509(a)-3(f) (gifts and contributions distinguished from gross receipts), 1.509(a)-3(g) (grants distinguished from gross receipts), 1.509(a)-3(h) (membership fees distinguished from gross receipts).

15. Note that under § 509(a)(2), the test is *more than one-third*. Under the one-third test of § 509(a)(1), the test is *at least* one-third.

16. The amount of the unusual grant will be excluded from the denominator in both the more than one-third, and the not more than one-third tests. But it will not be excluded from the numerator of the not more than one-third test because it would not have been included in the first place. Treas. Reg. § 1.509(a)-3(c)(3).

care and consultation. Charity has the following sources of revenue (in the thousands) in the indicated years:

SOURCE	Year 1	Year 2	Year 3	Year 4	Year 5	Year 6
Donations, gifts, grants	100	70	110	60	40	50
Membership fees	110	110	120	120	130	130
Related activities	80	70	80	80	80	60
Income from unrelated activities, less tax	100	120	130	70	120	110
Interest	10	20	10	20	10	20
Dividends	0	0	30	0	20	10
Rents	40	50	50	20	40	1000
Royalties	50	50	50	60	30	10
Capital gains	0	0	200	0	0	150
Donated services	150	60	100	70	50	30

1. For Year 5, will the organization meet the § 509(a)(2) public support test?

2. Is there any other route by which the organization can be classified as other than a private foundation?

3. Assuming the organization is classified as a public charity for Year 5 (based upon Years 1 to 4), will it be classified as a public charity in Year 6?

3. 509(a)(3) Organizations

CODE: §§ 509(a)(3); 4942(g)(4); 4943(f); 4958(c)(3); 4966(d)(4); 6033(l)

REGS.: §§ 1.509(a)-4(b)(1); 1.509(a)-4(c)–(j) [omit 1.509(a)–4(i)(4)]

The third non-private foundation organization is the "supporting organization," referred to in §§ 509(f), 4943 and 4966 as a Type I, II, or III organization. In essence, these are organizations that operate almost as a subsidiary of, and exclusively for, one or more organizations that are classified under subparagraph (1) or (2) of § 509. Thus, their publicly supported nature is derived from the fact that they are, in effect, accountable to another publicly supported organization. An organization is a § 509(a)(3) supporting organization if it:

> (A) is organized and operated exclusively for the benefit of, or to perform the functions, or to carry out the purposes of one or more publicly supported organization, and
>
> (B)(i) is operated, supervised, or controlled by, or in connection with such organizations,
>
> (ii) is supervised or controlled in connection with such organizations, or
>
> (iii) is controlled in connection with such organizations, and

(C) is not directly or indirectly controlled by a disqualified person, other than a foundation manager or a publicly supported organization.

Type I, II, and III supporting organizations are described in paragraph (B).

Type III organizations come in two flavors: functionally integrated and not functionally integrated. IRC § 4943(f)(5). The three types and two flavors result from 2006 legislation. The consequences of a supporting organization being of one Type or another arise mostly in connection with the § 4943 excise tax on excess business holdings.

A Type II or III supporting organization can also qualify to support a social welfare organization under 501(c)(4), labor and agricultural organizations under 501(c)(5), or trade associations under 501(c)(6).

To be organized in accordance with § 509(a)(3), a 509(a)(3) supporting organization's articles of organization must actually state a purpose for the benefit of, to perform one or more functions of, or to carry out one or more purposes of one or more specifically identified publicly supported organizations. The articles of organization may not expressly state that the supporting organization may benefit an organization that is not described in § 509(a)(1) or (2) nor expressly empower the supporting organization to engage in activities not specified in 509(a)(1) or (2). The articles of organization may simply state a purpose that is similar to, but not broader than, the stated purpose of its supported organization(s). That statement will suffice for purposes of the organizational requirement. Treas. Reg. § 1.509(a)-4(h)(1)(i).

When the supporting organization is either a Type I or Type II organization, its articles of organization may refer to the supported organization by reference to its class or purpose rather than name. In contrast, for Type III supporting organizations, each supported organization must be named in the 509(a)(3) organization's articles of organization. Treas. Reg. § 1.509(a)-4(d)(2).

The supported organization need not be named if two requirements are met:

(1) there has been a historic and continuing relationship between the supporting and supported organization, such that

(2) there has developed a substantial identity of interests between the two organizations.

Most alumni associations of established colleges and universities can benefit from this provision.

As we mentioned earlier, the relationship between the supported and the supporting organization is loosely analogous to that of a parent-subsidiary. The regulations require the supporting organization to be responsive to the needs of, and an integral part of, its supported organizations. "Operated, supervised, or controlled by" a supported organization refers to the fact that the supported organization exercises "a substantial degree of direction" over the supporting organization. Treas. Reg. § 1.509(a)-4(g)(1)(i). When a majority of the supporting organization's senior management is appointed or elected by the supported organization, the necessary degree of direction is presumed. *Id.* An organization is "supervised or controlled in connection with" a publicly supported organization only if the same persons control or manage both organizations.[17] Treas. Reg. § 1.509(a)-4(g)(1)(i).

Finally, an organization is considered "operated in connection with" a publicly supported organization only if it meets both the "responsiveness test" and the "integral part" test.[18] Treas. Reg. § 1.509(a)-4(i).

To meet the responsiveness test, the senior management of the publicly supported organization must have "significant voice" in directing the use of the supporting organization's income or assets. Treas. Reg. § 1.509(a)-4(i)(3)(iii). That "significant voice" must arise either because the supported organization has the power to appoint or elect one or more members of the supporting organization's senior management, at least one member of the supported organization's senior management also serves as a member of the supporting organization's senior management, or simply because the senior management of the supported and supporting organization maintain a close and continuous working relationship. Treas. Reg. § 1.509(a)-4(i)(3)(ii).

The integral part test is satisfied if the supporting organization is "significantly" involved in the operations of the supported organization, and the supported organization is dependent upon the supporting organization for the benefit or function the supporting organization provides. Treas. Reg. § 1.509(a)-4(i)(1)(iii), In addition, 2006 legislation added a statutory aspect to the "responsiveness" test in § 509(f)(1)(A). Essentially, Congress delegates to the Secretary authority to promulgate regulations requiring a "Type III" organization to supply reports to the supported organization. The further requirements of the "responsiveness" and "integral part" test are described in the case following this discussion.

Another requirement for § 509(a)(3) supporting organizations is that the supporting organization may not be directly or indirectly controlled by one or more disqualified persons. This does not mean that a disqualified person may not be on the organization's governing board. However, a disqualified person may not — alone or in conjunction with another disqualified person — possess 50% or more of the voting power with respect to the governing board. Treas. Reg. § 1.509(a)-4(j). In addition, a disqualified person — alone or in conjunction with another disqualified person — may not have the power to require or prevent the performance of any act that significantly affects the supporting organization's operations. *Id.* As examples, the regulations state that the power to direct which among several supported organizations is to receive the income attributable to a disqualified person's contribution,

17. The fact that the supporting organization pays all of its earnings to the supported organization is not sufficient to demonstrate commonality of control. Treas. Reg. § 1.509(a)-4(c)(3).

18. Although in general, all supporting organizations must be responsive to and an integral part of a publicly supported organization, only those supporting organizations seeking to qualify under the "operated in connection with" standard must meet specifically defined responsive and integral part tests.

or the presence of a veto power (alone or in conjunction with another disqualified person) represent prohibited control. (Disqualified persons are discussed in Chapter 17. In general, disqualified persons include major contributors and high-level managers.)

Finally, §509(f)(2) added a new requirement in 2006 that precludes Type I and Type III organizations from being controlled by donors. It does not, however, apply to a Type II supporting organization: one "supervised or controlled in connection with" a publicly supported organization.

Roe Foundation Charitable Trust v. Commissioner

T.C. Memo. 1989-566 (1989)

CLAPP, Judge:

* * *

Petitioner was established on or about January 1, 1983, and was funded with a $10 donation from Raymond O. and Evelyn A. Sawyer (Sawyers), who have provided in their wills that their estate of approximately $1 million will pass to the trust upon their deaths. Copies of the Sawyers' wills are not in the record. Since 1983, no additional funds have been donated. In addition to the expectancy under the Sawyers' wills, petitioner, if it receives its section 509(a)(3) exemption, also expects to be funded from public contributions.

Petitioner's creators and trustees at all times relevant to this case were the Sawyers, Stan A. Long, an accountant, and Maggie Ellis, then the annual president-elect of the Washington Community Action Agencies (WCAA). The WCAA is a consortium of salaried state agency executive directors who administer the daily needs of the Washington area charities, although not exclusively those which represent the needy aged. The annual president-elect of the WCAA will act as a trustee for the Roe Foundation. An attorney, Stephen Hansen, was listed as a trustee on the Form 1023 dated January 19, 1983, but unlike the other designated trustees, his signature does not appear on the trust instrument. Moreover, he was not listed as a trustee on the later submitted Form 1023 dated December 19, 1984.

The trust instrument provides in pertinent part that it is organized solely for charitable purposes and on its Form 1023 describes that its intended activity is "to supply funds, aid and assistance to aged persons who are poor and distressed and who are residents of the State of Washington," and that the funds, aid, and assistance will be given based on referrals from churches, senior citizens groups, and the WCAA.

* * *

On September 10, 1986, respondent issued its final adverse determination to petitioner as to its private foundation classification based on the following reasons:

> You fail to meet *section 509(a)(3)(A) of the Internal Revenue Code* because you are not organized and at all times thereafter operated, exclusively for

> the benefit of, or to perform the function of, or carry out the purposes of one or more specified organizations; and,
>
> You fail to meet section 509(a)(3)(B) of the Code because you are not operated, supervised, or controlled by or in connection with one or more organizations described in section 509(a)(1) or (2). You also fail to meet the integral and responsiveness test described in the regulations at section 1.509(a)-4(i); and,
>
> You fail to meet section 509(a)(3)(C) of the Code because you are directly and indirectly controlled by one or more disqualified persons.

Petitioner then brought this action under section 7428 for a declaratory judgment. The sole issue is whether petitioner is an organization described in section 509(a)(3) and, therefore, not a private foundation pursuant to section 509(a).

All section 501(c)(3) organizations are private foundations except those specified in section 509(a)(1) through (4). Petitioner claims that it is excluded from private foundation status because it is a supporting organization described by section 509(a)(3). The theory for creating this exception to private foundation status was that a close relationship between a supporting organization and another organization that is publicly supported insures adequate oversight of the supporting organization. As a result, there is no need to apply the extensive regulation of private foundations that the Code provides. *Quarrie Charitable Fund v. Commissioner*, 70 T.C. 182, 190 (1978), *aff'd*, 603 F.2d 1274 (7th Cir. 1979).

In order to qualify as a supporting organization an entity must meet all of three requirements. First, section 509(a)(3)(A) requires that the organization must be "organized, and at all times thereafter . . . operated, exclusively for the benefit of, to perform the functions of, or to carry out the purposes of one or more specified" publicly supported organizations. Second, section 509(a)(3)(B) requires the organization to be "operated, supervised, or controlled by or in connection with one or more" publicly supported organizations. Third, section 509(a)(3)(C) excludes organizations that are "controlled directly or indirectly by one or more disqualified persons." Petitioner argues that it satisfies all three requirements. Respondent argues to the contrary. Petitioner has the burden of proving that respondent's determination of private foundation status was incorrect. Rule 142(a). To do this, petitioner must establish that it satisfies the requirements of section 509(a)(3)(A), (B), and (C). Because the relationship between a supporting organization and its publicly supported organization for the purposes of section 509(a)(3)(B) may affect the issue of whether the supporting organization is organized exclusively to support the publicly supported organization pursuant to section 509(a)(3)(A), we first consider the section 509(a)(3)(B) issue. See *Cockerline Memorial Fund v. Commissioner*, 86 T.C. 53, 58 (1986); *Change-All Souls Housing Corp. v. United States*, 671 F.2d 463, 469 (1982).

Section 509(a)(3)(B) describes the nature and quality of the relationship that must exist between the supporting organization and the publicly supported organization.

Section 1.509(a)-4(f)(2), Income Tax Regs.,[19] sets forth three different types of relationships, one of which must be met in order to qualify for the section 509(a)(3) exception. Thus, a supporting organization may be (1) operated, supervised, or controlled by, (2) supervised or controlled in connection with, or (3) operated in connection with, one or more publicly supported organizations. Section 1.509(a)-4(f)(3), Income Tax Regs., provides that any one or more of these relationships must exist to insure that the supporting organization will (1) be responsive to the needs or demands of one or more publicly supported organization and (2) will constitute an integral part of, or maintain a significant involvement in, the operations of one or more publicly supported organizations.

"Operated, supervised, or controlled by" section 1.509(a)-4(f)(2)(i), Income Tax Regs.

Petitioner concedes it is not "operated, supervised, or controlled by" WCAA within the meaning of *section* 1.509(a)-4(f)(2)(i), Income Tax Regs.

"Supervised or controlled in connection with" section 1.509(a)-4(f)(2)(ii), Income Tax Regs.

Under this relationship test, there must be common supervision or control by the persons supervising or controlling both the supporting organization and the publicly supported organization. This is generally established by the control or management of each organization being vested in the same persons. "In such a situation, the supporting and publicly supported organizations are compared to brother and sister organizations subject to common control. Sec. 1.509(a)-4(h)." *Cockerline Memorial Fund v. Commissioner*, 86 T.C. at 59.

Respondent argues that the record fails to show who the persons are that control or manage the purported publicly supported organizations or that these persons are the same persons who control or manage petitioner. Respondent contends that petitioner has failed to establish in the record (1) who controls or manages the WCAA executive directors, (2) what relationship that organization has to the WCAA which petitioner purports to support, and (3) whether petitioner's trustees also control or manage these supported organizations.

Petitioner states that this special relationship exists pursuant to the regulation because the president-elect of the WCAA, whose agencies the foundation is assisting, will serve on petitioner's board of trustees. Petitioner contends that the Roe Foundation first made its intentions known to the State's Community Action Agencies almost 6 years ago when the trust was organized and Maggie Ellis, the then president-elect of the agency's executive board, became a trustee. Petitioner continues that the trust will assist the State of Washington to aid its needy aged by donating funds to the state agencies who administer these programs and are funded by

19. [4] Section 1.509(a)-4(f)(4), Income Tax Regs., gives a general description of the three types of relationships described in section 1.509(a)-4(f)(2), Income Tax Regs. These relationships are specifically described in section 1.509(a)-4(g), (h), and (i), Income Tax Regs.

the state, and that Maggie Ellis' willingness to serve as a trustee, who will have full voting power on all matters, is sufficient to create a common supervision or control.

We do not believe that petitioner's relationship with the WCAA constitutes the type of common supervision or control envisioned by section 1.509(a)-4(f)(2)(ii) and (a)-4(h), Income Tax Regs. The regulations specifically state that in the case of a supporting organization which is "supervised or controlled in connection with" the "distinguishing feature is the presence of common supervision or control among the governing bodies of all organizations involved, such as the presence of common directors." Sec. 1.509(a)-4(f)(4), Income Tax Regs. See also sec. 1.509(a)-4(h)(1), Income Tax Regs.

The Roe Foundation's relationship to WCAA falls short of the close relationship necessary to meet this test. This conclusion is highlighted by an example provided in the regulations. In Example (1), a philanthropist who has founded a school set up a trust into which he transferred all of the operating assets of the school, together with a substantial endowment for it. Under the trust, the same persons who control and manage the school also control and manage the trust. Under the circumstances, the trust is organized and operated for the benefit of the school and is "supervised or controlled in connection" with such organization under section 509(a)(3). The fact that the same persons control the school and the trust insures the trust's responsiveness to the school. See section 1.509(a)-4(h)(3), Example (1), Income Tax Regs. The mere presence of one trustee on petitioner's board from the WCAA fails to rise to the level of responsiveness required. We have no indication to what extent the president-elect will be in contact with each of the intended beneficiaries of the trust funds (i.e., the community organizations). Finally, nowhere is it indicated whether representatives from the individual beneficiaries of petitioner will be involved in any way with the Roe Foundation. Absent common control or management of the supported and supporting organizations, petitioner's relationship to the WCAA does not fall within section 1.509(a)-4(f)(4) and (a)-4(h), Income Tax Regs. We therefore next review whether the Roe Foundation is "operated in connection with" WCAA.

"Operated in connection with" section 1.509(a)-4(f)(2)(iii), Income Tax Regs.

Section 1.509(a)-4(f)(4), Income Tax Regs., provides that the distinguishing feature of the "operated in connection with" relationship is that the supporting organization is responsive to, and significantly involved in the operations of, the publicly supported organization as described in section 1.509(a)-4(i), Income Tax Regs. A supporting organization can satisfy this relationship test only if it meets the "responsiveness test" defined in section 1.509(a)-4(i)(2), Income Tax Regs., and the "integral part test" defined in section 1.509(a)-4(i)(3), Income Tax Regs. See section 1.509(a)-4(i)(1)(i), Income Tax Regs. It is the "operated in connection with" test that appears to be petitioner's primary basis for asserting its section 509(a)(3) status.

1. Responsiveness test

The "responsiveness test" is designed to insure that the supported organization will have the ability to influence the activities of the supporting organization. The "responsiveness test" can be met by one of two alternative methods. The first method of satisfying the responsiveness test is set out in section 1.509(a)-4(i)(2)(ii), Income Tax Regs., and is quite direct. This method requires the supporting organization to demonstrate that one of the following arrangements exist:

(a) One or more officers, directors, or trustees of the supporting organization are elected or appointed by the officers, directors, trustees, or membership of the publicly supported organizations;

(b) One or more members of the governing bodies of the publicly supported organizations are also officers, directors, or trustees of, or hold other important offices in, the supporting organization; or

(c) The officers, directors, or trustees of the supporting organization maintain a close and continuous relationship with the officers, directors, or trustees of the publicly supported organization.

Once one or more of the arrangements have been shown, petitioner must demonstrate that by reason of such arrangement the officers, directors, or trustees of the publicly supported organization have a "significant voice in the investment policies of the supporting organization, the timing of grants, the manner of making them . . . and in otherwise directing the use of the income or assets of such supporting organization." See sec. 1.509-4(i)(2)(ii)(d). The word "significant" means "likely to have influence," not control. *See Cockerline Memorial Fund v. Commissioner*, 86 T.C. at 60.

The alternative method of satisfying the "responsiveness test" provided by section 1.509(a)-4(i)(2)(iii), Income Tax Regs., requires that:

(a) The supporting organization is a charitable trust under State law;

(b) Each specified publicly supported organization is a named beneficiary under such charitable trust's governing instrument; and

(c) The beneficiary organization has the power to enforce the trust and compel accounting under State law.

Petitioner does not satisfy the first alternative to the responsiveness test. Although petitioner in its governing body includes the president-elect of the WCAA, the record fails to specify the exact role she will play in the foundation's policy making or in the selection of recipients of grants from the Roe Foundation. Petitioner has failed to indicate how the WCAA trustee will have a "significant" voice in any of the trust's activities and, in particular, in petitioner's investment policies or in directing the use of its income. In its application for exemption, petitioner states that "funds, aid, and assistance to aged, poor and distressed persons will be given based on referrals from churches, senior citizens groups, and the Washington Community Action Agencies." It thus appears the WCAA publicly supported organizations will provide only some of the referrals, but the ultimate decision of who receives the aid and how much aid will be made by petitioner's trustees, only one of whom directly represents the interests of the publicly supported organizations.

The record clearly illustrates this fact. The president-elect of the WCAA has only one out of a possible four votes. Petitioner alleges that there are five trustees, the fifth presumably being an attorney, Steve Hansen, such that the Sawyers will not have two of the four votes and not control the decision making of the trust. Petitioner's later Form 1023, however, fails to validate this as it omits Steve Hansen as a trustee. Moreover, his name does not appear on the trust document. In any case, the focus is not on whether the Sawyers have control but whether the supporting organization's representatives are "likely to have influence." Under the facts presented, we think not. Additionally, the trust fails to safeguard the WCAA's role in the trust's decision making activities. The fifth paragraph of petitioner's trust instrument specifically allows one of the four trustees to resign without the appointment of a new trustee, as long as petitioner has at least three trustees. Nowhere does the trust condition that a WCAA representative must always serve as a trustee. Thus, a time may come when no public charity individual is active on the trust committee. The facts on this record do not illustrate that the WCAA trustee has and will continue to have a significant voice in the foundation affairs.

Petitioner fails to satisfy the second alternative of the "responsiveness test." Although petitioner is a charitable trust under Washington State law, the second and third requirements of section 1.509(a)-4(i)(2)(iii), Income Tax Regs., are not met because petitioner's trust instrument fails to specifically name as beneficiaries any publicly supported organizations, and because under Washington State law of charitable trusts, the state's attorney general, not the beneficiaries (even assuming they are specifically identified), has the power to enforce the trust and compel an accounting, see Wash. Rev. Code Ann. sec. 11.110.090 et seq. (1986).

Petitioner argues that it meets the second alternative of the "responsiveness test" because the State of Washington is the named beneficiary, and the state has the power to enforce the trust through the state's attorney general. Petitioner argues that a broad reading of this section is necessary since the requirements of this section are met "when the language of the governing instrument is sufficiently unambiguous to leave no doubt as to the supported organization intended to be benefitted," citing *Nellie Callahan Scholarship Fund v. Commissioner*, 73 T.C. 626, 635 (1980), and *Goodspeed Scholarship Fund v. Commissioner*, 70 T.C. 515 (1978). These cases, however, deal with a different set of facts than is presented before us.

In *Goodspeed Scholarship Fund v. Commissioner*, 70 T.C. at 520, a will provided that the net income of a charitable trust be used for paying "the education . . . at Yale College of such graduates of Duxbury, Massachusetts, High School" as were chosen according to the procedures set forth in the will. Respondent argued that the governing instrument failed to name a publicly supported organization for purposes of the "organizational test" of section 1.509(a)-4(c)(1), Income Tax Regs., because the pupils themselves were clearly not within this meaning, and the trust was therefore a private foundation. We held that although the document failed to use the magic language "for the benefit of Yale University" because it was clear that this was the intent of the will language, the trust was a supporting organization under section 509(a)(3). 70 T.C. at 524.

In *Nellie Callahan Scholarship Fund v. Commissioner*, 73 T.C. at 628, the trust instrument stated that the income from the trust would be used each year "to finance, or aid in financing, the education of a pupil or pupils . . . from the . . . Winterset Community High School of Winterset, Iowa . . . to assist any of the eligible . . . graduates in attending any college or university . . . within the state of Iowa." In *Callahan*, we applied the same rationale to the "responsiveness test." We based our decision in part on Rev. Rul. 75-436, 1975-2 C.B. 217, which states:

> In granting scholarships to the graduating class of the public high schools, the trust is benefiting individual members of the charitable class benefited by the city [a sec. 170(c)(1) organization] through its public school system. Thus, the requirement of section 1.509(a)-4(e) of the regulations that the supporting organization be operated exclusively to support or benefit one or more publicity supported organizations is also satisfied. If, pursuant to the "operational test" of section 509(a)(3)(B), the payments to the high school students comprised an activity benefiting the school, then the high school should similarly be a named beneficiary under the "responsiveness test" because the "municipality (of which Winterset Community High School . . . is an integral part) . . . [was], the beneficiary organization. . . ." *Nellie Callahan Scholarship Fund v. Commissioner*, 73 T.C. at 636. The Court noted that:

> Under section 1.509(a)-4(e), Income Tax Regs., the making of payments to graduates of Winterset High School constitutes an activity which supports or benefits the high school for purposes of the operational test. . . . See sec. 1.509(a)-4(e)(1) and (2), Income Tax Regs. We fail to perceive the rationale underlying any different results in the operational test and the one before us. If, under the regulations, the making of payments to the high school graduates comprises an activity which benefits the high school for purposes of the operational test, then the high school should similarly be considered a named beneficiary under subdivision (iii) of the responsiveness test. [*Nellie Callahan Scholarship Fund v. Commissioner*, 73 T.C. at 636.]

We also determined that under the relevant state law, the trustees would be accountable to the local district court and required to make detailed annual report to the court, which would become part of the public record. The records could be examined by the school district in the event of default by the trustees.

We do not, however, find that the "responsiveness test" is met in the instant case. By stating that the Roe Foundation trust will make payments to "charitable organizations" defined as "corporations, trusts, funds, foundations, or community chests created or organized in the State of Washington, organized and operated exclusively for charitable purposes," it fails to include as a named beneficiary any specified publicly supported organization. The State of Washington is not a properly named beneficiary because it leaves doubt as to the precise supported organizations intended to be benefited. The fact that Washington State is a section 170(c)(1) organization does not remedy this defect. This section requires a showing that the supported organizations will have the ability to influence petitioners. To simply state that the WCAA and the State of Washington are one and the same for purposes of the "responsiveness test," goes beyond the "broad reading of the section" required under the case law. In each of the cited cases, a specific school and a specific graduating class were listed and the intended beneficiary. In this case, there are not enough facts to determine the intended beneficiaries. Had petitioner specifically named the WCAA in the trust instrument, it is still unclear whether this would strengthen petitioner's position. The record gives no indication whether the WCAA is a publicly supported organization or just the coordinator of the organizations which are publicly supported.

2. Integral part test

Section 1.509(a)-4(i)(3)(i), Income Tax Regs., provides that a supporting organization will be considered to meet the "integral part test" if it maintains a significant involvement in the operations of one or more publicly supported organizations and such publicly supported organizations are in turn dependent upon the supporting organization for the type of support which it provides. In order to meet this test, section 1.509(a)-4(i)(3)(ii) or (iii), Income Tax Regs., must be satisfied.

Section 1.509(a)-4(i)(3)(ii), Income Tax Regs., sets forth the first of the two ways in which the "integral part test" may be satisfied. Under this rule, the test will be satisfied if the activities engaged in for or on behalf of the publicly supported organizations are activities to perform the functions of, or to carry out the purposes of such organizations, and but for the involvement of the support organization, would normally be engaged in by the publicly supported organizations themselves. This rule generally applies only to situations where the supporting organization actually engages in activities that benefit the supported organization, such as performing a specific function for one or more publicly supported organizations. Sec. 1.509(a)-4(i)(3)(ii) and (a)-4(i)(5), Examples (1), (2), and (3), Income Tax Regs.

Section 1.509(a)-4(i)(3)(iii)(a), Income Tax Regs., sets forth the second way in which the "integral part test" may be satisfied. Under this rule, the test will be satisfied if:

> (iii)(a) The supporting organization makes payments of substantially all of its income to or for the use of one or more publicly supported organizations, and the amount of support received by one or more of such publicly supported organizations, is sufficient to insure the attentiveness of such organizations to the operations of the supporting organization. In addition, a substantial amount of the total support of the supporting organization must go to those publicly supported organizations which meet the attentiveness requirement....

All pertinent factors must be considered in determining whether the amount of support received by the publicly supported beneficiary organizations is sufficient to insure the attentiveness of such organizations to the operation of the supporting organization. These factors include the number of beneficiaries, the length and nature of the relationship, and the purpose to which the funds are put. Generally, the attentiveness of a beneficiary organization is motivated by reason of the amounts received from the supporting organization. The more substantial the amount involved as a percentage of the supported organization's total support, the greater the likelihood that the required degree of attentiveness is present. Section 1.509(a)-4(i)(3)(iii)(d), Income Tax Regs. The regulations specifically state, however, that in determining whether the amount received will be sufficient to insure attentiveness by the beneficiary organization "evidence of actual attentiveness by the beneficiary organization is of almost equal importance." (Emphasis added.) Section 1.509(a)-4(i)(3)(iii)(d), Income Tax Regs.

The first alternative of the "integral part test" clearly is not satisfied since petitioner has not demonstrated it is engaged in any activities or is performing any functions that, but for petitioner's involvement, would normally be engaged in by the publicly supported organization. In fact, the administrative record does not present any facts which demonstrate any significant involvement by petitioner in the affairs of the WCAA, or in any group of the WCAA. Nowhere in the record has petitioner shown in detail what its functions, purposes, or activities with the WCAA will be. The only functions listed in the Form 1023 are extremely broad, i.e., to provide funds, aid, and assistance to elderly and aged individuals who may be referred to petitioner by the purported publicly supported organizations. While petitioner has presented several letters from local area groups requesting funds for the activities once the trust is set up, petitioner has no funds to provide for the activities until the Sawyers die and pass their estate to the Roe Foundation. With no funds to speak of, petitioner is incapable of performing activities or functions which benefit anyone.

Next, petitioner argues it satisfies the second alternative. In order to establish that this second alternative of the "integral part test" is satisfied, the organization must demonstrate that (1) it has income and earnings available for support, (2) the amount of support it provides to each beneficiary organization, and (3) the amount of total support received by each beneficiary organization.

Respondent argues that the record in this case fails to establish any of these facts. The sum total of the financial information submitted by petitioner during the administrative process which started on January 19, 1983, shortly after petitioner was organized, and ended on September 10, 1986, the date of the final adverse determination, is as follows: (1) that the total income received by petitioner to the date of the determination was $10, which amount was received from its trustees and organizers, the Sawyers, at the time of the organization of the trust; (2) that funds for support may come from earnings of assets which the Sawyers may eventually (but had not yet at the time of determination) transfer to the trust in an amount which could approximate $1 million; (3) that petitioner anticipated public support during the first 2 years of operations "may well amount to $50,000 or more," when in fact it has shown petitioner had only $10 of support during this 2-year period; and (4) that petitioner's "expected figures" of public support may "well be as high as $50,000 per year" initially and "as much as $120,000 eventually."

Respondent points out that petitioner consistently has not provided any detailed financial information requested by respondent during the administrative process. Thus, the record contains no indication of where these projections come from, how they were determined, or how petitioner expects to achieve such optimistic results.

Petitioner argues that—

It is ludicrous to label a million dollar trust fund as incapable of producing at least a projected 5% return on investment, $50,000 per year, as "... pie in the sky ... having no basis in reality" and that that sum of money will not "assure attentiveness" by the supported organization especially when ... [petitioner has received] letters from potential donee agencies practically "begging to be funded either carte blanche or for specific projects."

None of the requirements of this test have been established by petitioner. Nowhere in the record are copies of the Sawyers' wills, and petitioner contends elsewhere in the record that the $50,000 is to be received by virtue of public donation, not return on investment. Petitioner is totally contradictory in its contentions. It has not been demonstrated it makes payments of substantially all of its income to the publicly supported organizations or that it will have the income to make any payments at any time in the near future. Petitioner's argument that respondent can always audit it in the future to ascertain whether it operates in compliance with the section 509(a)(3) requirements misses the point that petitioner's application for exemption fails to meet the section 509(a)(3) requirements. While an exemption application often deals with prospective transactions, absent any access to the Sawyers' wills, and absent any detailed information about the individual charities the trust seeks to benefit, or their relationships to the WCAA, we are unable to conclude that any funds other than currently nonexistent public funds will ever find their way into the Roe Foundation's war chest or where these funds will actually go. The organizations requesting aid were all under the impression that petitioner would shortly be funded by the Sawyers and, of course, would be responsive to letters by petitioner that a trust with over $1 million was to be created. However, no such trust is yet created.

The organizations which have met the "integral part test" have all involved situations where an actual trust had been created and funds actually expended for charitable causes. For example, in *Cockerline Memorial Fund v. Commissioner*, 86 T.C. 53 (1986), a scholarship fund was created by a testamentary trust pursuant to a will, and it was shown that substantially all of the income was actually paid to the colleges and universities it sought to benefit, the integral part test was satisfied. It was shown that the scholarship trust insured the attentiveness of the schools, many of which were small institutions and depended on the funds. In *Nellie Callahan Scholarship Fund v. Commissioner*, 73 T.C. 626 (1980), a decedent's will also set up a testamentary trust, which specified that the income of the trust was to be used to provide college scholarships for graduates of the local high school. Due to the small size of the high school, "the awarding of scholarships is an activity that is significant enough to insure that the high school will be attentive to petitioner's operation" within the meaning of section 1.509(a)-4(i)(3)(iii), Income Tax Regs. *Nellie Callahan*

Scholarship Fund v. Commissioner, 73 T.C. at 639. In each of these cases, the trust had funds to insure the attentiveness of the supporting organization. In the instant case, it is the promise of funds which attracts the organization's interest. This, however, falls far short of providing the actual attentiveness required to insure adequate monitoring of petitioner's activities.

For the reasons stated, petitioner fails the "integral part test" just as it fails the "responsiveness test." We conclude that petitioner was not "operated in connection with one or more publicly supported organizations," within the contemplation of section 509(a)(3)(B). Petitioner's relationship with the WCAA fails to create the close relationship necessary to remove its activities from the extensive regulation associated with private foundation status. We therefore do not have to determine whether petitioner meets section 509(a)(3)(A) or (C).

Decision will be entered for the respondent.

Cockerline Memorial Fund v. Commissioner

86 T.C. 53 (1986)

Simpson, Judge.

* * *

The petitioner, a testamentary trust, was created under the will of Mrs. Lois E. Cooley in 1968. Her will directed that the income from the trust should be used to:

> [provide] young people of the State of Oregon with funds to attend college and maintain themselves while attending college. It is my desire and request that in expending such fund and selecting persons to become the beneficiaries of such memorial fund, that the trustees give particular preference to students attending the Northwest [Christian] College at Eugene, Oregon, but shall be entirely free to use any portion of said income for the benefit of deserving young people who wish to attend other institutions of learning in the State of Oregon, . . .

Northwest Christian College (Northwest) is a private college closely related to churches variously known as the Disciples of Christ or the Christian Church. Full-time student enrollment at Northwest for the relevant years was: 1977, 431; 1978, 332; and 1979, 291.

Mrs. Cooley's will provides that the petitioner is to be managed by a board of trustees consisting of seven members. The president of Northwest is ex officio one of the members, and the manager of the Albany Branch of the United States National Bank of Portland (Oregon) is ex officio another member of the board. The remaining five members of the board were named in the will, and vacancies in such positions are to be filled by a vote of the other members. Each member of the board of trustees has an equal vote in the board's affairs. No board member, other than the president of Northwest, is required to be associated with any college or university. However, at the time of trial, each board member was a member of a church which supported Northwest and which was frequently visited by the president of Northwest.

The petitioner's board of trustees has total control over and responsibility for the petitioner's affairs....

A five-member scholarship committee selects, subject to approval by the board of trustees, recipients of grants from the scholarship applicants. The board has rarely, if ever, selected a recipient not recommended by the committee. No member of the board of trustees is a member of the committee. Committee members are nominated by the president and the financial aid officer of Northwest. At the time of trial, the financial aid officer and academic dean at Northwest were members of the scholarship committee, and it was customary for the committee to include such officials of Northwest and other persons interested in Northwest.

The scholarship committee meets at and operates out of Northwest. It receives applications, reviews application material, and ranks the applicants according to financial need and grade point average. All successful applicants must be residents of Oregon and accepted at a college or university in Oregon. The maximum total score for an applicant based on financial need and grade point average is 8, and scholarships are awarded on the basis of the highest scores. During the years at issue, students at Northwest were given a bonus of .25, but in the 1979–80 academic year, that bonus was increased to 2.00.

* * *

During the years in issue, Northwest received an average of two-thirds of the grants made by the petitioner. During the prior 3 years, it received an average of three-quarters of such grants. At the time of trial, Northwest received over 90 percent of the funds dispensed by the petitioner.

Annually, an average of 9 percent of Northwest's full-time students were awarded grants by the petitioner during the years at issue. The grants by the petitioner amounted to an average of 8 percent of Northwest's total financial aid for students, including Government grants and loans, and 55 percent of the reoccurring endowed funds available each year at Northwest. Endowed funds arise where, as here, there is an income-producing trust and only the income is distributed. Endowed funds are viewed very favorably by Northwest because there is greater certainty that the funds will be available in future years than with unendowed sources. At the time of trial, over 20 percent of the students at Northwest received grants from the petitioner. The grants for students attending other Oregon colleges or universities did not represent a significant portion of the student financial aid received by any of such colleges or universities.

The parties agree that the petitioner is an organization described in section 501(c)(3) and that it is exempt from the income tax. In 1970, the Commissioner determined that the petitioner was a private foundation. Years later, during a routine audit, it was determined that the petitioner had not requested advance approval of its grant-making procedures, as required of private foundations under section 4945(g). In 1979, the petitioner filed a request for the approval of such procedures, and in 1980, the Commissioner approved the request, retroactive to November 30, 1979. In 1983, the Commissioner issued a notice of deficiency determining the deficiencies at issue.

Opinion

Section 4945 imposes certain excise taxes on grants made to individuals by private foundations, unless the Commissioner has given his prior approval of the program for the grants in accordance with section 4945(g). The first issue for decision in this case is whether the petitioner is a private foundation and subject to such excise taxes. . . .

The petitioner is a section 501(c)(3) organization and, thus, presumptively a private foundation. Sec. 508(b). The petitioner claims that it is excluded from private foundation status because, during the years in issue, it was a supporting organization within the meaning of section 509(a)(3). . . .

The Commissioner concedes that the petitioner is not controlled by a disqualified person within the meaning of section 509(a)(3)(C). . . .

The petitioner contends that it is a supporting organization since it is "operated in connection with" the colleges and universities in Oregon. Sec. 1.509(a)-4(f)(2)(iii). In order for the relationship to exist, the petitioner must satisfy the requirements of the responsiveness and the integral part tests of section 1.509(a)-4(i) of the regulations.

The responsiveness test is designed to insure that the publicly supported organization will have the ability to influence the activities of the supporting organization. The responsiveness test requirements are set forth in section 1.509(a)-4(i)(2), Income Tax Regs. The relevant requirements, under the facts of this case, are found in subdivisions (*b*) and (*d*) of section 1.509(a)-4(i)(2)(ii). Under subdivision (*b*), at least one member of the governing body of a publicly supported organization must hold an important office in the supporting organization, such as a seat on the board of trustees. Subdivision (*d*) requires that the relationship between the organizations insures that the publicly supported organizations:

> have a significant voice in the investment policies of the supporting organization, the timing of grants, the manner of making them, and the selection of recipients by such supporting organization, and in otherwise directing the use of the income or assets of such supporting organization.

We hold that the petitioner satisfies the requirements of the responsiveness test. The president of Northwest is, by virtue of his office, a member of the board of trustees of Northwest and the board of trustees of the petitioner. Therefore, there is a common member of the governing bodies of both organizations, as required by subdivision (*b*) of the responsiveness test.

The Commissioner contends that because the president of Northwest holds only one of seven seats on the petitioner's board of directors, no publicly supported organization "controls" the activities of the petitioner and that, therefore, the petitioner does not meet the requirements of subdivision (*d*) of the responsiveness test. The plain language of the regulation undermines the Commissioner's argument. The regulation requires one or more publicly supported organizations to have a "significant voice" in the activities of the supporting organization. The word "significant" means "likely to have influence," not control. Webster's Third New International Dictionary 2116 (1981). Additionally, the regulations make it clear that the "operated in connection with" relationship does not require control of the supporting organization by any publicly supported organization. Sec. 1.509(a)-4(i), Income Tax Regs.

As stated in the petitioner's constitution and bylaws, the board of trustees has complete power over all facets of the petitioner's activities, including investment decisions and selection of the grant recipients. No provision is made for the exercise of power by any other group, other than those authorized by the board of trustees. The broad scope of authority given the board of trustees assures that the president of Northwest had the opportunity to exercise a significant voice in the affairs of the petitioner.

The facts indicate that Northwest did exercise a significant voice in the petitioner's affairs. Through the president's position on the petitioner's board of trustees, Northwest was able to participate in the decision-making process with regard to such important subjects as investments and scholarship recipient selection. Additionally, the evidence shows that Northwest dominated the scholarship committee. Indeed, as vacancies occurred, the president of Northwest and Northwest's financial aid officer, who was on the committee, proposed replacement members for approval by the board of trustees. The committee's meetings were held on the Northwest campus. Finally, for the years in issue, Northwest received an average of two-thirds of the funds distributed by the petitioner, and in later years, it received 90 percent of the petitioner's distributions.

The integral part test is described in depth in section 1.509(a)-4(i)(3), Income Tax Regs. It is designed to insure that the publicly supported organization will be attentive to the supporting organization, thereby acting to curb any abuses by the supporting organization of its reasons for tax exemption. The test requires that the supporting organization maintain a substantial involvement in the operations of the publicly supported organization by either performing an essential function for, or paying a substantial amount of money to, one or more publicly supported organizations. Sec. 1.509(a)-4(i)(3)(ii) and (iii). The record shows that the petitioner satisfies the requirements of the integral part test under section 1.509(a)-4(i)(3)(iii). The regulation requires that the supporting organization pay substantially all of its funds to publicly supported organizations and that the amount paid to at least one publicly supported organization be sufficient to insure the attentiveness of such publicly supported organization to the supporting organization's activities. The determination as to attentiveness should be made by reference to all the circumstances surrounding the relationship between the organizations, including "evidence of actual attentiveness" by the publicly supported organization. Sec. 1.509(a)-4(i)(3)(iii)(*d*).

At all relevant times, the petitioner paid substantially all of its income to colleges and universities in Oregon. Because these are publicly supported institutions, the first requirement is satisfied. Therefore, the petitioner must show only that the amount of funds paid was sufficient to insure the attentiveness of a publicly supported organization.

Taking into account all of the circumstances surrounding the relationship between the petitioner and Northwest, including the amount of funds distributed, the number of students affected, and the history and nature of the relationship, we find the requisite attentiveness on the part of Northwest. The funds paid to Northwest from the petitioner constituted an average of 8 percent of the scholarship funds at Northwest and affected 9 percent of the full-time students at Northwest. The president of Northwest testified that a reduction in funds from the petitioner would cause Northwest to expend efforts to obtain offsetting funds elsewhere. Additionally, the near-decade-long relationship between the petitioner and Northwest, together with the petitioner's reliance upon the Northwest-nominated scholarship committee, points to continuing attentiveness by Northwest to the operations of the petitioner. Finally, we believe that the Commissioner recognized the importance of the petitioner's funds to Northwest when the Commissioner stated in his brief that "a small private college such as Northwest would be understandably reluctant to lose the support of the petitioner's endowment."

Here, as under the responsiveness test, the Commissioner argues that the petitioner does not meet the criteria of the regulations because Northwest does not control the petitioner. The argument is erroneous because the integral part test focuses attention on the motivation of a publicly supported organization to be attentive to the supporting organization's activities. Control by the publicly supported organization is not required by the integral part test.

The purpose requirement, as set forth in section 509(a)(3)(A), requires that a supporting organization be organized and operated "exclusively" to support one or more "specified" publicly supported organizations. Paragraphs (c), (d), and (e) of section 1.509(a)-4, Income Tax Regs., describe the organizational and operational tests of section 509(a)(3)(A).

The elements of the organizational test are set forth in detail in section 1.509(a)-4(c). This regulation requires that the articles of organization of the supporting organization, in this case Mrs. Cooley's will, limit the purposes of the organization to supporting one or more publicly supported organizations and "specify" the organization to be benefited. No particular language is needed to satisfy the requirements. *Goodspeed Scholarship Fund v. Commissioner*, 70 T.C. 515, 524 (1978).

The relevant passage from the will of Mrs. Cooley states that the petitioner's funds are to be distributed "for the purpose of providing young people of the State of Oregon with funds to attend college." The colleges and universities in the State of Oregon are publicly supported organizations. However, the Commissioner maintains that because the petitioner substantially benefits students, who are not publicly supported organizations, the petitioner is not organized exclusively for the benefit of a publicly supported organization. This argument is directly contradicted by example (1) of section 1.509(a)-4(d)(2)(iii), Income Tax Regs., and we find it meritless. See *Nellie Callahan Scholarship Fund v. Commissioner*, 73 T.C. 626, 635–636 (1980).

Section 509(a)(3)(A) requires that the publicly supported organization be "specified." Paragraphs (g) and (h) of section 1.509(a)-4, Income Tax Regs., provide that supported organizations may be designated by class or purpose when the relationship between the publicly supported and supporting organizations is that of parent-subsidiary or brother-sister organizations. However, paragraph (d)(2)(i) of section 1.509(a)-4 takes the position that where the supporting organization is operated "in connection with" the publicly supported organization, as is the case here, the supported organization must be designated by name. An exception is made to such requirement by paragraph (d)(2)(iv) of section 1.509(a)-4, which states that the publicly supported organization will be sufficiently specified, even though not named in the supporting organization's articles, when there has been a "historic and continuing relationship" between the organizations and a "substantial identity of interests" between such organizations has resulted.

The petitioner contends that the required naming of the publicly supported organization where the supporting organization is operated "in connection with" the publicly supported organization, while allowing all other supporting organizations to identify the publicly supported organizations by class or purpose, is invalid because neither subparagraph (A) nor (B) of section 509(a)(3) draw such a distinction. However, we need not and do not pass on such contention since we are convinced that the petitioner satisfies the historic and continuing relationship exception described in section 1.509(a)-4(d)(2)(iv), Income Tax Regs. No specific time period is required to establish a historic and continuing relationship between the supporting and the publicly supported organizations. The existence of the relationship and the identity of interest between the organizations must be determined from the circumstances surrounding the interaction of the organizations. *Change-All Souls Housing Corp. v. United States*, 671 F.2d 463, 471–472 (Ct. Cl. 1982). Additionally, the requirements must be applied consistent with the stated legislative goal of not unduly interfering with supporting organizations which aid educational institutions. S. Rept. 91-552 (1969), 1969-3 C.B. 423, 462; H. Rept. 91-782 (Conf.) (1969), 1969-3 C.B. 644, 651.

The petitioner has maintained the historic and continuing relationship with the colleges and universities in Oregon. Since its inception in 1968, the petitioner, in accordance with Mrs. Cooley's will, has distributed all of its funds directly to colleges and universities in Oregon. Such funds were returned to the petitioner if the student upon whose behalf the funds were provided failed to enroll full-time or if the required 2.50 grade point average was not maintained. The petitioner has established a scholarship committee to recommend worthy students attending colleges or universities in Oregon. Additionally, the petitioner and Northwest, one member of the class of publicly supported organizations, have established a particularly close working relationship. Finally, we observe that both the petitioner and the colleges and universities in Oregon have as their ultimate goal the education of students in Oregon. These facts establish the type of relationship and the "substantial identity of interests" needed to determine that the petitioner is organized to benefit identifiable publicly supported organizations, thereby avoiding abuses which might arise where the beneficiaries are not identified in the articles of the supporting organization.

The Commissioner's final objection is that to qualify the petitioner as a supporting organization would be inconsistent with the congressional intent associated with the adoption of section 509. We disagree.

Private foundations were defined and subjected to extensive regulation by the Tax Reform Act of 1969, Pub. L. 91-172, 83 Stat. 487. The act was intended to combat the perceived abuse of tax exempt status where there is self-dealing between substantial contributors and their foundations, failure to distribute foundation income to charities, foundation ownership and control of private businesses, speculative investment of foundation funds, and the use of foundation money for programs or activities not within the scope of the tax exemption provisions. H. Rept. 91-413 (Part 1) (1969), 1969-3 C.B. 200, 213–228; S. Rept. 91-552, *supra*, 1969-3 C.B. at 440–464; H. Rept. 91-782, *supra*, 1969-3 C.B. at 644–651. The act imposes a series of excise taxes on private foundations. Secs. 4940 through 4945. Public charities are exempt from private foundation treatment and, consequently, the excise taxes, on the theory that public scrutiny arising from a foundation's dependence upon public funds will prevent abusive acts by the foundation. Supporting organizations are similarly excepted on the theory that scrutiny by the publicly supported organizations will prevent abuse by the supporting organization. *Quarrie Charitable Fund v. Commissioner*, 70 T.C. 182, 190 (1978), *aff'd*, 603 F.2d 1274 (7th Cir. 1979). The belief that scrutiny by a publicly supported organization, under the appropriate circumstances, is sufficient to guard against abuse by the supporting organization is embodied in section 509(a)(3). The provisions of that section are designed to insure that a supported organization has the ability and motivation to properly oversee the activities of the supporting organization. The close and continuous relationship between the petitioner and Northwest was of this type. It produced the type of close scrutiny which renders unlikely the congressionally feared abuses. In fact, as the Commissioner agrees, no such abuses have occurred.

In conclusion, we hold that the petitioner was a supporting organization within the meaning of section 509(a)(3) during the years in issue. As a supporting organization, the petitioner is not subject to the excise tax under section 4945(a)(1). Because we hold for the petitioner on this issue, we need not address the second issue raised by the petitioner.

Question

How is it that Cockerline Memorial Fund was successful in avoiding private foundation status while the Roe Foundation was not?

Chapter 16

Private Foundation Excise Taxes — The Audit Fee Tax

A. Introduction

The private foundation excise taxes' legislative history recounts a laundry list of abuses perpetrated by primary donors. These typically wealthy people, having been granted generous tax benefits for their endowment of charitable causes, were essentially caricatured as greedy people with secret agendas who were using the tax exemption for their own benefit. Congress believed that enough big donors were abusing the charitable contribution deduction and tax exemption for their own financial or political purposes that something should be done.

Thus, came the enactment of the private foundation excise taxes §§ 4940–4945. The initial tax (§ 4940), called the "audit fee tax," applies to every private foundation regardless of the activity or nefarious intentions — so long as there is sufficient taxable "net investment income." This audit fee tax is an excise tax imposed on the net investment income of most domestic private foundations. The tax is reported on Form 990-PF, Return of Private Foundation, and must be paid annually at the time for filing that return or in quarterly estimated tax payments if the total tax for the year is $500 or more.

In addition, the Internal Revenue Code imposes other excise taxes on private foundations, foundation managers, or other disqualified persons that engage in certain prohibited acts. These excise taxes are reported and paid on Form 4720, Return of Certain Excise Taxes Under Chapters 41 and 42 of the Internal Revenue Code. These remaining excise taxes fall into two general categories. The first category is of excise taxes that presume nefarious involvement of a primary donor, referred to as "disqualified person," to profit personally from the transaction — §§ 4941 (self-dealing) and 4943 (excess business holdings). Indeed, § 4941 bases itself on the notion that disqualified persons can hardly ever transact business fairly with the charity that benefits from their generosity. The other excise tax provisions (§§ 4942, 4944 and 4945) explicitly rely on the assumption that disqualified persons are somehow invariably behind the abuse to be prevented, whether the abuse is failure to distribute (§ 4942), making jeopardizing investments (§ 4944), or spending charitable funds for prohibited purposes (§ 4945). For example, § 4944 (which punishes a charity for risky investments) is, in part, based upon the notion that disqualified persons use charitable funds as "play money" to invest in highly speculative ventures.

Section 4945 depends on the belief that significant donors were bankrolling, under the guise of charity, those who furthered certain political causes. We begin by first discussing in this Chapter the general audit fee tax of § 4940. Then, we will move to Chapters 17 and 18 which address the other two categories of excise tax.

B. The Audit Fee Tax

CODE: §§ 4940, [omit 4940(b)], 4942(j)(3)–(4), 4942(g)(1)(A)–(B), 4942(f)

REGS.: §§ 53.4940-1(c)–(f)(1); 53.4942(a)-2(d); 53.4942(a)-2(c); 53.4942(b)-1(a)(1); 53.4942(b)-1(b)–(d); 53.4942(b)-2.

When Congress accepted the proposition that wealthy people were abusing charitable organizations, it also decided that the cost of preventive supervision and enforcement with regard to those organizations should not be paid by the taxpaying public. It therefore enacted § 4940, which imposes a generally unavoidable 1.39% tax on all private foundations, except certain "exempt operating foundations." In December 2019, Congress changed this tax rate from 2% to 1.39%. See Pub. L. 116-94, div. Q, title II, § 206(a), (b), Dec. 20, 2019, 133 Stat. 3246. Prior to 2020, § 4940(e) provided a complicated test that, if met, resulted in a reduced tax rate that applied when a foundation's qualifying distributions for the taxable year equal or exceed: (1) the fair market value of noncharitable assets (less acquisition indebtedness) multiplied by the "average percentage payout," (2) plus 1% of the net investment income. However, Congress eliminated the 4940(e) reduced tax in 2019 when it lowered the tax rate from 2% to 1.39%.

The 4940 audit fee tax is imposed on a private foundation's "net investment income." IRC § 4940(a). Net investment income is the private foundation's gross investment income, plus its "capital gain net income" less ordinary and necessary expenses related to the gross investment income and property held to produce such income. IRC § 4940(c)(1), (3). Gross investment income is the private foundation's exempt passive income[1] — interest, rents, dividends, royalties, and payments with respect to securities loans — while capital gain net income are gains from the sale or disposition of property used to produce (1) investment income or (2) unrelated business taxable income prior to its sale, if the sale or disposition gain is not otherwise included in unrelated business income. IRC § 4940(c)(4).

Expenses incurred to generate both net investment income and in pursuit of the private foundation's exempt purpose must be allocated between the different

1. These types of income are generally excluded from the definition of unrelated business taxable income. IRC § 512(b). To the extent, though, that the incomes are included in UBIT, they are excluded from "gross investment income." IRC § 4940(c)(2) and (c)(4)(A). A like rule applies to the deduction of any expenses taken into account in determining UBIT. Treas. Reg. § 53.4940-1(e)(1).

activities, and only the portion allocated to the net investment income will be deductible. Treas. Reg. § 53.4940-1(e).[2] A special rule limits the depreciation deduction to the straight-line method. IRC § 4940(c)(3)(B)(i). Finally, the organization may deduct losses from the sale of property used to generate investment or unrelated income only to the extent of the gains from such properties. Thus, the private foundation is entitled to neither a capital loss carryback nor carryover in the computation of its net investment income. IRC § 4940(c)(4)(C); Treas. Reg. § 53.4940-1(f)(3).

Another rule applies with respect to capital gain net income if a private foundation uses property in both an exempt activity and to produce income includible in determining net investment income. If the use of the property to produce passive income is merely "incidental" to its use in an exempt activity, none of the gain from the sale or disposition will be capital gain net income. Treas. Reg. § 53.4940-1(f)(1). If such use is "other than incidental," gain on the disposition must be allocated to the exempt and taxable use. The portion allocated to the taxable use is capital gain net income. *Id.*

A controversial issue has involved the meaning of "capital gain net income" for purposes of the audit tax. Until August 17, 2006, § 4940(c)(4)(A) provided: "There shall be taken into account only gains and losses from the sale or other disposition of property used for the production of interest, dividends, rents, and royalties, and property used for the production of income included in computing the tax imposed by section 511. . . ." Interestingly, the code refers to property "used" rather than property "held" for the production of income. This important distinction was the focus of multiple decisions involving the Zemurray Foundation. A 2006 amendment to the Code changed the § 4940(c)(4)(A) language to:

> There shall be taken into account only gains and losses from the sale or other disposition of property used for the production of gross investment income (as defined in paragraph (2)), and property used for the production of income included in computing the tax imposed by section 511 . . . .

In addition, the 2006 amendment changed the meaning of "gross investment income" to include not only "interest, dividends, rents, payments with respect to securities loans . . . and royalties," but also: "*income from sources similar to those in the preceding sentence.*"

Zemurray[3] involved a private foundation that held the naked ownership of timberland in Louisiana. The donor's widow held the usufruct—the right to enjoy the use and advantage of another's property short of the destruction or waste of its substance. A naked ownership in civil law jurisdictions is roughly comparable to a future interest in common law jurisdictions. Similarly, a usufruct is roughly

---

2. Although the regulations do not say so, presumably the allocation must be via a "reasonable" method.

3. *Zemurray Foundation v. United States*, 755 F.2d 404 (5th Cir. 1985).

comparable to a term interest. The usufructuary receives all the income, and the naked owner receives none. The *Zemurray* case focused on whether a naked ownership could ever be "used" for the production of income. The controversy also focused on the regulations, which broadly interpret the word "used" as being "*of a type which generally produces* [1] interest, [2] dividends, [3] rents, [4] royalties, or [5] capital gains through appreciation (for example, rental real estate, stock, bonds, mineral interests, mortgages, and securities)" (emphasis added). Treas. Reg. § 53.4940-1(f)(1).

This regulation departs from the literal language of the code in two respects. First, it changes "used" to "held," and second, it adds the category of being held for "appreciation." This broad reading works to increase tax liability in most cases and, therefore, as *Zemurray* demonstrated, has caused consternation among private foundations. Ultimately, the Circuit Court upheld the "held" language, but struck down the "appreciation" category. The court properly found that a Louisiana naked ownership in land cannot produce income other than appreciation.

In response, Congress amended § 4940, as provided above, to include income from sources "similar to" those actually listed. According to the Joint Committee Report accompanying the amendment:

> Such similar items include income from notional principal contracts, annuities, and other substantially similar income from ordinary and routine investments, and, with respect to capital gain net income, capital gains from appreciation, including capital gains and losses from the sale or other disposition of assets used to further an exempt purpose.[4]

With the amendment, *Zemurray* remains important only for its approval of the regulatory shift from "used" to "held" for the production of income. The court's striking down of the regulatory addition of "appreciation" as a source of income is apparently no longer valid. One might, however, criticize the amendment for failing to list the types of income in the Code, rather than burying them in a Committee Report. Clearly, the Report is critical of *Zemurray* and clearly it approves of the expansive regulation. However, one might fairly argue that "appreciation" is not "similar" to "interest, dividends, and royalties": the former involves the underlying property (the naked ownership interest in civil law jurisdictions) while the Code examples involve something separated from the property (the *usus* and *fructus* in civil law terminology). While we doubt the issue remains realistically open, we note that the language adopted by Congress is not consistent with the interpretation given it by the Joint Committee staff.

---

4. Joint Committee Report JCX-38-06 (for H.R. 4), prepared by the Staff of the Joint Committee on Taxation August 3, 2006.

Question

Private Foundation (not an operating foundation) had the following income in Year 1:

Dividends	$10,000
Rents	$50,000
Royalties	$100,000
Interest	$840,000
	$1,000,000

In addition, Private Foundation received a vacant lot as a donation on June 1, Year 1. On September 1, Year 1, Private Foundation sold the lot, realizing a gain of $1,000,000. The lot was in the middle of a very blighted neighborhood area with little prospect for residential or commercial use without substantial rehabilitation of the entire area. Private Foundation could not itself have engaged in an urban renewal project, but it sold the lot to a developer (who planned and had the financial ability) to redevelop the area. Assuming no deductions, what is Private Foundation's 4940 tax for Year 1?

As noted above, the audit fee tax does not apply to "exempt operating foundations." Operating foundations are defined in § 4942(j)(3). Thus, not only must the organization meet the § 4942 definition, but also the § 4940 "exempt" requirements. Section 4942 requires that a private foundation meet the (1) qualifying distribution test, and either (2) the asset test, (3) the endowment test, or (4) the support test. Those tests are described in Treasury Regulation § 53.4942(b)-2. *"Miss Elizabeth,"* a case involving § 4942 (which we reconsider in detail below), introduces the concept of "operating foundations" and discusses the qualifying distribution requirement and the endowment test. The discussion following the case briefly summarizes the § 4940 requirements necessary to achieve "exempt" operating foundation status.

Of significance in *"Miss Elizabeth"* was whether certain scholarships constituted qualifying distributions directly for the active conduct of the entity's purpose, as required by § 4942(j)(3). The government agreed the items were "qualifying distributions"; however, it disputed whether they satisfied the "direct" test.

The "Miss Elizabeth" D. Leckie Scholarship Fund v. Commissioner

87 T.C. 251 (1986)

GERBER, Judge.

On September 9, 1983, respondent issued a determination letter to petitioner, finding that the foundation is exempt from Federal income tax under section 501(c)(3) and that the foundation is a private foundation within the meaning of section 509(a). On November 29, 1983, respondent issued a final adverse ruling as to petitioner's status as an "operating foundation" within the meaning of section 4942(j)(3).

* * *

Petitioner was initially funded by a charitable contribution of investments worth $135,986.11, donated by Cheatham. All interest income generated by the trust assets is used to pay petitioner's administrative expenses and to provide scholarships.

Petitioner's sole source of income since the initial endowment has been interest earned on the endowment. Petitioner expects to earn $6,600 interest income annually, with projected annual expenses of $6,000 in scholarships and $600 in administrative expenses. The issue we must decide is whether petitioner qualifies as a "private operating foundation" under section 4942(j)(3). Respondent argues that the moneys petitioner spends on scholarships ($6,000 out of $6,600 income per year) are not "qualifying distributions . . . directly for the active conduct of the activities constituting the purpose or function for which it [petitioner] is organized and operated."[5] Sec. 4942(j)(3)(A). Thus, respondent argues, petitioner is not entitled to "private operating foundation" status. Furthermore, respondent contends that petitioner fails each of the three tests (the assets, endowment, and public support tests), one of which petitioner must pass to attain "operating status." Petitioner argues that its scholarship grants are qualifying distributions as required by section 4942(j)(3) and defined in section 53.4942(b)-1(b)(2)(ii), Foundation Excise Tax Regs., and that it meets the endowment test, thereby fulfilling all statutory requirements. . . .

We find that petitioner meets the requirements of section 4942(j)(3) and the regulations promulgated thereunder. Accordingly, petitioner is entitled to "private operating foundation" status.

Section 4942 is part of the detailed statutory provisions of the Tax Reform Act of 1969 which were designed to combat then existing abuses in the formation and operation of exempt organizations. One such abuse was the availability of a current deduction for the donor with a corresponding ability by the foundation to delay actual

5. [7] That the scholarships are qualifying distributions within the meaning of sec. 4942(j)(3) as defined in sec. 4942(g)(1) and (2) is not at issue. That the scholarships are made directly for the active conduct of the activities constituting the purpose or function for which petitioner is organized and operated is at issue. For convenience, however, we sometimes phrase the issue as simply whether the scholarships are qualifying distributions.

distribution for charitable purposes. This could occur when a private foundation invested in assets that produced no current income, and made no distributions. See S. Rept. 91-552 (1969), 1969-3 C.B. 423, 446, 447. Accordingly, section 4942 requires that certain private foundations make a minimum level of charitable distributions.

Section 4942(a)(1), however, exempts "operating foundations" from these requirements. Section 4942(j)(3) defines "operating foundations" as follows:

> (3) Operating foundation.—For purposes of this section, the term "operating foundation" means any organization—
>
> (A) which makes qualifying distributions (within the meaning of paragraph (1) or (2) of subsection (g)) *directly for the active conduct of the activities constituting the purpose or function for which it is organized and operated* equal to substantially all of the lesser of—
>
> (i) its adjusted net income (as defined in subsection (f)), or
>
> (ii) its minimum investment return; and
>
> . . .
>
> [B](ii) which normally makes qualifying distributions (within the meaning of paragraph (1) or (2) of subsection (g)) directly for the active conduct of the activities constituting the purpose or function for which it is organized and operated in an amount not less than two-thirds of its minimum investment return (as defined in subsection (e))
>
> * * *
>
> Notwithstanding the provisions of subparagraph (A), if the qualifying distributions (within the meaning of paragraph (1) or (2) of subsection (g)) of an organization for the taxable year exceed the minimum investment return for the taxable year, clause (ii) of subparagraph (A) shall not apply unless substantially all of such qualifying distributions are made directly for the active conduct of the activities constituting the purpose or function for which it is organized and operated.

Section 53.4942(b)-1(b)(1), Foundation Excise Tax Regs., enunciates the general rule that qualifying distributions are not made "'directly for the active conduct of activities' unless such qualifying distributions are used by the foundation itself, rather than by or through one or more grantee organizations which receive such qualifying distributions directly or indirectly from such foundation."

Section 53.4942(b)-1(b)(2), Foundation Excise Tax Regs., provides an exception to the general rule. That regulation considers "Payments to individual beneficiaries," and provides in pertinent part: [the court here quotes from Treasury Regulation 53.4942(b)-1(b)(2)(i)–(ii)(A); we omit the provision to preserve space, though readers may wish to pause and read the provision before reading proceeding].

The controversy centers on whether the foundation's granting of scholarships is a "qualifying distribution . . . directly for the active conduct of the foundation's exempt activities." We find that it is.

Respondent argues that the foundation merely screens and selects applicants. Petitioner, on the other hand, contends that it maintains a significant involvement in its exempt activity, and, therefore, the scholarship amounts should be considered as qualifying distributions. We agree with petitioner.

The determination of whether the scholarships made by petitioner constitute "qualifying distributions expended directly for the active conduct of the foundation's exempt activities," is a purely factual one, made on a qualitative basis. Sec. 53.4942(b)-1(b)(2), Foundation Excise Tax Regs. An exempt organization, such as petitioner, that uses more of its funds for scholarships than for any other purpose can still be considered a private operating foundation if it maintains a significant involvement in an exempt activity for which such scholarships are awarded. "Significant involvement" occurs if an exempt purpose of the foundation is to relieve poverty and its conditions among a poor class of persons, the making of such payments is direct, and the foundation has personnel who supervise and direct the activities described on a continuing basis. Sec. 53.4942(b)-1(b)(2)(ii)(A), Foundation Excise Tax Regs.

A careful review of the record is necessary to determine whether the foundation maintains a significant involvement in an exempt activity for which scholarships are awarded. Whether petitioner maintains a significant involvement is a factual determination. Sec. 53.4942(b)-1(b)(2), Foundation Excise Tax Regs. A primary objective of the foundation is to improve the county. This objective is sought to be accomplished by giving Butler County high school students a chance to receive a college education. The trust agreement sets forth the criteria by which the potential scholarship beneficiaries are to be selected. The most important consideration is need. After selection of the scholarship recipients, the board, on a volunteer basis, maintains contact with the recipients, assists them in finding summer jobs in Butler County, introduces them to officials, business, and professional leaders of the county, conducts county tours and compiles data and statistics promoting the county as a desirable place to live and work. Such activity hardly qualifies as mere selection, screening, and investigation of applicants. We believe that an exempt purpose of petitioner is to relieve poverty in a poor class of people through aiding needy students in Butler County to obtain a college education and through encouraging those students to return to the county, thus raising the standard of living. Accordingly, we find that under these facts, petitioner's program amounts to a "significant involvement" as defined by section 53.4942(b)-1(b)(2)(ii)(A), Foundation Excise Tax Regs.

In addition, petitioner meets the requirements of the endowment test.

Petitioner will satisfy the endowment test if it normally makes qualifying distributions directly for the active conduct of activities constituting its exempt purpose in an amount not less than two-thirds of its minimum investment return. Petitioner, therefore, must make qualifying distributions of approximately $4,533 to satisfy the test. Petitioner spends $6,000 each year in scholarships and $600 in expenses related thereto.

Petitioner, therefore satisfies the endowment test as stated under section 4942(j)(3)(B)(ii).

Accordingly, petitioner is qualified as a private operating foundation as defined by section 4942(j)(3).

Note: "Exempt" Operating Foundation Status and the Reduced Audit Fee Tax

To be an "exempt" operating foundation, an operating foundation must have met the §§ 170 or 509 public support test for at least 10 of its taxable years, and for the taxable year that it is seeking exempt operating foundation status, its governing board may have no more than 25% disqualified persons[6] and must be "broadly representative" of the community. IRC § 4940(d)(2). In addition, a disqualified person may not be an officer of the foundation during the taxable year for which it seeks exemption. *Id.*

Questions

1. Private Foundation (PF) earns the following amounts of income during the taxable year: $29,000 from an unrelated business, $142,000 in rents, $11,000 in dividends, $58,000 gain on the sale of stock. It also suffers a loss of $23,000 on the sale of a building that housed its administrative offices and spent $2,000 for investment advice.

   a. What is PF's 4940 tax for the year?

   b. What if the building on which a loss was suffered had been used as rental property that housed banks, accounting firms and law firms?

   c. What if PF received some valuable paintings and sculptures from a decedent's estate, none of which had any relation to its charitable purpose, and two months after receipt of the paintings, PF sold them at public auction for $800,000?

   d. Assume PF conducts a leadership institute in its community, whereby it conducts a six-week course through which it identifies promising persons in the community and trains them to be community leaders. The course provides instruction on public speaking, working with the media, accessing government, and community organizational skills. PF's assets for the taxable year and the past three years consist of an endowment fund worth $3,500,000 and a furnished building, from which it conducts classes and houses its administrative offices, worth $300,000. Approximately 70% of PF's support is derived from income on its endowment fund. In the taxable year and the past four years, PF has spent $250,000 annually to conduct its leadership course. Is PF liable for the 4940 tax?

---

6. For "exempt operating foundation" purposes, disqualified persons is defined more narrowly than under § 4946. For exempt operating foundation purposes, disqualified persons includes only (i) substantial contributors, (ii) 20% (or more) owner of entities that are substantial contributors, and (iii) § 4946(d) family members of the first two categories.

Chapter 17

Private Foundation Excise Taxes — Self Dealing and Excess Business Holdings

A. Disqualified Persons

CODE: §§ 4946; 507(d)(2)

REGS.: TREAS. REG. §§ 53.4946-1; 1.507-6

We begin consideration of the non-audit fee tax excise taxes with the definition of "disqualified persons" because of its relevance in applying these taxes. The basic definition of a disqualified person is easy enough to grasp. Though we have seen the phrase, "disqualified person" with respect to § 4958 (excess benefit transactions), the private foundation excise tax regime adopts a completely different definition of "disqualified person."

A "substantial contributor" — that is, a person, corporation, unincorporated enterprise, partnership, estate, or trust that contributes or bequeaths more than $5,000 to a private foundation in a taxable year — is a disqualified person if the contribution makes up more than 2% of the foundation's total gifts or bequests for the year. IRC §§ 507(d)(2); 4946(a)(1). In the case of a trust, the creator of the trust is always considered a "substantial contributor." *See* IRC § 507(d)(2)(A). Spouses are treated as a single unit for purposes of determining their amounts contributed or bequeathed. IRC § 507(d)(2)(B)(iii). Thus, if husband contributes $1,000 and wife contributes $6,000, both are treated as if they contributed $7,000. A public charity is excluded from disqualified person status for all purposes, and a private foundation is excluded from disqualified person but only for § 4941 (self-dealing) purposes. Treas. Reg. § 53.4946-1(a)(7).

Once a person becomes a substantial contributor, it is very difficult to shake that status. A person ceases to be a substantial contributor only if neither he/she nor any related person makes any contribution to the foundation or serves as a foundation manager at any time during the 10-year period ending at the close of the preceding taxable year. IRC § 507(d)(2)(C). Even if the substantial contributor does not make a contribution or serve as a foundation manager during the next 10 years, he or she will still be treated as a disqualified person unless the Service determines that his/her aggregate contributions, including contributions by related persons, are "insignificant" when compared to at least one other person. *Id.* "Foundation managers" are classified as disqualified persons even if they never contribute a dime to the foundation. IRC § 4946(a)(1)(B). A foundation manager is an officer, director, trustee, or any person holding powers or responsibility similar to those held by such persons. In addition, an employee with final authority or responsibility, whether officially or de facto, over an act or failure to act is a disqualified person with regard to that act or failure to act. IRC § 4946(b)(2).

The definition only gets more burdensome for the foundation from the initial starting point of identifying substantial contributors and foundation managers. All family members — very broadly defined as spouses, ancestors, descendants to the great-grandchild level, and spouses of those descendants — of substantial contributors or foundation managers are disqualified persons. IRC § 4946(a)(1)(D). Note that siblings of a disqualified person are not disqualified persons. If a corporation, partnership, unincorporated enterprise, or trust is a disqualified person, any person who owns 20% of the voting power (corporations), profit interest (partnerships) or beneficial interest (trusts) thereof is also a disqualified person, and any family member of a 20% owner is a disqualified person. IRC § 4946(a)(1)(C) and (D). The attribution rules of IRC § 267(c) apply (except with the broader definition of "family" discussed above) for purposes of determining the percentage of ownership held by any one person. A corporation, partnership, unincorporated entity, estate, or trust can also be a disqualified person even if it is not a substantial contributor. If disqualified persons (i.e., substantial contributors — foundation managers, family members, or 20% owners) own more than 35% of the voting power (corporations), profit interest (partnerships), or beneficial interest (trust, estate, or unincorporated enterprise), then the entity is a disqualified person. IRC § 4946(a)(1)(E)–(G).

For purposes of § 4943 (the excess business holding provision), a private foundation is a disqualified person with respect to another private foundation if the private foundations are "effectively controlled" by the same person or persons, or if substantially all the contributions are made to the foundations by the same disqualified persons (except 35% owned entities). The regulations incorporate the definition of control used for purposes of the transfer pricing regulation. The incorporated transfer pricing regulation states:

> *Controlled* includes any kind of control, direct or indirect, whether legally enforceable or not, and however exercisable or exercised, including control resulting from the actions of two or more taxpayers acting in concert or with a common goal or purpose. It is the reality of the control that is decisive, not its form or the mode of its exercise. A presumption of control arises if income or deductions have been arbitrarily shifted.

Treas. Reg. § 1.482-1(i).[1] "Substantially all" means 85% of all contributions and bequests ever received, and only persons who have made at least 2% of a foundation's

---

1. The regulations refer to § 1.482-1(a)(3), which cite relates to a prior version of the 482 regulations.

contributions or bequests are included in the "same person or persons" group. A "government official" is also a disqualified person, but only for purposes of § 4941 (regarding self-dealing). Treas. Reg. § 53.4946-1(g)(1) specifically enumerates those positions that fall within the definition of government official.

Question

There is only one method to really get a grasp on the definition of "disqualified persons" for purposes of the private foundation excise taxes—practice, practice, practice! The following question is not intended to make your life miserable, though we admit that it may have that effect. Our best advice—to complete the question and in practice: make an organizational chart.

ABB is a Foundation Manager of PF1. ABB owns 40% of XYZ Corporation, which is a substantial contributor to PF4. SJW is a Foundation Manager of PF2. SJW owns 40% of ABC Corporation, which is a substantial contributor to PF3. SJW is married to VKB, the daughter of ABB. PF1, PF2, PF3, and PF4 are unrelated private foundations. List any 4946 disqualified persons as to each private foundation.

B. The Self-Dealing Excise Tax

Code: § 4941

Regs.: §§ 53.4941(a)-1; 53.4941(d)-1; 53.4941(d)-2(f); 53.4941(d)-3

The prohibition against self-dealing is similar to, and has its roots in, the prohibition against private inurement. Recall that the prohibition against private inurement operates to prevent "insiders" from realizing valuable benefits from and at the expense of the organization. (Similar to the "first bite" rule applicable under § 4958, self-dealing cannot result from a transaction with a person who becomes a disqualified person solely as a result of the transaction. Treas. Reg. § 53.4941(d)-1.) Likewise, the prohibition against self-dealing is intended to prevent persons with significant financial influence over the private foundation from realizing valuable benefits as a result of their status. The significant difference, however, is that under § 4941, most (but not all) transactions between the organization and its disqualified persons—the private foundation analogue to "insiders"—are irrebuttably presumed to result in prohibited benefit. Those transactions will trigger the § 4941 sanction even though the transaction is fair, reasonable, and results in no discernable harm to the private foundation. Congress simply believes that in the context of private foundations, the strength of the conflict between the disqualified person's individual and fiduciary interests, coupled with the lack of public oversight, creates too high a potential for abuse. Thus, the prohibition against profit-taking is much more absolute in the private foundation setting than it is in the public charity setting.

A self-dealing transaction triggers an initial tax on the participating disqualified person equal to 10% of the "amount involved" for each year in the "taxable period."

IRC § 4941(a)(1). The "amount involved" is the amount paid to or by the private foundation, whichever is greater. Treas. Reg. § 53.4941(e)-1(b). In the case of unreasonable compensation, the "amount involved" is the amount by which the compensation exceeds a reasonable amount. IRC § 4941(e)(2). The taxable period includes all years, or parts of years occurring within the period measured from the date of the transaction and ending on the earliest of the date on which a notice of deficiency is mailed, an assessment is made, or the transaction is "corrected." IRC § 4941(e)(1). There is no time limit on making an assessment if the foundation does not file a tax return. IRC § 6501(c)(3). If the private foundation files the return, assessment must be made within three years from the date of filing. IRC § 6501(a). But if the return understates an excise tax by more than 25%, the period is extended to six years. The regulations provide very detailed "minimum standards" related to the definition of correction. Treas. Reg. § 53.4941(e)-1(c)(2)–(6). In general, however, a correction occurs when the transaction is "undone" to the extent possible and the private foundation's financial position is no worse than it would have been had the transaction not occurred. Treas. Reg. § 53.4941(e)-1(c)(1). Thus, "correction" involves rescinding the transaction (unless the property exchanged in the self-dealing transaction was later sold to a good faith purchaser) and turning over to the private foundation any gains realized by the disqualified person and traceable to the relevant property.

Any disqualified person (other than a government official), who participates in a self-dealing transaction, is strictly liable for the tax. A government official is liable only if he participates in the transaction knowing it to be prohibited under § 4941. Treas. Reg. § 53.4941(d)-2(d)(1). A foundation manager whose only participation in a self-dealing transaction is pursuant to his role as a foundation manager is not liable for the first-tier tax. IRC § 4941(a)(1). A foundation manager, however, is liable for a 5% tax if a tax is imposed on a disqualified person, but only if he knows that the transaction is prohibited and willfully and without reasonable cause participates in the self-dealing transaction. IRC § 4941(a)(2). If the transaction is not corrected within the taxable period, an additional excise equal to 200% of the amount involved is imposed on the disqualified person. IRC § 4941(b)(1). The foundation manager is liable for an additional tax equal to 50% of the amount involved if she refuses to agree to part or all of the undoing of the transaction. IRC § 4941(b)(2). Both the first and second tier tax that may be imposed on foundation managers are limited to $20,000. Self-dealing transactions are defined in IRC § 4941(d)(1)(A) through (F). In general, an act of self-dealing occurs through any transfer of value — i.e., a sale, exchange, leasing or loaning of property, money, goods, services, or facilities — between a disqualified person and an associated private foundation. In addition, a self-dealing transaction occurs when a disqualified person is allowed to use the private foundation's income or assets, whether for adequate consideration or not. Treas. Reg. § 53.4941(d)-2(d)(1). The code and regulation definitions are self-explanatory so we do not restate them in detail here.

Note, however, that consistent with general tax principles, there can be a "sale" of property to a private foundation when a disqualified person contributes encumbered property to a private foundation. IRC § 4941(d)(2). However, that rule applies only if the private foundation assumes the debt or takes the property subject to a debt that was placed on the property within 10 years of the contribution. A disqualified person may, of course, contribute—that is, a transfer for no charge—goods, services, or facilities, or the use of money without engaging in a self-dealing transaction. The goods, services, facilities, or interest-free use of money, however, must be used exclusively for an exempt purpose. IRC § 4941(d)(2)(B) and (C). A self-dealing transaction occurs, however, if by any circumstance, a disqualified person becomes a creditor or debtor of the associated private foundation (provided the debt is not interest free in cases involved a disqualified creditor). Treas. Reg. § 53.4941(d)-2(c)(1). For example, if a third party contributes a disqualified person's note to a private foundation, a self-dealing transaction occurs even though the disqualified person originally gave the note to the third-party contributor and not to the private foundation. That is, a prohibited debtor-creditor relationship need not arise solely by a straightforward lending of money by or to the private foundation.

In certain instances, an exchange of value between a private foundation and one of its disqualified persons will not be a self-dealing transaction. The first such instance is the private foundation's furnishing of goods, services, or facilities to a disqualified person, but only if the goods, services, or facilities are made available to the general public on no less favorable basis as they are made available to the disqualified person. IRC § 4941(d)(2)(D). The regulations specify that this exception will not apply if there is an insubstantial constituency (excluding disqualified persons) who use the goods, services, or facilities. Treas. Reg. § 53.4941(d)-3(b)(2). For example, if a private foundation has a collection of books held available to the public, but only a few members of the public actually use the books, the furnishing of the books to a disqualified person will not fit within the exception.

Another exception allows a private foundation to pay reasonable compensation and expense reimbursements to disqualified persons who provide personal services to the foundation. IRC § 4941(d)(2)(E). The services must be reasonable and necessary to the carrying out of the foundation's exempt purpose. Under the regulations, a private foundation may indemnify (directly or via liability insurance) a foundation manager against civil costs and liabilities without engaging in a self-dealing transaction if: (1) the indemnified expenses were reasonably incurred, and the manager did not act willfully and without reasonable cause with respect to the event giving rise to the liability or civil costs. Treas. Reg. § 53.4941(d)-2(f)(3). In other cases, indemnification can be provided against: (1) a penalty, tax, or correction expense, or (2) a liability arising from a foundation manager's unreasonable or willful act or failure, if in either case the foundation manager is not unreasonably compensated, taking into account all compensation plus the indemnification amount or premiums. Treas. Reg. § 53.4941(d)-2(f)(4).

The reasonable compensation exception does not apply to the payment of compensation to a government official. IRC § 4941(d)(2)(E). However, certain other payments to government officials—prizes or awards excludible under § 74 if the government official is selected from the general public, certain annuities, gifts or contributions not in excess of $25, and payments relating to employee training programs—do not constitute self-dealing transactions. IRC § 4941(d)(2)(G). In addition, a private foundation may reimburse government officials for domestic travel expenses, including meals and lodging, even if the amount is not deductible to the governmental employee. IRC § 4941(d)(2)(G)(vii).

The final exception involves exchanges of value between a private foundation that is a shareholder of a corporate disqualified person. If the private foundation transfers its stock to the corporate disqualified persons as part of a liquidation, merger, redemption, recapitalization, or similar corporate-shareholder transaction, it will not be an act of self-dealing so long as the terms of the transaction are the same for all shareholders in the class and the private foundation receives no less than fair market value. IRC § 4941(d)(2)(F). Thus, a disqualified person may redeem the private foundation shareholder's stock if the terms of the redemption are the same for all other shareholders of the same class of stock and the redemption price is equal to or greater than fair market value. The following cases highlight some of the more common issues arising under § 4941.

John W. Madden, Jr. v. Commissioner

T.C. Memo. 1997-395 (1997)

FAY, Judge:

* * *

Self-Dealing Transactions

Petitioner is a disqualified person, as defined by section 4946(a)(1), with respect to the Museum. Petitioner admits that on June 5, 1985, the Museum and petitioner engaged in a self-dealing transaction. He also admits that, on July 12, 1985, he and the Museum engaged in a self-dealing transaction. Petitioner concedes that he owes the first tier excise tax under section 4941(a)(1) on the self-dealing transactions.

The transactions involve payments made by the Museum for repairs to artwork owned by petitioner. In each case, petitioner was out of town when the transactions occurred. As noted supra, employees of the Company performed accounting services for the Museum. While petitioner was out of town, checks were issued from the Museum's bank account for services rendered to repair petitioner's artwork. Petitioner's daughter learned of the transactions a day or two after they occurred and corrected them immediately by having petitioner reimburse the Museum.

A third transaction at issue involves a $3,000 payment made by the Museum to Form, Inc. Form, Inc., is an association of artists who create large stone sculptures. The payment relates to art exhibition expenditures made pursuant to a contract with Form, Inc. However, the Company is the named party in the contract with Form, Inc., not the Museum.

Opinion

* * *

Issue 3. Payments to GMC

Section 4941 imposes an excise tax for acts of "self-dealing" that occur between a private foundation and a "disqualified person". Sec. 4941(a)(1). The parties agree that GMC is a "disqualified person" with respect to the Museum, a private foundation. For the purposes of this section, "self-dealing" includes the "furnishing of goods, services, or facilities between a private foundation and a disqualified person". Sec. 4941(d)(1)(C). However, section 4941(d)(2) provides several exceptions for certain arrangements that would otherwise constitute self-dealing transactions. Specifically, section 4941(d)(2)(E) provides:

> the payment of compensation (and the payment or reimbursement of expenses) by a private foundation to a disqualified person for personal services which are reasonable and necessary to carrying out the exempt purpose of the private foundation shall not be an act of self-dealing if the compensation (or payment or reimbursement) is not excessive . . .

Throughout the years at issue, the Museum contracted with GMC to perform general maintenance, janitorial, and custodial functions. Respondent maintains that payments to GMC for services performed are self-dealing transactions within the ambit of section 4941(d)(1)(C). Petitioner replies that these transactions fit within the exception in section 4941(d)(2)(E) as "personal services" which are reasonable and necessary to carry out the Museum's exempt functions. As might be expected, respondent disagrees.

The resolution of this issue depends solely on whether or not the functions that GMC performed fall within the definition of "personal services" of section 4941(d)(2)(E). Before making this determination, a review of the legislative history of section 4941 is helpful.

Prior to 1969, sections 501(a) and 503(a), (b), and (d) had imposed severe sanctions for transactions that resulted in the diversion of funds to a creator or substantial contributor of a tax-exempt organization. Further, in order to prevent tax-exempt foundations from being used to benefit their creators or substantial contributors, Congress had established a set of arm's length [sic] standards for dealings between the foundations and these disqualified individuals. H. Rept. 91-413 (Part 1), at 21 (1969), 1969-3 C.B. 200, 214.

Nevertheless, Congress noted that abuses involving tax-exempt organizations continued. Congress believed the abuses resulted from the significant enforcement problems posed by the arm's length [sic] standards. *Id.* Therefore, section 4941 was enacted as part of subchapter A of a new chapter 42 added to the Internal Revenue Code by the Tax Reform Act of 1969 (the 1969 Act), Pub. L. 91-172, sec. 101(b), 83 Stat. 487, 499.

One of the stated goals of the 1969 Act was to minimize the need for an arm's length [sic] standard by generally prohibiting self-dealing transactions. Specifically, the 1969 Act prohibited the following transactions between a foundation and a disqualified person: (1) The sale, exchange or lease of property; (2) the lending of money; (3) the furnishing of goods, services or facilities; (4) the payment of compensation to a disqualified person; (5) the transfer or use of foundation property by a disqualified person; and (6) payments to Government officials. S. Rept. 91-552, at 29 (1969), 1969-3 C.B. 423, 443. If the foundation and a disqualified person entered into a prohibited transaction, then the 1969 Act imposed various levels of sanctions.

The question before us is whether the functions performed by GMC qualify as "personal services" under section 4941(d)(2)(E). Thus, we must construe what activities Congress intended would qualify as personal services. At the outset, we can look to the regulations interpreting the statute. While those regulations do not define the term "personal services", they offer several examples of activities that constitute "personal services". *See* sec. 53.4941(d)-3(c)(2), Foundation Excise Tax Regs. The activities set out in the examples include legal services, investment management services, and general banking services. *Id.*

Respondent argues that the character of the services performed by GMC, namely maintenance, janitorial, and security, are different than those outlined in the regulations. We agree. The services in the regulations are essentially professional and managerial in nature. These types of services contrast with the nature of the services rendered by GMC.

GMC contends any activity is a service where capital is not a major factor in the production of income. Under this interpretation, as set out in the brief, "the sale of goods is not the rendering of personal services, but certainly all other services which assist the private foundation in carrying on its legitimate business are personal services." We cannot agree with GMC's interpretation of the statute. First, this position would nullify the prohibition against furnishing services contained in section 4941(d)(1)(C), because almost any service would be a "personal service" and fall within the exception. The statute draws an explicit distinction between a "charge" for "furnishing of goods, services, or facilities", see sec. 4941(d)(1)(C) and (2)(C), and the payment of "compensation" "for personal services", see sec. 4941(d)(1)(D) and (2)(E). GMC's argument equating a charge for services with compensation for personal services significantly erodes this distinction.

Second, GMC's interpretation of the term "personal services" contravenes congressional intent, as expressed in the above legislative history. We think it is clear that Congress intended to prohibit self-dealing. Consequently, any exceptions to the self-dealing transactions rules should be construed narrowly. We therefore reject GMC's broad interpretation of the term "personal services" and conclude that the janitorial services provided by GMC do not meet the definition of "personal services". Accordingly, we find that the payments made by the Museum to GMC constitute "self-dealing" within the meaning of section 4941(d)(1)(C), and, as a consequence, GMC is liable for the self-dealing excise tax under section 4941(a)(1).[2]

Issue 4. Excise Tax on Payments Made by the Museum to GMC

We shall next turn our attention to whether petitioner, petitioner's wife, and petitioner's daughter (the foundation managers)[3] are liable under section 4941(a)(2) for payments made to GMC by the Museum. In general, section 4941(a)(1) imposes an excise tax on the self-dealer for each self-dealing transaction. When an excise tax is imposed under section 4941(a)(1), then section 4941(a)(2) may impose excise taxes on the management of the foundation as well.

Thus, this tax is imposed only when (1) a tax is imposed under section 4941(a)(1), (2) the participating foundation manager knows that the act is an act of self-dealing, and (3) the participation by the foundation manager is willful and is not due to reasonable cause. Sec. 53.4941(a)-1(b)(1), Foundation Excise Tax Regs. Respondent must prove, by clear and convincing evidence, that the foundation managers participated knowingly in the self-dealing transaction. Sec. 7454(b); Rule 142(c).

We first turn to the regulations to provide the initial guidance in applying section 4941(a)(2). The regulations interpret what the statute requires for knowing participation. Section 53.4941(a)-1(b)(3), Foundation Excise Tax Regs., states:

> a person shall be considered to have participated in a transaction "knowing" that it is an act of self-dealing only if—
>
> (i) He has actual knowledge of sufficient facts so that, based solely upon such facts, such transaction would be an act of self-dealing,
>
> (ii) He is aware that such an act under these circumstances may violate the provisions of federal tax law governing self-dealing, and
>
> (iii) He negligently fails to make reasonable attempts to ascertain whether the transaction is an act of self-dealing, or he is in fact aware that it is such an act.

The regulations specify that the term "knowing" does not mean "having reason to know", but evidence that shows a person has a reason to know a fact is relevant in determining whether that person has actual knowledge of that fact. *Id.* These regulations were adopted in 1972, 3 years after the passage of the statute, and have not been substantially modified since that time. Therefore, we must give appropriate

2. [7] Respondent asserts that, if GMC is liable for the self-dealer excise tax, then it is also liable for the foundation self-dealing excise tax under sec. 4941(b)(1). GMC does not dispute this assertion. The parties have stipulated that the transactions at issue were not corrected within the taxable period.

3. [8] A separate excise tax was imposed on petitioner, on petitioner's wife, and on petitioner's daughter (the foundation managers). However, the legal issues and relevant facts are identical with respect to each of the foundation managers. For brevity, we will combine our examination of each tax into a single discussion and refer to the above-named parties collectively as the foundation managers where possible.

weight to the regulations in interpreting the statute. *Commissioner v. South Texas Lumber Co.*, 333 U.S. 496 (1948).

The parties have stipulated that the foundation managers were aware both that GMC was a disqualified person vis-a-vis the Museum, and that some transactions between a private foundation and a disqualified person are considered "self-dealing" under section 4941(d). Further, the parties have agreed that the foundation managers were aware self-dealing is defined as, inter alia, a direct furnishing of goods, services, or facilities between a private foundation and a disqualified person. In addition, the parties have agreed that the foundation managers were aware the Museum was making payments to GMC, and the managers did not oppose the making of these payments. On the basis of these facts, we conclude respondent has proven, by clear and convincing evidence, that the foundation managers possessed actual knowledge of sufficient facts concerning the transactions to establish the arrangements with GMC were self-dealing transactions.

Respondent has satisfied both the first and second requirements of section 4941(a)(2). First, we have concluded that, under section 4941(a)(1), an excise tax should be imposed on the payments from the Museum to GMC. Second, respondent has established that the foundation managers possessed sufficient "knowledge" concerning the self-dealing payments to GMC. Next, we shall evaluate whether the foundation managers made the payments willfully and without reasonable cause, the third requirement under section 4941(a)(2).

The regulations define "willful" participation by the foundation manager as conduct that is "voluntary, conscious, and intentional." Sec. 53.4941(a)-1(b)(4), Foundation Excise Tax Regs. On the basis of the facts, we conclude the foundation managers voluntarily and intentionally caused the Museum to enter into the transactions with GMC. Accordingly, we sustain respondent's determination that the participation of the foundation managers was willful.

Additionally, the foundation managers' participation in these transactions must not be due to reasonable cause. The regulations explain that "A foundation manager's participation is due to reasonable cause if he has exercised his responsibility on behalf of the foundation with ordinary business care and prudence." Sec. 53.4941(a)-1(b)(5), Foundation Excise Tax Regs. The foundation managers were aware that GMC was a disqualified person with respect to the Museum, and they were aware that tax laws prohibited self-dealing transactions. Nevertheless, they proceeded to contract with GMC to provide services to the Museum without first attempting to get advice from their counsel concerning the implications of these arrangements. This demonstrates a failure to exercise their responsibilities with ordinary business care and prudence.

Question

Assume that when the Greenwood Plaza South (GPS) partnership donated the amphitheater to the Museum, it became a substantial contributor. Assume also that Madden owns a 75% profit interest in GPS and an unrelated person owns the remaining profit interest. If Madden's daughter signs an agreement with Madden's partner's daughter allowing her to use the museum at fair rental for a business reception, is there a self-dealing transaction? If so, who is liable for the taxes that might be imposed?

The following decision is noteworthy because it actually applies the excise tax language in a light favorable to a taxpayer. According to the government, Courts should read the language of the taxes literally. At issue were the § 4941 provisions dealing with redemption of stock. If a disqualified person purchases stock from a Private Foundation, § 4941(d)(2)(F) excludes it from an act of self-dealing if the purchase is on the same terms available to all persons. In this case, however, the redemption plan excluded officers and directors of the disqualified persons. Why? Because SEC rules required it. As a result, the Court explained, the redemption plan was unworkable if § 4941 applied literally: purchases from the Private Foundation would never be on identical terms as every possible shareholder because some shareholder—namely insiders—had to be excluded from the plan.

Deluxe Corporation v. United States

885 F.2d 848 (Fed. Cir. 1989)

Newman, Circuit Judge.

In applying Code § 4941(d)(2)(F) to this situation, we cannot ignore that by operation of law securities transactions involving officers and directors are not treated identically to other transactions, whether or not they are nominally subject to the same terms. Although officers and directors may hold the same class of stock as other shareholders, due to their extensive regulation while they are officers and directors their behavior as shareholders is circumscribed, from the practical and legal viewpoint. *See, e.g., Reliance Electric Co. v. Emerson Electric Co.*, 404 U.S. 418, 422 (1972) ("the only method Congress deemed effective to curb the evils of insider trading was a flat rule taking the profits out of a class of transactions in which the possibility of abuse was believed to be intolerably great.... 'Such arbitrary and sweeping coverage was deemed necessary to insure the optimum prophylactic effect.'") (quoting *Bershad v. McDonough*, 428 F.2d 693, 696 (7th Cir. 1970)).

The failure of § 4941(d)(2)(F) to treat this distinction in its text does not mean that Congress intended to present a conflict with the securities laws, or otherwise to make § 4941(d)(2)(F) unworkable when the disqualified person is a corporation whose officers and directors may be shareholders. *See American Tobacco Co. v. Patterson*, 456 U.S. 63 (1982) ("Statutes should be interpreted to avoid untenable distinctions and unreasonable results whenever possible.")

The self-dealing rules were designed to protect assets dedicated to charitable purposes, and thus enjoying exemption from tax, from manipulation to the benefit of disqualified persons. *See, e.g.*, S. Rep. No. 552, *supra*, at 6, *reprinted* at 2032. The underlying theme of the self-dealing rules is to protect against abuse by insiders. The

Program's ban on participation by officers and directors was based on their position as insiders, not on their position as shareholders. The restraint against officers and directors is in harmony with, if not furtherance of, the statutory purpose of preventing those in positions of control of a disqualified person from using such position for prohibited purpose. The Program simply makes explicit what is implicit, and the exclusion of the Corporation's officers and directors from the Program is a reasonable response to the existence of laws and rules that affect any stock transaction by officers and directors. This exclusion does not affect the terms to which all shares are subject. It is not the shares that are under restraint, but these specific insiders, and only for as long as they are officers and directors.

We conclude that the intent of Congress to prohibit self-dealing is served by accommodating the impact of the securities laws on shareholding insiders. The text "subject to the same terms" does not require a corporation which is a disqualified person to include in a redemption program those shares held by its officers and directors. We hold that the express exclusion of such persons from participation in the Program does not negate compliance with Code § 4941(d)(2)(F). The Claims Court's ruling to the contrary was in error.

Estate of Bernard J. Reis v. Commissioner

87 T.C. 1016 (1986)

Opinion

This matter is before the Court on cross-motions for summary judgment. Each party alleges that if its or his respective motion for summary judgment is denied, factual issues will remain which preclude entry of summary judgment in favor of the other party. . . .

The issues in this case arise out of the widely publicized and much litigated Estate of Mark Rothko (hereinafter sometimes referred to as the estate). Mark Rothko was a well-known American abstract expressionist painter who died in 1970. Bernard J. Reis, decedent (Reis), was one of the executors of the Estate of Mark Rothko. Reis also was one of the directors of the Mark Rothko Foundation (the foundation). The foundation was established by Mark Rothko in 1967. In his will, after making certain specific bequests to family members, Mark Rothko bequeathed all of his remaining property to the foundation.

Reis also was an officer and employee of the Marlborough Gallery, Inc. (the gallery). In May of 1970, shortly after Mark Rothko's death, the executors of the estate, including Reis, entered into contracts on behalf of the estate with the gallery under which the paintings of Mark Rothko (which comprised the bulk of the estate's assets) could be sold only by the gallery or its affiliated corporations, offices of which were located throughout the world. The contracts were to last 12 years, and the gallery was to receive a commission of 50 percent of the proceeds from the sale of each painting.

* * *

Much of the legal relief sought by the surviving family of Mark Rothko was granted in the New York litigation. Reis and the other executors of the estate were removed, the contract with the gallery was voided, and monetary damages were awarded to the estate.

... Respondent's representatives audited the foundation and determined that Reis was liable for various self-dealing excise taxes under section 4941 for the years 1970 through 197 . . . , and additions to tax under sections 6651 and 6684 for the same years. . . . .

Petitioner's motion for summary judgment is based on the following three alternative legal arguments: (1) That section 4941(d)(1)(E) and the related provisions are so vague and imprecise that they are unconstitutional and void; (2) that the assets of the estate were separate and distinct from the assets of the foundation and therefore that any improper, non-arm's length conduct that occurred in administering the assets of the estate do not also constitute self-dealing in the use of the assets of the foundation; and (3) that whatever misuse of the assets of the foundation may have occurred, under the undisputed facts of this case, such misuse did not constitute self-dealing by Reis because the assets of the foundation were not used for the benefit of or transferred to Reis.

* * *

Constitutionality of the Self-Dealing Excise Taxes

Petitioner argues that in light of the large amounts of Federal excise taxes (e.g., the approximate $21 million at issue herein) that can be assessed against an individual for self-dealing with respect to the assets of a private foundation, it is particularly important that the statutory language be clear and precise. If ambiguous, petitioner argues that the Court should not be hesitant to void the statute as unconstitutional. Petitioner submits that subparagraph (E) of section 4941(d)(1) is so vague that it should be held unconstitutional.

Although based on slightly different reasons, the constitutionality of the self-dealing excise taxes of section 4941 and the underlying regulations previously have been upheld. *Rockefeller v. United States*, 572 F. Supp. 9, 12–14 (E.D. Ark. 1982), *aff'd per curiam* 718 F.2d 290 (8th Cir. 1983), *cert. denied*, 466 U.S. 962 (1984). A number of court opinions have discussed the statutory scheme of the self-dealing excise taxes, and each opinion has recognized those provisions as a valid legislative response to perceived abuses in the use of private foundations. *Gershman Family Foundation v. Commissioner*, 83 T.C. 217, 224–225 (1984); *Adams v. Commissioner*, 70 T.C. 373, 379 (1978); *Matter of Kline*, 403 F. Supp. 974, 978–979 (D. Md. 1975), *aff'd per curiam* 547 F.2d 823 (4th Cir. 1977). We find no basis for holding any of the provisions of section 4941 unconstitutional.

Estate Property versus Foundation Property

Petitioner contends that under New York law the paintings of Mark Rothko that were the subject matter of the May 1970 contracts entered into by Reis and the other executors on behalf of the estate and the gallery constituted, at that time, property of the estate, not assets of the foundation. Petitioner thus contends that regardless of the propriety of those contracts, as a matter of law, the contracts could not have constituted acts of self-dealing by Reis with respect to assets of the foundation.

Respondent contends that because the foundation was a beneficiary under Mark Rothko's will, the foundation had a vested beneficial interest in the property of the estate. Respondent contends that Reis' acts with respect to the property of the estate simultaneously and adversely affected the foundation's beneficial interest therein and thereby constituted an indirect use by or for the benefit of Reis of the assets of the foundation. Respondent cites section 53.4941(d)-1(b)(3), Excise Tax Regs., as authority for the general proposition that acts of self-dealing with respect to property of an estate also will be regarded as acts of self-dealing with respect to assets of a private foundation that has a beneficial interest in the property of the estate. For the reasons explained below, we agree with respondent on this issue.

Section 53.4941(d)-1(b)(3), Excise Tax Regs., clearly contemplates that the interest of a private foundation in the property of an estate, as a beneficiary thereof, will be treated as an "asset" of the private foundation under section 4941(d)(1)(E). Accordingly, acts of self-dealing with respect to property of an estate may also constitute acts of self-dealing with respect to assets of a private foundation which is a beneficiary of the estate. Section 53.4941(d)-1(b)(3), Excise Tax Regs., provides, however, an exception to what otherwise is considered acts of self-dealing if, among other requirements, the transaction is approved by a probate court and if the transaction reflects an exchange at fair market value.

Petitioner concedes that the contracts entered into between the estate and the gallery do not qualify for the exception allowed in the section 53.4941(d)-1(b)(3), Excise Tax Regs. The sales contracts were not approved by the probate court and the terms of the contracts apparently did not reflect the fair market value of the paintings. Petitioner argues, however, that because section 53.4941(d)-1(b)(3), Excise Tax Regs., is written in the negative form (i.e., because it explains what transactions are excluded from being treated as acts of self-dealing under section 4941), the regulation does not cover transactions that are to be treated as acts of self-dealing under section 4941. We disagree.

It is obvious to us that the only reason section 53.4941(d)-1(b)(3), Excise Tax Regs., takes a negative approach and describes certain exceptions to acts of self-dealing is that in the absence of those exceptions, such transactions would have been covered by section 4941. In other words, in light of the terms of section 53.4941(d)-1(b)(3), Excise Tax Regs., it is clear that transactions affecting the assets of an estate generally are treated also as affecting the assets of any private foundation which, as a beneficiary of the estate, has an expectancy interest in the assets of the estate.

As previously mentioned, the validity of section 53.4941(d)-1(b)(3), Excise Tax Regs., has been sustained. See *Rockefeller v. United States, supra*. The general purpose of the regulation was explained as follows:

> It logically follows that Congress would be concerned about the circumvention of an estate's assets which are earmarked for a private foundation, especially in a case such as this, where the bulk of the estate is bequeathed to a charitable trust. It is also reasonable to subject such an estate, in part, to the statutory checks which Congress has deemed fit for private foundations. [*Rockefeller v. United States*, 572 F. Supp. 9, 14 (E.D. Ark. 1982).]

In summary, regardless of whether the foundation is considered to have had a vested or merely an expectancy interest under New York law in the property of the Mark Rothko Estate, under section 4941 and the relevant Treasury regulations, the expectancy interest the foundation had in the estate is treated as an asset of the foundation, and transactions affecting property of the estate are treated as affecting assets of the foundation. Such transactions are excepted from the definition of acts of self-dealing under section 4941 only if they qualify for the exception described in section 53.4941(d)-1(b)(3), Excise Tax Regs., or under one of the other available exceptions (e.g., the exception for transactions which provide only incidental benefits to disqualified persons). Sec. 53.4941(d)-2(f)(2), Excise Tax Regs.

Benefit to Petitioner

Petitioner's third argument in support of its motion for summary judgment is that the alleged acts of self-dealing only could have benefited Reis in a nonpecuniary manner and that under any proper reading of section 4941, that section does not reach nonpecuniary benefits. We disagree.

The language of section 4941(d)(1)(E) does not suggest that it is limited to pecuniary benefits, and we find no basis for imposing such a limitation. Section 4941(d) enumerates in detail those categories of activities that will constitute acts of self-dealing. The purpose of that enumeration was to clarify what acts would be considered acts of self-dealing and to minimize the need to use subjective standards in evaluating potential acts of self-dealing. S. Rept. 91-552 (1969), 1969-3 C.B. 423, 442–443; *Rockefeller v. United States*, 572 F. Supp. 9, 12–13 (E.D. Ark. 1982).

Petitioner argues that respondent's interpretation of section 4941(d)(1)(E) is erroneous because it is too broad and fails adequately to distinguish between significant and insignificant personal benefits accruing to a disqualified person. We again disagree. Implicit in the statutory language of subparagraph (E) of section 4941(d)(1) is the requirement that the benefits accruing to the disqualified person be significant. That reading of the statute is supported by Treasury regulations which expressly provide that incidental or tenuous benefits accruing to a disqualified person will not constitute acts of self-dealing. See sec. 53.4941(d)-2(f)(2), Excise Tax Regs.

We also note that respondent contends that the benefits accruing to Reis as a result of the alleged acts of self-dealing were pecuniary in nature and were substantial. Although such allegation does not establish either of those facts, we must assume such facts to be true for purposes of deciding petitioner's motion for summary judgment. *Espinoza v. Commissioner*, 78 T.C. 412 (1982). If petitioner establishes in a subsequent trial herein that Reis, as a disqualified person, received tenuous benefits from his use of the assets of the foundation, section 53.4941(d)-2(f)(2), Excise Tax Regs., will protect petitioner from imposition of the self-dealing taxes.

For the reasons set forth above, petitioner's motion for summary judgment against respondent will be denied.

Respondent's Motion for Summary Judgment

Respondent argues that this Court, pursuant to Fed. R. Evid. 201, should take judicial notice of the specific findings of fact of the New York State courts in the New York litigation. Respondent argues that those findings constitute adjudicative facts of which this Court should take judicial notice and that they thereby are conclusively established for purposes of the instant proceeding. Respondent argues that those findings of fact establish that Reis was a disqualified person under section 4941, that Reis engaged in acts of self-dealing, and that the benefits accruing to Reis were direct and substantial. Accordingly, respondent argues that those findings properly may serve as the basis for a decision that petitioner is liable for the self-dealing taxes at issue herein.

In the New York litigation, among other improprieties, the contracts between the Mark Rothko Estate and the gallery were found to have been entered into on a nonarm's-length basis and the executors were found to have acted imprudently. With regard to the reason Reis, as an executor of the estate, agreed to the terms of the two contracts with the gallery, the New York State courts described the personal benefits accruing to Reis as a result of the contracts as follows:

> the prestige and status of Reis as a director, secretary and treasurer of MNY [Marlborough Gallery, Inc.] apart from his salary as secretary-treasurer provided by Lloyd's MNY, and his fringe benefits and perquisites, were quite important to Reis' life style. The court infers and finds that Reis was concerned and insistent on the continuation of this prestigious status. He was known and wanted to be known as a collector of valuable masterworks of many artists. [Reis] continued to sell some of his and his family's private collection for substantial sums through MNY before, during and after the critical period of these estate negotiations. Even though MNY appears to have used the same twenty percent formula for commissions for selling Reis' consigned paintings as for those owned by other collectors, the elaborate color catalogues and efforts of Marlborough promotion on behalf of Reis were extraordinary when compared to efforts in behalf of other collectors. Reis' and his immediate family's share of such sales by Marlborough of part of their private collections for about eight years before through two years after the May 21, 1970 estate contracts here complained of, aggregated for Reis and his family almost $1,000,000. Air tickets to and from Venice and Houston were supplied to Reis by MNY purportedly to help MNY promote the enhancement of Mark Rothko's work after his death. It would seem that this aspect, and other aspects of his part-time association with

> MNY, were amenities of a prestigious and undemanding nature which he did not wish to relinquish . . .

Respondent contends that the New York litigation was exhaustive and expensive and dealt with all aspects of Reis' acts as an executor of the estate, his acts as a director of the foundation, and his acts as an employee of the gallery. The issues in that litigation were hotly contested and Reis was represented by reputable New York counsel. In summary, in the interests of judicial economy, respondent beseeches this Court to conclude that Reis already has had his day (i.e., years) in court and should not be allowed to relitigate herein the facts relating to his acts as an executor of the Mark Rothko Estate, as a director of the foundation, and as an employee of the gallery.

* * *

This is a very old case. Much litigation arising out of the administration of the Mark Rothko Estate already has occurred. It certainly will be tedious if this Court is required to rehear any significant facts concerning the administration of the estate. No one would be more pleased than this Court if we simply could take judicial notice of the many opinions of the New York State courts and make evidentiary and ultimate findings of fact herein based solely on the findings of fact set forth in those opinions.

Although we can and do take judicial notice herein under rule 201 of the existence of the New York State court opinions concerning the Mark Rothko Estate, we cannot take judicial notice of the specific findings of fact set forth therein. Such findings do not satisfy the two tests of rule 201(b). They are not generally known to the public, nor are they so indisputable that their accuracy cannot reasonably be questioned. The mere fact that a court in one opinion makes findings of fact is not a basis for the same or another court in another proceeding to take judicial notice of those findings and to deem them to be indisputably established for purposes of the pending litigation. In the absence of the application of collateral estoppel, petitioner is not precluded from relitigating herein the facts relating to her acts as an executrix of the Mark Rothko Estate and as a director of the foundation. Because such facts remain in dispute herein, respondent's motion for summary judgment is premature and must be denied. Rule 121, Tax Court Rules of Practice and Procedure.

Appropriate orders will be issued.

Note on Indirect Self-Dealing

How did the contract in *Estate of Reis* result in a "transfer to, or use by or for the benefit of, a disqualified person?" We know that Rothko was a disqualified person (because he was a foundation manager), and we can understand that an expectancy can be viewed as a valuable right in property. But the contract providing for an exclusive listing of the paintings was with a corporation and Rothko was not an owner of the corporation. He was instead a mere employee (albeit an officer)! The Service and the Court apparently take a broad view of indirect self-dealing. Is this appropriate, given the wide net that the definition of "disqualified person" creates? It's bad enough that an unsuspecting relative of a substantial contributor might suddenly receive a big tax bill. Remember, the knowledge requirement applies only to foundation managers and government officials. In addition to strict liability, other disqualified persons must be concerned with an ill-defined category of "indirect self-dealing." The following excerpt tries to reduce some of the uncertainty.

Alvin J. Geske, Indirect Self-Dealing and Foundations' Transfer for the Use or Benefit of Disqualified Persons

12 Houston L. Rev. 379 (1975)[4]

* * *

III. Toward a Definition of "Indirect Self-Dealing"

A. In General

The concept of "indirect self-dealing" originates in § 4941(d)(1), which indicates that the term *self-dealing* includes any direct or indirect act described in § 4941(d)(1)(A) through (F). The regulations adopt this concept of "indirect self-dealing" in § 53.4941(d)-1(b), but no comprehensive definition of this term is attempted. Rather, the regulations set forth a number of safe harbors—that is, types of transactions that will not ordinarily be considered indirect self-dealing. Despite several protests that a comprehensive definition of the term *indirect self-dealing* should be contained in the final regulations,[5] the Treasury Department's basic approach in the final regulations remains the same as that in the proposed regulations, namely, that of providing only enumerated safe harbors and avoiding any attempt at a comprehensive definition.[6] This apparently leaves the taxpayer to the uncertainties of a facts-and-circumstances test.

Generally, the following three types of transactions may involve indirect self-dealing:

(1) Transactions that are step transactions or shams;

(2) Transactions between an organization in which a foundation has an interest and a disqualified person; and

(3) Certain transactions between a disqualified person and an estate in which the foundation has an interest.

The third category of transactions normally would be subsumed within the second category. But since it offers significant opportunities to correct otherwise faulty

4. Reprinted with permission.

5. [1] *E.g.*, Letter from The American Institute of Certified Public Accountants to Commissioner of Internal Revenue, July 14, 1971; Letter from the Massachusetts Co., Inc., to Commissioner of Internal Revenue, July 3, 1971; *cf.* Kurz, *The Private Foundation Provisions: The Purpose and Effect of Sections 4941, 4942, 4943,* 1973 N.Y.U. 31st Inst. on Fed. Tax. 1311, 1317–20.

6. [2] Treas. Reg. § 53.4941(d)-1(b) (1973).

estate planning, and since the regulations contain certain complex rules that apply solely to this type of transaction,[7] this category will be examined separately.

B. "Indirect" as a Protection Against Step Transactions or Shams

1. *In General*— Although case law in federal income taxation has developed doctrines such as "step transaction," "sham," "business purpose," and "form over substance" to prevent taxpayers from taking advantage of technicalities or loopholes in the statutory scheme, these doctrines are read much more narrowly in some areas than in others.[8] The specific proscription against "indirect" self-dealings as used in § 4941(d)(1) indicates a congressional intent that the self-dealing rules are to be construed not as mere formal requirements that can be avoided by careful planning and satisfaction of form, but rather as expressions of a broad general policy against dealings involving foundations and disqualified persons, which should be interpreted broadly to achieve this objective.[9] Only those types of transactions that are specifically excepted by the statute should be allowed.

The exact scope of the transactions proscribed by the term *indirect self-dealing* under these doctrines is not clear. Certainly an arrangement, such as a sale, by a private foundation made through a third person who is under a binding agreement to transfer the property to a disqualified person at a given price is prohibited.[10] It may be that, in such a case if the third party were free to sell or not to sell to the disqualified person, there would be no act of self-dealing. In that situation, somewhat like situations under § 4941(d)(2)(F), there is third-party participation which may act as insurance that the foundation is not being cheated.[11] Even if this approach is adopted, however, there may be differences depending upon the degree of unrelatedness of the third party. Thus, it may be relevant if the third party is, although not a disqualified person, a person who is under the influence of a disqualified person. Under such circumstances the Internal Revenue Service may well find a step transaction.

Since the regulations do not generally address problems concerning the meaning of "indirect" in terms of the "step transaction" or "sham" doctrines, an analysis of whether a particular set of facts presents such a problem will have to be made on a case-by-case basis as with the application of the sham and step-transaction doctrines generally.

---

7. [3] *Id.* § 53.4941(d)-1(b)(3).

8. [4] *Compare* Bazley v. Commissioner, 331 U.S. 737 (1947), *and* Gregory v. Helvering, 293 U.S. 465 (1935), *with* Commissioner v. Day & Zimmerman, Inc., 151 F.2d 517 (3d Cir. 1945).

9. [5] S. Rep. No. 552, 91st Cong., 1st Sess. 28–34 (1970).

10. [6] *Cf.* Davant v. Commissioner, 366 F.2d 874 (5th Cir.), *cert. denied*, 386 U.S. 1022 (1966). *See generally* B. Bittker & J. Eustice, Federal Income Taxation of Corporation's and Shareholders 14.101-.103 (3d ed. 1971).

11. [7] *Cf.* Treas. Reg. § 53.4941(d)-3(d) (1973).

2. *Grants to Intermediaries*— The only "step transaction" problems discussed in the regulations involve grants to government officials made through third parties. The regulations provide that an act of "indirect self-dealing" does not include

> a transaction engaged in with a government official by an intermediary organization which is a recipient of a grant from a private foundation and which is not controlled by such foundation . . . if the private foundation does not earmark the use of the grant for any named government official and there does not exist an agreement, oral or written, whereby the grantor foundation may cause the selection of the government official by the intermediary organization.[12]

The regulations further provide that "a grant by a private foundation is earmarked if such grant is made pursuant to an agreement, either oral or written, that the grant will be used by any named individual."[13] The regulations make it clear, however, that a grant by a private foundation is not an indirect act of self-dealing even though the foundation had reason to believe that certain government officials would derive benefit from the grant so long as the intermediary organization exercises control in fact over the selection process and actually makes the selection completely independent of the private foundation.

These principles are illustrated by example (3) of § 53.4941(d)-1(b)(8), which states that a private foundation can make a grant to a university (not controlled by the private foundation) for the purpose of conducting a seminar to study methods for improving the administration of the judicial system even though the foundation has reason to believe that government officials would be compensated for participating in the seminar so long as the university has completely independent control over the selection of the participants. If there is an agreement that a particular individual is to be selected or if the foundation has control over the final selection of any government official, the grant would be treated as having been made by the private foundation to the government official.[14] Nevertheless, a private foundation probably does have some discretion in negotiations concerning the class of qualified recipients, such as carrying on a discussion relating to the minimum requirements for potential grant recipients.[15]

C. Transactions Involving an Organization in Which a Foundation Has an Interest

1. *In General*— In addition to functioning to prevent the deliberate use of agents and intermediaries to circumvent the limits on direct transactions between foundations and disqualified persons, the prohibition against indirect self-dealing

12. [8] *Id.* § 53.4941(d)-1(b)(2).
13. [9] *Id.*
14. [10] *See id.* § 53.4945-4(a)(4)(iv).
15. [11] The "earmarking" standard relating to grants to government officials in § 53.4941(d)-1(b)(2) gives a foundation somewhat less freedom to play a role in selection of individual grantees than it has in the area of individual grants under § 4945. *See id.* § 53.4945-4(a)(4).

apparently also includes certain transactions involving organizations in which a foundation has an interest.[16] Such organizations may include corporations, sole proprietorships, partnerships, estates, and trusts. While the first sort of indirect self-dealing is probably governed by established tax principles relevant to many areas of tax law, the second category appears to be unique to the private-foundation context, unless it is considered to be merely an outgrowth of the concepts embodied in the attribution rules among related groups found in many places in the Code.[17]

In examining different types of foundation-organization relationships, two types of transactions are particularly significant: transactions between a disqualified person and the organization and transactions between the foundation and the organization. In discussing these two types of transactions, it is helpful to consider separately the following three general classifications of situations: (1) situations where the foundation controls the organization or where its interest combined with the interest of a disqualified person is required to control the organization; (2) situations where the organization is controlled by a disqualified person or persons even without the foundation's interest being needed for such control; and (3) situations in which neither the foundation, the disqualified persons, nor the foundation and disqualified persons combined control the organization.

It is clear that relationships of these types will continue to exist over a long period of time. Thus, during the transitional periods allowed by § 4943, foundations alone can own a majority of the voting power in organizations, including active business entities, and even thereafter can own a majority of the voting power in certain passive entities. Similarly, minority interests in businesses can be held indefinitely, and estates and trusts in which foundations have an interest will be a continuing problem. Since the regulations primarily address situations in which a private foundation controls another organization, it is appropriate to examine the scope of these organizations' permissible dealings.

2. *Transactions Involving Controlled Organizations*—The regulations indicate that there are two different types of organizations controlled by a private foundation for purposes of the indirect self-dealing rules.[18] The first type of controlled organization exists if the foundation or its manager or managers acting as representatives of the foundation "may, only by aggregating their votes or positions of authority, require the organization to engage in a transaction which if engaged in with the private foundation would constitute self-dealing."[19] The second type of organization that is deemed controlled by a private foundation for purposes of certain transactions is an organization that is subject to "combined control." The regulations provide that if a transaction would be an act of self-dealing if engaged in between a

16. [12] *Id.* § 53.4941(d)-1(b).

17. [13] *See, e.g.*, Int. Rev. Code of 1954, §§ 267, 318, 544 (attribution rules).

18. [14] Treas. Reg. § 53-4941(d)-1(b)(5) (1973).

19. [15] *Id.*

controlled organization and a private foundation, it is an act of self-dealing for that controlled organization to engage in such a transaction with any disqualified person

> if such disqualified person, together with one or more persons who are disqualified persons by reason of such a person's relationship (within the meaning of section 4946(a)(1)(C) through (G)) to such disqualified person, may, only by aggregating their votes or positions of authority with that of the foundation, require the organization to engage in such a transaction.[20]

This "combined control" concept makes clear what the proposed regulations had hinted at, namely, that for purposes of determining control where the foundation itself does not control the organization directly but can control it with certain disqualified persons, if there are two sets of disqualified persons who are not related to one another, only the amounts of control of the concerned set of disqualified persons will be counted in analyzing a transaction between the organization and disqualified persons.

A "combined control" situation is set out in example (6) of § 53.4941(d)-1(b)(8). This example states in part as follows:

> Private foundation P owns 20 percent of the voting stock of corporation W. A, a substantial contributor with respect to P, owns 16 percent of the voting stock of corporation W. B, A's son, owns 15 percent of the voting stock of corporation W. The terms of the voting stock are such that P, A, and B could vote their stock in a block to elect a majority of the board of directors of W. W is treated as controlled by P.[21]

Consequently, the sale of property by *W* to *A* or *B* (or to any party whose relationship to *A* or *B* makes him a disqualified person) would be an act of self-dealing, because W is controlled by a combination of *P*, *A*, and *B*. If there were another disqualified person with respect to P who was completely unrelated to *A* or *B* and who owned, for example, none of the voting stock of *W*, *W* would not ordinarily be regarded as controlled with respect to a sale to such a disqualified person.[22]

The regulations also state that the concept of "control" is control in fact and not just control by reason of holding majority voting power. The regulations provide that control exists if the foundation or the foundation and interested disqualified persons

> are able, in fact, to control the organization (even if their aggregate voting power is less than 50 percent of the total voting power of the organization's governing body) or if one or more of such persons has the right to exercise

20. [16] *Id.*

21. [17] *Id.* § 53.4941(d)-1(b)(8) ex. (6).

22. [18] However, W would be regarded as controlled by *P* if it could be shown that *P*'s block of stock alone was sufficient to constitute control of W (an unlikely factual showing with *A* and *B*, father and son, having a total of 31 percent of the voting stock).

veto power over the actions of such organization relevant to any potential acts of self-dealing.[23]

This "control in fact" approach protects against the fairly common situation where a party or parties who actually possess less than 50 percent of the voting power of an organization nevertheless actually control the organization. This approach may present problems, however, because of the uncertainty in determining whether under particular circumstances a party may have control with less than a majority of voting power. This problem appears to occur only in corporations and perhaps in widely held partnerships. The "control in fact" approach may, however, have another side. For instance, a disqualified person owning perhaps 30 percent of the voting stock of an organization of which the foundation owns 25 percent may be able to show that his 30 percent is in fact a control block and, as a result, there is no "combined control" problem with respect to transactions between the disqualified person and the organization.

The regulations also take the position that the controlled organization can be, for example, "any type of exempt or nonexempt organization" including public charities and operating foundations, social welfare organizations, and presumably any kind of profit-making organizations such as a regular corporation or partnership, as well as an estate or trust.[24]

3. *Transactions Between Foundation-Controlled Organizations and Disqualified Persons—*

The regulations provide certain safe harbors with respect to transactions between a disqualified person and an organization controlled by a foundation, including "combined control" cases, where the organization is not itself a disqualified person. One of these rules provides that there is no indirect self-dealing with respect to certain business transactions between a disqualified person and such a controlled organization. The requirements for this exception are: (1) that the business relationship was established before January 1, 1970; (2) the transaction was at least as favorable to the controlled organization as an arm's length [sic] transaction with an unrelated party; and (3) severe economic hardship would result either to the controlled organization or to the disqualified person if the transaction had to be engaged in with an unrelated party.[25] The severe economic hardship to the disqualified person must meet another requirement: such hardship must be geared to the unique nature of the product or services provided by the controlled organization.

This exception is illustrated by example (2) of § 53.4941(d)-1(b)(8), which deals with a situation in which a controlled organization manufactures electronic

23. [19] Treas. Reg. § 53.4941(d)-1(b)(5) (1973).

24. [20] *Id.* This provision indicates, however, that a private foundation will not be deemed to have control over another organization merely because it exercises expenditure responsibility, as required by § 4945(d)(4) and (h), with respect to grants or contributions to the organization.

25. [21] *Id.* § 53.4941(d)-1(b)(1).

computers and a disqualified person "owns the patent for, and manufactures, one of the essential component parts used in the computers."[26] This situation is held to satisfy the "severe economic hardship" test and, in the context of a pre-1970 agreement and market-level prices, is specifically permitted.

Another exception to indirect self-dealing included in the final, but not the, proposed, regulations involves certain transactions in the normal course of a retail business. This exception provides as follows:

> The term "indirect self-dealing" shall not include any transaction between a disqualified person and . . . [a controlled organization] or between two disqualified persons where the foundation's assets may be affected by the transaction if—
>
> (i) the transaction arises in the normal and customary course of a retail business engaged in with the general public,
>
> (ii) in the case of a transaction between a disqualified person and an organization controlled by a private foundation, the transaction is at least as favorable to the organization controlled by the foundation as an arm's length [sic] transaction with an unrelated person, and
>
> (iii) the total of the amount involved in such transactions with respect to any one such disqualified person in any one taxable year does not exceed $5,000.[27]

Another stated exception to indirect self-dealing is "a transaction involving one or more disqualified persons to which a private foundation is not a party in any case in which the private foundation, by reason of § 4941(d)(2), could itself engage in such a transaction."[28] This exception allows, for example, a controlled organization to pay a disqualified person (other than a government official) reasonable compensation for personal services.[29]

These provisions and examples could be taken to imply by negative inference that all other transactions between disqualified persons and controlled organizations are self-dealing. The fear that the Treasury Department might take such a position led many commentators to protest vigorously against the proposed regulations, which contained only the first of the three exceptions enumerated above.[30] The addition of the other two exceptions has allayed some fears of persons representing private foundations by indicating that disqualified persons can continue to be employed by controlled corporations, that such controlled organizations can probably continue to pay interest to disqualified persons with respect to pre-1970 indebtedness (at least

26. [22] *Id.* § 53.4941(d)-1(b)(8) ex. (2).
27. [23] *Id.* § 53.4941(d)-1(b)(6).
28. [24] *Id.* § 53.4941(d)-1(b)(7).
29. [25] *Id.*
30. [26] Refer to authorities cited note 42 *supra*.

until taxable years beginning after December 31, 1979),[31] and that such controlled organizations can engage in retail sales for limited amounts to disqualified persons. Nevertheless, some problems remain.

The regulations, for example, provide no clear answer as to whether a controlled corporation can pay dividends to those of its shareholders who are disqualified persons without the risk of self-dealing. As an analytical matter, the foundation does not appear to be harmed by the allowance of a payment of dividends to all shareholders on a nondiscriminatory basis. Although the law is not entirely clear in this area, it would appear that in this situation, and perhaps in many other situations, the issue in a potential indirect situation should be whether the foundation is harried or cheated by the transaction rather than whether the transaction should be absolutely banned. This is the basic approach in several of the stated exceptions to indirect self-dealing, namely, the "business-hardship rules,"[32] the "estate" rules,[33] and the retail-sales-in-limited-amounts rules.[34] Although this approach is contrary to the general attitude taken in attempting to ban direct self-dealing transactions generally, it appears to be supported by an analysis of § 4941(d)(1)(E), which is concerned in part with use of the assets of a private foundation for the benefit of a disqualified person.

Thus, an analysis of indirect self-dealing in the area of transactions involving an organization in which a foundation has an interest appears to reflect some tension between two conflicting concepts—first, the concept of banning transactions between disqualified persons and foundations absolutely regardless of the benefit or detriment to the foundation, a position which generally prevails in § 4941; and, second, an analysis of whether the foundation has been cheated, that is, whether foundation assets have been used by or for the benefit of disqualified persons.

The regulations intend some transactions between disqualified persons and controlled organizations (such as those mentioned in the immediately preceding seven paragraphs) to be governed by arm's length [sic] standards. On the other hand, some transactions between disqualified persons and controlled organizations are probably intended to be banned absolutely, such as sales of significant portions of the controlled organization's operating assets or loans to a disqualified person by a controlled organization.[35] Perhaps the general distinction between the types of transactions to be governed by the arm's length [sic] standards and the types to be

31. [27] Certain transitional rules relating in part to allowing the continuance of certain pre-1970 indebtedness until taxable years beginning after December 31, 1979 are contained in the Tax Reform Act of 1969 and Treas. Reg. § 53.4941(d)-4(c). *See* Tax Reform Act of 1969, Pub. L. No. 91-172, § 101(l)(2), 83 Stat. 533. These transitional rules may well protect indirect transactions also by analogy to § 53.4941(d)-1(b)(7).

32. [28] Treas. Reg. § 53.4941(d)-1(b)(1) (1973).

33. [29] *Id.* § 53.4941(d)-1(b)(3

34. [30] *Id.* § 53.4941(d)-1(b)(6).

35. [31] A clear case of a transaction that should fit under the "absolute ban" rule is a loan made after 1969 to a disqualified person by an organization in which a foundation holds 95 percent of the voting power.

governed by the absolute ban may be that the absolute ban is, except in the limited circumstances set out in the regulations and analogous situations, to apply to all transactions of large amounts and of a type that are outside of normal business relationships. In the absence of both of these factors, the appropriate rationale is whether arm's-length standards have been satisfied. Nevertheless, the allowance of certain arm's length [sic] transactions should not necessarily be interpreted to allow substantial further entanglement of the affairs of the controlled organization and disqualified persons. Thus, while a foundation-controlled organization should be allowed to initiate the employment of a disqualified person at a reasonable salary, it is certainly questionable whether new loans should be allowed. In particular, it seems clear that where the foundation alone controls the organization, no new loans should be allowed.

4. *Transactions Between Disqualified Persons and Organizations Controlled by Disqualified Persons in Which a Private Foundation Has an Interest*—There may be different problems involved where the organization is controlled by disqualified persons rather than by a foundation, but where the foundation has an interest in the organization. Since control means control in fact, the organization itself may or may not be a disqualified person depending on whether the disqualified persons have more than a 35 percent interest in the organization. In either case transactions between disqualified persons and the organization are covered only in one rather limited provision of the regulations. This provision allows sales at retail to disqualified persons provided that the amount is under $5,000 per disqualified person per year.[36]

It would seem to be impossible to play the game of negative inferences with these regulations. Negative inferences from the above-mentioned exception could be interpreted to mean that any other activity is impermissible. Negative inferences from exceptions that apply solely to the controlled organizations could, on the other band, be used to indicate that there are no indirect self-dealing problems in such transactions. Neither result is proper.

A proper interpretation of indirect self-dealing in such transactions would indicate that transactions should be closely scrutinized to determine whether or not the foundation was cheated by such transaction. This type of approach should allow normal business relationships to proceed smoothly but should prohibit such acts as a redemption of a portion of the disqualified person's shares at a price in excess of fair market value on the grounds that the foundation is being cheated, as some of its assets are being used for the benefit of a disqualified person.

5. *Transactions Between Disqualified Persons and Organizations Controlled by Neither Disqualified Persons Nor Private Foundations*—In the case of a transaction between a disqualified person and an organization in which a foundation has an interest but which is controlled by neither disqualified persons, the foundation, nor any combination thereof, it appears generally that there is no problem of indirect

36. [32] Treas. Reg. § 53.4941(d)-1(b)(6) (1973).

self-dealing.[37] Nevertheless, in certain cases it may be appropriate to apply the test of whether a foundation is being cheated to certain transactions outside the scope of normal business. Thus, for example, redemption of a disqualified person's stock at a premium or a sale to a disqualified person at less than fair market value by such an organization could result in the foundation's interest being reduced in value. This sort of situation would be particularly open to challenge where the other parties interested were, although not themselves disqualified persons, related in some way to disqualified persons, such as brothers or sisters.

6. *Transactions Between a Foundation and an Organization in Which a Foundation or Disqualified Persons Have an Interest*—The regulations contain one subparagraph that is relevant to the general area of transactions between a private foundation and an organization in which there are ownership interests of a disqualified person or persons but which are insufficient to make the organization itself a disqualified person. This provision states that a transaction between a private foundation and an organization that is not controlled by the foundation and that is not a disqualified person itself because disqualified persons own no more than

> 35 percent of the total combined voting power or profits or beneficial interest of such organization shall not be treated as an indirect act of self-dealing between the foundation and such disqualified persons solely because of the ownership interest of such persons in such organization.[38]

Although this provision protects certain types of transactions, it would appear to create more questions than it answers. Thus, for instance, the use of the words "solely because" indicates that if other factors are added to the 35-percent-or-less-ownership factor, an act of self-dealing may occur. The identity of such undesirable other factors, however, is left to speculation, except perhaps in the most obvious of cases. Perhaps what is called for in such instances is an application of the criterion of whether the foundation has been cheated. For instance, a sale of property to a private foundation for a price in excess of fair market value or a redemption of the foundation's stock for less than fair market value might well be regarded as a diversion of the foundation assets to other parties, including disqualified persons.

In respect to transactions between a foundation and a controlled organization (that is, one controlled by the foundation within the definition of the regulations), a most intriguing question is whether there is a negative inference to be drawn from the safe-harbor rules described above. It seems clear that if the organization is wholly owned by the foundation, no such inference would exist. In such a case the foundation is merely transferring assets or funds from one pocket to another. Similarly, there is probably no problem in any case where disqualified persons have no interest in the controlled corporation because there is no direct or indirect transaction between a foundation and the disqualified person. On the other hand, where

37. [33] *Cf. id.* § 53.4941(d)-1(b)(4).

38. [34] *Id.*

disqualified persons have any significant interest in the controlled organization, negative inferences from the regulations' statements may exist. The main question is what sort of analysis should be applied in evaluating these transactions—should they be regarded as absolutely banned or should the issue be whether there is a diversion of foundation assets to the benefit of disqualified persons? The correct answer would seem to be that the analysis applied should focus on whether the foundation is cheated, since Congress was aware of many relationships in which foundations control businesses. As the transitional rules contained in chapter 42 of the Code and § 101(*l*) of the Tax Reform Act indicate, Congress probably did not intend to hinder greatly the dealings of these organizations with their controlling foundations during the transitional periods. Instead, Congress appeared to be concerned with getting foundations out of business enterprises in a reasonable and orderly manner without great economic hardship.[39]

In cases where the transactions are between a foundation and an organization that is controlled by disqualified persons, the problems are less severe. If disqualified persons have more than 35 percent of the voting or beneficial interests, the transaction between the foundation and such organization will be a direct act of self-dealing. In the case where disqualified persons control the organization but have less than a 35 percent interest, there again is occasion to examine the "solely because" language of § 53.4941(d)-1(b)(4). There are several alternative interpretations. One alternative is that control itself might be sufficient to make any transaction bad and might overcome the "solely because" safe harbor. This interpretation, coupled with the absolute-ban analysis, could prohibit any transaction between the foundation and the organization. Here again it appears appropriate to apply the analysis of whether the foundation is cheated in transactions between the foundation and such an organization for the same reason as stated in the transaction between a foundation and a controlled organization.

Similarly, with respect to a transaction between a foundation and an organization controlled by neither the disqualified persons nor the foundation in a situation where both disqualified persons and the foundation have an interest in the organization (or perhaps even where merely disqualified persons have an interest in the organization), it appears that there is some danger of indirect self-dealing. It would be appropriate to apply the standard of whether the foundation has been cheated by the transaction or transactions rather than to have an absolute ban on such transactions for reasons similar to those stated above.

D. Transactions During the Administration of an Estate or Revocable Trust

The regulations contain a very significant provision excepting from the term *indirect self-dealing* certain transactions during the administration of an estate or

39. [35] *See* S. Rep. No. 552, 91st Cong., 1st Sess. 34 (1970).

with respect to a revocable trust.[40] It is important to note that this provision does not protect any disqualified person (including the estate or trust) from the direct self-dealing rules. Consequently, if an estate were a disqualified person by virtue of either its contributions to the foundation or the ownership of more than 35 percent of the beneficial interests in the estate by disqualified persons, it could not, for example, sell property to the foundation, because the sale would be a direct act of self-dealing.

Despite this limitation, the provision has substantial significance and should be examined in detail. It reads as follows:

The term "indirect self-dealing" shall not include a transaction with respect to a private foundation's interest or expectancy in property (whether or not encumbered) held by an estate (or revocable trust, including a trust which has become irrevocable on a grantor's death), regardless of when title to the property vests under local law, if—

(i) The administrator or executor of an estate or trustee of a revocable trust either—

(*a*) Possesses a power of sale with respect to the property,

(*b*) Has the power to reallocate to another beneficiary, or

(*c*) Is required to sell the property under the terms of any option subject to which the property was acquired by the estate (or revocable trust);

(ii) Such transaction is approved by the probate court having jurisdiction over the estate (or by another court having jurisdiction over the estate (or trust) or over the private foundation);

(iii) Such transaction occurs before the estate is considered terminated for Federal income tax purposes pursuant to paragraph (a) of § 1.641 (b)-3 of this Chapter (or in the case of a revocable trust, before it is considered subject to section 4947);

(iv) The estate (or trust) receives an amount which equals or exceeds the fair market value of a foundation's interest or expectancy in such property at the time of the transaction, taking into account the terms of any options subject to which the property was acquired by the estate (or trust); and

(v) With respect to transactions occurring after April 16, 1973, the transaction either—

(*a*) Results in the foundation receiving an interest or expectancy at least as liquid as the one it gave up,

(*b*) Results in the foundation receiving an asset related to the active carrying out of its exempt purposes, or

40. [36] Treas. Reg. § 53.4941(d)-1(b)(3) (1973).

(*c*) Is required under the terms of any option which is binding on the estate (or trust).[41]

This provision is much more detailed than the comparable provision in the proposed regulations, which allowed certain transactions during the administration of an estate. Under this provision in the proposed regulations, either the foundation or a disqualified person could purchase property from the estate or have the property interests within the estate adjusted subject to the following conditions:

(1) Possession by the administrator or executor of a power of sale of the property or power to reallocate the property;

(2) Probate court approval;

(3) Occurrence of the transaction before the estate is considered terminated for federal income tax purposes; and

(4) Receipt by the foundation of an amount which equals or exceeds fair market value.[42]

The provision in the final regulations is substantially more expansive in some respects and more restrictive in others. A significant expansion of the provision is its application to revocable trusts as well as to estates. This expansion has been made in order to allow the use of a revocable trust as a substitute for a will or as a partial substitute for a will and reflects a view that this portion of the federal tax law should be neutral between these alternative means of estate planning.

Another expansion contained in the final regulations is explicit allowance of the disposition of property pursuant to an option to which the property is subject when it is received by the estate or trust. An example of property that would be covered under this provision is corporate shares or a partnership interest subject to a cross-purchase agreement or a redemption agreement. Allowance of such a disposition while the estate is in administration may be helpful in avoiding potential excess-business-holdings problems or minimum-payout problems.

Another significant expansion of the scope of this provision is the allowance of court approval by a court other than a probate court. This expansion would appear to cover such situations as transactions involving estates that are under independent administration (such as some estates in Texas)[43] and to cover obtaining the requisite court approval where a court (other than a probate court) has jurisdiction over a revocable trust.

On the other hand, the final regulations add two significant limitations to the provision in the proposed regulations. The first is that the proposed regulations covered any "transaction with respect to property . . . held by an estate of which a private foundation is a beneficiary";[44] the final regulations, however, cover only

41. [37] *Id.*

42. [38] Proposed Treas. Reg. § 53.4941(d)-1(b)(3), 36 Fed. Reg. 10968, 10970 (1971).

43. [39] Tex. Prob. Code Ann. § 45 (Supp. 1974).

44. [40] Proposed Treas. Reg. § 53.4941(d)-1(b)(3), 36 Fed. Reg. 10968, 10970 (1971).

"transaction[s] with respect to a private foundation's interest or expectancy in property . . . held by an estate or revocable trust."[45] Under the proposed regulations, it was at least arguable that a foundation by virtue of a minuscule interest in an estate could pay liquid funds that it already held to purchase, for example, a large piece of unproductive land or some other "white elephant" from the estate. Thus, even though it were only a nominal beneficiary of the estate, it could be allowed to expend much more money than it would ever receive from the estate to acquire property that might be useless to it. The limitation of this exception to a private foundation's interest or expectancy in property held by the estate or trust should prevent such an undesirable result while still allowing the trustee or administrator to do some after-death tax planning, such as allowing the foundation to receive cash in lieu of its interest in a corporation that, if held by the foundation, would be excess business holdings, or to purchase with its expectancy property that would be particularly useful to the carrying on of the foundation's exempt purposes. Additionally, the final regulations insure that a foundation can be harmed by such a transaction in an amount that cannot exceed the value of its interest or expectancy in the estate — an amount that it did not bold prior to the decedent's death.

Another significant limitation added by the final regulations relates to the character of what the foundation could receive in lieu of the property specifically given, devised, or bequeathed to it.[46] These rules were made prospective to transactions occurring after April 16, 1973 (the date on which the regulations were filed by the Federal Register). Although the proposed regulations contain no limitations on the character of what the foundation could receive, the final regulations require that (unless covered by the option-agreement provisions) the foundation can receive only an interest or expectancy at least as liquid as the one it gave up or an asset that is related to the active carrying out of its exempt purposes. This limitation is designed to prevent a foundation from getting a white elephant, even within the limitations of the dollar value of its interest or expectancy, but it allows a foundation to acquire property that would be valuable in carrying out its exempt purposes, such as real property adjacent to the facilities of an operating foundation that operates a camp for underprivileged boys.

Thus, it can be seen that the estate rules, even as modified, offer a fertile field for post-death estate planning and correction of errors made in a testamentary disposition or a revocable trust. Particularly in the case of a will or trust executed after 1969, this provision may be the sole way to get closely held stock out of a foundation without having to sell or give it to unrelated parties.

A significant difficulty in utilizing this rule, however, is that it applies only to acts of indirect self-dealing and would not apply where beneficiaries of 35 percent of the estate are disqualified persons, since transactions then might well be direct acts of self-dealing. If the property interest has not vested in the foundation under local

45. [41] Treas. Reg. § 53.4941(d)-l(b)(3) (1973).

46. [42] *Id.*§ 53.4941(d)-1(b)(3)(v).

law, however, it is arguable that a transaction between the estate and a disqualified person would not be a direct act of self-dealing but rather a transaction that must be analyzed as a potential indirect act of self-dealing. Since the estate rules are safe harbors rather than an expression of the outer limits of permissible transactions, where the transaction between a disqualified person and an estate that is also a disqualified person involves unvested expectancies, it may be permissible either under the estate rules or by analogy to such rules. If the regulations do achieve this result, it appears to be undesirable, because great reliance is placed on the local property law rather than the substance of the situation. In fact, there would appear to be little difference between the situation in which property has not yet vested in the foundation and the situation in which property has vested in the foundation, although the latter situation would be treated as a direct act of self-dealing.

One plausible reason for this exception applying only to indirect acts of self-dealing is that the Treasury Department believes that it has much more leeway to define indirect acts of self-dealing because of the ambiguity of the term than it has with the unambiguous ban on direct acts of self-dealing. Additionally, there ordinarily may be less potential for abuse in the indirect area. Some persons, however, would still desire an extension of the exception to permit transactions between private foundations and estates that are disqualified persons, since such an extension would be helpful in allowing an orderly disentanglement of foundation interests from those of disqualified persons.[47]

IV. Conclusion

Section 4941(d)(1)(E) and the concept of indirect self-dealing present many traps for the unwary. The only way to avoid these potential problems is for foundations and disqualified persons to be extremely cautious in dealings not only with each other but also in situations that could in any way potentially affect the other.

The arm's length [sic] standard still retains considerable viability in potential indirect transactions even though, except in the areas of compensation for personal services, certain corporate transactions described in § 4941(d)(2)(F), and certain transitional-period transactions, it has very limited scope with respect to direct transactions between a private foundation and a disqualified person.

The estate rules are useful in situations where an estate (or revocable trust) is not a disqualified person, because they allow an estate of a private foundation's interest (or expectancy) in potential excess business holdings and unproductive assets to disqualified persons and also allow foundations to acquire, under certain circumstances, property that might be very useful in the performance of their exempt purposes. They also may apply in cases where an estate deals with a foundation or a disqualified person with respect to property interests that have not yet vested in the private foundation. Nevertheless, an extension of these rules to cover direct acts of self-dealing, either by statute or, if possible, by regulations, would be useful in

47. [43] *Cf.* S. Rep. No. 552, 91st Cong., 1st Sess. 34 (1970).

allowing private foundations to avoid the acquisition of property that might create excess business holdings or payout problems.

Questions

1. W is a taxable corporation engaged in computer manufacturing. Private Foundation, PF, owns 19% of W's voting shares. A, a disqualified person with respect to PF, owns 17%, and his wife, B, owns 15% of W. A and B also own 30% of Y, a retail computer store. W enters into a long-term contract with Y under which it will supply computer equipment to Y at wholesale prices for the next three years. Is this a self-dealing transaction? What if, instead of buying computers, W hires A to provide consultation with regard to the computer retail market?

2. Is there indirect self-dealing under the following circumstance? John is a disqualified person with respect to Private Foundation. John's son, Jr., owns 5% of the voting stock (the only class of stock) in Corporation X. Corporation X is a commercial educational management firm that manages and operates public school systems that are in financial distress. Essentially, states pay Corporation X a flat fee to operate the schools in an efficient manner. Corporation X makes a profit by operating the schools for less than the flat fee (the corporation gets to keep the excess). Thus, to the extent Corporation X can reduce the costs of operating the school system, it will be more profitable. One method Corporation X uses to reduce its costs is by encouraging donations to the school system. On June 1, Private Foundation donates $2 million to school system.

C. Excess Business Holdings

CODE: § 4943, omit 4943(c)(4)–(5)

REGS.: §§ 53.4943-6(a)–(b)

Senate Report 91-552

91st Cong., 1st Session

1969-3 C.B. 423, 449–450 (1969)

The use of foundations to maintain control of businesses appears to be increasing. It is unclear under present law at what point such noncharitable purposes become sufficiently great to disqualify the foundation from exempt status. Moreover, the loss of exempt status is a harsh sanction for having such holdings.

The Treasury Department in its 1965 study of private foundations included the following examples of where business, and not charitable, purposes appeared to predominate in foundation activities:

Example 1. The A foundation holds controlling interests in 26 separate corporations, 18 of which operate going businesses. One of the businesses is a large and aggressively competitive metropolitan newspaper, with assets reported at a book value of approximately $10,500,000 at the end of 1962 and with gross receipts of more than $17 million for that year. Another of the corporations operates the largest radio broadcasting station in the State. A third, sold to a national concern as of the beginning of 1965, carried on life insurance business whose total assets had a reported book value of more than $20 million at the end of 1962. Among the other businesses controlled by the foundation are a lumber company, several banks, three large hotels, a garage, and a variety of office buildings. Concentrated largely in one city, these properties present an economic empire of substantial power and influence.

Example 2. The B foundation controls 45 business corporations. Fifteen of the corporations are clothing manufacturers; seven conduct real estate businesses; six operate retail stores; one owns and manages a hotel; others carry on printing, hardware, and jewelry businesses.

Example 3. The C foundation has acquired the operating assets of 18 different businesses, including diaries, foundries, a lumber mill, and a window manufacturing establishment. At the present time it owns the properties of seven of these businesses. Its practice has been to lease its commercial assets by short-term arrangements under which its rent consists of a share of the profits of the leased enterprise. By means of frequent reports and inspections, it maintains close check upon its lessee's operations.

This is not simply a phenomenon of the past. Recently, a major newspaper carried the following advertisement:

> "Tax exempt organization will purchase companies earning $300,000 pre tax at high earnings multiple. Immediate action."

Those who wish to use a foundation's stock holdings to acquire or retain business control in some cases are relatively unconcerned about producing income to be used by the foundation for charitable purposes. In fact, they may become so interested in making a success of the business, or in meeting competition, that most of their attention and interests is devoted to this with the result that what is supposed to be their function, that of carrying on charitable, educational, etc. activities is neglected. Even when the foundation attains a degree of independence from its major donor, there is a temptation for the foundation's managers to divert their interest to the maintenance and improvement of the business and away from their charitable duties. Where the charitable ownership predominates, the business may be run in a way which unfairly competes with other businesses whose owners must pay taxes on the income that they derive from the businesses. To deal with these problems, the committee has concluded it is desirable to limit the extent to which a business may be controlled by a private foundation.

Congress enacted § 4943 to address the problems described in the preceding legislative history. Deceptively complex (the hidden complexity results primarily from the transition rules, which we attempt to summarize in a footnote below), § 4943 uses the familiar two tier excise tax to forcefully prevent private foundations from devoting undue time and attention to the operation of commercial enterprises. The first tax is equal to [10]% of the value of a private foundation's "excess business holdings" held during each year ending during the taxable period. IRC § 4943(a). If the private foundation does not divest itself of the excess holding by the end of the taxable period, a 200% tax is imposed. IRC § 4943(b).

Excess business holdings are measured by reference to the percentage of a "business enterprise" owned by a private foundation and its disqualified persons. IRC § 4942(c)(1) A business enterprise, however, does not include "functionally related businesses." IRC § 4943(d)(3). If the business enterprise is a corporation, the private foundation's holdings, when added to that of its disqualified persons, may not exceed 20% of the corporation's outstanding voting stock. If the corporation is effectively controlled[48] by a nondisqualified person, the aggregate limit is 35%. IRC § 4943(c)(2)(B). If the business enterprise is a partnership or joint venture, the aggregate limits are applied with respect to the profit interest therein (determined under § 704). IRC § 4943(c)(3); Treas. Reg. § 53.4943-3(c)(3). If the business enterprise is a trust or other unincorporated entity, the limits are applied to the "beneficial interest"—defined as a right to receive fixed distributions of profit, or if profit distributions are not fixed, a right to receive a portion of the assets upon liquidation. *Id.* Thus, the percentage actually or constructively owned by a disqualified person must be subtracted from 20% (or 35%, if a nondisqualified person effectively controls the business enterprise). The remaining excess, if any, is compared to the private foundation's "permitted holdings"—i.e., the amount a private foundation may own without being subject to tax under § 4943. Excess business holdings result when the private foundation actually or constructively owns more than the permitted holding.

If disqualified persons own 20% (by voting power) or more of a business enterprise, all of a private foundation's stock, profit, or beneficial interest is excess business holdings, except when the de minimis rule applies. That rule states that if a private foundation owns no more than 2% of a business enterprise, it will not be subject to tax even if disqualified persons own more than 18% of the business enterprise (i.e., even if the permitted holdings is less than 2%). IRC § 4943(c)(2)(C). But if the private foundation owns more than 2%, and that amount exceeds the permitted holdings, the total amount held by the private foundation is excess business holdings (not just the amount that exceeds 2%). Treas. Reg. § 53.4946-3(b)(4). Finally, if disqualified persons own less than 20% (or 35%) of the voting power, a private foundation's permitted holdings also include any nonvoting stock. If disqualified persons own more than 20% (or 35%) of the voting power in a business enterprise' voting stock, all voting and nonvoting stock held by an associated private foundation is considered excess business holdings. If disqualified persons do not own more

48. Treas. Reg. § 53.4949-3(b)(3)(ii) defines "effective control" as the "power to direct or cause the direction of the management and policies of a business enterprise" however that power comes about. *See also* Revenue Ruling 81-111, reprinted below.

than 20% (or 35%) of the voting stock in a business enterprise, all nonvoting stock is also "permitted holding."

There are two grace periods during which a private foundation can avoid the § 4943 excise tax.[49] The first grace period applies if the private foundation purchases excess business holdings, not knowing or having reason to know it was doing so, but disposes of such holdings within 90 days of the date on which it does know or have reason to know of the event that caused it to have an excess business holding. Treas. Reg. § 53.4943-2(a)(ii). For example, a private foundation buys stock in a business enterprise not knowing that a disqualified person(s) has previously purchased an amount of stock sufficient to cause the private foundation's purchase to result in excess business holdings. When the foundation learns of the prior acquisition or of facts from which it has reason to know of the prior acquisition, it then has 90 days to divest.

The rule will also apply when a disqualified person purchases or acquires stock or other business interest, which purchase or acquisition renders the foundation's prior ownership interest an excess business interest. For example, assume a foundation owns 18% of the stock in Corporation A on January 1, 2004. On March 1, 2004, disqualified person A purchases 10% of the stock in Corporation A. As a result of the purchase, foundation now has an excess business holding equal in value to 8% of Corporation A stock. It must divest within 90 days, not from the date of A's purchase, but from the date it knows or has reason to know of A's purchase.

---

49. A longer and more complicated grace period/transition rule applies to pre 1969 holdings: If a private foundation and disqualified persons owned more than the permitted holdings as of May 26, 1969, the permitted holding limit is increased to the amount actually held, but not in excess of 50%. IRC § 4943(c)(4)(A)(i). Thereafter, a complex, "3-phase" grace period applies during which the private foundation must gradually reduce its holdings to 35%. During the first stage, if the private foundation and disqualified persons own more than 95% of the voting stock of such a pre-enactment business enterprise, the amount of the private foundation's holdings greater than 50% will be considered owned by disqualified persons for twenty years (until May 26, 1989). If the aggregate ownership was less than 95% but more than 75%, the holdings were considered owned by disqualified persons for 15 years (until May 26, 1984). If the aggregate ownership was less than 75% but more than 50%, the holdings were considered owned by disqualified persons for ten years (until May 26, 1979). During the second phase—the 15 year period after the 20-, 15-, or 10-year period, a private foundation and disqualified person may own up to 50% of a pre-enactment held business enterprise. During the third phase—i.e., all time after the second phase—, a private foundation and disqualified persons may own up to 35% of the voting stock of a pre-enactment held business enterprise. Note that with regard to business holding not held on May 26, 1969, the 35% limit applies only if a nondisqualified person effectively controls the business enterprise. This requirement does not apply to pre-enactment enterprises and therefore the permitted holding limitation is 35% even if the enterprise is not effectively controlled by nondisqualified persons. Beginning with the second phase, the foundation may not own more than 25% of the combined 50% or 35% voting stock permitted to be owned by the foundation and its associated disqualified persons from the time disqualified persons own more than 2% of a pre-enactment business enterprise's voting stock.

The regulations provide one method by which to avoid the "reason to know" standard, and in doing so suggests one factor which would give a foundation a reason to know. If a private foundation sends out an annual survey to all disqualified persons inquiring about the disqualified person's actual or constructive holdings in business enterprises in which the foundation has an interest, the private foundation will not have a "reason to know" of holdings not reported on the annual survey. Treas. Reg. § 53.4946-2(d)(v)(B). Does this mean the foundation is better off not sending out an annual survey? Probably not. By negative implication, it might be argued that a foundation has reason to know of an event that caused it to have excess business holdings as of the date it should have made a proper inquiry of its disqualified persons as to their business interests.

The second grace period applies when a private foundation acquires what would otherwise constitute excess business holdings by means other than a purchase by the foundation or its disqualified person(s). The 5-year grace period is intended to apply when an excess business holding is acquired by gift, devise, bequest, legacy or intestate succession and will not apply if the excess business holding results from a purchase by either the foundation or its disqualified persons. IRC § 4943(c)(6). A business holding that would otherwise constitute excess business holdings, if acquired by gift or distribution, is treated as owned by disqualified persons for a period of five years beginning on the date the gift or distribution of property (in the case of acquisition by will or trust). *Id.* The holdings sheltered under this five-year rule thus do not result in taxation unless they are still owned by the private foundation after the five years elapses. The Service, though, may grant an extension of the five-year period if the holdings cannot be disposed of at a fair price due to market constraints, and despite the foundation's diligent efforts. IRC § 4943(c)(7). To obtain an extension, the foundation must submit a plan of disposition to both the Service and the state official with authority over charitable organizations, and the Service must determine that the plan "can reasonably be expected to be carried out" before the extended period. *Id.*

Revenue Ruling 81-111

1981-1 C.B. 509 (1981)

Issue

In the situations described below, is the 35 percent permitted holdings rule of *section 4943(c)(2)(B) of the Internal Revenue Code* applicable to the holdings of the private foundation?

Facts

P is exempt from federal income tax under section 501(c)(3) of the Code and is a private foundation under section 509(a). Corporations *M* and *N* each have outstanding 100*x* shares of voting stock, with each share entitling the holder thereof to one vote. *M* and *N* are business enterprises within the meaning of section 4943(d)(4) of the Code and section 53.4943-10(a) of the Foundation Excise Tax Regulations.

Situation 1.

P holds 15*x* shares of *M* voting stock, and disqualified persons with respect to *P*, within the meaning of section 4946(a) of the Code, hold 20*x* shares of *M* voting stock. The remaining 65*x* shares of *M* voting stock are held by *C*, who is not a disqualified person with respect to *P*. By virtue of *C*'s ownership of 65 percent of the *M* voting stock, *C* has elected a majority of the board of directors of *M*.

Situation 2.

P holds 15*x* shares of *N* voting stock, and disqualified persons with respect to *P* hold 20*x* shares of *N* voting stock. The remaining 65*x* shares of *N* voting stock are held by a large number of individuals, none of whom is a disqualified person with respect to *P*. There does not exist any voting trust, contractual arrangement, or other similar agreement between any of these individuals relating to their stock voting rights. None of these individuals alone has sufficient voting stock holdings in *N* to direct or cause the direction of the management and policies of *N*, nor has one of them historically elected the majority of *N*'s board of directors. *P*'s holdings of *N* stock are not protected by any of the special transitional rules of sections 4943(c)(4), (5), and (6) of the Code.

Section 53.4943-3(b)(3)(ii) of the regulations provides that the term "effective control" mean the possession, directly or indirectly, of the power to direct or cause the direction of the management and policies of a business enterprise, whether through the ownership of voting stock, the use of voting trusts, or contractual arrangements, or otherwise. It is the reality of control which is decisive and not its form or the means by which it is exercisable. Thus, where a minority interest held by individuals who are not disqualified persons has historically elected the majority of a corporation's directors, effective control is in the hands of those individuals. . . .

Analysis

In *Situation 1, C* holds a majority of the voting stock of *M*, and *C* has elected a majority of the board of directors of *M*. Under these circumstances, *P* has established that effective control of *M*, within the meaning of section 4943(c)(2)(B) of the Code and section 53.4943-3(b)(3)(ii) of the regulations, is in the hands of *C*. Thus, since the holdings of *P* and all disqualified persons do not exceed 35 percent of the voting stock of *M*, the 35 percent permitted holdings rule of section 4943(c)(2)(B) of the Code is applicable. It follows that *P* is not in an excess business holdings position with respect to its holdings of *M* voting stock.

In *Situation 2*, on the other hand, none of the individuals holding the 65 percent of *N* voting stock, not in the hands of the foundation or disqualified persons, alone has sufficient voting stock holdings in *N* to direct or cause the direction of the management and policies of *N*, nor has one of these individuals historically elected the majority of *N*'s board of directors. Also, none of these individuals has entered into any voting trust, contractual arrangement, or other similar agreement resulting in their combined control of *N*. Under these circumstances, *P* has not established that effective control of *N*, within the meaning of section 4943(c)(2)(B) of the Code and section 53.4943-3(b)(3)(ii) of the regulations, is in the hands of third persons who are not disqualified persons with respect to *P.*

Even if *P* were to establish that *P* and its disqualified persons cannot exercise effective control of *N* because of their minority voting stock interest in *N*, and that they have not, in fact, exercised effective control over *N*, the 35 percent rule would not be applicable. Section 4943(c)(2)(B)(ii) of the Code and the regulations thereunder require affirmative proof by a private foundation that some unrelated third party, or a group of third parties does, in fact, exercise effective control over the business enterprise in question.

Accordingly, the 35 percent permitted holdings rule of section 4943(c)(2)(B) of the Code is not applicable to *Situation 2.* Thus, because disqualified persons hold 20 percent of the *N* voting stock, *P* is in an excess business holdings position with respect to its 15 percent ownership of *N* voting stock.

* * *

David Bank, Foundations Divide Over Need to Diversify: Two High-Profile Progeny of H-P Adopt Different Strategies

Wall Street Journal, Feb. 14, 2002, at C1[50]

Small investors aren't the only ones who have a tough time deciding how much to diversify their portfolios. The two foundations established by the founders of Hewlett-Packard Co., while allied in their opposition to H-P's proposed acquisition of Compaq Computer Corp., have pursued opposite strategies for the huge endowments that pay for their charitable programs.

The endowment of the David and Lucile Packard Foundation, which holds stock only in H-P and a spinoff, Agilent Technologies Inc., soared to a peak of more than $18 billion in 2000, only to plummet to $6.2 billion at the end of last year. The William and Flora Hewlett Foundation has better weathered the downturn. In preparation for an infusion of H-P shares from the estate of Mr. Hewlett, who died last year, the foundation worked down its stake in H-P to just 2% of its portfolio. Including the shares in Mr. Hewlett's trust, H-P now makes up about half of the foundation's holdings. "As these installments come in, the foundation will gradually diversify," says Laurance Hoagland, Hewlett's chief financial officer. The foundation currently has an endowment of about $6 billion, including the Hewlett trust.

Spread your bets or hold tight? Like Hewlett and Packard, other foundations have split over how best to manage their endowments. Since a foundation's spending is generally figured as a percentage of its asset base, investment results directly affect organizations that rely on foundations for funding. The Packard Foundation, for

50. Reprinted with permission.

example, has slashed its grant-making to a budgeted $250 million this year from $615 million in 2000.

"The '90s was the decade of the one-stock foundation doing very, very well," says Sara Engelhardt, president of the Foundation Center in New York, an information clearing house for the industry. "When you have the stock market dropping, you're going to have people tell you, 'I told you so.'"

Packard isn't the only foundation being second-guessed. The Robert W. Woodruff Foundation in Atlanta, founded by the long-time chairman of Coca-Cola Co., keeps nearly 89% of its portfolio in Coke. The stock outperformed the Standard & Poor's 500-stock index for most of the 1990s, but has underperformed since 1998. The foundation's president, Charles McTier, isn't worried. "The stock has been good to the foundation over the years," he says.

Looking at the performance of large foundations, there is a lesson for small investors: By diversifying, you likely will avoid the lows—but also miss the highs—of concentrating your holdings in one stock.

"When you become a foundation, you take on an obligation to support good works," says Clay Singleton, vice president of Ibbotson Associates, an investment-research firm in Chicago. "Even diversified portfolios are going to wax and wane. But the added risk you take on by concentrating in one or two holdings puts the ability of the foundation to accomplish its mission at risk."

A 1969 tax change barred foundations from holding more than 20% of a company's shares, with some exceptions, but didn't directly require diversifications. Foundations are held to the same "prudent investor" guidelines that cover other trustees, but regulators have generally permitted single-stock portfolios when that was the expressed wish of the donor.

Those wishes sometimes pay off. In 1978, the Starr Foundation in New York was endowed with about $20 million in shares of American International Group Inc. from the estate of AIG's founder, Cornelius Vander Starr. The 60.2 million shares of AIG are now valued at about $4.4 billion. "I challenge you to find any index that has performed that well," says Florence Davis, the foundation's president.

The Lilly endowment, in Indianapolis, has nearly all of its holdings in Eli Lilly & Co. The Robert Wood Johnson Foundation, in Princeton, N.J., keeps about 63% of its holdings in shares of Johnson & Johnson Inc. After dropping in 2000, both Lilly and J & J have outperformed the S & P 500 in the past year.

Other foundations are lucky to have diversified. The Kresge Foundation, in Troy, Mich., was endowed with $60 million in stock by Sebastian S. Kresge, founder of S.S. Kresge Co. The $2.4 billion portfolio now has no holdings in Kmart Corp., as Kresge is now known. Kmart recently filed for bankruptcy protection from creditors.

Back in 1954, Henry Ford II, as president of Ford Motor Co. And chairman of the Ford Foundation's board, favored divestment of the foundation's 89.5% stake in the auto company. "If our industry went sour, it would not be able to meet its obligations," Mr. Ford said at the time. The Ford Foundation now says it holds no Ford shares.

Selling a large holding on the open market isn't easy. In January 2000, Bill Gates, chairman of Microsoft Corp., donated shares valued at $5 billion to his foundation, the nation's largest philanthropy. By the time the last of the shares were sold in September 2000, the foundation netted only $3.67 billion from the gift. Mr. Gates has contributed $21.7 billion in Microsoft shares to the foundation, based in Seattle.

Likewise, the new Gordon and Betty Moore Foundation, in San Francisco, is gradually diversifying from the 175 million shares of Intel Corp. set aside by Mr. Moore, Intel's co-founder. "Over the long term, we plan to reduce the single-stock risk of holding Intel," says Alice Ruth, the foundation's chief financial officer.

Some foundations have had better luck lately with their primary stock than with their diversified portfolio. Shares in Kellogg Co. made up about 72% of the $5.2 billion in assets of the W.K. Kellogg Foundation, in Battle Creek, Mich., as of Aug. 31. The Kellogg foundation suffered in the late 1990s as shares in the cereal maker languished. But the focus on Kellogg paid off between August 2000 and August 2001, when a rise in Kellogg's stock buffered other investments, which fell 11%.

The Hewlett Foundation's diversification plan dates to 1979, when Arjay Miller, former dean of the Stanford Business School and former president of Ford Motor, says he put his arm around Mr. Hewlett and told him, "Bill, H-P's a great stock, but the foundation has to diversify."

"It's just a prudent thing to do when you have fixed obligations." Mr. Miller says now. The foundation is selling H-P even as its chairman, Walter Hewlett, Mr. Hewlett's son, solicits proxies in opposition to the Compaq acquisition.

The foundation's strategy is a legacy of Mr. Packard himself, who expressed his preference for holding H-P in a letter written before his death in 1996. "H-P has certainly been an excellent investment for the foundation long term," says George Vera, Packard's chief financial officer. "Obviously, the more years that it underperforms, the more it makes sense to diversify."

Questions

1. Disqualified persons own 13% of the voting stock in Corporation A. Private Foundation owns 6.5% of the voting stock and 37% of the nonvoting preferred stock of Corporation A. Is Private Foundation liable for the excess business holding tax? If Foundation is liable for the tax, to whom could it transfer its holdings in order to avoid liability?

2. Assume the facts of Question 1. What if, on January 2, a disqualified person purchases another 10% of Corporation A voting stock? What effect does that purchase have on Private Foundation's ownership of the voting and nonvoting stock? What if, instead of a purchase by a disqualified person, the disqualified person inherits an additional 10% of Corporation A voting stock?

3. Assume the facts of Question 1, except that a disqualified person purchases 25% of the nonvoting preferred stock. Is the foundation liable for the excess business holding tax?

4. What if, instead of owning 6.5% of the voting stock and 37% of the nonvoting stock on the date of the purchase referred to in question 2, Private Foundation owned only 1.5% of the voting stock along with 37% of the nonvoting stock? Assume that Private Foundation's holding represent 1.8% of the total value of Corporation A's stock of all classes.

5. Assume the facts of Question 2. What if 70.5% of the voting stock not held by foundation or disqualified persons is held under a voting trust agreement?

6. What if Foundation A's charitable purpose involves environmental preservation and Corporation A manufactures a new type of diesel fuel filter to be used on trucks and buses?

John G. Simon, Private Foundations as a Federally Regulated Industry: Time for a Fresh Look?

27 Exempt Org. Tax Rev. 66 (2000)[51]

I. The Regulated Industry Regime

One would not expect lawyers specializing in nonprofit and tax exemption matters to look upon America's private foundations as a regulated industry. The matrix of code and regulations that rules the foundations emerged—at least explicitly—from concerns about obedience to fiduciary and charitable governance norms, rather than the conventional wellsprings for industry regulation. Thus, the foundations do not exhibit the hallmarks or the vices that typically beget industry regulation: they do not have the consumer-serving characteristics of airlines or hospitals, and they do not exhibit monopoly, scarcity, or other earmarks of "market failure"—or the negative health, safety, or environmental "externalities"—that call for public control.

Indeed, the foundations themselves do not regard themselves as an "industry." That term has connotations of commerce and the pursuit of profit that offend foundation persons (even those whose salaries were set with one eye on "comparable" business-sector executives). The Council on Foundations does not look on itself as a "trade association," and when this author once applied the word "cartel" to foundation conclaves that appeared to reach collective decisions on the goodness or badness of certain applicants, the reaction was one of bewilderment.

Whether or not the "industry" sobriquet fits the foundation world, and despite the strangeness of the regulated industry metaphor to members of the nonprofit bar, it is fitting that we examine the present legal treatment in regulated industry terms. The "regulated industry" term is used variably in the literature—sometimes to apply

51. Reprinted with permission of Tax Analysts.

to rate-regulated industries (e.g., public utilities or railroads or natural gas production), sometimes to apply to industries where entry and/or exit are controlled (e.g., broadcasting or airlines), sometimes to apply to industries whose goods or services are inspected and monitored in order to protect the public from health or financial hazards (e.g., pharmaceuticals, banking). What is true of all these "regulated industry" usages, whether they refer to federal or state regulation, is that they deal with instances in which a number of actors have enough common characteristics to be subjected to a common regulatory regime — clearly the case for the country's 45,000 foundations — and where that regime imposes a relatively intensive and/or extensive set of controls on the regulated actors. Consider then, in terms of intensivity or extensivity, the following controls imposed on foundations by the federal government:

A Highly Detailed Regulatory Corpus

The private foundation code, enacted by Congress largely in 1969, implemented by copious regulations, embraces not only the prohibitions set forth in sections 4941–4945 but also the section 4940 tax on investment income, the section 170(b)(1)(B) and section 170(e)(1)(B)(ii) restrictions on deductibility of gifts to foundations, the exemption application requirements of section 508(e), the termination tax of section 507(c) and the reporting and other disclosure provisions of sections 6033(c) and 6104(d).[52] This thicket of rules is comparable to other regulatory regimes in its comprehensiveness. It controls central aspects of entry and exit and of the financial, managerial and even programmatic activities of foundations, as described below.

Entry and Exit Controls

With respect to entry, while nonprofits over a certain size that wish recognition of tax-exempt status (except churches) must comply with the requirement of filing a Form 1023, the entry hurdle is a little higher for foundations: they must file regardless of size. Another aspect of entry control is also in place: the federal requirement that each foundation's state certificate of incorporation contain certain prohibitions (tracking code sections 4941–4945); this is not a difficult legal step — indeed, legislation in many states automatically inserts the mandated prohibitions into all certificates filed in those states — but it does reflect federal gatekeeping.

---

52. [1] All references in this paper that simply set forth a section number (e.g., section 170) refer to sections of the Internal Revenue Code of 1986, as amended. All of the provisions just cited in the text apply to "nonoperating foundations" (roughly speaking, grant-making foundations). "Operating foundations" (roughly speaking, foundations that mainly operate their own programs rather than make grants) (section 4942(j)(3)) are exempt from the deductibility restrictions (sections 170(b)(1)(A)(vii), (E)(i); section 170(e)(1)(B)(ii)) and the section 4942 payout rules (section 4942(a)(1)). Since nonoperating foundations are vastly more numerous — and represent a vastly higher level of assets and expenditures — than operating foundations (The Foundation Center, Foundation Giving (1999), p. 2, Table 1), references in this paper to "foundations" or "private foundations" will be to "nonoperating foundations," unless otherwise indicated.

With respect to exit, the fearsome termination tax penalties of section 507(c) make it impossible for a foundation to pass away quietly in the night when its work is done. One can understand the evasive techniques section 507(c) seeks to combat; the fact remains that it represents an outgoing barrier more formidable than the entrance gate.

Financial Controls

Output controls: The mandatory payout rules of section 4942 set a floor on foundation grants. That floor is further elevated by the way the section 4940 investment income tax works. As Eugene Steuerle states, "The excise tax on income is increased [from 1 percent to 2 percent] if payout in any one year falls below the average for previous years. Therefore, extra giving in one year merely raises the base on which the adequacy of future payouts will be assessed."[53]

Price controls: Here the controls are not imposed on prices charged by foundations (what would they be?), but on those paid by the suppliers of resources to foundations—i.e., the after-tax price paid by donors as the cost of contributing to foundations. Until recently, the after-tax price of a gift of appreciated property to a foundation (except a pass-through gift) greatly exceeded the price of giving the same property to a public charity; only basis could be deducted in the former case, compared to market value in the latter. Even now, that price disparity applies to a significant class of contributions: gifts of appreciated property that is not "qualified appreciated stock," a term referring to publicly-traded stock that is a capital asset in the donor's hands and does not represent more than ten percent of the issuer's equity (sections 170(e)(1)(B)(2), 170(e)(5)).[54] Moreover, contributions of any kind to a foundation are limited to a lower percentage of the donor's adjusted gross income than gifts to other *charities* (section 170(b)(1)(B)).

Investment controls: The investment practices and policies of foundations are shaped in important ways by (a) the general "jeopardizing investment" provisions of section 4944, which do not necessarily duplicate the investment standards of the state courts of equity in a foundation's home jurisdiction, and (b) the more particularized "excess business holdings" prohibitions of section 4943 (discussed later in Part II).

Transactional controls: Section 4941's self-dealing rules regulate the transactional activity between a foundation and its managers or related entities, as well as transactions between a foundation and certain government officials.

---

53. [2] Eugene Steuerle, *Foundation Giving: Will it Follow the Bubble Economy?*, Tax Notes, June 21, 1999, pp. 1797, 1798.

54. [3] The original, 1969, basis limitation on gifts of appreciated property was modified, to remove that limitation in the case of "qualified appreciated stock," a number of times—on each occasion with a sunset clause—until, finally, the Tax and Trade Relief Extension Act of 1998 made the "qualified appreciated stock" exception permanent, effective for gifts made after June 30, 1998.

Programmatic and Other Grantmaking Controls

Controls on "political" activity: These rules (a) effectively prohibit grants to influence legislation (section 4945(e)), without the "insubstantiality" escape hatch or the safe-harbor election enjoyed by non-foundations (sections 501(c)(3), 501(h), 4911), and (b) limit a foundation's ability to support voter registration (section 4945(f)), while not imposing most of these limits on public charities.

Controls on grants to individuals: Section 4945 requires pre-grant clearance from the IRS of a foundation's criteria for travel or study grants to individuals.

Controls on grants to non-public charities: Foundations must comply with a special set of "expenditure responsibility" procedures to accompany grants to most entities that are not public charities (section 4945(h)).

In addition to this extensive set of controls, other hallmarks of industry regulation obtain in the foundation field:

A Specialized Regulatory Agency

While the IRS is not, of course, an agency that exclusively regulates foundations, the personnel of the Exempt Organizations Branch, and the agents and examiners they train, specialize in nonprofit matters; moreover, processing foundation applications and audits occupies a disproportionate amount of the time of this cadre of personnel (in part because the section 4940 tax is justified as an auditing fee for foundations).

Enforcement Measures

Penalty Taxes: The excise taxes imposed by sections 4941–4945 on foundations and their managers operate for all the world like the fines imposed by regulatory agencies in other fields. The enactment of these penalty taxes/fines (for that is what they are) has spread to the world of public charities, where penalty taxes/fines are now in place for (a) violations of the lobbying ceilings that become operative if a charity files a section 501(h) election (section 4911); (b) engaging in certain forms of electoral activity (section 4955); (c) falling afoul of the recent "intermediate sanctions" legislation (section 4958). Reliance on penalty taxes/fines is, however, much more widespread in the regulation of foundations.

Triggering of State-Level Sanctions: As noted, section 508(e) requires that every foundation certificate include the prohibitions of sections 4941–4945, thus enabling the attorneys general and courts of every state to use state law sanctions to police this array of restrictions.

Detailed Reporting Requirements

Foundations are required to provide a higher level of reporting than other charities (compare Form 990 [public charities] with Form 990-PF [foundations]), and small foundations are not exempt from an annual reporting requirement, as are small public charities (section 6033(a)(2)).

Differentiated Treatment Targeted to Industry Subsets

Just as the airline subsectors are subjected to different levels and forms of regulation, so the foundation world has been disaggregated: operating foundations (defined in section 4942(j)(3)) are exempted from some of the provisions regulating non-operating foundations; a newer (1984) breed, "exempt operating foundations" (defined in section 4940(d)(2)), is exempt from some other provisions; and certain split-interest trusts (per section 4947) are subject, in some cases, to all of the private foundation provisions, in other cases to only some of them.

What all of these provisions construct is what Justice Stephen Breyer has called the "large . . . governmental presence" that accompanies industry regulation.[55] Moreover, even the avenues of escape from regulation resemble the exit patterns found in all or most other regulated industries. The legislative history and post-enactment history of the 1969 Tax Reform Act reveal three revered avenues of partial or total exit:

Exemptions

Congress over the years, in "bullet" provisions and otherwise, has provided special relief to many foundations from a variety of provisions (e.g., the excess business holdings provision in the case of one foundation that owns a celebrated resort hotel)—a form of ad hoc deregulation that may well be justified in individual cases but does not receive the public scrutiny it ought to have.

Avoidance or Evasion

I have used standard tax terminology to refer, respectively, to lawful and unlawful escape methods:

Avoidance: The use of section 509(a)(3) supporting organizations, community foundations, and donor-advised funds located within public charities, in order to preserve important measures of donor influence while avoiding private foundation treatment.[56] In all three of these categories, organizations have marketed these advantages with varying degrees of bluntness.

Evasion: Unlawful tactics to defeat regulation. I was shocked a few years ago, after all the effort that went into the 1969 compromise that saved voter registration activity for foundations (section 4945(f)), to hear program officers of foundations in a certain large city boast about how they had gotten around the voter registration rules by giving technically non-earmarked grants to a local church for the clear

---

55. [4] Stephen Breyer, Regulation and Its Reform (1982), p. 156.

56. [5] These mechanisms are discussed by Victoria Bjorklund in *Charitable Giving to a Private Foundation and the Alternatives, the Supporting Organization and the Donor-Advised Fund,* in N.Y.U. School of Law, Center on Philanthropy and the Law, Conference on Private Foundations Reconsidered (1999), which appears elsewhere in this issue. Robert Ferguson's paper at the same conference, *Avoiding Private Foundation Status: Escape Routes Based on Operations and Income,* also in this issue, discusses other "escape routes" that use the foundation definitional rules to arrive in public-charity-land or at least in the demi-monde of operating-foundation-land.

purpose of getting out the vote for a favored local candidate. (I protested both on grounds of law obedience and prudence; they were asking for all kinds of trouble. It was not clear to me that they were listening. I have not seen much of this behavior; I hope it is rare.)

Incremental Deregulation

Congressional level: In the years following 1969, Congress reduced (subject to conditions referred to above) the tax on investment income; cut back on payout requirements by eliminating the net investment income test; improved the deductibility of property gifts to foundations (but not in the crucial case of closely held stock); provided longer redemption periods under the excess business holding rules (but not enough to remove the disincentives referred to in Part III); and relaxed, quite modestly, the self-dealing provisions.[57]

Administrative level: The Treasury and the Service have engaged in what I think is, for the most part, a sophisticated and enlightened approach to the issuance of regulations under the 1969 Act. Treasury implementation of the anti-lobbying and jeopardizing investment rules (sections 4945(e), 4944), for example, has provided a mild form of interpretive deregulation in these two areas although the section 4944 regulations are marred by an internal contradiction.[58] Moreover, the Service has generally been thoughtful and sensitive to the needs of the foundation community in its rulings.

This review of the classic earmarks of industry regulation (and escape from regulation) that are encountered in the foundation field compels us to look upon the world of private foundations as a regulated industry.[59]

---

57. [6] These and other modifications for the period 1969–1984 are described in John D. Edie, *Congress and Foundations: Historical Summary*, in Teresa Odendahl (ed.), America's Wealthy and the Future of Foundations (1987). pp. 43–64.

58. [7] Compare Reg. section 53.4944-1(a)(2), third sentence (every investment to be appraised "taking into account the foundation's portfolio as a whole") with Reg. section 53.4944-(1)(c), Example (1) (appearing to ignore the "portfolio as a whole" approach).

59. [8] In one respect, American foundations are more heavily regulated than their counterparts in other countries, where the legal treatment is much less dense and detailed (partly a consequence of the fact that these foreign charities receive far less favorable tax treatment). For reviews of foreign legal systems, *see* Lester Salamon, The International Guide to Nonprofit Law (1997) and Thomas Silk (ed.), Philanthropy and Law in Asia (1999). In another respect, however, the foreign counterparts to American foundations—indeed, most other foreign charities—are more heavily regulated than U.S. entities because of the requirement of advance registration. Thus, "each country [in the Asia Pacific Region] uses some form of permission system . . . , requiring NPOs to overcome obstacles and restrictions before government approval is granted." Silk, *supra*, p. 20; *see also* Salamon, *supra*, p. 17.

Chapter 18

Private Foundation Excise Taxes — Mandatory Distributions, Jeopardizing Investments, Taxable Expenditures and Termination

A. Mandatory Distributions

CODE: § 4942, omit 4942(g)(4)

REGS.: §§ 53.4942(a)-2(c)(1)–(3); 53.4942(a)-3(a)(1)–(6); 53.4942(b)-3(b)(1)–(6); 53.4942 (a)-3(c); 53.4942(b)-1; 53.4942(b)-2 PROPOSED REGS.: §§ 53.4942 (a)-3(a)(5), 53.4942(a)-3(a)(6)

Another abuse Congress believed typical of private foundations was the failure to spend tax-exempt money for charitable causes. Congress believed that, in many instances, big donors set up tax-exempt charitable organizations and took charitable contribution deductions for amounts transferred to the organization, while the organization failed to actually distribute significant amounts toward its purported charitable cause. Prior law threatened to revoke tax exemption if a private foundation unreasonably accumulated its wealth. But Congress believed the "unreasonable accumulation" standard was too subjective to be of any real consequence. Section 4942 takes the opposite approach by objectively defining a minimum level of charitable expenditures that private foundations must make.

A private foundation that fails to make "qualifying distributions" equal to or greater than its "distributable amount" computed for each taxable year, by the close of the next taxable year, will be subject to an initial tax of 30% of the difference between its qualifying distributions and its distributable amount. The difference is referred to as "undistributed income." IRC § 4942(c). The 30% tax is imposed each year thereafter (on whatever difference remains in succeeding years) until qualifying distributions earmarked to that previous taxable year equal that taxable year's distributable amount, or until the close of the taxable period (whichever occurs first). Treas. Reg. § 53.4942(a)-1(a). The taxable period begins on the first day of each taxable year and ends when the Service mails a notice of deficiency or makes an assessment with respect to that taxable year. IRC § 4942(j)(1). If a first-tier tax is imposed and qualifying distributions earmarked for a taxable year do not equal or exceed the distributable amount for that year within 90 days of the close of the taxable period, the foundation is liable for a tax equal to 100% of the difference. IRC § 4942(b); IRC § 4961.

A private foundation's distributable amount is computed by taking 5% of the value (less acquisition indebtedness) of its noncharitable assets. This amount is referred to as the "minimum investment return." IRC § 4942(e). The distributable amount is the minimum investment return increased by any repayments of previous qualifying distributions, amounts received from the sale or disposition[1] of charitable assets, and set aside amounts that are no longer necessary to achieve the purpose for which the amount was set-aside, and decreased by any taxes imposed under Subtitle A and IRC § 4940 for the taxable year. IRC § 4942(d); 4942(f)(2)(C). Noncharitable assets are those assets not directly used, or held for use, in pursuit of a charitable purpose. Thus, charitable assets are not only those so used or held for use, but also investments that help achieve the organization's charitable goal (i.e., "program related investments") and investments in functionally related businesses. Qualifying distributions are amounts paid to accomplish a charitable purpose, to acquire an asset used or held for use in pursuit of a charitable purpose, reasonable and necessary administrative expenses related to the accomplishment of a charitable purpose, and certain amounts "set aside" to achieve a charitable purpose in the foreseeable future. Distributions to a controlled § 501(c)(3) organization or another private foundation are not qualifying distributions unless the recipient organization makes qualifying distributions equal to the distribution from the donor private foundation. IRC § 4942(g)(3). The distribution must be made by the close of the taxable year following the year in which the distribution was received and the donor organization must obtain records or evidence confirming the recipient's qualifying distribution. *Id.;* Treas. Reg. § 53.4942(a)-3(a)–(b)(6), (c)(1)–(4).

The § 4942 excise tax does not apply in two situations. First, the tax does not apply to an operating foundation. IRC § 4942(a)(1). Note, however, that the special requirements for operating foundations seeking exemption from the § 4940 (the "exempt operating foundation") tax do not apply for exemption from the IRC § 4942 tax. § 4942(a)(1). Second, the tax will not apply if undistributed income results solely from an incorrect valuation of the foundation's assets, provided the incorrect valuation was not willful and was due to reasonable cause. To avoid the tax resulting from a good faith, but incorrect valuation, the foundation must make a qualifying distribution equal to the shortfall within the "allowable distribution period." The allowable distribution period begins with the second taxable year after the taxable year and ends 90 days after the Service mails a notice of deficiency. IRC

1. A disposition may occur, for example, if property acquired for a future charitable is used for an unreasonable period of time (pending its conversion to that charitable use) in an income producing activity. When the period of time that it is used in an income producing activity becomes unreasonable, a disposition occurs. Treas. Reg. § 53.4942(a)-2(c)(3). The regulations state that using property for income for a period of no more than one year is generally reasonable. After that, no presumption applies. *Id.*

§ 4942(j)(2). The foundation must earmark the distribution to the taxable year for which the shortfall exists and must notify the Service that it has made the distribution to correct the shortfall. IRC § 4942(a)(2)(C)–(D). Qualifying distributions sometimes include amounts set aside for future use, as demonstrated in the following revenue ruling.

Revenue Ruling 74-450

1974-2 C.B. 388

A private foundation, which is exempt under section 501(c)(3) of the Code, was organized to restore and perpetuate wildlife and game on the North American continent, and to foster such activities by others. The foundation has for many years maintained a wildlife sanctuary on its own land and distributed excess income from its investments to other exempt charitable organizations.

Shortly after the beginning of the current taxable year, the foundation received a bequest of a contiguous tract of land formerly used for farming purposes which doubled its total land holdings. The trustees in control of the foundation's affairs thereupon committed a portion of this farm land for conversion into an extension of its wildlife sanctuary and the balance for conversion into a public park. The combined conversion project will entail extensive tree planting, the building of a large earthen dam, and the construction of various fences, roads, and other public service facilities. It would currently be possible for the foundation to have all the work required to complete the entire farm land conversion project performed under a single four-year contract at an agreed total price of 120x dollars, no more than about 15x dollars of which would become payable in either of the first two years.

The foundation's productive investments are currently yielding a net income of 45x dollars per year. Its current annual operating expenses, which include the cost of operating the present wildlife sanctuary and the excise taxes imposed under section 4940 of the Code, amount to 15x dollars. . . .

The application for Service approval further shows that the total work required to convert the farm land to use as a wildlife sanctuary and public park will take approximately 4 years. It also includes a duly authorized representation by the chairman of its board of trustees that, in any event, all income earmarked and set aside pursuant to the proposed plan will be fully expended within a five-year period commencing with the date of the foundation's initial set aside to convert its newly acquired farm land in the manner described above.

Under section 53.4942(a)-3(b) of the Foundation Excise Tax Regulations, specific projects of the kind that might qualify for a set-aside are those involving relatively long-term grants or expenditures that must be made in order to assure the continuity of particular charitable projects; for example, a plan to erect a building to house a direct charitable, educational, or other similar exempt activity of the foundation.

* * *

Consummation of the foundation's plan to convert its newly acquired farm land into an extension of its existing wildlife sanctuary and a public park will serve its charitable and educational purposes all of which come within section 170(c)(2)(B) of the Code. Such plan thus constitutes a "specific project" of the class for which an amount may be set aside and treated as a qualifying distribution under section 4942(g)(2), if such amount is further shown to meet the additional requirements of that statutory provision.

* * *

Entering into the above-described contractual agreement would commit the organization to a major unitary project costing substantially more than the foundation's total available income on an annual basis, notwithstanding the fact that a major part of the required disbursement would not fall due until after the entire project was well along towards completion. Therefore, the proposed undertaking is one which can be better accomplished by a set-aside than by the immediate payment of funds and that all current income items specifically earmarked and set aside on the accounting records of the foundation for use in fulfilling the above-described conversion plan and program will thereupon become eligible for treatment as qualifying distributions under section 4942(g)(2) of the Code with respect to any taxable year within which they are so set aside and as of the end of which they remain unexpended.

Note on Qualifying Distributions Under the "Cash-Distribution Test"

A private foundation that seeks to accumulate funds for a long-term project is best served when it can meet the so-called "suitability" test discussed in the previous two revenue rulings. If it cannot, though, the set aside might still be considered a qualifying distribution if the foundation meets the "cash-distribution" test set out § 4942(g)(2)(B)(ii). The cash distribution test is much more burdensome than the suitability test. To meet the cash distribution test, the foundation must have made aggregate cash or "equivalent" distributions in amounts equal to the sum of 20% of its distributable amount for the first taxable year of its "start-up" period, plus successive annual distributions increased by 20% per year until the fourth year of its start-up period. Treas. Reg. § 53.4942(a)-3(b)(3). The cash or equivalent distributions need not be made annually, so long as at the end of the start-up period, the total cash or equivalent distributions, Y, complies with the following equation:

$$Y = .20(x_1) + .40(x_2) + .60(x_3) + .80(x_4),$$

where x_b is the distributable amount for the indicated taxable year of the start-up period. Treas. Reg. § 53.4942(a)-3(b)(4)(i).

The start-up period begins in the taxable year after the year in which the foundation's distributable amount exceeds $500. After the start-up period, the foundation must make cash or equivalent distributions equal to 100% of its distributable amount each year, presumably just until the set-aside amount is actually spent. If the foundation fails (or failed) to meet the start-up period minimum distribution requirement or the full payment period minimum distribution requirement, the set aside will no longer be considered a qualifying distribution (unless it meets the suitability test) and the organization will never again be allowed to rely on the cash distribution test for approval of set asides. Treas. Reg. § 53.4942(a)-3(b)(6).[2] Thus, to get the benefit of the cash distribution test, the foundation must have a history of always making significant expenditures towards charitable purposes.

Questions

Private Foundation's charitable goal is to stimulate and encourage the construction of affordable housing for low-income families. For the taxable year, PF holds the following assets:

Assets	FMV
Stocks and Bonds in various computer tech firms	$2,500,000
Land on which to build a new headquarters, subject to a mortgage of $75,000	300,000
Office Equipment	450,000
Stock in Home Construction Business	100,000
Cash	$1,000,000
One Year Certificate of Deposit	$2,000,000

1. What is PF's minimum investment return for the taxable year? Assume the Home Construction Business is one that specializes in building affordable housing.

2. How does your answer change if the Certificate of Deposit represents a restricted fund to be used solely to build the new headquarters?

3. Assuming the CDs do represent a restricted fund, and PF's 4940 tax is $4,000 (2% of $200,000 worth of dividends) what is the distributable amount?

4. What if the land was purchased eight years ago and has been rented to a farmer ever since, pending construction of the new headquarters? What if the CD was purchased two years ago and has continually been rolled over into a new one-year CD and continues to earn interest?

5. What if revised estimates show that building will cost only $1.5 million instead of $2 million?

6. Private Foundation 2 seeks to provide low-cost financing to low- and middle-income, first-time home buyers. Private Foundation's sole activity is acting as guarantor for low- and middle-income buyers who seek to borrow money from conventional banks to purchase homes. If, during the taxable year, Private Foundation

2. And with a previous failure on its records, we suspect that any future request for set-aside approval under the suitability test will be strictly scrutinized.

makes a grant of $200,000 to Private Foundation 2, will the grant constitute a qualifying distribution? What if, in addition to guaranteeing home loans, Private Foundation 2 provides free, mandatory credit counseling and budgeting classes for low- and middle-income families whose loans are guaranteed by Private Foundation 2? Private Foundation 2's endowment is used as security for the loans for which it acts as guarantor; the earnings on the endowment are used to pay the costs of the credit counseling and budgeting classes.

B. Jeopardizing Investments

CODE: § 4944

REGS.: §§ 53.4944-1; 53.4944-3(a); 53.4944-5(b)

Another concern behind the statutory scheme relating to private foundations was that those who controlled the foundations were squandering tax-exempt wealth through aggressive and high-risk investments. Prior law allowed for the revocation of tax exemption when a private foundation's investment activities "jeopardized" the accomplishment of the purpose for which the foundation was granted tax exemption. As with provisions already studied, Congress believed that the threat of revocation was ineffective because the harshness of the sanction meant that it was unlikely to be applied. In addition, the foundation manager who pursued the risky investment suffered no personal liability (and thus, there was no negative reinforcement of such investment activity).

To correct this situation,[3] § 4944 and Treas. Reg. § 53.4944-1(b)(2)(i) require foundations and their managers to "exercise ordinary business care and prudence, under the facts and circumstances prevailing at the time of making the investment, in providing for the long- and short-term financial needs of the foundation to carry out its exempt purposes." There are no per se jeopardizing investments, but highly speculative investments, such as trading on margin, trading in commodity futures, oil and gas wells, puts, calls, straddles, and short sales will raise a suspicion of jeopardy, according to the regulations. Treas. Reg. § 53.4944-1(b)(2)(i).

Again, a two-tier system operates. First a tax equal to 10% of a jeopardizing investment is imposed on the foundation for each year (or part of a year) that a jeopardizing investment is held during the taxable period.[4] IRC § 4944(a)(1). A foundation manager who knowingly, willfully, and without reasonable cause participates in the

3. Many have noted, though, that there has never been significant evidence to prove that foundation managers were actually making such risky investments. Still, § 4944 is probably the most harmless of all the private foundation excise taxes since it only requires foundation managers to do what most would do in any event.

4. Similar to prior definitions of "taxable period," the taxable period for jeopardizing investments begins when the investment is made and ends on the earliest of (1) the mailing of a deficiency notice, (2) removal of the investment from jeopardy, or (3) the making of an assessment.

making of the investment is liable for a tax equal to 10% of the investment for each year (or part thereof), but not more than $10,000 per investment. IRC § 4944(a)(2); 4944(d)(2). As usual, the regulations over-define the terms "knowing" and "willful." A manager acts knowingly if she has actual knowledge of facts that would make the investment a jeopardizing one, is aware that under the circumstances the investment may violate § 4944, and is actually aware that it violates § 4944 or negligently fails to investigate whether the investment would violate that provision. Treas. Reg. § 53.4944-1(b)(2)(i). A manager acts willfully if her participation is "voluntary, conscious, and intentional." Treas. Reg. § 53.4944-1(b)(2)(ii). These terms appear to provide an out only if the manager acted under duress or by accident. The "advice of counsel" provision relating to self-dealing applies as well to shield a foundation manager from a finding of knowing or willful conduct. Treas. Reg. § 53.4944-1(b)(2)(v). In addition, though, a foundation manager may rely on the written advice of a qualified investment manager. *Id.*

If the investment is not "removed from jeopardy" within the taxable period, an additional tax equal to 25% thereof is imposed on the foundation and another 5% tax—that is, 5% of the amount still in jeopardy—is imposed on any foundation manager who refuses to so remove that part of the investment. IRC § 4944(b). The limit for the second tax on foundation managers is $20,000 per investment. IRC § 4944(d)(2). The second tax may be imposed on the foundation manager even if she was not liable for the first tax. Thus, a foundation manager that acts with reasonable cause with respect to what turns out to be a jeopardizing investment will avoid the first tax, but incur the second if she refuses to remove that investment from jeopardy. Treas. Reg. § 53.4944-2(c), Example 2.

An investment is "removed from jeopardy" when the foundation sells or disposes of it, and the proceeds from the sale or disposition are not jeopardizing investments. IRC § 4944(e)(2). For example, if a foundation makes a jeopardizing investment in a risky venture and then directly exchanges that interest for another highly speculative investment, there is a single continuing investment that has never been removed from jeopardy. Treas. Reg. § 53.4944-5(b)(2). If the foundation sells the first investment for cash or other non-jeopardizing investment, it has been removed from jeopardy. A second jeopardizing investment results (and a new taxable period begins) if the foundation uses the cash, for example, to purchase another risky investment. A removal from jeopardy can also be accomplished by a change in the terms of the jeopardizing investments (without an actual divestment thereof). For example, if a private foundation buys stock in a very poorly run corporation, it likely engages in a jeopardizing investment and the taxable period begins. If the corporation maintains its stock ownership, but requires the corporation to implement prudent business practices, it will have removed the investment from jeopardy and the taxable period will end (assuming it has not been sooner ended). Cf. Treas. Reg. 53.4944-3(a)(3)(i).

The excise tax for jeopardizing investments does not apply to "program related investments" no matter how risky. IRC § 4944(c); Treas. Reg. § 53.4944-3. Program related investments are investments: (1) made for the primary purpose of achieving an exempt purpose, (2) which do not have as a significant purpose the production of income or appreciation of property, and (3) which are not made to influence legislation or to intervene in political campaigns. *Id.* An investment meets the primary purpose requirement if it significantly furthers the accomplishment of an exempt purpose and would not have been made "but for" its relationship to the accomplishment of the purpose. For example, a tax-exempt environmental protection organization that buys stock in a corporation seeking to develop speculative, untried and untested technology that might result in quicker oil spill clean-ups will not be making a jeopardizing investment even if a prudent investor would not have purchased the stock. In addition, an investment in a functionally related business is also exempt from the § 4944 excise tax. Treas. Reg. § 53.4944-3(a)(2)(ii).

There are few judicial opinions and only one "precedential" IRS ruling[5] regarding § 4944. But the absence of interpretive authority provides us with an opportunity to raise two important practical considerations. The first is that practitioners, by necessity, frequently rely on non-precedential guidance in advising and assisting clients. Indeed, it is only a matter of good sense that an attorney would want to know the informally stated positions of those with enforcement authority over her area of practice. Students who pursue careers affecting charitable organizations will therefore quickly adopt the habit of paying attention to what Service officials say, not only in "private" correspondence to or with regard to individual taxpayers (i.e., in private letter rulings, technical advice memoranda, and closing agreements), but also in speeches, IRS training documents (such as the IRS Exempt Organization Continuing Education Textbook), and other internal legal memoranda (such as "general counsel memoranda" and "field service advice") between Service personnel and their attorney-advisors. The second important practical consideration, demonstrated in part by the following private letter rulings, is that oftentimes a transaction that triggers one excise tax will also implicate another excise tax or will cause the Service to open a broad investigation of the foundation's operations. The occurrence of one transaction may therefore have a devastating snowball effect even when the foundation is "innocent." The time and financial expense devoted to the Service's

5. Rev. Rul. 80-133, 1980-1 C.B. 258. In that ruling, the owner of a whole life insurance policy donated the policy to a private foundation. At the time of the donation, the policy was subject to a loan previously granted to the donor, and the donor had a life expectancy of ten years. The policy provided for a payment of the face amount, less the loan balance and interest thereon, to the foundation upon the death of the donor. According to the ruling:

> Instead of immediately surrendering the policy to the insurer for its cash surrender value, the foundation retained the policy as an investment and annually pays the premiums and interest due on the policy and policy loan, respectively. The combined premium and interest payments are of such an amount that, by the end of eight years, the foundation will have invested a greater amount in premiums and interest than it could receive as a return on this investment, i.e., the form of insurance proceeds upon death of the insured.

Because the investment would produce a foreseeable financial loss to the foundation, the Service ruled that the managers failed to "exercise ordinary business care and prudence" and therefore the payments with regard to the policy constituted a jeopardy investment.

inquiry (which can last for years) can be significant and debilitating. It is important, then, that a foundation have a "compliance" program designed to guard against prohibited transactions.

Question and Planning Exercise

Poverty Relief is 501(c)(3) private foundation dedicated to the relief of world hunger. During a recent Trustee Retreat, the Board heard presentations from The Center for Corporate Responsibility, a national organization that seeks to encourage investment in "socially responsible" corporations and businesses, as well as divestment from "socially irresponsible" corporations. Soon after the retreat, the Board adopted a resolution instructing its Finance Committee to sell its stock holdings in The Expensive Athletic Apparel Company, a corporation that sells high-end athletic apparel. For many years, the yield on the investment in EAA has averaged about 13%. The Board ordered divestment, nevertheless, because of EAA's use of child labor in foreign countries. By the same resolution, the Finance Committee was instructed to bring to the Board's attention three socially responsible corporations in which Poverty Relief might invest its moderately sized endowment.

At the next meeting, the Finance Committee presented a proposal to invest in several socially responsible corporations through International Biodiversity, Inc., (IB), a for-profit venture capital corporation. IB was formed for the purpose of financing and promoting the expansion of environmentally oriented businesses that will contribute to conservation and economic development in economically and/or environmentally sensitive areas of the world. IB will coordinate the funding efforts of socially conscience investors and then make direct investments in businesses that involve the sustainable use of natural resources, foster the preservation of biological diversity, or engage in organic agriculture with biodiversity linkages. The shareholders in IB include governments, international development aid agencies, and some private investors.

IB has twin goals. First, IB has a goal of at least 3% rate of return per investor. Because IB will not invest in corporations without a "social conscience" it cannot expect to achieve the higher rates of return that other venture capital firms provide investors. Second, IB must be able to demonstrate a clear environmental benefit through each investment. The 3% return is significantly less than the acceptable rate of return on international venture capital fund investments of comparable risk, and is well below the rate that Poverty Relief would have required prior to adopting a socially responsible investment strategy. An independent analysis would prove that the targeted rate here, 3%, taken as a factor by itself in a normal investment strategy would not compensate for the speculative nature of the investment and the overall risk associated with M's unique investment characteristics.

The investment guidelines IB will use are consistent with the objectives of the Global Environmental Facility of the World Bank and that these objectives are derived from the Convention of Biological Diversity, which is an international framework for habitat and direct species protection signed by the United States government and most of the home countries of businesses targeted for investment by IB. This objective is "conservation of biological diversity, the sustainable use of its components and fair and equitable sharing of the benefits arising out of the utilization of genetic resources."

IB's board of directors will appoint a special Investment Committee (IC). The IC will have up to six members. Two will be designated by the board of directors and will be employees of S's investment advisor, one shall be designated by IA and appointed by S's investment advisor and shall serve as long as N is a shareholder. S is a private foreign company whose primary focus is environmental activities. The board of directors has agreed to initially designate one person named by T. All investment decisions for M will be recommended by IA (described below) and will be approved by IC or by a majority of M's board of directors, if IC is unable to assemble a quorum, or if IC has failed to approve the three prior recommendations of IA. According to M's shareholders agreement, IA shall adopt and implement a written Environmental Management System (EMS) that is reasonably satisfactory to each of the shareholders of the Investment Advisor, and that is intended to assure that M's investments will be consistent with the World Bank Environmental Policies and Guidelines.

IA is a newly established organization owned jointly by Q, a § 501(c)(3) public charity that operates an investment fund and provides debt and equity financing to support environmentally-sound economic development in developing countries. IA will work with individuals and companies in the targeted countries to identify and evaluate projects for investment. It will then perform the necessary due diligence on all investments. This will include on-site review of the potential investments under environmentally sensitive guidelines. IA will then present the potential investment first to the Biodiversity Advisory Board (BAB) (described below) for comments and, pending positive review, to IC for approval. IA is also responsible for ensuring proper distribution of funds and for monitoring all financial and environmental aspects of each investment. IA will ensure that the expected guidelines will be properly applied to all investments. IA is also responsible for documentation in connection with any investments made by M, ensuring proper distribution of funds and for monitoring all financial and environmental aspects of each investment.

As noted above, IA will work with BAB, which is anticipated to include a broad range of individuals, scientists, government representatives, and representatives of not-for-profit organizations that have substantial experience in the environmental area. BAB is to provide counsel on biodiversity issues and on biodiversity-related investment eligibility guidelines. Poverty Relief has represented that there will be representatives from non-government organizations located in the areas within which investments are to be made. It is to include representatives from world-renowned environmental and investment organizations.

1. Are there any tax consequences from the Board's decision to divest from EAA, Inc.? Does that investment have any continuing relevance after divestment?

2. Please prepare an outline of an opinion regarding the Board's "socially responsible investment policy" in general and the proposal to invest its entire endowment in IB in particular. How might the Board eliminate any potential weaknesses in its position.

3. If your opinion is that the organization may adopt the policy and invest in IB and the Service later alleges that investing in IB constitutes a jeopardy investment, what is the potential liability to the organization and board members?

C. Taxable Expenditures

CODE: §§ 4945, IRC 74(a), 117(a)

REGS.: §§ 53.4945-2(a)(4)–(7), 53.4945-3(b)(1)–(2), 53.4945-4(a)(1)–(4), 53.4945-5(a)–(b)(3)

The final excise tax resulting from Congress' concern with private foundations is § 4945. The legislative history indicates that the provision results from the belief that private foundations were becoming "increasingly active in political and legislative activities." The involvement manifested itself, according to Congress, via lobbying activities as well as bribes (essentially) to or in support of influential persons involved in politics.[6] Thus, § 4945 employs the familiar two-tier system to punish foundations that engage in such activities.[7] A 20% tax is imposed on the foundation for each of its "taxable expenditures" and a 5% tax is imposed on any foundation manager who knowingly agrees to make the expenditure willfully and without reasonable cause. IRC § 4945(a)(2). The definitions of "knowingly," "willfully" and "reasonable cause" under IRC § 4945 are identical to the definitions applicable under the jeopardy investments prohibition. Treas. Reg. § 53.4945-1(a)(2)(ii)–(v). In addition, a foundation manager can gain a measure of protection by relying on the written advice of counsel, under a regulatory provision similar to that available under the self-dealing and jeopardy investment prohibition. Treas. Reg. 53.4945-1(a)(2)(iv).

"Taxable expenditures" are amounts spent for lobbying and political campaign activities, grants to individuals for travel and study, unless such grants are made pursuant to a procedure approved in advance by the Service, grants to non-public charities (except exempt operating foundations) over which the foundation does not exercise "expenditure responsibility," and grants made for noncharitable purposes.

6. Some might find the use of the word "bribes" to be a bit strong. But the legislative history suggests that suspicion and cynicism played no small part in the enactment of § 4945:It was also called to the committee's attention that existing law does not effectively limit the extent to which foundations can use their money for "educational" grants to enable people to take vacations abroad, to have paid interludes between jobs, and to subsidize the preparation of materials furthering specific "political viewpoints."Senate Report 91-552, 91st Cong., 1st Sess., 1969-3 C.B. 423, 455.

7. The purpose is to prevent such activities, but the effect of § 4945 is far broader than that since proof that the private foundation is supporting a political activity is unnecessary.

IRC § 4945(d) Fortunately, lobbying and campaign activities are essentially defined the same under IRC 4945 as they are under IRC § 4911 and IRC § 501(c)(3), respectively. Treas. Reg. § 53.4945-2(a). The same exceptions (nonpartisan analysis, technical advice, and "self-defense" communications) also apply. Treas. Reg. § 53.4945-2(d). The special "members-only" rule, however, does not apply under IRC § 4945. Thus, a communication that would not be grass roots lobbying under IRC 4911 because of the members-only rule, may be a taxable expenditure under IRC § 4945. In addition, voter registration drives are specifically included as prohibited campaign intervention, unless such activities comply with more stringent requirements not applicable to public charities. IRC § 4945(f); Treas. Reg. § 53.4945-3(b)(1). It may seem strange that a provision related to lobbying and political activities would concern itself with individual grants, but remember that the Congress believed that such grants were being used to support politically involved individuals under the guise of "education." Likewise, we have previously discussed the use of targeted voter registration drives to support a political candidate or party.

A grant made to a public charity might indirectly support lobbying activities, because a public charity is not entirely barred from engaging in such activities. Thus, to the extent a private foundation relieves the public charity from having to pay other expenses, the foundation may be viewed as financially supporting the public charity's lobbying activities. Enforcing this logic would impose tax on a foundation every time it made a grant to a public charity that engaged in any lobbying. The regulations provide, however, that general grants will not create vicarious liability if the grant is not earmarked for lobbying, and, if the grant is for a specific project, the amount thereof does not exceed the amount budgeted to accomplish the project (other than lobbying costs, if any). Treas. Reg. § 53.4945-2(a)(6). Grants to individuals that will constitute taxable expenditures unless the procedures for making such grants are approved by the Service before the grants are made. The approval procedures are discussed in the revenue procedures below. Grants subject to the pre-approval requirement include: loans, scholarships, fellowships, paid internships, prizes and awards, and program-related investments, but do not include taxable compensation paid to employees (even if the compensation is in the form of includible education expenses) or payments to consultants and advisors who provide personal services to assist the foundations with their projects or conferences.

A grant made to a public charity may also be funneled to an individual in a manner that implicates the concern regarding support of politically influential persons. For example, a private foundation may make a grant to a public charity and that public charity may use the grant to fund the travel or education of an individual. In such cases, the private foundation's grant will be considered a taxable expenditure by the private foundation unless the public charity recipient supervises the project for which the grant is made and controls the selection of the grantee (though the grantee may be selected with the foundation's input). Treas. Reg. § 53.4945-4(a)(4)(ii). Likewise, grants to governmental agencies that are to be used to fund the travel or study of an individual will not be taxable expenditures if the governmental agency obtains prior approval of a program that is consistent with a charitable purpose, requires the individual recipient to submit annual and final reports regarding the use of the grant, and requires the organization to investigate any improper diversions of the grant funds. § 53.4945-4(a)(4)(iii).

The regulations assume that a non-earmarked grant to a public charity or an exempt operating foundation will not be used for political purposes and therefore imposes no special requirements on such grants. Treas. Reg. § 53.4945-5(a)(1). But grants made to private foundations or taxable entities are taxable expenditures unless the grantor foundation exercises potentially burdensome "expenditure responsibility" over the grant. Treas. Reg. § 53.4945-5(b). Remember, all such grants must be made to achieve a charitable purpose or they will be taxable expenditures even if the foundation exercises expenditure responsibility. Treas. Reg. § 53.4945-6(a)–(b). Expenditure responsibility means that the grant is made after a "pre-grant" inquiry of the potential grantee, and under a written agreement requiring the recipient not to use the grant for legislative or political activity (either directly or via a grant to another organization that does not meet the individual travel/study or expenditure responsibility requirements), nor for any purpose other than charitable purposes clearly specified in the agreement. Treas. Reg. § 53.4945-5(b)(1). The agreement must require repayment of any portion of a grant that is diverted from the specified purpose. Treas. Reg. § 53.4945-5(b)(3)(i). The foundation must also require the grantee to submit annual and final reports regarding the use of the grant. Treas. Reg. § 53.4945-5(b)(3)(ii). Finally, the granting foundation must make an annual report to the Service with respect to each grant. Essentially, the report must contain the name and addresses of all grantees, the date, amount and purpose of each grant, the expenditures made by grantees, and whether the grantee diverted any of the grant funds to an improper purpose. Treas. Reg. § 53.4945-5(d)(2).

When the foundation meets its expenditure responsibility, it will normally not be considered to have made a taxable expenditure. Treas. Reg. § 53.4945-5(e)(3). However, if the grantee organization either fails to submit required reports or diverts the grant to an improper purpose, the granting foundation will have made a taxable expenditure unless (in addition to having complied in all other respects with the expenditure responsibility requirement) it takes reasonable steps to obtain the required report, or, in the case of a diversion, reasonable steps to recover the grant or insure its restoration and use for a proper purpose, obtain the grantee's assurance against recurrences, and impose extraordinary precautions on the grantee to prevent recurrences. Treas. Reg. § 53.4945-5(e)(1)–(2). In either case, the foundation must withhold any future payments to the grantee organization until the remedial steps are accomplished (i.e., the report is obtained, the funds are restored,[8] assurance is received, and extraordinary precautions are undertaken).

8. Only if the grantee has previously violated the proper use requirement must the private foundation withhold future payments until diverted payments are restored. Upon the first violation, the

The Tax Court, in 1989, considered two significant issues regarding "expenditure responsibility." It answered both in the negative.[9]

First, may a private foundation win by arguing "No harm, no foul?" In other words, if the grants are actually spent for proper purposes by the recipient, is the lack of proper oversight by the Private Foundation grantor acceptable? No, said the Court. Congress required oversight regardless of whether, in hindsight, the oversight was unnecessary in a particular case.

Second, does the existence of overlapping Officers and Directors between the grantor and grantee constitute the exercise of "expenditure responsibility"? No, said the Court. This may make the exercise easier to conduct; however, the mere existence of common employees and directors does not necessarily suggest the Private Foundation satisfied the statute.

As is quite obvious, the private foundation regulatory scheme is detailed and complex. Our study of that scheme is necessarily broad, because a more comprehensive study would require several more volumes of this book. Still, we want to end our study of the private foundation excise taxes by recommending a case that takes a *long* walk through the private foundation thicket—touching upon such other thorns as grants to foreign organizations, reliance on advice of counsel, correction, burden of proof, additional penalties, and several other details of the whole mess. The case is helpful but requires patience and perseverance. We suggest it be read lightly once and then again with greater concentration. Later, you should refer to the case as you study the private foundation excise taxes. The case, which comprises more than 30 pages, is not included in this book. It does not break new ground or establish any new law. We suggest it, however, as an example of what not to do—of the kinds of behavior (or lack thereof) that result not only in the imposition of an excise tax, but also in the application of penalties doubling the tax because of "knowing" violations. The case is: *John E. Thorne v. Commissioner*, 99 T.C. 67 (1992).

Student Teaching Exercise

Often, students do not realize that professors and practitioners are students, too. Indeed, the study of law is a lifelong pursuit and one never stops being a student, particularly with regard to tax law (though we admit to bias in this regard). When you complete your formal studies, you will most likely be required to return to class (i.e., continuing legal education courses) as a condition of maintaining a license to practice. The best way to understand an area of law is through teaching. And once your practice is well under way, you may seek or be called upon to teach a class related to your particular area of practice. To simulate such a real-world event, and to help with your understanding of taxable expenditures, assume you have been

private foundation must only take reasonable steps to achieve restoration (even if restoration is not actually accomplished).

9. *Hans S. Mannheimer Charitable Trust v. Commissioner of Internal Revenue*, 93 T.C. 35 (1989).

called upon to teach § 4945 to a group of attorney colleagues or a group of foundation executives. Draft two questions pertaining to § 4945 and be prepared to present them, along with a solution analysis to your class (i.e., your professor may ask you to display your question and analysis via whatever technological equipment is installed in your classroom).

Note: Abatement and Refund of Excise Taxes

A common characteristic underlying the private foundation excise taxes is that Congress is more concerned with altering behavior rather than raising revenue. This is seen in each section's imposition of a relatively light "warning tax" followed by a severe confiscatory tax only if the foundation and/or its managers stubbornly refuse to do things differently or correct the prior behavior. In fact, none of the second-tier taxes are imposed without a finding of fault of some sort on the part of the foundation and/or its managers. Even most of the first-tier warning taxes are ultimately subject to a finding of fault. All first-tier taxes except those imposed for self-dealing are to be forgiven (i.e., abated or refunded) if the event giving rise to liability was due to reasonable cause and not willful neglect, and is corrected within 90 days of the mailing of a notice of deficiency with respect to any such first-tier tax. IRC §§ 4962(a); 4963(e). All second-tier taxes, including those imposed for self-dealing, are subject to forgiveness if corrected with 90 days of the mailing of a notice of deficiency with respect to any such tax. IRC § 4963. Clearly, then, Congress would rather foundations and managers exhibit fidelity to the charitable goal. As we saw in *Thorton*, § 6684 imposes another penalty in an effort to finally end abusive behavior. It is as if Congress imposed an incredibly detailed and complicated regulatory scheme and then bends over backwards in order not to impose any sanctions for violations. This Sword of Damocles approach is exemplified one last time in § 507, to which we now turn.

D. The Termination Tax

Code: § 507

Regs.: §§ 1.507-1(a)–(b)(1); 1.507-2(a)(6)–(7), 2(b)(1)(i)–(iii); 1.507-2(d)–(e); 1.507-9

To this point, we have referred to the excise taxes as a series of "two-tier" penalties imposed for certain acts or failures to act. This focus on conduct carries forward to a "third tier" tax imposed under § 507. That provision recognizes that at some point, "enough is enough." Thus, the Service may involuntarily terminate the private foundation status of an organization if it knowingly engages in one "willful and flagrant act (or failure to act)" that results in the imposition of an excise tax, or if the organization knowingly engages in two or more willful acts (or failures to act) each of which gave rise to an excise tax.[10] Involuntary termination is by no means painless.

---

10. "Willfully" and "knowingly" are defined, for purposes of § 507(a), essentially the same as they are defined under § 4945.

If the Service is successful, the involuntarily terminated private foundation must essentially pay back the entire amount of tax benefit, with interest, reaped not only by the foundation (because of its tax exemption over the years of its existence) but also by all substantial contributors (because of their charitable contribution deductions) of the foundation. Treas. Reg. § 1.507-1(c)–(d). The third-tier penalty is limited, however, to the value of the foundation's net assets (i.e., gross value minus liabilities) as of the date of the willful and flagrant act or the first of the willful and repeated acts that results in the involuntary termination. Treas. Reg. § 1.507-7(a). If the value of the net assets is higher on the date that private foundation status is involuntarily terminated, then the value on that date serves as the limitation. *Id.*

Even when enough really is enough, a wayward foundation can still avoid the termination tax. The Service may abate the termination tax if, after assessment, the private foundation distributes all of its net assets to one or more public charities, each of which has been in existence as such for at least 60 consecutive months. IRC § 507(g). The distribution must comply with the rules applicable to a voluntary termination by distribution, which rules are discussed below. Treas. Reg. § 1.507-9(a). The Service may also abate the termination tax if, within one year of the date on which it notifies the "appropriate state officer" that the foundation is liable for the termination tax, the state officer certifies to the Service that court-ordered or approved corrective action has been initiated to assure compliance with the excise tax purposes and ensure the charitable use of the foundation's assets in compliance with the excise tax provisions.

The termination tax is inapplicable when a private foundation voluntarily terminates its private foundation status and meets the alternative requirements of § 507(b). The voluntary termination method is unavailable, though, to a foundation that has engaged in willful and repeated acts, or a willful and flagrant act giving rise to an excise tax.[11] A voluntary termination is achieved, in the first instance, when a private foundation distributes all of its net assets to a public charity that has been in existence as such for at least 60 consecutive months prior to the distribution. IRC § 507(b)(1)(A). To prevent the foundation from maintaining control over the assets so distributed, the regulations require that the distribution essentially be without conditions or reservations as to the use of the assets or the income therefrom. Treas. Reg. § 1.507-2(a)(6)–(7). Thus, the foundation must transfer all of its "right, title, and interest" in the assets to the public charity. Certain conditions, however, are not regarded as improper conditions. For example, a restriction on the use of assets to a purpose consistent with the recipient's charitable purpose is permissible. The regulations provide a laundry list of factors that should be considered in determining whether a transfer is with so many strings attached that it is not a transfer of all the foundation's right, title, and interest. Treas. Reg. § 1.507-2(a)(8).

11. The involuntary termination may have the same effect of the voluntary termination, however, if the involuntarily terminated foundation distributes all of its net assets to a public charity and the termination tax is thereafter abated.

The second method by which to achieve a voluntary termination is by operating as a public charity for a period of 60 months. Treas. Reg. § 1.507-2(b). This option, too, is unavailable to a foundation that has previously engaged in willful and repeated acts, or a willful and flagrant act. The 60-month period begins on the first day of any taxable year, prior to which notice has been given to the Service of the foundation's intent to voluntarily terminate its status. If, at the beginning of the 60-month period and at all times throughout, the foundation meets all the requirements of the public charity status it is seeking to attain, it will be treated as a public charity during the 60-month period and thereafter (assuming it continues to meet the requirements thereafter). If the foundation meets the requirements for less than the entire 60-month period, it will be treated as a public charity only for the taxable years during the 60-month period that it meets the requirements. A foundation seeking to terminate under the 60-month method may obtain an advance ruling that it is a public charity during the 60-month period, and thereby provide assurance to potential donors that their contributions will be deductible under the more favorable provisions applicable to public charity status.[12] The advance ruling will also mean that the foundation is treated as a public charity for purposes of §§ 4942 and 4945. Therefore, grants from other private foundations will more easily be treated as qualifying distributions, and private foundation grantors will be relieved of the expenditure responsibility requirements with respect to the recipient foundation during the 60-month period.

Note: Enforcement in a Practical Sense

The various excise taxes and potential termination tax are indeed harsh. Whether they actually deter improper behavior is open to question. Certainly, the government enforces the provisions at least occasionally, as they raise fairly modest amounts of revenue. Another potential method of enforcement applies to "controversial" organizations: competitors and people who disagree with their "controversial" views can judge them in the marketplace of the media, Internet, and blogs. Whether this informal enforcement is wise and whether it is good for society is debatable; however, anyone involved with private foundations in general—and controversial ones in particular—should pay heed not only to the Service, but also to public watchdogs. For several practical examples involving Boy Scouts, Girl Scouts, PTA Groups, and a large well-known private foundation, see Steven J. Willis, *People in Glass Houses*, 113 Tax Notes 477 (2006). The article argues that a private foundation can violate several excise tax restrictions and other fundamental rules governing the tax law of charities with apparent impunity. It thus illustrates the option of "competitor"-based enforcement of the law (public chastisement and embarrassment) rather than government enforcement.

12. The procedure for obtaining an advance ruling for the 60-month period and the effect of that advance ruling is essentially the same as the procedures and effects applicable for and of advance rulings issued to new organizations, except that a consent to extend the statute of limitations is mandatory (such a consent is not mandatory with regard to advance rulings to new organizations).

Chapter 19

Alternatives to Private Foundation Status

A. Overview

The underlying assumption of the private foundation regulatory scheme is that the person or persons who provide the organization's capital also control its operations. Thus, the assumption goes, "big donor" claims a generous tax deduction but then too often succumbs to the temptation to operate the recipient organization in a manner that is not necessarily for the public good. Because the organization is not the recipient of, nor dependent upon, support from the public, it need not be concerned with public opinion.

This theory and the resulting private foundation regulatory scheme essentially define all big donors solely by reference to the malevolent big donor. In the years since enactment of the private foundation regulatory scheme, responsible, well-meaning donors have sought alternatives in an effort to retain some degree of control over contributed funds without triggering the burdens of private foundation status. In general, these alternatives involve the interposition of an independent governing body between the big donor and the endowed organization with the big donor retaining significant influence over the organization. The exempt organization must also demonstrate that it is responsive to public opinion rather than a big donor's influence.

This Chapter considers some of the accommodations the Code and Service make for well-meaning donors who would otherwise suffer under the private foundation scheme right along with not-so-well-meaning donors. As you read, consider the extent to which the accommodations might make it easier for not-so-well-meaning donors to use the charitable contribution and tax exemption provisions for their own private goals. The questions that follow each section below are broadly designed to get you to think from a policy perspective concerning the desirability—from an equity and efficiency standpoint—of the whole private foundation regulatory scheme.

Caution: this Chapter covers some controversial topics. Many people view these "alternatives to private foundations status" as important developments in tax practice: as societal goods that help ensure proper use of charitable funds. Others see them differently: as cynical schemes to avoid the rigors of private foundation treatment by paying "rent" to public charities willing to sell (or rent) their public charity status. Effectively, the cynic might argue, these alternatives make private foundation status essentially elective, rather than the result of mechanical tests.

More stringent controls imposed by the 2006 legislation suggest that Congress, at the behest of the Treasury, has sided with the cynics.

We place alternatives to private foundations into six categories:

1. Preferred Private Foundations: pools, conduits, and private operating foundations.
2. Traditional Supporting Organizations for Public Charities.
3. Traditional Supporting Organizations for Social Welfare Organizations, Labor Unions, and Business Leagues.
4. Donor-Advised Funds.
5. Type I, II, and III Supporting Organizations (Other than B and C).
6. Community Trusts and Foundations.

The first category involves three different "preferred private foundations" described by § 170(e)(1)(F). They are private foundations and thus not true alternatives, but their preferred status is significant. Thus, they are each an "alternative."

The second and third categories are traditional "supporting organizations" described in 509(a)(3), generally covered in Chapter 15. They are public charities created and controlled by public charities or other publicly supported organizations. We covered them generally in Chapter 15 Part B.3, which dealt with 509(a)(3) organizations. We repeat some of the analysis here from a different angle so as to put them into context of other private foundation alternatives.

The fourth and fifth categories are the most useful alternatives to private foundations. They have similarities—some retained involvement—but also important differences. The fourth covers donor-*advised* funds, not to be confused with donor-*directed* funds (the first category). The fifth category is fundamentally a sub-group of categories two and three; however, § 4966[1] added them in 2006. We find them worthy of separate analysis.

The last category overlaps with the others. We list it separately because that appears to be how many practitioners and others in the field view them.

A full discussion of these categories might be book-length. This is a primer. Terminology in this area is critical, so take this slowly. The following discussion uses these terms of art:

- Pool
- Conduit
- Donor-Advised Fund (DAF)
- Donor-Directed Fund (same as a Pool)

1. IRC § 4966 (Section 1231(a) of the Pension Protection Act of 2006).

- Disqualified Person (three definitions)
- Described Person (multiple definitions)
- Sponsoring Organization
- Supported Organization
- Traditional Supporting Organization
- Type I Supporting Organization
- Type II Supporting Organization
- Type III Supporting Organization
- Functionally Integrated Type III Supporting Organization
- Non-Functionally Integrated (NFI) Type III Supporting Organization.

The following descriptions are intense. They assume the reader has knowledge of law generally, knowledge of tax law specifically, and knowledge of tax-exempt law more specifically. Probably the most important part is near the end of Part E describing how easy it is to become a sponsoring organization or donor-advised fund without intending to become one. Those are popular vehicles, but they are subject to two substantial excise taxes; as a result, one must be careful not to inadvertently become one.

B. Preferred Private Foundations: Pooled "Donor-Directed" Funds; Conduits; and Private Operating Foundations

Code: § 170(b)(1)(F)(i), (ii), (iii)

Reg.: § 1.170A-9(i)

This category comprises three types of preferred private foundation. So it is, technically, not an "alternative" to private foundation status. However, given that the preferences bestowed on these entities and the understanding of them that is required in order to appreciate the Donor-Advised Funds discussed below, we thought it advisable to include discussion of them here. We focus mostly on pools. Created in 1969 (long styled as 170(b)(1)(E)(iii) but more recently moved to 170(b)(1)(F)(iii)), a "pooled" common fund is a private foundation.

First, consider some background. Section 170(b)(1)(F) lists three types of preferred private foundations. Contributions to such entities are treated as if they were contributions to public charities for purposes of § 170(e) reductions and § 170(b) limitations. The types are:

- A private operating foundation per paragraph 4943(j)(3). This is a private foundation which actually operates as a charity, as opposed to funding other charities.

- A "conduit."[2] This is a private foundation which distributes 100% of its contributions within 2.5 months of the end of the year. Distributions must be "qualified" and records must be kept per § 4942(g) and (h).
- A "pool."[3] This is a private foundation which supports a 509(a)(1) public charity. It is similar to, but distinct from, both donor-advised funds or Type I, II, or III supporting organizations.

Multiple donors give to a pool, but individual "substantial contributors"[4] retain some rights regarding donations. Such a donor may annually designate how income from his/her donation is to be distributed. All fund income must be distributed annually within 2.5 months of the end of each fund year. All distributions must be to public charities which satisfy the 509(a)(1) public support test. Satisfying the 509(a)(2) test is insufficient. Also, the corpus of any donor's contribution must similarly be distributed (subject to the designation of the donor) within one year of the donor's death.

Such private foundations, along with private operating foundations under § 4943(j)(3) and "conduits" described in 170(b)(1)(F)(ii), are "preferred" as compared with other private foundations. Contributions to them are subject to the 170(b)(1)(A) limitations as well as to the more favorable 170(e)(1)(B) contribution reductions applicable to public charities. As a result, per § 170(e)(1)(B)(ii), contributions of appreciated real property are deductible at fair market value (subject to the arguable application of § 1250 reductions). Recall: a significant disadvantage of private foundation status is that contributions to private foundations are only deductible to the extent of 30% of the contributor's contribution base (roughly, adjusted gross income (AGI)), rather than to the extent of 50% of the contributor's contribution base for gifts to public charities. IRC § 170(b)(1)(B).[5] In addition, a deduction for a contribution of capital gain property to most private foundations is limited to the donor's basis in the contributed property. IRC § 170(e)(1)(B)(ii).

In contrast, cash contributions to a donor-directed fund use the 50% limit, IRC § 170(b)(1)(A)(vii), and contributions of capital gain property to a donor-directed fund are allowable up to the capital asset's fair market value, subject to the 30% limitation in § 170(b)(1)(C) (which limitation also applies to public charities). Thus, big donors who want to maintain control over their donations can use a donor-directed fund to achieve the same individual tax benefits available to donors who give up control.

This alternative to private foundation status, donor-*directed* funds, is actually only half an alternative and, indeed, may ultimately cast aspersions on the donor's

2. IRC § 170(b)(1)(F)(ii).

3. IRC § 170(b)(1)(F)(iii); Treas. Reg. § 1.170A-9(i).

4. Per Treas. Reg. § 1.170A-9(i), the § 509(a)(2) definition of substantial contributor applies.

5. Sixty percent through 2025 under the 2017 Tax Cuts and Jobs Act IRC 170(b)(1)(G)(i) and, potentially, 100% in 2020 as a result of § 2205 of the 2020 CARES Act. Pub. L. No. 116-136, § 2205, 134 Stat. 281 (2020).

motives. As discussed in greater detail below, one popular alternative to private foundation status is the 509(a)(3) supporting organization. A supporting organization may not be controlled by disqualified persons. Accordingly, if a disqualified person can designate recipients of the funds donated by the disqualified person to the supporting organization, the supporting organization fails the § 509(a)(3)(C) requirement and becomes a private foundation. *See* Treas. Reg. § 1.509(a)-4(j)(1). Some taxpayers avoid this result and keep public charity status through a donor-directed fund as described in § 170(b)(1)(F)(iii).

To summarize, the basic requirements for a donor-*directed* fund under § 170(b)(1)(F)(iii) are:

- a private foundation
- that pools all its donations in a way that meets the requirements of a § 509(a)(3) supporting organization
- except that major donors can annually designate income attributable to that donor's contribution to specific public charities.

Charitable causes may suffer somewhat from the diversion of charitable funds to the administrative costs associated with the fund's private foundation status (because the donor-directed fund is still a private foundation for all other purposes). The donor's motives might therefore be questioned because the retention of control does not affect the donor's tax deduction, but does decrease the amount of value that is transferred to charitable causes.

Question

What are the ethical and social responsibility issues created when Big Donor comes to your law office and asks you to advise him on the various ways he might be able to set up a charity with his tax deductible endowment and over which he can exercise direct or indirect control without having to deal with private foundation regulatory problems?

C. Traditional Supporting Organizations for a Public Charity[6]

CODE: § 509(a)(3)

This category comprises charities which are a subsidiary or brother/sister of a 501(c)(3). On its own, the parent[7] must satisfy either the 509(a)(1) or (a)(2) public charity test. On its own, the subsidiary—commonly called a satellite—qualifies as a

6. We use the term "public charity" as a charity which satisfies either the § 509(a)(1) or (2) public support tests plus churches, schools, and hospitals (per 170(b)(1)(A)(i) through (iii)).

7. IRC § 4966 (Section 1231(a) of the Pension Protection Act of 2006). (using the term parent or common parent).

501(c)(3), but does not satisfy a public support test. However, the satellite satisfies the following two tests from 509(a)(3)(B) and (C), which require that it:

> (B) is —
>
> > (i) operated, supervised, or controlled by one or more organizations described in paragraph (1) or (2) [the public support tests plus churches, schools, and hospitals],
> >
> > (ii) supervised or controlled in connection with one or more such organizations, or
> >
> > (iii) operated in connection with one or more such organizations, and
>
> (C) is not controlled directly or indirectly by one or more disqualified persons (as defined in section 4946) other than foundation managers and other than one or more organizations described in paragraph (1) or (2)[.]

IRC § 509(a)(3)(B) and (C).

To illustrate, a public charity may desire a special fund dedicated for particular purposes which it wants to operate as a separate entity. Perhaps it runs a thrift shop which it wants to incorporate separately for limited liability purposes. If it controls, supervises, or operates the separate entity (the satellite) as required by § 509(a)(3)(B)(i), (ii), or (iii), and if the separate entity is itself a 501(c)(3), then per 509(a)(3)(A), the subsidiary takes on the public charity status of the parent. This type of supporting organization is consistent with the integral part doctrine discussed in Chapters Six and Eight. Many organizations *operate* as one entity but have investment funds in a separate entity. They create, control, supervise, and operate the subsidiary. That would be a typical category two scenario with few important concerns in relation to this discussion which ultimately focuses on donor-advised funds.

D. Traditional Supporting Organizations for a Social Welfare Organization, Labor Union, or Business League

CODE: § 509(a)(3)

This category is very similar to the prior one. It comprises charities—also sometimes called satellites—which are either a subsidiary or brother/sister of a § 501(c)(4), (5), or (6) organization—a social welfare, labor union, or business league. Controlled by the parent (or a common parent), the subsidiary conducts activities which qualify it for 501(c)(3) status. If the satellite satisfies either 509(a)(1) or (2), it is a public charity; however, if the satellite itself cannot meet a public support test, it falls into this category. The parent or common parent must satisfy the § 509(a)(2) test if it were applicable. That test is inapplicable, because the parent is not a 501(c)(3). If the controlling, supervising, or operating entity satisfies the (a)(2) public support test—*not* the (a)(1)—then the satellite becomes a public charity per § 509(a)(3).

A common example would be a charitable scholarship fund controlled by a local bar association. The bar association would be a 501(c)(6) business league. As a result, both the § 509(a)(1) and (2) public support tests would be irrelevant: private foundation status only applies to § 501(c)(3) or former 501(c)(3) entities. The scholarship fund would satisfy the requirements of 501(c)(3) but might not satisfy either public support test in 509(a)(1) or (2). But the *bar association* might be able to satisfy the *509(a)(2)* public support test if it were required to do so (which it is not). If so, and if the requisite controls, supervision, or operations required by 509(a)(3)(B) exist, the subsidiary will be a public charity. Of note, the parent—the bar association in the example—must satisfy the 509(a)(2) test; satisfying the 509(a)(1) test is insufficient.

In an impressively brief and amazing cumbersome sentence, the flush language to subsection 509(a) allows for this type of supporting organization:

> For purposes of paragraph (3), an organization described in paragraph (2) shall be deemed to include an organization described in section 501(c)(4), (5), or (6), which would be described in paragraph (2) if it were an organization described in section 501(c)(3).

IRC § 509(a) (flush language).

E. Donor-Advised Funds

CODE: §§ 509(f); 4943(e); 4958(c)(2); 4966; 4967; 6033(k)

REG.: § 1.507-2(a)(7)

Though they have been around for quite some time, donor-*advised* funds (not to be confused with donor-*directed* funds, discussed above) have only recently been touted as a vehicle for the modern, and moderate, philanthropist. In essence, a donor-*advised* fund is just that—donors contribute to a fund (either segregated or mutual) from which grants are made to public charities. Funds grant donors the explicit right to *provide* advice and recommendations to the fund not only as to grant recipients, but also as to the amount and timing of grants made from their donation. And while a grant need not be made for some time after the donor actually contributes to the fund, the donor is entitled to a charitable contribution deduction immediately upon making the contribution. The fund's fiduciaries *need not* follow the donor's advice and recommendations, though as a practical matter, it might be expected that they will do so in the normal course of events. The latter observation, that the fiduciaries normally will follow the donor's advice and recommendation, is one source of regulatory concern.

A DAF is subject to the advice (really, suggestions which need not be followed) of a donor, but not to the common pool donor-directed fund distribution restrictions. They are not separate organizations; instead, they are a bank or investment account or perhaps a set of bookkeeping entries. They have a relationship with a public charity called the "sponsoring organization." As explained by Notice 2017-73:

> Section 4966(d)(2) defines a DAF as a fund or account owned and controlled by a sponsoring organization, which is separately identified by reference to contributions of a donor or donors, and with respect to which the donor, or any person appointed or designated by such donor (donor advisor), has, or reasonably expects to have, advisory privileges with respect to the distribution or investment of the funds. Section 4966(d)(2)(B) excepts from the definition of DAF any fund or account which makes distributions only to a single identified organization or governmental entity, or certain committee-advised funds that make grants to individuals for travel, study, or other similar purposes.
>
> Section 4966(d)(1) defines a sponsoring organization as an organization that: (1) is described in §170(c) (other than a governmental unit described in §170(c)(1), and without regard to the requirement under §170(c)(2)(A) that the organization be organized in the United States); (2) is not a private foundation (as defined in §509(a)); and (3) maintains one or more DAFs.

Typical donor-advised funds look very much like a typical private foundation, though on a smaller scale. Like non-operating private foundations, they conduct no active charitable operations themselves, but instead fund other operating charities. They also provide donors, even a primary donor, with an element of control similar, but not explicitly identical, to that available via a private foundation. Because that control is informal—in the sense that we might expect the fund to comply with the donor's recommendations though it is not required to do so—donor-advised funds historically have not been subject to the private foundation regulatory scheme. In the absence of any other specifically applicable authority, the Service applied Treas. Reg. § 1.507-2(a)(7) to determine whether a donor has retained so much control over the contribution that the donor-advised fund should be denied public charity status and instead be subjected to the private foundation regulatory scheme. If the several factors listed in the regulation indicate too much control, then the donor-advised fund is regulated as a private foundation under the theory that the donor is using the fund as a mere conduit to generate a charitable deduction from activities from which the donor receives personal benefits.

With this approach, then, the Service has partly resolved the questions concerning the proper form of regulating donor-advised funds. The lack of clear legislative authority essentially led the Service to select a "one or the other" approach (i.e., public charity or private foundation status), when perhaps a hybrid approach might have been better advised. After all, a donor-advised fund logically avoids private foundation status because it is not under a donor's explicit control. But as a practical matter, a donor-advised fund that ignores a donor's wishes as often as it follows those wishes is not likely to attract very many donors. It should be expected, therefore, that despite their formal documentation to the contrary, donor-advised funds necessarily concede the same sort of donor control available from private foundations. The potential for abuse seems no different with regard to a donor-advised fund than with a private foundation.

Donor-advised funds are a potentially dangerous alternative to private foundation status, so one must tread lightly with them. As recently as the 1980s, such organizations sometimes prompted criminal investigations because they essentially evaded the complex private foundation excise taxes imposed by §§ 4940 through 4946. For a fee, the controlling public charity would create the subsidiary entity or fund and then operate it consistently with 509(a)(3)(B)(i), (ii) or (iii). Often it would grant too much deference to the donor and thus violate 509(a)(3)(C).

Over time, donor-advised fund gained broad acceptance, but at the cost of substantial restrictions. Since 2006, they are covered by complex rules styled as excise taxes in §§ 4966, 4967, and 4943. Those sections arguably provide the long-sought middle-ground approach. Such funds present a legitimate alternative to private foundations.

If a client has very substantial funds which he/she wishes to donate to a charity for later use, an attorney may create a traditional private foundation—an entity which does not satisfy 509, 4943(j)(3) or 170(b)(1)(F)(iii). As a result, the client has a current charitable deduction[8] for future distributions under his/her control. But the organization will be subject to substantial reporting requirements through Form 990-PF and potentially onerous excise taxes found in §§ 4940 through 4945. It must carefully maintain the very complex lists of disqualified persons found in § 4946. This entity will come with substantial legal and accounting fees to insure it complies with those restrictions. The administrative costs can be substantial, so one might not use this route unless more than $1,000,000 (and arguably much more) in funds are available.

In the alternative a client can donate to an existing public charity—called a sponsoring organization per § 4966(d)(1)—which maintains a donor-advised fund, as defined in § 4966(d)(2). This avoids the substantial current and future legal/accounting fees as well as reporting requirements associated with private foundation status, because the entity is a public charity; however, it comes at the cost of loss of real control. The controlling public charity may consult with the fund donor regarding uses and distributions of the fund; however, it cannot give control to the donor. The intricate excise taxes associated with donor-advised funds found in §§ 4943, 4966, and 4967 are beyond what we can cover in depth herein. However, the private foundation excise taxes discussed in Chapters 16, 17 and 18 should give you a flavor for what's at stake. But be aware, the excise taxes for donor-advised funds are not for the faint of heart: they are complex and onerous. Many large public charities exist which will accept donor-advised fund contributions, at a cost, of course. If a practitioner and client want to create their own sponsoring public charity with donor-advised funds, they should be very careful. Pay heed to the following Code sections:

8. Per § 170(e), the deduction will generally be reduced to the donor's basis. Per § 170(b)(1)(B) and (D), the reduced deduction will be limited to at most 30% of the donor's contribution base.

4966— Excise tax imposed on sponsoring organization (20%) and fund managers (5%—capped at $10,000). Section 4966(c)(1)(A) requires that no distribution can be made to a "natural person" (a human). Section 4966(c)(1)(B) requires all distributions be for purposes described in § 170(c)(2)(B)—basic 501(c)(3) purposes. Further, the sponsoring organization must exercise § 4945(h) expenditure responsibility over the distribution, which involves oversight and record keeping.

4967— Excise tax imposed on non-complying advice of a donor or donor advisor or person related to them (125%) and on a fund manager who agreed to a non-qualifying distribution (10%). Section 4967 is even more consequential. It applies if a donor or donor advisor or a persons related to them receives—directly or indirectly—more than an incidental benefit from a distribution. Related persons include 35% controlled entities (using family attribution rules per paragraphs 4946(a)(3) and (4) and § 267) as well as family members. Family members include a person's "spouse, ancestors, children, grandchildren, great grandchildren, and the spouses of children, grandchildren, and great grandchildren" (per § 4946(d)) as well as the person's siblings and their spouses (per §§ 4967(d) and 4958(f)(7)).

4943(e)— Excise tax (10%) imposed on excess business holdings of a donor-advised fund. It uses a special definition of "disqualified persons."[9]

4958(c)(2)— Excise tax (25%) on "excess benefit transactions" of donor-advised funds. Section 4958(c)(2) greatly broadens the definition of "excess benefit transaction" for donor-advised funds to include any payment, not just excess ones. Paragraph (c)(2) provides:

---

9. The term "disqualified person" has many different definitions in the Code. Section 4946 defines it in relation to private foundations. Section 4958(f)(1) defines the term very differently in relation to public charities. Section 4958(f)(7) has a special definition of described persons for donor advised funds. Be careful, as section 4958(c)(3)(B) has a different definition of described person for supporting organizations, which can include a donor advised fund in which case, both definitions apply, albeit for different purposes. Section 4943(e)(2) uses the section 4958(f)(7) definition, but labels it as disqualified persons for donor advised funds. The language is cumbersome and differs facially from 4958(f)(7) but is substantively the same:

> (2) Disqualified person
>
> In applying this section to any donor advised fund (as so defined), the term "disqualified person" means, with respect to the donor advised fund, any person who is —
>
> (A) described in section 4966(d)(2)(A)(iii) ["a donor or someone selected by the donor who reasonably expects to have advisory privileges with respect to distribution or invested of a donation"],
>
> (B) a member of the family of an individual described in subparagraph (A), or
>
> (C) a 35-percent controlled entity (as defined in section 4958(f)(3) by substituting "persons described in subparagraph (A) or (B) of section 4943(e)(2)" for "persons described in subparagraph (A) or (B) of paragraph (1)" in subparagraph (A)(i) thereof).

(2) Special rules for donor-advised funds

In the case of any donor advised fund (as defined in section 4966(d)(2))—

(A) the term "excess benefit transaction" includes any grant, loan, compensation, or other similar payment from such fund to a person described in subsection (f)(7) with respect to such fund, and

(B) the term "excess benefit" includes, with respect to any transaction described in subparagraph (A), the amount of any such grant, loan, compensation, or other similar payment."

The definition of described "person" appears in subparagraph (f)(7). It includes:

- a donor (or any person appointed or designated by such donor) [who] has, or reasonably expects to have, advisory privileges with respect to the distribution or investment of amounts held in such fund or account by reason of the donor's status as a donor,
- a member of the family of such a person, and
- an entity controlled at a 35% or greater level by persons described above.

A non-donor-advised fund public charity can avoid § 4958 by ensuring it has no excess benefit transactions with anyone. That essentially requires transactions be at fair market value. In contrast, donor-advised funds must not only satisfy § 4958 generally, but they must avoid *any* transaction which involves a payment to a described person.

6684— Doubles 4966, 4967 and 4943(e) excise taxes if the non-compliance is not due to "reasonable cause" and if it is either repeated or "willful and flagrant."

508(f)— Requirement to notify Treasury if a sponsoring organization "maintains" or "intends to maintain" a donor-advised fund.

170(f)(18)— Disallows a 170(a) deduction for some contributions to donor-advised funds. The paragraph adds three important restrictions. *First*, the sponsoring organization must be described in 170(c)(1), which comprises many governmental units, or in (c)(2), which comprises 501(c)(3) entities. Other 170(c) organizations cannot be sponsoring organizations with DAFs. *Second*, the sponsoring organization cannot also be a Type III supporting organization (discussed below). *Third*, the contemporaneous written receipt required for most contributions must state the sponsoring organization has *exclusive legal control* over the contribution.

Our fear regards how easy it is to inadvertently create a donor-advised fund. For example, a church may have a donor who says: "I'll give you $25,000, but I want it used for specific purposes." The church may be tempted to accept the monies and to agree to regular consultations with the donor—who may expect them. That consultation risks the fund being a donor-advised fund and the church being a sponsoring organization subject to the donor-advised fund excise taxes and other restrictions listed above. If it is, the fund, the church, and church board members who participate may be subject to the taxes, which can be enormous. So, tread very carefully when accepting monies subject to the continuing advice of the donor. Intentionally creating a donor-advised fund or sponsoring organization is one thing, albeit not to be taken lightly; but, inadvertently creating one is dangerous. Thus, all public charities must be informed of these dangers by counsel.

As provided in § 4966:

> the term "donor advised fund" means a fund or account—
>
> (i) which is separately identified by reference to contributions of a donor or donors,
>
> (ii) which is owned and controlled by a sponsoring organization, and
>
> (iii) with respect to which a donor (or any person appointed or designated by such donor) has, or reasonably expects to have, advisory privileges with respect to the distribution or investment of amounts held in such fund or account by reason of the donor's status as a donor.[10]

Thus, to *avoid* being a sponsoring organization which has a donor-advised fund, one must ensure no donor or their designee *believe* they have advisory privileges regarding distributions or investment decisions. Students should heed this carefully. If you want to create a sponsoring organization with donor-advised funds, spend significant time with the intricacies and record keeping described above. If, instead, you want to avoid this potential nightmare, be very clear to your client that donors cannot have any continuing rights or expectations with regard to the use of their donations. And be sure the client follows that advice, understanding that membership on boards and committees can change frequently and the ability of lay persons to understand complex—and often counter-intuitive—legal matters is limited. You may find yourself repeating the advice frequently. If you are a board member, remember—errors and omissions insurance rarely, if ever, covers tax liabilities.

The following excerpt suggests that perhaps the private foundation rules are unnecessary altogether. The article appeared seven years prior to the enactment of § 4966.

10. IRC § 4966(d)(2)(A).

Gene Steuerle, Charitable Endowments, Advised Funds and the Mutual Fund Industry — Part Two

82 Tax Notes 129 (1999)[11]

Foundations face all sorts of rules, including minimum payouts for charitable purposes, excise taxes, and elaborate reporting requirements on income and activities. Charitable endowments placed in donor-advised funds at mutual funds, community foundations, and some trust companies do not. This inconsistency eventually may force policymakers to re-examine the laws relating to foundations and to charitable organizations in general. Whether Congress moves and in what direction, however, is uncertain. Lawmakers could treat non-operating foundations more like donor-advised funds or donor-advised funds more like non-operating foundations or simply let each part of the charitable sector evolve under its own set of rules and practices.

While the debate is proceeding, the long-term interests of the charitable community, as well as mutual funds, community foundations, and others offering donor-advised funds, would be well served by a little self-policing to minimize both the possibility and the hint of abuse. One of the basic rules applied to non-operating foundations is that they must pay out an average of 5 percent of their net worth annually. This anti-accumulation rule deters foundations from forever building up their power relative to other institutions in society, while ensuring that charitable causes are served currently. Donor-advised funds, on the other hand, technically face no payout requirement whatsoever, although Fidelity and others have been adopting voluntary rules ensuring minimum payouts. One important issue is whether a voluntary formula should even try to replicate a flawed foundation rule. Consider three examples:

- First, a new donor-advised fund just starting out might want to accumulate some assets so that it can achieve a longer-term purpose. For instance, it may want to accumulate monies for 20 years so that it can pay out the lump sum for a worthy cause. Or an endowment program may want to test market a few ideas of a donor before it is to receive a larger contribution on the donor's death. Should these programs be granted a more lenient rule on payouts in the near term than the rule that currently applies to non-operating foundations?
- Second, under one type of voluntary formula the payout of one donor-advised fund can be mingled with the payout of another donor-advised fund at the same mutual fund to determine whether some aggregate payout has been met. This type of approach might provide much simplicity, but at the same time it could grant significant leeway for a single donor-advised fund to keep a very

11. Reprinted with permission of Tax Analysts.

low payout rate for a long period of time. What type of back-up rule is required if a mingling formula is used?

- Third, and perhaps more importantly, the current foundation rule tends to encourage more payout when times are good and less payout when times are bad—just the opposite of what we might want if foundations are to serve the greatest needs of society over time. Simply adopting a foundation-like rule would merely replicate this behavior for donor-advised funds. Might it not be better to establish some longer-term rule to encourage higher payouts when societal needs are likely to be greater and lesser payouts in good times?

Whatever route is chosen, it is fairly clear that the absence of a payout implies that no charitable purpose is being served. Barring persistent diligence on the part of the mutual funds and the community foundations, Congress is likely itself to come up with a set of rules for donor-advised funds. Mutual funds, trust companies, and community foundations, therefore, should continue efforts at self-policing and should come up with simpler rules that they themselves voluntarily apply to their endowments. Admittedly, no group has enforcement power on other organizations, but by setting standards now, a precedent is established when and if Congress later decides to act.

A second set of rules that currently applies only to foundations is even more complex. The excise tax on investment income of foundations was put into the law with the stated intent, at least in some congressional documents, of financing the IRS's monitoring of the charitable sector. The money collected, however, has always been well in excess of the cost of all IRS efforts with regard to the exempt organization sector as a whole—even more in excess of the cost of policing the foundation subsector. Moreover, this money was never dedicated to the administrative function of the IRS's Employee Plans/Exempt Organizations operation but was instead transferred to general revenues. The recent IRS restructuring formally delinks this source of funding from the EP/EO function.

In many ways, this excise tax violates most standards of efficiency and equity and can only be understood as a penalty developed historically against the past abuses, real or perceived, of foundations. IRS officials, however, have given foundations high marks recently and have indicated that private foundations are less likely to be an area of the charitable sector requiring enforcement resources. While the excise tax is not huge, it is a nuisance, especially for smaller foundations. It violates standards of simplicity in taxation, which call for limits on the number of taxes imposed by the state. Its particular design creates all sorts of havoc with filing and other requirements. As only one example, Martin Sullivan and I demonstrated a few years ago that the current payout rule actually discourages paying out larger percentages of endowment in any year because one consequence is a higher—yes, a higher—tax in future years. That is, the formula penalizes a foundation if it does not pay out a percentage of assets currently in excess of what it paid out in the recent past. Pay out more now, and the foundation is more likely to pay a penalty in the future if that higher payout rate is not maintained.

Since the tax is hard to justify, there is not much of a case to be made (other than a legal bent for consistency) for extending it from non-operating foundations to the new forms of donor-advised funds. Note again that the types of charitable endowments that most mutual funds and community foundations support often involve little more than making contributions and paying out grants. If Congress is not willing to get rid of this tax but wants to provide consistent treatment, it might extend the benefits of nontaxation to those foundations that look no different from many of the simpler donor-advised funds. In effect, I am suggesting that any distinction here be made less on the basis of form of organization and more on types of activities of the organization.

A third area of difference sometimes cited involves the varying expenditure policies of donor-advised funds. For example, in some mutual fund operations there may be little investigation of the worthiness of a recipient organization. A list of charitable organizations from the IRS may be all that is cross-checked by a mutual fund, while the donor-advisors typically have no paid staff to advise them. In community foundations, on the other hand, there more likely are to be limits on how much control resides with the donor-advisor, while potential donees are often culled by community foundations to include only organizations in the region that are considered worthy of support. Differences here are in practice more than in law—a mutual fund could engage in significant checking, a non-operating foundation may check almost nothing, or vice-versa. Because of the inconsistency both within and across foundation and donor-advisor subsectors, it is especially difficult to think of a reform that might apply only to one or the other. It's also almost impossible to think of any rule that works. Certainly, requiring higher administrative expenses would not ensure better quality of grant-making.

A final source of distinction is that the elaborate filing requirements for foundations tend to be avoided by most donor-advised funds. Because of the ways these funds are set up, there usually can be no possibility of a disputed activity (such as self-dealing or excess business holdings); hence no extra filing requirement on the donor-adviser makes sense. That should serve as an incentive for Congress and the IRS to figure out when foundations might also meet a standard for simpler filing requirements, and to the foundation sector to seek intermediaries that could simplify their lives as the mutual funds are now doing for donor-advised funds.

On the other hand, some filing requirements—such as lists of grants and contributions paid or approved—probably should be made more uniform across the board. But those requirements should be made in a way that still holds the reporting burden on mutual funds and community foundations to a reasonable minimum.

Mutual funds have helped democratize endowment giving through donor-advised funds, laying open some exciting prospects for the future of philanthropy. Their expansion has also laid bare some of the differences in tax law treatment both between and among foundations and donor-advised funds, ranging from payout rates to excise taxes to expenditure policies to complexity of filing requirements. The positive development of donor-advised funds should be pushed off course neither by a drive toward consistent application of needlessly complex rules, as now apply to many non-operating foundations, nor by a laissez-faire attitude that would encourage abuse or the perception of abuse. This narrow path is one that the Congress, the Treasury, the IRS, non-operating foundations, community foundations, and the mutual fund industry must figure out how to walk together.

Questions

Read through the discussion of "independent governing body" in Treas. Reg. § 1.507-2(a)(7)(ii). How easy or difficult might it be for a Big Donor to create a governing body that satisfies the definition, while still achieving the sort of loyalty that would assure him or her that the governing body will follow Big Donor's "advice" with regard to when and how the fund should make charitable expenditures? Are there any other sources of law that will increase the likelihood that the governing body will actually be independent? Is the list of factors tending to show that the donor has retained too much control sufficient? By listing certain factors that do not support a finding that the donor has retained too much control, does the Service essentially provide a formula to assist Big Donor in achieving his or her goal?

F. Type I, II, and III Supporting Organizations

CODE: §§ 509(a)(2 & 3), 509(f), 4942, 4943, 4958, 4966(d)(4)

REG.: § 1.509(a)-4

This is where the real bizarreness of the code provisions kick in. Section 4966 mostly deals with donor-advised funds and sponsoring organizations; however, it also defines "supporting organizations" and divides them into three types: I, II, and III. Type III then divides into functionally related Type IIIs and non-functionally related Type IIIs. Section 509(f)(3) also defines "supported organization," which is similar to but distinct from "sponsoring organization." Consequences of these various statuses are less clear. But, first let us define them.

These things are "organizations" as opposed to mere funds or accounts, as in donor-advised funds. That said, one must remember a mere fund can be an entity for purposes of 501(c)(3), so the distinction has limits. Still, the 4966 reference to "organization" differs from the donor-advised fund reference to a fund. But a supporting organization can have funds, including donor-advised funds; hence, the distinction is a tad circular.

Types I and II Supporting Organizations

Section 4966(d)(4) technically defines "*disqualified*" supporting organization." In so doing, it defines the underlying term. Subparagraph (B) defines Types I and II:

(B) Type I and Type II supporting organizations

> An organization is described in this subparagraph if the organization meets the requirements of subparagraphs (A) and (C) of section 509(a)(3) and is —
>
> (i) operated, supervised, or controlled by one or more organizations described in paragraph (1) or (2) of section 509(a), or
>
> (ii) supervised or controlled in connection with one or more such organizations.[12]

Type I supporting organizations thus appear in 509(a)(3)(B)(i), Type IIs appear in § 509(a)(3)(B)(ii), and Type IIIs, as we will see, appear in 509(a)(3)(B)(iii). As explained in the preamble to TD 9605:

> Organizations described in section 509(a)(3) are known as supporting organizations. Supporting organizations achieve their public charity status by providing support to one or more organizations described in section 509(a)(1) or (2), which in this context are referred to as supported organizations.[13]

On the surface, supporting organizations seem to be straightforward paragraph 509(a)(3) entities, with the superficial difference of being described with a capital I, II, or III rather than a small (i), (ii), or (iii). We group them separately because of how they come about. The second and third category of private foundation alternatives described above (to be distinguished from *Type* I and II) have long existed. They arise because the parent entity desired them, created them, and likely controls, supervises, and operates them. Such ordinary, commonplace organizations present few issues. We list this category because into it we place organizations created by, for, or at the behest of donors who may seek continuing control.

In the case of the fifth category of private foundation alternatives—Type I and II supporting organization—donor(s) relinquish sufficient supervision and control over the entity or its operations. If they did not, the entities would be private foundations. They may themselves contain donor-advised funds and may themselves thus be a sponsoring organization. If so, they are subject to the § 4966 and 4967 excise taxes and other donor-advised fund restrictions. Similar to the situation with donor-advised funds, a Type I or II supporting organization must also be aware of several other provisions:

> **4942(g)(4)**— Though the § 4942 excise tax on private foundations does not apply to supporting organizations, it does affect them indirectly by affecting what constitutes a qualified distribution from a private foundation.

12. IRC § 4966(d)(4)(B).
13. T.D. 9605, 77 F.R. 76382–76400.

A distribution from a non-operating private foundation[14] is "disqualified" for purposes of the 4942 excise tax if:

(I) a disqualified person of the private foundation directly or indirectly controls such organization or a supported organization (as defined in section 509(f)(3)) of such organization, or

(II) the Secretary determines by regulations that a distribution to such organization otherwise is inappropriate.[15]

Traditional supporting organizations—the second and third alternatives to private foundations—can likely ignore this, though it applies to them. In those scenarios, close involvement with a disqualified person of a private foundation seems a remote situation. But, when a donor creates or has someone create a supporting organization, private foundation and disqualified person involvement seems plausible.

4943(f)— Though the § 4943 excise tax on the "excess business holdings" applies to some Type II supporting organizations, it does not apply to Type I organizations. Section 4943(f)(4) defines a "substantial contributor" with a combination of the § 4958 definition and the § 4946 definition of that term. As such, it is impressively complicated and extensive. Maintaining that list is a significant requirement for Type II supporting organizations.

4958(c)(3)— For supporting organizations, § 4958(c)(3)(A) greatly broadens the meaning of "excess benefit transaction" to include "any grant, loan, compensation, or other similar payment provided by such organization to a person described in subparagraph (B)" and "any loan provided by such organization to a disqualified person (other than an organization described in subparagraph (C)(ii))."

For this purpose, § 4958 does not use the main 4958 definition of "disqualified person." Instead, it applies to a special class of described persons:

(B) Person described

A person is described in this subparagraph if such person is —

(i) a substantial contributor to such organization,

(ii) a member of the family (determined under section 4958(f)(4)) of an individual described in clause (i), or

(iii) a 35-percent controlled entity (as defined in section 4958(f)(3) by substituting "persons described in clause (i) or (ii) of section 4958(c)(3)(B)" for "persons described in subparagraph (A) or (B) of paragraph (1)" in subparagraph (A)(i) thereof).[16]

---

14. Section 4942(j) defines a private operating foundation. Such foundations are "preferred" foundations in § 170(b)(1)(F) and are subject to different rules in 4942 and 4940.

15. IRC § 4942(g)(4)(a)(ii).

16. IRC § 4958(c)(3)(B).

The section defines a substantial contributor using the same language used by § 507(d), which § 4946 also uses. Of note, this special definition of excess benefit transaction does not apply to traditional (as opposed to Type II) supporting organizations: those which support a social welfare organization, labor union, or business league.

Notice the horrible complexity faced by a supporting organization. As a public charity, it must maintain the complex § 4958 list of disqualified persons. It must also maintain the very different and even more complex list of § 4946 disqualified persons for purposes of subsection 4942(g). The "supported organization" it relates to must also maintain the § 4946 disqualified persons list so that it can apply the § 509(a)(1) and (2) public support tests to avoid being a private foundation. The supported organization must further maintain the § 4958 main list, which may differ from the supporting organization list. The supporting organization must then maintain the list of § 4958(c)(3)(B) described persons, as well as (discussed below) the separate and different § 509(f)(2)(B) list of described persons. If either the supporting or supported organization is a sponsoring organization for a donor-advised fund, it must maintain the multiple lists required of a DAF. That complexity applies if the sponsoring organization is a Type I or II. If a Type III (discussed below), the complexity is greater.

> **509(f)–509(f)(2)(A)—** applies to all supporting organizations—Types I, II, and III. It disqualifies them from public charity status if they receive *any* gift or contribution from a described person. Paragraph (2) is styled as applying to "Organizations controlled by donors"; however, it actually applies to organizations receiving gifts from persons who control a "supported organization."[17] That is, if the entity the supporting organization supports is controlled by a described person who contributes anything to the supporting organization. The list of described persons is:
>
> (B) Person described
>
> A person is described in this subparagraph if, with respect to a supported organization of an organization described in subparagraph (A), such person is—
>
> (i) a person (other than an organization described in paragraph (1), (2), or (4) of section 509(a)) who directly or indirectly controls, either alone or together with persons described in clauses (ii) and (iii), the governing body of such supported organization,

17. IRC § 509(a)(3) defines a supported organization as a 509(a)(1) or (2) public charity:

> (A) for whose benefit the organization described in subsection (a)(3) is organized and operated, or
>
> (B) with respect to which the organization performs the functions of, or carries out the purposes of.

A supported organization differs from, though it is similar to, a sponsoring organization.

(ii) a member of the family (determined under section 4958(f)(4)) of an individual described in clause (i), or

(iii) a 35-percent controlled entity (as defined in section 4958(f)(3) by substituting "persons described in clause (i) or (ii) of section 509(f)(2)(B)" for "persons described in subparagraph (A) or (B) of paragraph (1)" in subparagraph (A)(i) thereof).[18]

Type III Supporting Organizations

At this point, the terminology is long-past confusing, but bear with us. Type III supporting organizations are ones operated in connection with a § 509(a)(1) or (2) public charity, as described in 509(a)(3)(B)(iii) and 4943(f)(5)(A):

> (A) Type III supporting organization
>
> The term "type III supporting organization" means an organization which meets the requirements of subparagraphs (A) and (C) of section 509(a)(3) and which is operated in connection with one or more organizations described in paragraph (1) or (2) of section 509(a).

Remember, Type I organizations are operated, supervised, or controlled *by* a public charity. The Treasury describes these as existing in a parent/subsidiary type relationship. Type II are supervised or controlled *in connection with* a public charity. The Treasury describes these as existing in a brother/sister type relationship with a common parent. Type III are *operated in connection with* a public charity. Thus, the Type III is neither operated *by* nor supervised or controlled in connection with a public charity: it is merely operated in connection with one.

Type III operating organizations fit into two main categories:

- Functionally integrated Type III supporting organizations
- Non-functionally integrated (NFI) Type III supporting organizations.

Section 4943 defines a "functionally integrated" Type III:

> (B) Functionally integrated type III supporting organization
>
> The term "functionally integrated type III supporting organization" means a type III supporting organization which is not required under regulations established by the Secretary to make payments to supported organizations (as defined under section 509(f)(3)) due to the activities of the organization related to performing the functions of, or carrying out the purposes of, such supported organizations.[19]

Standing alone, that definition is not helpful because it says so little and defers so much to the Treasury. It defines a FI Type III as one which is not required to make

18. IRC § 509(f)(2)(B).
19. IRC § 4943(f)(5)(B).

payments to supported organizations because it has activities "related to" the functions or purposes of the supported organizations. It does not, however, define such payments, let alone how an entity might have activities related to functions or purposes of another entity. Further, it does not say what happens if a Type III is not so "functionally related."

Treasury Regulations[20] from 2012, however, fill the gaps left by the incomplete Code definitions. A full explanation would take more space than we feel would be helpful. We can say three things:

- A Type III which meets the functionally integrated test is a public charity.
- A NFI Type III—a Type III which fails the functionally integrated test but which meets the payment test—is also a public charity.
- Other supporting organizations which fail the Type I and Type II requirements as well as 509(a)(1), (2), or (4) tests are private foundations.

Prior to 2006, a Type III supporting organization had to meet both a "responsiveness test" and an "integral part test." The responsiveness test had an alternative test based on state-law enforcement of support. The integral part test had two alternative tests: a "but for" test and a pay-out test. The main part of the responsiveness test continues. The integral part test is mostly supplanted by the "functionally integrated" rules and the NFI (non-functionally integrated) rules.

To be clear, while being a "functionally integrated" Type III supporting organization is preferable to not being one, being a NFI Type III supporting organization is not necessarily bad. A NFI is also a public charity, albeit subject to different rules. As bizarre as it may sound, the bad situation is being neither functionally integrated nor non-functionally integrated. Those "Type III" supporting organizations are private foundations.

As explained in TD 9605, the 2006 legislation made five important changes to Type III organizations:

(1) It removed the ability to rely solely on the alternative test for charitable trusts as a means of meeting the responsiveness test;

(2) To ensure that a "significant amount" is paid to supported organizations, it directed the Secretary of the Treasury to establish a new payout requirement for Type III supporting organizations that are not "functionally integrated" (with the term "functionally integrated" referring to Type III supporting organizations that are not required to meet a payout requirement due to their activities related to performing the functions of, or carrying out the purposes of, their supported organization(s));

20. Treas. Reg. § 1.509(a)-4.

(3) It required a Type III supporting organization to annually provide to each of its supported organizations such information as the Secretary may require to ensure that the supporting organization is responsive to the needs or demands of its supported organization(s);

(4) It prohibited a Type III supporting organization from supporting any supported organization not organized in the United States; and

(5) It prohibited a Type I or Type III supporting organization from accepting a gift or contribution from a person who, alone or together with certain related persons, directly or indirectly controls the governing body of a supported organization of the Type I or Type III supporting organization.[21]

Thus, Type III supporting organizations fit into the two categories, both of which are public charities, but which are subject to differing collateral consequences.

Functionally Integrated Type III— As explained in T.D. 9605:

> a Type III supporting organization is functionally integrated, and thus not subject to a distribution requirement, if it either: (1) engages in activities substantially all of which directly further the exempt purposes of the supported organization(s) to which it is responsive by performing the functions of, or carrying out the purposes of, such supported organization(s) and which, but for the involvement of the supporting organization, would normally be engaged in by the supported organization(s); or (2) is the parent of each of its supported organizations.[22]

Treasury Regulation § 1.509(a)-4(i)(4) provides additional explanation and examples.

Recall § 4946 imposes an excise tax on "taxable distributions" from donor-advised funds. Distributions to functionally integrated Type III supporting organizations are not "taxable distributions."[23] As explained above, the § 4943 excess business holdings tax applies to donor-advised funds. It also applies generally to Type III supporting organizations; however, it does not apply to functionally integrated Type IIIs.[24] As explained above, subsection 4942(g) indirectly affects Types I and II supporting organizations by disqualifying (for purposes of the excise tax) distributions to them from a private foundation. Although this also indirectly affects Type III supporting organizations, it does not affect functionally integrated Type IIIs.[25]

21. T.D. 9605, 77 F.R. 76382–76400.
22. *Id.*
23. IRC § 4966(c)(2)(A).
24. IRC § 4943(f)(3)(A).
25. IRC § 4942(g)(4)(A)(i).

Non-Functionally Integrated Type III— A non-functionally integrated Type III supporting organization must meet two requirements:[26] the distribution test and the attentiveness test. If it does, it is a public charity, albeit subject to more restrictions than a functionally integrated Type III.

Authority for the distribution test appears in subparagraph 509(f)(5)(B), which grants the Treasury Secretary authority to create it. Treasury regulations adopted in 2012 and amended in 2015 created the test. Generally, the Type III must annually distribute its "distributable amount" to one or more supported organizations.[27] The distributable amount is the greater of:

- 85% of its "adjusted net income"[28] for the prior year, or
- Its minimum asset amount.[29]

The "minimum asset amount" is 3.5%[30] of the aggregate fair market value of the organization's non-exempt use[31] assets (reduced by acquisition indebtedness[32] with respect to such assets).

The attentiveness test has four requirements, including its own distribution tests. Generally, the Type III must annually distribute at least one-third of its distributable amount to attentive supported organizations.[33] The other three requirements define how a supported organization can be attentive:

- The supported organization must have received at least 10% of its total support for the prior year from the supporting Type III.[34]
- The support received from the Type III must be "necessary to avoid the interruption of the carrying on of a particular function or activity of the supported organization."[35]
- Based on a variety of factors, the support received must be sufficient to ensure attentiveness.[36]

NFIs are subject to the § 4942, and 4943 consequences generally applicable to Type I and II organizations but which are inapplicable to functionally integrated Type IIIs. Distributions from them are also subject to the § 4966 excise tax.

---

26. Treas. Reg. § 1.509(a)-4(i)(5)(i)(A).
27. Treas. Reg. § 1.509(a)-4(i)(5)(ii)(A).
28. Treas. Reg. § 1.509(a)-4(i)(5)(ii)(B). The adjusted net income is "determined by applying the principles of § 4942(f) and § 53.4942(a)-2(d)." *Id.*
29. Treas. Reg. § 1.509(a)-4(i)(5)(ii)(C).
30. *Id.* The percentage was the subject of significant debate. It began as 5% in 2006.
31. Defined in Treas. Reg. § 1.509(a)-4(i)(8).
32. Per § 514(c)(1).
33. Treas. Reg. § 1.509(a)-4(i)(5)(iii)(A).
34. Treas. Reg. § 1.509(a)-4(i)(5)(iii)(B)(i).
35. Treas. Reg. § 1.509(a)-4(i)(5)(iii)(B)(ii).
36. Treas. Reg. §1.509(a)-4(i)(5)(iii)(B)(iii).

G. Community Trusts and Foundations

CODE: §§ 170(b)(1)(A); 509(a)(3); 4942(g)(4); 4943(f); 4958(c)(3); 6033(l)

REG.: § 1.170A-9(f)(10)–(12)

Community Foundation is an oft-used term. It is not really a separate alternative to what we describe above. It is arguably an antiquated term; however, practitioners, courts, and regulators use the phrase, so we must address it. A community trust or foundation, as the phrase is commonly used, is a public charity. It may be a common charity which accepts donations and has little continuing interaction with donors other than fundraising. Or it may be a sponsoring organization with multiple DAFs. Or it may be a supported organization with multiple Type I, II, or III supporting organizations. Or it may be a combination of all three. It is not, however, a separate alternative to private foundation status.

Thus, the most popular alternatives to private foundation status utilize a community trust in one way or another. A community trust is an entity—or more accurately, a group of entities—governed and operated in a manner that alleviates the concerns underlying the private foundation regulatory scheme. The trust must meet the § 170 public support test (either the 33⅓ percent test or the 10% facts and circumstances test) on an aggregate basis and must subject its several separately created component organizations to a common governing body and governing document. Thus, an organization that would otherwise be a private foundation (because it has only one donor) can achieve public charity status and its primary donor can continue to exercise significant control over its operations, provided that control is consistent with the requirements of the governing body and document. The governing body's requirements must be consistent with provisions in the regulations that seek to divest Big Donor of ultimate control.[37] In essence, Big Donor may exercise advisory authority over his or her fund, but that authority must be subject to a higher independent body's authority. By complying with the "component part" requirements of Treas. Reg. § 1.170A-9(f)(11)(ii), the organization will be treated as part of the community trust (i.e., as part of a public charity). If the organization were viewed in isolation, it would most likely be a private foundation. *See* Treas. Reg. § 1.170A-9(f)(12).

The following excerpts describe in greater detail the community trust and the use of a supporting organization in conjunction with a community trust. Note: the publication date is prior to the 2006 legislation and the 2012 regulations.

---

37. For example, a donor-directed fund would violate the requirement that a transfer not be subject to a material restriction as defined in Treas. Reg. § 1.507-2(a)(7). As a result, the fund could not be part of a community trust. Treas. Reg. § 1.170A-9(f)(12).

Christopher R. Hoyt, Pooled Income Funds of Community Foundations; IRS Swiftly Revokes Its Revenue Ruling

58 Tax Notes 1499 (1993)[38]

. . .

III. Structure and Operation of Community Foundations

A. Basic Structure

A community foundation is a § 501(c)(3) grant-making organization that is classified by the IRS as a public charity because it has passed the public support test.[39] It is basically structured as an amalgamation of funds, with each fund bearing the name of the donor (e.g., the "Richard and Jane Smith Fund") or the fund's charitable purpose (e.g., the "Symphony Endowment Fund"). Grants are made from each fund to carry out the charitable purposes specified by the founder of the fund at the time the fund was established. If no purpose was specified, grants are made for charitable purposes determined by the community foundation's governing body. Although most grants are usually made within the community foundation's geographic area, grants to national charities (particularly universities) are very common.

B. Categories of Funds

Community foundations usually divide their funds into four categories. The classification of any particular fund depends on the type of restrictions a donor imposed on the fund at the time that the fund was established. The four types of funds are:

1. "unrestricted fund," where the community foundation has complete discretion as to the charitable grants made from the fund,
2. "designated fund," from which amounts are distributed to a specific public charity,[40]
3. "field-of-interest fund," from which amounts are distributed for a specific charitable purpose described in § 170(c)(2) (such as health or education), and
4. "advised fund," where a designated person or committee can advise the community foundation on charitable dispositions.

---

38. Reprinted with permission of Tax Analysts.

39. [22] The public support test is used to determine whether a charity is a public charity or a private foundation. If it is a private foundation, the negative consequences described *infra* at n. 27, 28, and 29 would occur. Technically, a community foundation is classified as a publicly supported charity under section 509(a)(1) because it passed the public support test under section 170(b)(1)(A)(vi) and Treas. Reg. section 1.170A-9(e)(6), as modified by Treas. Reg. section 1.170A-9(e)(10).

40. [23] At the time that a fund is established, a donor can require a community foundation to make grants from that fund to any charity described in section 509(a)(1), 509(a)(2) or 509(a)(3). *See* Treas. Reg. section 1.170A-9(f)(11)(ii)(B) in conjunction with 1.507-2(a)(8)(iii)(B). Often these funds serve as endowment funds for the specified charities.

C. Multiple Trusts

Most of the newer community foundations are structured as corporations, so that each fund is essentially an accounting entry on the corporation's books (a "directly held fund"). However, the older (and usually wealthier) community foundations, such as the New York Community Trust and the Cleveland Foundation, are structured in the form of multiple trusts: each fund is usually held in a separate trust or corporation (a "component fund").

The regulations contain a special exception for community foundations that permits a trust or corporation to be treated as a component part of a community foundation for federal tax purposes, even though it will be treated as a separate trust or corporation under state law.[41] The effect of the regulations is to permit multiple charitable trusts and corporations to file a consolidated tax return. Because many community foundations were structured in the form of multiple trusts and most of these organizations were, as a whole, subject to public scrutiny since they continuously raised contributions from the general public,[42] the Treasury Department exempted these trusts from the private foundation taxes if certain conditions were met.

Normally a charitable grant-making trust or corporation is treated as a private foundation because it has only one donor (e.g., Jane Smith) or because its receipts consist solely of investment income (e.g., an endowment fund).[43] Charitable contributions to a private foundation are subject to reduced tax benefits, and the private foundation is subject to a series of excise taxes and administrative requirements.

However, if a trust or corporation is treated as a component part of a community foundation, then contributions to the trust or corporation qualify for the same advantageous tax benefits as a contribution directly to a public charity. In addition, the trust or corporation will not have to file any tax return or pay any private foundation excise taxes; instead, its financial transactions will be included on the Form 990 of the community foundation.[44]

---

41. [24] Treas. Reg. section 1.170A-9(f)(11)(ii).

42. [25] Treas. Reg. section 1.170A-9(f)(10). The rationale for treating public charities that regularly sought charitable contributions from the public differently from private foundations was succinctly explained by the Seventh Circuit Court of Appeals as follows: "The statutory definition of 'private foundation' reflects an underlying congressional philosophy which turns upon a very crucial distinction between organizations that are privately financed and those that depend upon the public for their support. In the latter case, the organization is subject to the discipline of public opinion. If it misbehaves, misuses its capital, or engages in questionable practices, the public will presumably learn about it, and by the simple expedient of cutting off contributions, correct that which has become offensive. "On the other hand, the institution that is privately financed is subject to no such corrective influence and therefore must be regulated in some other way." Quarrie Charitable Fund v. Commissioner, 603 F.2d 1274 (7th Cir. 1979), footnote 3.

43. [26] This is because it would fail the public support test.

44. [30] Private Letter Ruling 8621112 (Feb. 28, 1986). See also the last sentence of Treas. Reg. section 1.170A-9(e)(14)(i) that states that financial information of component funds is to be included on the community foundation's Form 990.

D. Requirements for Component Funds

For a trust or corporation to be a component part of a community foundation (a "component fund"), four conditions must be met:

1. the organizational documents of the community foundation must meet the "single-entity" requirements;[45]
2. the trust or corporation must subject itself to the common governing instrument of the community foundation;[46]
3. the community foundation must accept the contribution (this is a standard requirement for all charitable gifts); and
4. the fund may not be directly or indirectly subjected by the donor to any material restriction or condition (as that term is defined in the Treasury regulations) with respect to the transferred assets.[47] If a material restriction is imposed, then the trust or corporation will generally be treated as a private foundation[48] (with special rules for some trusts).[49] The regulations specifically recognize that each of the four categories of community foundation funds (unrestricted, designated, field-of-interest, and advised) can be administered in separate trusts or corporations.[50]

---

45. [31] Treas. Reg. section 1.170A-9(f)(11)(ii). These requirements are usually satisfied by provisions in the community foundation's organizational documents (e.g., articles of incorporation for incorporated community foundations or the governing trust instrument for those organized as trusts). Virtually every community foundation in the nation has organizational documents that comply with the single-entity requirements, even if it is structured as a single corporation with no component trusts or corporations (i.e., all funds are directly held funds).

46. [32] Treas. Reg. section 1.170A-9(f). Although this is not technically required by Treas. Reg. section 1.170A-9(e)(11)(ii), it is a practical necessity that the fund's instrument of transfer, trust instrument, or articles of incorporation subject it to the control of the community foundation by reference to the common instrument. The IRS suggested on the last page of GCM 38812 (Aug. 31, 1981) that the common instrument provisions should be considered a requirement for component fund status.

47. [33] Treas. Reg. section 1.170A-9(f)(11)(ii)(B). A material restriction is a restriction or condition that prevents a community foundation from "freely and effectively employing the transferred assets, or the income derived therefrom, in furtherance of its exempt purposes." Treas. Reg. section 1.507-2(a)(8). The definition is from the regulations that govern private foundation terminations. It is designed to determine whether a private foundation has transferred "all of its right, title, and interest in and to all of its net assets" to a public charity. Treas. Reg. section 1.507-2(a)(7).

48. [34] Treas. Reg. sections 1.170A-9(f)(14)(i) and 1.170A-9(f)(11)(ii).

49. [35] Some trusts might be subject to the rules of *section 4947. Section 4947* imposes on certain charitable trusts the same income and excise taxes that are imposed on private foundations, even though they do not meet all of the technical requirements to be a private foundation. It also addresses the tax treatment of some split-interest trusts (trusts that benefit both a charitable organization and a noncharitable purpose, such as charitable remainder trusts and pooled income funds).

50. [36] *See* Treas. Reg. section 1.170A-9(f)(11)(ii)(B) in conjunction with:
   1. Treas. Reg. section 1.507-2(a)(7)(iii)(A)—Unrestricted named funds.
   2. Treas. Reg. section 1.507-2(a)(7)(iii)(B)—Designated funds.
   3. Treas. Reg. section 1.507-2(a)(7)(iii)(B)—Field of Interest funds.
   4. Treas. Reg. section 1.507-2(a)(7)(iv)(A)(2)—Advised funds.

E. Gifts Are "to" a Community Foundation

The single-entity regulations provide that a gift to a separate trust or corporation will be treated as a gift "to" a community foundation if the trust or corporation qualifies as a component fund.[51]

Perhaps this result can best be illustrated by the following example:

> Liz Lofty established an endowment fund by contributing money to a charitable trust. She named The Bank as trustee. The Bank is instructed to distribute all of the trust's income each year to The Art Museum. The trust instrument provides that the trust will be governed by the articles of incorporation of The Community Foundation, and The Community Foundation has accepted the gift.
>
> The Community Foundation's principal responsibilities are the minimum required by the single-entity regulations:
>
> (1) to monitor disbursements from the trust and to see that the trustee complies with the terms of the trust instrument;
>
> (2) to exercise the "variance power" when appropriate:

The regulations define the variance power as the community foundation's power "To modify any restriction or condition on the distribution of funds for any specified charitable purpose or to any specified organization if in the sole judgment of the governing body such restriction or condition becomes, in effect, unnecessary, incapable of fulfillment, or inconsistent with the charitable needs of the community or area served."[52]

The variance power would be exercised if, for example, The Art Museum goes out of existence; and

> (3) to replace the trustee if there has been either (a) a breach of fiduciary duty or (b) an inadequate return on the investments.[53]

Even though a gift in trust for a charity is normally considered as having been made "for the use of" a charity rather than "to" a charity, the single-entity regulations make it clear that a contribution to a component fund (including a designated fund)[54] is treated as having been made "to" a community foundation.[55] Thus, under the facts in this example, establishing a fund to benefit The Art Museum is treated as a contribution "to" The Community Foundation rather than "for the use of" a charity. Consequently, the contribution and the trust's investment income enter into

51. [37] Treas. Reg. section 1.170A-9(f)(11)(ii) (the second-to-last sentence; the word "to" even appears in quotation marks in the regulation).

52. [38] Treas. Reg. section 1.170A-9(f)(11)(v)(B)(1).

53. [39] Treas. Reg. section 1.170A-9(f)(11)(v)(B)(2) and (3).

54. [41] Treas. Reg. section 1.170A-9(f)(11)(ii)(B) in conjunction with 1.507-2(a)(8)(iii)(B). *See* also the example contained in Treas. Reg. section 1.507-2(a)(8)(v), Example (3).

55. [42] Treas. Reg. section 1.170A-9(f)(11)(ii) (the second-to-last sentence).

the computation of The Community Foundation's public support test and the assets (even though they are held in a separate trust) are treated as a component part of The Community Foundation.[56]

Comment and Question

Agency theory holds that there is an efficiency loss in any agency relationship. Thus, the most efficient use of capital occurs to the extent that the owner of capital actually directs the uses to which the capital is put. To the extent an owner must rely on agents (e.g., employees or independent contractors), efficiency decreases. Agency costs are the costs a principal ought to incur to decrease efficiency losses inherent in the agency relationship. Thus, a principal might expend resources creating and enforcing an employee disciplinary code that punishes efficiency losses created by the divergence in interests between owner and employee (e.g., the owner seeks the most profit possible, employee seeks a peaceful workplace and therefore might not work as hard as the owner might, or as hard as he should). Agency costs are routinely incurred because they are viewed as cheaper than unintended agency losses. For example, it is cheaper to regulate employee conduct than it is to pay the higher costs of unchecked employee misconduct. If agency theory is correct, how much efficiency is lost by a private foundation regulatory scheme that essentially presumes that owners of charitable capital should be precluded from the exercise of control over the uses of that capital? Might there be a more efficient method of ensuring that Big Donor who controls or engages in transactions with the charity he or she endows will not use the charity for private gain?

---

56. [43] *See* Treas. Reg. section 1.170A-9(f)(11)(ii) (the second-to-last sentence) and GCM 38812 (Aug. 31, 1981).

PART FOUR

Non-Charitable Exempt Organizations

Chapter 20

Social Welfare Organizations

A. General Requirements for Social Welfare Organizations

CODE: § 501(c)(4), REVIEW § 4958

REGS.: §§ 1.501(c)(3)-1(c)(3); 1.501(c)(4)-1

Upon first reading the provision granting tax exemption to social welfare organizations, one might be compelled to ask, "what is the difference between a (c)(3) and a (c)(4)?" The most honest answer is that a (c)(4) is essentially a disfavored sibling of the (c)(3) without the ability to confer a charitable contribution deduction. The (c)(4) strives for the common good, just as a (c)(3), but fails in one respect or another to achieve all of the requirements attendant to (c)(3) status. One example that we have already seen in Chapter 6 involves health maintenance organizations (HMOs) that request (c)(3) status but are instead granted (c)(4) status. Section 501(c)(3) status is most often denied based upon a finding of private benefit. That (c)(4) is much less advantageous is proven by the fact that HMOs frequently litigate the denial of (c)(3) status after having been granted (c)(4) status.

The modern (c)(4) is most likely significantly involved in legislative or campaign activities, either directly or via a related § 527 organization. A 501(c)(4) organization can have substantial lobbying activities, but only insubstantial campaign intervention. Treas. Reg. § 1.501(c)(4)-1(a)(2)(ii). Moreover, a 501(c)(3) may establish a 501(c)(4) which, in turn, may establish a 527 organization. The 527 organization can then engage in campaign interventions to a degree not permitted to the (c)(4) — thus, through the 527 organization, the 501(c)(4) can engage in substantial campaign activities.

It makes little sense to try to categorize the innumerable activities that promote the "social welfare." "Social welfare" is as amenable to definition as "charity." Instead, it helps to simply list a sample of the types of organizations granted (c)(4) status. The following excerpt from an IRS training text is helpful in gaining a basic understanding of organizations that qualify for exemption under § 501(c)(4).

Note on IRS Exempt Organization CPE Program Textbook

Although entirely without binding authority, the Service's Exempt Organizations Continuing Professional Education Program Textbook (CPE text) is essentially "required reading" for exempt organization practitioners. And why not? Issued annually from 1979 to 2004, the articles are written by attorneys and other officials with daily responsibility to regulate and monitor the exempt organization community. Thus, the CPE text contains valuable insights on the internal thinking and ruminations of Service officials who occupy the front lines of enforcement. In many instances an article in a CPE text will persuade an examining agent that a client's position is correct. CPE texts are invaluable time savers because each article essentially constitutes a comprehensive legal memorandum on a particular subject—complete with citations and sometimes insights on the Service's litigation strategy in past cases. Readers may notice that the excerpt below from the 1981 CPE text does not contain a byline and thus we cannot know which Service official wrote the article nor does the Service official get the recognition he or she deserves.

Social Welfare: What Does It Mean? How Much Private Benefit Is Permissible? What Is a Community?

Internal Revenue Service, Exempt Organizations Continuing Professional Education Technical Instruction Program Textbook, Chapter G (1981)

1. Introduction

IRC 501(c)(4) provides, in part, for the exemption from federal income taxation of civic leagues or organizations not organized for profit but operated exclusively for the promotion of social welfare.

* * *

[501(c)(4) social welfare organizations and civic leagues] were first exempted from federal income tax by the Revenue Act of 1913. The Committee Reports are deficient in offering any reasoning behind the inclusion of this particular exemption.

There is no official Congressional or Service pronouncement construing the terms "civic league" or "social welfare" as embodied in section 501(c)(4). However, in *United States v. Pickwick Electric Membership Corp.*, 158 F.2d 272 (6 Cir. 1946), the Court stated that a civic organization is described as embodying "the ideas of citizens of a community cooperating to promote the common good and general welfare of the community." In *C.I.R. v. Lake Forest, Inc.*, 305 F.2d 814 (4 Cir. 1962), the court described a civic organization as being "a movement of citizenry or the community," whereas the court in *Erie Endowment v. United States*, 316 F.2d 151 (1963), while acknowledging the difficult task in arriving at a specific definition of "civic organization," stated that "the organization must be a community movement designed to accomplish community ends."

* * *

Organizations exempt under section 501(c)(4) are generally described in one of the following categories:

1. Nonprofit organizations that traditionally have been labeled in common parlance as social welfare organizations;

2. Organizations that may be performing some type of public or community benefit but whose principal feature is lack of any private benefit or profit;

3. Organizations that would qualify for exemption under section 501(c)(3) but for a defect in their organizational instruments or if they were not "action organizations."

Therefore, although social welfare generally denotes benefits to the community, beyond that there is disagreement as to a working definition of the term. In practice, section 501(c)(4) has been used by both the courts and the Service as a haven for organizations that lack the accepted essential characteristics of a taxable entity, but elude classification under other subparagraphs of 501(c).

2. Overlapping Relationship Between Section 501(c)(4) and Other Tax Exempt Sections of the Code

Because statutory history is lacking, with respect to the origins of section 501(c)(4), and statutory language is scant and couched in seemingly subjective terminology, the regulations' drafters and the courts have lacked clear guidance in this area. The predictable result has been a lack of uniformity in judicial decisions that contributes to more confusion and still more lack of uniformity. As a result, judicial inconsistency becomes both the cause for and effect of confusion under IRC 501(c)(4).

The concepts of social welfare and community benefits are present, to some extent, in virtually all other subparagraphs of section 501(c), perhaps most notably in (c)(3), (c)(5), (c)(6), (c)(7), (c)(8), (c)(9), (c)(12), (c)(17), and (c)(21). Consequently, the opportunities for confusion under section 501(c)(4) are compounded by the apparent overlap among these provisions. This overlap is less evident or important where the language of the subparagraph is precise, as is the case with 501(c)(17), or where there are few benefits to be gained by preferring one exempting provision over another. For these reasons it is the 501(c)(3)/(c)(4) overlap that is the greatest source of difficulty for the Service. This conflict and a few of the other overlapping subparagraphs of 501(c) are discussed below.

a. Section 501(c)(3)

The concepts of "social welfare" under section 501(c)(4) and "charity" under section 501(c)(3) are not mutually exclusive. Section 1.501(c)(4)-1(a)(2) of the regulations states that a social welfare organization that meets the definition of "charitable" in section 1.501(c)(3)-1(a)(2) and is not an "action" organization can qualify for exemption under section 501(c)(3). Conversely, section 1.501(c)(3)-1(c)(3)(v) of the regulations states that an "action" organization may qualify for exemption under section 501(c)(4) where it otherwise qualifies under section 501(c)(3). As a general rule, all organizations exempt under section 501(c)(3) could also qualify under section 501(c)(4), though the reverse is not true. *See* Rev. Rul. 80-108, 1980-16 IRB 8.

* * *

One of the major distinctions between section 501(c)(3) and 501(c)(4) organizations is the amount of activity that may be devoted to nonexempt purposes. The regulations under IRC 501(c)(3) provide that an organization will be regarded as operated "exclusively" for one or more exempt purposes only if it engages "primarily" in activities which accomplish one or more of the exempt purposes specified in section 501(c)(3). Section 1.501(c)(3)-1(c)(1).

* * *

For example, the regulations under section 501(c)(3) contain a prohibition against substantially engaging in legislative activities. No similar type of provision is contained in section 501(c)(4), and a 501(c)(4) organization may engage in germane legislative activities as its sole activity. See Rev. Rul. 67-293, 1967-2 C.B. 185. Neither does the statute expressly prohibit participation in political campaigns on behalf of a candidate, as does section 501(c)(3). Section 1.501(c)(4)-1(a)(2)(ii). However, the regulations under section 501(c)(4) do state that:

> "An organization is operated exclusively for the promotion of social welfare if it is primarily engaged in promoting in some way the common good and general welfare of the community . . . The promotion of social welfare does not include direct or indirect participation or intervention in political campaigns on behalf of or in opposition to any candidate for public office. Nor is an organization operated primarily for the promotion of social welfare if its primary activity is operating a social club . . . or is carrying on a business with the general public in a manner similar to organizations which are operated for profit." Section 1.501(c)(4)-1(a)(ii) of the regulations.

It can therefore be argued that the "primary" test, as employed in section 501(c)(4), may permit an organization lawfully to participate or intervene in political campaigns on behalf of or in opposition to campaigns for public office so long as its primary activities remain the promotion of social welfare. *See* Rev. Rul. 67-293, 1967-2 C.B. 185.

An organization exempt under section 501(c)(4) may often be presumed to have compromised. That is, such an organization may have settled for the somewhat less favorable status of 501(c)(4) as opposed to 501(c)(3) (lack of deductible contributions and reduced postage rates) in return for the somewhat greater freedom of action that 501(c)(4) status affords.

Despite some amount of overlapping between sections 501(c)(3) and (c)(4), there are substantial distinctions between the two subsections. Section 501(c)(4) contains no provision requiring that organizations meet the organizational tests similar to the ones contained in section 501(c)(3) for proper purposes or dissolution clauses.

* * *

The most important tax difference between classification as a section 501(c)(4) and a section 501(c)(3) organization is that contributions to section 501(c)

(4) organizations are not deductible under 170(c). An exception is that they are deductible when the contributions are deemed to be for the use of a political subdivision for exclusively public purposes. See section 170(c)(1) and Rev. Rul. 71-47, 1971-1 C.B. 92.

The principal advantage to classification as a social welfare organization, where the issue of deductibility of charitable contributions, lower postal rates, and liability for FICA or FUTA taxes are not at issue, is that such organizations are not held to the strict standards required of charitable organizations under section 501(c)(3). For example, a lobbying organization may not wish to be held to 501(c)(3) restrictions, even with the liberalized provisions under 501(h) and 4911. Before 1970, exemption under section 501(c)(4) presented an additional attraction: the unrelated business income tax rules did not apply.

B. The Community Benefit Requirement

If an organization's charter documents are written broadly enough, it can easily meet the qualification that it is operating for the "good of the community" or for the "public good." But in some instances, an organization's goals are explicitly directed toward a defined segment of the community. In some instances, conferring a benefit on a defined group may be necessary to confer the benefit on the "public." In still others, the benefit to the "public" may be insignificant to the point that it may reasonably be concluded that the organization is only interested in its own members' well-being. The following cases take up the distinction between community benefit and private benefit. Note how the doctrine is similar, if not identical, with regard to both (c)(3) and (c)(4) qualification.

Flat Top Lake Association, Inc. v. United States

868 F.2d 108 (4th Cir. 1989)

Widener, Hall, and Chapman, Circuit Judges. Widener, Circuit Judge, dissenting.

Hall, Circuit Judge: Flat Top Lake Association ("Flat Top" or "the Association") appeals an order of the district court granting summary judgment in favor of the United States in a civil action seeking a refund of income taxes. The district court concluded that Flat Top was not entitled to exemption from taxation as a social welfare organization pursuant to Section 501(c)(4) of the Internal Revenue Code, 26 U.S.C. § 501(c)(4). Finding no error in that determination, we affirm.

I.

Flat Top was organized in 1950 as a nonprofit corporation under state law by certain individuals, who wished to develop an artificial lake in the area near Beckley, West Virginia. The purpose of the Association as provided in the articles of incorporation was:

> To own, control, lease and sell real estate; to build, maintain and operate a lake and other recreational facilities for the pleasure and convenience of its members without profit upon a cooperative basis, and to do all other things necessary or incidental to the operation of a recreational and conservation project.

In furtherance of its stated goal, the Association acquired approximately 2,200 acres of land whereon it constructed a 230 acre artificial lake. The land surrounding the lake front was subdivided into lots and sold at $1,000 a lot. Access to the property was provided by a two-lane road also constructed by the Association. The road is not a public highway and bears a sign at the entrance to the development stating "Flat Top Lake Association, Private Property, Members Only."

The articles of incorporation and the Association bylaws provide that entry into the development property, and use of the lake or any other Association facilities is restricted to members and their guests. Membership is limited to persons over 21 years of age who own in their own names one or more lots in the development. Members must also pay annual dues and special assessments as levied by the Association's board of directors with the approval of the majority of the members.

At present there are 375 lots in the Flat Top Lake development owned by members. There are permanent structures on 240 of the lots and 80 families reside at Flat Top on a year-round basis. The remaining members use their lots as recreational facilities.

There are no schools, churches or commercial establishments within the bounds of Flat Top lake property, nor is commercial development permitted by the Association bylaws. Although Flat Top has the requisite number of residents to incorporate as a class four municipality under West Virginia law, it has chosen to continue to operate under statutes applicable to private corporations. The Association has, however, undertaken certain tasks of a quasi-governmental nature. It has constructed a bridge within the development, maintains certain common areas including the road, a park, and the lake itself, and provides waste disposal for residents. Finally, the Association has arranged for some law enforcement by obtaining the appointment of a conservator of the peace pursuant to West Virginia Code § 6-3-1. The conservator is paid by the Raleigh County Sheriff's Department which is in turn reimbursed by the Association.

From 1952 until 1979, the Association enjoyed exemption from federal taxation as a social welfare organization.[1] In 1979, however, the Regional Director of the Internal Revenue Service ("IRS") concluded that the Association could not qualify for exempt status because it did not benefit a "community" bearing a "recognizable relationship to a governmental unit." Reasoning that the Association existed only

1. [1] Exemption was originally granted pursuant to Section 101(8) of the Internal Revenue Code which corresponds to the present provision found at 26 U.S.C. § 501(c)(4).

for the private benefit of its members, the Director revoked the social welfare organization exemption retroactively to 1975.

The Association sought administrative review of the Director's adverse decision but the revocation of exempt status was affirmed by the Commissioner of the IRS on June 18, 1981. Thereafter, Flat Top, as required, filed returns and paid taxes for the years 1975-81.[2] Amended returns were subsequently filed again asserting exempt status and seeking a refund. After the refunds were denied, the Association filed the instant civil action seeking a judicial determination that it is and has been a tax exempt organization.

By memorandum opinion filed on October 14, 1986, the district court granted summary judgment in favor of the United States. The district judge noted that she was aware of no authority that authorized tax exemption for "a private association of home owners which restricts use of its facilities to the exclusive use of its members."

This appeal followed.

II.

At issue is the proper interpretation and application of section 501(c)(4) of the Internal Revenue Code, 26 U.S.C. § 501(c)(4) which provides a tax exemption for:

> Civic leagues or organizations not organized for profit, but operated exclusively for the promotion of social welfare, or local associations of employees, the membership of which is limited to employees of a designated person or persons in a particular municipality and the net earnings of which are devoted exclusively to charitable or recreational purposes.

The chief analytical difficulty lies in the need to formulate a workable definition of "social welfare." The IRS has attempted to advance the analysis by promulgating a regulation at 20 C.F.R. § 1.50(c)(4)-1 which defines a social welfare organization as one "primarily engaged in promoting in some way, the common good and general welfare of the *community*." (emphasis added) Unfortunately, the regulation itself is of limited value since it merely substitutes one amorphous term (i.e. "community") for another ("social welfare").

On appeal, the Association contends that the district court failed to recognize that in reality Flat Top Lake is a separate, distinct, definable "community" and urges our consideration of *Vecellio v. United States*, 196 F. Supp. 1 (D.W.Va.1961), in which the district court repeatedly described Flat Top Lake in those terms. Citing, *inter alia, Rancho Santa Fe Association v. United States*, 589 F. Supp. 54 (S.D. Cal.1984), and *Lake Petersburg Association v. United States*, 35 T.C.M. (P-H) 74,055 (1974), appellant argues that an organization that directs its efforts to the betterment of

2. [2] According to materials provided by the Association in connection with this appeal, it has paid the following amounts since the revocation of its exemption: 1975 $974.00, 1976 $994.00, 1977 $42.00, 1978 $51.00, 1979 $6.00, 1980 $1,232.40, 1981 $1,426.00, 1982 $2,837.00, 1983 $1,976.00.

all inhabitants of a community equally thereby serves the social welfare even if the benefits are not available to the public at large.

We acknowledge that the IRS has been something less than fully successful in establishing the precise limits of a Section 501(c)(4) exemption. We are further aware that some judicial decisions, most notably *Rancho Santa Fe, supra*, wherein the district court approved a social welfare exemption for an association serving a privately built housing development, do offer some support for appellant's position. Nevertheless, we find the Association's argument ultimately unsatisfying. Instead, we are persuaded as was the district court, that an organization that operates for the exclusive benefit of its members does not serve a "community" as that term relates to the broader concept of social welfare.

In 1972, the IRS recognized that "a neighborhood, precinct, subdivision, or housing development may constitute a community" for purposes of section 501(c)(4). See Rev. Rule 72-102, 1972-1 C.B. 149. Within two years, however, the IRS found it necessary to clarify that determination to avoid the claims for exemption advanced by home owners associations—private organizations formed by property owners in real estate developments, funded by member assessments and dedicated to the maintenance of the development. In Rev. Rule 74-99, 1974-1 C.B. 131, the IRS stated:

> A community within the meaning of section 501(c)(4) of the code and the regulations is not simply an aggregation of homeowners bound together in a structured unit formed as a integral part of a plan for the development of a real estate subdivision and the sale and purchase of homes therein. Although an exact delineation of the boundaries of a "community" contemplated by section 501(c)(4) is not possible, the term as used in that section has traditionally been construed as having reference to a geographical unit bearing a reasonably recognizable relationship to an area ordinarily identified as a governmental subdivision or a unit or district thereof.

Significantly, in 1976 Congress amended the Internal Revenue Code to create a specialized exemption for "homeowners associations" Tax Reform Act of 1976, Pub. Law No. 94-455, 90 Stat. 1520 § 2101. The legislative history of the new section 528 reveals Congress' assessment of the then existing law and particularly the scope of the social welfare exemption provided by section 501(c)(4).

> Under present law, generally a homeowner association may qualify as an organization exempt from federal income tax (under sec. 501(c)(4) of the Code) only if it meets three requirements (Rev. Rul. 74-99, 1974-1 C.B. 131). First, the homeowner's association must serve a "community" which bears a reasonably, recognizable relationship to an area ordinarily identified as a governmental subdivision or unit. Second, it must not conduct activities directed to the exterior maintenance of any private residence. Third, common areas or facilities that the homeowner's association owns and maintains must be for the use and enjoyment of the general public.

H. R. Rep. No. 94-658, 94th Cong., 1st Sess. at 326–32; S. Rep. no. 94-938, 94th Cong. 2d Sess. at 393.

The third prong in the summary demands attention in the instant case. Clearly Congress believed that an organization cannot serve social welfare if it denies its benefits to the general public. Implicitly, Congress recognized that a true "community" functions within a broader national fabric. Service to such a community thereby furthers the national interest by expanding potential, by opening opportunities to all citizens who may someday find themselves within the bounds of that particular community. Although it is unquestionably their right to do so, when a group of citizens elects, as have the inhabitants of Flat Top Lake, to separate themselves from society and to establish an entity that solely advances their own private interests, no potential for general social advancement is implicated. In many ways, exemption from taxation may be seen as a democratic commonwealth's method of acknowledging the conferral of a universal benefit. Wholly private activity, however meritorious, confers no such benefit which would render a compensatory exemption appropriate.

We have addressed this distinction between the advancement of private interest and the promotion of social welfare on at least one other occasion. In *C.I.R. v. Lake Forest, Inc.*, 305 F.2d 814 (4th Cir. 1962), we reversed the Tax Court's award of an exemption under 26 U.S.C. § 101—the predecessor of section 501(c)(4)—to an organization that operated a housing development as a means of providing low income housing to veterans. Reasoning that the work of the Lake Forest Corporation, although "unquestionably praiseworthy" was not directed to the benefit of the "public at large" nor of "a public character," we concluded that it was a "privately devoted endeavor" and not an exempt social welfare organization. *Lake Forest*, 305 F.2d at 818.

Admittedly, *Lake Forest* did not address the precise argument urged upon us by taxpayer in this case *i.e.* that an organization serving a private development also serves social welfare by granting benefits to all members of that development equally. At the core of *Lake Forest*, however, is the principle that society is an inclusive concept. An organization that bases its benevolence upon some exclusive characteristic of the recipient has moved away from benefiting society. That is certainly true when, as in the instant case, the beneficiaries of the taxpayer's efforts have consciously and deliberately sought to insulate themselves from contact with society around them.

To the extent that the district court decision allowing a section 501(c)(4) exemption in *Rancho Santa Fe, supra*, can be read to support the position asserted by the Association in this appeal, we reject its reasoning. We would note, in any event, that the factual circumstances presented in *Rancho Santa Fe* are dramatically distinguishable from the instant case. The housing development served by the organization claiming exemption therein was much larger than Flat Top and, in virtually every meaningful fashion, functioned as a public municipality. Access to the development by nonresidents was unrestricted and the use of a substantial portion of the development's recreational facilities by the general public was unlimited.

Unlike the inhabitants of Flat Top Lake, there was no indication that the inhabitants of Rancho Santa Fe sought to shut themselves off from society and to hold an outside world at arm's length [sic]. While the court in *Rancho Santa Fe* did believe that a development that attained "community" status could exclude the public at large and still obtain section 501(c)(4) exemption, that conclusion must be regarded largely as dicta in light of the actual nature of Rancho Santa Fe.

The determination of a "community" for section 501(c)(4) purposes will generally turn on the facts and circumstances of the individual case. See Rev. Rul. 80-63, 1980-1 C.B. 166. Nevertheless, the guiding focus must remain upon whether the would-be community is an active part of society or a private refuge for those who would live apart. In the instant case, Flat Top Lake Association has obviously done all within its power to create a wholly private environment for its members. It is not a community within the contemplation of section 501(c)(4) and cannot claim a tax exemption for benefiting itself.

III.

For the foregoing reasons, the judgment of the district court is affirmed.

AFFIRMED.

Widener, Circuit Judge, dissenting:

Because I think Flat Top Lake Association should not necessarily be excluded from the benefit of the exemption, I respectfully dissent.

The Association performs, as the majority recognized, "tasks of quasi-governmental nature" for the Association members and others. Those tasks include year-round water and sanitation services, snow removal from common areas, police protection, road and equipment maintenance and maintenance of the dam and other common areas. The Association is working with local authorities in considering construction of a sewage treatment plant. Further, it has promulgated a disaster relief plan in the event of failure of the dam, and it supplies a backup water supply to the nearby City of Beckley, a city of some 19,000 population.

The tax exemption was revoked because the IRS, with whom the district court and the majority have agreed, determined that the Association did not meet the definition of a "community" in order to qualify for the exemption because the Association "restricts the use of its facility to the exclusive use of its members." Public use is thus made the *sine qua non* of a § 501(c)(4) exemption.

The rationale of the decisions of the district court and the majority is misplaced, however, for, as I will demonstrate, the proper premise of the federal tax exemption for social welfare organizations is not based upon public use, as the majority holds, but upon the public benefit derived therefrom. The district court found explicitly that Flat Top Lake Association falls squarely within the language of 26 U.S.C. § 501(c)(4) as "a nonprofit organization" operated "for the promotion of social welfare." Since that finding of fact by the district court is even based on stipulation, I take it the matter is beyond question.

With all deference to the majority's view, I suggest that we are off the track. The correct approach to the question before us is not that taken in the majority opinion; rather, it is that set out in *Peoples Educational Camp Society, Inc. v. CIR*, 331 F.2d 923 (2d Cir.) (1964), in which the Second Circuit, in construing § 501(c)(4), stated:

> The exemption granted to social welfare and like organizations is made in recognition of the benefit which the public derives from their social welfare activities, *Trinidad v. Sagrado Orden*, 263 U.S. 578, 581 (1924), and we think it only fair to determine a particular organization's right to an exemption largely on the basis of the effect its operations have on the public.

Thus, we see that the Second Circuit, unlike ours, by its reliance on *Trinidad*, places the emphasis where it should be, on the public benefit resulting from the activity, not upon the public use thereof.

Using that analysis, there is no doubt that in this case either a judgment for the taxpayer is required, or at the least the question should be reconsidered on remand. There is no evidence in this record but that all the activities of the taxpayer benefit the public, for they directly affect the public purse by performing activities which the taxpayers otherwise would have to pay for. Even if it might be said that the district court did not approach the matter from the standpoint of public benefit rather than public use and should be afforded another opportunity to find facts, that opportunity should be offered; although, in this case, I see no use of it because the government does not suggest any activity undertaken by the taxpayer which does not benefit the public.

Questions

1. Why might the Service have changed its view of "community benefit," vis-a-vis homeowners' associations, from the view it held prior to *Rancho Santa Fe Association v. United States*, 589 F. Supp. 54 (S.D. Cal. 1984) (cited above in *Flat Top Lake Association*)?

2. Is there any difference between the private benefit doctrine as stated for purposes of § 501(c)(3) and § 501(c)(4)? Compare *Flat Top Lake Association* and *American Campaign Academy v. Commissioner*, 92 T.C. 1053 (1989) (text of case is in Chapter 12). Should there be a different standard of private benefit for the two categories of tax exemption?

3. The Service consistently adheres to the *Flat Top Lake Association* articulation of the private benefit doctrine for § 501(c)(4) purposes. Recall that HMOs that seek exemption under § 501(c)(3) are usually denied that status and instead granted exemption under § 501(c)(4). Do HMOs pass the private benefit test as defined in *Flat Top Lake Association*?

Note on Tax Exempt Homeowners' Associations: Section 528

Although the preceding cases are still relevant to the interpretations of "social welfare" and "community benefit," the enactment of § 528 settles the issue insofar as homeowners' associations are concerned. An association that receives at least 60% of its gross income from dues, fees, or assessments paid by owners is eligible for tax exemption if at least 90% of its expenditures are for the acquisition, management maintenance and upkeep of association property, or (with regard to Timeshare Associations) for activities conducted for timeshare owners. As explained below, however, tax exemption is only with regard to member dues, fees, and assessments. All other income is taxed at a flat 30% rate. Thus, 528 status is not as beneficial as 501(c)(4) status. In the latter instance, for example, most passive income — e.g., interest, royalties, and rents — is excluded from taxation. Still, the rule seems a fair trade because homeowners' associations are most concerned with preserving the value of members' homes (by enforcing covenants and sending notices around when the neighbor refuses to cut the grass!) as opposed to the "public good." The private inurement prohibition (but not the prohibition against excess benefit transactions) is explicitly applicable and the substantial lobbying prohibition is effectively made applicable by the requirement that at least 90% of the expenditures be devoted to the association's property.

Senate Finance Committee Report on P.L. 96-605 (Miscellaneous Revenue Act of 1980), pp. 18–19

Under present law, a qualified homeowners association (a condominium management association or a residential real estate association) may elect to be treated as a tax-exempt organization (Code sec. 528). If an election is made, the association will not be taxed on "exempt function income." Exempt function income means membership dues, fees, and assessments received from persons who own residential units in the particular condominium or subdivision and who are members of the association.

The association will be taxed, however, on income which is not exempt function income. For example, any interest earned on amounts set aside in a sinking fund for future improvements is taxable. Similarly, any amount paid by persons who are not members of the association for use of the association's facilities, such as tennis courts, swimming pools, golf courses, etc., is taxable. Further, any amount paid by members for special use of the association's facilities, the use of which would not be available to all the members as a result of having paid the membership dues, fees, or assessments required to be paid by all members of the association, will be taxable. For example, if the membership dues, fees, or assessments do not entitle a member to use the association's party room or to use the swimming pool after a certain time period, then amounts paid for this use are taxable to the association.

Deductions from nonexempt income are allowed for expenses directly related to the production of such income, and a $100 deduction against taxable income is provided so that associations with only a minimal amount of taxable income will not be subject to tax. However, a net operating loss deduction is not allowed, and the special deductions for corporations (such as the dividends received deduction) are not allowed.

* * *

The basic rationale for the tax treatment of homeowners associations in the Code is that activities which would not be taxed if engaged in by homeowners individually (for example, maintenance of their property or the payment of utility bills) should not be subject to tax when the individuals band together in an association.

* * *

The committee believes that the taxable income of a homeowners association should not be subject to tax at higher rates than the rates which would normally apply to such income if it were taxable to the members of the association. However, it would be too complicated to require a pass through of ratable portions of an association's income to its members. Consequently, the committee believes that it is appropriate to tax the income of homeowners associations at a flat rate of 30 percent, which may reasonably approximate the average marginal income tax rate of the members of these associations.

Under this provision, taxable income of a homeowners association will be taxed at a rate of 30 percent. This rate applies to both ordinary income and capital gains.

C. Credit Counseling Services

Code: §§ 501(q); 513(j)

Technical Explanation of H.R. 4 the "Pension Protection Act of 2006"

Joint Committee on Taxation
CMP 2006-JTX-0018, page 312

August 3, 2006.

JCX-38-06.

* * *

Title XII: Provisions Relating to Exempt Organizations

* * *

10. Establish additional exemption standards for credit counseling organizations (secs. 501 and 513 of the Code)

Present Law

Under present law, a credit counseling organization may be exempt as a charitable or educational organization described in section 501(c)(3), or as a social welfare organization described in section 501(c)(4). The IRS has issued two revenue rulings holding that certain credit counseling organizations are exempt as charitable or educational organizations or as social welfare organizations.

In Revenue Ruling 65-299, an organization whose purpose was to assist families and individuals with financial problems, and help reduce the incidence of personal bankruptcy, was determined to be a social welfare organization described in section 501(c)(4). The organization counseled people in financial difficulties, advised applicants on payment of debts, and negotiated with creditors and set up debt repayment plans. The organization did not restrict its services to the poor, made no charge for counseling services, and made a nominal charge for certain services to cover postage and supplies. For financial support, the organization relied on voluntary contributions from local businesses, lending agencies, and labor unions.

In Revenue Ruling 69-441, the IRS ruled an organization was a charitable or educational organization exempt under section 501(c)(3) by virtue of aiding low-income people who had financial problems and providing education to the public. The organization in that ruling had two functions: (1) educating the public on personal money management, such as budgeting, buying practices, and the sound use of consumer credit through the use of films, speakers, and publications; and (2) providing individual counseling to low-income individuals and families without charge. As part of its counseling activities, the organization established debt management plans for clients who required such services, at no charge to the clients. The organization was supported by contributions primarily from creditors, and its board of directors was comprised of representatives from religious organizations, civic groups, labor unions, business groups, and educational institutions.

In 1976, the IRS denied exempt status to an organization, Consumer Credit Counseling Service of Alabama, whose activities were distinguishable from those in Revenue Ruling 69-441 in that (1) it did not restrict its services to the poor, and (2) it charged a nominal fee for its debt management plans. The organization provided free information to the general public through the use of speakers, films, and publications on the subjects of budgeting, buying practices, and the use of consumer credit. It also provided counseling to debt-distressed individuals, not necessarily poor or low-income, and provided debt management plans at the cost of $10 per month, which was waived in cases of financial hardship. Its debt management activities were a relatively small part of its overall activities. The district court determined the organization qualified as charitable and educational within section 501(c)(3), finding the debt management plans to be an integral part of the agency's counseling function, and that its debt management activities were incidental to its principal functions, as only approximately 12 percent of the counselors' time was applied to such programs and the charge for the service was nominal. The court also considered the facts that the agency was publicly supported, and that it had a board dominated by members of the general public, as factors indicating a charitable operation.

A recent estimate shows the number of credit counseling organizations increased from approximately 200 in 1990 to over 1,000 in 2002. During the period from 1994 to late 2003, 1,215 credit counseling organizations applied to the IRS for tax exempt status under section 501(c)(3), including 810 during 2000 to 2003. The IRS has recognized more than 850 credit counseling organizations as tax exempt under section 501(c)(3). Few credit counseling organizations have sought section 501(c)(4) status, and the IRS reports it has not seen any significant increase in the number or activity of such organizations operating as social welfare organizations. As of late 2003, there were 872 active tax-exempt credit counseling agencies operating in the United States.

A credit counseling organization described in section 501(c)(3) is exempt from certain Federal and State consumer protection laws that provide exemptions for organizations described therein. Some believe that these exclusions from Federal and State regulation may be a primary motivation for the recent increase in the number of organizations seeking and obtaining exempt status under section 501(c)(3). Such regulatory exemptions generally are not available for social welfare organizations described in section 501(c)(4).

Congress recently conducted hearings investigating the activities of credit counseling organizations under various consumer protection laws, such as the Federal Trade Commission Act. In addition, the IRS commenced a broad examination and compliance program with respect to the credit counseling industry. On May 15, 2006, the IRS announced that over the past two years, it had been auditing 63 credit counseling agencies, representing more than 40 percent of the revenue in the industry. Audits of 41 organizations, representing more than 40 percent of the revenue in the industry have been completed as of that date. All of such completed audits resulted in revocation, proposed revocation, or other termination of tax-exempt status. In addition, the IRS released two legal documents that provide a legal framework for determining the exempt status and related issues with respect to credit counseling organizations. In CCA 200620001, the IRS found that "[t]he critical inquiry is whether a credit counseling organization conducts its counseling program to improve an individual debtor's understanding of his financial problems and improve his ability to address those problems." The CCA concluded that whether a credit counseling organization primarily furthers educational purposes:

> can be determined by assessing the methodology by which the organization conducts its counseling activities. The process an organization uses to interview clients and develop recommendations, train its counselors and market its services can distinguish between an organization whose object is to improve a person's knowledge and skills to manage his personal debt, and an organization that is offering counseling primarily as a mechanism to enroll individuals in a specific option (e.g., debt management plans) without considering the individual's best interest.

Under the Bankruptcy Abuse Prevention and Consumer Protection Act of 2005, Public Law 109-8, an individual generally may not be a debtor in bankruptcy unless such individual has, within 180 days of filing a petition for bankruptcy, received from an approved nonprofit budget and credit counseling agency an individual or group briefing that outlines the opportunities for available credit counseling and assists the individual in performing a related budget analysis. The clerk of the court must maintain a publicly available list of nonprofit budget and credit counseling agencies approved by the U.S. Trustee (or bankruptcy administrator). In general, the U.S. Trustee (or bankruptcy administrator) shall only approve an agency that demonstrates that it will provide qualified counselors, maintain adequate provision for safekeeping and payment of client funds, provide adequate counseling with respect to client credit problems, and deal responsibly and effectively with other matters relating to the quality, effectiveness, and financial security of the services it provides. The minimum qualifications for approval of such an agency include: (1) in general, having an independent board of directors; (2) charging no more than a reasonable fee, and providing services without regard to ability to pay; (3) adequate provision for safekeeping and payment of client funds; (4) provision of full disclosures to clients; (5) provision of adequate counseling with respect to a client's credit problems; (6) trained counselors who receive no commissions or bonuses based on the outcome of the counseling services; (7) experience and background in providing credit counseling; and (8) adequate financial resources to provide continuing support services for budgeting plans over the life of any repayment plan. An individual debtor must file with the court a certificate from the approved nonprofit budget and credit counseling agency that provided the required services describing the services provided, and a copy of the debt management plan, if any, developed through the agency.

Explanation of Provision

Requirements for exempt status of credit counseling organizations

The provision establishes standards that a credit counseling organization must satisfy, in addition to present law requirements, in order to be organized and operated either as an organization described in section 501(c)(3) or in section 501(c)(4). The provision does not diminish the requirements set forth recently by the IRS in Chief Counsel Advice 200431023 or Chief Counsel Advice 200620001 but builds on and is consistent with such requirements, and the analysis therein. The provision is not intended to raise any question about IRS actions taken, and the IRS is expected to continue its vigorous examination of the credit counseling industry, applying the additional standards provided by the provision. The provision does not and is not intended to affect the approval process for credit counseling agencies under Public Law 109-8. Public Law 109-8 requires that an approved credit counseling agency be a nonprofit, and does not require that an approved agency be a section 501(c)(3) organization. It is expected that the Department of Justice shall continue to approve agencies for purposes of providing pre-bankruptcy counseling based on criteria that are consistent with such Public Law.

Under the provision, an organization that provides credit counseling services as a substantial purpose of the organization ("credit counseling organization") is eligible for exemption from Federal income tax only as a charitable or educational organization under section 501(c)(3) or as a social welfare organization under section 501(c)(4), and only if (in addition to present-law requirements) the credit counseling organization is organized and operated in accordance with the following:

1. The organization provides credit counseling services tailored to the specific needs and circumstances of the consumer;

2. The organization makes no loans to debtors (other than loans with no fees or interest) and does not negotiate the making of loans on behalf of debtors;

3. The organization provides services for the purpose of improving a consumer's credit record, credit history, or credit rating only to the extent that such services are incidental to providing credit counseling services and does not charge any separately stated fee for any such services;

4. The organization does not refuse to provide credit counseling services to a consumer due to inability of the consumer to pay, the ineligibility of the consumer for debt management plan enrollment, or the unwillingness of a consumer to enroll in a debt management plan;

5. The organization establishes and implements a fee policy to require that any fees charged to a consumer for its services are reasonable, allows for the waiver of fees if the consumer is unable to pay, and except to the extent allowed by State law prohibits charging any fee based in whole or in part on a percentage of the consumer's debt, the consumer's payments to be made pursuant to a debt management plan, or on the projected or actual savings to the consumer resulting from enrolling in a debt management plan;

6. The organization at all times has a board of directors or other governing body (a) that is controlled by persons who represent the broad interests of the public, such as public officials acting in their capacities as such, persons having special knowledge or expertise in credit or financial education, and community leaders; (b) not more than 20 percent of the voting power of which is vested in persons who are employed by the organization or who will benefit financially, directly or indirectly, from the organization's activities (other than through the receipt of reasonable directors' fees or the repayment of consumer debt to creditors other than the credit counseling organization or its affiliates) and (c) not more than 49 percent of the voting power of which is vested in persons who are employed by the organization or who will benefit financially, directly or indirectly, from the organization's activities (other than through the receipt of reasonable directors' fees);

7. The organization does not own (except with respect to a section 501(c)(3) organization) more than 35 percent of the total combined voting power of a corporation (or profits or beneficial interest in the case of a partnership or trust or estate) that is in the trade or business of lending money, repairing credit, or providing debt management plan services, payment processing, and similar services; and

8. The organization receives no amount for providing referrals to others for debt management plan services, and pays no amount to others for obtaining referrals of consumers.

Additional requirements for charitable and educational organizations

Under the provision, a credit counseling organization is described in section 501(c)(3) only if, in addition to satisfying the above requirements and the requirements of section 501(c)(3), the organization is organized and operated such that the organization (1) does not solicit contributions from consumers during the initial counseling process or while the consumer is receiving services from the organization and (2) the aggregate revenues of the organization that are from payments of creditors of consumers of the organization and that are attributable to debt management plan services do not exceed the applicable percentage of the total revenues of the organization. For credit counseling organizations in existence on the date of enactment, the applicable percentage is 80 percent for the first taxable year of the organization beginning after the date which is one year after the date of enactment, 70 percent for the second such taxable year beginning after such date, 60 percent for the third such taxable year beginning after such date, and 50 percent thereafter. For new credit counseling organizations, the applicable percentage is 50 percent for taxable years beginning after the date of enactment. Satisfaction of the aggregate revenues requirement is not a safe harbor; all other requirements of the provision (and of section 501(c)(3)) pertaining to section 501(c)(3) organizations also must be satisfied. Satisfaction of the aggregate revenues requirement means only that an organization has not automatically failed to be organized or operated consistent with exempt purposes. Compliance with the revenues test does not mean that the organization's debt management plan services activity is at a level that organizationally or operationally is consistent with exempt status. In other words, satisfaction of the aggregate revenues requirement (as a preliminary matter in an exemption application, or on an ongoing operational basis) provides no affirmative evidence that an organization's primary purpose is an exempt purpose, or that the revenues that are subject to the limitation (or debt management plan services revenues more generally) are related to exempt purposes. As described below, whether revenues from such activity are substantially related to exempt purposes depends on the facts and circumstances, that is, satisfaction of the aggregate revenues requirement generally is not relevant for purposes of whether any of an organization's revenues are revenues from an unrelated trade or business. Failure to satisfy the aggregate revenues requirement does not disqualify the organization from recognition of exemption under section 501(c)(4).

Additional requirement for social welfare organizations

Under the provision, a credit counseling organization is described in section 501(c)(4) only if, in addition to satisfying the above requirements applicable to such organizations, the organization notifies the Secretary, in such manner as the Secretary may by regulations prescribe, that it is applying for recognition as a credit counseling organization.

Debt management plan services treated as an unrelated trade or business

Under the provision, debt management plan services are treated as an unrelated trade or business for purposes of the tax on income from an unrelated trade or business to the extent such services are provided by an organization that is not a credit counseling organization. With respect to the provision of debt management plan services by a credit counseling organization, in order for the income from such services not to be unrelated business income, it is intended that, consistent with current law, the debt management plan service with respect to such income (1) must contribute importantly to the accomplishment of credit counseling services, and (2) must not be conducted on a larger scale than reasonably is necessary for the accomplishment of such services. For example, the provision of debt management plan services would not be substantially related to accomplishing exempt purposes if the organization recommended and enrolled an individual in a debt management plan only after determining whether the individual satisfied the financial criteria established by the creditors for such plan, without (1) considering whether it was an appropriate action in light of the individual's particular needs and objectives, (2) discussing the disadvantages of a debt management plan with the consumer, and (3) presenting other possible options to such consumer.

Definitions

Credit counseling services

Credit counseling services are (a) the provision of educational information to the general public on budgeting, personal finance, financial literacy, saving and spending practices, and the sound use of consumer credit; (b) the assisting of individuals and families with financial problems by providing them with counseling; or (c) any combination of such activities.

Debt management plan services

Debt management plan services are services related to the repayment, consolidation, or restructuring of a consumer's debt, and includes the negotiation with creditors of lower interest rates, the waiver or reduction of fees, and the marketing and processing of debt management plans. . . .

D. Political Campaign and Lobbying Activities of IRC §§ 501(c)(4), (c)(5) and (c)(6) Organizations

Chapters 13 (Lobbying Restriction) and 14 (Political Activity Prohibition) of this book outline the various tax rules pertaining to lobbying and political campaigning by 501(c)(3) charities. As a complement to that discussion, the excerpt below discusses the tax rules on lobbying and political campaigning by 501(c)(4) social welfare organizations and other non-(c)(3) tax-exempt entities.

Political Campaign and Lobbying Activities of IRC 501(c)(4), (c)(5), and (c)(6) Organizations

John Francis Reilly & Barbara A. Braig Allen

Exempt Organizations Continuing Professional Education (CPE)
Technical Instruction Program FY 2003.
https://www.irs.gov/pub/irs-tege/eotopic103.pdf
2003 WL 23649724 (IRS)

Overview

Purpose

This article is intended to provide EO with information about the rules relating to the political campaign and lobbying activities of IRC 501(c)(4), (c)(5), and (c)(6) organizations.

* * *

A. General Rules Relating to Lobbying and Political Campaign Activities by IRC 501(c)(4), (c)(5), and (c)(6) Organizations

May IRC 501(c)(4), (c)(5), or (c)(6) Organizations Engage in Attempts to Influence Legislation (Lobbying)?

Yes. Organizations described in IRC 501(c)(4), (c)(5), and (c)(6) may engage in an unlimited amount of lobbying, provided that the lobbying is related to the organization's exempt purpose.

- This principle is enunciated in Rev. Rul. 61-177, 1961-1 C.B. 117, which holds that a corporation organized and operated primarily for the purpose of promoting a common business interest is exempt under IRC 501(c)(6) even though its sole activity is introducing legislation germane to such common business interest.
- Rev. Rul. 61-177 notes that there is no requirement, by statute or regulations, that a business league or chamber of commerce must refrain from lobbying activities to qualify for exemption.
- The rule set forth in Rev. Rul. 61-177 applies to organizations described in IRC 501(c)(4) and (c)(5) as well. *See* Rev. Rul. 67-293, 1967-1 C.B. 185, and Rev. Rul. 71-530, 1971-2 C.B. 237.

May IRC 501(c)(4), (c)(5), or (c)(6) Organizations Engage in Political Campaign Activities?

IRC 501(c)(4), (c)(5), and (c)(6) organizations may engage in political campaigns on behalf of or in opposition to candidates for public office provided that such intervention does not constitute the organization's primary activity.

- The regulations under IRC 501(c)(4) provide that promotion of social welfare does not include participation or intervention in political campaigns. Reg. 1.501(c)(4)-1(a)(2)(ii).

G.C.M. 34233 (Dec. 3, 1969) reaches the same conclusion with respect to labor unions described in IRC 501(c)(5) and business leagues described in IRC 501(c)(6).

- The G.C.M. contrasts support of a candidate for office with lobbying activities.
- The G.C.M. notes that the content of specific legislative proposals may be readily identified and related to the business or labor interests of the organizations. Therefore, business leagues and labor unions may engage in lobbying activities that are germane to their exempt purposes as their primary activity.
- However, "support of a candidate for public office necessarily involves the organization in the total political attitudes and positions of the candidate."

Because of this, the G.C.M. concluded that "this involvement transcends the narrower [exempt] interest" of the organization and could not be the primary activity of an organization described in either IRC 501(c)(5) or IRC 501(c)(6).

May IRC 501(c) Organizations Make Expenditures for IRC 527 "Exempt Function" Activities?

IRC 501(c) organizations may generally make expenditures for political campaign activities if such activities (and other activities not furthering its exempt purposes) do not constitute the organization's primary activity.

Examples:

- Social welfare organizations described in IRC 501(c)(4): (Rev. Rul. 81-95, 1981-1 C.B. 332—because organization's primary activities promote social welfare, its less than primary participation in political campaigns will not adversely affect its exempt status).

* * *

- Labor organizations described in IRC 501(c)(5): (Marker v. Schultz, 485 F.2d 1003 (D.C. Cir. 1973) and G.C.M. 36286 (May 22, 1975)).
- Business leagues described in IRC 501(c)(6): (G.C.M. 34233 (Dec. 3, 1969)).

Effect of Political Campaign Activity or Lobbying by an IRC 501(c) Organization on the Deductibility of Dues or Contributions to the Organization Under IRC 162

Dues or contributions to IRC 501(c)(4), (c)(5), and (c)(6) organizations may be deductible as business expenses under IRC 162.

Political campaign activity:

- Amounts paid for intervention or participation in any political campaign may not be deducted as a business expense. IRC 162(e)(2)(A).
- Lobbying:
- Amounts paid for direct legislative lobbying expenses at the federal and state (but not the local) level may not be deducted as a business expense.
- Grass roots lobbying expenditures also are not deductible.
- Amounts paid for contact with certain federal officials would not be deductible under IRC 162(e).

Amounts paid to an IRC 501(c) organization that are specifically for political campaign activities or lobbying, would not be deductible under IRC 162.

If a substantial part of the activities of the IRC 501(c) organization consists of political campaign activities or lobbying, a deduction under IRC 162 is allowed only for the portion of dues or other payments to the organization that the taxpayer can clearly establish was not for political campaign or lobbying activities. Reg. 1.162-20(c)(3).

Until 1993, no mechanism existed at the association level to ensure notification to members of the disallowance.

OBRA 1993

In 1993, Congress enacted the Omnibus Budget Reconciliation Act of 1993 (OBRA 1993).

- The Act disallowed the deduction for direct lobbying at the federal and state level as a business expense under IRC 162.
- Grassroots lobbying and political campaign activity continued to be nondeductible.

§ 13222 of OBRA 1993 amended IRC 6033, adding a new subsection to provide a system based on the disallowance of dues that builds in an incentive (or penalty) to ensure that associations notify their members.

The trigger is contained in IRC 6033(e), which imposes reporting and notice requirements on tax-exempt organizations incurring expenditures to which IRC 162(e) applies. IRC 162(e)(3) denies a deduction for the dues or other similar amounts paid to certain tax-exempt organizations to the extent that:

- The organization, at the time the dues are assessed or paid, notifies the dues payer that the dues are allocable to nondeductible lobbying and political expenditures of the type described in IRC 162(e)(1).
- Payments that are similar to dues include voluntary payments or special assessments used to conduct political campaign activities.

The reporting and notice requirements and proxy tax under IRC 6033(e) are discussed under "D. Disallowance and Notification — IRC 162(e) and 6033(e)."

Chapter 21

Labor, Agricultural and Horticultural Organizations

A. Labor Organizations

CODE: § 501(c)(5), 501(g), Skim 401(a)

REG.: § 1.501(c)(5)-1

1. General Rule Defining Labor Organizations

Tupper v. United States

134 F.3d 444 (1st Cir. 1998)

TORRUELLA, Chief Judge:

The trustees of both a multiemployer pension plan trust and an annuity plan trust appeal a judgment from the district court. The court held that during 1986, 1987, and 1988, when the plans had failed to meet the requirements of the Employee Retirement Income Security Act ("ERISA") and Internal Revenue Code ("I.R.C.") § 401(a), the trusts could not qualify as exempt from taxation as "labor organizations" under I.R.C. § 501(c)(5). We affirm.

Background

The Plumbing, Pipe Fitting and Heating Contractors Association of Brockton and Vicinity (the "Employers") and the Local Union 276 of the United Association of Journeymen and Apprentices of the Plumbing and Pipe Fitting Industry of the United States and Canada (the "Union") entered into collective bargaining agreements in 1959 and 1983 providing for the creation of a defined benefit pension plan and a money purchase annuity plan respectively (the "plans"). According to the plans, half of the trustees of each plan trust are appointed by the Employers and half by the Union. The trustees are currently John F. Tupper, Robert S. Norvish, Raymond F. Brierly, Louis M. Colombo, Edward F. Cruz, and Dennis J. Cruz (the "trustees"). The trusts are funded entirely by employer contributions and exist solely to provide pension and annuity benefits for plan participants and beneficiaries.

In 1974, after the pension plan had been in existence for fifteen years, ERISA was passed. *See* Pub. L. No. 93-406, 88 Stat. 829. ERISA resulted from a Congressional finding that pension benefits promised to employees were not being adequately protected. *See* ERISA § 2(a). Congress created a system of tax incentives and penalties in order to ensure protection of these funds. Pursuant to ERISA, a form containing certain information about a pension plan must be filed annually with the IRS in order to qualify the fund for tax exemption under I.R.C. § 401(a). *See* IRS Form 5500. The plans at issue in this case submitted these forms for 1986, 1987, and 1988.

An Internal Revenue Service ("IRS") audit for those three years revealed that the documents of the plans failed to meet the requirements of I.R.C. § 401(a) and found that the pension trust was not being operated in compliance with its plan. Consequently, the trustees paid over $450,000 in back taxes and then filed claims in federal court for refund, claiming entitlement to a tax exemption under various theories. All of those theories were eventually dismissed by the trustees' stipulation, save one somewhat novel claim which was the object of the district court's order and this appeal. The only question at issue in this case is whether the trusts, failing to meet ERISA standards, alternatively qualified for a tax exemption under I.R.C. § 501(c)(5) as "labor organizations."

The District Court of Massachusetts rejected a magistrate judge's recommendation that summary judgment be granted in favor of the trusts on this question, granting summary judgment in favor of the United States. This appeal followed.

Discussion

An award of summary judgment is reviewed *de novo. See United Nat'l Ins. Co. v. Penuche's, Inc.*, 128 F.3d 28, 30 (1st Cir. 1997). We view the entire record in the light most hospitable to the party opposing summary judgment, indulging all reasonable inferences in that party's favor. *See Ahern v. O'Donnell*, 109 F.3d 809, 811 (1st Cir. 1997). However, taxpayers must prove unambiguously that they are entitled to exemptions. *See United States v. Wells Fargo Bank* [88-1 USTC ¶13,759], 485 U.S. 351, 354 (1988). Therefore, if "doubts are nicely balanced" regarding the applicability of a tax exemption, the exemption must be accorded its more limited interpretation. *Troter v. Tennessee*, 290 U.S. 354, 356 (1933). Thus, while factual doubts must be resolved in favor of the trustees in this case, legal ambiguities must be resolved in favor of the United States. We proceed with these standards in mind.

It is tautological that, when asked to interpret a statute, a court first looks to the text of that statute. *See Strickland v. Commissioner, Me. Dep't of Agric.*, 48 F.3d 12, 17 (1st Cir. 1995). If our query is not answered by the text, we skeptically examine legislative history in search of an "unmistakable expression of congressional intent" before considering agency interpretations or other devices of construction. *See id.*

Thus, we begin our analysis with I.R.C. § 501(c)(5), which provides a tax exemption for "labor organizations." However, this term is not defined in the statute.[1] Further-

1. [1] Courts routinely look to other statutes when construing a particular statutory term, *see Friends of the Boundary Wilderness v. Robertson*, 978 F.2d 1484, 1490 (8th Cir. 1992). While the term "labor organization" is not defined anywhere in the I.R.C., the National Labor Relations Act ("NLRA") defines the term as "any organization of any kind, or any agency or employee representation committee or plan, in which employees participate and which exists for the purpose, in whole

more, the legislative history regarding this provision offers no insights into whether a pension trust established pursuant to collective bargaining and controlled jointly by the union and the employers was meant to be exempt from taxation. *See Stichting Pensioenfonds Voor de Gezondheid v. United States* [97-1 USTC ¶50,158], 129 F.3d 195, 198 (D.C. Cir. 1997) ("*Stichting*") (noting that the text and legislative history of I.R.C. § 501(c)(5) provide "little help" in understanding the scope of the term "labor organization").[2] In their briefs, both the United States and the trustees candidly acknowledge that we must look beyond the I.R.C. for guidance in this case.[3]

We next turn to the Treasury Department's Regulations that have been adopted in order to elaborate upon the definition of the term "labor organization" in 501(c)(5). These regulations provide as follows:

> The organizations contemplated by section 501(c)(5) as entitled to exemption from income taxation are those which:
>
> (1) Have no net earnings inuring to the benefit of any member, and
>
> (2) Have as their objects the betterment of the conditions of those engaged in such pursuits [i.e., labor], the improvement of the grade of their products,

---

or in part, of dealing with employers concerning grievances, labor disputes, wages, rates of pay, hours of employment, or conditions of work." *See* 29 U.S.C. § 152(5). The Supreme Court has held that this NLRA definition is susceptible to very broad interpretation. *See Marine Engineers Beneficial Ass'n v. Interlake S.S. Co.*, 370 U.S. 173, 181-82 (1962); *NLRB v. Cabot Carbon Co.*, 360 U.S. 203, 211 n.7 (1959). However, even a broad interpretation of this inclusive definition would not encompass the plans at issue. Nonetheless, we will continue with our analysis of the question presented by this case because we are hesitant to import definitions from statutes with unrelated or cross-purposes. *See General Dynamics Corp. v. Director, Office of Workers' Comp. Programs*, 585 F.2d 1168, 1170 (1st Cir. 1978). The I.R.C. and the NLRA have very different objectives. It is unclear whether Congress intended to exempt from taxation each organization and only those labor organizations which it felt necessary to regulate via the Taft-Hartley Act and the NLRA. Furthermore, neither party addressed the applicability of the NLRA definition to I.R.C. § 501(c)(5).

2. [2] In *Stichting*, the Court of Appeals for the District of Columbia Circuit recently addressed the same question posed here; i.e., whether a jointly-controlled employer-funded pension fund was exempt from taxation under § 501(c)(5) of the Internal Revenue Code. The court concluded that the plaintiff failed to unambiguously establish that such funds were "labor organizations" according to the Code. 129 F.3d at 200.

3. [3] The United States argues that the congressional debates of 1909 do hint at a desire to exempt only representational entities under § 501(c)(5). However, the history does not reveal an "unmistakable expression of congressional intent" on this point. *See Strickland*, 48 F.3d at 17. There is no evidence that Congress envisioned modern pension plans like the one at issue in this case during these debates. Furthermore, the United States' argument is unpersuasive in light of the numerous Revenue Rulings in which the IRS has consistently exempted various non-representational entities under this provision. *See* discussion *infra*. Furthermore, Congress has amended § 501(c) ten times since 1980 without ever clarifying the term "labor organization." *See* 26 U.S.C.A. § 501 (tracing these amendments). While "congressional inaction frequently betokens unawareness, preoccupation, or paralysis," *Zuber v. Allen*, 396 U.S. 168, 185-186 n.21 (1969), when a specific subsection has received repeated congressional attention without any revision or clarification of a term which has been consistently interpreted by an administrative agency, there is a presumption that Congress is familiar with and supportive of the agency's interpretation. *See Lorillard v. Pons*, 434 U.S. 575, 580 (1978); *Estey v. Commissioner, Me. Dept. of Human Services*, 21 F.3d 1198, 1214 (1st Cir. 1994) (Cyr, J. dissenting).

> and the development of a higher degree of efficiency in their respective occupations.

26 C.F.R. §1.501(c)(5)-1(a) (1997). If these regulations were applied consistently by the IRS, this case could be decided on the definition provided therein. Clearly the pension funds do not improve the grade of the workers' products or develop a higher degree of efficiency in the plumbing and pipefitting professions. However, while we accord due deference to all reasonable agency interpretations of a statute, *see Strickland*, 48 F.3d at 17, the IRS's interpretation of the I.R.C. is reflected in Treasury Regulations *together with Revenue Rulings. See* 26 C.F.R. §1.6661-3 (1997). An examination of the IRS Revenue Rulings interpreting §501(c)(5) reveals that these regulations are routinely applied so liberally as to render them virtually useless in the present case.

In its Revenue Rulings, the IRS has held that "[a]n organization which is engaged in activities appropriate to a labor union, even though technically not a labor union itself, may qualify for exemption under §501(c)(5)." Rev. Rul. 75-473, 1975-2 C.B. 213; *see also* Rev. Rul. 67-7, 1967-1 C.B. 137, 138 (same). Over the years, pursuant to §501(c)(5), the IRS has exempted a union stewardship trust, a union dispatch hall, and a union newspaper. *See*, respectively, Rev. Rul. 77-5, 1977-1 C.B. 145; Rev. Rul. 75-473, 1975-2; Rev. Rul. 68-534, 1968-2 C.B. 217. Much like the trusts at issue, it is difficult indeed to see how these entities "improved the grade of workers' products" and "developed a higher degree of efficiency in their respective occupations" in accordance with the Treasury Regulations. The plan trusts, like the examples above, have no net earnings inuring to the benefit of any member, and, in a sense, have as their objects the betterment of the conditions of the union members participating in the plans.[4] Against these background interpretations of the applicable Treasury Regulations, we must look elsewhere for guidance in deciding this case.

The trustees urge this court to consider General Counsel Memoranda ("GCMs") in order to establish that, pursuant to §501 (c)(5), the IRS has exempted entities similar to the plan trusts. GCMs are legal memoranda from the Office of Chief Counsel to the IRS prepared in response to a formal request for legal advice from

---

4. [4] In awarding summary judgment to the United States in *Stichting*, the D.C. District Court recognized a pattern in Revenue Rulings whereby non-representational entities which were not controlled by unions were not exempted under 501(c)(5). *See Stichting Pensioenfonds Voor de Gezondheid v. United States* [97-1 USTC ¶50,158], 950 F. Supp. 373, 377-378 (D.D.C. 1996), *aff'd* [97-2 USTC ¶50,917], 129 F.3d 195 (D.C. Cir. 1997). The D.C. Circuit did not address this "pattern" on appeal, and we are reluctant to draw any conclusions from the district court's analysis. The Internal Revenue Service has never held out control as a litmus test for the §501(c)(5) "labor organization" exemption. Moreover, in two Revenue Rulings discussed above, the Service exempted a jointly-supervised dispatch hall and an employer-controlled trust funding a stewardship organization under the provision. *See*, respectively, Rev. Rul. 75-473, 1975-2 C.B. 213; Rev. Rul. 77-5, 1977-1 C.B. 146. While one might argue that each of these examples has a stronger union "nexus" than the trusts in this case, we are unpersuaded that current regulations *require* a taxpayer seeking a §501(c)(5) "labor organization" exemption to be either a representational or union-controlled entity.

the Assistant Commissioner (Technical). *See Taxation With Representation Fund v. Internal Revenue Service* [81-2 USTC ¶9784], 646 F.2d 666, 669 (D.C. Cir. 1981). Completed GCMs are distributed to key officials within the IRS. *See id.* at 670. The Office of Chief Counsel retains GCMs, and indexes and digests them as an in-house research tool. *See id.* While the Internal Revenue Manual instructs IRS personnel not to use GCMs as precedents in the disposition of other cases, they may refer to GCMs for guidance in negotiations and in formulating a district office position on an issue. *See id.* (citing Internal Revenue Manual § 4245.3). Furthermore, GCMs are extensively cross-referenced and updated to reflect current agency policy. *See id.* at 682. As the D.C. Circuit has recognized, GCMs constitute the "working law" of the agency, and are thus of use to courts and taxpayers as a research tool providing a substantially consistent interpretation of the I.R.C. *See id.* at 683.

However, under the Treasury Regulations, GCMs do not establish precedent, and taxpayers cannot cite GCMs as authority against the United States in litigation. *See* 26 C.F.R. § 1.6661-3(b)(2) (1997) (unlike Revenue Rulings, GCMs are not "authority"). This is precisely what the trustees seek to do. GCMs may be looked to as a research tool by any interested court or party, but they are not authority in this court. *See Stichting* [97-2 USTC ¶50,917], 129 F.3d at 200. When a reasonable regulation has been instituted pursuant to proper administrative procedures, federal courts must accord deference to the regulation. *See Chevron v. Natural Resources Defense Council*, 467 U.S. 837, 843 (1984); *Cohen v. Brown University*, 101 F.3d 155, 195 (1st Cir. 1996), *cert. denied*, 117 S. Ct. 1469 (1997). We are thus precluded from considering GCMs in the manner urged by the trustees.[5]

Finding no definitive resolution of this issue in the text or history of § 501(c)(5), the Treasury Regulations, or precedential Revenue Rulings, we look at congressional treatment of jointly-controlled pension funds under other Internal Revenue Code provisions to see if the trustees' interpretation of the 501(c)(5) exemption is consistent with pronouncements about the taxation and regulation of such funds. Unfortunately for the taxpayers in this case, it is not.

In the Revenue Act of 1962, Pub. L. No. 87-834, § 25, 76 Stat. 960, Congress enacted a provision that allowed a particular pension plan to qualify retroactively under § 401(a). In so doing, the Senate Finance Committee stated that "[u]nder present law, a pension trust is qualified for income tax exemption only if it meets certain requirements relating to coverage of employees and nondiscrimination of contributions or

5. [5] In *Morganbesser v. United States* [93-1 USTC ¶50,082], 984 F.2d 560 (2d Cir. 1993), the Second Circuit addressed the same issue presented by this case and *Stichting*. The panel, with one judge dissenting, held that a jointly-controlled pension fund *was* entitled to a tax exemption under § 501(c)(5) as a "labor organization." The majority decision, however, relied on GCMs. As explained above, we cannot follow this course. *See also Stichting* [97-2 USTC ¶50,917], 129 F.3d at 200 (declining to follow *Morganbesser*'s reliance on "the precedentially dubious" GCMs). Furthermore, as the D.C. Circuit noted in *Stichting*, *id.*, *Morganbesser* did not mention the Supreme Court's directive that "[e]xemptions from taxation are not to be implied ... they must be unambiguously proved." *United States v. Wells Fargo Bank* [88-1 USTC ¶13,759], 485 U.S. 351, 354 (1988).

benefits." S. Rep. No. 87-1881, at 300, *reprinted in* 1962-3 C.B. 707, 837. This statement implies that Congress intended § 401(a) as the only umbrella under which pension trusts might shield themselves from tax liability.

Congress again spoke on this issue when enacting ERISA. The House Ways and Means Committee explained that employer-provided plans are "required to comply with the new coverage, vesting, and funding standards in order to qualify for the favored tax treatment [i.e. tax exemption] under the Internal Revenue Code." H.R. Rep. No. 93-807 at 3, 31, *reprinted in* 1974-3 C.B. (Supp.) 238, 266. At the very least, these statements reveal that Congress was not anticipating a section 501(c)(5) "end run" around § 401(a)'s requirements for employer-provided pension funds. At most, these statements imply an affirmative intent to exclude these plans from the 501(c)(5) exemption.

Furthermore, ERISA sections 413(a) & (b) specifically include multiemployer-funded pension plans established pursuant to collective bargaining agreements as entities covered under the regulation. It is hard to imagine that Congress would have painstakingly designed ERISA, choosing to use a conditional tax exemption as the primary incentive to ensure compliance, and at the same time would offer tax exemptions to all jointly controlled pension plans as "labor organizations" under § 501(c)(5). As the Supreme Court has stated, federal courts are "reluctant to tamper with an enforcement scheme crafted with such evident care as the one in ERISA" and we see no need to do so here. *Massachusetts Mut. Life Ins. Co. v. Russell*, 473 U.S. 134, 147 (1985).

Presented with no authority which clearly establishes an exemption under 501(c)(5) for the plan trusts at issue, and recognizing that such an interpretation would be at odds with, if not directly contrary to, the statements Congress has made regarding the proper taxation of such entities, we conclude that the trustees have failed to "unambiguously" establish their entitlement to a tax exemption. *See also Stichting*, 129 F.3d at 200 (reaching the same result).[6]

Conclusion

For the reasons stated herein, the order of the district court is *affirmed.*

Note

The Treasury Department eventually adopted the proposed regulation discussed in footnote 6 of *Tupper*, but it did not otherwise address the general criticism that IRC § 501(c)(5) provides no real standard or rule, or that the IRS has issued such a wide variety of revenue rulings (not implicating organizations disqualified under

6. [6] It is worth noting that Treasury Department Regulations have been proposed which would clarify the meaning of "labor organization" under § 501(c)(5). *See* 62 Fed. Reg. 40,447, 40,449 (1997) (adding proposed 26 C.F.R. § 1.501(c)(5)-1(b)(1)). Under the proposed regulations, pension funds would be explicitly excluded from the exemption. Thus, the primary dispute in *Stichting*, *Morganbesser*, and the present case may soon be definitively resolved.

Treas. Reg. § 1.501(c)(5)-1(b)) as to make any other substantive generalization nearly impossible. The only thing for sure is that the organization may not allow private inurement. It should be noted, though, that the prohibition against excess benefit transactions discussed in Chapter 11 does not apply to 501(c)(5) organizations.

In *Stichting Pensioenfonds*, mentioned in *Tupper* (footnote 4), the court discussed the unhelpful legislative history and the relationship between ERISA and IRC § 501(c)(5):

> Section 501(c)(5) of the Internal Revenue Code exempts labor organizations from taxation. The statute itself, though, does not provide a definition for the term "labor organization," and, therefore, the Court must look beyond the plain language of § 501(c)(5) to determine whether the Fund is a labor organization as that term is understood under § 501(c)(5).
>
> Neither does the legislative history of § 501(c)(5) and other relevant tax statutes provide the Court much help in determining a useful definition of labor organizations for purposes of applying § 501(c)(5). Congress first exempted labor organizations from the general corporate tax levied by the Tariff Act of 1909. Tariff Act of 1909, ch. 6, § 38, 36 Stat. 113. The phrase "labor organization" was included in the bill sent to the Senate Finance Committee, but the bill emerged from committee without it. 44 Cong. Rec. 4148 (1909). The committee found the phrase to be unnecessary, because labor organizations were believed to be covered by the wording "fraternal beneficiary societies, . . . operating under the lodge system and providing for the payment of life, sick, accident, and other benefits." 44 Cong. Rec. at 4148–49.
>
> Several labor unions, however, were concerned that the existing "beneficiary societies" language did not cover them since they did not provide life, sick, accident, and other benefits to their members. See e.g., 44 Cong. Rec. at 4154 (concern of the Brotherhood of Local Firemen that their organization would not be exempt). The phrase "labor organization" consequently was added to the statute to cover organizations that do not "make such provisions, and are not organized for those purposes." 44 Cong. Rec. at 4155. When the first income tax was instituted in 1913 under the Sixteenth Amendment, the phrase "labor organizations" was included with exempt entities. Tariff Act of 1913, ch. 16, § 11(G), 38 Stat. 172. This language has remained unchanged in every major revision since that time. . . .
>
> While far from determinative, this legislative history provides no support for the Fund's claim that the phrase "labor organization" encompasses a pension fund that exists only to provide retirement benefits for its members. In fact, the legislative history shows that the term "labor organizations" was added to the 1909 Tariff Act to cover entities that did not provide monetary benefits, but served other functions concerning the welfare of workers. The drafters more likely found that the provision of monetary

benefits was not a defining function of a labor organization, but, rather, was an activity engaged in by some labor organizations and not by others. On the other hand, the legislative history equally fails to prove that an association which only provides monetary benefits to its members cannot be a tax-exempt labor organization. The legislative history thus provides little help in defining "labor organizations."

* * *

The regulation promulgated by the IRS under this statute provides a brief description of a labor organization. It states:

> The organizations contemplated by section 501(c)(5) as entitled to exemption from income taxation are those which:
>
> (1) Have no net earnings inuring to the benefit of any member, and
>
> (2) Have as their objects the betterment of conditions of those engaged in such pursuits, the improvement of the grade of their products, and the development of a higher degree of efficiency in their respective occupations.

Treas. Reg. § 1.501(c)(5)-1(a). While traditional labor unions clearly fall within this definition, it is much less clear which nonunion entities constitute labor organizations under this regulation.

In this case, the "inurement" requirement of paragraph (1) is satisfied by the Fund because payments do not discriminate between similarly situated employees. The Court concludes, however, that the plaintiff has not shown that it meets the requirements of paragraph (2) of the regulation. The clauses within paragraph (2) are connected by an "and," which instructs that all three characteristics must be true of an organization in order to be found as a labor organization.

While the Fund, in providing retirement benefits, has as its object the betterment of the conditions of the employees, it does not have as its object the improvement of the grade of their products, nor the development of a higher degree of efficiency. In fact, the Fund has no authority to represent employees in the collective bargaining process, but, rather, has the limited authority to invest and manage the available funds to ensure the solvency of the pension fund, and to pay benefits to its members according to the rules governing it. Therefore, the regulation, on its face, excludes the Fund from classification as a tax-exempt labor organization.

* * *

E. Allowing Retirement Plans With Few Connections to Traditional Labor Organizations to Qualify for Tax Exemption as Labor Organizations Would Undermine the Legislative Intent of ERISA.

Judge Minor and the IRS have argued that granting exemptions to independent employee-funded retirement funds under § 501(c)(5) undermines the legislative intent of ERISA and opens the floodgates to pension plans wishing to avoid § 401(a) requirements while still retaining tax exemption. The *Morganbesser* majority and the plaintiff here dismiss this argument, asserting that an exemption under § 401(a) is still more favorable than an exemption under § 501(c)(5), and, thus, tax-exemption under § 501(c)(5) will not induce plans to avoid the rigorous requirements under ERISA.

The Court agrees that an exemption under § 401(a) is more favorable than an exemption under § 501(c)(5). Where a plan fails to qualify for an ERISA exemption, an employer may not immediately deduct its contributions and employees must immediately report contributions made on their behalf as income. See I.R.C. §§ 402(b), 404(a). The loss of those advantages when a plan does not comply with ERISA, however, is felt by the beneficiaries and the employer. There is no enforcement tool applicable to the plan itself if an exemption under § 501(c)(5) is allowed for such plans. *Morganbesser*, 984 F.2d at 567 (Minor, J., dissenting). The Court agrees with the *Morganbesser* dissent that Congress most likely did not seek to establish the weaker set of inducements for compliance with ERISA. ERISA is a proactive statute designed to encourage plans to adopt its rigorous requirements. If the Tax Code allows the § 501(c)(5) exemption for employer-funded plans, the plans may purposefully discriminate among employees, or fail in other ways to qualify under § 401(a), and still realize tremendous benefits as a tax-exempt organization. In discrimination cases, especially, sheltering retirement plans behind § 501(c)(5) frustrates congressional intent, and should not be permitted.

The following fact patterns are from various revenue rulings issued over the years. In each case, explain whether the organization qualifies for exemption under IRC 501(c)(5):

a. An apprenticeship committee was organized for the purpose of establishing standards of employment concerning apprentices in various skilled crafts. The committee establishes standards as to the appropriate wages to be paid the apprentices, the amount of time to be spent under a journeyman in learning a particular phase of work, and the number of apprentices who shall be employed in a trade by an employer. The committee aids in adjusting and settling disputes between the employer and the apprentice. The committee also establishes or cooperates with local boards of education in establishing supplemental classroom instruction pertaining to the apprentice's vocation. Committees of this type have been established pursuant to collective bargaining agreements or have been promoted by state encouragement of cooperation between employer and employee groups and are usually composed of an equal number of employer and employee representatives. They are organized in various forms, such as, corporations, associations, and trusts. Their operational expenses are met by various methods of financing, primarily by contributions from the employers and the labor union, although funds may be solicited from the public. These committees, whether established pursuant to state law or pursuant to a collective bargaining agreement, are the same.

b. The organization was formed to better the conditions of its members who are all engaged in a particular trade. It carries out its purposes by working for better wages and working conditions. Most of the members are employees. However, some members work for themselves rather than for the employers with whom the organization negotiates. The organization states that the self-employed are members since they believe that the organization's activities better their conditions.

c. The organization was formed to advance the interests of its members who are drivers, trainers, and horse owners engaged in harness racing in a specific geographic area. Most of the trainers and drivers are independent contractors and are self-employed . . . rather than employees. In addition to agreed amounts received from horse owners for feeding, caretaking, exercising, and managing a horse, or for driving a horse, the trainer and driver of a winning horse each get a percentage of the owner's purse. The organization negotiates with the operators of area raceways for larger purses, better hours, and safer operating conditions.

d. The organization was formed to promote the welfare of law enforcement officers by advancing programs for improved working conditions and mitigating the hazards inherent in law enforcement. It represents its members in matters of wages, hours of labor, and economic benefits. In addition, as a minor activity, it provides funds for counsel in cases where legal action is brought against members in connection with the performance of their official duties. Before any funds are distributed, a special committee evaluates the case to determine whether it involves the performance of official duties within the accepted standards of the profession. Income is derived from membership dues, and disbursements are made for office costs, employees' salaries, and legal fees.

e. A company was organized to provide employment to members of a certain labor union exempt from Federal income tax under section 501(c)(5) of the Code. It operates a business as its only activity and is owned and controlled by the union to which it turns over all of its profits.

f. The organization was formed to provide financial assistance to the members of a labor union who are involved in strikes or lockouts. It is controlled by the executive board of the union. Funds are derived from dues paid by members and disbursements are made to pay benefits to members who are not working as a result of a strike or lockout.

B. Agricultural and Horticultural Organizations

Tax exemption for agricultural and horticultural organizations, as might be expected, is not as controversial as the exemption for labor organizations. At one time, there was an issue as to whether the harvest of the seas was considered an agricultural pursuit. Congress resolved that issue with the enactment of § 501(g), which defines "agricultural" to include the harvesting of aquatic resources. Still, some of the rulings with regard to agricultural organizations demonstrate that there is a limit to the private benefit allowed with an exemption. In Revenue Ruling 66-105, 1966-1 C.B. 145, for example, the Service denied tax exemption after holding that the organization was being used as a direct marketing device for its cattle rancher members rather than to improve agricultural products or techniques. The demonstrated principle is that the permissible private benefit is only that which accrues to the labor, agricultural or horticultural sciences, and the conditions under which participants in those fields endeavor (from which the members may secondarily benefit). If the organization exists to primarily benefit the members and only secondarily to further or improve the science of labor, agriculture, or horticulture, it is denied tax exemption. Of course, stating the distinction is often easier than proving or demonstrating the distinction.

Chapter 22

Business Leagues

CODE: § 501(c)(6)

REG.: § 1.501(c)(6)-1

The exemption for business leagues, chambers of commerce, real estate boards, boards of trade, and professional football leagues is essentially an expanded version of the exemption provided to labor and agricultural organizations. The relevant, intertwined issues are: (1) whether the organization exists for the betterment of a whole industry, as opposed to a single or limited number of participants in the industry—is the organization representative of an entire industry or of a private party within that industry? and (2) whether the organization is engaged in a normal commercial activity rather than a noncommercial activity that works to the advantage of commercial activities conducted by others, including its own members. The following cases demonstrate how these issues arise in everyday practice.

National Muffler Dealers Assn., Inc. v. United States

440 U.S. 472 (1979)

MR. JUSTICE BLACKMUN delivered the opinion of the Court.

Petitioner, National Muffler Dealers Association, Inc. (Association), as its name indicates, is a trade organization for muffler dealers. The issue in this case is whether the Association, which has confined its membership to dealers franchised by Midas International Corporation (Midas), and its activities to the Midas muffler business, and thus is not "industrywide," is a "business league" entitled to the exemption from federal income tax provided by § 501(c)(6) of the Internal Revenue Code of 1954, 26 U.S.C. § 501(c)(6).

I

In 1971, during a contest for control of Midas, Midas muffler franchisees organized the Association under the New York Not-for-Profit Corporation Law. The Association's purpose was to establish a group to negotiate unitedly with Midas management. Its principal activity has been to serve as a bargaining agent for its members in dealing with Midas. It has enrolled most Midas franchisees as members.[1] The Association was successful in negotiating a new form of franchise agree-

1. [1] The trial court, in focusing on the Association's fiscal years ended November 30 in 1971, 1972, and 1973, found that 290 franchised Midas dealers were members of the Association. App. 18a.

ment which prevents termination during its 20-year life except for cause. It also persuaded Midas to eliminate its requirement that a customer pay a service charge when a guaranteed Midas muffler is replaced. And the Association sponsors group insurance programs, holds an annual convention, and publishes a newsletter for members.

The Association sought the exemption from federal income tax which § 501(c)(6) provides for a "business league." Treasury Regulation § 1.501 (c)(6)-1 states that the activities of a tax exempt business league "should be directed to the improvement of business conditions of one or more lines of business." In view of that requirement, the Internal Revenue Service initially rejected the Association's exemption application, stating that § 501(c)(6) "would not apply to an organization that is not industry wide."

The Association then (in October 1972) amended its bylaws and eliminated the requirement that its members be Midas franchisees. Despite that amendment, and despite the Association's announced purpose to promote the interests of individuals "engaged in business as muffler dealers," it neither recruited nor acquired a member who was not a Midas franchisee.

In 1974, after the Internal Revenue Service had issued a final rejection of the Association's exemption application, the Association filed income tax returns for its fiscal years 1971, 1972, and 1973, and, thereafter, claims for refund of the taxes paid with those returns. The 1972 claim was formally denied. Subsequent to that denial, and after more than six months had passed since the filing of the 1971 and 1973 claims, see § 6532 (a)(1) of the 1954 Code, the Association brought this suit in the United States District Court for the Southern District of New York asserting its entitlement to a refund for the income taxes paid for the three fiscal years. The District Court found: "There is no evidence that [the Association] confers a benefit on the muffler industry as a whole or upon muffler franchisees as a group." It then concluded that "Midas Muffler franchisees do not constitute a 'line of business,' "and held that the Association was not a "business league" within the meaning of § 501(c)(6), and thus was not entitled to the claimed refund.

The United States Court of Appeals for the Second Circuit affirmed. 565 F.2d 845 (1977). It confronted what it called the "lexicographer's task of deciding what is meant by a 'business league.'" *Id.*, at 846. Finding no direct guidance in the statute, the court applied the maxim *noscitur a sociis* ("[it] is known from its associates," BLACK'S LAW DICTIONARY 1209 (Rev. 4th ed. 1968)), and looked "at the general characteristics of the organizations" with which business leagues were grouped in the statute, that is, chambers of commerce and boards of trade. The court agreed with the Service's determination, in § 1.501 (c)(6)-1 of the regulations, that a business league is an "organization of the same general class as a chamber of commerce or

---

This was about 50% of the dealers. By the time of the trial in 1975, the Association included almost 80% of all Midas dealers. *Id.*, at 49a.

board of trade." Reasoning that it was the "manifest intention" of Congress by the statute "to provide an exemption for organizations which promote some aspect of the general economic welfare rather than support particular private interests," the court concluded that the "line of business" requirement set forth in the regulations is "well suited to assuring that an organization's efforts do indeed benefit a sufficiently broad segment of the business community." 565 F.2d, at 846–847. The court noted that any success the Association might have in improving business conditions for Midas franchisees, and any advantage it might gain through tax exemption, would come at the expense of the rest of the muffler industry, and concluded that the Association's purpose was too narrow to satisfy the line-of-business test.

The court explicitly refused to follow the decision in *Pepsi-Cola Bottlers' Assn.* v. *United States*, 369 F.2d 250 (C.A.7 1966). There, the Seventh Circuit, by a divided vote, had upheld the exempt status of an association composed solely of bottlers of a single brand of soft drink. It did so on the ground that the line-of-business requirement unreasonably narrowed the statute.

We granted certiorari to resolve this conflict. 436 U.S. 903 (1978).

II

The statute's term "business league" has no well-defined meaning or common usage outside the perimeters of § 501 (c)(6). It is a term "so general . . . as to render an interpretive regulation appropriate." *Helvering* v. *Reynolds Co.*, 306 U.S. 110, 114 (1939). In such a situation, this Court customarily defers to the regulation, which, "if found to 'implement the congressional mandate in some reasonable manner,' must be upheld." *United States* v. *Cartwright*, 411 U.S. 546, 550 (1973), quoting *United States* v. *Correll*, 389 U.S. 299, 307 (1967).

We do this because "Congress has delegated to the [Secretary of the Treasury and his delegate, the] Commissioner [of Internal Revenue], not to the courts, the task of prescribing 'all needful rules and regulations for the enforcement' of the Internal Revenue Code. 26 U.S.C. § 7805(a)." *United States* v. *Correll*, 389 U.S., at 307. That delegation helps ensure that in "this area of limitless factual variations," *ibid.*, like cases will be treated alike. It also helps guarantee that the rules will be written by "masters of the subject," *United States* v. *Moore*, 95 U.S. 760, 763 (1878), who will be responsible for putting the rules into effect.

In determining whether a particular regulation carries out the congressional mandate in a proper manner, we look to see whether the regulation harmonizes with the plain language of the statute, its origin, and its purpose. A regulation may have particular force if it is a substantially contemporaneous construction of the statute by those presumed to have been aware of congressional intent. If the regulation dates from a later period, the manner in which it evolved merits inquiry. Other relevant considerations are the length of time the regulation has been in effect, the reliance placed on it, the consistency of the Commissioner's interpretation, and the degree of scrutiny Congress has devoted to the regulation during subsequent re-enactments of the statute.

III

A

The history of Treas. Reg. § 1.501 (c)(6)-1 and its "line of business" requirement provides much that supports the Government's view that the Association, which is not tied to a particular community and is not industrywide, should not be exempt. The exemption for "business leagues" from federal income tax had its genesis at the inception of the modern income tax system with the enactment of the Tariff Act of October 3, 1913, 38 Stat. 114, 172. In response to a House bill which would have exempted, among others, "labor, agricultural, or horticultural organizations," the Senate Finance Committee was urged to add an exemption that would cover nonprofit business groups. Both the Chamber of Commerce of the United States and the American Warehousemen's Association, a trade association for warehouse operators, submitted statements to the Committee. The Chamber's spokesman said:

> "The commercial organization of the present day is not organized for selfish purposes, and performs broad patriotic and civic functions. Indeed, it is one of the most potent forces in each community for the improvement of physical and social conditions. While its original reason for being is commercial advancement, it is *not in the narrow sense of advantage to the individual, but in the broad sense of building up the trade and commerce of the community as a whole. . . .*" (Emphasis added.) Briefs and Statements on H. R. 3321 filed with the Senate Committee on Finance, 63d Cong., 1st Sess., 2002 (1913) (hereinafter Briefs and Statements).

The Chamber's written submission added:

> "These organizations receive their income from dues . . . which business men pay that they *may receive in common with all other members of their communities or of their industries* the benefits of cooperative study of local development, of civic affairs, of industrial resources, and of local, national, and international trade." (Emphasis added.) *Id.*, at 2003.

The Committee was receptive to the idea, but rejected the Chamber's proposed broad language which would have exempted all "commercial organizations not organized for profit." Instead, the Committee, and ultimately the Congress, provided that the tax would not apply to "business leagues, nor to chambers of commerce or boards of trade, not organized for profit or no part of the net income of which inures to the benefit of the private stockholder or individual." Tariff Act of Oct. 3, 1913, § IIG (a), 38 Stat. 172.

Congress has preserved this language, with few modifications, in each succeeding Revenue Act.

The Commissioner of Internal Revenue had little difficulty determining which organizations were "chambers of commerce" or "boards of trade" within the meaning of the statute. Those terms had commonly understood meanings before the statute was enacted.[2] "Business league," however, had no common usage, and in 1919 the Commissioner undertook to define its meaning by regulation. The initial definition was the following:

> "A business league is an association of persons having some common business interest, which limits its activities to work for such common interest and does not engage in a regular business of a kind ordinarily carried on for profit. Its work need not be similar to that of a chamber of commerce or board of trade." Treas. Regs. 45, Art. 518 (1919).

This language, however, proved too expansive to identify with precision the class of organizations Congress intended to exempt. The Service began to cut back on the last sentence of the material just quoted when, in 1924, the Solicitor of Internal Revenue invoked *noscitur a sociis* to deny an exemption requested by a stock exchange. He reasoned that, while a stock exchange conceivably could come within the definitions of a "business league" or "board of trade," it lacked the characteristics that a "business league," "chamber of commerce," and "board of trade" share in common and that form the basis for the exemption. Congress must have used those terms, he said, "to indicate organizations of the same general class, having for their primary purpose the promotion of business welfare." The primary purpose of the stock exchange, by contrast, was "to afford facilities to a limited class of people for the transaction of their private business." L. O. 1121, III-1 Cum. Bull. 275, 280–281 (1924). The regulation was then amended so as specifically to exclude stock exchanges. T. D. 3746, IV-2 Cum. Bull. 77 (1925).

In 1927, the Board of Tax Appeals, in a reviewed decision with some dissents, applied the principle of *noscitur a sociis* and denied a claimed "business league" exemption to a corporation organized by associations of insurance companies to provide printing services for member companies. *Uniform Printing & Supply Co. v. Commissioner*, 9 B. T. A. 251, *aff'd*, 33 F.2d 445 (CA7), cert. denied, 280 U.S. 591 (1929). In 1928, Congress revised the statute so as specifically to exempt real estate boards that local revenue agents had tried to tax. The exclusion of stock exchanges, however, was allowed to remain.

In 1929, the Commissioner incorporated the principle of *noscitur a sociis* into the regulation itself. The sentence, "Its work need not be similar to that of a chamber of commerce or board of trade," was dropped and was replaced with the following qualification:

> "It is an organization of the same general class as a chamber of commerce or board of trade. Thus, its activities should be directed to the improvement of business conditions or to the promotion of the general objects of one or

2. [10] Webster's New International Dictionary 245, 366 (1913), defined the terms as follows:

> board of trade: "In the United States, a body of men appointed for the advancement and protection of business interests. Cf. chamber of commerce."

> more lines of business as distinguished from the performance of particular services for individual persons." Treas. Regs. 74, Art. 528 (1929).

This language has stood almost without change for half a century through several re-enactments and one amendment of the statute.

During that period, the Commissioner and the courts have been called upon to define "line of business" as that phrase is employed in the regulation. True to the representation made by the Chamber of Commerce, in its statement to the Senate in 1913, that benefits would be received "in common with all other members of their communities or of their industries," *supra*, at 478, the term "line of business" has been interpreted to mean either an entire industry, see, *e.g., American Plywood Assn.* v. *United States*, 267 F. Supp. 830 (W.D. Wash. 1967); *National Leather & Shoe Finders Assn.* v. *Commissioner*, 9 T.C. 121 (1947), or all components of an industry within a geographic area, see, *e.g., Commissioner* v. *Chicago Graphic Arts Federation, Inc.*, 128 F.2d 424 (C.A.7 1942); *Crooks* v. *Kansas City Hay Dealers' Assn.*, 37 F.2d 83 (C.A.8 1929); *Washington State Apples, Inc.* v. *Commissioner*, 46 B. T. A. 64 (1942).

Most trade associations fall within one of these two categories. The Commissioner consistently has denied exemption to business groups whose membership and purposes are narrower. Those who have failed to meet the "line of business" test, in the view of the Commissioner, include groups composed of businesses that market a single brand of automobile,[3] or have licenses to a single patented product,[4] or bottle one type of soft drink. The Commissioner has reasoned that these groups are not designed to better conditions in an entire industrial "line," but, instead, are devoted to the promotion of a particular product at the expense of others in the industry.[5]

In short, while the Commissioner's reading of § 501(c)(6) perhaps is not the only possible one, it does bear a fair relationship to the language of the statute, it reflects the views of those who sought its enactment, and it matches the purpose they articulated. It evolved as the Commissioner administered the statute and attempted to give to a new phrase a content that would reflect congressional design. The regulation has stood for 50 years, and the Commissioner infrequently but consistently has interpreted it to exclude an organization like the Association that is not industry-wide. The Commissioner's view therefore merits serious deference.

3. [16] Rev. Rul. 67-77, 1967-1 Cum. Bull. 138, superseding I. T. 4053, 1951-2 Cum. Bull. 53 (to the same effect under prior law). Cf. Rev. Rul. 55-444, 1955-2 Cum. Bull. 258 (industrywide advertising program exempt).

4. [17] Rev. Rul. 58-294, 1958-1 Cum. Bull. 244.

5. [[19] *See* Rev. Rul. 76-400, 1976-2 Cum. Bull. 153, 154. *Cf.* Rev. Rul. 61-177, 1961-2 Cum. Bull. 117 (organization to improve members' competitive standing in various lines of business through lobbying exempt). . . .

B

The Association contends, however, that the regulation is unreasonable because it unduly narrows the statute. This argument has three aspects: First, the Association argues that this Court need not defer to the regulation because, instead of being a contemporaneous construction of the statute, it is actually contrary to the regulation first in force from 1919 to 1929. Second, it argues that the addition in 1966 of professional football leagues to the statutory list of exempt organizations makes a new view of *noscitur a sociis* appropriate. Third, it contends that, if the maxim applies here, the Court should reach out beyond § 501 (c)(6) and take into account the fact that the Association's bargaining function is much like that of a labor organization which would be exempt under § 501 (c)(5). We consider these arguments in turn.

1. As noted above, the Commissioner's first definition of "business league" provided that its work "*need not* be similar to that of a chamber of commerce or board of trade." Treas. Regs. 45, Art. 518 (1919) (emphasis added). The association contends that, because this language differs from the language that replaced it in 1929, the latter is not a "contemporaneous construction" to which this Court should defer, *Bingler* v. *Johnson*, 394 U.S. 741, 749–750 (1969), but is instead an arbitrary narrowing of the statute. It is said that the earlier language rejects the rule of *noscitur a sociis*, and that it is the earlier language that should be treated by the Court as truly authoritative.

Contemporaneity, however, is only one of many considerations that counsel courts to defer to the administrative interpretation of a statute. It need not control here. Nothing in the regulations or case law, see *Produce Exchange Stock Clearing Assn.* v. *Helvering*, 71 F.2d 142 (C.A.2 1934), directly explains the regulatory shift. We do know, however, that the change in 1929 incorporated an interpretation thought necessary to match the statute's construction to the original congressional intent. We would be reluctant to adopt the rigid view that an agency may not alter its interpretation in light of administrative experience. In *Helvering* v. *Wilshire Oil Co.*, 308 U.S. 90, 101 (1939), the Court acknowledged the need for flexibility and applied a 1929 regulation to a taxpayer even though the taxpayer had acted in reliance on an opposite interpretation incorporated in an earlier regulation. Here, where there is no claim that the Association ever relied on the Commissioner's prior view, the case for accepting the later regulation as authoritative is even stronger.

2. In 1966, Congress amended § 501(c)(6) by adding to the list of exempt organizations "professional football leagues (whether or not administering a pension fund for football players)." Act of Nov. 8, 1966, Pub. L. 89-800, § 6 (a), 80 Stat. 1515. The Association contends that a professional football league is not of the same general character as a chamber of commerce or board of trade, and that a new view of *noscitur a sociis* is appropriate, one that would include the Association within the exemption. This, of course, is the complement to the first argument.

Nothing in the legislative history of the amendment, however, indicates that Congress objected to or endeavored to change the Commissioner's position as to the class of organizations included in § 501 (c)(6). The purpose of the amendment was to forestall any claim that a football league's pension plan would be considered inurement of benefits to a private individual. Congressman Mills stated flatly that "no inference is intended by this change as to the application of section 501 (c)(6) to other types of organizations." 112 Cong. Rec. 28228 (1966).

Nor does the Association share characteristics in common with a professional football league that would necessarily entitle it to exemption even if a new view of *noscitur a sociis* were applied. The teams in a football league depend on mutual cooperation to promote a common business purpose. They need a league to provide uniform rules of play. A franchisee, however, does not need another franchisee in order to bargain with its franchisor, even though joint bargaining may make them more powerful. Also, it is not without significance that the 1966 amendment was part of a large statutory package which paved the way for a merger which created an "industrywide" professional football league. It can hardly be read to evince a congressional intent that other associations that are not industrywide should be afforded tax-exempt status.

3. The Association says that, if *noscitur a sociis* is to apply, then sound policy considerations support the reasonableness of searching for *socii* beyond the confines of § 501(c)(6). The Association draws a comparison to other exempt organizations, particularly labor unions that are exempt under § 501(c)(5). The Association says that, like a labor union, it exists to redress unequal bargaining power in the marketplace. Some States have special legislation protecting franchisee associations. Employer bargaining associations that deal with unions in a particular industry are exempt "business leagues." Rev. Rul. 65-14, 1965-1 Cum. Bull. 236, 238. It is argued that the Association meets all the regulation's requirements except the line-of-business test. Applying the thin logic of that requirement to tax a nonprofit organization like the Association, it is said, unreasonably will discourage joint action to improve shared business conditions and will yield only scant revenue to the Treasury. The Association concludes that it would be appropriate now to expand the "business league" exemption to embrace the modern phenomenon of franchisee associations that was unknown in 1913.

These arguments are not unlike those that persuaded the Senate to add the business-league exemption to the 1913 bill. See Briefs and Statements 2002–2003. Perhaps Congress would find them forceful today. The Association, however, needs more than a plausible policy argument to prevail here. Just last Term, in *Fulman v. United States*, 434 U.S. 528, 536 (1978), the Court upheld a regulation which had a "reasonable basis" in the statutory history, even though the taxpayer's challenge to its policy had "logical force." *Id.*, at 534, 536, and 540 (dissenting opinion). The choice among reasonable interpretations is for the Commissioner, not the courts. Certainly, *noscitur a sociis* does not compel the Commissioner to draw comparisons that go beyond the text of the Senate's amendment to the 1913 bill, particularly when the Senate Finance Committee, in drafting the amendment, rejected a broad proposal modeled on the same labor exemption the Association now wishes to incorporate.

In sum, the "line of business" limitation is well grounded in the origin of § 501 (c)(6) and in its enforcement over a long period of time. The distinction drawn here, that a tax exemption is not available to aid one group in competition with another within an industry, is but a particular manifestation of an established principle of tax administration. Because the Association has not shown that either the regulation or the Commissioner's interpretation of it fails to "implement the congressional mandate in some reasonable manner," *United States* v. *Correll*, 389 U.S., at 307, the Association's claim for a § 501(c)(6) exemption must be denied.

The judgment of the Court of Appeals is affirmed.

Questions

1. Why didn't National Muffler Dealers seek tax exemption under § 501(c)(5)? It engaged in a form of collective bargaining with Midas, similar to what we might envision of a classic labor union. Did it miss out on an opportunity for tax exemption as a labor organization?

2. In 2015, the National Football League (NFL) voluntarily relinquished its 501(c)(6) status, but it need not have done so under current law. It could have retained the exemption. Does it seem strange that the National Football League (NFL) would be singled out for tax exemption? On what theoretical basis should a professional football league, an organization that charges fairly high prices for everything from the broadcast rights to actual games to jerseys, hats, logos and anything else associated with the game of football, be granted exemption from tax? It should be noted, as well, that while the statute refers only to "professional football Leagues," other professional sports organizations — Major League Baseball, the Professional Golfers Association (PGA), the National Hockey League (NHL), and the Ladies Professional Golf Association (LPGA), to name a few — were also 501(c)(6) organizations. MLB relinquished its 501(c)(6) status in 2007, while the National Basketball Association never actually sought (c)(6) status.

In 2018, Congress considered, but eventually did not pass an amendment to § 501(c)(6) that would have removed tax exemption for professional sports leagues. President Trump, who once owned a football team — the New Jersey Generals — in a league that sought to compete against the NFL, and who (prior to becoming President) sued the NFL for antitrust violations when the United States Football League folded, supported the bill but perhaps not for the reasons it was proposed. President Trump's support for denying tax exempt status to professional sports leagues was, according to one of his Twitter posts, a reaction to the on-field protests made famous by San Francisco Forty-Niner quarterback Colin Kaepernick. Shortly after Kaepernick and other NFL players began kneeling during the playing of the National Anthem in 2016 to protest police brutality against people of color, the President tweeted, "Why is the NFL getting massive tax breaks while at the same time disrespecting our Anthem, Flag and Country? Change tax law!" Of course, the

NFL had given up its 501(c)(6) status two years before the President's tweet. In any event, Congress has never amended § 501(c)(6) to deprive professional sports leagues of exempt status.

Note on Definition of "Business League"

The definition of "Business League" under § 501(c)(6) and Treas. Reg. § 1.501(c)(6)-1 arose again in *National Prime Users Group, Inc. v. United States*, 667 F. Supp. 250 (D. Md. 1987). The taxpayer, an organization that provided communication between Prime Computer, Inc. and companies that used Prime Computer, Inc. equipment, claimed that it was a § 501(c)(6) Business League because its members came from a wide range of businesses and government agencies. The District Court held against the taxpayer, stating:

> In determining whether NPUG improves business conditions in one or more lines of business, as is necessary to qualify for exemption under § 501(c)(6), the Court must look to all of the circumstances of NPUG, including the primary objective of the corporation, its activities, and its membership. By directing its activities to users of Prime Computers, NPUG improves business conditions in segments of the lines of business represented by its members. Only those select businesses within an industry represented by NPUG's members which use Prime products benefit through NPUG's existence. Moreover, the primary objective of NPUG, as is evident in its corporate documents, prior to amendment, its Policy on Commercialism which remains unchanged since 1982, and the consistent focus of its activities, even after the amendments to the corporate documents, is to provide a method for the dissemination of information to and communication among users of Prime. Underlying all of this, of course, is the inherent benefit to Prime in marketing its products. Its activities provide a competitive advantage to Prime, at the expense of other computer manufacturers. No other computer company benefits, except incidentally, through the activities of NPUG. Indeed, NPUG's membership, purposes and activities are virtually identical to an organization denied exemption by the Internal Revenue Service in Revenue Ruling 83-164. There the organization was formed to develop and disseminate information pertaining to the electronic data processing equipment manufactured by the M Corporation. The membership was made up of representatives of diversified businesses that owned, rented or leased computers manufactured by M. As with NPUG, membership was also open to representatives of businesses that did not use M Computers. Conferences constituted the primary activity of the organization, with members of M attending to distribute information relative to M's equipment. The service concluded that the organization's primary activity was to promote the common business interests of users of one particular brand of computers and, therefore, did not qualify for exemption from federal income tax as a business league under § 501(c)(6).

667 F. Supp. 250, 255–56 (D. Md. 1987).

Engineers Club of San Francisco v. United States

791 F.2d 686 (9th Cir. 1986)

Tang, Circuit Judge.

Plaintiff/Appellee, the Engineers Club of San Francisco, filed suit in federal district court seeking reclassification as a business league under IRC § 501(c)(6), 26 U.S.C. § 501(c)(6). A business league classification would entitle Engineers Club to income tax refunds on its unrelated business income for the years 1978–81. The district court held that Engineers Club met the requirements of § 501(c)(6) and qualified as a business league. 609 F. Supp. 519. We reverse.

Facts

Engineers Club is a nonprofit corporation formed in 1912. According to its amended articles of incorporation, Engineers Club's purpose is:

> to provide an organization in which Engineers of all branches of the Profession may come together, and through which they may cooperate and foster the development of the Engineer Profession as a whole in California and incidentally and in aid of such main purpose to acquire by purchase, lease or otherwise and conduct suitable quarters for a meeting place for carrying out such purpose. Membership is open to and composed primarily of professional engineers.

Engineers Club leases space on the top two floors in an office building in downtown San Francisco. The facility consists of a large kitchen, meeting and dining rooms, a bar, a combination game-grill room, and a library-reading room. Administrative offices and storage rooms are located on other floors. The Club is open daily and serves lunch to its members and their guests.

The Club serves its members, and the professional societies to which they belong, by providing meetings and meeting space, logistical support, a location for operations, mailing service, telephone service, storage of records, and other facilities and services. Members of the Club may reserve Club facilities for their own purposes. Club facilities are mostly reserved for meetings and seminars conducted by the professional societies to which members belong. The professional societies are not charged a fee for the use of the facilities but only for the food, liquor or tobacco furnished. The entire membership of a professional society, including non-Club members, is invited to attend such events.

During the years in question, the Club was used by over twenty engineering societies and other organizations associated with the engineering profession. The meetings of the professional organizations are conducted primarily for the purpose of providing professional education and training to their members, and to disseminate information for the benefit of the profession as a whole. Toward this end many of the meetings are held outside normal business hours, or are specially scheduled when the members of the professional societies are in the San Francisco area. A significant number of meetings occur during the lunch hour or at dinner time and include the service of meals and beverages.

Since 1935, the Internal Revenue Service has classified Engineers Club as a "social club," exempt under IRC § 501(c)(7) from some income tax.[6] In November 1981, Engineers Club filed a written request with the IRS seeking reclassification as a business league retroactively to include fiscal years 1978–80. The IRS issued a ruling denying the exempt status in July 1982. The denial was timely protested and hearings took place in January 1983. The IRS issued a letter affirming its denial of the requested status in March 1983. Timely claims for refunds were filed with and denied by the IRS. Engineers Club filed suit in district court for reclassification and income tax refunds.

Discussion

* * *

Analysis

IRC § 501(c)(6) provides an . . . exemption for:

> Business leagues, chambers of commerce, real estate boards, boards of trade, or professional football leagues . . . not organized for profit and no part of the net earnings of which inures to the benefit of any private shareholder or individual.

According to the long-accepted regulatory definition, a "business league" is:

> An association of persons having some common business interest, the purpose of which is to promote such common interest and not to engage in a regular business of a kind ordinarily carried on for profit. It is an organization of the same general class as a chamber of commerce or board of trade. Thus, its activities should be directed to the improvement of business conditions of one or more lines of business as distinguished from the performance of particular services for individual persons. An organization whose purpose is to engage in a regular business of a kind ordinarily carried on for profit, even though the business is conducted on a cooperative basis or produces only sufficient income to be self-sustaining, is not a business league.

Treas. Reg. § 1.501(c)(6)-1 (1983). Having been left undisturbed despite numerous reenactments of identically-worded predecessors to I.R.C. § 501(c)(6), this definition is deemed to have been given the imprimatur of Congress and is thus entitled to the effect of law.

Thus, for an organization to achieve business league status, the requirements as stated in Treas. Reg. § 1.501(c)(6) must be met. Section 1.501(c)(6) requires a business

---

6. [1] Section 501(c)(7) confers tax exempt status but requires tax to be paid on unrelated business income.

league to be an association (1) of persons having a common business interest; (2) whose purpose is to promote the common business interest; (3) not organized for profit; (4) that does not engage in a business ordinarily conducted for profit; (5) whose activities are directed to the improvement of business conditions of one or more lines of business as distinguished from the performance of particular services for individual persons; (6) of the same general class as a chamber of commerce or a board of trade. The government concedes that Engineers Club is: (1) an association of persons having a common business interest; (2) one purpose of which is to promote that common business interest; and (3) the club is not organized for profit. Thus, Engineers Club meets requirements (1)–(3).

The district court based its determination that Engineers Club qualifies as a business league by applying a functional analysis to the "incidentalness" exception of requirement (4), the "Business Ordinarily Conducted for Profit" prohibition. Although a business league should not be engaged in a regular business of a kind ordinarily conducted for a profit, a business activity will not cost an organization its exemption as a business league if the activity is merely incidental to the main purpose of the organization. *Retailers Credit Association v. Commissioner*, 90 F.2d 47, 51, 19 A.F.T.R. (P-H) 800 (9th Cir. 1937).

We assume, without deciding, that the district court was not clearly erroneous in determining that the Engineers Club food and beverage service was incidental to the main purpose of the organization. We find, however, that the district court's "functional" test did not adequately address requirements (5) and (6). Our examination of these latter requirements leads us to conclude that Engineers Club fails to qualify for business league classification.

Particular Services for Individual Persons

Section 1.501(c)(6) requires that a business league be "directed to the improvement of business conditions of one or more lines of business as distinguished from the performance of particular services for individual persons." The district court failed to address this requirement.

In fact the club did and does provide particular services, chiefly food and beverage service, to its individual members. Although we recognize that the food and beverage service also confers a general benefit on the engineering profession, the food and beverage service, and particularly the luncheon trade, is a service performed for individual persons and organizations rather than the engineering profession as a whole.

Organizations frequently fail to qualify for business league status even though their activities confer collective benefits. For example, in *MIB, Inc. v. Commissioner*, 734 F.2d 71 (1st Cir. 1984), an insurance industry established non-profit corporation operated a computer storage and retrieval bank from which each member company could obtain, for a fee, data relevant to insurance sales. This service, the court said, may "confer[] a general benefit upon all members and act[] in the collective interest," *id.* at 78, chiefly as a deterrent to applicant fraud. Nevertheless, the court ruled that the organization failed to qualify as a business league. The collective benefit, although real, did not alter the fact that the rendered services were in form and substance "particular services for individual persons." *Id.* at 78. *See also, Contracting Plumbers Cooperative Restoration Corp. v. United States*, 488 F.2d 684, 688 (2d Cir.), *cert. denied*, 419 U.S. 827 (1974) (repair of city streets, although of benefit to entire trade and to public, nevertheless the "performance of particular service for individual members"); *Steamship Trade Association of Baltimore, Inc. v. Commissioner*, 757 F.2d 1494, 1498 (4th Cir. 1985) (incidental synergy not sufficient to overcome "performance of particular service for individual members" prohibition).

Same General Class as a Chamber of Commerce or a Board of Trade

Section 1.501(c)(6) also states that a business league "is an organization as the same general class as a chamber of commerce or a board of trade." Again, the district court failed to discuss this requirement.

In *MIB, Inc. v. Commissioner*, 734 F.2d at 78 n.5, the court noted:

> In *National Muffler Dealers Ass'n v. United States*, the Supreme Court traced the genesis, and confirmed the significance, of the sentence in the regulation that a business league "is an organization *of the same general class* as a chamber of commerce or board of trade." (Emphasis supplied.) Reference to these organizations is meant, under the principle of *noscitur a sociis*, to limit business league classification to organizations which share the same general characteristics.

The fact that an organization conducts professional programming of its own has long been an important consideration. Rev. Rul. 67-295; Rev. Rul. 70-244; Rev. Rul. 70-641; Rev. Rul. 71-504; Rev. Rul. 70-505. Engineers Club does not itself conduct professional programming; rather, it hosts the professional societies and groups to which its members belong. The absence of Club conducted professional programming suggests that any resemblance to a chamber of commerce or a board of trade is, at best, weak.

Conclusion

The district court's functional test ignores important language of treasury regulation 1.501(c)(6). In order to qualify for a business league classification, each and every requirement of 1.501(c)(6) must be met. On the facts before us, Engineers Club fails to qualify for business league status. The judgment of the district court is therefore

REVERSED.

Questions

Do the following described organizations qualify for exemption under § 501(c)(6)?

1. The association was organized for the mutual exchange of business information among its members; to facilitate the making of business contacts for its members; to encourage all types of trade expansion for the benefit of its members; and to encourage better business relations among its members. The bylaws of the association

provide that the membership shall be composed of persons, firms, associations, and corporations, each representing a different trade, business, occupation, or profession. With respect to the main activities of a member, no member shall be in competition with another member. An applicant shall not be denied membership in the association solely because the applicant's main activity is in conflict with the incidental activities of a member. Where the member is a firm or corporation, it is required to designate one of its executives as its representative in the association. The association holds weekly luncheon meetings; operates a central information service for the exchange, among members, of business information; encourages member cooperation and business efficiency; and operates an information service relating to sales and sales prospects. Each member submits a list of business acquaintances and agrees to furnish to other members letters of introduction to such acquaintances. Each member agrees to keep the association's members informed of business changes that may indicate potential markets for the sale of members' products.

2. The organization was formed to stimulate the development of, with free interchange of information pertaining to, systems and programming of electronic data processing equipment. Its membership is made up of representatives of diversified businesses who own, rent, or lease one or more digital computers, produced by various manufacturers, without regard to the identity of the manufacturer of any such computer. The organization holds semi-annual conferences, lasting from two to four days, at which operational and technical problems relating to computer use are discussed. Nonmembers are invited to attend the conferences and are encouraged to join as members. The organization does not provide counseling or other services to its members with respect to specific individual problems. The speakers at the conferences typically include both members as well as recognized professionals in the computer industry. In addition, manufacturers of computer equipment are invited to attend and disseminate current information relative to their equipment.

3. M was incorporated on February 27, 1987. M's stated purposes in its Articles of Incorporation include the promotion, through educational, cultural, and charitable activities, of understanding, dialogue, and bonds of friendship between the American people and the people of O; and to take other appropriate action in furtherance of such purposes. M's Articles also provide that M shall have three classes of members, academic, individual, and corporate; any individual, corporation, or foundation having an interest in promoting understanding, dialogue, and friendship between the American people and the people of O; the membership fee will be established by the Board of Directors and will be at such a level as to encourage a broad cross section of the interested public to become members. A later amendment to the Articles provided a fourth category of membership: non-profit organizations. M states that it is affiliated to three organizations: N, recognized as exempt under § 501(c)(6); P, recognized as exempt under § 501(c)(3); and Q, an independent non-profit organization, located in another country, whose purpose is to foster and promote commercial relationships between and among firms and businesspersons in that country and O.

In its application for recognition of exemption, M stated that it exists to provide a national focus of concern and resources to enhance relations between America and O; M was established with the participation of American friends of O to bring people and organizations from both countries together through programs and activities that widen cooperation and strengthen the ties of friendship and understanding between the United States and modern O. M stated that its activities would focus on individual and institutional efforts that involve people from both countries and their organizations, and that its efforts would include:

1. Organizing for better cooperation between the two cultures at the regional, state, and local levels in the United States;

2. Establishing cooperative exchanges between experts in the two societies in the scientific, health, and medical care areas;

3. Fostering cooperation between educational institutions in the United States and O to improve mutual understanding at all levels of education;

4. Developing and sponsoring exchange programs in the visual and performing arts;

5. Preparing and implementing programs involving people from both O and America from various fields that will address current social issues confronting both of the societies;

6. Developing a better understanding by people in both O and America of their respective economic systems in order to improve the economic cooperation between the two countries;

7. Preparing and disseminating information to the business communities that will improve the opportunities for trade and investment cooperation between O and the United States;

8. Exploring areas where benefits from technology exchanges can be derived to the mutual benefit of both O and the United States;

9. Organizing exchange programs between O and the United States that will foster a better mutual understanding of the similarities and differences in the two political systems; and

10. Developing programs, both exchange and educational, that will seek to bridge the cultural differences between the two peoples to achieve better cooperation and understanding across a broad spectrum of areas.

M's primary activity is to provide the required certification of origin ("clearing document" for shipment) to American suppliers of goods and services. These American suppliers export their goods and services to O, which requires the certifications, and the Consul General of O has designated M as a certifying agent for goods being exported from the United States to O. M states that it is the only authorized organization in the United States to certify commercial and legal documents related to transactions between the United States and O, and that documents certified by other organizations are not recognized by the Consulates of O in the United States. M's regulations for the certification of commercial and legal documents provide for certain certification fees, which provided more than 95% of M's total revenue for the year under examination.

In reply to a request from the Service for copies of promotional membership materials, M submitted a copy of a directory (first published in the year under examination) and a brochure that it provides to each member and prospective members. The directory states that joint membership in M and N is open on an annual fee basis to corporations and other business entities with commercial interests in O, as well as other interested organizations, institutions, and individuals. In its brochure, which includes a membership application, M states that it is its policy that whenever a client's account reflects a total payment of a certain amount or more, then a certain portion of such payment will be automatically allocated toward that client's annual membership fee. That portion is equal to a full dues payment for all members except corporations.

Chapter 23

Social Clubs

A. Basic Operational Requirements

Code: § 501(c)(7), (i)

Reg.: § 1.501(c)(7)-1

Clubs — country clubs, college fraternities and sororities, athletic clubs, university clubs, garden clubs, ski clubs, ballroom dancing clubs, flying clubs, cooking clubs, book clubs, and so many other groups organized to collectively engage in recreation or pleasure-type activities — are ubiquitous in society. Quite often, these clubs own, control, and generate substantial assets and revenues, primarily from dues, fees, and assessments collected from members. Social clubs are probably the quintessential form of mutual benefit organization. As we discover in the pages that follow, the tax code treats social clubs least favorably of all mutual benefit organizations. It is often asserted that the tax code is essentially a reflection of society's values. What does it say, then, about the worth of recreation and pleasure to our society that the Code would impose tax disadvantages on social clubs that are not imposed on labor unions or business leagues?

Revenue Ruling 58-589

1958-2 C.B. 266

Advice has been requested concerning the criteria or tests to be met in determining whether a social club can qualify for exemption from Federal income tax under the provisions of section 501(a) of the Internal Revenue Code of 1954.

Section 501(c) of the Code describes certain organizations exempt from income tax under section 501(a) and reads, in part, as follows:

> (7) Clubs organized and operated exclusively for pleasure, recreation, and other nonprofitable purposes, no part of the net earnings of which inures to the benefit of any private shareholder.

In making a determination whether an organization comes within the provisions of section 501(c)(7) of the Code, all facts pertaining to its form of organization, method of operation and activities should be considered. An organization must establish (1) that it is a club both organized and operated exclusively for pleasure, recreation and other non-profitable purposes and (2) that no part of its net earnings inures to the benefit of any private shareholder or individual. To meet the first requirement, there must be an established membership of individuals, personal contacts and fellowship. A commingling of the members must play a material part in the life of the organization. . . .

Section 1.501(c)(7)-1 of the Income Tax Regulations relating to the exemption of social clubs under section 501(a) of the Internal Revenue Code of 1954 reads as follows:

> (a) The exemption provided by section 501(a) for organizations described in section 501(c)(7) applies only to clubs which are organized and operated exclusively for pleasure, recreation, and other non-profitable purposes, but does not apply to any club if any part of its net earnings inures to the benefit of any private shareholder. In general, this exemption extends to social and recreational clubs which are supported solely by membership fees, dues, and assessments. However, a club otherwise entitled to exemption will not be disqualified because it raises revenue from members through the use of club facilities or in connection with club activities.
>
> (b) A club which engages in business, such as making its social and recreational facilities available to the general public or by selling real estate, timber, or other products, is not organized and operated exclusively for pleasure, recreation, and other non-profitable purposes, and is not exempt under section 501(a). *Solicitation by advertisement or otherwise for public patronage of its facilities is prima facie evidence that the club is engaging in business* and is not being operated exclusively for pleasure, recreation, or social purposes. However, an incidental sale of property will not deprive a club of its exemption [Italics supplied by Editors.]

It is clear under the foregoing regulations that a club which engages in business, such as making its social and recreational facilities available to the general public or by selling real estate, etc., may not be considered as being organized and operated exclusively for pleasure, recreation or social purposes. It is equally clear that activities by a social club such as the solicitation by advertisements or otherwise of public patronage of its facilities may be adverse to the establishment of an exempt status.

Therefore, to qualify for income tax exemption, a social club should not advertise its facilities for nonmember patronage since this would be prima facie evidence it was engaging in business. Likewise a social club should not engage in any type of business activity for profit which is designed to increase or which could result in an increase in net earnings inuring to the benefit of any shareholder or individual. Net earnings may inure to members in such forms as an increase in services offered by the club without a corresponding increase in dues or other fees paid for club support or as an increase in the club's assets which would be distributable to members upon the dissolution of the club.

However, this is not to say that a club will necessarily lose its exemption if it derives income from transactions with other than its bona fide members and their guests. A club will not be denied exemption merely because it receives income from the general public, that is, persons other than members and their bona fide guests, or because the general public on occasion is permitted to participate in its affairs, provided such participation is incidental to and in furtherance of its general club purposes and it may not be said that income therefrom is inuring to members. This is generally true where the receipts from nonmembers are no more than enough to pay their share of the expense.... Where, however, a club makes its facilities open to the general public and the purpose is to increase its funds for enlarging its club facilities or for otherwise benefiting its members, it is evident that it is not operating as an exempt social club within the intendment of section 501(c)(7) of the Code....

Similarly, where a club engages in income producing transactions which are not a part of the club's purposes, exemption will not be denied because of incidental, trivial or nonrecurrent activities such as sales of property no longer adapted to club purposes. *Santee Club* v. *White*, 87 Fed. (2d) 5. But in order to retain exemption a club must not enter into outside activities with the purpose of deriving profit. Section 1.501(c)(7)-1 of the Income Tax Regulations and *Santee Club* v. *White, supra.* If such income producing activities are other than incidental, trivial or nonrecurrent, it will be considered that they are designed to produce income and will defeat exemption....

Note

Even when § 501(c)(7) required that social clubs be "exclusively" operated for recreation or pleasure, the Service nevertheless allowed (in Revenue Procedure 71-17, set out immediately below) a diversion of up to 5% from purely recreational or pleasurable pursuits. That is, up to 5% of a social club's revenues could be derived from activities other than the provision of related services to members. In 1976, Congress amended § 501(c)(7) by replacing the "exclusively" standard with a "substantially" standard, thereby officially approving of the Service's approach. But Congress went even further than the Service by determining that "substantially" meant that at least 65% (as opposed to 95% required by the Rev. Proc. 71-17) of revenues must be derived from the provision of member services. Neither the statute nor the regulations, however, explicitly contain the requirement that at least 65% of a social club's revenues be derived from the exercise of its exempt social purposes. Instead, those standards are contained in the legislative history set out after Revenue Procedure 71-17. Despite whatever constitutional barriers there may be to legislation by committee report, the legislative history has essentially taken on the role of statutory law and can be ignored only at a social club's peril. Revenue Procedure 71-17 includes certain presumptions, however, that are still relevant to the determination of whether income is derived from the provision of services to members, or from the provision of services to nonmembers (and therefore subject to UBIT as well as affecting the determination of whether the organization is substantially operated for the recreation and pleasure of members).

Revenue Procedure 71-17

1971-1 C.B. 683

Section 1. Scope and Purpose

This Revenue Procedure sets forth guidelines for determining the effect gross receipts derived from use of a social club's facilities by the general public have on the club's exemption from Federal income tax under section 501(c)(7) of the Internal Revenue Code of 1954. These guidelines will be used in connection with the examination of annual returns on Forms 990 and 990-T filed by social clubs. This Revenue Procedure also describes the records required when nonmembers use a club's facilities and the circumstances under which a host-guest relationship will be assumed, which are relevant both for purposes of determining adherence to the exemption requirements and for computing exempt function income under section 512(a)(3) of the Code. However, this Revenue Procedure does not deal with other factors bearing on the exempt status of clubs.

Sec. 2. Background

.01 *General statement.*— Use of a club's facilities by the general public is significant for two reasons. It may indicate the existence of a nonexempt purpose; or, if not of sufficient substantiality to result in loss of exemption, it may make the club liable for unrelated business income tax. The term "general public" as used in this Revenue Procedure means persons other than members of a club or their dependents or guests. The member's spouse is treated as a member.

.02 *Nonexempt purpose.*— In the examination of information returns of clubs, the problem frequently is to determine under what circumstances and to what extent the fact that a club makes its facilities available to the general public is to be relied upon by the Service as indicating the existence of a nonexempt purpose.

Where a club makes its facilities available to the general public to a substantial degree, the club is not operated exclusively for pleasure, recreation, or other nonprofitable purposes.... However, this does not mean that all dealings with the general public are necessarily inconsistent with the club's purposes....

.03 *Unrelated business income tax.*— Clubs have been made subject to the tax on unrelated business income....

The unrelated business taxable income of a club is its gross income (excluding any exempt function income), less the allowable deductions directly connected with the production of the gross income (excluding exempt function income), both computed with the modifications specified. Section 512(a)(3)(A) of the Code.

Sec. 3. Guidelines

.01 *Minimum gross receipts standard.*— A significant factor reflecting the existence of a nonexempt purpose is the amount of gross receipts derived from use of a club's facilities by the general public. As an audit standard, this factor alone will not be relied upon by the Service if annual gross receipts from the general public for such use is $2,500 or less or, if more than $2,500, where gross receipts from the general public for such use is five percent or less of total gross receipts of the organization. This minimum gross receipts standard reflects the audit experience of the Service that gross receipts at or below this level do not, standing alone, usually demonstrate a nonexempt purpose. Even though gross receipts from the general public exceed this standard, it does not necessarily establish that there is a nonexempt purpose. A conclusion that there is a nonexempt purpose will be based on all the facts and circumstances, including but not limited to the gross receipts factor. This audit standard relates only to determinations of exempt status. There is no minimum audit tolerance with respect to unrelated business taxable income.

.02 *Meaning of the term "total gross receipts".* — For the purpose of the minimum gross receipts standard established in section 3.01 above, "total gross receipts" means receipts from normal and usual activities of the club including charges, admissions, membership fees, dues, and assessments. Excluded for this purpose are (a) initiation fees and capital contributions, (b) interest, dividends, rents, and similar receipts, and (c) unusual amounts of income such as amounts derived from nonrecurring sales of club assets.

.03 *Assumption as to status of non-members.*

1. Where a group of eight or fewer individuals, at least one of whom is a member, uses club facilities, it will be assumed for audit purposes that the nonmembers are the guests of the member, provided payment for such use is received by the club directly from the member or the member's employer.

2. Where 75 percent or more of a group using club facilities are members, it will likewise be assumed for audit purposes that the nonmembers in the group are guests of members, provided payment for such use is received by the club directly from one or more of the members or the member's employer.

3. Solely for purposes of section 3.03 1 and 3.03 2, above, payment by a member's employer will be assumed to be for a use that serves a direct business objective of the employee-member.

4. In all other situations, a host/guest relationship will not be assumed but must be substantiated. See section 4, below, for the records required.

Sec. 4. Recordkeeping Requirements

.01 With respect to the situation described in section 3.03 1, above, the records specified in section 4.03, below, need not be maintained by the club. However, the club must maintain adequate records to substantiate that the group was comprised of eight or fewer individuals, that at least one of them was a member, and that payment was received by the club directly from members or their employers. Where payment is made directly to the club by the member, the club is under no obligation to inquire about reimbursement.

.02 With respect to the situation described in section 3.03 2, above, the records specified in section 4.03, below, need not be maintained by the club. However, the club must maintain adequate records to substantiate that 75 percent or more of the persons in the group were, in fact, members of the club at the time of such use and that payment was received by the club directly from members or their employers. Where payment is made directly to the club by the member, the club is under no obligation to inquire about reimbursement.

.03 With respect to all other occasions involving use by nonmembers, the club must maintain books and records of each such use and the amount derived therefrom. This requirement applies even though the member pays initially for such use. In each instance the record must contain the following information:

1. The date;

2. The total number in the party;

3. The number of nonmembers in the party;

4. The total charges;

5. The charges attributable to nonmembers;

6. The charges paid by nonmembers;

7. Where a member pays all or part of the charges attributable to nonmembers, a statement signed by the member indicating whether he has been or will be reimbursed for such nonmember use and, if so, the amount of the reimbursement:

8. Where the member's employer reimburses the member or makes direct payment to the club for the charges attributable to nonmembers, a statement signed by the member indicating the name of his employer; the amount of the payment attributable to the nonmember use; the nonmember's name and business or other relationship to the member; and the business, personal, or social purpose of the member served by the nonmember use. (The use of club facilities must serve some personal or social purpose of the employee-member or some direct business objective of the employee-member; the mere use of club facilities for the accommodation of the member's employer does not serve a business, personal, or social purpose of the member.) If a large number of nonmembers are involved and they are readily identifiable as a particular class of individuals, the member may record such class, rather than all of the names; and

9. Where a nonmember, other than the employer of the member, makes payment to the club or reimburses a member and a claim is made that the amount was paid gratuitously for the benefit of a member, a statement signed by the member indicating the donor's name and relationship to the member, and containing information to substantiate the gratuitous nature of the payment or reimbursement.

.04 Failure to maintain such records or make them available to the Service for examination will preclude use of the minimum gross receipts standard and audit assumptions set forth in this Revenue Procedure.

* * *

Senate Report No. 94-1318, 2d Session

1976-2 C.B. 597

A. Social Clubs

1. Income From Nonmembers and Investment Sources

Present law

Among the present law categories of exempt organizations are social clubs and other somewhat similar nonprofit organizations, such as national organizations of college fraternities and sororities. Present law (sec. 501(c)(7)) provides that these organizations must be organized and operated exclusively for pleasure, recreation, and other non-profitable purposes with no part of the net earnings inuring to the benefit of any private shareholder. The regulations under this provision (Regs. §1.501(c)(7)-1(b)) state that a club which engages in business is not organized and operated exclusively for non-profitable purposes and, therefore, is not exempt.

Generally, the Internal Revenue Service has not challenged the exempt status of these organizations if the income derived from providing goods and services to persons other than members and their guests is small in relation to the total activities of the organization. Thus, as an audit tolerance, the Service has indicated that it generally will not disturb social clubs, certain fraternities and sororities, and employees' beneficiary if the club's annual income from outside sources either is not more than $2,500 or is not more than 5 percent of the total gross receipts of the organization. Where gross receipts from non-members dealings exceed this 5-percent figure, all facts and circumstances are taken into account in determining whether the organization continues to qualify for exempt status. In the case of investment income, the Service applies no percentage rule, but instead looks to whether a substantial part of the club's income is from investment sources. . . .

Reasons for change

In the Revenue Act of 1950, because of the competitive problem with taxable businesses, Congress imposed the regular income tax on the income certain tax-exempt organizations receive from active business enterprises which are unrelated to their exempt purposes. Social clubs, national organizations of college fraternities and sororities, and certain other types of tax-exempt organizations were not subjected to the unrelated business income tax imposed at that time.

In its consideration of the Tax Reform Act of 1969 [1969-3 C.B.], however, because many of the exempt organizations not subject to the unrelated business income tax were engaging in substantial business activity, Congress extended the unrelated business income tax to virtually all of the exempt organizations not already subject to that tax. As a result, social clubs and national organizations of college fraternities and sororities became taxable on all of their unrelated business income.

In addition, the 1969 Act extended the unrelated business income tax, in the case of these social clubs and national organizations of college fraternities and sororities, to cover investment income as well as unrelated business income. Investment income was made taxable in the case of these membership organizations because not to do so would have permitted them to provide recreational or social facilities and services out of revenues other than membership fees and as a result would have permitted individuals to devote investment income, free of tax, to personal activities.

Because of the personal nature of these organizations, the Internal Revenue Service in prior years developed the 5-percent test referred to above in determining whether a social club was properly exempt from tax. Not to have significantly limited the income which could be derived from nonmembers, under the conditions prevailing at that time, would have resulted in non-taxed income being devoted to the personal, recreational, or social benefit of the members of these clubs.

However, since the passage of the 1969 Act, this strict line of demarcation between the exempt and nonexempt activities of social clubs appears unnecessary. Since the passage of the 1969 Act all of the income derived from nonmembers as well as investment income is subject to tax, even though the organization itself is still classified as an exempt organization. Thus, while it is necessary to require that a social club must still be substantially devoted to the personal, recreational, or social benefit of members, the extent to which such a club can obtain income from nonmember sources can be somewhat liberalized. In view of these considerations the committee's bill clarifies existing law to permit somewhat larger amounts of income to be derived by exempt social clubs from nonmembers and also from investment income sources.

Explanation of provision

The first change made by the bill substitutes for the requirement of existing law that clubs which are exempt from tax under sec. 501(c)(7) must be organized and operated "exclusively" for pleasure, recreation, and other non-profitable purposes, the new requirement that "substantially all" of such a club's activities must be for these purposes.

The effect of this change is two-fold. First, it is intended to make it clear that these organizations may receive some outside income, including investment income, without losing their exempt status. Second, it is intended that a social club be permitted to derive a somewhat higher level of income than was previously allowed from the use of its facilities or services by nonmembers without the club losing its exempt status. The decision in each case as to whether substantially all of the organization's activities are related to its exempt purposes is to continue to be based on all the facts and circumstances. However, the facts and circumstances approach is to apply only if the club earns more than is permitted under the new guidelines. If the outside income is less than the guidelines permit, then the club's exempt status will not be lost on account of nonmember income.

It is intended that these organizations be permitted to receive up to 35 percent of their gross receipts, including investment income, from sources outside of their membership without losing their tax-exempt status. It is also intended that within this 35-percent amount not more than 15 percent of the gross receipts should be derived from the use of a social club's facilities or services by the general public. In effect, this latter modification increases from 5 percent (current audit standard: Rev. Proc. 71-17) to 15 percent the proportion of gross receipts a club may receive from making its club facilities available to the general public without losing its exempt status. This also means that a club exempt from taxation described in sec. 501(c)(7) is to be permitted to receive up to 35 percent of its gross receipts from a combination of investment income and receipts from nonmembers so long as the latter do not represent more than 15 percent of total receipts.

Gross receipts are defined for this purpose as those receipts from normal and usual activities of the club (that is, those activities they have traditionally conducted) including charges, admissions, membership fees, dues, assessments, investment income (such as dividends, rents, and similar receipts), and normal recurring capital gains on investments, but excluding initiation fees and capital contributions. However, where a club receives unusual amounts of income, such as from the sale of its clubhouse or similar facility, that income is not to be included in the formula; that is, such unusual income is not to be included in either the gross receipts of the club or in the permitted 35- or 15-percent allowances. On the other hand, where college fraternities or sororities charge membership initiation fees, but no annual dues, such fees will be included in their gross receipts, notwithstanding that initiation fees are ordinarily excluded. It is not intended that these organizations should be permitted to receive, within the 15- or 35-percent allowances, income from the active conduct of businesses not traditionally carried on by these organizations.

It is intended that a social club, national organization of a college fraternity or sorority, and any other organization exempt under section 501(c)(7), may receive the full 35-percent amount of its gross receipts from investment income sources (reduced by any amount of nonmember income, discussed above). This means that a national organization of a college fraternity or sorority that has no outside income from permitting the general public to use its facilities may receive investment income up to the full 35-percent amount of its gross receipts. On the other hand, in the case where a social club permits nonmembers to use its club facilities and receives 15 percent of its gross receipts from these nonmember sources, it may receive only up to 20 percent of its gross receipts from investment income.

In the case of the application of the unrelated business income tax to investment income of these organizations, present law (sec. 512(a)(3)) exempts that income which is set aside to be used for religious, charitable, scientific, literary, educational, etc., purposes (the purposes specified in sec. 170(c)(4)) or the reasonable cost of administration of these activities. For purposes of the 35-percent test, this exempt function income should be included in both the numerator and the denominator, and if this exempt function income causes the organization to exceed the 35-percent limit, the organization is to lose its exempt status (unless the facts and circumstances of the case warrant otherwise).

If an organization has outside income in excess of the 35-percent limit (or 15-percent limit in the case of gross receipts derived from nonmember use of a club's facilities), all the facts and circumstances are to be taken into account in determining whether the organization qualifies for exempt status. If it is determined that the organization is to lose its exempt status for that year, all of its income, even that received from its membership, is to be subject to tax in that year. In such a case the income received from the club's members (but only this income) could be offset by the cost of services and goods furnished the members (sec. 277).

Note

Section 277 applies to taxable non-profit membership organizations — essentially cooperatives that make services available to members on a cost or below-cost basis. One effect of § 277 is that a social organization that derives too great a percentage of its income from commercial or other unrelated activities may not effectively achieve tax exemption by "zeroing out" its commercial income through the use of losses incurred in providing recreation to its membership.

For example, in *Armour-Dial Men's Club, Inc. v. Commissioner*, 708 F.2d 1287 (7th Cir. 1983), a social club composed of employees of Armour-Dial, Inc. (a manufacturer of soap, detergents, and other cleaning items) conducted 10 social, recreational, and entertainment functions for its members each year. The costs to conduct the social functions exceeded the charges imposed on members and therefore the functions generated an economic loss to the club. The club was not tax-exempt, because the great bulk of its revenues were derived from the retail sale (apparently at discounted prices) of rejected Armour-Dial products (i.e., soap and other detergent items that were manufactured incorrectly or with flaws that made them unsuitable for normal retail sale). The club sought to deduct the losses from its social functions against the income generated from the sale of rejected soap and detergent products. Section 277 prevented the organization from doing so. Had it been able to do so, the club would essentially achieve the same result as tax exemption, under circumstances that would distort the tax base by allowing losses on personal activities to offset business income. *Cf.* IRC § 262. Except in certain cases, § 277 prohibits the pooling of gains and losses incurred in providing member services with income from normal commercial activities.

Question

Despite having been issued more than 60 years ago, Revenue Ruling 58-589 is still cited and relied upon by Service. Consider whether the following organization, discussed in a 2020 Private Letter Ruling, qualifies for exemption under IRC § 501 (c)(7):

The Organization's Constitution states your purpose is:

- To unite men and women through the common bond of fishing.
- To educate anglers and develop angling skills (emphasis on bass fishing).
- To strengthen student camaraderie.
- Promote sportsmanship through athletic competition and fellowship.
- Encourage good stewardship of our natural resources.
- To develop and train student athletes for participation in tournament angling.
- To participate in activities that enhance the future of the sport of angling.

You bring students together to enjoy the sport of bass fishing. The club is affiliated with C and competes in affiliated C sanctioned tournaments. Any club member may participate but must earn a spot through a tryout process. You will also teach fishing tactics to all levels of fishermen and will participate in community activities that enhance the future of bass fishing.

Annually, the club participates [and] competes in regional tournaments that involve travel, lodging, and operating expenses that are all provided out of pocket by club members, who compete in boat fields to qualify for that year's national championship event. Any purse money won goes back to the club for funding and support, not the angler's pockets.

You organize and run a tournament each spring where a percentage of funds is retained for club use. The remainder is paid out to top finishers. This tournament is an open invite, open to the public.

The club volunteers at youth and community fishing related events, including running and helping at local river clean-ups and youth fishing derbies to promote the sport of fishing and make such events possible due to limited manpower that the organizations who organize such events have. Personal travel expenses fall on the volunteers, and no form of income or payment to the club or to the volunteers is received. One event like this is expected each spring and fall. You also attend and operate a booth at a local fishing expo. Members attend the booth to distribute information, promote the annual tournament, help run games and a kid zone, and to sell branded apparel raising funds for the club.

Additionally, you hold regular meetings and work to promote the club through social media and other forms including advertising at D. The membership requirement for the club is that one must be a currently enrolled student at D.

While your Constitution indicates members pay a fee of e dollars, you have stated you have no non-member income because there are no club dues, and all income comes from companies and corporate sponsors that donate money to the club or fundraisers held by the club. The money received by the club is then used to pay for expenses at fundraiser events or given to club members to cover travel expenses. Your sources of income are listed as the annual tournament, apparel sales, crowd-sourced fundraising, sponsorships, purse money from competitions and outside donations.

B. Anti-Discrimination Requirement

CODE: § 501(i)

Section 501(i) provides that a § 501(c)(7) organization cannot be tax exempt if its "charter, bylaws, or other governing instrument" or "any written policy statement" provides for "discrimination against any person on the basis of race, color, or religion." The legislative history of § 501(i) (included below) indicates that Congress enacted this provision in response to a federal district court case involving a constitutional challenge to the validity of § 501(c)(7). *See McGlotten v. Connally*, 338 F. Supp. 448 (D.D.C. 1972). Despite the tremendous social implications of this congressional enactment, the legislative history states simply "in view of national policy, it is believed that it is inappropriate for a social club or similar organization described in § 501(c)(7) to be exempt from income taxation if its written policy is to discriminate on account of race, color, or religion." Of course, § 501(i) prohibits only the promuigation of "written policies" and some might argue is therefore purely symbolic because social clubs operate more by action than written documents.

Senate Report No. 94-1318, 2d Session

1976-2 C.B. 597

A. Social Clubs

* * *

4. Prohibition of Discrimination by Social Clubs, etc.

Present law

The Internal Revenue Code does not deal explicitly with the question of whether an income tax exemption for social clubs, etc. (i.e., organizations described in sec. 501(c)(7) which are exempt under sec. 501(a)), is incompatible with discrimination on account of race, color, or religion.

It has been held (*McGlotten v. Connally*, 338 F. Supp. 448 (D.D.C. 1972)) that, in light of the present statutory scheme of income tax treatment of social clubs, etc. (including their treatment under the unrelated business income tax provisions described above), discrimination on account of race is not prohibited under the Constitution in the case of an exempt organization merely because it is described in section 501(e)(7).

Also, the Supreme Court has affirmed (*Coit v. Green*, 404 U.S. 997 (1971)) a decision (*Green v. Connally*, 330 F. Supp. 1150 (D.C., D.C. 1971)) that discrimination on account of race is inconsistent with an educational institution's tax-exempt status (sec. 501(c)(3)) and also with its status as a charitable contribution donee (sec. 170(c)(2)).

Reasons for change

In view of national policy, it is believed that it is inappropriate for a social club or similar organization described in section 501(c)(7) to be exempt from income taxation if its written policy is to discriminate on account of race, color, or religion.

Explanation of provision

Under the bill, an organization otherwise exempt from income tax as an organization described in section 501(c)(7) is to lose its exempt status for any taxable year if, at any time during that year, the organization's charter, by-laws, or other governing instrument, or any written policy statement contains a provision which provides for discrimination against any person on the basis of race, color, or religion.

Question

S country club (the Club) in City X had been in existence for more than 150 years and, over the years, had developed a reputation as the top social, political and economic club in the City, membership in which was required for anybody wanting to "get ahead." For most of its history, its charter specifically limited membership to "White men." For two years after Congress enacted § 501(i), the Club maintained its written policy of limiting membership only to white men. After the Service threatened to revoke its exemption under § 501(c)(7), the Club amended it charter to remove the membership restriction. Nevertheless, the Club continued admitting only white men for the next 7 years, despite receiving applications from men and women of all races. In year 8, the Service conducts an examination of Club. The examining agent's report concluded there is "substantial evidence of actual discrimination, either in the selection of members or in the use of club facilities." Should the Club's exemption be revoked?

Chapter 24

States and State-Related Organizations

A. Introduction

An often-overlooked subject regarding federal tax exemption involves the tax status of states, political subdivisions, and the entities by which states and political subdivisions accomplish public functions. While there are no compiled statistics available we might safely assume that the largest group of tax-exempt organizations are states and their political subdivisions (state agencies, municipalities, counties, etc.). By what authority do states avoid paying federal income tax? And if a commercial entity is wholly owned by a state, does the entity also enjoy federal tax exemption? Certainly, the Constitution does not explicitly prevent the federal government from taxing the revenues derived by state governments. On the other hand, states are quintessentially charitable organizations in the generic sense of the phrase. States and their political subdivisions exist, under our system of government, for the purpose of locally providing for the common good. It would be ironic, indeed, if private organizations serving the public good were tax-exempt while states (which have a legal obligation to do the same, and necessarily lessen the burdens imposed on the federal government) were subject to taxation. In this part, we therefore look at two interrelated doctrines by which states are granted tax exemption: intergovernmental tax immunity — the constitutional notion[1] that the state sovereign is not subject to taxation by the federal sovereign and vice-versa — and Code § 115, the very briefly stated statute under which states and even some privately controlled entities are granted tax exemption.

1. As we will learn from comments made by the Supreme Court in *South Carolina*, as interpreted by *Michigan Educational Trust*, the doctrine of intergovernmental immunity is not explicitly stated in the Constitution. Instead, it is "implied" from the American system of government and is followed, insofar as state immunity is concerned, more as a matter of good policy rather than legal dictate. A stronger argument exists, however, for federal immunity from state taxation which is rather clearly grounded in the supremacy clause.

B. Intergovernmental Tax Immunity — States, Political Subdivisions, Integral Parts

While the doctrine of intergovernmental tax immunity is applied daily to the many state income-producing activities — ranging from the operation of parking lots, utility companies, lotteries and gambling casinos, liquor stores and prepaid tuition programs — its contours remain somewhat murky. The Supreme Court's broadest statement of the modern doctrine is contained in only two brief footnotes from *South Carolina v. Baker*, 485 U.S. 505 (1988):

> The sources of the state and federal immunities are, of course, different: the state immunity arises from the constitutional structure and a concern for protecting state sovereignty whereas the federal immunity arises from the Supremacy Clause. The immunities have also differed somewhat in their underlying political theory and in their doctrinal contours. Many of this Court's opinions have suggested that the Constitution should be interpreted to confer a greater tax immunity on the Federal Government than on States because all the people of the States are represented in the Federal Government whereas all the people of the Federal Government are not represented in individual States. *Helvering v. Gerhardt*, 304 U.S. 405, 412 (1938); *McCulloch v. Maryland*, 4 Wheat. 316, 435–436 (1819); *New York v. United States*, 326 U.S. 572, 577, and n. 3 (1946) (opinion of Frankfurter, J.). In fact, the federal tax immunity has always been greater than the States' immunity. The Federal Government, for example, possesses the power to enact statutes immunizing those with whom it deals from state taxation even if intergovernmental tax immunity doctrine would not otherwise confer an immunity. *See, e.g., Graves v. New York ex rel. O'Keefe*, 306 U.S. 466, 478 (1939). The States lack any such power. Also, although the Federal Government has always enjoyed blanket immunity from any state tax considered to be "on" the Government under the prevailing methodology, the States have never enjoyed immunity from all federal taxes considered to be "on" a State. *See infra*, at 523, and n. 13. To some, *Garcia v. San Antonio Metropolitan Transit Authority*, 469 U.S. 528 (1985), may suggest further limitations on state tax immunity. We need not, however, decide here the extent to which the scope of the federal and state immunities differ or the extent, if any, to which States are currently immune from direct nondiscriminatory federal taxation. It is enough for our purposes that federal and state tax immunity cases have always shared the identical methodology for determining whether a tax is "on" a government, and that this identity has persisted even though the methodology for both federal and state immunities has changed as intergovernmental tax immunity doctrine shifted into the modern era.

485 U.S. at 520 n.11 (1988).

> All federal activities are immune from direct state taxation, *see Graves*, 306 U.S., at 477, but at least some state activities have always been subject to direct federal taxation. For a time, only the States' governmental, as opposed to proprietary, activities enjoyed tax immunity, *see e.g., Helvering v. Powers*, 293 U.S. 214, 227 (1934); *South Carolina v. United States*, 199 U.S. 437, 454–463 (1905), but this distinction was subsequently abandoned as untenable by all eight Justices participating in *New York v. United States*, 326 U.S. 572 (1946). *See id.*, at 579–581, 583 (opinion of Frankfurter, J., joined by Rutledge, J.); *id.*, at 586 (Stone, C. J., concurring, joined by Reed, Murphy, and Burton, JJ.); *id.*, at 591 (Douglas, J., dissenting, joined by Black, J.). Two Justices reasoned that any nondiscriminatory tax on a State was constitutional, even if directly collected from the State. *See id.*, at 582–584 (Frankfurter, J., joined by Rutledge, J.). Four other Justices declined to hold that every nondiscriminatory tax levied directly on a State would be constitutional because "there may be non-discriminatory taxes which, when laid on a State, would nevertheless impair the sovereign status of the State quite as much as a like tax imposed by a State on property or activities of the national government. *Mayo v. United States*, 319 U.S. 441, 447–448 (1943). This is not because the tax can be regarded as discriminatory but because a sovereign government is the taxpayer, and the tax, even though non-discriminatory, may be regarded as infringing its sovereignty." 326 U.S., at 587 (Stone, C. J., concurring, joined by Reed, Murphy, and Burton, JJ.) (emphasis added) (the cited discussion from Mayo stressed the difference between levying a tax on a government and on those with whom the government deals); see also 326 U.S., at 588 ("Only when and because the subject of taxation is State property or a State activity must we consider whether such a non-discriminatory tax unduly interferes with the performance of the State's functions of government"). The four Justices then concluded that the tax at issue was constitutional even though directly levied on the State because recognizing an immunity would "accomplish a withdrawal from the taxing power of the nation a subject of taxation of a nature which has been traditionally within that power from the beginning." *Ibid.* We need not concern ourselves here, however, with the extent to which, if any, States are currently immune from direct federal taxation. See supra, at 517, n. 10. For our purposes, the important principle *New York* reaffirms is that the issue whether a nondiscriminatory federal tax might nonetheless violate state tax immunity does not even arise unless the Federal Government seeks to collect the tax directly from a State.

485 U.S. at 523 n.14 (1988). In 1994, the Sixth Circuit had occasion to consider the scope of state immunity from federal taxation. The resulting majority and dissenting opinions are both intellectually provocative.

State of Michigan v. United States

40 F.3d 817 (6th Cir. 1994)

David A. Nelson, Circuit Judge.

The question presented here is whether the United States Internal Revenue Code imposes a tax on investment income realized by the Michigan Education Trust. The trust is a state agency established to receive advance payments of college tuition, invest the money, and ultimately make disbursements under a program that lets its beneficiaries attend any of the state's public colleges or universities without further tuition cost.

The district court held the education trust liable for federal income taxes. We conclude that while Congress could, if it wished, tax the investment income of state agencies such as the education trust, it has not chosen to do so. Accordingly, we shall reverse the judgment of the district court.

I

The Michigan Education Trust, [was] created by an act of the Michigan legislature [as] ... "a public body corporate and politic." ... As such, the education trust is a public instrumentality of the state. The grant of corporate powers to such an agency makes it "a quasi corporation" under Michigan law. ...

The Michigan Constitution provides, ..., that each of the "agencies and instrumentalities of the executive branch of state government" must "be allocated by law" to one of the principal departments of the executive branch. .... Pursuant to this constitutional requirement, ... the education trust [is] "... within the department of treasury. ..."

Like many government agencies vested with corporate powers, the education trust has a board of directors by which such powers are exercised. ... The state treasurer is a member of the education trust's board ex officio, and the other board members (eight in number) are appointed by the governor with the advice and consent of the senate. ...

Although the education trust is "within" the treasury department, and although the state treasurer (who is the head of that department) serves as a member of the board, the board acts "independently" of the treasury department [and] ... assets of the education trust are not considered state money, common cash, or revenue of the state. ...

Trust assets may be invested in any manner the trust deems appropriate, and may be pooled for investment purposes with state pension funds and other investments of the state. ... It is state employees who invest education trust assets, and trust funds are paid out only through State of Michigan checks or warrants. All income of the education trust is exempt from state income taxes. ... Michigan's auditor general is responsible for auditing the books of the education trust, and the board must submit an annual accounting to the governor and leaders of the Michigan legislature. . . . Legal representation is provided to the education trust by the Attorney General of the State of Michigan.

The business of the education trust's board must be conducted in compliance with Michigan's Open Meetings Act, and the education trust is likewise subject to the state's Freedom of Information Act. . . . All education trust employees are members of the classified civil service of the state; as civil servants, they are subject to state civil service commission rules and regulations. Advance tuition payments collected by the education trust are deposited in a bank trust account under the name of the State Treasurer, State of Michigan, Agent for the Michigan Education Trust. Assets of the trust are earmarked for uses set forth in the statute, including the making of payments to state institutions of higher education on behalf of qualified beneficiaries. . . .

The Michigan attorney general's department has advised the board of the education trust that the trust is an "agency" of the State of Michigan. The attorney general's department has further advised that the members of the board are "public officers" for purposes of the Michigan Governmental Liability for Negligence Act.

Before we turn to the purposes for which the education trust was created, it will be useful to refer to a bit of early history. On July 13, 1787—two years before the Constitution of the United States was adopted and 50 years before the State of Michigan was admitted to the Union—Congress enacted the Northwest Ordinance. Captioned "An Ordinance for the Government of the Territory of the United States Northwest of the River Ohio," this landmark legislation—which was to have a profoundly important effect on the subsequent development of both state and national law—was the fundamental instrument of government for an area covering more than a quarter of a million square miles. The territory to which the ordinance applied included all of present-day Michigan, plus Indiana, Illinois, Wisconsin, Ohio, and part of Minnesota.

Article III of the Northwest Ordinance began with this famous sentence: "Religion, morality, and knowledge being necessary to good government and the happiness of mankind, schools and the means of education shall forever be encouraged." The framers of both of Michigan's 20th Century constitutions—the first adopted in 1908 and the second in 1963—included articles on education in which the opening language mirrored the language of the first sentence of Article III of the Northwest Ordinance. Thus Article VIII, § 1 of Michigan's present constitution, adopted without change from Article IX, § 1 of the constitution of 1908, perpetuates, as part of the state's basic law, the principle that "schools and the means of education shall forever be encouraged."

As part of Michigan's efforts to make "the means of education" available to its citizens, the state maintains an extensive system of public colleges and universities. (The University of Michigan and Michigan State University are but two of a rather long list of such institutions.) Financial support for these public colleges and universities comes from a variety of sources, including both appropriations from the legislature and tuition payments.

During the first half of the decade of the 1980s, tuition costs at Michigan's public institutions of higher education, like tuition costs at public and private colleges throughout the nation, increased at rates that many found alarming. (Over the decade as a whole, the average tuition at Michigan's four-year colleges and universities more than doubled.) In January of 1986, responding to concern about soaring tuition costs, Michigan's governor proposed in his State of the State Address that Michigan adopt a state-run prepaid tuition program "designed to help parents guarantee to their children the opportunity of a Michigan college education." 1986 Mich. Journal of the House 152. The Michigan Education Trust Act was the embodiment of that proposal.

The act contained an extensive set of legislative findings, beginning with one that the attentive reader will find familiar: "It is an essential function of state government to forever encourage schools and the means of education, as provided in section 1 of article VIII of the state constitution of 1963." . . . The legislature further found it to be "an essential function of state government to encourage attendance at state institutions of higher education," § 2(c); noted that "students in elementary and secondary schools tend to achieve to a higher standard of performance when the payment of tuition for their higher education is secured," § 2(h); and declared that "providing assistance to assure the higher education of the citizens of this state is necessary and desirable for the public health, safety, and welfare," § 2(i).

* * *

The manner in which the education trust operates is relatively simple in concept. Acting on behalf of the state and itself . . . , the trust enters into advance tuition payment contracts with parents, grandparents, or anyone else who wants assurance that tuition costs for a particular beneficiary will be covered when the time comes for the beneficiary to enter college. The purchaser pays the trust a stipulated sum—determined on the basis of various actuarial assumptions and forecasts—that reflects the number of years for which tuition is to be prepaid and the number of years remaining before the beneficiary (who must be a Michigan resident at the time of the contract) is expected to enter college.

The trust invests all of the funds so collected. If the beneficiary ultimately enrolls as a Michigan resident in a Michigan public college or university—and the contract does not guarantee that the beneficiary will be admitted, of course, although we are told that by January of 1993 more than 85 percent of the education trust beneficiaries who had graduated from high school had been admitted to a state college or university—the trust is obligated to use the funds it controls to pay the beneficiary's full tuition cost, whatever that cost turns out to be. If the beneficiary is no longer a Michigan resident, he is responsible for the difference between the in-state rate and the out-of-state rate.

If the beneficiary reaches the age of 18 and certifies that he will attend a private college within the state, or will attend a college outside the state, or has decided not to attend college at all, the trust is obligated to pay a refund (which, at the beneficiary's option, may go directly to a designated college or university) in an amount determined under a contractual formula covering that particular contingency. The refund formulas are designed to encourage attendance at some college, as opposed to not enrolling anywhere, but the trust does not promise to cover full tuition costs at any institution other than a public college or university in Michigan.

II

In 1988, before any advance tuition payment contracts had been entered into, the Treasurer of the State of Michigan requested a "no action" letter from the Securities and Exchange Commission. The state treasurer's letter to the SEC submitted that the education trust was a "public instrumentality" the contracts of which, if deemed to be securities, would be exempt from registration under the Securities Act of 1933 pursuant to § 3(a)(2) of that act, 15 U.S.C. § 77c(a)(2). The SEC responded favorably, the agency's corporate finance division stating that it would not recommend any enforcement action.

The state was also required to request a ruling from the Internal Revenue Service, pursuant to the following provision in the Education Trust Act: "An advance tuition payment contract shall not be entered into by the trust until the internal revenue service has issued a favorable ruling or opinion that the purchaser of the advance payment contract will not be considered actually or constructively to be in receipt of income." . . . Joined by a prospective participant in the advance tuition payment program, the Treasurer of the State of Michigan requested such a ruling by letter dated February 19, 1987. The letter also asked for a ruling that "the accrued investment income of the Trust is exempt from federal income taxation pursuant to either the Doctrine of Intergovernmental Tax Immunity or the provisions of Section 115(1) of the Code [26 U.S.C. § 115(1)]."

In Private Letter Ruling 88-25-027, dated March 29, 1988, the IRS responded with good news and bad news. The good news was that no income would be realized by the purchaser or the beneficiary when an advance tuition payment contract was executed — although income would be realized later on if the value of any subsequently-received educational services or refund exceeded the amount initially paid. The bad news, from the state's standpoint, was that the trust's investment income would be subject to federal income tax.

* * *

The education trust paid a federal income tax of $4,495 on investment income realized in the fiscal year ending September 30, 1988. A claim for refund followed. More than six months elapsed without a response. . . . and . . . the education trust, joined by the State of Michigan, commenced the present refund action . . .

... [T]he district court held the education trust liable for the taxes. The plaintiffs had argued that the Internal Revenue Code was not intended to apply to states or their instrumentalities, but the district court rejected this argument on the theory that the education trust is not an integral part of the State of Michigan. Section 115 was held inapplicable on either or both of two theories: the education trust is not a state or a political subdivision thereof, and the income of the trust does not "accrue" to the state in a bookkeeping sense....

III

The state and the education trust have now abandoned the argument that the federal government lacks constitutional authority to impose a tax on investment income produced in the operation of state programs such as that conducted by the education trust. This was an appropriate move, we believe. The broad constitutional immunity from federal taxation once thought to be enjoyed by states and their instrumentalities has been severely eroded with the passage of time, and several years ago the Supreme Court suggested that it is now an open question whether there is "any" extent "to which States are currently immune from direct non-discriminatory federal taxation." *South Carolina v. Baker*, 485 U.S. 505, 518 n. 11 (1988).

It used to be thought that public instrumentalities of a state were constitutionally immune from taxation insofar as they performed a "governmental function," as opposed to performing a proprietary or "business" function.... But the constitutionally-based governmental function/proprietary function test produced "uncertainty and instability" that finally led the Supreme Court to abandon it.... Accordingly, we are confident that today's Supreme Court would say that Congress is free to impose a non-discriminatory tax on the investment income at issue here if it wants to. The question we must decide is whether Congress has done so.

Section 11(a) of the Internal Revenue Code, 26 U.S.C. § 11(a), provides that "[a] tax is hereby imposed for each taxable year on the taxable income of every corporation." The education trust is only a "quasi corporation" under Michigan law, but the reference in § 11(a) to "every corporation" appears, on its face, to be very broad indeed. If one were to read § 11(a) in a vacuum, one might well conclude that the tax imposed by this section extends to the income of all government corporations, "quasi" or otherwise ...

The United States does not contend, of course, that § 11(a) should be read in a vacuum. As a matter of history, the appellee's brief acknowledges, this section has never been interpreted as imposing a tax on income earned directly by a state, a political subdivision of a state, or "an integral part of a State." ...

... Justice Rutledge urged that the Court apply a rule of construction "requiring that before a federal tax can be applied to activities carried on directly by the States ..., the intention of Congress to tax them should be stated expressly and not drawn merely from general wording of the statute applicable ordinarily to private sources of revenue." ... Justice Rutledge went on to say that "I should expect that

Congress would say so explicitly, were its purpose actually to include state functions, where the legal incidence of the tax falls upon the state." *Id.*

* * *

Congress has never adopted a "plain statement" . . . with regard to the investment income . . . of state colleges and universities or other public instrumentalities of the state. If Congress wants to tax the investment income of public bodies, it knows how to make the kind of "plain statement" necessary to impose such a tax.

The United States does not deny that the "plain statement rule" applies in the tax field. It argues, however, that the "rule obviously does not apply where, as here, the activities are carried on by an entity that is not a political subdivision of a state or otherwise an integral part thereof." This argument turns, of course, on the proposition that the education trust is not a political subdivision or otherwise an integral part of the State of Michigan. We are not persuaded, on the record before us, that this proposition is correct.

. . . In *Commissioner v. Shamberg's Estate*, . . . , and *Commissioner v. White's Estate*, . . . , the Second Circuit addressed the question whether the Port of New York Authority and the Triborough Bridge Authority were "political subdivisions" . . . . The court's answer, delivered in opinions written by Judge Augustus Hand, was "yes."

The pertinent treasury department regulations . . . said that "the term 'political subdivision' . . . denotes any division of the State or territory which is a municipal corporation, or to which has been delegated the right to exercise part of the sovereign powers of the State or Territory." The Port of New York Authority—"a body politic and corporate" through which the states of New York and New Jersey built and operated the George Washington Bridge, the Holland and Lincoln Tunnels, and other projects "operated in the interest of the public without profit to private persons," . . . —was held to fit this definition notwithstanding that the authority lacked the power to impose taxes, had no power to pledge the credit of either state, and was not subject to the debt limiting provisions of the state constitutions.

Judge Hand found support for this holding in the test laid down in an opinion given by Attorney General McReynolds . . . :

> "The term 'political subdivision' is broad and comprehensive and denotes any division of the State made by the proper authorities thereof, acting within their constitutional powers, for the purpose of carrying out a portion of those functions of the State which by long usage and inherent necessities of government have always been regarded as public." . . .

"The real criterion adopted by the Attorney General," Judge Hand observed, "seems to have been whether the activities of the subdivision were for a public purpose." . . .

Applying this criterion to the facts before us, we think it obvious that encouraging higher education by helping provide the means for attendance at Michigan's public colleges and universities—the basic function for which the education trust was established by the Michigan legislature—is at least as much a "public function" as building and operating bridges and tunnels. . . .

As we have seen, the treasury regulations quoted by Judge Hand in Shamberg defined a "political subdivision" as any division of the state which was either a municipal corporation or to which the right to exercise a part of the state's sovereign power had been delegated. . . .

In the case at bar, similarly, the education trust is a public agency explicitly authorized to exercise contracting powers "on behalf of the state" for a purpose that the Michigan legislature has declared "is necessary and desirable for the public health, safety, and welfare." The education trust has thus been empowered to exercise governmental functions on behalf of the State of Michigan, it seems to us, just as Judge Hand said the Triborough Bridge Authority had been empowered to do on behalf of the City of New York. And the education trust would qualify as a "political subdivision" under the regulations in any event, we believe, since, as "a public body corporate and politic," it is in a broad sense a "municipal corporation."

* * *

Whether a particular entity is an agency or instrumentality of a state or political subdivision . . . has long been determined by the Internal Revenue Service under Rev. Rul. 57-128, 1957-1 Cum. Bull. 311. This revenue ruling lists six factors to be considered:

> In cases involving the status of an organization as an instrumentality of one or more states or political subdivisions, the following factors are taken into consideration: (1) whether it is used for a governmental purpose and performs a governmental function; (2) whether performance of its function is on behalf of one or more states or political subdivisions; (3) whether there are any private interests involved, or whether the states or political subdivisions involved have the powers and interests of an owner; (4) whether control and supervision of the organization is vested in public authority or authorities; (5) if express or implied statutory or other authority is necessary for the creation and/or use of such an instrumentality, and whether such authority exists; and (6) the degree of financial autonomy and the source of its operating expenses.

* * *

The . . . Michigan Education Trust satisfies at least five of the criteria. (1) . . . the education trust is used for what the state legislature has determined to be a "governmental purpose." (2) . . . the education trust performs this function on behalf of the state. (3) . . . the education trust is solely a governmental entity; no private ownership interests are involved. (4) . . . the education trust is controlled by public appointees. (5) The functions performed by the railroad were delegated to it by the Metropolitan Transportation Authority, while the functions performed by the education trust would not even exist, of course, but for the enactment of the statute creating it.

With regard to the sixth criterion, financial autonomy, the appellant in *Rose* stressed the fact that although the railroad had received large operating subsidies from the state ever since the takeover, the state was not legally obligated to fund the railroad. The court acknowledged that this was true, but observed that "[the appellant's] argument ignores the fact that many governmental services are funded in the same manner." *Id.*

Whether Michigan's education trust will ultimately be able to continue operating without significant appropriations from the legislature remains to be seen. Michigan obviously hopes that such appropriations will never be necessary—and as in the case of the publicly-owned railroad and many similar governmental instrumentalities, there is no legal requirement that any operating deficits be covered by appropriations from the general funds of the state. If the education trust should ever find itself unable to fulfill the contractual commitments made by it on behalf of the state, however, there would undoubtedly be enormous pressure on the legislature to supply the necessary funds. This may not be enough to satisfy the sixth criterion, but viewing the six factors as a whole it seems to us that on balance they militate in favor of a conclusion comparable to that reached by the Second Circuit in *Rose*.

* * *

The education trust is not an integral part of the State of Michigan, the United States argues, both because the trust's corporate form of organization makes it "functionally independent" of the state and because the source and earmarking of its funds make it "fiscally independent." Neither branch of the argument is persuasive.

It is "immaterial," . . . that the Michigan legislature decided to create a public quasi corporation to receive and invest advance tuition payments instead of assigning this function to a traditional executive department not organized in corporate or quasi corporate form. The point can be illustrated, perhaps, with an example from the federal level. This country's postal service used to be operated by a traditional executive department; since the early 1970s, however, it has been operated by an "independent establishment," the United States Postal Service, organized along the lines of a government corporation. *See* 39 U.S.C. §§ 201 *et seq.* No one would ever have imagined that the income of the old Post Office Department was subject to taxation by either the United States or by individual states—and to suppose that the income of the new Postal Service is now subject to taxation merely because the Postal Service is "functionally independent" would be absurd. The Postal Service is as much an integral part of the United States as the Post Office Department was.

It is likewise immaterial that the funds of the education trust, like the funds of many public corporations, authorities, and similar establishments, come primarily from persons to whom the entity provides a service—and it is immaterial that such funds are earmarked for the benefit of those who receive the service. If the funds of the Postal Service come primarily from persons who buy stamps, the funds of the Tennessee Valley Authority from those who purchase power from that agency, and the funds of the Port of New York Authority from users of the authority's bridges and tunnels, it does not mean that the Postal Service, the Tennessee Valley Authority, and the Port of New York Authority are anything other than governmental in character. Neither is the governmental character of these agencies compromised in any way by the fact that the agencies' funds are earmarked—like highway trust funds and countless other restricted accounts of governmental bodies—for use in performing the functions that the agencies were created by law to perform.

It is true that the particular individuals who attend public colleges and universities in Michigan under the state's prepaid tuition program benefit directly from the program, while the rest of the citizenry benefits only indirectly. But much the same thing can be said of most government benefit programs, including the state student loan programs through which many students "post-pay" their tuition. Suppose the State of Michigan were to create a public quasi corporation to manage a revolving student loan fund for disadvantaged youths. If the investment income of such a body would not be held subject to taxation under existing law—and we are confident that it would not be, regardless of the body's "functional independence" and regardless of the earmarking of its assets—it is hard to see how the investment income of the education trust could be considered taxable.

Or suppose that the State of Michigan created a public quasi corporation to hold and invest state employees' pension funds. The only direct beneficiaries would be the employees themselves, and the agency, by hypothesis, would be functionally and fiscally independent of the general government. The notion that the pension agency would be treated as anything other than an integral part of the state strikes us as untenable—and the notion that the Michigan Education Trust is not an integral part of the State of Michigan is equally untenable, in our opinion. The education trust is an integral part of the state, and its investment income is not currently subject to taxation under § 11(a) of the Internal Revenue Code.

The foregoing analysis makes it unnecessary for us to reach the remaining issues raised on appeal, including the question whether the "very old and somewhat cryptic language" of 26 U.S.C. § 115 creates an exclusion for the education trust's income and the question whether the trust is a charitable, educational, or social welfare organization exempt from taxation by reason of 26 U.S.C. §§ 501(c)(3) or 501(c)(4).

The judgment of the district court is REVERSED, and the case is REMANDED with instructions to grant the refund.

Guy, Circuit Judge, dissenting.

I respectfully dissent. In doing so, I hasten to add that this is a difficult case, and principled arguments can be marshalled on either side of this issue. The court starts out by stating that "while Congress could, if it wished, tax the investment income of state agencies such as the education trust, it has not chosen to do so." My view is to the contrary. I believe that although Congress could exempt such income from taxation, it has not done so.

* * *

I also would place more of a political overlay on the analysis of these issues than does the court. However well intentioned it may sound to put into place a program guaranteeing parents affordable college tuition in the future for their children, the engine driving this program was in no small degree plain old partisan politics. Fifty-five thousand persons signed up for this program, and I assume that most of them were registered voters. At this point one might ask, so what? What does all of this have to do with whether or not the money earned on MET investments is taxable? The answer to this question is somewhat complex.

Parents who signed a contract with MET essentially were buying an annuity. They would put "X" dollars up front, and over time the interest earned on their investment would allow the fund to grow and keep pace with projected increases in college tuition. If it was this simple, why didn't parents just buy an annuity on the open market to accomplish the same result? The answer is that no private company could offer an annuity at the attractive price at which it was being offered by MET. MET was able to undercut the market for two reasons. First, in my view, MET proceeded imprudently on the assumption that its earnings would continue at the abnormally high rate that State investments had been earning. Second, unlike a private company, MET had the luxury of underestimating the rate of future tuition increases.

Now I realize that for a government official to overstate revenues and understate expenses is not a capital offense. If it were, death row would be even more crowded than it is. But for MET there were more immediate consequences than the possibility of an eventual deficit. MET was forced to deal almost immediately with a shortfall, and in 1990, only two years after its launch, MET stopped accepting applications and has never resumed.

Although the shortfall was primarily the result of less return on investment than anticipated and greater increases in tuition than contemplated, nothing could be done about these two factors. The only adjustment that hopefully could be made was to secure tax-exempt status, notwithstanding that MET had been told from the start by the IRS that it would not qualify for tax-exempt status, a ruling MET accepted. MET was forced by financial pressure to revisit this issue, however, and instituted this lawsuit. The district judge granted summary judgment in favor of the United States. For the reasons that follow, I am convinced that Judge Hillman was correct. The Florida program is an integral part of the state government, he said, because it is a state agency with a budget funded by state appropriations.").

I

With one limited exception,[2] Congress has never imposed a federal income tax upon sovereign states, their political subdivisions, or other entities that are an integral part of the state. This exemption is nowhere written in the tax code. Instead, this de facto exemption has applied since 1913 because the IRS has acknowledged

2. [7] Section 511(a) of the Code includes state colleges and universities in the group of organizations subject to the unrelated business income tax.

that states are not "corporations, associations, trusts or individuals" subject to income taxation under the Code. In considering the de facto tax-exempt status of state-created entities, the courts have used both the "sovereign power" test and the "integral part" test. Under either test, MET's petition for tax-exempt status under the de facto exemption fails.

The Internal Revenue Code does not define the term "political subdivision," but the term has been defined by Treasury regulations pertaining to the exemption of interest on state obligations as "any division of any State or local governmental unit which is a municipal corporation or which has been delegated the right to exercise part of the sovereign power of the unit." 26 C.F.R. § 1.103-1(b) (1992). Construing the regulation, courts have required entities seeking "political subdivision" status to be authorized to exercise at least one of three sovereign powers: the power of eminent domain, the power to tax, or the police power.

This "sovereign power" test was first recognized by the Second Circuit in two companion cases, *Commissioner v. Shamberg's Estate*, 144 F.2d 998 (2d Cir. 1944), *cert. denied*, 323 U.S. 792 (1945), and *Commissioner v. White's Estate*, 144 F.2d 1019 (2d Cir. 1944), *cert. denied*, 323 U.S. 792 (1945). In *Shamberg's Estate*, the court addressed whether interest on the New York Port Authority's bonds was excludable from gross income. The court found that the Authority was a political subdivision of New York and New Jersey because it was created by a contract between the two states and had maintained many sovereign powers, including the power of eminent domain and the police power. The Authority's police power included the power to subpoena, the power to issue orders and enforce orders against persons within its jurisdiction, and the power to maintain a uniformed police force. Although the Authority did not have the power to tax, the court found this did not jeopardize the Authority's tax-exempt status:

> Here the activities . . . are exercised for a public purpose by an agency set up by the states and given many public powers, though not of taxation or control through the suffrages of citizens. It minimizes its public and political character to treat such an agency as a private corporation merely because of the lack of taxing power which is only one of the attributes of sovereignty.

Shamberg's Estate, 144 F.2d at 1005.

In *White's Estate*, the court considered whether the Triborough Bridge Authority was a political subdivision for the interest on its bonds to be tax exempt. The court found that the Authority was a political subdivision of the State of New York because the Authority was "plainly a subdivision of state government empowered to exercise governmental functions on behalf of the City of New York. . . ." 144 F.2d at 1020. The Authority's powers included the power of eminent domain and the power "to make use of city agents, employees, and facilities, and to issue bonds for constructing the bridges." *Id.*

Other courts have followed this reasoning. In *Seagrave Corp. v. Commissioner*, 38 T.C. 247 (1962), the Tax Court recognized that an entity must be authorized to exercise a sovereign power to constitute a political subdivision. In rejecting several volunteer fire departments' claims that they were political subdivisions under the Code, the court held:

> The volunteer fire companies perform a public function in the sense that they perform the same function that is generally carried on by municipal fire departments. But the volunteer fire companies here involved ... [are] not created by any special statutes and they received no delegation of any part of the State's power. It is not enough that they perform a public service. They cannot be called a subdivision of the State unless there has been a delegation to them of some functions of local government.

Seagrave, 38 T.C. at 250. Likewise, later courts have held that the delegation of traditional sovereign authority is a crucial factor in determining whether an entity is a political subdivision.

* * *

I find this test helpful, but note that it should not be applied mechanically to grant or deny tax-exempt status to those entities that do or do not possess one of the three historic attributes of state sovereignty. For example, many public utilities have eminent domain powers, and many private colleges have private police forces. However, neither organization has been viewed as a candidate for tax-exempt status.

MET argues that it qualifies as a political subdivision of Michigan because: (1) it possesses the power of eminent domain; (2) it is created by statute for the specific purpose of carrying on a specified governmental program; (3) it has been delegated a part of the duty to foster education within the State, and among the police powers of Michigan is the constitutionally mandated and legislatively required power and duty to promote education within the State; and (4) it possesses the governmental powers of rule-making and conducting quasi-judicial hearings.

MET's assumption that it possesses the power of eminent domain is based on Mich. Comp. Laws Ann. § 213.23, which provides:

> Any public corporation or state agency is authorized to take private property necessary for a public improvement or for the purposes of its incorporation or for public purposes within the scope of its powers....

The United States argues that any "theoretical power" of eminent domain that MET possesses is inadequate to confer tax-exempt status upon it, for the Trust's purpose is to invest money and it therefore is "inconceivable" that the Trust would ever need to invoke its alleged power of eminent domain. I find it unnecessary to decide whether MET possesses eminent domain power under Michigan law, for, even if it did, possession of such power in this case would be insufficient to grant MET tax-exempt status.

MET does not have the power of taxation, nor does it benefit from legislative appropriation of funds. Any money that it has received from the State was in the form of a loan that MET paid back immediately. Moreover, the State does not guarantee the continued liquidity of the fund. If MET became actuarially unsound, purchasers of MET contracts could not rely on the State to meet MET's promise that children's tuition to state universities will be paid. In addition, despite MET's arguments to the contrary, it has not established that it possesses the police power. Although the promotion of higher education is a governmental, public function that has been assumed by the states, the maintenance of a prepaid tuition fund is not the type of responsibility historically borne by the states.

My conclusion that MET is not entitled to the de facto exemption is buttressed by MET's failure to meet the "integral part" test for considering entities who seek tax-exempt status. In deciding whether an entity is an integral part of a state, courts have relied on six factors:

> (1) whether it is used for a governmental purpose and performs a governmental function; (2) whether performance of its function is on behalf of one or more states or political subdivisions; (3) whether there are any private interests involved, or whether the states or political subdivisions involved have the powers and interests of an owner; (4) whether control and supervision of the organization is vested in public authority or authorities; (5) if express or implied statutory or other authority is necessary for the creation and/or use of such an instrumentality, and whether such authority exists; and (6) the degree of financial autonomy and the source of its operating expenses.

See Rose v. Long Island R.R. Pension Plan, 828 F.2d 910, 918 (2d Cir.1987) (quoting Rev. Rul. 57-128, 1957-1 C.B. 311), *cert. denied*, 485 U.S. 936 (1988).

It is unnecessary to define the extent to which MET must meet all of the elements of this list. Even if it were necessary only to fulfill a substantial part of the requirements, MET would fail to meet at least elements (3), (4), and (6). Substantial private interests are involved in MET, for (put in its best light) it was conceived primarily to alleviate parents' fears about the affordability of higher education. Private individuals, and not public actors, have the right to receive distributions from the Trust, either in tuition payments or in cash. In addition, MET is an independent entity that is not controlled or supervised by the State. MET's funds are not commingled with the State's general revenue fund, ensuring that the State cannot "raid" the Trust. MET, then, has significant financial autonomy from the State, since the State does not guarantee MET's promise to provide the tuition payments of those beneficiaries who enroll in Michigan's state colleges and universities. MET also does not receive financial assistance from the State, but instead relies on the income it receives from its investments to pay for operating expenses. Although MET, a state-created entity controlled by board members selected by the governor, has an undeniable connection to the State, its activities and funding arrangements indicate that it is not integral to the functioning of the State.

II

Section 115 provides in relevant part as follows:

Gross income does not include—

> (1) income derived from any public utility or the exercise of any essential governmental function and accruing to a State or any political subdivision thereof. . . .

26 U.S.C. § 115.

Plaintiffs contend that MET serves an essential governmental function, and the income earned eventually accrues to the State because much of it is used to make direct payments to Michigan public colleges and universities. The district court found that § 115 did not alter MET's tax status because the statute's accrual requirement was lacking in this case. Although I have no quarrel with that conclusion, I find that MET does not perform an essential governmental function and therefore does not meet § 115's standard for tax-exempt status. *See United States v. Maryland Savings-Share Ins. Corp.*, 400 U.S. 4, 7 n. 2 (1970).

The phrase "essential governmental function" was defined long ago by the Supreme Court:

> The true distinction is between the attempted taxation of those operations of the States essential to the execution of its governmental functions, and which the State can only do itself, and those activities which are of a private character. The former, the United States may not interfere with by taxing the agencies of the State in carrying out its purposes; the latter, although regulated by the State, and exercising delegated authority, such as the right of eminent domain, are not removed from the field of legitimate Federal taxation. *Flint v. Stone Tracy Co*, 220 U.S. 107, 172 (1911). *See also South Carolina v. United States*, 199 U.S. 437, 461 (1905) (limiting tax exemption to instrumentalities "of a strictly governmental character").

Plaintiffs contend that higher education in Michigan is an essential governmental function, and I agree. However, it does not necessarily follow that providing a tuition prepayment program for those state citizens who can afford it is an essential governmental function. *See Allen v. Regents*, 304 U.S. 439, 452 (1933) ("If it be conceded that the education of its prospective citizens is an essential governmental function of [a state], as necessary to the preservation of the State as is the maintenance of its executive, legislative, and judicial branches, it does not follow that if the State elects to provide the funds for any of these purposes by conducting a business, the application of the avails in aid of necessary governmental functions withdraws the business from the field of federal taxation."). Offering a program such as MET is not something that only the State itself can do. As noted earlier, investment of money is a quintessentially private function, and investment services similar to those of the Trust are available currently through private companies.

In addition, if the MET program were discontinued, the State of Michigan would be harmed, if at all, only indirectly. The money involved in this program is entirely independent of the State, and thus dissolution of the Trust would not result in any monies flowing out of Michigan's general fund—unless the state legislature chose to bail out the Trust. Importantly, however, a bail out is not required by statute. To the extent that the MET program makes Michigan public colleges and universities more attractive to prospective students, any shortfall in revenue from a decline in enrollments if MET were dissolved could be recouped through higher tuition and would not necessarily require additional appropriations from the Michigan legislature. MET does not serve an essential governmental function with such indirect and hypothetical injury to the State.

Plaintiffs respond by noting that MET is not an investment program, but instead guarantees prepaid tuition to state universities and colleges. I might take this argument more seriously if the State pledged its full faith and credit to the MET program, because then the State would suffer direct and measurable harm if the program failed. The State provides no such guarantee, however. Instead, the legislature at its discretion can decide to bail out the Trust if it becomes actuarially unsound. Thus, MET's pledge to purchasers is chimerical. It is not bottomed on any state guarantee, but rather on wise investment strategies and the correctness of its financial assumptions to ensure the continued soundness of its guarantee. I have already voiced my doubts on this subject.

* * *

I would affirm.

Note on IRS Objections to Michigan Education Trust

Our consideration of the intergovernmental tax immunity doctrine would not be complete without noting that the Service, with the vocal support of some thoughtful scholars, continues to proclaim that *Michigan Education Trust* is just plain wrong. The Service has repeated the same mantra, almost verbatim, in just about every private letter ruling on the subject of intergovernmental tax immunity issued since *Michigan Education Trust:*

> In *State of Michigan and Michigan Education Trust v. United States*, 40 F.3d 817 (6th Cir. 1994), rev'd 802 F. Supp. 120 (W.D. Mich. 1992), the court held that the investment income of the Michigan Education Trust (MET) was not subject to current taxation under section 11(a) of the Code. The court's opinion is internally inconsistent because it concludes that MET qualifies as a political subdivision of the State of Michigan (*Id.* at 825), that MET is "in a broad sense" a municipal corporation (*Id.* at 826), and that MET is in any event an integral part of the State of Michigan (*Id.* at 829). Moreover, the court's reliance on the factors listed in Rev. Rul. 57-128, 1957 C.B. 311, to reach its conclusion is misplaced. The revenue ruling applies to entities that are separate from a state. The factors in the revenue ruling do not determine whether an enterprise is considered to be a separate entity or an integral part of the state.

PLR 9809013 (Nov. 7, 1997). At least one commentator has better summarized the objections to *Michigan Education Trust*: (1) the Court in *Michigan Education Trust* incorrectly held that the trust was a political subdivision because the trust possessed none of the three powers (tax, eminent domain, and police) available to a true sovereign, (2) the trust does not satisfy the six-part test for "instrumentality" status and, even if it did, an instrumentality is tax exempt only if it is a political subdivision (possesses sovereign powers) or is actually controlled by the state (i.e., an integral part of the state, though not a political subdivision), and (3) the trust could not be an "integral part" of a state because in fact, it had an independent existence from the state (the state has insufficient control over the Trust) and the integral part test does not apply to an organization with such an independent existence (i.e., an organization that is not actually controlled by the state). *See* Ellen Aprill, *The Integral, the Essential, and the Instrumental: Federal Income Tax Treatment of Governmental Affiliates*, 23 Iowa J. Corp. L. 803, 824–28 (1998).

The Service's requirements for an entity to be considered a political subdivision, an instrumentality, or an integral part seem difficult to follow. However, the Service appears to base the ultimate decision of whether the federal government should tax a state-sanctioned or related entity on technical requirements that, in some instances, have no probative relevance to the constitutional notion of separate sovereigns being allowed to operate without undue interference from each other. Appearances aside, though, the technical requirements are oftentimes relevant to whether there is interference by one sovereign with the sovereign activities of another. We suggest that both sides, by relying on the technical labels and niceties, are unnecessarily obscuring the overall concern. Both sides can legitimately assert that the Michigan Education Trust does or does not meet whatever technical definition should be adopted to determine whether there is an important state activity that ought not to be impeded by federal taxation. However that debate is resolved, there is a strong factual predicate from which to conclude that Michigan Education Trust is essentially nothing more than a state-sanctioned, private organization that benefits private annuitants, rather than the state, per se. We admit, though, that the conclusion begs the question of how diverse must a benefit be before it is considered "public" as opposed to private. We have also asked, in an earlier context, whether charity can exist without a benefit *necessarily* flowing to poor people. In addition, Michigan's almost complete lack of financial interest or obligation suggests that no state function is burdened or otherwise put at risk by federal taxation. But then, to the extent citizens are unable to pay tuition costs, the state's financial burdens will increase and perhaps that realization support's a policy decision not to tax the Trust.

In 1996, Congress enacted § 529, which confirmed tax exemption for "qualified state tuition programs" (QSTP). In general, a QSTP was a state program under which a person could purchase tuition credits or contribute to a college tuition savings program. To be tax exempt, the program could accept contributions only in cash, had to impose penalties on withdrawals occasioned other than by incurring higher education expenses by the beneficiary, or death or disability of the beneficiary. In addition, no contributor or beneficiary could direct the investment of the funds deposited in the program, the program had to maintain separate accounts for each beneficiary, the program had to implement safeguards to prevent persons from depositing amounts in excess of that necessary to cover future higher education expenses. In 2001, § 529 was amended to allow private institutions to maintain exempt tuition savings accounts. All other requirements essentially remained the same.

C. State-Related Entities

CODE: § 115

Revenue Ruling 90-74

1990-2 C.B. 34

Issue

If political subdivisions of a state create, fund, and operate an organization to pool the casualty risks of the participating political subdivisions, is the income of the organization excluded from gross income under section 115(1) of the Internal Revenue Code?

Facts

X is a non-profit organization incorporated under the laws of State *A*. County governments may, under the laws of State *A*, form and become members of *X* to pool the casualty risks of the participating counties. The governing body of each county must authorize the county to join *X* and must designate an individual to represent the county at meetings of *X*. The board of directors, elected by and from the representatives of the counties, controls *X*.

Each member appropriates funds from its general revenues to pay to *X* an initial deposit and an annual fee based upon its size and its actuarially determined level of risk. *X* also receives investment income. *X* reimburses its members for any casualty losses. In the event of dissolution, *X* will distribute its assets to its members.

Law and Analysis

Section 115(1) of the Code provides that gross income does not include income derived from the exercise of any essential governmental function and accruing to a state or political subdivision.

The determination whether a function is an essential governmental function depends on the facts and circumstances of each case. Rev. Rul. 77-261, 1977-2 C.B. 45, concludes that the income of a fund, established under a written declaration of trust to pool the temporary investments of the state and its political subdivisions, is excludable from gross income under section 115(1) of the Code. The fund was authorized by state statute, managed by the state treasurer, and benefited only the state and its political subdivisions. The ruling states that the investment of funds is a necessary incident of the power of governmental entities to raise revenue and meet expenses.

Political subdivisions insure against casualty risks and other risks arising from employee negligence, workers' compensation statutes, and employee health obligations. Insuring against these risks satisfies governmental obligations. Any private benefit to employees from insuring against these various risks is incidental to the public benefit.

Pooling casualty risks through *X* instead of purchasing commercial insurance fulfills the obligations of the political subdivisions to protect their financial integrity. *X* is created under authority granted by the governing body of each participating county and State *A*. Except for the incidental benefit to employees of the participating political subdivisions described in the preceding paragraph, no private interests participate in or benefit from the operation of *X*. Accordingly, *X* performs an essential governmental function.

Section 115(1) of the Code also requires that the income accrue to a state or a political subdivision. In Rev. Rul. 77-261, a state and the participating political subdivisions had an unrestricted right to receive a proportionate share of the income earned by a joint investment fund. The ruling states that section 115(1) does not require that the income in question accrue only to a state or a single political subdivision and concludes that the income accrues under section 115(1), even though more than one governmental entity participated in the fund.

The income of *X* is used to reimburse casualty losses incurred by the counties or to reduce the annual fees that the member counties would otherwise be required to pay to the organization. The income of *X* does not benefit private interests. Furthermore, upon dissolution, *X* will distribute its assets to its members. Therefore, the income of *X* accrues to a political subdivision within the meaning of section 115(1) of the Code.

Holding

The income of an organization formed, operated, and funded by political subdivisions to pool their casualty risks is excluded from gross income under section 115(1) of the Code. Similarly, the income of an organization formed, operated, and funded by one or more political subdivisions (or by a state and one or more political subdivisions) to pool their risks in lieu of purchasing insurance to cover their public liability, workers' compensation, or employees' health obligations is also excluded under section 115(1) if private interests do not, except for incidental benefits to employees of the participating state and political subdivisions, participate in or benefit from the organization.

City of Bethel, Alaska v. United States

594 F.2d 1301 (9th Cir. 1979)

Before Wright, Goodwin and Anderson, Circuit Judges.

Anderson, J. This is an appeal from a tax refund action brought by City of Bethel, Alaska (Bethel), and Community Liquor Sales, Inc. (CLS). After a bench trial, the district court found that the revenue in question was exempt from federal income tax under section 115(a) of the Internal Revenue Code of 1954. We reverse because the revenue had not accrued to Bethel and therefore was taxable income to CLS.

Facts

For years Bethel has been plagued with alcohol-related problems. In 1965 the citizens of Bethel voted to prohibit the sale of alcohol in the City. The problems continued, however, for alcohol purchased legally elsewhere was readily available in Bethel. In 1966 the citizens voted to end prohibition.

To control the sale of alcohol, CLS was incorporated and licensed as the sole licit supplier of alcohol in Bethel. CLS was a nonprofit corporation managed by three trustees, all of whom served at the pleasure of the Bethel City Council. . . . CLS's profits, with minor exceptions, were retained to purchase inventory until CLS was dissolved in 1973 . . . . The assets of the corporation were then turned over to Bethel.

From 1967 through 1971, CLS filed returns and paid income tax on its net profits. During those years CLS and Bethel maintained wholly separate books and accounts. CLS did pay licensing and rental fees to Bethel, but CLS's profits were not listed as an account receivable or other asset on Bethel's financial statements.

Analysis

Section 115(a) exempts from income tax income "accruing to a State . . . or any political subdivision thereof. . . ." . . . CLS was a distinct legal entity. The income was never actually transferred to Bethel from CLS, nor do any bookkeeping entries reflect that the income was owed to Bethel. The Eighth Circuit has held, and we agree, that a right *en futuro* to receive the assets of a corporation upon dissolution cannot be equated to present accrual of the income. . . . Through its power of appointment, Bethel did control CLS, but control of a corporation does not automatically cause the income to accrue to the controlling entity. . . . In Bear Gulch the court held that a corporation's retained earnings do not accrue to a government entity for purposes of section 115(a) even though the corporation's stock is wholly owned by the government entity. Here, Bethel could have exercised its control to effect accrual by having the trustees distribute CLS's profits to the City, but it never did.

If the income had been transferred to Bethel coffers and then expended to finance CLS's operations, a different result might follow, for then the money undeniably would have accrued to Bethel. Instead, the income was retained by CLS and shown as an asset on its financial statements. No offsetting debit to Bethel was reflected in CLS's financial records, nor did Bethel's financial records reflect any right to receive income from CLS. Inasmuch as the two entities were operated separately and reported their income separately, the income of one cannot be said to be the income of the other without more. Here, the income was never received by the City, and there is no indication either the City or CLS recognized a present obligation to the City from CLS. No matter what expectation the City might have had that it would receive distributions from CLS, the amounts of those receipts could not be fixed with any reasonable certainty until the distributions were actually made. Therefore, there is no basis for inferring accrual as that term is ordinarily defined.

* * *

REVERSED.

Questions

1. If the income had actually accrued to the City, would it have been exempt?

2. If your answer to Question 1 is "no" what change could be made to ensure that the income is exempt?

3. In a few states, Pennsylvania, New Hampshire, Oregon, Utah, Vermont, Washington, and Idaho, for example, wines and distilled liquor can only be purchased from state-owned "Wine and Spirit" stores. Can the federal government impose income taxes from the sale of wine and spirits on those states? If so, has the federal government waived its right to do so in IRC § 115?

D. Native American Governing Bodies

CODE: § 7871(a), (d)

Section 7871 implicitly recognizes that Native American societies are essentially sovereign and that their governing bodies exercise powers normally associated with the sovereign. Thus, the same theory or policy upon which states are tax exempt should apply to Native American governing bodies. Note, however, that § 7871 does not confirm that such bodies are exempt from income taxes. Instead, the provision works to include Native American governing bodies in several provisions that impose tax benefits or duties vis-a-vis states. Neither, though, is there a provision explicitly exempting states from income taxes. As with states, Native American governing bodies enjoy income tax exemption by virtue of the Service's decision not to impose taxes on those bodies (and, of course, Congressional acquiescence to that decision). Note, also, that subdivisions of Native American governing bodies can also achieve tax exemption, just as with subdivisions of states.

25 U.S.C. § 477. Incorporation of Indian Tribes; Charter; Ratification by Election

The Secretary of the Interior may, upon petition by any tribe, issue a charter of incorporation to such tribe: Provided, that such charter shall not become operative until ratified by the governing body of such tribe. Such charter may convey to the incorporated tribe the power to purchase, take by gift, or bequest, or otherwise, own, hold, manage, operate, and dispose of property of every description, real and personal, including the power to purchase restricted Indian lands and to issue in exchange therefore interests in corporate property, and such further powers as may be incidental to the conduct of corporate business, not inconsistent with law, but no authority shall be granted to sell, mortgage, or lease for a period exceeding twenty-five years any trust or restricted lands included in the limits of the reservation. Any charter so issued shall not be revoked or surrendered except by Act of Congress.

Private Letter Ruling 200207013

November 14, 2001

This letter is in response to your request for a ruling that the Authority is a political subdivision of Tribe within the meaning of 7871(d) of the Internal Revenue Code.

Facts and Representations

You make the following factual representations. Tribe is listed as an Indian tribal government in Rev. Proc. 2001-15, 2001-05 I.R.B. 465, which lists Indian tribal governments that are to be treated as states for certain federal tax purposes pursuant to 7701(a)(40) and 7871(a). Authority is not included in the list of political subdivisions of an Indian tribal government . . .

Authority provides general governmental services to the tenants of the area within the physical boundaries of the Authority, including police, fire, emergency roads, sewer, water, land use planning, and other standard governmental services. On Date 1, Tribe enacted the Act, which authorizes Tribe to grant charters for municipal corporations to be located within the Reservation. On Date 2, pursuant to the Act, Tribe chartered Authority as a municipal corporation of the Authority. Pursuant to its charter, Authority is designated as a political subdivision of Tribe and is authorized to exercise the following powers within its physical boundaries: taxing and police powers, as well as the power of eminent domain.

The Board of Directors of Authority consists of a president and two board members elected by the Board of Directors of Tribe. The president and board members may be removed in the same manner as they are elected. Authority must file with the Board of Directors of Tribe on an annual basis a full report of its financial activities.

Law and Analysis

The Indian Tribal Governmental Tax Status Act . . . added provisions to the Internal Revenue Code that pertain to the tax status of Indian tribal governments. For two years beginning in 1983, Indian tribal governments were to be treated as states for some federal tax purposes. . . .

Section 7701(a)(40)(A) defines the term "Indian tribal government" as the governing body of any tribe, band, community, village, or group of Indians, or (if applicable) Alaska Natives, which is determined by the Secretary, after consultation with the Secretary of the Interior, to exercise governmental functions. Section 7871(a) treats an Indian tribal government as a state for certain specified tax purposes. In the legislative history to 7871(a), Congress indicated that this provision of the Code will not apply to any Indian tribal government unless it is recognized by the Treasury Department, after consultation with the Interior Department, as exercising sovereign powers. The legislative history provides that sovereign powers include the power to tax, the power of eminent domain, and police powers (such as control over zoning, police protection, and fire protection).

* * *

Indian tribes possess inherent sovereignty except where it has been limited by treaty or statute, or by implication as a necessary result of their dependent status. Indian tribes are viewed as having certain inherent powers, including the power to tax and administer justice, whether they choose to take actions to exercise them or not. A written constitution or other governing document is not a prerequisite for the exercise of inherent sovereign powers. . . .

Section 7871(d) provides that for purposes of 7871(a), a subdivision of an Indian tribal government shall be treated as a political subdivision of a state if (and only if) the Secretary of the Treasury determines (after consultation with the Secretary of the Interior) that such subdivision has been delegated the right to exercise one or more of the substantial governmental functions of the Indian tribal government.

* * *

Section 2.03 of Rev. Proc. 84-37 provides that a subdivision of an Indian tribal government that has been delegated one of the generally accepted sovereign powers may qualify as a political subdivision of a state as provided under 7871(d). Section 2.03 indicates that the generally accepted sovereign powers of states are the power to tax, the power of eminent domain, and the police power. Tribe is a federally recognized Indian tribe. Pursuant to the Act, Tribe chartered Authority as a municipal corporation of the Authority. The charter was reviewed and approved by the BIA. Pursuant to its charter from Tribe, Authority is designated as a political subdivision of Tribe and is authorized to exercise taxing and police powers, as well as the power of eminent domain. The portion of each power delegated to Authority is not insubstantial.

This office has consulted with the United States Department of the Interior regarding Tribe and Authority. The United States Department of the Interior has opined that Tribe has effectively delegated to Authority the power of eminent domain and the power to tax. Accordingly, after consultation with the Secretary of the Interior, we conclude that, within the meaning of 7871(d), Authority has been delegated the power to exercise one or more of the substantial governmental functions of Tribe. Therefore, for purposes of 7871, Authority will be treated as a political subdivision of a state.

Conclusion

Pursuant to 7871(d), Authority will be treated as a political subdivision of an Indian tribal government (Tribe). Accordingly, Authority will be treated as a political subdivision of a state for purposes of 7871.Except as specifically stated above, no opinion is expressed regarding the consequences of this transaction under any provision of the Code or regulations thereunder.

This ruling letter is directed only to the taxpayer who requested it. Section 6110(k)(3) provides that it may not be used or cited as precedent.

Revenue Ruling 94-16

1994-1 C.B. 19

Issue

Is income earned by an Indian tribe or tribal corporation from the conduct of a commercial business subject to federal income tax?

Facts

Situation 1. Tribe T, a federally recognized Indian tribe, conducts an unincorporated commercial business both on and off T's reservation.

Situation 2. Tribe U incorporates itself as Corporation X under section 17 of the Indian Reorganization Act of 1934, 25 U.S.C. section 477 (1993) (IRA). X conducts a commercial business both on and off U's reservation.

Situation 3. Tribe V organizes Corporation Y under the law of State S. V is the sole shareholder of Y, which conducts a commercial business both on and off V's reservation.

Law and Analysis

Section 1 of the Internal Revenue Code imposes a tax on the taxable income of individuals, trusts and estates. Section 11 imposes a tax on the taxable income of corporations.

Section 61 of the Code provides that gross income means all income from whatever source derived, unless otherwise provided by law. Section 63 defines taxable income as gross income minus deductions.

Revenue Ruling 67-284, 1967-2 C.B. 55, 58, modified on another issue by Rev. Rul. 74-13, 1974-1 C.B. 14, holds that Indian tribes are not taxable entities. The revenue ruling further holds that tribal income not otherwise exempt from federal income tax is includible in the gross income of the Indian tribal member when distributed to, or constructively received by, the tribal member.

Revenue Ruling 81-295, 1981-2 C.B. 15, relying on *Mescalero Apache Tribe v. Jones*, 411 U.S. 145, 157, n. 13 (1973), holds that an Indian tribal corporation organized under section 17 of the IRA shares the same tax status as the Indian tribe and is not taxable on income from activities carried on within the boundaries of the reservation.

However, a corporation organized by an Indian tribe under state law is not the same as an Indian tribal corporation organized under section 17 of the IRA and does not share the same tax status as the Indian tribe for federal income tax purposes. Generally, the choice of corporate form will not be ignored. . . .

Because an Indian tribe is not a taxable entity, any income earned by an unincorporated tribe, regardless of the location of the business activities that produced the income, is not subject to federal income tax. An Indian tribal corporation organized under section 17 of the IRA shares the same tax status as the tribe. Therefore, any income earned by such a corporation, regardless of the location of the business activities that produced the income, is not subject to federal income tax. However, a corporation organized by an Indian tribe under state law does not share the same tax status as the tribe for federal income tax purposes and is subject to federal income tax on any income earned, regardless of the location of the business activities that produced the income.

Accordingly, Tribe T in Situation 1 and Corporation X in Situation 2 are not taxable entities and are not subject to federal income tax on any income earned from their business activities. Corporation Y in Situation 3 is a taxable entity and is subject to federal income tax on all income earned from its business activities.

Holding

An unincorporated Indian tribe or an Indian tribal corporation organized under section 17 of the IRA is not subject to federal income tax on the income earned in the conduct of commercial business on or off the tribe's reservation. However, a corporation organized by an Indian tribe under state law is subject to federal income tax on the income earned in the conduct of the commercial business on and off the tribe's reservation.

This revenue ruling deals only with federal income taxes. It does not affect the application of other federal taxes, such as employment taxes and excise taxes (including excise taxes on wagering), to Indian tribes or tribal corporations.

Ramsey v. United States

302 F.3d 1074 (9th Cir. 2002), cert. denied, 540 U.S. 812 (2003)

Overview

TROTT, CIRCUIT JUDGE: The United States appeals the district court's grant of summary judgment in favor of Kip R. Ramsey ("Ramsey") awarding him a refund of federal heavy vehicle and diesel fuel taxes, penalties and interest. The government argues that Ramsey's prior federal lawsuit challenging a similar Washington state tax is not controlling, and that the district court erred by deferring to it. . . . As in his prior suit, Ramsey claims that the 1855 Yakama Treaty exempts him from all taxes burdening his use of the public roads. We agree that the Treaty is the relevant starting point, but we disagree with Ramsey's gloss on its interpretation. The federal standard requires a definite expression of exemption stated plainly in a statute or treaty before any further inquiry is made or any canon of interpretation employed. Applying the federal standard to this case, we find no "express exemptive language" in the relevant Treaty provision. Thus, we reverse the district court's decision and remand for entry of summary judgment in favor of the United States.

Background

Ramsey is a member of the federally recognized Yakama Indian Tribe ("Yakama"). He lives and works on the Yakama Reservation. He is the sole owner of Tiin-Ma Logging, which cuts timber only on the reservation. Ramsey hauls his lumber to off-reservation markets using diesel fuel trucks that exceed 55,000 pounds gross vehicle weight.

Section 4481 of the Internal Revenue Code . . . ("heavy vehicle tax") requires that Ramsey pay a tax on his trucks that exceed 55,000 pounds. Section 4041 ("diesel fuel tax") mandates that Ramsey pay tax on diesel fuel. See 26 U.S.C. § 4041. For the period between 1986 and 1993, Ramsey was assessed and paid $460,702.55 in federal heavy vehicle and diesel fuel taxes, penalties and interest.

Ramsey disputed the assessed taxes and requested a refund from the Internal Revenue Service ("IRS") claiming the federal taxes were preempted by the Treaty with the Yakamas, June 9, 1855, 12 Stat. 951 (1859) ("Treaty"). In particular, Article III, paragraph 1 of the Treaty reads:

> If necessary for the public convenience, roads may be run throughout the said reservation; and on the other hand, the right of way, with free access from the same to the nearest public highway, is secured to them; as also the right in common with citizens of the United States, to travel upon all public highways.

12 Stat. at 952–53. Ramsey argued that the Treaty exempted the Yakama from paying fees to use the public highways, citing as authority his successful challenge to a similar, state-imposed, highway-related tax in *Yakama Indian Nation v. Flores*, 955 F. Supp. 1229 (E.D. Wash. 1997), which we affirmed in *Cree v. Flores*, 157 F.3d 762 (9th Cir. 1998) (*Cree II*). Unswayed, the IRS denied Ramsey's request for a refund.

Ramsey filed suit in district court to settle the refund dispute. On cross motions for summary judgment, the district court held, based on *Cree II*, that the Yakama were exempt from federal taxes for the use of public highways. The district court entered judgment in favor of Ramsey. The United States appealed.

Discussion

* * *

B. Tax Exemption Analysis — Federal and State Standards

Ramsey argues that this case is controlled by *Cree II*'s exemption of the Yakama from state heavy vehicle taxes. In the alternative, Ramsey argues that the "in common with" language in the highway use provision of the Treaty creates an exemption from the federal heavy vehicle and diesel fuel taxes.

Application of Cree II

Ramsey's argument begins with *Cree v. Waterbury* . . . in which several Yakama Indians who operated logging companies, including Ramsey, claimed that Article III of the Treaty precluded application of Washington's heavy vehicle tax to the Yakama. The district court agreed with the Yakama, but based its decision on the Supreme Court's construction of the "in common with" language in the Treaty's fishing rights provision without analyzing separately the "in common with" language in the highway use provision....

On appeal, this Court concluded that "state tax laws applied to Indians outside of Indian country, such as those at issue here, are presumed valid 'absent express federal law to the contrary.' ... We remanded the case and instructed the district court to "examine the Treaty language as a whole, the circumstances surrounding the Treaty, and the conduct of the parties since the Treaty was signed in order to interpret the scope of the highway right." ... The district court was to determine if the Treaty prohibited state heavy vehicle taxation of the Yakama based on the Treaty's language and the parties' intent when they signed the Treaty.

On remand, the district court considered extrinsic evidence of the Yakama's understanding of the treaty and found that the Treaty, as understood by the Yakama, "unambiguously reserved to the Yakamas the right to travel the public highways without restriction for purposes of hauling goods to market." ... In the alternative, the district court found that even if the Yakama's right to travel was not so unambiguously expressed in the Treaty, the Indian-friendly canons of construction required that it should be read in the Yakama's favor.... We affirmed on these latter grounds in large part because the state offered no evidence to suggest that the parties to the Treaty intended to limit the Yakama's broad reading of this right....

In this case, the United States agrees that if *Cree II*'s interpretation of the Treaty is equally applicable to both state and federal taxes, Ramsey would be exempt from federal road use taxes. The government argues, however, that the *Cree II* analysis is inapplicable to federal taxes because there is a different standard for exemptions from federal taxation. We agree.

In fact, this Court recognized a distinction between the standard for state tax exemptions and federal tax exemptions in *Cree I*:

> The State argues that the fees "implement federal highway financing policy" and that consequently, the fees are valid unless the Treaty creates a "definitely expressed" exemption. *The State presents no authority for this court to find that the state-imposed truck fees should be judged according to the standard for federal fees.* 78 F.3d at 1403 n. 4 (emphasis added) (citation omitted).

The different standards stem from the state and federal government's distinct relationships with Indian tribes. The federal government has plenary and exclusive power to deal with tribes.... States, on the other hand, interact with the tribes in a more limited capacity. A state's regulatory authority over tribal members is limited by the tribal right of self-government and the preemptive effect of federal law.... For this reason, all citizens, including Indians, are subject to federal taxation unless expressly exempted, ... while a state's authority to tax tribal members is limited depending on the subject and location of the tax....

The applicability of a federal tax to Indians depends on whether express exemptive language exists within the text of the statute or treaty. The language need not explicitly state that Indians are exempt from the specific tax at issue; it must only provide evidence of the federal government's intent to exempt Indians from taxation. Treaty language such as "free from incumbrance," "free from taxation," and "free from fees," are but some examples of express exemptive language required to find Indians exempt from federal tax.

Only if express exemptive language is found in the text of the statue or treaty should the court determine if the exemption applies to the tax at issue. At that point, any ambiguities as to whether the exemptive language applies to the tax at issue should be construed in favor of the Indians. In *Karmun v. Commissioner* [84-2 USTC §10,003] 749 F.2d 567, 569 (9th Cir. 1984), we noted that "[n]otwithstanding the canon of interpretation that resolved ambiguities in statutes and treaties in favor of Indians, we have recognized that the intent to exempt income of Indians from taxation must be clearly expressed." In addition, we stated that "[p]olicy considerations by themselves are insufficient to justify the implication of a tax exemption absent express exemptive language." . . . Therefore, when reviewing a claim for a federal tax exemption, we do not engage the canon of construction favoring the Indians unless express exemptive language is first found in the text of the statute or treaty. Only if such language exists, do we consider whether it could be "reasonably construed" to support the claimed exemption. . . .

When a court interprets a state's taxation of Indian's off-reservation activities, the court determines if there is an express federal law prohibiting the tax. The federal law must be interpreted in the light most favorable to the Indians, and extrinsic evidence may be used to show the federal government's and Indians' intent. Unlike the federal standard, there is no requirement to find express exemptive language before employing the canon of construction favoring Indians.

In *Cree II* this court implemented the Indian-friendly canon of construction and analyzed the history of the Treaty and the understanding of the Yakama to find an "express federal law" which exempted the Yakama from state taxation. *Cree II*, 157 F.3d at 769. We held that the Yakama Treaty should be interpreted "to guarantee the Yakamas the right to transport goods to market over public highways without payment of fees for that use." *Id.* Ramsey argues that *Cree II*'s Treaty interpretation, finding an "express federal law" exempting the Yakama from state heavy vehicle taxes, controls this case when looking for "express exemptive language" to exempt the Yakama from similar federal taxation. *Cree II*'s interpretation, however, is not binding on the question of *federal* taxation because the initial inquiry when exempting Indians from *federal* taxes is whether the federal law in question contains express exemptive language at all. The canon of construction favoring the Indian when ambiguities are present in a statute or treaty does not come into play absent such language.

* * *

2. Application of the Federal Standard

Applying the federal standard, we hold that the relevant Treaty provision contains no "express exemptive language." The Treaty simply states that "free access from the [reservation] to the nearest public highway, is secured to [the Yakama]; as also the right, in common with the citizens of the United States, to travel upon all public highways." 12 State at 953. This provision does not provide express language from which we can discern an intent to exempt the Yakama from federal heavy vehicle and diesel fuel taxation. The only exemptive language in the Treaty is the "free access" language. "Free access," however, does not modify the right to travel upon the public roadways. Indeed, the clause granting the Yakama the "right, in common with citizens of the United States, to travel upon all public highways" contains no exemptive language. "In common with" does not express an intent to exempt the Yakama from taxes. Thus, there is no express exemptive language in the Treaty to exempt the Yakama from the generally applicable, federal heavy vehicle and diesel fuel taxes. Absent any express exemptive language to the contrary, the taxes at issue apply to the Yakama, and the district court's judgment in favor of Ramsey must be reversed and summary judgment entered into in favor of the United States.

Conclusion

Ramsey's prior federal case, analyzing a state's heavy vehicle tax and the Yakama Treaty, is not binding in this lawsuit dealing with a similar federal tax. When the Treaty is analyzed under the federal standard, there is no express language exempting the Yakama from the heavy vehicle and diesel fuel taxes, nor can we find any broader exemptive language that could be reasonably construed as encompassing such an exemption. Thus, we remand for entry of summary judgment in favor of the United States.

Questions

1. Assume A, a state, operates a lottery and earns substantial revenues.

    a. If the lottery is conducted through A's Department of Treasury, may the federal government impose an income tax on the revenues? If the federal government taxes all gambling winnings but is silent as to state gambling winnings, will the lottery be exempt?

    b. If each political subdivision of A may conduct a lottery, will the lottery be exempt from income tax in the absence of a federal statute specifically taxing the lottery?

    c. If the lottery is conducted through a statutorily created corporation, whose board is elected by voters every four years, that may sue or be sued in its own name, to which the state's full faith and credit has not been pledged and is under no public constraint or oversight other than that all proceeds must be paid over to the Department of Treasury, will the lottery be exempt from federal income tax?

    d. If only the state may conduct lotteries and it does so through a corporation organized pursuant to the state's general corporation law under a charter that requires the net revenues to be paid over to the Department of Treasury on an annual basis, will the corporation's revenues be exempt from tax? What if the corporation pays its officers exorbitant salaries?

By 2000, more than 200 Indian tribes operated casinos employing more than 300,000 people. In 2001, those gaming facilities grossed nearly $13 billion annually, none of which was subject to federal taxation. Mark Cowan, *Leaving Money on the Table(s): An Examination of Federal Income Tax Policy Towards Indian Tribes*, 6 FLA. TAX REV. 345 (2004). Is this good social, economic, or political policy?

PART FIVE

Taxation of Exempt Organizations — Unrelated Business Income Tax

Chapter 25

Unrelated Business Income Tax—In General

Read, but do not yet study, the following provisions:

CODE: §§ 511(a)–(b); 512(a)(1), 512(b), 512(c); 513(a), (c), Skim § 514

The unrelated business income tax (UBIT) is a primary source of statutory and regulatory complexity relating to the tax law of charities and other exempt organizations. However, the complexity is caused primarily by the dense detail of the provisions and number of issues pertaining to UBIT, rather than by an inherent substantive difficulty. The code provisions comprising UBIT, §§ 511–514, are long and detailed, even by tax standards. Those already detailed provisions are further interpreted by lengthy regulations, not to mention reams of technical advice memoranda and more caselaw, probably, than any other substantive area pertaining to tax-exempt organizations. Despite all of that, UBIT jurisprudence is still characterized by uncertainty and recurrent policy debate.

With the complexity and uncertainty pertaining to UBIT in mind, we begin with a very well-written synopsis, in hopes of orienting the reader and thereby making the subsequent detailed study easier. Although the synopsis was written and delivered to Congress in 1987, it still gives an accurate and helpfully broad overview of UBIT. Obviously there will have been some changes in the statistical data cited; students may easily update that data from publicly accessible sources. We note changes to substantive law in footnotes or later in this and subsequent chapters.

After this synopsis in this chapter, in the two following chapters (Chapters 26 and 27) we undertake a detailed study of the three findings necessary for the imposition of UBIT—(1) the conduct of a trade or business, which is (2) regularly carried on, and (3) not substantially related to the achievement of the purpose for which tax exemption has been granted. In the following chapter (Chapter 28), we look at issues pertaining to the allocation of deductible expenses to unrelated trade or business income and UBIT of controlled entities. In Chapter 29, we look at the unrelated debt financing provisions contained in § 514, and we finish in Chapter 30 with a discussion of special UBIT Rules.

Statement of O. Donaldson Chapoton

Deputy Assistant Secretary (Tax Policy) Department of the Treasury
Before the Subcommittee on Oversight of the Committee on
Ways and Means U.S. House of Representatives[1]

Mr. Chairman and Members of the Committee:

I am pleased to have the opportunity to present the Treasury Department's views concerning the appropriate tax treatment of income-producing activities of exempt organizations.

The exemption of charitable, religious, and educational organizations from tax has been a part of federal law since 1894 when the first federal act imposing a general tax on the income and profits of corporations was enacted. Many other tax exemption provisions, including those for labor unions, trade associations, and social clubs, were enacted over seventy years ago. Despite, or perhaps because of, the long history of tax exemptions in the federal income tax law, there is little guidance in the legislative record as to the rationale for exempting particular organizations from tax.

Over the years, the exempt sector has grown enormously in both size and diversity. Moreover, many exempt organizations have come gradually to derive much or all of their income from sources other than donations. These changes have not only increased the importance of tax exemption to the exempt sector, but have also tended to blur the historical differences in activities and funding between exempt and taxable organizations.

As more fully explained below, on two previous occasions, Congress has addressed the taxation of income-producing activities of exempt organizations in a comprehensive manner. In 1950, largely in response to concerns about unfair competition between exempt organizations and taxable businesses, Congress enacted the unrelated business income tax ("UBIT"). In 1969, Congress revisited the area and expanded application of the UBIT.

In the 1980s, the income-producing activities of exempt organizations have again become matters of concern. The small business community has complained that current rules are insufficient to protect them from unfair competition. Others have questioned the rationale for the exemption of certain activities under current law.

1. Committee on Ways and Means Serial No. 100-74, p. 24-42, May 9, 1988, https://congressional-proquest-com.proxy.library.vanderbilt.edu/congressional/docview/t29.d30.hrg-1988-wam-0016?accountid=14816.

1

I. Background

A. General Description of Tax-Exempt Organizations

The Code does not prohibit tax-exempt organizations (other than private foundations) from engaging in business activities for profit. If such business activities are related to the tax-exempt purpose of the organization, such as the sale by a museum of reproductions of its art collection, any profit from such business is exempt from tax. If such a business is unrelated to the exempt purpose of the organization, however, such as the operation of a manufacturing facility by a university, any profits from the unrelated business are subject to income tax, generally to the same extent as the profits of a taxable business. The fact that an organization is required to pay tax on its unrelated business income does not, in general, affect the organization's tax-exempt status. Nonetheless, if the operation of an unrelated business becomes the primary purpose of a tax-exempt organization, and its exempt function becomes a secondary purpose, the organization will cease to qualify for tax exemption under the Code.

* * *

D. Funding for the Nonprofit Sector

Most nonprofit organizations finance their activities through a number of sources: government grants, private donations, fees for services, operation of businesses and investments yielding income such as interest, dividends, rent, or royalties. The relative reliance on these different revenue sources differs greatly among subsectors of the nonprofit community. For example, while religious organizations rely mainly on private contributions, health service organizations rely on fees and charges for most of their funding, and social service organizations rely most heavily on government grants.

* * *

There is some evidence that nonprofits have increased their reliance on income-producing or commercial activities in recent years. IRS Master File data show that, in 1946, organizations exempt under section 501(c)(3) obtained 59 percent of their support from business receipts, interest, dividends, rents, royalties, sales of assets and miscellaneous sources other than government grants, private contributions, dues, and assessments; 71 percent from such sources in 1975; and 78 percent in 1983.

* * *

E. The Unrelated Business Income Tax (UBIT)

As noted above, tax-exempt organizations are required to pay income taxes on their unrelated business income. In fiscal year 1985, approximately 24,000 nonprofits, or three percent of all tax-exempt organizations on the IRS Master File of Exempt Organizations, filed Form 990-T in order to report unrelated business income tax liability. In fiscal year 1986, the number of exempt organizations filing

Form 990-T increased to over 32,000. The amount of unrelated business tax revenue also increased, from about $30 million in fiscal year 1985 to $53 million in fiscal year 1986.

Data for 1984 indicate that most unrelated businesses have a small amount of gross unrelated business income. . . .

The amount of tax reported on Form 990-T, however, does not present a complete picture of tax paid by exempt organizations on unrelated businesses. Many exempt organizations operate unrelated businesses in taxable subsidiaries which file corporate income tax returns. Under current reporting requirements, it is not possible to identify the returns of taxable corporations owned by exempt organizations or to correlate such returns with those of their parents. Thus, no data are available with respect to the amount of tax paid by subsidiaries of exempt organizations.

II. Current Law

A. Historical Development

Prior to 1950, the law was unclear as to the taxation of unrelated business activities of tax-exempt organizations. Under the "destination of income" rule, the majority of courts had held that a tax-exempt organization did not lose its tax exemption by virtue of the conduct of an unrelated business so long as the profits from the business were dedicated to charitable purposes. In fact, a "feeder" organization that engaged exclusively in commercial, non-exempt activities was treated as exempt from tax so long as all the profits from the organization were distributed to an affiliated charitable organization. The majority view was thus that the destination of income, not its source, was the appropriate test for tax exemption. Because of the liberality of the destination of income rule, prior to 1950 a number of charitable organizations, carried on unrelated businesses—businesses that often competed directly with taxable companies.

In 1950, Congress responded to the operation by exempt organizations of unrelated businesses by enacting a tax on such organizations' unrelated business income. The legislative history of the Revenue Act of 1950 indicates that Congress was primarily concerned with the issue of "fair competition." Both the House and Senate reports state that:

> The problem at which the tax on unrelated business income is directed is primarily that of unfair competition. The tax-free status of [section 501(c)] organizations enables them to use their profits tax-free to expand operations, while their competitors can expand only with the profits remaining after taxes. Also, a number of examples have arisen where these organizations have, in effect, used their tax exemptions to buy an ordinary business. That is, they have acquired the business with little or no investment on their own part and paid for it in installments out of subsequent earnings—a procedure which usually could not be followed if the business were taxable.

As part of the Revenue Act of 1950, Congress also enacted the "feeder organization" provision, which provides that an organization carrying on a trade or business for profit shall not be exempt under section 501 on the ground that all of its profits are payable to another exempt organization.

In addition to directly operating a commercial enterprise, some tax-exempt organizations engaged in a transaction which became popular during the late 1940s — the "sale and lease-back" of a taxable business to an exempt organization. In such transactions, a charitable organization would acquire a property (such as real estate) from a business, often borrowing to finance the entire acquisition, and would then lease the property back to the seller under a long-term lease. The result of the transaction was that the seller received capital for use in its business, the seller's taxable income was substantially reduced by the deductible rent, and the charity received the difference between the rental payments and its loan amortization payments, with little or no money down.

The House and Senate reports identified three principal objections to sale and lease-back arrangements. First, the tax-exempt organization was trading on its exemption because the only contribution it made to the sale and lease-back was its tax exemption. Second, the lease-back transactions, if unchecked, would result in tax-exempt entities owning the bulk of the commercial and industrial real estate in the country. Third, the exempt organization that entered into the sale and lease-back and either paid an above-market price for the property, or charged below-market rent for the use of the property, had in effect sold part of its tax exemption. In response to these objections, Congress imposed the tax on unrelated business income on income from the long-term rental of debt-financed real property and personal property leased in connection with it.

Notwithstanding the changes made by the Revenue Act of 1950, many tax-exempt organizations continued to engage in unrelated commercial activities. Such activities were permissible under the law because first, a number of tax-exempt organizations as churches, social clubs, and fraternal beneficiary societies were not subject to the tax on unrelated business income and second, because the tax on rental income from debt-financed real property did not apply to leases of five years or less. The tax on debt-financed real property was avoided by so-called *Clay Brown* transactions — "bootstrap acquisitions" similar to the sale and lease-back transactions described earlier.

In response to the continued involvement of charitable organizations in unrelated businesses, Congress in 1969 revisited this area of the law and made several significant changes. First, the rules regarding debt-financed property were expanded to include all debt-financed property unrelated to the exempt purpose of the organization, with no exception for short-term leases. Second, the tax on unrelated business income was expanded to apply to all exempt organizations, except certain U.S. instrumentalities created and expressly granted tax-exemption by a specific Act of Congress. Third, the investment income of social clubs and voluntary employees' beneficiary associations was subjected to tax, based on the rationale that an exemption for investment income constituted an unwarranted subsidy of recreational or personal activities. Fourth, any rent, interest or royalties paid by an 80-percent controlled subsidiary to a tax-exempt parent was included in unrelated business taxable income of the parent in an amount reflecting the portion of the subsidiary's income that would be unrelated business income if earned directly by the tax-exempt parent organization. The controlled subsidiary rule was imposed to discourage charitable organizations from "renting" part of their physical plants to taxable subsidiaries, thereby reducing or eliminating the taxable income of the subsidiaries. And fifth, Congress clarified the definition of the term "trade or business" to include activities carried on within a larger aggregate of similar activities. Thus, the sale of advertising in a magazine published by an exempt organization could be treated as an unrelated business, even though publication of the magazine was the organization's exempt function.

Each of the changes made by the Tax Reform Act of 1969 had the effect of tightening the rules with respect to the unrelated business activities of charitable organizations, helping to ensure that such organizations paid tax on income from business activities unrelated to the purpose for which they were granted tax exemption.

During the early 1980s, a number of charitable organizations again became involved in leasing transactions with taxable entities although with a different twist from the sale and lease-back transactions described earlier. Due to the investment tax credit and accelerated depreciation, certain types of property were effectively subject to a negative rate of tax, generating credits or losses that would offset income from the other investments. Because tax-exempt organizations could not benefit from these tax incentives directly, a number of exempt organizations, including schools, city governments, federal agencies, and foreign governments, sold part of their asset to taxable businesses that could make use of the tax incentives and would then lease the property back on a long-term basis. As part of the Tax Reform Act of 1984, Congress sought to discourage such transactions by providing that property used by a tax-exempt entity (including foreign and domestic governments) is not eligible for tax incentives such as the investment tax credit and accelerated depreciation.

Subsequent to the 1969 Act, exceptions were created to the debt-financed property rule for certain real estate investments. In 1980, with respect to pension trusts, in 1984 with respect to educational institutions, and in 1986 with respect to real property title holding companies, the general rule was modified, to exclude from the debt-financed property rules the acquisition of real estate with debt so long as certain requirements were met.

B. Structure of the Unrelated Business Income Tax

In general, the UBIT is imposed on the unrelated business taxable income ("UBTI") of organizations that are otherwise exempt from tax under Code section 501(a). Tax-exempt trusts are taxed at individual tax rates and all other exempt organizations are taxed at corporate rates.

The term "unrelated trade or business" means any trade or business that is regularly carried on and is not substantially related, aside from the need of the organization for funds, to the performance of the purpose for which the organization was granted exempt status.

Specifically excluded from the term "unrelated trade or business" is any trade or business (1) in which substantially all the work is performed by volunteers; (2) which is carried on by a section 501(c)(3) organization or a state or city college or university primarily for the convenience of its members, students, patients, officers, or employees; or (3) which is the selling of donated merchandise. Certain trade show and similar activities are also specifically excluded, as are services furnished by certain cooperative hospital service organizations, the rental of telephone poles by cooperative telephone or electric companies, the rental of mailing lists to certain other exempt organizations, and the distribution of low-cost articles incidental to soliciting charitable contributions. Conducting bingo games is also specifically excluded so long as bingo is legal under state law and is not ordinarily conducted on a commercial basis.

UBTI is defined as the gross income derived from any unrelated trade or business less deductions directly connected with the carrying on of such trade or business, subject to certain modifications.[2]

Among the most significant of the modifications are the following:

1. All dividends, interest, payments with respect to loans of securities, and annuities are excluded.

2. Royalties (including overriding royalties), whether measured by production or by gross or taxable income, are excluded.

3. Rent from real property, and rents from personal property leased with real property if the rents attributable to the personal property are only an incidental amount of the total rents received or accrued under the lease, are excluded. If more than 50 percent of the rent under a lease is attributable to personal property, then none of the rent, whether attributable to the real property or the personal property, qualifies for the exclusion. . . . .

4. All gains or losses from the sale, exchange or other disposition of property other than the sale of property of a kind properly includable in inventory and property held primarily for sale to customers in the ordinary course of a trade or business are excluded. . . . Also excluded are all gains on the lapse or termination of options to buy or sell securities written by the organization in connection with its investments activities.

5. Income from various research activities also is excluded. All income from research performed for the United States, a State, or a political subdivision of a State is excluded. In the case of a college, university, or hospital and in the case

2. ["Modifications" are further discussed in Chapter 28. — Eds.]

of an organization operating primarily for the purpose of carrying on fundamental research that makes the results of its research freely available to the public, all income derived from research is excluded, regardless of for whom performed.

6. A "specific deduction" of $1,000 is allowed from unrelated business taxable income for all tax-exempt organizations. . . .

As noted earlier, the modifications for interest, royalties, annuities and rents do not apply to an 80-percent controlled subsidiary to the extent it is engaged in a trade or business unrelated to the exempt purpose of the parent organization.

* * *

The provisions pertaining to "unrelated debt-financed income" represent an exception to the general rules in that a charitable organization can have unrelated business taxable income under this section, regardless of whether it is engaged in a trade or business.[3]

The section provides that to the extent any property held for the production of income is debt-financed, the income from the property is subject to tax.

There are a number of exclusions from the definition of debt-financed property, including the following: (1) property the use of which is substantially related to the exempt purpose of the organization, (2) property used for research activities, the income from which is specifically excluded from tax under section 512, and (3) property used in certain other trades or businesses, the income from which is excluded under section 513. . . .

A final, and very significant, exception to the debt-financed income rules is an exception, added in 1980 and subsequently amended, for the acquisition of real estate by "qualified organizations," namely, educational institutions, pension trusts, and real property title holding companies exempt under section 501(c)(25). Section 514(c)(9) provides that the term "acquisition indebtedness" does not include debt incurred by a qualified organization to purchase real property so long as certain conditions are met. . . . The elaborate requirements of section 514(c)(9) were designed, in part, to prevent charitable organizations from entering into the type of "bootstrap" acquisitions that were common prior to the Tax Reform Act of 1969.

III. Tax Policy Considerations

A. Rationale for Tax Exemption of Nonprofit Organizations

As described above, the legislative record provides little direct evidence as to the original rationale for the exemption of certain organizations from tax. Moreover, the current diversity in activities and funding of the exempt sector suggests that the scope of tax exemption under current law reflects a variety of policy considerations. . . .

3. ["Unrelated debt financed income" is further discussed in Chapter 29. — Eds.]

The broadest segment of the exempt sector, however, including specifically those organizations engaged in the educational, health and charitable activities identified in section 501(c)(3) (public charities), draw substantial revenues from sources that could, at least in concept, be subject to income tax. Tax exemption for these organizations may, in part, reflect historical circumstances, but is more importantly based on the same tax policy principles that support an income tax deduction for charitable contributions. Taxes are imposed to fund the activities of government, and represent a removal of resources from private hands to support the broad, public purposes served by government. Although public charities are privately operated and controlled, their exempt activities are restricted to those deemed to serve the general public interest. An organization that provides food and shelter for the poor, or that encourages education, the arts or humanities, is serving the same general resources purposes with which government itself is concerned. Thus, resources dedicated to the activities of such organizations may be viewed as similar to funds transferred to and used for the general purposes of government. For this reason, income transferred through a charitable contribution or earned directly by a public charity may appropriately be exempted from tax.

* * *

B. The Problem of Competition

As described above, Congress adopted the unrelated business income tax primarily because of its concern with "unfair" competition between tax-exempt organizations and taxable businesses. Some competition between tax-exempt and taxable activities is inevitable, however, and could not be eliminated without repealing altogether the tax exemption for nonprofit organizations. A nonprofit hospital will compete with for-profit hospitals for patients, and in providing its patients with food, drugs or medical devices will compete with taxable businesses offering the same products. Similarly, in maintaining student dormitories, an exempt university will compete with local businesses offering meals and housing. Because the hospital and university are not subject to tax, they may be able to provide goods or services at a lower cost than their taxable competitors or to expand more rapidly to attract additional students or patients. Although this may leave the exempt organization with a competitive advantage over its taxable counterpart, this advantage is an intended consequence of the societal decision to encourage the exempt functions performed by these organizations.

Competition between taxable and tax-exempt organizations becomes of greater concern, however, when the good or service provided by the tax-exempt organization is further removed from the organization's core purposes. We may not be concerned that a state university's tax exemption extends to the sales of textbooks through the student bookstore, since the product is essential to the school's educational function and may be irregularly or incompletely supplied by private businesses. If the same student bookstore, however, also sells clothes, appliances and other consumer goods, the activity moves further from the university's educational function, and involves products which in general are amply supplied by the private sector. Extending the university's tax exemption to sales of these products may only displace taxable businesses in an area where private markets are working effectively.

C. Accountability

As indicated above, the privilege of tax-exempt status affords substantial benefits and, at least with respect to public charities, may be justified because of the public, quasi-governmental purposes served by their activities. Because nonprofit organizations are privately controlled, however, their activities are not subject to the public review or scrutiny that applies to the actions of government. It is thus necessary that the tax system ensure that non-profit organizations are operated for the purposes that support their exemption.

At present, the responsibility for ensuring that nonprofit organizations are accountable for the benefits of tax exemption in large part rests on the enforcement activities of the Internal Revenue Service. Through the return and audit process, the Internal Revenue Service is in a position to review the activities of nonprofit organizations and the purposes for which their funds are spent. In addition to focusing on an exempt organization's use of funds, however, the tax system may improve accountability by encouraging particular sources of funding. Thus, rules limiting the scope of tax exemption may appropriately encourage an exempt organization to concentrate on activities and investments that do not distract from its exempt function. This channeling function may be served by the current law rules subjecting nonprofit organizations to tax on their unrelated business activities. Although the earnings from an unrelated business activity may go equally to serve the organization's exempt purposes, the unrelated activity may divert management resources or otherwise cause the organization to lose sight of its exempt function. In the same vein, the current law rules exempting passive investment income, whether or not related to a nonprofit organization's exempt function, effectively encourage investments that will not directly engage the organization in purely commercial activity.

There are of course limits on the extent to which the tax laws can be used to ensure accountability of tax-exempt organizations. For example, determining whether contributed funds are used wisely and efficiently is not a function of the tax law. Such accountability might be aided by fuller public disclosure required by the rules or by state authorities.

IV. Analysis of Current Law

Our analysis of current law is divided into four parts: (1) income from business activities, a category that includes all activities that consist of charging a fee for goods or services; (2) "passive" investment income such as dividends, interest, annuities, royalties and rents; (3) research activities, a class of business activities that are specifically excluded from UBTI under certain circumstances; and (4) joint ventures with taxable entities.

A. Business Activities

1. Fee-for-Service Activities that Constitute Basis for Exempt Status

A necessary threshold question in examining the income-producing activities of exempt organizations is what basic activities merit the privilege of tax exemption. Many currently exempt organizations are principally engaged in the provision of goods or services for a fee, similar in many respects to taxable, for-profit businesses. Routine examples include hospitals, schools, and organizations for the performing arts.

. . . [T]ax exemption for the income of such organizations should reflect a societal judgment that the goods or services they provide are in the public interest and would not be adequately supplied by market forces alone. The substantial benefits of tax exemption make it important, moreover, that such judgments be reexamined in light of changes both in the exempt and for-profit sectors.

2. The Unrelated Business Income Tax

. . . [T]he UBIT provisions impose a tax on a trade or business regularly carried on by an exempt organization if it is not substantially related to the organization's exempt purpose.

a. The "substantially" test

[T]he test of present law for determining whether or not a trade or business regularly carried on is exempt from tax is whether the business is substantially related to the exempt purpose of the organization, aside from the need for funds. Treasury regulations elaborate upon the meaning of the term "substantially related" by requiring that the business activity have a substantial causal relationship to accomplishment of the organization's exempt purposes. Thus, the activity which generates income must "contribute importantly" to the accomplishment of the exempt purposes for which the organization was formed, a determination that depends in each case upon the facts and circumstances involved. Examples of activities ordinarily viewed as "substantially related" include school-sponsored athletic events and university publication of scholarly works.

The regulations further provide that the sale of products resulting from the performance of exempt functions does not constitute an unrelated trade or business if the product is sold in substantially the same state as on completion of the exempt function. Thus, the sale of milk by a scientific organization that maintains an experimental dairy herd would not constitute an unrelated trade or business, but the sale of ice cream would. Similarly, the regulations provide that to the extent a business is conducted on a larger scale than reasonably necessary to accomplish the organization's exempt purpose, income from the activity is taxable.

Although the "substantially related" test raises a number of administrative and compliance concerns, which are discussed below, we believe the standard, as interpreted by the regulations, has conceptual merit. As previously noted, tax exemption may appropriately be granted for activities that are socially important and would not be adequately supplied by market forces alone. Assuming an organization merits exemption under this standard, tax-exemption should appropriately extend to that collection of activities that are substantially or integrally related to the organization's exempt functions. Thus, for example, a university's tax exemption should extend to the provision of dormitory housing, given the university's significant interest in maintaining a campus and assuring students of standard, affordable housing with reasonable access to university facilities. On the other hand, tax exemption might appropriately be denied to a university-maintained student record store, which ordinarily would simply duplicate private sector businesses without importantly advancing the school's educational purposes.

Our primary concern with the "substantially related" test is whether in practice it has been useful in distinguishing activities entitled to exemption from those that are not. The general concepts enunciated in the regulations inherently require facts and circumstances determinations that are not likely to achieve consistency among different exempt organizations. The practical result appears to be an *ad hoc* test that, in many cases, offers inadequate guidance to the courts, exempt organizations, and revenue agents. Moreover, to the extent the relatedness standard has provided guidance, there are indications it has been applied in an overly generous manner. Some courts appear to have found the requirement that an activity contribute importantly to an organization's exempt purpose satisfied where the activity contributes simply in some way to that purpose.

Our concerns in this area are heightened by evidence, albeit inconclusive, that some exempt organizations are aggressively seeking tax-exempt income-producing opportunities. For example, an increasing number of publications and seminars are advising exempt organizations of ways to increase their revenues through the operation of related businesses. Moreover, as stated above, current data suggest that exempt organizations are relying to an increasing extent on income-producing activities as a source of revenue.

b. Exceptions to the definition of an unrelated business[4]

There are number of exceptions to the definition of an unrelated business, including businesses carried on by volunteers; businesses carried on by public charities and state schools primarily for the convenience of members, students, patients, officers or employees; and businesses involving the sale of donated property.

4. In a reversal of the original proposed regulations, the revised proposal regulations eliminate the "tainting rule" that rendered revenues from sponsorships taxable if, within the same media, profit-seekers also presented stereotypical advertisement related to the sponsorship message. Compare Prop. Treas. Reg. §1.513-4 (c)(2) (original proposed regulations), 58 Fed. Reg. 5687, 5690 (1993) and Notice of Proposed Rulemaking, 65 Fed. Reg. 11012-14 (March 1, 2000) (eliminating "tainting rule"). Notice of Proposed Rulemaking, 65 Fed. Reg. 11012, 11014 (proposed sponsorship) is advertising. Prop. Treas. Reg. §1.513-4 (c)(2)(iv), 65 Fed. Reg. 11012, 11017 (2000). Thus, so long as sponsorship language is kept separate from advertising language, the revenues attributable to sponsorship will not be taxed.

(1) Businesses operated by volunteers

The exception for businesses operated by volunteers was part of the original unrelated business income tax enacted in 1950. Although the Committee Reports do not state the reason for the exception, there are a number of considerations that, while not entirely satisfactory, provide some justification for the exception. First, Congress was concerned with unfair competition. It may have viewed the requirement that substantially all the work be performed by volunteers as an inherent limitation on the growth and competitive strength of such organizations. On the other hand, one could argue that the use of volunteer labor would itself constitute unfair competition because it would lower the costs of the business. Second, Congress may have been concerned that general rules for computing taxable income were not appropriate for businesses conducted by volunteers. In concept, a salary payment and offsetting charitable contribution could be imputed between the organization and the volunteer. Failure to reduce the organization's taxable income for the imputed cost of its labor arguably overtaxes the organization's income. Although an overly broad response, tax exemption for volunteer activities prevents such possible overtaxation. Finally, Congress may have viewed the provision simply as a means of exempting small fundraising activities, such as a weekly fish fry sponsored by a veteran's organization or a craft shop operated by a church.

(2) Convenience of members, etc.

The legislative history of the Revenue Act of 1950 indicates that the exception for businesses carried on primarily for the convenience of members, students, patients, officers or employees prevented the taxation of dining halls and dormitories operated by educational institutions. A hospital cafeteria serving primarily patients and employees also would fall under this exception. Although we agree that dining halls, dormitories and hospital cafeterias should generally be exempt from tax, such businesses would in most instances be treated as substantially related to the exempt purpose of the organization and hence not require a special exception. The convenience exception might be asserted to protect other cases, however, such as university-sponsored travel services or student stores offering clothing and records, that probably would not merit tax exemption under the substantially related standard.

(3) Donated property

The exception for businesses selling donated property was designed to prevent thrift shops operated by exempt organizations from paying income tax on the sale of donated property. Although there exists competition between taxable and tax-exempt thrift shops, we believe most exempt thrift shops would generate little, if any, taxable income, and that the exception is justified on grounds of administrative convenience. The recipient of donated property generally takes a basis in the property equal to the lesser of the donor's basis or fair market value. Since most donated property of the type sold in thrift shops has depreciated in value, basis would usually equal fair market value, which ordinarily would also be the price at which the property was sold.

c. Computation of UBIT

To the extent an exempt organization is taxable on an unrelated business, present law generally taxes the unrelated business in the same manner as if the business were carried on by a taxable entity.

(1) Allocation of expenses

The proper allocation of expenses between related and unrelated businesses is one of the most difficult issues that arises in determining an exempt organization's unrelated business taxable income. Unrelated business taxable income is defined as gross income derived from an unrelated business less allowable deductions "directly connected" with the carrying on of such business. In interpreting this language, the regulations provide that an item of deduction not only must satisfy the general requirements of deductibility for a trade or business, but must also have a "proximate and primary relationship" to the carrying on of a business. Where facilities and personnel are used both to carry on exempt activities and to conduct unrelated trade or business activities, the regulations provide that expenses, depreciation and similar items (as, for example, items of overhead) shall be allocated between the two uses on a reasonable basis.

(2) The fragmentation rule

Another problem area with unrelated businesses carried on directly by exempt organizations is the application of what is sometimes referred to as the "fragmentation" rule — the rule that any activity carried on for the production of income can constitute an unrelated business even if it is part of a larger aggregate of activities, some of which are related to the exempt purposes of the organization.

The difficulties with the fragmentation rule are most evident in the tax treatment of retail businesses such as museum gift shops. Under present law, for example, a museum is required to make an item-by-item determination of which sales by its gift shop constitute a related business (for example, sales of reproductions) and which constitute an unrelated business (sales of souvenirs).

3. Unrelated businesses carried on by subsidiaries

It is not uncommon for an exempt organization desiring to engage in an unrelated business to operate the business through a taxable subsidiary. The subsidiary is an independent taxpaying entity that is subject to the same tax rules as if it were owned by a taxable entity or by individual shareholders. Dividends paid by the subsidiary to the tax-exempt parent are treated in the same manner as any dividend received by the parent — they are specifically excluded from tax on unrelated business income.

Two important issues regarding the use of taxable subsidiaries include first, the treatment of rents, royalties, interest and annuities received from a "controlled" subsidiary and, second, the effect of subsidiaries on the determination of whether a charitable organization is operated for the primary purpose of carrying on an unrelated trade or business.

a. Controlled subsidiaries[5]

There are a variety of non-tax reasons for an exempt organization to make use of taxable subsidiaries, including concerns about commercial liability and the desire to have the taxable business operated and accounted for separately from the primary exempt activity. There are also tax reasons for utilizing a taxable subsidiary. Chief among these is the ability to make tax deductible payments to the parent that reduce the subsidiary's taxable income but are not taxed to the parent because of the specific exclusions for interest, rent, annuities or royalties. If an exempt organization directly carries on the unrelated business of manufacturing sweatshirts embossed with the organization's logo, for example, the organization is taxed on its gross income less deductions "directly connected" with the business. But if the organization were to drop the sweatshirt business into a taxable subsidiary, with a minor interest held by another taxpayer, the subsidiary would be free to pay to the parent organization rent for the use of its building, a royalty for the use of the logo, and interest on money loaned to the subsidiary by the parent. These payments, which could not be used to reduce taxable income if the business were carried on directly by the exempt organization, are deductible by the subsidiary and excluded from the taxable income of the exempt organization.

b. "Primary purpose" test

As described earlier, regulations under section 501(c)(3) of the Code provide that a section 501(c)(3) organization can engage in a business as a substantial part of its activities so long as the operation of the business is in furtherance of the organization's exempt purpose and the organization is not organized or operated for the primary purpose of carrying on an unrelated business. Thus, if a charitable organization carried on an unrelated business with a million dollars of net revenue each year, but made comparatively small expenditures for carrying on the purpose for which it was granted tax exemption, it would cease to qualify as a section 501(c)(3) organization.

The question arises whether the above result should be any different if the organization instead puts the unrelated business into a subsidiary. Although operation of an unrelated business in a subsidiary may protect the exempt organization from liabilities of the business and otherwise require less direct and active involvement, we do not believe it eliminates concern that the unrelated business could supplant the organization's exempt function as its primary purpose. As is common in the taxable sector, management of a subsidiary may be fully integrated with that of its parent. Although we are not aware of cases in which an unrelated business has been transferred to or formed in a subsidiary in order to avoid the primary purpose test, we believe consideration should be given to a rule that in appropriate cases aggregates the activities of an exempt organization and its subsidiaries for this purpose.

5. ["Controlled subsidiaries" are discussed in detail in Chapter 28. — Eds.]

B. "Passive" Income

1. In General

The definition of unrelated business income excludes dividends, interest, annuities, royalties and rents (collectively referred to as "passive" investment income). In explaining the continued exemption for passive investment income at the time the UBIT was enacted in 1950, Congress stated that such income had long been recognized as proper for charitable and educational organizations and was not likely to generate competitive problems for taxable businesses.

a. Public charities

As discussed above tax exemption for income earned by public charities can be justified on the grounds that the income will be used to support organizations, as identified in section 501(c)(3), deemed to act for the general public good. We believe this rationale appropriately extends to passive investment income of public charities. Moreover, we do not believe the concerns justifying a tax on an exempt organization's unrelated business activities apply with respect to passive investments. Although we recognize that the line between a passive investment and an active business is at times very thin, an exempt organization's investment of capital in a taxable business should not generally raise concerns over unfair competition. Moreover, we believe the exemption for passive investment income may appropriately encourage exempt organizations to avoid deeper commercial involvements and the potential distractions and conflicts they present. Thus, although we have some concerns, as discussed below, about the current law rules defining passive investment income, we think tax exemption for such income earned by public charities is appropriate.

* * *

2. Royalties

The exclusion of royalties from UBTI raises issues in addition to those discussed above with respect to passive income generally. The statute excludes "all royalties . . . whether measured by production or by gross or taxable income from the property." Although neither the statute nor the regulations define the term "royalties" for purposes of the passive income exception, there is authority for treating essentially any payment for the right to use intangible property as a royalty for tax purposes.

Because of the exceedingly broad definition of a royalty and because the statute allows payments to be measured by taxable income, the exception for royalty income permits exempt organizations to use licensing agreements to obtain a portion of the profits of an unrelated business without incurring tax liability. For example, if an organization sold tote bags bearing its logo, the sales would be taxed as an unrelated trade or business. If, however, the organization licensed the right to use its logo to a third party in exchange for a share of taxable income, the organization's income would be treated as tax-free royalty income, notwithstanding the fact that the organization in essence would be sharing in the net profits of the business. This would be the result even if the organization retained the right to approve the quality or style of the products. It is difficult to justify these results from a tax policy perspective. In cases where the organization shares in the net profits of a business, as opposed to the gross income or receipts, it is more akin to a partner in an active business than to a passive investor.

Another concern with the exclusion for royalties is that in many cases, such as where the organization licenses the right to use its name or trademark, the licensing agreement is in essence an endorsement of a commercial product. The regulations provide that where goodwill or other intangibles generated by the performance of an organization's exempt functions are exploited for a commercial purpose, the resulting income is unrelated business income, unless the commercial activities themselves contribute importantly to accomplishment of the organization's exempt purpose. The regulations provide as an example of such unrelated business income an exempt scientific organization which enjoys an excellent reputation in the field of biological research and exploits its reputation by selling endorsements of various items of laboratory equipment to manufacturers. The organization, however, could effectively endorse the same products and avoid tax liability by licensing the right to use its name or trademark instead of actively endorsing the equipment.

* * *

Chapter 26

UBIT — The "Trade or Business" Requirement

A. In General

CODE: §§ 511(a); 512(a)(1), (a)(5), (a)(6), (a)(7), (c)(1); 513(a)

REGS.: § 1.513-1(a)–(b)

An activity will not produce unrelated business income unless that activity is a "trade or business." This chapter explores what is a "trade or business" for purposes of the unrelated trade of business income tax.

United States v. American Bar Endowment

477 U.S. 105 (1986)

JUSTICE MARSHALL delivered the opinion of the Court.

The first issue in this case is whether income that a tax-exempt charitable organization derives from offering group insurance to its members constitutes "unrelated business income" subject to tax under §§ 511 through 513.

* * *

I

Respondent American Bar Endowment (ABE) is a corporation exempt from taxation under § 501(c)(3) of the Code, which, with certain exceptions not relevant here, exempts organizations "organized and operated exclusively for . . . charitable . . . or educational purposes." ABE's primary purposes are to advance legal research and to promote the administration of justice, and it furthers these goals primarily through the distribution of grants to other charitable and educational groups. All members of the American Bar Association (ABA) are automatically members of ABE. The ABA is exempt from taxation as a "business league" under § 501(c)(6).

ABE raises money for its charitable work by providing group insurance policies, underwritten by major insurance companies, to its members. Approximately 20% of ABE's members participate in the group insurance program, which offers life, health, accident, and disability policies. ABE negotiates premium rates with insurers and chooses which insurers shall provide the policies. It also compiles a list of its own members and solicits them, collects the premiums paid by its members, transmits those premiums to the insurer, maintains files on each policyholder, answers members' questions concerning insurance policies, and screens claims for benefits.

There are two important benefits of purchasing insurance as a group rather than individually. The first is that ABE's size gives it bargaining power that individuals lack. The second is that the group policy is experience-rated. This means that the cost of insurance to the group is based on that group's claims experience, rather than general actuarial tables. Because ABA members have favorable mortality and morbidity rates, experience-rating results in a substantially lower insurance cost. When ABE purchases a group policy for its members, it pays a negotiated premium to the insurance company. If, as is uniformly true, the insurance company's actual cost of providing insurance to the group is lower than the premium paid in a given year, the insurance company pays a refund of the excess, called a "dividend," to ABE. Critical to ABE's fundraising efforts is the fact that ABE requires its members to agree, as a condition of participating in the group insurance program, that they will permit ABE to keep all of the dividends rather than distributing them pro rata to the insured members.

It would be possible for ABE to negotiate lower premium rates for its members than the rates it has charged throughout the relevant period, and thus receive a lower dividend. However, ABE prices its policies competitively with other insurance policies offered to the public and to ABE members. In this way ABE is able to generate large dividends to be used for its charitable purposes. In recent years the total amount of dividends has exceeded 40% of the members' premium payments. ABE advises its insured members that each member's share of the dividends, less ABE's administrative costs, constitutes a tax-deductible contribution from the member to ABE. Thus the after-tax cost of ABE's insurance to its members is less than the cost of a commercial policy with identical coverage and premium rates.

In 1980 the Internal Revenue Service (IRS) advised ABE that it considered ABE's insurance plan an "unrelated trade or business" and that the profits thereon were subject to tax under §§ 511–513.

II

We recently discussed the history and structure of the unrelated business income provisions of the Code in *United States v. American College of Physicians*, 475 U.S. 834 (1986). The Code imposes a tax, at ordinary corporate rates, on the income that a tax-exempt organization obtains from an "unrelated trade or business . . . regularly carried on by it." §§ 512(a)(1), 511(a)(1). An "unrelated trade or business" is "any trade or business the conduct of which is not substantially related . . . to the exercise or performance by such organization of its charitable, educational, or other purpose," § 513(a). The Code thus sets up a three-part test. ABE's insurance program is taxable if it (1) constitutes a trade or business; (2) is regularly carried on; and (3) is not substantially related to ABE's tax-exempt purposes. Treas. Reg. § 1.513-1(a), 26 CFR § 1.513-1(a). ABE concedes that the latter two portions of this test are satisfied.

Its defense is based solely on the proposition that its insurance program does not constitute a trade or business.

A

In the Tax Reform Act of 1969, Congress defined a "trade or business" as "any activity which is carried on for the production of income from the sale of goods or the performance of services," § 513(c). The Secretary of the Treasury has provided further clarification of that definition in Treas. Reg. § 1.513-1(b) (1985), which provides: "in general, any activity of [an exempt] organization which is carried on for the production of income and which otherwise possesses the characteristics required to constitute 'trade or business' within the meaning of section 162" is a trade or business for purposes of 26 U.S.C. §§ 511–513.

ABE's insurance program falls within the literal language of these definitions. ABE's activity is both "the sale of goods" and "the performance of services," and possesses the general characteristics of a trade or business. Certainly the assembling of a group of better-than-average insurance risks, negotiating on their behalf with insurance companies, and administering a group policy are activities that can be — and are — provided by private commercial entities in order to make a profit. ABE itself earns considerable income from its program. Nevertheless, the Claims Court and Court of Appeals concluded that ABE does not carry out its insurance program in order to make a profit. The Claims Court relied on the former Court of Claims holding in *Disabled American Veterans v. United States*, 650 F.2d 1178, 1187 (1981), that an activity is a trade or business only if "operated in a competitive, commercial manner." *See* 4 Cl. Ct., at 409. Because ABE does not operate its insurance program in a competitive, commercial manner, the Claims Court decided, that program is not a trade or business. The Court of Appeals adopted this reasoning.

The Claims Court rested its conclusion on four factors. First, it found that "the program was devised as a means for fundraising and has been so presented and perceived from its inception." 4 Cl. Ct. at 409. Second, the Court found that the program's phenomenal success in generating dividends for ABE was evidence of noncommercial behavior. The court noted that ABE's insurance program has provided $81.9 million in dividends in its 28 years of operation, and concluded that such large profits could not be the result of commercial success, but must proceed from the generosity of ABE's members. Third, and most important, in the court's view, was the fact that ABE's members collectively had the power to change ABE's conduct of the insurance programs so as to drastically reduce premiums. That the members had not done so was strong evidence that they sought to further ABE's charitable purposes by paying higher insurance rates than necessary. Fourth, because ABE did not underwrite insurance or act as a broker, it was not competing with other commercial entities.

It appears, then, that the Claims Court viewed ABE as engaging in two separate activities — the provision of insurance and the acceptance of contributions in the form of dividends. If so, the unspoken premise of the Claims Court's decision is that ABE's income is not a result of the first activity, but of the second. There is some sense to this reasoning; should ABE sell a product to its members for more than that product's fair market value, it could argue to the IRS that the members intended to pay excessive prices as a form of contribution, and that some formula should be adopted to separate the income received into taxable profits and nontaxable contributions. Even if we viewed it as appropriate for the federal courts to engage in such a quasi-legislative authority, however, there is no factual basis for the Claims Court's attempt to do so in this case.

B

We cannot agree with the Claims Court that the enormous dividends generated by ABE's insurance program demonstrate that those dividends cannot constitute "profits." Were ABE's insurance markedly more expensive than other insurance products available to its members, but ABE nevertheless kept the patronage of those members, we might plausibly conclude that generosity was the reason for the program's success. The Claims Court did not find, however, that this was the case. ABE prices its insurance to remain competitive with the rest of the market. Thus ABE's members never squarely face the decision whether to support ABE or to reduce their own insurance costs.

The Claims Court concluded that "such profit margins [as ABE's] cannot be maintained year after year in a competitive market." *Id.*, at 410. The court apparently reasoned that ABE's staggering success would inevitably induce other firms to offer similar programs to ABA members unless that success is the result of charitable intentions rather than price-sensitive purchasing decisions. It is possible, of course, that ABE's members genuinely intend to support ABE by paying higher premiums than necessary, and would pay those high premiums even if a competing group insurance plan offered very low minimums. But that is by no means the only possible explanation for the market's failure to provide competition for ABE. Lacking a factual basis for concluding that generosity is at the core of ABE's success, we can easily view this case as a standard example of monopoly pricing. ABE has a unique asset — its access to the ABA's members and their highly favorable mortality and morbidity rates — and it has chosen to appropriate for itself all of the profit possible from that asset, rather than sharing any with its members.

The argument that ABE's members could change the insurance program and receive the bulk of the dividends themselves if they so desired is unconvincing. Were ABE to give each member a choice between retaining its pro-rata share of dividends or assigning them to ABE, the organization would have a strong argument that those dividends constituted a voluntary donation. That, however, is not the case here. ABE requires its members to assign it all dividends as a condition for participating in the insurance program. It is simply incorrect to characterize the assignment of dividends by each member as "voluntary" simply because the members theoretically could band together and attempt to change the policy.

Again, the Claims Court put too much weight on an unsupported assumption. It found that the program was "operated with the approval and consent of the ABA membership," *ibid.*, observing that the program had met with "surprisingly little dissent," *id.*, at 411, even though there were "ample" opportunities for members to change policies with which they disagreed, *ibid.* We believe that those facts cannot carry the weight that the Claims Court put on them. Perhaps each member that purchases insurance would, given the option, pay excessive premiums in order to support ABE's charitable purposes; however, that is not the only possible explanation for the members' failure to change the program. Any given member might feel that the potential savings in insurance costs are not sufficient to justify the effort required to mount a challenge to ABE's leadership. Many might not want to "make waves" and upset a program that generates tax-free income for ABE and charitable deductions for their fellow members. The members' theoretical ability to change the program, therefore, is at best inconclusive.

The Claims Court also erred in concluding that ABE's insurance program did not present the potential for unfair competition. The undisputed purpose of the unrelated business income tax was to prevent tax-exempt organizations from competing unfairly with businesses whose earnings were taxed. H. R. Rep. No. 2319, 81st Cong., 2d Sess., 36 (1950); see *United States v. American College of Physicians*, 475 U.S., at 838. This case presents an example of precisely the sort of unfair competition that Congress intended to prevent. If ABE's members may deduct part of their premium payments as a charitable contribution, the effective cost of ABE's insurance will be lower than the cost of competing policies that do not offer tax benefits. Similarly, if ABE may escape taxes on its earnings, it need not be as profitable as its commercial counterparts in order to receive the same return on its investment. Should a commercial company attempt to displace ABE as the group policyholder, therefore, it would be at a decided disadvantage.

The Claims Court failed to find any taxable entities that compete with ABE, and therefore found no danger of unfair competition. It is likely, however, that many of ABE's members belong to other organizations that offer group insurance policies. Employers, trade associations, and financial services companies frequently offer group insurance policies. Presumably those entities are taxed on their profits, and their policyholders may not deduct any part of the premiums paid. Such entities may therefore find it difficult to compete for the business of any ABE members who are otherwise eligible to participate in these group insurance programs.

The only valid argument in ABE's favor, therefore, is that the insurance program is billed as a fundraising effort. That fact, standing alone, cannot be determinative, or any exempt organization could engage in a tax-free business by "giving away" its product in return for a "contribution" equal to the market value of the product. ABE further contends that it must prevail because the Claims Court found that ABE's profits represent contributions rather than business income; ABE argues that we may not upset that finding unless it is clearly erroneous. Cf. *Carter v. Commissioner*, 645 F.2d 784, 786 (C.A.9 1981) (question of profit motive for purposes of § 162 is one of fact). The undisputed facts, however, simply will not support the inference that the dividends ABE receives are charitable contributions from its members rather than profits from its insurance program. Moreover, the Claims Court failed to articulate a legal rule that would permit it to split ABE's activities into the gratuitous provision of a service and the acceptance of voluntary contributions, and we find no such rule in the Code or regulations. Even if we assumed, however, that the court's failure to attach the label "trade or business" to ABE's insurance program constitutes a finding of fact, we would be constrained to hold that finding clearly erroneous.

IV

We hold that ABE's insurance program is a "trade or business" for purposes of the unrelated business income tax. We further hold that the individual taxpayers have not established that any portion of their premium payments to ABE constitutes a charitable contribution. Accordingly, we reverse the judgment of the Court of Appeals and remand to that court with instructions to reverse the judgment of the Claims Court with respect to ABE and to affirm the judgment of the Claims Court with respect to the individual taxpayers.

It is so ordered.

Justice Powell and Justice O'Connor took no part in the consideration or decision of this case.

Justice Stevens, dissenting.

The charitable work of the American Bar Endowment is funded, in large part, through a procedure in which the Endowment provides insurance policies for participating American Bar Association members, and the members assign the dividends to the ABE. The primary question presented is whether that assignment of dividends is taxable as an unrelated "trade or business." "The problem at which the tax on unrelated business income is directed . . . is primarily that of unfair competition." The unrelated business tax was adopted in 1950, and substantially revised in 1969. It is useful to recall the kind of situation that gives rise to the unrelated business tax. Perhaps the best known case involved the C.F. Mueller Company. The Mueller Company was a longstanding macaroni concern. It was acquired and operated for the benefit of the New York University School of Law, and its profits were donated to the University. The Internal Revenue Service claimed that the macaroni company's profits should be taxable, like any other competitive macaroni company, to avoid giving this competitor an unfair advantage. Although longstanding precedent seemed to be against the Commissioner, the Tax Court was sufficiently concerned about the implications that it agreed with the Commissioner. Ultimately, the Court of Appeals reversed, relying on precedent; by that time, however, Congress had acted and imposed a tax on unrelated business income. See *C.F. Mueller Co. v. Commissioner*, 190 F.2d 120 (C.A.3 1951).

In considering the ABE insurance fundraising, then it is appropriate to assume that, if the ABE were funded by operating a normal macaroni company and receiving an unfair competitive advantage from its tax exemption, it would be a "trade or business" within the Act and taxable. On the other hand, it is equally clear that, if the ABE simply provided insurance for ABA members at very low cost, and sent the insurance dividends with an urgent request that the dividends be assigned to the Endowment, the arrangement would not be a "trade or business," and would not be taxable. The central issue in this case is thus whether the ABE's insurance program should be viewed as akin to the macaroni company, and thus a "trade or business," or as akin to the dividend assignment request, and thus not a "trade or business."

I believe that the ABE's activities are far closer to the latter than the former for two reasons. First, there is no danger of unfair competition, the problem that the unrelated business tax addresses. Second, the program has functioned as a charitable fundraising effort, rather than as a business.

I

An understanding of the purpose of the unrelated business income tax exposes a basic error in the Court's analysis. As noted, that purpose is to protect commercial enterprises from the unfair competition that may be generated by the operation of competing businesses by tax-free organizations. There is no evidence in the record, despite more than three weeks of trial and numerous witnesses, to support the notion that the Endowment's provision of insurance to its members has had any competitive impact whatsoever. The Court relies on a parade of hypotheticals to justify its conclusion that there is some effect on competition. The Court is, however, unable to point to a single piece of evidence in the record to justify its conclusion about the effect on competition. The trial judge scoured the record for evidence pointing to a harmful effect on competition, and found none.[1]

---

1. [4] In its oral opinion at the end of the trial, the Claims Court emphasized the absence of a "Ronzoni" — the macaroni-selling competitor who had been harmed by New York University's tax-free entry into the business:

> "The unrelated business income tax was passed to avoid a certain kind of evil.... So you go back and look at what evil there is in the market. What was Congress trying to do ... when the ... tax was passed, and one comes to the frequently-asked QUESTION, 'Who is Ronzoni.'
>
> "Now, nobody has really satisfactorily pointed to Ronzoni for me. I have been listening for three weeks of trial and nobody came up and said, 'Here, this is Ronzoni, this is the competitor that will be adversely affected in the manner in which Congress feared there would be adverse effects when it slapped Mueller Macaroni Company on the wrist, or basically said you cannot do that, you cannot use your ... tax exempt status to make profits.[']
>
> * * *
>
> "And ... perhaps other witnesses and other economists, on a different record, somebody will be able to point out to me Ronzoni in this ... picture, but I have tried very hard, and looking at the policies of the tax, the policies of the unrelated business income tax, I have not been able to find the evils that Congress sought to alleviate by passing that tax." App. 507–509.

In the published opinion, the Claims Court incorporated its earlier oral opinion, 4 Cl. Ct. 404, 405, n. 1 (1984), and reiterated that the record did not support a finding of a harmful effect on competition:

The absence of evidence in the record, rather than the Court's ruminations about possibilities and likelihoods, should control our analysis.

The legislative history further underscores the fact that the ABE insurance operation poses none of the possible effects on competition that the unrelated business tax was intended to address. Congress has twice made clear that insurance programs by other nonprofit organizations are not subject to the unrelated business tax. When Congress substantially revised the unrelated business tax in 1969, the accompanying legislative history emphasized that the group insurance policies provided by fraternal organizations were not intended to be subject to the unrelated business tax. Similarly, when a question arose concerning the taxability of income from insurance programs administered by veterans' organizations, Congress enacted legislation to ensure that the insurance income would not be taxed. Indeed, Congress found the taxation of the veterans' insurance operations so contrary to its intent that it took the unusual step of making the 1972 amendment fully retroactive to 1969.

The Government argues that these developments actually support its position because the need for congressional attention, and the emphasis on the "substantially related" prong for the fraternal societies, reveal that, without such attention, and without such a substantial relationship, the activity should be presumptively taxable. Particularly when the general legislative purpose of preventing unfair competition is considered, however, these legislative developments have a different significance. For they highlight the fact that the "market" in which the ABE is competing, even temporarily leaving aside the complete absence of evidence of harm to competitors, is itself already partially exempt from the unrelated business income tax provisions, and the possible threat to competition becomes all the more hypothetical and remote.

Ironically, moreover, the tax-exempt alternative suggested by the Government would have a far more obvious effect on competition than the ABE's current fund-raising process. For the ABE would then be offering insurance rates dramatically lower than those available elsewhere. If speculation of the kind indulged in by the majority is appropriate, that speculation surely should include the realization that the tax-exempt alternative—in which the ABE would merely recover its actual costs of managing the program and return all of the premium refunds to the individual policyholders—would attract more than the 20% of the ABE membership that currently hold ABE policies; it would appeal to those who simply want an insurance bargain rather than those who also want to make a charitable contribution.

"The absence of any identifiable business over which the ABE is able to gain an unfair advantage supports the conclusion that its activities are not commercial and therefore not a business. At the very least, it suggests that nothing in the policies underlying the [unrelated business tax] requires that the Endowment's activities be taxed. . . ." *Id.*, at 414.

It is not completely surprising that a consideration of the purpose of the unrelated business tax in light of the record developed at the extensive trial leads to a conclusion that the ABE's program should not be taxed. For the Government itself initially held such a view. Furthermore, the ABE's insurance program was initiated in 1955 as a pioneering, and widely publicized, effort in charitable fundraising. When Congress revamped the unrelated business tax in 1969, there was no suggestion that it was intended to apply to this venerable and successful program, and the IRS did not so interpret it until several years later. In short, a proper consideration of the purpose of the unrelated business tax leads to a conclusion that the ABE's insurance program is not a "trade or business."

II

Not only does the ABE program completely fail to raise the concerns against which the unrelated business tax is directed, but it is also operated as a charitable fundraising endeavor.

The learned trial judge expressly found, after hearing a good deal of evidence, that the assignment of the dividends was the result of charitable intentions, rather than a commercial transaction. First, he found that, since the program's inception, for three decades, the ABE has trumpeted the insurance program as a charitable fundraising activity, and that it has been so understood. The trial court emphasized that even members who testified against the ABE viewed the insurance program as strictly a charitable fundraising effort. Second, the court specifically found that the reason for the Endowment's enormous profits was the charitable intent of the members. Finally, the court emphasized that, all of the factors of the program, taken together, compel the conclusion that the ABE procedure was operated as, and understood to be, charitable fundraising rather than a business.

Notwithstanding the Court of Appeals' explicit endorsement of the trial judge's findings, this Court speculates that the members' assignment of their premium refunds was not "voluntary" because the assignment was a condition to participating in the insurance program. This speculation rests on a remarkably unrealistic appraisal of the intelligence and independence of the lawyers who participate in the ABE program. Those who elected to buy the insurance and contribute the premium refunds to the Endowment clearly understood the legal consequences of the transaction, and were free to purchase insurance elsewhere if they did not want to make the requested charitable contribution.

The Court's opinion also seems to rest on the notion that the ABE members who purchased insurance were somehow coerced by a monopolist. But this is absurd. There is nothing in the record to suggest that the insurance policy offered by the ABE to its members was so attractive that the ABE could foist some unwanted condition upon its members. After all, only 20% of the membership purchased the policies. This transaction has none of the earmarks of an improper tying arrangement.

Finally, the Court states that "there is no factual basis" for an assumption that the large revenues generated by the insurance program were the result of the members' charitable motivation rather than the market value of the insurance package, see *ante*, at 112–113. But this is what the Claims Court found:

> "I am persuaded that if the American Bar Association Plan were not viewed as a fundraising enterprise and were not viewed by the overwhelming majority of the membership as something to be tolerated as, to be sure, an economic expense but one for the good of the profession, and for the greater good of society, that it would not exist, it could not have existed, it could not have survived, it would not have survived to today. And at least on the basis of this record those are my findings on that point." App. 505. *See also* 4 Cl. Ct. 404, 405, n. 1 (1984) (incorporating oral findings of fact).

I believe that we are bound by that ruling. The Court's suggestion to the contrary notwithstanding, rejecting that finding would run afoul of the "two court rule," would decide the case on a ground expressly disavowed by the Government, and would conflict with the record. That finding, combined with the other findings and with a proper analysis of the purpose and scope of the unrelated business tax, requires a conclusion that the ABE has been operated as a charitable fundraising effort, rather than as a commercial business.

III

The ABE's program poses no harm to competitors and has been operated as a charitable fundraising activity. Depending on its members' agreement to assign their dividends, it is far less like the operation of a competitive macaroni company than like the provision of insurance as a service with a request for the dividends. In my opinion, the Court of Appeals and the Chief Judge of the Claims Court were both quite correct in concluding that, on the basis of the record generated at the vigorously contested trial, the tax that the Government seeks to collect in this case was not the kind of tax that Congress intended to impose. Accordingly, I respectfully dissent.

Questions

1. Reread footnote 4 in Justice Stevens' dissent. Does the majority opinion answer the question, "Who is Ronzoni?" If so, how does it do so?

2. What would be the effect on the Service's ability to collect the unrelated business income tax if it actually had to prove the existence of "Ronzoni"? Would requiring the Service to do so be a good thing or a bad thing as a matter of policy?

American Academy of Family Physicians v. United States

91 F.3d 1155 (8th Cir. 1996)

Before FAGG, WOLLMAN, and MURPHY, Circuit Judges.

FAGG, Circuit Judge.

The Internal Revenue Service (IRS) appeals the district court's grant of a tax refund to the American Academy of Family Physicians (Academy). The IRS contends the Academy, a tax-exempt organization, is required to pay federal income tax on certain payments it received through its sponsorship of group insurance plans. We conclude the payments are not taxable, and affirm.

The Academy is a national association of family physicians that was organized to represent the interests of family physicians and to promote quality health care. The Academy is exempt from federal income tax as a business league under 26 U.S.C. § 501(a), (c)(6). The Academy created the American Academy of Family Physicians Foundation (Foundation) to serve as the Academy's charitable arm. The Foundation is exempt from federal income tax as a scientific and educational foundation. *See id.* § 501(a), (c)(3).

The Academy owns and sponsors group disability, medical and life insurance plans that are available to Academy members and their employees. The Principal Mutual Life Insurance Company (Principal) underwrites the policies. The policies were initially administered by an individual, and when he died, he bequeathed the business of administering the policies to the Foundation. The Foundation then created AAFP Insurance Services, Inc. (ISI), a separate corporation, and turned over administration of the insurance plans to ISI. ISI is a for-profit corporation that pays federal income tax on its profits from administering the insurance plans and distributes dividends to the Foundation, which owns all ISI's stock. The Academy provides its membership lists to ISI for fair market value. ISI reports twice a year to an Academy committee, and must obtain the committee's approval before making any changes to the policies.

The Academy members who elect coverage under the group policies pay premiums to Principal. Principal sets aside part of the premium payments as reserves to pay future claims, and Principal controls the investment of the reserves. The group policies require Principal to turn over to the Academy any reserve funds remaining after the policies have been terminated and all the claims have been paid, whenever that might occur. In the meantime, whether the insurance plans are profitable for Principal or not, the policies require Principal to make annual payments to the Academy for Principal's use of the reserves, based on a fixed percentage of the insurance reserves. Principal paid the Academy over $600,000 a year during the Academy's 1984 to 1987 fiscal years. The issue on appeal is whether these annual payments are taxable.

The IRS contends the payments are taxable under 26 U.S.C. § 511, which provides that an organization entitled to a tax exemption under § 501(a), like the Academy, still must pay income tax on its "unrelated business taxable income." *See id.* § 511(a)(1)–(2)(A). Unrelated business taxable income is income the organization earns by regularly carrying on a trade or business that is not substantially related to the purposes or functions entitling the organization to its § 501(a) tax exemption. *Id.* §§ 512(a)(1), 513(a). Here, the IRS concluded Principal's payments to the Academy were compensation for the Academy's sponsorship of the group insurance plans, and the payments qualified as unrelated business taxable income. The IRS determined the Academy had improperly failed to pay tax on the payments received from 1984 to 1987. The Academy paid the back taxes and interest assessed by the IRS and then brought this refund action, contending the Academy's participation in the insurance plans did not constitute a trade or business under § 513 and the payments from Principal were interest, a type of income specifically excluded from unrelated business taxable income, *id.* § 512(b)(1). Relying on the parties' extensive factual stipulations, the district court decided the Academy's insurance activities were not a trade or business, granted the Academy summary judgment, and ordered a tax refund. The district court did not reach the interest issue.

In reviewing the district court's decision, we must first determine the meaning of the phase "trade or business" in § 513. Section 513(c) defines a trade or business as "any activity which is carried on for the production of income from the sale of goods or the performance of services." Treasury Regulation § 1.513-1(b) clarifies this statutory definition by providing that "trade or business" has the same meaning in § 513 as it does in 26 U.S.C. § 162, the Internal Revenue Code section permitting business expense deductions. *United States v. American Bar Endowment*, 477 U.S. 105, 110 (1986). The standard test for whether an activity is a trade or business under § 162 is whether the activity "'was entered into with the dominant hope and intent for realizing a profit.'" *Id.* at 110 n. 1. In other words, "the taxpayer's primary purpose for engaging in the activity must be for income or profit." *Commissioner v. Groetzinger*, 480 U.S. 23, 35 (1987). In keeping with these interpretations of § 162, several courts of appeals have adopted a profit motive test to determine whether an activity is a trade or business for purposes of the unrelated business income tax. *American Bar Endowment*, 477 U.S. at 110 n. 1. "'The existence of a genuine profit motive is the most important criterion ... a trade or business.'" *Professional Ins. Agents*, 726 F.2d at 1102.

In addition to the profit motive requirement, the income-producing activity of a tax-exempt organization must have the general characteristics of a trade or business. *American Bar Endowment*, 477 U.S. at 110–11. Specifically, some courts of appeals have recognized that an exempt organization must carry out extensive business activities over a substantial period of time to be engaged in a trade or business, and we agree with the reasoning of these cases. *See Zell v. Commissioner*, 763 F.2d 1139, 1142 n. 2 (10th Cir. 1985) (interpreting "trade or business" in § 162); *Professional Ins. Agents*, 726 F.2d at 1102 (interpreting §§ 162 and 513). Contrary to the IRS's position, requiring extensive commercial activities is consistent with *American Bar Endowment*, in which the Supreme Court held the American Bar

Endowment's (ABE's) group insurance program was a trade for business or purposes of § 513(c) and triggered the unrelated business income tax, see 477 U.S. at 119.... The ABE' Assembled a Group of Better-Than-Average insurance risks and negotiated on their behalf with insurance companies, *id.* at 111, compiled lists of ABE members and solicited them, collected premiums for the insurer, maintained files on each policyholder, answered members' questions about the policies, and screened claims for benefits, *id.* at 107.

Moreover, the ABE's significant business activity was important to the Supreme Court's analysis. The Supreme Court decided the ABE's insurance activities met the definition of a trade or business because they involved both the sale of goods and the performance of services, and "possessed the general characteristics of a trade or business." *Id.* at 110–11. Indeed, the ABE was engaging in the same kind of commercial activities that taxable organizations perform to earn a profit. *Id.* at 111. Recognizing that "the undisputed purpose of the unrelated business income tax was to prevent tax-exempt organizations from competing unfairly with businesses whose earnings were taxed," the Supreme Court described the ABE's insurance program as a classic example of "the sort of unfair competition that Congress intended to prevent." *Id.* at 114. Having examined Supreme Court and court of appeals precedents, we conclude we must consider both the Academy's motive for participating in the insurance plans and the nature and extent of the Academy's participation during the relevant tax years.

In our view, the Academy did not have the profit motive required for a trade or business. *Id.* at 110 n.1. The IRS contends the Academy was earning a profit because the payments from Principal to the Academy were essentially "a brokerage fee for [the Academy's] delivering its members to the insurance company as premium-paying customers." This contention is unsupported by the record and goes against the grain of the parties' stipulations.

The stipulations show the payments were not compensation for services rendered and were not profit in a commercial sense. As we have already explained, the parties stipulated the group policies entitled the Academy to receive the excess reserves after the policies' termination. Thus the Academy had a recognizable interest in the reserves Principal was holding. The parties also stipulated Principal was required to make the annual payments to the Academy as "interest on [the] insurance reserves for Principal's use of the reserves." Appellant's App. at 148. These annual payments were based on a specified, annual, fixed percentage of the insurance reserves, and were generated by Principal's investment of the reserves. Further, the parties stipulated the interest on the insurance reserves was payable without regard to the profitability of the group insurance plans. Based on these stipulations, the annual payments were neither brokerage fees nor other compensation for commercial services, but were the way the parties decided to acknowledge the Academy's eventual claim to the excess reserves while Principal was still holding and using the reserves. We need not decide whether the payments were interest within the meaning of § 512(b)(1) as the Academy asserts, because the stipulated record persuades us the payments were not compensation for commercial services performed by the Academy and were not profit for purposes of the unrelated business income tax.

Besides finding no profit motive, we also conclude the Academy's involvement in the insurance plans was not extensive and did not "possess[] the general characteristics of a trade or business." *American Bar Endowment*, 477 U.S. at 110–11. At most, the Academy purchased the group policies offering coverage to its members, sold its membership lists to ISI for fair market value, allowed Principal and ISI to use the Academy's endorsement, and kept track of the policy provisions to make certain the insurance products the Academy sponsored would meet the needs of its members. The IRS stipulated that ISI handled the promotion, marketing, and administration, and Principal processed the insurance applications and made decisions about coverage. The Academy had no administrative or underwriting responsibilities. The parties' stipulations make clear the Academy was not engaged in the kind of activities that concerned the Supreme Court in American Bar Endowment. While the ABE negotiated with an insurance company and performed numerous administrative tasks, 477 U.S. at 107, 111, the Academy neither carried on a tax-free business nor sought a competitive edge for the group insurance program for a profit and passed its after-tax profits on to the Foundation (in the form of dividends) to support the Foundation's charitable work. ISI paid income tax like all other competing commercial entities. Although the Academy made group coverage available by assembling its members into a group and purchasing the policies, the Academy consistently acted like an insurance customer, not an insurance company, and ISI took the active, profit-making role. We conclude the Academy's involvement in the group policies was not significant enough to constitute a trade or business and expose the Academy to income tax.

Contrary to the IRS's view, "not every income-producing and profit-making endeavor constitutes a trade or business." *Groetzinger*, 480 U.S. at 35. The Academy's sponsorship of a group insurance program administered in its entirety by an unrelated, non-exempt corporation with no competitive advantage over other taxable organizations does not translate into taxable business activity for the Academy. Even if Principal made the payments to the Academy for the Academy's sponsorship—and the parties' stipulations show otherwise—the payments would not be taxable. For purposes of this case, it does not matter whether the payments were brokerage fees, gratuities to promote goodwill, or interest, because the Academy was not engaged in business activity for a profit and the unrelated business income tax does not apply. We affirm the judgment of the district court.

Questions

1. Do the facts below describe a trade or business for purposes of the unrelated business income tax? Articulate your reasons.

> A volunteer fire department qualified as a § 501(c)(3) organization raised funds to support its fire-fighting activities by receiving the proceeds from the operation of tip jars. Tip jars are a gambling device in which patrons

purchase sealed pieces of paper containing numbers, series of numbers, or symbols, which may entitle them to cash or other prizes.

Under the terms of the County Ordinance that governed tip jars, the "operator" of the tip jars must jointly apply with a non-profit organization for a County permit. To obtain a permit, the applicants must establish:

- the bona fide non-profit status of the sponsoring organization,
- that the non-profit organization will receive a minimum of seventy percent (70%) of the proceeds from a tip jar after the winnings are paid but before any operating expenses are deducted, and
- that the operator will not receive more than thirty percent (30%) of the proceeds after winnings are paid.

The 501(c)(3) organization limited its contribution to jointly applying for the gaming permit and purchasing the tip jar tickets. In his undisputed affidavit, the organization's president stated that the fire department has no access to the operator's books and records regarding the operation of tip jars.

2. In 2017, as part of the Tax Cuts and Jobs Act, Congress amended IRC § 274 to disallow deductions to taxable entities for the cost of "qualified transportation fringe" benefits to employees. Qualified transportation fringe benefits include such things as free bus passes, van pools, free or reduced parking and other commuting expenses. Simultaneously, Congress adopted § 512(a)(7) essentially requiring exempt organizations to treat as unrelated business income the *expenses* incurred by exempt organizations that provided qualified transportation to employees. The provision stated:

> Increase in unrelated business taxable income by disallowed fringe.—
>
> Unrelated business taxable income of an organization shall be increased by any amount for which a deduction is not allowable under this chapter by reason of section 274 and which is paid or incurred by such organization for any qualified transportation fringe (as defined in section 132(f)), any parking facility used in connection with qualified parking (as defined in section 132(f)(5)(C)), or any on-premises athletic facility (as defined in section 132(j)(4)(B)). The preceding sentence shall not apply to the extent the amount paid or incurred is directly connected with an unrelated trade or business which is regularly carried on by the organization. The Secretary shall issue such regulations or other guidance as may be necessary or appropriate to carry out the purposes of this paragraph, including regulations or other guidance providing for the appropriate allocation of depreciation and other costs with respect to facilities used for parking or for on-premises athletic facilities.

What do you think Congress' rationale was for requiring exempt organizations to pay tax on the expenses the exempt organization actually paid for qualified transportation fringe benefits? A hint: the rationale was related to the idea that exempt organizations enjoyed an unfair business advantage over taxable entities after IRC § 274 disallowed the deduction for taxable entities.

In any event, the provision was met with a sustained outcry, particularly from larger exempt organizations such as colleges, universities, and hospitals. Two years later, the provision was repealed retroactively by the Taxpayer Certainty and Disaster Relief Act of 2019 (P.L. 116-94).

B. The Fragmentation Rule

CODE: § 513(c)

REGS.: § 1.513-1(b), (c)(2)(ii)

We know from our study of the "exclusively operated" requirement that an exempt organization may engage in a noncharitable activity on an insubstantial basis without losing its tax exemption. We also know that the unrelated business income tax was originally imposed in response to the "destination of income" doctrine and to prevent "unfair competition" (whatever that may be). The classic paradigm for unfair competition, of course, involves an exempt organization that operates a normal commercial business that is entirely separate from the exempt activity in a profit-seeking manner (e.g., a macaroni factory). In such cases, it is understandable to think that an exempt organization can "corner the market" because of the tax exemption advantage. But what about the case where the exempt organization is performing an unquestionably charitable service, and the assets and functions attendant to that service lend themselves to commercial use on a part-time basis or on a scale that is entirely dependent upon the effective and primary performance of the exempt activity? If the performance of an exempt function creates the opportunity to fund additional commercial activities, and the exempt organization takes advantage of that opportunity, is there "unfair competition" such that UBIT should be imposed? To pose the issue in more familiar and concrete terms, if an exempt law school publishes a law review and sells advertising space in that law review, is the law school unfairly competing with *Time Magazine* or *Newsweek* such that the law school's advertising revenue should be taxed?

One can make a strong argument that the answer is "no" because the editorial content is not created, manipulated, and published with the goal of attracting the widest possible audience (which is what advertisers seek). Section 513(c) specifically rejects that argument. It eliminates the argument that an activity is not a trade or business merely because it is performed as a subpart of a larger activity that unquestionably furthers an organization's tax-exempt activities. Thus, selling advertising space will not lose its identity as a trade or business merely because the space is sold only in a tax-exempt law review. A bookstore operated primarily for the convenience of a tax-exempt university's students and employees is nevertheless engaged in a potentially taxable trade or business if it sells items to non-students. In effect, both the advertising space and the sale of goods to non-students is considered separately from the sale of the editorial material and the sale of goods to students and employees. This "fragmentation" rule is discussed further in the case that follows.

United States v. American College of Physicians

475 U.S. 834 (1986)

JUSTICE MARSHALL delivered the opinion of the Court.

A tax-exempt organization must pay tax on income that it earns by carrying on a business not "substantially related" to the purposes for which the organization has received its exemption from federal taxation. The question before this Court is whether respondent, a tax-exempt organization, must pay tax on the profits it earns by selling commercial advertising space in its professional journal, The Annals of Internal Medicine.

I

Respondent, the American College of Physicians, is an organization exempt from taxation under § 501(c)(3) of the Internal Revenue Code. The purposes of the College, as stated in its articles of incorporation, are to maintain high standards in medical education and medical practice; to encourage research, especially in clinical medicine; and to foster measures for the prevention of disease and for the improvement of public health. The principal facts were stipulated at trial. In furtherance of its exempt purposes, respondent publishes the Annals of Internal Medicine (Annals), a highly regarded monthly medical journal containing scholarly articles relevant to the practice of internal medicine. Each issue of the Annals contains advertisements for pharmaceuticals, medical supplies, and equipment useful in the practice of internal medicine, as well as notices of positions available in that field. Respondent has a longstanding policy of accepting only advertisements containing information about the use of medical products, and screens proffered advertisements for accuracy and relevance to internal medicine. The advertisements are clustered in two groups, one at the front and one at the back of each issue.

In 1975, Annals produced gross advertising income of $1,376,322. After expenses and deductible losses were subtracted, there remained a net income of $153,388. Respondent reported this figure as taxable income and paid taxes on it in the amount of $55,965. Respondent then filed a timely claim with the Internal Revenue Service for refund of these taxes, and when the Government demurred, filed suit in the United States Claims Court.

The Claims Court held a trial and concluded that the advertisements in Annals were not substantially related to respondent's tax-exempt purposes. 3 Cl. Ct. 531 (1983)....

The Court of Appeals for the Federal Circuit reversed. 743 F.2d 1570 (1984). It held clearly erroneous the trial court's finding that the advertising was not substantially related to respondent's tax-exempt purpose.... We granted the Government's petition for certiorari, 473 U.S. 904 (1985), and now reverse.

II

The taxation of business income not "substantially related" to the objectives of exempt organizations dates from the Revenue Act of 1950.... The statute was enacted in response to perceived abuses of the tax laws by tax-exempt organizations that engaged in profit-making activities. Prior law had required only that the profits garnered by exempt organizations be used in furtherance of tax-exempt purposes, without regard to the source of those profits. See *Trinidad v. Sagrada Orden de Predicadores*, 263 U.S. 578, 581 (1924); *C.R. Mueller Co. v. Commissioner*, 190 F.2d 120 (C.A.3 1951).... As a result, tax-exempt organizations were able to carry on full-fledged commercial enterprises in competition with corporations whose profits were fully taxable. See Revenue Revision of 1950: Hearings before the House Committee on Ways and Means, Vol. I, 81st Cong., 2d Sess., 18–19 (1950) (hereinafter cited as 1950 House Hearings) (describing universities' production of "automobile parts, chinaware, and food products, and the operation of theatres, oil wells, and cotton gins"). Congress perceived a need to restrain the unfair competition fostered by the tax laws. See H.R. Rep. No. 2319, 81st Cong., 2d Sess., 36–37 (1950).

...The 1950 Act struck a balance between its two objectives of encouraging benevolent enterprise and restraining unfair competition by imposing a tax on the "unrelated business taxable income" of tax-exempt organizations. 26 U.S.C. § 511(a)(1).

...Whether respondent's advertising income is taxable, therefore, depends upon (1) whether the publication of paid advertising is a "trade or business," (2) whether it is regularly carried on, and (3) whether it is substantially related to respondent's tax-exempt purposes.

III

A. Trade or Business

Satisfaction of the first condition is conceded in this case, as it must be, because Congress has declared unambiguously that the publication of paid advertising is a trade or business activity distinct from the publication of accompanying educational articles and editorial comment.

In 1967, the Treasury promulgated a regulation interpreting the unrelated business income provision of the 1950 Act. The regulation defined "trade or business" to include not only a complete business enterprise, but also any component activity of a business. Treas. Reg. § 1.513-1(b)...). This revolutionary approach to the identification of a "trade or business" had a significant effect on advertising, which theretofore had been considered simply a part of a unified publishing business. The new regulation segregated the "trade or business" of selling advertising space from the "trade or business" of publishing a journal, an approach commonly referred to as "fragmenting" the enterprise of publishing into its component parts:

"[Activities] of soliciting, selling, and publishing commercial advertising do not lose identity as a trade or business even though the advertising is published in an exempt organization periodical which contains editorial matter related to the exempt purposes of the organization." 26 CFR § 1.513.1(b) (1985).

In 1969, Congress responded to widespread criticism of those Treasury regulations by passing the Tax Reform Act of 1969, Pub. L. 91-172, 83 Stat. 487 (1969 Act). That legislation specifically endorsed the Treasury's concept of "fragmenting" the publishing enterprise into its component activities, and adopted, in a new § 513(c), much of the language of the regulation that defined advertising as a separate trade or business:

> Advertising, etc., activities . . . an activity does not lose identity as a trade or business merely because it is carried on . . . within a larger complex of other endeavors which may, or may not, be related to the exempt purposes of the organization.

26 U.S.C. § 513(c). The statute clearly established advertising as a trade or business, the first prong of the inquiry into the taxation of unrelated business income.

[Editors' note: The portion of this case that addresses "substantially related" is excerpted and included later in this chapter.]

. . . In this case . . . we have concluded that the Court of Appeals erroneously focused exclusively upon the information that is invariably conveyed by commercial advertising, and consequently failed to give effect to the governing statute and regulations. Its judgment, accordingly, is

Reversed.

Questions

Large Urban University (LU) operates a bookstore on campus as a separate corporation from which students may purchase texts, supplies, and other materials required for their classes. In addition to books and supplies, the bookstore sells clothes, toothpaste, and other personal hygiene items, compact discs, computers, and various other items that would also be found in a large department store such as Target or Wal-Mart. Of course, the bookstore is not the least bit competitive with those mega stores. Most of the bookstores sales are to students, faculty, and staff of LU, but entry to the bookstore is not limited to LU students, faculty, and staff. In fact, the bookstore manager welcomes all customers. On football weekends, for example, the bookstore operates under extended hours in hopes of selling to the increased pedestrian traffic on campus, many of whom have no affiliation with the university other than their presence on campus to see the "big game." Recently, the bookstore received an "audit comment" from its outside auditors. The auditors noted that the bookstore has not been filing Form 990-T (Return of Unrelated Business Income). The manager, waving a determination letter, informed the auditor that the bookstore was tax-exempt by virtue of its relationship to the university, but the auditor refused to retract the audit comment. The manager, who prides himself on running a smooth, profitable operation, has called you and angrily asked you for an opinion and explanation regarding the comment. How do you respond?

C. The Corporate Sponsorship Exception

CODE: § 513(i)

REGS.: § 1.513-4

In an attempt to address the question of corporate sponsorship, the Service issued Technical Advice Memorandum 9147007 — known as the "Cotton Bowl" ruling. In that ruling,[2] the Service concluded that the Cotton Bowl Athletic Association realized taxable advertising income ($1.5 million) from payments made to the association by its corporate sponsor, Mobil Oil. The Service viewed the transaction as one involving a payment of money in return for valuable services — advertising — rather than a gift in exchange for a "mere acknowledgement" of Mobil's generosity. In essence, the Cotton Bowl Athletic Association agreed to rename the Cotton Bowl football event the "Mobil Cotton Bowl Classic" and to display the corporate sponsor's name and logo on each player's jersey, on the game scoreboard, and on various conspicuous places on the field. In addition, the Association would require any broadcaster to refer to the event as the "Mobil Cotton Bowl Classic." One commentator described what viewers would see thusly:

> For anyone not familiar with the Mobil Cotton Bowl, here is what you see and hear when you turn on your television set New Year's Day. First, you are told you will be watching the "Mobil Cotton Bowl Classic." Then, as the announcers talk about the teams, you are shown the football field, with the name of the game — Mobil Cotton Bowl Classic — emblazoned on the 50-yard line, the Mobil logo at each 30-yard line, and the name "Mobil Cotton Bowl" filling each end zone. Each time the game score is flashed on the screen it is accompanied by the heading Mobil Cotton Bowl.

Paul Streckfus, *IRS' Pre-Inaugural Gift for Charities*, 58 TAX NOTES 384 (1993). As many, many commentators noted, what Mobil Oil received in exchange for its payment to the Cotton Bowl Association was substantively no different than what it might have received had it purchased advertising time on the network that broadcast the game. That is, as a matter of substance, the Cotton Bowl Association sold advertising space and should have been taxed on the revenues under § 513(c).

Despite its intuitive correctness, the Service's conclusion that the Association was selling advertising space was almost universally condemned. Powerful members of the exempt organizations' community spearheaded an intense lobbying and

---

2. The Service eliminated all of the identifying details in the TAM and therefore rendered it almost nonsensical. However, within weeks, Tax Notes and other respected tax journals reported the details of the transaction. The details reported in the text above are taken from those reports.

letter-writing campaign. Part of the lore of tax-exempt jurisprudence holds that an attorney representing an exempt organization was overheard bragging that "as long as there were three Texans on the House Ways and Means Committee, the Cotton Bowl would never be taxed." *Id.* at 385. And indeed, when the Service soon thereafter began to retreat from the Cotton Bowl ruling, its spokespeople candidly admitted that it was doing so in the face of imminent congressional action that would overturn the conclusion. The anticipated congressional action soon arrived in the form of § 513(i).

Under the regulations, a qualified sponsorship payment (whether cash, services, or property) requires no expectation that the payor will receive a substantial return benefit other than the use and association of the payor's logo, products and established slogans, with the charitable recipient's activities. Treas. Reg. § 1.513-4(c)(1). If the payment amount is contingent upon the degree of public exposure to the sponsored event, it is not a qualified sponsor payment. Treas. Reg. § 1.513-4(e)(2).

Although advertising comes in many guises (subtle *and* crass), § 513(i)(2)(A) and the regulations nevertheless draw a distinction between use or acknowledgement and advertising. A communication (no matter how conveyed) will constitute potentially taxable advertising if it includes messages containing "qualitative or comparative language, price information, or other indications of savings or value, an endorsement, or an inducement to purchase, sell, or use such products or services."[3] Treas. Reg. § 1.513-4(c)(2)(v). A use or acknowledgement, on the other hand, may contain any number of messages that create brand or vendor awareness but that do not explicitly persuade the consumer to purchase the sponsor's products. Treas. Reg. § 1.513-4(c)(2)(iv) contains a laundry lists of permissible messages that includes the display and distribution of the sponsor's products at the organization's event (e.g., the display distribution of a sponsor's sports drink at a youth football game). While a sponsor may be identified as the organization's "exclusive sponsor," the grant of an exclusive right to distribute the sponsor's products (e.g., exclusive pouring rights) is considered a substantial return benefit. Treas. Reg. § 1.513-4(c)(2)(vi)(B).[4]

The prohibition against persuasive speech is weakened by a provision in the statute and regulations that allows the display of the sponsor's "established slogan" even though the slogan may contain qualitative messages. Treas. Reg. § 1.513-4(c)(2)(iv). Thus, if a sponsor's established slogan is, "Ford Motor Cars. For the Best Ride of Your Life!" the display of the slogan is not considered advertising. *Cf.* Treas. Reg. § 1.513-4(f), Example 9. The rub, of course, is determining whether a slogan is

---

3. The phrase, "substantial return benefit" includes more than just advertising. It also includes privileges, services, or facilities and granting the payor rights to use the organization's intangible assets (such as a patent or logo). Treas. Reg. § 1.513-4(c)(2)(i). Certain low cost items do not constitute a "substantial return benefit." Treas. Reg. § 1.513-4(c)(2)(ii).

4. That the organization is found to have provided a "substantial return benefit" does not end the inquiry. To be taxable, the provision of that benefit must still meet the other requirements of the unrelated business income tax.

"established." Neither the statute nor the regulations give any indication of how to make that determination.

A single message that contains both an acknowledgement and advertising is considered advertisement. On the other hand, a sponsor may communicate several different messages at a single event. Those that otherwise constitute use or acknowledgement are not deemed advertisement merely because they appear at the same sponsored event or in the same publication. Remember, though, just because a message constitutes advertisement does not mean that the income earned by publishing the message is taxable. The activity must still meet the other two requirements for taxation.

Questions

A state university conducts a well-attended, three-day track and field event each spring at an outdoor athletic facility owned by the university. The athletic facility is bounded on all sides by streets owned by the city. All of the approximately 85,000 fans attending the event over the three-day period must use one of the city streets to get to and leave the track and field arena. In exchange for a $50,000, sponsorship payment, the university agrees to display the logo and products of "Cola," a well-known soft drink maker. The manufacturer's logo and products are on display at and distributed from approximately 30 different places throughout the facility. In addition, the logo is affixed to the shirts and warm-up suits of all participants. The university sells the television rights to the event to a national broadcaster. In addition to buying stereotypical advertising time from the broadcaster, the cola manufacturer purchases $20,000 worth of billboard space on the four streets bordering the facility and displays stereotypical advertisement on each billboard, and for $40,000 it hires a blimp displaying Cola's logo and the statement, "Cola tastes better than Un-Cola" to fly over the facility.

1. What are the tax consequences to the university from the receipt of the $50,000 payment?

2. What if, in addition to the facts stated above, the arrangement provides that state university will not allow any other soft drink manufacturer to sell products during the event and prohibits any participant from displaying the logo of any other soft drink manufacturer on his or her uniform?

3. What if, in addition to the display of logos and products, the sponsor also purchases, for an additional $10,000, billboard space within the arena on which it displays the message "Cola is better than any other soft drink. Drink some today!"

4. What if, in addition to the display of logos and products, the university also provides free admission to the event for all of sponsor's 100 employees and the price of admission (for all three days) to the general public is $40.00 per person? How much, if any, of the $50,000 payment would be potentially taxable?

5. What if, for an additional $10,000, state university agrees to place the sponsor's logo and established slogan, "Cola Kills Your Thirst: Drink More of It!" in the official program magazine sold at the event?

Chapter 27

UBIT — The "Regularly Carried on" Requirement

A. In General

CODE: § 512(a)(1)

REGS.: § 1.513-1(c)

As we have seen in the prior two chapters, Congress and the courts are very generous with exempt organizations when it comes to the imposition of the unrelated business income tax. Tax exempt organizations avoid the tax from activities that are not a trade or business (Chapter 26). Further, tax exempt organizations also avoid the tax on income from business activities that are not regularly carried on. The materials below explore what makes a trade or business regularly carried on so that income from these activities subject tax-exempt organizations to UBIT.

National Collegiate Athletic Association v. Commissioner

914 F.2d 1417 (10th Cir. 1990), non-acquiescence, AOD 1991-015 (1991)

SEYMOUR, Circuit Judge.

The National Collegiate Athletic Association (NCAA), the petitioner in this case, appeals from the decision of the tax court, which determined a deficiency of $10,395.14 in unrelated business income tax due for the 1981–1982 fiscal year. On appeal, the NCAA challenges the court's conclusion that revenue received from program advertising constituted unrelated business taxable income under I.R.C. § 512. . . . We reverse.

I.

The NCAA is an unincorporated association of more than 880 colleges, universities, athletic conferences and associations, and other educational organizations and groups related to intercollegiate athletics, for which it has been the major governing organization since 1906. The NCAA is also an "exempt organization" under section 501(c)(3) . . . , and hence is exempt from federal income taxes. One of the purposes of the NCAA, as described in the organization's constitution, is "to supervise the conduct of . . . regional and national athletic events under the auspices of this Association." Pursuant to this purpose, the NCAA sponsors some seventy-six collegiate championship events in twenty-one different sports for women and men on an annual basis. The most prominent of these tournaments, and the NCAA's biggest revenue generator, is the Men's Division I Basketball Championship. The tournament is held at different sites each year. In 1982, regional rounds took place at a variety of sites, and the Louisiana Superdome in New Orleans was the host for the "Final Four," the tournament's semifinal and final rounds. In that year, the Championship consisted of forty-eight teams playing forty-seven games on eight days over a period of almost three weeks. The teams played in a single-game elimination format, with each of the four regional winners moving into the Final Four.

The NCAA contracted with Lexington Productions, a division of Jim Host and Associates, Inc. ("Host" or "Publisher"), in 1981 to print and publish the program for the 1982 Final Four games. The purpose of such programs, according to the NCAA's then-director of public relations, is

> to enhance the experience primarily for the fans attending the game.... [It also] gives the NCAA an opportunity to develop information about some of its other purposes that revolve around promoting sports [as a] part of higher education and demonstrating that athletes can be good students as well as good participants.

The "Official Souvenir Program" for the 1982 Final Four round of the tournament was some 129 pages long. Advertisements made up a substantial portion of the program, some of which were placed by national companies.

The Commissioner mailed the NCAA a notice of deficiency in which he determined that the NCAA was liable for $10,395.14 in taxes on $55,926.71 of unrelated business taxable income from the program advertising revenue. The NCAA petitioned the tax court for a redetermination of the deficiency set forth by the Commissioner. The tax court determined that this revenue was unrelated business taxable income, and that it was not excludable from the tax as a royalty.

* * *

III.

Section 511 of the Code imposes a tax on the unrelated business taxable income of exempt organizations. Section 512(a)(1) of the Code defines the term "unrelated business taxable income" as "the gross income derived by any organization from any unrelated trade or business ... regularly carried on by it...." The term "unrelated trade or business" means "any trade or business the conduct of which is not substantially related ... to the exercise or performance by such organization" of its exempt function. I.R.C. § 513(a). Under the heading "Advertising, etc., activities," section 513(c) provides that "the term 'trade or business' includes any activity which is carried on for the production of income from the sale of goods or the performance of services.... An activity does not lose identity as a trade or business merely because it is carried on ... within a larger complex of other endeavors which may, or may not, be related to the exempt purposes of the organization." I.R.C. § 513(c).

The NCAA's advertising revenue therefore must be considered unrelated business taxable income if: "(1) It is income from trade or business; (2) such trade or business is regularly carried on by the organization; and (3) the conduct of such trade or business is not substantially related (other than through the production of funds) to the organization's performance of its exempt functions." Treas. Reg. § 1.513-1(a). If a taxpayer shows that it does not meet any one of these three requirements, the taxpayer is not liable for the unrelated business income tax.

The NCAA concedes that its program advertising was a "trade or business" not "substantially related" to its exempt purpose. The only question remaining, therefore, is whether the trade or business was "regularly carried on" by the organization. The meaning of the term "regularly carried on" is not defined by the language of the statute. Accordingly, we turn to the Treasury Regulations for assistance.

Section 1.513-1(c) of the Treasury Regulations provides a discussion of the phrase "regularly carried on." The general principles set out there direct us to consider "the frequency and continuity with which the activities productive of the income are conducted *and* the manner in which they are pursued." Treas. Reg. § 1.513-1(c)(1) (emphasis added). As a cautionary note, the regulations emphasize that whether a trade or business is regularly carried on must be assessed "in light of the purpose of the unrelated business income tax to place exempt organization business activities upon the same tax basis as the nonexempt business endeavors with which they compete." *Id.*

The regulations then move beyond the general principles and set out a process for applying the principles to specific cases. The first step is to consider the normal time span of the particular activity, and then determine whether the length of time alone suggests that the activity is regularly carried on, or only intermittently carried on. *See id.* § 1.513-1(c)(2)(i). If the activity is "of a kind normally conducted by nonexempt commercial organizations on a *year-round* basis, the conduct of such [activity] by an exempt organization over a period of only a few weeks does not constitute the regular carrying on of trade or business." *Id.* (emphasis added). As an example of a business not regularly carried on, the regulations describe a hospital auxiliary's operation of a sandwich stand for only two weeks at a state fair. In contrast, the regulations deem the operation of a commercial parking lot every Saturday as a regularly-carried-on activity. *Id.*

If the activity is "of a kind normally undertaken by nonexempt commercial organizations only on a *seasonal* basis, the conduct of such activities by an exempt organization during a *significant portion* of the season ordinarily constitutes the regular conduct of trade or business." *Id.* (emphasis added). The operation of a horse racing track several weeks a year is an example of a regularly-conducted seasonal business, because such tracks generally are open only during a particular season. *Id.*

A primary point of contention in this case is whether the NCAA's advertising business is normally a seasonal or year-round one, and whether it is intermittent or not. The tax court noted that the Commissioner looked at the short time span of the *tournament*, concluded that it was as much a "seasonal" event as the operation of a horse racing track, and then argued that the time involved in the tournament program advertising made it a regularly carried on business. The court observed that the NCAA, which did not agree with the Commissioner's "season" conclusion, also focused on the tournament itself in contending that the event's short time span made the activity in question intermittent. The tax court rejected these arguments as "placing undue emphasis on the tournament itself as the measure for determining whether petitioner regularly carried on the business at issue.... Although sponsorship of a college basketball tournament and attendant circulation of tournament programs are seasonal events, the 'trade or business' of selling advertisements is not."

We agree that to determine the normal time span of the activity in this case, we should consider the business of *selling advertising space*, since that is the business the Commissioner contends is generating unrelated business taxable income. There is no dispute that the tournament itself is substantially related to the NCAA's exempt purpose and so, unlike the horse racing track, it should not be the business activity in question. Since the publication of advertising is generally conducted on a year-round basis, we conclude that if the NCAA's sale of program advertising was conducted for only a few weeks, that time period could not, standing alone, convert the NCAA's business into one regularly carried on.

The tax court held, and the Commissioner argues, that the amount of preliminary time spent to solicit advertisements and prepare them for publication is relevant to the regularly-carried-on determination, and that the length of the tournament is not relevant. This position is contrary to the regulations and to existing case law. The language of the regulations alone suggests that preparatory time should not be considered. The sandwich stand example in the regulations, for instance, included a reference only to the two weeks it was operated at the state fair. *See* Treas. Reg. § 1.513-1(c)(a)(i). The regulations do not mention time spent in planning the activity, building the stand, or purchasing the alfalfa sprouts for the sandwiches.

The advertising here was solicited for publication in a program for an event lasting a few weeks. While the length of the tournament is irrelevant for purposes of assessing the normal time span of the business of selling advertising space, we hold that, contrary to the tax court's conclusion, the tournament must be considered the actual time span of the business activity sought to be taxed here. The length of the tournament is the relevant time period because what the NCAA was selling, and the activity from which it derived the relevant income, was the publication of advertisements in programs distributed over a period of less than three weeks, and largely to spectators. Obviously, the tournament is the relevant time frame for those who chose to pay for advertisements in the program. This case is unlike *American College of Physicians, 475 U.S. at 836*, where advertisements were sold for each issue of a monthly medical journal. Accordingly, we conclude that the NCAA's involvement in the sale of advertising space was not sufficiently long-lasting to make it a regularly-carried-on business solely by reason of its duration.

The next step of the regulation's analysis is to determine whether activities which are intermittently conducted are nevertheless regularly carried on by virtue of the manner in which they are pursued. In general, according to the regulations, "exempt organization business activities which are engaged in only discontinuously or periodically will not be considered regularly carried on if they are conducted without the competitive and promotional efforts typical of commercial endeavors." Treas. Reg. § 1.513-1(c)(2)(ii). As an example of an activity not characteristic of commercial endeavors, the regulations refer to "the publication of *advertising in programs for sports events* or music or drama performances." *Id.* (emphasis added). The NCAA places considerable emphasis on this latter sentence and criticizes the tax court, which stated only that there was insufficient evidence from which the court could draw conclusions on the manner of Host's conduct of its advertising activities. As the NCAA stresses, the tax court did not distinguish the 1982 Basketball Championship from the "sports events" referred to in the regulation above.

The difficult question of whether the NCAA's advertising is of the type envisioned as commercial in nature, or instead as consistent with that connected to the "sports events" referred to in the regulations, is not one which we must answer now, however. For the final step in the process spelled out by the regulations requires us to consider whether, promotional efforts notwithstanding, an intermittent activity occurs "so infrequently that neither [its] recurrence nor the manner of [its] conduct will cause [it] to be regarded as trade or business regularly carried on." Treas. Reg. § 1.513-1(c)(2)(iii). We conclude that the advertising here is such an infrequent activity. The programs containing the advertisements were distributed over less than a three-week span at an event that occurs only once a year. We consider this to be sufficiently infrequent to preclude a determination that the NCAA's advertising business was regularly carried on.

Our conclusion is buttressed by the regulation's admonition that we apply the regularly-carried-on test in light of the purpose of the tax to place exempt organizations doing business on the same tax basis as the comparable nonexempt business endeavors with which they compete. *See* Treas. Reg. § 1.513-1(c)(1). The legislative history of the unrelated business income tax also convinces us that we must consider the impact an exempt organization's trade or business might have on its competition. The tax was a response to the situation prevailing before 1950, when an exempt organization could engage in any commercial business venture, secure in the knowledge that the profits generated would not be taxed as long as the *destination* of the funds was the exempt organization. The *source* of those funds did not affect their tax status. *See, e.g., Trinidad v. Sagrada Orden de Predicadores*, 263 U.S. 578, 581 (1924); *C.F. Mueller Co. v. Commissioner*, 190 F.2d 120, 121 (3d Cir. 1951); *see also American College of Physicians*, 475 U.S. at 837–38. As more and more exempt organizations began acquiring and operating commercial enterprises, there were rumblings in Congress to do away with the perceived advantage enjoyed by these organizations. The case which most forcefully brought this point home was that involving the C.F. Mueller Co. That company, a leading manufacturer of macaroni products, was in 1947 acquired and organized for the purpose of benefiting the New York University's School of Law, a tax-exempt educational institution. *See C.F. Mueller*, 190 F.2d at 121. This acquisition prompted an outcry from a number of sources.

In President Truman's 1950 message to Congress, for example, he stated that "'an exemption intended to protect educational activities has been misused in a few instances to gain competitive advantage over private enterprise through the conduct of business . . . entirely unrelated to educational activities.'" Primarily to "restrain the unfair competition fostered by the tax laws," Congress imposed a tax on the business income of exempt organizations, but only on that income substantially unrelated to the organization's exempt purposes. *See* Revenue Act of 1950, Pub. L. No. 814, § 301, 64 Stat. 906, 947.

Although we have observed that the purpose of the unrelated business income tax was to prevent unfair competition between companies whose earnings are taxed and those whose are not, it is not necessary to prove or disprove the existence of actual competition. *See United States v. American Bar Endowment*, 477 U.S. 105 (1986). But analyzing the business in question in terms of its possible effect on prospective competitors helps to explain why an activity can occur "so infrequently" as to preclude a designation as a business regularly carried on. While the operation of a parking lot on a weekly basis occurs sufficiently frequently to threaten rival parking lot owners, the hospital auxiliary's annual sandwich stand is too infrequent a business to constitute a threat to sandwich shop owners. The competition in this case is between the NCAA's program and all publications that solicit the same advertisers. The competition thus includes weekly magazines such as *Sports Illustrated* and other publications which solicit automobile, beverage, photocopier, and fried chicken advertisements, to name a few. Viewed in this context, we conclude that the NCAA program, which is published only once a year, should not be considered an unfair competitor for the publishers of advertising. Application of the unrelated business tax here therefore would not further the statutory purpose. We hold that the NCAA's advertising business was not regularly carried on within the meaning of the Code.

The decision of the tax court is REVERSED.

State Police Association of Massachusetts v. Commissioner

125 F.3d 1 (1st Cir. 1997) (cert. denied 1998)

Selya, Circuit Judge.

In this case, the Commissioner of the Internal Revenue Service (the Commissioner) issued a deficiency notice to the State Police Association of Massachusetts (the Association) for income taxes allegedly due but unpaid. When the Association protested, the Tax Court sided with the Commissioner. . . . The Association appeals, contending that the Tax Court erred both in finding that the deficiency assessment was timely and in holding that certain of the Association's activities gave rise to liability for unrelated business income tax. We affirm.

I. Background

The Association is a labor organization, and, as such, is exempt from income taxes under 26 U.S.C. § 501(c)(5) (1994). The purpose of the organization is to represent its members in bargaining over the terms and conditions of their employment and to promote a fraternal spirit among members. Virtually all the troopers who are eligible to join the Association do so.

During the years at issue, the Association published an annual yearbook, known as The Constabulary. The yearbook consisted of photographs, articles, display advertisements, and a business directory. We describe *infra* the sales effort (which the Association in more salubrious times called the "earnings program") and the mechanics of publication and distribution. It is enough for now to say that the earnings program proved to be aptly named: gross receipts related to the publication of The Constabulary for the years at issue totaled $8,788,211. Of this amount, the Association retained somewhat over 40% (the precise percentage varied from year to year, and is of no consequence here). The Association paid no tax on the income.

It is said that all good things come to an end. Federal law requires that an otherwise tax-exempt organization must pay federal income tax on income derived from business ventures which are not substantially related to its tax-exempt purpose(s). *See* IRC § 511. After due investigation, the Commissioner concluded that the Association had violated this stricture because the sale of advertising in The Constabulary yielded taxable income. Acting on this conclusion, the Commissioner issued a deficiency notice seeking $1,352,433 in taxes due for the tax years ended April 30, 1986 through April 30, 1989, the three months ended July 31, 1989, and the tax years ended July 31, 1990 and 1991, along with additions to tax and penalties totaling $711,075.

Displeased by this turn of events, the Association brought suit in the Tax Court *under* IRC § 6213(a) to obtain a redetermination of the taxes allegedly due. It claimed that, for certain tax years, the notice of deficiency had been issued beyond the applicable limitation period; and that, on a broader plane, the activity cited by the Commissioner—the solicitation, sale, and publication of display ads and listings in The Constabulary—did not constitute an unrelated trade or business regularly carried on, and that, therefore, the income derived from that activity was exempt from tax. The Tax Court rejected both of these and sustained the Commissioner's determination of the existence and extent of the deficiency (although it eliminated the additions to tax and the penalties). This appeal ensued.

* * *

III. The Merits

The gravamen of the Commissioner's case is the charge that the activity undertaken in connection with publication of The Constabulary generated unrelated business taxable income. The allegation that an activity engaged in by a tax-exempt organization gives rise to unrelated business taxable income requires proof of three components. The Commissioner must demonstrate (1) that the activity comprises a trade or business, (2) which is regularly carried on, and (3) which is not substantially related to the organization's tax-exempt purpose. *See United States v. American Bar Endowment*, 477 U.S. 105, 110 (1986); *see also* IRC § 513(a).

* * *

C.

The Association's final contention is that, even if its activities comprise a business attributable to it, that business was not carried on regularly. To buttress this contention, the Association makes two separate, but related, arguments.

Its first assertion rests on the decisions in *National Collegiate Athletic Ass'n v. Commissioner*, 914 F.2d 1417 (10th Cir. 1990) (NCAA), and *Suffolk County Patrolmen's Benevolent Ass'n v. Commissioner*, 77 T.C. 1314 (1981). These decisions are inapposite. In each instance, the advertising activity was tied to the program for a specific event. *See NCAA*, 914 F.2d at 1420 (collegiate basketball tournament); *Suffolk County*, 77 T.C. at 1316 (vaudeville show). Thus, resolution of those cases depended on Treas. Reg. §1.513-1(c)(2)(ii), which specifically provides that "publication of advertising in programs for sports events or music or drama performances will not ordinarily be deemed to be the regular carrying on of business." That regulation is of no assistance here because the Tax Court found specially that the Association's publication of The Constabulary was not linked to the occurrence of a specific event and the Association has not challenged that finding in this venue.

We hasten to add, moreover, that the mode of analysis used in NCAA and Suffolk County cannot be employed here. Because those cases each involved a particular event, they looked to the time frame of the event in determining the regularity with which the business was carried on. *See NCAA*, 914 F.2d at 1422–23; *Suffolk County*, 77 T.C. at 1322–24. In a case like this one, where the publication of an ad book is not pegged to a particular event, a court must assay the activities which collectively comprise the business, and look to the overall time frame in which they occurred. For present purposes, that means the time frame in which the Association solicited, sold, and published advertising. *See* Treas. Reg. §1.513-1(b) (noting that the activities of soliciting, selling, and publishing advertising collectively constitute a business). Those activities persisted for approximately 46 weeks a year. This is more than sufficient regularity by any standard.

The Association next argues that it did not regularly engage in a business because it did not carry on the advertising activity with the same entrepreneurial zeal that might typify a commercial operator. But this is an ill-conceived comparison. Although the purpose behind the unrelated business income tax is to create a more level playing field between taxed and tax-exempt enterprises, competitive similarities are not the only factors to be taken into account. The applicable regulation stipulates that the activity in question must be judged "in light of the purpose" of the tax, but it does not require that either actual competition or competitive equality be shown. Treas. Reg. §1.513-1(c)(1).

In this instance, the Association carried on its activities in a systematic and well-organized fashion, with a clearly defined profit motive. Given the limitations of clear-error review, we cannot disturb the lower court's finding that the Association's activities were sufficiently regular to bring them within the ambit of the regulation.

IV. Conclusion

We need go no further. While the Association makes several other arguments, none requires discussion; each of them is either adequately treated in the Tax Court's opinion, or obviously incorrect, or both. It suffices to say that the Commissioner's determination of the tax due and owing rests on a sturdy factual and legal foundation.

Affirmed.

Questions

1. X, a § 501(c)(3) organization, conducts an annual golf tournament and an annual charity ball. The sole purpose of the two events is to raise funds for a wild animal preservation project. A souvenir program that includes (1) editorial articles regarding the environment and wild animals and (2) advertising published each year in connection with the golf tournament. X solicits advertising during a nine-month period before the tournament. One or more of X's paid employees sells advertising on an ongoing basis during this period.

a. What are the tax consequences from the operation of the golf tournament and annual charity ball?

b. What are the tax consequences from the receipt of advertising revenue?

2. Are the revenues derived by M under the following fact situation taxable as unrelated business income?

M's main fund-raising activity is a concert series held each spring and fall. Typically, each concert series is performed by the same performer over a two- or three-day weekend at different locations throughout P. Sometimes there are two performances on the same day. In year 2 there were a total of eight separate performances and in year 3 there were 10 performances. At each of the shows, an introduction is made stating that the show is brought to the attendees by M. M represents that this introduction "emphasizes the wonderful job that the firefighters are doing on the streets."

In January, year 1 M first engaged the services of N to assist with fund-raising, as reflected in a contract between the two parties. M granted and extended to N the use of its good name, goodwill, and cooperation to stimulate the sale of tickets and advertising, and its complete cooperation in the presentation of six events. Aside from the contractual agreement, there are no ties whatsoever between M and N. N provided a campaign manager to direct a campaign for the sale of admission tickets in connection with these events. All sales work was done by this campaign manager and/or his employees. The telemarketers identify themselves as being from N, but calling on behalf of M.

Aside from ticket sales, N was responsible for arranging the logistics of each concert series, including contracting for the artists, renting an appropriate facility, and providing insurance and security. The preparation and solicitation for each of the spring and fall concerts usually takes up to six months.

The persons who are contacted are solicited for a donation to M, which is not tax deductible. For each donation of $12.50, the donor receives one voucher, which resembles an admission ticket. M represents that only about 10–15% of the solicited donors attend the entertainment events. Upon agreeing to donate to M, the donor is informed that he or she will be receiving a voucher or vouchers, along with an invoice and a thank-you letter. The invoice prominently identifies M along with its address and telephone number. The thank-you letter identifies M as the recipient of the ticket revenues and is signed by the President of M. The vouchers have imprinted on their face "(M) Proudly Presents . . ."

M's representatives advised that the $12.50 amount on the voucher is a suggested amount; M will be "grateful" to receive as little as $5.00 from individuals in poorer areas of P. Upon receipt of payment, M (through N) will send out a thank-you letter with M's logo and an explanation of the organization's goals with respect to public safety and legislation. Sixty percent of the individuals who agree to purchase vouchers make good on their donations. This leaves a sizable minority who may attend the concerts free of charge because N mails out the vouchers before receiving any payment. If no payment is received, a reminder will be sent out in 10 to 15 days, but still if no check is received, then N will make no further effort to collect the amount. Likewise, no attempt is made to collect on a bounced check. M's representatives characterized the above practices as completely "non-commercial" in nature.

All solicited monies were made payable to M and were mailed or delivered each week to N. These monies were deposited into a joint bank account that was mutually agreed upon by M and N. Both organizations approved any disbursements from the bank account — all checks required the signatures of two individuals, one from M and one from N. Following their deposit into the joint bank account, 40% of the gross receipts were disbursed for payment of wages to the campaign manager and his staff.

Gross receipts from the concerts were also used by N to pay all direct and indirect costs related to the production of the show, including rent, insurance, postage, and printing. The remainder of the receipts were divided equally between M and N. Under the terms of the contract between M and N, M had no risk of loss with respect to any concert event. In the event of a deficit, N was solely responsible for the payment of any resulting liability. For the taxable period in question, no such losses have been borne by N. For the two taxable years (2 and 3), M received approximately $463x and $578x, respectively, as its profits share from the concert events, with an equal allocation to N.

B. The "Substantially Related" Requirement

CODE: § 513(a)

REGS.: §§ 1.513-1(d)(1)-(3)

United States v. American College of Physicians

475 U.S. 834 (1986)

JUSTICE MARSHALL delivered the opinion of the Court.

[Editors' note: The facts of this case are included in an earlier section of this chapter that discusses the fragmentation rule aspect of the trade or business requirement.]

III.

* * *

B. Substantially Related

According to the Government, Congress and the Treasury established a blanket rule that advertising published by tax-exempt professional journals can never be substantially related to the purposes of those journals and is, therefore, always a taxable business. Respondent, however, contends that each case must be determined on the basis of the characteristics of the advertisements and journal in question. Each party finds support for its position in the governing statute and regulations issued by the Department of the Treasury.

In its 1967 regulations, the Treasury not only addressed the "fragmentation" issue discussed above, but also attempted to clarify the statutory "substantially related" standard found in § 513(a). It provided that the conduct of a tax-exempt business must have a causal relation to the organization's exempt purpose (other than through the generation of income), and that "the production or distribution of the goods or the performance of the services from which the gross income is derived must *contribute importantly* to the accomplishment of [the exempt] purposes." Treas. Reg. § 1.513-1(d)(1), 26 CFR § 1.513-1(d)(2) (1985) (emphasis added). In illustration of its new test for substantial relation, the Treasury provided an example whose interpretation is central to the resolution of the issue before us. Example 7 of Treas. Reg. § 1.513-1(d)(4)(iv) involves "Z," an exempt association formed to advance the interests of a particular profession and drawing its membership from that profession. Z publishes a monthly journal containing articles and other editorial material that contribute importantly to the tax-exempt purpose. Z derives income from advertising products within the field of professional interest of the members:

> Following a practice common among taxable magazines which publish advertising, Z requires its advertising to comply with certain general standards of taste, fairness, and accuracy; but within those limits the form, content, and manner of presentation of the advertising messages are governed by the basic objective of the advertisers to promote the sale of the advertised

> products. While the advertisements contain certain information, the informational function of the advertising is incidental to the controlling aim of stimulating demand for the function of any commercial advertising. Like taxable publishers of advertising, Z accepts advertising only from those who are willing to pay its published rates. Although continuing education of its members in matters pertaining to their profession is one of the purposes for which Z is granted exemption, the publication of advertising designed and selected in the manner of ordinary commercial advertising is not an educational activity of the kind contemplated by the exemption statute; it differs fundamentally from such an activity both in its governing objective and in its method. Accordingly, Z's publication of advertising does not contribute importantly to the accomplishment of its exempt purposes; and the income which it derives from advertising constitutes gross income from unrelated trade or business.

§ 1.513-1(d)(4)(iv), Example 7.

The Government contends both that Example 7 creates a *per se* rule of taxation for journal advertising income and that Congress intended to adopt that rule, together with the remainder of the 1967 regulations, into law in the 1969 Act. We find both of these contentions unpersuasive.

Read as a whole, the regulations do not appear to create the type of blanket rule of taxability that the Government urges upon us. On the contrary, the regulations specifically condition tax exemption of business income upon the importance of the business activity's contribution to the particular exempt purpose at issue, and direct that "[whether] activities productive of gross income contribute importantly to the accomplishment of any purpose for which an organization is granted an exemption depends *in each case* upon the facts and circumstances involved," § 1.513-1(d)(2) (emphasis added). Example 7 need not be interpreted as being inconsistent with that general rule. Attributing to the term "example" its ordinary meaning, we believe that Example 7 is best construed as an illustration of one possible application, under given circumstances, of the regulatory standard for determining substantial relation.

The interpretative difficulty of Example 7 arises primarily from its failure to distinguish clearly between the statements intended to provide hypothetical facts and those designed to posit the necessary legal consequences of those facts. Just at the point in the lengthy Example at which the facts would appear to end and the analysis to begin, a pivotal statement appears: "the informational function of the advertising is incidental to the controlling aim of stimulating demand for the advertised products." The Government's position depends upon reading this statement as a general proposition of law, while respondent would read it as a statement of fact that may be true by hypothesis of "Z" and its journal, but is not true of Annals.

We recognize that the language of the Example is amenable to either interpretation. Nevertheless, several considerations lead us to believe that the Treasury did not intend to set out a *per se* statement of law. First, when the regulations were proposed in early 1967, the Treasury expressed a clear intention to treat all commercial advertising as an unrelated business. See Technical Information Release No. 889, CCH 1967 Stand. Fed. Tax Rep. para. 6557. When the regulations were issued in final form, however, following much criticism and the addition of Example 7, they included no such statement of intention. 32 Fed. Reg. 17657 (1967). Second, a blanket rule of taxation for advertising in professional journals would contradict the explicit case-by-case requirement articulated in Treas. Reg. § 1.513-1(d)(2), and we are reluctant to attribute to the Treasury an intention to depart from its own general principle in the absence of clear support for doing so. Finally, at the time the regulations were issued, the 1950 Act had been interpreted to mean that business activities customarily engaged in by tax-exempt organizations would continue to be considered "substantially related" and untaxed. *See* Note, *The Macaroni Monopoly: The Developing Concept of Unrelated Business Income of Exempt Organizations*, 81 HARV. L. REV. 1280, 1291 (1968). A *per se* rule of taxation for the activity, traditional among tax-exempt journals, of carrying commercial advertising would have been a significant departure from that prevailing view. Thus, in 1967 the idea of a *per se* rule of taxation for all journal advertising revenue was sufficiently controversial, its effect so substantial, and its statutory authorization so tenuous, that we simply cannot attribute to the Treasury the intent to take that step in the form of an ambiguous example, appended to a subpart of a subsection of a subparagraph of a regulation.

It is still possible, of course, that, regardless of what the Treasury actually meant by its 1967 regulations, Congress read those regulations as creating a blanket rule of taxation, and intended to adopt that rule into law in the 1969 Act. The Government appears to embrace this view, which it supports with certain statements in the legislative history of the 1969 Act. For example, the Government cites to a statement in the House Report, discussing the taxation of advertising income of journals published by tax-exempt organizations:

> "Your committee believes that a business competing with taxpaying organizations should not be granted an unfair competitive advantage by operating tax free unless the business contributes importantly to the exempt function. It has concluded that by that standard, advertising in a journal published by an exempt organization is not related to the organization's exempt functions, and therefore it believes that this income should be taxed." H.R. Rep. No. 91-413, pt. 1, p. 50 (1969).

Similar views appear in the Senate Report:

> "Present law. — In December 1967, the Treasury Department promulgated regulations under which the income from advertising and similar activities is treated as 'unrelated business income' even though such advertising for example may appear in a periodical related to the educational or other exempt purpose of the organization.

> "General reasons for change. — The committee agrees with the House that the regulations reached an appropriate result in specifying that when an exempt organization carries on an advertising business in competition with other taxpaying advertising businesses, it should pay a tax on the advertising income. The statutory language on which the regulations are based, however, is sufficiently unclear so that substantial litigation could result from these regulations. For this reason, the committee agrees with the House that the regulations, insofar as they apply to advertising and related activities, should be placed in the tax laws." S. Rep. No. 91-552, p. 75 (1969).

Based on this language, the Government argues that the 1969 Act created a *per se* rule of taxation for advertising income. The weakness of this otherwise persuasive argument, however, is that the quoted discussion appears in the Reports solely in support of the legislators' decision to enact § 513(c), the provision approving the fragmentation of "trade or business." Although § 513(c) was a significant change in the tax law that removed one barrier to the taxation of advertising proceeds, it cannot be construed as a comment upon the two other distinct conditions — "regularly carried on" and "not substantially related" — whose satisfaction is prerequisite to taxation of business income under the 1950 Act. Congress did not incorporate into the 1969 Act the language of the regulation defining "substantial relation," nor did the statute refer in any other way to the issue of the relation between advertising and exempt functions, even though that issue had been hotly debated at the hearings. *See, e.g.*, Tax Reform, 1969: Hearings before the House Committee on Ways and Means, 91st Cong., 1st Sess., 1113, 1118, 1192, 1241 (1969). Thus, we have no reason to conclude from the Committee Reports that Congress resolved the dispute whether, in a specific case, a journal's carriage of advertising could so advance its educational objectives as to be "substantially related" to those objectives within the meaning of the 1950 Act.

It is possible that the Committees' discussion of advertising reflects merely an erroneous assumption that the "fragmentation" provision of § 513(c), without more, would establish the automatic taxation of journal advertising revenue. Alternatively, the quoted passages could be read to indicate the Committees' intention affirmatively to endorse what they believed to be existing practice, or even to change the law substantially. The truth is that, other than a general reluctance to consider commercial advertisements generally as substantially related to the purposes of tax-exempt journals, no congressional view of the issue emerges from the quoted excerpts of the Reports. Thus, despite the Reports' seeming endorsement of a *per se* rule, we are hesitant to rely on that inconclusive legislative history either to supply a provision *not* enacted by Congress, or to define a statutory term enacted by a prior Congress. We agree, therefore, with both the Claims Court and the Court of Appeals in their tacit rejection of the Government's argument that the Treasury and Congress intended to establish a *per se* rule requiring the taxation of income from all commercial advertisements of all tax-exempt journals without a specific analysis of the circumstances.

IV. Important Contribution to Tax Exempt Purpose

It remains to be determined whether, in this case, the business of selling advertising space is "substantially related" — or, in the words of the regulation, "contributes importantly" — to the purposes for which respondent enjoys an exemption from federal taxation. Respondent has maintained throughout this litigation that the advertising in Annals performs an educational function supplemental to that of the journal's editorial content. Testimony of respondent's witnesses at trial tended to show that drug advertising performs a valuable function for doctors by disseminating information on recent developments in drug manufacture and use. In addition, respondent has contended that the role played by the Food and Drug Administration, regulating much of the form and content of prescription-drug advertisements, enhances the contribution that such advertisements make to the readers' education. All of these factors, respondent argues, distinguish the advertising in Annals from standard commercial advertising. Respondent approaches the question of substantial relation from the perspective of the journal's subscribers; it points to the benefit that they may glean from reading the advertisements and concludes that that benefit is substantial enough to satisfy the statutory test for tax exemption. The Court of Appeals took the same approach. It concluded that the advertisements performed various "essential" functions for physicians and found a substantial relation based entirely upon the medically related content of the advertisements as a group.

The Government, on the other hand, looks to the conduct of the tax-exempt organization itself, inquiring whether the publishers of the Annals have performed the advertising services in a manner that evinces an intention to use the advertisements for the purpose of contributing to the educational value of the journal. Also approaching the question from the vantage point of the College, the Claims Court emphasized the lack of a comprehensive presentation of the material contained in the advertisements. It commented upon the "hit-or-miss nature of the advertising," 3 Cl. Ct., at 543, n. 3, and observed that the "differences between ads plainly reflected the advertiser's marketing strategy rather than their probable importance to the reader." *Id.*, at 534. "[Any] educational function [the advertising] may have served was incidental to its purpose of raising revenue." *Id.*, at 535.

We believe that the Claims Court was correct to concentrate its scrutiny upon the conduct of the College rather than upon the educational quality of the advertisements. For all advertisements contain some information, and if a modicum of informative content were enough to supply the important contribution necessary to achieve tax exemption for commercial advertising, it would be the rare advertisement indeed that would fail to meet the test. Yet the statutory and regulatory scheme, even if not creating a *per se* rule against tax exemption, is clearly antagonistic to the concept of a *per se* rule *for* exemption for advertising revenue. Moreover, the statute provides that a tax will be imposed on "any trade or business the *conduct* of which is not substantially related," 26 U.S.C. § 513(a) (emphasis added), directing our focus to the manner in which the tax-exempt organization operates its business. The implication of the statute is confirmed by the regulations, which emphasize the "manner" of designing and selecting the advertisements. See Treas. Reg. §1.513-1(d)(4)(iv), Example 7, 26 CFR §1.513-1(d)(4)(iv), Example 7 (1985). Thus, the Claims Court properly directed its attention to the College's conduct of its advertising business, and it found the following pertinent facts:

> "The evidence is clear that plaintiff did not use the advertising to provide its readers a comprehensive or systematic presentation of any aspect of the goods or services publicized. Those companies willing to pay for advertising space got it; others did not. Moreover, some of the advertising was for established drugs or devices and was repeated from one month to another, undermining the suggestion that the advertising was principally designed to alert readers of recent developments..... Some ads even concerned matters that had no conceivable relationship to the College's tax-exempt purposes." 3 Cl. Ct., at 534 (footnotes omitted).

These facts find adequate support in the record. Considering them in light of the applicable legal standard, we are bound to conclude that the advertising in Annals does not contribute importantly to the journal's educational purposes. This is not to say that the College could not control its publication of advertisements in such a way as to reflect an intention to contribute importantly to its educational functions. By coordinating the content of the advertisements with the editorial content of the issue, or by publishing only advertisements reflecting new developments in the pharmaceutical market, for example, perhaps the College could satisfy the stringent standards erected by Congress and the Treasury. In this case, however, we have concluded that the Court of Appeals erroneously focused exclusively upon the information that is invariably conveyed by commercial advertising, and consequently failed to give effect to the governing statute and regulations. Its judgment, accordingly, is

Reversed.

Afro-American Purchasing Center Inc.

T.C. Memo. 1978-31

TANNENWALD, Judge:

* * *

Petitioner, Afro-American Purchasing Center, Inc. (hereinafter petitioner or AAPC), is a nonprofit corporation organized in 1964 and existing under the laws of the State of New York with its principal place of business in New York, New York, at the time of the filing of the petition herein. It filed information returns for the years in question with the district director of internal revenue, New York, New York.

In 1963, the United States Agency for International Development (AID) determined that inadequate training of procurement officials in countries receiving AID assistance hindered the progress of AID financed projects and necessitated waivers of AID requirements that assistance funds be used to purchase goods manufactured in the United States. AID decided that a program should be established that would assist recipient nations in satisfying their procurement needs in United States markets and would educate officials of such nations in procurement methods. Based upon a study prepared by Ohio State University, it was decided that a new corporation should be formed to carry out this program. AID thereupon caused AAPC to be formed, named its initial board of directors and worked closely in planning AAPC's operations. In addition, during petitioner's fiscal years 1966 and 1967, AID made grants to AAPC totaling $170,000, to help establish AAPC and to enable it to commence its activities.

Petitioner's Certificate of Incorporation provides:

> The purpose for which the Corporation is formed is:
>
> To establish, assist, aid and encourage the maintenance and improvement of educational and training facilities to develop the abilities, skills and techniques of African nationals or residents, including personnel of African governments, in the methods, procedures and sources of supply for world-wide purchasing, procurement, supply management and supply operations.

The certificate further provides that no one is to receive any pecuniary profit from petitioner's operations (excepting reasonable compensation for services rendered to AAPC); that no part of petitioner's net earnings is to inure to any private member or individual; that no substantial part of petitioner's activities is to consist of attempting to influence legislation; that petitioner is not to participate in any political campaign on behalf of any candidates for public office; and that all of petitioner's assets will be distributed to an organization described in section 501(c)(3) upon petitioner's dissolution.

The parties have stipulated that petitioner implemented the foregoing provisions by operating in the following fashion and with the consequences indicated:

> 5. AAPC performs various educational functions and conducts several different programs designed to meet its educational purposes.
>
>> (a) AAPC conducts a formal, structured eight-month educational training program wherein the student-trainees are usually selected by the AID Office of Internal Training on the recommendation of their respective foreign governments. Occasionally, trainees are accepted to participate in this program upon the recommendation of other governmental or quasi-governmental agencies such as the United Nations, Branch for Training and Fellowships.
>>
>> (b) After selection, trainees participate in a one-week orientation program in Washington, conducted by the AID Office of Internal Training where representatives of AAPC are generally present.
>>
>> (c) Next, the trainees are assigned to formal classroom training at Fordham University for a special academic program designed and developed by AAPC, AID and Fordham to meet the objectives of AAPC. AAPC generally monitors all stages of the formal classroom work, specifies

the subject matter of the training courses, approves the professors, and discusses the curriculum to be covered with the professors during the training program.

(d) In this phase, students cover such subjects as International Trade Relations and Procedures, Inventory Control, Supply Management and Purchasing Functions, including negotiation techniques and contract administration.

(e) Although some of the courses and material presented in the special Fordham program is available to full time matriculated students, none is available to nonmatriculated students not enrolled on a regular basis at that university other than AAPC trainees.

(f) Many of the courses and material presented in the Fordham program were specially designed and are only available to AAPC trainees. Moreover, only AAPC trainees are eligible to enroll and participae in this special program as such.

(g) Upon the conclusion of this course, the trainees are directly assigned to AAPC where they are thoroughly tested by AAPC to insure their understanding of the formal instruction and are prepared to begin on-the-job training. When necessary, special tutoring is arranged by AAPC's instructor staff.

(h) The trainees are then assigned to work on a simulated purchasing exercise wherein they are responsible to do all the work (make analysis, review specifications, prepare sample bids, obtain quotations from manufacturers, and inquire about shipping and payment arrangements) in connection with a procurement implementation project that had already been carried out by AAPC.

(i) The students are next assigned to work with AAPC staff members on all stages of an actual procurement cycle. The students, under the guidance of AAPC's staff, handle all facets of the purchasing cycle from the preparation of specifications to the payment of invoices.

(j) During the on-the-job training period, conferences are conducted by AAPC specialists and various experts from American industry and universities. Visits to purchasing departments of various companies in the United States, as well as with financial and freight forwarding company representatives, are arranged.

(k) In addition to the formal eight-month educational program, AAPC also designs and administers special programs designed to meet the educational needs of certain less-developed nations in particular circumstances, usually at the request of the United States Government. Examples of such special programs include:

(i) programs for architects and contractors of schools and public buildings from underdeveloped nations;

(ii) seminars and discussion groups for groups ranging from dock superintendents to commercial delegations who desire to compare various commercial methods; and

(iii) education of local maintenance people in the underdeveloped nations relating to the care and maintenance of the materials and supplies procured by AAPC.

(1) From time to time, AAPC has hosted high officials from various African underdeveloped nations and has established special one-month courses for them to acquaint them with AAPC's program.

6. During the years here in question, more than 80% of the salaries paid by AAPC are paid to individuals directly involved with the educational purposes of, and the educational program conducted by, AAPC. All of such individuals do not spend 100% of their time on such matters.

7. During the years here in question, approximately 25% of the time of AAPC's staff was spent in direct contact with trainees in connection with actual on-the-job training.

8. Actual procurement activity is essential to the successful achievement of AAPC's educational purposes and to the viability of its entire educational and training program.

9. AAPC's procurement activities also result in the support of other essential services and policies of the United States Government, the burden of which would otherwise fall on the United States Government and its agencies.

(a) Virtually all of AAPC's procurement activities are in connection with AID-financed foreign origin procurement.

(b) AAPC provides an alternative non-governmental procurement organization to the United States General Services Administration ("GSA") capable of effectively handling AID-financed foreign origin procurement at the lowest cost.

(c) AAPC encourages and facilitates purchases of domestic goods by foreign nations.

(d) AAPC lessens the burden of foreign governments, charitable organizations and, on occasion, has assisted Embassies of the United States Government, by more efficiently utilizing funds appropriated by the United States.

10. AAPC procurement activities at no time was operated in the same manner as a commercial, profit-seeking corporation in that:

(a) AAPC purchases only for governments, quasi-government agencies and certain non-profit charitable institutions (such as the Peace Corps and certain foreign universities);

> (b) AAPC has not, does not, and pursuant to a resolution adopted by the board of directors will not, purchase for private commercial interests, domestic or foreign;
>
> (c) The procurement fee scales charges by AAPC are substantially lower than those charged by commercial enterprises that are comparable and by GSA;
>
> (d) The salaries paid to employees of AAPC are reasonable for non-profit organizations.
>
> (e) AAPC does not, and does not plan to, solicit business, advertise in any commercial media or employ any public relations officer.

The question to be resolved herein is whether, during its fiscal years 1969 and 1970, petitioner qualified as an organization exempt from tax under section 501(c)(3). Respondent concedes that to the extent of its educational activities, petitioner was organized and operated for an exempt purpose and has stipulated that "[A]ctual procurement activity is essential to the successful achievement of AAPC's educational purposes and to the viability of its entire educational and training program." Essentially, respondent's position is that procurement activity is not usually an exempt function and that petitioner's procurement activity was the primary purpose of its operations, thereby depriving petitioner of its exempt status. In other words, respondent contends that a non-exempt tail was wagging an otherwise exempt animal. Petitioner counters with the assertion that its procurement activity was an integral and essential part of its educational program and that, however, such type of activity may be characterized in another context, it does not affect petitioner's exempt status—in short, the procurement activity functioned as the normal appendage to an exempt animal. Alternatively, petitioner argues that, under the circumstances herein, its procurement activity in and of itself constituted an exempt function on the ground that it lessened the burdens of government.

We address ourselves first to the main point of contention between the parties, namely, the role of petitioner's procurement activities in relation to its concededly exempt educational purposes. In so doing, we have been handicapped by petitioner's attempt to seek refuge in the stipulated facts and respondent's complacent reliance on the fact that the burden of proof is on the petitioner. The consequence of this procedural scenario is that we must reach our decision without the benefit that might have flowed from testimony as to the details of petitioner's operations—particularly its procurement activities during the years in issue. We have done the best we can with the limited record before us and concluded that, on balance, petitioner has carried its burden of proving (see Rule 142, Tax Court Rules of Practice and Procedure) that the conduct of its procurement activities was not its primary purpose and that accordingly it should prevail.

Section 1.501(c)(3)-1(e)(1), Income Tax Regs., provides that an organization otherwise satisfying the requirements of section 501(c)(3) will not be denied an exemption where "it operates a trade or business as a substantial part of its activities, if the operation of such trade or business is in furtherance of the organization's exempt purpose of purposes and if the organization is not organized or operated for the primary purpose of carrying on an unrelated trade or business, as defined in section 513." The pertinent regulations under section 513 are contained in section 1.513-1(d) as follows:

> (2) Type of relationship required. Trade or business is "related" to exempt purposes, in the relevant sense, only where the conduct of the business activities has causal relationship the achievement of exempt purposes (other than through the production of income); and it is "substantially related," for purposes of section 513, only if the causal relationship is a substantial one. Thus, for the conduct of trade or business from which a particular amount of gross income is derived to be substantially related to purposes for which exemption is granted, the production or distribution of the goods or the performance of the services from which the gross income is derived must contribute importantly to the accomplishment of those purposes. Where the production or distribution of the goods or the performance of the services does not contribute importantly to the accomplishment of the exempt purposes of an organization, the income from the sale of the goods or the performance of the services does not derive from the conduct of related trade or business. Whether activities productive of gross income contribute importantly to the accomplishment of any purpose for which an organization is granted exemption depends in each case upon the facts and circumstances involved.
>
> (3) Size and extent of activities. In determining whether activities contribute importantly to the accomplishment of an exempt purpose, the size and extent of the activities involved must be considered in relation to the nature and extent of the exempt function which they purport to serve. Thus, where income is realized by an exempt organization from activities which are in part related to the performance of its exempt functions, but which are conducted on a larger scale than is reasonably necessary for performance of such functions, the gross income attributable to that portion of the activities in excess of the needs of exempt functions constitutes gross income from the conduct of unrelated trade or business. Such income is not derived from the production or distribution of goods or the performance of services which contribute importantly to the accomplishment of any exempt purpose of the organization.

As we see it, the foregoing regulations establish three levels of possible tax impact:

> (1) a trade or business which is sufficiently causally related, both in type and volume, to the exempt functions of an organization qualified under section 501(c)(3) so as neither to jeopardize its exemption or justify the imposition of the unrelated business tax under sections 511 through 515. In this context, the fact that the trade or business involved is commercial in nature is immaterial. See section 1.513-1(d)(4)(iv), Example (5) Income Tax Regs.

> See also *Squire v. Students Book Corp.*, 191 F.2d 1018, 1020 [41 AFTR 194] (9th Cir. 1951).
>
> (2) a trade or business which, although sufficiently causally related in type to an organization's exempt function, is conducted at such a level as to expose the organization to the unrelated business tax but not so as to justify the denial of the organization's exemption. Cf. *Iowa State University of Science & Tech. v. United States*, 500 F.2d 508 [34 AFTR 2d 74-5541] (Ct. Cl. 1974);
>
> (3) a trade or business which, although ostensibly causally related in type to an organization's exempt function, is carried on in such a volume that it constitutes the primary purpose of the organization so that such organization should not be accorded exempt status. See *American Institute For Economic Research v. United States*, 302 F.2d 934 [9 AFTR 2d 1426] (Ct.Cl. 1962).

In the instant case, the issue presented by category (2) above is not before us. Respondent has not made any claim that petitioner is subject to the unrelated business tax on the commissions derived from its procurement activities. Accordingly, we do not reach the question whether petitioner's procurement activities reached such a level that the income therefrom should be at least partially considered subject to the unrelated business tax. Cf. *Santa Barbara Club v. Commissioner*, 68 T.C. 200, 203 (1977); sec. 1.513-1(d)(3). In so stating, we are not unmindful that the lines of demarcation among the three above-mentioned categories are not always clearly discernible, so that some of the ingredients of a determination with respect to liability of an exempt organization for the unrelated business tax are at least tangentially involved in determining the applicability of categories (1) and (3).

Nor do we have to determine whether petitioner necessarily falls within category (1) in order to be exempt. In the context of the issue placed before us, petitioner's position herein should be sustained if we decide that it does not fall within category (3). While the evidence is far from conclusive, we are satisfied on the basis of the record before us, that petitioner has carried its burden of proof on this score.

Initially, we note that more than 80 percent of the salaries paid by AAPC were paid to individuals directly involved in the educational program conducted by it, and approximately 25 percent of the staff time was spent in direct contact with the students in connection with actual on-the-job training. It is reasonable to infer that additional staff time was expended on preparation for such direct contact, and the support services ancillary to the training.

In addition to the efforts spent directly on the on-the-job training, AAPC supervised the formal instruction at Fordham University, tested the trainees upon completion of that program, arranged special tutoring where necessary, and conducted special educational programs which offered instruction in various facets of procurement and commercial processes. The time expended on these matters was in furtherance of AAPC's educational purposes.

A significant portion of the procurement, (aside from that portion in which trainees actively participated) appears to have been reasonably necessary for the accomplishment of petitioner's educational goals. First, as part of the training process, trainees were assigned to work on a simulated purchasing exercise based upon a procurement implementation project that had earlier been performed by AAPC. Second, the educational program envisioned instruction in general principles of procurement, and practices and procedures specific to the countries to which the trainees would return.

It is reasonable to infer that, to satisfy these educational goals, petitioner needed a backlog of projects suitable as training exercises for individuals from numerous African countries, and a variety of current projects from such countries for their on-the-job training. Thus it appears that more projects were required that would be necessary for general training of the trainees.

In sum, petitioner's procurement activities ostensibly furthered its educational and training program. On-the-job training, an integral element of the program, required an ongoing procurement operation to which the students could be assigned. At the very least, such training gave trainees valuable experience which would better prepare them for handling procurement on their return to their native lands. In the context of the stipulated facts herein, to the extent that petitioner's procurement activity might be considered unrelated, it was secondary in purpose to petitioner's organization and operation. Compare *Scripture Press Foundation v. United States*, 285 F.2d 800 [7 AFTR 2d 489] (Ct.Cl. 1961). Accordingly, we hold that petitioner is entitled to an exemption from taxation under section 501(c)(3) for the years in issue. In view of our conclusion, we do not reach the issue presented by petitioner's alternative argument.

Decision will be entered for petitioner.

Questions

1. Determine whether, under the following fact situation, the operation of a pharmacy is substantially related to the organization's exempt purpose.

> Hospital was established in year 15 to provide hospital and other related services to its members. It is located in Hale Center, Texas, a small town of about 2,250 people. Prior to year 7, Hale Center had been served by a resident doctor. From year 7, when the doctor died, until year 15, when Hospital was established, Hale Center lacked medical services. During that period, another doctor also lived and provided care to residents of Hale Center, but she could not stand the isolation and soon left. The establishment of Hospital both provided a physical facility in which patients could be treated and served as an inducement to doctors to practice in Hale Center. Toward this end, Hospital offered to provide a doctor who would work on its staff with furnished offices in the hospital, complete nursing assistance, and a bookkeeping and billing service for the benefit of his private practice. Although

it is undisputed that the cost of such facilities and services would normally consume 40% of a doctor's fees, Hospital offered these services in return for five percent of a doctor's collected fees. Moreover, the hospital made certain that its own services, such as x-ray, laboratory facilities and a pharmacy, were available to its doctors' private patients. Thus, if a doctor wanted a patient who had come in for an office visit to be x-rayed, the doctor would refer that patient to the hospital, which would take the x-ray and bill the patient.

The pharmacy makes sales to hospital patients, to private patients of the doctors located in the hospital, and to the general public. The bulk of these sales consists of prescription drugs. Only a small percentage of the pharmacy's income is derived from the sale of nonprescription items. The pharmacy neither advertises nor uses display areas to attract customers. It maintains only a counter where orders can be placed. A small cardboard sign, which the state requires to be displayed, is the pharmacy's only identifying mark.

Note on Commercial Exploitation of an Exempt Function

If a charitable organization develops more pest-resistant vegetables as part of its exempt mission to improve farming techniques, will it compete unfairly with commercial sellers if it uses its research tomatoes to make and sell spaghetti sauce? What if a charitable organization uses its fine arts theatre to show educational films during the day, but Hollywood movies at night? Is it competing unfairly with the local movie theaters?

It would seem silly to require an organization devoted to developing and improving a certain product to simply discard or give away the product once the new techniques have been perfected and the test product is no longer needed. For that reason, perhaps, the regulations specifically state that "ordinarily, gross income from the sale of products which result from the performance of exempt functions does not constitute gross income" from an unrelated trade or business. Treas. Reg. § 1.513-1(d)(4)(ii). Our hypothetical spaghetti sauce seller might therefore rely on that regulation, adding also that its sale of spaghetti sauce is limited by its research agenda, which effectively prevents the organization from competing with commercial sellers. Both arguments would fail.

The regulation provides that the sale of exempt function products will be considered a related activity only if the product is "sold in substantially the same state it is in on completion of the exempt function." *Id.* In other words, the tomatoes cannot be used in the manufacture of some other product without the sale of that other product generating potentially taxable income. Although the organization may be correct in pointing out that the limitation caused by using only research tomatoes prevents it from effectively competing with commercial sellers, the regulations nevertheless treat the activity as unrelated. Remember, we do not need to prove that Ronzoni exists.

It is easier to see why the regulations potentially tax our second organization's use of its facility in a non-exempt commercial activity. Treas. Reg. § 1.513-1(d)(4)(iii).

That the building is also used to further an exempt function does not lessen whatever unfair competition is caused by using the building in a nonexempt commercial endeavor. We cannot say, as perhaps we can with the disposition of exempt function products, that the commercial use of the building is an inevitable consequence of, and is limited by, the pursuit of the exempt function.

Finally, the regulations also consider the commercial exploitation of an organization's intangibles as not substantially related to an exempt function and thus potentially taxable. Treas. Reg. § 1.513-1(d)(4)(iv). However, as we will see in more detail later, income from the exploitation of an organization's intangibles via a royalty arrangement is excluded from taxation by statute, though the sale of the intangibles is not substantially related to an exempt function.

Beginning in the late 1980s and early 1990s, the commercial travel industry began to complain that charitable organizations (primarily educational organizations) were unfairly cutting into the commercial travel business by offering travel packages, seminars, and tours billed as "educational" or otherwise related to the organization's exempt function. The unfairness, as with all activities deemed unrelated, was said to arise because the offering organizations paid no tax on the revenues derived from such activities so long as the activity was indeed related to the organization's exempt purpose. Thus, a university that offers "Semester at Sea" programs where students attend classes on board a ship cruising the Caribbean can avoid taxation on the revenues it charges the students because the activity is not unrelated to the university's educational mission. The commercial travel industry complained that many such programs offered very little substance related to the exempt purpose and were simply a commercial means by which universities and other organizations raised money from alumni and other patrons. The commercial travel industry wanted the Service to crack down on such travel activities. After a number of years, the Service finally issued Treasury Regulations § 1.513-7. Those regulations can hardly be viewed as a crackdown and many in the commercial travel industry were disappointed when the regulations were finalized. In fact, the regulations essentially provide a simple roadmap for organizations that wish to conduct such programs without realizing unrelated taxable income—perhaps the opposite effect of what was sought by the commercial industry. Essentially, a travel program must include organized activities, such as meetings, seminars, classes, and other activities easily recognized as related to the exempt purpose (e.g., organized outings to historical sites). Probably a majority of the organized activities should be mandatory (i.e., participants required to attend) and an organization would be well-advised to keep records concerning those mandatory activities and attendance. Provided the program includes a fair amount of mandatory activities related to the organization's exempt purpose, it may also include plenty of time and opportunity for fun and frolic. All in all, the burdens imposed by Treasury Regulation Section 1.513-7 seem light and, much to the chagrin of the commercial travel industry, the regulation should make it safer (by eliminating uncertainty) for organizations to offer travel programs without fear of taxation.

Chapter 28

UBIT — Modifications, Deductions and Controlled Entities

A. In General

Code: § 512(a)(1), (b)

Regs.: §§ 1.512(a)-1(a); 1.512(b)-1(a)–(c)

Section 512(b) identifies a number of modifications that are to be implemented in computing unrelated taxable income. Some modifications, such as the exclusion of dividends, interest, and royalty payments under § 512(b)(2), are based on the notion that certain activities do not implicate the concerns underlying the unrelated business income tax. Other modifications, like the inclusion of debt-financed income under §§ 512(b)(4) and 514 and the inclusion of passive income from a controlled entity under § 512(b)(13), are rather antagonistic toward charitable organizations. The rules pertaining to debt-financed income and passive income from controlled entities were originally imposed in response to a sense that exempt organizations were abusing their tax exemptions by engaging or assisting in tax avoidance transactions with or by taxable persons or entities. Most of the modifications were discussed earlier in Deputy Assistant Secretary Chapoton's overview in Chapter 25, and so we do not further summarize them here. Instead, we begin in the first part of this chapter by focusing on passive income received from a controlled corporation and two of the most significant modifications — the exclusion of rental and royalty income. The second part of the chapter examines UBIT deductions. Finally, Chapter 29 focuses on unrelated debt-financed income.

B. The Royalty Modification

Reg.: § 1.512(b)-1(b)

The royalty modification might reasonably be labeled "the exception that swallows the rule." For example, an educational organization will normally realize unrelated taxable income from the sale of sports beverages to the general public. However, if the organization develops and patents a formula for a sports beverage, it may grant a commercial entity the right to exploit the patent in exchange for periodic royalty payments which are excluded from taxation under § 512(b)(2). Likewise, an exempt organization can indirectly participate in the regular sale of

T-shirts or the marketing of credit, by licensing the use of its logo, or the likeness of its school mascot for a fee. If the organization sold T-shirts or offered credit to the general public directly, it would incur unrelated taxable income. Moreover, commercial entities that exploit their intangible assets — for example, Nike, Inc. — must pay taxes on the income derived, whether that income is derived directly or through a royalty arrangement. Perhaps because royalties allow organizations to do indirectly without taxation what they could do directly only with taxation, the Service has sought to limit the scope of the royalty modification, primarily by arguing that many purported royalty arrangements actually involve payments for services or evidence of a joint venture in which the tax exempt organization actively participates. These efforts have been spectacularly unsuccessful.

Sierra Club Inc. v. Commissioner

86 F.3d 1526 (9th Cir. 1996)

Wiggins, Circuit Judge:

Sierra Club, Inc., a tax-exempt organization under I.R.C. § 501(c)(4), must pay taxes on "unrelated business taxable income" ("UBTI") under I.R.C. §§ 511-13. I.R.C. § 512(b)(2), however, excludes "all royalties" from UBTI, thus rendering the royalty income of a tax-exempt organization non-taxable. The Commissioner of Internal Revenue ("Commissioner") contends that the Tax Court erred in determining on summary judgment that Sierra Club's income from the rental of its mailing lists and from participation in an affinity credit card program constituted "royalties" and therefore was not taxable....

I.

The income Sierra Club received from the following two business arrangements is at the center of this dispute.

A. Mailing List Rentals

[*Editors' summary of facts:* For its own internal purposes, Sierra club developed and maintained lists of its members, donors, supporters and catalogue purchasers. Sierra Club was the sole owner of these mailing lists. Sierra Club retained Triplex Marketing ("Triplex") to maintain and update the lists as needed. Sierra Club also inserted "seed names" in its mailing lists to protect against abuse and unauthorized use of the lists.

Sierra Club also rented the names from its mailing lists to other organizations. Sierra Club retained Names in the News ("Names") and Chilcutt Direct Marketing ("Chilcutt") as list managers to administer and oversee the rental of its lists. Sierra Club set the rates for the rentals, retained the right to review requests for rental, to approve all proposed mailing material and mailing schedules. Names and Chilcutt promoted the rental of the lists through solicitations, personal sales calls, advertising and seminars. Thus, any entity wishing to rent Sierra Club's lists placed an order with Chilcutt or Names; and Chilcutt or Names then forwarded the order to Sierra

Club. Sierra Club would then fill the list rental order through Triplex, which would organize the list in accordance with the criteria requested by the renter. Triplex billed Names or Chilcutt for these services and Names or Chilcutt in turn billed the list renter for these costs. Names and Chilcutt (and its individual list broker) received commissions from Sierra Club of twenty to thirty percent of the base price of the list (the cost of renting the list excluding the Triplex service charges).

In the tax years 1985, 1986, and 1987, Sierra Club received $142,636, $317,579, and $452,042 respectively for the rental of its mailing lists.]

* * *

B. Affinity Credit Card Program

[*Editors' summary of facts:* On February 20, 1986, Sierra Club entered into an agreement with American Bankcard Services, Inc. ("ABS"). Under the agreement, ABS would offer Sierra Club members a bankcard with the name "Sierra Club" on the front of the card and Sierra Club's logo on the back. In addition, Sierra Club would continually solicit and encourage its members to use this bankcard.

ABS agreed to pay Sierra Club a monthly "royalty fee." ABS also agreed to develop, subject to Sierra Club's approval, promotional and solicitation materials for the card program and bear the cost of such materials. The agreement explicitly did not establish an agent/principal relationship between ABS and Sierra Club. Sierra Club also agreed not to authorize the issuance of other affinity cards by any other bank during the terms of its agreement with ABS.

On June 15, 1986, ABS sent its initial solicitations, on Sierra Club letterhead with a Sierra Club return address and signed by Sierra Club's president, to Sierra Club members for the credit card program. The letters were mailed using Sierra Club's non-profit postage permit. ABS paid standard commercial rates for advertisements in *Sierra* magazine. Sierra Club members sent their credit card applications to Chase Lincoln and either Chase Lincoln or ABS answered customer questions about the program.

For the tax years 1986 and 1987, Sierra Club received $6,021 and $303,225 respectively from the credit card program.]

C. The Tax Court

* * *

The Tax Court held that the rental income from the mailing lists constituted royalties. In reaching this decision, the court defined royalties as "'payments for the use of intangible property rights'" and thus not limited solely to passive income....

The parties then filed cross-motions for summary judgment on the issue of whether the income from the affinity credit card program constituted royalties as well.... [T]he Tax Court held that the "consideration received by [Sierra Club] on account of its participation in the affinity credit card program was for the use of intangible property ([Sierra Club's] name, logo, and mailing list)." ... Accordingly, the court concluded that the income derived from licensing Sierra Club's name and logo to ABS and granting ABS permission to use Sierra Club's mailing lists for solicitation was royalty income.

The Commissioner appeals both decisions of the Tax Court.

II.

* * *

B.

The crux of the parties' dispute is how to define "royalties" for the purpose of I.R.C. § 512(b)(2). A tax-exempt organization under I.R.C. § 501(c) must pay taxes at normal corporate rates on "unrelated business taxable income." I.R.C. § 511(a). UBTI is defined as "the gross income derived by any organization from any unrelated trade or business . . . regularly carried on by it, less the deductions allowed . . . both computed with the modifications provided in subsection (b)." I.R.C. § 512(a)(1). Section 512(b)(2) provides that "there shall be excluded all royalties (including overriding royalties) whether measured by production or by gross or taxable income from the property, and all deductions directly connected with such income."

"Royalties" as used in § 512(b)(2) is not further defined by statute or by regulation.

* * *

Black's Law Dictionary provides a definition of a royalty as

> compensation for the use of property, usually copyrighted material or natural resources, expressed as a percentage of receipts from using the property or as an account per unit produced. A payment which is made to an author or composer by an assignee, licensee or copyright holder in respect of each copy of his work which is sold, or to an inventor in respect of each article sold under the patent. Royalty is share of product or profit reserved by owner for permitting another to use the property.

Black's Law Dictionary 1330–31 (6th Ed. 1979).

From the above, we can glean that "royalty" commonly refers to a payment made to the owner of property for permitting another to use the property. The payment is typically a percentage of profits or a specified sum per item sold; the property is typically either an intangible property right—such as a patent, trademark, or copyright—or a right relating to the development of natural resources.

Revenue Ruling 81-178, relied upon by the parties, supports defining royalty as a payment which relates to the use of a property right. It states that "payments for the use of trademarks, trade names, service marks, or copyrights, whether or not payment is based on the use made of such property, are ordinarily classified as royalties for federal tax purposes." Rev. Rul. 81-178, 1981-2 C.B. 135. Thus, according to Revenue Ruling 81-178, by definition, "royalties do not include payments for personal services."

The parties agree that the above definition of royalty is correct—up to this point. The Commissioner argues that "royalty" must be further defined, claiming that a payment for the use of intangible property is not necessarily a royalty *unless* the subject of the payment is "passive in nature." Sierra Club, on the other hand, contends that any payment for the use of an intangible property right constitutes a royalty. For the following reasons, we hold that under § 512(b)(2) "royalties" are payments for the right to use intangible property. We further hold that a royalty is by definition "passive" and thus cannot include compensation for services rendered by the owner of the property.

First, the circuits that have considered whether or not income received by a tax-exempt organization constitutes royalties under § 512(b)(2) have consistently excluded income received as compensation for services—income that is not "passive"—from royalty income. In *Disabled American Veterans v. United States*, 650 F.2d 1178 (Ct. Cl. 1981) ("DAV I"), the Court of Claims upheld the Tax Court's determination that DAV's income from the rental of its donor lists to other organizations was not royalty income under § 512(b)(2). *Id.* at 1189. The court reasoned that § 512(b) as a whole "excludes from taxation the conventional type of passive investment income traditionally earned by exempt organizations (dividends, interest, annuities, real property rents)." *Id.* Because DAV's rental of its donor lists was "the product of extensive business activity by DAV" (such as preparing rate cards, sending the rate cards to list brokers, sorting the lists, and providing the information on magnetic tape or labels), the court held that the list rental income did "not fit within the types of 'passive' income set forth in section 512(b)." *Id.*

* * *

This distinction between payments for services and payments for the right to use an intangible property right is supported by Rev. Rul. 81-178. The ruling discusses and applies the exclusion of royalty income from UBTI in two factual scenarios. In the first, a tax-exempt organization of professional athletes solicits and negotiates licensing agreements which authorize the use of the organization's trademarks, trade names, service marks, as well as its members' names, photographs, likenesses and facsimile signatures; under the terms of the agreements, the organization has the right to approve the quality and style of the use of the licensed product. In the second, the same organization solicits and negotiates agreements to endorse the products and services offered by the other party to the agreement; the agreements require personal appearances by the members of the organization. The ruling states that the income generated by the agreements in the first situation is royalty income within the meaning of § 512(b). However, the income received in the second situation is not royalty income because the agreements "require the personal services of the organization's members in connection with the endorsed products and services." Rev. Rul. 81-178, 1981-2 C.B. 135.

Lastly, differentiating between passive royalty income and income which is compensation for services comports with the purpose of I.R.C. §§ 511–513. As discussed by the Commissioner, the imposition of the tax on unrelated business income was in response to a concern that tax-exempt organizations were competing unfairly with taxable businesses. Certain categories of income, however, were excluded from UBTI because "[the] committee believed that they are 'passive' in character and are not likely to result in serious competition for taxable businesses having similar income." S. Rep. No. 2375, 81st Cong., 2d Sess., 28, 30–31 (1950).[1] The purpose of the tax on UBTI to prevent unfair competition coupled with the exclusion of income believed to be "passive" in character from that tax provides additional support for excluding payment for services from royalty income.

Sierra Club, in arguing that Congress intended to exclude *all* royalty income from UBTI, not simply royalty income passively derived, points to legislative history that states:

> All dividends, interest, annuities, and royalties, and the deductions directly connected therewith, are excluded from the concept of unrelated business net income. This exception applies not only to investment income, but also to such items as business interest on overdue open accounts receivable.

S. Rep. No. 2375, 81st Cong., 2d Sess. at 108. We agree with Sierra Club that the legislative history, as well as the language of the statute, indicates that Congress intended to exclude "all royalties." Acknowledging this, however, does not aid in determining whether by definition "all royalties" *means* payments (for the use of a property right) that are passive in nature.

Sierra Club also claims that in order for the exception to UBTI to apply, the royalty income must be derived from an unrelated business activity, or it would not be taxable as UBTI in the first place. Thus, if the exclusion of royalties from UBTI were only meant to encompass passively derived royalties, § 512(b)(2) would never apply. In other words, because a trade or business is defined to *exclude* passive activities, a tax-exempt organization must be engaged in an active trade or business before a royalty could possibly be taxed under § 511.

This last argument highlights why royalties should be defined as "passive" only to the extent that a royalty cannot be compensation for services. Sierra Club could be engaged in a trade or business such as manufacturing t-shirts. The income from selling the t-shirts would be taxable as UBTI. However, if Sierra Club copyrighted the designs on its t-shirts and then licensed the designs to a t-shirt manufacturer in exchange for a one percent royalty fee on gross sales, the royalty fees would be excluded from UBTI under § 512(b)(2).

---

1. [16] H.R. Rep. No. 2319, 81st Cong., 2d Sess., 36, 38 (1950), also states:

> The tax applied to unrelated business income does not apply to dividends, interest, royalties (including, of course, overriding royalties), rents (other than certain rents on property acquired with borrowed funds), and gains from sales of leased property. Your committee believes that such "passive" income should not be taxed where it is used for exempt purposes because investments producing incomes of these types have long been recognized as proper for educational and charitable organizations.

Thus, to the extent the Commissioner claims that a tax-exempt organization can do *nothing* to acquire such fees (*e.g.*, providing a rate sheet listing the fee charged for use of each copyrighted design or retaining the right to approve how the design is used and marketed), the Commissioner is incorrect. However, to the extent that Sierra Club appears to argue that a "royalty" is any payment for the use of a property right—such as a copyright—regardless of any additional services that are performed in addition to the owner simply permitting another to use the right at issue, we disagree.

In sum, we hold that "royalties" in § 512(b) are defined as payments received for the right to use intangible property rights and that such definition does not include payments for services.

III.

Given the above definition of royalties, we must now decide whether the district court erred in granting summary judgment on the issue of whether the payments received by Sierra Club for one-time rentals of its lists constitute "royalties" or payments for services performed by Sierra Club.

The facts upon which the Tax Court based its decision are as follows. Sierra Club maintained its mailing lists in furtherance of its tax exempt function; it hired Triplex to perform the task of maintaining the lists on a computerized data base. It also contracted with Chilcutt and Names to administer the rental of the lists. Sierra Club set the rates for the list rentals and retained the right to approve the content and date of the mailings of a list user. Chilcutt and Names were paid a commission for its services that was taken from the fee that the list user paid for the rental. Chilcutt and Names forwarded orders for list rentals to Sierra Club, which in turn had Triplex fulfill those orders. Triplex invoiced Chilcutt and Names for services such as sorting and providing labels; these charges were ultimately billed to the list user.

* * *

On these facts, the Tax Court held that it was undisputed that the income Sierra Club received for the rental of the lists was compensation for the use of its unique property—the mailing lists.

Here, Sierra Club contracted with others to perform those services that the Court of Claims held constituted "extensive business activity" in *DAV I*. The government argues that it does not matter that Sierra Club paid others to perform services such as sorting by zip code and providing the names on labels—Sierra Club was still in the business of selling and marketing its mailing lists. Sierra Club, on the other hand, correctly points out that it did not participate in any of the business activities that could be considered providing services. It did not market its lists, sort the lists, provide the lists on labels, or provide any other service to the list users. Nor did it pay Triplex to perform these services. Triplex billed Names and Chilcutt for these services, who in turn billed the list renter.

Moreover, Sierra Club did not pay Names and Chilcutt to market the lists; rather, Names and Chilcutt received a commission from each rental. Nonetheless, the Commissioner argues that this commission was deducted from the list rental fee, and therefore was the equivalent of Sierra Club paying Names and Chilcutt to provide marketing services. Accordingly, the Commissioner would have us hold that any active effort to market intangible property—such as the right to use the names on the mailing lists—converts what was a royalty into a non-royalty, because the payment is obtained by active rather than passive conduct.

We find Sierra Club's position more persuasive. Sierra Club did not itself perform the services relating to the rental of mailing lists. Nor did it market the mailing lists. It did nothing more than collect a fee for the rental of its mailing lists. Thus, Sierra Club's activities with regard to the mailing list rentals were far less substantial than the activities other courts have found to prevent a claim that income was royalty income. To hold otherwise would require us to hold that any activity on the part of the owner of intangible property to obtain a royalty, renders the payment for the use of that right UBTI and not a royalty.

We therefore affirm the Tax Court's grant of partial summary judgment on this issue because the income received by Sierra Club from the list rentals was royalty income and not payment for services.

IV.

We now address whether, given the definition of "royalties" discussed above, the district court erred in granting summary judgment on the issue of whether the income from the affinity credit card program constituted "royalties." Because the Tax Court improperly resolved disputed factual issues in favor of Sierra Club, rather than viewing the evidence in the light most favorable to the Commissioner, we reverse the Tax Court's grant of partial summary judgment and remand to the Tax Court for findings of fact regarding whether Sierra Club's income from the affinity card program constituted royalties under § 512(b).

To begin, we note that the agreements between Sierra Club, ABS, Concept I, and Chase Lincoln provide a sufficient basis for reversing the grant of summary judgment in favor of Sierra Club. We agree with the Tax Court that the agreements were unclear regarding what the parties were contracting for—Sierra Club's services or the use of Sierra Club's logo, mailing lists, and name. However, the Tax Court resolved any disputes as to the interpretation of the agreements in favor of Sierra Club.

For example, the Sierra Club Bankcard Agreement states that Sierra Club "agrees to cooperate with ABS on a continuing basis in the solicitation and encouragement of [Sierra Club] members to utilize the Services provided by ABS." This clause would permit a factfinder to infer that Sierra Club agreed to perform endorsement services—not simply to license its name and logo and permit the use of its mailings lists, as the Tax Court concluded. Similarly, the Sierra Club Bankcard Agreement nowhere states that Sierra Club agreed to license its name and logo to ABS and yet the Tax Court concluded that such a licensing was intended by the parties.

The agreements aside, the Commissioner points to facts which the Tax Court could have interpreted as evidence that Sierra Club performed services for ABS, Chase Lincoln, and its members in connection with the credit card program. For example, ABS used Sierra Club's postal permit to send the initial solicitation materials to Sierra Club members. In determining that the use of the permit did not demonstrate that Sierra Club provided a service to ABS, the Tax Court relied upon ABS' explanation that the use of Sierra Club's permit was a mistake. However, ABS only characterized the use of the permit as a "mistake" because in using the permit the mailing had to be spread out through the entire month. However, a factfinder could infer that Sierra Club permitted ABS to use the permit as part of its agreement to cooperate with the solicitation of its members.

As yet another example, the Commissioner points to Sierra Club's actions once ABS failed to perform under the agreement: Sierra Club reimbursed its members for ABS' dishonored checks, and subsequently assumed ABS' responsibilities. Although a factfinder could find that Sierra Club only did so to protect its members and its reputation, a factfinder also could infer that Sierra Club was providing its members with a service, in conjunction with ABS, and that once ABS defaulted, Sierra Club took over its duties.

In sum, the Tax Court failed to view the facts regarding the affinity credit card program in the light most favorable to the Commissioner. Therefore, we reverse the grant of partial summary judgment on the issue of whether the income generated by the affinity credit card program was royalty income and remand this issue for trial before the Tax Court. As a consequence, the Tax Court failed to recognize that there remain genuine issues of material fact as to whether the payments Sierra Club received in connection with the program were payments for services.

Note on Remand of Sierra Club

On remand, the Tax Court held that the income from the affinity program was within the definition of "royalty" and therefore excluded from UBTI. 77 TCM 1569 (1999). With respect to ABS' use of Sierra Club's non-profit mailing permit and the argument that such use showed that Sierra Club was compensated for services, the Court found that all mailings were ABS' (an entity not entitled to the non-profit rate). The Court further stated, "ABS' use of the mail permit was unlawful. Because it involved an unlawful action, we hesitate to classify it as cooperation under the SC-ABS agreement."

Ironically, *Sierra Club, Inc.* might be viewed as evidence that the Service had finally proven its point. Readers might note that the Ninth Circuit essentially adopted the Service's argument on the law (i.e., that royalties constitute payments for the use of property alone, but not for any non-passive related activities connected with the use of property). Thus, the Service's efforts to limit the scope of the royalty modification failed in *Sierra Club, Inc.*, and many cases before that, not on the law but on the facts. *See, e.g., Mississippi State University Alumni, Inc. v. Commissioner,*

T.C. Memo. 1997-397; *Oregon State University Alumni Association, Inc. v. Commissioner*, T.C. Memo. 1996–34, *aff'd*, 193 F.3d 1098 (9th Cir. 1999); *Alumni Association of the University of Oregon v. Commissioner*, T.C. Memo. 1996–63, *aff'd*, 193 F.3d 1098 (9th Cir. 1999). To avoid taxation, organizations simply limited their participation in any royalty agreement to providing use of the property and retaining final approval authority.

In December 1999, the Service finally announced that it would no longer seek to tax royalty income under its "all or nothing approach," (that is, if any portion is for services, the entire payment is taxable) but would instead seek to identify any portion of a purported royalty payment that was really made as compensation for services and tax that portion alone. We think well-advised (and even not so well-advised) organizations will easily avoid this approach as well.

Question

Is the income derived under the following circumstances excluded under the royalty exception?

A is a non-profit corporation generally recognized as exempt from federal income tax under 26 U.S.C. § 501(c)(3). From year 3 through year 6, A entered into an agreement with B, an Arizona publishing company, to publish "The A-Train" magazine three times a year. Two separate agreements (two years each) covered the four years. Both agreements were titled "Royalties and Licensing Agreement."

B paid A $25,200 each year to publish the magazine, as well as a percentage (26% under one of the two-year agreements, and 27% under the other) of the money received from the advertising published in the magazine. Over the course of the four years, A received a total of $876,697 from the publication of the magazine.

B bore all the costs of producing and distributing the magazine and solicited all the advertising, but B's solicitors indicated they were calling "on behalf of the A Charitable Association." B controlled the funds received from the advertisers, but the checks were made payable to A. The front cover of the magazine bore the inscription "The Official Publication of the A." A "President's Message" written by A's elected president appeared in each issue of the magazine. A provided its membership list to B, and B distributed copies of the magazine free of charge to A members, to advertisers who paid at least $100 for ads, and to each A state legislator.

A's Vice President of Public Relations (a part-time, voluntary position) devoted approximately 250 to 300 hours a year to a variety of projects sponsored by A, including magazine-related activities. The Vice President reviewed B's sales presentations, and reviewed the pre-publication copy of the magazine for accuracy and suitability of the use of A's name. The Vice President also wrote to A's members, encouraging them to take photographs and write articles about A activities, and to submit them to A for inclusion in the magazine. The Vice President spent about 15–20 hours each year on magazine-related activities.

C. Passive Income from Controlled Entity

Code: §§ 512(b)(13); 318(a)(1)–(a)(4); 337

Reg.: § 1.512(b)-1(l)

As we have seen, the motivation for the unrelated business income tax was to eliminate an unfair advantage allegedly enjoyed by charitable organizations that engage in commercial activities. However, as briefly noted in *Sierra Club, Inc. v. Commissioner*, Congress believed that certain passive activities—collecting interest, dividends, royalties, and rents—do not unfairly compete with commercial entities. Thus, these types of income are excluded from unrelated business income. As a result, charitable organizations may indirectly participate in a commercial endeavor without taxation through ownership of stock, lending of money, licensing of intangible property, or rental of real property. In these cases, we might argue that there is no unfair advantage, because the entity that pays income to the charitable organization is ordinarily subject to tax on its net income regardless of whether the debtor, licensee, or lessee is a charitable or for-profit organization. If the user is a charitable organization, it will pay tax on any unrelated business in which the property is used and, of course, a for-profit organization will likewise pay tax on the income derived from use of the money or property. Thus, the charitable organization will derive after-tax income, just like any other entity engaged in a for-profit activity.

Nevertheless, Congress believed that when a charitable organization derives passive income from a "controlled entity," the charitable organization does indeed enjoy an unfair advantage. For example, a charitable organization might conduct a taxable activity through use of a subsidiary, but instead of contributing property for use in that taxable activity, the charitable organization may rent or license the property to the subsidiary for an amount that approximates the total gross income derived from the activity. The rental or license fee is taken as a deduction under § 162, thereby reducing the subsidiary's taxable income to zero. At the same time, the charitable organization excludes the rental or royalty payment under § 512(b)(1) or (2). This strategy works to the extent that the rental or royalty payment absorbs the subsidiary's leftover income after all other deductions.

Note on Charities Controlling a Subsidiary

Many charities have subsidiaries. They may acquire an existing organization, or they may create a controlled subsidiary hoping to limit liability for a particular activity, operate an unrelated business without jeopardizing the parent's tax exempt status, or foster special projects. Section 512(b)(13) describes the treatment of interest, rents, royalties, and annuities received by the parent (the controlling charity) from the controlled subsidiary. These rules apply notwithstanding the general § 512(b) (1), (2), and (3) rules excluding interest, rents, royalties, and annuity payments.

1. Control.

Clause 512(b)(13)(D)(i) defines control as:

- For a corporate subsidiary, more than 50% of the stock, considering both voting power and value.
- For a partnership subsidiary, more than 50% of either the profits or capital interest.
- In all other cases, more than 50% of the beneficial interests.

Clause (D)(ii) applies § 318 attribution rules to determine ownership or beneficial interests.

Prior to 1997, the control threshold was set at 80%. That provided a fairly simple loophole: the controlling charity could reduce its ownership stake to 79%, retain actual control, and be exempt from § 512(b)(13). As a result, it could easily wipe out what would otherwise be unrelated income. Congress reduced the ownership threshold to the 50% level; thus, to escape the (b)(13) rules, the controlling charity must release actual control.

Unfortunately, Treas. Reg. § 1.512(b)-1(l), written soon after the original 1969 enactment, refers to the pre-1997 statute both for the control test and also for the mechanics of how the paragraph works. Prior to 1997, § 512(b)(13) contained multiple double negatives and was notoriously difficult to decipher. The 1997 amendments did not change the substance of the provision (other than the control threshold), but they did re-phrase the rules in a reasonably straightforward manner. Thus, we caution readers against using the Treasury Regulations until Treasury gets around to updating them.

2. What § 512(b)(13) Applies to.

The paragraph only deals with interest, rents, royalties and annuity payments. Specifically, it does not affect the treatment of dividends.

Under general § 512(b)(1), (2), and (3) rules, interest, rents, royalties, annuity payments and also dividends received by a charity would escape tax. The first four would also be deductible by the subsidiary, reducing its income (if it were a taxable subsidiary) or potentially reducing its unrelated income (if it were an exempt subsidiary). Thus, without (b)(13), the subsidiary could reduce taxable income by paying interest, rent, royalties, or annuity payments to a parent, which would then exclude the receipts. Congress wisely considered that an unacceptable loophole and closed it in 1969.

Dividends, however, are not deductible and thus would not impact a subsidiary's income. Thus, excluding them from the charitable parent's income was justified.

3. Types of Subsidiaries.

A controlling charity can have two very different types of subsidiary it controls:

- A tax-exempt subsidiary.
- A for-profit subsidiary.

That is clear on the face of the statute, as it has separate mechanical provisions for the treatment of interest, rents, royalties, and annuity payments for each type of subsidiary. We have—to our dismay—heard many students (and practitioners) ask whether a charity "is permitted to own or control a for-profit subsidiary." Yes, indeed it can. That answer is crystal clear. That is half the purpose of § 512(b)(13)—to deal with certain payments from a controlled for-profit subsidiary to a charitable parent. If control were not possible, half the purpose of § 512(b)(13) would not exist.

Remember, charities may invest their funds. They can own stocks and bonds—including those issued by general business corporations and publicly traded—and generally exclude the interest and dividends they receive. That is the general purpose of § 512(b)(1) and (2). For-profit corporations paying those dividends or interest (or royalties and rents) are taxable; thus, the activities producing the income are taxed. Such entities deduct interest, rents and royalties under general, long-standing deduction sections, such as §§ 162 and 163. A problem arises, however, if a charity controls the for-profit entity paying the interest, rents and royalties (or a tax-exempt subsidiary that uses interest and royalty payments to reduce unrelated income). Without § 512(b)(13), a parent could easily arrange for the subsidiary to pay sufficient non-taxable, but still deductible by the subsidiary, interest and royalties to eliminate any tax on what should be taxed.

4. Mechanics for Controlled Exempt Subsidiary.

If the subsidiary is also exempt from tax, § 512(b)(13) applies only to the extent the interest, rent, royalty and annuity payments reduce unrelated business taxable income of the subsidiary. Consider an example.

Suppose a charity operates an unrelated trade or business with regular profits of $100,000 per year. It would pay tax on the $100,000. Without § 512(b)(13), it could create a tax-exempt subsidiary which had, as an insubstantial part of its activities, the operation of the unrelated business. The subsidiary would have $100,000 of income, rather than the parent. But, the parent could then (again, absent § 512(b)(13)) charge $25,000 in royalties for use of its intellectual property (which the parent retained) and $50,000 in rent for use of property the unrelated business needed, and another $25,000 in interest for loans needed to capitalize the unrelated activity. The subsidiary could deduct each of those items under § 162, resulting in zero income taxed to the subsidiary.

In such a case—again, absent § 512(b)(13)—the controlling exempt parent would exclude the interest, rent and royalties under § 512(b)(1), (2), and (3). As a result, the unrelated trade or business would escape tax altogether. Since 1969, controlling parents of an exempt subsidiary must include interest, rent, royalties and annuity payments which are deductible by the controlled exempt subsidiary against unrelated income.

A 1997 amendment reduced the control threshold to eliminate the then often-used loophole of the parent owning merely 79% of the subsidiary. Post-1997, the threshold is 50%. Thus, a charity can still exclude interest, rent, royalties and annuity payments from other charities even if those payments reduce the payors' unrelated income; however, that is only possible if the recipient does not control the payor, using the fairly broad definition of control, coupled with § 318 attribution rules and § 512(b)(13)(F) related person rules.

5. Mechanics of a Controlled Non-Exempt Subsidiary.

The mechanics for a controlled for-profit subsidiary are quite similar to those for an exempt subsidiary. Because a for-profit subsidiary is not subject to UBIT, it cannot have unrelated business taxable income; hence, the statute requires a different statement of the rule, with the same result. It applies to interest, rents, royalties and annuity payments which reduce the income of the subsidiary to the extent such income would be unrelated income if the subsidiary were exempt for the same purpose as the parent.

Consider two examples. Parent is an exempt hospital. It owns 100% of two for-profit subsidiaries. Subsidiary A manufactures and sells macaroni. Subsidiary B operates a for-profit hospital identical to Parent (other than not being exempt).

If Subsidiary A were exempt for the reasons Parent is exempt—if it were a hospital—manufacturing and selling macaroni would be an unrelated trade or business. Thus, any interest, rents, royalty and annuity payments from Subsidiary A to Parent are taxable to Parent. They continue to be deductible to Subsidiary A.

If Subsidiary B were exempt for the reasons Parent is exempt—if it were a charitable hospital—its activities of operating a hospital would not be an unrelated trade or business. As a result, § 512(b)(13) does not apply; thus, Parent may exclude any interest, rent, royalty or annuity payments received from Subsidiary B.

6. Merger of a For-Profit Subsidiary.

Section 337 applies to the liquidation of a for-profit subsidiary controlled by an exempt parent. It requires the subsidiary to recognize all gains and income which would result if it sold all its assets for fair market value immediately prior to the merger with the parent.

This provision is one practitioners must understand if they represent a charity with a for-profit subsidiary. Such ownership is essentially forever. A merger will not be tax-free; instead, it will be a taxable event as if they sold the subsidiary assets, trigging gains on appreciated property, and depreciation recapture. Avoiding it is very difficult, if not impossible.

Thus, a charity considering the purchase of a for-profit entity which operates a potentially exempt activity should proceed with caution. For example, an exempt hospital might consider buying a for-profit hospital, or an exempt school might consider buying a for-profit school. They can certainly do so and continue to operate the for-profit subsidiary which will be taxable. Interest, rents, royalties and annuity payments to the parent will be deductible by the subsidiary and excludable by the parent. But the two entities must continue as separate entities with all collateral legal obligations and consequences which normally flow from that. The subsidiary must have its own board of directors, respect corporate formalities, carry its own insurance and generally do all the things a for-profit business must do. The two must carefully avoid a constructive liquidation, as that would trigger § 337. They likely can never merge.

Lawyers advising such an acquisition should ensure the clients understand corporate formalities. Experience teaches us that clients will be tempted to become lax about such things over time, effectively treating the two entities as one. This book does not focus on mergers and acquisitions, let alone constructive liquidations. But be forewarned: laxity with corporate formalities involving a for-profit sub (especially one which does the exact same activity as the parent) can trigger a huge tax under § 337. The acquiring parent should consider whether purchasing the assets of the entity might not be a better long-term strategy than locking itself into forever owning a for-profit subsidiary.

Questions

The best way to approach this question is by first making a diagram showing the relationship between the parties.

1. The National Geographic Society, Inc., a § 501(c)(3) organization, produces a show for PBS titled, "National Geographic Explorer." Historically, the show has been funded by a corporate sponsor at a cost of $5 million dollars per episode. Recently, however, it has become more difficult to obtain sponsors willing to undertake the rising costs of the show. National Geographic, however, wishes to continue the show because it is an effective means of providing public education on the environment. Because of the inability to obtain sponsors, National Geographic decides to produce five episodes of the show itself and sell them to the Discovery Channel, a taxable cable network. To protect its tax exemption from liability, National Geographic decides to create a wholly owned subsidiary. The subsidiary will produce the shows and sell them to the Discovery Channel. National Geographic transfers several assets that it would otherwise use itself to produce the show to National Sub 1 in return for all of the stock of National Sub. Thereafter, National Geographic transfers all of the National Sub 1 stock to National Sub 2, another newly created corporation, in exchange for all of National Sub 2's stock. Thus, National Sub 2 becomes the 100 percent owner of National Sub 1. National Sub 1 thus becomes a "second tier" subsidiary of National Geographic. National Geographic rents space to National Sub 1. In addition, National Geographic grants an exclusive license to National Sub 1, allowing National Sub 1 to use the name "National Geographic Society" and National Geographic's membership lists with respect to the production and marketing of the episodes, as well as other activities. In addition to producing the five episodes for the Discovery Channel, National Sub produces one-hour-long fictional motion pictures that it sells to another entertainment network.

a. Suppose that in Year 1, National Sub 1 has the following amounts of income and expenses:

Income:	$5,000,000
Income from sale of 5 episodes to Discovery Channel	$3,500,000
Income from sale of 1 motion picture	$1,500,000
Expenses:	
Rent paid to National Geographic	$250,000
Royalties	$750,000

1. How much of the $1,000,000 rents and royalties paid by National Sub 1 to National Geographic, if any, must National Geographic include as unrelated business income?

2. What if National Geographic incurred $50,000 in deductible expenses with regard to the office space rented to National Sub 1?

b. What if National Sub 1 was exempt under IRC § 501(c)(3) and its total taxable income was $4,000,000, $3,000,000 of which was derived from the five episodes and $1,000,000 from the motion picture?

c. What if National Geographic sold 52% of its stock in National Sub 2 to an unrelated third party prior to receiving rents and royalties from National Sub 1?

D. Deductions

CODE: § 512(a)(1)

REG.: § 1.512(a)-1(a)–(c)

Until now, we have essentially dealt with determining gross unrelated taxable income. Of course, UBIT is imposed only on net taxable income. Section 512(a)(1) defines unrelated taxable income (UBTI) as the gross unrelated trade or business income "less the deductions allowed by this chapter which are directly connected with the carrying on of such trade or business." Thus, UBTI is determined by: (1) aggregating the total unrelated income from all activities, (2) aggregating the total deductions authorized by other provisions of the Code that are directly connected with those activities; and (3) netting the two amounts. Because all unrelated income is aggregated and all deductions directly connected therewith are likewise aggregated, expenses generated from one activity may be deducted against another. *See* Treas. Reg. § 1.512(a)-1(a).

The regulations state that to be directly connected, expenses must "have a proximate and primary relationship to the carrying on of that business." Treas. Reg. § 1.512(a)-1(b). Expenses incurred exclusively in pursuit of the unrelated trade or business obviously meet this requirement. *Id.* Expenses that benefit both an unrelated and a related activity, however, must be allocated between the two activities, and the amount allocated to the related activity will be nondeductible. Treas. Reg. § 1.512(a)-1(c). Thus, as demonstrated in the following case, charitable organizations have an incentive to select an allocation method that results in the greatest amount possible of deductions allocated to the unrelated activity.

1. Directly Connected Expenses

Rensselaer Polytechnic Institute v. Commissioner

732 F.2d 1058 (2d Cir. 1984)

Pratt, Circuit Judge:

The issue before us is not only one of first impression; it is also of considerable financial significance to many of our colleges and universities. When a tax-exempt organization uses one of its facilities, as in this case a fieldhouse, for both tax-exempt purposes and for the production of unrelated business income, what portion of its indirect expenses such as depreciation may it deduct from its unrelated business income pursuant to I.R.C. § 512 (1982)? May it allocate those expenses, as prescribed by Treas. Reg. § 1.512(a)-1(c), on any "reasonable" basis? Or must it first establish, as the commissioner here argues, that the expense would not have been incurred in the absence of the business activity? Finding no conflict between the regulation and the statute and finding no error in the determination of the tax court that RPI's method of allocation was reasonable, we reject the commissioner's position and affirm the tax court's judgment, which approved apportioning the fieldhouse's idle time in proportion to the hours devoted to exempt and not exempt uses.

The facts are undisputed. Rensselaer Polytechnic Institute (RPI) is a non-profit educational organization entitled to tax-exempt status under I.R.C. § 501(c)(3). It owns and operates a fieldhouse which it devotes to two broad categories of uses: (1) student uses, which include physical education, college ice hockey, student ice skating, and other activities related to RPI's tax-exempt educational responsibilities; and (2) commercial uses, which include activities and events such as commercial ice shows and public ice skating, that do not fall within its tax-exempt function. For fiscal year 1974, the net income from commercial use of the fieldhouse constituted "unrelated business taxable income" which was subject to taxation under I.R.C. § 511(a)(1).

The dispute is over the amount of unrelated business tax due from RPI for 1974 and, since there is no disagreement over the gross income, $476,613, we must focus on the deductible expenses. The parties have classified RPI's applicable deductible expenses in three groups.... For the year in question direct expenses amounted to $371,407, and the parties have always agreed to their deductibility.

... [N]either side has appealed that part of the decision below which (a) found the total variable expenses to be $197,210; and (b) allocated them on the basis of actual use, as claimed by RPI, rather than total availability, as claimed by the commissioner.

This appeal involves the third group, "fixed expenses", which do not vary in proportion to actual use of the facility. The amounts of fixed expenses incurred with respect to the fieldhouse were stipulated to be:

Salaries and fringe benefits	$59,415
Depreciation	29,397
Repairs and Replacements	14,031
Operating Expenditures	1,356
	$104,199

Narrowly stated, the issue is how these fixed expenses should be allocated between RPI's dual uses: the exempt student use and the taxable commercial use. RPI contends it is entitled to allocate the fixed expenses on the basis of relative times of actual use. Thus, in computing that portion of its deductible expenses, RPI multiplies the total amount of fixed expenses by a fraction, whose numerator is the total number of hours the fieldhouse was used for commercial events, and whose denominator is the total number of hours the fieldhouse was used for all activities and events — student and commercial combined.

The commissioner argues that the allocation of fixed expenses must be made not on the basis of times of actual use, but on the basis of total time available for use. Thus, he contends the denominator of the fraction should be the total number of hours in the taxable year. In practical terms, the difference between the two methods of allocation amounts to $9,259 in taxes.

Below, the tax court agreed with RPI's method of allocating on the basis of actual use, finding it to be "reasonable" within the meaning of Treas. Reg. § 1.512(a)-1(c). The commissioner appeals, contending (a) that the tax court's otherwise reasonable allocation based on actual use does not satisfy the statutory requirement that in order to be deductible an expense must be "directly connected with" the unrelated business activity; (b) that the cases the tax court relied on below, dealing with allocation of home office expenses between business and personal use, are inapposite; and (c) that strict application of the "directly connected with" language of the statute is "necessary to prevent serious abuse of the tax exemption privilege."

* * *

Recognizing . . . the unfair competitive advantage that freedom from income taxation could accord tax-exempt institutions that entered the world of commerce, congress, in 1950, extended the income tax to the "unrelated business income" of certain tax-exempt institutions, including educational corporations. Pub. L. No. 81-814, § 301, 64 Stat. 906, 947 (1950) (codified at I.R.C. §§ 511–513). Its objective in changing the law was to eliminate the competitive advantage educational and charitable corporations enjoyed over private enterprise, without jeopardizing the basic purpose of the tax-exemption. *See* H.R. Rep. No. 2319, 81st Cong., 2d Sess. 36–38; S. Rep. No. 2375, 81st Cong., 2d Sess. 28–30.

With this historical background in mind, we turn to the applicable statute and regulations. Section 512 of the code defines as "unrelated business taxable income" gross income derived from unrelated business activities less deductions "directly connected with" such activities. Treas. Reg. § 1.512 (a)-1(a) further defines the term "directly connected with", and provides that "to be 'directly connected with' the conduct of unrelated business for purposes of section 512, an item of deduction must have proximate and primary relationship" to that business. Two subsequent subsections of that regulation define "proximate and primary relationship" in the context of (a) items that are attributable solely to the unrelated business, Treas. Reg. § 1.512(a)-1(b); and (b) as in this case, item's that are attributable to facilities or personnel used for both exempt and unrelated purposes, Treas. Reg. § 1.512(a)-1(c). The latter regulation provides:

> (c) *Dual use of facilities or personnel.* Where facilities are used both to carry on exempt activities and to conduct unrelated trade or business activities, expenses, depreciation and similar items attributable to such facilities (as, for example, items of overhead), *shall be allocated between the two uses on a reasonable basis.* Similarly, where personnel are used both to carry on exempt activities and to conduct unrelated trade or business activities, expenses and similar items attributable to such personnel (as, for example, items of salary) *shall be allocated between the two uses on a reasonable basis.* The portion of any such items so allocated to the unrelated trade or business activity is *proximately and primarily related to that business activity, and shall be allowable as a deduction in computing unrelated business taxable income* in the manner and to the extent permitted by section 162, section 167 or other relevant provisions of the Code.

Treas. Reg. § 1.512(a)-1(c) (emphasis added).

Thus, when allocated "on a reasonable basis", expenses attributable to such facilities or personnel—which expressly include such "indirect expenses" as depreciation and overhead—are by definition "proximately and primarily related" to the business. They are therefore "directly connected with" the unrelated business activity and expressly made deductible by the regulation.

Under this regulation, therefore, the critical question is whether the method of allocation adopted by RPI was "reasonable". The tax court found that it was, and, giving due regard to its expertise in this area we see no error in that conclusion. Apportioning indirect expenses such as depreciation on the basis of the actual hours the facility was used for both exempt and taxable purposes sensibly distributes the cost of the facility among the activities that benefit from its use. In addition, the method is consistent with that followed by the tax court in the most common dual-use situation, home office deduction cases. *See Browne v. Commissioner*, 73 T.C. 723 (1980); *Gino v. Commissioner*, 60 T.C. 304, *rev'd*, 538 F.2d 833 (9th Cir. 1976), *cert. denied*, 429 U.S. 979 (1976).

Indeed, the commissioner does not claim that RPI's allocation method is factually unreasonable, but instead contends solely that the method is not "reasonable", because by permitting depreciation during "idle time", when the fieldhouse is not being used at all, it contravenes the statutory requirement that deductible expenses be "directly connected with" RPI's unrelated business activities. By advancing this argument, however, the commissioner ignores his own definition of the concept "directly connected with" included in Treas. Reg. § 1.512(a)-1(a) discussed above. In addition, the commissioner would have us adopt a more stringent interpretation of "directly connected with" in § 512 than has been applied for over sixty years to the same concept in the commissioner's regulations governing the deductibility of ordinary and necessary business expenses. *See* Treas. Reg. § 1.162-1(a). Moreover, the logical extension of his position would require the commissioner to deny depreciation deductions to all businesses for those periods when their assets are idle. Such a view, however, would contravene the basic concepts underlying the commissioner's elaborate regulations governing depreciation generally. *See* Treas. Reg. § 1.167(a)-1 et seq.

For an expense to be "directly connected with" an activity, the commissioner argues that it must be one that would not have been incurred in the absence of the activity. But whether or not the fieldhouse is actually put to any business use, depreciation of the facility continues. We cannot accept the commissioner's argument, therefore, because it would in effect eliminate entirely all deductions for indirect expenses such as depreciation, a result that is not required by statute and that is directly contrary to the regulation.

The commissioner relies on *Pittsburgh Press Club v. United States*, 579 F.2d 751 (3d Cir. 1978), to support his argument that indirect expenses that would have been incurred regardless of business use may not properly be deducted from unrelated business income. That case, however, arose under § 501(c)(7), which prohibited an exempt social club from engaging in any business activities. It is inapplicable here, because RPI, as an exempt educational institution, is permitted by statute to engage in unrelated business activities. The issue before us is not whether a business was carried on, but what is the proper allocation of indirect expenses, such as depreciation, between two uses, one a taxable business use and the other tax-exempt.

Furthermore, to apply the statute as the commissioner interprets it would not fulfill the congressional purpose of placing private enterprise on an equal level with competing businesses run by tax-exempt institutions, but would place RPI at a competitive disadvantage. Unlike business enterprises, it would be unable to allocate any of its indirect expenses to those periods when the fieldhouse was not being used at all.

Some concern has been expressed that RPI's allocation method would provide an incentive for educational institutions to abuse their tax-exempt status. The argument is a red herring. Use of educational facilities for producing unrelated business income is not tax abuse; on the contrary, as we have pointed out above, such non-exempt activities have been consistently permitted and, since 1950, expressly approved by congress. Moreover, should the trustees of a particular tax-exempt educational institution so pervert its operations that the institution no longer "engages primarily in activities which accomplish . . . [its exempt purposes]", Treas. Reg. § 1.501(c)(3)-1(c)(1), the commissioner has adequate remedies available to correct any abuse or even terminate the exemption.

The judgment appealed from is affirmed.

MANSFIELD, Circuit Judge (Dissenting):

I respectfully dissent.

Rensselaer Polytechnic Institute ("RPI") is a tax-exempt institution only because it has dedicated itself and its property in perpetuity to "charitable" and "educational purposes." 26 U.S.C. § 501(c). Its unrelated business income less "deductions . . . which are directly connected with the carrying on of such trade or business" is taxable. 26 U.S.C. §§ 501(b), 512(a). We are here asked to permit the college to deduct from its commercial business income fixed expenses that would normally be allocated on a time basis to periods when the college's property is *not* being used for trade or business but for its educational purposes.

In my view such expenses are not "directly connected" with the institution's commercial business activities within the meaning of § 512(a) and are therefore not deductible from its business income. On the contrary, they are attributable to time when the facilities exist for educational purposes. Indeed, it could reasonably be argued that since RPI would, absent part-time use of its fixed assets for commercial purposes, be required to absorb all depreciation of such assets, no such depreciation is "directly connected" with its commercial business operations. See *Pittsburgh Press Club v. United States*, 579 F.2d 751, 761 (3d Cir. 1978). RPI represented in its petition to the Tax Court that "the main function of the fieldhouse is to provide a suitable facility necessary to allow petitioner to carry out *its total educational responsibilities*." (Emphasis added). Although some allocation may be permissible, I do not believe RPI should be allowed to give its commercial use any credit for time when its facilities exist for educational use. To do so would give a tax-exempt institution an unfair tax advantage over commercial institutions. The majority reaches this result only by what appears to be a misinterpretation of the governing statute and regulations.

In my view the fundamental error underlying the majority's decision is its assumption that tax-exempt institutions are governed for tax deduction purposes by the same standards as those governing taxable businesses. That assumption conflicts with legislative intent, economic reality, and the express wording of the pertinent statute and regulations. When Congress in 1950 passed legislation subjecting tax-exempt organizations to income tax on unrelated business income, it was concerned both with removing the unfair competitive advantage enjoyed by tax-exempt institutions and with assuring that the unrelated business income would produce a fair amount of revenue for the public fisc. However, it was confronted with inherent differences between regular taxable business and a non-profit university engaged mainly in educational activity and only partially in income-producing commercial activities. These differences precluded a wholesale transfer and application to a university of the same deduction principles as those governing regular commercial businesses.

In the case of a commercial business devoted solely to making a profit, its entire operation is subject to a tax on its income. Regardless of how it chooses to allocate its business expenses between divisions, the net income from all divisions is taxable. The IRS therefore has no quarrel with a "reasonable" allocation of deductible expenses between branches of the operation. The tax-exempt university, on the other hand, is fundamentally different in that one of its "divisions"—the educational function—is not subject to taxation. The university will therefore always have an incentive to minimize the allocation of expenses attributed to the educational function, and correspondingly to maximize the deduction for unrelated business activity. This incentive, which is not present in the ordinary business setting, requires a stricter standard of deductibility for tax-exempt organizations than for purely profit-seeking firms. The government cannot, in the case of an educational institution engaged in unrelated commercial business activity, afford to take the same relaxed approach as with wholly-taxable businesses and to accept any allocation the taxpayer may deem "reasonable."

Thus, the majority achieves parity only in the most superficial sense. The identical rule of deductibility is imposed, but it is imposed on organizations that have different characteristics and are therefore affected differently by the same rule. To whatever extent Congress sought to place wholly taxable and exempt organizations on the same footing, it was concerned not with such technical legal tests but with the real after-tax situations of the two different types of organization. Yet the majority's approach, which claims to provide equal treatment, actually leaves the tax-exempt organizations with the very advantage that the majority claims Congress was trying to eliminate.

That Congress adopted a narrower test of deductibility for the tax-exempt organization is clearly reflected in the statute. 26 U.S.C. § 512 allows such an organization to take those "deductions allowed by this chapter *which are directly connected with*" its unrelated business income (emphasis added). The italicized language is imposed as an *additional* requirement for tax-exempt institutions not faced by purely profit-oriented businesses.

* * *

For these reasons, I would reverse the Tax Court's decision.

2. Expenses from an Exploited Exempt Activity

REG.: § 1.512(a)-1(d)–(f)

As a general proposition, the regulations at Treas. Reg. § 1.512(a)-1(d) hold that, when an unrelated activity is dependent upon or made possible by the conduct of the exempt activity, all incurred expenses are nondeductible. A primary example is the sale of advertising space in a university law review.

The apparent rationale for nondeductibility is that expenses are incurred primarily to further the exempt activity (e.g., expenses incurred to create editorial content) and therefore do not have a "proximate and primary" relationship with the unrelated activity. As suggested by the dissent in *Rensselaer Polytechnic Institute*, the government could completely deny deductions for these expenses. The regulations, however, provide a special rule when the unrelated activity is of a kind carried on for profit by taxable organizations, and the exempt activity is of a kind normally conducted by taxable organizations in pursuit of the unrelated activity. Again, the sale of advertising space in a periodical provides an example. When both conditions are met and the exempt activity produces a net loss, the amount of the loss is deducted against net income (i.e., gross income less directly connected deductions) from any unrelated trade or business activity that exploits the exempt activity. Treas. Reg. § 1.512(a)-1(d)(2). The unrelated activity loss may only be taken to the extent of the net income from the exempt activity. If the exempt activity loss exceeds the net income from related exploiting activities, it may not be further deducted against other unrelated trades or business not dependent on the exploited activity. *Id.*

Assume, for example, that Activity 1 is an exempt activity that produces $100 in income but generates $300 in expenses. If Activity 2 is an unrelated activity that exploits Activity 1 and generates net income of $100, $100 of the $200 exempt activity's net loss may be deducted against the $100 gross unrelated income. The remaining $100 is lost. If Activity 3 is unrelated and also exploits Activity 1, generating $100 of gross income, the remaining $100 may be deducted against the income from Activity 3.

The regulations explain in detail how the general deduction and exploited activity deduction rules apply to advertising. In keeping with the general aggregation rule, the regulations state that when an advertising activity produces a net loss (taking into account directly connected expenses only), the loss may be deducted against any other unrelated activity. Thus, expenses directly connected to the conduct of the advertising activity (as opposed to expenses related to the exploited exempt activity) are fungible and may be deducted against any other unrelated activity. Treas. Reg. § 1.512(a)-1(f)(2)(i). However, if the unrelated advertising activity produces a net gain, and the exploited exempt activity produces a net loss, the loss is deductible against the net advertising gain, but only to the extent thereof. Any loss in excess of the net gain is not fungible and may not be deducted against any unrelated activity that does not exploit the exempt activity. Treas. Reg. § 1.512(a)-1(f)(2)(ii). The tax result in any case may be derived from these two rules. The regulations, however, go further and provide more detail as to how the two rules determine the taxability of unrelated advertising income.

One method of following the regulation's technique is by first identifying the relevant categories of income and expenses:[2]

1. Total periodical income. Total periodical income is gross advertising income plus circulation income. Treas. Reg. § 1.512(a)-1(f)(3)(i).
2. Gross advertising income. Gross advertising income is essentially the total payments received from advertisers. Treas. Reg. § 1.512(a)-1(f)(3)(ii).
3. Circulation income. Circulation income is the revenue received from subscribers or recipients of the periodical, including reprint and republishing fees. If members are entitled to a subscription, a portion of each member's dues must be included in circulation income. Determination of the portion is discussed in the *AMA* case, following this note. Treas. Reg. § 1.512(a)-1(f)(3)(iii).
4. Total periodical costs. Total periodical costs include direct advertising costs plus readership costs. Treas. Reg. § 1.512(a)-1(f)(6)(i).
5. Direct advertising costs. Direct advertising costs include expenses, depreciation and similar items directly connected with the sale and publication of advertising. Treas. Reg. § 1.512(a)-1(f)(6)(ii).
6. Readership costs. Readership costs include expenses, depreciation, and similar items directly connected with the production and distribution of the readership content of the periodical. Treas. Reg. § 1.512(a)-1(f)(6)(iii).

After the amounts in each category are determined, the computation of UBTI is made in accordance with whichever of the following rules apply:

1. If gross advertising costs exceed direct advertising income, the excess is deductible against any other unrelated activity. Treas. Reg. § 1.512(a)-1(f)(2). This is consistent with and may be derived from the aggregation rule, which applies whenever an unrelated activity produces a loss without regard to expenses benefiting both exempt and non-exempt activities.
2. If the circulation income of the periodical equals or exceeds the readership costs, then the unrelated business taxable income is the excess of the gross advertising income of the periodical over direct advertising costs. Treas. Reg. § 1.512(a)-1(f)(2)(ii)(a). This is consistent with and may be derived from the rule that expenses of an exploited activity are deductible against a related exploiting activity only to the extent that the exploited exempt activity operates at a loss (and then only to the extent of the income from the exploiting activity). Because there is no loss under this rule, UBTI is determined simply by netting gross advertising income and direct advertising costs.

2. The following descriptions are quite general and are not intended to fully summarize the relevant definitions. As always, the student must closely examine the relevant provision to gain a complete understanding.

3. If the readership costs exceed the circulation income [i.e., the exploited exempt activity operates at a loss], the unrelated business taxable income is the excess, if any, of the total periodical income over the total periodical costs. Treas. Reg. § 1.512(a)-1(f)(2)(ii)(b). That is, exempt activity expenses are deductible only to the extent of exempt activity income plus net exploiting activity income.

Once again, we refer readers to the useful examples in Treasury Regulation Section 1.512(a)-1(f)(2)(iii). We caution, however, that Example (4) gets to the correct result, but contains an incorrect articulation regarding the deductibility of the readership costs. If you can identify and explain the error without referring to the footnote, you should be confident in your understanding of the deduction rules.[3]

American Medical Association v. United States

887 F.2d 760 (7th Cir. 1989)

CUDAHY, Circuit Judge.

This case involves the allocation of income and expenses between a charitable organization's tax-exempt activities and its taxable business endeavors for purposes of computing the charity's "unrelated business income tax" under 26 U.S.C. sections 511 to 513. The American Medical Association (the "AMA"), a tax-exempt charitable organization, filed suit in the Northern District of Illinois seeking a refund for the tax years 1975 through 1978. The AMA argued that the Internal Revenue Service (the "IRS") had improperly calculated its income from the non-exempt unrelated business of publishing advertising in the organization's publications. The district court substantially agreed with the AMA's statutory and regulatory arguments, and ordered the United States to pay the AMA the full amount of the refund requested. We affirm in part and reverse in part.

I.

The AMA is a tax-exempt membership organization under section 501(c)(6) of the Internal Revenue Code. Its charitable function is "to promote the science and art of medicine and the betterment of public health." In aid of this purpose the AMA publishes the *Journal of the American Medical Association* ("JAMA") and the *American*

3. Example (4) assumes $30,000 in direct advertising costs, $40,000 in gross advertising income (for a net $10,000 unrelated advertising income), $60,000 circulation income, $90,000 readership costs, (for a net loss of $30,000 from the exploited exempt activity) $100,000 total periodical income, and $120,000 total periodical costs. Since the advertising activity operates at a gain of $10,000 and the exploited exempt activity operates at a loss of ($30,000), the readership costs are deductible only to the extent they exceed the income from the exempt activity (i.e., $30,000) and then only to the extent of net unrelated advertising income (i.e., $10,000). Thus, the readership costs are deductible to the extent of $10,000 in computing unrelated taxable income, rather than $70,000 as stated in the regulation. Technically, $60,000 of the readership costs are nondeductible because they relate to the exempt activity (and are therefore not directly connected to the advertising activity), and $20,000 are nondeductible because they exceed the net income from the advertising activity. If, as the regulation concludes, $70,000 of the readership costs were actually deductible in computing unrelated business taxable income, the organization would have a net loss of ($60,000).

Medical News ("AM News"). Most of the AMA's members pay annual dues to belong to the organization. Between 1975 and 1978, AMA members received JAMA and AM News at no additional cost as a benefit of membership.

JAMA and AM News both contain articles of relevance to the practice of medicine. But the journals also contain paid advertising. During the relevant period the AMA sent complimentary copies of JAMA and AM News to targeted groups of physicians who make up an especially desirable audience for firms likely to advertise in the journals. The parties stipulated that the AMA's sole purpose in engaging in this complimentary "controlled circulation" was to increase advertising revenues. Many of the AMA's dues-paying members were also on the controlled circulation list and therefore would have been entitled to receive JAMA and AM News even if they were not AMA members. However, the AMA apparently did not inform these physicians that they were entitled to complimentary copies of the journals. Nor did the AMA refund any portion of these physicians' membership dues in recognition of the fact that they need not have paid for the periodicals.

Between 1975 and 1978, the AMA placed a portion of the membership dues it received in an "association equity" account, which was intended to serve as a reserve fund to offset any deficit which might occur in future years if the association's revenues were insufficient to cover expenses. The amounts deposited in the association equity account remained on the AMA's books as a reserve until 1985, when the AMA withdrew some of these funds to compensate for a shortfall in its revenue.

There is no dispute that the editorial or readership content of the two periodicals furthers the AMA's charitable mission, and therefore any revenue attributable to the publication and distribution of articles in JAMA and AM News is exempt from taxation. And the AMA has admitted that the advertising in JAMA and AM News is a business endeavor unrelated to the AMA's charitable purpose, and is therefore taxable. This case presents several question involving the allocation of income and expenses between the exempt and taxable aspects of JAMA and AM News, and the allocation of membership dues between these periodicals and the AMA's other (exempt) activities.

The statutory scheme applicable to these journals is fairly straightforward. Section 511 of the Code provides that the "unrelated business taxable income" of a charitable organization is subject to the tax applied to corporate income under section 11. Section 512(a)(1) defines "unrelated business taxable income" as

> the gross income derived by any organization from any unrelated trade or business (as defined in section 513) regularly carried on by it, *less the deductions* allowed by this chapter *which are directly connected with the carrying on of such trade or business....*

(emphasis added). Finally, section 513(a) defines an "unrelated trade or business" as

> any trade or business the conduct of which is not substantially related (aside from the need of such organization for income or funds or the use it makes

> of the profits derived) to the exercise or performance by such organization of its charitable . . . purpose or function constituting the basis for its exemption under section 501. . . .

In a provision added in 1969, and significantly titled "Advertising, etc., activities," section 513(c) further explains:

> the term "trade or business" includes any activity which is carried on for the production of income from the sale of goods or the performance of services. For purposes of the preceding sentence, an activity does not lose identity as a trade or business merely because it is carried on within a larger aggregate of similar activities or within a larger complex of other endeavors which may, or may not, be related to the exempt purposes of the organization.

The Supreme Court construed these provisions in *United States v. American College of Physicians*, 475 U.S. 834 (1986). *American College* involved a charitable organization's medical journal which, as here, contained both articles which furthered the organization's exempt function and paid advertisements. The Supreme Court held that section 513(c) clearly indicated Congress' intent to treat advertising in an otherwise tax-exempt publication as a separate "trade or business," which may be taxable if the "conduct of [the advertising business] is not substantially related . . . to the . . . performance by such organization of its charitable . . . purpose." *Id.* at 839–40. To determine whether the advertising content of a journal is "substantially related" to the organization's educational mission, the IRS must look to the manner in which the advertising is selected and displayed; i.e., whether only advertising of new technologies or medications is allowed, whether the charity coordinates the subject matter and content of the ads, etc. *Id.* at 848–50. The organization's tax exemption extends to its publication of advertising only if the advertisements "contribute[] importantly" to the charity's exempt purpose. *Id.* at 847; *see also United States v. American Bar Endowment*, 477 U.S. 105, 109–16 (1986).

American College specifically endorsed the so-called "fragmentation" principle, whereby a charitable organization's publications are divided into two components: (1) the tax-exempt publication of the journal's "editorial" or "readership content"; and (2) the taxable enterprise of selling and publishing advertising. The United States and the AMA agree on these general principles; in fact, the AMA has even conceded that the advertisements in JAMA and AM News are not "substantially related" to the AMA's educational mission, and therefore constitute an "unrelated" business under *American College*. The parties' disagreement centers on the application of the "fragmentation" principle to the facts of this case.

The IRS has adopted detailed regulations which govern the allocation of revenues and expenses between a journal's exempt editorial and non-exempt advertising activities. Regulation 1.512(a)-1(f)(6) provides for division of a periodical's costs into two categories:

> (ii)(a) The direct advertising costs of an exempt organization periodical include all expenses, depreciation and similar items of deduction which

> are directly connected with the sale and publication of advertising.... The items allowable as deductions under this subdivision do not include any items of deduction attributable to the production or distribution of the readership content of the periodical.
>
> * * *
>
> (iii) The "readership" costs of an exempt organization periodical include expenses, depreciation or similar items which are directly connected with the production and distribution of the readership content of the periodical.... Readership costs include all the items of deduction attributable to an exempt organization periodical which are not allocated to direct advertising costs under subdivision (ii).
>
> * * *

26 C.F.R. §1.512(a)-1(f)(6). "Direct advertising costs" are fully deductible from gross advertising income, Reg. (f)(2)(i); "readership costs" are only deductible from gross advertising income to the extent they exceed circulation income. Reg. (f)(2)(ii)(b). "Circulation income," in turn, is defined as

> the income attributable to the production, distribution or circulation of a periodical (other than gross advertising income).... Where the right to receive an exempt organization periodical is associated with membership... in such organization for which dues... are received (hereinafter referred to as "membership receipts"), circulation income includes the portion of such membership receipts allocable to the periodical (hereinafter referred to as "allocable membership receipts").

Reg. 1.512(a)-1(f)(3)(iii). Regulation (f)(3)(iii) goes on to explain that "allocable membership receipts" should generally represent the amount which a taxable organization would have charged for the periodical in an arm's length [sic] transaction with the member. The regulation refers taxpayers to regulation (f)(4) "for a discussion of the factors to be considered in determining allocable membership receipts." Regulation (f)(4) provides three methods for determining the share of membership receipts which should be deemed to constitute a member's payment for the right to receive the periodical. Only the third method of calculating allocable membership receipts is applicable to JAMA and AM News. That method is described as a "pro rata allocation."

> Since it may generally be assumed that membership receipts and gross advertising income are equally available for all of the exempt activities (including the periodical) of the organization, the share of membership receipts allocated to the periodical, where [methods 1 and 2] do not apply, shall be an amount equal to the organization's membership receipts multiplied by a fraction the numerator of which is the total periodical costs and the denominator of which is such costs plus the costs of other exempt activities of the organization.

Reg. 1.512(a)-1(f)(4)(iii). Therefore, the amount of dues to be allocated to circulation income under the pro rata allocation method equals total membership receipts multiplied by the ratio of total periodical costs to the costs of all exempt activities.

The AMA raises a number of challenges to the validity of these allocation rules, and to the IRS's application of these principles in this case. However, before discussing the AMA's arguments in detail, it is worth noting that the AMA's goal throughout this litigation has been to reduce, to the maximum extent allowable, its tax liability from its "unrelated" advertising business.[4] Therefore, the AMA would like to decrease the amount of its (taxable) advertising income by *increasing* the expenses (labeled "direct advertising costs") which are fully deductible from advertising income. And, since any loss attributable to the readership content of JAMA and AM News is also deductible from advertising income (in something of a departure from strict application of the "fragmentation" principle), the AMA is also interested in producing a loss on the readership side of the journals. Such a loss may be created, in part, by decreasing the amount of circulation income derived through the allocation of membership dues to circulation income in the form of a hypothetical subscription price which members pay (as part of their total membership dues) for the right to receive the journals.

The AMA argues, most generally, that the allocation regulations are invalid because the IRS did not comply with the notice and comment requirements of the Administrative Procedure Act (the "APA") in promulgating the rules. In the alternative, the AMA urges that the regulations are invalid because they conflict with the statutory provisions governing the unrelated business income tax.

The AMA also makes a series of fact-specific arguments. First, it argues that membership dues which were placed in the "association equity" reserve account, and which were not employed to cover current expenses in the tax years in question, should not have been included in "membership receipts" for the purpose of determining the allocation of membership dues to circulation income. The AMA's next two arguments relate to its practice of distributing complimentary copies of JAMA and AM News as part of its "controlled circulation." The AMA argues, first, that the cost of producing the articles in these complimentary copies (which would normally be considered "readership costs" and deductible only from tax-exempt circulation income) should be considered "direct advertising costs" since the AMA's sole purpose in distributing these copies was to promote its advertising business. Second, the AMA argues that the dues of physicians who were AMA members, but who were entitled to receive the journals anyway due to their membership in the control groups, should not be included in allocable membership receipts, since it is absurd to suggest that these physicians paid for a journal which they would have received free of charge in any case.

4. [2] Of course the AMA is entitled to seek to minimize its tax liability to the fullest extent permitted by law. *Gregory v. Helvering*, 293 U.S. 465, 468–69 (1935), aff'g, 69 F.2d 809, 810 (2d Cir. 1934) (L. Hand, J.); *Yosha v. Commissioner*, 861 F.2d 494, 497 (7th Cir. 1988).

The district court accepted the AMA's arguments in substantial part. The court held that the costs of producing the editorial content of journals distributed free of charge to promote the AMA's advertising business were "direct advertising costs" directly deductible from advertising income. The court also ruled that the dues placed in the AMA's "association equity" account should not have been considered current membership receipts, and therefore no portion of these payments should have been allocated to circulation income in the year received. Finally, the court ruled, contrary to the AMA view, that the dues received from AMA members who were also members of the control group were to be included in the dues allocated to circulation income.

* * *

III.

The AMA contends that the allocation rules are inconsistent with the Code sections governing the unrelated business income tax. The regulations establish a dichotomy between "direct advertising costs" and "readership costs"; readership costs (those expenses associated with the production and distribution of the editorial content of a periodical) are not fully deductible from advertising income. The AMA argues that the readership content of its journals contributes to the production of advertising revenue; to the extent the regulations prohibit the deduction of readership costs directly from advertising income, they are inconsistent with the statutory mandate that expenses "directly connected with" an unrelated business should be fully deductible. *See* § 512(a)(1). The AMA also contends that the allocation rules are invalid because they ignore competitive factors in allocating membership receipts to circulation income. According to the AMA the overriding purpose of the unrelated business income tax was to equalize competition between taxable and tax-exempt entities operating similar enterprises; to the extent the regulations prohibit the AMA from demonstrating that the subscription price charged by its competitors is lower than the result of the pro rata allocation method, the regulations impermissibly depart from the "competition-equalizing" purpose of the statute.

* * *

The regulations related to the deductibility of a periodical's expenses generally parrot the statutory language. The statute states that expenses are fully deductible from taxable income if they are "directly connected with" the conduct of the unrelated business; the regulation similarly provides that "direct advertising costs," which are fully deductible, are those costs which are "directly connected with the sale and publication of advertising." Reg. 1.512(a)-1(f)(6)(ii)(a). So far, there would not appear to be any problem.

However, the regulation goes on to state that "readership costs," (those costs which are "directly connected with the production and distribution of the readership content of the periodical"), are *only* deductible from advertising revenues to the extent that those costs exceed circulation income; *i.e.*, only to the extent that the editorial side of the journal produces a "loss." Reg. 1.512(a)-1(d)(2), (f)(1). These are the provisions with which the AMA vigorously disagrees. For as the AMA sees things, the readership content of a journal contributes to its publisher's ability to sell advertising — a journal with high-quality articles is presumably more widely read and advertisers are accordingly more likely to place ads for their products in such a periodical. By failing to take account of the symbiotic relationship between advertising and editorial content, the regulation impermissibly fails to allow the deduction of costs which are in reality "directly connected with" the sale and publication of advertising.

While the AMA's argument is perhaps minimally plausible, we do not believe the AMA has carried the heavy burden of demonstrating that the IRS's contrary approach is "plainly inconsistent" with the tax code. First, we note that the AMA's position here is somewhat ironic — the AMA has been accorded a tax exemption for the readership content of its journals because the publication of a periodical furthers the organization's charitable purposes by disseminating knowledge to its members. The AMA (and many other tax-exempt organizations) initially argued that even the *advertising* revenue of its periodicals was tax exempt, because the advertising subsidized the readership content of the journal and thereby contributed to the organization's exempt purposes. That position was ultimately defeated by the addition of section 513(c) to the Code, and the decision in *United States v. American College of Physicians*, 475 U.S. 834 (1986). The AMA now essentially reverses its position, portraying its journals as, in large part, vehicles for advertising, and seeks to have a portion of editorial costs deducted directly from taxable advertising income.

Certainly, the AMA makes a valid point that the editorial content of its journals contributes in some manner to the success of the advertising business. Presumably few AMA members would read, and therefore few advertisers would advertise in, a journal which was one-hundred percent advertising. However, it is entirely plausible to label this general benefit which the articles confer on the advertising "indirect" (and therefore not fully deductible from advertising revenue), especially when advertising is viewed (as it must be under the "fragmentation" principle, *see* section 513(c) of the Code) as a separate and independent enterprise. The costs of producing the readership content of the AMA's journals is most directly connected with the editorial "business" of the journals; these costs are attributable only indirectly to the other business (advertising) which the AMA also conducts within the confines of a single periodical. *See* Reg. 1.512(a)-1(a) ("to be 'directly connected with' the conduct of unrelated business for purposes of section 512, an item of deduction must have proximate and primary relationship to the carrying on of that business"). If two businesses occupy a single building, and one business increases its sales volume, thereby increasing the customer traffic through the common building, benefitting the second, independent enterprise, we would without hesitation label the effect on the latter business "indirect." The situation of the AMA's publications is identical — the AMA essentially carries on two separate businesses "under the same roof"; when one business does well and increases the allure of the building as a whole to customers, the effect on the second business is "indirect" and therefore the first enterprise's expenses are not immediately deductible from the latter's income. It is certainly reasonable for the IRS to have concluded that, in general, "readership costs" of the AMA's periodicals are not "directly connected with" the conduct of the AMA's advertising business.

The AMA argues that the Second Circuit's decision in *Rensselaer Polytechnic Institute v. Commissioner*, 732 F.2d 1058 (1984), requires that the AMA be allowed to deduct some portion of readership costs from advertising income. *Rensselaer* involved a fieldhouse operated by a tax-exempt educational institution. The fieldhouse was used for both tax-exempt, student events (*e.g.*, college athletics), and for commercial functions, such as commercial ice shows. The staging of commercial events at the fieldhouse constituted an "unrelated business." The allocation question before the Second Circuit involved certain "fixed costs" of operating the structure—repairs, depreciation, salaries of fieldhouse personnel, etc. The court held that those fixed expenses should be allocated to the school's tax-exempt and taxable businesses based on the number of hours for which the fieldhouse was used for each activity, since the fixed costs were attributable to both student and commercial events. *Id.* at 1061–62; *see also Disabled Am. Veterans v. United States*, 704 F.2d 1570, 1573–74 (Fed. Cir. 1983).

Rensselaer is distinguishable from this case. *Rensselaer* involved the cost of goods or services which actually benefited both the tax-exempt function and the unrelated trade or business. *Rensselaer* would control the present case if the AMA wished to apportion the costs of a printing press, paper stock or employees used in both the editorial and advertising businesses based on the extent to which each business employed the common resource. Such an apportionment would clearly be proper, since the expense benefited both activities in some measure.

But *Rensselaer* does not address the independent question whether, assuming costs are directly tied to only one activity, those costs may *still* be deductible from the other activity, because the activities themselves benefit each other in some undefined fashion. In *Rensselaer* the school did not argue that a portion of the costs of its student functions should be deducted from its taxable income because staging student events promoted commercial leasing by demonstrating to the entertainment industry that the fieldhouse was an attractive venue fully capable of handling major events. (As a factual matter, such an argument might well be accurate—commercial promoters would doubtless be hesitant to stage a major entertainment event in a stadium which was seldom used, and with which the local audience was unfamiliar.) We have no doubt that, if such an argument *had* been presented, the Second Circuit would have rejected it for the same reasons we reject the AMA's argument here—while one activity may benefit the other in some generalized way, that beneficial effect is more properly viewed as only "indirectly connected" to the benefited business.

The AMA also contends that the regulations are invalid because they ignore the situation of the AMA's taxable competitors in determining the portion of membership dues receipts to be allocated to circulation income. The AMA argues that the approach of the regulations is inconsistent with the fundamental purpose of the unrelated business income tax, which was to equalize competition between taxable and tax-exempt organizations plying the same trade. The AMA argues that this "competition-equalizing" goal can be attained only by placing the AMA's journals on the "same [*i.e.*, identical] tax basis" as its commercial competitors. The simple answer to this argument is that, although the equalization of competition was indeed a major goal of the unrelated business tax, Congress never intended to place tax-exempt organizations on a tax basis identical to that of their commercial competitors. Congress instead endorsed the "fragmentation" principle, whereby a charity's periodicals are divided into two components. In light of Congress' adoption of the "fragmentation" concept, it is not possible to place the AMA's journals on an identical footing with competing publications. Taxable publications labor under no "fragmentation" requirement; there is no need for a taxable publisher to segregate its income or expenses into components, some taxed, others not. A commercial publisher is taxed on all aspects of its business. Therefore, although it is certainly instructive to recall the purposes underlying the enactment of the unrelated business income tax, direct analogies to the tax treatment of commercial publishers are of limited assistance in deciding specific allocation questions involving tax-exempt organizations.

* * *

VII.

For the foregoing reasons the judgment of the district court is

AFFIRMED IN PART AND REVERSED IN PART.

Chapter 29

Unrelated Debt Financed Income

A. Background and History

The best way to gain an understanding of any tax code provision is to understand the prototypical transaction to which it relates. This is especially true with respect to a complex provision, such as IRC § 514. We therefore begin our consideration of the unrelated debt-financed income provision with an examination of one of the landmark cases pertaining to charitable tax exemption.

Commissioner v. Brown

380 U.S. 563 (1965)

MR. JUSTICE WHITE delivered the opinion of the Court.

* * *

Clay Brown, members of his family and three other persons owned substantially all of the stock in Clay Brown & Company, with sawmills and lumber interests near Fortuna, California. Clay Brown, the president of the company and spokesman for the group, was approached by a representative of California Institute for Cancer Research in 1952, and after considerable negotiation the stockholders agreed to sell their stock to the Institute for $1,300,000, payable $5,000 down from the assets of the company and the balance within 10 years from the earnings of the company's assets. It was provided that simultaneously with the transfer of the stock, the Institute would liquidate the company and lease its assets for five years to a new corporation, Fortuna Sawmills, Inc., formed and wholly owned by the attorneys for the sellers. Fortuna would pay to the Institute 80% of its operating profit without allowance for depreciation or taxes, and 90% of such payments would be paid over by the Institute to the selling stockholders to apply on the $1,300,000 note. This note was noninterest bearing, the Institute had no obligation to pay it except from the rental income and it was secured by mortgages and assignments of the assets transferred or leased to Fortuna. If the payments on the note failed to total $250,000 over any two consecutive years, the sellers could declare the entire balance of the note due and payable. The sellers were neither stockholders nor directors of Fortuna but it was provided that Clay Brown was to have a management contract with Fortuna at an annual salary and the right to name any successor manager if he himself resigned.

Fortuna immediately took over operations of the business under its lease, on the same premises and with practically the same personnel which had been employed by Clay Brown & Company. In 1957, because of a rapidly declining lumber market, Fortuna suffered severe reverses and its operations were terminated. Respondent sellers did not repossess the properties under their mortgages but agreed they should be sold by the Institute with the latter retaining 10% of the proceeds. Respondents returned the payments received from rentals as the gain from the sale of capital assets. The Commissioner, however, asserted the payments were taxable as ordinary income and were not capital gain within the meaning of I.R.C. 1939, §117(a)(4) and I.R.C. 1954, §1222(3). These sections provide that "the term 'long-term capital gain' means gain from the sale or exchange of a capital asset held for more than 6 months. . . ."

* * *

Having abandoned in the Court of Appeals the argument that this transaction was a sham, the Commissioner now admits that there was real substance in what occurred between the Institute and the Brown family. The transaction was a sale under local law. The Institute acquired title to the stock of Clay Brown & Company and, by liquidation, to all of the assets of that company, in return for its promise to pay over money from the operating profits of the company. If the stipulated price was paid, the Brown family would forever lose all rights to the income and properties of the company. Prior to the transfer, these respondents had access to all of the income of the company; after the transfer, 28% of the income remained with Fortuna and the Institute. Respondents had no interest in the Institute nor were they stockholders or directors of the operating company. Any rights to control the management were limited to the management contract between Clay Brown and Fortuna, which was relinquished in 1954.

Whatever substance the transaction might have had, however, the Commissioner claims that it did not have the substance of a sale within the meaning of §1222(3). His argument is that since the Institute invested nothing, assumed no independent liability for the purchase price and promised only to pay over a percentage of the earnings of the company, the entire risk of the transaction remained on the sellers. Apparently, to qualify as a sale, a transfer of property for money or the promise of money must be to a financially responsible buyer who undertakes to pay the purchase price other than from the earnings or the assets themselves or there must be a substantial down payment which shifts at least part of the risk to the buyer and furnishes some cushion against loss to the seller.

To say that there is no sale because there is no risk-shifting and that there is no risk-shifting because the price to be paid is payable only from the income produced by the business sold, is very little different from saying that because business earnings are usually taxable as ordinary income, they are subject to the same tax when paid over as the purchase price of property. This argument has rationality but it places an unwarranted construction on the term "sale," is contrary to the policy of the capital gains provisions of the Internal Revenue Code, and has no support in the cases. We reject it.

* * *

"A sale, in the ordinary sense of the word, is a transfer of property for a fixed price in money or its equivalent," it is a contract "to pass rights of property for money,— which the buyer pays or promises to pay to the seller . . .". Compare the definition of "sale" in § 1(2) of the Uniform Sales Act and in § 2-106(1) of the Uniform Commercial Code. The transaction which occurred in this case was obviously a transfer of property for a fixed price payable in money.

* * *

In the actual transaction, the stock was transferred for a price payable on the installment basis but payable from the earnings of the company. Eventually $936,131.85 was realized by respondents. This transaction, we think, is a sale, and so treating it is wholly consistent with the purposes of the Code to allow capital gains treatment for realization upon the enhanced value of a capital asset.

The Commissioner, however, embellishes his risk-shifting argument. Purporting to probe the economic realities of the transaction, he reasons that if the seller continues to bear all the risk and the buyer none, the seller must be collecting a price for his risk-bearing in the form of an interest in future earnings over and above what would be a fair market value of the property. Since the seller bears the risk, the so-called purchase price *must* be excessive and *must* be simply a device to collect future earnings at capital gains rates.

We would hesitate to discount unduly the power of pure reason and the argument is not without force. But it does present difficulties. In the first place, it denies what the tax court expressly found—that the price paid was within reasonable limits based on the earnings and net worth of the company; and there is evidence in the record to support this finding. We do not have, therefore, a case where the price has been found excessive.

Secondly, if an excessive price is such an inevitable result of the lack of risk-shifting, it would seem that it would not be an impossible task for the Commissioner to demonstrate the fact. However, in this case he offered no evidence whatsoever to this effect; and in a good many other cases involving similar transactions, in some of which the reasonableness of the price paid by a charity was actually contested, the Tax Court has found the sale price to be within reasonable limits, as it did in this case.

Thirdly, the Commissioner ignores as well the fact that if the rents payable by Fortuna were deductible by it and not taxable to the Institute, the Institute could pay off the purchase price at a considerably faster rate than the ordinary corporate buyer subject to income taxes, a matter of considerable importance to a seller who wants the balance of his purchase price paid as rapidly as he can get it. The fact is that by April 30, 1955, a little over two years after closing this transaction, $412,595.77 had been paid on the note and within another year the sellers had collected another $238,498.80, for a total of $651,094.57.

Furthermore, risk-shifting of the kind insisted on by the Commissioner has not heretofore been considered an essential ingredient of a sale for tax purposes. In

LeTulle v. Scofield, 308 U.S. 415, one corporation transferred properties to another for cash and bonds secured by the properties transferred. The Court held that there was "a sale or exchange upon which gain or loss must be reckoned in accordance with the provisions of the revenue act dealing with the recognition of gain or loss upon a sale or exchange," *id.*, at 421, since the seller retained only a creditor's interest rather than a proprietary one. "That the bonds were secured solely by the assets transferred and that, upon default, the bondholder would retake only the property sold, [did not change] his status from that of a creditor to one having a proprietary stake." *Ibid.* Compare *Marr v. United States*, 268 U.S. 536. To require a sale for tax purposes to be to a financially responsible buyer who undertakes to pay the purchase price from sources other than the earnings of the assets sold or to make a substantial down payment seems to us at odds with commercial practice and common understanding of what constitutes a sale. The term "sale" is used a great many times in the Internal Revenue Code and a wide variety of tax results hinge on the occurrence of a "sale." To accept the Commissioner's definition of sale would have wide ramifications which we are not prepared to visit upon taxpayers, absent congressional guidance in this direction.

* * *

There is another reason for us not to disturb the ruling of the Tax Court and the Court of Appeals. In 1963, the Treasury Department, in the course of hearings before the Congress, noted the availability of capital gains treatment on the sale of capital assets even though the seller retained an interest in the income produced by the assets. The Department proposed a change in the law which would have taxed as ordinary income the payments on the sale of a capital asset which were deferred over more than five years and were contingent on future income. Payments, though contingent on income, required to be made within five years would not have lost capital gains status nor would payments not contingent on income even though accompanied by payments which were.

Congress did not adopt the suggested change but it is significant for our purposes that the proposed amendment did not deny the fact or occurrence of a sale but would have taxed as ordinary income those income-contingent payments deferred for more than five years. If a purchaser could pay the purchase price out of earnings within five years, the seller would have capital gain rather than ordinary income. The approach was consistent with allowing appreciated values to be treated as capital gain but with appropriate safeguards against reserving additional rights to future income. In comparison, the Commissioner's position here is a clear case of "overkill" if aimed at preventing the involvement of tax-exempt entities in the purchase and operation of business enterprises. There are more precise approaches to this problem as well as to the question of the possibly excessive price paid by the charity or foundation. And if the Commissioner's approach is intended as a limitation upon the tax treatment of sales generally, it represents a considerable invasion of current capital gains policy, a matter which we think is the business of Congress, not ours.

The problems involved in the purchase of a going business by a tax-exempt organization have been considered and dealt with by the Congress. Likewise, it has given its attention to various kinds of transactions involving the payment of the agreed purchase price for property from the future earnings of the property itself. In both situations it has responded, if at all, with precise provisions of narrow application. We consequently deem it wise to "leave to the Congress the fashioning of a rule which, in any event, must have wide ramifications."

Affirmed.

Mr. Justice Harlan, concurring.

Were it not for the tax laws, the respondents' transaction with the Institute would make no sense, except as one arising from a charitable impulse. However the tax laws exist as an economic reality in the businessman's world, much like the existence of a competitor. Businessmen plan their affairs around both, and a tax dollar is just as real as one derived from any other source. The Code gives the Institute a tax exemption which makes it capable of taking a greater after-tax return from a business than could a nontax-exempt individual or corporation. Respondents traded a residual interest in their business for a faster payout apparently made possible by the Institute's exemption. The respondents gave something up; they received something substantially different in return. If words are to have meaning, there was a "sale or exchange."

* * *

Therefore I concur in the judgment to affirm.

Mr. Justice Goldberg, with whom The Chief Justice and Mr. Justice Black join, dissenting.

The essential facts of this case which are undisputed illuminate the basic nature of the transaction at issue. . . . In essence respondents conveyed their interest in the business to the Institute in return for 72% of the profits of the business and the right to recover the business assets if payments fell behind schedule.

At first glance it might appear odd that the sellers would enter into this transaction, for prior to the sale they had a right to 100% of the corporation's income, but after the sale they had a right to only 72% of that income and would lose the business after 10 years to boot. This transaction, however, afforded the sellers several advantages. The principal advantage sought by the sellers was capital gain, rather than ordinary income, treatment for that share of the business profits which they received. Further, because of the Tax Code's charitable exemption and the lease arrangement with Fortuna, the Institute believed that neither it nor Fortuna would have to pay income tax on the earnings of the business. Thus the sellers would receive free of corporate taxation, and subject only to personal taxation at capital gains rates, 72% of the business earnings until they were paid $1,300,000. Without the sale they would receive only 48% of the business earnings, the rest going to the Government in corporate taxes, and this 48% would be subject to personal taxation at ordinary rates. In effect the Institute sold the respondents the use of its tax exemption, enabling the respondents to collect $1,300,000 from the business more quickly than they otherwise could and to pay taxes on this amount at capital gains rates. In return, the Institute received a nominal amount of the profits while the $1,300,000 was being paid, and it was to receive the whole business after this debt had been paid off. In any realistic sense the Government's grant of a tax exemption was used by the Institute as part of an arrangement that allowed it to buy a business that in fact cost it nothing. I cannot believe that Congress intended such a result.

* * *

Note

Identifying and substantiating the exact harm caused by the "bootstrap" transaction exemplified in *Clay Brown* is no easy task. Early commentators assumed that the harm was in allowing a business owner to illegitimately convert ordinary income into capital gains. Because the rental payments were: (1) made from the corporate lessee's earnings, thereby "zeroing" out the lessee's income otherwise taxable at ordinary rates, (2) exempted from tax when received by the exempt lessee, (3) and subsequently paid to the "former" owners as part of the exempt organization's purchase price, the substantive effect was that earnings escaped taxation under ordinary rates but were instead taxed at capital gains rates. But the seller could have (and still can) obtain capital gain treatment with a taxable buyer, though in cases involving a taxable buyer the rents collected from the lessee (and therefore the payments to the buyer) would have been diminished by taxation at ordinary rates. The harm, then, was not that the former owners were being taxed at capital gains rates, but that the corporate "buyer" was not being taxed at ordinary rates on income used to purchase a valuable asset. In part, the tax exemption redounded to the benefit of a taxable person (the seller). Because Congress has apparently condoned the capital gains treatment for a seller in either event, the Court considered the Service's attempt to deny the existence of a sale altogether as "overkill." Essentially, the Service was focusing on the wrong consequence. More recently, some commentators have suggested that the harm caused by exempt organizations engaging in leveraged transactions results from the organization's severing its dependence on public support. As a result, according to the theory, the organization will no longer be accountable to the public.

When the bootstrap transaction first came to Congress' attention, it responded by enacting an earlier version of § 514, commonly referred to as the "Business Lease" provision. The provision would have taxed the rents earned by the *Clay Brown* buyer at ordinary rates (thereby restoring the corporate tax base to its status quo ante, but not denying capital gain treatment to the seller), but for a provision that exempted all rents payable under a lease not exceeding five years. The legislative history articulates the harm Congress sought to prevent:

> As implied by its name, a lease-back involves the purchase of a property by a tax-exempt organization, and the leasing of the property, usually to the same business from which the property was purchased....

> In many cases the exempt organization, in buying the property, does not use its own funds to make the payment, but borrows the purchase price and pays off the loan plus the interest charges thereon by applying part or all of the rental income received for a period of years to this purpose.
>
> * * *
>
> There are three principal objections to the lease-back arrangements where borrowed funds are used. First, the tax-exempt organization is not merely trying to find a means of investing its own funds at an adequate rate of return but is obviously trading on its exemption, since the only contribution it makes to the sale and lease is its tax exemption. Therefore, it appears reasonable to believe that the only reason why it receives the property at no expense to itself is the fact that it pays no income tax on the rentals received.
>
> The second objection to the lease-back is that it is altogether conceivable that if its use is not checked, exempt organizations in the not too distant future may own the great bulk of the commercial and industrial real estate in the country. This, of course, would lower drastically the rental income included in the corporate and individual income-tax bases. The fact that under present law an exempt institution need not use any of its own funds in acquiring property through lease-backs — borrowed funds may represent 100 percent of the purchase price — indicates that there is no limit to the property an exempt institution may acquire in this manner. Such acquisitions are not in any way limited by the funds available for investment on the part of the exempt institution. This explains why particular attention should be given to lease-backs which involve the use of borrowed funds. Where an exempt organization uses its own funds, expansion of its property holdings through the lease-back device must necessarily proceed at a much slower pace.
>
> A third reason for proposing the taxation of lease-backs is the possibility which exists in each case that the exempt organization has in effect sold part of its exemption. This can occur either by the exempt organization paying a higher price for the property or by charging lower rentals than a taxable business could charge. Proof, of course, is difficult to obtain because the purchase price, or rental charge which a taxable business would agree to pay, is unknown.

S. Rep. No. 2375, 81st Cong., 2d Sess. 31–33 (1950). The five-year exception to the business lease provisions allowed exempt organizations to continue engaging in *Clay Brown* transactions. From 1952 to 1965, for example, Loyola University of Los Angeles was involved in 24 bootstrap transactions, resulting in an approximately $10 million decrease in tax revenues to the government.[1] Finally, Congress closed

1. *University Hill Foundation v. Commissioner*, 51 T.C. 548 (1969). The government's *Clay Brown* type challenge failed, but the case was later reversed on other grounds. 446 F.2d 701 (1971).

the loophole in 1969 and in the process greatly broadened the tax on leveraged, income-producing properties. The following excerpt from the 1969 legislative history nicely summarizes the main provisions of present law 514. The footnotes do not appear in the legislative history but were added by the authors for further detail. As always, an in-depth study of the code and regulations is necessary for a complete understanding.

B. The Mechanics of IRC § 514

CODE: §§ 512(b)(4), 514(a)–(c)(7), 514(e)

TREAS. REGS.: §§ 1.514(a)-1(a)(1), 1.514(a)-1(a)(3)(i), 1.514(b)-1(a), 1.514(b)-1(b)(1), 1.514(b)-1(d)(1)–(2), 1.514(c)-1(a)(1)

Tax Reform Act of 1969

S. Rep. N. 552, 91st Cong.
1st Sess. 63-67 (1969)

Explanation of provision:

Both the House bill and the committee amendments provide that all exempt organizations' income from "debt-financed" property, which is unrelated to their exempt function, is to be subject to tax in the proportion in which the property is financed by the debt. Thus, for example, if a business or investment property is acquired subject to an 80 percent mortgage, 80 percent of the income and 80 percent of the deductions are to be taken into account for tax purposes. As the mortgage is paid off, the percentage taken into account diminishes. Capital gains on the sale of debt-financed property also are taxed in the same proportion.

The bill defines debt-financed property to be all property (e.g., rental real estate, tangible personal property, corporate stock) which is held to produce income and with respect to which there is an "acquisition indebtedness" at any time during the taxable year (or during the preceding 12 months, if the property is disposed of during the year).

The House bill would except from this definition the following: (1) property where all of its use is related to the exercise or performance of the organization's exempt function; (2) property where all of its income is already subject to tax as income from the conduct of an unrelated trade or business, (3) property where all of its income is derived from research activities excepted from the present unrelated business income tax; and (4) property where all of its use is in a trade or business exempted from tax because substantially all the work is performed without compensation, the business is carried on primarily for the convenience of members, students, patients, etc., or the business is the selling of merchandise, substantially all of which was received as gifts (sec. 513(a)(1), (2), (3)).

The committee approves of these exceptions but believes that they are somewhat too limited. Where the use of the property is "related," the House bill provides an exemption only if it is "all" related. The committee amendments exempt from the tax income from property where "substantially" all of its use is substantially related to its exempt purpose. In addition, if less than substantially all of its use is related, then the term debt-financed property is not to include the property "to the extent" that its use is related to the organization's exempt purpose or to the purpose described in (3) or (4) above, or where the income from the property is unrelated business income. The committee believes that its amendments provide a more appropriate test of what constitutes related.

The committee also provided that where a debt-financed building is owned by an exempt holding company (or other exempt organization) and used by any related exempt organization, the property of the holding company (or other exempt organization) is not to be classified as debt-financed property to the extent it is used by the related exempt organization (whether or not a section 501(c)(3) organization) in the performance of its exempt functions. The committee believes that this amendment is appropriate since it is consistent with the purposes and functions of the exempt organization.

Both the committee and the House versions of the bill provide that the tax on the unrelated debt financed income is not to apply to income from real property, located in the neighborhood of the exempt organization, which it plans to devote to exempt uses within 10 years of the time of acquisition. A more liberal 15-year rule is established for churches and it is not required that the property be in the neighborhood of the church.[2]

Under the bill, income producing property is considered to be debt-financed property (making income from it taxable) only where there is an "acquisition

2. Editor's Note: The "neighborhood land" exception requires that the land be in the organization's neighborhood, which the regulations define as (1) any property contiguous with property owned and used by an organization in the performance of its exempt purpose, or which would be contiguous except for the interposition of a thoroughfare, stream, railroad, or similar property, or (2) property within one mile of property owned and used in an exempt purpose, but only if the facts and circumstances make the acquisition of contiguous property unreasonable. Treas. Reg. § 1.514(b)-1(d)(ii). Even if the exception originally applies, it will not apply after the fifth year unless the land has actually been converted to an exempt purpose or the organization establishes to the Service' satisfaction that such conversion is reasonably certain. IRC § 514(b)(3)(B). The organization will be entitled to a refund of taxes (for all years within the 10 (or 15) year period that it paid taxes, not just those after the fifth year) if it ultimately converts the land to an exempt purpose use within the 10 (or 15) year period. IRC § 514(b)(3)(D). In addition, the exception will exclude income from buildings on the land at the time the land is acquired only if and so long as the organization intends to demolish or remove the building as part of its intended exempt purpose use of the land. IRC § 514(b)(3)(C). Income from a building on neighborhood land is taxable as UDFI from the time the organization abandons its intent to demolish or remove the building. IRC § 514(b)(3)(C). Finally, the neighborhood land exception will not exclude income from any building (the use of which is not otherwise excepted from taxation) erected after the land's acquisition or any building on the land subject to a business lease, as defined under old section 514. IRC § 514(b)(3)(C)(ii)–(iii).

indebtedness" attributable to it. Acquisition indebtedness exists with respect to property whenever the indebtedness was incurred in acquiring or improving the property, or the indebtedness would not have been incurred "but for" the acquisition or improvement of the property. Thus, for example, where a church has a portfolio of investments with no debt, and subsequently incurs a debt to construct a church related building, such as a seminary, such debt will not be considered acquisition indebtedness with respect to the investment portfolio.

If an indebtedness is incurred after the property is acquired or improved, it would not be "acquisition indebtedness" unless its incurrence was reasonably foreseeable at the time of the acquisition or improvement. If property is acquired subject to a mortgage, the mortgage is to be treated as an acquisition indebtedness incurred by the organization when the property is acquired.

The bill excepts from the term "acquisition indebtedness" property subject to indebtedness which an exempt organization receives by devise, by bequest, or, under certain conditions, by gift. This exception permits organizations receiving such property a 10-year period of time within which to dispose of it free of tax or to retain it and reduce or discharge the indebtedness on it with tax-free income. The bill also would not treat the extension, renewal, or refinancing of an existing indebtedness as the creation of a new indebtedness. Further, the term acquisition indebtedness does not include indebtedness which was necessarily incurred in the performance or exercise of the purpose or function constituting the basis of the organization's exemption—such as the indebtedness incurred by a credit union in accepting deposits from its members. Special exceptions are also provided for the sale of annuities and for debts insured by the Federal Housing Administration to finance low and moderate income housing.

The committee intent is that property acquired under a life income contract is not to be treated as debt-financed property if none of the payments received by any life beneficiary are treated for tax purposes as the proceeds of a sale or exchange of part or all of the property transferred to the exempt organization. Under a life income contract, an individual transfers property to a trust or a fund subject to a contract providing that the income is to be paid to the donor, or to other private persons, for a period of time (generally for life) with the remainder interest going to charity. These life income contracts do not represent the type of obligation intended to be treated as "acquisition indebtedness."

The computation of unrelated debt-financed income (the amount subject to tax) is determined by applying to the total gross income and deductions attributable to debt-financed property the fraction:

$$\frac{\text{average acquisition indebtedness for the taxable year}}{\text{average adjusted basis of the property during the taxable year}}$$

For purposes of the numerator of the fraction, acquisition indebtedness is to be averaged over the taxable year. The averaging mechanism precludes an exempt organization from avoiding the tax by using other available funds to pay off the indebtedness immediately before any fixed determination date. If debt-financed property is disposed of during the year, "average acquisition indebtedness" would mean the highest acquisition indebtedness during the preceding 12 months. Without such a rule, an exempt organization could avoid tax by using other resources to discharge indebtedness before the end of one taxable year and dispose of property after the beginning of the next taxable year.[3]

For purposes of the denominator of the fraction, adjusted basis would be the average adjusted basis for the portion of the year during which the property is held by the exempt organization. The use of average adjusted basis is for purposes only of determining the fraction. Where property is disposed of, gain or loss will, as usual, be computed with reference to adjusted basis at the time of disposition.[4]

The percentage used in determining the taxable portion of total gross income also is to be used to compute the allowable portion of deductions "directly connected with" the debt-financed property or the income from it. The direct connection requirement is carried over from present law (sec. 512). In general the bill allows all deductions that would be allowed to a normal taxpayer, to the extent consistent with the purpose of the bill and the nature of the special problems to which they are directed. For example, net operating loss and charitable contribution deductions would be allowed, subject to the limitation imposed by existing law on organizations taxable on unrelated business income (e.g., the percentage limitations on the charitable deduction are computed with reference only to the organization's unrelated business income, not its total income).

The deduction for depreciation would be restricted to the straight-line method, however. Accelerated depreciation ordinarily has the effect of deferring tax on income from depreciable property. However, under the bill, an exempt organization would become a taxpayer with respect to debt-financed property only for a limited period of time — while acquisition indebtedness remains outstanding — and would during that time be taxed on a declining proportion of its income from this property. In that setting, accelerated depreciation can be used for more than mere tax deferral; it can be used to reduce the total amount of the tax payable or, in some situations, eliminate tax altogether. It accomplishes that result by enlarging deductions in early years, in which the taxes would otherwise be high because of the large amount of indebtedness outstanding. To the extent that the useful life of the property is longer than the term of the indebtedness, acceleration of depreciation shields otherwise taxable income by means of deductions shifted from periods in which no tax at all would be paid. Hence, the bill's limitation of depreciation to the straight-line method is necessary to make this approach meaningful.

3. Editors' Note: *See* Treas. Reg. §1.514(a)-1(a)(1)(iii) and -1(a)(3)(ii).

4. Editors' Note: *See* Treas. Reg. §1.514(a)-1(a)(2)(i).

If property is used partly for exempt and partly for nonexempt purposes, the income and deductions attributable to the exempt uses are excluded from the computation of unrelated debt-financed income, and allocations are to be made, where appropriate, for acquisition indebtedness, adjusted basis, and deductions assignable to the property.

* * *

Southwest Texas Electrical Cooperative, Inc. v. Commissioner

67 F.3d 87 (5th Cir. 1995)

Jerry E. Smith, Circuit Judge:

Southwest Texas Electrical Cooperative, Inc. ("petitioner"), received a low-interest federal loan to finance an improvement of its facilities. At the time of construction, petitioner needed and withdrew only one-half of the approved loan amount; it later withdrew the remainder, however, and invested it in Treasury Notes. The Tax Court found that interest income from the Treasury Notes is debt-financed and therefore subject to federal taxation. We affirm.

I.

Petitioner, a tax-exempt rural electrical cooperative, received a $5.148 million loan from the Rural Electrification Administration ("REA") to finance an expansion and upgrade of its facilities. The REA permitted petitioner to draw on the approved loan funds only as reimbursement for construction costs it had already incurred. Petitioner made six REA loan draws from September 1983 through June 1985, totaling $2.574 million. Although petitioner was entitled to withdraw the remaining $2.574 million by July 1986, it chose not to do so, in part because its financial condition had improved and in part because further debt would have had a negative effect on its financial indicators.

The REA notified petitioner in March 1989 that its eligibility for the remaining approved funds would expire in August 1989. Petitioner requested the $2.574 million in early May 1989 and received it on May 16, 1989, at an interest rate of five percent. Petitioner's motivations for borrowing the funds included uncertainty over whether it could receive another REA loan and the costs it had already incurred in applying for the loan. Petitioner placed the borrowed funds in its General Fund Account on May 17, 1989, and withdrew $2,575,735.25 from that account the next day to purchase two United States Treasury Notes paying more than nine percent interest.

Petitioner received interest income on the Treasury Notes in the amount of $146,096.61 in 1989 and $230,938.49 in 1990. It also incurred related expenses (including interest payments on the REA loan) of $86,222.29 in 1989 and $134,812.53 in 1990. Petitioner reported that it had no taxable income in 1989 and 1990; the Commissioner of Internal Revenue ("the Commissioner") disagreed and assessed deficiencies for those years, contending that the interest income from the Treasury

Notes, less related expenses, is taxable as business income unrelated to petitioner's tax-exempt purpose. The Tax Court upheld the deficiencies.

II.

A.

The parties agree that (1) petitioner is generally exempt from federal income tax under 26 U.S.C. § 501(a); (2) 26 U.S.C. §§ 501(b) and 511(a) require petitioner to pay taxes on its "unrelated business taxable income"; and (3) interest income counts as "unrelated business taxable income" when it is both earned on property that is not substantially related to petitioner's tax exempt purpose, see 26 U.S.C. §§ 512(a)(1) and 513(a), and debt-financed. *See* 26 U.S.C. §§ 512(b)(4) & 514(a). The parties further agree that the improvement of petitioner's facilities is substantially related to its tax-exempt purpose, and the purchase of Treasury Notes is not. Accordingly, the question presented is whether the $2.574 million in debt financing should be attributed to the facilities or to the purchase of the Treasury Notes.

Petitioner contends that the debt financing should be attributed to the facilities. The REA approved the loan for the sole purpose of financing construction. Under the terms of the loan agreement, petitioner expended general operating funds for the construction and received corresponding reimbursement from the REA. Petitioner argues that the legislative history of 26 U.S.C. § 514 evidences an intent to permit non-profit organizations to make tax-free investments with their own funds, taxing passive investments only when they are made with borrowed funds. Because the REA releases funds only upon proof of completed construction, taxing investments made with general funds only because those funds have been replenished by REA loans could have the effect of taxing investments that Congress intended to exempt.

The Commissioner conceded at oral argument that the REA loan proceeds would be attributable to the construction and not the Treasury Notes if petitioner had drawn on the loan proceeds at the time of construction. The Commissioner argues that petitioner lost this tax advantage by its lengthy delay in drawing on the loan, however. Other circuits have found that § 514 taxes income from a passive investment when a taxpayer borrows money for the purpose of making such an investment; the Commissioner argues that this case falls within those holdings because petitioner made the loan draw three and one-half years after completing construction and immediately invested the proceeds in Treasury Notes.

B.

We review the Tax Court's legal conclusions *de novo*. We defer to its fact findings unless they are clearly erroneous.

This is a case of first impression. While other circuits have held or assumed that indebtedness incurred for the purpose of making passive investments is attributable to those investments, reimbursement loans arguably present a different question. The parties agree that a taxpayer that receives loan funds before incurring construction expenditures can use the loan proceeds to finance construction directly while simultaneously investing its own money tax-free; a similar taxpayer that receives loan funds only after incurring construction expenditures must use its own money to pay construction bills and then use the reimbursement funds for the investment. If we were to hold broadly that the latter investment is debt-financed *merely* because the specific dollars used to make it are traceable to a lender, we would grant different tax consequences to similar transactions.

C.

We need not resolve the difficulties presented by reimbursement loans, however, because petitioner's arguments amount to an attempt to restructure this transaction after the fact. As noted above, petitioner's Treasury Notes are subject to federal taxation only if they are debt-financed. Property is debt-financed if it is held to produce income and there is an "acquisition indebtedness" attributable to it. *See* 26 U.S.C. § 514(b)(1). "Acquisition indebtedness" is defined as follows:

> The term "acquisition indebtedness" means, with respect to any debt-financed property, the unpaid amount of—
>
> (A) the indebtedness incurred by the organization in acquiring or improving such property;
>
> (B) the indebtedness incurred before the acquisition or improvement of such property if such indebtedness would not have been incurred but for such acquisition or improvement; and
>
> (C) the indebtedness incurred after the acquisition or improvement of such property if such indebtedness would not have been incurred but for such acquisition or improvement and the incurrence of such indebtedness was reasonably foreseeable at the time of such acquisition or improvement.

26 U.S.C. § 514(c)(1).

Petitioner made a business decision to finance the remaining construction by spending its own funds, not by drawing on the remainder of the approved loan; petitioner subsequently decided to borrow the remainder and invest it in Treasury Notes. Accordingly, petitioner incurred the indebtedness not for financing the construction, but for making arbitrage profits on federal lending and borrowing rates.

Petitioner contends that § 514(c)(1)(C) attributes the indebtedness to the facilities because petitioner would not have been eligible for the loan but for the construction. Although petitioner is correct that the indebtedness *could not* have been incurred but for the construction, it does not follow that the indebtedness "*would not* have been incurred but for" the construction. *See* § 514(c)(1)(C) (emphasis added). In fact, the record shows that petitioner not only would not have incurred the debt for the construction, but that in fact it did not.

Conversely, the indebtedness must be attributed to the Treasury Notes, as it "would not have been incurred but for such acquisition." *See* § 514(c)(1)(B). Petitioner argues that because its primary motivation for taking the loan was to secure financing for future (and presumably tax-exempt) monetary needs, purchase of the Treasury Notes was not a "but for" cause of the indebtedness. Petitioner concedes that it drew on the loan only after deciding to invest the proceeds in Treasury Notes, however. Petitioner's additional motivations are irrelevant, as it incurred indebtedness with the intention of immediately investing it in Treasury Notes.

Petitioner's further contention that the Treasury Notes were purchased from general funds, not indebtedness, is unavailing. Petitioner cannot evade taxes by depositing funds in a bank account before forwarding them to their intended use. *See* 26 C.F.R. §1.514(c)-1(a)(2) (example 2) (providing that when working capital is reduced by a non-exempt investment, any indebtedness needed to restore working capital to the amount necessary to conduct tax-exempt operations is attributed to the non-exempt investment).

III.

Years after deciding that its construction projects did not require further federal financing, petitioner received federal funds at five percent interest and immediately invested them for more than nine percent interest. While such arbitrage is an excellent business opportunity, it is not exempt from federal taxation.

The decision of the Tax Court is AFFIRMED.

Gundersen Medical Foundation, Ltd. v. United States

536 F. Supp. 556 (W.D. Wis. 1982)

Opinion and Order

Facts

1. The plaintiff, Gundersen Medical Foundation Ltd. (the Foundation), is a nonstock corporation organized in 1944 . . . with its principal place of business in LaCrosse.

* * *

5.1 The exempt purpose of the Foundation is to provide programs of medical education at the technical, undergraduate, postgraduate and continuing medical education levels in LaCrosse, Wisconsin. It is also the purpose of the Foundation to sponsor medical research programs incident to and as a complement to its educational functions.

6. The Gundersen Clinic Ltd. (the Clinic) is a private corporation also located in LaCrosse, Wisconsin. The Clinic is not and never has been a tax-exempt organization.

7. The LaCrosse Lutheran Hospital (the Hospital) is an organization exempt from federal income taxes under section 501(c)(3) of the Code. The Hospital has a capacity of 350 beds.

8. The Foundation owns certain land and buildings in LaCrosse, Wisconsin. The real estate owned by the Foundation is adjacent to LaCrosse Lutheran Hospital.

9. In 1967 the Foundation expanded one of the buildings it owned which housed the Clinic. The cost of this expansion was primarily financed with funds borrowed from the Northwestern Mutual Life Insurance Company. . . .

10. For some time prior to and during the years in suit (1970–1974), the Foundation leased the facilities it owned to the Clinic. The facilities include both the building and the personal property . . . in the building.

11. The real estate and personal property are leased by the Foundation to the Clinic at fair market rental value. . . . The funds generated by the rental payments, after payment of expenses for the equipment and the mortgage, are used to support the Foundation's educational and research programs, and the payment of stipends to residents and interns.

12. The Internal Revenue Service determined that during the years in suit, a certain portion of the lease payments made to the Foundation by the Clinic was unrelated business income under sections 511 and 514 of the Code, and therefore taxable. That is, the position of the Service was that of the Foundation's income from the leased, debt-financed property, a certain portion was unrelated to the exempt function of the Foundation.

13. However, the Service excluded certain amounts of the lease payments from unrelated business income. That is, the Service conceded that a part of the use of the leased premises was substantially related to the Foundation's exempt function and purposes, namely, medical education and research. The percentage deemed to be so substantially related varied with each year in suit.

* * *

21. The entire bundle of medical activity engaged in by the medical staff of the Clinic throughout the building leased by the Foundation, and with the use of the equipment leased by the Foundation and located within the leased building, will be referred to as Bundle A. Included within Bundle A are two sub-classes of medical activity. Bundle A(1) consists of that medical activity engaged in by the medical staff of the Clinic, in which the students of the Foundation do not participate either as actors or observers. Bundle A(2) consists of that medical activity engaged in by the medical staff of the Clinic, in which the students of the Foundation do participate either as actors or as observers. In terms of diagnosis and treatment of patients and related activity, there is no difference in kind between the medical activity engaged in by the medical staff of the Clinic in Bundle A(1) and that in Bundle A(2).

The purpose of the Clinic in engaging in the medical activity by its staff in Bundle A(1) is profit-making. With respect to the medical activity of the Clinic staff in Bundle A(2), both profit-making and the promotion of the education of the students of the Foundation are purposes of the Clinic.

The exclusive purpose of the Foundation in arranging for its students to participate in Bundle A(2) is to provide programs of medical education . . . and to sponsor medical research programs incident to and as a complement to the Foundation's educational functions. With respect to the medical activity of the Clinic staff in Bundle A(1), the exclusive purpose of the Foundation is also the promotion of the education of its students, but only by indirection . . . Thus, the quality of the education received by the Foundation's students in the course of their participation in Bundle A(2) is enhanced by the medical activity of the Clinic staff in Bundle A(1). As to neither Bundle A(1) nor Bundle A(2) is profit-making a purpose of the Foundation.

The Foundation does not cause the happening of any part of the medical activity of the staff of the Clinic in Bundle A. The Foundation and the Clinic are both actors who cause the happening of the education of the Foundation's students in the course of their participation in the medical activity of the Clinic staff in Bundle A(2).

21.1 The education of the Foundation's students takes place throughout the facilities of the LaCrosse Lutheran Hospital and throughout the facilities leased by the Foundation to the Clinic. The Foundation's students' clinical education occurs in the course of treatment of patients who come to the Clinic and to LaCrosse Lutheran Hospital. Virtually every part of the facilities leased to the Clinic, including diagnostic, treatment, conference and office areas is used in the educational process, and the Foundation's students are excluded from no part of the facilities leased to the Clinic.

* * *

23. The large number of patients treated by the Clinic provides an unusual opportunity for medical education. . . .

24. The Foundation's programs make available a wide range of specialization and experience to its students. . . .

25. It would not be possible to accomplish the Foundation's exempt purpose of providing medical education in the LaCrosse area without the existence and operation of a large and sophisticated outpatient clinic treating hundreds of thousands of patients, such as the Gundersen Clinic. The Gundersen Clinic is the only one of this type in the LaCrosse area.

Opinion

Whether correct or incorrect, the theory upon which the United States assessed the deficiencies against the Foundation was comprehensible. That theory is summarized in the following paragraph.

As of 1970 through 1974, the Foundation was correctly classified as exempt from federal income tax as an organization described in section 501(c)(3) of the Code. Among the various purposes which may qualify organizations for exemption under section 501(c)(3), one is recognized in section 170(b)(1)(A) (ii), namely, the purpose of an educational organization which normally maintains a regular faculty and curriculum and normally has a regularly enrolled body of pupils or students in attendance at the place where its educational activities are regularly carried on. As of 1970 through 1974, the Foundation was correctly classified, also, as a section 170(b)(1)(A)(ii) educational organization. Under section 514(b)(1)(A)(ii) of the Code, the rent received by the Foundation from the Clinic was exempt from taxation to the extent that use of the leased real and personal property was substantially related (aside from the need of the Foundation for income or funds) to the exercise of the Foundation's section 170(b)(1)(A)(ii) educational purpose. The extent of the use so substantially related to that purpose was comparatively small. The balance of the rent was taxable to the Foundation as income.[5]

* * *

In its final post-trial brief, the United States contended the focus must be on the reason why the Foundation borrowed money from the Northwestern Mutual Life Insurance Company in about 1967 to expand one of the buildings and to purchase medical equipment. The United States argued: "The key issue, defendant submits is whether the debt resulting from the expansion of the facilities and the purchase of medical equipment was incurred to advance the profit motives of the Clinic or the non-profit purpose of the Foundation."

* * *

Foundation assumed to have been a Section 170(b)(1)(A)(ii) organization

The statutory framework (as of 1970 through 1974) is that a foundation organized and operated exclusively for an educational purpose (section 501(c) (3)) is generally exempt from taxation on its income (section 501(a)), but is nevertheless taxable on its unrelated business income (section 511(a)(1)). Unrelated business income means income from any unrelated trade or business regularly carried on by the foundation (section 512(a)). Unrelated trade or business, in turn, means any trade or business the conduct of which is not substantially related to the exercise or performance by the foundation of the educational purpose constituting the basis for its exemption (section 513(a)). The receipt of certain so-called "passive" forms of income, including rental income, is generally not taxable (section 512(b)(3)). However, if the property from which the rental income is realized is "debt-financed property," the rental income is taxable, unless the property is property "substantially all the use of which is substantially related (aside from the need of the organization for income or funds) to the exercise or performance by such organization of its ... educational ... purpose or function constituting the basis for its exemption under section 501. ..." Section 514(b)(1)(A)(i). If "substantially all the use" of such property is not so substantially related, the rental income from it is nevertheless free of taxation "to the extent that its use is so substantially related. ..." Section 514(b)(1)(A)(ii).

In the present case, for the years in question, the leased property was "debt-financed" in the sense that it was property which was held by the Foundation to produce income and with respect to which there was an acquisition indebtedness.

5. [2] The portion of the rental income determined by the Service to be exempt, classified year by year and as between real and personal property, is shown at finding number 13, above. For brevity, in this opinion I will use the determination for the 1970 real property rental: 22% exempt and 78% nonexempt.

Section 514(b)(1). But to the extent that its use was "substantially related (aside from the need of the (Foundation) for income or funds) to the exercise of its . . . educational . . . purpose or function," which constituted the basis for its exemption under sections 170(b)(1)(A)(ii), 501(c)(3), and 501(a), the property was not "debt-financed," and to that extent the rental income was not taxable.

As a section 170(b)(1)(A)(ii) organization, this Foundation's purpose or function was the purpose or function of an educational organization which normally maintains a regular faculty and curriculum and normally has a regularly enrolled body of pupils or students in attendance at the place where its educational activities are regularly carried on. Based upon the findings of fact I have made, above, substantially all the use of the leased real property and personal property was related to the exercise or performance by the Foundation of this section 170(b)(1)(A)(ii) purpose or function.

This is true whether the extent of such use is measured in time or in space. See Treas. Reg. 1.514(b)-1(b)(ii) and (iii). See, particularly, findings 21, 21.1, 23, and 25. . . .

However, it is not sufficient that the use was related to the exercise or performance by the Foundation of its exempt purpose or function. The use must have been substantially related. Treasury Regulations aid in defining substantiality. Section 1.514(b)-1(b)(1), which deals with debt-financed income, declares that guidance is to be found in regulations dealing with the definition of unrelated trade or business. That is, a trade or business in which the Foundation might engage directly is analogous, in this respect, to activities which might be engaged in by a lessee in debt-financed property leased by the Foundation. Treas. Reg. 1.513-1(d)(2) provides:

> Trade or business is "related" to exempt purposes, in the relevant sense, only where the conduct of the business activities has causal relationship to the achievement of exempt purposes (other than through the production of income); and it is "substantially related," for purposes of section 513, only if the causal relationship is a substantial one. Thus, for the conduct of trade or business from which a particular amount of gross income is derived to be substantially related to purposes for which exemption is granted, the production or distribution of the goods or the performance of the services from which the gross income is derived must contribute importantly to the accomplishment of those purposes. . . .

With respect to the use I have labeled as Bundle A(2) in finding 21—medical activity engaged in by the medical staff of the Clinic, in which the students of the Foundation participated either as actors or as observers-the relationship was surely substantial. These medical activities of the Clinic staff were a cause of the development of knowledge and skill among the students, and they were a substantial cause. They contributed importantly to the accomplishment of that purpose of the Foundation.

But with respect to the use I have labeled as Bundle A(1)—medical activity engaged in by the medical staff of the Clinic, in which the students of the Foundation did not participate-the question of substantiality is more difficult. The causative role of the Bundle A(1) activities was real: (a) increasing the skills of, adding breadth and depth to the knowledge of, the teachers; and (b) creating and maintaining a volume and variety of medical activity, a cross-section of which was educationally richer for the students than would have been a cross-section of a smaller, more familiar fare. While real, however, in both respects this causative role was indirect in its impingement on the education of the Foundation's students. . . .

The uncertainty with respect to the substantiality of the relationship between Bundle A(1) activities and the section 170(b)(1)(A)(ii) purpose and function of the Foundation is virtually completely removed, however, by reason of examples provided by Congress and the Treasury, and by Treasury rulings.

First, section 514(b)(1) of the Code provides:

> (Substantially) all the use of a property shall be considered to be substantially related to the exercise or performance by an organization of its . . . educational . . . purpose or function constituting the basis for its exemption under section 501 if such property is real property subject to a lease to a medical clinic entered into primarily for purposes which are substantially related (aside from the need of such organization for income or funds or the use it makes of the rents derived) to the exercise or performance by such organization of its . . . educational . . . purpose or function constituting the basis for its exemption under section 501.

The specificity of Congressional focus on leases by educational organizations to medical clinics is remarkable. . . . It is unlikely Congress supposed that the students of the lessor-educational organizations would play a role, either as participants or as observers, in every bit of the profit-making medical activity which would occur within the leased premises. Yet nowhere in this specific reference is there recognition of a need to compare Bundle A(1) to Bundle A(2), so to speak. The Congressional language is strongly suggestive that however dominant Bundle A(1) might be in a particular case, "substantially all the use of the property shall be considered substantially related. . . ."

This express Congressional guidance is echoed in Treas. Reg. 1.514(b)-1(c)(1), relating to leases of real property to medical clinics. The regulation provides an example:

> For example, assume that an exempt hospital leases all of its clinic space to an unincorporated association of physicians and surgeons who, by the provisions of the lease, agree to provide all of the hospital's out-patient medical and surgical services and to train all of the hospital's residents and interns. In this situation, the rents received by the hospital from this clinic are not to be treated as unrelated debt-financed income.

Obviously, it is a hospital rather than an educational foundation which is the lessor in the example, although the training of the hospital's residents and interns by the clinic staff is a close parallel to the training of the Gundersen Foundation's students by the Clinic staff. The truly persuasive point of the example, however, is that there is no qualification expressed concerning the total volume of the medical services provided by the clinic within the leased space, as compared with that portion which is responsive to the needs of the hospital's patients for out-patient medical and surgical services or that portion which is responsive to the hospital's need for training of its residents and interns. . . .

Rev. Rul. 464 involved facts resembling those in the example just quoted from Treas. Reg. 1-514(b)-1(c)(1). An exempt hospital leased an adjacent, recently-constructed, mortgaged office building to physicians who were members of the hospital's medical staff, so that the physicians could carry on their private medical practices in the leased building. The Service held that the rents received by the hospital were not unrelated business income. . . . The Service found no need to determine what portion of the total volume of medical services provided by the lessee-physicians within the leased space was rendered to patients of the hospital. . . .

Fortified by the Congressional language in section 514(b)(1) of the Code and by the administrative construction of the Code, I conclude that substantially all the use of the real and personal property . . . was substantially related to the exercise or performance by the Foundation of its educational function as a section 170(b)(1)(A)(ii) organization.

* * *

The "motives" test

It becomes obvious that the true contention of the United States must be that the test to be applied is not, after all, the presence or absence of a substantial relationship between the use made of the leased space and equipment, on the one hand, and the exempt purpose and function of the Foundation, on the other. The true contention of the United States is that the test to be applied is that stated in its final post-trial brief: "whether the debt . . . was incurred to advance the profit motives of the Clinic or the non-profit purpose of the Foundation." This formulation of the test sets abuzz a swarm of questions. It seems to accept that the Foundation was organized and operated exclusively for educational purposes (as it must accept that proposition in light of the position of the Service that the Foundation was a section 501(c)(3) foundation). But the inquiry is not to be directed to the nature of the use made of the leased space and equipment. Indeed, it is not the lease, but rather the mortgage loan, which is to be focused upon. It is not the terms of the mortgage loan, however, but rather the motives of some participant or participants in the loan transaction to which attention is to be directed. Perhaps the emphasis of government counsel on the motives for incurring the debt was inadvertent, and that what is meant is the motives for entering into the whole arrangement, including the mortgage loan and the lease. I will assume so.

* * *

Of course, in a given case, an apparently non-profit lessor-foundation may be in truth a profit-making alter ego of a profit-making lessee-clinic. The record here does not show that this Foundation was powerless to entertain a motive other than the motives of persons who controlled both the Foundation and the Clinic. No such finding has been requested by the United States. I have found as fact that this Foundation was governed by a board, a majority of whose members were not employed by the Clinic; and that the board was selected by a vote of members, a majority of whom were not employed by the Clinic. Moreover, a finding that the Foundation and Clinic were a single entity, sharing a single set of motives, would contradict the position of the United States in its November 2, 1979 revocation letter and its final post-trial brief: that the Foundation was organized and operated exclusively for educational purposes (Section 501(c)(3)) while the Clinic was not.

I conclude that the applicable test is the substantiality of the relationship between the use made of the leased property and the educational purpose or function constituting the basis for the Foundation's exemption under section 501(c)(3). Applying that test, I conclude that substantially all the use of the real and personal property leased by the Gundersen Foundation to the Clinic was substantially related to the exercise or performance by the Foundation of its educational function as a section 501(c)(3) organization. Section 514(b)(1)(A)(i). Specifically, I conclude that in terms of both time and space, more than 85% of the use of said property was substantially devoted to the exercise or performance by the Foundation of the said educational function. Treas. Reg. 1.514(b)-1(b)(1)(ii).

Order

It is ordered that judgment be entered granting plaintiff the relief sought in its complaint. Counsel for plaintiff are directed to submit a proposed form of judgment not later than April 23, 1982.

Note

There are, admittedly, many confusing aspects about *Gundersen Medical Foundation, Inc.* The opinion leads us to conclude that the confusion results from the government's last change in its substantive argument. However, we focus here on just one point. The court points out that if substantially all the use of property is substantially related to the organization's exempt purpose, then the property is not debt-financed property even though there is an outstanding acquisition indebtedness with respect to the property. In essence, the statute and regulations define "debt financed property" as much by the use of the property as they do by whether there was money borrowed to buy the property. The court implies that a better approach is to label the property in accordance with the debt — i.e., debt-financed — and then exempt the income because the use of the property is in furtherance of an exempt purpose.

The reason for the code and regulation approach seems related to the need to trace borrowed money through one or more pieces of property. "Acquisition indebtedness" is defined as debt that would not exist *but for* the acquisition of certain property. The debt need not be formally connected to that certain property. For example, if an organization borrows money to buy property, and substantially all of the property is used in a manner substantially related to an exempt purpose, the income will not be taxed. If the organization then sells the property for its full fair market value, but does not extinguish the debt using the proceeds instead to buy additional property the use of which is not related (or otherwise exempt from taxation under IRC § 514), the organization might be viewed from a substantive standpoint as engaging in the following four-step transaction:

1. Borrowing money
2. Buying exempt purpose property with a FMV equal to the amount of borrowed money
3. Selling the exempt purpose property for its FMV, but not paying the debt off
4. Buying more property with the money received, the use of which is not for an exempt purpose and which is not in any way encumbered by the original debt.

Ultimately, the second unrelated property could not have been purchased but for the original borrowing. The regulations, at 1.514(c)-1(a)(4), hold that the first piece of property is not debt-financed property because it is used in an exempt manner. But the second piece of property is debt financed because it is not used in an exempt manner *and* its acquisition was ultimately made possible by not repaying the original debt, though the original debt was incurred some time before the acquisition of the nonexempt property and related to a related use property.

It might, indeed, be less confusing if the Service followed the Court's implication (all leveraged property the acquisition of which was made possible by borrowing somewhere along the way, is debt-financed, though income from such property is exempt if the property is used in an exempt manner). After all, the Service's approach is merely a particularized application of the definition of "acquisition indebtedness" as debt (whether incurred before or after the acquisition of certain property, tangible or intangible) that would not have been incurred, or continue to exist, but for the acquisition of that certain property. *See* Treas. Reg. § 1.514(c)-1(a)(2), Example 3.

In Example 3, Regulation 1.514(c)-1(a)(2), the transaction is a different variation of our deconstructed substantive example:

1. Exempt organization sells property used exclusively in its exempt purpose for $1 million cash plus a $2 million note paying 10% interest.
2. The new owner of the previously exempt property pays interest on the note to the tax exempt organization. This interest is not taxed to the exempt organization.
3. The new owner uses the previously exempt property for a non-exempt purpose.
4. The exempt organization borrows $2.5 million to construct a new property. The new property will be used exclusively in the organization's exempt purpose.

Suddenly, after step four, there is debt-financed property and the organization incurs a tax liability with regard to the property it sold in step 1.

In the regulation example, the Service logically concludes that had the organization not acquired the mortgage note for the sale of the first property, it would not have had to borrow $2.5 million for purchase of the second property. Put another way, the acquisition of the note would not have been possible (in light of the organization's foreseeable needs) but for the subsequent, foreseeable borrowing. It may take a little time to see the logic in this brain teaser. The questions that follow are designed to help.

Planning Exercise

1. Your client, a § 501(c)(3) organization, operates a museum to exhibit the history of nuclear weapons. Anticipating the need for expansion, the museum would like to purchase 10 acres of land near its existing facility for future use. The price of the land is $1,000,000. The organization would like to borrow $600,000 for the purchase. During the period prior to expansion, it plans to lease the property to an unrelated parking facility. The law firm partner would like a list of issues raised by this acquisition. Please explain the options and tax consequences. In particular, the partner has asked you to find out whether the tract of land contains any buildings and, if so, what the organization plans to do with them. Why does the partner need to know this? What other facts do both you and the partner need to know to fully analyze the proposed transaction?

2. Your client, a private high school exempt under § 501(c)(3), has a large investment in mutual funds that earn dividends. The endowment is actually owned and controlled by a separate supporting organization (a § 509(a)(3) organization) controlled by the high school. The endowment includes monies donated and invested over the past five years as part of a building campaign in which the organizations raised money for a new gymnasium. The donations amounted to $2,000,000. The funds in which the entire $2,000,000 were invested are now worth $5,000,000. The entire endowment is worth $25,000,000. Rather than liquidating some of the mutual funds, the high school's Board decides to borrow $3,000,000 from First National Bank to build the gymnasium. One of the Board members is the President of FNB and was able to arrange a construction and permanent financing loan at 6.5% interest, which the Board considers a very good rate. In the year the high school borrows the $3,000,000 it also receives a 5% dividend of $250,000 on the mutual funds. What are the tax consequences?

C. Advanced Application: Leveraged Real Estate Partnerships

Internal Revenue Code § 514(c)(9) provides a complicated, limited, but very important exception to the definition of "acquisition indebtedness." Before considering its detail, it is helpful to understand the context in which it was enacted. The Tax Code is sometimes referred to as a complicated reflection of American values.

One such American value is property ownership. The Tax Code contains many tax benefits and exceptions based upon property ownership. Moreover, real estate is generally considered one of the safest of long-term investments available. Thus, certain charitable organizations—primarily large universities and pension plans—often seek to invest in leveraged (i.e., debt financed) real estate. The unrelated debt-financed rule distorts the normal economic decision to do so—the imposition of tax encourages the educational organization or pension fund to look for other, tax-free places in which to invest what are normally substantial endowments.

So it should come as no surprise that § 514(c)(9) excludes from the definition of "acquisition indebtedness" debt incurred by educational organizations (and their support organizations), exempt pension plans, and exempt title holding companies to acquire or improve real property. The acquisition or improvement of real property as an investment strategy is apparently of sufficient import that it is not to be impeded by the imposition of taxation. Recall, though, that the tax avoidance in *Clay Brown* revolved around a property transaction. To prevent the exception from reviving that tax avoidance, the exception is subject to several requirements that are best understood in light of *Clay Brown*.

First, the price for the acquisition or improvement of the real property must be fixed and determinable as of the date of the acquisition or completion of the improvement. The amount payable with respect to the indebtedness cannot be dependent upon revenues, income, or profit derived from the real property and the real property may not be subject to a lease-back, nor may financing be provided by the seller.

If the real property is held by a partnership, the exception will not apply unless the above requirements are met and all the partners are educational organizations described in § 170(b)(1)(A)(ii), exempt pension plans described in § 401, or title holding companies described in § 501(c)(25). If any of these partners have unrelated business income tax from any source, the exception will not apply. If not all the partners are educational organizations, pension plans, or title holding companies—or if one or more such partners is liable for UBIT—any indebtedness attaching to the real estate will be acquisition indebtedness with respect to all charitable partners (even those not otherwise liable for UBIT) unless all the allocations to the exempt partners are "qualified allocations."

It is relatively rare that a real estate investment partnership will be composed entirely of tax-exempt organizations, none of whom are liable for UBIT. Thus, this exception is of little use and the partnership might then try to qualify under the "qualified allocation" rule. A qualified allocation is one that allocates the same distributive share of income, gain, loss, deduction, or credit to the charitable organization during the entire time the organization is a partner, and meets the substantial economic effect test of § 704(b)(2). IRC § 514(c)(9)(E)(i). The problem, of course, is that the qualified allocation requirement—that allocations to exempt partners be identical throughout the life of the partnership—interferes with the flexibility and business realities that most partnerships need and face. Thus, the qualified allocation exception is also not feasible for most partnerships.

If a partnership has partners other than educational associations, exempt pension plans, or title holding companies (or one or more of such partners is liable for UBIT), and does not wish to, or cannot, comply with the qualified allocations rule, the charitable partners may still avoid unrelated debt-financed income with regard to leveraged real estate held by the partnership if all partnership allocations, beginning on the date the partnership holds leveraged real estate, meet both the fractions rule as well as the substantial economic effect test.

In essence, the fractions rule is a second substantial economic effect test imposed in an effort to prevent the shifting of income made possible by the fact that one or more partners have no tax liability (i.e., the partner is a "zero bracket" taxpayer). Indeed, the fractions rule regulations rival the substantial economic effect regulations with respect to complexity. Before getting to those regulations, consider the following example provided by a former Treasury official in support of the fractions rule:

> Assume that a taxable entity and [a] tax-exempt organization form a partnership to acquire property for $1 million, that all depreciation deductions are allocated to the taxable partner, and that any gain on the sale of the property is allocated to the taxable partner to the extent of his depreciation deductions and then divided equally between the partners. Assume that the property is sold after 20 years. Under current law, the partnership would be required to use 40-year straight line depreciation and thus the taxable partner would have taken depreciation deductions of $500,000 by the time of the sale. If 40-year straight line depreciation is an accurate measure of true economic depreciation, then in theory the building would be sold for $500,000 ($1 million less $500,000 depreciation) and no gain would be realized. In that case, the entire sales proceeds would be allocated to the tax-exempt partner and the taxable partner would have suffered a true economic loss of $500,000. In practice, however, because of inflation and because 40 years may not represent true economic depreciation for some buildings, the building could be expected to be sold for more than its basis. Thus, for example, if the building was sold for $1 million, the gain of $500,000 would be allocated to the taxable partner. In this case, the taxable partner would have received the benefit of deducting depreciation allowances in the early years which would be offset by gain deferred until the later years. Because there is a common expectation that real estate will not decline, in nominal value, the gain on the property will equal or exceed depreciation deductions.

Unrelated Business Income Tax: Hearings Before the Subcommittee on Oversight of the Committee on Ways and Means, House of Representatives, 100th Cong., 1st Sess. 31 (June 22, 1987) (Statement of O. Donaldson Chapoton, Deputy Assistant Secretary (Tax Policy), U.S. Department of Treasury) at page 2.

A note of explanation is in order with regard to the example. A partnership is tax-exempt (that is, no tax is actually imposed on a partnership), but the partners who engage in a trade or business via the partnership are taxable (unless the partners themselves are tax exempt). IRC § 701. The partnership generates items of income and deduction (such as depreciation) that "pass through" to the partners. IRC § 703-04. The partners pay taxes on their share of income earned by the partnership and claim a share of the deductible items incurred by the partnership. Because individual partners have differing tax attributes, allocations can be structured to shift tax benefits from one partner to another.

In the example above, the partners allocate all of the depreciation deductions to the taxable partner and this results in a shifting of tax benefit (depreciation deductions) to that party. The exempt partner is no worse off because it is a zero bracket taxpayer having no tax liability and therefore no need for any part of the depreciation deduction. This sort of tax shifting can be accomplished any time one partner has no tax liability (for example, if one partner is insolvent and the allocation relates to discharge of indebtedness income), or a lower tax rate than another partner.

By resort to a complicated set of "substantial economic effect" (SEE) regulations enacted under § 704, the Service can disregard an allocation, *inter alia*, if the allocation is made solely for tax avoidance purposes. In the example above, the allocation would not violate the SEE regulations because of certain presumptions.

The facts existing at the time the allocation scheme is adopted must be such as to allow a prediction that the allocation will have no effect on the economic arrangement between the parties, aside from the tax consequences. Treas. Reg. § 1.704-1(b)(2). We might assume, as did the example's author, that the property will appreciate in value resulting in a gain upon a later sale. Because the gain will be allocated back (i.e., "charged back") to the taxable partner to the extent of the prior depreciation deductions, the taxable partner will pay the same amount of tax whether the depreciation deductions are allocated equally (with a corresponding equal allocation of gain) or disproportionately as the parties have done (with a corresponding disproportionate allocation of gain). The sole benefit from the disproportionate allocation would be a tax benefit—i.e., the deferral of tax liability for some number of years. Thus, the allocation shifts income (i.e., income is increased to the tax-exempt partner in the early years because that partner claims no depreciation deduction) and has no effect on the economics between the parties.

Nevertheless, the SEE regulations create a presumption that the property will actually decrease in value by an amount equal to the depreciation. Treas. Reg. § 1.704-1(b)(2)(iii)(c). Thus, we cannot assume at the time the allocation scheme is adopted that there will be a sufficient amount of gain to charge back to the taxable party. Instead, we must assume that the taxable party will suffer an economic loss. Thus, the allocation is respected even though we know better!

Internal Revenue Code § 514(c)(9), implemented by the regulations at § 1.514(c)-2, is designed to thwart the assignment of income that the substantial economic effect rule allows. The following excerpt explains the basic workings of the rule. After the excerpt, we will return to the example above to see whether the rule works.

William B. Holloway, Jr., Structuring Real Estate Investment Partnerships with Tax-Exempt Investors

87 Tax Notes 1517 (2000)

II. Summary of UBTI

* * *

C. Real Estate Exception — *Section 514(c)(9)*

Section 514(c)(9) . . . provides an exception from the debt-financed property rule for the acquisition and improvement of real property (the "Real Estate Exception"). This exception allows a tax-exempt entity to debt-finance real property and not be subject to UBTI with respect to the income earned from such real property if the tax-exempt entity is a qualified organization and certain other requirements are met. A qualified organization ("QO") is (i) a qualified trust under section 401 (i.e., a pension or profit-sharing plan), (ii) an educational organization meeting certain requirements under section 170(b)(1)(A)(ii) and its affiliated support organizations, and (iii) a title-holding company exempt from tax under section 501(c)(25).

* * *

III. The Disproportionate Allocation Rule

A. Background

Congress added section 514(c)(9)(E) in 1988 for the purpose of preventing the use of partnerships to permanently or temporarily transfer tax benefits from tax-exempt partners to taxable partners under the Real Estate Exception. The IRS subsequently issued Notice 90-41 and final regulations on May 11, 1994. No guidance after the final regulations exists with respect to section 514(c)(9)(E).

B. Summary of the Rule

While some people refer to section 514(c)(9)(E) as the "Fractions Rule," a more correct reference is to the Disproportionate Allocation Rule. In fact, referring to it as the "Fractions Rule" is technically incorrect since section 514(c)(9)(E) requires the compliance with two requirements — the Fractions Rule Requirement and the Substantial Economic Effect Requirement. In general, the Fractions Rule Requirement requires that a QO never receive an allocation of overall partnership income greater than its smallest share of overall partnership loss. On the other hand, the Substantial Economic Effect Requirement requires all partnership allocations to have substantial economic effect under section 704(b)(2). While deceptively simple at first glance, these two requirements provide a formable challenge to all who struggle with them, even in the simplest of cases.

C. Fractions Rule Requirements

The first requirement for complying with the Disproportionate Allocation Rule is the fractions rule requirement (the "Fractions Rule Requirement"). The Fractions Rule Requirement requires a partnership to establish that the allocation of items to a QO partner cannot result in that QO partner having a percentage share of overall partnership income for any tax year greater than that QO partner's "fractions rule percentage." A QO partner's fraction rule percentage is the QO partner's percentage share of overall partnership loss for the tax year for which that QO partner's percentage loss share will be the smallest. Thus, the Fractions Rule Requirement requires that a QO partner never be allocated a percentage share of "overall partnership income" for any tax year greater than that QO partner's lowest percentage share of "overall partnership loss" for any tax year.

> Example 2: Fractions Rule Percentage. QO and TP form a partnership in which QO receives an allocation of overall partnership loss of 30 percent for year 1, 25 percent for year 2, and 20 percent for year 3 and thereafter. QO's fraction rule percentage is 20 percent; thus, QO can never be allocated more than 20 percent of overall partnership income in any tax year if the partnership intends to meet the Fractions Rule Requirement.

The Fractions Rule Requirement must be satisfied not only on an actual basis for each tax year of the partnership commencing with the first tax year of the partnership in which the partnership holds debt-financed real property and has a QO as a partner, but also on a prospective basis. Thus, in cases other than the temporary exclusions discussed in Section III.C.1.b. of this report and subsequent changes to the partnership agreement that result in violations of the Fractions Rule Requirement, a failure to comply with the Fractions Rule Requirement for any tax year after the partnership holds debt-financed real property and has a QO as a partner causes the partnership to be unable to use the Real Estate Exception to the debt-financed property rule for any tax year of its existence. This draconian cliff effect is further amplified by the fact that the Fractions Rule Requirement is applied on an overall partnership basis. Thus, if partnership allocations to one QO fail to satisfy the Fractions Rule Requirement, that QO partner and all other QO partners in the partnership will be subject to the debt-financed property rule, even if the allocations to those other QO partners would otherwise have complied with the Fractions Rule Requirement.

1. Overall partnership income and loss. Because of the prospective application of the Fractions Rule Requirement, it is imperative to fully understand what constitutes "overall partnership income" and "overall partnership loss." Overall partnership income is the amount by which the aggregate items of partnership income and gain for the tax year exceed the aggregate items of partnership loss and deduction for the year. Conversely, overall partnership loss is the amount by which the aggregate items of partnership loss and deduction for the tax year exceed the aggregate items of partnership income and gain for the year. In general, a partnership includes those items of income, gain, loss, and deduction (including expenditures described

in section 705(a)(2)(B)) that increase or decrease partners' capital accounts under Treasury regulation section 1.704-1(b)(2)(iv) in computing overall partnership income and loss. Tax items allocable under section 704(c) or with respect to revaluations of property under Treasury regulation section 1.704-1(b)(2)(iv)(f)(4), however, are not included in computing overall partnership income or loss, although they may be relevant in applying the antiabuse rules.

While the Treasury regulations broadly define overall partnership income and loss, the Treasury regulations also reduce the breadth of the definition by excluding numerous allocations from the computation of overall partnership income and loss. Some of these exclusions apply during the entire life of the partnership, while others apply only until an actual allocation is made.

* * *

Let's see how IRC § 514(c)(9) would apply to the example discussed above. Assume that in addition to a $25,000 depreciation deduction each year ($1,000,000 divided by 40-year useful life), the partnership also incurs deductible expenses of $25,000 during each of the first ten years. It has no income or gain for the first four years. The partnership's overall loss in year one through four is therefore $50,000 (the excess of loss and deduction over income and gain). Treas. Reg. 1.514(c)-2(c)(1).

In years four through ten the partnership earns $60,000 per year from the building. After taking into account its expenses and depreciation ($50,000) for those years, the partnership has overall partnership income of $10,000. Assume also that all items other than depreciation are allocated equally. Thus, the exempt partner's "fraction rule percentage" is 25% since of the $50,000 overall partnership loss, only $12,500 (one half the deductible expenses, or 25% of overall partnership loss) is allocated to the exempt partner.

The fractions rule states that beginning in the year that the partnership has leveraged real estate, an allocation to an exempt partner cannot result in that partner receiving more than 25% of overall partnership income. In years four through ten, when the exempt organization is allocated $30,000 (50%) of the partnership's gross income of $60,000, and $12,500 of the deductible expenses (for a net $17,500 income allocation) the partnership will violate the fractions rule because the allocation results in the exempt partner having a greater than 25% share of the overall partnership income. All allocations of income from the building—not just those in the profitable years—will therefore result in unrelated debt-financed income to the exempt partner. In effect, the government recoups from the exempt partner the tax avoided by the taxable partner.

Chapter 30

Special UBIT Rules for Membership Organizations

A. Introduction

CODE: § 512(d)

The exemption of member organizations, such as labor unions, presumes that the main source of revenues for such organizations — dues — are not to be taxed. This presumption provides opportunity for tax avoidance by allowing member organizations to, in effect, sell unrelated goods and services while labeling the price thereof "dues." In the late 1980s and early 1990s the Service caught wind of these schemes and began to question whether persons receiving such goods or services were really "members" or were simply the organizations' customers with respect to unrelated transactions. In a series of cases, the Service successfully swept aside the form — "dues paid for member benefits" — and imposed tax consequences on the substance — the unrelated sale of goods and services to ordinary customers.

Unrelated Business Taxable Income of Labor Organizations

Rev. Proc. 95-21
1995-1 C.B. 686

Sec. 1. Purpose

The purpose of this revenue procedure is to establish when associate member dues payments received by an organization described in section 501(c)(5) will be treated by the Service as gross income from the conduct of an unrelated trade or business under section 512.

Sec. 2. Background

An organization exempt from tax under section 501(a) as an organization described in section 501(c)(5) is subject to the unrelated business income tax imposed by section 511(a). Section 501(c)(5) organizations often receive dues payments not only from members that are accorded full privileges in voting for the directors of the organization but also from associate members that are accorded less than full or no voting privileges. Whether associate member dues payments are treated as gross income from the conduct of an unrelated trade or business under section 512 is determined in accordance with the following section.

Sec. 3. Treatment of Associate Member Dues Payments

The Service will not treat dues payments from associate members as gross income from the conduct of an unrelated trade or business unless, for the relevant period, the associate member category has been formed or availed of for the principal purpose of producing unrelated business income. For purposes of this revenue procedure, unrelated business income is income from the sale of, or the provision of access to, goods or services produced by an activity which constitutes a trade or business, regularly carried on, and not substantially related to the organization's exempt purposes other than through the production of income. Consequently, other than where the statute or regulations specifically provide a method of allocating a portion of dues payments to unrelated business taxable income, the Service will treat dues payments from associate members as not including gross income from an unrelated trade or business if the associate member category has been formed or availed of for the principal purpose of furthering the organization's exempt purposes.

In applying this revenue procedure, the Service will look to the purposes and activities of the organization rather than of its members.

National League of Postmasters of the United States v. Commissioner

86 F.3d 59 (4th Cir. 1996)

Lay, Senior Circuit Judge:

The National League of Postmasters ("the League") is a tax-exempt labor organization under 26 U.S.C. § 501(c)(5). The Commissioner determined deficiencies in the League's federal income taxes from 1987 to 1990 on the basis that dues and service fees the League received in relation to certain members, known as "League Benefit Members" ("LBMs"), were not "substantially related" to any of the League's tax-exempt purposes. See 26 U.S.C. § 513(a). The Tax Court upheld the Commissioner. We affirm.

Factual Background

In August of 1987, the League formed a new class of membership called "League Benefit Members" ("LBMs"). The League maintains that the dues and service charges related to LBMs, unlike a former class of membership, "Limited Benefit Members," are tax-exempt. From 1987 to 1990, LBMs received several benefits, including access to the League's health insurance plan; a quarterly newsletter; certain employment-related group legal services (if the member did not otherwise have access to binding arbitration); and the right to participate in the League's travel, credit card, eyewear, and long-term care insurance programs. At the same time, the League expanded the focus of its legislative and administrative lobbying from issues related solely to postal services to include issues concerning "the overall working conditions and retirement benefits of all Members." J.A. 7-78. In addition, the League provided that the new class of LBMs, who accounted for roughly half of the League's total membership, could elect one member to the League's executive board, otherwise composed of nine active postmasters. The elected LBM representative was also the only LBM delegate out of five hundred total delegates to the League's annual national convention. Before the Tax Court, the League stipulated that its activities with respect to the LBMs constituted a "trade or business" and were "regularly carried on" during the years in question. See 26 U.S.C. § 512(a)(1). The Commissioner stipulated that income from the League's activities with respect to the other members, essentially active and retired postmasters, was tax exempt. Thus, the only issue presented in this case is whether the League conducted its activities with respect to LBMs in a manner "substantially related" to the League's tax-exempt purposes such that the income derived from those activities is tax exempt. See 26 U.S.C. § 513(a).

Discussion

* * *

The League's tax-exempt purposes are defined in part by regulation, which provides that a tax-exempt labor organization must have as its object "the betterment of the conditions" of those engaged in labor. See 26 C.F.R. § 1.501(c)(5)-1(a)(2). In addition, as the District of Columbia Circuit did in *American Postal Workers Union v. United States*, 925 F.2d 480, 482, 288 U.S. App. D.C. 249 (D.C. Cir. 1991), we also look to the League's articles of incorporation, which define the League's purposes as follows:

> Section 1. Provide a vehicle through which members may assist one another in matters connected with their career employment in the United States Postal Service;
>
> Section 2. Advance the proficiency of personnel in providing postal service promptly, reliably and efficiently to individuals and businesses in all areas of the nation;
>
> Section 3. Consult with the management of the United States Postal Service on policies which concern the welfare, happiness and morale of employees;
>
> Section 4. Improve the conditions under which individual members work, having concern for salaries, hours of employment, working environment, adjustment of grievances and labor disputes;
>
> Section 5. Cooperate with other groups and levels of postal management in the achievement of common goals;
>
> Section 6. Encourage contact among members in social, operational and professional relationships; and
>
> Section 7. Engage in any other activity not inconsistent with the laws of the District of Columbia.

The League contends that Section 4 of its statement of purpose—"improve the conditions under which individual members work, having concern for salaries, hours of employment, working environment, adjustment of grievances and labor disputes" — is sufficiently broad to cover non-postal federal employees. We find, however, that the League's articles, as the League's name suggests, reflect an overriding purpose to improve the working conditions of postmasters, and, to a lesser extent, other postal employees. The statement of purpose fails to provide for the betterment of conditions for all federal employees. It is patently clear that the articles as a whole focus on postmasters and other postal employees. Under basic principles of construction, the general words in Section 4 apply only to those of the same class (postal workers) as set forth in the other sections. However, assuming that Section 4 can be read to encompass all federal employee members, and that it thus constitutes a valid tax-exempt purpose, we nonetheless find the League's activities in regard to LBMs not substantially related to any such purpose.

First, we deem it highly dubious that the League's generalized provision of health insurance benefits to federal employee members, including retired federal employees, is substantially related to improving the working conditions of LBMs. The Commissioner has allowed tax-exempt treatment for the provision of health insurance to a labor organization's members. See Rev. Rul. 62-17, 1962-1 C.B. 87, 87–88. In the present case, however, the Tax Court found the provision of health insurance was not substantially related to the League's exempt purposes because the League marketed the health insurance in a commercial manner, much like competitor for-profit health plans, and the health plan was available to retired federal employees who had not been members of the League prior to retirement. In such circumstances, the Tax Court found the health benefits were not substantially related to improving the working conditions of LBMs.

Moreover, it is now clear that the "provision of insurance benefits to persons who are not members in any other sense cannot be substantially related to a [labor organization's] tax-exempt purposes." In distinguishing American Postal Workers and Postal Supervisors, the League contends the overall bundle of benefits provided to LBMs — group legal services, communications, lobbying, and voting rights — made them bona fide League members. As such, the League argues, their dues should be tax-exempt. We disagree.

Although it is possible that LBMs joined the League for reasons other than to obtain access to the League's health insurance plan, the League failed to show how many LBMs opted not to participate in the League's health plan. In light of the history of LBMs, as the offspring of the Limited Benefit Members whose sole benefit was the League's health plan, supra, it was incumbent upon the League to show that LBMs acted as bona fide League members in some manner more substantial than as health benefit purchasers. . . . Without such a showing by the League, the Commissioner could reasonably suspect that the League was evading the Commissioner's earlier decision to tax the dues and service fees of so-called "members" whose only membership benefit was health insurance. . . .

Moreover, we think the Tax Court properly found the other benefits in the League's bundle of benefits were not substantially related to the League's tax-exempt purposes of improving the working conditions of the League's members.... First, the Tax Court found that although some LBMs obtained assistance in employment-related disputes through the group legal services contract, it was of no value to many LBMs who either were retired, and thus had no need for employment-related legal assistance, or were covered by binding arbitration agreements, and thus were ineligible for the League's group legal services. Second, the Tax Court found the League's newsletter for LBMs was used primarily as an advertisement for the health and other commercial benefits available to LBMs, rather than as a means to communicate important labor news to federal employee members.... Third, the Tax Court found any lobbying on issues of concern to federal employees was either incidental to its lobbying efforts on behalf of postmasters or otherwise too generalized to constitute a substantial relationship to the working conditions of LBMs.... Fourth, the Tax Court found the limited voting rights provided to the LBMs were effectively diluted by other changes in voting which maintained the power of postmasters to control the League's agenda. Upon our review of the record, we find no error in the Tax Court's findings.

The League argues, however, that the Tax Court erred by examining whether its activities actually improved the working conditions of LBMs in some tangible, quantitative manner rather than whether its activities were designed to improve the working conditions of LBMs or were consistent with such a purpose. Under the regulations, a taxpayer must show that an organization's income-generating activities have a substantial "causal relationship to the achievement of exempt purposes" or "contribute importantly to the accomplishment of those purposes." 26 C.F.R. § 1.513-1(d)(2) (emphasis added). Thus, to the extent that the Tax Court looked for evidence of actual improvement in the working conditions of LBMs, we think such an inquiry was proper....

Under these circumstances, the Tax Court properly found the dues of LBMs and related service charges not substantially related to any of the League's tax-exempt purposes, and we affirm the Tax Court's decision.

AFFIRMED.

Note on Small Dues

Shortly after the Service issued Revenue Procedure 95-21, Congress enacted § 512(d). Section 512(d) provides that if a 501(c)(5) charges membership dues that do not exceed an inflation-adjusted $100, then in "no event shall any portion of such dues be treated as derived by such organization from an unrelated trade or business by reason of any benefits or privileges to which members of such organization are entitled." *See* IRC § 512(d). The inflation adjusted amount for 2020 is $171. In Revenue Procedure 97-12, the Service explains that "if required annual dues exceed [the inflation adjusted amount] per member, the entire dues payment will be subject to the principles of Rev. Proc. 95-21." *See* Rev. Proc. 97-12, 1997-1 C.B. 631.

Questions

1. Are the revenues from the associate members received under the circumstances described below derived from an unrelated trade or business?

> Labor is recognized as exempt from federal income tax as a Labor Union described in § 501(c)(5) of the Code. Labor was established to: (1) promote the interest and welfare of its members, (2) raise the standards of the plumbing industry, (3) foster a cooperative spirit between Labor and plumbing suppliers, and (4) represent members in their contacts with local, state, and national governments. Labor states that to accomplish these purposes, it: (a) periodically sponsors institutes and seminars designed to aid its members in keeping abreast of recent innovations as well as improving their businesses and assuring future success; (b) gives status reports on legislation and proposed changes in existing laws that might affect members' jobs, at both state and federal levels, and assistance in dealing with special problems or situations with individual departments, bureaus, or officials in state and federal government; (c) sponsors two membership meetings a year to hear speakers, to meet with industry representatives, and to get to know fellow members on a business and social level; (d) publishes a monthly bulletin containing industry news, changes in regulations and legislation, and information of general interest; and (e) endorses a group insurance, life and major medical for both owners and employees, and insurance for property, liability, and Worker's Compensation.
>
> The revision of Labor's bylaws under which it was operating during the majority of the year under examination provides that active membership is limited to persons engaged in the plumbing trade. The bylaws also provide that associate membership is open to all persons, firms, and corporations engaged in the transportation of plumbing products, and to plumbing equipment manufacturers, dealers, and representatives. The bylaws specifically state that associate members shall be extended all privileges of Labor except to vote at regular or special meetings, to hold office, and to attend business meetings. The bylaws were amended during the year in question, among other matters, to state specifically that associate members shall be extended all privileges of membership, including attendance at business meetings, except the privilege to hold office and to vote.
>
> Labor states that during the year under examination, approximately 33 percent of its members were associate members, and that it has a very stable membership base; Labor has a retention rate of 90 percent among its associate members. Although there is no restriction on associate members being on one or more of the seven standing committees, only approximately five percent of the committee members were associate members for the year under examination. The attendance roster for Labor's fall convention in that year shows that approximately 25 percent of the attendees were

associate members. Approximately 20 percent of the exhibitors at that convention were associate members.

Labor also states:

> Since plumbers are our regular members and suppliers are our associate members, it can be readily seen that from our founding, Labor has considered that one of our principal purposes is to promote good working relationships between regular members and associate members. This we try to accomplish by encouraging our associate members to participate in Labor activities such as our conventions, our trade show, and as members of our standing committees and ad hoc committees that we create from time to time for specific purposes. One of the reasons for having a diverse associate membership is that it gives the Labor staff an opportunity to become well acquainted with the principals of firms in various fields whom we can depend upon to provide quality products and services.... it is always our goal with every associate member to encourage their participation in Labor activities to the maximum extent possible.

Labor's active members pay dues on a sliding scale with 11 gradations, based on the annual sales of the member's individual business. The amounts range from a low of $100.00 (for organizations with less than a certain amount in annual sales), to $1,000.00 (for organizations with more than a certain amount in annual sales). Labor's associate membership dues are a particular amount (less than the third lowest gradation of active membership dues) for certain major organizations and an amount equal to the second lowest gradation of active membership dues for all other associate members. For the year under examination, associate member dues constituted less than 20 percent of the total membership dues. Other income items for that year consisted of program service revenue (conventions and seminars), promotional rebates and reimbursements, interest on savings, and gross amount from sale of assets. Labor's income from interest on savings that year was more than Labor's income from associate member dues.

Labor states that, for the most part, the only matter on which regular votes are taken is the annual election of officers and directors at the yearly fall conventions. Labor states that these votes are made by voice, and because both active and associate members are present at these meetings, Labor has no way of knowing whether associate members were voting or not. In an exception to this general practice, during the fall convention in the year under examination, Labor's members also voted on changes in the Articles of Incorporation and the bylaws. In this matter, in addition to the voice vote, Labor also conducted a mail ballot for all regular members not in attendance at the convention, at the direction of Labor's legal counsel.

Labor's correspondence file for the year under examination contains several requests concerning the availability of Labor's mailing/membership list. Labor's standard response was that the membership list was not for sale, but that a copy could be obtained by becoming an associate member; a folder describing Labor's major functions, which included a membership application, was sent with the response. The membership application folder does not differentiate between active and associate members (except to show the dues structure and to state the fact that active members are automatically members of a national federation), and states that Labor's benefits include education, insurance, government liaison, two membership meetings a year (the Spring convention and the annual meeting in the fall), and bulletins.

One of Labor's correspondence file responses stated that Labor did not accept paid advertising in its monthly publication; it also stated that Labor published free classified advertising and public information articles for members each month. During the year under examination, the free classified advertising in each of the 12 bulletins comprised five percent or less in the majority of the individual bulletins and never comprised more than nine percent.

Labor states that the health insurance plan that it endorses for its regular members is not available to most of its associate members because the carrier solicits business primarily from plumbers and not suppliers.

2. Does Labor's making available its mailing lists solely to members, including associate members raise any issues with regard to whether Labor is entitled to continued tax exemption?

B. Unrelated Business Taxable Income of Social Clubs

CODE: § 512(a)(3)

Portland Golf Club v. Commissioner of Internal Revenue

497 U.S. 154 (1990)

JUSTICE BLACKMUN delivered the opinion of the Court.

This case requires us to determine the circumstances under which a social club, in calculating its liability for federal income tax, may offset losses incurred in selling food and drink to nonmembers against the income realized from its investments.

Petitioner Portland Golf Club is a nonprofit Oregon corporation, most of whose income is exempt from federal income tax under § 501(c)(7) of the Internal Revenue Code of 1954, 26 U.S.C. § 501(c)(7). Since 1914 petitioner has owned and operated a private golf and country club with a golf course, restaurant and bar, swimming pool, and tennis courts. The great part of petitioner's income is derived from membership dues and other receipts from the club's members; that income is exempt from tax. Portland Golf also has two sources of nonexempt "unrelated business taxable income": sales of food and drink to nonmembers, and return on its investments.

... Petitioner received investment income in the form of interest in the amount of $11,752 for fiscal 1980 and in the amount of $21,414 for fiscal 1981. It sustained net losses of $28,433 for fiscal 1980 and $69,608 for fiscal 1981 on sales of food and drink to nonmembers. Petitioner offset these losses against the earnings from its investments and therefore reported no unrelated business taxable income for the two tax years. In computing these losses, petitioner identified two different categories of expenses incurred in selling food and drink to nonmembers. First, petitioner incurred *variable* (or direct) expenses, such as the cost of food, which varied depending on the amount of food and beverages sold (and therefore would not have been incurred had no sales to nonmembers been made). For each year in question, petitioner's gross income from nonmember sales exceeded these variable costs. Petitioner also included as an unrelated business expense a portion of the *fixed* (or indirect) overhead expenses of the club — expenses which would have been incurred whether or not petitioner had made sales to nonmembers. In determining what portions of its fixed expenses were attributable to nonmember sales, petitioner employed an allocation formula, described as the "gross-to-gross method," based on the ratio that nonmember sales bore to total sales. When fixed expenses, so calculated, were added to petitioner's variable costs, the total exceeded Portland Golf's gross income from nonmember sales.

On audit, the Commissioner took the position that petitioner could deduct expenses associated with nonmember sales up to the amount of receipts from the sales themselves, but that it could not use losses from those activities to offset its investment income. The Commissioner based that conclusion on the belief that a profit motive was required if losses from these activities were to be used to offset income from other sources, and that Portland Golf had failed to show that its sales to nonmembers were undertaken with an intent to profit. The Commissioner therefore determined deficiencies of $1,828 for 1980 and $3,470 for 1981; these deficiencies reflected tax owed on petitioner's investment income.

Portland Golf sought redetermination in the Tax Court. That court ruled in petitioner's favor. The court assumed, without deciding, that losses incurred in the course of sales to nonmembers could be used to offset other nonexempt income only if the sales were undertaken with an intent to profit. The court, however, held that Portland Golf had adequately demonstrated a profit motive, since its gross receipts from sales to nonmembers consistently exceeded the variable costs associated with those activities. The court therefore held that "petitioner is entitled to offset its unrelated business taxable income from interest by its loss from its nonmember food and beverage sales computed by allocating a portion of its fixed expenses to the nonmember food and beverage sales activity in a manner which respondent agrees is acceptable."

The United States Court of Appeals for the Ninth Circuit remanded. The Court of Appeals held that the Tax Court had applied an incorrect legal standard in determining that Portland Golf had demonstrated an intent to profit from sales to nonmembers. The appellate court relied on its decision in *North Ridge Country Club v. Commissioner*, 877 F.2d 750 (1989), where it had ruled that a social club "can properly deduct losses from a non-member activity only if it undertakes that activity with the intent to profit, where profit means the production of gains in excess of all direct and indirect costs." *Id.*, at 756. The same court in the present case concluded: "Because Portland Golf Club could have reported gains in excess of direct and indirect costs, but did not do so, relying on a method of allocation stipulated to be reasonable by the Commissioner, we REMAND this case to the tax court for a determination of whether Portland Golf Club engaged in its non-member activities with the intent required under *North Ridge* to deduct its losses from those activities." Because of a perceived conflict with the decision of the Sixth Circuit in *Cleveland Athletic Club, Inc. v. United States*, 779 F.2d 1160 (1985), and because of the importance of the issue, we granted certiorari. 493 U.S. 1041 (1990).

II

Virtually all tax-exempt business organizations are required to pay federal income tax on their "unrelated business taxable income." The law governing social clubs, however, is significantly different from that governing other tax-exempt entities. As to exempt organizations other than social clubs, the Code defines "unrelated business taxable income" as "the gross income derived by any organization from any unrelated trade or business (as defined in section 513) regularly carried on by it, less the deductions allowed by this chapter which are directly connected with the carrying on of such trade or business." 26 U.S.C. § 512(a)(1). As to social clubs, however, "unrelated business taxable income" is defined as "the gross income (excluding any exempt function income), less the deductions allowed by this chapter which are directly connected with the production of the gross income (excluding exempt function income)." § 512(a)(3)(A). The salient point is that § 512(a)(1) (which applies to most exempt organizations) limits "unrelated business taxable income" to income derived from a "trade or business," while § 512(a)(3)(A) (which applies to social clubs) contains no such limitation. Thus, a social club's investment income is subject to federal income tax, while the investment income of most other exempt organizations is not.

This distinction reflects the fact that a social club's exemption from federal income tax has a justification fundamentally different from that which underlies the grant of tax exemptions to other nonprofit entities. For most such organizations, exemption from federal income tax is intended to encourage the provision of services that are deemed socially beneficial. Taxes are levied on "unrelated business income" only in order to prevent tax-exempt organizations from gaining an unfair advantage over competing commercial enterprises.... Since Congress concluded that investors reaping tax-exempt income from passive sources would not be in competition with commercial businesses, it excluded from tax the investment income realized by exempt organizations.

The exemption for social clubs rests on a totally different premise. Social clubs are exempted from tax not as a means of conferring tax *advantages*, but as a means of ensuring that the members are not subject to tax *disadvantages* as a consequence of their decision to pool their resources for the purchase of social or recreational services. The Senate Report accompanying the Tax Reform Act of 1969, 83 Stat. 536, explained that that purpose does not justify a tax exemption for income derived from investments:

> Since the tax exemption for social clubs and other groups is designed to allow individuals to join together to provide recreational or social facilities or other benefits on a mutual basis, without tax consequences, the tax exemption operates properly only when the sources of income of the organization are limited to receipts from the membership. Under such circumstances, the individual is in substantially the same position as if he had spent his income on pleasure or recreation (or other benefits) without the intervening separate organization. However, where the organization receives income from sources outside the membership, such as income from investments . . . upon which no tax is paid, the membership receives a benefit not contemplated by the exemption in that untaxed dollars can be used by the organization to provide pleasure or recreation (or other benefits) to its membership. . . . In such a case, the exemption is no longer simply allowing individuals to join together for recreation or pleasure without tax consequences. Rather, it is bestowing a substantial additional advantage to the members of the club by allowing tax-free dollars to be used for their personal recreational or pleasure purposes. The extension of the exemption to such investment income is, therefore, a distortion of its purpose.

S. Rep. No. 91-552, p. 71 (1969).

In the Tax Reform Act of 1969, Congress extended the tax on "unrelated business income" to social clubs. As to these organizations, however, Congress defined "unrelated business taxable income" to include income derived from investments. Our review of the present case must therefore be informed by two central facts. First, Congress intended that the investment income of social clubs should be subject to federal tax, and indeed Congress devised a definition of "unrelated business taxable income" with that purpose in mind. Second, the statutory scheme for the taxation of social clubs was intended to achieve tax *neutrality*, not to provide these clubs a tax advantage: Even the exemption for income derived from members' payments was designed to ensure that members are not disadvantaged as compared with persons who pursue recreation through private purchases rather than through the medium of an organization.

III

Petitioner's principal argument is that it may deduct losses incurred through sales to nonmembers without demonstrating that these sales were motivated by an intent to profit. In the alternative, petitioner contends (and the Tax Court agreed) that if the Code does impose a profit-motive requirement, then that requirement has been satisfied in this case. We address these arguments in turn.

A

We agree with the Commissioner and the Court of Appeals that petitioner may use losses incurred in sales to nonmembers to offset investment income only if those sales were motivated by an intent to profit. The statute provides that, as to social clubs, "the term 'unrelated business taxable income' means the gross income (excluding any exempt function income), less the deductions *allowed by this chapter* which are directly connected with the production of the gross income (excluding exempt function income)." § 512(a)(3)(A) (emphasis added). As petitioner concedes, the italicized language limits deductions from unrelated business income to expenses allowable as deductions under Chapter 1 of the Code. In our view, the deductions claimed in this case—expenses for food, payroll, and overhead in excess of gross receipts from nonmember sales—are allowable, if at all, only under § 162 of the Code.... Section 162(a) provides a deduction for "all the ordinary and necessary expenses paid or incurred during the taxable year in carrying on any trade or business." Although the statute does not expressly require that a "trade or business" must be carried on with an intent to profit, this Court has ruled that a taxpayer's activities fall within the scope of § 162 only if an intent to profit has been shown.... Thus, the losses that Portland Golf incurred in selling food and drink to nonmembers will constitute "deductions allowed by this chapter" only if the club's nonmember sales were performed with an intent to profit.

* * *

We see no basis for dispensing with the profit-motive requirement in the present case. Indeed, such an exemption would be in considerable tension with the statutory scheme devised by Congress to govern the taxation of social clubs. Congress intended that the investment income of social clubs (unlike the investment income of most other exempt organizations) should be subject to the same tax consequences as the investment income of any other taxpayer. To allow such an offset for social clubs would run counter to the principle of tax neutrality which underlies the statutory scheme.

Petitioner concedes that "generally a profit motive is a necessary factor in determining whether an activity is a trade or business." Petitioner contends, however, that by including receipts from sales to nonmembers within § 512(a)(3)(A)'s definition of "unrelated business taxable income," the Code has defined nonmember sales as a "trade or business," and has thereby obviated the need for an inquiry into the taxpayer's intent to profit. We disagree. In our view, Congress' use of the term "unrelated *business* taxable income" to describe all receipts other than payments from the members hardly manifests an intent to define as a "trade or business" activities otherwise outside the scope of § 162. Petitioner's reading would render superfluous the words "allowed by this chapter" in § 512(a)(3)(A): If each taxable activity of a social club is "deemed" to be a trade or business, then *all* of the expenses "directly connected" with those activities would presumably be deductible. Moreover, Portland Golf's interpretation ignores Congress' general intent to tax the income of social clubs according to the same principles applicable to other taxpayers. We therefore conclude that petitioner may offset losses incurred in sales to nonmembers against investment income only if its nonmember sales are motivated by an intent to profit.

Losses from Portland Golf's sales to nonmembers may be used to offset investment income only if those activities were undertaken with a profit motive—that is, an intent to generate receipts in excess of costs. The parties and the other courts in this case, however, have taken divergent positions as to the range of expenses that qualify as costs of the non-exempt activity and are to be considered in determining whether petitioner acted with the requisite profit motive. In the view of the Tax Court, petitioner's profit motive was established by the fact that the club's receipts from nonmember sales exceeded its variable costs. Since Portland Golf's fixed costs, by definition, have been incurred even in the absence of sales to nonmembers, the Tax Court concluded that these costs should be disregarded in determining petitioner's intent to profit.

The Commissioner has taken no firm position as to the precise manner in which Portland Golf's fixed costs are to be allocated between member and nonmember sales. Indeed, the Commissioner does not even insist that any portion of petitioner's fixed costs must be attributed to nonmember activities in determining intent to profit. He does insist, however, that the *same* allocation method is to be used in determining petitioner's intent to profit as in computing its actual profit or loss. In the present case the parties have stipulated that the gross-to-gross method provides a reasonable formula for allocating fixed costs, and Portland Golf has used that method in calculating the losses incurred in selling food and drink to nonmembers. The Commissioner contends that petitioner is therefore required to demonstrate an intent to earn gross receipts in excess of fixed and variable costs, with the allocable share of fixed costs being determined by the gross-to-gross method.

Although the Court of Appeals' opinion is not entirely clear on this point, that court seems to have taken a middle ground. The Court of Appeals expressly rejected the Tax Court's assertion that profit motive could be established by a showing that gross receipts exceeded variable costs; the court insisted that *some* portion of fixed costs must be considered in determining intent to profit. The court appeared, however, to leave open the possibility that Portland Golf could use the gross-to-gross method in calculating its actual losses, while using some *other* allocation method to demonstrate that its sales to nonmembers were undertaken with a profit motive.

We conclude that the Commissioner's position is the correct one. Portland Golf's argument rests, as the Commissioner puts it, on an "inherent contradiction." Petitioner's calculation of actual losses rests on the claim that a portion of its fixed expenses is properly regarded as attributable to the production of income from nonmember sales. Given this assertion, we do not believe that these expenses can be ignored (or, more accurately, attributed to petitioner's exempt activities) in determining whether petitioner acted with the requisite intent to profit. Essentially the same criticism applies to the Court of Appeals' approach. That court required petitioner to include *some* portion of fixed expenses in demonstrating its intent to profit, but it left open the possibility that petitioner could employ an allocation method different from that used in calculating its actual losses. Under that approach, some of petitioner's fixed expenses could be attributed to exempt functions in determining intent to profit and to nonmember sales in establishing the club's actual loss. This, like the rationale of the Tax Court, seems to us to rest on an "inherent contradiction."

Petitioner's principal response is that § 162 requires an intent to earn an *economic* profit, and that this is quite different from an intent to earn *taxable income*. Portland Golf emphasizes that numerous provisions of the Code establish deductions and preferences which do not purport to mirror economic reality. Therefore, petitioner argues, taxpayers may frequently act with an intent to profit, even though the foreseeable (and, indeed, the intended) result of their efforts is that they suffer (or achieve) tax losses. Much of the Code, in petitioner's view, would be rendered a nullity if the mere fact of tax losses sufficed to show that a taxpayer lacked an intent to profit, thereby rendering the deductions unavailable. In Portland Golf's view, the parties have stipulated only that the gross-to-gross formula provides a reasonable method of determining what portion of fixed expenses is "directly connected" with the nonexempt activity for purposes of computing *taxable income*. That stipulation, Portland Golf contends, is irrelevant in determining the portion of fixed expenses that represents the *actual economic cost* of the activity in question.

We accept petitioner's contention that § 162 requires only an intent to earn an economic profit. We acknowledge, moreover, that many Code provisions are designed to serve purposes (such as encouragement of certain types of investment) other than the accurate measurement of economic income. A taxpayer who takes advantage of deductions or preferences of that kind may establish an intent to profit even though he has no expectation of realizing taxable income. The fixed expenses that Portland Golf seeks to allocate to its nonmember sales, however, are deductions of a different kind. The Code does not state that fixed costs are allocable on a gross-to-gross basis irrespective of economic reality. Rather, petitioner's right to use the gross-to-gross method rests on the club's assertion that this allocation formula reasonably identifies those expenses that are "directly connected" to the nonmember sales, § 512(a)(3)(A), and are "the ordinary and necessary expenses paid or incurred" in selling food and drink to nonmembers. Language such as this, it seems to us, reflects an attempt to measure economic income—not an effort to use the tax law to serve ancillary purposes. Having calculated its actual losses on the basis of the gross-to-gross formula, petitioner is therefore foreclosed from attempting to demonstrate its intent to profit by arguing that some other allocation method more accurately reflects economic reality.

IV

We hold that any losses incurred as a result of petitioner's nonmember sales may be offset against its investment income only if the nonmember sales were undertaken with an intent to profit. We also conclude that in demonstrating the requisite profit motive, Portland Golf must employ the same method of allocating fixed expenses as it uses in calculating its actual loss. Petitioner has failed to show that it intended to earn gross income from nonmember sales in excess of its total (fixed plus variable) costs, where fixed expenses are allocated using the gross-to-gross method. The judgment of the Court of Appeals is therefore affirmed.

Atlanta Athletic Club v. Commissioner

980 F.2d 1409 (11th Cir. 1993)

Cox, Circuit Judge:

Atlanta Athletic Club (the "Club") appeals a United States Tax Court ruling that the Club must recognize and report as unrelated business taxable income a $2.3 million gain from the sale of land. The Club argues that the gain qualifies for nonrecognition under I.R.C. § 512(a)(3)(D) because the Club used the property for its members' recreation and reinvested the sale proceeds in recreational facilities. The Tax Court found that the Club did not directly use the property for recreation within the meaning of § 512(a)(3)(D). . . . Thus, according to the Tax Court, nonrecognition was unavailable under the statute. We find that the Club directly used the property for recreation, and we reverse the Tax Court's ruling.

Background

The Club is a private social organization that owns and operates recreational facilities for members and their guests. It is exempt from federal income tax as a social club under I.R.C. § 501(c)(7). In 1964 the Club bought 617.1 acres of land at its present location in northern Fulton County, Georgia. A highway divided the property into a 425.6-acre eastern tract (the "Eastside Property") and a 191.5-acre western tract (the "Westside Property"). The Club held all of the land for two decades before selling 108 acres of the Westside Property in 1984.

From the start, the Eastside Property was the hub of the Club's activities. It is there that the Club built its golf courses, clubhouse, swimming pool and tennis courts. On the other hand, the Club did little to develop the Westside Property across the highway. The Club constructed a slag road on the Westside Property in 1976 to accommodate public and member parking for a professional golf tournament. After the tournament, Club members began jogging on the slag road. The Club also built a jogging track with a pine bark surface on the Westside Property, but drainage problems quickly forced members to abandon the track. The Club once stocked a lake on the Westside Property with fish. Other than mowing grass in the open areas, the Club made no other effort to improve the Westside Property for recreational uses.

When it decided to sell part of the Westside Property, the Club for the first time divided the parcel into three tracts: A, B and C. The 1984 sale of the 108 acres in tracts A and B brought the Club a $2.3 million gain. The Club retained tract C.

The parties have stipulated that the Club spent its $2.3 million gain to construct a new tennis center and renovate the clubhouse on the Eastside Property. The money was reinvested within the time limits specified by § 512(a)(3)(D).[1]

The Club deferred payment of income tax on the gain for its taxable year that ended March 31, 1985, in the belief that § 512(a)(3)(D) allowed nonrecognition of the full amount. The Commissioner . . . disagreed. The Commissioner determined that the nonrecognition provision did not apply because the Club did not directly use tracts A and B for the Club's exempt function (i.e., the pleasure and recreation of Club members). Treating the $2.3 million gain as unrelated business taxable income, the Commissioner assessed a $658,063 deficiency against the Club. The Club petitioned the Tax Court to redetermine the deficiency.

Club members and employees testified before the Tax Court that the Westside Property was the site of a number of activities through the years. Among the events were "pasture parties," Easter egg hunts, fishing tournaments, kite-flying contests, hot-air balloon rides and organized foot races.[2] Many members jogged on the property, and some members used the area for archery practice and to fly model airplanes.

To counter this testimony, the Commissioner relied largely on the Club's monthly newsletters and other documents from the 1970s and 1980s. The Commissioner argued that some of the organized events described by the Club's witnesses were held either on the Eastside Property or on the portion of the Westside Property retained by the Club, not on tracts A and B.

The Tax Court ruled in favor of the Commissioner, stating that it was "not convinced" by the testimony of the Club's witnesses. The Tax Court determined that, at most, individual members merely jogged across tracts A and B on their own initiative. Jogging "was not an activity directly sponsored by the Club as part of its

---

1. [1] The statute provides, in pertinent part:

(D) Nonrecognition of gain.—If property used directly in the performance of the exempt function of an organization . . . is sold by such organization, and within a period beginning 1 year before the date of such sale, and ending 3 years after such date, other property is purchased and used by such organization directly in the performance of its exempt function, gain (if any) from such sale shall be recognized only to the extent that such organization's sales [sic] price of the old property exceeds the organization's cost of purchasing the other property.

2. [3] The general manager of the Club at the time of the Tax Court hearing, Allan Christopher Borders, said annual pasture parties that began in the late 1970s were held on what was later designated as tract A. Borders said kite-flying contests each spring were always held on tract A. Club member Lewis E. Reeves said an annual "5K" (3.1-mile) run took contestants across all three tracts, although the start and finish were on tract C. Reeves said he was in charge of the kite-flying contest one year, and that it was held on tract A. The Club's athletic director, Wiley R. McGriff, testified that an annual one-mile run for children crossed from tract C into tract A. McGriff recalled pasture parties on tract A. James E. Petzing, a former general manager of the Club, said fishing tournaments were held at the lake on tract A for four or five years in the early 1970s.

exempt function." Therefore, "such activity [was] not sufficient to establish that the Club directly used Tracts A and B for exempt functions."

* * *

Issue

The issue before this court is whether the Tax Court erred in finding that tracts A and B of the Westside Property were not "used directly" by the Club, within the meaning of I.R.C. § 512(a)(3)(D), to provide pleasure and recreation for Club members.

* * *

Discussion

* * *

The statute speaks in terms of use rather than intent. Therefore, the Tax Court correctly observed that the Club's various plans for the land were irrelevant. The analysis must concentrate on the ways in which the Westside Property was or was not "used directly." This process entails factual findings as to the activities that occurred on tracts A and B of the Westside Property, and legal conclusions as to whether those activities constituted sufficient recreational uses by the Club.

After hearing the Club's witnesses and reviewing the documentary evidence, the Tax Court found as a fact that "the only activities which may have occurred on Tracts A and B were running and jogging." In reaching this conclusion, the Tax Court disregarded significant portions of the testimony from the Club's witnesses. The Tax Court stated that, "in light of the evidence," it was "not convinced from the testimony of members that the Club held activities on Tracts A and B."

We do not read the Tax Court's "not convinced" remark to mean that the court rejected all testimony by the Club's various witnesses as incredible. The Tax Court accepted the same witnesses' testimony that many members individually used the property. If the Tax Court did discount extensive portions of the testimony, it articulated no reasons for rejecting such testimony as incredible and none are apparent from the record. Most of the testimony about specific activities on tracts A and B conflicts with nothing in the documentary evidence, and the Commissioner called no witnesses to dispute the recollections of the Club's witnesses.

* * *

Because nothing in the record contradicts the Club's evidence in many significant respects, we are left with a definite and firm conviction that the Tax Court mistakenly determined that no Club-sponsored events occurred on what eventually became known as tracts A and B. We hold that the Tax Court clearly erred in this regard.

We begin our interpretation of a statute with "the plain language of the statute itself." "Absent unusual circumstances we are bound by the plain meaning of the language Congress has enacted." The plain language at issue here consists of the words "used directly." The statute does not define "used directly," and the words are not terms of art. Finding no unusual circumstances, "we are not at liberty, notwithstanding the apparent tax-saving windfall bestowed upon taxpayers, to add to or alter the words employed to effect a purpose which does not appear on the face of the statute."

The Commissioner seeks to equate direct use with dominant use. According to the Commissioner, "incidental use of the property for a club-sponsored function, or by club members for recreational pursuits of their own, would not satisfy the language or purpose of Section 512(a)(3)(D)." Even if all of the activities listed by the Club's witnesses occurred on the property in question, the Commissioner would deny nonrecognition because "the dominant if not exclusive use of that unimproved land was for investment." There are two problems with the Commissioner's approach: First, whether the Club ever planned to hold the Westside Property as an investment goes to the Club's intentions rather than to any actual uses of the property. Second, the statute in no way qualifies the concept of direct use to require that such use be dominant as well as direct.

The Commissioner has offered other, slightly varying interpretations of the statute. Before the Tax Court, the Commissioner contended that "used directly" means "'in actual, direct, continuous, and regular usage.' "The statute, however, says nothing about continuity or regularity. On this appeal, the Commissioner argues that nonrecognition under § 512(a)(3)(D) "is available only for gain realized from the sale of property, such as a clubhouse, tennis court, swimming pool, or golf course, that forms an integral part of the exempt functions of a social club." Once again, the Commissioner would qualify the statute's plain language. Moreover, the Commissioner offers no objective standard for determining which activities are "integral" to a social club's broad function to provide for the pleasure and recreation of its members. It is certainly conceivable that joggers derive as much pleasure and recreation from their pastime as golfers do from their rounds on the links.

* * *

In an attempt to overcome the statute's plain language, the Commissioner resorts to the legislative history of § 512(a)(3)(D). Specifically, the Commissioner cites a Senate Finance Committee report that illustrates the operation of § 512(a)(3)(D) by referring to the sale of a clubhouse and the reinvestment of the gain in a larger clubhouse. *See* S. Rep. No. 91-552, 91st Cong., 1st Sess. . . . . By using a clubhouse as an example, however, the committee did not pretend to limit the statute's coverage in a way not apparent on the face of the statute itself. Likewise, the committee mentioned "securities" as an example of investment property that would produce a taxable gain for a social club. This does not mean that securities are the only type of income-producing property that would subject a club to the federal tax.

"The law is well settled that a statute must be interpreted according to its plain language unless a clear contrary legislative intent is shown." We find nothing in the legislative history, much less any indication of a clear intent, to support the notion that the words in § 512(a)(3)(D) have other than their ordinary meaning.

The Commissioner warns that viewing the Club's "desultory activities" on the Westside Property as direct recreational uses would open the statute to abuse. Other organizations "would have an easy route to avoid tax on investment profits from real estate." (*Id.*) Nevertheless, Congress enacted this tax provision; if it is too generous, the power to tighten it also rests with Congress. As the old Fifth Circuit remarked about another tax law, "It may be that the statute gives an undeserved benefit to a particular class of taxpayers. . . . [But] we can no more grant relief to the Government from hardships than we could to a taxpayer."

Conclusion

The Club bought tracts A and B with members' funds. Nothing in the record contradicts the bulk of the Club's evidence that the Club used the property for its members' pleasure and recreation. We hold that the Club's activities on the Westside Property constituted direct uses of the property for the pleasure and recreation of Club members within the meaning of § 512(a)(3)(D). The Club reinvested its gain from the sale of tracts A and B in other property that members also used for pleasure and recreation. The reinvestment occurred within a period beginning one year before and ending three years after the sale of tracts A and B. Therefore, under § 512(a)(3)(D), the Club's $2.3 million gain from the sale of the property should not be recognized for federal income tax purposes.

We REVERSE the decision of the Tax Court.

Questions

The Beach Tennis and Golf Club is exempt from taxation under § 501(c)(7). For the taxable year, the Club has the following amounts of income:

Income:	
Membership Fees	$350,000
Fees for Member's use of Tennis Courts and Green Fees	$150,000
Dividends	$100,000
Rental of Tennis Courts to General Public and Green Fees Paid by General Public	$200,000
Revenues from use of Restaurant by members	$150,000
Revenues from use of Restaurant by nonmembers	$50,000
Total	$1,000,000

1. How much gross unrelated income does the Club have? What if the dividend income is set aside to support a scholarship fund for deserving students in the community?

2. Assume the dividend income is not set aside. Is the Club's exemption safe from challenge?

3. How would your answer change to the previous questions if the Club's provision of tennis courts, golf course, and restaurant meals to the general public resulted in losses of $200,000 and $50,000 (rather than gains of those amounts).

4. How much gross unrelated income would the Club have if, during the taxable year, it sold one of its golf courses for $400,000 and two years later purchases a health club for member use, paying $320,000?

PART SIX

Charitable Giving

Chapter 31

Deductible Charitable Contributions

A. Introduction

CODE: § 170(a), (b), (c), (d), (e)(1), (e)(7)

Charitable Contributions — for *income tax* purposes — involve four main issues:

1. Was the recipient a proper entity?
2. Was the transfer a "completed" "gift"?
3. Was the gift a present or future interest?
4. How much is deductible currently and can any excess be carried over?

This Chapter focuses mostly on issue 4: how much of a charitable contribution is deductible or carried over. We cover the first two questions only briefly.

Question 3 is beyond the coverage of this edition. Also, we limit coverage to income tax issues. Charitable contribution issues for gift tax or estate tax purposes involve very similar inquiries as do those for income tax. Be careful, however, as §§ 2055, 2106, and 2522 — which deal with Subtitle B taxes — differ in subtle, but important ways from § 170, which deals solely with Subtitle A (income) tax. A close side-by-side examination of the various sections should illuminate the differences.

Again, the following discussion covers the income tax consequences of a charitable contribution.

B. Was the Recipient a Proper Entity?

Section 170(c) lists five types of entities capable of receiving deductible contributions:

1. **States, possessions, political subdivisions, the United States and the District of Columbia.** This category mostly — but not completely — overlaps with § 115 status.

2. **"Charitable organizations."** This category mostly — but not completely — overlaps with § 501(c)(3) entities.

3. **War Veterans posts.** This category mostly — but not completely — overlaps with § 501(c)(19).

4. **Domestic Fraternal Societies.** This category mostly—but not completely—overlaps with § 501(c)(10). Note: it does not include college fraternities and sororities, which are themselves exempt under § 501(c)(7) as social clubs. Contributions to social clubs are not deductible under § 170(c).

5. **Cemetery Organizations.** This category mostly—but not completely—overlaps with § 501(c)(13).

Category 2—Section 170(c)(2) organizations—overlaps almost entirely with § 501(c)(3) and thus is the most important group: the group we refer to as "charities." The differences between section 170(c)(2) and 501(c)(3) are mostly cosmetic, as the punctuation differs while the substance is the same.

Each section lists corporations, community chests, funds, and foundations. Section 170(c)(2) then adds the category of trusts. Thus, some recipient formality is necessary; however, it need not involve a legal entity: a mere *fund* (if controlled by a tax-exempt entity) can receive income tax deductible contributions. The fund category is useful in two scenarios:

(1) Those involving small amounts of money.

(2) Those involving "sloppiness" in organization.

Because creation of a corporate entity requires significant paperwork and fees—at least to the tune of several hundred dollars—the costs may not be justified for small or short-term fundraising projects. However, if the creator is itself tax-exempt other than under § 501(c)(3) (and thus § 170(c)(2)), it can create a mere fund, which will qualify for both §§ 501(c)(3) and 170(c)(2) purposes. Such a fund needs to have no more formality than a separate bank account.

The fund organizational structure is not advisable for relatively large amounts or long-term, regular fundraising projects. However, it is available and thus can be useful after the fact. For example, a bar association (*i.e.*, a § 501(c)(6) organization) or labor union (*i.e.*, a § 501(c)(5) organization) might raise funds for a charitable purpose, such as a scholarship fund. Properly advised, the creator would probably establish a separate corporation or trust for state-law purposes: this would clarify the legal status of the charitable entity separate from the non-charitable entity (the bar association or labor union). Often, however, such entities are less than perfectly advised and they might plausibly raise money for charitable purpose without realizing that contributions to bar associations and labor unions are not tax deductible. Hindsight, however, can clean up the problem, assuming the funds raised were adequately segregated—a realistic assumption. In such a case, counsel can properly claim the separate charitable fund was just that: a *fund*, which can qualify for both §§ 501(c)(3) and 170(c)(2) purposes on its own.

Corporate status, however, is the most likely format used, and trusts are probably second. Community chests are not a type of legal entity and thus are unlikely ever to constitute a real category—most such recipients are likely incorporated. The same is true of the category "foundation." That is not a legal entity in most jurisdictions;

hence, those things called "foundations" are likely either corporations or trusts. Formal creation under a state not-for-profit act is typical, but not required: even a business corporation may qualify as tax-exempt if it satisfies the various organizational and operational requirements discussed in Chapters 2 through 6.

Section 170(c)(2) also imposes a "domestic" requirement on charities: they must be "created or organized in the United States or in any possession thereof, or under the law of the United States, any State, the District of Columbia, or any possession of the United States." While a foreign (non-domestic) charity may be *exempt* from U.S. income taxes — *no domestic requirement appears in § 501* — contributions directly to it are *not deductible* in the United States. All is not lost, however, as the existence of a U.S. entity to accept the contribution is normally all that is required.

For example, a school organized in Paris — if it has U.S. income — may be exempt under § 501(c)(3) and thus exempt from U.S. income taxes. A contribution to it, however, is not deductible. The Parisian school could, nevertheless, create a related entity in the United States for the purpose of receiving tax-deductible U.S. contributions that are to be used in Paris. Those contributions will normally satisfy § 170(c). These are essentially the facts of *Bilingual Montessori School v. Commissioner*, 75 T.C. 480 (1980). The case involved a single entity, with presence both in the United States and France, rather than two separate entities; however, that formality is unlikely important.

A related "domestic use" requirement appears in the flush language to § 170(c)(2):

> A contribution or gift by a corporation to a trust, chest, fund, or foundation shall be deductible by reason of this paragraph only if it is to be used within the United States or any of its possessions. . . .

The above passage is easily misread, so be careful: it applies only to *corporate* gifts to *non*-corporate tax-exempt entities. Thus, a gift from General Motors to American Tax Exempt Trust is deductible by General Motors.

In *Holder v. Humanitarian Law Project*, 561 U.S. 1 (2010), several tax-exempt organizations challenged 18 U.S.C. § 2339B, which makes it unlawful to give material support to terrorist organizations. The tax-exempt organizations wanted to provide conflict resolution training. They claimed that prohibiting their ability to provide the training was a burden on their free speech and right of association. The Supreme Court held that § 2339B does not suppress ideas or opinions in the form of pure political speech. "Rather, Congress has prohibited 'material support,' which most often does not take the form of speech at all. And when it does, the statute is carefully drawn to cover only a narrow category of speech to, under the direction of, or in coordination with foreign groups that the speaker knows to be terrorist organizations."

Rev. Rul. 66-79, 1966-1 CB 48 — IRC § 170

The Internal Revenue Service has been requested to clarify Revenue Ruling 63-252, C.B. 1963-2, 101, with respect to the deductibility of contributions to a domestic charitable corporation which may solicit contributions for a specific project of a foreign charity in the manner presented below.

X Corporation is a domestic charitable organization formed under the nonprofit laws of the state of Y. It is exempt from Federal income tax as being organized and operated exclusively for charitable, educational, and scientific purposes described in section 501(c)(3) of the Internal Revenue Code of 1954. Contributions to it are deductible since it is an organization described in section 170(c)(2) of the Code.

The corporation's charter provides, in part, that in furtherance of its educational, scientific, and charitable purposes it shall have the power to receive and allocate contributions, within the discretion of the board of directors, to any organization organized and operated exclusively for charitable or educational purposes within the meaning of section 501(c)(3) of the Code.

In contrast to the broad generality of the purposes stated in its charter, the name X corporation suggests a purpose to assist a named foreign organization. The individuals who organized X corporation had become interested in furthering the work of the named foreign organization, a corporation organized and operated in a foreign country exclusively for charitable, scientific, and educational purposes. The individuals concerned, who are United States citizens not acting on behalf of the foreign organization, did not wish X corporation to function simply as a fund raising medium for the foreign organization. Instead, they were interested in raising funds for specific projects, such as scientific research projects, to be carried out by the foreign organization, or individuals connected with the foreign organization, pursuant to grants previously reviewed and approved by the board of directors of X corporation.

The bylaws of X corporation provide, in part, that: (1) The making of grants and contributions and otherwise rendering financial assistance for the purposes expressed in the charter of the organization shall be within the exclusive power of the board of directors; (2) in furtherance of the organization's purposes, the board of directors shall have power to make grants to any organization organized and operated exclusively for charitable, scientific or educational purposes within the meaning of section 501(c)(3) of the Code; (3) the board of directors shall review all requests for funds from other organizations, shall require that such requests specify the use to which the funds will be put, and if the board of directors approves the request, shall authorize payment of such funds to the approved grantee; (4) the board of directors shall require that the grantees furnish a periodic accounting to show that the funds were expended for the purposes which were approved by the board of directors; and (5) the board of directors may, in its absolute discretion, refuse to make any grants or contributions or otherwise render financial assistance to or for any or all the purposes for which funds are requested.

The bylaws also provide that after the board of directors has approved a grant to another organization for a specific project or purpose, the corporation may solicit funds for the grant to the specifically approved project or purpose of the other organization. However, the board of directors shall at all times have the right to withdraw approval of the grant and use the funds for other charitable, scientific or educational purposes.

In accordance with the provisions of its charter and bylaws, X corporation at times solicits contributions which are to be used to provide grants to the foreign organization mentioned above, or to individuals connected with such foreign organization, for specific purposes approved by X corporation's board of directors in accordance with its bylaws. At all times all of the pertinent facts, including the fact that the board of directors may withdraw its approval of a particular grant even after it has been made, are available to any contributor not previously informed of such facts should the contributor so request either before or after a contribution has been made. The corporation refuses to accept contributions so earmarked that they must in any event go to the foreign organization.

Section 170(a) of the Code provides, in part, that there shall be allowed as a deduction any charitable contribution as defined in subsection (c), payment of which is made within the taxable year.

Section 170(c) of the Code defines a charitable contribution as meaning, in part, a contribution or gift to or for the use of a corporation, trust, or community chest, fund or foundation which is organized and operated exclusively for religious, charitable, scientific, literary, or educational purposes or for the prevention of cruelty to children or animals. However, the organization must be created or organized in the United States or in any possession thereof, or under the law of the United States, any State or Territory, the District of Columbia, or any possession of the United States.

Revenue Ruling 63-252, C.B. 1963-2, 101, discusses the deductibility of contributions by individuals to a charity organized in the United States which thereafter transmits some or all of its funds to a foreign charitable organization. Example (4) of that ruling concerns a domestic organization described in section 170(c) of the Code which makes grants to a foreign organization for purposes which the domestic organization has reviewed and approved as in furtherance of its purposes. Contributions to the domestic organization are not earmarked in any manner for a foreign organization and the use of such contributions is subject to control by the domestic organization. For these reasons, the domestic organization is considered to be the recipient of such contributions within the meaning of section 170(c)(2) of the Code.

Under the provisions of its charter and bylaws, X corporation may make grants to any organization organized and operated exclusively for charitable, scientific, or educational purposes within the meaning of section 501(c)(3) of the Code. An organization described in that section can be either a domestic or a foreign organization. The operations of X corporation bring it within the purview of example (4) of Revenue Ruling 63-252 except for the manner in which it may solicit contributions for its foreign grants. This raises a question as to whether the contributions are earmarked for the foreign organization so as to prohibit a deduction under section 170 of the Code.

Revenue Ruling 62-113, C.B. 1962-2, 10, holds that where gifts to an organization described in section 170(c) of the Code are not earmarked by the donor for a particular individual, the deduction will be allowable where it is established that a gift is intended by the donor for the use of the organization and not as a gift to an individual for whose benefit the amount given may be used by the donee organization. The test in each case is whether the organization has full control of the donated funds, and discretion as to their use, so as to insure that they will be used to carry out its functions and purposes.

In the instant case the domestic corporation may only solicit for specific grants when it has reviewed and approved them as being in furtherance of its purposes. Furthermore, under the terms of its bylaws the domestic corporation may make such solicitations only on the condition that it shall have control and discretion as to the use of the contributions received by it. Therefore, contributions received by the domestic organization from such solicitations are regarded as for the use of the domestic corporation and not for the organization receiving the grant from the domestic organization.

Accordingly, contributions paid to the domestic organization under the circumstances described above are deductible, for Federal income tax purposes, in the manner and to the extent provided by section 170 of the Code.

Revenue Ruling 63-252 is hereby amplified.

Rev. Rul. 69-80, 1969-1 CB 65 — IRC § 170

Advice has been requested as to the deductibility, under section 170 of the Internal Revenue Code of 1954, of a contribution made by a commercial corporation to a domestic charitable corporation that uses the contribution in a foreign country.

X corporation, a domestic commercial corporation, made an unrestricted charitable contribution to Y corporation, a domestic charitable corporation described in section 170(c)(2) of the Code. Y will use the contributions from X, as well as other funds, to further its charitable projects in a foreign country. Y has full control of all of the donated funds and discretion as to their use.

Section 170 of the Code provides, in material part, as follows:

(a) "Allowance of Deduction." —

> (1) "General rule. — There shall be allowed as a deduction any charitable contribution (as defined in subsection (c)) payment of which is made within the taxable year. A charitable contribution shall be allowable as a deduction only if verified under regulations prescribed by the Secretary or his delegate."

"Charitable Contribution Defined."—For purposes of this section, the term "charitable contribution" means a contribution or gift to or for the use of—

"A corporation, trust, or community chest, fund, or foundation"—

(A) "created or organized in the United States or in any possession thereof, or under the law of the United States, any State or Territory, the District of Columbia, or any possession of the United States";

(B) "organized and operated exclusively for religious, charitable, scientific, literary, or educational purposes or for the prevention of cruelty to children or animals";

(C) "no part of the net earnings of which inures to the benefit of any private shareholder or individual; and"

(D) "no substantial part of the activities of which is carrying on propaganda, or otherwise attempting, to influence legislation."

"A contribution or gift by a corporation to a trust, chest, fund, or foundation shall be deductible by reason of this paragraph only if it is to be used within the United States or any of its possessions exclusively for purposes specified in subparagraph (B)."

While the last sentence in section 170(c)(2) denies a deduction for a charitable contribution by a corporation to a trust, chest, fund, or foundation if it is used outside the United States or any of its possessions, that sentence contains no limitation as to deductions by a corporation for charitable contributions to a domestic charitable corporation. Thus, the statute does not preclude the deductibility of contributions to a domestic charitable corporation which uses its funds for a charitable purpose in a foreign country.

Accordingly, in the instant case the X corporation is entitled to a charitable contribution deduction, subject to the limitations of section 170(b)(2) of the Code, for contributions to Y corporation even though Y uses the contributions in a foreign country.

C. Was the Transfer a "Completed" "Gift"?

Two words are operative in the above question: *completed* and *gift*. The issue of completion covers methods of accounting—cash or accrual. The gift issue distinguishes a gift—which is required for deductibility—from other transfers, such as payments for services or products.

1. "Completed" Gifts and Methods of Accounting

As a general rule, charitable contributions are deductible only on the cash method. In other words, the taxpayer must actually *pay* the amount for that amount to be deductible: a mere promise to pay, such as a pledge, will not suffice. This is true even for accrual method taxpayers. A small exception exists for accrual method corporations. For them, the accrual of a charitable contribution is permissible, conditioned on payment occurring within 2.5 months of the year-end. IRC § 170(a)(2).

What constitutes "payment" is another issue. According to Treasury Regulations, delivery of a present interest in property effectuates payment. Similarly, delivery of a contributor's check constitutes payment, assuming the check ultimately clears. Treas. Reg. § 1.170A-1(b). Contributions of future interests of tangible personal property, however, are not considered "paid" until either all intervening interests have expired or until such interests are held by persons other than the contributor (or by persons related to the contributor). IRC § 170(a)(3).

2. What Is a "Gift"?

In 1960, the Supreme Court decided the classic *Duberstein* decision defining a "gift" as a transfer resulting from detached and disinterested generosity. *Commissioner v. Duberstein*, 363 U.S. 278 (1960). The Court also adopted a "primary purpose" test under which the dominant or primary motive of the transferor controls the characterization of a transfer. Pursuant to the test, a trier of fact must classify all transferor motives into either gift or non-gift categories. Then, the larger category controls.

For example, if a transfer were motivated 70% by compensatory motives and 30% by donative intent, it constitutes compensation in full. Whether such an all-or-nothing approach should (or even does) truly apply in the employment context is debatable, as is the question of whether motives can be adequately quantified. Arguably, mixed-purpose transfers should be apportioned into their component parts, each to be characterized to the extent motivated by gift or compensation.

In the charitable arena, however, no such "all-or-nothing" controversy exists: mixed-purpose transfers must indeed be apportioned. To the extent motivated by "detached and disinterested generosity" they constitute charitable contributions, potentially deductible under § 170. To the extent they constitute the purchase of property or services, they are non-deductible. Two separate tax provisions effectively require apportionment.

Section 6115 covers the disclosure requirements for charitable recipients of *quid pro quo* contributions. Such entities must disclose to the contributor the portion that is deductible. For example, if a person "contributes" $250 for a ticket to a banquet, only a portion of the "contribution" is indeed a gift. The charitable recipient must subtract from the $250 price the fair market value of contributor benefits, such as a meal or entertainment. The remaining portion is deductible. Failure to disclose the deductible portion results in a penalty owed by the charity.

Section 1011(b) specifically requires basis apportionment for bargain sales to charity. Treas. Reg. § 1.1011-2(b) clarifies the process. First, the contributor must compute the ratio of the amount realized to the fair market value of the transferred property.

That portion (the ratio times the basis) of the basis then applies to the portion sold, with the remaining basis applying to the portion donated.

For example, suppose a taxpayer sold to a church for $4000, stock with a fair market value of $10,000 and a basis of $4,000. Forty percent of the transfer constitutes a sale (4000 sale price divided by the 10,000 fair market value) and sixty percent constitutes a donation. Thus, forty percent of the $4000 basis applies to the sale (40% of $4000 equals $1600) and sixty percent of the basis applies to the donation (60% of $4000 equals $2400). The sale thus produces taxable gain of $2400 ($4000 amount realized minus $1600 basis). The donation comprises a gift of appreciated capital gain property with a value of $6000 and a basis of $2400.

a. Ebben

Ebben v. Commissioner of Internal Revenue

783 F.2d 906 (9th Cir. 1986)

. . . We hold that a transfer by gift of encumbered property to a charity is a "sale" under section 1011(b).

. . . Taxpayers concede that the amount of the encumbrance on the property contributed to charity is an "amount realized." *See Estate of Levine v. Commissioner*, 72 T.C. 780, 789–91, *aff'd*, 634 F.2d 12, 15 (2d Cir. 1980). Taxpayers also concede that the contribution to charity is a disposition of property which causes the amount of the encumbrance to be an "amount realized" by the taxpayers on such disposition. Thus, taxpayers realized $544,584 from the transfer of the property to Pitzer because the college took the land subject to a note and deed of trust in that amount. But taxpayers contend that "not every disposition of encumbered property to a charity is a 'sale' to the extent of the encumbrance, but will be considered a 'sale' only where the taxpayer directly or indirectly realized a benefit from such encumbrance." Taxpayers then limit "benefit" to *receipt of cash* when a loan is placed on the property prior to the contribution or *deduction of depreciation* with respect to the amount of the encumbrance which had been included in taxpayers' basis under *Crane v. Commissioner*, 331 U.S. 1, 67 S. Ct. 1047, 91 L. Ed. 1301 (1947). We hold that every contribution of mortgaged property to charity is a "sale" and basis is computed under section 1011(b).

* * *

Under this paragraph, taxpayers realize taxable gain because the amount realized ($544,584) exceeds the allocated basis ($506,679).

* * *

Taxpayers assert that because section 1011(b) uses the word "sale" rather than the term "sale or other disposition" used elsewhere in the Code, Congress intended to limit the scope of section 1011(b) to cases in which the taxpayer received a benefit such as cash on mortgaging the property or depreciation deduction with respect to the property prior to transferring it to the charity.

The Supreme Court in *Commissioner v. Tufts*, 461 U.S. 300, 307–310, 103 S. Ct. 1826, 75 L. Ed. 2d 863 (1983), however, established that taxation on relief from debt under *Crane* does not depend on any theory of economic benefit and applies to situations in which no depreciation deductions have been taken.

* * *

When the taxpayers in this case gave the subject property to Pitzer College, which took the property subject to the debt, it was as if the taxpayers had been paid with cash borrowed by Pitzer College from the mortgagee on a nonrecourse basis, and then had used the cash to satisfy their obligation to the mortgagee. "When a taxpayer receives a loan, he incurs an obligation to repay that loan at some future date. Because of this obligation, the loan proceeds do not qualify as income to the taxpayer. When he fulfills the obligation, the repayment of the loan likewise has no effect on this tax liability." *Tufts*, 461 U.S. at 307. But when someone else relieves him of his obligation to pay the loan, it is as though the taxpayer had received cash and the transfer of the encumbered property to the charity is the equivalent of a sale without regard to any tax benefit theory.

* * *

The tax court, in a decision unanimously reviewed by the full court, has specifically held that a gift of encumbered property to a charity is a "sale" as that term is used in section 1011(b). *Guest v. Commissioner*, 77 T.C. 9 (1981). The taxpayer in *Guest* donated mortgaged property to a charity. The court held that the gift resulted in taxable gain and the basis used to determine gain was an allocated basis calculated under section 1011(b). *Guest*, 77 T.C. at 24–26 & n.12.

The tax court concluded that there was a sale under section 1011(b) "we are convinced that [taxpayer's] charitable contribution of the properties must . . . be treated as a sale or exchange." *Guest*, 77 T.C. at 25. In reaching this conclusion, the tax court relied on *Freeland v. Commissioner*, 74 T.C. 970, 981 (1980). "We believe the holdings of *Crane* and subsequent cases decided in the light of *Crane* mandate the conclusion that *relief* from indebtedness, even though there is no personal liability, is sufficient to support a sale or exchange." The *Guest* court then concluded that section 1011(b) applies "to both sales and exchanges, despite the sole use of the word sale in the statute." 77 T.C. at 25 (citing Treas. Reg. §§ 1.1011-2(a)(1) & 1.1011-2(a)(3)).

The IRS has consistently interpreted "sale" in section 1011(b) to include gifts of mortgaged property to a charity. Treasury Regulation § 1.1011-2(a)(3) states:

> If property is transferred subject to an indebtedness, the amount of indebtedness must be treated as an amount realized for purposes of determining whether there is a sale or exchange to which section 1011(b) and this section apply, even though the transferee does not agree to assume or pay the indebtedness.

Taxpayers contend that this regulation should be read to cover only "disguised sales," rather than all gifts of mortgaged property. A disguised sale occurs when the taxpayer mortgages the property just prior to giving it to a charity. In such a case, the donor receives the cash proceeds of the loan and the charity receives the property subject to the debt. However, the Commissioner in Rev. Rul. 81-163, 1981-1 C.B. 433, made it clear he did not intend to limit the regulation to disguised sales.

* * *

Taxpayers maintain that the IRS's interpretation of section 1011(b) in Treas. Reg. §1.1011-2(a)(3) exceeds the scope of the statute. Our review of the Commissioner's regulations is strictly limited. We may set aside Treas. Reg. §1011-2(a)(3) only if it is not a reasonable interpretation of section 1011(b).

* * *

The plain language of section 1011(b) applies to sales to a charitable organization. Neither the code nor the regulations, however, define the word sale directly.[1]

* * *

In the absence of specific direction from Congress, we find that the Commissioner's regulation interpreting section 1011(b) is reasonable.... The congressional mandate embodied in section 1011(b) is to offset the "combined effect... of not taxing the appreciation and at the same time allowing a charitable contributions deduction for the appreciation." H.R. Rep. No. 413, 91st Cong. 1st Sess. 53, *reprinted in* 1969-3 C.B. 200, 234. Treasury Regulation §1.1011-2(a)(3) thus harmonizes with the origin and purpose of section 1011(b).[2]

---

1. [11] Treasury Regulation §1.1002-1(d) defines "sale" indirectly: "Ordinarily, to constitute an exchange, the transaction must be a reciprocal transfer of property, as distinguished from a transfer of property for a money consideration only." But this definition adds little to the petitioners argument beyond an appeal to common sense that the word "sale" means for money consideration.

2. [13] The Commissioner introduced Treas. Reg. §1.1011-2(a)(3) twelve years ago. Our research discloses no substantial criticism of the Regulation during this period. When Treas. Reg. §1.1011-2(a)(3) was first offered for notice and comment, one commentator concluded that the Regulation was "too broad." Whitaker, *Dealing with Outright Gifts to Charity in Kind*, 30th Annual N.Y.U. Inst. on Fed. Taxation 45 (1972). The author's argument, however, is mainly directed at cases in which the donor transfers encumbered property and agrees to pay the debt. *Id.* at 73–75. That is not the case before us. To the extent the article criticizes sale treatment for gratuitous transfers of encumbered property without an agreement to repay the debt, it merely offers an alternative interpretation of §1011(b) which the Commissioner properly rejected. A rule excluding such transfers from §1011(b) would lead to odd results. If any cash were involved in the transaction, say $100, the contribution would be a bargain sale and hence an allocated basis would be used. The amount realized would have to include the $100 and the amount of nonrecourse debt. *See Crane*, 331 U.S. at 1. It is difficult to justify why a contribution without the $100 receipt of cash should receive a different basis under §1011(a). Treas. Reg. §1.1011-2(a)(3) is therefore a reasonable interpretation of §1011(b) in light of *Crane* and its progeny.

Petitioners claim that *Ebben* would be the first case to apply an allocated basis for calculating gain from a gratuitous transfer is misguided. Their assertion apparently stems from an incorrect footnote in Cunningham, *Payment of Debt with Property—The Two-Step Analysis after Commissioner v. Tufts*, 38 Tax Lawyer 575, 616 n.255 (1985). The author asserts that only *Ebben* uses an allocated basis among recent cases that raise this issue. However, the author reaches this conclusion by incorrectly stating that *Guest* relied on a full basis. We note that the tax court in *Guest* concluded

On balance, the cases, Treasury regulations, and revenue rulings support the tax court's conclusion that taxpayers realized gain. Accordingly, we hold that a charitable contribution which entails relief from nonrecourse indebtedness is a "sale" within the meaning of section 1011(b).

AFFIRMED in part and REVERSED in part.

BEEZER, Circuit Judge, concurring in part and dissenting in part.

... I cannot conclude that Congress intended every transfer of encumbered property to a charity to be deemed a "sale," regardless of whether there is any indicia of a "sale," such as a direct economic benefit received by the transferor.

If Congress had intended section 1011(b) to have so broad an application, Congress would not have adopted the narrow term "sale" in its drafting of this statutory provision. By contrast, in several other sections of the Internal Revenue Code, when Congress intended a provision to govern other types of transfers, the language "sale or other disposition" has been enacted. *See, e.g.*, §§ 1001(a), 1001(b), 1011(a).

* * *

b. United States v. American Bar Endowment

The following decision is important for two reasons: its discussion of the unrelated business income tax *and* its discussion of mixed-motive transfers involving charities. The case thus also appears, in part, in Chapter 25, dealing with unrelated business taxable income. The portion of the case affecting charitable deductions appears below.

Initially, the facts may appear to be essentially identical with those of the $250 banquet ticket hypothesized above. Members of the American Bar Association may purchase life insurance through a program sponsored by the American Bar Endowment. Prior to the decision, such life insurance purchasers paid substantially *more* for the insurance coverage than what market forces might justify, just as the hypothetical banquet ticket purchaser paid far more than the meal and entertainment value. Nevertheless, the hypothetical banquet sales result in a part purchase/part donation analysis, while the ABE insurance sales resulted in a pure sales analysis: none of the excessive amount paid for the insurance was deductible by the purchasers.

Why would the Supreme Court reach such an anomalous result? The answer lies in a careful reading of the facts. The type of insurance policy involved resulted in annual dividends for policyholders, effectively reducing the price substantially. Traditionally, under such a group policy, the policyholders would receive the dividends.

---

that "petitioners adjusted bases for calculating his gain ... should be determined under § 1011(b), and his gain is equal to the difference between the outstanding mortgages and that portion of his adjusted bases which bears the same ratio to the adjusted bases as the amount of the mortgages bears to the fair market value of the properties." 77 T.C. at 25–26. Our decision today follows this same allocation formula.

The ABE, however, required policyholders to "donate" the annual dividends to the entity. It then asserted that such "contributions" were tax deductible. Thus, policy purchasers indeed paid substantially more than what market forces might have justified; however, they paid exactly what was demanded. Compared to non-group policies, or policies with some other groups, the premiums were less expensive because of the perceived longevity of bar association members. In that light, policy purchasers did not pay more than fair value. Further, the Court questioned whether a "required donation" was indeed a donation motivated by detached and disinterested generosity . . . or was it merely a price paid motivated by the desire to purchase insurance.

United States v. American Bar Endowment

477 U.S. 105 (1986)

JUSTICE MARSHALL delivered the opinion of the Court.

The first issue in this case is whether income that a tax-exempt charitable organization derives from offering group insurance to its members constitutes "unrelated business income" subject to tax under §§ 511 through 513 of the Internal Revenue Code (Code), 26 U.S.C. §§ 511–513. The second issue is whether the organization's members may claim a charitable deduction for the portion of their premium payments that exceeds the actual cost to the organization of providing insurance.

Respondent American Bar Endowment (ABE) is a corporation exempt from taxation under § 501(c)(3) of the Code, which, with certain exceptions not relevant here, exempts organizations "organized and operated exclusively for . . . charitable . . . or educational purposes." ABE's primary purposes are to advance legal research and to promote the administration of justice, and it furthers these goals primarily through the distribution of grants to other charitable and educational groups. All members of the American Bar Association (ABA) are automatically members of ABE. The ABA is exempt from taxation as a "business league" under § 501(c)(6).

ABE raises money for its charitable work by providing group insurance policies, underwritten by major insurance companies, to its members. Approximately 20% of ABE's members participate in the group insurance program, which offers life, health, accident, and disability policies. ABE negotiates premium rates with insurers and chooses which insurers shall provide the policies. It also compiles a list of its own members and solicits them, collects the premiums paid by its members, transmits those premiums to the insurer, maintains files on each policyholder, answers members' questions concerning insurance policies, and screens claims for benefits.

There are two important benefits of purchasing insurance as a group rather than individually. The first is that ABE's size gives it bargaining power that individuals lack. The second is that the group policy is experience-rated. This means that the cost of insurance to the group is based on that group's claims experience, rather than general actuarial tables. Because ABA members have favorable mortality and morbidity rates, experience-rating results in a substantially lower insurance cost.

When ABE purchases a group policy for its members, it pays a negotiated premium to the insurance company. If, as is uniformly true, the insurance company's actual cost of providing insurance to the group is lower than the premium paid in a given year, the insurance company pays a refund of the excess, called a "dividend," to ABE. Critical to ABE's fundraising efforts is the fact that ABE requires its members to agree, as a condition of participating in the group insurance program, that they will permit ABE to keep all of the dividends rather than distributing them pro rata to the insured members.

It would be possible for ABE to negotiate lower premium rates for its members than the rates it has charged throughout the relevant period, and thus receive a lower dividend. However, ABE prices its policies competitively with other insurance policies offered to the public and to ABE members. 761 F.2d 1573, 1575 (CAFC 1985). In this way ABE is able to generate large dividends to be used for its charitable purposes. In recent years the total amount of dividends has exceeded 40% of the members' premium payments. *Ibid.* ABE advises its insured members that each member's share of the dividends, less ABE's administrative costs, constitutes a tax-deductible contribution from the member to ABE. Thus the after-tax cost of ABE's insurance to its members is less than the cost of a commercial policy with identical coverage and premium rates.

* * *

III.

Section 170 of the Code provides that a taxpayer may deduct from taxable income any "charitable contribution," defined as "a contribution or gift to or for the use of qualifying entities," § 170(c). The individual respondents contend that the excess of their premium payments over the cost to ABE of providing insurance constitutes a contribution or gift to ABE.

Many of the considerations supporting our holding that ABE's earnings from the insurance program are taxable also bear on the question whether ABE's members may deduct part of their premium payments. The evidence demonstrates, and the Claims Court found, that ABE's insurance is no more costly to its members than other policies—group or individual—available to them. Thus, as we have recognized, ABE's members are never faced with the hard choice of supporting a worthwhile charitable endeavor or reducing their own insurance costs. A payment of money generally cannot constitute a charitable contribution if the contributor expects a substantial benefit in return. S. Rep. No. 1622, 83d Cong., 2d Sess., 196 (1954); Singer Co. v. *United States*, 449 F.2d 413, 196 Ct. Cl. 90 (1971). However, as the Claims Court recognized, a taxpayer may sometimes receive only a nominal benefit in return for his contribution. Where the size of the payment is clearly out of proportion to the benefit received, it would not serve the purposes of § 170 to deny a deduction altogether. A taxpayer may therefore claim a deduction for the difference between a payment to a charitable organization and the market value of the benefit received in return, on the theory that the payment has the "dual character" of a purchase and a contribution. *See, e.g.*, Rev. Rul. 67-246, 1967-2 Cum. Bull. 104 (price of ticket to charity ball deductible to extent it exceeds market value of admission); Rev. Rul. 68-432, 1968-2 Cum. Bull. 104, 105 (noting possibility that payment to charitable organization may have "dual character").

In Rev. Rul. 67-246, supra, the IRS set up a two-part test for determining when part of a "dual payment" is deductible. First, the payment is deductible only if and to the extent it exceeds the market value of the benefit received. Second, the excess payment must be "made with the intention of making a gift." 1967-2 Cum. Bull., at 105. The Tax Court has adopted this test, see *Murphy v. Commissioner*, 54 T.C. 249, 254 (1970); *Arceneaux v. Commissioner*, 36 TCM 1461, 1464 (1977); but see *Oppewal v. Commissioner*, 468 F.2d 1000, 1002 (CA1 1972) (expressing "dissatisfaction with such subjective tests as the taxpayer's motives in making a purported charitable contribution" and relying solely on differential between amount of payment and value of benefit). The Claims Court applied that test in this case, and held that respondents Broadfoot, Boynton, and Turner had not established that they could have purchased comparable insurance for less money. Therefore, the court held, they had failed to establish that the value of ABE's insurance to them was less than the premiums paid. *4 Cl. Ct., at 415–417.* Respondent Sherwood demonstrated that there did exist a group insurance program for which he was eligible and which offered lower premiums than ABE's insurance. However, Sherwood failed to establish that he was aware of that competing program during the years at issue. Sherwood therefore had failed to demonstrate that he met the second part of the above test—that he had intentionally paid more than the market value for ABE's insurance because he wished to make a gift.

The Court of Appeals, in reversing, held that the Claims Court had focused excessively on the taxpayers' motivation. In the Court of Appeals' view, the necessary inquiry was whether "the transaction was . . . of a business and not a charitable nature," considering all of the circumstances. 761 F.2d, at 1582. The Court of Appeals therefore remanded for redetermination under that standard. We hold that the Claims Court applied the proper standard. The sine qua non of a charitable contribution is a transfer of money or property without adequate consideration. The taxpayer, therefore, must at a minimum demonstrate that he purposely contributed money or property in excess of the value of any benefit he received in return. The most logical test of the value of the insurance respondents received is the cost of similar policies. Three of the four individual respondents failed to demonstrate that they could have purchased similar policies for a lower cost, and we must therefore assume that the value of ABE's insurance to those taxpayers at least equals their premium payments. Had respondent Sherwood known that he could purchase comparable insurance for less money, ABE's insurance would necessarily have declined in value to him. Because Sherwood did not have that knowledge, however, we again must assume that he valued ABE's insurance equivalently to those competing policies of which he was aware. Because those policies cost as much as or more than ABE's, Sherwood has failed to demonstrate that he intentionally gave away more than he received.

... We ... hold that the individual taxpayers have not established that any portion of their premium payments to ABE constitutes a charitable contribution....

D. Was the Gift a Present or Future Interest?

This issue largely involves Charitable Lead Trusts and Charitable Remainder trusts, topics which are traditionally covered in a course on the income taxation of trusts and estates. We therefore exclude coverage in this edition.

E. What Is the Amount Currently Deductible or to Be Carried Over?

Once we determine, in response to the above questions, that the taxpayer made a completed gift of a present interest to a proper charity, the remaining analysis is largely mechanical. The mechanics involve 11 steps:[3]

Section 170 Charitable Contribution Deduction Computation Steps

Step 1: Treas. Reg. § 1.170A-1(c)

- Start with the fair market value of the property donated.

Step 2: § 170(e)(1)(A)

- Subtract any potential non-long-term capital gain.

Step 3: § 170(e)(1)(B)(i)(I)

- Subtract 100% of any potential long-term capital gain if the transfer is a gift of unrelated tangible personal property given to a public charity or to a section 170(b)(1)(F) private foundation.

Step 4: § 170(e)(1)(B)(i)(II)

- Subtract 100% of any potential long-term capital gain if the transfer is a gift of tangible personal property but (1) is sold, exchanged, or disposed of by the donee before the last day of the taxable year and (2) the donee has not made a 170(e)(7)(D) certification with respect to the property.

3. A Step 10 limitation does not affect the Step Nine computation. *E.g.*, Treas. Reg. § 1.170A-8(f) Examples 2, 5, 15(b). This regulation is consistent with the clause 170(b)(1)(B)(ii) parenthetical providing that the (b)(1)(B) computation [Step 9] is "determined without regard to subparagraph (c) [Step 10]." A clause 170(b)(1)(C)(iii) election affects the subparagraph (b)(1)(B) [Step 9] computation. *E.g.*, Treas. Reg. § 1.1 70A-8(f) Example 15(a). This appears inconsistent with the clause 170(b)(1)(B)(ii) parenthetical: because the election is permitted under subparagraph (C), a literal reading of the statute would not allow the election to affect the § 170(b)(1)(B) computation. Nevertheless, the regulation example is quite clear.

Step 5: § 170(e)(1)(B)(ii)

• Subtract 100% of any potential long-term capital gain if the transfer is a gift to a private foundation other than one described in § 170(b)(1)(F).

Step 6: § 170(e)(1)(B)(iii)

• Subtract 100% of any potential long-term capital gain if the transfer is a gift of a patent, copyright, trademark, trade name, trade secret, know-how, software, or similar property, or applications or registrations of such property.

Step 7: § 170(e)(1)(B)(iv)

• Subtract 100% of any potential long-term capital gain if the transfer is a gift of taxidermy property by the person who prepared, stuffed, or mounted the property or by a person who paid for preparation, stuffing, or mounting.

Step 8: § 170(b)(1)(A) flush language

• Limit the amount of contributions to 50% of the taxpayer's contribution base if they are either to a public charity or to a § 170(b)(1)(F) private foundation. Carryover the remainder of such contributions for five years per § 170(d). Note that special rules apply for tax years covered by the 2017 Tax Cut and Jobs Act and the 2020 CARES Act. From 2021 to 2025 the 50% limit climbs to 60%. In 2020, the limit can hit 100%.

Step 9: § 170(b)(1)(B)

• Limit any contributions to private foundations other than those described in § 170(b)(1)(F) to the lesser of:

• 30% of the contribution base, or

• 50% of the contribution base minus the amount from step 8. Note the increased limits discussed above for years 2020 to 2025.

• Carryover the remainder for five years.

Step 10: § 170(b)(1)(C)

• Limit the contributions from step 8 to 30% of the contribution base if the contributions involve capital gain property and Steps 3 through 7 did not cause a reduction. Carryover the remainder for five years. Do not change Step 9.

Or

• Elect § 170(b)(1)(C)(iii) to apply to all contributed capital gain property. If you elect, do not apply the 30% limitation in this Step 10, but go back to steps 4 through 7.

Step 11: § 170(b)(1)(D)

• Limit the contributions from Step 9 to the lesser of:

• 20% of the contribution base,

Or

- 30% of the contribution base minus the Step 10 amount (if no § 170(b)(1)(C)(iii) election was made).
- Carryover the remainder for five years.

Consider the following example to illustrate the eleven steps:

Example Illustrating 11 Steps to Calculating Charitable Contribution Deduction

Taxpayer, an individual engaged in a trade or business of oil and gas exploration, donates to a hospital, the following property:

- $100,000 cash.
- A generator with an adjusted basis of $100,000, a fair market value of $300,000, an original cost of $275,000, a holding period of more than one year and prior depreciation of $175,000.
- Land with a basis of $100,000, an original cost of $100,000, a fair market value of $500,000, and a holding period of more than one year.

Note: In applying the steps, remember that reductions (under Steps 2, 3, and 5) are permanent, but limitations (under Steps 8 through 11) result in carryovers.

Step 1: Fair Market Value.

Prior to 1969, the fair market value of charitable contributions was deductible. This resulted in substantial problems, particularly involving taxpayer created property such as art. For example, a painter could deduct the $5000 fair market value of a painting, which cost him $10 to paint. Congress saw such examples as abusive and thus enacted § 170(e), which reduces the amount of such a contribution to the taxpayer's $10 basis. Nevertheless, the first step in computing the amount of a charitable contribution begins with the fair market value of the property contributed. Treas. Reg. § 1.170A-1(c).

Thus, taxpayer's initial contribution amount is $900,000:

Cash	$100,000
Generator	300,000
Land	500,000
Total	$900,000

Step 2: § 170(e)(1)(A): Universal *Reduction* for *Non*-long-term Capital Gain

Section 170(e)(1)(A) provides that the amount of the contribution must be reduced by:

- the amount of gain which would *not* have been long-term capital gain . . . if the property contributed had been sold by the taxpayer at its fair market value (determined at the time of such contribution) (emphasis added).

Paragraph 170(e)(3) lists several types of contributions that escape part of the Step Two reduction. For example, corporate gifts of appreciated inventory actually used by the public charity recipient are potentially reduced by only one-half the appreciation rather than the full appreciation.

Clearly, the Section has no impact on the cash donation, which continues to be valued at $100,000. The property contributions, however, are subject to possible reduction in amount. Taxpayer must hypothetically sell each asset, characterize any resulting gain, and then subtract from the contribution amount any non-long-term capital gain.

Had the generator been sold for its $300,000 fair market value, it would have generated $200,000 gain: the excess of the value over its adjusted basis. Because the taxpayer used it in a trade or business, the generator would be § 1231 property, resulting in § 1231 gain. The flush language to paragraph 170(e)(1) provides, however:

> For purposes of applying this paragraph (*other than* in the case of gain to which section 617(d)(1), 1245(a), 1250(a), 1252(a), or 1254(a) applies), property which is property used in the trade or business (as defined in section 1231(b)) shall be treated as a capital asset. (Emphasis added).

Thus, the potential $200,000 of § 1231 gain is treated as capital gain, which in this case is long-term and thus not subject to Step Two reduction (because of the holding period greater than one year). Section 1245, however, overrides both § 1231 and the above quoted language. Had taxpayer sold the generator, it would have resulted in $175,000 of depreciation recapture under § 1245, which is characterized as ordinary income. Thus, only the remaining potential $25,000 of gain is actually treated as potential long-term capital gain.

Ultimately, the taxpayer reduces the contribution amount for the generator to $125,000: the $300,000 fair market value minus the $175,000 potential non-long-term capital gain.

The land, in contrast, has no Step Two reduction. Had it been sold for fair market value, the land would have generated $400,000 of gain, all of which would have been treated as long-term capital gain. Of course, had the land been held for less than one-year, or had it been inventory, the potential gain would not have been than long-term capital gain, resulting in a Step Two reduction of the full $400,000.

Thus, after Step Two, taxpayer's contribution amount is:

Cash	$100,000
Generator	125,000
Land	500,000
Total	$725,000

Step 3: §170(e)(1)(B)(i)(I): Public Charity *Reduction*

Section 170(e)(1)(B) reduces the amount of the contribution by:

> the amount of gain which would have been long-term capital gain if the property contributed had been sold by the taxpayer at its fair market value (determined at the time of such contribution).
>
> This reduction *does not* apply to contributions of tangible personal property, if the use by the donee is *related* to the purpose or function constituting the basis for its exemption under §501.

§170(e)(1)(B)(i)(I) (emphasis added).

Clearly, intangible property is not subject to this reduction. Thus, gifts of securities to public charities (and to some private foundations) are deductible at fair market value, subject to a Step Two reduction if they were held only short-term. Likewise, the gift of land—because it comprises *real* (not personal) property—escapes this potential reduction.

The gift of the generator, however, falls within the ambit of Step Three: it involves tangible personal property with potential long-term capital gain (the $25,000 potential §1231 gain) if it were sold rather than donated.

An important inquiry involves whether the gift is *related* to the purpose for which the recipient is exempt. If the generator were indeed related to the reason the recipient hospital is exempt, Step Three results in no reduction in the amount of the contribution.

If, instead, the generator were unrelated, then Step Three would result in a reduction equal to the potential long-term capital gain (or §1231 gain) if the property were sold rather than donated. Combined with Step Two, this would effectively reduce the amount of the contribution to the taxpayer/donor's adjusted basis (all potential gain would either be long-term capital gain—reduced in Step Three—or not long-term capital gain—reduced in Step Two).

Treas. Reg. §1.170A-4 provides limited guidance regarding how a donor might prove related use. Certainly, a taxpayer will rarely want to donate appreciated tangible personal property to a public charity for an unrelated use: the loss of deduction amount would be unjustifiable. If a charitable recipient could not assure the donor that it would indeed use the donated property in a related manner, the donor would be well-advised to find another charitable recipient. Such a large number of charities exist in the United States that most any property should be of use to some entity.

While the above hypothetical facts do not suggest whether the hospital recipient would indeed use the oil field generator, such a use is easily imaginable considering the need for a continuous supply of electricity. Assuming the taxpayer were well-advised, he would have received assurances of such a use in advance of the donation, obviating the risk of a Step Three reduction.

Thus, after Step Three, taxpayer's contribution amount remains at:

Cash	$100,000
Generator	$125,000
Land	$500,000
Total	$725,000

Step 4: § 170(e)(1)(B)(i)(II): Related Property Reduction for Property Sold Before Close of Taxable Year.

This provision does not apply in our situation. But it does suggest the need to get a letter from the donee organization stating that (1) the property is indeed related to the exempt purpose, (2) the donee organization will complete the necessary § 170(e)(7)(D) certification, and (3) the property will not be sold or otherwise disposed of prior to the close of the taxable year or for three years thereafter. See § 170(e)(7).

Step 5: § 170(e)(1)(B)(ii): Private Foundation *Reduction*

As quoted in Step Three, § 170(e)(1)(B) reduces the amount of the contribution by:

> the amount of gain which would have been long-term capital gain if the property contributed had been sold by the taxpayer at its fair market value (determined at the time of such contribution).

In Step Three, this reduction applied to unrelated tangible personal property. Pursuant to § 170(e)(1)(B)(ii), the reduction for potential long-term capital gain applies to most donations (with some exceptions) to most *private foundations.*

> (ii) to or for the use of a private foundation (as defined in § 509(a)), other than a private foundation described in subsection (b)(1)(F),

Clearly, this reduction applies regardless of whether the donated property is related or unrelated, tangible or intangible, personal or real. Effectively, it reduces the contribution amount to basis for contributions to most private foundations. This is a significant example of how private foundations are disfavored as compared to public charities.

Subparagraph 170(b)(1)(F) lists some favored private foundations—particularly private operating foundations. These entities not only receive treatment comparable to public charities under § 170(e), but they also receive more favorable treatment (compared to most private foundations) under §§ 170(b)(1)(A) and 4940.

Paragraph 170(e)(3) lists several types of contributions that escape part of the Step Two reduction. For example, contributions of "qualified appreciated stock" to a private foundation may be deductible at fair market value rather than basis.

The above facts provide for a *hospital* recipient. Such an entity is described in § 170(b)(1)(A)(iii) and thus automatically qualifies as a public charity under § 509(a)(1). As a result, all three contributions to it escape a Step Five reduction.

If, instead, the recipient were a disfavored private foundation, the contribution amount for the generator would drop to its $125,000 basis and the contribution amount for the land would drop to its $100,000 basis. In the case of the land, which is very substantially appreciated, the Step Five reduction would be particularly harsh. Hence, the donor was well-advised to contribute that property to a public charity. In the case of the generator, which was less significantly appreciated, the Step Five reduction is important, but not overwhelming.

Thus, after Step 5, taxpayer's contribution amount remains at:

Cash	$100,000
Generator	125,000
Land	500,000
Total	$725,000

Step 6: § 170(e)(1)(B)(iii): Reduction for intellectual or intangible properties.

Since there was no intellectual or intangible property donated, this provision does not apply.

Step 7: § 170(e)(1)(B)(iv): Reduction for Taxidermy Property

There was no gift of stuffed animal heads and the like so this provision does not apply.

Step 8: § 170(b)(1)(A): Public Charity *Limitation*

Section 170(b)(1)(A) limits the total amount of public charity contributions:

> to the extent that the aggregate of such contributions does not exceed 50% of the taxpayer's contribution base for the taxable year.

Section 170(b)(1)(H) defines contribution base as:

> adjusted gross income (computed without regard to any net operating loss carryback to the taxable year under § 172).

Specifically, this limitation applies only to contributions *to* a public charity, as opposed to *for the use of* a public charity. Although § 170(e) defines the term charitable contribution as including gifts both *to* and *for the use of* various charities, only those *to* public charities receive the favorable 50% adjusted gross income limitation.

Also, for this purpose, we are using the term "public charity" extra broadly: as including not only actual public charities, but also § 170(b)(1)(F) private foundations. This is the same group of private foundations excluded from the harsh Step Five reduction; hence, while they are not technically public charities, they receive *some* public charity benefits.

Amounts limited by Step Eight are not lost (as is the case with Steps Two, Three, and Five reductions); instead, they may be carried over for five years. Section 170(d) provides complicated carryover provisions for amounts limited by Step Eight. In contrast, Steps Nine, Ten, and Eleven carryover provisions are found elsewhere. In general, carryovers last for five years, after which they disappear. They retain their character—as contributions to public charities or to private foundations and of personal versus real, tangible versus intangible, and related versus unrelated property. Any reductions which occurred in the year of contribution are permanent and thus affect carryover years as well.

In the respective carryover year, current contributions are deducted first, followed by the oldest to the youngest carryover amounts. Thus, if a taxpayer has a five-year-old carryover and a two-year-old carryover to the current year, he would first deduct current contributions. If he then had not consumed the entire 50% of his contribution base, he would deduct the five-year-old carryover amount (assuming it was to a public charity). Any amount not deducted would be lost. If, after deducting the carryover he continued to have any remaining allowance amount, he could deduct the two-year old carryover.

Within the current year, two different ordering rules apply:

1. Cash is deducted first. Hence, if anything is carried over, it is first comprised of property contributions rather than cash.

2. Non-capital gain property is deducted before capital gain property. I.R.C. § 170(b)(1)(C)(i).

In the above example, the taxpayer's adjusted gross income was $1,500,000, which also was his contribution base. Fifty percent of that amount is $750,000. Each of the three contributions made were *to* a hospital, which qualifies as a public charity under § 170(b)(1)(A)(iii). Hence, Step Eight does not limit the deductibility of the three contributions.

Thus, after Step Eight, taxpayer's deduction amount is:

Cash	$100,000
Generator	125,000
Land	500,000
Total	$725,000

Step 9: § 170(b)(1)(B): Private Foundation *Limitation*

Section 170(b)(1)(B) limits private foundation contributions (plus contributions merely *for the use of* public charities) to the lesser of:

(i) 30 percent of the taxpayer's contribution base for the taxable year, or

(ii) the excess of 50 percent of the taxpayer's contribution base for the taxable year over the amount of charitable contributions allowable under subparagraph (A).

Clearly, private foundation contributions are thus disfavored (at least those to other than (b)(1)(F) private foundations). Also, clearly, public charity contributions are to be deducted first, with private foundation contributions consuming only the remaining contribution base. Remember, such *limited* private foundation contributions are also those subjected to the harsh Step Five permanent *reduction* to basis amount.

Any amount limited by Step Nine may be carried over for up to five years. The specific rules governing such carryovers appears in § 170(b)(1)(B) flush language. Such carryovers retain their character as private foundation contributions in succeeding years. They are also subject to the § 170(d) carryover ordering rules.

In the above example, the taxpayer's contribution base was $1,500,000. Thirty percent of that amount is $450,000. But, the taxpayer made public charity contributions in the amount of $725,000. Fifty percent of his contribution base was $750,000, which exceeds the public charity contribution amount by only $25,000. Because $25,000 is less than $450,000, the Step Nine limitation is only $25,000.

The facts did not mention any private foundation contributions. If the taxpayer were to make any, he could, at most, deduct $25,000, with any excess amount to be carried over for up to five years.

Thus, after Step Nine, taxpayer's deduction amount remains:

Cash	$100,000
Generator	125,000
Land	500,000
Total	$725,000

Step 10: § 170(b)(1)(C): Public Charity *Limitation* or *Election* of *Reduction*

Section 170(b)(1)(C) furthers limits contributions to public charities (again including favored private foundations under § 170(b)(1)(F)). The limitation is very complicated.

First, it does not affect Step Nine; hence, the above Step Nine private foundation limitation amount of $25,000 remains even if Step Ten substantially limits public charity contributions.

Second, the Step Ten limitation applies only to contributions of capital gain property not already reduced in Step Three. It does not apply to cash contributions or to contributions of non-capital assets or non-section 1231 assets. It also does not apply to contributions of intangible property, real property, or property unrelated to the recipient's exemption: such contributions would have been subjected to the Step Three reduction and thus escape the Step Ten reduction. In other words, Steps Three and Ten are mutually exclusive. Or, a third way of saying it: §§ 170(b)(1)(C) and (e)(1)(B) are mutually exclusive: if Step Three reduces the contribution amount to basis, Step Ten does not apply.

Third, the donor may elect not to h[illegible] Ten apply to any property. The cost of the election, however, is that Step T[illegible] then apply to all property.

In the above example, the cash contribution escapes Step Ten limitation. The land and generator contributions, however, trigger the limitation. The land was real property donated to a public charity. The generator comprised related tangible personal property donated to a public charity. As such, Step Three did *not* apply to either, which was good news: the contribution amounts did *not* drop to basis. The cost of that good news, however, is that Step Ten applies.

Thirty percent of the taxpayer's $1,500,000 contribution base is $450,000. The amount of public charity contributions of capital gain property to which Step Three did not apply was $125,000 (the generator, as reduced in Step Two) plus $500,000 (the land). This is thus limited in current deductibility to $450,000. The excess $175,000 is carried over for up to five years per § 170(b)(1)(C)(ii). The carryover retains its character as a gift to a public charity of capital gain property that escaped Step Three.

As explained above, this Step Ten limitation does not affect Step Nine. The maximum amount currently deductible by the hypothetical taxpayer for private foundation gifts remains at $25,000—it *does not* increase to $200,000. Treas. Reg. § 1.170A-8(f) Examples 2, 5, 15(b). This regulation is consistent with the clause 170(b)(1)(B)(ii) parenthetical providing that the 170(b)(1)(B) computation (*i.e.*, Step Nine) is "determined without regard to subparagraph (c) (*i.e.*, Step Ten)."

Thus, if the Step Ten limitation applies, the taxpayer's deduction amount is $550,000: the cash of $100,000 plus $450,000 of capital gain property contributions. His carryover amount is $175,000 of capital gain property to a public charity to which Step Three did not apply.

The taxpayer, however, has a choice. Section 170(b)(1)(C)(iii) permits him to elect to apply the Step Three reduction and thus escape the Step Ten limitation. If he were to do so, the generator contribution would drop to its basis of $100,000 and the land contribution would drop to its basis of $100,000. The full $300,000 contribution amounts (cash plus generator plus land) would satisfy the Step Eight limitation amount. Step Nine would then be re-computed. The private foundation contribution limitation would be the lesser of 30% of the contribution base ($450,000) or the excess of 50% of contribution base ($750,000) minus the Step Eight amount (now $300,000). Both limitations would then be $450,000, which would be the Step Nine limit.

Although the facts did not hypothesize a private foundation gift, consider a cash contribution of $450,000. Without the § 170(b)(1)(C)(iii) election, the taxpayer would have deducted $25,000 to the private foundation and $550,000 to the public charity for a total of $575,000. He would have also had a private foundation carryover of $425,000 and a public charity carryover of $175,000. In the alternative, he could elect to apply Step Three to the land and generator. In such a case, he could deduct only $300,000 to the public charity, but he could then deduct $450,000 to the private foundation. He would have no carryovers.

Which should he choose: $575,000 current deduction with a $600,000 carryover (private plus public) *or* $750,000 current deduction with no carryover? The answer is unclear without further information. Assuming the taxpayer is young (he'll live long enough to use the carryovers) and wealthy (he'll have sufficient contribution base to use the carryovers), the non-election option appears better, even though it results in a smaller current contribution. If, instead, the taxpayer is elderly, ill, or perhaps already dead, rendering the value of the potential carryover nearly or absolutely worthless, the larger current deduction is preferable.

Of note, the election applies to all subject property during the year—the taxpayer cannot choose to apply it to some, but not all, eligible contributions. Also, once the election applies, the amount of the subject contributions is permanently reduced, even if the contribution is carried over to a year without an election. Third, if a contribution not subject to an election is carried over to a year of an election, the election reduction applies not only to current contributions, but also to the carryovers used.

Step 11: § 170(b)(1)(D): Private Foundation *Limitation*

Section 170(b)(1)(D) further limits private foundation contributions to the lesser of:

> (I) 20 percent of the taxpayer's contribution base for the taxable year, or
>
> (II) the excess of 30 percent of the taxpayer's contribution base for the taxable year over the amount of the contributions of capital gain property to which subparagraph (C) applies.

This limitation is further evidence of the disfavor to which private foundation contributions are subject. Also, as above, any contributions so limited may be carried over for up to five years.

In the above example, the Step Eleven limitation would likely be zero, which is the lesser of 20% of the contribution base ($300,000) or zero ($450,000 minus the $450,000 non-election contribution of capital gain property to the public charity).

If the hypothetical taxpayer were to make the Step Ten election, the Step Eleven limitation would rise to $300,000. Twenty percent of the contribution base would still be $300,000, and the secondary limitation would be $450,000 (30% of contribution base minus zero contributions to which subparagraph C applied—zero, because the election was to apply to § 170(e)(1)(B) and not § 170(b)(1)(C)). The $300,000 amount is less than $450,000, and thus applies.

Problems

1. *Percentage Limitations.* For Year 1, John has Gross Income of $200,000 and Adjusted Gross Income of $180,000. He has no net operating loss carryovers.

> a. What is the maximum amount he can deduct for charitable contributions made during Year 1?
>
> b. What is the maximum amount he can deduct for charitable contributions to Private Foundations (other than those described in § 170(b)(1)(F)) during Year 1?

c. What is the maximum amount of he can deduct for contributions of "capital gain property" during Year 1?

d. What is the maximum amount he can deduct for contributions of "capital gain property" to Private Foundations (other than those described in § 170(b)(1)(F)) during Year 1?

2. *Carryovers*. For both Year 1 and Year 2, Jim had a "contribution base" of $300,000. He had no charitable contribution carryovers from years prior to Year 1. During Year 1, he gave $200,000 cash to a "public charity" [a school] described in § 170(b)(1)(A)(ii) and no other contributions for either year.

a. How much may he deduct for Year 1? For Year 2?

b. Suppose Jim also gave $150,000 cash to the school during Year 2. How does this affect his charitable contribution carryover? When does the carryover expire? See § 170(d) for carryovers of non-capital gain contributions to public charities.

c. Suppose, instead, Jim gave $100,000 cash to the school in Year 1 and $100,000 cash to a Private Foundation (not described in § 170(b)(1)(F)) and also $150,000 cash to the school in Year 2.

d. Suppose, instead, Jim gave $150,000 cash each year to the school plus undeveloped land with a fair market value of $100,000. How much could he deduct in Year 1 and Year 2 and what would be the amount, nature and time limits on any resulting carryovers?

3. *Amount of Contributions*. For Year 1, Jane had a "contributions base" of $450,000. She donated the following items to a school, described in § 170(b)(1)(A)(ii) [automatically a Public Charity per § 509(a)(1)]. Pursuant to § 170(e), what is the amount of each contribution? How much can she deduct for Year 1? What is the amount and nature of her carryover, if any? [Do not concern yourself with § 170(b)(1)(C) for now].

a. Cash of $50,000.

b. Undeveloped land, held for investment, with a basis of $10,000 and a fair market value of $50,000.

c. Shares of stock in General Motors, with a basis of $20,000 and a fair market value of $30,000.

d. Share of stock in ABC.com, with a basis of $100,000 and a fair market value of $10,000.

e. Office equipment with an original cost of $25,000, a fair market value of $7,500, and a basis of zero (reflecting depreciation of $25,000). [Query: would it matter if the basis reduction resulted from a § 179 election rather than § 169 depreciation?]

f. Artwork with an original cost of $25,000 and a fair market value of $100,000. [Query: does it matter what the school plans to do with the artwork? *See* § 170(e)(1)(B)(i).]

g. Personal services, performed by her, with a value of $10,000 and associated with out-of-pocket expenses incurred by her of $500.

h. Inventory with a fair market value of $20,000 and a basis of $5,000.

i. Her personal use automobile with an original cost of $40,000, a fair market value (reflecting its real condition) of $2,000, and a "Blue Book" value of $6,000 (reflecting average condition).

j. How would your answers change if all the donations were to a Private Foundation (not described in § 170(b)(1)(F))? *See* § 170(e)(1)(B)(ii).

4. *Election.* Taxpayer, with a contribution base of $100,000, made two gifts. He gave a public charity capital gain real property with a fair market value of $50,000 and a basis of $40,000. He gave $30,000 cash to a private foundation.

5. *Bargain Sale.* Ann sold a building and land to a public charity for $270,000. The total Fair Market Value was $360,000. Her Adjusted Basis was $160,000. Prior depreciation was $40,000. What are the tax consequences to Ann?

6. *Complicated Problem.* During Year 1, D, a calendar-year individual taxpayer, made a charitable contribution to a church of $8,000, consisting of $5,000 in cash and $3,000 in vacant land. The land had an adjusted basis of $500. For Year 1, D's contribution base was $10,000. D had no carryovers of charitable contributions from prior years. During Year 2, D gave a contribution of $10,000 in vacant land to the church. The land had an adjusted basis of $9,900. D had a year Year 2 contribution base of $25,000. You are asked to determine D's charitable deduction for Year 2.

7. *Very Complicated Problem.* Taxpayer made two contributions during the taxable year: one to a hospital and one to a private foundation not described in § 170(b)(1)(F). To the hospital, he gave oil field generating equipment with a fair market value of $750,000, an adjusted basis of $250,000, and an original cost of $500,000. To the private foundation, he gave securities with a fair market value of $300,000 and an adjusted basis of $100,000. He had a contribution base of $1,000,000 and no carryovers of charitable contributions. What may he deduct for income tax purposes?

8. *Foreign Gifts.* Alphonse gave $100,000 to a French school. He had a contribution base of $200,000. May he take an income tax deduction?

a. Suppose, instead, the gift was to a Delaware subsidiary of the French school.

b. Suppose, instead, Alphonse, Inc. made the contribution to the Delaware subsidiary.

c. Considering *Bilingual Montessori School v. Commissioner,* 75 T.C. 480 (1980), and Rev. Rul. 66-79, how much presence should the foreign entity have in the U.S.? May it be a mere subsidiary of a foreign entity, or should it actually control the foreign operations? What other factors are important?

9. *Contributions from Non-Citizens.* Juan, a citizen of Uruguay, donated $15,000 of U.S. income to a Puerto Rican charitable corporation. What are the U.S. tax consequences? Consider §§ 170(c)(2), 2522(a), 2055(a)(2), and 2522(b)(2).

10. *Corporate Contributions.* ABC, Inc., a for profit C corporation, had $1,000,000 taxable income during Year 1. It gave land with a fair market value of $500,000 and a basis of $100,000 to a Public Charity described in § 170(b)(1)(A)(iii). This was its only charitable contribution for the year. How much may it deduct?

a. Would your answer change if the contribution were to a Private Foundation not described in § 170(b)(1)(F)?

b. Suppose ABC, Inc. had no assets other than the land: what would be the tax consequence of the donation? Consider § 337 and Treas. Reg. § 1.337(d)-4. Would it matter whether the charity owned any of the stock in ABC?

Chapter 32

Foreign Charities and Cross Border Giving

A. Introduction

Today's world is increasingly characterized by international trade. Groups such as the World Trade Organization are actively and continuously working to eliminate geographic, legal, and cultural barriers to economic trade. As a result, borders are becoming increasingly irrelevant to human interactions. That growing irrelevance of borders applies no less to the universe of charitable organizations and charitable givers. But still, as one author notes below, laws relating to charity are still essentially "landlocked" and inconsistent across differing jurisdictions. It doesn't take much knowledge of high economic theory to conclude that differing legal structures interfere with the efficient operation of altruistic organizations and individuals in the global environment. The consequences are not merely theoretical. One country's qualification laws might seriously impede or thwart altogether efforts of altruistic individuals in another country designed to respond to humanitarian crises. Despite these axiomatic observations — ones made by many observers — neither the United States nor the world community have taken significant steps towards dismantling legal barriers to international operations of charities and charitable givers. What might account for the reluctance to eliminate barriers to international charitable activity, even as countries work to eliminate barriers to profit making activities? We offer one possible rationale below.

Whatever the rationale, we presently live in a world of nations each of which jealously guards its prerogatives with regard to the regulation of charities within their borders. Time and space do not allow us to survey all the differing laws so we limit our study to the manner in which the United States regulates the international aspects of charities and charitable organizations. The following excerpt addresses (1) the income tax consequences of giving to foreign organizations by individuals and corporations, and (2) the U.S. domestic law treatment of foreign organizations.

B. Technical Rules Relating to Deduction of Contributions to and U.S. Tax Exemption for Foreign Organizations

Harvey P. Dale, Foreign Charities[1]

48 Tax Lawyer 655 (1995)

* * *

I. Introduction

One of the most knowledgeable observers of international nonprofit activity recently wrote:

> A striking upsurge is under way around the globe in organized voluntary activity and the creation of private, nonprofit or nongovernmental organizations. From the developed countries of North America, Europe and Asia to the developing societies of Africa, Latin America and the former Soviet bloc, people are forming associations, foundations and similar institutions to deliver human services, promote grass-roots economic development, prevent environmental degradation, protect civil rights and pursue a thousand other objectives formerly unattended or left to the state.

The scope and scale of this phenomenon are immense. Indeed, we are in the midst of a global "associational revolution" that may prove to be as significant to the latter twentieth century as the rise of the nation-state was to the latter nineteenth. The upshot is a global third sector: a massive array of self-governing private organizations, not dedicated to distributing profits to shareholders or directors, pursuing public purposes outside the formal apparatus of the state. The proliferation of these groups may be permanently altering the relationship between states and citizens, with an impact extending far beyond the material services they provide.[2]

The enormous scope of this international activity has given rise to an urgent need for support from U.S. individuals and organizations. The legal—and particularly the federal tax—structure regulating such giving, however, is ancient and bizarre. It serves more to constrain than to guide or assist. It is in great need of overhaul. This Article attempts to describe, and then to criticize, the current U.S. rules.

* * *

There are only approximately 1,000 foreign organizations listed as charitable in the I.R.S. Master File of Nonprofit Entities. Only a few of them file returns with the Service. In 1985, the foreign charitable organizations that did file returns reported

1. We have edited this article.—Editors.

2. [1] Lester M. Salamon, *The Rise of the Nonprofit Sector*, Foreign Affairs, July-Aug. 1994, at 109. For a description of, and the preliminary results of, a significant international project headed by Prof. Salamon and designed to shed some empirical light on the global role of the third sector, see Lester M. Salamon & Helmut K. Anheier, The Emerging Sector: An Overview (1994).

total revenue of $3.9 million ($2 million of which came from contributions) and total assets of $7 million. A recent sample of grantmaking by the largest U.S. foundations showed that just over ten percent of total giving—amounting to over $500 million—went either to foreign recipients or to domestic recipients for international purposes.

The Conference Board estimates that "[o]ver the past [ten] years, companies in the United States have increased their contributions to foreign countries by more than 500 percent." The "steep rise" from 1981 through 1990 "did not continue," and foreign contributions from such companies "appear to be flattening." Nevertheless, the median aggregate foreign donations made by reporting U.S. companies rose from less than $100,000 in 1981 to $429,000 in 1991.

These figures vastly understate the number and size of foreign charities for several reasons. Virtually no foreign charities apply to the Service for a determination letter or file information returns; the I.R.S. Master File is seriously inaccurate; and data is sparse and unreliable on the nonprofit universe generally and on foreign charities in particular.

* * *

In an increasingly interconnected global economy, international charitable activities have also grown rapidly. The collapse of communism and the emergence of nascent free markets in many previously socialist states have also provoked growing interest in foreign charities. Despite this, only a few articles and secondary sources address the relevant tax and other issues raised.

This Article will consider, in turn, (1) the U.S. tax treatment of U.S. donors (individuals, corporations, trusts and estates, private foundations, and public charities) to foreign charitable organizations; (2) the U.S. tax treatment of foreign charities themselves; and (3) certain non-tax constraints on giving to foreign 501(c)(3) entities.

II. Treatment of U.S. Donors

A. Individuals

When a U.S. individual contributes money or property to a charity, there may be income, gift, excise, estate, or generation-skipping tax consequences.

1. Income Tax

The principal provision for income tax purposes is section 170, which includes a definition of "charitable contribution." For foreign charities, section 170(c)(2) is central. It includes "a contribution or gift to or for the use of . . . [a] corporation, trust, or community chest, fund, or foundation" which meets four statutory criteria:

> (1) The donee must be "created or organized in the United States or in any possession thereof, or under the law of the United States, any State, the District of Columbia, or any possession of the United States;"
>
> (2) The donee must be "organized and operated exclusively for religious, charitable, scientific, literary, or educational purposes, or to foster national

or international amateur sports competition . . . or for the prevention of cruelty to children or animals;"

(3) The donee must avoid the proscription against private inurement; and

(4) The donee must avoid the prohibitions against political campaign activity and excessive lobbying.

The first criterion is pivotal. Prior to 1938, there was no such geographical limitation for individual charitable contributions in the Code. The Revenue Act of 1935, which first gave corporations an income tax charitable contributions deduction, contained two geographical limitations: no corporate deduction was allowed either for gifts to foreign-organized donees or, generally, for foreign use of donated property or money. The Revenue Act of 1938 imposed the first of these geographical limitations (but not the second) on individual charitable contribution deductions; it provided that no deduction was available unless the recipient was a "domestic" organization. This restriction was not inadvertent. The legislative history said:

> The bill provides that the deduction . . . be also restricted to contributions made to domestic institutions. The exemption from taxation of money or property devoted to charitable and other purposes is based upon the theory that the Government is compensated for the loss of revenue by its relief from financial burden which would otherwise have to be met by appropriations from public funds, and by the benefits resulting from the promotion of the general welfare. The United States derives no such benefit from gifts to foreign institutions, and the proposed limitation is consistent with the above theory. If the recipient, however, is a domestic organization the fact that some portion of its funds is used in other countries for charitable and other purposes (such as missionary and educational purposes) will not affect the deductibility of the gift.

In the case of a corporation, contributions or gifts . . . to or for the use of a domestic corporation, or domestic trust, or domestic community chest, fund, or foundation, organized and operated exclusively for . . . charitable . . . purposes . . . (but in the case of contributions or gifts to a trust, chest, fund, or foundation, only if such contributions or gifts are to be used within the United States).

The quoted language contains bad history, because there is no indication that the tax exemption, afforded since the end of the nineteenth century, was predicated on the quid pro quo rationale. It contains bad philosophy, because the quid pro quo rationale for tax exemption is quite defective. Indeed, the Service itself has expressed doubts about the quoted language on that ground, stating:

> It would seem to be at least very doubtful, however, that the well-recognized propriety of treating trusts for the advancement of religion as charitable can be adequately explained or justified on this [quid pro quo] basis in view of the broad constitutional restrictions in regard to the separation of church and state affairs that apply with respect to all levels of government in this

> country. Somewhat the same general situation likewise appears to obtain with respect to the virtually universal recognition of a charitable status for any trust which is exclusively engaged in relieving poverty or in advancing education among the residents of foreign lands.

* * *

The legislative history also contains bad logic, because it makes no sense to deny the deduction on the basis of where the donee is organized but to permit it even if the funds are expended abroad. Nevertheless, the place-of-organization restriction has been part of the Code since 1938.

It should be noted that the 1938 legislative history, quoted above, conceded that a domestic donee was permitted to use "some portion of its funds" abroad. The relevant regulations now read: "A charitable contribution by an individual to or for the use of an organization described in section 170(c) may be deductible even though all, or some portion, of the funds of the organization may be used in foreign countries for charitable or educational purposes."[3] Thus, although the Code absolutely bars income tax deductions for an individual's gifts directly to foreign charities, there is no restriction whatsoever on the foreign use of funds by U.S. charities. Furthermore, it is clear that, in pursuit of its mission, a domestic charity can properly make charitable gifts to a foreign charity.[4]

An obvious question arises: is a U.S. individual donor entitled to an income tax deduction for contributions to a U.S. donee made with the expectation that the U.S. donee, in turn, will re-grant the funds to a foreign charity? The seminal authority is Revenue Ruling 63-252, which discusses five examples. In the first three examples, no income tax deduction is permitted because the U.S. charity has no discretionary authority, and must transmit certain funds to the foreign charity. In example 4, because the U.S. charity reserves the power to review and approve grants from its general funds to the foreign charity, the ruling permits the U.S. individual donor to claim a tax deduction. In example 5, the U.S. charity is itself active in a foreign country, where it also sometimes uses its own subsidiary foreign charity for administrative convenience, but subject to complete control by the U.S. parent. Once again, the ruling permits a tax deduction. The crucial language in the ruling is:

---

3. [30] Regs. §1.170A-8(a)(1). *See also* Rev. Rul. 63-252, 1963-2 C.B. 101 (confirming that section 170(c)(2)(A) "does not restrict the area in which deductible contributions may be used"). *Accord* Rev. Rul. 71-460, 1971-2 C.B. 231 (charitable organization remains tax exempt even if all of its activities are outside of the United States); Bilingual Montessori School of Paris, Inc. v. Commissioner, 75 T.C. 480, 485 (1980) (individual allowed income tax deductions for gifts to a U.S. organization even though all of its activities were carried out abroad). This position is longstanding. *See, e.g.*, (approving charitable status for an organization formed to provide war memorials in European countries); (approving charitable status for an organization providing a water supply system in Lebanon). *See also* G.C.M. 30645 (Apr. 30, 1958).

4. [31] Rev. Rul. 63-252, 1963-2 C.B. 101; Rev. Rul. 66-79, 1966-1 C.B. 48; Rev. Rul. 69-80, 1969-1 C.B. 65; Rev. Rul. 75-65, 1975-1 C.B. 79.

> [I]f an organization is required for other reasons, such as a specific provision in its charter, to turn contributions, or any particular contribution it receives, over to another organization, then in determining whether such contributions are deductible it is appropriate to determine whether the ultimate recipient of the contribution is a qualifying organization.... [I]t seems clear that the [geographical] requirements of section 170(c)(2)(A) ... would be nullified if contributions inevitably committed to go to a foreign organization were held to be deductible solely because, in the course of transmittal to the foreign organization, they came to rest momentarily in a qualifying domestic organization. In such cases the domestic organization is only nominally the donee; the real donee is the ultimate foreign recipient.

Revenue Ruling 63-252 has been widely misunderstood. The Service does not require, for example, that the domestic entity look about to see which particular foreign donee deserves the funds it receives. The Service well understands that a U.S. intermediate donee — often referred to as a "friends of" organization — will give only to a particular named foreign entity. It does require:

(1) that the U.S. intermediate donee not be bound to deliver the funds to the foreign entity by virtue of a charter or by-law provision;

(2) that gifts by the U.S. intermediate donee to the foreign entity be within the charitable mission and purpose of the U.S. entity; and

(3) that the U.S. intermediate donee exercise some appropriate level of scrutiny over the foreign donee to make sure that it, in turn, is an eligible charity within the meaning of section 501(c)(3) (the so-called "foreign equivalency" test).[5]

It is extremely difficult to justify the place-of-organization restriction. The rationale in the relevant legislative history is both inadequate and erroneous. No such restrictions apply for purposes of the gift or estate tax charitable deduction. In a world in which charity increasingly crosses — and ought to cross — national borders, U.S. donors should not be forced to resort to formalisms, such as "friends of" organizations, in order to provide needed support abroad. Although an intermediate U.S. — organized donee may be administratively helpful, making it easier for the Service to obtain and audit documents and records, there are other more suitable methods available to the Service to obtain foreign-located documents and information. The easiest would be to require more detailed substantiation of foreign-targeted charitable deductions under already-existing Code provisions.

---

5. [35] There should be no requirement that the governing board of the U.S. charity have a different composition or different members than that of the foreign charity. Although the Service has never so stated explicitly, and although many practitioners advise to the contrary, there is some evidence that board member overlaps are not fatal. Private Letter Ruling 9129040 approved charitable status for a U.S. "friends of" organization that had seven directors, three of whom had to be approved by the foreign charity, and two of whose directors had to be present to constitute a quorum and had to vote in favor of any by-law amendments. P.L.R. 9129040 (Apr. 23, 1991).

* * *

b. *Bilateral Income Tax Treaties.* Three of our bilateral income tax conventions permit an income tax deduction for a direct gift by a U.S. person to a foreign charity. Under Article 22(2) of the U.S. — Mexico tax treaty, a U.S. individual is explicitly granted a deduction for a direct gift to a Mexican charity so long as the donee is subject to a Mexican law that provides standards "essentially equivalent" to the United States law regulating charitable organizations.[6]

* * *

Mexico has already adopted legislation which is intended to be "essentially equivalent" to the relevant U.S. law, and the United States has agreed that it does provide "essentially equivalent standards" for Mexican organizations within its coverage (but not including churches).

Under certain circumstances, U.S. individuals can also get a deduction for direct gifts to a Canadian charity. Article XXI(5) of the Canada-U.S. tax treaty, however, does not rely on Canadian legislation, but rather applies U.S. standards to the Canadian donee. Procedures to establish that a Canadian entity does qualify under U.S. standards are set forth in Revenue Procedure 59-31, 1959-2 C.B. 949. Section 3.02 of that Revenue

* * *

On September 23, 1994, the U.S. Senate finally consented to the adoption of the 1975 U.S. — Israel tax treaty, including Article 15A (from a 1980 protocol) permitting U.S. individuals a deduction for direct contributions to charities organized in Israel. . . . As in the Canadian case, the treaty does not rely on Israeli legislation to set standards for eligible donees; it applies U.S. standards.

For both Canada and Mexico, U.S. percentage limitations on the charitable deduction apply; for Israel, however, the percentage limitation is fixed by the treaty at twenty-five percent. In all three treaties, the relevant limitations are calculated by reference solely to the donor's income from sources within the foreign treaty state (*i.e.*, Mexico, Canada, or Israel).

* * *

Future U.S. bilateral tax treaties are unlikely to contain similar provisions. The Senate has expressed grave concern about using the treaty process to grant charitable contribution deductions which otherwise would be denied under section 170(c)

---

6. [52] Congress historically has been reluctant to extend the charitable deduction by treaty, and rejected a similar provision in Article 22 of the Brazil-U.S. tax treaty. Income Tax Treaty, Dec. 30, 1994, U.S.-Brazil, Tax Treaties (CCH) P1503.23, Tax Treaties (WGL) P21,501. For a general discussion, see Zack D. Mason, *Foreign Charitable Contribution Deductions: A Shift in U.S. Tax Treaty Policy?*, 7 Exempt Org. Tax Rev. 624 (1993). *See also* Milton Cerny, *Cross-Border Grant Making and the U.S.-Mexico Tax Treaty*, 10 Exempt Org. Tax Rev. 875 (1994); Milton Cerny, *U.S.-Israel Tax Treaty*, 10 Exempt Org. Tax Rev. 1156 (1994); Thomas A. Troyer, *EO Practitioners Alerted to Importance of U.S. — Mexico Tax Treaty*, 10 Exempt Org. Tax Rev. 877 (1994).

(2)(A). Thus, for example, the Senate Foreign Relations Committee Report on the U.S.-Mexico Income Tax Treaty states:

> A provision requiring the granting of deductions for contributions to treaty country charities is found in only one currently effective U.S. income tax treaty—the treaty with Canada—and in one income tax treaty that is not yet in force—the treaty with Israel. The Committee enunciated strong concerns with respect to those provisions, and made it clear that future treaties containing similar provisions would be closely scrutinized.
>
> As has been previously pointed out with respect to the Canadian and Israeli treaties, the Committee is concerned with granting deductions to U.S. persons by treaty in cases where the Congress has chosen not to do so under the ... Code. The Committee does not believe that the practice of allowing tax deductions to U.S. persons for contributions to charities in foreign countries should be expanded by the treaty process.

* * *

The Treasury Department appears to agree. Under questioning from Senator Sarbanes at a hearing before the Senate Foreign Relations Committee on October 27, 1993, Assistant Secretary of the Treasury Samuels stated:

> [I]n those very limited cases [of Canada and Mexico], I think, given the relationships with the countries, that it is appropriate. But I do agree with you, Senator, and your question that it is something that we do on an exceptional basis and not as a general part of our policy.

* * *

D. Private Foundations

Because domestic private foundations are exempt from taxation, the deductibility of their grants, gifts, or donations is not an issue. Private foundations do have other tax concerns, however, which affect their ability to make grants to foreign charities.

Private foundations are subject to the rules of Subchapter A of Chapter 42 of the Code, which were added in 1969. Among other requirements, private foundations must meet certain distribution-of-income rules to avoid penalty taxes. In general, they must make annual "qualifying distributions" in an amount equal to five percent of their net assets. "Qualifying distributions" include amounts "paid to accomplish one or more purposes described in section 170(c)(2)(B)," but generally do not include amounts paid to a non-operating private foundation. Thus, a private foundation must determine (1) whether its grants are paid for section 170(c)(2)(B) purposes, and (2) whether the donee is a non-operating private foundation.

As to the first test, it should make no difference to the U.S. private foundation whether a grant is being made to a domestic or a foreign donee. The second test, however, imposes a special burden on a U.S. foundation making grants to a foreign charity: determining whether the foreign charity is a non-operating private foundation. The regulations make clear that the U.S. donor is not prevented from making a grant merely because the foreign charity has not applied for and received a determination letter from the Service establishing its status. Instead, the regulations require the distributing U.S. foundation to make its own "good-faith determination" of the donee's organizational status.[7] The regulations explain that the:

> "[G]ood faith determination" ordinarily will be considered as made where the determination is based on an affidavit of the donee organization or an opinion of counsel (of the distributing foundation or the donee organization) that the donee is an organization described in section 509(a)(1), (2), or (3) or 4942(j)(3).

For many years, that was the state of the law. Private foundations had to make such good faith determinations whenever considering grants to foreign charities. No private foundation could rely on the good faith determination of another private foundation, even as to the same foreign donee. Furthermore, the details of compliance with the good-faith standard proved to be complex, time-consuming, and expensive.

The "taxable expenditures" rules[8] impose similar burdens on U.S. private foundations making grants to foreign charities. Section 4945(d) defines as a "taxable expenditure," subject to penalty taxes, any grant made by a private foundation unless:

> (A) such [donee] organization is described in paragraph (1), (2), or (3) of section 509(a) or is an exempt operating foundation (as defined in section 4940(d)(2)), or
>
> (B) the private foundation exercises expenditure responsibility with respect to such grant in accordance with subsection (h), . . .

In addition, this section treats as a "taxable expenditure" any grant made "for any purpose other than one specified in section 170(c)(2)(B)." The regulations provide two separate tests to guide the domestic foundation in making the relevant determinations:

---

7. [142] Regulations section 53.4942-3(a)(6)(i) provides:Distributions for purposes described in section 170(c)(2)(B) to a foreign organization, which has not received a ruling or determination letter that it is an organization described in section 509(a)(1), (2), or (3) or 4942(j)(3), will be treated as a distribution made to an organization described in section 509(a)(1), (2), or (3) or 4942(j)(3) if the distributing foundation has made a good faith determination that the donee organization is an organization described in section 509(a)(1), (2), or (3) or 4942(j)(13).

8. [145] Regulations section 53.4942-3(a)(6)(i) provides:

> Distributions for purposes described in section 170(c)(2)(B) to a foreign organization, which has not received a ruling or determination letter that it is an organization described in section 509(a)(1), (2), or (3) or 4942(j)(3), will be treated as a distribution made to an organization described in section 509(a)(1), (2), or (3) or 4942(j)(3) if the distributing foundation has made a good faith determination that the donee organization is an organization described in section 509(a)(1), (2), or (3) or 4942(j)(13).

> (1) With respect to expenditures described in section 4945(d)(4), the private foundation can make a "good faith determination that the grantee organization is an organization described in section 509(a)(1), (2), or (3)."
>
> * * *
>
> (2) With respect to expenditures described in section 4945(d)(5), the private foundation is protected if the donee is a section 501(c)(3) organization.[9] In the case of a foreign donee, the domestic foundation may make a "reasonable judgment . . . [that] the grantee organization is an organization described in section 501(c)(3)."

The good faith determination is made in virtually the same manner as for the qualifying distribution test. And, as in the case of qualifying-distribution determinations, the burdens of complying with the taxable-expenditure determinations—whether based on good faith or reasonable judgment—were substantial.

After several years of effort, the Service and the foundation community worked out a simplified method of compliance. In Revenue Procedure 92-94, the Service removed most—but not quite all—of the relevant thorns from the feet of U.S. private foundations. The revenue procedure applies:

> [I]f the grant is made by a domestic private foundation to a foreign organization that does not have [a] . . . Service ruling letter recognizing its exemption under section 501(c)(3), or classifying it as a public charity under section 509(a)(1), (2), or (3), or as a private operating foundation under section 4942(j)(3).

A domestic private foundation that follows the requirements of this revenue procedure will be protected against the imposition of excise taxes under both sections 4945 and 4942:

> If the requirements of this revenue procedure are met, a grant to a foreign grantee will be treated as a grant to an organization that is described in section 501(c)(3) or section 4947(a)(1), . . . and, that is either a public charity within the meaning of section 509(a)(1), (2), or (3), or a private operating foundation under section 4942(j)(3).

9. [149] Regulations section 53.4945-6(c)(2)(i) protects the donor if either it makes the grants to a section 501(c)(3) organization (other than one testing for public safety), or it "is reasonably assured" that the grant will be used for section 170(c)(2)(B) purposes, it undertakes to maintain the grant in a separate fund, and it complies with the expenditure responsibility provisions. Note that the status of the donee as a section 501(c)(3) organization relieves the donor of all of the more rigorous policing rules. In transmitting the Treasury Decision dealing with these regulations, while still in proposed form, the Commissioner wrote to the Assistant Secretary of the Treasury: "However, it appears to be an unreasonable administrative burden on the Service as well as the foreign organizations to require such organizations to obtain rulings or determination letters in situations where their only connection with the United States might be as recipient of a grant from a United States private foundation." T.D. 7233 (Oct. 4, 1972).

Revenue Procedure 92-94 allows both the reasonable judgment and good faith determinations to be made based on a "currently qualified affidavit" from the grantee. The affidavit need not have been prepared for the particular U.S. donor; thus, once a proper affidavit has been executed, it will, so long as it remains "currently qualified," protect all domestic private foundations making grants to the same foreign charity. In general, an affidavit will be "currently qualified" as to non-financial data so long as the underlying facts have not changed. If, however, financial data are important (*e.g.*, because the foreign grantee needs to demonstrate widespread public support for purposes of avoiding private foundation status), the affidavit will only be "currently qualified" if it reflects the grantee's "latest complete accounting year."

Although Revenue Procedure 92-94 significantly eases the burdens of U.S. private foundations interested in international grantmaking, it does not completely eliminate them. In addition to the "currently qualified affidavit" requirement, certain other tests must be met. First, not surprisingly, the affidavit may not protect a donor with actual knowledge that it is unreliable. Second, foreign schools must comply with U.S. standards for racial nondiscrimination. This second requirement was ratified for domestic schools by the Supreme Court in *Bob Jones University v. United States*, and has created some interesting problems — discussed below — in its application to foreign circumstances.

E. Public Charities

Because they are not subject to any of the Chapter 42 restrictions, public charities making contributions to foreign charities have a much easier row to hoe than do private foundations. Nevertheless, even public charities have important concerns about the charitable status of foreign donees.

For example, if a foreign donee does qualify under section 501(c)(3) standards, the domestic public charity may make donations to it without requiring any accounting. If the foreign donee does not so qualify, however, the domestic public charity would risk its own exemption if it transferred funds to the donee without verifying that the foreign donee used the funds for section 501(c)(3) purposes. As a recent Service publication states:

> [I]f a domestic organization, otherwise qualified under [section] 501(c)(3), transmits its funds to a private organization not described in [section] 501(c)(3) and fails to exercise, or has too little, discretion and control over the use of such funds to assure their use exclusively for charitable purposes, the domestic organization forfeits its qualification for exempt status because it cannot demonstrate that it is operated exclusively for charitable purposes, and contributions to it are not deductible.[10]

Thus, providing funds only to foreign donees that meet section 501(c)(3) standards (*i.e.*, that satisfy the so-called "foreign equivalency" test) may spare U.S. public

10. [168] IRS CPE § 92, *supra* note 33, at 233.

charities from a section 501(c)(3) version of expenditure responsibility. However, the regulations prescribe no good-faith or reasonable-judgment standards for making such determinations, and Revenue Procedure 92-94 provides no direct assistance.[11]

III. Treatment of Foreign Charities

A. In General

1. Tax-Exempt Status

Section 501(c)(3) contains no geographical restrictions. It is clear beyond question that foreign-organized entities may qualify under that paragraph. The Service has explicitly confirmed this in Revenue Ruling 66-177, 1966-1 C.B. 132 which reads, in its entirety:

> The fact that an organization has been formed under foreign law will not preclude its qualification as an exempt organization under section 501(a) of the Internal Revenue Code of 1954 if it meets the tests for exemption under that section.

Two questions remain: (1) how are U.S. standards for charitable status applied to foreign organizations; and (2) what procedural requirements, if any, affect foreign entities desiring so to qualify?

The first question has several interesting answers. The Service generally applies all relevant U.S. standards for section 501(c)(3) status to foreign entities. Thus, for example, they must be both organized and operated for charitable purposes. The former sometimes causes difficulties for foreign organizations which do not routinely put provisions in their "articles" addressing the proper charitable treatment of their assets on dissolution. Furthermore, the legal restrictions on inurement, private benefit, excessive lobbying, and political campaign activities are all applicable to foreign entities.

The Service also applies the public policy behind the *Bob Jones* decision to foreign organizations. Thus, foreign "schools" are expected to comply with Revenue Procedure 75-50, which requires every school to "show affirmatively both that it has adopted a racially nondiscriminatory policy as to students that is made known to the general public and that since the adoption of that policy it has operated in a bona fide manner in accordance therewith." More specifically, each school must include an appropriate nondiscriminatory statement "in its charter, bylaws, or other governing instrument, or in a resolution of its governing body"; include a similar statement "in all its brochures and catalogs dealing with student admissions, programs, and scholarships"; publicize its policy in "a newspaper of general circulation that serves

11. [170] Of course, counsel for public charities may attempt to rely on Revenue Procedure 92-94 as a useful analogy for their clients. By its own terms, however, the revenue procedure does not apply unless "the grant is made by a domestic private foundation." Rev. Proc. 92-94, 1992-2 C.B. 507, § 3.

all racial segments of the community" or via "the broadcast media . . . if this use makes such nondiscriminatory policy known to all segments of the general community" and take certain other steps. Each school "must certify annually, under penalties of perjury . . . that . . . the school has satisfied the applicable requirements of . . . this Revenue Procedure."

Clearly, few foreign schools comply with these requirements. The Service sometimes has been willing to waive some or all of them. For example, the Service confirmed the tax-exempt status of several foreign schools despite their non-compliance with various portions of Revenue Procedure 75-50, when each in fact had a racially-nondiscriminatory policy, the local law made it potentially illegal to maintain statistics by race, and their student bodies were racially mixed. The Service first stated that "the declared Federal policy against racial discrimination in education . . . is applicable to the subject foreign schools in the determination of their exempt status." It then analyzed the submissions of the foreign schools, including their statements that some of the Revenue Procedure 75-50 requirements would be illegal, unusual, embarrassing, or inappropriate in their respective circumstances. It concluded:

> We do recognize, however, that situations may arise where foreign law or practice may render compliance with certain provisions of [Revenue Procedure] 75-50 illegal or impractical in a particular country. In those cases, compliance with the provisions of [Revenue Procedure] 75-50 giving rise to the illegality or impracticality may be excused, but only after a showing by the foreign school of a reasonable basis for excusing compliance. The burden is on the organization to show such a reasonable basis.

This flexibility is reflected in Revenue Procedure 92-94, which permits the foreign charity's "currently qualified affidavit" to "explain any basis for the grantee school's failure to comply with one or more of the provisions of [Revenue Procedure] 75-50."

If a foreign organization, otherwise qualified under section 501(c)(3), violates some provision of foreign law — *e.g.*, a law requiring racial segregation — will that impact its U.S. tax status? It is clear that violations of U.S. law will result at least in the loss of tax exemption if the violations are not inadvertent and the law in question is not merely "regulatory." This is true even if the violations occur outside of the U.S. However, there is no authority bearing on an organization's ability to continue to qualify under section 501(c)(3) if the violation relates only to a provision of foreign law. The Service has called this an open question and has directed that any such issue be brought to the National Office for technical advice.

The Service has been inconsistent about whether foreign charities need to apply for recognition of their exempt status. For domestic charities, the rules are straightforward. With exceptions not here relevant, the Code requires that an organization apply to the Service within twenty-seven months of its organization for recognition of charitable status. The statute provides two apparent sanctions for failure to comply with this notice requirement: the offending charity "shall not be treated as an organization described in section 501(c)(3)," and donors to it will be denied a charitable contribution deduction. Because donors to foreign charities are denied such deductions in any event, only the first sanction appears to threaten foreign charities.

For several reasons, however, the apparent threat is illusory. First, the Service encourages tardy charities to apply for section 501(c)(4) status to cover the earlier period, and routinely grants such applications. In most cases, section 501(c)(4) status provides exactly the same tax-exempt benefits to the entity as section 501(c)(3). Furthermore, in the instances in which section 501(c)(4) status is not identical—*e.g.*, when the organization has outstanding section 103 bonds, or would become liable for state sales taxes, or has been contracting with state or local governments under rules requiring section 501(c)(3) status—the Service sometimes has been willing to grant section 501(c)(3) status retroactively, notwithstanding the charity's failure to file the notice in a timely fashion.

The Code itself exempts most foreign organizations from filing a notice. Section 4948(b) reads:

> Section 507 (relating to termination of private foundation status), section 508 (relating to special rules with respect to section 501(c)(3) organizations), and this chapter (other than this section) shall not apply to any foreign organization which has received substantially all of its support (other than gross investment income) from sources outside the United States.

* * *

Although section 4948(b) would appear to cover virtually all foreign charities, the Service has on occasion suggested that it applies only to foreign private foundations. Not only is that a narrow reading inconsistent with the statutory language, but, even if it is accepted, the section 4948(b) exemption may apply, because the Code contains a presumption that any organization which fails to notify the Service under section 508(a) is a private foundation. Thus, a silent foreign public charity would be presumed to be within section 4948(b) even if that section is narrowly read as applying only to foreign private foundations.

Although Service personnel sometimes assert that no foreign public charity can qualify under section 501(c)(3) if it fails to make a timely filing, in other instances the Service recognizes that both foreign public charities and foreign private foundations may indeed so qualify without filing a notice. The latter view should prevail, not only for the reasons urged above, but because it is completely foolish to assume that any meaningful number of foreign charities will even be aware of, much less choose to comply with, any requirement to file with the United States Internal Revenue Service.

* * *

2. Income Tax Consequences

A foreign organization that qualifies under section 501(c)(3) is "exempt from taxation under this subtitle," which includes all of the income tax provisions and the Chapter 3 withholding tax provisions. Thus, the Service confirmed as early as 1922 that a foreign charity was not liable for tax on U.S.—source bond interest received by it, and no withholding of tax was required. The Service has restated that early precedent several times. Each of these rulings, however, requires the foreign charity to notify the withholding agent of its exempt status, and each "suggests" doing so in language which refers to the Service's determination of the foreign charity's exempt status.

Because a foreign charity may qualify under section 501(c)(3) without asking the Service for any such determination, it would seem that no tax (and no withholding) should be imposed on such "silent" foreign entities. No authority was found bearing on this question, however. In other analogous situations, the regulations provide for making good-faith determinations of the charitable status of the silent entity, but no such regulations appear to cover this general case. Nevertheless, if the withholding agent is prepared to rely on its own analysis of the exempt status of a silent foreign charity, it should be protected if that judgment can be substantiated.

* * *

B. Foreign Private Foundations

1. Tax-Exempt Status

Because private foundations are a subset of section 501(c)(3) entities, the rules generally covering foreign charities also apply to foreign private foundations. Although even the Service agrees that section 4948(b) exempts foreign private foundations from filing under section 508, two consequences flow to a foreign private foundation that either fails to meet the "substantially all" test of section 4948(b) or engages in a prohibited transaction: (1) the section 508(a) notice requirements will apply, and (2) exempt status will be lost completely unless the foreign organization has certain provisions in its governing instrument covering mandatory distributions of income, self-dealing, excess business holdings, jeopardizing investments, and taxable transactions.

* * *

C. Policy Challenges Regarding Cross Border Giving and Multinational Charities

Penina Kessler Lieber, 1601–2001: An Anniversary of Note

62 U. Pitt. L. Rev. 731 (2001)

* * *

Globalization and technology are critical forces in today's world. Their impact on civil society has been extensive, necessitating that civil society establish a transnational agenda to insure its sustainability. While much has been written about sustainability in terms of policy and funding, less attention has been paid to the important role that law plays in providing support for civil society, its institutions and its programs. From that perspective, the real question may be: Does civil society have in place a legal infrastructure that is adequate, relevant and capable of furthering its stability and capacity for growth? It does not. Although the institutions, funding streams and volunteer reserves of civil society are internationalizing, the laws that control it are still overwhelmingly domestic. In other areas of international private tax and business law, geographic barriers are being dismantled; in the area of transnational civil society, however, the laws remain landlocked. Few coherent legal principles apply cross-border or from country to country. Few legal standards or norms transcend their borders. Like the Tower of Babel, the confusion is exacerbated-not only by cultural and historic differences, but by the nature of diverse legal systems (common law, civil law, former Socialist law, Asian law, religious law), which impose legal variants on basic aspects of civil society's practice and principle. These disparities include such basics as legal definitions/classifications, rules of formation/operation, legal personality/capacity, financial administration, public supervision/regulation, dissolution and tax treatment. Additional issues of state sovereignty and lost revenues add to the din. The need for coherent laws, standards and policies is not limited to the developing or the newly democratized states. The same question of adequacy applies to all countries, albeit in the context of existing law rather than emerging law.

One of the most pressing legal problems affecting civil society in 2001 derives from the inconsistent tax treatment of NGOs. Because charitable giving is the lifeblood of civil society, the question of tax treatment goes to the heart of the sector's sustainability. Without adequate tax incentives, it is unrealistic to assume that charitable dollars from individual donors, private foundations and/or corporate philanthropic programs will continue to generate enough funds to support the vast needs of newly independent or third world nations. Even though an increasing number of multinational corporations are now internationalizing their "corporate citizenship" activities, many companies still experience discomfort at the prospect of pouring corporate dollars into foreign communities without assurances of adequate accountability and without beneficial tax treatment. As a result, even the most sophisticated corporate philanthropists choose to rely on intermediary agencies for foreign charitable giving, despite corresponding administrative costs and decreased control.

Legal inadequacies continue to plague the deductibility rules of cross-border giving under the Internal Revenue Code. This is somewhat ironic given the progressive stance of Congress with respect to other aspects of section 501(c)(3), charitable exemption law. Still held hostage by the "geographic limitation rule" of Section 170 of the Internal Revenue Code. American donors are limited in the way they can make deductible, charitable contributions to foreign recipients. The rule is a product of the Depression mentality of the mid-late 1930's, when America was still focused inward on national recovery, had a New Deal domestic agenda and an isolationist foreign policy. In 1938, the Rule probably made good sense because it encouraged charitable giving domestically where the benefits were most needed. The Rule, however, continues its archaic control in a world that is very different from that of the 1930's. Since 1938, the Internal Revenue Service has tried repeatedly to ease the Rule by regulations and informal guidance. Similarly, the courts have wrestled with the Rule, although to a lesser degree, producing a body of case law that is small and narrow in scope. According to the Geographic Limitation Rule, American donors who wish to take a charitable deduction for a contribution to a foreign cause must do indirectly what they cannot do directly. The inconsistencies are obvious. The Rule allows the use of domestic intermediary organizations, but prohibits the use of "conduits." It disallows "earmarking," but promotes the use of "Friends of" organizations. The Rule endows the terms "discretion and control" with semi-magical properties and elevates form over substance.

The problem of inconsistent tax treatment is even more daunting in other countries, where there is no congruity between the legal rules on foundations and the fiscal policies that apply to them. This can be seen in matters of defined public benefit, tax exemptions and tax credits/deductibility. Rules of deductibility vary widely from country to country. They range from unlimited ceilings to 50% or 1%, 5% or 10% of pre-tax income and are often qualified by the nature of the charitable activity. The problem has not been resolved by either diplomatic intervention or by treaty. Ironically, there is not a single NGO-specific bilateral tax treaty, and only a handful of treaties or conventions even address the issue of cross-border reciprocity for charitable contributions. Although the United States has ratified three bilateral tax treaties granting reciprocity for charitable deductions, these treaties continue to retain foreign source income requirements, decreasing the efficacy of the deduction. Congress has been unwilling to enlarge the availability of treaties in this area.

Informal international efforts to develop a consistent tax policy have met with limited success. In 1970, the International Standing Conference on Philanthropy (Interphil) proposed a draft convention on the tax treatment of nonprofit organizations to the Council of Europe. The Council took no action on the proposal, although it later incorporated some of the provisions into the Convention on the Recognition of the Legal Personality of International Non-Governmental Organizations (1991). The impact of this document, however, is limited because its focus is directed at the single issue of possession of legal personality; it is silent on the broader issue of applicable law. Despite efforts to mobilize collective resources of NGO's affected by the inhospitable tax climate, little concrete progress has been made at the United Nations, Council of Europe and Organization of Economic Cooperation and Development (OECD), where the reluctance of member nations remains the status quo. Apparently, nongovernmental tax concerns plummet to the bottom of the list of international priorities when contrasted with security, health and commercial issues.

Note

What are the socio-political reasons why governments might be reluctant to eliminate barriers to international charitable activities? The following law review article excerpt seeks to answer the question we posed at the beginning of the chapter—why do governments maintain barriers to international charitable activity—by reference to a case study regarding China's transition to a market economy and its reluctance to encourage an independent charitable sector. Do you agree or disagree with the arguments?

Earlier, the Article briefly noted the opinion of one Chinese scholar who candidly admitted the unlikelihood that a true, independent sector will emerge in China because organizations that traditionally comprise the independent sector contain "threatening elements." An understanding of the phrase "independent sector" as that phrase is used in Western society, explains much of the apparent Chinese antipathy against Western-style altruistic organizations. The phrase implies that society may be divided into distinct sectors, one of which, the "independent sector," is populated by charities and other nonprofit organizations. The independent sector is loyal to no particular authority or philosophy except the accomplishment of "good works" and the diffusion and decentralization of authority. The other two sectors, government and business, compete with each other and with the independent sector for influence in the tripartite society. For reasons related to the monopolization and maintenance of power, the governmental sector seeks (but rarely attains) total allegiance and reacts suspiciously and defensively to criticism, whether implicit or explicit. The governmental sector pursues its own social theory, however just or unjust that theory may seem to those outside of the governmental sector. Authoritative governments attack, discredit and destroy social theories that are not in accord with their own, and just as often attacks methodologies that are not in accord with their own.

Darryll K. Jones, The Neglected Role of International Altruistic Investment in the Chinese Transition Economy

36 Geo. Wash. Int'l L. Rev. 71, 126–33 (2004)

* * *

The independent sector considers itself morally superior to the other sectors. Participants in the independent sector decry the mad pursuit of profit that ultimately benefits, or seems to benefit, only a few winners. Ironically, the independent sector seeks the sort of Utopia that China previously sought via the iron rice bowl. The independent sector is more similar to the governmental sector than to the business sector. Despite any similarities, though, the independent sector is nonetheless fiercely independent and it disdains the very essential characteristics of government, which are the concentration of power and the standardization of methodology. The independent sector is instead governed by principled expediency and particularized methodology with regard to the accomplishment of goals that are sometimes consistent with government goals. The independent sector is, almost by definition, invariably critical of government methodology, especially insofar as the allocation of power and influence within society are concerned.

* * *

The existence of an independent sector represents many ideals of Western democratic society. Western style independent sectors implicitly advocate the superiority of a society that believes in the sharing and diffusion of power, freedoms of speech, belief, dissent, and association. Observers, however, have noted that China seeks both economic democracy and also concentrated and centralized governmental power. China's gradual approach to transitioning from a planned to a market economy is motivated by a metaphorical desire to have its cake and eat it too. Some economists believe that a market economy can truly exist only within the context of a democratic political society and that, inevitably, China's strategy will fail. China's twenty-year transition process challenge's that conventional wisdom.

China refers to its new economic order as "market socialism" or "socialism with Chinese characteristics." The existence of a truly independent sector is either completely anathema to market socialism or at least much more threatening to market socialism than is the existence of a relatively unregulated, but closely supervised, business sector. The threat exists because the independent sector, idealized, represents an alternative sovereign that answers to discovered moral principle — the environment is to be protected at all costs, profits should give way to affordable housing, or social order does not justify the death penalty, to name a few such principles. The independent sector cannot be "bought out" the way business eventually will; it seemingly has no ultimate goal for which it will trade its critical and alternative nature. China might successfully incorporate Western economic theory and still maintain its present governmental structure, that is, China may indeed achieve market socialism — by allowing for the gradual emergence of a business sector while also maintaining its present form of government. It is unlikely, however, that China can maintain a centralized authoritative government alongside a Western-style independent sector.

* * *

The final barrier from a Chinese viewpoint is one that is particular to U.S. altruistic investment. Despite the many instances in which the Chinese and U.S. governments have engaged in tension-reducing, cooperative endeavors, the Chinese government still sometimes views and portrays the United States as an aggressive "hegemon," bent on forcing the international community to conform to U.S. desires. By some accounts, the Chinese government views U.S. international engagements, regardless of how benevolent a specific engagement may appear to or actually be, as merely a means to achieve an ultimately hegemonic goal. U.S. altruistic investment in China therefore presents a very particularized threat to the Chinese governmental sector. Consequently, U.S. altruistic investors, unlike altruistic investors from other countries, will have to overcome a Trojan horse syndrome of sorts in order to gain legitimacy in China.

* * *

Table of Cases

Table of Statutes and Regulations

Federal Materials

United States Constitution

United States Code

Code of Federal Regulations

Table of Agency Decisions

Index

[References are to sections.]